D1241559

MULTINATIONALS UNDER FIRE

Multinationals Under Fire

UNDER FIRE

Lessons in the
Management of Conflict

THOMAS N. GLADWIN
INGO WALTER
New York University

A Wiley–Interscience
Publication
JOHN WILEY & SONS

New York Chichester
Brisbane Toronto

Library of Congress Cataloging in Publication Data:

Gladwin, Thomas N.
     Multinationals under fire.

  "A Wiley–Interscience publication."
  Includes bibliographical references and index.
     1.   International business enterprises—Management.
2. International business enterprises—Social aspects.
I.   Walter, Ingo, joint author.   II.   Title.

HD69.I5G54   658.1′8   79-21741
ISBN 0-471-01969-0

Printed in the United States of America

10 9 8 7 6 5 4 3

for Annie and Jutta

PREFACE

Nationalization and expropriation. Sabotage, assassination, and kidnapping. Apartheid, repression and torture. Labor participation in management decisions, export of jobs, and technology drain. Consumerism and environmentalism. Tax-avoidance and exchange controls. Bribery and extortion. Social responsibility, accountability, and disclosure. Shareholder suits, management shakeups, and executive suicide. These are some of the "buzzwords" of conflict management in multinational companies that are facing an increasingly bewildering array of issues outside the comfortable rules of the marketplace. And the game is changing, often with breathtaking speed. The multinational enterprise is perhaps the most controversial economic institution of our time—those who manage it perhaps the most beleaguered. Top corporate executives tell us that enormous chunks of their time are spent on conflict management. "Tending the store" demands new talents, and skills written off as trivial less than a decade ago will, we submit, prove critical for multinational corporate survival in the years immediately ahead.

This book is about a lot of highly controversial topics—issues that many managers would prefer not to discuss at all and others wish would just go away. Neither is in the cards. The issues exist, they will grow, and they must be dealt with. In this book we attempt to identify and diagnose these issues and propose ways of coping with them that are both intellectually defensible and managerially feasible.

The organization of the volume is straightforward. We begin by describing the entire context of nonmarket conflict facing the multinational firm through the experience of five multinationals. We then develop a system for effective diagnosis and management of such conflict in Chapters 2 and 3, and proceed to discuss each of the major sources of conflict in Chapters 4 through 14. Some of these chapters are long, but try as we might, we found no shortcuts. In each case we attempt to apply our conflict management model. The final chapter focuses on international control of multinational enterprises and how such firms can effectively organize themselves for conflict management.

The book tackles another question as well—can a behavioral scientist and an economist collaborate without fatalities, and in so doing, produce something useful? We have had many conflicts. What good is writing about conflict without experiencing it first-hand? We tried to practice what we preach and "manage" our conflicts constructively. We are still talking to each other. Our wives are too. Whether we have succeeded in our broader objective is left for the reader to judge.

Needless to say, many people have helped us along the way, most particularly our MBA and PhD students at NYU. Russell S. Werner did much of the underlying research for the chapter on marketing conflict. Craig L. Kaiser performed yeoman service in developing conflict case studies on pressures for national ownership and control, and on the extension of national law and political influence through the multinational enterprise. And Kenneth M. Krieger assisted with the analysis of the patterns of MNE conflict with respect to the natural environment. To each, we owe a rather significant debt of gratitude.

Another group of individuals read and commented on parts of the manuscript. These include Robert G. Hawkins, Duane Kujawa, William R. Dill, Raymond Vernon, George S. Dominguez, Joseph Bertotti, Donald Guertin, Richard Levich, and Tracy Murray, although none are responsible for errors or commission in the final product. James Bodurtha, Judith Ugelow, Janis Bromfeld, and Maura Spielmann assisted with the editorial work. Monica Kaufmann and Jutta Walter compiled the index—an heroic task in itself. Financial assistance at various junctures during the course of the project was provided by the Ford, Rockefeller, and Alcoa Foundations, the New York University Project on the Multinational Corporation in the United States and World Economy, and the Deutsche Forschungsgemeinschaft. Besides NYU, the work was done at the Centre d'Etudes Industrielles in Geneva, the University of Aberdeen in Scotland, and the Universität Mannheim in Germany. To all we owe sincere thanks. And no one contributed more than Marion Epps, who shepherded the volume through the writing, editorial, and production stages with her legendary efficiency.

Thomas N. Gladwin
Ingo Walter

New York City
September 1979

CONTENTS

TABLES

EXHIBITS

CHAPTER 1
THE ARENA OF CONFLICT

How Multinationals Get That Way   1
The Challenge of Conflict Management   4
A Tale of Five Multinationals   6
The Issues   9
When and Where?   26
The Opponents   30
The Tactics   37
So What?   40

CHAPTER 2
THINKING ABOUT CONFLICT MANAGEMENT

Two Dimensions of Conflict Behavior   46
Competition   48
Avoidance   52
Collaboration   55
Accommodation   58
Compromise   61

CHAPTER 3
DESIGNING A CONFLICT MANAGEMENT STRATEGY

Deciding When to Fight   66
When to Work With the Opposition   74
Putting It All Together   79
Mixed Strategies   82
Rolling With the Punches   84

CHAPTER 4
TERRORISM

The Challenge of Terrorism   94
What is Terrorism?   95
Effects of Terrorism   114

Coping With Terrorism   119
The Future   128

CHAPTER 5
HUMAN RIGHTS—THE ISSUES

What are Human Rights   131
The Status of Human Rights   136
Multinationals and Human Rights   142
The Human Rights Movement   147
Tactics of the Human Rights Movement   151

CHAPTER 6
HUMAN RIGHTS—THE CONFLICTS

Lending to Repressive Nations   167
Circumventing Sanctions   175
Buying from Repressive Nations   182
Selling to Repressive Nations   186
Collaborating with "Illegal" Governments   192
Expanding in Repressive Nations   200
Withdrawing from Repressive Nations   206
Managing the Challenge of Human Rights   212

CHAPTER 7
MONKEYS IN THE MIDDLE

International Boycotts   221
Competition Policy   232
Political Control of Trade   237
Multinational Oil Companies and the 1973 Crisis   246
Extraterritoriality and Conflict Management   257

CHAPTER 8
OWNERSHIP AND CONTROL

Why Control?   258
Boundaries of Control   260
Home Country Controls   261
Entry Controls   264

Operating Controls   273
Financial Controls   278
Terminal Controls   285

CHAPTER 9
QUESTIONABLE PAYMENTS

What, How, and For Whom?   298
Gains and Losses   301
Explaining QPs   304
What's Been Done About QPs?   318
QPs and Conflict Management   326

CHAPTER 10
MARKETING CONFLICT

Multinational Marketing, Consumer Interests, and Public Policy   332
Product Conflict   338
Price Conflict   349
Promotion Conflict   356
Conclusions   371

CHAPTER 11
LABOR RELATIONS

National Bargaining   375
Multinational Bargaining   378
Industrial Democracy   390
Expatriate Employees   404
Disadvantaged Groups   409
Conclusions   422

CHAPTER 12
THE NATURAL ENVIRONMENT

The Setting   425
Pollution Havens   430
Patterns of Environmental Conflict   435
The Seveso Incident   461
Managing Environmental Conflict   466

CHAPTER 13
TECHNOLOGY

Definitions, Forms, and Effects   470
Technology and the Multinational Enterprise   474
Technology Transfer: Forms and Competitive Effects   475
Technology Adaptation   480
Technological Dependence   484
Technology Pricing   486
Barriers to Technology Transfer   489
The Nuclear Technology Imbroglio   490
Summary   500

CHAPTER 14
ECONOMICS AND FINANCE

Sources of Economic Conflict   502
Dimensions of Economic Interaction   507
Problems of Impact Assessment   510
Dimensions of Economic Conflict   511
Questions of Risk and Leverage   542

CHAPTER 15
MULTINATIONAL CONFLICT MANAGEMENT

The Challenge of Conflict   544
International Politics and Conflict Management   546
Why and Hows of International Control   549
The Contingency Approach Revisited   555
Implementation of Conflict Management   557
Adapting the Organization   565
Conflict Management in the Years Ahead   572

NOTES   575

INDEX   647

TABLES

TABLES

1-1 Issue Distribution in Multinational Corporate Conflict, 1969–1978   13
1-2 Timing of Multinational Corporate Conflict, 1969–1978   27
1-3 Location of Multinational Corporate Conflict, 1969–1978   29
1-4 Issue-Locus in Multinational Corporate Conflict, 1969–1978   30
1-5 Types of Opponents in Multinational Corporate Conflict, 1969–1978   35
1-6 Opponent Tactics in Multinational Corporate Conflict, 1969–1978   38–39
5-1 "Freedom House" Political and Economic System Correlates of Comparative
     Freedom   138–139
5-2 Human Rights Proxy Resolutions, 1976–1978   158–160
7-1 Crude Oil Sources for Major Multinational Oil Companies   256
8-1 Takeovers of U.S. Foreign Direct Investment Interest by Type and by Coun-
     tries, 1962–1977   294–295
12-1 Composition of Environmental Conflict Sample   436
12-2 Issues in Environmental Conflict   438–439
12-3 Opponents in Environmental Conflict   442–443
12-4 Tactics of Opponents in Environmental Conflict   446–447
12-5 Resolution Mechanisms Used in Environmental Conflict   452–453
12-6 Outcomes and Duration of Environmental Conflict   456–457
12-7 Matrix of Correlation Coefficients Between Composite Variables in Environ-
     mental Conflict   459
13-1 Pattern of Limitations on Access to Technology by Developing Countries   488

EXHIBITS

1-1 Issues in Multinational Corporate Conflict   10–11
1-2 The Roster of Opponents   31–32
1-3 The Arsenal of Tactics   36
2-1 Two-Dimensional Model of Conflict Behavior   47
3-1 Determinants of Appropriate Conflict Behavior   79
3-2 Sequential Patterns of Conflict Behavior   87
4-1 A Contingency Explanation of Terrorism   98
4-2 Geographic Distribution of International Terrorist Incidents by Category,
     1968–1976   111
4-3 Arguments Favoring Resistance and Accommodation to Terrorist Demands
     126–127
5-1 "Freedom House" Rankings of Comparative Freedom—1979   140–141
5-2 Potential Impacts of Multinational Corporate Activities on Human Rights
     144–145
5-3 Selected Tactics of the Human Rights Movement and Their Impact on Multina-
     tionals   152
6-1 Organizations and Institutions Participating in the Bank Campaign of the Com-
     mittee to Oppose Bank Loans to South Africa   171
6-2 Sample Bank Proxy Statement   172

6-3 Proxy Statement of the Management of Standard Oil Company of California
203
6-4 "An Experiment in South Africa"   210–211
9-1 Explaining Questionable Payments of Multinational Corporations   306
10-1 Major Accusations Levied at Marketing Strategy Elements   335
10-2 Code of Ethics and Professional Standards for Advertising, Product Information
and Advisory Services for Breast-Milk Substitutes   365
10-3 Abbott Laboratories (Infant Formula Shareholder Resolution)   367
12-1 The Environmental Problem–Policy Cycle   426–427
12-2 Constructive Management of Environmental Conflict: A Contingency Model
449
14-1 Interactions Between an MNE and Home and Host Economies   508
14-2 Categories of Restrictive Business Practices   532
15-1 Determinants of Appropriate Conflict Behavior   556
15-2 Incentives and Task Systems for Constructive Conflict Management   558
15-3 Framework for Analyzing MNE Conflict Management   567

1 *THE ARENA OF CONFLICT*

This book is about conflict. Not the textbook competition of the marketplace where the rules of the game are understood and concepts of winning and losing are part of the intellectual baggage all of us carry around. Not even the messier conflict that increasingly preoccupies managers in dealings outside the market with government and pressure groups solely at the national level. At least here the political and social elements giving rise to conflict are part of a more or less coherent national decision system that managers can comprehend and, more importantly, influence. Our concern is with conflict of a different sort, a veritable managerial nightmare where the rules of the game are often incoherent, ambiguous, redundant and ever-changing. Where an attempt to resolve conflict in the here and now often leads to even greater conflict in another place or another time. Where managers are often trapped in conflicts not of their own making. And where "good" and "bad" solutions are often indistinguishable at the time managerial decisions have to be made.

The stuff of which conflict facing managers of multinational companies is made turns out to be as fascinating as it is troublesome. Bribery and corruption, human rights, terrorism, labor participation in management, ecology, consumerism, political boycotts, tax avoidance, and technology transfer are a few of the many dimensions that we shall be looking at.

Our perspective is distinctly managerial. Our objective is to explain where conflict originates, how it affects the multinational enterprise, how to forecast it and analyze its consequences, and how to design ways of managing it. And so the book is long and heavily documented—which may itself be a cardinal sin in trying to communicate with managers. But superficiality has no place in coming to grips with the kinds of subjects that concern us here. In this introduction, however, we shall be content to describe the bewildering array of conflicts that face multinational firms, and to offer some reasons why coping with them is so very difficult.

HOW MULTINATIONALS GET THAT WAY

It is hardly necessary to spend a great deal of time describing the multinational enterprise (MNE)—what it is, what it does, and how it affects nations, groups, and individuals.[1] The multinational is certainly the most intensively researched and debated international economic institution of our time. The World Council of Churches considers it the economic equivalent of evil. The Swiss man in the street, in an opinion poll not long ago, viewed it as the second most serious threat to his personal security, after the military might of the Soviet Union. A prominent French journalist some years ago termed it "the American challenge" to European economic sovereignty in the 1970s. Only a decade later, two British journalists considered it the vehicle by which "the European revenge" will be carried out against the hegemony of United States-based firms in the 1980s.[2] Corporate executives have termed it the greatest force for world peace in modern times, a veritable United Nations of international cooperation and solidarity, a promoter of international economic interdependence, and a force for the erosion of national political rivalries and their evolution into war. Economists, as usual, see costs and benefits in the existence of the MNE, with the "bottom line" depending on who you are, but most would agree that the overall impact of multinationals on world income and output has been decidedly positive.

For our purposes, we shall take the broadest possible definition of the multinational enterprise—any firm that maintains a production, assembly, or sales and service presence in two or more countries. Students of multinationals will differ about whether the definition ought to be so all-inclusive. But the kinds of problems we shall be discussing bear on management of any firm that fits this description.

There are many measures that purport to describe the multinationalization of a firm, including percentage of total sales accounted for by majority-owned foreign affiliates, percentage of earnings attributable to foreign operations, percentage of new capital investment destined for overseas facilities, and the like. By virtually any such measure the "multinationalization" of American companies has been dramatic, and companies like Exxon, IBM, General Motors, Eastman Kodak, and Citicorp all have experienced large and growing shares of offshore activity over the years. The same kind of phenomenon can be observed among non-American multinationals, whose offshore growth has often come somewhat later, such as Volkswagen, SKF, Hoffmann-La Roche, British Petroleum, Unilever, Philips, Olivetti, BASF, and others.[3]

There are many explanations about how firms become multinational.[4] A simple view is that the return on investment, adjusted for market imperfections and risk, is simply higher abroad than it is at home, so companies would be foolish not to allocate capital to foreign rather than domestic ventures. Another explanation considers multinationals to have superior technologies, marketing, management, and information, all of which are internal to the firm and confer on it certain monopolistic advantages that purely local firms simply do not have. This then gives the subsidiary of a multinational in a particular market a built-in competitive edge over local rivals. Still others see the MNE as a product of diversification pressures that are basically "horizontal"—national firms find that domestic expansion in an industry is blocked by competitors or by antitrust laws, so they find it opportune to expand overseas in the same line of business, which they know well. Then there are those who view multinationalization in part as a matter of management's reaction to what its competitors are doing in industries dominated by a few large firms. So in the rubber industry, or banking, or chemicals, if one of the industry leaders sets up shop in a new market, others are often close behind.

One major school of thought has associated the development of MNEs with the so-called "product cycle." A new product is developed in a technologically leading economy, gradually is accepted in the domestic market and—as volume builds and unit costs drop—eventually becomes a major export item. Sooner or later the technology embodied in the product becomes relatively standard and available abroad, and foreign suppliers themselves begin to produce for the local market, perhaps for export to third countries, and even back to the home country itself, eroding the home country's markets for the product. To retain the benefits of product innovations, the innovating firms can themselves go abroad, that is, become multinational. In the process, of course, they may also serve to speed up the product cycle.

Another set of theories attributes the growth of multinationals to attempts at diversification. In the simplest case, by diversifying its operations across a number of different countries—putting its eggs in many baskets—a firm can reduce its exposure to certain kinds of risks and thus, for a given level of profitability, raise the value of its shareholders' investments. Similarly, by buying stock in a multinational firm whose earnings are derived from operations in several countries, an individual shareholder can diversify his assets and reduce his exposure to risk. And then there are myopic investors who would not want the exchange risk in investing in stocks and bonds of foreign firms denominated in foreign currencies but who happily invest in equities and debt of multinationals (denominated in local currency) not realizing that they are doing precisely the same thing. Such capital market imperfections and diversification characteristics are often said to give multinationals a decisive edge in raising funds in home-country, host-country, and international capital markets over purely domestic firms, thus providing the wherewithal and a competitive advantage that lead to multinationalization.

Others take a decidedly different approach. Multinationals, according to the "behavioral process view," are largely products of managerial responses to chance stimuli, new opportunities, competitive threats, sunk costs, and the like. Managers, in this view, are not necessarily "economic men," but may be maximizing something other than shareholder profits—the size of the firm, market share, sales, personal power, whatever. These complex motivations, along with simple inertia, may bias managers to become increasingly multinational even if this does not always make sense from a profit and loss point of view. Economists tend to challenge this view, however, maintaining that departure from profit-maximizing behavior will soon be reflected in a falling stock price, shareholder dissatisfaction, stock-market analyst pessimism, unfriendly takeover bids, and similar unpleasant events which could easily cost the manager his job.

A totally different explanation is provided by the Marxists, who consider the rise of multinational firms a consistent extension of conventional Marxist theory. Profits in the mature capitalist countries are alleged to be falling, and must be bolstered by heavy investments abroad, particularly in Third World or "periphery" countries. The governments of capitalist "center" countries fully realize their dependence on exploitation of Third World resources, and work hand in glove with the multinationals to further their interests abroad. And so multinationals are viewed as essentially political instruments of capitalist exploitation, fostering economic imperialism and hegemony abroad and creating what the Latin Americans call "*dependencia*" of the poor periphery countries on the rich center states. At the same time, multinationals reinforce the position of the powerful elites in host countries, facilitate their oppression of the masses, and make income distribution worse than it already is. As usual, class struggle, solidarity, "wars of national liberation," and revolution in both home and host countries are offered as ways to break the vise-like grip of the multinationals. Ignored, however, is the fact that three-fourths of all MNE activities are carried out among the capitalist developed countries themselves, that those developing countries most "successful" in creating growth in real incomes and elevating levels of living are also most heavily involved with multinationals, and that Communist countries themselves seek out multinationals to carry out projects considered important for economic progress.

Finally, there is the essentially economic argument that multinationals represent a new and more efficient vehicle for securing the benefits of an improved global resource allocation. We know, for example, that international trade is hampered by all sorts of tariffs, nontariff barriers, exchange controls, and so on. By leapfrogging these distortions and setting up shop inside the protected market, multinationals substitute international flows of labor, capital, and know-how for international trade, thus producing very similar resource-allocation benefits. Moreover, free markets with arms-length transactions between independent buyers and sellers work best when there are large numbers of participants on both sides, when information and transaction costs are low, when products are homogeneous, when cheating is virtually impossible, and so on—stocks, foreign exchange, wheat and pork bellies, for example, are traded in relatively efficient markets. But international trade today consists increasingly of computers, aircraft, petroleum, parts and components, and similar products where few of these characteristics seem to hold. It also consists of pure know-how which would have to be divulged to the buyer in order for him to decide whether or not to buy and what price to pay, thus losing its value to the seller. For these kinds of internationally traded goods and services, then, *intrafirm* transactions via the MNE may actually be more efficient than arms-length transactions via the market. Just like countries, the multinational may have an "institutional comparative advantage" which, with the shifting composition and growing complexity of international trade, partly explains the prominence of the MNE as an organizational form in today's world economy.

So conflict goes down to the very roots of the multinational enterprise and the conceptual reasons for its existence, and our earlier examples of vastly differing views of multinationals often have a very deep ideological basis. The result is that the MNE debate often degenerates into a clash of value judgments, political posturing, and outraged fingerpointing. The range and sensitivity of specific conflicts—which occur largely outside the marketplace—that managers must cope with on a daily basis serve to amplify and inflame the underlying disagreements that are always just below the surface.

THE CHALLENGE OF CONFLICT MANAGEMENT

Within the multinational corporate context, it is important to distinguish between "conflict" and "competition." Competitors, whether striving for market share by heavy advertising in Western Europe or bidding for telecommunications contracts in the Third World, are indeed engaged in activities that are in some sense incompatible—the probability of satisfaction for one decreases as the probability for the other increases. But competition according to established rules does not involve direct action by one party to interfere with the ongoing activities of the other. Conflict, on the other hand, requires direct resistance as well as direct attempts to injure, hinder, neutralize, or eliminate the other party. Competition may lead to conflict when such interference or resistance occurs—

to use an analogy, this happens in a track meet when one runner intentionally trips another at the starting line.

Conflicts occur at many levels—individual, group, division, organization, nation, and the like. Our focus is not with role conflicts of individual MNE managers, or interpersonal conflicts among executives, or even intraorganizational conflicts within a firm, such as those which often arise among area or product division interests within a complex global structure. Our interest is in conflict between the organization and its external environment. We view MNEs as open systems that survive to the extent that they are effective in the management of external demands, particularly those of interest groups upon which they depend for a continuing flow of resources and support.[5] Meeting these demands, coping with external constraints, and acquiring and maintaining resources, basically depend on the firm's ability to manage conflicts. Effective conflict management, we believe, is the key to a MNE's survival. It is not conflict itself that is dangerous, but rather its mismanagement.[6]

The number and range of conflicts involving multinationals have increased haphazardly but steadily over the years and are bound to expand still further. Some believe that the external world has grown deeply and chronically hostile to MNEs. Managing purely domestic conflicts is quite different and far less complex than the challenge confronting an enterprise in a multinational business environment, both in kind and in degree.[7] The MNE is forced to confront a host of conflict issues *in addition* to those encountered in the national environment, and the penalties for failures of conflict resolution can be much more severe. The enterprise operates in multiple economic, political, and social settings, each with a different historical pattern of development, set of current values and institutions, and national goals. Not only does the problem of aligning business policy with prevailing social objectives confront the firm in a different way in each national setting, making more difficult or even precluding a consistent set of company policies, but acceptable business behavior in any one country may also run counter to public policy or group interests elsewhere. MNEs sometimes cannot escape being used as political tools and hostages by competing interests, and are often trapped like "monkeys in the middle" in conflicts not of their own making. They almost always face an inherent dual standard in host countries, with conflicts involving multinationals viewed more seriously than identical conflicts involving indigenous enterprises. Conflict in multinational operations involves new actors and issues, overlapping jurisdictions, elements of ethnocentrism and nationalism, physical and psychological distance, and often severe differences among opponents.

The short and long run consequences of multinational corporate conflict can be profound, both for the firm itself and for the other protagonists, third parties, and the larger social, political, and economic environment. Gains or losses relating to the immediate conflict issue get distributed, precedents get established, freedoms and options get realigned, internal changes occur within the participants, long-term effects are felt in the relationship between the parties involved, reputations get established in the eyes of various interested audiences, and so on.

The nature of conflict involving the world's multinationals raises an immense challenge. But it is evident from various tragic episodes in recent years that many MNEs, as well as their opponents, know little about how to cope with conflict constructively. To repeat, the point is not necessarily to eliminate or prevent conflict—the real issue is how to make conflicts productive, or at least how to prevent them from becoming destructive.[8] We are concerned with the function of "conflict management," one that we believe is best accomplished by means of a "contingency approach." The basic idea is that there is no one best way to manage all conflicts, but not all approaches are equally effective. The "best" strategies and techniques for dealing with conflicts will vary according to the circumstances or situation. Given certain combinations of contingencies—for example, the company's stake in the outcome, relative power position, quality of relations with the opposing party, degree of goal incompatibility—one can specify approaches to conflict management that are likely to be more effective than others. The contingency approach thus identifies various types of "if–then" relationships and makes general recommendations for managerial practice that are closely related to the situation involved. The approach depends critically on the conceptual skills of managers, diagnosing and understanding the various types of situations the firm may confront, and bringing about a proper "match" between a particular situation and type of conflict-handling behavior. The approach, of course, does not pretend to be a cure-all. We do believe, however, that the approach is a good deal more sophisticated and integrated than traditional notions of coping with conflicts, and that it can help multinationals improve their overall conflict-management track records.

A TALE OF FIVE MULTINATIONALS

Let us now move from the abstract to the concrete. This book deals with the conflicts involving hundreds of multinationals. To describe the arena of conflict, it is useful to look in some depth at the conflict experience of a handful of more or less representative multinational companies. How has the challenge of conflict during the past decade confronted Dow Chemical, Gulf Oil, F. Hoffmann-La Roche, International Telephone & Telegraph and Rio Tinto–Zinc?

Dow Chemical Company was organized in 1897 to extract chemicals from the native brine deposits of central Michigan. From a provincial, midwestern bromine producer, the company over the years has become one of the world's major multinationals. Dow is sometimes called "the chemical company's chemical company" because of its production of huge amounts of bulk chemicals (about 60% of its output).[9] More than 2000 products and services are offered by Dow world-wide. The company's employees in 1978 numbered 53,500, its total assets $8.79 billion, and its total sales $6.89 billion, making it the third largest chemical company in the United States, after Du Pont and Union Carbide, and the seventh largest in the world. In 1978 approximately 47% of its sales and 50% of its assets were outside the United States. Dow was perhaps the most expansion-minded of all chemical companies in the 1970s, with growth averaging 23% a year in the early part of the decade and capital expenditures averaging more than $1 billion a year during the period 1976–1979. It has also been one of the most profitable chemical producers in the United States, and perhaps the world, in recent years. Its strategy has emphasized "aggressive growth," a heavy research orientation, careful husbanding of its superior technology, backward integration into raw materials at home, and "conquering new frontiers" or untapped markets overseas. The company's operations are decentralized into relatively autonomous units—in the United States, Canada, Europe, Latin America and the Pacific—each with a president and area headquarters. A relatively small world headquarters group operates out of Midland, Michigan. Dow's strong, goal-oriented management team is highly respected in business and financial circles. Carl Gerstacker, an outspoken defender of multinational enterprise, was Chairman of the Board from 1960 to 1976. Leadership in 1979, after the bomb-shell resignation of Chairman Zoltan Merszei, was firmly in the hands of Paul F. Oreffice, President and Chief Executive Officer. According to one report, "Over the years Dow has built up an informal management style that has given it the flexibility to react quickly to change . . . in all they undertake, Dow's top ex-ecutives show a willingness to assume big risks in order to reap even bigger rewards."[10] Dow's corporate philosophy encompasses a belief in the firm's "abili-ty to shape the future;" as such, Oreffice noted in 1979 that the company was pointed for a "golden era" in the 1980s.[11]

Gulf Oil Corporation traces its history back to the fabled Spindletop, Texas discovery in 1901. It became a major international corporation in the postwar years by tapping the vast oil reserves of Kuwait.[12] Gulf was once a member of the "Seven Sisters" of the international oil industry, but today might be consid-ered a "stepsister" because of its losses of overseas oil concessions. The company was founded by the wealthy and influential Mellon family, which still controls about one-fifth of the firm's stock. Gulf is an integrated petroleum concern, mainly engaged in the production, purchasing, transportation, refining, and marketing of crude oil petroleum and natural gas, although it considers itself a "total energy company" and has been diversifying into related areas such as chemicals, coal, oil shale, uranium and other minerals. Gulf had sales of $18.07 billion in 1978, placing it behind Exxon, Mobil, Texaco, and Standard Oil of California in the United States petroleum industry. It had 58,300 employees worldwide in 1978 with operations in about 100 nations—51% of its sales and 39% of its assets were outside the United States in that year. Gulf's overall financial record has been the worst of any of the big oil companies, with major declines in earnings experienced in the 1970s.

The company has recently turned homeward for its natural resources, for its principal investment and diversification opportunities, and for its future earn-ings. In 1975 Gulf was restructured from a vertically integrated company into seven separate operating and service divisions that could be examined and man-aged independently. Corporate headquarters in Pittsburgh provides coordina-tion, evaluation, control, and planning functions for these divisions. Company management in the 1970s has suffered from a lack of direction, time-consuming political scandals, and Mellon family interference. Robert R. Dorsey was Gulf's chairman from 1972 until 1976, when he was ousted in a bribery scandal and replaced by Jerry McAfee, who told his stockholders in 1978 that Gulf has found that its "road to the future is strewn with quite a few more potholes than we'd bargained for."[13] The company motto has been "Gulf People: Meeting the Chal-lenge."

International Telephone and Telegraph Corporation was founded by Sos-thenes Behn in 1920 as a holding company for Caribbean telephone utilities, and today is involved in five distinct major worldwide businesses: (1) Telecommuni-cations and electronics (28% of 1977 sales), (2) engineered products (26%), (3) consumer products and services (19%), (4) insurance and finance (21%), and (5) natural resources (6%). The company has 379,000 employees and operates in more than 80 nations—52% of its sales revenues of $15.26 billion, and 45% of its assets of $14.03 billion were outside the United States in 1978. ITT's rapid growth was achieved through a series of acquisitions during the "go-go years" of the 1960s, and 250 acquisitions were made between 1961 and 1971. The architect of the company's growth was Harold S. Geneen, who "has been compared to Gen. George Patton, to Alexander the Great, and to Napoleon. He has been called a great leader of men, but also a corporate autocrat who treated sovereign governments as ITT subsidiaries and who, given the chance, would have bought up the world."[14] The "Geneen Machine" became known for its tightly centralized organization, careful planning, hunger for growth, fiercely loyal executives, checks and balances financial reporting system, creative accounting, action-oriented decisions, "no-surprise scenarios," and "get-it-done-I-don't-care-how" philosophy.[15] Geneen relinquished the chief executive's chair (but not the chairman's) at yearend 1977 to Lyman C. Hamilton, Jr., who subsequently was pushed out by ITT's board in favor of Rand V. Araskog in July of 1979. Tarnished by scandals, the company has faced the task of correcting its image in the business community and with the general public as the "most vilified corporation in the Western world."[16] ITT has promoted itself as "an uncommon company."[17]

F. Hoffmann-La Roche & Co. A.G. was founded in 1896 in Basel, Switzerland. Today the company is the world leader in vitamin and tranquilizer manufacturing. Its overall interests comprise pharmaceuticals (60% of 1975 turnover), vitamins and chemicals (20%), aromatic and flavors (10%), cosmetics, diagnostic reagents and apparatus, bioelectronic equipment, and audio-visual medical teaching aids. As of 1975 the company manufactured in 40 countries, marketed its products in 100[18]. 41,826 people were employed in 1978. Its five largest operating companies today are located in the United Kingdom, the United States, Switzerland, West Germany, and Japan. Its sales in 1978 were $2.73 billion and its assets were $5.31 billion. The company is generally acknowledged to be the world's largest and most profitable ethical (prescription) drug manufacturer, with a 1976 profit margin of 9.29%. Roche is also regarded by its competitors as the leader in research and development, one that insists on paying for its impressive $300 million a year worldwide research program out of current profits. The company is closely held, with effective control still firmly in the hands of the founder's family. All financing has been done internally—no debt has appeared on Roche's books since 1920. The firm's worldwide organization is divided between two holding companies: 1) F. Hoffmann-La Roche & Co. in Basel, which is responsible for business operations in continental Europe, North Africa, and the Middle East, and 2) SAPAC Corporation Ltd. (Société Anonyme de Produits Alimentaires et de Cellulose), a unique corporate entity set up during the Hitler era with a registered office in New Brunswick, Canada, a headquarters in Montevideo, Uruguay, and its principal operating installation in Nutley, New Jersey. SAPAC is responsible for business operations in all English speaking countries, South America, and Asia. From 1965 to 1978 both holding companies were headed by Adolf W. Jann as chairman and president. He was replaced upon retirement by Fritz Gerber as chairman and Alfred Hartmann as chief executive.[19] Roche has long had a reputation as one of the world's most enigmatic, secretive, conservative and introverted multinationals.[20]

Rio Tinto-Zinc Corporation Ltd. was founded by the Scottish merchant banker Hugh Matheson in 1873 to resuscitate the great Spanish Rio Tinto copper mines in the Province of Huelva, which had been mined since earliest history. Until 1954, when control of the mines reverted to Spanish hands, the story of Rio Tinto was always colorful and often violent. The English colony at the mines recreated their homeland in miniature, importing Victorian customs and prejudices ". . . even to the extent of not running the company's passenger-trains on Queen Victoria's birthday."[21] Rio Tinto merged with Consolidated Zinc in 1962, and since then has grown to become one of the world's principal international mining conglomerates. The group has interests in almost every metal and fuel, including aluminum, borax, coal, copper, gold, industrial and agricultural chemicals, iron ore, lead, oil, silver, specialty steels, tin, uranium, and zinc. It is active on all six continents, employing 50,600 worldwide, with the bulk of its turnover derived from Australia, New Zealand, the United Kingdom, Canada, the United States, Papua New Guinea, South Africa, and Namibia. Group sales in 1978 were $3.75 billion, assets were $5.61 billion, and net income were $170 million. RTZ supports its operations and expansion with brilliant international finance, and the company has been described as "a sort of merchant bank, using its knowledge of the ways and workings of international finance to get the money for mining."[22] RTZ views mining as "a slow and patient game,"[23] and in recent times has invariably chosen to share the burden of capital costs and political risks of large mining projects with international and/or local partners. Based in London, RTZ's headquarters coordinates the group's activities and provides a range of financial, consulting, environmental, legal, planning, and taxation services. The company was led by Sir Val Duncan as chief executive officer from 1950 until his sudden death in December 1975. He once noted that "we are very politically minded in RTZ, not party politically minded, but on an international basis."[24] Responsibility for the company in the late 1970s was in the hands of Sir Mark Turner as chairman and Alistair Frame as chief executive.

With background profiles of the five multinationals in mind, we can now briefly scan the reported external conflicts in which these companies have been involved over the past decade.[25] In all, we identified 650 separate conflicts during the 1969–1978 period for the five firms. Gulf led with 259 or 40% of the total collection, followed by ITT with 183 (28%), Dow with 125 (19%), RTZ with 42 (6.4%), and Roche with 41 (6.3%). Perhaps coincidentally, the figures correlate rather closely with the relative size of the firms—of combined total sales revenues for 1978, Gulf's share was 38%, ITT 32%, Dow 15%, RTZ 9%, and Roche 6%. We shall use these 650 conflicts to describe briefly the arena of multinational corporate conflict—the issues, timing, location, opponents, and tactics involved in disputes during a more or less representative ten-year period.

THE ISSUES

Myriad issues give rise to multinational corporate conflict. Exhibit 1–1 organizes them into nine subjects: terrorism, human rights, politics, questionable payments, marketing, labor relations, environment, technology, and economics/finance. The specific issues listed within each subject area represent examples drawn from our survey of the conflict experience of Dow, Gulf, ITT, Roche and

Exhibit 1-1
Issues in Multinational Corporate Conflict

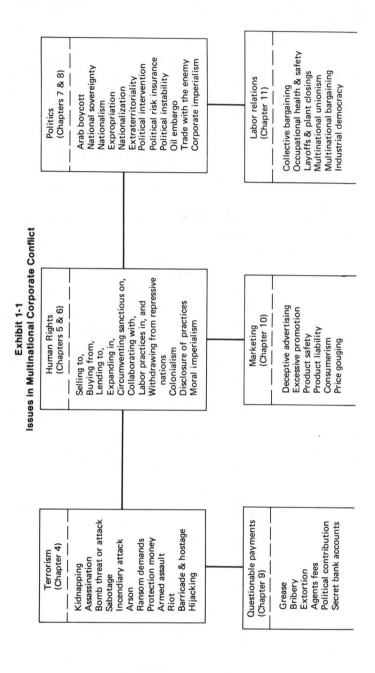

Terrorism
(Chapter 4)

Kidnapping
Assassination
Bomb threat or attack
Sabotage
Incendiary attack
Arson
Ransom demands
Protection money
Armed assault
Riot
Barricade & hostage
Hijacking

Questionable payments
(Chapter 9)

Grease
Bribery
Extortion
Agents fees
Political contribution
Secret bank accounts

Human Rights
(Chapters 5 & 6)

Selling to,
Buying from,
Lending to,
Expanding in,
Circumventing sanctions on,
Collaborating with,
Labor practices in, and
Withdrawing from repressive
  nations
Colonialism
Disclosure of practices
Moral imperialism

Marketing
(Chapter 10)

Deceptive advertising
Excessive promotion
Product safety
Product liability
Consumerism
Price gouging

Politics
(Chapters 7 & 8)

Arab boycott
National sovereignty
Nationalism
Expropriation
Nationalization
Extraterritoriality
Political intervention
Political risk insurance
Political instability
Oil embargo
Trade with the enemy
Corporate imperialism

Labor relations
(Chapter 11)

Collective bargaining
Occupational health & safety
Layoffs & plant closings
Multinational unionism
Multinational bargaining
Industrial democracy

10

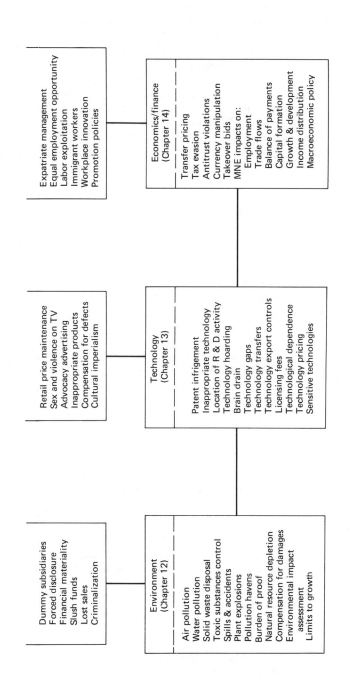

Environment (Chapter 12)	Technology (Chapter 13)	Economics/finance (Chapter 14)
Dummy subsidiaries Forced disclosure Financial materiality Slush funds Lost sales Criminalization	Retail price maintenance Sex and violence on TV Advocacy advertising Inappropriate products Compensation for defects Cultural imperialism	Expatriate management Equal employment opportunity Labor exploitation Immigrant workers Workplace innovation Promotion policies
Air pollution Water pollution Solid waste disposal Toxic substances control Spills & accidents Plant explosions Pollution havens Burden of proof Natural resource depletion Compensation for damages Environmental impact assessment Limits to growth	Patent infrigement Inappropriate technology Location of R & D activity Technology hoarding Brain drain Technology gaps Technology transfers Technology export controls Licensing fees Technological dependence Technology pricing Sensitive technologies	Transfer pricing Tax evasion Antitrust violations Currency manipulation Takeover bids MNE impacts on: Employment Trade flows Balance of payments Capital formation Growth & development Income distribution Macroeconomic policy

RTZ, along with others found in the many battles involving multinationals discussed in the chapters ahead. Exhibit 1-1 also notes the chapters in which each of the general issue areas are addressed and can serve as a "road map" for the rest of the book. The characteristics of the issues at stake (i.e., extent to which they are intangible, ideological, over precedents, complex, zero-sum in nature, and so on) importantly determine the intensity of the struggle, the duration of conflict, and the general difficulty of reaching agreement.[26]

Table 1-1 surveys the 650 conflicts involving the five firms according to the primary type of issue involved. For the group as a whole, 29% of the conflicts were economic or financial in nature. These, along with political, environmental, and questionable payments conflicts accounted for nearly three-quarters of all the battles. The remainder were scattered among terrorism, human rights, marketing, labor relations, and technology. The relative composition of issues, however, varied widely from firm to firm. More than half of Dow's conflicts during 1969–1978 involved questions of environmental and labor relations (mainly occupational safety and health). A majority of Gulf's conflicts were of the questionable payments and economics/finance variety. The same proportion of ITT's conflicts were political or economics/finance in nature. About 56% of Roche's conflicts were over marketing practices alone. Nearly half of RTZ's disputes were environmental or political in nature. In relative shares, ITT was the leader on terrorism and politics, RTZ on human rights, Gulf on questionable payments and economics/finance, Roche on marketing and technology, and Dow on labor relations and ecology. What follows is a sample collection of conflict cases drawn from the experience of our five representative multinationals, for each of the nine topical issues that have been identified. A quick scanning enables one to appreciate the truly diverse and pervasive challenge of conflict confronting multinationals. Each entry notes the multinational involved, main opponent, issue, location, and year of emergence. Along with each listing we also note the kinds of pertinent questions that later chapters will address.

Terrorism

Gulf vs. RASD: Sabotage of Gulf's refinery in Rotterdam—reportedly by Europeans operating on a contract from RASD, an underground counterintelligence organization believed to be controlled by Al Fatah (the Netherlands, 1971).

ITT vs. Descamisados Peronistas Montoneros: Kidnapping of Vincente Russo, Director General of ITT's subsidiary, U.S. Standard Electric of Argentina—released after reported ransom payment of $100,000 (Argentina, 1972).

ITT vs. Weathermen Underground: Time-bombing of the Latin American Section of ITT's corporate headquarters in New York City in retaliation for "ITT crimes . . . committed against Chile"—demolishing four rooms (U.S., 1973).

Gulf vs. Weathermen Underground: Bombing of the upper floors of Gulf's international headquarters in Pittsburgh causing $350,000 damage—followed

Table 1-1 Issue Distribution in Multinational Corporate Conflict: 1969-1978[a]
(650 conflicts involving Dow, Gulf, ITT, Roche and RTZ; % rounded off)

Firm	Terrorism	Human Rights	Politics	Questionable Payments	Marketing	Labor Relations	Environment	Technology	Economics/ Finance
Dow	1	6	6	2	2	22	34	7	20
Gulf	2	7	14	18	2	6	11	1	39
ITT	9	3	26	15	5	4	4	2	32
Roche	5	0	0	0	56	7	15	12	5
RTZ	2	14	22	2	0	12	24	5	19
All Five	4	6	15	12	7	9	15	3	29

[a]Data for first-half of 1978 only.

the next day by a bomb threat because of "crimes" by Gulf, including financing of the Portuguese in the war in Angola (U.S., 1974).

Dow vs. Popular Resistance Organized Army: Bombing of Dow's plastics factory in Laurion by group protesting U.S. government backing of military rule in Greece—killing two demolition experts (Greece, 1974).

ITT vs. Unidentified Terrorists: Bombing of three buildings in Rome housing offices of ITT subsidiaries—leaflets at the scene said "ITT organized the coup d'état in Chile and it is made up of Fascist and reactionary elements" (Italy, 1974).

ITT vs. Unidentified Terrorists: Fire set to the electronics warehouse of Face-Standard near Milan, a local ITT communications subsidiary, in revenge, according to leaflet, for ITT's role in Chile—resulting in about $9 million property damage (Italy, 1974).

RTZ vs. Bougainville Separatist Movement: Rioters stormed through RTZ's Bougainville copper mine, temporarily seizing control, causing an estimated $120,000 in damage, and putting the mine out of operation (Papua New Guinea, 1975).

Gulf vs. "A Jewish Militant": Gasoline pump hoses in ten Gulf service stations in Northern New Jersey were cut by vandals—a man identifying himself as "a Jewish Militant" claimed responsibility for incidents in retaliation for Gulf's "enormous monetary contributions to the Arab propaganda effort" (U.S., 1975).

Roche vs. "Commando 10th of July": Bombing of Basel home of Rudolf Rupp, Vice Director of Roche, and threats to other executives—in retaliation for 1976 dioxin cloud incident in Seveso, Italy, and Roche's "poisonous products" (Switzerland, 1977).

Why have multinationals like our five representative firms been among the preferred targets of terrorism in a great many of the nations in which they operate? Just what is terrorism, and what motivates and facilitates its occurrence? What kinds of demands do terrorists typically make of their MNE victims? How has terrorism in this decade affected executive life and corporate operations? What response options are open to MNEs? What arguments favor resistance versus accommodation to terrorist demands? What of the future—has the battle only just begun? These and other questions about this gruesome dimension of modern international corporate life are addressed in Chapter 4.

Human Rights

Dow vs. Medical Committee for Human Rights: Legal challenge to Dow's refusal to include in its annual proxy statement a shareholder proposal suggesting a charter amendment prohibiting Dow's manufacturing of napalm (U.S., 1969).

Gulf vs. Council for Christian Social Action of the United Church of

Christ: Council passed a resolution denouncing Gulf's support of Portuguese colonialism and called for a credit card turn-in and boycott of Gulf products (U.S., 1970).

Gulf vs. Southern Africa Task Force of the United Presbyterian Church in the U.S.A.: Shareholder resolution requesting Gulf to "cease operations in colonially held territories"—rejected by shareholders in vote at annual meeting (U.S., 1971).

RTZ vs. Counter-Information Services: Publication of "The Rio Tinto-Zinc Corp. Ltd. Anti-Report" dealing, among other issues, with RTZ's involvement in Namibia (U.K., 1972).

Gulf vs. Black Students at Harvard University: Six-day seizure of University Administration building to protest Gulf's collaboration with Portuguese rule in Angola and University's decision not to divest its Gulf stockholdings (U.S., 1972).

RTZ vs. Commissioners of the Church of England: Divestment of £1.5 million of RTZ equity because of dissatisfaction with the policies of RTZ regarding Southern Africa (U.K., 1972).

ITT vs. Church Project on U.S. Investments in Southern Africa: Shareholder resolution calling for disclosure by ITT of details of its South African operations—withdrawn after ITT agreed to voluntary disclosure (U.S., 1973).

Gulf vs. Pan African Liberation Committee: Full page "Boycott Gulf" ads placed by committee in *Jet* and *Ebony* and anti-Gulf activities intensified in black communities in protest of Gulf's Angolan operations (U.S., 1973).

ITT vs. United Presbyterian Church, U.S.A., et al.: Shareholder resolution asking ITT to establish corporate policy that it would not make or renew any contracts "to sell, lease, or service electronic equipment which may be used for military or police purposes to the government of the Republic of South Africa . . ." (U.S., 1976).

Dow vs. Michigan State University: A program of "prudent divestiture" adopted by the University's Trustees regarding stockholdings in companies doing business in South Africa, unless the firms were taking steps to pull out—Dow, in response, announced that it would not reduce operations there and asked if the University wished to continue receiving grants from the company (U.S., 1978).

Multinationals today have come face to face with a powerful popular movement concerned with cruelty, injustice and oppression. At the extreme, the question is even asked whether there is some sort of symbiotic relationship between MNEs and repressive dictatorships. What are human rights? Are they "political-civil" or "economic-social," or both? What is the current status of human rights around the globe? How can one assess the direct and indirect effects of MNE activity on human rights? What are the goals, actors, and tactics of the human rights movement? How and why have MNEs chosen to handle conflicts over human rights in the way they have? What impact has the human rights crusade actually had on MNEs? How is the human rights challenge facing MNEs likely to evolve? What guidelines might be useful in formulating appropriate corporate policies and responses? Conflict management in this troublesome area is considered in Chapters 5 and 6.

Politics

ITT vs. Chilean President Salvadore Allende: Speech by Allende before the U.N. General Assembly charging that his country was the victim of "serious aggression," that ITT and Kennecott Copper had "dug their claws into my country," that "ITT . . . launched a sinister plan to prevent me from acceding to the presidency," and that "before the conscience of the world I accuse the ITT of attempting to bring about civil war in my country. This is what we call imperialist action" (U. S., 1972).

Dow vs. Chilean Government: Government's takeover of Dow's 70%-owned Petroquimica and 100%-owned Quimica Chilena on grounds that Dow failed to supply its markets during the transport strike that paralyzed the nation (Chile, 1972).

ITT vs. Senate Foreign Relations Subcommittee on Multinational Corporations: Two-year inquiry regarding the extent to which MNEs influence U.S. foreign policy, with ITT's activities in Chile the leadoff case in its study—the Subcommittee concluded that ITT "overstepped the line of acceptable corporate behavior" by seeking to enlist the help of the CIA (U.S., 1973).

RTZ vs. Newfoundland Government: Threat by Newfoundland Premier Frank Moores to nationalize Brinco Co. Ltd. if RTZ refused to sell its 40.2% interest in the subsidiary to the government—Brinco and its partners subsequently agreed to sell the government its interest in Churchill Falls Labrador Corp., developer of a major hydroelectric project (Canada, 1974).

Gulf vs. Ford Administration and State Department: Pressure on Gulf to suspend its oil operations in Cabinda, Angola, and to place royalties destined for the Soviet-backed Popular Movement for the Liberation of Angola in escrow—Gulf had received payment demands from all three factions vying for political control in Angola (U.S., 1975).

ITT vs. Portuguese Government: ITT cut off all financial support to its Portuguese subsidiaries due to considerable financial losses and a progressive loss of effective management control attributable to wage increases required by law after the 1974 revolution, a purge of management personnel, and lack of support from local banks and the Portuguese government (Portugal, 1975).

RTZ vs. U.S. Justice Department and U.S. District Court in Richmond: Attempts by Westinghouse Electric in the courts of the U.K. to obtain evidence from RTZ in connection with the breach of contract proceedings by 13 U.S. utilities against Westinghouse—RTZ resisted such efforts strongly, even to the extent that the RTZ executives concerned pleaded Fifth Amendment against self-incrimination protection; RTZ's stand was reinforced by the intervention of the British government and vindicated when the House of Lords ruled in RTZ's favor (U.K., 1977).

Gulf vs. American Jewish Congress: Shareholder resolution calling for disclosure of Gulf's practices in regard to the Arab boycott of Israel—Gulf negotiated an agreement with the AJC to provide such information, removing the need for a shareholder vote on the issue (U.S., 1977).

Dow vs. Central Michigan University: After actress Jane Fonda spoke at the University and denounced big business in general (and Dow in particular) as constituting a "new group of rulers, tyrants," Dow's President Paul F. Oreffice fired off a letter to CMU officials stating that the firm had cut off its $70,000 annual contribution to the University—Dow stated it would not resume contributions "until we are convinced our dollars are not expended in supporting those who would destroy us" (U.S., 1977).

RTZ vs. South-West Africa People's Organization: Negotiations regarding acceptability of operating terms and conditions at RTZ's Rossing uranium mine, near Walvis Bay, to a black government after independence (Namibia, 1977).

What are the sources of political conflict involving multinational corporations, nation states, and international relations? How have MNEs been affected by efforts to extend national control in such areas as antitrust, economic boycotts, and East-West trade? To what extent have MNEs been caught in webs of overlapping jurisdictions? How have they fared in the Arab economic war against Israel and, more recently, Egypt? To what degree have home governments attempted to use their MNEs as instruments of foreign policy? What are the politics of ownership and control? How do controls vary as between their entry, operating, financial, and terminal forms? What has nationalism meant for multinationals? What can be learned from the nationalization and expropriation experience of this decade? Has overt political interference on the part of MNEs been widespread? These and other political questions are considered in Chapters 7 and 8.

Questionable Payments

RTZ vs. Local Press: Criticism of offering shares at an attractive price to selected politicians (including the Prime Minister) and journalists during a new public flotation by Comalco, a joint venture of Conzinc Riotinto of Australia and Kaiser (Australia, 1970).

ITT vs. Columnist Jack Anderson: Disclosure of memo from ITT Chief Lobbyist Dita D. Beard that linked Justice Department settlement of antitrust action against ITT on 31 July 1971 to a pledge of $400,000 from ITT subsidiary Sheraton Corp. of America for funding of 1972 Republican National Convention in San Diego, California (U.S., 1972).

ITT vs. Belgian Government: Frank Perperin, Managing Director of ITT subsidiary, Bell Telephone Manufacturing Co. of Antwerp, charged with having bribed high official of Belgian state phone service with $39,000 since 1966 to get consideration on equipment contracts—convicted in 1975 (Belgium, 1974).

Gulf vs. Senate Foreign Relations Subcommittee on Multinational Corporations: Hearings held on Gulf's overseas questionable payments and political contributions—Robert R. Dorsey, Gulf's Chairman, itemized the secret payments (U.S., 1975).

Gulf vs. Bolivian Government: Government demanded that Gulf disclose details of bribes allegedly paid in the 1960s to Bolivian officials or face cutoff of remaining payments from nationalization of Gulf's operations in 1969— after Gulf revealed $460,000 in such payments the government rejected the charges that the late President Barrientos received any money, jailed Gulf's representative in the country, called for an OAS condemnation of Gulf's "sordid activities," and convicted Gulf's chairman in absentia (Bolivia, 1975).

Gulf vs. Conference of Presidents of Major American Jewish Organizations: Conference approved a boycott of Gulf because of the firm's contribution of $50,000 to an anti-Zionist Arab propaganda campaign in the U.S.— Gulf's chairman publicly apologized, stating that "the contribution in question was regrettable, and you may be certain it will not happen again" (U.S., 1975).

Dow vs. Securities and Exchange Commission: SEC began a non-public inquiry in an effort to satisfy itself about the completeness and accuracy of Dow's internal investigation and disclosures regarding questionable payments—Dow had disclosed $3.1 million in such payments (U.S., 1976).

ITT vs. Congregation of the Passion, et al.: Shareholder resolution requesting a special report on ITT's "political involvement, political contributions, and questionable payments in Chile"—the Congregation stated that "ITT has hidden the truth from its shareholders and the public long enough regarding its involvement in the internal political affairs of Chile; 3.65% of ITT's shareholders voted for the resolution in 1977 and 3.69% in 1978 (U.S., 1977).

Gulf vs. Church Women United, et al.: Shareholder resolution asking Gulf to establish policy that would prohibit "contributions or grants to any political party or for any purpose that could be reasonably construed to be political to the Republic of Korea"—the resolution was withdrawn when Gulf agreed to adopt such a policy (U.S., 1978).

ITT vs. Securities and Exchange Commission: Complaint filed by the SEC against ITT, accusing it of making "many millions of dollars" in payoffs to foreign government officials and employees of commercial customers from 1970 through 1975, and also of engaging in a "deficient" internal investigation of its payments—ITT sought for months to suppress the complaint on grounds that its release (which provided details of about $8.7 million in alleged foreign payments) would harm the overseas business of the firm; the company settled the protracted litigation brought by the SEC in August 1979 by agreeing to a court order calling for improved accounting procedures, a reinvestigation of the firm's overseas payments, and a ban on future violations of federal securities law (U.S., 1978).

Hundreds of multinationals have experienced conflicts over questionable payments in recent years. Just what are questionable payments? Who have been the primary givers and takers of international payoffs? What forms, sizes, and shapes have QPs taken? What are the effects of QPs on firms, and home and host nations, and why all the excitement? Why do QPs come about? Do home nations "push" and host nations "pull" QPs out of MNEs? Are some industries and firms more payoff-prone than others? What has been done, and what remains to be done about QPs? How have MNEs been affected by QP revelations and the new anti-bribery laws and regulations? These irksome questions are considered in Chapter 9.

Marketing

Roche vs. "Action for Children's Television": Public criticism of vitamin producers' "deceptive and dangerous" advertising on childrens' TV programs—Roche, Miles Laboratories and Bristol Myers agreed to end ads in response to public pressure (U.S., 1972).

ITT vs. Federal Trade Commission: Charges against (ITT subsidiary) Continental Baking for deceptively advertising Wonder Bread for ten years as nutritionally unique—a few years later another FTC complaint was brought against Continental for making false claims in the advertising of its Fresh Horizons bread, which contained wood fiber (U.S., 1972).

Dow vs. Federal Trade Commission: Charges against Dow and other chemical companies of falsely advertising flammable plastics as nonflammable or self-extinguishing (U.S., 1973).

Roche vs. U.K. Monopolies Commission: Order requiring drastic price cuts on its Librium and Valium tranquilizers sold in the country (U.K., 1973).

Gulf vs. Federal Trade Commission: Charges against Gulf of violating the Truth in Lending Act by failing to tell its credit card customers that the cost of credit was hidden in the price of merchandise advertised through the mail (U.S., 1975).

Roche vs. EEC Antitrust Directorate: Complaint issued against Roche charging it with improper practices (e.g., loyalty rebates and binding customers to exclusive arrangements with the company) in marketing its vitamin products in the EEC—upon appeal, the European Court of Justice in 1979 found Roche guilty of abusing its dominant position and imposed a fine (Belgium, 1975).

Roche vs. Government of Brazil: Registration procedures tightened for drugs of foreign origin because of concerns about multinationals selling drugs banned abroad, engaging in excessively costly advertising, pushing harmful or ineffective drugs, and dominating the industry (Brazil, 1975).

ITT vs. Center for Science in the Public Interest: ITT subsidiary's Hostess products placed on the Center-sponsored Food Day "Terrible Ten" junk food list (U.S., 1976).

Roche vs. Canadian health authorities: Concern about the Canadian public's growing habit of treating stress with mood-altering drugs such as Librium and Valium prompted authorities to set up a special investigating committee—a resulting report, entitled *The Cost of Tranquility* noted that "the rising popularity of tranquilizers is disturbing" (Canada, 1976).

Gulf vs. Senate Judiciary Subcommittee on Administrative Practice and Procedure: Subcommittee subpoena of large amounts of material from Gulf and three other oil firms and their advertising agencies on companies' use of "image" and political advertising (U.S., 1978).

Should products banned in a multinational's home nation be sold by that firm abroad? How has the consumer movement evolved around the world, and what has this meant for MNEs? How are governments, via legislation and regulatory agencies, attempting to influence MNE marketing practices? How are antitrust policies impinging on pricing and distribution policies? What new concepts and principles are emerging in regard to product liability? Just how far do MNEs' liability and accountability extend for the safety and effectiveness of their products? What are some of the classic multinational corporate battles over product, promotion, pricing and distribution practices? How have the firms involved behaved? These are typical of the questions addressed in Chapter 10.

Labor Relations

RTZ vs. Trades Union Congress, et al.: Finding of high levels of lead in the blood of workers employed at the zinc-lead smelter of (RTZ subsidiary) Imperial Smelting Corp., at Avonmouth—led to a two month shutdown of the plant which earlier had been described as a "showpiece of British technology" (U.K., 1971).

ITT vs. International Metalworkers Federation and International Union of Food, Drink and Allied Workers' Associations: Drive begun to launch an international ITT trade council (Switzerland, 1972).

Roche vs. International Federation of Chemical and General Workers' Unions: Federation charged that Productos Roche in Madrid arbitrarily fired 70 workers after the predominantly female workforce of 3,000 voted to strike for a wage increase and increased work schedule—Federation stated it would continually spotlight Roche, the "world's most secretive company" (Spain, 1973).

Dow vs. United Steelworkers Local 12075: Rejection by Local of Dow's offer on a new contract and resulting strike of 5,300 hourly workers at the company's Midland, Michigan complex—the 177-day strike involved malicious destruction of property, rock throwing, mass picketing, violence, intimidation and coercion by USW members against company (U.S., 1974).

Dow vs. Plant Maintenance Workers: Two-day strike at Dow's plant in Lejona, near Bilbao, protesting government's execution of five Basque urban guerrillas (Spain, 1975).

Roche vs. Montclair Chapter of National Organization for Women: Charges of discrimination against women in Roche's Nutley, New Jersey facility, particularly among semiskilled and hourly workers—Roche signed an affirmative action agreement with the State's Civil Rights Divsion in 1976 and in 1979 signed an equal-opportunity agreement with the U.S. Labor Department giving low-paid female employees more than $1 million for back pay and other wage adjustments (U.S., 1976).

Gulf vs. Loretto Literary and Benevolent Institution: Shareholder resolution requesting Gulf to provide a full written report on labor conditions in its Korean operations—the Loretto group charged that conditions for workers were "questionable" and that trade union rights were "greatly abridged" (U.S., 1977).

ITT vs. International Metalworkers Federation: Nomination of Mr. Werner Thonnessen, an Assistant General Secretary at the IMF, for supervisory board membership under Germany's Mitbestimmung system at (ITT affiliate) Standard Elektrik Lorenz (West Germany, 1977).

Dow vs. Occupational Safety and Health Administration, et al.: OSHA's stringent standard limiting worker exposure to the pesticide DBCP (dibromochloropropane) found to cause sterility and possibly cancer in workers handling the material—Dow subsequently stopped producing DBCP, noting that "there would be no incentive to resume production" because the expenditures needed to comply with the OSHA standards would mean that "nobody could compete with foreign producers" (U.S., 1977).

Gulf vs. Anti-Defamation League of B'nai B'rith: Charge by the League that Gulf and five other U.S. oil companies have discriminated against employment of Jews in their corporate headquarters (U.S., 1978).

A wide variety of conflicts are associated with labor relations, or more broadly, human resource management, in multinational corporate operations. How do settings for collective bargaining over wages and working conditions differ around the world? What difficulties are associated with layoffs in many host nations? What complaints have labor unions expressed regarding MNEs? What features of the MNE limit a national union's bargaining power? Is multinational unionism likely to become a reality? What are the prospects for international bargaining? What challenges does the "industrial democracy" movement present for MNEs? How should conflicts over expatriate employees be handled? What special problems are posed by drives for equal employment opportunity among disadvantaged groups? How have MNEs been handling conflicts over employment of females, racial and religious minorities, and older workers? What kind of labor practices have MNEs employed in nations such as South Africa? These kinds of questions are addressed in Chapter 11.

Environment

Gulf vs. Italia Nostra, et al.: Opposition over the environmental impacts of Gulf's proposed oil refinery near Milan—pressures led Gulf to shift the location of the refinery to Bertonico, about 40 miles away (Italy, 1969).

Dow vs. Province of Ontario: Government suit for damages from mercury discharge into St. Clair River and Lake St. Clair from Dow Chemical of Canada's plant in Sarnia—in an out-of-court settlement in 1978 Dow agreed to pay $400,000 to the government and fishermen (Canada, 1971).

Gulf vs. Rozenburg Municipality: Order to close Gulf's new $40 million, 300,000 metric tons/year ethylene plant in the Europoort district of Rotterdam because the plant "emits too much carbon and smoke, and bothers residents with its flares and noise" (Netherlands, 1971).

RTZ vs. Authors Richard West and Amory Lovins: Publication of two books critical of RTZ's impact on the environment, *River of Tears: The Rise of the Rio Tinto Zinc Corp. Ltd.* by West and *Eryri: the Mountains of Longing* by Lovins (U.K., 1972).

Dow vs. Lejona Associations, et al.: Protests over air pollution from proposed $10 million insecticide plant which Dow planned to build in Lejona, near Bilbao—Dow was chosen as a protest target because it was "a multinational with an anonymous face" (Spain, 1974).

Dow vs. Bay Area Air Pollution Control District, et al.: Permits delayed and denied because of expected air pollution from proposed $500 million petrochemical complex in Solano County, California—Dow withdrew after spending $4 million battling more than a dozen regulatory agencies in a futile attempt to obtain 65 approvals needed for the plant that would have employed 1000 workers (U.S., 1975).

Roche vs. Lombardy Regional Authorities and Area Residents: Compensation for damages caused by the poison dioxin gas cloud released by Roche's subsidiary, ICMESA, at Seveso—Roche, by mid-1979, had reportedly paid out $25 million for cleanup work and compensation to victims (Italy, 1976).

ITT vs. Environmental Protection Agency: ITT Rayonier charged with delay in installing pollution control equipment at its pulp mill at Port Angeles, Washington in order to comply with EPA control standards (U.S., 1977).

Dow vs. Sao Paulo State Environmental Protection Agency: Agency prohibition on the production, formulation, and use of dioxin-containing materials, thus blocking some output at Dow's recently completed $6 million agricultural chemical plant at Franco da Rocha (Brazil, 1977).

RTZ vs. Aboriginal Tribesmen: Environmental opposition to many of Conzinc Riotinto of Australia's diamond claims associated with its jointly owned Ashton project in the Kimberly region of Western Australia (Australia, 1978).

When asked about environmentalists or governments that attempt to block the company's development plans, Dow's former chairman Zoltan Merszei once snapped: "Screw 'em . . . unless we are really wanted, to hell with them. There are plenty of investment opportunities in the world."[27] Just how have MNEs been coping with issues of job creation versus clean air, energy development versus wilderness preservation, risks versus costs, growth versus no-growth, hypotheses versus facts, and present versus future generations? What role is environmental legislation and opposition playing in MNE investment and production decisions? Are we witnessing "locational flight" on the part of pollution-intensive MNEs to "pollution havens"? What kinds of issues, opponents, tactics, resolution mechanisms, and outcomes have been associated with the hundreds of environmental battles involving MNEs? What environmental policy trends now confront MNEs? Should home country environmental regulations be imposed on firms exporting or investing overseas? What kinds of environmental guidelines and organizational arrangements are appropriate for MNEs? The difficult challenges of ecological conflicts are assessed in Chapter 12.

Technology

Roche vs. Department of Health and Social Security: Roche opposition to granting of compulsory licenses to Berk Pharmaceuticals Ltd. and DDSA Pharmaceuticals Ltd. to produce Librium (U.K., 1970).

Dow vs. Dutch State Mines: DSM's refusal to grant a license to Dow for rights to the Ziegler high-density polyethylene process—DSM eventually agreed "not to stand in the way" (Netherlands, 1971).

RTZ vs. Kaiser Aluminum: Dispute over technological and labor problems at aluminum smelter joint venture at Anglesey—Kaiser forced by RTZ and British Insulated Callenders Cables to increase its shareholdings and thus its share of losses (U.K., 1972).

Dow vs. Japanese Chlorine and Caustic Producers: Opposition to Dow's plans to build a 360,000 tons/year chlorine and caustic soda complex in Japan by local producers fearing a loss of their markets because of Dow's superior technology—Dow's behavior in Japan described by Japan Soda Industry Association Managing Director as "provocative and irritating to Japanese businessmen who respect mutual reliance and trust" (Japan, 1974).

Roche vs. Zenith Laboratories: Roche complaint filed against Zenith charging infringement of Librium patent and trademark and unfair competition—Roche won suit for patent infringement (U.S., 1975).

ITT vs. Brazilian Government: Requirement imposed on ITT to sell control of its Standard Electrica S.A. manufacturing facility to local partners as a condition for gaining permission to introduce a new switching system in the country (Brazil, 1975).

Dow vs. Italian Communist Party Economist, Eugenio Peggio: Criticism of Dow for "dismantling" the research and sales operations of its 70%-owned drugmaking subsidiary, Gruppo Lepetit S.A., and placing them under the Dow umbrella, with the result that "if Dow decides to leave, what is Italy left with?"—according to Peggio those multinationals that "devour and dismember Italian companies for their own benefit" will be opposed (Italy, 1976).

ITT vs. French Government: "Frenchifying" pressure on ITT to sell its 68% controlling interest in Le Matériel Téléphonique to Thomson CSF in order "to have the control of sensitive telecommunications and electronic manufacturing facilities in domestic hands" (France, 1976).

Dow vs. Brazilian Industrial Development Council: Two and a half years of negotiations over conditions and incentives for a Dow research and development center outside São Paulo (Brazil, 1976).

Gulf vs. Carter Administration: Willingness of the Administration to abandon the half-built commercial nuclear waste reprocessing plant at Barnwell, South Carolina, on which Gulf, Allied Chemical and Shell had already spent $250 million (U.S., 1977).

Technology is both a key to the economic power and influence of the MNE on the world economy and a source of a great many of the conflicts that surround it. Just what is technology, and what forms does technology transfer take? What are the international competitive and trade effects of technology transfer via MNEs? Do MNEs transfer "inappropriate technology" to developing countries? Who decides what is appropriate? What are the constraints on technology adaptation? What are the arguments for and against research and development centralization and decentralization? How is MNE technology priced? How have technology transfers been constrained by home-country export controls? These kinds of knotty questions are considered in depth in Chapter 13.

Economics/Finance

ITT vs. General Biscuit Co: ITT's bid to take over General Biscuit of Antwerp opposed by Biscuit's Belgian Directors—General Biscuit raised capital 15% by selling stock to friendly corporation (Belgium, 1970).

ITT vs. Justice Department: Consent decree to settle antitrust litigation requiring ITT to divest itself within two years of its holdings in Canteen Corp., the Fire Protection Division of Grinnell Corp., and a third unit to be chosen later—in all about $1 billion in annual sales (U.S., 1971).

Roche vs. Secretary of State for Social Services: Demand for repayment by Roche of "excessive" profits made on past sales of Librium and Valium in the U.K. to the National Health Service (U.K., 1973).

RTZ vs. Government of Papua New Guinea: Demands for renegotiation of terms of the Bougainville copper mining agreement, partly as a consequence of extraordinarily large profits earned during the $550 million mine's first year of operation (Papua New Guinea, 1973).

Gulf vs. Nelson Bunker Hunt and two of his brothers, Herbert and Lamar: Antitrust claims brought against Mobil, Gulf and 10 other oil firms alleging that they conspired to deprive the Hunts of crude oil to which they were entitled under the Libya Producers Agreement of 1971 (the Hunt oil fields were nationalized in Libya in 1973)—in 1978 a U.S. district judge in Manhattan dismissed the antitrust claims (U.S., 1974).

Dow vs. Ina Industrija Nafte of Zagreb: Delicate negotiation of conditions for construction of a $750 million joint venture petrochemical complex on the Adriatic island of Krk, off Rijeka—Dow demanded and won concessions never before given to a Western company (Yugoslavia, 1975).

Dow vs. Local Brindisi Prosecutor: Charges by prosecutor that Dow's partially owned subsidiary, Gruppo Lepetit S.A., was illegally exporting currency from Italy via its pricing of a family of antibiotics named Rifampicin—Lepetit's managing director was arrested and jailed on the charges (Italy, 1977).

RTZ vs. Indonesian Government: Negotiation of final terms of key mining contract covering copper and other mineral development in northwest Sulawesi—bargaining had proceeded sporadically since 1972, and the 30-year contract agreed upon was the first to be settled under Indonesia's so-called third-generation mineral exploration and production contract conditions announced in 1976 (Indonesia, 1977).

Gulf vs. Westinghouse Electric Corp.: Damage suit brought by Westinghouse against Gulf, RTZ and 27 other uranium producers charging price fixing and market allocation by the international uranium cartel—Gulf in 1978 countersued charging Westinghouse with seeking to monopolize the uranium, nuclear fuel and power reactor businesses; Gulf's chairman charged Westinghouse with trying to hide its "greed or managerial mistakes" in the nuclear power business by raising a "uranium cartel smokescreen" (U.S., 1977).

Dow vs. Iranians Bank: After the small Iranian bank defaulted on an interbank deposit, sending an ominous tremor through the entire international financial system, Dow Banking Corp. (Dow's Zurich-based subsidiary) sued to block the foreign accounts of the bank and recoup its losses—a tardy payment of principal and back interest by Iranians put the two banks back on friendly terms (U.S. and U.K., 1978).

Economic and financial conflict is fundamental to the very character of the MNE and covers an extremely broad spectrum of both very specific and sweeping topics. What economic objectives drive the actions of MNEs, home and host governments, and economic interest groups? How do these objectives clash? What are the linkages between MNEs and national economies? How do MNE activities affect capital formation and levels of market competition prevailing in these economies? Do MNEs export home country jobs through "runaway plants"? Do they use variable transfer pricing among their subsidiaries to avoid taxes? Are MNEs responsible for the growth of monopoly and restrictive business practices? Do MNEs make more difficult the execution of economic policy by national governments? These and many other forms of economic conflict are reviewed in Chapter 14.

WHEN AND WHERE?

Multinational corporate conflict is of course nothing new. All of the five sample firms have experienced plenty of conflict all along. Here are some highlights. RTZ's predecessor, the Rio Tinto Co., suffered from rumors of financial malpractice and troubles with left-wing workers in Spain during the late 1800s. More than 100 demonstrators were shot dead in the first major strike against the company in 1887, and further clashes in the 1920s caused Rio Tinto to become a symbol of exploitative foreign capitalism in the eyes of Spanish leftists.[28] Rio Tinto miners led the anti-Franco forces in southern Spain when the civil war broke out. "With their defeat, the company formed an uneasy relationship with the Fascists, agreeing to ship ore to Germany for the Nazi arms industry. This earned them the hatred of the Left without winning the sympathy of the anti-Semitic Right who disapproved of the French Rothschild money involved (and which is still involved) in financing the company."[29]

Roche suffered sizeable losses of assets in the Russian revolution of 1917. In the 1950s it was a target of the highly publicized investigation by the U.S. Senate Committee headed by Senator Estes Kefauver into pricing and other practices in the pharmaceuticals industry. Gulf in the late 1920s and early 1930s found itself enmeshed in lengthy disputes in acquiring Colombian and Kuwaiti concessions. Gulf's prospects for obtaining Iranian oil were very much at stake when the U.S. Central Intelligence Agency helped to overthrow Premier Muhammad Mossadegh in 1953, who two years earlier had initiated a nationalization of the country's oil industry.[30] As for Dow, the company had produced mustard gas during World War I without public outcry. But Dow became one of the principal corporate targets of the anti-Vietnam War movement in the latter part of the 1960s because of its production of napalm. Pressure by the peace movement took the form of countless campus demonstrations throughout the nation, harassment of Dow's campus recruiters, picketing at corporate offices, threatening phone calls and letters to Dow employees, raucous stockholder meetings, and a relatively unsuccessful boycott of Dow's consumer products.[31]

ITT's early history under its founder Sosthenes Behn involved many confrontations with nationalism and government insistence on controlling domestic communications. According to one observer, Behn wove a web of corruption and compromise in order to hold his system together that "left idealism in ruins, and his company with deep kinks in its character."[32] ITT aroused the suspicion of the United States government in regard to its dealings with foreign governments, and part of the Federal Communications Act in the 1930s was aimed against it. Behn's collaboration with Nazi Germany before the war caused the U.S. State Department to have grave doubts about the company's loyalties. Divestment and expropriation struggles marked ITT's history in the 1940s in countries like Spain, Rumania, Argentina, and China—Cuba, Peru, Brazil and many others came along in the 1950s and 1960s.

But our interest lies with more recent history. Table 1–2 shows the distribution of the 650 reported conflicts involving the five multinationals according to year of emergence. The peak years were 1975 and 1977. Almost two-thirds of the conflicts emerged during the period 1973–1977.

Table 1–2 also shows that the composition of issues at stake in the conflicts

Table 1-2 *Timing of Multinational Corporate Conflict: 1969-78*
(650 conflicts involving Dow, Gulf, ITT, Roche and RTZ; % rounded off)

	1969	1970	1971	1972	1973	1974	1975	1976	1977	1978[a]
All Conflicts	4	9	5	11	13	10	16	12	15	5
2. Issue										
Terrorism	0	8	0	8	36	20	16	4	8	0
Human Rights	13	22	8	16	14	11	8	5	3	0
Politics	5	7	5	14	12	16	17	13	10	1
Questionable Payments	0	4	1	9	13	7	29	20	12	5
Marketing	2	10	2	10	31	2	14	19	3	7
Labor Relations	5	10	9	5	9	10	14	7	17	14
Environment	5	10	11	9	6	4	13	14	22	6
Technology	9	9	9	14	0	9	14	18	18	0
Economics/Finance	4	7	4	11	13	11	16	10	19	5
3. Area										
North America	5	8	5	10	13	9	15	12	17	6
Europe	3	10	4	11	21	12	15	16	5	3
Latin America	8	11	6	13	8	10	21	13	10	0
Asia-Oceania	0	13	6	6	10	9	13	9	31	3
Africa	0	0	0	0	18	18	28	9	18	9
Middle East	6	6	0	29	6	12	29	12	0	0
4. Firm										
Dow	6	10	8	6	8	11	14	10	16	11
Gulf	5	6	3	5	12	10	23	13	18	5
ITT	4	10	6	21	16	10	10	12	9	2
Roche	2	10	0	7	32	3	12	24	5	5
RTZ	0	12	10	19	7	7	12	5	26	2

[a]Data for first-half of 1978 only.

27

varied from year to year, reflecting the influence of social movements, fads, and domino-effects. On a global basis however, the issues were quite durable, with conflicts emerging in each one practically every year. But the temporal distributions varied widely. Conflicts erupted in a rather concentrated fashion in Africa and the Middle East, but were more spread out in the other four regions.

Conflicts involving multinationals undoubtedly occur in every society in which they operate, but vary widely in content, frequency, intensity, forms of expression, and duration. This is perhaps largely attributable to the diverse economic, social, political, and institutional contexts in which multinational companies function. A variety of factors may be important in the origin, course, and consequences of multinational corporate conflicts: 1) *economic factors* such as income and unemployment levels, rates of economic growth, and national dependences on particular industries; 2) *social factors* such as the existence of third-party roles, availability of communications channels, degree of media attention, prevailing value orientations, and education and literacy levels; 3) *political factors* such as the existence of concerned citizen lobbies and political parties, the agenda of current political issues, openness of the political system, and levels of ideological or intellectual activism; and 4) *institutional factors* such as the nature of government regulations, presence of legal uncertainties or jurisdictional ambiguities, availability of formal protest mechanisms, access to the judicial system, and prior institutional experience with similar conflicts. In short, conflict may vary considerably as a product of the different contexts found in different nations.

Table 1-3 provides location data for the 650 conflicts under study. Two-thirds of the disputes occurred in North America, 14% in Europe, 10% in Latin America, and 10% in Asia-Oceania, Africa and the Middle East combined. The 66% share for North America is higher than the share of combined physical assets of the five firms in his region in 1977, which was approximately 54%. In regard to issues, more than three-quarters of the conflicts over human rights, questionable payments, labor relations, and economics/finance emerged in North America, as did a majority of the marketing and environmental disputes. In contrast, a majority of the battles over terrorism, politics, and technology occurred outside North America. Table 1-3 also shows that the regional distribution of conflicts remained relatively stable from year to year.

Viewing multinational corporate conflicts in terms of the nations where they emerge is only one part of the overall location picture. A different and perhaps more valuable perspective emerges from their "issue locus"—that is, whether the conflict emerged in the company's home nation over a purely domestic matter, in the home nation over a foreign matter, in a host nation on a domestic matter, or in a host or third nation over a foreign matter. Conflicts are considered to be over "foreign matters" when the overseas behavior of the MNE was at issue or when foreign transactions, opponents or reactions were significantly involved. Church group protests in the United States regarding labor practices of American firms in South Africa, or disputes with the Securities and Exchange Commission in the United States over disclosure of questionable payments made abroad are considered to be home-nation conflicts over foreign matters, for example.

Table 1-4 shows that 42% of the 650 conflicts of the five sample firms occurred in their home nations over purely domestic concerns. About 21% took

Table 1-3 *Location of Multinational Corporate Conflict: 1969-1978*
(650 conflicts involving Dow, Gulf, ITT, Roche and RTZ; % rounded off)

	North America	Europe	Latin America	Asia-Oceania	Africa	Middle East
1. All Conflicts	66	14	10	5	2	3
2. Issue						
Terrorism	28	40	24	4	0	4
Human Rights	81	19	0	0	0	0
Politics	40	8	28	8	8	8
Questionable Payments	76	3	13	8	0	0
Marketing	61	33	2	2	2	0
Labor Relations	79	19	0	2	0	0
Environment	70	23	1	5	1	0
Technology	41	36	9	14	0	0
Economics/Finance	78	6	7	4	1	4
3. Year						
1969	69	10	17	0	0	4
1970	62	16	13	7	0	2
1971	70	12	12	6	0	0
1972	64	14	12	3	0	7
1973	64	23	6	4	2	1
1974	63	17	9	5	3	3
1975	63	13	12	4	3	5
1976	64	19	10	4	1	2
1977	76	5	6	11	2	0
1978[a]	84	10	0	3	3	0

[a]Data for first-half of 1978 only.

place at home but focused on aspects of the firms' activities overseas. Host-country disputes over domestic issues accounted for 27%, while the remaining 10% occurred in host or third countries but were focused on activities of the MNEs outside of these nations. Table 1–4 shows that the issue locus varied considerably among issues. Battles over marketing, labor relations, environment, technology, and economics/finance were predominantly "domestic" in orientation, whether in home or host countries. Disputes over human rights, in contrast, were almost exclusively "foreign" in content, as were 61% of the disputes over questionable payments. The battles over terrorism and politics were spread evenly between domestic and foreign classifications.

The data presented in Table 1–4 also reveal an important change in the nature of conflict as experienced by the five sample multinationals. During the period 1969–1972, about one-fifth of the conflicts emerging in home and host countries were concerned with the firm's foreign activities. But during the 1975–1978 period, this figure was two-fifths. In other words, the content of the issues in conflict over the decade had grown increasingly international. This is probably the result of growing economic interdependence, improved global communications, intergovernmental linkages, and a greatly increased propensity on the part of citizen lobbies, politicians and regulators to concern themselves with events and conditions abroad. The veil which used to insulate MNEs from attacks in one nation for their behavior in others has progressively been lifted. Of the five firms, Table 1–4 shows that ITT, RTZ and Gulf were each the victim of this

Table 1–4 *Issue Locus in Multinational Corporate Conflict: 1969–1978*
(650 conflicts involving Dow, Gulf, ITT, Roche and RTZ; % rounded off)

	In Home Nation on Domestic Matter	In Home Nation on Foreign Matter	In Host Nation on Domestic Matter	In Host or Third Nation on Foreign Matter Matter
1. All Conflicts	42	21	27	10
2. Issue				
Terrorism	12	20	48	20
Human Rights	3	89	0	8
Politics	3	32	52	13
Questionable Payments	34	41	5	20
Marketing	47	2	42	9
Labor Relations	67	7	21	5
Environment	72	2	21	5
Technology	22	14	50	14
Economics/Finance	55	14	24	7
3. Year				
1969	52	17	31	0
1970	47	16	31	6
1971	59	15	20	6
1972	46	19	25	10
1973	42	15	35	8
1974	41	17	33	9
1975	35	20	32	13
1976	31	23	30	16
1977	40	31	14	15
1978[a]	47	37	16	0
4. Firm				
Dow	56	9	30	5
Gulf	40	28	21	11
ITT	49	24	19	8
Roche	0	5	73	22
RTZ	17	21	50	12

[a]Data for first-half of 1978 only.

transparency and transnationalism in about one-third of their respective conflicts.

THE OPPONENTS

Who are the principal opponents of multinationals in their conflicts outside the marketplace? The answer, according to the data, is just about everybody. Exhibit 1–2 provides a sample listing of some of the many individuals, groups, or organizations that have struggled with one or more of the five sample firms over the past decade. Perhaps no other institution in recent history comes close to the MNE in engendering such a diverse array of antagonisms. Questions of conflict of interest have of course varied tremendously in extent and substance.

Characteristics of the opponents have also varied greatly—in ways critically

Exhibit 1-2

The Roster of Opponents

A sample listing of some of the individuals, groups or organizations which came into conflict with one or more of the following multinationals during 1969–1978: Dow Chemical, Gulf Oil, Hoffmann-La Roche, International Telephone & Telegraph, and Rio Tinto-Zinc

I. CITIZEN LOBBY

A. **Environmental**—e.g., Friends of the Earth Ltd., Sierra Club, Italia Nostra, Papua-New Guinea Conservation Society, Bürgerverein of Butzfleth.

B. **Religious**—e.g., American Jewish Congress, Interfaith Center on Corporate Responsibility, World Council of Churches, Church Commissioners of the Church of England, Task Force on Southern Africa of the United Presbyterian Church in the U.S.A.

C. **Human Rights**—e.g., Medical Committee for Human Rights, American Committee on Africa, Toronto Committee for the Liberation of Portugal's African Colonies, ITT Boycott–South Africa Committee, National Association for the Advancement of Colored People.

D. **Social Action**—e.g., Council on Economic Priorities, Gulf Boycott Coalition, Project on Corporate Responsibility, National Organization of Women, Counter Information Services.

E. **Consumer**—e.g., Action for Children's Television, Medical Association of Rio de Janeiro, North Jersey Federation of Senior Citizens, Ralph Nader, Center for Science in the Public Interest.

F. **Community**—e.g., Crow Indians of Montana, Lejona Associations of the Basque Region, Citizens of Rozenburg (the Netherlands), Residents of Flagler Beach (Florida), Aboriginal Tribesmen of the Kimberly Region of Western Australia.

G. **University**—e.g., Central Michigan University, Stanford University, Black Students at Harvard University, Students at the University of Michigan, Students at the University of Wisconsin.

II. REGULATORY

A. **Antitrust**—e.g., U.S. Justice Department, U.K. Monopolies Commission, West German Federal Cartel Office, Australian Trade Practices Commission, U.S. Federal Trade Commission.

B. **Finance**—e.g., U.S. Securities and Exchange Commission, U.S. Internal Revenue Service, U.S. Treasury Department, U.K. Price Commission, U.S. Overseas Private Investment Corporation.

C. **Welfare**—e.g., U.K. Department of Health and Social Security, U.S. Food and Drug Administration, U.S. Equal Employment Opportunity Commission, U.S. Consumer Product Safety Commission, British Race Relations Board.

D. **Environment**—e.g., São Paulo State Environmental Protection Agency, U.K. Department of the Environment, U.S. Environmental Protection Agency, U.S. Occupational Safety and Health Administration, San Francisco Bay Area Air Pollution Control District.

E. **Natural Resources**—e.g., Canadian National Energy Board, Michigan Natural Resources Department, U.S. Federal Energy Administration, U.S. Federal Power Commission, U.S. Nuclear Regulatory Commission.

F. **Commerce**—e.g., Japan Ministry of International Trade and Industry, Australian Foreign Investment Board, Canadian Foreign Investment Review Agency, Brazilian Industrial Development Council, U.K. Department of Trade and Industry.

III. POLITICAL

A. Heads of State—e.g., Chilean President Salvadore Allende, Philippines President Ferdinand E. Marcos, Argentine President Isabel Peron, Bolivian President Hugo Banzer Suarez, U.S. President Jimmy Carter.

B. Political Parties—e.g., South Korean Democratic Republican Party, Italian Communist Party, U.K. Labour Party, United Popular Action Movement in Chile, Australian Labour Party.

C. Legislative Bodies—e.g., U.S. Senate Foreign Relations Subcommittee on Multinational Corporations, U.S. Senate Watergate Committee, U.K. House of Commons, Brazilian Congress, Kuwait National Assembly.

D. International Bodies—e.g., EEC Commission, U.N. General Assembly, European Parliament, Organization of American States, Organization of Petroleum Exporting Countries.

E. Nationalist/Separatist Groups—e.g., Popular Movement for the Liberation of Angola, National Front for the Liberation of Angola, Basque Separatists, South-West Africa Peoples Organization, Bougainville Secessionist Movement.

F. Terrorist Groups—e.g., Descamisados Peronistas Montoneros, Tupamaros, Weather Underground, Commando 10th of July, LAOS-8 (Greek Popular Resistance Organized Army).

IV. COMMERCIAL

A. Corporations—e.g., Westinghouse Electric Corp., Berk Pharmaceuticals Ltd., Consumers Power Co., General Biscuit Co. of Antwerp, Price Waterhouse & Co.

B. Labor Organizations—e.g., U.K. Trades Union Congress, International Metalworkers Federation, United Steelworkers, United Farm Workers Organizing Committee, Oil, Chemical and Atomic Workers International Union.

C. Press—e.g., Jornal do Brasil, A Luta (Portuguese Socialist Newspaper), Columnist Jack Anderson, Richard West (author of *River of Tears* about RTZ), Anthony Sampson (author of *The Sovereign State of ITT*).

D. Victims of Accidents, etc.—e.g., Residents of Seveso (Italy), Residents of Santa Barbara (California), Vietnam War Veteran Paul Reutersham, Area landowners near nuclear weapons plant at Rocky Flats (Colorado), California Warehouseman Frank Arnett.

E. Other—e.g., South Korean Businessman Park Tung Sun, Lewis D. and John J. Gilbert of Corporate Democracy, Inc., Former Roche employee Stanley Adams, Certified Public Accountants.

affecting the development, course, and resolution of the disputes involved. Some were small and others very large; some were novices and others old hands at waging conflict; some were poor and others rich; some were ad hoc and unorganized, while others were long established and highly structured; some were obsessed with a single issue, while others dabbled in multiple issues; some had entire armies at their disposal, while others had only typewriters; some were out for a little fun and excitement, while others were willing to die for their cause. We could go on with other distinctions regarding knowledge, skills, access to the media, intelligence networks, internal cohesiveness, risk taking propensity, image, reputation, and the like. All of these can be viewed as resources, as potential ingredients of power which in given situations have enabled some of the MNEs' opponents to obtain the outcomes they desired at the expense of the five multinationals.

Exhibit 1–2 classifies 24 types of opponents into four general categories: citizen lobby, regulatory, political, and commercial. Although any classification system tends to be imperfect, we believe this one does capture the essence of four different (albeit overlapping) incentive systems that lead to conflicts with MNEs. *Citizen lobbies* tend to have deep-seated and ideological convictions, thus often producing greater rigidity in their conflict behavior and transforming conflicts with MNEs into eternal struggles over fundamental "truths." Their desire is typically for outcomes consonant with their own interpretation of the "public interest." *Regulatory agencies* are generally empowered to carry out mandates entrusted to them by either legislative or executive branches of government. In some nations the same administrative agency may set the rules, investigate infractions, prosecute the accused party, judge his guilt, and assess penalties. The foremost organizational goal of such an agency, particularly in the United States, is nonreversal of its actions by the legislature or courts, and thus confirmation that it is doing its job properly.

Politicians, wherever they are, constantly strive to come into, or remain in power. In a democracy this means keeping the voters happy. In a dictatorship it entails keeping the revolutionaries at bay or seizing power. Politicians in power are thus motivated to extract additional benefits from MNEs. For those out of power a common trick is to fix the blame on MNEs for undesirable states of affairs, to emphasize the economic and political disadvantages of relying on foreign-owned firms, and to play on strong aspirations for freedom and independence. Finally, *commercial bodies* tend to come into conflict with MNEs almost exclusively when matters of direct economic self-interest are at stake. Whether it is a labor union seeking increased wages, an accident victim seeking compensation, a local businessman seeking to appropriate domestic opportunities, or another MNE seeking to protect its patents from infringement, the same "economic" logic is involved. Crossing the fuzzy border from competition to conflict with an economic rival is often essential to protect the firm's ability to acquire and maintain a favorable position in the market.

Our focus so far has been on single opponents, but over half of the 650 conflicts examined in our survey were multi-party affairs. ITT's long-standing dispute over political intervention in Chile, for example, pitted the company against President Salvador Allende, the Chilean Senate, the U.S. Senate Foreign Relations Subcommittee on Multinational Corporations, columnist Jack Anderson, the CIA, the U.S. Overseas Private Investment Corporation, British author Anthony Sampson, former U.S. Ambassador to Chile Edward M. Korry, the U.S. Department of Justice, a Federal Grand Jury, the U.S. Securities and Exchange Commission, the U.N. General Assembly, many church groups, minority shareholders, students on many university campuses, employees of Phillips-Van Heusen Corp., "People's Coalition Against ITT," "ITT Boycott Committee," Ad Hoc Committee for Chilean Solidarity, Australian Labour Party, terrorists in the United States, Argentina, Italy, Switzerland, West Germany, and France, and many other groups and organizations.

As we have observed, an increase in the number of parties to a multinational corporate dispute generally enhances the chances of communications failure, increases the difficulty of coordination, reduces the range of alternative solutions acceptable to all parties, and consequently increases the amount of time needed for resolution. Conflicts initially involving many parties do show a persistent tendency, however, to reduce to simpler two-party conflicts via coalitions and blocs. Often parties who see themselves as sharing a common disadvantage at the hands of MNEs join forces and unify their resources in order to maintain or increase their individual strength. Multinationals, as we shall see in later chapters, just as often strive to prevent the formation of coalitions among opposing parties.

It is also important to note that in addition to the direct protagonists, audiences and/or third parties were involved in a good portion of the conflicts involving the five sample multinationals. The known presence of interested and significant "audiences" critically shaped the behavior of the parties in the disputes. Hoffman-La Roche, for example, in its disputes with British regulatory agencies over pricing of Librium and Valium, knew that every move was being closely watched by concerned antitrust and health regulators in many other countries.

It is also clear that third parties have greatly influenced the course of many MNE conflicts. Third parties entered the observed conflicts in several broad categories—as possessors of superior powers to impose a settlement (judges, arbitrators), as reconcilers of disparate interests (fact-finders, conciliators, mediators), and as expert counsel to one or the other contending parties (attorneys, consultants, special envoys). The mere availability of such parties probably creates pressures toward agreement. More directly, however, the interventions which neutral third parties initiate often generate significant pressures toward the reduction of differences between the opposing parties—by improving communications and understanding, by helping to identify the issues, by setting the circumstances for confronting the issues, by correcting distortions of fact, by pressing for fairness and equity, and by making settlements acceptable to the parties in conflict.

Let us now take a look at the facts concerning the four major types of opponents which confronted Dow, Gulf, ITT, Roche, and RTZ during a decade of conflict. For each of the 650 conflicts, we identified the single most important opponent confronting each multinational and classified that opponent as a citizen lobby, regulatory, political, or commercial actor according to the groupings shown in Exhibit 1-2. Table 1-5 reveals the distribution of actors across all conflicts, as well as the issues, areas, years, and firms involved.

One third of all the five firms' battles were with regulatory agencies, while just a bit less were fought with politicians. Commercial interests and citizen lobbies each accounted for about one fifth of all the conflicts. These statistics radically change, however, when specific issues are considered. Citizen lobbies, for example, were the dominant force on human rights and were also significantly involved in some other areas such as environmental protection and questionable payments. Regulatory agencies, on the other hand, managed during the decade to get their hands into almost everything, but particularly into matters of marketing, environment, and economics/finance. The "politicians" as defined in Exhibit 1-2 had a monopoly on terrorism and a two-thirds share of political squabbles. Despite being the main recipients of the largesse, politicians were also heavily involved in condemning questionable payments when they were exposed. The commercial interests, as one might expect, spent most of their time fighting MNEs over the predominantly commercial issues of technology, labor relations, and economics/finance. The fact that certain issues in large measure

Table 1-5 *Types of Opponents in Multinational Corporate Conflict: 1969-1978*
(650 conflicts involving Dow, Gulf, ITT, Roche and RTZ; % rounded off)

	Citizen Lobby Actors	Regulatory Actors	Political Actors	Commercial Actors
1. All Conflicts	18	33	28	21
2. Issue				
Terrorism	0	0	100	0
Human Rights	91	3	3	3
Politics	12	14	67	7
Questionable Payments	26	28	38	8
Marketing	14	70	9	7
Labor Relations	14	31	0	55
Environment	34	54	5	7
Technology	4	23	23	50
Economics / Finance	3	37	24	36
3. Area				
North America	22	39	14	25
Europe	21	29	26	24
Latin America	0	5	95	0
Asia-Oceania	13	25	37	25
Africa	0	18	82	0
Middle East	0	0	100	0
4. Year				
1969	28	24	31	17
1970	25	33	22	20
1971	26	32	18	24
1972	24	22	29	25
1973	15	42	34	9
1974	19	28	34	19
1975	14	26	36	24
1976	15	34	31	20
1977	16	36	20	28
1978[a]	13	53	9	25
5. Firm				
Dow	14	48	11	27
Gulf	18	27	36	19
ITT	20	30	32	18
Roche	12	59	12	17
RTZ	33	7	31	29

[a]Data for first-half of 1978 only.

attracted only one or two types of actors implies a certain specialization of labor in the attack on multinationals. The wider involvement of three or four types of actors seen on other issues suggests considerable complexity for MNEs who must contend with sometimes radically different opponent incentives in regard to the same general issue.

Table 1-5 also shows that citizen challenges to business authority confronted the five firms only in industrial nations. Countries such as the United States, Canada, Britain, Holland, Sweden, and West Germany in particular witnessed a pluralist uprising in the early 1970s that was marked by a profusion of groups willing to undertake the often difficult and expensive task of opposing multinational corporate policies.[33] Regulatory and commercial opponents were also con-

Exhibit 1-3

The Arsenal of Tactics

Legal—Criminal and civil suits, indictments, complaints, injunctions, subpoenas, arrests, grand jury investigations, consent decrees.

Legislative—Hearings, parliamentary investigations, legislation, statutes, inquiries, ordinances, referenda, committee reports.

Administrative—Administrative orders, agency clearances, setting of standards, bans and prohibitions, executive decrees, regulatory probes, seizures of assets, cease and desist orders.

Financial—Shareholder resolutions, stock divestitures, disclosure requirements, registration requirements, proxy fights, cash tender offers, takeover bids, stock trading suspensions.

Economic—Strikes, strike authorizations or threats, boycotts, patent infringements, extortion, rejections of bids and offers, hard bargaining, whistle blowing.

Communicative—Public speeches, publications, research reports, petitions, open letters, editorials, advertisements, lobbying.

Symbolic—Demonstrations, picketing, banners and posters, marches and parades, slogans and caricatures, harassment of speakers, counter-recruitment efforts, sit-ins.

Violent—Bombings, kidnappings, assassinations, sabotage, incendiary attacks, hijackings, armed assaults, threats of violence.

centrated in the industrialized home and host nations. Conflicts of the five firms in the developing areas of Latin America, Asia, Africa, and the Middle East, however, were predominantly fought with politicians—heads of state, senior cabinet ministers, revolutionary and terrorist groups. The evidence suggests that the most diverse groups of potential opponents of MNE activities are found in the advanced democratic nations, particularly those exhibiting "participatory activism" on the part of citizens. One might also conclude that there is a tendency for all kinds of conflicts to become politicized in developing nations.

The distribution of the different types of opponents facing the five multinationals over time (year the conflict emerged) is also shown in Table 1-5. Citizen lobbies accounted for about one quarter of the conflicts in the period 1969-1972, but their relative role then dropped and stabilized at about 15%. Politicians initiated about one-third of the conflicts during the 1973-1975 period—those years when the debate over the "global reach"[34] of MNCs was raging full bloom in such forums as the United Nations and the United States Senate. During the next three years it appears that regulators moved into the driver's seat in conflict with the five multinationals. These figures are generally consistent with the classic "social issue life cycle" hypothesis—citizen lobbies often cause an issue to receive increasing awareness, expectations build, and demands for action get politicized, and ultimately standards regarding the issue may be codified in law or regulation.[35]

The data show that Gulf, ITT, and RTZ each tangled with politicians in about a third of their conflicts. The same three companies also encountered the largest relative exposure to citizen lobbies. Dow and RTZ, mainly because of their ownership and labor relations policies, experienced the greatest relative shares of conflicts with commercial opponents. Hoffmann-La Roche and Dow each tangled with regulators in at least one-half of their external battles.

THE TACTICS

Harold S. Geenen told his company's stockholders in the early 1960s that ITT had "in its time met and surmounted every device employed by governments to encourage their own industries and hamper those of foreigners, including taxes, tariffs, quotas, currency restrictions, subsidies, barter arrangements, guarantees, moratoriums, devaluations . . . yes and nationalizations."[36] If a listing of devices employed by opponents of ITT were made today, it would surely have to be much longer. The tactics used against multinationals have been as varied as the groups using them and the issues involved. Exhibit 1–3 provides a breakdown of eight general categories of tactics that we discovered opponents have used in their battles with our five sample multinationals.

As part of our survey of the conflicts of Dow, Gulf, ITT, Roche, and RTZ, we classified each of the 650 battles according to the primary tactic employed by the main opponent involved. The results, using the classification scheme of Exhibit 1–3, appear in Table 1–6. Administrative and legal tactics dominated the overall battleground, appearing in more than one-half of the conflicts. The kinds of tactics employed varied widely from one issue to the next. Terrorism, by definition, involved violence exclusively. Human rights controversies were marked by communicative, financial (proxy resolutions and stock divestitures), and symbolic tactics. Administrative interventions marked the political and marketing conflicts that confronted the five firms in one-half of the cases. Economic tactics (e.g., strikes) dominated the labor relations scene. And conflicts over questionable payments, environmental protection, technology, and economics/finance all involved strong legal-administrative tactics. We should note, however, the wide variety of tactics brought to bear on most of the issues.

Regulatory opponents naturally tended to employ administrative and legal means, while commercial opponents used economic and legal devices. The citizen lobby and political groups, on the other hand, appeared to employ a wider range of tactics. The geographic data in Table 1–6 dramatically reveal the litigiousness in North America—90% of all conflicts involving legal tactics occurred in the United States alone. As many have observed, litigation seems to have become America's secular religion—access to the courts to redress political grievances or sue for damages has become a widely accepted, relatively easy, and rather quick-impulse aspect of American life. Although 11% of the conflicts in Europe involved litigation, a much greater share of the battles there saw the use of administrative and communicative devices—a combined 60% for Europe versus 38% for North America. In the Third World, the primary tactics employed by opponents were administrative and economic. The composition of tactics confronting the five firms as a group throughout the world, however, remained relatively stable over the ten years studied.

The data on the five multinationals presented in Part 6 of Table 1–6 reveal some significant differences in the composition of tactics each of the firms confronted. Gulf and ITT found themselves enmeshed in litigation over bribery, acquisitions, antitrust and other matters, to a greater extent than the other three

Table 1-6 *Opponent Tactics in Multinational Corporate Conflict: 1969–1978*
(650 conflicts involving Dow, Gulf, ITT, Roche and RTZ; % rounded off)

	Legal	Legislative	Administrative	Financial	Economic	Communication	Symbolic	Violent
1. All Conflicts	24	5	31	5	14	15	2	4
2. Issue								
Terrorism	0	0	0	0	0	0	0	100
Human Rights	3	0	3	24	11	40	19	0
Politics	10	7	51	3	5	19	5	0
Questionable Payments	32	12	17	13	10	16	0	0
Marketing	28	5	51	0	2	12	2	0
Labor Relations	7	2	28	3	43	15	2	0
Environment	31	3	38	2	2	23	1	0
Technology	32	4	23	0	23	18	0	0
Economics / Finance	37	4	30	4	20	4	1	0
3. Opponent								
Citizen Lobby	15	1	2	21	7	41	13	0
Regulatory	36	0	61	1	1	1	0	0
Political	5	16	38	0	14	12	1	14
Commercial	41	0	2	5	37	15	0	0
4. Area								
North America	33	6	26	7	11	12	3	3
Europe	11	0	32	2	16	28	1	10
Latin America	5	5	58	0	13	9	0	10
Asia-Oceania	3	3	35	0	28	28	0	3
Africa	0	0	46	0	36	18	0	0
Middle East	6	12	47	0	29	0	0	6

5. Year

1969	27	7	28	7	14	14	3	0
1970	15	2	38	2	16	18	5	4
1971	38	3	23	6	15	15	0	0
1972	25	6	17	7	10	29	3	3
1973	21	5	38	2	8	13	2	11
1974	14	5	31	6	13	17	6	8
1975	26	5	33	3	17	10	2	4
1976	29	6	34	4	15	10	1	1
1977	27	5	29	8	15	13	1	2
1978[a]	31	3	34	9	13	10	0	0

6. Firm

Dow	16	2	42	2	20	14	3	1
Gulf	28	6	30	5	16	11	2	2
ITT	28	6	24	9	7	14	3	9
Roche	19	0	54	0	5	15	2	5
RTZ	14	10	17	2	17	38	0	2

[a]Data for first-half of 1978 only.

39

firms. RTZ was the target of considerable communicative abuse—one observer has noted that "no British company has been more attacked by leftwing radicals and conservationists than RTZ . . . "[37] But as Sir Val Ducan, RTZ's former chairman, once wryly remarked, "Taking the wealth out of the soil is an emotional business and it is only too easy for political and nationalistic feelings to run high."[38]

Roche in 54% of its external battles, and Dow in 42% of its conflicts, had to contend with administrative tactics associated with the growing blanket of government regulation and red tape that has covered their industries in recent years. In the pharmaceutical industry, Roche, of course, has not been alone. The entire industry, according to a recent report of the British industry-backed office of Health Economics, has been "subjected to growing public criticism and political pressure" and forced into a state of seige in all European Economic Community (EEC) countries. The suggested reason for this is that "if profit in any shape or form is already regarded with suspicion, then criticism is bound to increase when the profit in question is made 'at the expense of the sick' and when, to cover the risks of research, it is also higher than the average in other industries."[39] Dow, for its part, has been a leader in the fight against the regulatory morass that has emerged in Washington, D.C., sometimes nicknamed "malfunction junction." In 1975 Dow Chemical U.S.A. began to calculate the cost of federal regulations and their impact on the firm's operations, dividing the costs into three categories: "appropriate," "questionable," and "excessive." Dow's total regulatory costs in the United States in 1976 were $186 million, equivalent to about 5.5 cents on each dollar of sales. Those classified as "questionable" or "excessive" totaled $83 million in that year. Regulatory costs in 1977 jumped to $268 million, equivalent to seven cents on every United States sales dollar.[40] According to Dow President Paul F. Oreffice, "Regulation is the single most inflationary thing" affecting Dow, "government overintervention is threatening to ruin" America, and "the days when business people can sit back in the bushes and not participate in the public decision-making process are over" but, of course, "taking a high profile always has its risks."[41]

SO WHAT?

Our introductory tour of the arena of multinational corporate conflict is almost over. We have surveyed the issues, timing, location, opponents, and tactics involved in MNE conflict through the experience of five major multinationals. But perhaps the most critical question still remains—so what? Why should we care? What is the bottom-line?

The course and outcomes of conflict can entail major resource losses. Examples include Gulf's loss of oil concessions in Venezuela, Ecuador, and Kuwait as a result of government takeovers—which along with the loss of Iranian production due to political unrest in 1978–1980 caused Gulf's own international crude-oil supplies in the late 1970s to be "tight as hell" in the words of Chairman McAfee—lost production from strikes at ITT and RTZ facilities in the United States and Europe, and lost markets for chemical products of Dow or pharmaceutical products of Roche due to government bans on use or production for health or environmental reasons. Corporate property can also be lost through patent infringement, sabotage and accidents, bombings, and arson. ITT can attest to property damage in the millions of dollars from terrorist attacks on its facilities in such cities as Montevideo, Buenos Aires, New York, Rome, Milan, West Berlin, Zurich, Nuremberg, Beirut, and Paris. Along with losses of existing resources, the acquisition of future resources can be seriously impaired by conflict. Whether it is a Dow petrochemical venture in Japan, an RTZ mining concession in Indonesia, or offshore oil drilling by Gulf off the United States East Coast, long delays in receiving approval inevitably result in higher construction costs, lost market opportunities, and tied-up capital and manpower. Resource acquisition plans can also be totally stymied by conflict, with sizeable corporate funds expended in unproductive efforts. Dow's shelving of plans for a petrochemical complex in California and for a chlorine/caustic soda plant in Japan due to regulatory delays and obstruction are cases in point.

Conflicts can be costly in still other ways. Ransom payments to get back a kidnapped executive or extortion payments to corrupt officials to protect corporate assets can add up. So can damage payments, such as the millions of dollars of compensation shelled-out by Roche to victims of the poisonous gas cloud emitted in 1976 by a subsidiary at Seveso, Italy, or to the families of French children killed or permanently handicapped in 1972 by a French-made talc containing a Roche subsidiary's hexachlorophene. Fines, settlements, and legal fees can also be considerable. In August of 1978, for example, Gulf agreed to pay the United States Treasury $42.4 million in settlement for alleged overcharges of customers. Other payments by Gulf have involved fines for operating a currency laundering scheme that supported the company's illegal political gifts, back wages to minority and women employees denied promotions in its Texas refinery, compensation for damages from an oil well blowout at Santa Barbara, and fines for illegal gratuities paid to an Internal Revenue Service agent who supervised the auditing of Gulf's books. Legal fees like those associated with ITT's defense against countless antitrust suits regarding acquisitions represent another important cost of conflict.

One of the most serious consequences of conflict is that it often consumes a disproportionate amount of top management time and attention. A remarkable amount of time was consumed at Dow over the napalm issue, at ITT over Chilean intervention, and at Roche over Librium/Valium pricing in the United Kingdom. Gulf's top management was almost totally consumed in 1975 by conflicts over questionable payments abroad, political contributions at home, takeovers in Kuwait and Venezuela, suspension of operations in Angola because of civil war, possible merger terms of Rockwell International Corporation, contributing to a pro-Arab propaganda campaign in the United States, and so on.[42]

Conflicts can result in badly tarnished public images due to constant front page exposure, muckraking columns and editorials, diatribes on the floors of the UN or national legislatures, sensationalist books, and so on. At various points during the last decade, for example, Dow became known as a "prime Vietnam war beneficiary," RTZ as a "destroyer of the environment," Gulf as the "epitome of corruption," Roche as a "conscienceless profiteer at the expense of the sick," and ITT as "evil incarnate." Partly as a result of unsavory disclosures and widely publicized investigations in 1972–1973, the price of ITT stock went from $60 in August 1972 to about $35 in August 1973, and down further to $20 in July 1974. The company lost the investment community's support, and its stock decline caused a number of merger proposals to fall apart. In an attempt to change its unfavorable image, ITT embarked on a $6.4 million ad campaign in mid-January 1974.[43] The company's ability to turn its image around was greatly hampered, however, by a preoccupation of citizen lobbies and governmental agencies with what former President Hamilton in 1979 labeled "the far past"—wave after wave of allegations about past foreign payments and prior involvement in Chile continued to dominate shareholder meetings throughout the 1970s. Gulf likewise recognized its scandal-damaged image problem. In 1976 Chairman McAfee announced that the greatest challenge facing the company was "to restore our confidence in ourselves and our credibility with others."[44]

As McAfee's statement implies, the human element in organizations can easily be debilitated by conflict. Employee morale can sink under the burden of repeated revelations of wrongdoing. Constant streams of harsh public criticism, shareholder resolutions, demonstrations, consumer boycotts, and negative press can generate stress among employees, sometimes leading to low job satisfaction, reduced organizational commitment, and even poor performance. Executive stress can set in as a result of high levels of uncertainty or ambiguity concerning conflict outcomes. Frustration is likely to arise among executives whose missions get aborted, products discontinued, or projects shelved. Leadership is naturally disrupted when, for example, managers are arrested and thrown into jail (Dow in Italy), kidnapped by terrorists (ITT in Argentina), or ousted by boards of directors (Gulf's ouster of four top executives, including its chairman, for their roles in domestic and overseas payoffs). Finally, external conflicts may at times induce internal dissention within the firm. Almost from the first flurry of scandal at ITT in the early 1970s, fires reportedly raged between Mr. Geneen and his board. According to a former high-level ITT executive: "The board plagued him for years to give up [the job of] chief executive . . . everybody in the company knew it. There were the external pressures, street opinions and the scandals—they all made the board nervous."[45]

Our focus on the consequences of conflict has been on economic losses, conflict costs, tarnished images, and organizational disruption. But all is not negative. Multinational corporate conflict can also be legitimate, productive, and desirable for both individuals and organizations. The mere fact that Dow and Roche have been among the most profitable firms in their respective industries worldwide over the past decade dramatizes this point. Conflict is often a necessary condition for the attainment of corporate goals. Just as resources may be lost as a result of conflict, they can also be gained. And conflict can often be highly enjoyable, providing managers with a sense of excitement, intrigue, adventure, and challenge. As Adolf W. Jann, former chairman of Roche, once noted, "there is a certain pleasure in fighting, particularly in fighting back . . . a Roman cohort has nothing in comparison to our fighting team and spirit."[46] According to an expert on management style, "A key thing about Harold Geneen is his incredible taste for conflict . . . I know of no one who allows as much heat to build as this man."[47]

Many kinds of positive effects can flow from limited or controlled conflict.[48] It can foster internal cohesiveness, prevent stagnation, help clarify objectives, direct managerial attention to needed changes, and arouse motivation among employees to solve problems. Conflict may also stimulate curiosity, provide an hospitable environment for creativity, and result in better decisions because of the need to offer supporting evidence and arguments. The resolution of conflict can clarify positions of strength in the current power structure, open up new and lasting communication channels, and result in a reduction of tension by serving as a vehicle for catharsis. It lies at the root of personal, organizational, and societal change. It pinpoints needed modifications in organizational and managerial processes. It determines the direction of social change, and in effect defines social welfare. Precedents are established and standards of business conduct are clarified. Conflict can thus be viewed as a stimulant that, if held within bounds, can be the source of much progress.

Conflict in multinational corporate operations can thus be functional, dysfunctional, or both at the same time. The "best" MNE is not necessarily the one that is conflict-free—it is more likely one that is characterized by some "functional" level of external conflict. Our view is that proper management can significantly reduce the negative effects and enhance the positive effects of conflict.

It is important to note here that multinationals, including our five sample firms, have often badly mismanaged conflict. They have frequently misread the nature of conflict situations—under- or overestimating the amount of power at their disposal, misconceiving the real stakes riding on the conflict outcome, falsely defining occasions that might have permitted mutual gain as situations of pure "zero-sum" conflict, misinterpreting the quality of the firm's relationship with an opposing party, thereby missing useful communications opportunities, and so forth. Faulty diagnosis has often led multinationals to adopt inappropriate strategies and tactics in conflict.

Multinational corporate behavior, as in the case of ITT-Chile, has occasionally been unnecessarily arrogant, heavy-handed, and ruthless. In other cases it has been downright illegal or morally repugnant, with easily uncovered shenanigans backfiring and soiling the entire landscape of international business. Corporate executives have at times overreacted, wildly shooting from the hip. With narrow vision, they have occasionally failed to consider the impact abroad of measures taken in one nation, responses of competitors, or implications for the future.

Conflict emergence and escalation can often be attributed to misperception or biased perception among corporate executives. Insulated in their cloistered corporate headquarters, senior executives in companies like ITT or Roche may well have developed myopia and misunderstanding of new outside pressures. Such firms can become victims of "group-think"—the deterioration of mental efficiency, reality testing, and moral judgment that results from group pressures and excessive loyalty.[49] Executives operating under a "seige mentality" will tend to be suspicious of all outsiders and their motives and engage in stereotyped thinking. The danger in stereotyped views, of course, is that they can be self-confirming. A given multinational, for example, may expect social action groups to be wholly untrustworthy and therefore treat them (and any overtures they might make) with suspicion, thereby helping to elicit from them the very negative, hostile, and untrustworthy behavior that the firm suspected in the first place.

Many of the cases examined in the pages ahead reveal that multinationals have often been inadequately prepared to handle conflicts, particularly those associated with major crises or disasters, with poor communications that have served to intensify and perpetuate them. Consider the following:

At Gulf, company policy dictated that any communications with the press be cleared through the corporate secretary, a process that, at the minimum, required several days. As problems intensified, however, this policy became an Achilles' heel. Faced with picketing, protests, and a suddenly interested and unsympathetic press, Gulf managers either said nothing at all (strictly observing company policy) or reflected it, in effect believing it wasn't any of the public's business, which contributed to suspicions and hostilities between "them" and "us." Even senior managers, unused to dealing with reporters and unsure of how much they could say, missed frequent opportunities to explain misconceptions about the industry or to contribute to public understanding of problems. Operating managers were at a particular disadvantage. Isolated in their local communities and not authorized to discuss company policy, they found themselves besieged by environmentalists, social activists, consumer protectionists, and other special interest groups.[50]

Still other mistakes have resulted from failures to adapt corporate behavior in response to the dynamics of conflict situations. Some multinationals have fallen victim to processes of gradual and unwitting commitment. They have become locked into positions of excessive demands or insufficient concessions, thus making it less likely that the conflicts would be resolved cooperatively. Cases in point might include Gulf's stonewalling on questionable payments at home and abroad, Roche's vociferous and rigid challenge of the British government order to cut its tranquilizer prices, ITT's belligerence and lack of candor regarding intervention in Chile, Dow's unrelenting insistence on hoarding its superior chlorine/caustic soda technology in Japan, and RTZ's dogged determination to explore for minerals in Britain's most beautiful national park. Multinationals have often chosen to remain deadlocked in costly and unproductive conflicts, rather than to cut their losses and move on to greener pastures.

To summarize, we began this chapter by noting that multinational corporate conflict appears *inevitable*, given that MNEs operate in an environment of multiple interest groups that place conflicting demands on them. Such conflict is *different*, both in kind and in degree, form purely domestic conflict because of unique features both of the MNE itself and of the interdependent global system in which the conflict occurs. As a result, the disputes are often far more *complex*. And given the probable course of world events, it is likely that frequency and intensity of conflicts involving MNEs will be *increasing*. Our survey of the experiences of five major multinationals during a recent decade revealed that the challenge of conflict has been truly *diverse* and *pervasive* with respect to the kinds of issues, opponents, tactics, and areas involved. The structure of conflict was found to be growing increasingly *transnational* through time. And lastly we noted that multinational corporate conflict can be *consequential*, in both destructive and constructive ways, and that it has often been *mismanaged*. Our nine italicized words describe the "arena of conflict." We turn next to the ways multinationals can deal with conflict situations.

2 *THINKING ABOUT CONFLICT MANAGEMENT*

For many, "Life is just one damned thing after another." For multinational enterprises like Dow Chemical, Gulf Oil, Rio Tinto-Zinc, Hoffmann-La Roche, and International Telephone and Telegraph, "Life is just one damned conflict after another." Given the actors, issues, and outcomes in the game of multinational enterprise conflict, we need a coherent way of thinking about the problem in order eventually to learn how to diagnose and manage it constructively.

The first and perhaps most important lesson is that there are no simple cookbook approaches to dealing with conflict in multinational corporate operations—no panaceas, no foolproof strategies, no one best answer. Management is constantly bombarded by academics and consultants with just such "how to" approaches. Simplistic and often shortsighted prescriptions for "more joint ventures," "more fade-out arrangements," "more communication," "more social responsibility," "more disclosure," "more cooperation," "more morality," and the like dominate the literature. But none of these by themselves could possibly eliminate or resolve all the conflicts MNEs encounter—the profiles in the previous chapter show that conflicts in multinational operations are simply too heterogeneous, complex, dynamic, and uncertain.

A wide variety of corporate strategies and tactics exist that may be appropriate for dealing constructively with conflict. To use a currently fashionable expression in business policy and organizational behavior, "it all depends." What an enterprise should do is contingent upon the particular circumstances found in a specific conflict situation. Only after the situation has been properly diagnosed in a contingency framework by competent managers will certain normative guidelines appear plausible. Only a quack prescribes the same medicine for all patients. The professional first makes a careful assessment, then draws on his knowledge of available alternative actions and their effects, and only then does he prescribe. This contingency viewpoint forms the basic logic of our conflict management approach. It does not pretend to provide a foolproof guide to coping with all conflicts, everywhere, and for all time. A "science" of rational conflict management will probably never exist. The approach does, however, suggest some working themes concerning the usefulness of different types of managerial behavior under different conditions. As other observers have found: "The general tenor of the contingency view is somewhere between the simplistic, specific principles and complex, vague notions. It is a mid-range concept which recognizes the complexity involved in managing [conflict] but uses patterns of relationships and/or configurations of subsystems in order to facilitate improved practice."[1]

Our model provides a basis for analyzing situations of conflict in international business and for identifying behavioral strategies and tactics that are most likely to obtain outcomes consistent with the attainment of MNE goals. Our perspective is thus purely managerial. The basic task is determining which strategies and kinds of behavior are most functional or appropriate given the desired outcomes and notions of feasibility. How useful different kinds of behavior are, of course, ultimately has to be judged according to long-run corporate objectives. Our model assumes rationality—that multinationals will make choices calculated to maximize their own long-term gains and minimize their losses—and much of the framework is well grounded in systematic theory and research, representing a blending of economics, political science, social psychology, game theory, and organizational behavior. The model is simplified and emphasizes central features and determinants, but can accommodate a proliferation of specific detail if required. By laying out the range of behavioral options available in handling conflict, identifying the key variables relevant in the diagnosis of conflict situations, and suggesting functional linkages among behaviors and situations, we hope that the model will help managers of multinationals to cope more constructively with that inevitable stream of "one damned conflict after another."

TWO DIMENSIONS OF CONFLICT BEHAVIOR

The overwhelming majority of studies on conflict have treated conflict behavior as a "unidimensional" variable, ranging from uncooperative at one extreme to cooperative at the other. But the "uncooperative-cooperative" dichotomy greatly oversimplifies the more complex range and richness of behavioral options available to a multinational enterprise in conflict.[2] When a MNE meets a conflict situation, it is likely to have at least two basic considerations in mind.[3] One is a concern for producing *results*, that is, getting a satisfactory outcome from, or resolution to, the disagreement. Another is concern for the *relationship* that the MNE needs or wants with the opposition. A firm's behavior in dealing with conflict is likely to be determined in large measure by the emphasis it places on each of these concerns. With this in mind, we have adapted a well-known two-dimensional model of conflict behavior.[4] The conflict-management scheme, as viewed from the perspective of one multinational enterprise, is illustrated in Exhibit 2-1.

The term "cooperativeness" defines the extent to which management is willing to help satisfy the concerns or interests of the other party (or parties) with which it is in conflict. As the figure shows, this dimension can be viewed as a continuum, with very uncooperative behavior (hostile, distrustful, unhelpful, stubborn) at one end of the scale and very cooperative behavior (friendly, trustful, helpful, complaisant) at the other. Increased cooperativeness implies greater attention to, acceptance of, concern for, communication about, interaction with, and efforts to meet the needs and desires of the other party.

The term "assertiveness" refers to the extent to which management is willing to take a high profile in order to satisfy its own concerns or interests in a conflict. This can likewise be viewed as a continuum, extending from very unassertive behavior (passive, weak, lethargic, nonaggressive) at one extreme to very assertive behavior (active, strong, vigorous, aggressive) at the other. Increased assertiveness implies greater confidence and initiative, persistent determination, and energetic pursuit of the firm's own ends. This typically entails greater investment of organizational time, manpower, and other resources, and is often embodied in a distinct managerial "style" of the enterprise.

Exhibit 2–1
Two-Dimensional Model of Conflict Behavior*

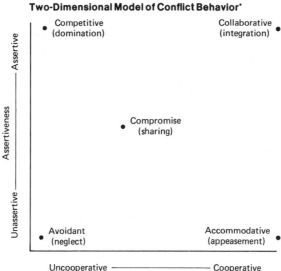

*Source: Kenneth W. Thomas, "Conflict and Conflict Management," p. 900, in Marvin D Dunnette, ed., *Handbook of Industrial and Organizational Psychology* (Chicago: Rand McNally, 1976).

There is, of course, an infinite variety of possible combinations of the two dimensions. Analytical emphasis can be given, however, to the five "pure" combinations corresponding to the corners and midpoint of the grid shown in Exhibit 2–1, which represent the extremes of what may be viewed as behavioral "zones." The five distinct modes or styles of handling conflict, together with their preferred outcomes, are as follows[5]: *Competing,* with the hope of achieving domination, is assertive and uncooperative. *Avoiding,* in order to neglect or withdraw from a conflict, is unassertive and uncooperative. *Accommodating,* for the purpose of appeasing the other party, is unassertive and cooperative. *Collaborating,* with the desire to fully integrate and satisfy the concerns of both parties, is assertive and cooperative. *Compromising,* in order to "split the difference" in bargaining, is intermediate in both assertiveness and cooperativeness.

It should be noted that there is no one-to-one correspondence between behavioral modes and the desired outcomes, and that the five conflict-handling styles only represent ways of *coping with* conflict, not necessarily ways of *resolving* conflict. Only collaboration and sharing represent conflict resolution processes in the sense of joint satisfaction of the opposing parties. Each of the conflict-handling modes has been variously described and investigated in detail.[6] It is our belief that all of them are essential to a multinational enterprise, at one time or another, for any effective overall program of managing conflict. We shall examine each of these five "pure" modes in a real world context in order to set the stage for a discussion of major types of conflicts facing multinationals where the model may be usefully applied. In the next chapter, we shall explore how these "pure" modes can be utilized, both simultaneously and sequentially, in the course of successfully managing a single conflict. We shall also explore the conditions under which each may be appropriately employed.

COMPETITION

A competitive (relatively assertive and uncooperative) way of handling conflict is often exhibited by MNEs when the goal is to overpower or suppress their adversaries. The aim is generally to dominate—that is, to fully obtain the specific outcome that the enterprise desires even at the expense of one or more other parties. The emphasis is on ending open conflict by creating a victor and a vanquished. Competition thus seeks only to *control* the open expression of conflict. It does not attempt to *resolve* its underlying causes. Aggressiveness, belligerence, stubbornness, obfuscation, and polarization often characterize behavior in the competitive mode. Here are a few cases—many of which will be elaborated upon later—where multinational corporate behavior has been predominantly competitive:

Case 1. In May of 1974, the "Third World Action Group" (TWAG) based in Bern, Switzerland published a pamphlet entitled "Nestlé Kills Babies." This adaptation of the London-based "War On Want" publication, *The Baby Killer,* charged that in less developed areas of the world, the promotion and use of powdered infant formula in lieu of breast feeding contributed to infant mortality and malnutrition. Nestlé Alimentana of Vevey, Switzerland sued TWAG for libel, and the trial began in Bern in November of 1975. The trial stimulated great interest and focused attention around the world on Nestlé's marketing practices and the infant formula issue. Nestlé won what may be regarded as a victory in the libel action, but the Swiss presiding judge emphasized that his decision was "not an acquittal of Nestlé."[7] The company thereafter became the target of a massive worldwide protest movement which included a well-organized "Boycott Nestlé" campaign.

Case 2. On September 8, 1975, the Westinghouse Electric Corporation announced that because the price of uranium had increased so rapidly, it would be unable to supply 65 million pounds of the nuclear reactor fuel that it was obligated to deliver to 27 utilities under long-term contracts. The utilities quickly sued Westinghouse for breach of contract. With potentially more than $2.5 billion in damages at stake, Westinghouse's defense was that unexpected events—including alleged cartel price-fixing—inflated the price of uranium and restricted supplies, thus calling into play the "commercial impracticality" clause of the U.S. Uniform Commercial Code. In a counteraction, Westinghouse brought an antitrust suit in Chicago on October 15, 1976, charging 29 domestic and foreign uranium producers with forming a cartel, fixing prices, refusing to sell to Westinghouse, and charging Westinghouse discriminatory prices. Those sued included Gulf Oil and Anaconda based in the United States, Rio Tinto-Zinc in Great Britain, Noranda Mines and Denison Mines in Canada, Uranerzgesellschaft in Germany, Nufcor in South Africa, Queensland Mines and Ranger Export Development Co. in Australia, and the Paris-based Groupement d'Interet Economique pour la Commercialisation de l'Uranium. "It's going to turn out to be a world-wide scandal, and we're going to prove it," said Westinghouse.[8] The dispute turned into one of the "thorniest legal imbroglios" in modern times and is likely to keep a horde of lawyers fully employed well into the late 1980s.

Case 3. Boeing Co. disclosed in 1976 that it had paid about $70 million to foreign consultants since 1970 but contended that it had done nothing illegal. As part of its investigation of corporate bribery, the U.S. Securities and Exchange Commission pressed Boeing to disclose the names of agents and consultants who had received the payments. A clash ensued, with Boeing refusing to disclose "proprietary and confidential information that could cause substantial, irreparable harm to Boeing if released." Boeing gained the support of the U.S. Department of State, which in a document filed with the U.S. Court of Appeals stated that disclosure of the names "could reasonably be expected to cause damage to the foreign relations of the United States"—a judicial protective order covering most details of the company's foreign payments was obtained. It became known, however, that the Boeing consultants were officials or persons closely associated with the governments of Argentina, Brazil, India, Saudi Arabia, Iran, Libya, Sudan, and United Arab Emirates, among others. Boeing settled SEC charges that its questionable overseas payments violated federal securities laws in 1978. The company also agreed to a far-reaching consent order with the Federal Trade Commission that prohibits payoffs to "anyone" abroad—an agreement more restrictive than the Foreign Corrupt Practices Act, which only makes it illegal for American firms to bribe foreign government officials.[9]

Case 4. Sixty-three major United States-based MNEs and banks joined together to form the Emergency Committee for American Trade (ECAT) during the early 1970s. Along with the U.S. Chamber of Commerce and the National Association of Manufacturers, ECAT mounted an aggressive lobbying campaign during 1971–1974 against the AFL-CIO backed "Hartke-Burke" bill that would have, among other things, imposed mandatory import quotas, removed foreign tax credits, and granted the President of the United States powers to prohibit exports of capital and technology. In 1975 and 1976, many of the companies and industry groups involved assembled a new coalition, called the "Special Committee for U.S. Exports." A powerful lobbying effort was organized to fight tax legislation that would have eliminated an export tax incentive arrangement, the Domestic International Sales Corporation (DISC).[10]

Case 5. India's Foreign Exchange Regulation Act, which came into force in 1973, required foreign companies to reduce their equity stake in Indian operations to between 40% (in low priority areas) and 74% (in exports and high technology), with 100% foreign ownership possible only if production was exclusively for export. In the summer of 1977, India's new Industry Minister, George Fernandes, demanded that Coca-Cola turn over its "know-how" to a new India-controlled soft drink company that would take over Coca-Cola's business in the country. The American company would be granted a 40% share in the new enterprise. Coca-Cola announced that it was willing to form an Indian company with 40% equity, but only if it could retain 100% ownership of another company controlling quality and dispensing its secret concentrate. Coke's formula—based on an ingredient called "7X" which provides the distinctive flavor—has been one of the world's most closely guarded commercial secrets for over 90 years. The Indian government refused Coca-Cola's offer, insisting that the formula absolutely had to be turned over so the government could control operations of the firm. India's hard-line approach was matched by Coca-Cola's insistence that it would never deliver the secret of its formula, which according to gossip is kept in a Georgia bank vault and is known to no more than ten people in the world. With little chance of compromise and nonrenewal of Coca-Cola's import license for concentrate ingredients, Coke pulled out and, to paraphrase its advertising jingles, would no longer "add life" or "teach the world to sing in perfect harmony," in India.[11]

Case 6. On April 6, 1972, Enka Glanzstoff, the fiber subsidiary of the Dutch chemical firm Akzo, announced plans to close fiber plants in the Netherlands, Belgium, West Germany, and Switzerland, affecting some 5000 to 6000 employees. When Enka tried to close a polyester plant in the Dutch town of Breda, it ran into fierce resistance. Unions in Belgium and Germany supported the Dutch workers who had seized the plant, and when public opinion turned against Akzo, it cancelled the plan. Three years later, in 1975, when Enka was reportedly losing $400,000 per day, Akzo again announced plans to close operations in three countries, eliminating 3100 jobs before the end of 1976 and phasing out an additional 3000 by the end of 1977. On the advice of McKinsey & Co., Akzo decided to avoid trouble spots such as the Breda plant. Akzo's two major Dutch and German unions, inspired by the International Federation of Chemical, Energy and General Workers Unions, called for discussions with the company to be held only on an international basis, hoping to set a precedent in multinational labor cooperation against multinational firms. Dutch Prime Minister Joop den Uyl publicly called on Akzo to consult with the unions on an international level, an action that brought an enraged letter from the Akzo Board blasting his "one-sided and emotional . . . distrust of international companies." Akzo steadfastly refused to talk on a multinational level, and successfully "busted" the front organized by Charles Levinson of the International Federation by appealing to desires of small Dutch unions who did not want an all out confrontation during a recession. Akzo was thus able to handle the plant closings through its labor unions in each separate country. By late 1977, Akzo was 17,000 employees slimmer and was creeping back toward profitability.

Case 7. In a 1976 pamphlet entitled "The Oil Conspiracy," the Center for Social Action of the United Church of Christ charged that Mobil Oil was supplying petroleum to Rhodesia "through a series of fictitious South African companies." When the Center disclosed its charges in a public meeting assisted by the People's Bicentennial Commission, Mobil heatedly denied charges of violating United States sanctions against trade with the then white-ruled Rhodesia, and characterized the Commission as a "far left organization." In September of 1976, Mobil's chief legal officer appeared before the Senate Foreign Relations Committee and described the entire episode as an "artful blend of fact and fiction" and a "skillfully contrived publicity scheme" for political ends. Mobil's management in 1977 refused to support a resolution by the United Church Board for World Ministry of New York that would have required the company to make certain that its petroleum products were not being sent to Rhodesia through Mobil's operations in South Africa. Mobil declared that it was unable to investigate the charges because of the South African Official Secrets Act. In May of 1977 the United States Treasury announced that after a lengthy investigation it was unable to determine if Mobil was guilty of violating the American trade embargo because the South African government denied the United States agency access to documents of Mobil's South African affiliate. But after an official commission in the U.K. forced Shell and British Petroleum to admit that they had participated in a secret scheme to ensure Rhodesian supplies, the U.S. Treasury Department renewed its investigation of possible sanctions violations by Mobil and Caltex in late 1978.[13]

Case 8. On November 29, 1962, the French and British governments signed an agreement to jointly design and develop a supersonic airliner which came to be known as the Concorde. Scheduled supersonic passenger service by Air France and British Airways—from Paris to Rio de Janeiro and London to Bahrain—started on January 21, 1976. Authorization for a 16-month test of passenger flights into Washington's Dulles International Airport and New York City's Kennedy International Airport was obtained on February 4, 1976. Within weeks, in response to massive protest against noise levels from Kennedy area residents and their political representatives, the New York State legislature and the Port Authority of New York and New Jersey (the airport operator) barred landing at New York pending a six-month study of tests elsewhere. With the New York-Europe route representing by far the most lucrative market for the Concorde, and with Air France and British Airways facing massive deficits in their supersonic operations, the two companies began a fierce onslaught to obtain Kennedy landing rights. Legal maneuvers challenging the constitutionality of the Port Authority's ban, public relations efforts with New York City residents, and diplomatic pressures at the highest levels were initiated. On April 22, 1977, French President Valéry Giscard d'Estaing met with American Secretary of State Cyrus R. Vance to urge acceptance of the Concorde. On September 15, 1977, French Prime Minister Raymond Barre took the case for Concorde landing rights directly to President Carter in a meeting at the White House. The year 1977 was also marked by a cascade of court proceedings, demonstrations, and angry charges, both in and out of court. On October 17, 1977, the U.S. Supreme Court lifted the 19-month-old ban, climaxing the long and bitter struggle. A program of trial flights at Kennedy, followed by regular commercial service, began shortly thereafter.[14]

These cases and many others presented in later chapters show that competitive behavior can take a wide variety of forms. It can involve outright rejection of demands such as Coca-Cola's over its secret formula in India, Akzo on multinational labor bargaining, and Mobil on investigation of oil supplies to Rhodesia. As we shall see later on, it can also include appeals to higher authorities along the lines of Copperweld's plea to the United States Congress for help in preventing its takeover by Société Imetal of France, General Telephone and Electronic Corporation's campaign of protest to United States agencies over alleged bribery on the part of Hughes Aircraft in Indonesia, or the filing of a complaint by Alcoa, Reynolds, and Kaiser with the International Center for the Settlement of Investment Disputes in a bauxite tax battle with Jamaica. Strenuous lobbying like that of ECAT with United States legislators over Hartke-Burke, or Boeing with the U.S. State Department over disclosure demands of the SEC, is another form of the competitive mode. So is the initiation of diplomatic intervention by the home government, as in the case of the Concorde. Formal litigation also comes into play, ranging from Nestlé's Swiss libel action to the Westinghouse antitrust suit against the alleged uranium cartel. One would also include the "hot mineral" suits brought by MNEs in third countries against governments that have allegedly unlawfully expropriated their property; for example, Kennecott versus Chile, British Petroleum versus Libya, Compagnie Française des Petroles versus Algeria, and Anglo-Iranian Oil Co. versus Iran, as discussed in Chapter 7. Finally, at the extreme, we could also include blatant direct political involvement along the lines of United Fruit in Guatemala in the 1950s, Union Minière in Katanga in the 1960s, or ITT in Chile in the 1970s. We shall discuss some of these cases in greater detail in the chapters to follow.

The competitive mode chiefly relies on a strategy of power and tactics of coercion, leverage, threat, and deception. Without the opposing party's trust as an asset, power is essentially limited to the coercive type, which tends to be rather costly in physical and business resources.[15] Contingent and noncontingent threats are often employed to deter or compel responses by the opponent.[16] Strong commitments are usually made to fixed positions or preferred alternatives, thus limiting flexibility. Cards are played close to the vest, and available communications channels and opportunities often go unused—or their use may be designed to mislead or intimidate the other party. A "dialogue of the deaf" gives rise to espionage or other techniques to obtain information. Deliberate confusion and obfuscation are inherent and perhaps necessary in the competitive mode. Generally, few attempts are made to recognize and separate conflicts over facts from conflicts over differences in values and attitudes. "Put your foot down where you mean to stand" and "nice guys finish last" are the watchwords of such win-lose power struggles.

AVOIDANCE

An avoidance—relatively unassertive and uncooperative—style of handling conflict is generally employed by MNEs when they want to steer clear of something considered harmful or undesirable for the enterprise. The objective is typically to refrain or retreat from involvement in conflicts and thus direct organizational efforts to greener pastures. This orientation often involves withdrawal, indifference, passivity, evasion, ignorance, apathy, flight, reliance on fate, and isolation.[17] Here are some examples of multinational corporate behavior that appear to be predominately avoiding in nature:

Case 1. More than 4000 businessmen, many associated with multinational firms, have been kidnapped worldwide since 1974 by political terrorists and nonideological gangsters who have been active in many nations, including West Germany, France, Italy, Northern Ireland, Mexico, Venezuela, Colombia, Uruguay, and Argentina. During 1973 the executive kidnap rate in Argentina was 10 per month, with executives from multinationals such as Ford Motor, Kodak, The First National Bank of Boston, and British American Tobacco entering the statistics. As a result, Exxon, Ford Motor, and General Motors, among other firms, quietly pulled most of their American executives out of Argentina in 1974. By the time the Isabel Peron regime was toppled, only a handful of American businessmen were working in Buenos Aires.[18]

Case 2. The Control Data Corporation announced on October 25, 1977—just after a wave of repressive moves by the South African government against blacks and their sympathizers—that "at the present time, our company does not consider it appropriate to enlarge our investments in South Africa."[19] CDC thus became one of the rare American companies to adopt, at least on a temporary basis, a policy of non-expansion in South Africa, where it employs just 150 workers. The company's statement came in response to an inquiry from the United Church Board for World Ministries, which had been urging companies to withdraw from South Africa. CDC thus avoided future conflict with American church groups.

Case 3. Automation Industries Inc., a United States-based systems engineering, testing, and technical-services company, admitted to the SEC that it had made $900,000 in questionable payments overseas. When asked months later by a reporter how the crackdown on bribery had affected its sales, the company reported that its payments problem had been resolved. It had "simply got out" of perhaps the most payoff-prone region in the world; it had "terminated business in the Mideast." About the same time, Lockheed Chairman Robert W. Haack reported that his company had lost "an eight-figure contract" because it refused to buy a new Mercedes for a foreign purchasing agent. Other MNEs reporting lost sales as a result of refusing to make questionable payments include Dow, ITT, Union Carbide, Abbott Labs, and many American construction firms.[20]

Case 4. Jacobs A. G. Zürich, a Swiss-based holding company, announced a plan in 1977 to split the ownership of its coffee plant at Bremen, West Germany, between the existing German subsidiary and a new Swiss affiliate. This restructuring would reduce the staff of the German company from 2800 to less than 2000. Under the new worker participation law in Germany (*Mitbestimmung*) which came into effect in 1978, only companies employing 2000 or more employees are required to fill half of the seats on their supervisory boards with worker representatives. Jacobs' plan was interpreted as a move by Europe's leading coffee company to evade the new law's requirements.[21]

Case 5. During 1977, Canadian Industries (an Imperial Chemical Industries affiliate), the Canadian subsidiary of Standard Brands, Bank of Montreal, Bell Canada, Canadian Pacific, Northern Telecom, Royal Bank of Canada, Combustion Engineering, and Alcan, moved some of their operations and personnel out of Québec and into other Canadian provinces. Besides this exodus, many prominent firms remaining in Québec were reportedly reluctant to expand. The jitters were induced by statements attributed to Premier René Levesque and his independence-minded Parti Québecois, which took control of the Québec government in late 1976. The issues generating uncertainty included the new language law mandating French as the "language of work," nationalization of industries such as asbestos, and most important, the drive for separation which could isolate Québec companies from the rest of Canada.[22] By 1979, dozens of other firms, including such MNEs as Allis Chalmers, Du Pont, Bristol Myers, and British Airways had moved or decided to move important offices out of the province.

Case 6. In the fall of 1964, Goodyear refused to sell a modern synthetic rubber plant to Rumania on the grounds that "even to a dedicated profit-making organization, some things are more important than dollars. Take the best of the U.S. and the free world for example. You can't put a price tag on freedom . . . Goodyear stood firmly on the side of freedom, as a foe of aggression." In January of 1965, however, Firestone announced that after extensive negotiations it had worked out a preliminary contract with Rumanian officials for building a synthetic rubber plant. In the months that followed, Firestone found itself subjected to unusual competitive pressures and a nuisance boycott campaign conducted by the Young Americans for Freedom, a conservative political organization. Demonstrations, pickets, letters, and handbills emerged around the United States with slogans such as "when red wheels are rolling, the name is known as Firestone." On April 20, 1965, Firestone announced that it had "terminated negotiations for a contract to design and equip a synthetic rubber plant in Rumania."[23]

Case 7. During the period 1962 to 1972, Australians had watched American and British interests take over 21 local food companies. On April 27, 1972, the International Telephone and Telegraph Corporation announced that it was to make a bid for all of the issued shares of Frozen Food Industries Ltd., a Melbourne-based snack food manufacturer. All but one of the Frozen Food directors recommended that shareholders accept the offer, and Australia's leading financial daily declared "ITT's chances of success in its FFI bid appear assured." Less than one week later ITT hastily postponed its bid, pending the government's clarification of its policy on foreign direct investment in Australia. The outcry from the one dissenting director of FFI and the Australian and Labour Democratic Parties against ITT had been enormous.[24]

Case 8. In the mid-1950s, the Shell Oil Company began to look for a new location for a refinery on the Atlantic coast of the United States. The company found its preferred site in an area called Blackbird Hundred on the shore of the Delaware Bay in the state of Delaware. A bitter struggle to get the agricultural land rezoned for heavy industrial use was waged in 1961. Shell won the battle, but as one journalist commented, "This was a pyrrhic victory, for in the court of public opinion Shell had lost the war." Ten years later, in January of 1971, Shell announced that it planned to start construction of a $200 million refinery at its Blackbird Hundred site in 1973. The environmentally-oriented Governor Russell W. Peterson swiftly promised to do everything he could "to see that the refinery is not built" in Delaware. The emotional controversy over the project precipitated the passage of Delaware's 1971 Coastal Zone Act, banning heavy industry from a strip about two miles wide along the State's coast, where Shell's property was located. Subsequently, the company's local attorney announced: "Faced with the prospect of extensive litigation to challenge the validity of the arguably invalid provisions of the Act, or waiting a long-term shift in the pendulum of hysteric public opinion generated by Mr. Peterson's shameful and disreputable 'To hell with Shell' campaign, Shell naturally chose not to exacerbate the then clearly inhospitable climate in Delaware. Accordingly, in order to meet anticipated long-range East Coast energy supply requirements, Shell was forced to seek an alternative site in the Delaware Valley, and has acquired property along the Delaware River in New Jersey . . ."[25]

The avoidance mode is probably the most common method of dealing with conflicts in multinational operations, but paradoxically it is also the least evident since most instances of such behavior are not readily observable. Avoidance takes many forms. One is departing from situations where potential conflict is expected, like Jacobs' organizational restructuring in order to avoid *Mitbestimmung*, or the exodus of firms from Québec. Other examples include shelving of projects in Argentina during the early 1970s by Cities Service, Exxon, and Dow Chemical as a result of surging nationalism and political instability, or the quiet reductions in exposure by a number of multinationals in France during 1976–1977 in expectation of an election victory by the nationalization-minded "Union de la Gauche" in March 1978. Another variation of withdrawal is fleeing the scene of actual conflicts, such as ITT disconnecting in Australia on frozen foods, Firestone terminating negotiations with Rumania, Automation Industries getting out of the Middle East, Shell moving to New Jersey, and General Motors pulling expatriate managers out of terror-ridden Argentina.

Surely the most prevalent form of avoidance is abstinence. Countless MNEs have eschewed investments in nations or regions with high social or political conflict potential, rejected takeover or merger bids for fear of antitrust action, shunned deals requiring large bribes to government officials, postponed needed price increases during government freezes, withheld new products, technologies, or advertising campaigns for fear of consumerist or environmentalist outcries, avoided closing plants or laying off workers in order to bypass union and government protest, and so on. Examples include the Control Data and Goodyear cases reported above, as well as other cases, discussed later, where American firms operating in Canada complied with the U.S. Trading with the Enemy Act by refusing to sell flour and office furniture to Cuba, drugs to North Vietnam, or trucks and aluminum to the People's Republic of China. One could also point to the sidestepping of public opposition in the New England region of the United States over oil refineries and subsequent location of refineries in the Canadian Atlantic Provinces by firms such as Texaco and Gulf Oil Company. The common practice of European multinationals of setting up shop in the Deep South and Appalachian regions in the United States, where organized labor is weakest, could also be noted.

In addition to withdrawal and abstinence, some more subtle forms of avoidance can be recognized. For example, a multinational may refuse to be drawn into controversy by attempting to maintain strict neutrality. Or a firm may "decide not to decide" and deflect or displace conflict onto other actors—as when a company tries to convince an adversary that its battle is really with someone else. Or the enterprise may try to insulate itself from conflict, as Coca-Cola has done with its worldwide franchise system. By operating through a system of nominally independent bottlers, the company can legally claim not to be responsible for the unpopular actions—bribery and unfair labor practices, for example—of its franchisees. The system thus allows Coca-Cola to at least partly disassociate itself from conflicts and keep its image more or less untarnished.[26]

Whatever the form of avoidance, the common thread is "distancing." Segregation is sought so that opposing sensibilities do not come into play in the same place or at the same time. Although avoidance is sometimes only a product of indecision or timidity, the goal is to eventually attain a conflict-free state of affairs. Communication in the avoidance mode is naturally at a minimal level—"silence is golden" and "no news is good news." Behavior is low-profile, designed to escape attention and minimize interaction with actual or potential adversaries.

COLLABORATION

A collaborative (relatively assertive and cooperative) way of dealing with conflict is occasionally used by MNEs when the objective is to satisfy the concerns of both themselves and other parties. The aim is to integrate all of the parties' respective concerns through collaborative effort. Conflicting interests are directly confronted, and joint optimization of those interests is sought. Collaboration is not a *rejection* of conflict, but rather its *conversion* into direct problem solving.[27] As a result, corporate behavior is often proactive, synergistic, trusting, and innovative. Consider the following:

Case 1. Often working with the governments involved, a number of MNEs have engaged in product innovation for the special conditions and technological needs of developing nations. Some have learned how to "invent backwards" in order to provide "appropriate" technology. Ford Motor, for example, developed a special "developing nations tractor," and in competition with General Motors pushed a "Basic Transportation Vehicle", designed for easy assembly plus maximum utility and durability for developing Asian markets. Colgate-Palmolive invented a hand-operated washing machine and Exxon devised a simplified kerosene stove. A hand-cranked developing-country cash register was "reinvented" by National Cash Register, while Coca-Cola attempted to market a drink in the third world that is nutritious as well as refreshing.[28]

Case 2. At the 1977 annual meeting of Skandinaviska Enskilda Banken—the heart of the Wallenberg banking and industrial empire in Sweden—a significant employee profit-sharing plan was approved. The plan called for the bank's 7200 employees to be allocated a specific amount of money from each years' profits. These funds would be placed in a central fund and used to acquire shares in the bank. The plan was thought to represent a precursor of similar programs throughout Swedish industry, since it represented a response to the highly controversial labor-backed Meidner Program, which called for the creation of trade-union controlled funds to acquire corporate shares in a similar fashion. According to the Bank's Chairman, "We will be forced to accept some kind of profit-sharing system in the future . . . It's best that we take the first moves and lead development in the proper direction."[29]

Case 3. During the mid-1970s, both the U.S. Department of Justice and many United States-based multinationals came to believe that the world economic situation was changing so fast that existing antitrust guidelines did not answer a number of knotty questions pertaining to exports and operations overseas. One uncertainty was how to deal with state monopolies, such as those in Eastern Europe, or with buyers like those in Mexico who were following detailed national economic plans, or with monolithic consortiums of traders, manufacturers and financial institutions, such as the huge Japanese *Zaibatsu*. In a drive to make sure that fear of antitrust prosecution was not restraining exports by American firms, the Justice Department called upon major corporations to identify possible antitrust problems in their export business. Monsanto, Union Carbide and Hercules were among firms that sat down with Justice Department lawyers in an attempt to constructively resolve such potential problems.[30]

Case 4. Over the years, a number of European-based enterprises have accepted, or even encouraged, talks and agreements with their unions on a multinational basis. Glaverbel, the Belgian glass company controlled by the French group BSN-Gervais Danone, for example, signed a formal protocol in 1975 with trade unions from five European nations. The agreement promised to spread employment fairly among these countries and to set up a joint international committee that would meet twice a year to monitor implementation of the accord. In the fall of 1977, officials of the International Metalworkers Federation (IMF)—a worldwide labor organization—and local Swedish unions met with SKF Industries management at the company's headquarters to talk about changes in the way the company allocates production among the countries in which it operates. Talks with IMF officials on investment and production plans and their effects on employment also took place in 1977 with Volvo in Eindhoven, Holland. Volvo's managing director and trade unionists from Sweden, Belgium, and Holland attended. Other firms that have held talks with international union officials include Philips, Brown-Boveri, Nestlé, and Dunlop Pirelli.[31]

Case 5. In response to a mutually recognized need for close working contacts of a consultative nature between the United Nations Environment Programme (UNEP) and the world's multinational petroleum firms, 19 oil companies and six industry associations created the International Petroleum Industry Environmental Conservation Association (IPIECA). In response to joint concerns of the United States government and the chemical industry regarding the urgent need for better information regarding the health and environmental effects of chemical products, the Chemical Industry Institute of Toxicology (CIIT) was established in the United States in 1975. The aims of CIIT are to facilitate communications, develop new testing methods, and conduct toxicological studies on large volume, nonproprietary chemicals to determine their safety, especially under long term exposure. The eleven charter members were Air Products, Allied Chemical, Dow Chemical, Diamond Shamrock, Eastman Kodak, DuPont, Exxon Chemical, Monsanto, Shell Chemical, Stauffer Chemical and Union Carbide.[32]

Case 6. The economy of Guyana is heavily dependent on two products, sugar and bauxite. During the 1960s, the sugar industry was dominated by Booker Sugar Estates, a subsidiary of Britain's Booker McConnell Ltd., and the bauxite industry was dominated by the Demerara Bauxite Company, a subsidiary of Canada's Alcan Aluminium Ltd. Faced with intensifying nationalistic pressures, Booker embarked upon a comprehensive program to win Guyanese acceptance by drastically increasing its contribution to the local economy. Working closely with government departments, the company promoted the formation of new business ventures, encouraged the expansion of independent cane farming, helped develop local government infrastructure, sought local equity participation, progressively "Guyanized" its management, and generally attempted to reduce the industry's traditional paternalism. Alcan, which did not engage in such a program, was suddenly nationalized on February 23, 1971. Booker's efforts to embody Guyanese goals in its corporate strategy allowed the company to operate unscathed until the summer of 1976, when a government takeover was negotiated.[33]

Case 7. On April 7, 1967, Freeport Indonesia Inc.—a subsidiary of Freeport Minerals Corp.—and the government of Indonesia signed a "work contract" regarding development of a copper mine in the remote Irian Jaya mountains. With the government anxious to begin exploiting its copper resources, Freeport was granted liberal tax concessions. The $200 million copper mining venture began operations in 1973. At the inauguration ceremonies Indonesia's President Suharto said: "I also trust that the mining activities in this area will not forget to pay attention to ways to assist the community around this project in achieving its progress." This was a special challenge for Freeport because the local population consisted of 1500 members of the Amungme mountain tribe, who prior to the project had lived almost totally unexposed to Indonesian or any other outside culture. Freeport, working with the government and a consulting firm specializing in social action programs, developed and implemented a major program to assist the local tribe in improving its health and living conditions, and to help promote income producing, self-sustaining enterprises based on existing agriculture. Two hundred tribesman have been employed and modern hygiene, medical facilities, nutrition, improved housing, and education have been introduced in the villages.[34]

Case 8. Long before the environmental storm broke in the United States, AMAX Inc. committed itself to working with, not against, environmentalists in the planning of its projects. While planning its $500 million Henderson molybdenum mine in the Rocky Mountains near Empire, Colorado, for example, the company launched a unique "Experiment in Ecology" in 1967. AMAX management set up a joint committee of company executives and representatives from a local citizens group, the Colorado Open Space Coordinating Council. The purpose was to find ways in which the ore could be mined and a mill operated with minimal harm to the environment. The committee met periodically over a seven-year period to discuss, monitor and make suggestions about the development of the Henderson ore body. The cooperative effort, and the many innovative aspects of the resulting project design, received wide acclaim from environmentalists around the country. After ten years of development and an estimated $100 million in expenditures to avoid environmental problems, the Henderson mine came on stream in 1976.[35]

Whether it be Skandinaviska Enskilda Banken and its employees, Freeport Minerals and the Amungme mountain tribe, AMAX and the Colorado Open Space Coordinating Council, or Booker McConnell and the Guyana government, the same principle seems to be at work—the harmonization or integration of interests along the lines of a "positive sum game." The same is true of token efforts of Ford, General Motors, Coca-Cola, and other multinationals such as the Netherlands-based Philips N.V., to devote some resources to the special technological problems of developing areas. Total collaboration in international business is still a relatively rare phenomenon, but we shall explore in later chapters numerous cases exhibiting some of its features.

A problem-solving and teamwork orientation is a common element in the collaborative mode. The joint efforts of corporate and public officials and citizen groups in AMAX's "Experiment in Ecology," the United States Justice Department's efforts to reduce antitrust uncertainties in corporate export operations, and the programs of Freeport Minerals in Indonesia or Bookers in Guyana are illustrative. Another element is the sincere attempt to build credibility, to listen, and to develop empathy but not necessarily agreement in working with other parties. Here the close consultation between UNEP and IPIECA, and union talks on a multinational basis with Volvo, Brown Boveri, SKF, and Glaverbel serve as examples.

Collaboration in its complete form entails open and honest sharing of all relevant information between the parties. Such candid and full disclosure enables the parties to go beneath the surface to the real underlying issues involved in a particular conflict. As compared to other conflict-handling modes, two-way communication is at a maximum level. Mutual understanding and trust are the keys to agreement. Attempts to influence the other side tend to be limited to persuasion.

The joint problem-solving process generally consists of three steps: (1) identifying the essential or underlying concerns of each party, (2) searching for alternatives and identifying their consequences for each party, and (3) identifying the alternative that seems most satisfactory.[36] Conflicts of interest, and the issues at stake within them, are employed as springboards for the creation of new, perhaps previously undefined or unanticipated solutions.[37] There is a willingness to reformulate a problem, to look at it from different perspectives, and to search far and wide for potential solutions. Emotions, reservations, and doubts are examined and worked through. Conflicts over facts are recognized and separated from conflicts over values. Intense discussions are not allowed to degenerate into personality clashes or public posturing. There is usually coordination of effort, division of labor, role-specialization, and a task-achievement orientation. The working proverb is "come, let us reason together."

ACCOMMODATION

An accommodative, relatively unassertive and cooperative style of coping with conflict tends to be exhibited by MNEs when their primary objective is to satisfy the concerns of other parties, but not necessarily their own, in a particular conflict situation. The aim is to preserve, promote or reestablish accord, harmony, and acceptance within the relationship—to attain a state of "peaceful coexistence." The focus is on appeasement. Conflicts are smoothed over, even though they may remain beneath the surface at a reduced level of intensity. Accommodative behavior is often characterized by acquiescence, benevolence, compliance, empathy, and adaptation.

Case 1. The Bank of America, the largest United States commercial bank, announced in November of 1976 that it would stop giving any assistance to the Arab boycott of Israel. The bank disclosed that it had instructed all of its branches in 45 different countries to stop immediately the processing of letters of credit and other documents containing boycott provisions. It thus became the first enterprise to spell out its compliance with a new State of California anti-boycott bill.[38]

Case 2. Left-wing Peronist Montonero guerrillas in Argentina kidnapped Franz Metz, the industrial director of the local Mercedes-Benz affiliate, in November of 1975. He was released five weeks later after the German company reportedly paid a ransom of $5 million, reinstated 119 workers who had been fired, and published advertisements in newspapers in Europe, Washington, D.C., and Mexico denouncing the "economic imperialism" of multinational enterprises in developing nations.[39]

Case 3. In an attack on French Prime Minister Raymond Barre's austerity program limiting wage increases to 6.5%, the Confederation Générale du Travail (CGT) and Confederation Française Démocratique du Travail (CFDT) took over an automotive components plant of General Motors France near Paris in April of 1977. GM obtained a court injunction to remove the 1000 plant occupiers, but then quickly backed away from a direct confrontation. Convinced that a confrontation might trigger student-labor violence of the May 1968 variety, GM France executives opted for a pacifying approach. Operating out of make-shift offices in hotels and cafés, the executives initiated low-key talks aimed at placating the strikers and getting them back to work.[40]

Case 4. When the Indonesian restaurant "Ramayana" first began catering to New York City diners, *The New York Times* declared that it was "one of the most opulent and agreeable restaurants to open in Manhattan in a good number of years." Only later did it become known that the shareholders of the million-dollar restaurant included MNEs such as Exxon, Mobil, Cities Service, Phillips Petroleum, Union Oil, Atlantic Richfield, Armco Steel, Monsanto, Gulf & Western, Schlumberger, Hughes Tool, Mitsui, Mitsubishi and C. Itoh of Japan, and Banque de Paris et Pays-Bas (BNP) of France. All had acquiesced to the purchase of stock in Ramayana's parent company after some not-so-subtle arm twisting by officials of Indonesia's national petroleum enterprise, P.N. Pertamina. The shakedown of companies doing (or hoping to do) business in Indonesia was masterminded by Major General Ibnu Sutowo, head of Pertamina until he was placed under arrest in 1976.[41]

Case 5. In September of 1977 Exxon faced charges by the U.S. Securities and Exchange Commission that the Corporation and the former head of its Italian affiliate had made $56.5 million in questionable payments overseas since 1963 and then covered them up. At the same time that the SEC complaint was filed in Federal Court in Washington, D.C., Exxon consented to the charges and released new details about $1.3 million in questionable payments that it made in more than a dozen foreign countries over the previous 14 years. Exxon agreed to a permanent injunction barring it from further violation of Federal securities laws.[42]

Case 6. In what some have labeled a far-reaching change in corporate posture and others call a public relations whitewash, 12 major United States-based multinationals disclosed in February of 1977 that they had agreed to support six principles "aimed at ending segregation" and "to promote fair employment practices" in South Africa. The firms were American Cyanamid, Burroughs, Caltex Petroleum, Citicorp, Ford Motor, General Motors, International Business Machines, International Harvester, 3M, Mobil, Otis Elevator, and Union Carbide. The declaration was in large measure the result of 18 months of missionary work among large companies by the Rev. Leon Sullivan, Minister of the Zion Baptist Church in Philadelphia and also a Director of the General Motors Corporation. By mid-1979 almost half of the 280 American firms operating in South Africa had provided their endorsement.[43]

Case 7. In the early 1970s the Brazilian government argued that foreign pharmaceutical firms operating in Brazil were performing little or no research and were discovering nothing patentable. As a result it was denying these companies patent protection and was not allowing them to collect royalty payments from their majority owned affiliates in Brazil. In response to government aspirations for R & D in Brazil and hints of leniency for cooperating firms, Johnson & Johnson set up a Research Institute for Endemic Diseases in July of 1971. Established in Sâo José dos Campos, the laboratory was the first to be set up by a major private company in Brazil to undertake research on tropical diseases.[44]

Case 8. In the early 1970s some of the richest oil fields in the North Sea were discovered in the Shetland Basin by multinational oil firms such as Shell, British Petroleum, Conoco, Burmah, Exxon, and Total. It became evident to the residents of the Shetland Islands, some 100 miles due west, that the oil firms would be seeking permission to pipe the oil ashore at Shetland, the nearest possible landing point. From there it would be carried by tanker to points south in the United Kingdom for refining and marketing. But very few of Shetland's 19,000 inhabitants wanted oil development to encroach on their unique way of life. Seizing the initiative, the Shetland County Council decided to weld the needs of the oil companies into a shape which would fit those of the Island's residents. Through the astute political action of Ian Clark—known in Britain as "the scourge of the oil companies"—a unique piece of private legislation was pushed through Parliament in 1974 which gave the Council wide-ranging rights to control and participate in oil-related development on the Island. Among other things, the Council insisted that all facilities be concentrated in one location, Sullom Voe, and that the Shetlanders receive inflation-hedged royalties from every barrel of oil coming into the new terminal. With the Shet-land landfall and tanker terminal vital to the economic exploitation of perhaps the most lucrative fields in the North Sea, the oil companies were in no position to argue, and yielded at almost every turn to the Council's demands. The $1.3 billion project became known as "Sullen Woe."[45]

Accommodative behavior can take the form of words or deeds. Our examples are mostly of the latter variety. Some of the cases are in reality capitulation—British Petroleum and others acceding to the belligerent demands of the Shet-land County Council, the many foreign companies knuckling under to the quasi-extortion of Maj. Gen. Ibnu Sutowo so that he could open his adventure in New York dining, and Mercedes-Benz surrendering to the ransom demands of the Argentine Montonero kidnappers. Other cases constitute propitiation, that is, the admitting of fault and making amends to allay hostile feeling. Exxon's consent to SEC charges of bribery and coverup, and Bank of America's decision to halt its compliance with the Arab boycott are cases in point.

Still other cases have involved placating the opposition, often with anxious overtures and concessions. General Motors pacifying the workers illegally occupying its plant near Paris or Johnson & Johnson meeting Brazilian demands for an R & D lab might be included here. So would Exxon management's recent support of a shareholder resolution, submitted by a group of churches, calling for reams of data on the company's stripmining operations.[46]

A final form of accommodation through deeds is conciliation, or attempts to win over an opponent by displaying a willingness to be just or fair. One might include here the "critical mass" of more than a hundred American firms endorsing Rev. Sullivan's six principles on South Africa. These have been criticized, however, as representing merely a token "lowest common denominator" and a case of "too little, too late."[47] Perhaps a more substantive example would be the *de facto* recognition, against the local government's wishes, of black labor unions in South Africa by Ford Motor, the Anglo-Dutch Unilever group, and SKF of Sweden, all in response to government or shareholder demands back home.

In addition to actual deeds, attempts to gain harmony and stability can also proceed by means of soothing persuasion. Disputes can be "smoothed over." Similarities and common interests among parties can be accentuated and the importance of differences can be minimized. Negative feelings can be withheld, shaded, or played down so as to make things seem less complicated and more acceptable. Opponents can sometimes be cajoled or coaxed into agreement by focusing on how good things are, compared with how bad they might be. Protest can also be "absorbed" by legitimating the energies of the rebellious.[49]

Whatever the technique, the objective of both active and passive accommodation is to attain a state of peace. Relevant proverbs here include "turn the other cheek," "let's come together," "pour oil on troubled waters," and "nice guys don't fight."

COMPROMISE

Compromise, a moderately assertive and cooperative way of handling conflict, is commonly used by MNEs when their objective is to settle what they and other parties must give and take, or perform and receive, in a particular transaction. The aim is to "split the difference" and obtain moderate, albeit incomplete, satisfaction for each side. Through processes of bargaining, negotiation, and compromise, the parties compete and cooperate with each other in order to reach a mutually satisfactory agreement. Compromise is typically characterized by reciprocity, mixed motives, and attitudes of "give and take."

Case 1. Numerous multinationals operating in France found themselves at the bargaining table in the mid-1970s as a result of the government's strategy of bringing high-technology industries, considered important for national economic independence, under French control. The government was quite effective in bringing pressure to bear because of its role as chief controller or customer in high-technology markets. By promising first claim on governmental data-processing business, the government in June of 1975 persuaded Honeywell Inc. to reduce its holding in its French affiliate from 66% to 45% and to merge the company with Compagnie Internationale pour l'Informatique (CII). As the main customer of nuclear reactors, the government pressured Westinghouse in December of 1975 into selling its 45% share of Framatome, France's only builder of nuclear power plants, to it for $25 million. With a $7 billion modernization of France's telephone system in the works, the government prevailed upon ITT to offer its entire 68% interest in Le Matériel Téléphonique to the French electronics conglomerate Thomson-CSF for $160 million. As part of the deal, ITT retained another wholly-owned French subsidiary which was promised sizable government business.[50]

Case 2. During 1976–1977 the American Jewish Congress negotiated agreements with a number of major United States-based multinationals regarding the Arab boycott of Israel. Gulf Oil, Bethlehem Steel, Goodyear Tire & Rubber, Standard Oil of California, and Tenneco were among those who agreed with the AJC to provide requested information about boycott practices and/or to revise corporate policies. Bethlehem Steel added to its existing policy of nondiscrimination a statement demanded by the AJC prohibiting the issuance of "negative certificates of origin"—documents stating that a product was not made in Israel. Tenneco accepted a provision that "no U.S. person may discriminate against a U.S. individual . . . in order to comply with, further or support a foreign boycott." The AJC withdrew its shareholder resolutions on the Arab boycott from all of the firms with whom it reached such agreements.[51]

Case 3. After years of vacillating, the Supervisory Board of Volkswagenwerk AG unanimously approved a $250 million investment for a Rabbit assembly plant in the United States on April 23, 1976. In making and implementing this decision, VW's management had to engage in intricate bargaining. The government of Lower Saxony, which owns 20% of VW, had to be convinced that the project would not increase unemployment in the company's German operations. Likewise concerned about layoffs, VW's unions—which held one-third of the seats on VW's board—had refused to go along with the United States move in 1974. Numerous concessions, involving employment guarantees, no re-imports from the United States back to Germany and the like, reportedly were needed to overcome union recalcitrance. VW started a virtual auction among many states in the U.S. for its bounty of an estimated 5000 new jobs, enlarged tax revenues and other benefits. The victory went to Pennsylvania Governor Milton J. Shapp, who devised a hefty $200 million-plus financing package for VW. The company also had to negotiate a price for Chrysler's partially built auto plant at New Stanton. VW ran into the wrath of the U.S. Environmental Protection Agency on hydrocarbon emissions from the proposed plant's paint-spraying operations. Through a complex offset agreement VW was permitted to add some pollution to the local airshed contingent upon the State reducing emissions from existing sources. VW hired an all-American management team, which quickly fought and won a battle with VW headquarters on the design of the assembly line. Tensions developed between Volkswagen of America, the traditional VW import marketer, which feared being swallowed up, and the new assembly subsidiary, Volkswagen Manufacturing Corporation of America. In October of 1977, a coalition of black organizations charged that VW had failed to carry out an equal opportunity and affirmative action plan for the hiring of minority employees. About the same time, the residents of New Stanton began to express concern about the type of "element" VW would be bringing into the community. After the assembly plant opened, a festering labor dispute developed, with unauthorized strikes occurring in 1978 and 1979 that required contract renegotiations.[52]

Case 4. Negotiations for the release of kidnapped executives have been tedious and delicate for a number of MNEs. Exxon bargained for 144 days for the release of Victor E. Samuelson, General Manager of Exxon Argentina, before Marxist guerrillas accepted a ransom of $14.2 million. Luchino Revelli-Beaumont, the head of Fiat France was abducted in Paris by the "Committee for Socialist Revolutionary Unity" and held for 89 days in 1977. During the three months of complex negotiations, the original ransom demand of $30 million was reduced to $2 million. Revelli-Beaumont's family, with Fiat's support, refused to capitulate to the initial demands of the kidnappers or to abdicate its negotiating position to government officials. In fact, the efforts of French, Swiss, and Italian police were deliberately thwarted by activities of the family, its intermediaries, and Fiat. From experience in Italy and Argentina, Fiat had learned to run such matters its own way. Communications with the gang were conducted through small ads, Swiss bankers, and secret meetings. One day in July, by the lakeside in the middle of Geneva, a man from Credit Suisse handed over the money to a "passer-by," who jumped into a moving car and took off. Three days later, policemen found Revelli-Beaumont sitting on a park bench in Versailles.[53]

Case 5. During 1970–1971 B.F. Goodrich and Goodyear fought a bitter takeover battle for the Dutch tiremaker, Rubberfabriek Vredestein N.V. Goodrich won, but over the years failed to make anything of Vredestein, renamed International B.F. Goodrich Europe B.V. It experienced $5.5 million loss in 1975 and a $1.9 million loss during the first half of 1976. Goodrich attempted to reorganize the profitless non-tire section of Vredestein, which would have meant firing 762 of the 4700 employees. The unions protested the layoffs, which brought the Dutch government into the dispute. Negotiations ambled along until Goodrich, fed up over the slow pace, delivered an ultimatum. In June of 1976 offered to sell Vredestein to the government, and announced it would sell off or close down if no agreement could be reached. The pace quickened, with negotiating teams flying back and forth between Akron and The Hague. In October, the Dutch government purchased 49% of the Goodrich subsidiary. An additional 2% was sold to a Dutch foundation which, subject to a favorable tax ruling, would acquire Goodrich's remaining interest for a nominal fee over the next ten years.[54]

Case 6. Egypt, with a very troubled economy and a desperate need of foreign investment, began in the fall of 1977 to capitalize on a rather unique incentive. In exchange for new investments in the country by foreign firms, it offered to try to get them deleted from the 22-nation Arab League boycott list. As part of its new "open-door" investment policy, the Cairo government in September approved a joint venture between American Motors Corporation and the government to assemble utility vehicles, and another by Coca-Cola Company to develop citrus groves. In October the government approved a joint venture with Ford Motor to assemble medium-sized trucks and to manufacture diesel engines in Egypt. Coca-Cola's deal, which the company saw as a "major breakthrough," had required 13 months of intensive negotiations. Ford had been negotiating with Egypt on its venture for several years. Because of their operations in or with Israel, Coca-Cola and Ford had been on the Arab boycott list since 1966, and American Motors since 1970. All three carefully pointed out in their project announcements that their Egyptian joint ventures would in no way affect their existing ties with Israel. For that reason it appeared that at least one of the deals might backfire. Mohammed Mahgoub, a Sudanese and chief administrator of the Arab boycott, lashed out at Egypt for agreeing to the deal with Ford. He warned that trucks and diesel engines produced by the new Ford Middle East Company would be banned in Arab markets. The whole basis of Egypt's negotiating strategy collapsed, of course, in 1979 when the Arab League decided to ostracize Egypt in retaliation for President Sadat's abandonment of a united Arab front against Israel. Western MNEs, particularly banks, were placed in the uncomfortable position of having to treat Egypt as a virtual pariah or risk Arab hostility. Coca-Cola, however, after finally ironing out some loose ends in its long negotiations to reenter Egypt, began heavy advertising and distribution of Coke in Cairo in July 1979. Ford Motor's $145 million project, on the other hand, had gone nowhere as of fall 1979 since Arab capital had not materialized due to the Egypt-Israel peace settlement. [55]

Case 7. During 1977, the insistence of the International Business Machines Corporation on 100% control of its foreign subsidiaries was being challenged in Brazil, Nigeria, Indonesia and India. In a major drive to enforce its Foreign Exchange Regulation Act of 1973, the Indian government informed IBM in 1975 that it would have to divest 60% of its equity to local shareholders in all units of the company that were not manufacturing solely for export. In April of 1976 IBM counterproposed the creation of two companies. One would run IBM computer service bureaus in which the company would retain only 40% of the equity. It would retain full ownership of the other, producing $10 million worth of data processing equipment entirely for export and *also* market and service imported computers inside India. The government did not like this last provision, but in early September of 1977 it reported that it might make concessions to IBM and accept its "compromise proposal." IBM had also thrown in a number of "sweeteners", including an integrated circuit card assembly and testing facility and a measurement and analyzing lab, both government operated, an IBM-equipped research center for "projects of national significance," and a provision making IBM patents available to Indian organizations. Negotiations continued, but as a result of intense internal debate the government apparently concluded that there could be no relaxation of the regulations for IBM alone—especially since ICL, the British computer firm operating in India, had fully bowed to the government's wishes. The government formally rejected IBM's proposal in November of 1977. As a result, IBM announced on November 15th that it would dismantle its manufacturing and marketing operations in India. Frank Cary, IBM's chairman, called the Indian outcome "a great disappointment to us."[56]

Case 8. At the end of October 1975, John Riccardo, Chairman of Chrysler Corporation, disclosed in a Detroit press conference that the company had lost $254.6 million during the first nine months of 1975. He also disclosed that some losing operations might have to be abandoned and that the British subsidiary, which lost $42.5 million in 1974 and $33 million during the first half of 1975, was the leading candidate. On November 3rd over dinner in London, Riccardo presented Prime Minister Harold Wilson with three options: (1) the British unit could be liquidated·as of the end of the year, (2) the government could completely nationalize the subsidiary, or (3) the government could take a majority interest in the operation. Chrysler's ultimatum and the tight time schedule were widely viewed as heavy-handed blackmail. When the government responded in early December with an offer of $70 million in aid, Chrysler threatened to withdraw entirely unless the offer was increased. In December the government finally decided that it could not accept the loss of 21,000 jobs, the serious balance of payments effects, and the loss of an important contract to supply knockdown vehicles for assembly in Iran. After a month and a half of tense negotiations and considerable controversy among British labor union leaders, politicians, and businessmen, the Labor government agreed to a $360 million package of direct aid, loans, and loan guarantees to subsidize the company's losses and provide funds for new-car development. Chrysler's financial weakness had given it great bargaining strength. The *Detroit News* called Chrysler's achievement "a triumph of negotiations." In 1978, however, Chrysler was forced to sell its European operations to Peugeot-Citro-ën.[57]

Compromise is perhaps the most commonly used and widely accepted way of handling conflicts in multinational operations. Procedurally, compromise can take many forms, ranging from bilateral negotiations to mediation and arbitration which involve third-party intervention.[58] The common aim is to reach agreement among the parties on how to divide or split the pie subject to bargaining. This process can be achieved in just a few days or weeks, or it may drag on for years, as many of the cases we shall review later on will illustrate. From the point of view of incentives, there are really two types of bargaining: (1) benign or positive bargaining, which involves the offering of rewards in return for improvements in the firm's own position, and (2) malign or negative bargaining, which involves the offering of punishments in return for not obtaining an improved position.[59] The latter is typified by Chrysler's tense 1975 negotiations with the British government and Goodrich's imbroglio with the Dutch government over the fate of Vredestein in 1976. The former is illustrated by the 1977 deals of Ford Motor and Coca-Cola with Egypt, and Volkswagen's bargaining with German labor union in regard to its United States investment plans.

The compromise approach can thus involve use of positive (promises and rewards) or negative (threats and punishments) incentives. Both can be employed simultaneously, as illustrated by the French government's use of sticks and carrots in its "Frenchification" of Honeywell, Westinghouse, and ITT affiliates. Multinationals engaged in compromise must also frequently contend with a "dilemma of goals."[60] As dramatically brought home by cases like the Fiat kidnap and ransom, an MNE pushing for an agreement must chart a course between two distinct risks: (1) In driving too hard for an agreement which maximizes its own gain, being too tough, it may provide the other party with so unsatisfactory an outcome that it refuses to settle or abandons the relationship. (2) In not driving hard enough for a preferred agreement, being too soft, it may end up providing the other side with too good an outcome, thereby settling for less than necessary and possibly setting a damaging precedent.

The give-and-take in the process of compromise, whereby originally divergent positions are brought closer together, is possible only if each participant is at least partially ignorant of his opponent's true intentions. Whether it is IBM and the Indian government, VW and the Governor of Pennsylvania, or Tenneco and the American Jewish Congress, a compromise relationship can be sustained only if each party selects a middle course between the extremes of complete openness and total deception. Each side must be able to convince the other of its integrity without endangering its own bargaining position. In the process of exchanging offers and counteroffers, each party tries to acquire information about the other's true preferences and intentions, while disclosing only selective information about his own. A certain flexibility or tentativeness is also needed in the process of compromise so that positions can be shifted without being wrong, losing face, or appearing inconsistent. Offers and counteroffers continue to be made until the parties reach a mutually acceptable settlement concerning the division or exchange of one or more specific resources—or, if unsuccessful, terminate interaction as in the case of IBM in India. As seen from the concessions involved in many of our cases, all of the parties usually give up something, and keep or gain something. As the proverb goes, "half a loaf is better than none."

Having outlined a way of thinking about specific instances of conflict involving multinational enterprises, the following chapter will review four key contingencies which in combination appear to determine which of the five modes of handling conflict reviewed above is likely to be most appropriate in a given conflict situation. With the *modes* of this chapter and the *contingencies* of the next, our model for diagnosing and constructively managing conflicts that confront MNEs will then be complete.

3 *DESIGNING A CONFLICT MANAGEMENT STRATEGY*

Having developed the basic theme of a contingency logic—embodying such options for the firm as competition, avoidance, accommodation, collaboration and compromise with respect to the opposing interests in any given conflict situation—we can now identify the contingencies which determine the desirability and feasibility of utilizing these various modes in specific conflict situations. Let us turn back for a moment to the two underlying dimensions of *assertiveness* and *cooperativeness* in the basic model introduced in the last chapter and examine some factors that are relevant to each.

DECIDING WHEN TO FIGHT

When confronted with an actual or potential conflict, how should management of a multinational enterprise go about deciding how assertive to be? What should determine the level of material and human resources it is willing to invest in the hope of obtaining a particular conflict outcome that fully satisfies its needs? The answers appear to rest both on the "desirability" and "feasibility" of obtaining such a satisfactory outcome. Desirability is primarily a product of the *stakes* the enterprise places on the outcome. Feasibility, on the other hand, is principally a matter of the relative *power* of the enterprise to bring about the outcome.

Stakes

The stakes of a multinational enterprise in any given conflict depend on the amount of perceived gain or loss associated with particular results. Stakes are high when a great deal can be won or lost. Just how much does obtaining a specific outcome that represents total satisfaction of corporate interests really matter? How much would be jeopardized or forfeited if the outcome went completely against the firm? Stakes are a product of the expected difference in value between an outcome which totally fulfills the interests of the enterprise and an outcome which totally frustrates them. The factual determination of stakes is usually a very complex task and involves assessment of gains and losses, tangible and intangible factors, and short-term and long-term considerations including the setting of precedents. Stakes can indeed be subjectively estimated, but perhaps never rigorously defined in complete detail.

Probably the most important factor to a multinational enterprise in determining stakes is its global strategy. The potential outcome of a given conflict can be gauged according to its impact on (a) the corporate capabilities which underlie the company's strategy, (b) the economic basis of that strategy, and (c) the requirements for effective implementation of the strategy, such as degree of control. Conflict outcomes which weaken the heart of a strategy—damaging the firm's distinctive competence, competitive edge, or unique capabilities—are likely to be those which the enterprise will most want to avoid. On the other hand, outcomes that greatly strengthen the essential requirements for satisfactory pursuit of its corporate strategy are likely to be those which the firm will most enthusiastically seek. Stakes are likely to be highest, in other words, when the outcome of a conflict either threatens to severely erode or promises to significantly bolster a multinational's "advantages." These include technological superiority, control of goods or factor markets, and economies of scale.[1]

Large and complex multinational enterprises, of course, often pursue multiple strategies in different product and geographic divisions. Drawing on past research, however, it seems possible to distinguish between different kinds of strategies and to show how the stakes, and thus conflict behavior, profoundly depend on the specific nature of these various strategies.[2] Firms which concentrate on exploiting technological leads, such as IBM, usually consider it essential to maintain an exceptionally strong R & D program, high quality standards, tight control of technological skills, and close supervision of marketing strategy. Commenting on Indian demands for majority ownership in 1977, for example, an IBM spokesman announced that the company believed that "such equity dilution would seriously impair its ability to manage an international high-technology company requiring sharing of resources and know-how across national borders.[3] Or consider General Electric, which during the mid-1970s was under considerable pressure to share control of high-technology products like diesel locomotives and power-generating equipment with host-country partners. The company consistently refused, stating that trade secrets were involved and that product quality must be upheld.[4]

Other multinationals pursue strategies of high technology, but believe themselves to be broad-based enough not to fear an invasion of corporate know-how or quality control. Technological leads by such firms may be exploited in many product lines and in many markets, although technological preeminence in any one area may not be assured. With such diversity, the firms see themselves as comparatively efficient in the development of innovative leads. The need for tight control of production and marketing is not so critical as in the case of IBM or GE, for example. In conflicts over ownership, patents, quality control, and so on, stakes are rarely preceived as a matter of life and death. Honeywell, Westinghouse, ITT, and L.M. Ericsson have been able to relax while being "Frenchified" in France, knowing that greener pastures in products and markets lay right around the corner.

Some firms pursue strategies in the international marketplace involving technologies that possess a relatively modest rate of innovation or relatively little differentiation among competing producers. As in the aerospace industry, contact with foreign markets primarily takes the form of exports, often facilitated by overseas agents. The economic returns to firms such as Boeing or Lockheed must be based on one-shot or sporadic sales arrangements, with no presumption of large-scale continuing income over an extended period of time. It is not hard to understand why Boeing and Lockheed clashed with the SEC in 1976–1978 over disclosure of the names of the government officials overseas who accepted more than $100 million in "agents fees" from the two companies between 1970 and 1975. Identifying such beneficiaries could have seriously harmed each firm's billion dollar backlog of unfulfilled orders, presumably by causing embarrassed foreign governments to cancel contracts. Disclosure also could have upset future marketing efforts by destroying each firm's network of highly placed agents and consultants upon which their future overseas prospects depend.

Multinationals in the oil, copper, aluminum, and chemicals industries tend to pursue strategies resting on the advantages of large scale. The success of these capital-intensive firms depends on the maintenance of barriers to entry into the industry, the coordination of decisions at various stages of production, security in raw materials supply, and stability in the demand for their products. These are the "jugular veins" of the natural resource industries, and whenever governments, producer cartels such as the Organization of Petroleum Exporting Countries (OPEC), or even independent firms take action which threatens the corporate need for stability, the stakes are likely to be viewed as high. This is why, for example, Exxon, Texaco, Gulf, Mobil, Standard Oil of California, Standard Oil of Indiana, Shell, and Atlantic Richfield so vigorously opposed the U.S. Federal Trade Commission's antitrust complaint that the eight firms had maintained "a noncompetitive market structure in the refining of crude oil into petroleum products," east of the Rockies in the United States. At stake is "vertical divestiture," with the companies possibly broken apart to separate control of crude oil production and transportation from refinery and marketing.[5]

Many multinationals in the food and pharmaceutical industries rely on strategies based on the exploitation of advanced managerial and marketing skills. Strong trade names are often supported by copious promotional expenditures. Tight control of the marketing programs is usually viewed as absolutely essential. And so when the global image of Nestlé's product line was severely threatened by the book titled *Nestlé Kills Babies*, the company saw no choice but to sue for libel in an effort to clear its name. And when the Indian government attempted to gain control of Coca-Cola's most fundamental commercial asset— its secret formula—the company was compelled to forcefully resist.

A final type of strategy to consider is that which exploits a multinational scanning capability and a well-integrated and efficient global logistics system. The automobile and electronics industries quickly come to mind. Economic returns are achieved from low-cost production locations and effective global marketing. Tight internal control is needed to tie together this kind of multinational network, and a substantial capacity for flexibility and mobility in production is required. So Chrysler resisted British government incomes policy pressures in 1971 and granted an inflationary wage increase to its British workers— the increased wage costs were less important, from a global point of view, than the disruption of output for the American small-car market.[6] And Volkswagen, in convincing its German unions to allow it to set up a plant in the United States, was in the final analysis fighting a battle to remain in the American market— VW's market share in the United States had deteriorated from 6% in 1971 to 2% in 1976. With increased Japanese competition, higher wage costs in Germany, and prices driven inexorably higher by the 70% appreciation of the deutsche Mark against the dollar since 1969, the need for cost-saving local production was compelling.

When any of this series of strategic requirements of multinationals are endangered by conflict outcomes, the result is a perception of high stakes. Conversely, when essential strategic elements are not affected by outcomes of conflict, then stakes are likely to be perceived as lower by multinational corporate managers. Besides these strategic determinants, which will tend to vary from industry to industry, there are a number of other considerations that also enter into the assessment of stakes.

One is the financial condition, present and prospective, of the firm. If the enterprise is very well off, it may be prepared to offer more concessions to its opponents. But when close to collapse, such as Lockheed, Chrysler, and Montedison in the mid-1970s, or when reducing the massive deficits of the Concorde depend on New York City landing rights, or when corporate survival is probably at stake, as with Westinghouse and the uranium dilemma, the ability and desire to make concessions decline dramatically. Another factor involves precedents that may be established, in the eyes of interested observers, by the conflict outcome. Akzo in 1972 and 1975 did not want to set the precedent of accepting multinational union bargaining; Hoffmann–LaRoche knew in 1973 that if it cut drug prices and refunded "excessive" profits in Britain, it would be forced to do the same elsewhere (see Chapter 10); an IBM joint venture in India would have brought similar demands abroad; and Alcan was hesitant to yield to Guyana's demands for renegotiation in 1971 in part because management considered the resulting nationalization to be less costly than the contagion effects in other bauxite-producing nations that would surely follow a precedent-setting accommodation in Guyana.[7] Another factor tending to increase stakes is accountability to third parties—joint venture partners, industry associations, and the like. Multinationals are often induced by accountability to exhibit greater loyalty, commitment, and advocacy of the positions preferred by their constituents.

A number of other factors may serve to reduce the perceived stakes. One is insurance, as is provided to American companies by the Overseas Private Investment Corporation against seizure of overseas property by foreign governments, or inability to repatriate profits, or damage to property by acts of war. Kidnap insurance, which in 1978 ran about $50,000 in annual premiums for $1 million in coverage, can also reduce financial vulnerability and thus the stakes in executive abductions. Another stakes-reducing factor is the existence of options: ITT could abandon its takeover of Frozen Foods in Australia and Control Data could forego expansion in South Africa because many alternative acquisitions and markets were available to each. Multinationals naturally treasure such flexibility. That is why the Emergency Committee for American Trade so vigorously fought the Hartke-Burke bill, which would have served to reduce multinationals' freedom to operate in other countries and generally to integrate their operations on a worldwide basis. A third factor which may tend to reduce stakes is the joint ownership of many capital-intensive facilities, such as aluminum smelters, copper mines, oil fields, natural gas pipelines, and petrochemical complexes, by a number of rival firms. Such consortia tend to create a common cost structure and common exposure to risk for the firms involved. If a consortium facility is blocked by environmentalists or expropriated by a nationalist government, competitive relationships remain more or less intact among the rivals. So losing a conflict does not necessarily set one firm back in relation to its competitors.

In regard to all such considerations, management must also factor in "temporal urgency." This has been defined as "the pressure to minimize costs associated with delaying a settlement, e.g., a decision must be reached to cope with immediate threats from the [external] environment, or direct monetary costs are charged for time taken in reaching a decision, or opportunities of superior employment of effort are foregone."[8] Time-limits for multinationals in conflicts may be self-imposed or introduced by third parties, and they may be explicit or implicit, flexible or rigid. Their mere presence, however, may have important effects on the nature of a conflict. As time pressures increase, perceived stakes in obtaining the most desirable outcome may decrease. Increasing urgency increases "decision costs,"[9] and to minimize this effect, the firm may soften its demands, reduce its aspirations, or increase its concessions.[10] Time pressures increase the importance of reaching agreement, and thus may alter the willingness of the firm to settle a dispute.

Strategic requirements, financial conditions, precedents, available options, and urgency all help determine the significance that a multinational enterprise will attach to a desired conflict outcome. These factors will thus also determine the amount of corporate resources that management is willing to invest in the conflict. When the stakes are perceived to be high, it seems logical that an enterprise will want to be assertive in the pursuit of the desired outcome, and it should be willing to expend considerable time and energy in either fighting like hell (competition) or in extensive problem-solving together with the other party (collaboration). When the stakes are low, however, it may make sense to be unassertive, that is to do nothing (avoidance) or simply to go along with the other side's position (accommodation). With low stakes, great outlays of corporate energy simply may not make sense. Finally, with intermediate stakes it may be in the best interest of the firm to devote a moderate amount of energy to striving for compromise.

Relative Power

Power, perhaps the core concept of social science, is a very complex factor indeed. It is a "relational" concept—a multinational's power does not reside exclusively within the firm itself, but rather in the relationship it has with its external environment. In any given conflict, therefore, the power position of the enterprise will be a joint function of its own characteristics and the characteristics of the situation in which it finds itself.[11] The key point is that a multinational's power position is rarely constant across all situations, and the firm's potential leverage can vary greatly from one conflict to another.

Following conventional social science terminology, we can formally define power as the ability of one party to move another party through a range of outcomes.[12] The greater a multinational's power, the broader the range of outcomes—positive and negative—through which it can push another actor such as a labor union or a national government. So the firm and its opposition have *equal* power to the extent that each can move the other through an equivalent range of outcomes, and *unequal* power to the extent that one can move the other through a broader range of outcomes. The relative power picture of a multinational enterprise in a given conflict situation can thus be viewed as a continuum extending from high (significant power advantage) at one end, to equal in the center, and low (significant power disadvantage) at the other end.

A multinational has several potential bases of power available to it for mobilization in various conflict situations. Social scientists have singled out six common bases of power or influence: informational, referent, legitimate, expert, reward and coercive.[13] The enterprise can exert *informational influence* if it can provide information not previously known to the other party or if it can point out contingencies about which the other has little or no awareness. The firm can utilize *referent influence* if it can emphasize its common interests with the other party and attempt to engender feelings of solidarity. It can exert *legitimate influence* if it can convince the other party that it is justified in making a particular demand based on "oughts" of various kinds—rules, precedents, reciprocity, fair play, and the like. The multinational can use *expert influence* if it is able to convince the other party it possesses superior knowledge or ability. It can use *reward influence* if it is able to promise rewards or benefits, such as prospects of new investment, for the other party where it is clear that the reward depends on a conflict outcome that is favorable to the enterprise. Finally, it can use *coercive influence* if it is able to deal out punishments or negative incentives such as pulling out if the conflict is not favorably resolved from management's point of view.

The ingredients of power, both the firm's and the opposition's, include size, membership, financial base and potential resources, leadership quality, managerial capacity, prestige, image, reputation, communication and persuasion skills, access to the media, degree of organization, amount of cohesiveness and unity, prior experience in waging conflict, intensity of commitment, degree of trust and legitimacy, knowledge, expertise, risk-taking propensity, intelligence network, and available options.

But merely studying the ingredients of power is not enough. The emphasis must be on "effective power." One observer has stated that "effective power depends upon the following key elements: (1) the control or possession of resources to generate power, (2) the awareness of the resources one possesses or controls, (3) the motivation to employ these resources to influence others, (4) skill in converting the resources into usable power, and (5) good judgment in employing this power so that its use is appropriate in type and magnitude to the situations in which it is used."[14] And so management must examine both the *ingredients* of power and the *effectiveness* with which they can be brought to bear, both for the firm and the opponents confronted in a particular conflict situation.

Another important determinant of relative power is *coalition formation*. A coalition is the unification of the power or resources of two or more parties for the purpose of maintaining or increasing their individual strength, thus improving their chances of obtaining a desired conflict outcome.[15] There seems to be a general tendency for such coalitions to form in multinational corporate conflicts. Whether it be OPEC joining against the multinational oil companies, unions from three nations joining against Akzo, creation of the Emergency Committee for American Trade, developing nation governments allying themselves with local businessmen, more than 150 firms endorsing the Rev. Sullivan's six principles on South Africa, or a dozen foreign oil companies battling the government of Indonesia, the same principle is at work. Coalitions are especially likely to form in multi-party conflicts when power is distributed—or perceived to be distributed—in such a way that one or more of the parties views itself as disadvantaged or vulnerable with respect to obtaining a particular outcome and does not consider it fruitless to join forces with another party with complementary objectives. Coalition formation appears to be inhibited, however: (1) when the combined initial weights or resources of the weaker parties are considered simply insufficient to offset those of the more powerful parties; (2) when a more powerful party effectively blocks the formation of alliances among weaker parties; and (3) when sources of external contention among would-be partners are sufficiently intense that seemingly advantageous coalitions are avoided.[16]

Still another thing that must be kept in mind is the site of the conflict. Waging conflict on one's own territory is a potential source of strength that can increase both assertiveness and "winning" outcomes for the "home team". Multinationals play most of their conflicts "away;" their opponents have the advantage of contending on "home" territory. Indigenous opponents are thus more familiar with the local environment and also enjoy the legitimate right to control and manipulate it. The foreign enterprise, as a guest, may be constrained in its assertiveness by a need for caution in the unfamiliar environment. And since it lacks legitimate rights of manipulation, it is often externally viewed as occupying subordinate status and may therefore be compelled to behave less assertively or even deferentially toward its host.

The multinational firm, however, draws its strength from a number of well-known and somewhat special sources. One is assistance from the parent government. American influence in the Middle East to gain entry for American oil companies, United States Marine landings in Central America to bolster United Fruit, promulgation of the Hickenlooper amendment, the CIA cooperation with ITT in Chile are stories frequently used to illustrate this kind of strength. But times are changing. As we have seen time and again, divergent interests, fragmented policies, diplomatic constraints, and the like dramatically reduce the opportunities multinationals have for enlisting the powers of one government in their struggles against another. And so multinationals have to some extent become more vulnerable as governments have found them easier to attack without fear of intergovermental retaliation.

Multinational corporate power is also strengthened by the existence of options, whether they are utilized or not. We have seen how Chrysler and Goodrich, with mobility options not available to their adversaries, were able to weaken the negotiating positions of labor unions and governments they confronted. Another strength is geographic dispersion of production: enterprises that rely on well-diversified supply sources are less vulnerable to embargoes and nationalizations, and perhaps more resilient in conflicts in general, than are firms which rely on a single source. Occidental Petroleum, for example, in its negotiations with Libya in 1973 found itself more dependent on that country than any of the other oil firms involved; as a result it was in the weakest position to resist the government's demands.[17]

Multinationals also gain strength from market dominance which can reduce the ability of governments to reach out for alternative sources of technology or capital. The entry of new rivals into an industry serves to dilute the power of the established leaders. With a proliferation of local and foreign rivals, governments can more easily shop around. But when there is not much else being offered in the marketplace multinationals can have surprising power. Witness the mad rush by more than two dozen American states attempting to capture Volkswagen's assembly plant in the early 1970s, or the more recent competition among the Netherlands, Germany, Ireland, France, Belgium, Spain, and Britain to win Ford's $313 million, 2500-jobs Fiesta engine plant. After months of intense maneuvering and top level political wooing, the Ford plant finally ended up in Wales, receiving the equivalent of at least $63 million in British government grants, plus other benefits.[18]

Another source of power can come into play especially in natural resource based industries. Consider the case of Kennecott in Chile. Responding to an acute sense of vulnerability, the company worked out a sophisticated external defense based on transnational market and credit networks. The idea was that when and if nationalization occurred, the Chilean government would jeopardize its standing with credit institutions on several continents if it failed to provide adequate compensation.[19] Similar programs to minimize risk and involve third parties in the face of a declining position of power have been employed by ASARCO, Freeport Minerals, Rio Tinto-Zinc, AMAX, and Roan Selection Trust.[20] In manufacturing industries, similar power can be achieved by breaking down the production process so finely that expropriation or nationalization becomes meaningless. A government's expropriation of a "screwdriver" type electronics components assembly operation, which is merely putting imported parts together for export, would yield precisely nothing.

One observer has pointed to perhaps the most important single source of power: "Multinational enterprises that perform a unique function, such as providing access to some difficult technology or some otherwise inaccessible foreign market, have generally been less vulnerable to government pressures, while subsidiaries whose withdrawal is thought to entail very little national loss have been more vulnerable."[21] Multinationals attain power through a degree of indispensability, that is, by possessing something unique to offer or withhold when a conflict arises. IBM for example, despite a few chinks in its armor in countries such as Iran, India, Brazil, Indonesia, and Nigeria, still retains enormous bargaining power because of its technological uniqueness.

If the content of power is complex, it is also the primary determinant of the feasibility of different types of conflict behavior. High relative power, by definition, increases a multinational's chances of procuring the conflict outcomes it wants, and a clearly superior power position is likely to favor relatively assertive behavior in conflict situations. This may either take the form of an unabashedly competitive stance, or one of collaboration, where the firm's problem-solving resources imply a position of strength and reduced risk. When there is equal power, or only a moderate difference in the relative power of the protagonists, the conditions seem right for bargaining and compromise. And when the multinational's power is very low it will probably be unable to compel the other side to negotiate. If weak and vulnerable, unassertive behavior (avoidance or accommodation) may be more appropriate. This assumes, of course, that the option of attempting to increase relative power—through efforts to increase one's own power or reduce the other side's—has been rejected as not feasible or excessively costly.

WHEN TO WORK WITH THE OPPOSITION

Outcome *stakes* and relative *power* thus appear to be the prime factors that should determine a multinational's assertiveness level in a particular conflict. But this is only half of the picture. The multinational also has to be concerned with deciding how cooperative to be. Why should a multinational enterprise be concerned with the desires of its opponents? To what extent should it be willing to undertake efforts to meet these desires and why? As with assertiveness, there seem to be two critical factors that affect the desirability and feasibility of cooperative behavior. *Desirability* is primarily a function of the "interest interdependence" between the multinational enterprise and the other parties—for instance, whether the attainment of the firm's and its opponent's goals are positively or negatively correlated. *Feasibility*, on the other hand, is principally a matter of "relationship quality" between the enterprise and the other parties—for example, whether relations are trusting and friendly or suspicious and hostile. Divergent interests give rise to competitive or "object-centered" conflict, while poor relations give rise to hostile or "opponent-centered" conflict.[22]

Interest Interdependence

Interests among parties in a relationship can be purely convergent (common), purely divergent (different), or both convergent and divergent at the same time. Convergence or divergence of interests arise from interdependence of goals, means, or both. Cooperativeness in conflict situations is encouraged or facilitated to the extent that goals and means are positively interdependent, while uncooperativeness is likely to emerge if goals and means are negatively interdependent. A purely cooperative situation has been defined as one in which "the goals of the participants are so linked that any participant can attain his goal if, and only if, the others with whom he is linked can attain their goals."[23] In a purely uncooperative situation, on the other hand, the goals are linked in such a way that one party can reach its goals only if the others do not—"in a cooperative situation the goals are so linked that everybody 'sinks or swims' together, while in the competitive [uncooperative] situation if one swims, the other must sink."[24]

The above conceptions define the extremes of goal interdependence which may exist in a relationship between a multinational enterprise and its opponents in a conflict situation. We have briefly scanned some cases in the previous chapter that approach purely cooperative situations such as Ford Motor and Asian governments on the "Basic Transportation Vehicle," Control Data and the United Church Board for World Ministries on nonexpansion in South Africa, Coca-Cola and the government of Egypt on investment in citrus groves in exchange for help in getting off the Arab boycott list, and Skandinaviska Enskilda Banken and its 7200 employees on profit-sharing and employee ownership. Cases approaching the purely uncooperative situation might encompass Air France/British Airways and residents living near Kennedy airport over Concorde landing rights, Boeing versus the SEC on disclosure of payoff recipients, Goodrich and the Dutch government over the shutting down of its Vredestein plant, "Big Oil" versus the FTC on divestiture, or Coca-Cola versus the government of India on release of its secret formula. Although multinationals occasionally experience some conflicts characterized by such extreme divergence or convergence of interest, the most common situations are likely to be those containing a mix of both convergent and divergent goals. Most of the conflicts considered in this book appear to be "mixed-motive" in character, with the relative strength of cooperative and uncooperative interests varying from case to case.

Although goal interdependence is obviously of primary importance in determing the degree of cooperation possible in a particular conflict relationship, we should note that "means interdependence" may also be involved in conflict. Means interdependence exists when the methods, procedures or instruments that one party needs in order to reach its goal affect the means available to the other. A multinational often finds, for example, that even though both it and the opposition are in general agreement on a common goal such as resource development, there may be disagreements on how it should be accomplished—fast versus slow, one extractive method versus another. Our examples of Shell/British Petroleum versus Shetland County Council, the AMAX molybdenum mine in Colorado, Tenneco versus the American Jewish Congress, the Ramayana restaurant in New York, and the Rev. Leon Sullivan's principles on South Africa, surveyed in Chapter 2, were all essentially conflicts over means, not goals.

The sources of goal and means incompatibility primarily include differing need and value structures in the context of joint dependence on common pools of resources. Struggles to acquire exploitation rights over such resources, as we have seen, take many forms. Multinationals affect a wide range of politically sensitive areas in the nations where they operate, including growth, employment, prices, technological progress, income distribution, taxation, dependence on external markets, pollution control, balance of payments, national security, competitive position in world markets, reliance on foreign resources, and so on. Actions that are perceived to threaten these interests are likely to represent points of incompatibility. Developing-nation governments may perceive multinational enterprise activity as harmful to their search for national identity, autonomy, and choice. As for labor organizations, the multinational may threaten their desire for a dominant and unassailable negotiating position. Social action groups may view the multinational as harming the interests of human rights, quality of life, or consumer protection. The ways in which multinational corporate interests may also diverge from the interests of opponents like local businessmen, military planners, out-of-office political parties, and international organizations will receive attention in the chapters ahead.

Perhaps the most fundamental source of diverging interests and resulting tensions is incompatibility between the global perspective of the multinational enterprise and the national perspective of most of the institutions with which it interacts. We normally view the world in terms of macroeconomic policy at the national level, setting the conditions within which the microeconomic functions of the firm are carried out. But we now have the global microeconomics of multinationals influencing the formation and effectiveness of macroeconomic policy at the national level. As one observer points out: "The most honest corporate manager allocating resources rationally with a transnational perspective is bound to have conflicts of interest with the most reasonable of statesmen whose rationality (and democratic responsibility) is bounded by national frontiers."[25] And so the multinational has interests that extend beyond the border of any single country. Each affiliate of an enterprise has what might be termed a double personality:

> It is an entity created under the laws of the country in which it operates, responsive to the sovereign that sanctions its existence. Yet at the same time, as a unit in a multinational network, each affiliate must also be responsive to the needs and strategies of the network as a whole. The multiplicity of influences to which any affiliate of a multinational enterprise is potentially exposed preoccupies national leaders, creating fertile ground for speculation and a sense of foreboding about their effects on the national economy.[26]

Conversely, multinational managers worry about the problems that arise from overlapping national jurisdictions, particularly their affiliates being used as political tools, conduits, and hostages by competing soverign states.

Resource scarcity, incompatible needs, multinational versus national perspectives, and overlapping jurisdictions are thus some of the basic causes of interest-divergence. We should also note a number of factors, however, that can serve to modify the amount of divergence that is perceived or acted upon. For instance, the social environment within which a particular multinational corporate conflict occurs may generate pressures for the reduction of differences between opposing parties. These ambient social pressures pushing for convergence (and thus cooperative behavior) include established traditions of cooperation, social norms, legal and moral restraints, public opinion, moral suasion from formal authorities, and the availability or presence of interested third parties such as conciliators, mediators, arbitrators, and fact-finders.[27] These pressures can push a multinational firm and an opposing party in a conflict in two directions: "toward deference to norms of fairness, social responsibility, reciprocity, and equity of exchange; and toward the search for alternatives to their preferred positions."[28]

A multinational enterprise is likely to be best able and most highly motivated to facilitate the need satisfaction of another party when *both* goals *and* means are positively interdependent. Here, coordination of convergent interests through collaborative effort seems appropriate. A relatively high level of cooperative behavior may also be useful when positive goal-interdependence is coupled with independence or even negative interdependence of means. When interests between the enterprise and the other party are convergent in some respects, but divergent in others, the situation will obviously involve mixed motives. A combination of cooperative and uncooperative behavior, ultimately resulting in compromise, will probably be in order. Here divergent and convergent interests, in regard to both goals and means, can be traded off against each other. Finally, a multinational will be least motivated to cooperate in situations where there is negative interdependence with respect to both goals and means. Interests here are totally opposed, and competing or avoiding conflict behavior is likely to be necessary. Uncooperative behavior may also be functional when goals are negatively interdependent but means are independent, or when means are negatively interdependent but goals are independent.[29]

Relationship Quality

Conflicts in multinational corporate operations may occur even when there is no perceived or actual divergence in goals or means among the parties. This is because emotional hostilities may exist as a result of prior relations and attitudes. Whether or not objective conflict of interest exists, the quality of a multinational's relations with an opposing party will help determine the amount of cooperativeness that is useful or possible.

A positive relationship will generally foster mutual trust, recognition of the legitimacy of the other party's interests, open communications, and an increased willingness to respond helpfully to the other party's needs. Examples we have briefly mentioned in Chapter 2 would include Booker McConnell and the government of Guyana during the 1960s, AMAX and the Colorado Open Space Coordinating Council in their "Experiment in Ecology," Freeport Minerals and the government of Indonesia on social programs for the Amungme tribe, the Reverend Sullivan and many of the companies endorsing his principles, and a few of the European multinationals which have openly accepted talks with international labor bodies.

A negative relationship, on the other hand, may give rise to suspicion, a low level and quality of communications, increased sensitivity to differences and threats, and a readiness to exploit or respond negatively to the other's demands. Cases here would include Nestlé and the Third World Action Group, Hoffmann-La Roche and the United Kingdom Monopolies Commission, Coca-Cola and the Indian government, ITT and Senator Church's Foreign Relations Committee, Shell and Delaware's Governor Russell W. Peterson, Akzo and unions in three countries, the Emergency Committee on American Trade and the AFL-CIO on Hartke-Burke, Mobil and the People's Bicentennial Commission, Firestone and the Young Americans for Freedom and so on.

The key idea here is a rather crude law of social relations: "Characteristic processes and effects elicited by a given type of social relationship (cooperative or uncooperative) tend also to elicit that type of social relationship."[30] In other words, cooperative relations breed cooperative behavior, while uncooperative relations breed uncooperative behavior.

Positive and negative relations and attitudes can emerge in many ways. Negative relations can result from isolation, stereotypes, failure or disillusionment in prior conflicts, mutual ignorance, awareness of dissimilarity in values, racial differences, distorted perceptions, institutional barriers between the parties, and so on. In many countries, ideologies and values may reject the multinational enterprise as an institution. Socialism as an ideological commitment, and concepts of capitalist exploitation, imperialism and class struggle will naturally place a burden on constructive conflict resolution. So will anti-American, anti-German, or anti-Japanese paranoia. The notorious, excessive, corrupt, or repugnant behavior of a handful of mutinationals can erode the foundation of mutual trust needed for positive relations. Many groups promote a poor image of MNEs. For example, the World Council of Churches declared its vehement opposition to multinationals in 1977 on the grounds that they were accomplices of "repressive states, predatory local elites and racism," and thus pillars of a system that "oppresses, excludes and exploits."[31]

Perhaps the foremost sources of negative relations for multinationals are ethnocentrism and nationalism. Ethnocentrism is "that view of things in which one's own group is the center of everything, and all others are scaled and rated with reference to it. Each group nourishes its own pride and vanity, boasts itself superior, exalts its own divinities, and looks with contempt upon outsiders. Each group thinks its own folkways are the only right ones, and if it observes that other groups have other folkways, these excite scorn."[32] Ethnocentrism reflects an inability to appreciate the viewpoint of others whose cultures have, for example, a different morality, religion or language. Ethnocentric attitudes, whether held by managers of a multinational enterprise or their opponents, express an unwillingness or inability to see the common problems that face all societies and that lie beneath variations in social and cultural traditions.

Nationalism, an extension of ethnocentrism, is a rather elusive concept that can be described as "a fusion of patriotism with a consciousness of nationality . . . or the individual's identification of himself with the 'we-group' to which he gives supreme loyalty."[33] Nationalism adds a strong emotional component to many conflicts involving multinationals.[34] It promotes devotion, often chauvinistic, to one's nation as a conscious emotion. It involves a sense of common political and economic interests or aspirations. It causes people to seek joint protection from perceived external threats and dependence. As one observer notes: "It is extremely unlikely that one can come to grips effectively with the pressures and conflicts inherent in the international movement of capital, skills, technology, and goods without an appreciation of the essential nature of nationalism and the cluster of interests represented in that notion."[35]

As the cultural anthropologist Margaret Mead demonstrated years ago, some cultures encourage a cooperative, trusting orientation toward people, while others foster competition, distrust and hostility.[36] Besides such cultural factors, many other things can lead to positive rather than hostile relations between multinationals and their opponents in conflict situations. These include experiences of successful prior interactions, perceived similarity in beliefs, values and attitudes, loyalties to a superordinate community and its institutions, mutual allegiances and memberships, cross-cutting identifications, free and continuing exchange of members, recognitions of existence and legitimacy, good communications, and importantly, concerns of the parties about their ability to work together in the future, particularly if such an association is perceived as unavoidable.

The number, salience, and importance of existing negative and positive bonds between a multinational enterprise and its conflict protagonists will determine the mutual attraction or identification between them. An enterprise is likely to exhibit high cooperativeness (in the form of collaboration or accommodation) when relations are open, friendly, and trusting. Uncooperative behavior (competition or avoidance), on the other hand, is most likely when relations are characterized by hatred, suspicion, distrust, and hostile attitudes. Finally, moderate levels of cooperativeness as expressed through compromise behavior are perhaps most probable, all else being equal, when relations are mixed or indifferent.

PUTTING IT ALL TOGETHER

Exhibit 3–1 summarizes our discussion of the key determinants of appropriate behavior in multinational corporate conflicts. The framework suggests that in any given conflict, the behavior likely to be most functional is a product of the interaction of four parameters: outcome stakes, relative power, interest interdependence, and relationship quality. As continuums, there is an infinite set of values (extending from low to high or negative to positive) which each of these four variables might have. This is, of course, also true for cooperativeness and assertiveness. The five points on the grid represent the extremes of what may be envisioned as behavioral "zones"—a competitive zone, an avoidance zone, a collaborative zone, an accommodative zone, and a compromise zone. It is our view that most multinationals have already encountered, and will continue to encounter, conflict situations of a relatively pure form, where the four situational

Exhibit 3–1
Determinants of Appropriate Conflict Behavior

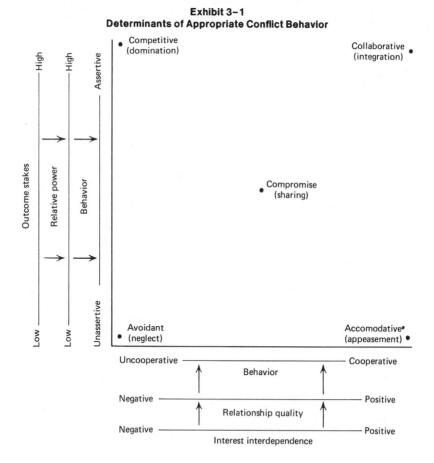

variables combine to unambiguously recommend behavior that is most appropriate—for example, stakes and power both high, and interests and relations both negative, thus calling for competitive behavior. Most multinationals have surely also experienced conflict situations where the four variables combine to suggest contradictory behavior, for example, where stakes are perceived to be high but power is relatively low, or where relations with another party are positive but the issues involved represent a mix of divergent and convergent interests. These mixed and ambiguous situations may require mixed behavior, as we shall argue below.

We should emphasize that the four situational variables are perhaps not equally important. The two related to "desirability," outcome *stakes* and interest *interdependence*, are probably much more important in assessing a conflict situation than the two variables related to "feasibility," relative *power* and relationship *quality*. In other words, the "motivational structure" of the conflict is probably a more important determinant of desired conflict behavior and outcomes than that of the "capability structure." This is because capabilities are more readily changeable than basic underlying motives.

We should also note certain linkages among the situational variables that may ease the task of analysis. Negative interest *interdependence* and negative relationship *quality*, for example, may be directly correlated. As a prominent sociologist noted many years ago, "it is expedient to hate the adversary with whom one fights, just it is expedient to love a person whom one is tied to."[37] It has also been shown experimentally that parties who dislike one another are apt to emphasize or develop incompatible goals.[38] Perhaps *stakes* and *power* are also linked. As the stakes in a conflict outcome increase, so does the incentive to utilize every source of power that may be available. High stakes provide the motivation to enhance one's relative power by increasing one's share of resources at the base of power and the effectiveness in using them, by finding allies, by decreasing the resources or increasing the costs of the other party.

Our framework suggests that a *competitive* (assertive, uncooperative) mode of handling conflict is likely to be appropriate for a multinational enterprise when its stakes and power are relatively high, and when interest independence and relations are relatively negative. The objective is domination. Competing in a militant way is likely to be useful only in very rare situations. Less extreme versions of "tough battling," however, may be necessary when conflict is felt to be inevitable and agreement impossible. Competing may be the only alternative against opponents who take advantage of noncompetitive behavior. It may also be vital in the face of totally unreasonable governmental, union, or action-group demands on matters where the firm's welfare is at stake and it knows for sure that it is right.

An *avoidance* (unassertive, uncooperative) mode of handling conflict is likely to be appropriate for a multinational when its stakes and power are relatively low, and when interest interdependence and relations are relatively negative. The objective is withdrawal or neglect. Avoidance can be useful to a multinational firm in many kinds of situations, for example:

1. When it does not wish to recognize the existence or legitimacy of a certain party.
2. When time is needed to let other parties cool down and regain perspective.
3. When alternate projects, sources, and markets are readily available.
4. When is seems fruitless to join forces with another party in pursuit of a desirable outcome.
5. When the issues in conflict are trivial and represent only minor annoyances.

6. When more important battles are pressing.
7. When potential disruption and negative publicity seem to outweigh the benefits of conflict resolution.
8. When more time is needed to gather information or to prepare for the struggle.
9. When others can resolve the conflict more effectively.
10. When the issues involved seem tangential to the principal conflict or symptomatic of other issues.[39]

A *collaborative* (assertive, cooperative) mode of handling conflict is likely to be appropriate for a multinational when its stakes and power are relatively high, and when interest interdependence and relations are relatively positive. The objective is integration. Collaboration is effective when the multinational and the other party want to achieve a mutually desired objective, but differ over the means; it is less useful in conflicts over basic goals or differing value systems. It can be especially valuable when the objective is to learn or to merge insights from groups with different perspectives. It can serve to gain commitment by incorporating divergent concerns into a consensus. It can help to work through feelings which have previously interfered with relationship. And it just may be necessary if both sets of concerns are too important to be compromised.

An *accommodative* (unassertive, cooperative) mode of handling conflict is likely to be appropriate for a multinational when its stakes and power are relatively low, and when interest interdependence and relations are relatively positive. The objective is appeasement. Accommodation is desirable when harmony and stability—"peaceful coexistence"—is deemed especially important. It makes sense when issues are more important to others than to the firm itself, and when giving-in is feasible from a cost point of view. Judicious accommodation can help to avoid substantial delays. It can serve to minimize loss when the firm finds itself outmatched and losing the battle. It can be useful when uncooperative behavior would mean the loss of cooperation of significant third parties. It can be necessary when the enterprise finds that it has been wrong. And it can be useful when organizational energy is needed for other conflicts where the stakes are higher.

Finally, a *compromise* (moderately assertive and cooperative) mode of handling conflict is likely to be appropriate for a multinational when its stakes are moderate and its power advantage or disadvantage is slight, and when interest interdependence and relations are mixes of positive and negative elements. The objective is to "split the difference"; to share the outcome of the conflict. Sharing is particularly useful where conflicts involve differences in goals, attitudes, and values. It works well when many issues, assigned different priorities by the two parties, are involved. It makes sense when goals are important, but not worth the effort or potential delays involved with more assertive modes of behavior. It can produce expedient solutions under time pressure and can provide temporary settlements to complex issues. And, it can be a primary backup when collaboration or competition are unsuccessful.

As we have suggested, it will generally be rare to find conflict situations that unambiguously call for either "pure" competition, avoidance, collaboration, accommodation, or compromise. Most conflict situations faced by multinationals are likely to be more complex and ambiguous. This means that behavioral approaches to conflict management likewise will have to be mixed, both simultaneously and sequentially. A wide variety of "hybrid" types of behavior, composed of elements partially drawn from two or more of the "pure" approaches, may have to be employed. These would correspond conceptually to points on our assertiveness-cooperativeness grid that fall elsewhere than the four corners or the exact center.

MIXED STRATEGIES

It is often necessary or useful for a multinational enterprise to employ different behavioral modes simultaneously in a single conflict. This can be done either on an issue or on actor basis. One of the major reasons why many multinational corporate conflicts become so protracted, and why participants become so unyielding, is that the bones of contention often become fused into a monolithic whole that is not easily broken apart. Each side comes to view the issues as so interconnected, and the resulting complex as so overwhelming, that the give-and-take process of compromise and concession appears impossible. The same phenomenon occurs when opposing coalitions come to be viewed as monolithic entities.

The likelihood of reaching a satisfactory solution to a conflict can often be increased by separating or "fractionating" the large issues involved into smaller and more workable ones.[40] Issues in a multinational corporate conflict can be manipulated—sized up or down, hooked together, broken apart, or stated in different language. They can be differentiated in terms of their importance and relatedness. When these subsets are formed, different conflict management modes can be applied. Some issues can be avoided, others compromised, still others subjected to intense competition, and so on. Creative issue-control can help alleviate the negative effects of excessive commitment that are often associated with attempts to resolve large or all-encompassing conflicts. Fractionation and application of multiple conflict-management behavior can often restructure a competitive zero-sum, "winner-take-all" conflict into one that includes give and take, a certain degree of cooperation, and a nonzero-sum outcome.

The parties with whom a multinational is in conflict can also be "fractionated." This is often necessary when the enterprise simultaneously confronts multiple parties whose interests in the conflict are divergent. Faced with contradictory and ambiguous pressures, the multinational frequently becomes the "monkey in the middle."[41] Pressed in different directions, the firm often has no choice but to handle the various parties in different ways. These kinds of situations can arise when protagonists are located within the same host or home nation, as well as when they are located in different nations.

Consider how Owens-Illinois got caught in the middle in Venezuela, and Ford Motor in the United Kingdom. As we shall see in Chapter 4 seven armed guerrillas of the Argimiro Gabalden Revolutionary Command kidnapped William F. Niehous, the general manager of the Venezuelan subsidiary of Owens-Illinois in 1976. The terrorists demanded, as conditions for the release of Niehous, that the company pay its workers compensation for past exploitation, distribute food packages to needy families, and place a lengthy manifesto denouncing the Venezuelan government and the company in local and foreign newspapers. On the third demand the company ran into a roadblock—the long standing policy of the government of President Perez not to allow guerrilla propaganda of any kind to appear in the local press. Owens-Illinois decided to ignore the government's warnings and ran the manifesto in *The New York*

Times, London Times, and *Le Monde.* Enraged by the action, the Perez regime abruptly announced it would expropriate the Venezuelan subsidiary of Owens-Illinois because it had "offended the dignity of the country and promoted the subversion of our constitutional order."[42] Although the government's nationalization plans were quietly dropped three years later and Niehous was soon after rescued, it had appeared back in 1976 that the company's gamble of simultaneously accommodating the terrorists and competing with a tough political leader had backfired.

We shall see in Chapter 14 how Ford Motor found itself repeatedly squeezed between British government pressure to hold wage increases below anti-inflation guidelines and union pressure to obtain much greater wage increases throughout the 1970s. Ford's 1971 wage settlement paved the way for the breakdown of the Heath government's attempt at voluntary pay restraint, and its 1974 settlement defied the national "social contract." Both of these wage deals led to accelerated wage inflation, since they set the pace for the rest of the automotive and engineering industries. In the fall of 1977, Ford found itself confronting Prime Minister Callaghan's policy of a 10% ceiling on wage increases, with sanctions threatened if the pay policy was blatantly ignored. Ford also faced union demands for 15% on pay plus 10% in fringe benefits. Given past experience one observer at that point noted that "the future of the government's pay policy in the private sector now lies in Ford's hands."[43] Not wanting a damaging strike and doubting the credibility of government sanctions—particularly because the company had recently announced its new engine plant for Wales—Ford once again breached the government's ceiling and settled with its workers for 12% plus fringe benefits. The British government grumbled a bit in public, but privately may well have been delighted that the settlement did not go much higher.

There are countless other cases calling for simultaneous utilization of different conflict-handling modes by multinationals in conflicts with more than one opponent in a particular nation. But more interesting and unique to conflicts facing multinational enterprises are situations calling for different modes of behavior applied to different parties in *different* nations. Because of their "double identity" and questions of overlapping and conflicting jurisdiction, multinationals often find themselves wedged between the hauling and shoving of parties in different countries whose interests point in fundamentally different directions.

Consider these cases involving simultaneous *competition* and *accommodation:* DuPont, confronted with depressed prices for acrylic fibers in Europe, upset the Dutch in 1977 by deciding to close down its plant at Dordrecht, but at the same time met the anxious wishes of the Secretary of State of Northern Ireland by agreeing to keep its plant at Londonderry open. Metal Box faced indignation in Israel by deciding to sell out its stake in Israel Can Co., but in doing so yielded completely to the pressure of its multinational food company customers that were being boycotted in Arab markets because of their use of blacklisted Metal Box cans. Volkswagen angered the Brazilian government during the recession of 1975 when it reassigned an export production order from its Brazilian subsidiary back to its German plants to appease workers at home. And numerous American-based multinationals have incurred the wrath of church, student, and labor groups at home by submitting to the demands of the South African government that black African trade unions not be recognized.

Perhaps the most provocative cases of this sort involve the extraterritorial application of American anti-trust or export-control laws. The application of the U.S. Trading With the Enemy Act in jurisdictions of other sovereign states has given rise to numerous *causes célèbres* with United States–based multinationals caught squarely in the middle. This Act authorized the President to regulate and control transactions with Communist countries and to embargo trade with countries like the People's Republic of China, North Korea, Vietnam, and Cuba. We shall examine in Chapter 7 how Fruehauf's majority-owned subsidiary in France found itself sandwiched between conflicting United States and French government positions in 1965 in regard to the shipment of truck trailers to the Peoples Republic of China. In Canada, cases over the years have involved Ford Motor, Rayonier, Alcan Aluminium, Fairbanks-Morse, MLW Worthington, American-owned flour milling companies, and drug companies on proposed sales of various goods to Cuba, Vietnam, or the Peoples Republic of China.[45] In many of these cases the multinationals have found themselves competing with, and antagonizing, Canadian interests as a result of their submission to pressure from the American government.

We should not leave the impression that multinationals employ mixed modes simultaneously only when forced to do so. In many conflicts the enterprise may find it particularly advantageous to use different conflict-handling modes with different parties. The strategy of "divide and conquer" has been employed throughout the ages. Using mixed modes, the multinational will often be able to block the formation of powerful opposing alliances. Coalitions may be prevented or broken down by the formation of countercoalitions and concomitant coalitions, or by instigating division or contention among weaker parties. We have already noted how Boeing found it useful to collaborate with the U.S. State Department while competing with the SEC on disclosure of overseas recipients of questionable payments. How Akzo busted the labor union front orchestrated by the International Chemical Workers Federation by obstinately refusing to negotiate on a multinational basis on the one hand, and carefully persuading small Dutch unions to agree to talks on a national basis on the other. How Fiat found it fruitful to thwart the search by French police for the kidnapped head of its local subsidiary, while simultaneously engaging in direct negotiations with the kidnappers and thus talking down the ransom price. How Ford Motor in early 1977 accommodated some human rights groups by pledging its support of the Rev. Sullivan's six principles on South Africa, and at the same time resisted a shareholder resolution filed by church organizations demanding that the company withdraw from South Africa. And how Westinghouse, in a fight for survival, filed suit against some two dozen uranium producers alleging existence of an international cartel, while reaching negotiated settlements out of court with some of the utilities that had sued the company for failure to deliver uranium called for in supply contracts.

ROLLING WITH THE PUNCHES

Conflicts are dynamic. They usually do not appear suddenly. Rather, they pass through a series of progressive stages as tension builds. Stages of conflict development include latent conflict, perceived conflict, intensifying conflict, manifest conflict, conflict resolution or suppression, and conflict aftermath.[46] Conflicts do not necessarily pass through all of these stages, and each party in a conflict may not be at the same stage at the same time. During these various stages, the conflict may either escalate or de-escalate, expand or contract, and speed up or slow down. Conditions related to stakes, power, party relations, and interest interdependence can thus fluctuate from one time period to the next. Such changing conditions, of course, call for changing modes of behavior on the part of the multinational enterprise.

Alterations in situational variables over time can often be consciously attempted by the parties in conflict. Values, beliefs, and perceptions can be altered by means of communication. The quality of a relationship may be improved by means of skillful public relations programs. The power balance may be shifted using efforts to increase the resources that underlie an enterprise's power or the effectiveness with which these resources of power are employed. Coalitions can be formed to offset an initial power disadvantage. Perceptions of the stakes involved in a conflict can be modified by altering variables such as availability of options or decision deadlines. Perceptions of interest interdependence can be changed by developing satisfactory substitutes for the goals in question, by bringing into play third-party intervention, by reformulating the issues involved, and by introducing "superordinate" goals or common threats that outweigh the existing hostility and divergent goals.[47]

Stakes, power, interests, and relationships may thus change during the course of a conflict as a consequence of explicit efforts initiated by the parties involved. They may also shift—especially over the longer term—as a result of inevitable changes in circumstances not completely under the control of one or more of the parties. This is perhaps best illustrated by the inevitable cycles that seem to be involved in the bargaining strength of multinational enterprises and governments of developing nations on natural resource exploitation. Many have noted the common pattern, often labelled the "obsolescing bargain," by which terms of original agreements in oil, bauxite, copper, iron ore, timber, and so on tend to become politically obsolete over time.[48]

As we shall examine in Chapter 8, this tends to be translated into changing external control pressures by national governments. Changing circumstances bearing on bargaining power and perceived interests make existing contractual provisions grossly unrealistic. The position of the multinational enterprise vis-à-vis a national government may weaken over time, for example, because of:

1. Relative easing of barriers to entry within the industry—for instance, "independents" entering the international oil industry—which increases the options available to a resource-rich host nation.
2. Diffusion over time of the firm's original managerial or technological know-how to local competitors.
3. Improvements in the governments's relative negotiating and administrative skills as a function of growing experience and education of its civil servants.
4. Pressures on government policy makers by out-of-power political adversaries calling for a tightening of terms.
5. Precedent-setting agreements established with other firms in the industry that are more favorable to the government, either within the country or in another country where similar circumstances prevail.
6. Reversals in perceptions of risk and return on the part of either the government or the enterprise, or both.

The parties often view the undertaking of a major resource development project, for example, as a relatively risky affair. But after the capital has been sunk and the initial risks have been overcome, the attitudes usually change. The enterprise may now perceive the project as offering more promise than before. The government, with the project now "captured," often comes to view the original terms of the agreement as much less reasonable. Knowing that the terms needed to retain the enterprise can now be less generous than those needed to attract it in the first place, it presses for renegotiation. As one economist has noted: "Lamentations and exhortations are unlikely to change the dynamics of this cycle, which is based on a sharp break from a situation of great uncertainty, asymmetries and little transnational corporation commitment, to a situation of much more information, symmetry as well as large transnational corporation investments *in situ.*"[49]

Sequential use of different conflict-handling modes by multinationals may thus be required by necessity or design. Exhibit 3–2 illustrates sixteen potential paths of behavior change. Numerous paths may be used in any one conflict, although it should be noted that the course of many conflicts may be determined largely by the "language of opening moves."[50] Initial behavior in the form of offers, gestures, and moves is critical in the creation of the psychological setting that may prevail throughout much of the conflict. It is at this stage that rules and norms are first implanted, issues such as trust and toughness are considered for the first time, and each party's preferences, intentions, and perceptions are exposed. The first behavioral mode selected by a multinational enterprise, then, is likely to be the most important one, although some movement away from these opening positions may well be required.

From a normative point of view, many would recommend that a multinational enterprise initially attempt to employ the *collaborative* mode of handling conflict whenever possible. This is because outcomes of such behavior are likely to approximate most closely outcomes that are substantively "fair" or in the "public interest," and that are arrived at by procedurally "equitable means"— the assumption here is that over the long term, the interests of the enterprise will be maximized if they coincide with perceptions of public interest. But joint problem-solving efforts are fragile and may break down. Thus, path 1 (collaborate-compromise) in Exhibit 3–2 may be needed to resolve remaining issues. If the breakdown is severe enough and if the enterprise finds itself in a weak bargaining position, then path 2 (collaborate-accommodate) may be necessary to maintain a positive working relationship with the other party. If the multinational's power base is strong and the relationship is viewed as expendable, then path 3 (collaborate-compete) may represent a last resort when problem-solving efforts uncover completely irreconcilable interests.

When a multinational enterprise is confronted by a sudden issue that is associated with the expression of intense and aggressive feeling, the *accommodative* mode may be very useful as a starting point. If the desire to fully understand and empathize with the other party is sincere, it may serve to reestablish a relationship that can eventually employ either compromise (path 4) or possibly even collaboration (path 5). Accommodation may facilitate influence by gradations—the "foot-in-the-door" technique—or even induce guilt or obligation in the other party, making it less able to resist the more uncooperative or assertive influence attempts that follow.

Exhibit 3–2
Sequential Patterns of Conflict Behavior

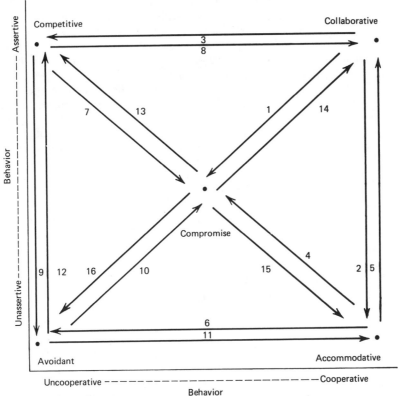

The switch from accommodation to avoidance (path 6) may be necessary when the enterprise is pushed too far or when things just don't work out. As we shall note in Chapter 11, Philips N.V. used to meet with the European Metalworkers Federation (EMF), and representatives of its European employees. But when EMF wanted to include an official of the International Metalworkers Federation (IMF), a worldwide, rather than European body, the company cried off.[51] As another example, there was the case of Polaroid Corp. and South Africa, which will be discussed in Chapter 5. In 1971 demonstrations, sit-ins and an attempted product boycott in the United States led Polaroid to acquiesce to some of the demands of the Polaroid Workers' Revolutionary Movement. The company required its independent distributor in South Africa to improve wages and job opportunities for blacks and barred sales of its products to the South African government, but in November 1977 it pulled out altogether after it confirmed reports from exiled black activists that its distributor had been selling film to the government in violation of the 1971 understanding. [52]

Competitive opening behavior on the part of a multinational may be necessary to bypass "premature cooperation" which leads to a superficial, unsatisfactory, or unstable agreement before the underlying issues in a conflict have really been worked through. Competition, with its threat of losses, may occasionally be a necessary precondition to motivate the parties to engage in a cooperative process. By starting tough, the enterprise acquires options associated with being a "reformed sinner." It can thus systematically soften its position by making positive concessions, either in part (path 7) or in full (path 8). Texaco and Standard Oil of California, for example, after their oil concessions in Libya were nationalized in 1973–74, took their cases to the International Court of Justice, contending that Libya had not lived up to the terms of their concessions. In May of 1977, the court ruled that Libya should abide by the concession agreement. The ruling led to negotiations resulting in a settlement under which each company would receive crude oil valued at $76 million in compensation.[53] Without the leverage of the international arbitration proceedings, the process of genuine bargaining might never have occurred. Finally, we should note that with competitive behavior, the enterprise always has the option to "leave the field" when the going gets too rough or too costly (path 9). Examples here that we reviewed earlier would include Firestone's termination of its Rumanian rubber plant deal as a result of the protest organized by the Young Americans for Freedom, and Shell Oil's departure from the state of Delaware after the bitter "To Hell with Shell" campaign of environmentalists.

Avoidance behavior, as we have explored, often makes sense for openings when stakes and power are low and interests and relationships are negative. But all of these variables change over time. For an extreme case consider Coca-Cola and Portugal. The soft drink had been opposed by the Portuguese government for fifty years on grounds that it was a symbol of American degeneracy and a habit-forming drug. But in mid-January of 1977, Portugal announced that it would allow the manfacture of Coca-Cola within the country.[54] Many other conflicts involving multinationals represent only hot emotions of the moment. If the enterprise backs off and lets the situation cool down (avoidance), it is possible that a basis may emerge at a later time for meaningful dialogue and negotiation (path 10). When the relationship improves or interests converge, a transition to accommodation may be appropriate (path 11). If the stakes go up or the power balance reverses, then a switch to competition (path 12) may become the logical course of action.

When might it make sense to move away from an opening position of willingness to *compromise?* When negotiations are moving slowly or leverage is needed, the enterprise may well find it expedient to introduce some threats into the picture (path 13). This behavior is typified by Goodrich's delivery of an ultimatium to the Dutch government during negotiations over the future of its money-losing Vredestein affiliate, or Alcoa, Reynolds and Kaiser asking the World Bank's International Centre for the Settlement of Investment Disputes to begin arbitration proceedings on the unilateral tax boost of the Jamaican Government in May of 1974. The actions of Kennecott, Anglo-Iranian Oil Company, British Petroleum, Nelson Bunker Hunt, and Compagnie Française des Petroles in their "hot mineral" battles with expropriating governments would also fall under this heading.

At other times the very experience of "good faith" bargaining and development of mutual trust between a multinational and another party may allow compromise behavior to be converted into collaboration (path 14). At still other times, a decline in power or desire to maintain a particular relationship may call for a movement towards accommodation (path 15). A classic case here would be that of the oil majors and OPEC. With the entry of lean and hungry independents into the Middle East, the leading firms lost their ability to set the terms of doing business. As a result, decisions that were the product of compromise in the 1950s and 1960s became products of accommodation in the 1970s. Finally, if bargaining fails to produce an acceptable agreement, the multinational enterprise always has the option of leaving the scene (path 16). IBM's refusal to bow to the demands of the Indian government after a long search for a workable compromise, and subsequent decision in late 1977 to dismantle its manufacturing and marketing operations in that country, provide an example of this final path.

In the chapters that follow, we shall explore a variety of kinds of conflicts confronting the management of multinational enterprises. In each case, we shall carefully explore the underlying nature of the conflict itself, and how it bears on the MNE. In each case as well, we shall attempt to apply our contingency model of conflict management in order to test its usefulness as a diagnostic and prescriptive tool in what are often highly sensitive and troublesome situations.

4 TERRORISM

Buenos Aires, May 1973: After seven years of floundering military government, the military junta led by President Lanusse had voluntarily decided to step down. A new Peronist government headed by Dr. Hector J. Campora would take office on May 25th, with the greatest popular mandate in 20 years. The revered former dictator Juan D. Peron would soon be returning home from 17 years in exile, the four year old "state-of-siege" decree of the military was to be lifted at last, and a "wide and generous" amnesty proclaimed for political prisoners. Many hoped that the reintroduction of democratic civilian rule would bring an end to mounting urban violence and usher in a long-awaited era of political stability and economic progress. Instead, Argentina quickly sank deeper into a political, social, and economic quagmire. Intent on a comprehensive socialist revolution, many of Argentina's young intellectuals were growing increasingly disenchanted with the moderate line espoused by President-Elect Campora. Pleas to young Peronist left-wingers and Marxists to lay down their arms were being ignored, and Argentina became engulfed by a wave of kidnapping, assassinations, bombings, and robberies. Multinationals operating in the country—such as Ford Motor Company, with 8500 employees producing over 47,000 cars and trucks, and a commitment in Argentina dating back to 1916—were among the chief victims.

May 22nd: The manager of Ford's analysis department, Luis Giovanelli, and supervisor of industrial relations Noemi Baruj de la Rin, were leaving the Ford complex in the Gen. Pachecho area of Buenos Aires. Without warning, their cars were blocked at the plant gate. In what was apparently a bungled kidnap attempt, two gunmen riding in a pickup truck panicked and sprayed machine gun fire into both cars. Rin survived; Giovanelli died a month later. Within hours, the August 22 Unit of the Peoples Revolutionary Army (Ejercito Revolucionario del Pueblo—ERP) claimed responsibility for the attack. A non-Peronist, Trotskyite group with about 500 members, ERP had developed into Argentina's most active, well-armed and efficient urban guerilla organization.[1] Ford Argentina and several newspapers were notified that further attacks would be made on Ford employees unless the company supplied over $1 million in new ambulances to the various Argentine states and directed donations to area hospitals. Ford's management was faced with the choice of extorted charitable contributions or threats of further violence.

May 23rd: Ford's vice-president of Asian, Pacific, and Latin American automotive operations, Edgar R. Molina, issued a statement in Dearborn, Michigan that "we have no idea what precipitated the attacks." Yet Ford wasted no time in surrendering. Molina's statement also announced that "Ford Argentina has responded affirmatively and expressed its willingness to meet the demands

. . . we believe under the circumstances we have no choice but to meet the demands."[2]

May 24th: Following negotiations with the ERP—in which the Argentine government apparently had "absolutely not participated"—Ford announced that the company would give an ambulance to each of 22 provincial hospitals, turn over medical supplies and equipment to children's hospitals in Buenos Aires and the province of Catamarca, and distribute food and school supplies in slum areas of the capital.[3] Reactions to Ford's decision from other foreign companies operating in Argentina ran the gamut from resignation to criticism. One executive noted: "This has become the price of doing business here. Companies will just have to try to figure out whether the profits are worth the investment in security, blackmail, and worries." Another took a different view: "This amounts to buying protection just like you would from any gangster group. . . . I think there is a limit beyond which a company should not give in."[4]

May 25th: Campora was inaugurated, and called for a "real political and social truce." Despite a wide-ranging amnesty program for political prisoners, including many convicted urban guerrillas, the ERP vowed to continue its attacks against businesses and the armed forces. Campora's moderate program was denounced as a "national unity between the army oppressors and the oppressed, between exploitative businessmen and the exploited workers."[5]

May 28th: The Argentine subsidiary of Otis Elevator Company received a telephone call from someone claiming to be a member of ERP, who threatened that an Otis executive would be killed unless the company granted all of its workers a 100% wage increase and distributed $500,000 in food, clothing, and medical supplies to slum residents and hospitals in Argentina.

June 1st: Otis countered with resistance. The company announced: "We are convinced that no organization wishes to close a source of employment for 1200 persons and their families."[6] Before adopting this stance, however, Otis executives and their families had been relocated to São Paulo, Brazil. Otis had provided a new model.

June 7th: The Argentine subsidiary of General Motors received a similar threat. GM promptly transferred 16 of 22 expatriate families out of the country and announced that it would not comply with terrorist demands that it rehire 1000 workers laid off in 1968.

June 20th: Former president Juan D. Peron returned home, only to be greeted at the airport by an outbreak of shooting between leftist and rightist followers, which killed 20 and wounded 400.

August 11th: Twenty-five Coca-Cola Export Company executives and their families began leaving Argentina after the company refused to pay a $1 million extortion demand. The MNE response pattern of resistance coupled to precautionary avoidance was beginning to catch on. With the Ford extortion model evidently of limited value, the terrorists increased reliance on the classic technique of kidnapping. During the Argentine winter executives of the following multinationals were abducted and subsequently released after the payment of "revolutionary taxes" collectively totalling more than $7 million: First National City Bank of New York, Bank of Italy, Firestone Tire and Rubber, Sylvania, Coca-Cola, British American Tobacco, and Acrow Steel.

October 12th: Peron, suffering from a bad heart condition, was inaugurated on his 78th birthday. As many expected, he had orchestrated the resignation of his "puppet," Campora, soon after his return, and was elected President of Argentina on September 23rd with 61% of the popular vote. His inauguration was preceded and followed by a wave of political assassinations growing out of factional struggle within the Peronist movement. ITT's Sheraton Hotel and the Bank of America branch in Buenos Aires had been bombed a few days earlier. The next five weeks saw the kidnapping of a British banker, an Austrian industrialist, and David W. Wilkie, President of Amoco Argentina, a subsidiary of Standard Oil of Indiana.

November 22nd: Ford again became a victim. As John A. Swint, American general manager of Ford's Transax parts subsidiary located in Cordoba, was on his way to the plant, his car and another one carrying bodyguards were blocked on the road by four cars and trucks. Fifteen well-dressed gunmen sprayed both cars with machine gun fire. Swint, his chauffeur, and one of his two bodyguards were killed instantly. A week later a Peronist guerilla group, called the Peronist Armed Forces (Fuerzas Armadas Peronistas—FAP) claimed responsibility for the murders. Ford Argentina soon received written threats that its executives and their families would be "knocked off one by one" and that its main plant in a suburb of Buenos Aires would be blown up.[7]

November 28th: Ford secretly chartered an aircraft and flew 22 foreign executives and their families to Montevideo, Uruguay. Some continued to the United States and others to Europe. Ford's exit mirrored executive departures at Otis Elevator, GM, Coca-Cola, and Kodak. IBM, meanwhile, had permanently moved operations out of Argentina. A few days later Tom Drake, the general sales and marketing manager of Ford Argentina, commented on his homecoming: "Ford decided it would be in our best interests."[8]

December 5th: Argentine troops armed with machine guns and automatic rifles took up positions around Ford's plants. The Ford attack and departure had aroused panic within the foreign community still residing in Argentina and spurred the Peron government to take action. American and other foreign auto makers had met with Interior Minister Benito Llambi, and on December 3rd he proclaimed that protection would be provided to any foreign plant that requested it—protective security measures would be provided by the Gendarmeria Nacional, the para-military force which guards the nation's frontiers and strategic installations. The company announced the next day that with this new protection it would gradually bring some of its executives back to Argentina.

December 6th: With the automakers now heavily guarded, the terrorists switched to petroleum. Seven men carrying submachine guns casually strolled into the cafeteria at Exxon's Esso refinery in Campana, 90 miles north of Buenos Aires, and abducted manager Victor S. Samuelson. Slogans painted on the canteen walls indicated that the job had been done by the outlawed ERP.

December 11th: The ERP demanded a $10 million "Santa Claus" ransom "as a partial reimbursement to the Argentine people for the copious riches extracted from our country by the company in long years of imperialist exploitation."[9] Samuelson was being held in a "peoples jail" and would soon be "submitted to trial" on unspecified charges. Complex negotiations between Esso Argentina and the ERP began, reportedly using two former Argentine federal policemen to handle most of the direct contacts. Constant touch was maintained with Exxon headquarters in New York, and the Argentine government was frequently consulted. The negotiations reached a critical impasse several times. The company reportedly rejected the initial demand of $10 million as being too high and offered $7 million. The guerrillas responded by sending Esso a written death sentence and indicated that Samuelson's body would be found draped in an American flag unless the offer was increased. Indeed, ERP raised its ransom demand to $14.2 million, the additional $4.2 million to take the form of food, clothing, and building materials for flood victims in northern Argentina. Exxon rejected the new demands and the talks collapsed.

February 14th, 1974: In a clandestine press conference held by the ERP, one of the guerrilla leaders spoke about the negotiations for Samuelson's release: "His company says it is willing to pay but it fears it will have problems with the Argentine government . . . but we told them we were confident they would figure out a way to get around those problems." In regard to the size of the demands, "we are certain that all the big foreign companies have already figured ransom demands into their budgets. We know the money is well within Esso's budget."[10]

February 25th: According to the Buenos Aires *Herald,* "at the 11th hour . . . a series of frantic telephone calls linked top management in the United States with local executives. They all agreed that they could not go to bed that night conscious of the fate that awaited Samuelson. Urgent efforts were made to re-establish contact with the guerrillas—and by a stroke of luck, the news that the company was prepared to resume negotiations reached a contact."[11] The message reportedly arrived just as Samuleson was being transported from the "peoples prison" to the site where he was to be executed.

March 11th: At a rendezvous with ERP guerrillas, an Esso representative handed over 142,000 $100 bills packed in brief cases in the trunk of a car. The representative asked the guerrillas to sign a receipt, which produced only a scrawled obscenity. The Argentine government had strongly objected to the $4.2 million aid-in-kind for flood victims, so Esso convinced the terrorists to accept this portion in the form of cash. As another condition for Samuelson's release, Esso was required to publish an advertisement in some 40 Argentine newspapers detailing the original demands, criticizing its own "exploitation" of workers, and justifying the payment as "an indemnification." Only three of 12 newspapers in Buenos Aires published the ad; the other nine feared reprisals by the Argentine government, since the press had previously been forbidden to mention ERP's name or its messages. The left-wing newspaper *El Mundo,* which did run the ad on its front page, was soon closed down by the government and criminal proceedings were ordered against its publishers and editors.[12]

April 29th: Samuelson was released at the home of a doctor in the suburbs of Buenos Aires. Weeks had passed with no word about his fate. Some feared a terrorist doublecross. Others speculated that the terrorists were merely experiencing difficulty changing dollars into Argentine pesos on the limited black market. Still others felt that Argentine terrorists were preoccupied—during the Samuelson negotiation period, executives of Peugeot, Pepsico, and McKee Tecsa had been kidnapped and ransomed, the Fiat personnel chief and a Brazilian industrialist were assassinated, a U.S. Information Service official was seriously wounded, and the director of the Argentine affiliate of Lloyds International Exchange Bank of London was kidnapped and released. After a cup of tea and a reunion with Esso officials, Samuelson boarded a plane for the United States, traveling under an assumed name. On his arrival in Miami the next day, he merely told awaiting reporters: "I'm very happy and I am well . . . I'm anxious to get back to my family."[13] A few days later at a news conference he had a simple comment: "It was not an experience I'd recommend to anybody."[14]

June 12th: ERP announced that $5 million, a part of the ransom obtained for the release of Samuelson, had been provided to Uruguayan, Chilean, and Bolivian insurgent groups by way of the "Junta de Coordinación" which had been formed to direct the "joint struggle" in five countries of Latin America.[15] Paradoxically, one of the world's largest multinational corporations, may thus have provided start-up financing for one of the world's largest multinational terrorist networks.

THE CHALLENGE OF TERRORISM

A report of the U.S. Central Intelligence Agency, completed in July 1977, estimated that 1152 acts of international and transnational terrorism were committed during the period January 1, 1968, through December 31, 1976, of which 391 victimized American citizens or property.[16] In 1976, three out of five terrorist incidents that were directed against American citizens or facilities abroad victimized United States-based multinationals or their employees. Dr. Charles A. Russell, a former chief in the U.S. Air Force's Directorate of Counter-Intelligence, using a data base of 1800 terrorist episodes occurring during the period January 1, 1970 to November 1, 1977, offers some additional findings.[17] His data base, which excludes actions in Northern Ireland, Israel, and the United States, shows that during the period studied, 512 persons were killed, 551 wounded, and 363 kidnapped. Eighty percent of the kidnappings were successful, 78% of the incidents had occurred in the last three years, and 43% of the victims were businessmen. More than $146 million in known ransoms had been paid during this period. Over two-thirds of the assassinations had taken place in the last three years—390 victims were involved in 257 incidents; 38% of them occurred in Latin America and 46% in Western Europe. Of the assassination victims, 17.2% were businessmen, slightly more than diplomats, who accounted for 15.7%. Business enterprises, especially American-owned, were the focus of terrorist bombs in half of the 924 bombings recorded in Russell's data base.

Statistics of course are cold and impersonal, and given the subject, highly imperfect—hence the "Argentine chronology" with which this chapter began, showing a small "slice" of terrorist activities affecting multinational enterprises.

A scanning of terrorist incidents over the past decade or so indicates clearly that business concerns—particularly MNEs—have been preferred targets of numerous forms of terrorism in a great many nations. Multinationals, according to many observers, have become a favorite "instrumental target" of terrorists because of public allegations—frequently advanced by governmental spokesmen, religious organizations, and "public interest" groups—that they are responsible for various societal ills, because they have symbolic propaganda value as agents of imperialism, and because of their high "embarrassment quotients" for national governments.[18] The CIA has concluded that "because of the tighter security measures that have been introduced at U.S. military and diplomatic installations, the continuing lure of potentially lucrative ransom and extortion payments, and the symbolic value of U.S. firms (e.g., as "capitalist foreign exploiters" of the local working class), there is a real danger that terrorist attacks on the U.S. business community abroad will become even more frequent in the future.[19]

In raw numbers the price tag of terrorism for MNEs to date, in terms of executives lost, property damaged, and ransom paid, has hardly been astronomical. But the threat, while often exaggerated, is very real indeed. And so are its consequences for multinationals. In the opinion of many experts, MNEs continue to appear naked, vulnerable, and ill-prepared to respond to terrorism. They cannot afford to neglect this complex and controversial menace or the problems it poses for society or themselves. This chapter draws on the vast amount of literature that has recently emerged on the subject of terrorism in order to provide a broad survey of the problem and some approaches to coping with this grisly challenge of modern international business.[20]

WHAT IS TERRORISM?

A universally accepted and comprehensive definition of terrorism does not exist, and probably never will. Wide disagreements exist on a number of counts and, as the old political maxim goes, "one man's terrorist is another man's freedom fighter." Third World and communist states have consistently argued that terrorism is not subversive to international order *if* it is directed towards the liberation of oppressed peoples. By definition, therefore, "terrorism should only cover acts committed for personal gain or out of caprice of non-political purposes."[21] Other questions about the meaning of terrorism include the following: (1) Should acts of psychopaths and criminals be included along with acts of crusaders? (2) Should "terror from above," as variously practiced by regimes in Uganda, Chile, Ethiopia, East Germany, and the Soviet Union, be included with "terror from below?" (3) Should acts of terror during wartime such as the atomic bomb at Hiroshima be included? (4) Should acts which occur during guerrilla warfare, mass insurrection, liberation struggles, revolutionary or counter-revolutionary action be included? (5) Should distinctions be made between domestic, transnational, and international acts of terrorism?

The boundaries which separate terrorism from other forms of violence are indeed fuzzy. Some have argued that it is the amorality of terror—the use of indiscriminate murder and other violence without moral scruples or regard for the degree of suffering of the victims—which distinguishes it from other forms of violence.[22] Indeed, "depersonalization" of victims to regard them as simple instruments of oppressors rather than human beings has become a standard component of terrorist dogma, intended to remove moral scruples from the act of killing. Others consider "terrorism to be violence aimed at the people watching. Fear is the intended effect, not a by-product. That, at least, distinguishes terrorist tactics from muggings, and other common forms of violent crime that may terrify but are not terrorism."[23] Symbolic expression appears to be fundamental—terrorism is "the purposive use of violence by the precipitator(s) against an instrumental target in order to *communicate* to a primary target a threat of violence so as to coerce the primary target into behavior or attitudes through intense fear or anxiety in connection with a demanded power (political) outcome."[24] It has variously been described as "armed propaganda," "propaganda by deed," "a symbolical act," "politics by violence," "an insurrectional strategy," "high-leverage violence," and "an ultimate form of protest."[25] Amid this diversity, one must concur that "any definition of political terrorism venturing beyond noting the systematic use of murder, injury, and destruction or the threats of such acts toward achieving political ends is bound to lead to endless controversies."[26] We should note, however, that our concern in this chapter rests with terror from below directed specifically against multinational enterprises, whether by "crusaders, criminals, or crazies,"[27] as apart from "regimes of terror" (that is, terror from above), which is considered in our next two chapters on human rights.

Terrorism is certainly not new. As many scholars have demonstrated, this sort of violence has been around for a long time, and has known no boundaries of nation or ideology.[28] Terrorists stalked and claimed their victims in ancient times. One of the earliest known movements was the "Sicarii," a sect active in the zealot struggle in Palestine during the first century. Ten centuries later the "Assassins," an offshoot of the Ismailis in Egypt, were galvanized by Messianic hope and political terrorism. Terrorism owes its name and subsequent conceptual flowering, however, to the French Reign of Terror (1793–1794). Russian men and women of the 19th Century "Narodnaya Volya" (people's will) lobbed bombs at the Czar's officials. They were followed in Europe by radical nationalist groups employing terrorism, such as the Irish "Sinn Fein" against the English in the 1920s, and Armenians and Macedonians against the Turks. The United States had its Molly Maguires in the Pennsylvania coal fields, and the assassins of Presidents Garfield and McKinley. Then there were the exploits of Menahem Begin's "Irgun Zvai Leumi" in the British-mandated territory of Palestine in the 1940s, including murder of kidnapped British soldiers, the King David Hotel bombing that cost 100 lives, and the Deir Yassin massacre. The Nationalist Liberation Front (FLN) employed random terrorism in the 1950s to help free Algeria of French domination.

Much has changed since the anarchist era of 80 years ago, when dynamite was hailed as the "ultimate destroyer." The weapons and techniques are more sophisticated today. Attacks seem to have become more impersonal, more indiscriminate. There is more "remote-control" support from established governments, a great deal more international collaboration among terrorists, and there are many more so-called "third-country" operations. And there is the historically unprecedented role of the electronic media in dramatizing terrorist acts.

Like terrorism itself, its causation in the present-day context is terribly complex and not fully understood. No simple explanation exists and generalizations tend to be of limited value—the search for a universal explanation that applies without contradiction to such diverse groups as the Argentine People's Revolutionary Army, Japanese Red Army, Black Panther Party, Irish Republican Army, Red Brigades, Baader-Meinhof Gang, Fatah, and South Moluccans has been and will continue to be a fruitless endeavor. It seems clear that terrorist groups have developed quite independently in very different social, political, and cultural environments, and each one can truly be understood only by careful reference to the specific environment in which it originated. Such a detailed diagnosis would constitute a monumental effort—there are at least 140 clearly defined terrorist organizations active in the world today. Nor would it be particularly useful to the multinational corporate executive who needs to consider the problem of terrorism from the standpoint of the enterprise as a whole.

A mid-range approach exists, however, between fine detail and vague generalization. One can define conditions under which terrorism seems to occur. By gathering and integrating a number of elements that various experts and scholars have suggested are relevant to the explanation of terrorism, one can begin to view the phenomenon as a matter of "contingencies." Utilizing what essentially amounts to a system of interconnected hypotheses (some confirmed and others not), one can rather quickly develop a feel for those circumstances or situations in which terrorism is most likely to flourish. At the same time we can pinpoint the particular groups or nations for which these factors seem to apply.

Such a "contingency" scheme is represented in Exhibit 4–1. It shows *Terrorist Actions* (box 4) as a product of three groups of variables: (1) *Origins*, factors that lie at the roots of terrorism itself; (2) *Objectives*, factors that conspicuously serve to inspire acts of terrorism; and (3) *Facilitators*, factors that imply a presence of support or an absence of impediments by outside agents. Terrorism can thus be viewed as a product of interactions between basic and proximate motivation and facilitation. The scheme suggests that, given the presence of one or more origins, these may get translated into one or more objectives. The latter, in turn, may find expression in acts of terrorism if the environment facilitates the implementation of these acts—that is, if contextual conditions do not thwart their occurrence. Terrorism directed against multinationals, therefore, can take many different paths—originating for different reasons, finding inspiration in different demands, being facilitated in different ways, and occurring at different times, in different forms, and with different degrees of intensity.

Origins of Terrorism

The roots of terrorism are varied, deep, and often interrelated, and we should note that the motives of terrorists may not necessarily be connected with observable "objective" conditions. As one observer has warned, "given the irrationality of the acts in question . . . it is surely a mistake to look for rational motivation."[29] Still, it seems useful to examine some of the correlations with objective factors that seem to make sense.

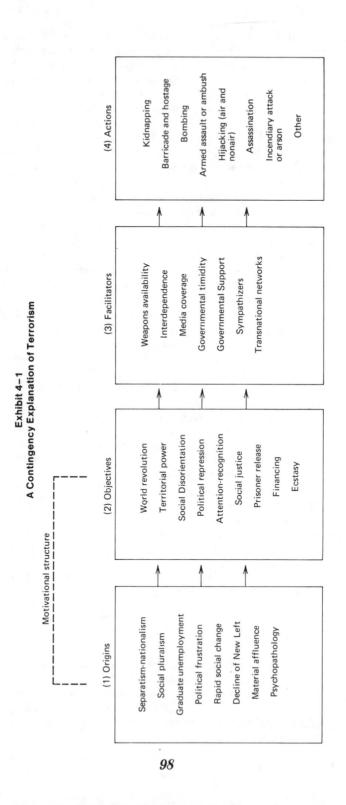

Exhibit 4-1
A Contingency Explanation of Terrorism

Motivational structure

(1) Origins

Separatism-nationalism

Social pluralism

Graduate unemployment

Political frustration

Rapid social change

Decline of New Left

Material affluence

Psychopathology

(2) Objectives

World revolution

Territorial power

Social Disorientation

Political repression

Attention-recognition

Social justice

Prisoner release

Financing

Ecstasy

(3) Facilitators

Weapons availability

Interdependence

Media coverage

Governmental timidity

Governmental Support

Sympathizers

Transnational networks

(4) Actions

Kidnapping

Barricade and hostage

Bombing

Armed assault or ambush

Hijacking (air and nonair)

Assassination

Incendiary attack or arson

Other

Separatism–nationalism. Countries with submerged nationality problems frequently fall prey to terrorism—"freedom fighting." Whether it is Ulster, Palestine, Québec, Corsica, Eritrea, Brittany, or the Basque region of Spain, movements for regional autonomy or separation have often turned to terrorism to "soften up" the national government, or after political action has failed. One finds in these cases "a great many ambitions and aspirations held by those with little leverage, which under present circumstances cannot be achieved and yet cannot be abandoned by the faithful."[30] One also finds strong relationships between terrorism and the effects of war, changes in frontiers, and displacement of persons. The deep-seated bitterness and frustration of Palestinian refugees is a case in point. Terrorism has also featured prominently in a great many anti-colonialism struggles—in this decade, for example, in Angola, Namibia, and Mozambique.

Social pluralism. Racial, religious, cultural, and linguistic pluralism within countries can often be associated with the use of terror. Indeed, since World War II the most common cause of violence involving states has not been external wars but internal ethnic or secessionist conflict.[31] Ethnic violence involving protracted or intermittent terrorism by minority groups involved American Blacks in the 1960s, and continues today with Catholics in Northern Ireland, East Indians in Guyana, Germans in Italy, French in Canada, and even French/Italians in Switzerland.[32] Nor can the impact of religious fanaticism in this context be ignored, especially in the Middle East, Ulster, the Basque region, and Croatia.

Social inequalities are frequently mentioned as the main factors responsible for the spread of terrorism. Institutionalized discrimination against minorities—whether Catholics in Northern Ireland or French in Canada—has often reinforced seccessionist demands and created swamps of misery in which hatred and fanaticism breed. Yet mass social grievances and class struggles have rarely led to terrorism. One observer had concluded: "As experience shows, societies with the least political participation and most injustice have been the most free from terrorism in our time."[33]

Graduate unemployment. Ernst Halperin has argued that terrorist movements in Latin America have expressed "the despair of young members of the administrative class, radicalized and alienated from society by the deterioration of their prospects in countries of stagnant economy."[34] Especially in Uruguay and Argentina, the upsurge of terrorism occurred in the last decade against backgrounds of serious economic crisis where university graduates could not find jobs and thus became an "academic proletariat." The same phenomenon has also been widespread in Italy. Economic difficulties linked to labor problems, lagging productivity, and recession, along with protective policies of unions towards workers already on the payroll, led to a situation where more than one million university and high school graduates failed to find their first jobs. They have been labeled "marginals" by the Italian press, live on the fringe of society, and feel rejected by it. Some of them have turned to terrorism.

The concept of "relative deprivation," as a "perceived discrepancy between the goods and conditions of life which members of a group believe are their due and the goods and conditions which they think they can in fact get and keep," nicely captures the essence of the Italian, Uruguayan, and Argentinian situations.[35] Still, terrorism often arises in the absence of economic stagnation and massive youth unemployment. It emerged at the time of economic prosperity, for example, in Northern Ireland, Northern Spain, Brazil, West Germany, and Japan.

Political frustration. Many observers contend that groups tend to opt for terrorism when they face unresolved grievances and when they perceive no other way of registering protest and affecting change. In Italy, Spain, Argentina, and France, for example, radicals seem to have found it hard to express their discontent inside the political system. In Italy, as the Communist Party became a pillar of the establishment by striking a deal with the governing Christian Democrats, a political no-man's land emerged to the left of the Communists. Much of Italy's terrorism has emerged from this barren territory. Other observers like to make a connection between political oppression and terrorism. In Brazil, for example, we have seen minor movements challenging the established regime, which have variously been suppressed by the authorities.

Rapid social change. In a gloomy book, *It Happened in Italy: 1968–1977*, Alberto Ranchey, a leading Italian journalist, has linked terrorism to the country's rapid socio-economic transformation and the tensions caused by it. "Enormous strains developed while Italian society hurtled from the agricultural and patriarchal to the urban and industrial in a fraction of the time that such other Western nations such as Britian and France had for the process." Rapid socioeconomic development and mass South-North migration dissolved ties, disrupted existing controls, disoriented newcomers to the cities, and produced a generation of half-educated students in crammed Italian universities.[36] The pace of socioeconomic change has also been noted as a factor in the case of West German terrorism. One political scientist has argued that young middle class German guerrillas were "spoiled by the rapidity of change in a technological world and by a permissive education that created revolutionary impatience."[37] Along with such change has come an erosion of established institutions of authority—the loss of a sense of relevance, combined with a loss of authority by democratic governments since the early postwar years.[38]

Decline of the New Left. When the rapid decline of the fortunes of the so-called "New Left" set in during the late 1960s, a few of its adherents evidently moved into terrorism. "Thus, more or less simultaneously, the United Red Army developed in Japan out of *Zengakuren*, the extreme student organization; the American SDS gave birth to Weathermen; and some of the German students of the far left founded the *Rote Armee Fraktion* (Baader-Meinhof) and the *Bewegung 7. Juni*. There were smaller groups in Italy (*Brigate Rosse*) and in England (*Angry Brigade*)."[39] Some of the terrorists of the 1970s can thus be traced back to the protestors of the 1960s—civil rights and the Vietnam war in the United States, archaic regulations and extreme crowding in European universities, and the like. A few observers trace modern terrorism to the hippies and yippies of the so-called counter-culture of the late 1960s, which advocated a total rejection of conventional societal norms. The "deeply romantic idealism that will stop at nothing to prove itself,"[40] which characterizes many of today's terrorists, might have flowered during that time.

Material affluence. "I am sick and tired of all that caviar-gobbling," Susanne Albrecht, the daughter of a well-to-do Hamburg lawyer, is supposed to have complained just before she became the prime suspect in the murder of Jürgen Ponto, Chairman of the Board of the Frankfurt-based Dresdner Bank and a friend of her father. Terrorism in West Germany is seen by some as "affluence crime" (*Wohlstandskriminalität*), and Chancellor Schmidt told the *Bundestag* in October of 1977 that many young people detest the mindless enjoyment of material well-being in a country with a very high standard of living, and are searching for a deeper meaning to life.[41]

Many have noted that most terrorists in western democracies tend to be young members of the middle and upper-middle classes. They seem to represent the bored children of a smugly affluent, materialistic bourgeoisie. For them, terrorism constitutes adventure and thrills, and a way of protesting the anonymous and consumer oriented character of modern society. In Europe, much has been made of the hypothesis that Germany's terrorists are "Hitler's Children,"[42] the logic being that the youth are protesting the guilt of the parental Nazi generation which, because of the Hitler experience, was obsessed after the War with material satisfaction at the expense of other human values. But the *London Economist* argues that "to link the emergence of terrorism in Germany to the country's Nazi past is unreasonable."[43]

Psychopathology. Two past leaders of Japan's Red Army were diagnosed by Japanese psychiatrists as catatonics, blank to the normal range of human feeling.[44] And in the early 1970s a psychiatrist argued that the typical American skyjacker was a suicidal schizophrenic, deeply frustrated in his private life, who was excited by violence and tended to regard the threat of death as a stimulus rather than a deterrent.[45] Others insist that terrorists are psychologically disturbed and their "grievances" not amenable to rational accommodation,[46] and that "amelioration of political grievances will do little good if the terrorists are in fact moved by a death wish."[47] Harvey Schlossberg, a psychiatrist who has trained the New York City Police Department's anti-terrorist unit, contends that many urban terrorists are compensating for inadequate personalties: "If they cry and stamp their feet, no one pays attention. But by taking hostages, in a matter of minutes the whole world is watching. This helps overcome their ego deficit."[48]

Much has been made of the anger, hatred, free-floating aggression, sadomasochism, paranoia, identity crises, unhappy childhoods, disorders of the inner ear, overt suicidal tendencies, and obsession with martyrdom which in different degrees seem to characterize quite a number of terrorists. After a thorough review of the evidence, however, one expert has concluded that "generalizations about the 'terrorist personality' are of only limited assistance . . . of little validity because so much depends on the political and social conditions in which terrorism has occurred, on the historical and cultural context, on the purpose and character of the terror, and, of course, its targets."[49]

Terrorist Objectives

With an idea of some of the sources from which terrorism perhaps springs, a next step might be to look more closely at the surface—to examine the objectives and demands that terrorists usually flaunt before their victims and audiences. These motives differ widely from case to case, and can be combined in a variety of ways.

World revolution. "Reduced to its most simple expression, the substance of the terrorist discourse is as follows: there are good and bad deaths, bourgeois lives and proletarian lives, and 'respect for life' is worth nothing when confronted with the political imperative of expediting the revolution."[50] If one reads the communiques and sloppily written leaflets of groups such as the Red Army Factions of Germany and Japan, the American Weathermen, or Italy's Red Brigades, one finds a good bit of talk about simultaneous "world revolution," solidarity with "oppressed masses" of the Third World, and the need to destroy the "islands of wealth" in the advanced West. Contempt for the sterile, gray Communism of the East is equally common. They seek to bring down all society and replace it with an uncharted millenium.

Terrorists the world over talk vaguely about anti-imperalism, anti-capitalism, anti-fascism, anti-Zionism, anti-Americanism, and so on, often using such terms almost synonymously. And so multinational corporate executives taken hostage are usually branded "imperialist agents" or "capitalist exploiters." When Germany's Red Army Faction decided to strike a symbol of capitalism, they went for the very top, abducting and murdering Dr. Hanns-Martin Schleyer, President of the West German Confederation of Employers Associations and also President of the Federation of West German Industries. "The top boss in the country," stated a German newspaper. After his murder, the terrorists announced that their targets from then on would be "capitalist profiteers and their lackeys."

It is easy to make too much of terrorist doctrine, however. Terrorist groups frequently lack any coherent political ideology or strategy whatsoever. They tend to be believers in deeds not words. Carlos Marighella, a Brazilian guerrilla leader, laid down in his *Minimanual for the Urban Guerrilla* the basic principle that "the urban guerrilla's basic reason for existence, the condition in which he acts and survives, is to shoot."[51] And in the coffee houses of German university towns, terrorists are called *Spontis,* for spontaneous radicals who do not bother with ideology but simply want to destroy. Elsewhere, as in the Middle East and Latin America, terrorist groups have deliberately kept their political programs vague in order to appeal to the widest possible spectrum both domestically and internationally.

Territorial power. The great majority of the world's terrorists are probably not nihilists. Many have rather limited and specific political goals. The Popular Front for the Liberation of Palestine wants to destroy the "Zionist State." The Eritrean Liberation Front wants to create a new nation. Rhodesian terrorists want to displace the existing regime. The Provos of the Irish Republican Army want to expel the British. The Kurds of Iran want regional autonomy. The Sandinist Front of National Liberation in Nicaragua pushed to overthrow Somoza. And the South Moluccan extremists in the Netherlands have attempted to bring Dutch government pressure to bear on Indonesia. And so it goes for the Jewish Defense League, Armenian Liberation Front, Euskadi ta Azkatasuna (Basque Homeland and Liberty), Front de Libération du Québec, Cuban National Liberation Front, and Montoñeros. Most of these nationalist, particularist, or separatist groups might be lumped into one category called "territorials,"[52] working primarily for independence and power in their particular region or state.

Social disorientation. Whether territorial or nihilistic, social disorientation is a proximate objective of terrorism, "removing the underpinnings of the order in which his targets live out their daily lives."[53] Goals falling under this umbrella include discrediting legitimate political authority, eroding popular support for the established political leadership, and destroying the opposition's morale. These are achieved by promoting extreme fear, uncertainty, polarization, and generally by destroying normality—always there is the effort to demonstrate that public authorities are powerless to enforce law and order. The Tupamaros of Uruguay, for example, became masters at showing up the government's vulnerability, and the Italian Red Brigade at intimidating the judicial system.

Political repression. One observer has noted that terrorism can serve as "a political catalyst—as a means of initiating a vicious cycle of terror and counterterror that will alienate popular support from the government."[54] The announced aims of the Red Army Faction in West Germany, for example, have been to expose "revisionists" and "reformists," to "intensify the contradictions of the system," and to "force the enemy to transform the political situation of the country into a military one."[55] The logic is straightforward. Terrorists believe that liberal democratic states such as West Germany are in reality fascist police states that are unaware of the fact. The revolutionary task thus becomes tricking governments into unmasking themselves. By outraging the putatively revolutionary masses with indiscriminate acts of violence, the terrorists hope to provoke brutal police repression and suspension of civil liberties. This then "will lead to political conditions propitious to revolutionary agitation and organization aimed at overthrowing the government."[56]

Attention-recognition. Terrorism can be viewed as "a form of mass communication . . . theirs is a campaign that needs publicity in order to succeed, and therefore they have come to operate within the ambit of contemporary public relations and communications arts: The world of cinema, camp fashion, and pop art, in which deadlines and prime-time are the chief realities and in which shock value is the chief virtue."[57] The functions of self-advertisement include underground morale boosting, humiliating the target, mass educating of the public, and gaining recognition of the cause. Terrorists crave attention and recognize well the paramount importance of the mass media. Hence outrages are often carefully staged, and foreign rather than local firms and senior rather than junior executives are frequently chosen as targets. Foreign involvement and "captains of industry" guarantee increased publicity, especially internationally.

The thirst for attention also accounts for the frequent demand that MNEs place full-page advertisements publishing the terrorists' manifesto in the local and foreign press as a condition for the release of a hostage executive. Owens-Illinois bought a space for the Argimiro Gabaldón Revolutionary Command, which had kidnapped the general manager of its Venezuelan subsidiary. In *The New York Times*, *The Times* of London, and *Le Monde*, it denounced itself as a "meddler" in the affairs of Venezuela and a "plunderer" of the Venezuelan people.[58] Daimler-Benz A.G. denounced the "economic imperialism" of multinationals in developing countries in a number of widely-read foreign dailies under orders from Argentine Montoñeros holding Franz Metz, the company's industrial director in Argentina; and Philips N.V. in late 1978 paid out more than a half million dollars to place a guerrilla tract denouncing the "murdering, persecuting, imprisoning" regime running El Salvador in 40 newspapers around the world—the "ransom in print" had been demanded by the Armed Front of National Resistance as one condition for the release of Fritz Schuitema, the head of Philips' subsidiary in El Salvador.[59]

Social justice. Dow Chemical plants were bombed during the Vietnam War because it was a supplier of napalm to the American military. In 1970 the National Liberation Alliance called for the confiscation of Swiss bank accounts of rich Brazilians as a condition for the release of the Swiss Ambassador to Brazil, Giovanni Bucher. In 1971, the People's Revolutionary Army in Argentina received a pledge of better pay and working conditions in the local Swift & Company meat packing plant as a condition for the release of its manager Stanley Sylvester. In 1972, Philips was barraged by bombs and bomb threats in Holland as a protest against the firm's defense contracts. In 1974, facilities of ITT in Italy, West Germany, France, and the United States were bombed in revenge for the company's political activities in Chile. In 1975, nuclear power plants of Electricité de France were bombed. In 1976, meat and poultry company executives were kidnapped by masked gunmen protesting the high price of meat in Italy. In 1977 the home of a Hoffmann-LaRoche senior executive in Switzerland was bombed in retaliation for an industrial accident at a subsidiary near Seveso in northern Italy the year before that contaminated 1000 acres with poison gas. And in 1979, saboteurs slipped into an industrial plant in La Seyne-sur-Mer, France, and bombed nuclear reactor equipment bound for Iraq, Belgium, and West Germany—a group claiming responsibility said they had "neutralized machines, dangerous to human life" and thus protected humanity from future "Harrisburg catastrophies."

Such incidents indicate that a certain proportion of terrorism is fired by a sense of "social conscience." Rather than passively accepting what they beleive to be immoral corporate conduct, or working through established channels to change corporate policies, terrorists often take matters into their own hands using symbolic attack. As noted earlier, terrorists have also assigned to themselves "Robin Hood" roles, often demanding ransoms in the form of food and other goods and services for the poor.

Prisoner release. On March 21, 1972, guerrillas of the People's Revolutionary Army, dressed in police uniforms, kidnapped Dr. Oberdan Sallustro, head of the Fiat Concord plant in Argentina. The terrorists quickly issued half a dozen communiques demanding the release of 50 "political prisoners." The military government of President Alejandro Lanusse firmly and quickly rejected the demand and rushed through an emergency decree to prevent private companies or individuals from submitting to "acts of extortion."[60] With the government's resistance, Fiat desperately tried to convince ERP to accept instead an unspecified ransom, a pledge to remove police from its Cordoba plant, $1 million in food and clothing for poor school children and a reinstatement of 250 employees who had been dismissed. The terrorists stood firm, insisting on release of their colleagues. On April 10th the police discovered the kidnappers' hideout in Buenos Aires, and as they began closing in, Sallustro was murdered by his captors.

Liberation of captured confederates has always been a top priority for terrorists. Over the years, aircraft hijacking and diplomat abduction have been the most popular techniques of securing prisoner release. Take Brazil during 1970, for example: A Japanese consul-general was released in exchange for five detainees in March, a German Ambassador released in exchange for 40 prisoners in June, and in December, the head money for a Swiss Ambassador amounted to 70 prisoners.[61] But executives have also been used in prisoner release. In October of 1975, for example, the IRA captors of Dr. Tiede Herrema, manager of Akzo's Ferenka metals plant in Limerick, Ireland, threatened to kill him unless three prominent IRA gunmen were released by the Irish government. And in September of 1977, the Red Army Faction in West Germany demanded the liberation of 11 of their hard-core colleagues, held in the maximum security Stammheim prison on the outskirts of Stuttgart, as the prime condition for the release of Dr. Hanns-Martin Schleyer.

Financing. Terrorists need money. Large sums are required to finance clandestine headquarters, hideouts, getaway cars, weapons purchases, travel, and "Robin Hood" distribution schemes. According to official estimates, the terrorist group that kidnapped and eventually murdered Schleyer spent nearly $100,000 on the six vehicles used, a number of "safe houses" around Cologne, and the place where he was held for six weeks in September and October of 1977.[62] The annual cash income of various terrorist groups has been estimated as follows: In 1970, the Tupamaros of Uruguay and the Alliance for National Liberation in Brazil each took in $5–10 million; in 1974, the People's Revolutionary Army of Argentina gathered $50–100 million. In 1975, Fatah in the Middle East accumulated $150–200 million, while PFLP, PDFLP and Saiga (smaller terrorist groups in the Middle East) collectively stole and extorted $20–30 million; also in 1975, the provisionals and regulars of the IRA in Ulster brought in $1–3 million.[63] Such funds are variously collected through abductions, robberies, donations, and protection rackets. In Latin America the bulk of such funds was acquired from foreign and domestic corporations—in one shot, for example, the Montoñeros of Argentina collected $60 million in ransom for the release of Jorge and Juan Born, co-owners and directors of the Argentine-based multinational grain firm Bunge and Born Ltd. Maj. Gen. Richard L. Clutterbuck, one of England's leading authorities on terrorism, offered this rationale in a recent interview: "Business seems more ready to pay up than governments. Governments have certain political restraints. It is politically disadvantageous for a leader to look weak. On the other hand a firm will probably assess the situation along strictly commercial lines and will pay if it cuts its losses."[64]

In attacks on MNE executives or facilities, the dividing line between politics and crime is hardly clear-cut. Appearances can be deceptive. A few years back, a representative of Douglas Aircraft was shot at the Bank of America in Beirut by ordinary bank robbers posing as *Fedayeen*. In Italy hardened gangsters regularly use revolutionary language as a cover and employ idealistic young stooges in their crimes. Indeed, many violent acts directed against corporations are criminal acts in the conventional sense, with no politics involved whatsoever. Snatching businessmen for profit has thrived in Sicily, Sardinia, and Southern Italy for centuries. Italian newspapers periodically print box scores showing how well the "cottage industry" of kidnapping is doing.[65] Elsewhere, the kidnappers who extorted a ransom of $4.16 million in October of 1977 for Dutch real estate executive Maurits Caransa were described by him as "just criminals" who wanted "a lot of money," not "butchers with political motives." And the abductors in Paris of Baron Edouard-Jean Empain, head of the Belgian-French Empain-Schneider industrial group, in January of 1978, were also only in it only for the money—this time, however, crime didn't pay, for the Baron was released by his captors in a frenzied panic after hard-line French authorities ambushed gang members attempting to retrieve $8.6 million at a phony ransom drop on a highway near Paris and captured the kidnappers' leader.

Ecstasy. Many believe that "ecstasy" is characteristic of all terrorist groups. Ecstasy may include elements of "frenzy," "irrationality," "exhilaration," or literally "standing outside oneself," that is, "standing outside the limits of ordinary consciousness or to stand free of the restraints and limits of every day behavior."[66] "What matter the victims provided the gesture is beautiful?"[67] For some terrorists, violence has indeed come to be an end in itself. Twenty years ago the psychiatrist and revolutionary writer Frantz Fanon, who championed the cause of Algerian independence, stated that "at the level of individuals, violence is a cleansing force. It frees the native from his inferiority complex and from his despair and inaction."[68] Today there are ideologists of both the extreme right and left who believe collective violence to be intrinsically creative, liberating, and "cathartic."[69]

Facilitators of Terrorism

We come now to our third and final set of variables that are relevant to the explanation of terrorism. As the U.S. Central Intelligence Agency has concluded: "The problem of transnational terrorism would not have mushroomed to its present dimensions were it not for the concurrent convergence and acceleration of a number of changes in the global environment that had begun to take shape much earlier."[78] These changes have made it possible for terrorists to carry out their deeds, either by providing assistance or by being unable to thwart them—factors that "grease the skids" of international terrorism.

Weapons availability. As one observer notes, "the persistence of terrorism is undoubtedly closely related to the availability of weapons."[71] Terrorists seem to be able to acquire some of the most modern arms in national arsenals—recoilless rifles, high-yield explosives, grenade launchers, heat-seeking missiles, ingenious timing and detonating devices, and perhaps eventually nuclear weapons. Such sophisticated weaponry can be stolen—for example, 15 light anti-tank weapons were lifted from an American Army maneuver in southern Germany in late 1976—purchased from unscrupulous international arms dealers, or perhaps more generally, supplied directly by governments friendly to the terrorist groups. Modern technology enables the terrorist to destroy at relatively greater distances, with greater effect, and in greater safety.

Interdependence and centralization. Contemporary society and multinational companies have become highly vulnerable to the terrorist's deed. Global and technological interdependence and centralization have provided terrorists with new and potentially disruptive targets for attack. Such "exposed jugulars" include electronic communications networks, computer nerve centers, municipal reservoirs, transportation hubs, power grids, pipelines, supertankers, and jumbo aircraft. We have come to depend increasingly on conveniences provided over a distance—for example, power systems, water from central storage systems, air in sealed-window buildings from central ventiliation systems, and the like. Disruption of ordinary activities can thus readily be achieved by disruption at one stage or "pressure point" of the transmission links involved. Complex industrial processes and sophisticated social facilities appear to present soft and extraordinarily fragile targets for terrorist outrages. And the mobility offered by modern jet travel allows the terrorist to strike almost anywhere in the world and then to move quickly to safe asylum.

Media coverage. Publicity is not only an end of terrorist activity, it is also a tool. The media, always inclined to give wide publicity and to sensationalize acts of violence, are the terrorists' natural ally. "The success of a terrorist operation depends almost entirely on the amount of publicity it receives . . . in the final analysis, it is not the magnitude of the terrorist operation that counts but the publicity; and this rule applies not only to single operations but to whole campaigns."[72] Maximum publicity of violent spectaculars enables the terrorist to create an atmosphere of fear and alarm. This causes people to "exaggerate the apparent strength of the terrorist movement and cause, which means that their strength is judged not by their actual numbers or violent accomplishments, but by the effect these have on their audience."[73] The terrorists' publicity goals are made all the easier because modern communications ensures them a worldwide audience—satellite communications gives the terrorist almost instant access to the world's living rooms.

Governmental timidity. Modern democratic societies provide a historically unprecedented degree of freedom that can be taken advantage of by terrorists. The means of social control and repression at the disposal of totalitarian and authoritarian states are just not available in liberal democracies. Governments are naturally reluctant to act sternly when it means closing down legal freedoms. And so planning and carrying out terrorism is relatively easy, when severe constraints are placed on clandestine operations and counterintelligence activities by governmental agencies, when security at airports or prisons is lax, and (as in Italy), when the police are demoralized and the judicial system delay-ridden and virtually without deterrent.

Democratic governments are timid in other ways as well—"The politics of international terrorism are such that many countries are still more willing to condone it than to condemn it."[74] Many governments are reluctant to commit themselves to a tough stance that might invite retribution, either by terrorist groups or by nations sympathetic to the terrorists' cause. Western governments, including the United States, have been unwilling to impose serious sanctions against countries that grant asylum to terrorists, and then set them free for another round of terror—in 1978, however, the United States began holding up or barring exports of military goods to Libya, Iraq, South Yemen, and Algeria because of these nations' "support for terrorist activities." Aware that imprisoning terrorists invites new acts of terrorism, especially the seizure of hostages in order to secure the release of jailed cohorts, governments in Paris, Bonn, Vienna, and elsewhere have often allowed acts of terrorism to go unpunished. The fact is that the vast majority of terrorists captured, arrested, or imprisoned during the last decade are now free.

The relative immunity from reprisal enjoyed by terrorists and the governments that aid them has taken much of the risk out of terrorism. And international efforts to deal with the problem have been weak and ineffective. Numerous anti-terrorism resolutions and conventions (noted below) have been adopted. But most are innocuous and little more than declarations of intent. Global collaboration to control terrorism remain a chimera.

Governmental support. A number of Communist regimes and developing-country governments clearly enjoy watching the industrial democracies squirm in the face of terrorism. Although some have recently reconsidered their positions, during the 1970s the list according to the CIA has included Libya, Cuba, the Soviet Union, China, North Korea, Algeria, South Yemen, Tanzania, Congo, Zaire, Egypt, Syria, Iraq, and a somewhat reluctant Lebanon.[75] They have provided terrorists in various degrees with funds, arms, false documents, training facilities, havens, and other operational support. The most active patrons of international terrorism seem to be Libya's Moamer Qaddafi, who has bankrolled numerous operations including the snatch of OPEC ministers, and Cuba's Fidel Castro, who has played Godfather to many Latin American terrorist groups and fostered a liaison network between them and European terrorist organizations. Algeria has provided refuge and assistance to North American terrorist groups, and to the Basque ETA and most African and Middle East groups. Some senior intelligence officials believe the Kremlin has been active in encouraging terrorists to concentrate on West Germany in an attempt to disrupt its government and undermine its citizens' confidence in democracy. Modern terrorism, in this view, is a form of "warfare by remote control."

Sympathizers. Besides governments, terrorists often find support in other quarters as well. In some cases, as in Northern Ireland, Spain, or the Middle East, general citizen support flows from ancient ethnic or religious hatreds. In Uruguay, left-wing Tupamaros paradoxically found support among the middle class hard-pressed by socialist economic policies. In West Germany, an estimated 1000 to 6000 committed radicals have provided hard-core terrorists with food, money, and safehouses. The goals, if perhaps not the means, of German and Italian guerrillas find sympathy from university professors, churchmen, young students, and left-wing intellectuals, who show a remarkable inclination to suspend disapproval and search for mitigating circumstances that justify terrorist actions. The Göttingen students organization, for instance, expressed its joy over the murder of Dresdner Bank Chairman Jürgen Ponto in its school newspaper.[76] All over Europe, following the October 1977 apparent suicides of three leaders of the Baader-Meinhof gang in their maximum security cells at Stammheim, leftists praised them as martyrs and bombed German-owned auto showrooms and businesses to avenge their death.

Support has taken other forms as well. In 1977 a young financier from one of

Argentina's most prestigeous banking families was accused of having managed large sums of ransom money for the left-wing Montoñero guerrillas.[77] In 1978, the Italian police announced that they arrested a Franciscan priest, a former high police officer, a retired civil servant, a shipowner, and nine other well-to-do businessmen, lawyers and society women on charges of having helped kidnappers rechannel more than $6 million of ransom money so that it could not be traced.[78] Swiss, Italian, and Middle Eastern financial "gnomes" have for years been suspected of an active role in the "recycling and laundering" of terrorist ransom money, buying banknotes from the groups at 70% or less of their face value.

Transnational networks. Finally, there are linkages and alliances among terrorist groups themselves. Such networks can be of considerable practical value to terrorists. In Western Europe, Latin America, and the Middle East terrorist groups have often provided one another with arms, safe-houses, technical information, and other operational support. This has enabled them to effectively carry out "third country operations"—the Palestinians committed 153 such operations affecting 16 foreign countries between 1967 and 1975. There is some evidence that elaborate "exchange attack systems" and "joint action commitments" have been concluded among groups of various nationalities. American Weathermen, IRA gunmen, West German radicals, and members of the Turkish Dev Genc have all received combat training at one time or another in armed Palestinian camps in Lebanon, Syria, and South Yemen. Joint operations have also developed, such as the Black September cooperation with Baader-Meinhof, and the Popular Front for the Liberation of Palestine with the Japanese Red Army.

Many worry that some sort of a "Terrorist International" may be evolving. Evidence supporting the existence of such a central command and control structure remains weak. Argentine, Bolivian, Chilean, Paraguayan, and Uruguayan terrorist groups did form a "Junta de Coordinación Revolucionaria" in 1974, which was initially financed, as noted above, by the overflowing coffers of the People's Revolutionary Army of Argentina. The Junta was designed to provide joint funding, strategy and tactics, arms purchases, and operations in Europe. But recently it appears to have fallen on hard times. Some of its leaders are thought to have fled to Europe.[79] The *London Times* reported in October of 1977 that the Junta had set up a headquarters in Paris that "has become a kind of clearing house for international terrorism" which raises funds (some of them from Cuba), forges passports and identity papers, and publishes elaborate training manuals dealing with subjects like guerrilla warfare, terrorist tactics, bomb manufacturing, and the endurance of torture.[80] As such, it seems to represent only a "service organization" and not really a central command structure.

Forms of Terrorism

The purpose of terrorism, as Lenin observed, is to terrify. The "weapons of fear" or "deeds of propagnada" are multifarious and are often used jointly in a single incident. Individually, terrorist techniques vary in their economy, facility, degree of risk, bargaining dimensions, and psychological-political effectiveness.

The U.S. Central Intelligence Agency offers the following useful categorization of incident types: kidnapping, barricade and hostage, bombing, armed assault or ambush, hijacking (air and non-air), assassination, incendiary attack or arson, and "other." Exhibit 4–2 shows the distribution of 1152 international terrorist incidents in the CIA's data-base which occurred during the period 1968–1976, 391 of which victimized United States citizens or property. In order to be included in this data-base, an incident had to represent a "threat or use of violence for political purposes when (1) such action is intended to influence the attitude and behavior of a target group wider than its immediate victims and (2) its ramifications transcend national boundaries—as the result, for example, of the nationality or foreign ties of its perpetrators, its locale, the identity of its institutional or human victims, its declared objectives, or the mechanics of its resolution."[81] It thus includes the great bulk of the incidents which have victimized multinational corporations in their foreign operations.

Kidnapping. Twelve percent of the total incidents during the nine year period consisted of kidnappings, of which almost half victimized American citizens or property. Almost two thirds of the abductions took place in Latin America. The peak year for this form of terrorism was 1973, when more than 500 persons were kidnapped in Argentina, 178 of whom were businessmen, and 29 of whom were foreigners and thus are included in the CIA statistics. Worldwide, it seems that auto companies and banks have been the most frequent targets of kidnapping. Fiat of Italy, in fact, probably holds the record for employees abducted. One British financial executive in Argentina, Charles A. Lockwood, holds the dubious distinction of having been kidnapped in Buenos Aires twice, in June of 1973 and July of 1975. Family members of executives, like J. Paul Getty III in 1973 and Patty Hearst in 1975, have also frequently fallen victim to kidnapping.

Barricade and hostage. Barricade-and-hostage operations are perhaps the most risky of terrorist methods, and accounted for only 3% of the total incidents during 1968–1976, of which 14% victimized United States property or citizens. They reached a peak in 1975 with nine incidents, mostly at embassies and banks in the Middle East and Europe. A few examples involving businesses include the following: In January 1971, 14 leftist guerrillas held 12 persons hostage for nearly eight hours while breaking into a vault of the National Development Bank in Buenos Aires, escaping with $450,000. In October 1973, five members of the Lebanese Socialist Revolutionary Organization raided and seized a Bank of America branch in Lebanon for 25 hours before police and army officials stormed the building, with four people killed and 16 injured. In October 1975, police discovered the hideout in Monasterevin, Ireland of IRA gunmen holding Akzo's Herrema, and a three week nerve-racking siege ensued before a release was negotiated. And in March 1976, two American executives of the Firestone plant in Portugal were held hostage for nearly 80 hours by leftist workers at the plant. A similar case occurred in El Salvador in August 1979, when 30 angry female employees took the head of the American-owned Apex Textile Company hostage and held him and other executives for weeks in the seized factory—the company was accused of "trampling the rights and interests of workers" in the country.

Exhibit 4-2
Geographic Distribution of International Terrorist Incidents by Category, 1968–1976

Region	Total Number of Incidents	Kidnapping	Barricade and Hostage	Bombing	Armed Assault or Ambush	Hijacking Air & Non-Air	Assassination	Incendiary Attack or Arson	Other
North America	131	3	1	81	10	22	3	10	1
Western and NATO Europe	451	14	15	255	37	21	22	67	20
Middle East and North Africa	132	9	9	46	26	21	10	1	10
Sub-Saharan Africa	41	17	2	6	7	6	1	0	2
Asia	54	7	2	8	9	17	4	7	0
Latin America	317	87	6	98	28	44	23	17	14
USSR/ Eastern Europe	19	0	0	2	1	15	0	0	1
Pacific and Australia	6	0	0	4	1	0	0	1	0
Transregional	1	0	0	1	0	0	0	0	0
Total:	1152	137	35	501	119	146	63	103	48

Source: "International Terrorism in 1976," RP 77-10034U, (Washington, D.C.: U.S. Central Intelligence Agency, July 1977), p. 13.

Bombing. Explosions accounted for a whopping 43% of the world's terrorist incidents in 1968–1976, a third of which affected American citizens or property; 50% took place in Europe and 20% occurred in Latin America. Bombings accounted for 62% of all terrorist episodes in North America and 57% in Europe. Their number rose steadily during the 1970s from 15 in 1971 to 126 in 1976. Bombs have been directed at individual executives, such as a three-pound bomb that was planted by "The Tribunal" under the car of Philips Board member Jan Bavinck in Holland in 1972; at groups of executives, as in the case of letter bombs that were sent from India to British businessmen named in the Zionist Yearbook in 1972; at aircraft, like the Tel Aviv-bound Swissair Convair 990 blown up in the air in 1970 by Popular Front for the Liberation of Palestine, killing all 47 passengers; at ships, such as the Greek charter vessel "Sanya" bound for Haifa and sunk in Beirut harbor in 1973 by a terrorist bomb; and at commerical facilities, like the explosion at the National Bank of Argentina in Milan, which killed 16 people and wounded 90 in 1969.

Bomb attacks on industrial facilities include the sea terminal of the Trans Alpine Oil pipeline at Trieste, Italy in 1972, an arms plant in West Berlin in 1973, a Shell Oil Refinery in Singapore in 1974, the North Sea Oil pipeline in Scotland in 1975, the Margnac uranium mine in France in 1976, a Fiat warehouse in Turin in 1977, and the Trans-Alaska oil pipeline in 1978, and the pipeline system feeding Iran's big Abadan oil refinery in 1979. Bomb campaigns affecting multiple targets have included some hundred bombings by the Front de Libération du Québec in the Montreal area during 1968 and 1969; the "Revolutionary Force" bombings of the New York offices of IBM, Mobil Oil, and General Telephone and Electronics within a 20 minute period in March 1970, claiming that the targets were "enemies of all human life"; and the widespread bomb attacks by the Armed Forces of National Liberation for Puerto Rico (FALN) on "imperialist banks" in New York City in October 1974, numerous corporations, banks and government offices in Chicago, New York, and Washington in October 1975, and a number of "Yankee Imperialist" multinationals in New York in August 1977. During the fall of 1977, a wave of "Union del Pueblo" bombings hit multinational corporate offices in Mexico and the aforementioned "reprisal" wave of bombs planted by Italian terrorists hit West German auto showrooms and businesses in Italy. A number of Alfa Romeo dealerships were simultaneously bombed in Italy in April 1978 and 32 bombs were set off outside French banks on Corsica in March 1979.

Armed assault. Armed attacks and ambushes accounted for 10% of incidents identified by the CIA, 37% of which involved American citizens or property. Most occurred in Europe, the Middle East, North Africa, and Latin America, reaching a peak of 29 episodes in 1973 and dropping slightly thereafter. Many involved bank robberies. Occasionally, terrorists have seized whole towns (the Argentine Montoñeros took over the town of La Calera and robbed its banks in June of 1970) or radio and TV stations in order to broadcast proclamations, factories in order to harangue workers, cinemas to propagandize moviegoers, and newspaper offices to force the tabloids to print terrorist manifestos. The Baader-Meinhof Gang relied heavily on "Bonnie-and-Clyde" bank robberies in Germany to raise money for its cause. This was reflected in the United States in the famous photograph of Patty Hearst holding a machine-gun during a Symbionese Liberation Army robbery of the Hibernia Bank in San Francisco in August of 1974. In 1977 the home of a Goodyear executive in suburban Buenos Aires was assaulted with machine-gun fire and pipe-bombs. Pan Am's Intercontinental Hotel in Istanbul was strafed with machine-gun fire by the Turkish Peoples Liberation Front. A railway project was raided in Zaïre by the Front for the Liberation of the Enclave of Cabinda—tunnels were destroyed, bridges blown up, and three French technicians abducted. And the Mauritanian iron mining center near Zouerate was attacked by Polisario guerillas using mortar and small arms fire, killing two French citizens and abducting six technicians. In 1978, four persons were killed and six wounded in two attacks that took place at a B.F. Goodrich rubber plantation in the Philippines by Muslim rebels.

Hijacking. Hijacking, both air and non-air, accounted for 13% of terrorist incidents during 1968–1976, of which 21% victimized United States property or citizens. This form of terrorism was fairly evenly distributed around the world, and reached a peak in 1970 with 47 cases, dropping steadily to five in 1975 and nine in 1976. In a number of the airline episodes, the planes were subsequently destroyed by the terrorists on the runways—three commerical aircraft were blown up at Dawsons Field in Jordan in September of 1970 by the Popular Front for the Liberation of Palestine, causing damage of $20 million; Japan Airlines jumbo jets were blown up in Benghazi and Tripoli, Libya in 1973 and 1974; a British Airways VC10 was blown up at Schiphol Airport in Holland in 1974; and an Air France plane was destroyed in Ajaccio in 1976. Using such incidents, the Popular Front for the Liberation of Palestine has allegedly been successful over the years in extorting protection money from several Western airlines providing scheduled service to Israel.[82] The Greek ship "Vori" was seized at the port of Karachi by three "Moslem International Guerrillas" in 1974 with the master and chief held hostage, and in 1972 it was rumored that the Black September organization had planned to hijack a supertanker at sea and sit on it for weeks, if necessary, in order to extort a ransom from one of the "Seven Sisters."[83]

Assassination. Six percent of the international terrorist incidents during the nine-year period consisted of assassinations, over a third of which involved American targets. Thirty-five percent of the murders took place in Europe and another 37% in Latin America. The number of victims has risen gradually over the years, from three in 1971 to fifteen in 1976. Most of the victims have been diplomats and multinational corporate executives. Domestic victims in Italy, Argentina and elsewhere have included judges, prosecutors, police officials, journalists, politicians, and trade union leaders. The corporate victims have included an El Al manager in Italy and two Ford Motor company executives in Argentina in 1973; a Fiat Chief of Personnel in Argentina in 1974; two Bendix Corporation executives in Argentina, the President of Chevron Oil Italiana in Italy, the President of Credit Lyonnais in France, and three executives of Rockwelll International in Iran in 1976, the Managing Director of DuPont in Northern Ireland, the Chairman of the Dresdner Bank in West Germany, a Director of Daimler-Benz in West Germany and the Technical Director of Peugeot in Argentina in 1977, the Chairman of Egypt's leading newspaper *Al Ahram* in Cyprus and Baron Charles Victor Bracht, one of the wealthiest industrialists in Europe, in Belgium, in 1978 and the head of the Texaco affiliate in Colombia in 1979. Mention should also be made of the rash of "knee-capping" attacks on corporate executives in Italy during 1978–1979—a few of the MNEs affected included Montedison, Pirelli, and the Chemical Bank of New York.

Incendiary attack. Nine percent of the terrorist incidents involved arson or incendiary attack—44% of them victimized United States-owned property and 65% occurred in Europe. This virtually risk-free form of terrorism reached a peak in 1976 with 44 incidents. A few of the multinational corporate targets hit over the years have included the General Motors office building in Montevideo, Urguay in 1969; the Isla Vista, California branch of Bank of America in 1970; Caltex-Mobil oil tanks in Lebanon in 1973; a Pan Am aircraft waiting to take off at Rome's airport in 1973; ITT's electronics warehouse near Milan in 1974; an Electricité de France nuclear power plant at Fessenheim in 1975; Fiat's Rivolta works in Turin in 1976; the Lufthansa German Airlines office in Genoa, Italy in 1977; and the car of George Link, the American manager of the Oil Service Company of Iran, in Anwaz in late 1978 during the Iranian revolution.

Other. Finally, four percent of the international incidents have consisted of a wide variety of other forms of terrorism, mainly sabotage, where 39% victimized American property or citizens. In 1978, for example, a few crates of Israeli-grown oranges bound for Europe were injected with mercury, touching off a wide scare and causing storekeepers in many parts of Western Europe to clear Israeli oranges from their shelves and cancel further orders. Letters to the Dutch and West German governments, attributed to the "Arab Revolutionary Army–Palestinian Commando," said "it is not our aim to kill the population, but to sabotage the Israeli economy, which is based on suppression, racial discrimination and colonial occupation."[84]

EFFECTS OF TERRORISM

The physical consequences of terrorist action must be viewed in the following context:

> By itself, terror can accomplish nothing in terms of political goals; it can only aim at obtaining a response that will achieve those goals for it . . . Terrorism is the weapon of those who are prepared to use violence but who believe that they would lose any contest of sheer strength. All too little understood, the uniqueness of the strategy lies in this: that it achieves its goals not through it acts but through the response to its acts. In any other such strategy, the violence is the beginning and its consequences the end of it. For terrorism, however, the consequences of the violence are themselves merely a first step and form a stepping stone toward objectives that are more remote.[85]

Terrorists thus practice a "high-leverage" form of violence. "Because the impact of their activity has been magnified by the publicity it has received and by its interactions with other destabilizing trends and forces, its disruptive effects have been grossly disproportionate to the resources employed by the terrorists as well as to the actual damage done in terms of the cost of life and property." [86]

Executive Life

The lives of executives have probably been most severely disrupted by terrorism in Italy and Argentina. In 1973 *The Economist* reported that MNE executives in the latter country were leading "wretched lives," while *Newsweek* wrote that life for businessmen had become "practically unbearable–a nerve-racking, mind-boggling experience."[87] A well-known American executive told *Business Week* in 1974 that "life is miserable for Americans in Buenos Aires now. Every move I make I have two guards with me. My wife and I hardly ever go out socially anymore. Actually, nobody goes out much. You can see it at night in the dining room at the American Club. That was a very popular dinner spot, but now it's almost deserted . . . I planned to stay here when I retire—but not now."[88] In 1976, Harry Leshinsky, President of Chrysler Fevre Argentina, one of the few American businessmen still in the nation, stated: "I thank God each morning I get to this office safely."[89] For some, terrorism has meant reduced personal freedom and a permanent loss of privacy, the constant presence of bodyguards; alteration of daily work patterns; travel in bullet-proof cars and convoys; life in walled compounds uncomfortably isolated from neighbors and friends; withdrawal from public life, publicity and political discussion; curtailment of social life; endurance of security checks; outward signs of insecurity, stress and paranoia (all reducing effective performance); and in some cases the carrying of weapons. At the 1976 annual meeting of W.R. Grace and Company in Boston, Chairman J. Peter Grace pushed aside his jacket while he was speaking—just enough that reporters saw a gun tucked under his belt.[90]

Corporate Operations

Despite waves of terrorism, for the majority of firms the disruption of basic activities has been relatively marginal. Some, however, have lost customers—the Dutch railroad estimates it lost the equivalent of $6.5 million to $8.7 million in 1977 because of fears raised by South Moluccan assaults on trains. Others have lost profits—a $1.5 million ransom paid by Kodak in Argentina wiped out all the profits it had made there in one recent year. Still others have experienced a drop in the price of their shares—the stock price of Lufthansa slumped several points when the Red Army Faction threatened in 1977 that "for each murdered comrade we will blow up one Lufthansa plane in flight . . . all should know that, beginning November 15, death flies with them on a German plane."

Some firms have had to shut down their plants. Bombings and violence caused American-owned Petroquimica Argentina to close down completely in 1975. Some have had to cancel business plans, as when Mackey International Airlines dropped plans to resume regular flights to Cuba after its offices were bombed in Florida by Cuban-exile terrorists. Others have shut down transport facilities, and even the 800 mile Trans-Alaska pipeline was closed down for 20 hours in February 1978 by a terrorist bomb blast. Still others have suffered sizeable material losses—ITT lost $12 million when terrorists set fire to its Milan electronics warehouse in 1974 and Honeywell lost $2 million in a similar warehouse firebombing in Italy in 1978.

Personnel matters have also been affected. Firms have lost key senior executives—Ponto had turned Dresdner Bank into the most aggressive of the German banks and had yet to groom a successor before he was murdered. Many have experienced high rates of absenteeism—as in Northern Ireland plants during severe periods of unrest—or have lost employee time during evacuations, as has often been felt by New York City corporations. Some have changed hiring practices—during an active period in Argentina, many firms began to hire people mostly over the age of 30, to prevent young subversives from infiltrating the companies. Some have increased salaries—as when Coca-Cola classified Buenos Aires a hardship post in 1974 and began awarding its expatriate employees an "environmental allowance" equal to about 10% of base pay—and speeded promotion of nationals. In Argentina, opportunities for promotion increased markedly as foreign firms replaced expatriates with local managers.

Finally, relations with governments have also been affected. Relations between Fiat and the Argentine government, for example, became extremely strained in 1972 when the government attempted to prevent the company from negotiating with the People's Revolutionary Army for the release of Dr. Sallustro. And the Venezuelan government in 1976 ordered Owens-Illinois to sell its holdings to the state when the company defied the government's order banning negotiations with, and publication of the manifesto of, terrorists who had abducted William F. Niehous, manager of the company's operations in the country. In March 1979, however, with Niehous still missing and Owens-Illinois now adhering to official policy, the government quietly dropped its nationalization plans. Four months later, Niehous was rescued unharmed after policemen, looking for cattle rustlers in an isolated jungle area of Southeastern Venezuela, accidentally came upon a hut where the guerrillas had held him captive for more than three years—the longest kidnapping in recent history.

Social Consequences

Terrorism affects styles of living and social patterns in many ways. As in Northern Ireland, it may embitter relations between neighboring ethnic or religious groups, creating or intensifying mutual hatred and suspicion. Political relations between groups can become so poisoned that all normal bargaining, search for compromise, or even limited cooperation becomes treason and betrayal. As in West Germany in 1977, terrorism can evoke a combination of fear and morbid fascination, as a cloud of anguish, self-doubt, anger, and uncertainty settles over public life.

Predictably, terrorism often leads to polarization and sloganeering—"if you're not with us, you're against us." In Holland, the Fascist Volksunie reemerged publicly in 1977 in an attempt to exploit resentment at the terrorism by South Moluccans. In Germany a spiral of mutual suspicion between cultural radicalism and political conservatism developed with calls for government to "clean up the swamp" of terrorists, liberal lawyers, leftist intellectuals, and sympathizers. Terrorism inevitably leads to demands for "law and order," with wide support for more and more police, and tough judicial measures including harsh sentences for convicted terrorists. Following the FALN bombing at the Mobil Oil building in New York City in August 1977, Mayor Abe Beame called for a resumption of the death penalty as "a deterrent to terrorism." In October 1977, London's *Daily Express* urged "Hang them all and hang them high." And sometimes opponent groups take matters into their own hands. Right-wing murder squads have arisen in Spain, Italy, Argentina, Brazil, and Guatemala to avenge left-wing terrorist outrages.

Economy

Most national economies have not been seriously affected by terrorism. A few have indeed encountered some adverse economic effects. For example, informed guesses put the 1977 cost of preventing terrorism in West Germany alone at hundreds of millions of dollars.[91] Ultimately, such costs will be passed on to tax payers, shareholders, and consumers. Tourism has also been affected: Uruguay, once known as the "Switzerland of Latin America," experienced a marked decline in tourism in the early 1970s, as did the Virgin Islands, Italy, Portugal, Spain, Lebanon, Jamaica, and Bermuda later on. In Northern Ireland tourism in 1977 was down almost two-thirds since 1968. Northern Ireland also lost 66,300 people during the period 1970–1975 through emigration. Even New York City has not been unaffected–within the oil industry alone, Atlantic Richfield, Shell Oil, Cities Service, Continental Oil, and Texaco have moved their headquarters out of the City in recent years. Mobil, which had suffered numerous bomb attacks, decided to move its United States Marketing and Refining Division out of the City in 1979 and announced that "a growing number of Mobil employees are reluctant to accept assignments in Mobil's New York City offices, even when such assignments would clearly enhance their careers."[92] Terrorist bombings are certainly not alone behind these moves, probably falling well behind high taxes, poor governmental services and transportation, middle class exodus, street crime, and urban filth as reasons. But the tight security one encounters at the new corporate suburban and exurban "campuses" indicates concern for a better defense against terrorism.

The Argentine Republic used to appear on every list of "countries of the future." That picture certainly did not describe the spectacle of Argentina during the Peronist period. And recently an Italian Undersecretary of the Interior announced that the new terrorism has weakened the "economic potential of the country." A West German Finance Minister listed terrorism as a factor contributing to "German industry's lack of confidence in the future and its reluctance to invest."[93] Certainly the worst economic damage directly attributable to terrorism has occurred in Northern Ireland. Roy Mason, the British Labor Government's Secretary of State for Northern Ireland, published a leaflet in 1976 that said: "Thousands of men and women are out of work in Ulster today and many of them have the terrorists to thank for being on the dole queue. Violence has cost us dearly in the job-creation drive."[94] Attracting foreign investment has proved to be especially difficult, with Northern Ireland securing only one new American investment during 1970–1977, a small synthetic fibers plant.

Politics

As Laqueur has noted: "Terrorism always engenders grossly exaggerated notions about its political effectiveness."[95] It is true that in years past, Irish (1920s), Irgun (1940s), and Algerian (1950s) terrorists did achieve political success in the warring days of the British and French colonial period. But contemporary terrorists have rarely triggered major revolutions or toppled governments. Uruguay's Tupamaros did help to transform a country with a long democratic tradition into a military dictatorship, and Argentina's Montoñeros and Peoples Revolutionary Army did contribute to the overthrow of Isabel Peron's quasi-democratic regime. Yet in neither case were the results quite what the terrorists expected, and in both instances, economic and political crises were also involved.

More generally, we do see a close connection between terrorism and human rights. As one observer sees it:

> Between state terrorism and individual terrorism a diabolical spiral starts, making one the source of the other. On the one hand, he who says that the .38 pistol represents the only possible politics and who, at the instant in which he says it, creates the very condition which justifies him. On the other hand, he who answers that we must respond to individual terrorism with repression and who, in supporting it, makes his decree into a necessity.[96]

In Latin America especially, terrorism from below produced massive and far more effective terror from above. In Brazil, Uruguay, and Argentina, essentially uncontrolled counter-insurgency forces—"death squads"—employed what amounted to a "shotgun approach," which "did away with due process, civilized criminal proceedings, personal freedom, and respect for the physical integrity of suspects."[97] The innocent frequently suffered along with the terrorists, and a Uruguayan officer reportedly told Amnesty International in 1976 that "practically all prisoners were tortured with drugs, beatings and electroshocks regardless of age or sex."[98]

More recently, many in Western Europe have grown concerned about alleged "anti-libertarian" trends in West Germany, citing the emergence of repressive legislation isolating prisoners (*'Kontaktsperre'*), loyalty programs banning radicals from public service employment (*'Berufsverbot'*), security oriented political programs, limitations on court appearance of "sympathetic" lawyers, and increased police powers. Others conclude that "a balanced view of West Germany would have to acknowledge that its political institutions have proven strong and flexible under great strain, that the political parties have behaved with restraint and responsibility—in the face of intolerable rumblings from below."[99] Yet it is hard to dispute that terrorism, wherever it occurs, is an anti-democratic force. Society has to respond, and the response invariably strains at the bonds of a free society.

Terrorism has also strained international relations, and the CIA has concluded that internationalized terror "promises to impinge more directly on U.S. interests and options with respect to a broad range of critical issue areas, including both East-West and North-South relations, the politically and economically sensitive questions of arms sales and the transfer of advanced technology, and the resolution of problems associated with the dependence of Western industrialized countries on foreign energy sources."[100] Others argue that the Soviet Union is gaining a great deal from terrorism in the West, and that the problem has generally weakened the coherence of the Western Alliance.

In sum, the impact of terrorism on humanity is "intrinsically evil", according to British author Paul Johnson, because of its "seven deadly sins": It is a "deliberate and cold-blooded exaltation of violence over all other forms of political activity"; it requires a "deliberate suppression of the moral instincts of man"; it is a "rejection of politics as the normal means by which communities resolve conflicts"; it "actively, systematically, and necessarily assists the spread of the totalitarian state"; it can "destroy a democracy . . . but it cannot destroy a totalitarian state"; it "exploits the apparatus of freedom in a liberal society and thereby endangers it"; and finally, it "saps the will of a civilized society to defend itself . . . it attempts, in short, to induce civilization to commit suicide".[101]

COPING WITH TERRORISM

Given the causes, characteristics, and effects of the terrorist challenge, what are the response options facing management of multinational enterprise? Clearly, the first line of defense is governmental and intergovernmental action and reassertion of the rule of law. As we have seen, though, there are always failings in society's defenses against terrorist actions, and this opens up the need for individuals, firms, and other institutions to assume a certain degree of responsibility for their own safety. For multinational firms that operate in an exposed way in many countries the problem of security against terrorist attack is clearly amplified and compounded. While complete security is impossible, available techniques do provide a useful set of options in response to international terrorism.

The Role of Governments

Recent years have seen a number of advanced nations creating cabinet-level task forces, increasing surveillance operations, tightening airport and prison security, establishing special anti-terror police units, budgeting more funds for internal security, and passing new legislation to increase penalties for conspiratorial crimes, speed court proceedings, and increase police powers. But as we have seen, liberal democracies are faced with an insoluble dilemma between protecting individual liberty and preserving public security. Draconian police crackdowns, Uruguayan or Brazilian style, or martial law, Turkish or Philippine style, are simply unacceptable in the liberal states in which multinationals do the bulk of their business. Constitutional restraints make such stern responses impossible. Tragically, such "police state" suppression is probably the only truly effective way to stamp out terrorist violence as many of today's military dictatorships and Communist totalitarian states have demonstrated.

"Terrorism is a worldwide problem that therefore must be solved within a worldwide framework," said former West German President Walter Scheel in September 1977.[102] Such a framework is eminently desirable but politically unfeasible. Since 1963, six major international conventions dealing with aspects of terrorism have in fact been adopted: the 1963 Tokyo Convention concerning offenses committed on board aircraft, the 1970 Hague Convention on the unlawful seizure of aircraft, the 1971 Montreal Convention concerning the suppression of unlawful acts against the safety of civil aviation, the 1971 OAS Convention on preventing and punishing acts of terrorism directed at diplomats, the 1973 United Nations Convention on the prevention and punishment of crimes against diplomats, and the 1976 Luxembourg Resolution of the European Community on measures to combat international terrorism.[103]

Some believe that these protocols have resulted in some progress in coping with air piracy and diplomatic kidnapping. But not all are yet in force, some nations have not acceded to them, various signatories have not carried out their responsibilities, and the emasculation process in reaching international agreements has made some of them little more than declarations of intent. Hence while "the various international conventions to combat terrorism may be of considerable interest to international lawyers and insurance agents, they are of no practical importance."[104] Another observer points out: "Clearly, few of the major underlying causes . . . appear amenable to international or national judicial or political measures. It would be naive to expect any new international convention or resolution to have a discernible effect upon the intensity or frequency of acts of terrorism."[105]

Given the continuing divergence of state views of justifiable versus illegal political violence, rights of political asylum, and perceptions of political repression, the international response to terrorism will remain weak and ineffective. The doors to terrorists will remain open as long as some states allow acts to go unpunished and others who act as facilitators remain immune to world public opinion or diplomatic persuasion. And so multinational enterprises will continue to be subject to the risks and fears of terrorist violence. The root causes are unlikely to be ameliorated, the motives are likely to remain, the facilitators will continue to function, and MNEs will have to depend, to a large degree, on self-defense.

Governmental inability to insulate individuals and firms from terrorist action has spawned a dynamic and profitable growth industry. Seminars abound covering the do's and don'ts for executives who might be subjected to a terrorist attack. Such seminars in the United State have been sponsored by the American Bar Association, the Georgetown University Center for Strategic and International Studies, the World Trade Institute, and Probe International. Topics covered at a recent Bar Association "Terror Conference" included corporate behavior in a terrorist environment, urban warfare, assassination, bomb threats, terrorist credibility, executive kidnapping, negotiating and bargaining, countermeasures, "victimology" and hostage behavior, strengths and weaknesses of terrorists, descriptions of various terrorist groups (their links and funding, their methodology and tools, and selection of targets and victims), emerging terrorist trends and tactics, effective response and incident management, development of effective anti-terrorist programs, nuclear and biological blackmail, and the like.[106]

Along with seminars and consultants, a boom in the security service business has also erupted. During 1977, West Germany's 400 or so licensed security companies hired thousands of additional guards and their revenues were estimated to have exceeded $1 billion. In the wake of terrorist outrages, such firms clustered like vultures around multinational firms. In the U.S. many of the new or expanded firms were not really qualified to provide proper security. As one veteran of the business put it: "Detective agencies that were doing divorce investigations last year are now offering corporate security."[107]

There are no magic formulas which can insulate a multinational's executives or facilities from danger. At best, managing the challenge of terrorism can only be a matter of piecemeal coping, not comprehensive solution. Consistent with the main thrust of our argument in Chapters 2 and 3, a contingency approach combining sound "security management" and "crisis management" is needed. Situations of terrorist threat can vary widely in terms of (a) the power balance—for example, terrorist group versus a MNE-government coalition, (b) the stakes involved—for example, magnitude of the danger faced or damage which could be done, (c) the quality of the relationship—for example, that which develops between corporate and terrorist representatives during negotiations, and (d) interdependence of interests—for example, the importance attached to hostage survival or common desires concerning the size and form of ransoms.

One can safely predict, however, that a situation calling for a collaborative strategy will never arise. Furthermore, although relative power and outcome stakes might vary over a wide spectrum from low to high, it will usually be the case that relationship quality and interest interdependence are fundamentally negative. In regard to our conflict management model, therefore, it appears that coping with terrorism calls for management behavioral options falling within the "avoidance-competition-accommodation" triangle.

Security Management

The first line of defense against terrorism is a high standard of security. No security system can be foolproof. As noted, there is no absolute protection against determined and highly intelligent terrorists. But a variety of precautionary security measures can serve limited but sometimes effective deterrent and demotivating purposes. Management can authorize adequate corporate funds and manpower for executive security, insurance, facility security, advance planning, and external consultants and security services. They can also shape policies which attempt to reduce the likelihood of encounters with terrorist groups.

Executive security. Many MNEs have focused mainly on taking precautions to protect senior executives, generally while they travel between home and office, and while they are out of town or abroad and considered most vulnerable. Thousands of executives located in "high risk" cities such as Buenos Aires, Mexico City, Cologne, Düsseldorf, Hamburg, Paris, Nice, Milan, Rome and New York are now accompanied by at least one bodyguard. Wiry Yugoslavs appear to be preferred in West Germany, while former agents of the FBI seem to be favored in the United States. Such protection for a single executive round-the-clock generally requires four expert "gorillas" and in 1978 cost up to $120,000 a year depending on the city involved.

Some experts note that bodyguards offer both advantages and disadvantages.[108] On the plus side, they can provide an emotional sense of security that is indispensable for effective executive performance, serve as a sufficient deterrent to discourage amateur, conventional, or "casual" kidnappers, and foil actual attempted kidnappings or assaults. The use of bodyguards, however, may actually cause violence during an attempted kidnapping resulting in injury or death, deflect the kidnappers away from the executive and toward unprotected members of his family, and in any event be no match for a determined and resourceful group of abductors. On the latter point, it is useful to recall that the presence of three bodyguards and an armed chauffeur did not help Hanns-Martin Schleyer when his motorcade was halted and ambushed by 10 to 15 members of the Red Army faction at a crossroads during the evening rush hour in Cologne on September 5, 1977—in the exchange of 300 shots all of his guards were killed and Schleyer was successfully abducted. Nor did it help Italian ex-Premier Aldo Moro, whose five bodyguards were slain during his abduction in March 1978.

In addition to armed escorts, a variety of other precautions can be taken. Special security briefings can be held for executives traveling or being transferred overseas. DuPont and Gulf Oil are among the many MNEs that now do so.[109] Executives who are likely targets can keep travel plans secret and change them at the last minute, discreetly book themselves in economy class on commercial flights, carry miniature transmitters that can be used to alert a monitoring unit to trouble, decline to make appointments until a few days or hours ahead of time, vary their schedules frequently, avoid solitary walks and talks with strangers, avoid ostentation, publicity, and unsolicited invitations, make speeches behind bullet proof glass or at gatherings subject to tight security arrangements, travel under assumed names, ride in armored limousines, vary routes to and from work, install tight electronic security, guards, and watchdogs at their residences, have their wives and children escorted by bodyguards, have chauffeurs trained in "defensive driving" to avoid terrorist ambushes, install personal mail screening devices, take weapons training, and personally carry guns. As this unending list of possibilities implies, though, executives can indeed be protected physically, but at the same time destroyed spiritually.

Insurance. The spread of international terrorism has brought a boom in sales of political risk and kidnapping insurance. Such policies, of course, serve to reduce the firm's financial vulnerability to acts of violence but do little to remedy the human costs. *Business Insurance* magazine has estimated that some 25% of the Fortune 500 firms in the United States have kidnap policies. [110] Many insurance companies offer coverage for actual kidnapping, kidnapping threats, and loss of ransom payments in transit to kidnappers. One type of policy generally offered by insurance firms requires the insured enterprise to name the specific executives to be covered—a typical policy covering a $1 million ransom demand on an executive in Argentina during 1973 cost $40,000. Group policies which cover numerous executives in particular regions or job categories can also be purchased. The annual premiums for corporate-type policies depend on the number of persons to be insured, the size and reputation of the enterprise, and the geographic areas for which coverage is to apply [111] Worldwide kidnap insurance covering all overseas executives can serve to spread the risk and lower average premiums.

Individual executives can also purchase kidnap insurance policies on their own. But if the policy is owned by the company, premium costs are tax deductible in most countries, as are ransom payments, under cost-of-business doctrines. This, however, may not apply to the cost of personal kidnap insurance. [112] For obvious reasons, multinationals are reluctant to discuss whether or not they are protected by kidnap insurance. Some policies, in fact, require the existence of the policy to be kept strictly confidential. This is also true for political risk insurance, for which Lloyds of London is by far the largest supplier. Such policies are by no means always profitable for the insurers—$35 million was lost in a single day when the Palestinians blew up three planes at Dawsons Field in 1970.[113]

Facility security. In addition to insurance and security covering key executives, multinationals can also take other precautions on behalf of all their employees, plants, and other productive assets. Bombers, arsonists, saboteurs, and kidnappers usually take the path of least resistance. No amount of financial, human, or technological resources can make a corporate facility totally secure, but a high standard of security can encourage terrorists to pick easier targets. The most difficult problem is controlling access to existing plants or office buildings. Here the firm can employ perimeter guards and dogs, protective fencing and lighting, briefcase and package inspection, photo badge identification systems, electronic security checks, personal escorts for visitors, sophisticated alarm and communications systems, and the like.

Measures can also be taken inside plants and offices. Corporate headquarters in some parts of the world have been turned into modern fortresses, complete with mailroom metal detectors, locked washrooms, card-key elevator systems, self-locking doors, bomb scare evacuation routes, stairwell inspections, employee background checks, closed-circuit television surveillance of sensitive areas, and hidden executive escape hatches. [114] Access to executive suites has recently been limited in many firms in order to reduce the probability of unauthorized visits. At the headquarters of Citicorp in New York City, for example, a bullet-proof, sliding glass partition was recently installed in front of the senior executives' suite. Such security is not cheap—according to one estimate, American companies spent $7.1 billion on security at home and abroad in 1978 [115]

Avoidance. Given the limitations of security systems, the best protection against terrorism may be a low profile. "This is particularly important for foreign subsidiaries, which can be camouflaged under a different name (where corporate pride allows that). In trouble areas visiting executives will have to learn to be more discreet about photographs in the press, the use of brightly painted company planes, and so on."[117] "Terrorists typically view top-level executives as symbols of the corporate entities they represent, and so it may be risky for chief executives to be featured in advertising campaigns or engage in highly visible controversial public policy debates where the incidence of terrorism is high. More generally, "the terrorists' favorite corporate targets tend to be those whose activities can most easily be reconciled with a conspiracy theory of multinational string-pulling." [117] Multinationals that keep their noses clean by avoiding political meddling, pollution incidents, discrimination cases, labor troubles, arms production, and so on are thus less likely to become targets.

Terrorist avoidance can take other forms as well. We noted earlier that foreign executives flocked across the River Plate to the comparative safety of Uruguay or even São Paulo, Brazil, often commuting to work in Buenos Aires by air, during the period of intense terrorist activity in 1973—1975. As noted, multinationals such as Kodak, Exxon, Coca-Cola, Otis Elevator, General Motors, Cities Service, and Ford Motor at least temporarily transferred their expatriates back home. In Cordoba Province Fiat closed down a railroad equipment plant because worker violence posed a threat to management's safety.[118] Petroquimica

Argentina (PASA) closed down the country's biggest petrochemical operation for the same reason. And IBM permanently moved its operations elsewhere. As the chief executive of another American firm reasoned: "When our profits have been overtaken by ransom payments, we'll simply cut our losses and get out."[119]

At the extreme, multinationals can simply forego business in countries where terrorism is a particular problem. A London-based security firm, Argen Information Systems, often advises companies against going into areas where their offices and personnel cannot be adequately protected. In late 1977, South America, West Germany, Ireland, and Italy were ranked as high-risk areas.[120]

Advance planning. In view of all the activity, it is perhaps surprising that few multinationals have developed any concrete programs, or even guidelines, for dealing with terrorism. Even the very best security, insurance coverage, or low-profile measures cannot prepare an enterprise to deal with actual terrorist threats or attacks once they occur. And it is quite common to find corporate executives confused, in disarray, and unable to make a decision or communicate effectively with terrorists. Terrorism does not always strike "the other guy," and there is clearly a need to formulate, *in advance*, specific policies and procedures to be followed in the event that an incident occurs. The same kind of contingency plans that are standard practice for handling major industrial accidents, oil spills, or natural disasters, are just as needed here—systematic "crisis management" programs at both headquarters and affiliate levels.

According to one writer, "The most comprehensive program of this type now in use is the one that Motorola Teleprograms Inc. (MTI), a security firm 80% owned by Motorola Inc., has set up for a number of multinational corporations. The major objective of the MTI program is to provide corporate personnel with a system in which they can use traditional management skills rather than relying on an intuitive or emotional response. It recommends that a crisis team be formed consisting of 5 to 10 managers from various disciplines in the company."[121]

The point is to use the kinds of management skills that provide the multinational's competitive edge in the marketplace and apply those skills to the management of terrorist crises. Crisis management teams should be headed by a senior executive—but not the President or Chairman—and composed of public relations, security, financial, legal, personnel, and intelligence experts. Such a team can intitiate intelligence surveys to learn about terrorist plans and developments in the high risk nations where the company operates. It can perform or commission target analyses, as through terrorist eyes, to decide which aspects of the firm's business operations might be most easily or severely disrupted. It can study all aspects of potential terrorism situations and carefully work out contingency plans for dealing with each. It can recommend that the Board of Directors adopt a confidential policy on whether ransom or extortion money should be paid and, if so, how much. A crisis center or "war room" can be established and permanently staffed, particularly in "hot spot" areas. Team effectiveness can be tested and enhanced by means of simulated incidents. And the unit should be able to swing into action as soon as a case suddenly breaks, thus eliminating the confusion which often occurs at such times. As one observer has concluded, "setting up a plan to deal with potential terrorist actions would probably cost a company several hundred thousand dollars. Considering the threat to life and the corporate upheaval an actual attack could cause, as well as the millions in extortion money that terrorist groups are demanding, it would seem a cheap price to pay for being prepared."[122]

Crisis Management

A senior executive is kidnapped. A threat of assassination, sabotage, or bombing is received. A plant is occupied and workers seized. A plane or ship is hijacked. It is not a hoax. Demands are made. How should MNE management react?

In terms of our conflict management model, avoidance and collaboration are out. The options remaining available fall on the diagonal zero-sum continuum, with "competition" at one extreme, "accommodation" at the other, and soft and hard bargaining in between. Assertive and uncooperative competition would mean standing firm—stubbornly refusing to accept or negotiate the demands of the terrorists. Unassertive and cooperative accommodation would mean capitulation—giving in to the demands in order to get the hostage back or to prevent the threatened violence.

Whether the multinational's response can be characterized as either one of these polar alternatives once again depends on the stakes, power, relationships, and interests involved. Some of the factors, values, and assumptions that may be useful in assessing the conflict situation at hand are listed in Exhibit 4-3. One set of factors represents arguments in favor of resistance; the other points to accommodation. They reveal the horrible intellectual and pragmatic dilemmas that confront executives in terrorist incidents. The fact is that each approach has its advantages and disadvantages. Yet despite the dilemmas, a decision must still be made.

The flexible response. Most writers on the subject contend that one should never give in to blackmail, since this will simply produce more crimes. But in the real world, with the life or death of a fellow executive at stake, "never" is too strong a word. Like every man, every multinational has its price. And if the penalties of resistance can be raised high enough, any enterprise will be pressed to give in. From our reading of the evidence, it seems that multinationals in this decade have quickly accommodated to demands of terrorists in about 50% of all cases, "split the difference" through bargaining in another 40%, and had the nerve to resist only in the remaining 10%. It's easy for the "Monday Morning Quarterback" to criticize the preponderance of acquiescence as indicating a gutless desire for momentary gains at the expense of long term strategic losses— to suggest that the gains of capitulation go to the firm itself but the costs must be borne largely by other individuals and firms who subsequently fall victim to terrorist extortion. But the critic typically has never experienced the pain and anguish of those confronted with life or death decisions nor, of course, has he suffered the harrowing experience of a terrorist hostage or victim.

It is impossible to lay down a general rule. No two terrorist situations are likely to be exactly the same. An uncompromising stance may make sense in one instance, one of rapid concession in another, and one of patient bargaining in still another. Each case of terrorism has its own unique characteristics and each has to be dealt with on its own merits by the kind of crisis management team

Exhibit 4–3
Arguments Favoring Resistance and Accommodation to Terrorist Demands

ARGUMENTS FAVORING RESISTANCE

1. Capitulation will only serve to encourage further terrorist acts via contagion and demonstration effects. Resistance will weaken and dishearten terrorists and reduce their expectations.

2. It is morally wrong to give in to demands of groups that have engaged in terrorist atrocities and murdered the innocent.

3. Giving in will place other executives in constant jeopardy. A life lost now may well prevent a greater number of lives being lost later.

4. Giving in to the original set of demands may only result in the terrorist making additional demands before the hostage is released.

5. There is no absolute guarantee that the terrorists will keep their part of the bargain if the demands are satisfied.

6. If the full demands are met this time around, they may simply escalate in similar incidents that follow.

7. Payment of ransom or extortion demands will supply the terrorists with funds that can be used for purchase of more arms and so on, thus improving their future effectiveness.

8. Some governments prohibit the payment of ransom and accommodation may thus be against the law.

9. Accommodation which violates government wishes or which involves publication of anti-government proclamations may lead to government reprisals against the firm.

10. Some corporate assets, when all is considered, are just not worth the outrageous ransom sums occasionally demanded.

ARGUMENTS FAVORING ACCOMMODATION

1. Firms have a moral duty and financial obligation to protect the lives of their executives, especially when they are assigned to parts of the world where their safety may be threatened.

2. Refusal to bargain or meet demands could have a devastating impact on the morale of other employees who might also be potential targets. Executives will leave the company when they realize their safety is not assured.

3. For humanitarian reasons, the safety of the hostage must be secured at all costs. After all, senior executives are not equipped for, and should not be placed in the position of, making life or death decisions.

4. The contagion hypothesis rests on shaky evidence. Some firms which have once given in to terrorist demands have not been victimized by further incidents.

5. Governments possess a monopoly on the organized use of force. Corporate victims cannot act as vigilantes. If the government so chooses, the "force option" may not be available.

6. In most nations the firm can deduct ransom payments and kidnap insurance premiums as business expenses. Furthermore, the ransoms demanded may be infinitessimal relative to financial resources readily available.

7. Even if the firm gives in, the police may subsequently capture and arrest the perpetrators, and recover at least part of the ransom.

8. Terrorists will rarely doublecross the firm as they have their own credibility to protect. If they renege on their part of the agreement, they can be sure that future victims will be less likely to concede.

9. If the demands take a "Robin Hood" charity form, the firm is then in a disconcerting position. Refusal to aid in fulfilling a charitable goal could result in adverse publicity.

10. Accommodation may achieve tranquility, at least temporarily. And it may serve to get the firm's name out of the news faster than a drawn-out stand of resistance.

suggested earlier employing what might be termed a "flexible response position."[123]

It would be futile, perhaps even dangerous, to prescribe specific sets of crisis management behavior. But observations on hostage survival and studies of bargaining experience with terrorists do produce some general patterns and guidelines.[124] Experts naturally advise that the firm's executives should not panic or overreact and that the existence of a competent "crisis management" team can help to avoid this. Top management must be involved from the outset so that effects on employees and their families, stockholder reactions, public image consequences, relations with the host government, costs which can be borne, and impact on future operations can be taken into account in an integrated and systematic way.

Effective response depends first and foremost on the availability of solid intelligence. Much depends on the firm's ability to accurately estimate the situation in terms of the nature of the demands and threats, the credibility of the threats, and the mental state of the terrorists:

> Data obtainable at the site of an incident can provide clues as to how the corporation should conduct negotiations. Relevant considerations may include previous behavior of the group in similar situations, logistical constraints, age and sex of the perpetrators, existence of communication with the group's headquarters, choice of the governments' negotiation team representative or intermediary, size of the attack force, number of terrorist groups involved in the incident, choice of targets in terms of their symbolic value, as well as the nationalities of the victims, targets and terrorists.[125]

Deciding whether the firm is dealing with mercenaries, the insane, political representatives, free-lance revolutionaries, or some combination, has crucial implications for the possibility of side payments, and the rationality and the predictability of terrorist behavior.

Negotiating with terrorists is especially difficult because of such factors as the high degree of uncertainty involved, possible irrationality and panic, the lack of outcomes or bargains that both parties regard as legitimate, the difficulty of making binding promises to one another, and the often necessary use of third-party intermediaries. Frequently the situation is a fluid one, since rationality and motivation of the terrorists—and also perhaps of the firm and government—are likely to change over time. Patience, persuasion, and firmness appear to be assets. As experience in many cases has shown, terrorist demands are indeed often "negotiable" and many firms have been successful at "talking down" ransoms. Experts recommend "playing for time," employing every circumstance as a basis for further negotiation, and putting back, if possible, the deadlines terrorists impose. With time, a quite close relationship can grow up between the terrorists and the hostage they have abducted, "humanizing" him and cutting down the possibility that death threats will actually be carried out. Stretching out the time may also produce a terrorist psychological let-down.

Good relations with the host government and its police forces is often desirable, but governmental aid can sometimes be counterproductive. For one thing, the goals of the firm and the government may be potentially incompatible or may follow different priorities—as for example between hostage release, deterrence of potential terrorism, and punishment of the terrorists. Furthermore, competition and mistrust may exist among governmental authorities. Involvement of the MNE home government can also misfire. Probably one of the worst mistakes a multinational can make is that of simply turning the problem over to the authorities. Use should be made of them, but they should not be given carte blanche to negotiate or to make "force option" decisions.

THE FUTURE

Should many of the genuine political and social grievances which motivate—and resources which facilitate—terrorism be reduced, it is quite likely that the intensity and frequency of international terrorism would decline markedly. Many MNE executives yearn for the late 1950s and 1960s which marked both the rapid growth of multinationals and relative freedom from terrorist activities aimed at business firms. But the outlook for eradicating major tensions or closing key doors to terrorism is not at all bright. As Walter Laqueur somberly concludes, ". . . there will always be disaffected and alienated people claiming that the present state of affairs is intolerable and there will be aggressive people more interested in violence than in liberty and justice."[126] Another author adds, "there always will be an absolutist faction which holds individual life in contempt, which justifies ends over means, which clutches at martyrdom for no matter how tawdry a cause."[127]

On the day in 1977 when Dr. Hanns-Martin Schleyer's corpse was found in the trunk of an abandoned green Audi in the French town of Mulhouse, his killers sent a message to the far-left Paris daily *Liberation* announcing: "The battle has just begun." One can hope they are wrong, but cannot overlook the possibility that terrorism may persist and evolve in ways that could pose threats more grave than anything experienced to date. We now face the danger of terrorist organizations acquiring even more lethal weapons of violence and mass destruction. This could take the form of biological pathogens or chemical and radiological threats. With nuclear proliferation difficult to control, it seems almost inevitable that eventually a terrorist group will manufacture or steal a small nuclear explosive device. An authoritative report to the Energy Policy Project of the Ford Foundation has concluded that the threat of nuclear theft and blackmail "must be taken seriously."[128] The potential leverage of nuclear terrorists over governments and corporations would be unprecedented. "Society may be spared the dilemma, but if the emergency arose countermeasures could involve a degree of state control and repression hitherto unknown in any democratic society except at a time of war."[129]

For "transnational enterprise," the final showdown with "transnational terrorism" may be yet to come. Multinationals will continue to operate in the shadow of other people's deadly quarrels. And with the great symbolic value of such firms, their vulnerability, massive resources, controversial nature, and reputation of quickly meeting demands, their popularity as terrorist targets is likely to remain high. Multinationals will thus continue to need a mix of security-oriented avoidance and crisis-oriented accommodation, bargaining, or resistance. Nonetheless, the more multinationals are able on balance to take an increasingly hard line on terrorist demands, the greater the likelihood that terrorism against them will gradually be reduced in scale.

5 HUMAN RIGHTS
—THE ISSUES

Should IBM stop selling or leasing its computers to Latin American governments which could use them to combat opposition forces and possibly abridge human rights? Should Bank of America stop making loans available to the military government of Chile? Should Coca-Cola establish minimum labor standards required of all its bottlers around the world to prevent abuses by its franchise holders in particular countries? Should Rio Tinto Zinc and Newmont Mining have paid taxes on their Namibian operations to the UN Council for Namibia rather than to the government of South Africa, which the UN says "illegally" occupied the territory? Should Union Carbide and U.S. Steel make no further capital commitments in South Africa, and should Ford and General Electric shut down their present South African operations as quickly as possible unless and until apartheid is scrapped and full political rights are given to the majority of the population?

These are but a few of the tough operational questions related to human rights that MNEs have recently had to face. A few companies encountered such problems a decade or more ago, but strident interrogation on a multitude of issues really did not begin until the mid-1970s when a combination of events brought the issue of human rights into sharp and urgent focus. Multinationals today have come face-to-face with a powerful popular movement concerned with cruelty, injustice, and oppression. To some, this movement reflects a genuine concern with human dignity and individual freedom. To others, it seems little more than trendy, faddish "radical chic" among North American and European liberals.

However well intentioned, the human rights movement has not always been careful with the consistency of its logic or the realism of its demands. MNEs have had to contend with sanctimonious outpourings of indignation and self-righteousness, as well as hypocritical, selective applications of morality. And the human rights activities of citizen groups and private institutions have generally been far ahead of the often ambiguous and contradictory positions and policies of governments. Like many of the other problems discussed in this book, human rights is an issue where MNEs are pressed to look beyond legal and quasi-legal analysis in determining appropriate conduct.

As public sensitivity to human rights violations has grown, the involvement of multinationals has come under increasing scrutiny and challenge. In the process, MNEs have often come to be viewed as morally bankrupt allies of reprehensible regimes. The frequently shrill and emotional debate has generally focused on whether the involvement of MNEs with governments that ostensibly violate human rights supports or counteracts such violations. In its extreme form, the question is raised whether indeed there is some sort of symbiotic relationship between MNEs and repression. The issues are certainly complex, laden with ideology and propaganda, and often shrouded by a lack of reliable information. And there are questions of state sovereignty versus foreign intervention, idealism versus realism, gradualism versus immediate change, and symbolism versus substance. The resulting paradoxes, dilemmas, and riddles have often been hard to reconcile.

Some multinationals have found the intrusion of human rights into management affairs abrasive and unwelcome, and have responded with cynicism. Some MNE executives have strongly defended the right of their firms to do business anywhere in the world, regardless of human rights violations of political regimes—their responsibility being to their shareholders and not to political ideas. Some have pleaded that they are ill-equipped to measure or even identify the civil and political effects of their activities—improving human rights requires information and competence which they do not, and perhaps should not, possess. Logical or not, such arguments have been drowned out by the roar of critics who refuse to tolerate corporate indifference to the human condition. In their view, MNEs can no longer divorce themselves from brutality and injustice, and so human rights has become a matter of serious corporate concern.

The growing moralization and politicization of international business poses serious dilemmas for multinational managers, fraught with ethical predicaments and tangled choices. MNEs are being called on to act consciously as agents of a broad social and political reform, and at the same time are viewed by others as agents of moral imperialism and cultural arrogance. They are being pressured on moral grounds to violate such basic principles as "full compliance with laws of the land," "respect for local customs," and "abstinence from interference in local politics." Perhaps nowhere else is the MNE caught so dangerously in the middle. In the South African case, for example, MNEs have been barraged by pressures of church groups, labor unions, students, and politicians in home and third nations, and at the same time have been subject to countervailing legal pressures from the South African government.

Most multinationals have yet to develop a coherent, effective response to the challenge of human rights. Management's basic task is to strike the right balance in specific situations between the interests and ideals of its many stakeholders. The problem is so complex that our discussion of human rights conflict facing multinational enterprise is rather extensive, and is presented in two parts. In this chapter we consider the concept of human rights and its evolution through time, the linkages between economic and human rights variables, and the development of private and public human rights pressures that are increasingly bearing on the MNE. The following chapter will focus on the specific effects of the human rights offensive on multinational corporate operations and ways of dealing with it effectively.

WHAT ARE HUMAN RIGHTS

Jimmy Carter painfully discovered not long after his election to the presidency that "defining human rights is a hazardous business."[1] This is not because the phrase is meaningless. On the contrary, it has too many meanings. These meanings, while "not necessarily incompatible," and "in practice always overlapping," are often incoherently muddled.[2] British political theorist Maurice

Cranston notes: "Human rights is a twentieth-century name for what has been traditionally known as natural rights or, in a more exhilarating phrase, the rights of man. Much has been said about them, and yet one may still be left wondering what they are."[3]

Human rights are an ancient concept, as old as the earliest notions of law and justice. The Code of Hammurabi proclaimed in 1750 B.C. "that the strong might not oppress the weak and that they should give justice." In ancient Greece, residents of certain cities enjoyed such rights as freedom of speech and equality before the law, and Stoic philosophers formulated concepts of "natural law" and "natural rights," which superseded the obligations and regulations imposed by human rulers. By 450 B.C., the Roman Republic had established the Law of the Twelve Tables, which guaranteed all citizens rights and duties. But perhaps the most powerful infusion of human rights principles emerged from Judeo-Christian values: "Love thy neighbor as thyself" became a central tenet of Western religion.

The Magna Carta in 1215 defined and guaranteed the legal rights of all Englishmen and were extended by the Habeas Corpus Acts of 1640 and 1670 and the English Bill of Rights in 1689. In the late 1600s the philosopher John Locke became the leading writer on the subject with works dealing with the rights of life, liberty, and property. Across the Atlantic, Locke's reasoning was embodied in the Bill of Rights adopted in Virginia by the representative convention in June of 1776, and a month later thirteen American states issued the Declaration of Independence, stating: "We hold these truths to be self-evident: that all men are created equal; that they are endowed by their Creator with certain inalienable rights; that among these are life, liberty, and the pursuit of happiness." The United States Constitution of 1789 defined these rights in greater detail. In France, meanwhile, the *Déclaration des Droits de l'Homme et du Citoyen* issued in 1789 by the Constituent Assembly paralleled in many respects the Anglo-American model. In the 1800s concern for individual rights was expressed in such multinational peace agreements as Vienna (1815) and Berlin (1878), and human rights considerations were an important thread of concern during the peace settlement discussions at Versailles in 1919. Throughout, human rights remained mainly a question of domestic jurisdiction, well beyond the reach of international law.

World War II changed all that. When the United Nations was created, one of its first and most important tasks was, in the words of Winston Churchill, "the enthronement of human rights." The UN Charter signed on June 26, 1945, stated that the organization was "to reaffirm faith in fundamental human rights, in the dignity and worth of the human person, in the equal rights of men and women and of nations large and small . . . "[4] Articles 55 and 56 of the Charter obligated all UN members to promote such rights.

On December 10, 1948, the UN General Assembly adopted the Universal Declaration of Human Rights, still preeminent among the many international conventions and declarations dealing with this subject.[5] As a declaration, it did not require ratification by member nations, nor was it intended to place legally binding obligations on member nations. Rather, it merely set forth a "common standard of achievement for all people and all nations." Articles 1–21 of the Declaration elaborate the classical notion of political and civil rights by spelling out such things as the right to freedom of movement; the right to own property;

the right to life, liberty, and security of person; the right not to be held in slavery, arbitrarily detained, or subjected to torture; the right to equality before the law and to a fair trail if accused of crime; the right to marry; the right to religious freedom; the right to free speech and peaceful assembly; and the right to asylum. Articles 22–30, however, introduce a new set of rights related to economic and social needs—the right to social security; the right to education; the right to equal pay for equal work; the right of everyone to a "standard of living . . . adequate for the health and well-being of himself and his family"; and such novelties as the right to rest, leisure, and "periodic holidays with pay." In the debate, the Western democracies had lobbied for the traditional political and civil rights, while both the Communist and nonaligned countries had argued for the new economic and social rights.

The general principles proclaimed in the 1948 Declaration were eventually translated into precise legal language (with detailed elaborations of exceptions, limitations, and restrictions) in the form of two separate convenants adopted by a substantial majority of the UN General Assembly in December 1966. One was entitled the "International Convenant on Civil and Political Rights" and the other the "International Convenant on Economic, Social and Cultural Rights."[6] Rather weak enforcement machinery in the form of a Human Rights Committee was provided for the first Covenant, but none was contemplated for the second. Both came into force in 1976, after ratification by 35 governments. By late 1977, 44 governments had ratified the civic-political Covenant and 46 the economic-social-cultural one. President Carter signed both on October 4, 1977, but each must be ratified by two-thirds of the U.S. Senate before coming into force in the United States—possibly a formidable legislative task, considering that after more than three decades the Senate has yet to ratify the UN Genocide Convention.

Efforts to protect human rights at the international level have been under-way outside the United Nations as well. Under the auspices of the Council of Europe, foreign ministers of 15 European states signed a "European Covenant for the Protection of Human Rights and Fundamental Freedoms" in 1950 and added further rights in 1952. These included the traditional political and civil rights, notably the rights of life, liberty, and security of person; freedom from torture and slavery; the right to a fair and public trial; the right to privacy; freedom of thought, conscience, and religion; freedom of expression and assem-bly; the right to form trade unions; and the right to marry.[7] The London *Econo-mist* has called this "the most uncontentious assertion of fundamental rights available."[8] The Covenant, which came into force in 1953, set up two interna-tional legal institutions, the European Commission for Human Rights and the European Court of Human Rights, thus providing individuals, groups, and states with unprecedented opportunities to draw on the assistance of these institutions when they feel there has been a violation of rights.

Elsewhere, the revision of the Charter of the Organization of American States (OAS) in 1967 provided for the protection of human rights in the Ameri-cas and created the Inter-American Commission on Human Rights.[9] The Perma-nent Arab Commission on Human Rights was created by the Arab League Council, but has never considered anything other than Israel. The creation of an African Commission on Human Rights was suggested in 1961 but never got beyond the proposal stage.

Given this background, one scholar has noted that "the debate on human rights can be conceptualized in part as a struggle between eighteenth century libertarian persuasions and nineteenth century egalitarian beliefs—that is, from a vision of human rights having to do with the right of individual justice before the law to a recognition of the rights of individuals to social security and equitable conditions of work and standards of living."[10] And so, a rather basic question is whether human rights are "passive and negative," "active and positive," or both. Whatever they are, can they be inalienable, universal, and timeless? Can one envisage standards that can be applied to all countries with equal relevance and integrity?

It is true that "a common legacy of democratic and socialist systems, of libertarian and egalitarian frameworks, is the assumption that there is such a goal as human rights."[11] Besides those cited earlier, respect of man is written into the founding documents of almost every nation on earth. Although such nominal "legal rights" may not in fact be enforced—Article 125 of the Soviet Constitution guarantees its citizens by law freedom of speech, press, assembly, and street demonstrations—it is still true that all nations have found it necessary to give some recognition to the existence of rights.

Rights in any given culture can and do change substantially over time. The evolution of human rights in the United States, for example, has gone from religious freedom through the Bill of Rights, the abolition of slavery, universal suffrage, the four freedoms, the civil rights movement, and the war on poverty to the Equal Rights Amendment of today. Just as rights differ over time, logic suggests that they will also tend to differ over space, in line with differing cultural, political, economic, juridical, and social systems. As one author has noted, "the character of nature of human rights is determined in the crucible of a specific sociopolitical culture."[12] Yet others flatly reject this notion, maintaining that basic "principles of morality are minimal precisely because they are universal," and that fundamental political and civil rights can and should be enjoyed by "all people at all times and in all situations."[13] The debate over universality is likely to go on indefinitely.

The debate over whether rights are political-civil or economic-social-cultural will also drag on. Owing to its traditions, the Western world tends to concentrate on civil and political freedoms—"civil" essentially pertaining to the rights of an individual *vis-à-vis* his government, and "political" relating to the right to participate in government. These rights attach themselves to the individual. They are "passive" in the sense that only protective legislation is needed, and "negative" since they are essentially prohibitions on government interference with the individual. They can be recognized and they can be measured.

Yet critics, mostly from the Third and Communist worlds, maintain that this individualistic, laissez-faire, "freedom and duty" concept is inappropriate to the cultures, conditions, and values of non-western nations. African leaders at a 1973 seminar in Tanzania concluded, for example, that there was "no point in talking about human rights as long as serious economic problems have not been solved" —they pronounced international covenants on political-civil rights to be "alien to African reality."[14] Moreover, the idea of economic, social, and cultural rights has become increasingly popular. In 1978, Iran's representative to the International Monetary Fund and the World Bank argued that "nearly a billion human beings in the Third World lack minimum requirements of food, health care, housing and functional literacy. To the extent that the basic needs of these vast masses of human beings are unmet, their 'human rights' in a larger context are certainly not adequately safeguarded."[15] And Robert S. McNamara, head of the World Bank, believes that "among the most fundamental of human rights are the rights to minimum acceptable levels of nutrition, health and education."[16] Such rights are often collective in nature. They are "active" in the sense that they require government or private action, and they are "positive" in that the emphasis is on material satisfaction.

Others strenuously object to economic and social rights being considered true "human rights." To them, they are pseudo rights: "There is simply no meaning to something like the 'right' to social security, to an 'adequate' standard of living, to periodic holidays and pay. . . . At best these 'rights' are utopian goals; at worst they are totalitarian slogans to be used as excuses for denying actual political rights."[17] Irving Kristol argues that the notion of such rights is a foolish doctrine—"the principle is that a welfare state is always and everywhere better than a non-welfare state; that the more comprehensive a welfare state, the better; and that the right to a broad range of government services is absolute, whether the nation can afford them or not, and whether the people want them or not."[18] One writer cautions that there "is a danger in men's hearts prevailing over their heads," and that "a philosophically respectable concept of human rights has been muddled, obscured, and debilitated in recent years by an attempt to incorporate into it specific rights of this new kind."[19] In this view, such economic and social rights are not practicable, not justifiable, and not universal. They thus belong to the "twilight world of utopian aspirations."[20] They are "ideals," "virtues," "basic needs," and "standards of achievement," but they are not genuine universal human rights.

We can hardly end the debate. Still, a choice has to be made if we are to say anything sensible about human rights and MNEs. We side with those who believe that human rights are essentially political and civil in nature. This does not mean, however, that economic and social needs or ideals can be cast aside.[21] Indeed, they are complementary and mutually reinforcing. Economic and social progress, for example, by bringing about higher standards of living and redistributing wealth and power, typically results in increased demands for, and acquisition of, political and civil freedoms. Economic and social decline, on the other hand, often leads to widespread unemployment, deprivation, misery, and despair, producing in its turn the growth of popular resistance movements, civil unrest, and terrorism that are then met by the authorities with increased repression of political freedoms and suspension of civil liberties.

One can also trace direct relationships flowing in the opposite direction, from human rights to human needs. Political freedoms of action, self expression, and association can provide individuals and groups with opportunities for initiative and access to resources. As experience has frequently shown, such economic "freedoms," and the improved economic and social welfare that derive therefrom, are likely to be at their peak only when political rights are safeguarded and sanctioned. Conversely, when civil and political rights fade—as with the increased oppression in South Africa in 1976–1977—the satisfaction of human needs is likely to be undermined by harsh economic policies, reduced flows of foreign investment and credit, and resulting widespread unemployment.

Some argue that relationships can also be the reverse, that is, that a certain amount of political repression may be necessary in poor or backward countries in order to ensure maximum economic and social progress.[22] Are we to condemn outright countries like Brazil, Singapore, the Philippines, Nigeria, and South Korea, where a political price may have had to be paid for economic progress? But others maintain that " . . . the argument that would place full stomachs ahead of political and civil freedom as though there were a tradeoff fails because there simply is no tradeoff."[23] Even the most poverty stricken tend to demand both bread and freedom, as was shown dramatically in the electoral affirmation of democracy by India's 620 million people in 1977. As the victorious Janata Party pointed out before the election: "History is replete with instances when those who conspire against the rights of people attempt to undermine freedom by portraying it as a luxury. They conceal the fact that fundamental freedoms are weapons that the poor need to fight tyranny. Bread cannot be juxtaposed against liberty. The two are inseparable."[24] Whether this faith is borne out depends on India's economic performance in the next few years.

Our focus in this chapter will be on both the *direct* relationships between multinational corporate activities and human rights, and also on the *indirect* relationships which flow from corporate activities through human needs and on to human rights. And we restrict ourselves only to the linkages between multinationals and human rights, which is indeed only a partial analysis of how MNEs relate to the welfare of people in countries where they operate.

THE STATUS OF HUMAN RIGHTS

Only a handful of nations come close to observing the complete list of political and civil rights we have identified. Studies by the U.S. State Department of human rights in over 100 nations receiving United States aid paint a rather bleak picture, with reported rights violations in all but a few non-western countries.[25] Freedom House, a New York-based private research organization that has been monitoring civil and political liberties in the world for 38 years, reported in 1979 that 35.1% of the world's population was "free," 24.7% "partly free," and 40.2% "not free."[26] Exhibit 5–1 shows the results of its 1979 survey in the form of rankings on political rights and civil liberties.°

Freedom House has also attempted to explore the economic and political correlates of its rankings, and Table 5–1 shows a matrix of political and economic systems into which each nation can be roughly positioned. The aforemen-

---

°Since 1973 Freedom House has published the highly regarded "Comparative Survey of Freedom" which uses a list of uniform standards to judge how free people in various nations of the world are, and to track whether they are advancing or declining on the freedom scale. A variety of questions are asked of a data base gathered on each nation to determine the relative presence or absence of political and civil freedoms—these are basically defined in the manner in which they have been traditionally understood in the constitutional democracies of the world.[27] Using multiple criteria, each nation is ranked separately on political rights and civil liberties on a seven point scale, with a rating of (1) meaning most free and (7) least free. To reach an overall judgment on the status of freedom in a nation—i.e., whether it is "free (F)" "partly free (PF)" or "not free (NF),"—the two rankings on political rights and civil liberties are combined. Nations averaging a ranking of 1 or 2 are generally rated "free," 3, 4, or 5 as "partly free," and 6 or 7 as "not free."

tioned freedom ratings are set off against prevailing political systems, which extend from democratic multiparty systems to traditional or military nonparty systems, with dominant and one-party systems in-between. The analysis purports to show that freedom is directly related to the existence of multiparty systems: "the further a country is from such systems, the less freedom it is likely to have."[28] With regard to economic systems, nations are characterized as ranging from capitalist to socialist, with mixed systems in-between and subcategories provided for industrial and preindustrial levels of development. Here the conclusion is "that freedom can apparently exist fairly well in all economic systems except the strictly socialist. Capitalist states can be free or unfree; socialist states can only be unfree."[29]

Human rights violations resulting in "partly free" or "not free" assessments occur for a wide variety of reasons, often in the name of such things as economic progress, counterinsurgency, public order, national emergency, preparedness for meeting outside aggression, national policies of self reliance, egalitarianism, and anti-communism. And sometimes they are fundamental to the prevailing social order—the "dictatorship of the proletariat" in Communist dogma simply precludes certain freedoms taken for granted elsewhere. One observer sums it up as follows:

> There is a worldwide growing abuse of human rights, with violations of international standards so widespread that we are, indeed, facing a global human rights crisis. The causes are not hard to find. Communist governments based on mass, highly ideological movements pay lip service to human rights, but maintain tight control. In the newly independent nations of Africa, single-party dominance has been accomplished by constraints on the political activities of other parties and organizations. In Latin America, increasing polarization between the right and the left has led to higher levels of violence, with rightist governments sanctioning torture and killing. In some countries, regression in the observance of human rights is occurring as rulers seek to perpetuate their power. In other countries, tensions arising from racial, religious, or linguistic differences often lead to increasing repression on the part of the government.[30]

From the perspectives of the multinational enterprise, then, what are the "human rights hotspots"? To start with, it should be noted that only a very small percentage of the business of the world's multinationals is conducted with nations that, according to the above criteria, violate human rights. If one compares statistics on United States foreign direct investment with the national rankings on civil liberties developed by Freedom House, for example, an estimated 85% of all American foreign investment is located in nations designated as "free" (columns 1 and 2 in Exhibit 5-1), 12% is in "partly free" nations (columns 3, 4, and 5), and only 3% is in the "not free" countries.[31] If one considers total domestic and foreign investments by American companies, an estimated 95% is located in nations designated as "most free"(column 1).°

° It is tempting to speculate that non-American MNEs have a much greater share of their overseas investments located in "partly free" and "not free" countries (e.g., in Africa and Asia) as compared to American-based multinationals, although this may be changing with the surge of foreign investment in the United States.

Table 5-1 "Freedom House" Political and Economic System Correlates of Comparative Freedom

POLITICAL		MULTIPARTY		DOMINANT-PARTY
ECONOMIC		Centralized	Decentralized	
CAPITALIST — Industrial		Bahamas F; Barbados F; Colombia F; Costa Rica F; Djibouti F; Dominica[4] F; Dominican Republic[4] F; France[3] F; Greece F; Grenada F; Iceland F; Ireland F; Italy[1] F; Japan F; Luxembourg F; Mauritius F; New Zealand[3] PF; Spain F; Surinam F; Trinidad & Tobago F; Upper Volta[3] F	Australia F; Belgium F; Canada F; Cyprus PF; Germany (W)[3] F; Lebanon PF; Switzerland F; United States F	El Salvador[1] PF; Korea (S) PF; Malaysia PF
CAPITALIST — Preindustrial		Fiji[4] F; Gambia[4] F; Guatemala PF; Lesotho PF; Morocco PF; Papua New Guinea[3] F; Solomon Islands[2] F	Botswana F	Nicaragua[1/4] PF; Transkei[5] PF
CAPITALIST-STATIST — Industrial		Malta F; South Africa PF; Sri Lanka F; Turkey[4] F; Venezuela F	Brazil[1/3/4] PF	China (Taiwan) PF; Mexico PF; Singapore PF
CAPITALIST-STATIST — Pre-industrial		Bangladesh[1] PF; Rhodesia[4] PF	India F	Indonesia[1/4] PF; Paraguay[1/3/4] PF
CAPITALIST-SOCIALIST — Industrial		Austria F; Denmark F; Finland F; Guyana PF; Israel F	Jamaica F; Netherlands F; Norway F; Portugal F; Sweden F; United Kingdom F	Egypt[3/4] PF; Senegal[3/4] PF; Syria[1/4] PF
CAPITALIST-SOCIALIST — Pre-industrial				
SOCIALIST — Industrial				
SOCIALIST — Preindustrial				Iraq[1/3/4] NF

Notes
1. Military dominated.
2. Party relationships analogous to this category.
3. Close decision on capitalist-to-socialist dimension.
4. Close decision on industrial/preindustrial dimension.
5. Over 50 percent of income from remittances of persons working in South Africa.

Source: Raymond D. Gastil, "The Comparative Survey
of Freedom—IX," No. 49 (January–February 1979), p. 12.

ONE-PARTY			NONPARTY	
Socialist	Communist	Nationalist	Military	Traditional
			Chile[1/3] NF	Jordan[1] NF
Sierra Leone PF		Cameroon[1] NF	Chad[1] NF	Bhutan[3] PF
		Central African	Ecuador[1] PF	Maldives PF
		Empire[1] NF	Honduras[1/4] PF	Nepal[1] PF
		Gabon NF	Niger[1] NF	Swaziland PF
		Haiti NF	Thailand[1/3] PF	Tonga PF
		Ivory Coast[4] NF	Uganda[1] NF	Tuvalu F
		Kenya PF	Yemen (N)[1/3] NF	Western Samoa PF
		Liberia PF		
		Malawi NF		
		Philippines[2/3/4] PF		
Libya[1/3] NF			Argentina[1] NF	Bahrain PF
			Ghana[1/4] PF	Iran[4] PF
			Panama[1/3] PF	Kuwait PF
				Nauru F
				Qatar PF
				Saudi Arabia NF
				U.A.Em. PF
		Comoro Islands[2/3] PF	Mauritania[1] NF	Oman NF
		Zaire[1] NF	Nigeria[1/3/4] PF	
			Pakistan[1] PF	
Tunisia[4] NF	Poland[3] PF	Seychelles[3] PF	Uruguay[1] NF	
	Yugoslavia[3] NF			
Afghanistan[3] NF		Madagascar[1/3] PF	Bolivia[1] PF	
Burma[1] NF		Mali[1] NF	Peru[1/4] PF	
Burundi[3] NF		Rwanda[1/3] NF		
Congo[1/3] NF		Sudan[1] PF		
Somalia[1/3] NF		Togo[1] NF		
Zambia[3] PF				
Algeria NF	Albania NF			
	Bulgaria NF			
	China (Mainland) NF			
	Cuba NF			
	Czechoslovakia NF			
	Germany (E) NF			
	Hungary NF			
	Kampuchea NF			
	Korea (N) NF			
	Mongolia NF			
	Rumania NF			
	USSR NF			
	Vietnam NF			
Angola NF	Laos NF		Ethiopia[1/3] NF	
Benin[1/3] NF				
Cape Verde Is.[3/4] NF				
Equatorial Guinea[4] NF				
Guinea NF				
Guinea-Bissau[3] NF				
Mozambique NF				
Sao Tome and				
Principe[3] NF				
Tanzania NF				
Yemen (S) NF				

139

Exhibit 5-1

"Freedom House" Ranking of Comparative Freedom—1979

Ranking of Nations by Political Rights

Most Free 1	2	3	4	5	6	Least Free 7
Australia	Botswana	Cyprus	Bangladesh	Bolivia	Algeria	Afghanistan
Austria	Colombia	Guatemala	Bhutan	China (Taiwan)	Argentina	Albania
Bahamas	Djibouti	Malaysia	Brazil	Ecuador	Bahrain	Angola
Barbados	Dominica	Morocco	El Salvador	Egypt	Cameroon	Benin
Belgium	Dominican Republic		Guyana	Indonesia	Cape Verde Is.	Bulgaria
Canada	Fiji		Lebanon	Kenya	Chad	Burma
Costa Rica	Finland		Mexico	Korea (S)	Chile	Burundi
Denmark	Gambia		Senegal	Lesotho	China (Mainland)	Central African Emp.
France	Greece		Western Samoa	Madagascar	Cuba	Congo
Germany (W)	Grenada			Maldives	Gabon	Czechoslovakia
Iceland	India			Nicaragua	Ghana	Equatorial Guinea
Ireland	Israel			Nigeria	Guinea-Bissau	Ethiopia
Luxembourg	Italy			Panama	Honduras	Germany (E)
Netherlands	Jamaica			Paraguay	Hungary	Guinea
New Zealand	Japan			Peru	Iran	Haiti
Norway	Malta			Philippines	Ivory Coast	Iraq
Sweden	Mauritius			Qatar	Jordan	Kampuchea
Switzerland	Nauru			Rhodesia	Kuwait	Korea (N)
United Kingdom	Papua New Guinea			Singapore	Liberia	Laos
United States	Portugal			South Africa	Libya	Mali
Venezuela	Solomon Is.			Sudan	Malawi	Mongolia
	Spain			Syria	Mauritania	Mozambique
	Sri Lanka			Tonga	Nepal	Niger
	Surinam			Transkei	Oman	Rumania
	Trinidad & Tobago			United Arab Emirates	Pakistan	Somalia
	Turkey			Zambia	Poland	Togo
	Tuvalu				Rwanda	Uganda
	Upper Volta				Sao Tome & Principe	USSR
					Saudi Arabia	Vietnam
					Seychelles	Yemen (S)
					Sierra Leone	Zaire
					Swaziland	
					Tanzania	
					Thailand	
					Tunisia	
					Uruguay	
					Yemen (N)	
					Yugoslavia	

Note: The Comoro Islands are omitted from this table because of insufficient information.

Ranking of Nations by Civil Liberties

Most Free						Least Free
1	**2**	**3**	**4**	**5**	**6**	**7**
Australia	Bahamas	Bolivia	Bahrain	Argentina	Algeria	Afghanistan
Austria	Dominican Republic	Botswana	Bangladesh	Cameroon	Burma	Albania
Barbados	Fiji	Colombia	Bhutan	Chile	Burundi	Angola
Belgium	Finland	Djibouti	Brazil	Egypt	Cape Verde Is.	Benin
Canada	France	Dominica	China (Taiwan)	Hungary	Chad	Bulgaria
Costa Rica	Gambia	Ecuador	Cyprus	Indonesia	China (Mainland)	Central African
Denmark	Germany (W)	Grenada	El Salvador	Iran	Congo	Emp.
Iceland	Greece	Guyana	Ghana	Ivory Coast	Cuba	Equatorial Guinea
Ireland	India	Honduras	Guatemala	Kenya	Czechoslovakia	Ethiopia
Japan	Israel	Jamaica	Lebanon	Korea (S)	Gabon	Guinea
Luxembourg	Italy	Kuwait	Lesotho	Madagascar	Germany (E)	Kampuchea
Netherlands	Malta	Malaysia	Liberia	Maldives	Guinea-Bissau	Korea (N)
New Zealand	Nauru	Nigeria	Mauritius	Nepal	Haiti	Laos
Norway	Papua New Guinea	Senegal	Mexico	Nicaragua	Iraq	Mali
Sweden	Portugal	Spain	Morocco	Pakistan	Jordan	Mongolia
Switzerland	Solomon Is.	Sri Lanka	Peru	Panama	Libya	Mozambique
United Kingdom	Surinam	Tonga	Rhodesia	Paraguay	Malawi	Somalia
United States	Trinidad & Tobago	Turkey	Seychelles	Philippines	Mauritania	Uganda
	Tuvalu	Upper Volta	Thailand	Poland	Niger	Vietnam
	Venezuela			Qatar	Oman	Yemen (S)
	Western Samoa			Rwanda	Rumania	
				Sao Tome	Saudi Arabia	
				& Principe	South Africa	
				Sierra Leone	Syria	
				Singapore	Tanzania	
				Sudan	Togo	
				Swaziland	USSR	
				Transkei	Uruguay	
				Tunisia	Zaire	
				United Arab		
				Emirates		
				Yemen (N)		
				Yugoslavia		
				Zambia		

Note: The Comoro Islands are omitted from this table because of insufficient information.

January–February/1979/Number 49

Still, the issue of multinational corporate involvement has been raised in connection with dozens of alleged human rights violators. A handful of these have received the lion's share of attention, and the extent to which this connection finds its way into the press, shareholder resolutions, and legislative initiatives seems to depend on a number of factors. These include the quantitative significance of corporate activity involved (for example, Brazil), the foreign policy concerns of the firms' home governments (United States and United Kingdom on South Africa), the amount of attention accorded by organizations such as the United Nations or Amnesty International (Chile), the extent to which atrocities (Uganda, Cambodia, Vietnam) or injustices (Indonesia, Philippines, South Korea, Argentina) are involved, and in general the amount of media-attracting sensationalism, terror, and radical changes which are in evidence. Moreover, the attention and morality appear to be selective, and not simply a direct function of the level of injustice or amount of corporate activity at stake.[32]

Multinational corporate involvement has been singled out during the 1970s rather infrequently in relation to human rights conditions in Iran, Saudi Arabia, Turkey, Morocco, Ethiopia, Guinea-Bissau, Spain, and Greece. It has also been given minimal attention in connection with Eastern Europe, the Soviet Union, and China. Moderate human rights attention has been directed to corporate involvement with such nations as Indonesia, Thailand, South Korea, the Philippines, Panama, Guatemala, Nicaragua, Haiti, Angola, and Uganda. Rather considerable attention has been given to Argentina, Chile, Uruguay, and Brazil, as well as Namibia, Rhodesia, and South Africa. Our estimate is that over half of the attention on the issue of multinationals and human rights has focused on South Africa alone. According to Senator Dick Clark, "what sets South Africa apart from other countries which have equally oppressive and, in some cases, quantitatively worse records of human rights violations is that (1) South Africa's policies are based on race as the sole criterion of discrimination, (2) its human rights violations have been made 'legal' through legislative and regulatory actions that have institutionalized racism into the fabric of society, and (3) it policies are justified in the name of defending the Free World, of which South Africa claims to be a member."[33]

MULTINATIONALS AND HUMAN RIGHTS

How can one assess the impact of multinational corporate activity on human rights? Assessing short-run effects and long-run consequences is a terribly complex task.[34] Analysis must be done on a "with" (multinational corporate activity) and "without" basis, and complex feedback interactions have to be studied. The most serious problem is that *we simply do not know* what many of the interrelationships are between economic, political, social, and human rights variables or what will happen to them if a proposed corporate action is undertaken. Some of them are obscure because of gaps in information and research. Others we can know only as probabilities. Still others we may *never* know with any confidence, since they may depend heavily upon assumptions about the behavior of other actors (for example, government bodies or local firms). And so the effects of multinationals on human rights cannot be predicted with very much certainty or precision.

Exhibit 5–2 provides a conceptual framework for thinking about the potential human rights consequences of MNE activities. The scheme draws on the analogy of throwing a pebble into a pond. Here we throw multinational corporate activities—capital, products, technology, investment, management, etc. as noted in Block I of Exhibit 5–2—into a particular host-nation human rights environment. The MNE's "ripples" are the various interactions with the host nation's economic, social, and political systems which, in turn, produce positive or negative human rights consequences. No single corporate action, by itself, can be neutral. Moreover, we know that most multinational involvements consist of a complex "package" of activities from which different kinds of human rights impacts may result.

The framework suggests that some MNE effects may influence human rights conditions directly. Others may follow an indirect route, first influencing human needs and subsequently producing human rights consequences. In general, the *direct* effects are the ones most often emphasized by critics of multinationals, whereas the *indirect* effects are typically stressed by the multinationals themselves—the critics seem to concentrate on the "visible foot," while the multinationals put their faith in the "invisible hand."

Although some of the "effects related to rights" presented in Block II of Exhibit 5–2 which may or may not flow from any given corporate activity could potentially help to increase the observance of human rights in host nations, many of them, according to critics, would tend to have the opposite result. In this view, multinational involvement tends to "buttress" or "perpetuate" repressive regimes, and the firms themselves are often viewed as profiting from injustice and exploitation of oppressed labor, assisting governments to attain defensive or "strategic" self-sufficiency, providing symbolic and material means of repression, constraining the diplomatic options of home governments, gaining advantage from martial law, or helping regimes to weather storms of popular protest and resistance.[35] The presence of the multinational is viewed as the product of a "favorable investment climate" generally associated with a stable political or social system rather than one undergoing radical change, and political stability is often maintained by containing civil rights, muzzling the press, banning trade unions, restricting population movements, and so on.

At the extreme, the critics see a symbiotic relationship between MNEs and repressive dictatorships and local elites. One recent study, for example, examined the historical links between the investment policies, official American support, and human rights records of 10 allegedly repressive regimes. They found that each regime's accession to power was followed by changes in investment policies designed to lure more foreign capital, including incentives, tariff reductions or exemptions, and stepped up pressure on labor movements. Such policies were in turn successful in attracting increased American economic and military assistance and financial resources. The study concludes:

> The pattern revealed is clear, persistent, rational and ugly. Human rights have tended to stand in the way of the satisfactory pursuit of U.S. economic interests—and they have, accordingly, been brushed aside systematically. U.S. economic interests in the Third World have dictated a policy of containing revolution, preserving an open door for U.S. investment, and assuring favorable conditions of investment. Reformist efforts to improve the lot

Exhibit 5-2
Potential Impacts of Multinational Corporate Activities on Human Rights

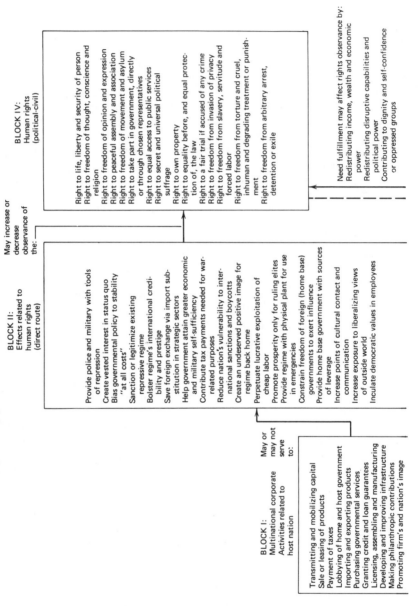

BLOCK I:
Multinational corporate
Activities related to
host nation

May or
may not
serve
to:

Transmitting and mobilizing capital
Sale or leasing of products
Payment of taxes
Lobbying of home and host government
Importing and exporting products
Purchasing governmental services
Granting credit and loan guarantees
Licensing, assembling and manufacturing
Developing and improving infrastructure
Making philanthropic contributions
Promoting firm's and nation's image

BLOCK II:
Effects related to
human rights
(direct route)

Provide police and military with tools
of repression
Create vested interest in status quo
Bias governmental policy to stability
"at all costs"
Sanction or legitimize existing
repressive regime
Bolster regime's international credi-
bility and prestige
Save foreign exchange via import sub-
stitution in strategic sectors
Help government attain greater economic
and military self-sufficiency
Contribute tax payments needed for war-
related purposes
Reduce nation's vulnerability to inter-
national sanctions and boycotts
Create an undeserved positive image for
regime back home
Perpetuate lucrative exploitation of
cheap labor
Promote prosperity only for ruling elites
Provide regime with physical plant for use
in emergencies
Constrain freedom of foreign (home base)
governments to exert influence
Provide home base government with sources
of leverage
Increase points of cultural contact and
communication
Increase exposure to liberalizing views
of outside world
Inculcate democratic values in employees

May increase or
decrease
observance of
the:

BLOCK IV:
Human rights
(political-civil)

Right to life, liberty and security of person
Right to freedom of thought, conscience and
religion
Right to freedom of opinion and expression
Right to peaceful assembly and association
Right to freedom of movement and asylum
Right to take part in government, directly
or through chosen representatives
Right to equal access to public services
Right to secret and universal political
suffrage
Right to own property
Right to equality before, and equal protec-
tion of, the law
Right to a fair trial if accused of any crime
Right to freedom from invasion of privacy
Right to freedom from slavery, servitude and
forced labor
Right to freedom from torture and cruel,
inhuman and degrading treatment or punish-
ment
Right to freedom from arbitrary arrest,
detention or exile

Need fulfillment may affect rights observance by:
Redistributing income, wealth and economic
power
Redistributing disruptive capabilities and
political power
Contributing to dignity and self-confidence
or oppressed groups

144

Exhibit 5-2 (continued)

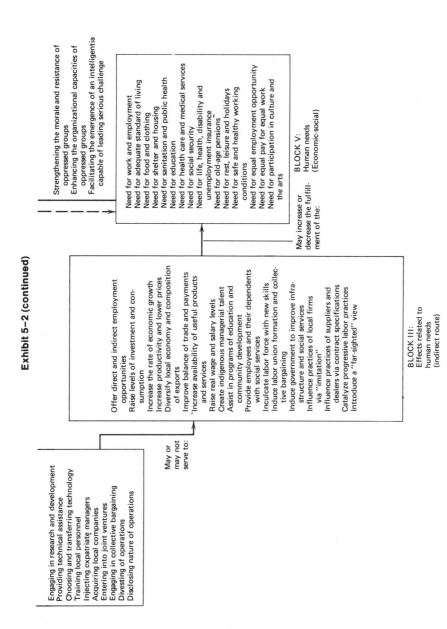

Engaging in research and development
Providing technical assistance
Choosing and transferring technology
Training local personnel
Injecting expatriate managers
Acquiring local companies
Entering into joint ventures
Engaging in collective bargaining
Divesting of operations
Disclosing nature of operations

May or
may not
serve to:

Offer direct and indirect employment opportunities
Raise levels of investment and consumption
Increase the rate of economic growth
Increase productivity and lower prices
Diversify local economy and composition of exports
Improve balance of trade and payments
Increase availability of useful products and services
Raise real wage and salary levels
Create indigenous managerial talent
Assist in programs of education and community development
Provide employees and their dependents with social services
Inculcate labor force with new skills
Induce labor union formation and collective bargaining
Induce government to improve infrastructure and social services
Influence practices of local firms via "imitation"
Influence practices of suppliers and dealers via contract specifications
Catalyze progressive labor practices
Introduce a "far-sighted" view

BLOCK III:
Effects related to
human needs
(indirect route)

Strengthening the morale and resistance of oppressed groups
Enhancing the organizational capacities of oppressed groups
Facilitating the emergence of an intelligentia capable of leading serious challenge

Need for work and employment
Need for adequate standard of living
Need for food and clothing
Need for shelter and housing
Need for sanitation and public health
Need for education
Need for health care and medical services
Need for social security
Need for life, health, disability and unemployment insurance
Need for old-age pensions
Need for rest, leisure and holidays
Need for safe and healthy working conditions
Need for equal employment opportunity
Need for equal pay for equal work
Need for participation in culture and the arts

May increase or
decrease the fulfill-
ment of the:

BLOCK V:
Human needs
(Economic-social)

of the poor and oppressed, including the encouragement of independent trade unions, are not conducive to a favorable climate of investment. [36]

What about the indirect effects? Block III of Exhibit 5–2 shows that corporate activities can have a range of economic and social impacts on the fulfillment of human needs or desires. Corporate involvement in this way can open up new opportunities, widen areas of individual choice, provide employees with a range of social services, expose local businessmen to competition and society in general to progressive or "liberal" ideas, aid victims of repression, catalyze structural change, and broadly improve economic and social well-being.[37] Economic development and higher levels of living may then create a set of pressures favorable to human rights. In this view, the demands of the modern industrial order can serve to gradually break down repression by making it increasingly costly and by subjecting the regime to pressures for change engendered by redistributed economic power and political leverage, rising expectations, and the emergence of an intelligentsia capable of leading serious challenge. This "evolutionary reform" argument in regard to South Africa has been summarized by a Goodyear executive as follows:

> Economic growth will accelerate change. Economic growth will accelerate the rate at which blacks assume more responsible positions in the economy and in the process acquire greater self-confidence, greater disposable income, and greater expectations, all of which will in turn accelerate social change. Economic growth means greater emphasis upon industry and mechanized agriculture, and the inevitable growth of the black urban population. These developments give the blacks increasingly disruptive power over the economy, and at the same time, lead toward "detribalization," which facilitates their organization in support of *black* causes, as opposed to Zulu, Xhosa or Tswana causes. Economic growth will in fact diminish the government's ability to maintain the status quo.[38]

In our own view, generalizations concerning the impact of multinational corporations on human rights are not particularly useful. There are no magic answers. Individual circumstances are governing, and each case has to be assessed on its merits, with informed empirical analysis and careful cost-benefit judgments. As one observer notes, "There are, in sum, enough persuasive arguments on all sides of this complex issue to caution against adopting a position of rigid moral certitude."[39]

It is clear that multinational corporate activities are not and cannot be neutral with respect to human rights. We do not share the easy piety of some corporate executives who maintain that such activities are automatically agents of benevolent change—even economic utopia is not an automatic passport to political equality. Indeed, "economic growth and greater control and oppression are not necessarily contradictory."[40] It is hard to ignore the views of numerous sophisticated observers who have concluded, for example, that despite the massive postwar flow of foreign direct investments and credits to South Africa, the infusion "has had marginal material benefits for blacks and has strengthened the grip of the whites. Over the years, the income gap between whites and blacks in South Africa has widened, the political rights of blacks have diminished, and the drift toward greater authoritarian control by the central government has accelerated."[41] But it is equally hard to ignore views—although predisposed to a gradualist, "reform and communications" approach—that multinationals can indeed nudge governments along the path to wider observance of human rights. Those who call for MNEs to cut all ties with countries alleged to violate human rights must realize that they are also calling for the removal of possibly the most significant (albeit non-violent) single mechanism of liberation available in the world today.

THE HUMAN RIGHTS MOVEMENT

As Archibald MacLeish wrote during the American Bicentennial, "the cause of human liberty is now the one great revolutionary cause. . . . " The human rights movement facing multinationals is indeed pervasive in scope.

The United States Government

Both national and international public-sector organizations are deeply involved in the human rights movement. As described below, actions affecting MNEs have been undertaken by an array of national governments including the United States, Canada, the United Kingdom, Japan, Sweden, Nigeria, and the Netherlands. Contrary to popular opinion, the global human rights drive in the United States did not begin with President Carter. The actual framework by which American policy has evolved was the result of liberal-oriented Congressional actions in the early and mid-1970s, usually in opposition to the desires of the Nixon and Ford Administrations. Human rights in relation to Southern Africa have long been a concern of the Congressional Black Caucus. Congressional initiatives were also taken by such leading human rights advocates as Representatives Don Fraser, Tom Harkin, Edward Koch, Mike Harrington, Stephen Solarz, and Berkley Bedell, and Senators Edward Kennedy, Alan Cranston, George McGovern, James Abourezk, and Dick Clark.[42] And it is easy to overlook the fact that the American tradition of "making the world safe for democracy" has very strong human rights overtones dating back centuries over time.

It is fair to conclude, though, that Jimmy Carter was responsible for making human rights a central theme of American foreign policy. After pressing the issue vigorously in the 1976 presidential campaign, not surprisingly finding that it struck a responsive chord in the electorate, he vociferously reiterated it in the early months of his administration. He pledged to "restore the moral authority of this country in its conduct of foreign policy" and pledged an "undeviating commitment" to the advancement of human rights abroad.[43] However, by raising high expectations he left himself open to charges of inconsistency and hypocrisy. He overestimated the world's readiness to accept his moral crusade, and the clumsy implementation of his initial human rights policy served to damage American relations with allies and adversaries alike. Strong criticism at home and abroad forced the Carter Administration to turn to a "cumbersome, tortured process of semantic squirming, selective amnesia and outright rationalization."[44] Subsequently, the Administration settled down to a less assertive approach to the issue, in effect transforming the crusade into a bureaucracy. Attacks on important allies were softened and a policy of "principled pragmatism" was introduced. According to Carter, however, the initial crusade made human rights an issue that "no government on earth can ignore." He also made it an issue that no MNE can ignore.

International Organizations

In theory, quite a bit of machinery exists for the protection of human rights at the international level. In practice, much of it has been ineffective. The European Economic Community has issued a "code of conduct" for European multinationals operating in South Africa and has begun to infuse human rights concerns into its trade policies. The Council of Europe, with its European Commission on Human Rights and European Court on Human Rights, has been relatively influential. The Inter-American Commission on Human Rights of the Organization of American States (OAS) has done some excellent work, but has experienced difficulties with governments ignoring its requests for information, access, and recommendations, and the OAS General Assembly until recently gave only perfunctory attention to its reports.

The United Nations system has many units concerned with human rights, but most have had little impact so far.[45] The UN Commission on Human Rights has the poorest track record of all, basically because nearly three-quarters of the member states are themselves accused of violating the rights of their citizens. For a long period the Commission refused to accept individual complaints. It does now, but little concrete action ever emerges because procedures are so slow. With the notable exceptions of South Africa, Israel, and Chile the Commission has been more concerned with covering up rather than exposing human rights violations. Except for countries in the United Nations political doghouse, governments are simply unwilling to point fingers at one another.

In the United Nations system other units concerned with human rights include the Commission's Subcommittee on Prevention of Discrimination and Protection of Minorities, the Human Rights Committee established in 1976 to implement the International Covenant on Civil and Political Rights, the Committee of 24 concerned with colonial independence, the Committee on Apartheid, the Council for Namibia, the Committee on the Elimination of Racial Discrimination, and even the Centre on Transnational Corporations. Most of these have been little more than "talking shops," but have in a sense provided legitimacy for many liberation movements.

Finally, a number of specialized UN agencies also have a specific interest in the protection of specific human rights: International Labor Organization (ILO), United Nations Educational, Scientific and Cultural Organization (UNESCO), World Health Organization (WHO), and Food and Agricultural Organization (FAO). The ILO's activities in the human rights area have been fairly effective, but its morality has been selective, pursuing violations in some states and granting immunity for the same violations in others—one of the reasons why the United States withdrew from that organization.

Private Organizations

The great bulk of all agitation on the human rights issue as it affects MNEs has come from nongovernmental organizations, some of which have emerged within the allegedly repressive countries themselves—the Southwest Africa People Organization in Namibia, the late Stephen Biko's "Black Consciousness" movement in South Africa, out-of-power politicians in nations such as the Philippines, and Roman Catholic bishops in Brazil and Chile. Most agitation, however, has arisen far away from the scene, in North America and Western Europe.

Human rights groups and organizations come in all shapes and sizes, and number in the hundreds. Some have been in existence for a long time, while others are ephemeral. For some, human rights is their primary purpose, for others it is a side issue. For some, the commitment to enhancing human rights around the world is deep and permanent, for others it appears transient. Some are large in size with professional staffs and huge budgets, while others are run on a shoestring with only voluntary help. Some operate on the scene and at some risk in countries where human rights violations occur, but most operate from a comfortable distance with little to lose whichever way events turn. The movement as a whole seems to possess great resiliency and staying power, and the groups within it find great strength in community, with considerable cross-contacts and coalition-formation.

The human rights movement is motivated by a mix of religious, civil, ethnic, racial, economic, and humanitarian concerns. For example, the United States Catholic Conference believes that "work for justice is essential to the Church, pertaining to its innermost nature and mission."[46] The Episcopal Church sees the necessity "to use its economic power for Godly purposes in the framing of a more just and equitable society. . . . "[47] The World Council of Churches has found "theological and Biblical justification for attacking economic structures which appear to inhibit the growth of social and economic justice."[48] Still other churchmen have found guidance by asking themselves: "Which side do you think Jesus would take?"[49]

Church groups in the United States and Britain, and to a lesser extent in Canada, the Netherlands, Belgium, and Scandinavia, have generally been in the forefront of specifically corporate-related protests. The National Council of Churches in the United States set up its Corporate Information Center in New York in 1971 to engage in analysis, interpretation, and action campaigns around the question of American corporate involvement with governments violating human rights. In 1972 the Episcopal Church, the United Church of Christ, the United Presbyterian Church in the U.S.A., the American Baptist Convention, and the United Methodist Church jointly formed the "Church Project on U.S. Investment in Southern Africa" to concentrate on questions concerning corporate involvement in that part of the world.[50] A year later the National Council of Churches established the Interfaith Center on Corporate Responsibility to coordinate shareholder campaigns for 14 Protestant denominations and more than 150 Roman Catholic religious communities that have combined shareholdings of more than $2 billion. The Center provides sophisticated current data on almost every human rights issue involving MNEs in order to guide member churches in the use of their leverage as shareholders to change corporate policies. Other religious-based groups in the United States focusing on human rights include the Office of International Justice and Peace of the United States Catholic Conference, the American Friends Service Committee, Liberty to the Captives, and the Clergy and Laity Concerned (CALC). CALC is the most action-oriented interfaith peace and justice organization in America, has a special "U.S. Power and Repression Program," and maintains a Human Rights Coordinating Center in Washington. Active church social action groups in other countries include the Working Group Betaald Antwoord in Holland, the Christian Concern for Southern Africa in Britain, and the Task Force on the Churches and Corporate Responsibility in Canada.

Then there is the World Council of Churches in Geneva, which has established a Fund to Combat Racism providing grants to Southern African liberation movements, and through the years has actively protested multinational corporate involvement in that area. In 1977, the Council's central committee adopted a resolution calling on its 293 member churches' congregations of 1.2 billion people to oppose the multinationals' "controversial" policies throughout the world. As we have already noted, the World Council believes MNEs are accomplices of "repressive states, predatory local elites and racism," and thus pillars of a system that "oppresses, excludes and exploits."[51]

Along with church groups, an estimated 200 to 300 nonsectarian organizations exist in the developed countries alone, and work on questions of colonialism, apartheid, liberation, and human rights.[52] In England the Anti-Apartheid Movement has been the main action group fighting minority rule in Southern Africa, while the Halesmere Group and "End Loans to South Africa" have attacked British multinationals. Groups in other nations include the Toronto Committee for the Liberation of Southern Africa in Canada, Anti-Apartheid Bewegung in West Germany, Anti-Apartheid Movement in Ireland, Committee Against Racial Exploitation in Australia, Comité Contre le Colonialisme et l'Apartheid in Belgium, and the Centre Europe-Tiers Monde in Switzerland. In the United States, the Council on Hemispheric Affairs and the North American Congress on Latin America focus on human rights questions in the Americas, while the American Committee on Africa, founded in 1953, informs and mobilizes people to work for policies that support African people in their "struggle for independence."[53]

Mention should also be made of groups composed of exiles and/or their supporters working for human rights "back home." In the United Kingdom, for example, one finds the Namibia Support Committee, Zimbabwe Solidarity Committee, Mozambique and Guinea Information Centre, and Angola Solidarity Committee. In the United States, there are the Friends of the Filipino People, American Friends of Brazil, Friends of Haiti, Operation Namibia, Union of Thais in the U.S., Campaign for Political Prisoners in Indonesia, and National Chile Center.

Another set of groups focuses on the interaction of foreign policy and human rights. The Coalition for a New Foreign and Military Policy, based in Washington, united 33 national religious, peace, labor, professional, and social action organizations in an effort to develop a "non-interventionist, humanitarian, and open U.S. foreign and military policy." Efforts in the same area are undertaken by the Friends Committee on National Legislation, Center for International Policy, Campaign for a Democratic Foreign Policy, and Americans for Democratic Action. All engage in research, lobby on human rights, monitor legislation, produce newsletters, and so forth. Freedom House, cited earlier, conducts and publishes research, and provides advisory services in an effort to strengthen free institutions in the United States and around the world.

A variety of other private organizations are also involved in the human rights movement at the national level, especially in regard to the role of MNEs. These include the press, pension funds, foundations, labor unions, civil rights groups, student groups, and university faculties—human rights, especially regarding South Africa, have been one of the hottest issues on American campuses in recent years. Organizations with massive portfolios of multinational corporate stocks and bonds, such as the Ford, Rockefeller, and Carnegie Foundations; pension funds such as the Teachers Insurance and Annuity Association and the College Retirement Equities Fund; and many colleges, seminaries, and universities, have all been involved in issues of human rights as a result of their "socially responsive" investment policies. Many of these investors are provided with information on human rights issued by the Washington-based Investor Responsibility Research Center, and regularly raise shareholder resolutions at annual meetings.

A number of "liberal" unions have withdrawn deposits from banks making loans to South Africa. The United Automobile Workers pressed auto companies to withhold investments in Chile. The International Longshoreman and Warehouse Workers Union in 1977 resolved "to implement means through which the union will stop all handling of goods to or from South Africa and Rhodesia." And there are the black civil rights groups in the United States—in 1977 the National Association for the Advancement of Colored People (NAACP) adopted the position of opposing further investment in South Africa by American corporations. In 1978 the group decided to call for the total withdrawal of American businesses from South Africa. Other black organizations concerned with human rights abroad include the Phelps-Stokes Fund, the National Black Coalition on Southern Africa, and the "Emergency Coalition for Human Rights in South Africa," organized in response to the Soweto riots of October 1977.

Nongovernmental organizations at the international level are also involved. Amnesty International won the 1977 Nobel Peace Prize for its work on behalf of political prisoners. Some concerned nongovernmental organizations with UN consultative status include the International League for Human Rights, the International Commission of Jurists, the International Rescue Committee, and the International Committee of the Red Cross. These organizations regularly raise the issue of human rights violations, illuminate specific cases, and recommend policies which governments might pursue. The International Defense and Aid Fund for Southern Africa provides financial support to the families of political prisoners. The International Confederation of Free Trade Unions and its rival the World Federation of Trade Unions have initiated boycotts against South African goods, supported labor union formation in South Africa, and provided monetary assistance.

TACTICS OF THE HUMAN RIGHTS MOVEMENT

The tactics employed against multinationals in the human rights movement are as varied as the groups involved. Exhibit 5–3 lists some of the major tactics in the arsenals of nongovernmental and governmental organizations and provides a model of how their use may affect multinational corporate involvement with

Exhibit 5-3
Selected Tactics of the Human Rights Movement and Their Impact on Multinationals

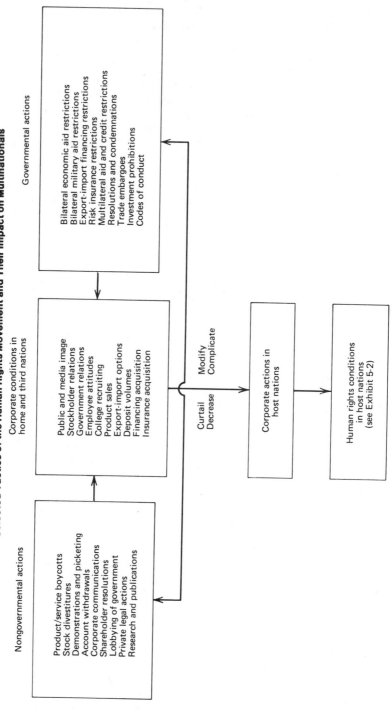

Nongovernmental actions

Product/service boycotts
Stock divestitures
Demonstrations and picketing
Account withdrawals
Corporate communications
Shareholder resolutions
Lobbying of government
Private legal actions
Research and publications

Corporate conditions in home and third nations

Public and media image
Stockholder relations
Government relations
Employee attitudes
College recruiting
Product sales
Export-import options
Deposit volumes
Financing acquisition
Insurance acquisition

Governmental actions

Bilateral economic aid restrictions
Bilateral military aid restrictions
Export-import financing restrictions
Risk insurance restrictions
Multilateral aid and credit restrictions
Resolutions and condemnations
Trade embargoes
Investment prohibitions
Codes of conduct

Curtail
Decrease

Modify
Complicate

Corporate actions in host nations

Human rights conditions in host nations (see Exhibit 5-2)

nations allegedly violating human rights. Some of the tactics of nongovernmental groups are quire traditional, other are innovative. Some are employed selectively on a small scale, others are mounted on a large-scale, comprehensive basis. They are often combined in any given battle, and the overall strategies within which they are utilized range from moderate to radical and revolutionary.

Governmental bodies, as shown on Exhibit 5–3, also possess a whole panoply of policy instruments for use in the human rights drive. These range from relatively painless symbolic acts to tough economic steps. One study identified 41 graduated and different actions that the United States might take against South Africa on human rights grounds.[54] We should note that nongovernmental and governmental actions are closely linked, with the stimulation going both ways. In most cases, private action against MNEs in the human rights area usually precedes governmental action, but the opposite is occasionally true as well. And multinationals, of course, are often hit simultaneously from both sides.

Exhibit 5–3 also reveals the essentially "transnational" structure of pro-human rights pressures with which a multinational must contend. Almost all of the tactics of governmental and nongovernmental organizations are directed at the firm *in home and third nations*, and not directly at the firm's management in the host countries allegedly violating human rights. The object is typically to influence management's thinking and decisionmaking at the corporate headquarters level by raising the perceived costs and reducing the perceived rewards associated with involvement in "repressive nations." This can be done, for example, by actions which tarnish the corporation's public image, reduce the firm's attractiveness to investors, diminish the firm's ability to acquire financing or risk insurance, upset minority employees in domestic plants, place constraints on the firm's ability to make sales or investments, and the like. These pressures, in turn, may serve to curtail, reduce, modify, or complicate the firm's involvement in the targeted nation. We thus come full circle back to the nature of actions taken by a multinational in a host nation and their human rights consequences, as outlined earlier in Exhibit 5–2. It may be useful to examine the specific tools that human rights organizations typically employ.

Nongovernmental Actions

Boycotts. Consumers in the United States and Western Europe have been urged to boycott a wide range of products and services in the name of human rights. A few of these include the South African Krugerrand, Angolan Coffee, Outspan Oranges, ITT and Gulf Oil products, Del Monte Sardines, and banking at Barclays, First National Boston, Maryland National, and Amsterdam-Rotterdam Bank N.V. The reasoning ranges from Del Monte fishing for sardines "illegally" in the waters off Namibia, to the various banks making loans to South Africa, to ITT representing—in the view of the South Africa Committee of the Congregation for Reconciliation—"America's Number One Corporation Supporting Apartheid" and the "World's Most Irresponsible Corporation."[55] Some groups have persuaded cities to pass resolutions prohibiting purchases from "offending" companies. The city of Gary, Indiana, for example, approved a resolution in 1976 to boycott Control Data, IBM, ITT, and Motorola because of their South African ties. As noted, they have also persuaded unions such as the

Longshoremen to pass resolutions against the handling of cargo to or from Southern Africa, and some shipments of Rhodesian chrome were in fact turned away by the dockers.

Stock divestitures. Campaigns to force universities and churches to divest themselves of stock in companies operating in such areas as Angola, Namibia, Rhodesia, and South Africa have been going on for over a decade. Toward the end of the 1960s, students and faculty pressed Princeton University's trustees to sell its $127 million of holdings in firms operating in South Africa. This campaign was unsuccessful, as was the one at Harvard University demanding divestment of $17.5 million worth of Gulf Oil shares because of the company's role in Angola—a fact-finding committee at Harvard had concluded that divestment would have "no practical effect in advancing the independence of black Angolans."[56] Through the years, however, anti-apartheid divestiture campaigns have been at least partially successful at such campuses as Oberlin College, Hampshire College, University of Wisconsin, Columbia University, Indiana University, Tufts University, Boston University, University of Massachusetts, University of Oregon, Smith College, Ohio University, and Antioch College. At Wisconsin, the State Attorney General told the University's regents that the law prohibits them from knowingly investing in any company that condones discrimination.[57] Campaigns have raged at more than 50 other campuses, with most large universities successfully arguing against stock divestiture, mainly on grounds that such action would only be symbolic and would risk millions in income and alumni/corporate gifts. The Regents of the University of California, for example, decided not to sell its $550 million of stock in companies doing business in South Africa on grounds that it would breach its fiduciary responsibility.[58]

Demonstrations. Marches, rallies, picketing, sit-ins, vigils, demonstrations, and street theater performances have been employed sporadically by protestors to dramatize the issues and obtain press coverage. Administration buildings were occupied at Princeton in 1969 and Harvard in 1972 when the trustees refused to sell their holdings in companies with ties to Southern Africa. During the spring of 1977 more than 700 students were arrested on campuses during South Africa-related demonstrations—294 of these arrests occurred at Stanford University when students staged a sit-in to protest the University's refusal to vote its proxies in Ford Motor Company against further investment in South Africa.[59] Demonstrations in 1978 and 1979 occurred on many campuses, including Harvard, Stanford, Oregon, and Brandeis. Informational picketing and vigils have frequently accompanied shareholder meetings. In the early 1970s, for example, blacks and liberal church leaders picketed Gulf Oil's meetings, chanting "Gulf Kills" and urging people to turn in their Gulf credit cards. Demonstrations have often taken place outside corporate headquarters, with targets including such firms as the Halling Vicker Corporation in London, Newmont Mining in New York, and Fluor Corporation in Los Angeles. Local branches of banks with loans to South Africa and coin dealers selling Krugerrands have also had to contend with informational pickets.

Account withdrawals. A favorite tactic employed against Dutch, British, Canadian, and American banks accused of supporting repression through loan activity has been the symbolic withdrawal of deposits. Such campaigns have been encouraged and/or orchestrated by the American Committee on Africa in the United States, Betaald Antwoord in Holland, "End Loans to Southern Africa" in Britain, and the World Council of Churches throughout Europe.[60] The campaigns have attracted support of liberal trade unions, churches, politicians, and individuals. One observer believes that this tactic "has had a remarkable effect, because of the sensitivity of banks to public attitudes and the punitive actions of groups and individuals."[61]

Corporate communications. Much of the protest activity of nongovernmental human rights organizations takes place behind the scenes in the form of letters, phone calls, and frequent meetings with officials of target corporations. The United Church Board of Canada, for example, has engaged in discussions with a number of corporations about human rights questions, five banks on their lending policies to South Africa and Chile, Falconbridge on its involvement in Rhodesia and Namibia, Noranda on its proposed involvement in Chile, Alcan on its involvement in South Africa, and Brascan on its involvement in Brazil.[62] In Holland the active ecumenical group Betaald Antwoord has held talks aimed at effecting withdrawal from South Africa with the boards of Philips, Hollandse Beton Groep, Bos Kalis/Westminster Dredging Group, Unilever, Estel Steel Corporation, Royal Dutch Shell, AKZO, and Algemene Bank Nederland.[63] Numerous university and college boards in the United States, such as at Harvard, Cornell, Amherst, Dartmouth, and Swarthmore, have written to companies with South African interests in which they hold stock urging them to follow progressive labor practices and asking them for information about such practices. And literally thousands of meetings have been held between church groups and MNEs in the United States on matters related to shareholder resolutions on human rights issues. The aim of such negotiations has often been to reach substantive agreement that would prevent the need for public resolutions and motions at annual meetings.[64] As one human rights activist notes: "We have found sometimes . . . just raising the issue is enough to get management to make changes. It doesn't get the publicity, but it's more of a success."[65]

Proxy resolutions. Perhaps the most influential tactic employed against American multinationals on issues of human rights has been shareholder proxy resolutions. The proxy resolution is the legal means by which institutional and individual investors may submit proposals to corporations on issues that speak to the immediate interests of the corporation.[66] If the company believes that a resolution is irrelevant or, in legal terms, "beyond the power of the company to effectuate," it can ask the SEC to have the resolution tossed out. If the firm does not do so, or if the SEC refuses its request, then the resolution must be voted on at the annual shareholders meeting of the firm. A 3% vote in favor is necessary under SEC regulations for the resolution to be introduced a second time. It needs a 6% vote in the third year, and 10% thereafter to survive.

The great bulk of proxy resolutions related to human rights have been submitted by church groups, and have often received the support of institutional investors such as foundations, universities, pension funds, and insurance companies. The first human rights resolutions were submitted in 1971, when the Episcopal Church filed with General Motors urging stockholders to vote on the withdrawal of the company from South Africa, and the United Presbyterian Church filed a similar resolution urging Gulf Oil to withdraw from Angola. Since that time there have been more than 180 resolutions related to issues of human rights. Table 5–2 lists those filed during the period 1976–1978. Although the proxy resolution process is much more difficult, if not impossible to use against non-American multinationals, British churches did set a precedent in 1976, when for the first time a stockholder resolution was filed with Midland Bank requesting an end to future loans to South Africa. Others have followed, including a resolution to Shell on Rhodesian sanctions-busting in 1979.

Without management endorsement, such resolutions almost always go down to ignominious defeat. But proxy voting is not an end in itself, and very few campaigners ever actually seek to win "the vote." The aim is to make management aware of the ethical implications of their decisions, and to argue them in open forum, as well as to force disclosure of information from the corporation. In this sense the tactic has been extraordinarily successful.

Lobbying government. Nongovernmental groups also directly influence the policies and actions of governmental bodies by lobbying and presenting petitions to legislators, writing to government agencies, testifying at hearings, conducting and publishing research, issuing press releases, and prompting governmental investigations and legal proceedings. For example, local groups helped prompt an investigation in the state legislature of California-based firms' involvements in South Africa. Similar action triggered discussions in the Massachusetts state legislature of the New England Power Company's use of South African coal. A report by the Center for Social Action of the United Church of Christ, implicating Mobil Oil in the sale of petroleum products through South Africa to Rhodesia, led to a lengthy investigation by the U.S. Treasury Department. Findings and reports of Amnesty International, the International Commission of Jurists, and the International League for Human Rights have led to hearings and proceedings in many countries, as well as in the United Nations.

Members of the Coalition for a New Foreign and Military Policy have closely monitored human rights legislation, developed educational and organizing materials, mobilized constituent pressure, and coordinated the work of groups in Washington in the human rights field. Combining grass roots constituent organizing with coordinated lobbying, the Coalition has been influential in the passage of human rights legislation. Multinationals have thus been indirectly affected by nongovernmental groups through their influence on government.

Governmental Actions

Bilateral foreign aid. Annual foreign aid appropriations by western governments provide a large, if diverse, chunk of business for MNEs. Aid programs provide manufacturers with billions of dollars in sales each year, shipping companies with a sizeable portion of their total revenues, and assorted research and technical organizations with hundreds of overseas contracts. The importance of such business varies widely among firms, of course, but human rights restrictions on aid programs could significantly affect multinationals in industries supplying military hardware, aircraft, chemicals and fertilizers, machinery and equipment, and motor vehicles. Such restrictions began to emerge in the United States in 1973, when the Subcommittee on International Organizations of the House Committee on International Relations began to hold hearings on the proper role of human rights in United States foreign policy. During the 94th Congress, the Subcommittee conducted a total of 40 hearings on human rights in 18 different nations.

These efforts generated a very tentative human rights provision in the Foreign Assistance Act of 1973 which declared: "It is the sense of Congress that the President should deny any economic or military assistance to the government of any foreign country which practices the internment or imprisonment of that country's citizens for political purposes." Although Congress encountered Administration resistance to its legislative initiatives on human rights, a series of provisions did begin to emerge, each one more forceful and detailed than the last.[67]

Section 116 of the International Development and Food Assistance Act of 1975 established that no economic assistance may be provided "to the government of any country which engages in a consistent pattern of gross violations of internationally recognized human rights, including torture or cruel, inhuman, or degrading treatment or punishment, prolonged detention without charges, or other flagrant denial of the right of life, liberty, and the security of person, unless such assistance will directly benefit the needy people in such country." Passed by a surprising 74 vote margin, this "Harkin amendment" offered a potent new tool for injecting human rights considerations into United States foreign policy.

Section 301 of the International Security Assistance and Arms Export Control Act of 1976, by amending Section 502B of the Foreign Assistance Act of 1961, extended the Harkin amendment to cover American military aid programs. This Act also established within the State Department a Coordinator for Human Rights and Humanitarian Affairs who would have the primary responsibility for maintaining information on the status of human rights around the world and reporting to the Congress through the Secretary of State on human rights practices of American aid recipients and arms purchasers.

On March 12, 1977, the first State Department report on human rights conditions in 82 aid-recipient countries was made public. A week or so later the Brazilian government reacted with anger to the rather mildly critical remarks on Brazil in the report. It immediately rejected $50 million in American military assistance credits proposed for fiscal year 1978, renounced the long-standing mutual assistance pact with the United States, and expressed resentment against "unacceptable and tendentious commentaries and judgments." Brazil was soon joined in the protest against United States "moral imperialism" by El Salvador, Argentina, Guatemala, Uruguay, and Chile, all of which symbolically turned down American aid.

Bilateral aid cuts by Congress and/or the Carter Administration because of human rights violations during 1976–1977 were made for Argentina, Ethiopia, Uruguay, Chile, Brazil, El Salvador, and Guatemala. Because of political and military considerations, 1978 military aid to rights violators was reduced only in the case of Nicaragua. The Carter Administration was promptly criticized for its new "kid gloves" treatment of violations on the part of major aid recipients and arms purchasers such as South Korea, the Philippines, and Indonesia. But the Administration's approach had clearly changed, relying on positive incentives

Table 5-2 Human Rights Proxy Resolutions 1976–1978

Year	Corporation	Resolution	Sponsor	% Vote or Action Taken
1976	Avon	Equal Employment Opportunity Disclosure	Unitarian Universalist Assoc., et. al.	withdrawn
1976	Celanese	Equal Employment Opportunity Disclosure	Joan Hull	5.27
1976	Chrysler	Equal Employment Opportunity Disclosure	Sisters of St. Ursula	withdrawn
1976	General Motors	Expansion and Worker Rights in Chile	United Church Board for World Ministries, et. al.	2.0
1976	Gillette	Equal Employment Opportunity Disclosure	Sisters of Loretto	withdrawn
1976	Goodyear	South African Operations Disclosure	United Methodist Church, et. al.	2.4
1976	IBM	Report on sales in South Africa	National Council of Churches, et. al.	2.2
1976	ITT	Sales Policy on South Africa	United Presbyterian Church, et. al.	withdrawn
1976	Kennecott	South African Expansion	Christian Church (Disciples), et. al.	3.6
1976	Merck	Equal Employment Opportunity Disclosure	C. Victoria Babish	withdrawn
1976	Midland Bank	Loans to South Africa	End Loans to South Africa	6.2
1976	Motorola	Disclosure of South Korean Labor Practices	Reformed Church in America, et. al.	.91
1976	Newmont	Equal Employment in Namibia	United Church of Christ, et. al.	3.2
1976	Phelps Dodge	South African Operations Disclosure	Atonement Friars	withdrawn
1976	Southern Co.	Prohibit South African Coal Importation	United Church Board for World Ministries	4.2
1976	Standard Oil (Calif.)	South African Expansion	United Methodist Church	2.1
1976	Texaco	South African Expansion	United Methodist Church, et. al.	2.3
1976	Union Carbide	Rhodesian Chrome Importation	United Church Board for World Ministries, et. al.	1.9
1976	Warner Lambert	Equal Employment Opportunity Disclosure	Barbara C. Garris	5.16
1977	AMAX	Namibia Operations Disclosure	Episcopal Church	withdrawn
1977	Bank America	Loans to Chile	Unitarian Universalist Association	5.9
1977	Castle & Cook	Overseas Labor Practices	United Church Board for World Ministries, et. al.	3.2
1977	Citicorp	Loans to South Africa	United Presbyterian Church, et. al.	2.4
1977	Coca-Cola	Labor Practices In Guatemala	Sisters of Providence	withdrawn
1977	Continental Illinois	Loans to South Africa	Adrian Dominican Sisters, et. al.	1.63
1977	First Chicago	Loans to South Africa	Adrian Dominican Sisters, et. al.	1.65
1977	Ford	Withdrawal from South Africa	United Presbyterian Church, et. al.	1.8
1977	Ford	Foreign Military Sales Disclosure	Unitarian Universalist Association	withdrawn
1977	General Electric	Foreign Military Sales Disclosure	United Methodist Church, et. al.	2.4
1977	General Electric	Withdrawal from South Africa	United Methodist Church, et. al.	1.8
1977	General Motors	Withdrawal from South Africa	American Baptist Home Mission Society, et. al.	withdrawn
1977	General Motors	Labor Practices in Chile	United Methodist World Division, et. al.	withdrawn
1977	Goodyear	Withdrawal from South Africa	United Methodist Church	1.95
1977	Kennecott	No Expansion in South Africa	Episcopal Church, et. al.	4.4
1977	Kresge	Equal Employment Opportunity Disclosure	Unitarian Universalist Association, et. al.	withdrawn

158

Year	Company	Issue	Sponsor	Vote
1977	Manufacturers Hanover	Loans to South Africa	United Church of Christ, et. al.	3.3
1977	Midland Bank	Loans to South Africa	End Loans to South Africa	N.A.
1977	Mobil	Rhodesian Oil Supply	United Church Board for World Ministries	1.75
1977	Mobil (Montgomery Ward)	Equal Employment Opportunity Disclosure	Adrian Dominicans	withdrawn
1977	Morgan (J.P.)	Loans to South Africa	Episcopal Church	2.8
1977	Newmont	Namibia Operations Disclosure	United Church Board for World Ministries	3.36
1977	Olin	Disclosure of South African Arms Sales	Sisters of Charity of St. Vincent de Paul, et. al.	withdrawn
1977	Phelps Dodge	No Expansion in South Africa	Reformed Church in America, et. al.	2.6
1977	Southern Co.	South African Coal Importation Disclosure	United Church Board for World Ministries, et. al.	5.9
1977	Standard Oil (Calif.)	Withdrawal from South Africa	United Methodist Church, et. al.	2.97
1977	J.P. Stevens	Equal Employment Opportunity Disclosure	United Methodist Church, et. al.	5.59
1977	Texaco	Withdrawal from South Africa	United Christian Missionary Society, et. al.	3.7
1977	Textron	Foreign Military Sales Disclosure	Sisters of Mercy (Brooklyn), et. al.	14.5
1977	Union Carbide	No Expansion in South Africa	American Baptist Home Mission Society, et. al.	3.2
1977	United Brands	Overseas Labor Practices	Dominican Fathers (St. Albert the Great)	2.5
1978	Bank America	Loans to Chile	Sisters of Mercy (Chicago), et. al.	3.45
1978	Bank America	Loans to South Africa	Sisters of Mercy (Chicago), et. al.	4.69
1978	Castle & Cook	Overseas Labor Practices	United Church Board for World Ministries, et. al.	2.9
1978	Citicorp	Disclosure of South African Loans	United Methodist Church, et. al.	4.6
1978	Coca-Cola	Equal Employment Opportunity Disclosure	Nazareth Literary and Benevolent Association	withdrawn
1978	Coca-Cola	Labor Practices in Guatemala	Marianists (N.Y.), et. al.	withdrawn
1978	Continental Illinois	Disclosure of South African Loans	United Church Board for World Ministries, et. al.	8.19
1978	Control Data	Sales to South African Government	United Presbyterian Church	4.5
1978	Crocker National	Loans to South Africa	United Presbyterian Church	(no vote)
1978	Eastman Kodak	Disclosure of Sales to South African Government	United Presbyterian Church	4.5
1978	First Chicago	Disclosure of South African Loans	Adrian Dominican Sisters, et. al.	4.45
1978	First National Boston	Loans to South Africa	United Church Board for World Ministries, et. al.	8.2
1978	General Electric	Equal Employment Opportunity Disclosure	Episcopal Church, et. al.	1.8
1978	General Electric	Foreign Military Sales	United Church Board in World Ministries, et. al.	1.8
1978	IBM	Criteria for Sales to Repressive Government	United Church Board for World Ministries, et. al.	2.12
1978	Kennecott	South African Operations Disclosure	Episcopal Church, et. al.	withdrawn
1978	Kimberly Clark	Withdrawal from South Africa	American Baptist Home Mission Society, et. al.	filed late
1978	Manufacturers Hanover	Loans to South Africa	United Church Board for World Ministries, et. al.	5.51
1978	Minnesota Mining & Mnfg.	Withdrawal from South Africa	National Council of Churches, et. al.	1.9
1978	Mobil (Montgomery Ward)	Equal Employment Opportunity Disclosure	United Church Board for World Ministries, et. al.	withdrawn
1978	Mobil	Rhodesian Oil Supply	United Church Board for World Ministries, et. al.	3.25
1978	Morgan (J.P.)	Disclosure of South African Loans	Episcopal Church, et. al.	4.38
1978	Motorola	Withdrawal from South Africa	Haverford College, et. al.	1.6
1978	Newmont	Namibia Operations Disclosure	United Church Board for World Ministries, et. al.	3.0
1978	Northrup	Foreign Military Sales	Dominican Congregation of Our Lady of the Rosary, et. al.	4.33
1978	Phelps Dodge	Withdrawal from South Africa	Franciscan Sisters of Perpetual Adoration, et. al.	5.31

Table 5-2 (continued)

Year	Corporation	Resolution	Sponsor	% Vote or Action Taken
1978	Rosario Resources	Disclosure of Nicaraguan Operations	Province of St. Joseph–Capuchin Order	withdrawn
1978	Southern Co.	South African Coal Importation Disclosure	Nazareth Convent & Academy Corporation, et. al.	5.4
1978	Standard Oil (Calif.)	Rhodesian Oil Supply	United Methodist Church, et. al.	4.15
1978	J.P. Stevens	Equal Employment Opportunity Disclosure	United Methodist Church, et. al.	3.92
1978	Texaco	Rhodesian Oil Supply	United Church Board for World Ministries, et. al.	2.97
1978	Texaco	Withdrawal from South Africa	United Presbyterian Church, et. al.	2.18
1978	Textron	Foreign Military Sales	Sisters of Mercy (Brooklyn), et. al.	3.8
1978	Union Carbide	No Expansion in South Africa	United Church Board for World Ministries, et. al.	5.08
1978	United Brands	Overseas Employment Practices	Dominicans–Province of St. Albert the Great, et. al.	1.54
1978	United States Steel	No Expansion in South Africa	Episcopal Church	5.7

Source: *The Corporate Examiner*, various issues.

such as offers of foreign aid rather than on public criticism or the threat of aid cutoffs, to induce nations to improve their records on human rights.[68]

It should be noted that United States aid to the developing countries flows through at least 15 faucets, only four of which are the traditional, visible foreign aid agencies that must clear their operations with the Congress—the Agency for International Development, the Peace Corps, P.L. 480-Food for Peace, and the Military Assistance Program.[69] The other eleven are national and international public financial institutions ranging from the International Monetary Fund and World Bank to the Export-Import Bank to the Overseas Private Investment Corporation. Each is a separate, semi-autonomous revolving fund that may occasionally be replenished by Congress. Their operating decisions are not subject to prior Congressional review, and such decisions in fiscal year 1976 accounted for 69% of the total United States foreign aid bill.[70] In 1977, Congress began to confront the fact that the bulk of foreign aid was outside its control, thus limiting its leverage in the human rights field.

Export financing and risk insurance. Campaigns began in Washington in 1977 to infuse human rights considerations into the policies of the Export-Import Bank (Eximbank) and the Overseas Private Investment Corporation (OPIC), both of which primarily service multinational corporations and banks. Eximbank is a self-sustaining export financing and insurance agency of the United States whose basic purpose is to facilitate American sales of goods and services abroad. It assumes commercial and political risks that cannot be undertaken by exporters or private financial institutions and offers loans with longer maturities than are generally available for private financing. It receives no appropriated funds or tax revenues, but has authority to borrow directly from the U.S. Treasury in amounts up to $6 billion at any one time. In addition to direct loans, Eximbank provides guarantees to United States commercial banks financing export sales.

A campaign to stop Eximbank financing of sales to South Africa was begun by the American Committee on Africa, American Friends Service Committee, Clergy and Laity Concerned, and Coalition for a New Foreign and Military Policy. In fiscal year 1977, Eximbank had granted $172.3 million in loan guarantees and insurance for export sales to South Africa, mostly advanced mining equipment, and its total exposure in South Africa, was around $200 million early in 1978. As compared to 1971, Eximbank's coverage of South African risk had grown by a factor of five. Perceiving a pattern whereby the United States was "slapping South Africa's wrist while still greasing the palm," the Congressional Black Caucus and a number of liberals in Congress in late 1977 called for an end to Eximbank financing of South Africa. Sweden and Denmark had cut off export credits to South Africa ten years earlier and the Canadian government had announced in 1977 that it was ceasing all but the most minor South African operations of its Export Development Corporation. The House Banking Committee in April 1978 approved a proposal to bar Eximbank credit guarantees for business activity in South Africa unless the President determined that "significant progress toward majority rule" was being made in that country. The restriction was softened by the full House in June 1978 when it instead adopted a proposal that would allow Eximbank to extend guarantees only if the recipient American firm had endorsed and proceeded with the implementation of a program to promote racial equality.[71]

OPIC is a United States government agency within the State Department which insures equity investments of American multinational corporations in the developing countries against political risks such as expropriation, currency inconvertibility, and war, revolution, or insurrection. On June 30, 1976, OPIC had a world exposure of $3.2 billion, approximately 90% of which insured the 100 largest American corporations. OPIC operations are covered by the 1975 Harkin amendment, requiring termination of U.S. bilateral aid to "gross and consistent" violators of human rights, unless such aid benefits the needy. Critics charged in 1977 that OPIC was ignoring this mandate, that its programs were not really promoting development that would benefit the needy, and that between 1974 and 1976 60% of the dollar volume of OPIC insurance had been issued for projects in six repressive nations—Brazil, the Philippines, South Korea, Indonesia, Taiwan, and the Dominican Republic. They also alleged that, during the same period, 41 percent of OPIC's insurance had gone to just 11 American multinationals. Stating that OPIC only benefits the large multinationals at home and most repressive developing nations abroad, a broad-based lobbying effort was begun in 1977 to have the Congress put OPIC out of business by not renewing its legislative mandate.[73]

Multilateral foreign aid and credits. More than a decade ago the U.S. Congress asked that foreign aid be channeled increasingly through multilateral lending agencies for the purpose of taking politics out of foreign assistance and allocating aid on the basis of need only. With the drive for human rights, however, a coalition of human rights liberals and anti-foreign-aid conservatives began to pull back on that commitment and in 1976 started a drive to "politicize" multilateral aid decisions. Chile served as a source of inspiration. While the Congress and President Carter were slashing bilateral aid to Chile in 1976, the World Bank, Inter-American Development Bank, and International Monetary Fund were at the same time increasing their aid to support Chilean reconstruction. President Pinochet thus was able to spurn $27.5 million in bilateral American aid while receiving $283.2 million in fiscal 1976 from the multilateral institutions and Eximbank.[73]

During 1976, Congress enacted legislation instructing United States executive directors of the Inter-American Development Bank and the African Development Fund "to vote against any loan, any extension of financial assistance, or any technical assistance to any country which engages in a consistent pattern of gross violations of internationally recognized human rights . . . unless such assistance will directly benefit the needy people in such country." Despite the strenuous objections of the Carter Administration, which wanted to retain flexibility, and World Bank President Robert S. McNamara, who did not wish to accept funds under such restrictions, similar but slightly milder language was attached as Section 701 of the Authorization for International Financial Institutions Act of 1977, which covered United States funding for the World Bank, International Development Association, International Finance Corporation, and the Asian Development Bank.

One of the human rights groups, the Center for International Policy, encouraged the restrictive legislation by reporting that many of the world's "most repressive" governments (Argentina, Brazil, Chile, El Salvador, Guatemala, Haiti, Nicaragua, Uruguay, South Korea, Indonesia, the Philippines, Thailand,

Zaïre, and Ethiopia) were scheduled to receive $2.9 billion in World Bank loans in fiscal 1979, out of a total of $9 billion.[74] The Center also noted a "close correlation between the onset of repression in the 1970s and disproportionate aid increases in World Bank loans," with financing expected to rise more than twice as fast in nations such as Argentina, Chile, the Philippines, and Uruguay as in all other recipient countries. It is too early to tell what impact the new U.S. human rights restrictions may eventually have—the U.S. Director of the World Bank has only 22.6% of the vote. McNamara stated in April of 1978 that "we have not in this institution allowed our lending policy to be determined by civil rights considerations, whether they be civil rights considerations in leftist or rightist governments."[75] By mid-1979 the United States Administration had still not drawn up guidelines on the human rights question for the American representative at the World Bank to follow. In their absence, the voting pattern had been inconsistent. Twenty-three loans had been vetoed by the representative (many of them to Chile and Vietnam), but all were approved by the Board. Opposition by the United States had thus failed to block the loans, but had simply aroused resentment among the other World Bank Board members.[76]

In late 1977 the human rights movement also began to focus on the policies of the International Monetary Fund. In 1976, IMF credits to South Africa reached a record $366 million, and another $98 million was approved in 1977 as a stand-by credit authorized in 1976 was drawn down. Responding to criticism that the IMF was financing apartheid, Thomas Leddy, a United States representative to the IMF said: "We have never cast a political vote in the IMF . . . while the World Bank has human rights amendments, the IMF doesn't. Our purpose is to sustain the world monetary system, which is vital to the existence of the U.S., and we are not about to upset that system."[77] In January of 1978, an amendment was proposed in the House Banking Committee requiring the United States to "take all necessary steps to insure" that the IMF's economic stabilization programs meet "basic human needs" and do not promote human rights violations.[78]

In addition to Congressional predisposition to such moves, it is clear that President Carter's initially strident "high profile" approach to human rights questions contributed greatly to the growing politicization of international economic institutions. The backlash could have been predicted. But now that the fat is in the fire it seems clear that the service of human needs in developing countries will be made much more difficult with uncertain gains for human rights.

In 1978 the drive to inject human rights concerns into multilateral aid programs spread to Western Europe. The EEC Commission approved a new negotiating strategy for the next Lomé Convention to replace the present "association" agreement with 53 African, Caribbean, and Pacific (ACP) states which expired at the end of 1979. The Commission proposed that aid to any ACP nation that violates fundamental human rights would be blocked—except for aid which meets the people's real needs, as opposed to those of the regime in power. But because few of the 53 member nations would qualify for aid if human rights were defined as political or democratic in nature, the Commission decided to define them more narrowly as the right to life, liberty, and security of person, and the right not to be subjected to torture. In addition, the Commission proposed that the Community would no longer provide tariff-free access to the EEC market for nations that inhumanely exploit their workers.[79]

Resolutions and condemnations. Much of the activity of intergovernmental organizations on questions of human rights has taken the form of rhetorical condemnations and nonbinding resolutions. The United Nations has been limited to moral pronouncements by a decided lack of enthusiasm for concrete action—depending on the case involved—on the part of either Western or Third World governments. The main targets have been South Africa, Rhodesia, Israel, and Chile, with South Africa alone bearing the brunt of hundreds of condemnations or resolutions over the past eighteen years in language that through time has become ever more shrill and intemperate. In October of 1977 the UN Security Council strongly condemned South Africa for resorting to "massive violence and repression" against its black people and other opponents of apartheid. Two months later the UN General Assembly adopted a record number of 14 (nonbinding) resolutions condemning apartheid, which variously criticized economic collaboration with South Africa, condemned military assistance, expressed concern over the plight of political prisoners, urged a boycott by the international sports community, censured Israel for its economic relations with South Africa, and called for the imposition of an oil embargo and a cessation of foreign investments. The motion to end foreign investment was approved 120 to 0, with 5 abstentions.[80] On the Namibian question, the UN Security Council in 1972 called on nations to "use all available means" to make sure that their "nationals and corporations conform in their policies of hiring Namibian workers to the basic provisions of the Universal Declaration of Human Rights."[81]

In other areas, the UN Economic and Social Council in 1974 called upon the government of Chile to "take all necessary steps to restore and safeguard basic human rights and fundamental freedoms in Chile, particularly those involving a threat to human life and liberty." During each of the next three years, the General Assembly adopted a resolution condemning human rights violations in Chile and urging the reestablishment of democracy. For multinationals, such condemnations or resolutions are not inconsequential. They often crystallize international opinion and occasionally serve as a prelude to binding national and international governmental action. They also tend to reinforce private nongovernmental actions in the form of shareholder resolutions, boycotts, stock divestitures, and similar steps discussed earlier.

Trade embargoes. Restrictions or embargoes on trade with countries charged with violating human rights have been adopted multilaterally or unilaterally only in a few special cases. A voluntary embargo against the sale of military weapons to South Africa was adopted by the United Nations in 1963, and at the same time the United States imposed its own mandatory embargo on exports of arms and ammunition. The effectiveness of the United Nations resolution was undercut for years by the policies of France and Israel, and to a lesser extent by Italy and West Germany. After the Soweto riots in October of 1977, the UN Security Council ordered a worldwide mandatory embargo on the supply of military materiel.[82] Given South Africa's 75% self-sufficiency in arms production, the measure was essentially symbolic. But the fact that Western governments were willing to agree on even limited mandatory sanctions was significant. The United States also took new unilateral measures at the time, extending its own embargo to include all goods and technical data to the police and military of South Africa and Namibia. Prime Minister Vorster's reaction to all of this was "we are not governed from overseas," and in November 1977 the South African government invoked sections of the National Supplies Procurement Act that gives the government the right to order foreign-owned plants to produce strategic materials that become unavailable from overseas suppliers.

After the Unilateral Declaration of Independence by Rhodesia in 1965, Britain persuaded the United Nations to first impose selective mandatory economic sanctions in 1966 and subsequently, in 1968, impose comprehensive mandatory sanctions, banning virtually all commodities originating from or destined for its former colony. But over the years Rhodesia managed to beat the sanctions, primarily with the help of South Africa and Mozambique and by covert activities of Japanese, French, British, German, Portuguese, and Italian companies and the Soviet Union.[83] The United States modified its adherence to the sanctions after passage of the Byrd Amendment in 1971, which provided for American importation of Rhodesian chrome until it was repealed in 1977. In 1978, the U.S. Congress also embargoed trade with Uganda while the Amin regime remained in power. In general, however, it appears that trade embargoes rarely prove effective in bringing nations to their knees, at least in the near term.

One other trade-related restriction that should be noted is the Jackson-Vanik Amendment, which was attached to Title IV of the U.S. Trade Act of 1974. Directed primarily at the Soviet Union, the amendment prohibits most-favored-nation (MFN)° status for any "nonmarket economy country" which (1) denies its citizens the right or opportunity to emigrate, and (2) imposes more than a nominal tax on emigration or on the visas and other documents required for emigration. At the same time the U.S. Congress placed a ceiling of $300 million on Eximbank credits to the Soviet Union. For both reasons, the Russians shortly thereafter renounced the 1972 United States-Soviet trade agreement, and trade thereafter essentially stagnated. In 1979, however, the United States opened talks with both China and the Soviet Union with a view to granting each MFN status. The Administration's policy in relaxing trade restrictions was one of "evenhandedness," motivated by the joint desires to normalize relations with China and give some recognition to the much improved emigration policy of the Soviet Union.

Investment prohibitions and restrictions. Following Rhodesia's Unilateral Declaration of Independence in 1965, the British government required U.K. firms to sever all ties with their Rhodesian affiliates. Some, however, continued to supply important services, often through their subsidiaries in South Africa. The United States government adopted a policy in the early 1970s to "officially discourage investment by American corporations in Namibia" and to withhold "protection of such investments against claims of a future lawful government of Namibia," although this did not appear to have much effect. The Japanese government has prohibited direct investment in South Africa, but this has not prevented the mushrooming of many other forms of involvement on the part of Japanese banks, trading companies and multinational firms.[84] Sweden, in 1979, became the first western nation to enact a law prohibiting companies from

---

°MFN status permits the country in question to sell products in the U.S. market under normal tariff rates. Non-MFN status means that the much higher tariffs existing in the depression years of the early 1930s would apply.

making new investments in South Africa. A new twist to investment restrictions was also introduced by Nigeria in late 1977, when it announced that any company seeking to invest in Nigeria would have to satisfy the authorities that it did not do business with the South African government and would not be expanding its investment in South Africa.[85] The Nigerian government nationalized the interests of British Petroleum in August 1979 on these grounds. Iraq, in a similar manner, threatened to cut off supplies of crude oil to multinational oil companies not complying with a boycott of Rhodesia and South Africa.

In addition to investment restrictions, a number of governmental bodies have issued codes of conduct on human rights which their multinationals are asked to follow. In 1973, the U.S. State Department circulated a set of "fair employment guidelines" to some 300 American companies operating in South Africa. In 1974, a Commons' Committee in the United Kingdom issued a code of conduct which asks companies operating in South Africa to supply information on the wages and working conditions of their black employees. Of 184 British companies with major South African interests, all but six have complied. The Canadian government announced that it would be issuing a "code of ethics" by which Canadian companies operating in South Africa would be asked to eschew racial discrimination in wage rates, promotions, working conditions, collective bargaining, and other employment practices.[86] The most sweeping code of this kind to emerge in recent years was adopted by the Foreign Ministers of the EEC member countries in September of 1977. The aforementioned code of conduct for EEC firms operating in South Africa calls on them to recognize black trade unions and practice collective bargaining, pay minimum wages 50 percent above basic needs, and institute training programs to ensure that equal pay for equal work promises are meaningful.[87] Firms operating under the code are required to publish a yearly report on the steps they have taken to implement it. Although the code has no statutory force and must rely on moral suasion, a proviso was added that companies which fail to conform can be penalized at home.

In this chapter we have attemped to outline the nature of the human rights issue as it confronts the multinational enterprise. We have stressed the definitional complexity of human "rights" and their linkages to economic progress or human "needs." The interactions of MNE operations and human rights are both direct and indirect. Sometimes they are clear-cut but often they are obscure. Perhaps most troublesome of all, sometimes there are tradeoffs between "rights" and "needs." Given the nature of the problem, we have traced through the many conduits of human rights pressures on policy and planning in both the public and private sector. The effects are substantial and growing. In the following chapter we shall identify the concrete implications for multinational companies and suggest ways of effective conflict-mangement in this troublesome area.

6 HUMAN RIGHTS
—THE CONFLICTS

Having examined in a general way the meaning, status, and development of human rights pressures around the world, the ways in which multinational corporate activities may affect them, and the actors and tactics of the transnational movement attempting to shape multinational corporate conduct in this area, we can now turn to some specific case histories of human rights conflict and attempt to learn how they might be effectively managed.

Although the hundreds of human rights conflicts in recent years involving MNEs could be categorized in a number of ways—by country, by industry, by time period, and so forth—it is probably most useful from a conflict management perspective to categorize cases on the basis of the strategic or operational activity of the multinational enterprise involved. The seven principal kinds of conflicts we have identified are as follows:

1. Lending to repressive nations;
2. Circumventing economic sanctions;
3. Buying from repressive nations;
4. Selling to repressive nations;
5. Collaborating with "illegal" governments;
6. Expanding investments in repressive nations;
7. Withdrawing from repressive nations.

An eighth dimension of human rights conflict confronting management of multinational enterprise involves labor practices in countries like South Africa, where labor relations and human rights issues are closely interrelated. This question is discussed in some detail in Chapter 11.

LENDING TO REPRESSIVE NATIONS

Believing that sizeable loans to the Chilean military government by Canadian and American banks in 1976 had provided "undeserved legitimacy and international respectability while the Junta represses Chilean opposition and violates human rights" the Unitarian Universalist Association filed the following resolution with the Bank of America in 1977: "Be it therefore resolved that the shareholders request the Board of Directors to establish the following as a policy of the corporation—the corporation and its affiliates or subsidiaries shall not make or renew any loan guarantees or credit to the present government of Chile or any of its agencies or instrumentalities." [1] The resolution received 5.9% of the vote at the 1977 meeting and was again reintroduced by religious groups in 1978 and 1979. Other banks receiving similar shareholder resolution demands to halt loans to Chile in 1979 included Chemical New York, Citicorp, First Chicago and Wells Fargo. Bankers Trust received one concerning loans to Nicaragua.

Certainly the bulk of concern in lending to repressive regimes over the years has centered on South Africa. A U.S. Senate Foreign Relations Committee report showed that major American banks had outstanding loans and credits worth $2.2 billion with South Africa as of mid-1977. The report also concluded that "international credit provided the margin of funds needed by South Africa in the 1974–76 period to finance its military buildup, its stockpiling of oil, and its major infrastructure projects in strategic economic sectors such as transportation, communications, energy, and steel production, all of which are related to security needs."[2] Multinational banks have been attacked for helping the South African government remain indifferent to international and internal human rights pressures by permitting the government to attain greater economic and strategic self-sufficiency. The banks have also been charged with creating a vested interest in stability at the price of oppression, with encouraging further Western corporate involvement, with limiting the diplomatic options of governments such as the United Kingdom and the United States, with providing moral legitimacy to South Africa, and with bolstering apartheid. Of all the conflicts over the impact of multinationals on human rights, the latter is certainly the one that has run the longest and been most visible internationally. It has also been the most ambitious and best organized campaign orchestrated by human rights activists. And because of the sensitivity of banks to public attitudes the campaign has also been regarded as one of the most "successful" although, as we shall see, this can be argued.

After the killing of 69 Africans at Sharpeville in 1960, several religious organizations launched a campaign to halt foreign bank loans to the South African government. In 1966 the American Committee on Africa and the World Student Christian Federation formed the Committee of Conscience Against Apartheid to campaign against a consortium of 10 American banks that were providing a $40 million revolving credit to the South African government—Bank of America, Chase Manhattan, Citibank, Manufacturers Hanover, Morgan Guaranty, Chemical Bank, Bankers Trust, Irving Trust, Continental Illinois, and First National Bank of Chicago.[3] The campaign attracted the support of American churches, community organizations, student groups, Congressmen, and private individuals, as well as the United Nations. Tactics ran the gamut from letters of protest, delegations to the banks, questions at shareholder meetings, and withdrawal of accounts to picketing, leaflets, and demonstrations.[4] Perhaps the most significant action was the United Methodist Board of Missions' vote to remove a $10 million investment portfolio from Citibank management. Together with other organizations, an estimated $23 million in funds were withdrawn from the 10 target banks. In November of 1969 the banks did not renew the revolving credit arrangement with the South African Ministry of Finance. The banks denied that public pressure had been responsible. They announced that South Africa simply no longer needed the funds. Nonetheless, the "bank campaign" model had thus been firmly established, to be resurrected on a much larger scale a decade later.

In mid-1973 copies of confidential bank documents were leaked to the U.S. National Council of Churches by sources within European-American Bank (EAB) in New York. The Council's Corporate Information Center subsequently published them under the title: "The Frankfurt Documents—Secret Bank Loans to the South African Government."[5] They revealed that EAB—controlled by six major European banks—had raised $210 million from banks in the United States, Canada, Europe and Japan to provide secret loans to the South African government and its agencies starting in 1970. Ten American banks were involved, and had contributed approximately $70 million of the total. Based on this revelation the Council's Interfaith Center on Corporate Responsibility (ICCR) began a multifaceted "bank campaign" primarily involving local protests, and by 1976 eight of the ten American banks had either withdrawn their loans or promised to become involved no further. Banks that withdrew included Merchants National Bank and Trust Co. of Indianapolis, Wells Fargo Bank of San Francisco, and Maryland National Bank of Baltimore. Those committing themselves to no further loans included City National Bank of Detroit, Central National Bank of Chicago, Wachovia Bank and Trust of North Carolina, and First National Bank of Louisville.[6] All were either community or regional banks, with very small stakes in the deal ($2 million on average) and presumably highly susceptible to local public pressures. Human rights activists hailed the EAB campaign as a signal victory despite its trivial importance in the overall picture of bank lending. The campaign did inspire, however, the Subcommittee on African Affairs of the Committee on Foreign Relations of the U.S. Senate to hold hearings in September of 1976 to examine U.S. lending to South Africa and the services of the Export–Import Bank.[7]

The EAB loans revealed in the "Frankfurt Documents" also inspired a well-coordinated international camapign on the issue. In Canada the United Church of Christ, the Anglican Church of Canada and the "Task Force on the Churches and Corporate Responsibility" made presentations and attended the annual general meetings of the Bank of Montreal, the Royal Bank of Canada, The Canadian Imperial Bank of Commerce, and the Toronto Dominion Bank. Efforts to end the loans of major Canadian banks to South Africa, however, were unsuccessful. In Europe the World Council of Churches (WCC) played a major role in campaigning against South Africa loans of European banks. After largely unproductive conversations with the European owners of EAB, the executive council of the WCC decided that none of its funds would be deposited with EAB or its shareholders—Deutsche Bank, Société Générale, Midland Bank, Amsterdam-Rotterdam Bank N.V., Société Général de Banque S.A. (Belgium), and Creditanstalt-Bankverein (Austria).[8]

In Holland, a campaign was launched by the Working Group Betaald Antwoord and other groups against the Amsterdam-Rotterdam Bank for its South African loans. The bank faced hostile questions from depositors, severe criticism from the WCC, interrogations in the Dutch Parliament and in the media, as well as calls for a boycott by church groups and three Dutch parliamentary parties unless it stopped dealing with South Africa.

In England, a similar set of actions was undertaken by the Anti-Apartheid Movement and others against Midland Bank and Barclays. An "End Loans to Southern Africa" group (ELTSA) was formed in April 1974 specifically to campaign against Midland's involvement in the EAB loans. ELTSA issued press reports and articles, organized pickets and street theater at the bank headquarters, had questions asked at the annual meeting, and planted counterfeit bank deposit forms overprinted "Deposit on Apartheid" in bank branches.[9] The group made history in 1976 by filing the first shareholder resolution ever presented to a registered British company or bank on a moral issue. The resolution called on the Midland directors to cease making loans to South Africa and had the backing of the Church of England Commissioners, the Methodist Church, and the Greater London Council. At the company's annual meeting the resolution received 6.2% of the shareholder votes and was regarded as a moral victory by its sponsors. Lord Armstrong, Chairman of Midland, had told the meeting that if political considerations were allowed to influence financial decisions, then "international business could rapidly become impossible."[10] Six days later the anti-apartheid activists turned out in force at the annual meeting of Barclays and barraged its chairman with questions about the bank's involvement in South Africa.[11]

Back in the United States, the bank campaign rose to new levels in intensity in 1977 with the formation in New York of the "Committee to Oppose Bank Loans to South Africa," sponsored by the American Committee on Africa. The campaign began officially in June 1977 with the objective of forcing banks to grant no further loans to South Africa and to publish an explicit policy which would prohibit such loans. Forty-seven banks that had made loans to South Africa were targeted, including Citibank, Chase Manhattan, Manufacturers Hanover, Morgan Guaranty, Continental Illinois, First National Bank of Chicago, Bank of America, and First National Bank of Boston; the rest were smaller regional banks. Tactics were to include shareholder resolutions, picketing, leaflets, information packets, slide shows, press releases, workshops, account withdrawals, and so forth. During 1977 the coalition picked up the support of more than 150 church groups, action groups, trade unions, members of Congress, and private individuals. A list of some of the organizational participants is given in Exhibit 6–1. By the end of 1977 campaigns were well underway against banks in New York City, Rochester, Boston, Chicago, San Francisco, and Philadelphia, and were beginning in Milwaukee, Madison, and Minneapolis. [12] Shareholder resolutions regarding loans to South Africa were filed by Protestant denominations and Catholic orders with Citicorp, Continental Illinois, First Chicago, Manufacturers Hanover, and J.P. Morgan.° The operative clause in the resolutions directed at the first three banks read:

> The Corporation and its affiliates or subsidiaries shall not make or renew any loans to the government of the Republic of South Africa or any of its agencies or instrumentalities or to any companies for operations in the Republic of South Africa, unless and until the South African government has committed itself to ending the legally enforced form of racism called apartheid and has taken meaningful steps toward the implementation of full political, legal and social rights for the majority population (African, Asian, Coloured).[13]

They failed to receive more than 3.3% of the vote at any of the five shareholder meetings. The position of the banks, which the great majority of shareholders endorsed, is typified in the proxy statement of Continental Illinois Corporation shown in Exhibit 6–2.

°Citicorp and J.P. Morgan are the holding companies for Citibank and Morgan Guaranty, respectively.

Exhibit 6-1

Organizations and Institutions Participating in the Bank Campaign of the Committee to Oppose
Bank Loans to South Africa (November 22, 1977)

Ad Hoc Committee Against Bank Loans to South Africa, (Rochester, New York)
African Agenda
American Committee on Africa
American Friends Service Committee (National)
American Friends Service Committee (Midwest)
Americans for Democratic Action
Asociacion Puertorriguena de Artistas y Tecnicos
Black Students Organization—Columbia University
Black Theology Project
Boston Coalition for the Liberation of Southern Africa
Center for International Education
Chicago Southern Africa Bank Campaign Coalition
Church of the Intercession
Clergy & Laity Concerned
Coalition of Concerned Black Americans
District 65 Distributive Workers of America
District Council 1707, AFSCME, AFL-CIO
District 1199 National Union of Hospital & Health Care Employees, AFL-CIO
Furriers Joint Council of New York
Institute for Education in Peace & Justice
Institute for Sport and Social Analysis
International Longshoremen & Warehouse Workers Union, Local 6
International Union, United Automobile & Aerospace Workers (UAW)
Internews
Minnesota Committee on Southern Africa
Namibia Peace Center
National Lawyers Guild
Northern California Interfaith Committee on Corporate Responsibility
Pan African Students Organization in America (PASOA)
Philadelphia Namibia Action Group
Potomac Association, Central Atlantic Conference, United Church of Christ
Resist
Robert R. Moton Institute
Rochester Peace & Justice Education Center
San Antonio Committee Against Mercenary Recruitment
South Africa Freedom Day Coalition
Southern Africa Committee
Stop Bank of America Banking on Apartheid Campaign
The East Organization, New York
United Church of Christ Commission for Racial Justice
United Electrical, Radio and Machine Workers of America (UE)
Washington Office on Africa
Women's International League for Peace & Freedom

Source: Committee to Oppose Bank Loans to South Africa.

Other campaign activities in 1977 included anti-bank loan demonstrations
and picketing at bank locations in New York, Chicago, and Boston, a "national
day of withdrawal"—"a run on the banks" on behalf of South African freedom—countless meetings with bank management representatives, and the acquisition of endorsements from the NAACP, leaders of seven national trade
unions and seven New York-area locals, and various Congressmen. An estimated
$30–35 million was withdrawn from the target banks. The Furriers Joint Coun-

Exhibit 6–2
Sample Bank Proxy Statement

**Management recommends a vote *against*
this resolution for the following reasons:**

The Corporation shares with all responsible Americans a repugnance of apartheid which is a denial of basic human rights. In the opinion of management, however, the economic boycott called for by the above proposal will not contribute to the elimination of apartheid and would clearly endanger the prospects for the non-whites whom the proponents seek to assist.

Informed observers believe that the promotion of trade and investment and the support of economic development within South Africa by American and other foreign interests will prove to be one of the most important contributions toward correcting the problem of apartheid and that no progress will be made through the construction of barriers. The Corporation has also adopted this policy and in recent years has made loans to corporations doing business in South Africa to support international trade, including U.S. exports, and to assist economic development. In addition, several black African nations also trade with South Africa. There are increasing signs that technical modernization and broadening of the industrial base in South Africa have had a beneficial effect and have produced a liberalization of the government's policy of apartheid. Leaders in both the public and private sectors now recognize black workers as indispensable to the country's economic progress. Management believes that continued financial assistance by major U.S. commercial banks, especially in the private sector, will further contribute to this process.

Further, the requested boycott is absolute and the standards under which financing could be reinstituted are vague. The Corporation's loan policy with respect to South Africa is closely monitored and regularly reviewed by management in light of current developments. Management believes that no useful purpose would be served by restricting the Corporation's flexibility in this area. The boycott would also preclude the Corporation from complying with existing legal commitments to renew certain loans thereby possibly subjecting it to lawsuits for damages.

The United States government maintains normal diplomatic relations with the government of South Africa. By financing American exports to South Africa, the Corporation is supporting United States foreign policy. It would be improper for the Corporation to make its own foreign trade policy by deciding under what conditions it will do business with South Africa.

For these reasons management is of the opinion that the proposal should be rejected and accordingly a vote AGAINST is recommended.

Source: Proxy statement of the management of Continental Illinois Corporation regarding stockholder proposal on South African loans filed by the Adrian Sisters of the Adrian Dominican Generalate for a vote at the spring 1977 annual meeting.

cil, for example, announced in June the termination of a $10 million pension fund account with Manufacturers Hanover. The United Radio, Electrical and Machine Workers Union closed down a $4 million payroll account with Chase Manhattan. The United Automobile Workers Executive Board said it would make no further deposits in banks lending to South Africa. And the National Council of Churches called on its 30 denominations to "undertake" to withdraw all their funds from financial institutions that deal with the government of South Africa or businesses there.[14] The National Council itself voted to withdraw $6 million from Morgan Guaranty and $5 million from Citibank.

The responses of target banks to the campaign pressures were mixed, but no major United States bank flatly stated that it would no longer lend money to any borrowers in South Africa. However, David Rockefeller, Chairman of the Board of Chase Manhattan issued the following statement at the bank's annual meeting in April 1977:

> In the Chase code of ethics adopted this year we state, "Strict attention should be given to the legal, moral and social implications of all loan and investment decisions on a global basis. We should seek to avoid business with identifiably harmful results, and assure that we always carefully evaluate the long-term, as well as short-term, meaning of our decisions." In South Africa this approach has resulted in a lending policy which specifically excludes loans that, in our judgement, tend to support the apartheid policies of the South African government or reinforce discriminatory business practices. Conversely, we are willing to consider loan proposals for projects of a productive nature which we believe will result in social and economic benefits for all South Africans. We recognize that this general policy requires a high degree of subjective judgement when applied to specific instances. These guidelines are reviewed on a quarterly basis in order to give recognition to changing circumstances in a fluid environment. Currently we are not extending loans to Namibia, the homelands or the border industries. General purpose loans to the government or to parastatal institutions are also discouraged.

Indeed, the ICCR decided not to file a shareholder resolution against Chase on the basis of Rockefeller's statement and prior talks with bank officers. With this gingerly selective policy, Chase became the first major bank to apply social criteria in its South African loans. A member of Clergy and Laity Concerned, however, was unrelenting. "This statement is a sop. The policymakers at Chase refuse to recognize the systemic and institutionalized racism which characterizes the South African society. No loan can 'result in social and economic benefits for all South Africans' as long as the system built upon the doctrine of apartheid remains intact."[15] Indeed, a week after Rockefeller made his proclamation, Chase's senior official in South Africa was quoted by a Johannesburg newspaper as saying: "We're just carrying on as before, and we'll shortly be moving to bigger premises."[16]

Inquiries to other leading banks elicited a variety of responses: A spokesman for Bank of America said in the Fall of 1977 that "we do not condone apartheid in South Africa. However, through a prudent lending policy we believe we can assist in stimulating economic trade and development fundamental to the betterment of local economic conditions." A spokesman for Crocker National Bank said loans were judged on the "ability of the borrower to repay and the purpose for which the loan is to be used" rather than on whether the bank liked the recipient country's political stance. A spokesman for First National Bank of Chicago said the bank would not sever relations with South Africa, because "we do not believe you can influence a relationship by cutting off all relations with a country."[17] Morgan Guaranty announced it would continue to make creditworthy loans "anywhere in the world we are permitted to." Citibank said it would "continue to moderate" its business involvement with South Africa. First National Bank of Boston said it had reduced the terms of prospective loans to South Africa from five years to three. And Manufacturers Hanover and Continental Illinois indicated that they would not make loans that supported apartheid but would still consider making loans which did not.[18] EAB said it would no longer grant credit to South Africa except for the financing of current trade.[19]

Pressure on banks outside the United States also continued, with church actions beginning in Belgium, Switzerland, and Scandinavia. In Canada the Toronto-Dominion Bank, Canadian Imperial Bank of Commerce, Royal Bank of Canada, and Bank of Montreal were subject to renewed pressure by churches, unions, and the Toronto Committee for the Liberation of Southern Africa. In England, the ELTSA action group gathered 106 individuals holding 900,000 shares and sponsored another resolution to the annual meeting of Midland Bank. Midland stated that it would no longer lend to the South African government. In the wake of vigorous protest, Barclays International requested its South African affiliate to withdraw $11.5 million from Government defense bonds—to which its managing director responded "we are sure our customers and the public will appreciate the difficult international business and political climate in which we operate at the present time."[20] In the Netherlands, after considerable public pressure, the Amsterdam Rotterdam Bank made public its decision to make no further loans to the South African government or its agencies until "essential changes" occurred. The Algemene Bank Nederland also assured the WCC that it would refuse loan requests from the South African government or its agencies until "legally enforced racism" has been abolished.[21]

.The campaign against loans to South Africa did not let up. Shareholder resolutions asking for no new loans to the government were filed in 1978 with Bank of America, Crocker National, First National Bank of Boston, and Manufacturers Hanover. Resolutions demanding a report on current loans to the South African government were filed with Citicorp, Continental Illinois, First Chicago, and J. P. Morgan.[22] The church sponsors were most successful with their resolution at First National Bank of Boston, which received 7.7% of the proxy votes cast but was strongly opposed by management on the grounds that shareholder determination of lending policies would set a dangerous precedent.[23] Perhaps the most important event was Citicorp's reversal of its long-standing policy and its disclosure in March 1978 that it had called a halt to the granting of loans to the South African government and to government owned or operated companies: "Citicorp is limiting its credit selectively to constructive private sector activities that create jobs and which benefit all South Africans." It added that it "would regard tangible progress away from apartheid as a positive factor in its risk evaluation."[24] *The New York Times* thereupon commented that "Citibank's action is certain to be noted by other leading banks and could be influential in shaping the attitudes of banks that do business with South Africa."[25] Indeed, a week later Chemical Bank disclosed—following demonstrations at several of its Manhattan branches—that it had had a corporate policy since 1974 prohibiting loans to the government of South Africa and state-owned entities.[26] A quite different policy was announced by Bank America Corporation on the following day. President A. W. Causen said his bank would continue doing business in that country and defended its right to do business anywhere in the world, regardless of political systems, if its investment can be protected and there is no prohibition by the United States government.[27]

In Britain, Midland Bank announced in March that it would further limit its lending to South Africa by financing only "identifiable" trade with Britain.[28] The Nigerian government ordered its public agencies to withdraw their funds immediately from the Nigerian subsidiary of Barclays Bank because of its interests in South Africa—a new wrinkle in the bank campaign—and also directed one-third of the bank's non-Nigerian employees to leave the country within a month. Some observers interpreted this as "a clear warning to all British companies that one day soon they will have to choose between black Africa and South Africa."[29]

By late 1978, international banks had all but ceased granting medium term loans to South Africa, although short term credit continued. A rather cynical cartoon in the South African *Financial Mail* shows nine "bank" sharks seated along a table. The chairman wraps up a strategy session with: "That's agreed then, gentlemen: on moral grounds we won't invest in Johannesburg . . . until there's some money to be made!" Many would conclude that the *de facto* cessation of medium-term lending reflected falling loan demand and standard commercial banking prudence, as political developments in 1976 and 1977 adversely affected South Africa's creditworthiness and increased "country-risk." One securities firm concluded that "the faltering economic situation, increasing polarization of black leadership, the social legislation of the white government, and clear indications of the willingness of certain major powers to intervene on behalf of one side or the other all have elevated the risk of violent confrontation."[30] Moreover, many of the major banks had already approached their lending limits to South Africa as a result of the large commitments made in 1974–1976.

Yet it is hard to dismiss completely the effects of adverse publicity and chanting pickets in motivating some banks—particularly those with only a marginal interest at stake and a major retail business—to cut off or restrict their involvement with South Africa. But for the big international banks with large stakes in South African business it seems that in 1977–1978 human rights "virtue" happened to coincide with economic "necessity," and that this considerably eased the problem of bending with the winds of human rights pressure. That pressure continued in 1979 with shareholder resolutions on loans to South Africa filed with Bank America, Citicorp, Continental Illinois, First Chicago, First National Boston, INA, Manufacturers Hanover, Merrill Lynch, J. P. Morgan and Wells Fargo.

CIRCUMVENTING SANCTIONS

"Sanction-busting," the evasion of United Nations or home-country economic restrictions on countries like Rhodesia and South Africa, has been a particularly contentious issue for certain multinationals in the defense, metals, and petroleum industries. The nature of the Rhodesian and South African sanctions was discussed in the previous chapter.[31] And we have already noted that embargoes have seldom been demonstrably effective anywhere—"Commerce has too many benefits to be so easily snuffed out by political fiat."[32] Both Western multinationals—sometimes with the explicit or implicit approval of their home governments—and Communist state trading organizations have found numerous ways to circumvent the spirit and intent even of the UN embargoes. And in some cases companies have found ways to "legally" contravene the intent of home-government policy on sanctions. And so in the case of Southern Africa the critics have charged MNEs with providing the white minority governments with an economic lifeline, thus delaying settlements for black majority rule. Curiously, there are few critics of Communist trading organizations doing precisely the same thing.

Here we shall examine three cases of sanctions-busting. In the first, the focus is on Union Carbide and the long battle over importation of Rhodesian chrome into the United States in contravention of UN economic sanctions. The second explores the controversy over oil supplies to Rhodesia, allegedly via "paper-chases" created in South Africa by multinational oil companies such as Mobil, Shell, and British Petroleum. The third case briefly reviews the prosecution of Olin Corporation on charges of selling arms and ammunition to South Africa in violation of the 1963 American weapons embargo. Of all the human rights conflicts considered in this chapter, the sanctions-busting cases probably have the highest profile. Multinationals operating in South Africa and Rhodesia have been both hard-pressed by groups in home and third countries and counter-pressured by the local governments' tough commercial and security laws.

The three cases we shall discuss highlight the problems and limitations of internal management control systems. Actions of a few employees somewhere in an MNE's global organization can take place without the knowledge of senior officials and may indeed violate corporate policies, thus damaging the entire organization—conglomerates like Olin may be most susceptible to such problems. The cases also reveal the behavioral imperatives of the highly competitive arms, oil, and metals trade and the hard choices confronting both executives and legislators when access to strategic raw materials is involved. Finally, the cases illustrate the impact of multinational corporate stakes changing over time— nations and corporations alike seem to be most willing to do what is "morally right" when the economic sacrifice is not too great.

Union Carbide and Rhodesian Chrome

In 1966, the UN Security Council imposed selective mandatory sanctions on Rhodesia banning the import and export of specific commodities, one of which was chrome. Rhodesia has two-thirds of world metallurgical chromite reserves, the high-quality ore most suited for the production of ferrochrome for use in steelmaking. With selective sanctions proving ineffective, the Security Council in 1968 imposed comprehensive mandatory sanctions banning virtually all commodities originating from or destined for Rhodesia.

Union Carbide, with two subsidiaries (Rhodesian Chrome Mines Ltd. and African Chrome Mines Ltd.) producing most of Rhodesia's chrome ore and another subsidiary (Union Carbide Rhomet Ltd.) producing ferrochrome, was seriously affected by the sanctions. Although some of the adverse impact was lessened by massive stockpiling in Mozambique just before the boycott took effect and by requesting "hardship" exemptions from the U.S. Treasury Department for chrome imports into the United States, the future outlook for Carbide's operations appeared bleak. American industry began buying much more chrome ore from the Soviet Union—with clear indications that the Russians were themselves buying ore from Rhodesia in direct violation of the UN sanctions—the price of which, however, climbed 188% from 1966 to 1971. And American producers were finding it difficult or impossible to pass on the price increase.

Although the United States government had been indicting and convicting firms and their officers for violating the Rhodesia trade embargo, and a host of groups were calling for still more severe sanctions, Union Carbide began a vigorous lobbying campaign in the U.S. Congress to abolish or relax American enforcement of the sanctions in regard to chrome. Foote Minerals Co., another American producer operating in Rhodesia, and the Rhodesian Information Service were also active in the campaign. In Congressional hearings in 1971, spokesmen for Union Carbide's Ferroalloys Division stressed the dangers of United States reliance on the Soviet Union "for more than 50 percent of its supplies of a critical and strategic material" and predicted that continued enforcement of the embargo might result in "employee layoffs in the ferroalloys and steel industries."[33]

The campaign stressing dependence on Russia and rapidly rising prices paid off in 1971 with passage of the "Byrd Amendment" (Sec. 503 of the Military Procurement Act of 1972). The amendment, sponsored by Virginia Independent Senator Harry F. Byrd, made it illegal for the President to block the importation of any strategic material that might otherwise have to be obtained from a Communist source. The legislation made the United States the only UN member government other than South Africa to be openly in violation of the sanctions. In early 1972, Union Carbide and Foote Minerals resumed importing Rhodesian chrome.

A coalition including legislators, church groups, black organizations, and unions became increasingly vociferous in their opposition to the Byrd Amendment. Union Carbide's 1972 shareholders meeting was picketed by a group of demonstrators protesting the company's role in breaking UN sanctions. Inside the meeting, representatives of several religious organizations condemned the company's implicit support of the Ian Smith régime: "Today we have a strange reversal of roles. Demonstrators for law and order, led by a judge, are protesting in the streets outside while the international law breakers meet here" stated one representative of the American Friends Service Committee. The chairman of the House Subcommittee on African Affairs, Charles Diggs, attended the meeting "to express the outrage of the Congressional Black Caucus and indeed of a growing number of black Americans all over this country that Union Carbide could be an accomplice in breaking international sanctions against Rhodesia."[34] A few weeks later, the Congressional Black Caucus and a number of other organizations sought an injunction against further Rhodesian chrome imports and nullification of the Byrd amendment. A District Court Judge, however, refused to issue such an injunction.[35]

Criticism of Union Carbide and efforts to repeal the Byrd Amendment continued for the next five years. Attempts to have the law withdrawn failed to achieve majority support in both Houses of Congress in 1972, 1973, and 1975. Carbide's position in countless Congressional hearings was that repeal would result in a sharp rise in chrome prices and would cripple the American ferrochrome industry because of the lower quality of ores that would be available. Foote Minerals, with stakes much smaller than those of Carbide, decided in late 1973 to leave the field and sold its Rhodesian properties.

In 1976 the United Church Board for World Ministries and two other religious organizations filed a proxy resolution with Carbide asking the company to set policy prohibiting importation of any chrome ore from Rhodesia "until such time as governmental power is transferred to the African majority and international economic sanctions against Rhodesia have been lifted." The resolution sponsors maintained that it was in the best interests both of the company and Rhodesia's African population "to withdraw any economic support for white racism . . ."[36] Carbide's position, as it had been for many years, was that its presence was bringing benefits to all segments of the population. The shareholder resolution received only 1.9% of the vote.

Things changed drastically in 1977. Less than three weeks after Jimmy Carter's inauguration his administration opened an all-out drive for repeal of the Byrd Amendment in the belief that by adding to the pressure on the minority Rhodesian government repeal would help accelerate negotiations for turning over political power to the black majority. Carter also had in mind a friendly signal to the black-ruled nations of Africa, and he did not want to be embarrassed in an upcoming speech on human rights before the UN General Assembly.[37] With vigorous White House lobbying, the House and Senate acted quickly, and in March passed identical bills amending the UN Participation Act of 1945 that in effect would repeal the Byrd Amendment. President Carter signed the bill into law on March 18th and thereby reimposed the embargo against Rhodesian chrome, placing the United States in compliance once again with UN economic sanctions.

American manufacturers of stainless steel and other alloys, the chief users of chrome, were opposed to the policy shift but put up only modest resistance. The stakes had changed. Industry's dependence specifically on Rhodesian chrome had declined, dropping from about half of total use to less than 15%. One reason was heavy investment by American specialty steel producers in technology that permitted greater use of high-carbon ferrochrome smelted from low-grade ores available outside Rhodesia—this particular technological advance was the argon oxygen decarbonization process developed by the Linde division of Union Carbide. Another reason for the weak resistance was the substantial expansion of chrome mining and smelting capacity in such countries as Brazil, Turkey, and particularly South Africa. With the stainless steel industry in the post-recession doldrums and prices stagnant, the steelmakers also could no longer cite the argument of a tight chrome market, which had served them well in previous years.[38]

Views on the repeal were mixed. Senator Dick Clark of Iowa, who piloted repeal through the Senate, stated that the United States was in a position to do "what is politically and morally right without economic sacrifice."[39] Professor John Hutchinson of UCLA saw repeal of the Byrd Amendment as "an act of national evasion and disservice, irrelevant to the liberation of Rhodesia, an act of propitiation to bad law and raucous hypocrites in the U.N."[40] Others saw it as symbolism at the 11th hour, expecially since former Prime Minister Ian D. Smith had already publicly committed himself to a transition to majority rule within a two-year period. Rhodesian officials were undismayed— they remained confident that they could divert their chrome exports to other markets and that some would continue to reach the United States despite the renewed boycott. As for Union Carbide, the general manager of the company's Rhodesia Chrome Mines Ltd., Geoffrey B. Blore, maintained, "We have been expecting this."[41] Two years later, after the election that brought black Methodist bishop Abel Muzorewa to power in Zimbabwe–Rhodesia, the United States Senate voted to lift the economic sanctions—President Carter, however, refused to go along, on the basis that in his view the election had been neither fair or free.

Mobil Oil and Shipments to Rhodesia

How the former Ian Smith government obtained its oil supplies during the Rhodesian trade embargo is undoubtedly the biggest sanction-busting story thus far. Answers to the question of how the Smith regime might have obtained the oil it needed for more than a decade began to emerge publicly in 1976, when the Center for Social Action of the United Church of Christ released a 50-page report entitled *The Oil Conspiracy* which alleged that Mobil Oil Corporation's South African subsidiary had played an important role in circumventing economic sanctions against Rhodesia since 1966.[42] The Center had obtained its data from OKHELA, a clandestine organization of whites in South Africa opposed to apartheid. The report contained alleged photocopies of Mobil documents showing that some executives of Mobil's wholly-owned South African affiliate conspired to secretly supply Mobil Oil products to Rhodesia—the main recipient of these products being Mobil Oil Southern Rhodesia, also a wholly-owned subsidiary. According to the documents, both Mobil affiliates conspired with the Rhodesian government to supply petroleum. In order to conceal the flow, the parties allegedly set up an elaborate "paper chase," including false billing, phony mail drops, bogus accounts with existing South African firms, and dummy corporations. An internal company memorandum dated September 2, 1968, allegedly states that the paper chase was set up to "involve and complicate this matter to a far greater degree than pertains at present in the hope that it will discourage an investigation."[43]

Although the report focused on Mobil, it also charged that Shell, British Petroleum,

Caltex, and Total of France had set up similar procedures to funnel oil products into Rhodesia. The Center's report was released in June 1976 at a Washington press conference staged by the People's Bicentennial Commission, a group which had previously offered a cash reward for information leading to the arrest and conviction of corporate executives for criminal activities. The Center refused the reward but utilized the facilities of the Commission to secure wide media coverage for its charges. According to one report: "At first Mobil heatedly denied the charges, concentrating its fire on the People's Bicentennial Commission and characterizing it as a 'far-left organization.' Mobil later issued a more moderate statement in which it said that it was conducting its own investigation of the charges." [44]

In September of 1976 the Senate Foreign Relations Subcommittee on African Affairs held hearings on "South Africa: U.S. Policy and the Role of U.S. Corporations." [45] The United Church of Christ's representative testified that American oil companies were supplying Rhodesia in violation of United States law and presented the Committee with a series of documents purporting to offer substantive proof of a conspiracy to violate sanctions. In reply, Mobil's chief legal officer stated categorically that the company had not violated any law pertaining to sanctions against Rhodesia. In the first place, it was not a violation of American sanctions for Mobil South Africa to supply oil to Rhodesia because it was incorporated under the laws of South Africa, its management was South African, and it had to obey the laws of South Africa, in the same way as any American subsidiary of a foreign corporation had to obey United States laws. Moreover, Mobil had enforced a company policy of prohibiting sales to Rhodesia and no such sales had taken place. Finally, he contended that the charges probably represented a "skillfully contrived publicity scheme" for political ends and that the entire episode was "an artful blend of fact and fiction" designed to "hoodwink" institutions such as the United Church of Christ and the United States Senate. [46]

The Subcommittee Chairman noted that the allegations against Mobil raised the question of whether American firms had control of company policies of their subsidiaries and whether it was possible to ensure that the policies and intentions of United States foreign policy are followed by American firms. The South African Official Secrets Act had in fact prevented Mobil Oil in New York from questioning officers or inspecting records of its wholly-owned South African affiliate. The manager of the affiliate had refused to provide parent company investigators with comments on the United Church of Christ allegations for fear of prosecution under South African law. South African government officials had clearly instructed Mobil that it must comply with its law, that it was long-standing government policy to require sales to willing and able buyers, and that it prohibited use of "destination commitments" on the final point of sale of traded products. This policy applied to all dealings with all customers domiciled in South Africa, and could be discussed only on a government-to-government basis since it was a matter of official policy. Mobil's South African affiliate also declined to provide information requested in an Administrative Order served on Mobil by the U.S. Treasury. As a result, the Treasury Department reported in May of 1977 that it could not determine whether Mobil had violated the United State trade embargo because it could not gain access to the files of Mobil's affiliate. In response, Mobil issued a statement that it was "pleased that the Treasury Department found no evidence that the company violated United States law." [47]

With the issue in limbo from a United States government point of view the action moved elsewhere. The United Church Board for World Ministries filed a proxy resolution with Mobil asking its board of directors to "take all measures necessary to insure that no Mobil products are supplied, directly or indirectly, to Rhodesia, and that no bulk sales of products are made to buyers who do not offer verifiable guarantee that said products are not destined for resale or transfer to Rhodesia." [48] Mobil's shareholders overwhelmingly voted down the resolution at the 1977 annual meeting, and five days later the Church body announced that it was taking the unusual step of submitting another resolution a year in advance, calling on Mobil to stop the alleged "illegal" shipments to Rhodesia.

In late May 1977 the Lonrho Trading Company, the British-based multinational which had once been the exclusive supplier of oil to Rhodesia, filed suit in London against 29 oil companies for allegedly supplying fuel to the white Rhodesian government in defiance of United Nations sanctions. Defendants in the High Court action included Mobil, Standard Oil Company of California, Texaco, Shell Oil, British Petroleum, and Total. Lonrho had halted oil shipments to Rhodesia by cutting its pipeline from neighboring Mozambique, and now contended that the companies it was suing took over the business. Alleged losses were reported as amounting to $170 million, and Lonrho's suit asked damages for breach of contract, unlawful interference with contract, conspiracy, negligence, and unlawful acts causing loss and injury. A spokesman from Mobil responded that "we don't think it's a matter for serious consideration. We have gone back and investigated both here and in Africa and have found no indications that Mobil products have been sent to Rhodesia."[49] Lonrho's suit was referred to arbitration in 1978.

Lonrho's motives in this unprecedented action were viewed by observers as complex: "Clearly the company wants financial compensation for the heavy losses which have piled up since the pipeline was closed. But it has also been pointed out that [President Tiny] Rowland became determined to take the oil companies to court for sanctions-busting after the British Government Department of Trade report last July [1976] branded Lonrho for having been more closely involved with mining operations in Rhodesia 'than was consistent with the terms of U.K. sanctioned legislation.' Finally, it also appears that Lonrho is cultivating the Zimbabwe nationalists in an attempt to win their goodwill for the day when Rhodesia wins majority rule."[50]

Lonrho's charges and high court writs, combined with pressure from Zambia, Nigeria, and Zimbabwe nationalists, led the British Foreign Secretary, Dr. David Owen, to set up an official inquiry to look into allegations of sanctions-busting by British oil companies. In this connection, the Haslemere Group of human-rights activists in London released a detailed submission on sanctions-busting by Shell and BP providing—as in the Center for Social Action report on Mobil—considerable unpublished material obtained from informants within the oil and shipping companies in Southern Africa. The same "paper-chase" arrangements were documented. The government's Bingham Commission subsequently found that Shell and BP had indeed secretly been aiding Rhodesia to obtain oil through intermediaries and that the British government cooperated with the scheme. The Bingham report caused a sensation in the British press which dubbed the scandal "oilgate"—"Tiny" Rowland emerged as the "Deep Throat."[51]

In August 1977 the Zambian government issued summonses against 17 Western oil companies it was suing for nearly $6.4 billion in damages for allegedly supplying Rhodesia with oil in defiance of United Nation sanctions and to the detriment of Zambia. President Kenneth Kaunda pointed out that "the time has come for the oil companies to choose between Ian Smith and cooperation with Africa."[52] Kaunda's logic was that the continued oil supply to Rhodesia had prolonged the Smith regime's stay in power and severly damaged the Zambian economy. The Zambian government's legal action was reportedly based on information supplied by Lonrho. Along with Zambia, the Nigerian government also took a strong stand on sanction-busting, threatening in the spring of 1977 to freeze the assets of Shell and BP for continuing to supply Rhodesia. In October of 1977, Lt. Gen. Olusegun Obasanjo, Nigeria's head of state, in a dinner speech to businessmen in New York, warned "we are . . . screening all foreign contractors and business firms with a view to discriminating against all those who have business relations with Rhodesia and South Africa. . . . Such business firms are however free to discontinue this relationship or at the least do nothing to expand it, if they feel their bread is better buttered on our side. Investors and businessmen are hardheaded calculators and I will leave you to decide and choose between doing business with us or with the racist regimes in Southern Africa."[53] The Nigerian government's first major action came in August 1979 when it nationalized British Petroleum's remaining oil interests in the country in retaliation against the British practice of "exporting North Sea oil to the 'apartheid regime' in South Africa and replacing it with oil imported from Nigeria."[54]

The Zambian, Nigerian, and Lonrho actions were interpreted by some observers as a call for a ban by the parent multinational oil companies on supplies to their South African subsidiaries. A committee of the UN Security Council, after months of deliberations, issued an interim report in November 1977 recommending legal action against oil companies whose subsidiaries continued to defy United Nation sanctions by providing oil to Rhodesia. The report also recommended that the arms embargo against South Africa be expanded to include an oil embargo.[55]

In the spring of 1978, the United Church Board for World Ministries and other religious organizations filed shareholder resulutions with Mobil, Texaco, and Standard Oil of California on the Rhodesian oil supply issue. The Mobil and Standard Oil proposals asked for the establishment of policy that the volume of oil shipments into South Africa be reduced by at least one-third in order to insure full compliance with the spirit of the United Nations and United States ban on sales to Rhodesia.[56] Mobil's management came out solidly against the shareholder resolution, which received a vote of 3.25%. The same resolution was filed with the three oil companies again in 1979 following issuance of the British Bingham report which fully implicated all three.

Olin and South African Weapons Shipments

Along with Rhodesia, sanctions-busting has also been at issue in the case of South Africa. American weapons producers were supposedly sidelined by President Kennedy's 1963 conversion of the voluntary United Nation embargo into a mandatory one for American firms. With the United States out of the picture, however, producers from France and Israel quickly and actively filled the void. The United Nations resolution was also undercut to a lesser extent by Italian and German producers, whose governments' enforcement of sanctions appeared to be weak. And in 1976 it became known that American arms manufacturers had also been unable to resist temptation. United States export controls were being circumvented both by transshipment through "third country" outlets and sales by subsidiaries or licensees abroad. Colt Industries announced that it had illegally shipped certain arms and ammunition through "third country" channels to South Africa—but that the sales were conducted by employees against corporate policy and without the knowledge of senior management. A former Colt export manager was sentenced to a year in prison after pleading guilty to illegal arms sales, and asserted that other armaments producers regularly transshipped munitions to South Africa while the American government generally "acquiesced" in these transactions.[57]

In March 1978, following an 18-month investigation, a Federal Grand Jury handed up a 21-count felony indictment charging Olin Corporation with violating the United States embargo in effect since 1963. It accused Olin, through its Winchester International firearms unit, of falsifying records to hide shipments of 21,000 rifles and 20 million rounds of ammunition to South Africa from 1971 through mid-1975.[58] Olin conceded that such shipments had indeed been made—through arms dealers in Mozambique, Spain, Greece, and Austria—but like Colt insisted that the sales were made by a few junior level employees without the knowledge of top management.

With religious group shareholders demanding disclosure, other shareholders filing suit for civil damages, and black workers angry at the Winchester division, Olin opted for "getting it over with" as quickly as possible. Over the strenuous objections of the prosecuting attorney, on March 21, 1978, Olin pleaded "nolo contendere," and this was accepted by the Federal judge, who noted that this was tantamount to an admission of guilt. Olin thus faced a maximum fine of $510,000 on all 21 counts of the indictment. Nine days later, the judge ordered Olin to pay the $510,000—not to the U.S. Treasury, as was customary, but to charity programs in New Haven, Connecticut, as "reparations" for the company's illegal arm sales. "A financial fine is not enough," said the judge, for "these violations could reflect on the credibility of the United States in the eyes of the world."[59] In effect, for allegedly assisting in the denial of political and civil rights in South Africa, Olin was sentenced to assist in the meeting of economic and social needs of disadvantaged blacks in the United States. This did not sit well with 20 local civil rights groups who proposed that the charity instead be used to aid black South Africans as the aggrieved parties in the illegal arms sales.

BUYING FROM REPRESSIVE NATIONS

Consider the plight of the American or European who enjoys sardines for lunch, tries to hedge against inflation by buying gold coins, and buys electricity from utilities in Florida using low-sulfur coal. If the sardines are the protein-rich Pilchard variety harvested in Namibian waters, canned in Namibia and merchandised by Del Monte in the United States, then the Namibia Action Group asserts that this person has been indirectly causing malnutrition in Namibia, eating stolen property, bolstering a contract labor system, and legitimizing South Africa's illegal occupation of Namibia.[60] If the gold coins are South African Krugerrand sold by brokerage houses and coin dealers, then according to the American Committee on Africa he has been "buying the blood of black miners" and strengthening the Apartheid system in South Africa. If the low sulfur coal being burned by utilities is supplied by the Southern Company from stocks imported from South Africa, then in the view of a number of religious groups, this person has been giving "a clear sign of support and approval for the racist South African government as it continues its repression of Black opponents to apartheid."[61] The list goes on and on from Chilean wines, Argentine or Uruguayan beef, Brazilian leather goods, and Philippine sugar to Russian vodka, Polish ham, Angolan oil, and Israeli orange juice. Whether the issue comes up depends on the existence of human-rights pressure groups interested in the country involved.

The human rights movement rarely accuses the consumers of sin. Instead, it is the companies involved that are the targets of protest. To illustrate, we shall review the campaigns against Ugandan coffee and the South African Krugerrand. The Krugerrand initiative was targeted at the grassroots level and had some success in reducing promotion but apparently not sales of the coin among very inflation-conscious buyers. The Ugandan coffee campaign raised the profile of the human rights question in the United States to new and controversial levels in 1977–1978, culminating in the trade embargo of 1978 which lasted until the Amin regime was overthrown in 1979.

The Ugandan Coffee Connection

For the first time in history, a serious movement to legislate economic sanctions against a non-belligerent state was initiated in both houses of Congress. The Ugandan coffee case raised the issue of deviating from international trade commitments for political reasons. The willingness of a considerable number of U.S. Congressmen to boycott Ugandan coffee indicates that when it comes to human rights, long-standing trade commitments are not viewed as sacronsact and inviolable. In the new era, international economic policy and politics are not largely on separate "tracks" but are frequently inseparable—especially when the stakes involved are low, for unlike the Rhodesian chrome case the Ugandan action could be considered a virtually painless "cheap shot." As one author has noted, "virtue that is costless is scarcely distinguishable from opportunism."[62]

Richard H. Ullman noted in *Foreign Affairs* in 1978 that "in any contemporary lexicon of horror, Uganda is synonymous with state-become-slaughterhouse. The most conservative estimates by informed observers hold that President Idi Amin Dada and the terror squads operating under his loose direction have killed 100,000 Ugandans in the seven years he has held power. Some estimates run as high as 300,000."[63] In Amin's reign of terror "every precept in the human rights canon has been violated, every appeal for moderation ignored,"[64] and according to President Carter, the allegedly wholesale violence in Uganda "disgusted the entire civilized world."[65] Most members of the United Nations and Organization of African Unity, however, remained silent. Western governments ended technical and financial aid and withdrew diplomatic representatives in the mid-1970s, and in 1977 a movement arose to go further and cut all remaining commercial ties linking Uganda with the United States.

Revelations about the commercial "Ugandan Connection" involving American companies indicated, for example, that Textron's Bell Helicopter division was training Ugandan police in Texas, Page Airways was selling Amin jet aircraft, Harris Corporation was providing a satellite communication system and various United States charter airlines were keeping Uganda's planes airborne or flying for Uganda under contract. [66] The most important connection, however, was with coffee dealers. During 1977 Uganda earned some $750 million for its green coffee exports, reaping considerable benefit from the rise in world coffee prices brought about by frosts in Brazil. The coffee, as Uganda's only export of significance, accounted for over 90% of Uganda's foreign exchange. One-third (the cheaper *robusta* type used for instant coffee) was imported by the United States, another one-fifth by the United Kingdom, and virtually all of the rest by West Germany, France, Italy, Japan, and the Netherlands. Ugandan supplies amounted to about 5–6% of American coffee imports in 1977, worth about $300 million.

According to one observer describing the situation in 1978, "Uganda's coffee is grown almost entirely by peasant smallholders, not on plantations. Growers are required to sell their beans to the state marketing board, and are paid, at a price set by the board, in vouchers redeemable only in nearly worthless Ugandan shillings. Sometimes they are not even paid at all. Their crop is simply seized. Thus Amin's regime, and not the growers, receives all the foreign exchange. Amin uses it to pay off loans from Libya and other Arab countries, to buy weapons (mostly from the Soviet Union), and to supply his army, police and civil service with luxury goods. The latter are particularly important to his hold on power: Amin uses lavish material rewards to purchase loyalty. Thus there is a direct relationship between foreign purchases of Uganda's coffee and Amin's murderous regime."[67]

To service the American market, six people were employed by the Ugandan Coffee Marketing Board in New York—33 major United States coffee companies and lesser known coffee distributors purchased more than 242 million pounds of Ugandan coffee in 1975–1976. The "big five" were the Folger Coffee Company (a subsidiary of Procter & Gamble) with 53.8 million lbs., General Foods (Maxwell House) with 45.7 million lbs., Saks International with 21.8 million lbs., ACLI Sugar Company with 21.3 million lbs., and Nestlé with 20.5 million lbs.[68] One of the first calls for a boycott of Ugandan coffee came from Franklin H. Williams, President of the Phelps Stokes Fund, which operates programs that aid education in Africa and the United States. In August of 1977 he called for "a flood of protest letters from consumer groups, human rights organizations, and individuals to the largest corporate purchasers of Ugandan coffee, declaring a boycott of their products unless they cease that practice . . . ."[69] In September, 76 Congressmen introduced legislation to cut off all American trade with Uganda. The legislative package had three parts: (1) a bill to prohibit the importation of any Ugandan products into the United States, (2) a bill to amend the Export Administration Act of 1969 to prohibit the exporting of American goods to Uganda, and (3) a bill to amend the International Coffee Agreement Act of 1968 to establish a ban on Ugandan coffee imports into the United States.[70] The logic was not to reform Amin, since he was viewed as beyond redemption, but to destroy him. In the words of one Congressman: "At the very least, a trade ban will serve to put distance between our nation and Amin's reign of terror. At best, a trade ban will hasten Amin's downfall and raise the prospects of a better day in the country once known as 'the Pearl of Africa'."[71]

American coffee companies naturally began to get nervous. In November 1977 the President of Maxwell House met State Department officials in Washington and urged the government to provide clarification of United States policy. "He was firmly rebuffed and told that it was the responsibility of each individual company to make up its own mind about whether or not it should buy Ugandan coffee."[72] Shortly thereafter the President of the National Coffee Association, representing the entire domestic industry, wrote to Secretary of State Vance and Congressman Don J. Pease—the leading advocate of trade sanctions—stating that "the violations of human rights occurring under the government of President Idi Amin are abhorrent and morally repugnant and have caused pressures on members of the association to desist from purchasing Ugandan coffee."[73] Rather than respond firm by firm—which would pose a risk to some coffee traders of losing sales through having their prices undercut by others who might refuse to join the embargo— and rather than risk being charged with antitrust violations for collusion in a privately-organized boycott, the Association asked the Administration and Congress "to declare and implement a uniform national policy" that would bind the entire industry.[74] Spokesmen for Folger and General Foods said they would comply with any government ban on Ugandan coffee. A Nestlé spokesman warned that a ban would "strengthen the hand" of Latin American nations that had jacked up coffee prices.[75]

In the winter of 1977–1978 strong opposition arose to the Congressional initiative revolving around "whether or not the richest and most powerful of sovereign states is justified in using its economic power unilaterally to force the government of a smaller and weaker state to alter the way it treats its own subjects."[76] The Carter Administration said it was opposed to a unilateral American embargo of Ugandan coffee, giving as reasons the dubious effectiveness of sanctions, noninterference in international trade, security of American missionaries in Uganda, and the possibility that Amin would try to exploit the boycott to his own advantage. Black U.S. Congressmen began to see a "double standard" at work, as white liberals were espousing "the cause of an embargo against Uganda, where the United States has few economic or strategic interests, without linking it to similar sanctions against South Africa, where those interests are manifestly entrenched."[77] Conservatives and businessmen began to grow worried about the concept of using trade as a political lever and the possibility that the Ugandan action might open the floodgates to other trade bans, with South Africa the next likely target—a boycott would set "a dangerous precedent for more of the same political manipulation of international trade in less egregious cases."[78]

But the opponents of the boycott were caught protesting against "motherhood" —what answers could possibly be given to Congressman Pease's question: "Are American coffee companies prepared to do business with a genocidist like Amin or Hitler if the price is right?"[79] In mid-1978 the House International Relations Committee recommended a trade embargo against Uganda, but refused to propose binding legislation. Shortly thereafter, the Folger Coffee Company, General Foods, and the American division of Nestlé stopped buying Ugandan beans. In July the trade embargo was passed by Congress. A year later, Amin had been thrown out by an invasion from Tanzania, national reconstruction had begun, and the boycott had been lifted.

The Krugerrand Campaign

One of the liveliest anti-import conflicts related to human rights has centered on sales of South African Krugerrand in the United States. The Krugerrand is the most popular gold coin in the world and contains exactly one ounce of gold, its value determined by the world gold price. The coins are legal tender in South Africa, but are mostly sold overseas, particularly in the United States to customers who are looking for a convenient way to hold gold. According to the International Gold Corporation, the New York-based marketing arm of South African gold producers, about 3.3 million Krugerrand were sold worldwide in 1977, up from three million the year before.[80] Demand is fostered through mass-media advertising, with $4 to $7 million reportedly spent to promote sales during the fall of 1977 in the United States alone. Advertising themes include "the world's best way to own gold" and "a hedge against inflation or the devaluation of paper money."

Starting in the mid-1970s a number of anti-apartheid groups, including the American Committee on Africa, began a campaign to halt American sales of the coin, which they consider a "symbol of apartheid." The logic of the protest was explained as follows: "Buying the Krugerrand is like buying the blood of black miners in South Africa. . . . Essentially it's providing critical foreign exchange by which South Africa is able to buy arms and anything else it needs to keep its system going."[81] Working with local groups across the nation, the organization provided anti-Krugerrand literature and helped organize protest actions. Targets included coin dealers, department stores, banks, brokerage houses, newspapers, and television stations. Tactics during 1977 included demonstrations, petitions, counter-advertising, picketing, and letter-writing.

One of the principal targets was Merrill Lynch, the nation's largest brokerage house, whose offices in half a dozen American cities were picketed in 1977 by protestors. In Los Angeles, "a young black woman laid in a coffin outside a Merrill Lynch office while her associates paraded back and forth, chanting and dropping gold coins into the coffin."[82] In January of 1978 Merrill Lynch halted sales of the gold coins, insisting that the decision "was a business judgement we made based on the demand for coins. Demand for gold coins didn't meet our earlier expectations."[83]

In October 1977, demonstrators from the Steven Biko Memorial Committee, Boston Coalition for the Liberation of Southern Africa, and other groups sharply questioned a panel of industry executives about Krugerrand television ads during a National Association of Broadcasters meeting in Boston. A week later the three major United States television networks' flagship stations in New York notified the Doyle Dane Bernbach advertising agency that they would not, for the time being, accept commercials for the coin.[84] Local protests also caused television stations in Chicago and Boston to discontinue Krugerrand advertising.

Local efforts caused the city councils of Dayton, Denver, San Antonio, Portland, and Chicago to pass resolutions opposing sales of the Krugerrand. Among banks, Continental Illinois discontinued selling them and First National of Chicago stopped promoting them. After some very noisy demonstrations, such department stores as Abraham & Strauss (Brooklyn), Mays (Cleveland), and Carson Pirie & Scott (Chicago) stopped sales in 1977. A Carson official declared: "From a merchandising point of view, we decided it wasn't worth it and bowed out."[85] Some newspapers rejected ads for the coins, with one publisher stating: "I'll be damned if I will let my pocketbook dictate to my conscience."[86] Still, in 1977–1978 it appeared that many Americans, especially small investors, were more concerned about hedging against inflation than opposing apartheid in South Africa. Despite the protests, 1977 Christmas sales of the Krugerrand in the United States reached record levels. In 1978 and 1979 investors were buying up gold coins at a brisk pace. To meet the rising demand, South Africa doubled output so that coins were accounting for 30% of its gold production.[87] With the gold coin business booming and the Krugerrand under pressure, the Engelhard Minerals and Chemicals Corporation entered the market with its own coin, called the American Gold Prospector, with an advertising campign stressing its "American origins."[88]

SELLING TO REPRESSIVE NATIONS

In the controversy over multinationals and human rights there is probably no allegation more emotionally explosive or worthy of damnation in the eyes of critics than multinationals' selling and supplying the "means of repression" abroad. After an ostensibly objective review of evidence, the Institute for Policy Studies concluded that United States agencies and firms in the fields of weaponry and computers "are deeply involved in the supply of repressive technology and techniques to many of the world's most authoritarian regimes. . . . Corporations are providing arms, equipment, training, and technical support to the police and paramilitary forces most directly involved in torture, assassination, and incarceration of civilian dissidents."[89]

This view holds that by standing at the supply end of a pipeline of technology flowing to the internal security forces of such countries as Argentina, Brazil, Chile, Ethiopia, Indonesia, Iran, Uruguay, the Philippines, South Korea, and Thailand, American producers "have become the western world's principal merchants of repression."[90]

Multinationals generally respond to this sort of indictment with a number of different arguments. One is that they cannot be held responsible for the ultimate use to which their products are put. And to the best of their knowledge, the products are being used for legitimate purposes. Moreover, it is unfair to single out particular products like computers for attack, since virtually every kind of product can conceivably be put to repressive uses. Too, there is a legitimate need for police and antiterrorist activity which has little or nothing whatever to do with human rights, yet the equipment needed is the same. American producers typically argue that if they refused to sell the products or technology, then companies from other countries would, and that their sales do not violate United States law and comply fully with governmental regulations and licensing requirements—even direct supply to the internal security forces of politically-allied foreign governments is in accordance with home government foreign policy. Such sales are justified by the governments of France, Britain, and West Germany as well as the United States as being essential to the protection of national security interests, survival of the existing alliance system, and benefiting the balance of payments particularly in an era of costly oil imports. If indeed human rights are to be added as another vital interest built into foreign policy, then it should be the job of governments, and not private firms, to make the tradeoffs involved and set any limits needed. Critics should thus pursue their concerns through standard political channels and not directly with the firms involved.

Criticism of the relationship between arms producers and governments and the propriety of supplying weapons to developing countries, repressive regimes, and potential war zones is not something new. During the Vietnam war for example, Honeywell came under heavy pressure from the peace movement for its production of antipersonnel weapons and Dow Chemical for its manufacture of napalm. From 1968 to 1972 the two firms were the target of many marches, rallies, boycotts, picketing, and several hundred university demonstrations against their campus recruiting and corporate policies. In the mid-1970s, religious groups began to focus closely on the "commerce of death."[91] These groups campaigned to stop production of the B-1 Bomber, with General Electric, Boeing, and Rockwell International the targets of protest and shareholder resolutions. Strong pressures against manufacture and export of arms have also grown in Europe—Sweden was the first nation to pass legislation prohibiting arms deliveries to countries "where human rights are being systematically repressed."[92]

On human rights grounds the agitation has not in most cases been focused on supply of weapons, tanks, fighter aircraft, and warships that are intended and mainly suitable to help countries defend themselves against external attack. The real protest has centered on counterinsurgency gear or other items designed primarily for internal uprisings or suppression of dissident groups. These include riot control gas, pistols and revolvers, ammunition, cannisters of MACE, armored cars, counterinsurgency planes, helicopters, riot guns, "Shock-Batons," patrol cars, trucks, radios, electronic surveillance systems, data processing equipment, and so on. Customers have included the secret police forces of countries like Chile and Iran and a good deal has evidently been sold indirectly through government-to-government sales programs such as the Military Assistance Program of the U.S. Department of Defense, International Narcotics Control Program of the U.S. State Department, and the now disbanded Public Safety Program of the U.S. Agency for International Development.[93] Increasingly, however, American producers have dealt directly with foreign buyers under the commercial sales program of the United States government.

The focus of protest action is not limited to hardware provided by such firms as Rockwell, Fairchild, Cadillac Gage (a subsidiary of Ex-Cell-O), Smith & Wesson, Colt Industries, Federal Laboratories, High Standard, Remington Arms, Winchester International, Cessna, Ford Motor, Textron, General Electric, Northrop, IBM, Control Data, and the like. It is also on the so-called "white collar mercenary" training, managerial and technological assistance, and other "military technical services" provided to foreign governments. Examples here include the Vinnell Corporation providing $77 million worth of training and technical assistance to the Saudi Arabian National Guard, Bell Helicopter training Amin's Ugandan pilots in Forth Worth or helping to develop the Shah's now defunct Iranian Sky Cavalry Brigade, Computer Sciences Corporation providing training to South Vietnamese police technicians in various data processing operations, Federal Laboratories conducting chemical weapons and riot control seminars for foreign law enforcement personnel, and Colt Industries building M-16 rifle factories in South Korea and the Philippines.[94]

Foreign Military Sales Disclosure

In December 1977 the American Committee on Africa protested to President Carter against the planned sale of six civilian Cessna aircraft to South Africa, objecting that the planes ordered for use in crop-dusting could also be used by volunteer paramilitary air commandos in counterinsurgency surveillance operations against black nationalist forces opposing the white minority government.[95]

Such protests against specific export sales by human rights groups have been relatively rare. The main actions in the arms field have instead been aimed at forcing disclosure and modifying general corporate policies. For instance, an assortment of Protestant and Catholic religious groups filed shareholder resolutions in 1977 with Ford, General Electric, Northrop, and Textron. Asserting that "the international arms trade is out of control," and worried about "the possibility of company personnel being involved in support of the aggressive or repressive activities of foreign governments," the groups asked the four firms to disclose a range of information on their foreign military sales. They also asked each for "a description of the social, ethical and political criteria which the corporation has used to determine whether to accept or refuse specific requests for foreign military equipment."[96]

General Electric, in its proxy-statement response to the resolution, announced the existence of a top-level corporate policy committee which had "established review procedures and internal decision authority on proposed contracts for the export of military equipment." Based on that response the Episcopal Church and two other religious groups filed another shareholder resolution in 1978 asking the GE committee to: "(1) evaluate the human rights situation in any country with which a contract is contemplated, reviewing available information from public and private sources; (2) establish criteria below which a country cannot fall and still remain a General Electric customer; (3) decline any sale to a country which does not meet these minimal standards; and (4) communicate to shareholders the criteria established and publish annually a list of the countries with which military sales/servicing agreements are in effect."[97] In 1978 religious groups also re-filed with Northrop and Textron the same sales disclosure resolution made the year before, since at the 1977 annual meetings the shareholder votes had been 3.8% and 14.5% respectively.

Computers and Human Rights

The use of photographic, electronic, and data processing equipment for repressive purposes has long been a major theme of anti-apartheid groups. We have already noted how, in 1971, Polaroid Corporation was pressured into establishing a policy prohibiting sales to the South African government. In 1977, when it discovered that its Johannesburg distributor had secretly violated the prohibition and allowed Polaroid products to be used in the government's program of enforcing Apartheid, Polaroid had no choice but to cut off all shipments. This motivated ten religious and academic organizations to file a resolution with Eastman Kodak in 1978 and again in 1979 asking the company to ban the sale of all photographic equipment to the South African government in order "to eliminate any possibility that our company's photographic products might be used, even inadvertently, to assist in the repression of South Africa's black population."[98] ITT was persuaded in 1976 by the United Presbyterian Church U.S.A. and other groups to make the precedent-setting announcement that it would no longer seek contracts with the South African military or police. Based on this model, religious groups submitted a resolution to Motorola in 1978 asking the company, among other things, to "terminate at once" all sales of radios and electronic equipment that might be used to repress black citizens. Other examples involving such firms as Ford Motor, Fluor, Caterpillar Tractor and GM could be listed. But perhaps the most interesting questions center on the human rights concern related to computer sales to South Africa, the Soviet Union, and Latin America.

IBM and South Africa

In 1972 and again in 1973, IBM was one of the companies chosen by the "Church Project on Investments in Southern Africa," an ecumenical coalition, in its efforts to learn about the role of American companies in that area.[99] The investigation indicated that IBM computers were being used by South Africa's Department of Defence, Council for Scientific and Industrial Research, National Airways, Department of Prisons, major communication networks, and the Department of Interior's "book of life project"—that is, the system of compulsory identification documents used for social control.[100] In the early 1970s IBM executives argued consistently that their equipment was not being used for harmful purposes by the military.

In November of 1974 a two-day open hearing concerning IBM's activities in South Africa was held in New York under the auspices of the National Council of Churches. Representatives from a number of organizations gave testimony, including the company itself. According to one observer present at the hearing, "Few participants questioned IBM's employment and labor practices in South Africa. However, many panelists saw a serious issue in IBM's sale of computer products to the South African government, because these might easily be used for repressive and military purposes."[101] IBM spokesmen stressed the company's compliance with United States law and positive contributions to the welfare of South African employees.

As a result of the hearing fourteen Protestant and Catholic groups filed a shareholder resolution with IBM in 1975 requesting the company to stop sales and service of computers to the South African government. The resolution drew considerable press notice and attracted the support of prominent black Americans and U.S. Congressmen. IBM formally opposed the resolution, saying that it "would be tantamount to proposing IBM withdraw from that country."[102] At the 1975 annual meeting a church spokesman charged that "computers enable the South African government to maintain and even perfect apartheid." Chairman Frank T. Cary's response was that IBM was opposed to apartheid, that the company did not believe the system was supported by computers, that it was setting a constructive example in South Africa, and that the establishment of criteria for determining sales with the government would not change apartheid.[103] The resolution drew only 1.7% of the shareholder's votes.

The pressure on IBM continued nevertheless. In the Fall of 1975 an article appeared in a church publication commending IBM's concerns about the use of its products and potential invasions of privacy in the United States, but charged that "unfortunately, IBM's sensitivity to the social implications of its products seems to stop at the water's edge."[104] In early 1976, fifteen religious groups submitted a shareholder resolution to IBM asking the company to disclose the nature of its computer, sales to the South African government, and to disclose the potential use of products to strengthen control over the black majority, to build military strength or capability, and to expand police functions. The vote for the resolution at the annual meeting was 2.2%.

In September of 1976, IBM's vice-chairman told the Senate Foreign Relations Subcommittee on African Affairs that he recognized that IBM products could be used in ways inimical to individuals and society, but that this had not been the case in South Africa. IBM had been scrupulous in monitoring the end-use of its products and was satisfied that they had not been used in ways inimical to respect for human dignity. He stressed that no IBM computers sold to the South African government were being used for security functions or military purposes, and denied that IBM's involvement with the passbook or "Book of Life" project contributed to the oppression of people who have to carry them. He stated that IBM did not use moral criteria in its business transactions, but acknowledged that in transactions with any government there is a risk that a computer may be used in ways which IBM might not approve.[105]

At the 1977 annual stockholders' meeting of IBM, Chairman Cary, in answer to a question about the use of computers "in facilitating repression," stated: "We would not bid any business where we believe that our products are going to be used to abridge human rights." He went on to say that the company had investigated each instance brought to its attention where there was any reason to believe that IBM computers might be used for repressive purposes and found no such use.[106] Church groups rejoiced that a very significant change had evidently been made in IBM's thinking—after five years of discussion the company had "publicly accepted moral responsibility" for the use of which its customers put their computers. Control Data Corporation had earlier announced that its own sense of responsibility would not permit it "to provide a computer system for any purpose that abridges human rights and dignity." Burroughs later announced that it would "direct its employees against knowingly selling its equipment for use for repressive purposes."[107]

South Africa is not the only situation in which computer companies have encountered criticism on human rights grounds. Another is the Soviet Union, where computer technology is allegedly being used for social control purposes and rumors persist that the KGB (secret police) has sophisticated data banks to keep track of dissidents and others—Aleksandr Solzhenitsyn urged the United States to stop providing the Soviets with technology that could easily be used by the KGB to implement subjugation of political dissidents.[108] Although the export control process for computers to Communist countries by the Office of Export Administration of the Commerce Department is somewhat clouded on the matter, until 1978 it appeared that no American exports to Communist nations had been denied because of human rights concerns. They have, of course, been blocked on grounds of potential military applications.[109]

In 1975 IBM filed an application to sell a 370/158 computer to Intourist, the official Soviet tourist agency. In October of that year a conservative group, Young Americans for Freedom (YAF), picketed IBM installations and urged Commerce to deny the application. According to the YAF, the system might be diverted for use to keep track of political dissidents, intellectuals, writers, persecuted minorities, and even Western tourists and news reporters. In August 1976, Commerce approved a license for IBM to sell a $4.95 million computer system to Intourist, but did not approve the model 370/158 as requested. Instead Commerce told IBM it could only export its model 370/145, with one-sixth the speed and one-fourth the memory of the 158. The more powerful computer, in the view of the Export Administration Office, would have run the risk of diversion to unauthorized uses.[110]

In the early 1970s, the Socialist countries of Eastern Europe were viewed by western computer companies as the next—perhaps last—of the great growth markets. Control Data Corporation (CDC) was one company with ambitious marketing ideas for the area, and as recently as June of 1976 one of its executives told a House Subcommittee that an $8 to $10 billion market opportunity awaited American companies over the next ten years, which by 1985 could produce export sales in excess of $2 billion per year and 100,000 additional jobs at home.[111] CDC, however, became involved in some rather heated debates on the issue, particularly the proposal to sell two computers, a Cyber/76 and a Cyber/12, to the Russians. With national security interests at stake and the United States government balking, CDC's president was quoted as saying: "Our biggest problem isn't the Soviets, it's the damn Defense Department."[112] In mid-1978, Sperry Rand became one of the first computer firms to be denied an export permit specifically on human rights grounds—involving a Univac system for use in coverage of the 1980 Moscow Olympics—in retaliation for the conviction of Soviet dissidents (the denial was eventually reversed, see Chapter 7). With human rights considerations now being added to national security concerns, it appears that the export problems of computer companies are only now really beginning and United States export policies are likely to become more restrictive, more ambiguous and more erratic in their application.

Latin America has also been an area for conflict on computers and human rights. A 1977 article in the reputable trade journal *Computer Decisions* was entitled "Would You Sell a Computer to Hitler?," with a subtitle "Latin American dictatorships are using computers as tools of repression. It appears that American equipment makes it possible to automate 'the final solution'."[113] It charged that security agencies in some Latin American countries were using computers to keep track of dissidents and to pinpoint individuals for arrest, interrogation, and possibly even assassination. Chile's secret police force was reported to possess American computer hardware, as were the police forces in Argentina, Brazil, and Uruguay. Evidence was also provided that the four nations had linked up their systems with each other in order to permit instantaneous exchange of data on terrorist and dissident activities across national boundaries.

The same issue had previously been raised with IBM by the National Council of Churches. In April of 1975 NCC representatives at IBM's annual meeting had tried to convince the company to halt its planned installation of a 370/145 computer at the University of Chile in Santiago, claiming that it would be used by the police and not the University. IBM Chairman Cary responded that "we don't think the installation of a computer on the campus of the University of Chile has any sinister implications at all."[114] IBM subsequently initiated an investigation and found that the computer was being used for payroll purposes, processing student aptitude tests, enrollment statistics and college applications, and to the best of its knowledge, "no other applications."

A few weeks after the *Computer Decisions* article was published, however, the State Department declared its intention to develop policy that would lead to control over the way American computers are used abroad: "In cases where there is reason to believe the computer could be used in the suppression of human rights, the State Department will recommend denial of the export license."[115] It apparently did so in the case of a Rockwell International computer ordered by the Chilean government in the winter of 1977. And from the floor of the Senate in February 1977 Senator Edward Kennedy called for an inquiry into the way the United States had allegedly allowed its computers to be misused by dictators.

In March of 1977 *Computer Decisions* reproduced a section of an IBM report disclosing that the police of Rio de Janeiro were apparently planning to order two IBM computers which would be used for, among other things, storing files on "political activists."[116] IBM admitted, following publication of the document, that it was authentic, but stated that the system was never ordered. It did not say whether Brazilian police had other, similar systems.[117] With the momentum rolling, 19 religious groups filed a resolution with IBM in 1978 requesting the Board of Directors to undertake the following steps: (1) Initiate an investigation into the use of IBM computers in Argentina, Brazil, Chile and Uruguay to assess whether these computers are being used in any way that aids police repression or abridges human rights. (2) Develop criteria for the sale, leasing and maintenance of IBM computers to minimize their possible use for repressive purposes in countries where civil liberties and human rights have no adequate constitutional protection. (3) Develop a program of implementation to insure that the criteria are being followed. This should include follow-up steps if IBM products and/or services are being misused. Options to be examined should include the cessation of service and maintenance of computers. The results of the investigation, the development of criteria and implementation of the plan were to be reported back to the shareholders.[118] Only 2.12% of the company's shareholders voted in favor of the resolution.

COLLABORATING WITH "ILLEGAL" GOVERNMENTS

Analogous to "collaborating with the enemy" during wartime, numerous multinationals have found themselves emeshed in conflicts because of their involvement in "illegally or colonially occupied and repressively administered territories." The illegal regimes in question have been those exercising authority in Zimbabwe-Rhodesia and Namibia (South-West Africa). The colonial regimes in recent times were those of the Portuguese in Angola, Mozambique, and Guinea (Bissau). Cuba has initiated action in the United Nations to have Puerto Rico put in the same category. "Collaboration" with illegal regimes, in the view of the United Nations, has been interpreted as covering "any observance of laws and regulations passed by the illegal regimes; the violation of United Nations sanctions; the payment of taxes or royalties; the supply of arms to the illegal regimes or conducting public relations activities on their behalf; establishing joint ventures with the illegal authorities and supplying them with technology; or undertaking any activities that facilitate the survival of the illegal regimes and their maintenance in power."[119] A similar conception has existed in regard to multinationals aiding or abetting colonial regimes.

Conflicts over "collaboration" have usually triggered considerable controversy, confusion, and political perils for multinationals, which have often found themselves on rather shaky legal ground. They have generally attracted a wide range of international participants, spectators, and kibitzers. Firms have sometimes been in direct contravention of home-government policies and international-organization resolutions. They have also been pressed between the incompatible demands of the authorities in *de facto* control of particular territories and those with *de jure* standing. In some cases, they have been forced to go beyond the normal purview of private companies and choose among political claimants to the contested arena. And so private diplomacy conducted simultaneously with numerous parties has often been unavoidable. Fearing nationalization of industry and expropriation of property when liberation governments come into power, some firms in extractive industries have chosen to extract and stockpile minerals at a prodigious rate during the period before independence. But most multinationals have attempted to avoid, or withdraw from, high-risk political situations involving illegal or colonial occupation. Only those with a great deal to lose, illustrated by the Gulf Oil Angola and Newmont Mining Namibia cases examined below, have chosen the perilous route of hanging on in the face of prolonged and widespread protest.

Gulf Oil and Angola

The involvement of multinationals in the last important vestiges of European colonialism in Africa was an issue that attracted considerable attention on human rights grounds in the 1960s and early 1970s. Much of it was focused on Portuguese colonialism in Angola, Mozambique, and Guinea (Bissau), where African guerrilla groups had begun fighting anticolonial wars in the early 1960s. When African nationalists moved militarily in Angola during 1961, for example, Portugal responded by sending in 50,000 troops in an attempt to crush the movement. Tens of thousands of Angolans fled the country and the UN General Assembly warned Portugal in a 1962 resolution to cease its activities. Portugal ignored the resolution and instead chose throughout the 1960s to apply heavy force to the escalating independence struggle. More than any other, one multinational, Gulf Oil, came under a great deal of criticism for its "support" of the colonial regime in Angola.

Gulf had begun exploration in 1954 in Cabinda, a small enclave separated from Angola by a sliver of Zaïre, and received its first drilling concession from Portugal in 1957. In 1961 the company was forced to suspend operations when insurgents successfully captured 90% of the enclave, but it returned after Portugal retook the area. Gulf struck oil in 1966 and began production in 1968. By 1970 the company had invested more than $150 million in the project, and in 1971 it achieved its production goal of 150,000 barrels of oil per day. Gulf executives saw the operation as "one of the major growth areas of the Corporation."[120] Indeed, by 1973 its investment had risen to $210 million and Angolan oil accounted for 6% of Gulf's profits and from 8% to 10% of the company's sales, world production, and proven reserves.[121]

In the late 1960s and early 1970s Gulf's involvement in Angola became the target of severe protest from such groups as the Committee of Returned Volunteers, Gulf Boycott Coalition, Center for Social Action of the United Church of Christ, Interfaith Center on Corporate Responsibility, American Committee on Africa, Pan-African Liberation Committee, Toronto Committee for the Liberation of Portugal's African Colonies, London Committee for Freedom in Mozambique, Angola and Guinea, and the United Nations. Gulf was charged with aiding colonialism by providing Portugal with: (1) tax and royalty payments since 1954, (2) foreign exchange contributing to financial stability and war-related purchases, (3) a strategic resource helping to make Portugal safe from economic sanctions and oil embargoes, (4) a contractual relationship that indirectly influenced United States policy toward support for Portugal's African wars, and (5) a positive image of Portuguese colonialism in America.[122] Gulf generally responded to such charges by claiming that it was politically neutral and was contributing to economic development in Angola.

In the Fall of 1969 a number of religious and political groups organized the core of an educational campaign on the role of American corporations in supporting colonial rule in Southern Africa. At Gulf's 1970 stockholders' meeting a group of prominent citizens called for Gulf to withdraw from Angola. In June 1970 the Ohio Conference of the United Church of Christ passed a resolution opposing Gulf's support of Portuguese colonialism and asked its members to turn in their credit cards and cease buying Gulf products. The company responded by threatening a lawsuit against the church body, but the Conference reaffirmed its stand and was joined by the Council for Christian Social Action of the United Church of Christ. In 1971, the Southern Africa Task Force of the United Presbyterian Church filed a shareholder resolution requesting Gulf "to cease operations in colonially held territories." Later that year the Gulf Boycott Coalition was formed in Dayton, Ohio, and succeeded in getting that city to cancel its gasoline contract with Gulf for city vehicles, even though Gulf was the low bidder.[123]

In early 1972, black students at Harvard University took over the administration building and demanded that Harvard divest itself of Gulf stock because of the company's role in Angola. The university responded by sending an official to Angola to inspect Gulf's installation, and on his return wrote a report favorable to Gulf—the university did not divest its stock.[124] In April 1972 the Council for Christian Social Action of the United Church of Christ filed a shareholder resolution seeking disclosure from Gulf regarding tax payments to Portugal and other information. Gulf's management opposed the resolution, but announced its intention to publish detailed information on its Cabinda operation later in the year. Gulf did so in June 1972 arguing that:

> Withdrawal from our contract would simply leave the government with all the revenue from a well-established oil field which the government is fully capable of operating or could contract to another company. In either event, the government would not be deprived of revenue. In fact, its revenue would increase substantially. . . . Gulf is making a special effort to hire and upgrade black nationals and in many other ways to make a meaningful contribution to the improved social and economic condition of the people of Angola. Management believes that real progress for Angolans lies in more, rather than fewer skills and jobs; in more, rather than less education; in more, rather than less medical services. And we believe Gulf's operations are providing a major contribution to this progress.[125]

Gulf's disclosure was praised by some church groups but others, such as the Council for Christian Social Action, responded by saying "We believe that employment practices in Angola have never been *the real issue*. The major issue at stake is the charge of the Council and other church bodies that Gulf is assisting Portugal to maintain its colonies in Africa . . . We conclude that the continued Gulf presence in Angola prolongs the agony of a people tortured by Portuguese colonialism whose rights to independence must not be obstructed by U.S. business or official policy. . . . We continue to urge Gulf to withdraw from Angola."[126]

In 1972 and 1973 Gulf was a prominent target in the African Liberation Day marches in Washington. In 1973, the Pan-African Liberation Committee placed full page "Boycott Gulf" ads in *Jet* and *Ebony* magazines, and anti-Gulf actions intensified in the American black community. Gulf responded by hiring a black public relations firm, Zebra Associates, Inc., and making large grants to black religious organizations including one of $50,000 to the Southern Christian Leadership Conference. Gulf also offered expense-paid visits to Angola to various stockholders, black clergy, civil rights leaders and the national black newspaper publishing association.[127] Some of the company's public relations efforts backfired, however, producing further condemnations and accusations of "trying to buy off" the opposition.

Following the Arab oil embargo of November 1973 the scramble for new sources of petroleum led to Angola, with the involvement of Exxon, Amoco, Occidental Petroleum, Sun Oil, Amerada Hess, Cities Service, and others.[128] Exxon had ignored a 1973 shareholder resolution requesting that it establish a committee to investigate the implications of involvement in Angola. In early 1974 a number of church groups filed another resolution with Exxon requesting that it cease operating in Guinea-Bissau under oil concessions received from the Portuguese. At the same time, the United Church of Christ Center for Social Action filed a resolution with Gulf requesting the company to disclose information about Cabinda reserves, shipments, contractual revisions, and the company's position regarding the Arab oil embargo.

All of this shareholder agitation was made irrelevant when the Armed Forces Movement, originating among junior military officers, staged a coup in Portugal and overthrew the Caetano government in April 1974. The primary cause of the revolt was the refusal of the government to give up the nation's overseas colonies despite the continued high cost in men and money to fight the independence movements. The coup installed General Antonio de Spinola as Provisional President, promising sweeping domestic reform and peace to the colonies. The new junta dismissed the governors of Angola and Mozambique, offered an immediate ceasefire to the guerrillas, and promised "self determination through referendum and independence." In August the Portuguese government signed an agreement granting independence to Guinea (effective September 1975) and in September 1974 Portugal agreed to the independence of Mozambique, effective the following June. Although Portugal itself was undergoing severe political crises at the time with numerous changes of government, the group in power in January 1975 signed an agreement setting November 11, 1975, as the date for Angolan independence and total withdrawal of Portuguese troops. The agreement called for election of a Constituent Assembly, which in turn would choose a President. A coalition provisional government was established, but within months warfare broke out among the three main independence groups: FNLA (National Front for the Liberation of Angola), MPLA (Popular Movement for the Liberation of Angola), and UNITA (National Union for the Total Independence of Angola). Combat between the Soviet-Cuban backed MPLA and the other factions supported by the United States, China, South Africa, and Zaïre led Portugal to declare martial law on May 15, 1975. But heavier fighting erupted in June and by July the bloody civil war had claimed more than 3000 lives. Portuguese troops frequently battled to protect the 350,000 Portuguese citizens in Angola and a massive airlift to evacuate refugees was begun in early August.

Gulf Oil, meanwhile, had attempted to remain neutral and work with whomever seemed to be in charge. But neutrality became extraordinarily difficult when all three factions in the civil war began making demands for payment of $10 per barrel on Gulf's 150,000 daily barrels of output from its wells off Cabinda. By July, the enclave of Cabinda was firmly controlled by the MPLA, as was the capital city of Luanda and about one-quarter of Angola. Contractually obligated, Gulf made payments totaling $116 million to the Banco Angola in Luanda in September and October of 1975. By this time the govermental coalition had shrunk to just one faction, the Soviet-Cuban backed MPLA. Gulf's funds were thus being used to finance a regime that the American government was opposing. The U.S. Central Intelligence Agency had in fact been funneling more than $30 million in funds and materiel to the socialist and moderate factions.

During the period, Gulf had been conferring frequently at high levels in the U.S. State Department about what to do. By December of 1975 Gulf found itself in a real quandry over whether to continue its tax and royalty payments to the MPLA[129]—$95 million was due in Luanda on December 31st and another $30 million by January 15th. The contending factions within Angola were making conflicting requests and the Ford Administration was urging Gulf to shut down its operations and withhold payments. Gulf feared, however, that if the payments were frozen, the MPLA would retaliate by holding its Cabinda employees hostage. Desperately in need of a way out of the political impasse, Gulf's management announced on December 22nd that it had temporarily suspended Angolan operations, withdrawn most of its foreign personnel, and decided to place future tax and royalty payments in escrow. Gulf's statement said that "border warfare and continued civil war in Angola . . . made it impossible for the movement of personnel, supplies and equipment necessary for the maintenance of operations there." The taxes and royalties due Angola would "become payable to the state of Angola when it has a government that is in control of the territory and population, and this government has been recognized by the world community."[130]

A few weeks later, Prime Minister Lopo do Nascimento, head of the government set up by the MPLA, charged that the United States—by pressuring Gulf to suspend operations and withhold royalties—was "waging economic war on Angola." The Prime Minister declared that "we are not going to let Gulf asphyxiate us, we are not prepared to let the oil remain in the ground while we need capital for our people."[131] He also threatened to get help from other countries in operating the fields if Gulf did not quickly resume operations. This response led Gulf to open indirect talks with Luanda through the Nigerian head of state. Gulf's President announced that "we would have no trouble working with any government in Angola."[132]

The stakes involved were summarized by one observer as follows: "The company has a strong incentive for seeking an accommodation with the MPLA because recent nationalizations of affiliates in Kuwait and Venezuela have converted Gulf from a seller to a net buyer of crude and cut its profit margin to just 22 cents per bbl. on oil purchased from those countries. The 150,000 bbl. per day of more profitable, low-sulfur crude from Cabinda last year accounted for 20% of the oil processed by Gulf in the U.S. The company figures that the shutdown cost it $19 million in the last two weeks of 1975, and a continued loss of Cabinda oil would lower Gulf's profits by at least 10%. The MPLA, for its part, badly needs the nearly $500 million that Angola earned from oil royalties and taxes last year."[133]

By mid-February 1976, the MPLA had taken over most of Angola and received recognition from the Organization of African Unity and from Western European nations and Canada. The United States was still withholding formal recognition because of the issue of Cuban troop involvement. Nonetheless, Secretary of State Henry Kissinger gave Gulf the go-ahead in early February to release to the Luanda regime the $125 million in oil tax revenues that Gulf placed in escrow in December and January at the request of the State Department.[134] The Administration then gave Gulf its approval to resume normal operations in Angola, and the company opened direct negotiations with the Luanda government in an attempt to cement ties. Subsequently, Angolan civil strife continued sporadically, with periodic allegations of widespread allegations of human rights violations by MPLA and its Cuban allies in attempts to stamp out UNITA and FNLA insurgency. Unlike its earlier problems, however, Gulf has not had to contend with vehement protests of American human rights groups this time around for its support of the existing regime. Evidently they are selective.

Newmont Mining, AMAX, and Resource Exploitation in Namibia

Local bushmen call the mineral-rich but barren territory of Namibia "the land God made in anger," and perhaps the exploitation of the land's natural wealth—which has thrust a number of multinationals into bitter confrontations during the last decade—is a reflection of that anger. Namibia is populated by 722,000 blacks and 99,000 whites and was formerly known as South-West Africa. It was colonized by Germans after 1884 and occupied by the South African army during World War I. In 1920, South Africa was awarded a fiduciary trust to administer the territory under a mandate from the League of Nations. Under this mandate, South Africa was to prepare the territory for eventual self-determination. In the 1950s and 1960s it became apparent to the League's successor, the United Nations, that South Africa was not fulfilling its obligations under the mandate. On October 27, 1966, the United Nations General Assembly voted to terminate South Africa's mandate and to place the territory under the direct responsibility of the United Nations under the Council for Namibia, a 25-country group formally established in 1967. South Africa refused to recognize UN jurisdiction or to allow the Council to visit the territory, and the South-West African Peoples' Organization (SWAPO) initiated an armed struggle on August 26, 1966 in the form of a sporadic, low-intensity guerrilla war in the northern areas of the territory. In 1968–1969, South Africa passed legislation that divided tribal areas into Bantustans and effectively made the territory a fifth province of the Republic. In 1970, the UN Security Council responded by passing resolutions declaring South Africa's actions illegal and requesting member states to refrain from relationships which would imply recognition of South African authority over Namibia.

The American government responded to the UN actions by adopting the following policy effective May 20, 1970:

(1) The United States will officially discourage investment by U.S. nations in South-West Africa; (2) U.S. nationals who, nevertheless, invest in South-West Africa on the basis of rights acquired through the South African government since adoption of U.N. General Assembly Resolution 2145 (XXI) (October 27, 1966) will not receive United States government assistance in protection of such investments against claims of a future lawful government of South-West Africa; and (3) Export-Import Bank credit guarantees and other facilities will not be made available for trade with South-West Africa.[135]

United States policy did not suggest that existing investments be withdrawn, or that current operations be curtailed.

On June 21, 1971, the International Court of Justice in an advisory opinion affirming the position taken by the United Nations ruled that South Africa's occupation of the international territory was illegal, that it was under obligation to withdraw, and that all other states had legal obligations to recognize the invalidity of the South African administration and to refrain from any action lending support or assistance to the illegal administration. This ruling inspired the United Nations Association, an unofficial group chaired at the time by Cyrus Vance, to issue a report at the end of 1971 recommending that the Internal Revenue Service stop granting income tax credits to American firms operating in South-West Africa for taxes paid to the South African government. Granting tax credits, according to the Association, was "inconsistent with our sharply defined national policy, and probably contrary to law."[136]

Attention was also focused on Namibia by an unprecedented strike of black workers against the government-run migratory contract labor system in December 1971. More than 30,000 workers walked off their jobs and crippled the economy. Tsumeb Corporation Ltd., the largest employer of contract labor in Namibia, was seriously affected by the walkout of about 80% of its African labor force. Tsumeb, controlled 65% by Newmont Mining and AMAX (but managed by Newmont), accounted in the early 1970s for 80% of Namibia's production of base metals. The mining operation also accounted for approximately 90% of the total United States investment in the territory. As such, Newmont and AMAX became the prime targets of widespread protest beginning in early 1972.

The American Committee on Africa summarized the charges against U.S. corporate involvement as follows:

(1) U.S. companies give direct support to the South African government in Namibia by the taxes they pay; (2) U.S. companies in Namibia strengthen the economy of South Africa by injecting large amounts of capital and developing significant sources of foreign exchange and earnings; (3) U.S. companies in Namibia operate in areas strategically vital to the continuation of white domination by force . . . thus reduc-

ing South Africa's vulnerability to international sanctions and boycotts; (4) U.S. economic involvement in Namibia serves to legitimize the illegal South African government, and inevitably brings about a closer integration of the South African economy with those of the West . . . ; and (5) Finally, because U.S. interests in Namibia are heavily concentrated in the extractive industries, the problem is particularly urgent, since resources are being depleted and the benefits of exploitation are nonrenewable.[137]

In February of 1972 various Members of Congress issued a statement denouncing Newmont and AMAX for abusing "the captive African population" of Namibia and calling on them to stop paying taxes to South Africa and to negotiate contracts directly with African workers. In the same month a group of black leaders and churchmen held a demonstration outside the New York City offices of Newmont, protesting its operations in Namibia. The Episcopal Churchmen for South Africa also filed shareholder resolutions with Newmont and AMAX asking that the companies disclose a range of information and "recognize the U.N. as the lawful authority in Namibia" by refusing to cooperate with the South African government and negotiating with the United Nations for the right to continue operating in the country. They also requested that Tsumeb profits be put in escrow until it was determined if the companies could "incur liabilities" for operating under South Africa's "exploitative, racially discriminatory" labor laws.[138] The UN Security Council passed a resolution in March 1972 calling on countries to "use all available means" to make sure that their "nationals and corporations conform in their policies of hiring Namibian workers to the basic provisions of the Universal Declaration of Human Rights."[139]

Newmont asked the SEC to omit the Episcopal shareholder resolution from its proxy statement for the annual meeting, stating in its brief that "it is erroneous to infer that normal business operations . . . are illegal and should be suspended merely because of a challenge under international law." The resolution, in Newmont's view, sought "to involve the corporation in a partisan role in matters heretofore, and still, strenuously contested between member states of the United Nations." AMAX, in its brief to the SEC, stated: "The question of who governs South West Africa, now also known as Namibia, is clearly a political matter." The opinion of the World Court and UN votes, in the company's view, were "political claims in the international arena and are well beyond the scope of any commercial corporation and normal business operation."[140]

The SEC decided not to disallow the resolutions and at the two companies' annual meetings they each received less than 3% of the stockholder vote. At its meeting, Newmont's board chairman announced adjournment before the resolution had been discussed, but following protest from churchmen he was forced to reconvene the session. AMAX management also opposed the resolution, stating that "in the opinion of management the annual meeting of shareholders is not the place for airing grievances or the solicitation of general information about the politics of countries within which the company has investments and the reactions of local companies to political factors in those countries."[141] During the AMAX meeting, SWAPO's observer at the United Nations declared: "The future lawful government of Namibia will be most eager to deal with foreign interests in Namibia according to their prior exploitation and discriminatory and repressive practices in collaboration with the illegal occupying apartheid regime. . . . I must remind you in the strongest possible terms that your company is reaping huge profits on the backs, sweat, tears and blood of my people."[142]

In 1973 the South African government began to sense increasing reluctance on the part of some multinationals to invest or become further involved in Namibia's natural resource sector. An oil exploration consortium involving Gulf Oil and five other firms had withdrawn following the opinion of the International Court of Justice, and Phelps Dodge had withdrawn in 1972. The South African government thus decided to further encourage foreign investment by liberalizing regulations for mining and prospecting concessions in Namibia.[143] Meanwhile, various Congressmen attempted to persuade the Treasury Department to disallow—on the jurisdictional ruling of the ICJ—tax credits to American corporations operating in Namibia. After a lengthy investigation, the Tax Policy Division ruled against this request on the grounds that the payment of taxes to any authority, de facto or otherwise, does not represent in any way recognition of that authority, and that under law if companies are paying such a tax they are entitled to nondiscriminatory treatment on the part of the American tax authorities.

The Episcopal Churchmen for South Africa again filed resolutions in 1973 with Newmont and AMAX urging the companies to withdraw from Namibia. The United Church of Christ filed another resolution with Newmont urging the company to adhere to "principles of fair employment" in international operations. In August 1973, eleven shareholders filed a lawsuit charging that the Tsumeb subsidiary of AMAX operated "illegally and immorally" and that AMAX directors were wasting company assets by allowing Tsumeb to pay taxes to South Africa—the suit asked that the court order taxes to be paid instead to the UN Council for Namibia. AMAX responded that issues "concerning the legitimacy of governments cannot be resolved by private litigation nor unilaterally by private companies. Such questions can only be settled among the governments involved. For these reasons we feel the suit is without merit."[144]

Newmont in its 1974 Annual Report stated that "age, sex, religion, race, and national origin are not criteria for hiring, training, advancement, compensation, other benefits, or membership in representative workers' organizations." Church shareholders saw this policy statement as an affirmation of their demands for worldwide equal employment opportunity. The most significant action that year, however, was the UN Council for Namibia Decree No. 1 of September 27, 1974 for the protection of the natural resources. This decree stated that no person or corporate body may explore, process, or export any Namibian natural resources without the permission of the UN Council for Namibia and that concessions granted by the South African government in Namibia were null and void. Furthermore natural resources taken from Namibia without the consent of the UN Council for Namibia, and the ships carrying them, were subject to seizure by or on behalf of the Council. Persons or corporations contravening the decree could be liable for damages by a future independent Namibian government. UN General Assembly Resolution 3295 of December 13, 1974 requested all states to insure full compliance with the provisions of the decree. The United States abstained on the resolution.[145]

This decree, along with the three-year efforts of several national church groups, played an important role in the withdrawal of five major American oil firms from exploration operations off the coast of Namibia during late 1974 and early 1975. In 1973, church groups had filed shareholder resolutions with Phillips Petroleum and Continental Oil requesting that they "not conduct exploration, mining or drilling activities in Namibia, either directly or through affiliates and shall wind up any operations currently underway in that country as expeditiously as possible."[146] The same resolutions were refiled with Phillips and Continental in 1974, and also were presented to Getty Oil and Standard Oil of California, making the usual arguments for withdrawal: (a) that the investments strengthened the illegal government and its occupation and violated international law; (b) that since the companies did not have valid concessions, they might be liable under international law to the future lawful government in Namibia for the value of any oil exported; (c) and that their presence in Namibia might adversely affect relations with other independent African governments from whom they had obtained concessions.

As withdrawal resolutions were about to be submitted once again in 1975, Continental Oil, Phillips Petroleum, and Getty Oil, comprising one consortium, and Texaco and Standard Oil of California, partners in a second venture, all announced they would pull out, despite favorable preliminary exploration results.[147] Getty cited "political changes that appear in the offing." Another cited "unresolved questions of sovereignty." Socal insisted it had made "purely a commercial decision." In May of that year *Business Week* reported that "one large U.S. corporation is currently negotiating the sale of its minority interest in a rich copper lode laced with other metals [in Namibia]. Confesses the company's chairman: 'we're scared to death of the political situation.' "[148] Yet at their respective annual meetings, the board chairmen of AMAX and Newmont each denied making this remark and neither admitted that he was worried about the United Nations decree. In November of 1975, however, the magazine reported that AMAX was taking the first steps toward getting rid of its holdings in two lucrative but sensitive mining operations in southern Africa—its 29.6% share of Tsumeb Corporation in Namibia and 17.3% equity in a copper operation in South Africa. AMAX had commissioned the investment banking firm of Kuhn, Loeb & Company to make a study of the properties with a view to selling them off. AMAX was apparently acting alone, since Newmont denied any efforts to get rid of its share in Tsumeb.[149]

In January of 1976 the UN Security Council unanimously adopted Resolution 385 demanding that South Africa accept elections in Namibia under UN supervision, and called on the government to take specific steps toward Namibia's self-determination and independence. Rio-Tinto Zinc's development of the Rossing uranium mine in Namibia was attacked by the left wing of the Labour Party in Britain, Falconbridge Nickel Mines' labor practices at the Oamites copper mine were criticized by the Canadian Task Force on the Churches and Corporate Responsibility, and Newmont was presented with another shareholder resolution asking for disclosure. Barclays Bank and Standard Bank also came under attack for their operations in Namibia. Peter Katjavivi, a senior SWAPO representative, stated that the relationship of the British banks "with other foreign enterprises investing in Namibia facilitates their operations, the transfer of their profits, and the payment of taxes to the South African regime. . . . When Namibia is free, the Namibian people will remember who were their friends and who were their enemies in the long struggle against the South African occupation."[150] And the head of SWAPO warned "we do not speak about nationalization. But those companies that are there illegally now and which are not only giving taxes to the South African government but also bringing in arms and ammunition to that government—those companies' right to be in Namibia will be reconsidered."[151]

In 1977 the Episcopal Church filed a resolution with AMAX asking for a report which would provide information about its operations in Namibia. The shareholder resolution was withdrawn after AMAX management agreed to issue such a report and to present the church's concerns to the board of Tsumeb Corporation. Newmont received a similar proposal from the United Church Board for World Ministries, but refused to release information. In an open letter to Newmont shareholders, the Philadelphia Namibia Action Group demanded that the company "Stop investing in apartheid! Stop investing in the exploitation of black labor! Stop defying the U.N. resolutions and World Court opinion on the illegal South African control on Namibia! Stop ignoring the official U.S. policy of discouraging firms from investing in Namibia!"[152]

In 1979, a transition from South African control to independence was underway in Namibia. But the politics of that transition remained highly dubious. South Africa was defying a plan for unsupervised elections, and a Western plan for a peaceful settlement in Namibia was on the verge of collapse. The West was still backing SWAPO, whose leader stated: "The question of black majority rule is out. We are not fighting even for majority rule. We are fighting to seize power in Namibia, for the benefit of the Namibian people. We are revolutionaries."[153] The political threat to MNEs operating in "God's angry land" remained considerable.[154]

EXPANDING IN REPRESSIVE NATIONS

Numerous attempts have been made to dissuade multinationals from investing or expanding in repressive nations. Again, the great bulk of the concern has centered on South Africa and Chile. Critics have generally charged that new capital investment provides significant economic support, international credibility, and moral legitimacy to the repressive regimes, and that foreign investments inevitably increase home country financial, and therefore political, commitments to the present structures of racism or martial law. We shall examine investment moratorium campaigns directed against a few multinationals here—well-publicized cases that reveal both "competitive" and "accommodative" response patterns on the part of target firms. We should also note, however, that many multinationals have confronted the issue of investing in a country allegedly violating human rights on an internal and unpublicized basis, which has often resulted in conflict-avoidance-oriented policies of either delaying or opting not to make the capital commitments in question.

Expansion in South Africa

Calls for a moratorium on new investment in South Africa have emanated from many church, political and institutional organizations over the years. For example, in 1976 the Christian Institute of South Africa called for a halt to further investment because:

(1) strong economic pressure is of vital importance in bringing about as peaceful a solution as possible; (2) investment in South Africa is investment in apartheid, and thus immoral, unjust, and exploitative; (3) attempts to change the situation through pressure by investors have proved inadequate; (4) the argument that economic growth can produce fundamental change has proved false; and (5) many black organizations have opposed foreign investment in South Africa, and we believe this would be the opinion of the majority of South African Blacks if their voice could be freely heard. Blacks accept that the consequent economic recession and unemployment would cause them suffering, but argue that this would be for a limited period by contrast with the unending suffering caused by the continuation of apartheid.[155]

Similar calls in 1977 and 1978 were made by Senator Dick Clark of the U.S. Senate Foreign Relations Committee, the U.N. General Assembly, and even the Teachers Insurance and Annuity Association - College Retirement Equities Fund.[156] In December of 1977 a poll by Louis Harris showed that a majority of the Americans interviewed who expressed an opinion favored "preventing all new U.S. business investment in South Africa."[157]

In 1975 Caltex, a joint venture of Texaco and Standard Oil Company of California, announced a $134 million expansion of its Cape Town oil refinery in South Africa. Because of the size and timing of the investment proposal, as well as the strategic importance of petroleum products to South Africa's military forces, the Caltex expansion was singled out for special attack by the American Committee on Africa and the Interfaith Center on Corporate Responsibility.[158] In the Spring of 1976 the World Division Board of Global Ministries of the United Methodist Church filed shareholder resolutions with Texaco and Socal requesting their Boards of Directors to establish the following corporate policy: "Neither the Corporation nor any of its affiliates shall expand its operations in the Republic of South Africa." The vote at Texaco's meeting was 2.2% in favor and at Socal it was 2.1%. The logic of Socal management is given in the corporation's proxy statement shown in Exhibit 6-3.

A number of other multinationals have also confronted and opposed shareholder and other pressure-group demands to abstain from investing in South Africa. Kennecott, which announced plans in 1975 to enter a $300 million mining and smelting operation near Richards Bay—an area which the Zulu people claim is part of their homeland—was asked by church groups in 1976 to establish a corporate policy to "not, directly or through affiliates, invest in, plan for, or conduct any mining, smelting or refining operations in the Republic of South Africa or in Namibia as a co-investor or in a joint venture with any agency of the South African government and shall promptly terminate any such plans now underway."[159] This resolution obtained 3.6% of the shareholder vote in 1976 and a reintroduction in 1977 achieved 4.4%. In 1978 the company was asked by resolution to report on the then-established operation.

In 1975 the British Labour Party opposed the granting of permission to British Steel Corporation to extend its involvement in South Africa in the form of a new chrome plant in the Transvaal. In 1977 Phelps Dodge was asked by three religious groups to establish a policy that "neither the corporation nor any of its affiliates or subsidiaries shall expand its operations in the Republic of South Africa."[160] Union Carbide, which announced plans to put a new $50 million ferrochrome plant on the border of a Bantustan, was asked by church shareholders in 1977 and again in 1978 not to expand in South Africa "unless and until the South African government has committed itself to ending the legally enforced form of racism called apartheid and has taken meaningful steps toward the achievement of full political, legal and social rights for the majority population (African, Asian, Coloured)."[161] In 1978 The Episcopal Church presented a similar resolution to United States Steel, which received a vote of 5.7%.[162] American Cyanamid, Borg Warner and Exxon were confronted with such resolutions in 1979.

Not all multinationals have resisted demands to halt expansion. Given rather dismal economic conditions in South Africa in the mid-1970s, one survey of American companies with direct investments there found that over half did not plan further investments in the next five years.[163] A number of these firms adopted public policies limiting their involvement. The Norton Company stated that because of the "dramatic" situation in South Africa it had decided against further investment there, while Gulf Oil announced it would not do business in a country that maintained discrimination as an official policy.[164] Seagram Company, Ltd. backed out of a $10 million distillery venture with South Africa's Stellenbosch Wines in Kwazulu when Canadian church groups charged that it would strengthen racial policies.[165]

Ford Motor Company in its 1976 annual report stated that any future investment in South Africa would include an assessment of the company's progesss in upgrading the labor standards of blacks. General Motors announced in 1977 that because of "disturbances and political uncertainties . . . in the midst of recession . . . the corporation has no present need for, and has no intention of, further expanding its productive capacity in South Africa. The single most important factor in the creation of a more promising investment climate in South Africa is a positive resolution of the country's pressing social problems, which

Exhibit 6-3
Proxy Statement of the Management of Standard Oil Company of California Regarding Stockholder Proposal on Expansion of Operations in South Africa Filed by the World Division Board of Global Ministries, United Methodist Church for a Vote at the Spring 1976 Annual Meeting

Your Directors do not agree with the foregoing proposal and recommend a vote AGAINST it for the following reasons:

In each investment decision in which it is involved, the Company makes every effort to be certain that all relevant factors receive full consideration. This is true not only of social, political, and economic implications, but of such other matters as environmental effects and full compliance with U.S. policy and law, and—where applicable—foreign legal requirements as well. All of these factors were considered in connection with Caltex's Cape Town Refinery expansion.

The Company is aware, of course, that a number of people in this country and elsewhere hold the view that the continued presence of American companies or their affiliates in South Africa is somehow inconsistent with the best interests of the United States or of the nonwhite community in South Africa. The Company does not doubt the sincerity with which these views are held, but it does not agree with their validity. Caltex activities in South Africa certainly are consistent with U.S. law and policy, and they make a positive contribution toward the achievement of meaningful social objectives so far as the South African nonwhite community is concerned. One can, of course, argue over the extent of this contribution, but the Company is satisfied that the nonwhite community would suffer more than any other element of South African society if Caltex were to withdraw from its commercial activities in that country. At the same time, it is important to remember that the continued presence of Caltex in South Africa should not be viewed as an endorsement by either Standard Oil Company of California or Caltex of all of the South African government's policies.

Caltex South Africa's employment practices are governed by South African laws, and in the event of any conflicts between those laws and equal employment opportunity practices, the Company must be guided by the former. However, Caltex South Africa consistently follows the practices of:

Firstly, always hiring on the basis of ability, and not race;

Secondly, always paying the rate for the job and promoting on merit;

Thirdly, ensuring that all its Benefit Plans and Programs are the same for all employees regardless of race; and

Fourthly, making a conscientious, continuing and successful effort to advance its less skilled workers to positions of responsibility by such means as job training and financially assisting in non-company conducted education programs. In this connection, some 40% of Caltex South Africa's total black staff today occupy positions previously held by whites. It can be expected that the refinery expansion will afford even greater opportunity for this effort.

The Arms Embargo against South Africa adopted by the United Nations in 1963 does not include petroleum products. Further, the Company has been advised that it would be a crime under South Africa's law were Caltex South Africa to undertake a commitment not to supply petroleum products to the South African Government.

Thus, in management's opinion, adoption of this resolution would not be in the best interests of those South Africans whom the proponents seek to assist, nor of the Company, nor of its stockholders.

It is recommended that stockholders vote AGAINST this proposal.

have their origin in the apartheid system."[166] In October of 1977 Control Data Corporation, citing recent human rights developments in South Africa, announced that "at the present time, our company does not consider it appropriate to enlarge our investment in South Africa.[167] And in December of 1977 Gulf & Western Industries announced, following pressure from the Interfaith Center on Corporate Responsibility, that the "continuation of the South African government's policies" made investment in the country, "increasingly unattractive" and that it had thus refused to invest in a major mining venture.[168]

Returning to Chile

In the mid-1970s the United Nations General Assembly repeatedly expressed its distress at "the constant flagrant violations of human rights, including the institutionalized practice of torture, cruel, inhuman or degrading treatment or punishment, arbitrary arrest, detention and exile . . . that continue to take place in Chile."[169] Reports of such organizations as the International Labor Organization and the United Nations Commission on Human Rights documented that freedom of expression and freedom of association, as well as the right to work, to hold trade union elections, to bargain collectively, and to strike were all either heavily restricted or denied in Chile. These conditions led many concerned groups around the world to take "the position that any sort of economic assistance to Chile, without the prior restoration of human rights, simply postpones the day when liberty will return, and strengthens the hand of a regime notorious for its repression."[170]

In late 1974 the Chilean government invited bids from fourteen foreign automobile manufacturers to participate in a reorganized automotive assembly industry. In August of 1975 the government announced that General Motors, Renault-Peugeot, and Fiat had been selected to contractually participate in the restructuring. Concerned about human rights violations in Chile, church investors asked GM in a letter of September 15th to guarantee rights of company workers, including "employment without regard to political or religious backgrounds, free establishment and operations of labor unions, and the recognition by the company of collective bargaining."[171] The United Auto Workers joined in, and asked GM to make present and future operations in Chile contingent on that government's commitment to honor basic worker's rights. When the company did not issue a final decision on these requests by January 1976, more than 15 church groups holding over $7.5 million in GM stock cosponsored a shareholder resolution for the spring annual meeting, listing three preconditions of GM's continuing operations or expansion in Chile. These were "that the company should be exempted from the restrictions of the government's blacklisting of hundreds of thousands of Chilean workers; that GM employees may freely choose the labor unions, if any, which they wish to represent them; and that any unions chosen by GM employees are free to present union concerns to management and may negotiate contracts, with recognition of the rights to strike."[172] The resolution also contained a statement requesting the GM Board of Directors to consider terminating all company operations in Chile within the next year if the government did not recognize and implement these minimal rights for all GM employees.

In 1976 a ten-year agreement was signed between GM and the Chilean government, granting the company the right to operate, and during 1976 GM sold 4000 vehicles in Chile, including 1300 light-duty Chevrolet trucks assembled at its Arica plant, 1600 imported passenger cars—primarily the Brazilian-sourced GM Chevette—and another 1100 imported trucks. GM Chile's 1976 sales represented about 30% of total motor vehicle sales in the country.[173] Believing that the resumption of GM's Chilean operations was helping to "legitimize the repressive policies of the Junta and the denial of worker's rights" and providing "the Junta with badly needed foreign investment necessary for maintenance of its economic and political power," six church groups filed a resolution in 1977 asking GM to report on its experience in its first year of renewed operations, including relations with employees and an assessment of the economic situation in Chile.[174]

In April of 1977 GM responded with a three-page report on its Chilean operations contained in its *Public Interest Report for 1976.* The company disclosed that it had raised the question of human rights on several occasions with leading Chilean government officials who had stressed that the suspension of the right to strike and negotiate wages were necessary in order to control the serious inflation that was preventing Chile from achieving a desired rate of economic growth. Despite the suspensions, GM concluded "that, as a practical matter, its Chilean employees have most of the same rights normally enjoyed by union members in the United States, even though not all of these rights are legally guaranteed at this time." The company also noted its appreciation for "the concern of some groups over the Chilean government's apparent lack of commitment to democratic practices. We are also aware, however, that we are a guest in that nation, subject to its laws. General Motors does not believe that it could, or should attempt to, force its will on Chile, or any other sovereign nation." But so as "to contribute to the economic and human progress of the people of Chile . . . GM Chile will continue to treat its employees fairly and. . . will, through appropriate channels, continue to express its views to the Chilean government regarding the rights of our employees, and human rights in general."[175]

In 1977 Chile's Bureau of Private Enterprise advertised in the American media that Chile was a "Safety Zone for Foreign Investors." It stressed "tranquility and stability in all sectors of the labor force" and "an undeniable guarantee of personal safety to foreign executives and their families and staff in internal conditions of social calm and peaceful coexistence, with a complete absence of any kind of radical violence, in contrast with the situation in many other parts of the world."[176] Such conditions and the government's plan to bring industry under private control had earlier inspired the return of Dow Chemical Company and Firestone Tire and Rubber Company. In December of 1977, Exxon Minerals International acquired the state-owned Disputada de las Condex copper mines for $107 million.[177] In January 1978 the Goodyear Tire and Rubber Company acquired Corso-Insa, Chile's biggest tire maker, for $34 million.[178] Insa, formerly owned by General Tire & Rubber Company, had been nationalized in 1975 amid a financial and tax evasion scandal. *Business Week* reported in February 1978 that "U.S. corporations continue to show a renewed interest in investing in Chile, where most have feared to tread since the late President Salvador Allende's wave of nationalizations in the early 1970s." A few pages later in the same issue an article entitled "Chile's Junta Flouts Carter on Human Rights" noted that Chile's president, General Augusto Pinochet, was dealing out harsh new repressive measures.[179] In March 1978, Diamond Shamrock confirmed that it had offered to buy the assets of Chile's government-owned Petroquimica Chilena for $12.2 million.[180] The following month a $150 million loan to the government from a group of international banks led by Morgan Guaranty Trust Company provided another sign of returning foreign confidence in Chile's resurgent economy—by mid-1979 there were 324 foreign projects totaling $2.5 billion in the pipeline.[181]

WITHDRAWING FROM REPRESSIVE NATIONS

Demands for withdrawal of operations from repressive nations raise our final set of issues related to human rights. As noted earlier, various multinationals have been asked to close up shop and walk away from their investments in Angola and Namibia. But the bulk of the calls for divestment have been directed at firms operating in South Africa. Targets for disengagement pressure have included a few multinationals based in Canada, France, Switzerland, West Germany, Sweden, and the Netherlands, but a much larger number headquartered in the United States. Human rights groups have argued as usual that multinational corporate presence in South Africa serves to bolster the racist status quo of apartheid and white minority rule—that despite changes in wages, benefits, and working conditions in many foreign-owned subsidiaries, no measureable steps have been taken by the South African government toward black enfranchisement and full human rights. In their view, the pressures exerted by multinationals have been minimal in alleviating injustice. The only thing that will hasten the collapse of white minority rule and transform the apartheid system in its entirety is economic strangulation and, the argument goes, such a shock can only be orchestrated if multinationals disengage *en masse.*

Multinationals have typically responded with the "progress through economic growth" argument. Virtually every firm confronted with the call for pullout argues that more can be accomplished for South African blacks by remaining than by leaving; that withdrawal of investments would be an empty symbolic gesture. In the corporate view, it is highly doubtful that withdrawal would have any tangible impact in changing the system for the better, and indeed the opposite might occur if the disinvestment serves to harden white Afrikaner intransigence.[182] Of course it is true that "no one can really prove whether pressure for change is better applied by staying or leaving."[183]

The South African Withdrawal Campaign

In 1971 the Executive Council of the Episcopal Church filed a shareholder resolution with General Motors, requesting that the company withdraw its investment from South Africa. This was the first action of its kind, and the resolution received front-page coverage by the media. GM's management opposed the proposal and it received a scant 1.29% of the shares voted at the annual meeting. A dramatic highlight occurred at the annual meeting, however, when GM chairman James M. Roche unexpectedly announced that the Reverend Leon Sullivan,

GM's first black board member, would speak in favor of the Episcopal resolution. In an eloquent and impassioned speech, Mr. Sullivan said that while he was "encouraged" by the Corporation's efforts to improve opportunities for minorities in the United States, "American industry cannot morally continue to do business in a country that so blatantly and ruthlessly and clearly maintain such dehumanizing practices against such large numbers of people . . . I want to see GM out of the contemporary unparalleled oppressive situation that exists there. I want General Motors to ring free for everybody."[184] This was believed to be the first time that a GM director had ever spoken against a management policy at an annual meeting. The following year Mr. Sullivan again pleaded: "Get out so they can change the system. Stay if being there changes the system. But of all things change the system. That is my concern."[185]

Given the emergence of a substantial debate within the ecumenical movement of the Christian churches over South African reform from within versus withdrawal, calls for disengagement moved from the floor of stockholder meetings into pamphlets and articles during the period 1973 to 1976. But the 1976 student uprising in Soweto and the wave of unrest that swept South Africa in the second half of that year gave new prominence to moral arguments against multinational corporate involvement, and calls for withdrawal began to mount. They reached a crescendo in 1977, when in October the South African government engaged in stepped-up repression, banning individuals and organizations involved in opposing the country's apartheid policies. Groups such as the NAACP and others in the United States adopted or strengthened formal policies calling for total withdrawal of American businesses from South Africa in order to bring about the collapse of the apartheid system. [186]

During 1977–1979 the following firms received shareholder resolutions calling for withdrawal: Ford Motor, General Electric, General Motors, Goodyear, Standard Oil of California, Phillips Petroleum, Texaco, Kimberly Clark, 3M Company, Union Carbide, Motorola, and Phelps Dodge. All were asked to terminate their present operations in South Africa as expeditiously as possible "unless and until the South African government has committed itself to ending the legally enforced form of racism called apartheid and has taken meaningful steps toward the achievement of full political, legal and social rights for the majority population (African, Asian, and Coloured)."[187]

Under mounting attack, each of the companies dug in its heels and refused to withdraw. GM stressed that "the necessary social and economic changes in South Africa cannot be furthered if General Motors simply withdraws from the country . . . We've been there over 50 years, and we plan to be there for a long time to come."[188] A Goodyear official said he could foresee nothing that would suggest a withdrawal from South Africa.[189] A General Electric spokesman said that the request of activist groups "to get out because they say our presence supports apartheid" would not influence its decision making.[190] GE was asked to debate the issue with a coalition of church groups, but declined the invitation and elected to stand on what it believed to be "a straightforward and clear statement of position." The company, which was attacked bitterly by the Interfaith Center on Corporate Responsibility,[191] believed it "had been able to make considerable progress by working quietly in an environment of nonconfrontation with the South African government."[192] Henry Ford II, after meeting with Prime Minister John Vorster in January 1978, said at a news conference: "Our policy is that we are remaining in South Africa. . . . It is our opinion that we do more for the people of South Africa by staying here, and by providing equal opportunities."[193] On the same day a senior executive of the Bavarian Motor Works made a similar commitment at the opening of a BMW multiracial training center in Pretoria.[194]

Polaroid's Experiment and Exit

On October 5, 1970, signs appeared on bulletin boards at the headquarters of Polaroid Corporation in Cambridge, Massachusetts, demanding that the company cease doing business in South Africa. Several days later two black employees of Polaroid, speaking for the "Polaroid Revolutionary Workers' Movement" (PRWM), voiced the same demand in a noisy mid-day demonstration outside the firm's headquarters. The PRWM demanded that the company end its activities in South Africa, publicly denounce apartheid, and contribute its cumulative South African profits to African liberation groups. The main target of protest was the company's furnishing of photographic materials for use in the passbook system.[195]

Polaroid, under the leadership of "part scientist and part humanitarian philosopher" Dr. Edwin H. Land, had enjoyed a reputation for being a pacesetter in both race relations policies and community relations programs. The company was sensitive to the PRWM criticism and at first responded by stressing that it had no direct investment in South Africa—it operated through a local distributor, Frank & Hirsch Pty. Ltd. Sales to the country amounted to less than one-half percent of Polaroid's annual revenues. On October 21 Polaroid's management announced a complete ban on the direct or indirect sale of identification systems and all photographic equipment to departments of the South African government. PRWM labelled the new policy "an insult," and began organizing a coalition to launch a boycott of Polaroid products both in the United States and overseas.

An "ad hoc" committee of 14 black and white employees was then set up to study the business in South Africa and to recommend appropriate action. Dr. Land warned the task force in an hour-long talk that giving in to the demands of "a couple of revolutionaries who don't believe we mean what we say" would inevitably lead to "a whole series of new demands, and there is no doubt that management would not meet them. I do not want to run a company based on demands rather than participation."[196] The task force decided to send a team of American Polaroid employees, two blacks and two whites, to evaluate working conditions and to poll the feelings of black South Africans as to what they would have the company do. The fact-finding committee was not obstructed by the South African government, and from 11 days of meetings and interviews its members became convinced that Polaroid should stay on in South Africa and work for reform from within. With these inputs, the larger task force then fashioned a one-year experimental program to be undertaken in the company's South African operations.

On January 11, 1971, the company held a press conference at its headquarters and released a statement on its conclusions and future course of action, which also formed the text of an advertisement that was published two days later in seven major American dailies and 20 black weeklies. As shown in Exhibit 6–4, this manifesto of what came to be known as the "Polaroid Experiment" announced the company's intention to stay in South Africa, give up its government contracts, help reform the system by pressuring its local distributor to dramatically upgrade wages and benefits for black employees, and contribute to African education.

Reactions were swift, sharp, and decidedly mixed. Initial comments ran the gamut from "what Polaroid says it has done and hopes to do is most commendable—it is perhaps the most intelligent thing yet attempted by an American industry" all the way to "the full page ad by Polaroid, condescending to do business in South Africa, sets a new high in arrogance."[197] The response of the PRWM was to reject the solution, characterizing the experiment as a "paternalistic act of charity" and a "trick," and reiterate the threat "to enforce an international boycott against Polaroid until it completely disengages from South Africa or until South Africa is liberated in the name of the people."[198] George Houser, Executive Director of the American Committee on Africa, urged rejection of the Polaroid approach arguing that "U.S. business operations in South Africa, no matter what programs they espouse that are designed to modify apartheid and help blacks, have not produced and will not produce any effect on a system grounded on the principle of race discrimination and separation."[199] Many gradualist church groups, however, were pleased with the plan and saw the prospect of change and reform for blacks in South Africa. "The Pretoria government, for its part, took the Polaroid announcement with equanimity, even going so far as to praise the company for its action."[200]

A year after the "Polaroid Experiment" began, the company asked the South African Institute on Race Relations to assist in assessing its impact.[201] With a positive evaluation, the experiment was extended another year, and then indefinitely. Over the years black wages were increased considerably and employment opportunities were upgraded in the operations of Frank & Hirsch. Almost half a million dollars were given to various black scholarship funds and other programs in the period 1971–1977. Perhaps most importantly, the wide publicity given to the Polaroid effort initiated a dialogue on the need for change and the role of multinationals in this process. The effort focused increased concern among other foreign investors about the wages and working conditions of black employees.

Polaroid had convinced Frank & Hirsch to make a practice of hiring politically involved blacks, including Winnie Mandela, a banished activist. Another was Indrus Naidoo, a member of the African National Congress for many years, who had completed a ten-year prison sentence for sabotage. Working in the shipping department, Naidoo discovered that the company was secretly making "substantial shipments" of film, cameras, and sunglasses to military headquarters outside Pretoria and to several Bantu Reference Bureaus that issue passbooks.[202] Naidoo managed to make a photocopy of a shipping order which revealed that products were being sent directly to the ultimate government purchaser packed in unmarked cartons and loaded on unmarked vans, while the invoices were forwarded to Muller Pharmacy in downtown Johannesburg. A member of the New York-based American Committee on Africa who had met him on a visit in 1975 received a copy of the delivery order from Naidoo. He subsequently passed on the document to the *Boston Globe* in the fall of 1977 and the newspaper, after communicating with Naidoo (by then in Europe), presented the evidence to Polaroid.

The company immediately sent two representatives, including its export sales manager, to Johannesburg to investigate. They examined the books of Frank & Hirsch and discovered that the distributor had indeed been in continuous violation of the 1971 agreement not to sell to the government. Polaroid management was described as "shocked," and "angry" at the revelations.[203] Then on November 21, 1977—only five days after receiving the information from the *Boston Globe*—Polaroid issued a statement reiterating its abhorrence of apartheid, reviewing the firm's accomplishments, and shutting off supplies to Frank & Hirsch. The statement concluded: "With the termination of this distributorship, we do not plan to establish another one."[204] Polaroid's management declined any further comment.

Polaroid had no other choice but to withdraw from South Africa as quickly as possible. A mockery had been made of its widely publicized "Experiment," and it was highly vulnerable both to another internal "revolution" and to an external smear and boycott campaign. With no manufacturing operations or sales offices at stake, and with trade amounting to only about $4 million annually, the loss of business would be trivial. Besides, the business climate in South Africa was deteriorating and some company officials had reportedly been feeling uneasy about their South African involvement even before the Frank & Hirsch affair.[205] So the choice now was clear and easy.

Exhibit 6-4
An Experiment in South Africa

Polaroid Corporation Advertisement in *The New York Times*, January 13, 1971.

Polaroid sells its products in South Africa as do several hundred other American companies. Our sales there are small, less than one half of one percent of our worldwide business.

Recently a group has begun to demand that American business stop selling in South Africa. They say that by its presence it is supporting the government of the country and its policies of racial separation and subjugation of the Blacks. Polaroid, in spite of its small stake in the country, has received the first attention of this group.

We did not respond to their demands. But we did react to the question. We asked ourselves, "Is it right or wrong to do business in South Africa?" We have been studying the question for about ten weeks.

The committee of Polaroid employees who undertook this study included fourteen members—both black and white—from all over the company. The first conclusion was arrived at quickly and unanimously. We abhor *apartheid*, the national policy of South Africa.

The *apartheid* laws separate the races and restrict the rights, the opportunities and the movement of non-white Africans. This policy is contrary to the principles on which Polaroid was built and run. We believe in individuals. Not in "labor units" as Blacks are sometimes referred to in South Africa. We decided whatever our course should be it should oppose the course of *apartheid*.

The committee talked to more than fifty prominent South Africans both black and white, as well as many South African experts. They heard from officials in Washington. They read books, papers, testimony, documents, opinion, interpretation, statistics. They heard tapes and saw films.

They addressed themselves to a single question. What should Polaroid do in South Africa? Should we register our disapproval of *apartheid* by cutting off all contact with the country? Should we try to influence the system from within? We rejected the suggestion that we ignore the whole question and maintain the status quo.

Some of the black members of the study group expressed themselves strongly at the outset. They did not want to impose on the black people of another country a course of action merely because *we* might feel it was correct. They felt this paternalistic attitude had prevailed too often in America when things are done "for" black people without consulting black people.

It was decided to send four of the committee members to South Africa. Since this group was to include two black and two white members, it was widely assumed they would not be granted visas. They were.

It was assumed if they ever got to South Africa they would be given a government tour. They were not.

It was assumed they would not be allowed to see the actual conditions under which many Blacks live and would be prevented from talking to any of them in private. They did see those conditions in Soweto and elsewhere. And with or without permission they met and talked to and listened to more than a hundred black people of South Africa. Factory workers, office workers, domestic servants, teachers, political leaders, people in many walks of life. They also talked to a broad spectrum of whites including members of all the major parties.

Their prime purpose in going to South Africa was to ask Africans what they thought American business should do in their country. We decided the answer that is best for the black people of South Africa would be the best answer for us.

Can you learn about a country in ten days? No. Nor in ten weeks. But our group learned one thing. What we had read and heard about *apartheid* was not exaggerated. It is every bit as repugnant as we had been led to believe.

The group returned with a unanimous recommendation.

In response to this recommendation and to the reports of the larger study committee, Polaroid will undertake an experimental program in relation to its business activities in South Africa.

For the time being we will continue our business relationships there (except for sales to the South African government, which our distributor is discontinuing), but on a new basis which Blacks there with whom we talked see as supportive to their hopes and plans for the future. In a year we will look closely to see if our experiment has had any effects.

First, we will take a number of steps with our distributor, as well as his suppliers, to improve dramatically the salaries and other benefits of their non-white employees. We have had indications that these companies will be willing to cooperate in this plan.

Our business associates in South Africa will also be obliged (as a condition of maintaining their relationship with Polaroid) to initiate a well-defined program to train non-white employees for important jobs within their companies.

We believe education for the Blacks, in combination with the opportunities now being afforded by the expanding economy, is a key to change in South Africa. We will commit a portion of our profits earned there to encourage black education. One avenue will be to provide funds for the permanent staff and office of the black-run Association for Education and Cultural Advancement (ASECA). A second method will be to make a gift to a foundation to underwrite educational expenses for about 500 black students at various levels of study from elementary school through university. Grants to assist teachers will also be made from this gift. In addition we will support two exchange fellowships for Blacks under the U.S.–South African Leader Exchange program.

Polaroid has no investments in South Africa and we do not intend to change this policy at present. We are, however, investigating the possibilities of creating a black-managed company in one or more of the free black African nations.

Why have we undertaken this program? To satisfy a revolutionary group? No. They will find it far from satisfactory. They feel we should close the door on South Africa, not try to push it further open.

What can we hope to accomplish there without a factory, without a company of our own, without the economic leverage of large sales? Aren't we wasting time and money trying to have an effect on a massive problem 10,000 miles from home? The answer, our answer, is that since we are doing business in South Africa and since we have looked closely at that troubled country, we feel we can continue only by opposing the *apartheid* system. Black people there have advised us to do this by providing an opportunity for increased use of black talent, increased recognition of black dignity. Polaroid is a small economic force in South Africa, but we are well known and, because of our committee's visit there, highly visible. We hope other American companies will join us in this program. Even a small beginning of co-operative effort among American businesses can have a large effect in South Africa.

How can we presume to concern ourselves with the problems of another country? Whatever the practices elsewhere, South Africa alone articulates a policy exactly contrary to everything we feel our company stands for. We cannot participate passively in such a political system. Nor can we ignore it. That is why we have undertaken this experimental program.

POLAROID CORPORATION

The significance of the withdrawal for both South Africa and the anti-apartheid movement was purely symbolic. Because Polaroid's "Experiment" had induced a ripple effect in 1971, a number of observers wondered whether the withdrawal in 1977 would also set a precedent. But as of mid-1979, Polaroid's disengagement from South Africa was the only one publicly attributed to grounds of human rights. As noted earlier, a number of other multinationals had also pulled up stakes or scaled down their involvement, although all had claimed economic reasons. Some examples in the period 1976–1978 included Chrysler merging its ailing subsidiary into a South African company and reducing equity participation from full ownership to 24.9%; ITT selling its South African telephone company to a local electronics concern and retaining a 36% interest; Weyerhaeuser selling its interest in four shipping container plants in the Republic to a former partner, Barlow Rand Ltd., because the operation lacked "growth potential"; and Phelps Dodge selling 51% of its wholly-owned subsidiary, the Black Mountain Mineral Development Company, to Gold Fields of South Africa; British MNEs reducing their investments in South Africa during this time included Racal, General Electric, British Leyland, United Dominions Trust, Guardian Royal Exchange Assurance and Reed International.[206]

In late 1977 *The Economist* reported that for reasons of economic self-interest, the need for a clean image, and pressure from labor, church, and student groups, about 15% of the 400 American companies were considering pulling out.[207] At about the same time the Investor Responsibility Research Center warned that "to those increasingly disturbed by events in South Africa, and to those who don't see sufficient progress toward intermediate objectives, withdrawal may become a dominant objective."[208] One observer noted: "In the end business is likely to be moved by business considerations, and that is fair enough. Doing business in South Africa will make it harder to operate elsewhere, and will run up against union and other protest at home. The stability of South Africa will appear increasingly doubtful. The logic of events is moving, and should move, toward American economic withdrawal."[209]

MANAGING THE CHALLENGE OF HUMAN RIGHTS

Having completed a detailed survey of some of the many conflicts that have confronted MNEs in recent years over human rights in seven different operational categories (also see our section on labor practices in repressive nations in Chapter 11), an integration and evaluation of the entire range of experience is necessary in order to draw out lessons for the constructive management of the human rights challenge. How and why have multinationals chosen to handle conflicts over rights in the way they have? What impact has the crusade against multinationals had in actually influencing the observance of human rights around the world? How is the human rights challenge facing multinationals likely to evolve, and what guidelines might be useful in formulating appropriate corporate policies and responses?

Handling Human Rights Conflicts

From the perspective of our contingency model of conflict management introduced in Chapters 2 and 3, it is evident that MNEs have employed a wide range conflict-handling methods in dealing with battles over human rights. Reliance on *assertiveness* and *cooperativeness* has varied from issue to issue, from firm to firm, and from time to time in regard to the same issue. As with many other types of conflict examined in this book, however, very little use has been made of the *collaborative* mode. This is probably because integration and joint optimization of the concerns of all parties in human rights disputes has simply not been feasible. In most human rights conflicts, the multinational firm has been simultaneously confronted with contradictory demands from two or more parties typically based in two or more countries—for example, a church group at home and the allegedly repressive regime in the host nation. Joint problem solving and teamwork is obviously impossible in cross-cultural and multiparty conflicts involving totally divergent sets of interests.

Avoidance. The simple fact—as noted in the previous chapter—that more than 90% of all American corporate investment is located in nations designated by Freedom House as "most free" on civil liberties implies that *avoidance* may have been widely used by multinationals in regard to involvement with nations violating human rights. Or the correlation may be largely spurious, with most American investment located in the highly-developed market-economy countries of Western Europe, Canada, Japan, Australia, and New Zealand which also happen to be liberal democracies. Although not readily apparent, one could conclude that hundreds of explicit or implicit decisions have been made by corporations to steer clear of potential human rights conflicts. New investment and expansion plans in "human rights hotspots" may have been delayed or shelved, levels of involvement may have been reduced, and a few operations may have closed down entirely. Governmentally-imposed economic sanctions against arms sales certainly have been abided by, positions of strict neutrality have been maintained, and low profile strategies have been pursued by MNEs on human rights grounds. Repressive nations—particularly those involving illegal or colonial occupation—have been viewed as high-risk political situations by companies. They have been especially avoided when "greener pastures" (alternative projects, markets, raw material sources) have been readily available, when home governments have issued unambiguous embargoes on trade and investment with them, and when multinationals have been strongly motivated to avoid encounters with radical and aggressive pressure groups targeting their fire on these nations.

Competition. Our survey revealed relatively frequent use of the *competitive* mode by multinationals in human rights struggles. Examples of tough battling with the hope of eventual domination include: (1) IBM's refusal to stop selling to the South African government, (1) Newmont's unwillingness to disclose information on its mining operations in Namibia, (3) Union Carbide's vigorous lobbying to have the United States embargo on Rhodesian chrome abolished and not reinstated, (4) Bank of America's strenuous defense of its right to do business anywhere in the world regardless of political systems, (5) Mobil Oil South Africa's rebuff to parent company and U.S. Treasury investigators seeking data regarding alleged oil supplies to Rhodesia, (6) Gulf Oil's pro-active public relations blitz against charges of aiding Portuguese colonialism in Angola, and (7) the flat rejections by most major European and North American banks of demands to formally restrict their loans to alleged human rights violators, and by most weapons manufacturers to restrict their export sales on human rights grounds.

Some common threads seem to underlie this diversity of competitive behavior. The company's stakes have generally been perceived as high in each case. The economic sacrifice entailed in meeting pressure group demands, whether in the form of lost markets, raw material sources, market share, or capital investment, has often been viewed as being rather large. Some firms have hung on in the face of prolonged protest out of fear of the precedents that might be established and restrictions on management flexibility that might result if they gave in. Still others have stressed that the actions demanded by human rights groups might preclude them from complying with existing legal commitments and potentially subject them to lawsuits for damages. The demands of pressure groups have also frequently been viewed as very unreasonable and totally divergent from the interests of the firm. And in most of the cases we have discussed, the MNEs have only been confronted with relatively weak, highly emotional and sometimes radical nongovernmental organizations such as church groups. Meaningful dialogue has often been hard to establish given strong elements of mutual distrust and hostility.

Accommodation. In contrast with relatively assertive and uncooperative competition, other cases have revealed multinationals employing the opposite conflict-handling behavior in the form of the *accommodative* mode. Some examples drawn from our survey would include: (1) Polaroid's withdrawal from South Africa in 1977, (2) major American coffee companies such as Folger and General Foods stopping their importation of Ugandan coffee in 1978, (3) IBM, Mobil, Burroughs, and many other firms acquiescing without a fight to demands for disclosure of information on their operations in allegedly repressive nations, (4) Control Data and ITT deciding not to provide their products to the police and military in South Africa, (5) Olin's plea of no contest to charges of illegally supplying arms and ammunition to South Africa, (6) the withdrawal of major oil firms from exploration activities off the coast of Namibia, (7) numerous banks' withdrawal from government lending in South Africa; (8) Merrill Lynch's halting of Krugerrand sales, and (9) manufacturing firms adopting policies of not expanding in South Africa.

These and other cases of accommodation in human rights conflicts, with perhaps one or two exceptions, reveal a major common factor—the economic sacrifice entailed was relatively small. "Virtue" was essentially costless. In each case, critical strategic elements were not affected by giving in to pressure groups demands; the volume of sales, bank lending or the supply of raw materials foregone was insignificant, and alternative options for the firm were readily available. And the particular circumstances of accommodation were often convenient; the interests of the firms and the pressure groups, albeit for different reasons, were basically compatible. Given South Africa's deteriorating credit-worthiness and escalating political risk in 1977–1978, for example, few banks or manufacturing firms were interested in increased levels of involvement. In addition to low stakes and convergent interests, a number of these cases also revealed high susceptibility on the part of the firms involved to public pressures and sanctions (that is, low "power") in the form of product or service boycotts, unassailable proof of wrongdoing, shaky legal positions, and potential reprisals from third-country governments.

Compromise. Between the extremes of competition and accommodation, of course, many multinationals have resorted to the *compromise* mode to handle human rights conflicts. To cite just a few of the many cases of bargaining included in our survey, one could note: (1) the compromises announced by Citicorp, Chase Manhattan, Manufacturers Hanover, and Continental Illinois resulting in a halt in loans to the South African government but a continuation of selective credit for "constructive" private sector activities in that country; (2) the efforts of General Motors to guarantee employee rights in Chile to the extent necessary to deflect withdrawal pressure from union and church groups at home; (3) Polaroid's refusal to withdraw from South Africa in 1971 but instead to embark on its classic "Experiment"; and (4) the large number of negotiations that have resulted in firms agreeing to issue disclosure reports in exchange for withdrawal of shareholder resolutions that would have required embarrassing votes and discussions at annual stockholder meetings. The interests of the multinationals and pressure groups in all of these cases have been convergent in some respects and divergent in others. Outcomes have been arrived at through moderately assertive and cooperative behavior utilizing processes of bargaining give and take.

Mixed forms of conflict behavior. Finally, like other types of conflict, multinationals have found it necessary to use mixed modes in handling human rights conflicts, both simultaneously and sequentially. We have stressed that human rights conflicts are typically multiparty in nature, where the firm simultaneously faces two or more protagonists whose interests are often completely divergent. Wedged between the hauling and shoving of these opposed stakeholders, the multinationals have had to handle the various parties—and/or the issues of concern to each—in different ways. Gulf Oil in its Angolan conflict, for example, had to simultaneously and delicately thread its way between the countervailing demands of the United States and Portuguese governments, church groups in half a dozen countries, and the three liberation groups struggling for power within Angola. Surviving the affair required the concurrent use of *competing, compromising*, and *accommodating* modes of behavior for different actors and different demands. In addition to the simultaneous use of mixed modes, Gulf also varied its behavior in different phases of the long conflict.

Conflicts over human rights are dynamic, and many of the cases we surveyed revealed sequential use of different conflict management techniques: (1) Union Carbide, after nearly a decade of resistance, hardly raised a fuss when the U.S. Congress moved to repeal the Byrd Amendment in 1977. (2) IBM, after five years of struggle with church groups, finally accepted moral responsibility for the use to which its customers put their computers in a public statement in 1977. (3) Polaroid in 1971 compromised with demands for withdrawal from South

Africa with an innovative program and an end to governmental sales, and in 1977 accommodated *anticipated* pressures when it was discovered that its distributor had violated the earlier agreement. (4) Banks such as Citicorp, Chase Manhattan, Midland, and Amsterdam-Rotterdam reversed their long-standing policies on loans to South Africa after years of resistance to human rights action group demands. In each case the situation had changed—the stakes involved in meeting the demands had declined and/or previously opposing interests had grown more compatible.

The Impact on Human Rights

Given the nature of the human challenge to multinationals discussed in the previous chapter and their responses to it considered here, what is the "bottom line"? How effective has all of this effort been in actually improving the observance of human rights around the world? The evidence so far is not very promising. It may, of course, be too early to really see results—in the words of President Carter, one "cannot expect quick and easy results in the struggle for human rights, a struggle which has been going on for many centuries."[210] And with regard to MNEs the human rights crusade is still very much in its evangelical phase, with heavy amounts of empty rhetoric, moral indignation, and indeed double standards, but very little real change in human rights as a result. Many of the results have been more symbolic than practical and serve mainly, to borrow a phrase from Andrew Young, to "make liberals feel good," both in Europe and North America.[211]

In 1977–1979 we did see some modest relaxation of human rights violations in nations such as Bolivia, Ghana, Nigeria, Peru, Chile, Indonesia, South Korea, Thailand, the Philippines, and Brazil. Here and in other countries some political prisoners were released, some states of siege were lifted, there were some limitations in the use of torture, some on-site investigations by international organizations were permitted, some expanded freedom of the press and labor organizations was evidenced, and some signs of return to civilian rule emerged.[212] Some of these changes were little more than cosmetic efforts to lessen external pressure, however, and in none of these countries was the basic apparatus giving rise to the alleged human rights violations dismantled. And it is of course difficult to say how many of these changes would have occurred anyway, in the absence of the global human rights crusade or the involvement of multinationals therein. With the exception of Chile's junta, which apparently relaxed its social controls slightly out of fear of not being able to attract multinational corporate investment and bank loans, it is difficult to pinpoint where the nongovernmental arm-twisting of multinationals has had any effect in nudging governments along the path to broader observance of human rights. The social and economic costs of repression—in relations with other countries, international development agencies, and multinational corporate involvement—are apparently not yet greater than the perceived costs of relieving repression. If and when multinational corporate activities and multinational bank lending truly become contingent on the relaxation of repression, by whatever means, human rights concessions could become more than token.

Though well-intentioned, the human rights crusade against MNEs has to some extent been counterproductive. The deep and prolonged recession in Southern Africa, in part perhaps caused by multinational corporate retrenchment, has only served to stiffen the "laager" defensive mentality of the ruling Afrikaners and heighten antagonism toward reform. South African blacks have had to bear the brunt of the recession in the form of increased unemployment and perhaps more, rather than less, apartheid. Those who feel singularly virtuous for playing a role in reducing the flow of investment and loans to South Africa must accept part of the blame for any suffering which has resulted. And the way decolonization has been pursued in Angola and Mozambique, and now perhaps Namibia, has served to plunge these areas into economic chaos and decline, installed socialist governments with historically abysmal track records in "delivering the goods" of economic progress, and driven out human skills as well as physical capital. In the name of political and civil rights, outsiders may have served to injure basic human needs.

The human rights action groups, for their part, respond with the logic that although short-run effects may indeed be retrogressive, in the long run the prevailing regimes would not otherwise be likely to yield. They also appear to understand that human rights rhetoric tends to inflame emotions and lead to unfulfilled expectations on the part of the victims of repression. While usually accomplishing little in the short term, these inflammatory conditions are viewed as essential to the long run cause of human rights. To some extent this may be true, but the pursuit of justice sometimes leads to consequences contrary to those intended. Those who maintain that short-run misery must be borne in order to topple illegal or repressive regimes in Africa, for example, seem to base their views more on hope than experience. The African continent offers precious little evidence that free institutions inevitably follow the collapse of former regimes. In many cases the transition has only amounted to a switch from "white repression to black repression," and at times "to even harsher restrictions on personal liberty."[213] We must learn that in some cases, no matter what we do, our actions will have little or no impact on human rights. We must learn how to resist that strong temptation, in Stringfellow Barr's classic phrase, "to do good against people."

The Managerial Challenge

So far, the costs to multinationals of the human rights challenge have not really been significant. Little business, with the exception of sales in parts of Latin America, has been lost and no major signs of a harmful backlash have emerged abroad.[214] But what of the future? It is futile to try to predict the precise role that the pursuit of human rights will play in international affairs in the years ahead, although we are certain that it will be an enduring feature. The idea has been growing for decades and simply cannot be "delegitimized." Human rights have come to be established in the aspirations of people around the world. Polls in Western Europe and North America reveal that the goal of human rights remains exceedingly popular politically. Bureaucracies have been established within governments with the mission of ensuring that concern for rights is factored into policy-making—human rights is the "soul of our foreign policy," said President Carter in December, 1978.[215] The intensity of concern exhibited by "ethical institutional investors" is not likely to fade away in the absence of what they consider to be genuine reforms. And given the steady growth of global economic interdependence, we see nothing on the horizon that would serve to halt this rising international consciousness. Concern for basic human rights and its impact on multinational corporate activities is here to stay.

How may the human rights movement involving multinationals develop in the near term? It will likely continue to be one where private protest precedes unambiguous expressions and regulations of governments. It will also continue to be selective, determined in large measure by an interaction of media attention, nature and degree of repression, and the amount of home-country involvement over which leverage might be applied. As a result, it will also continue to be hypocritical, with massive attention to cases like Chile where change is in the cards and economic leverage exists, but largely silent in cases like East Germany where human rights violations are just as serious—indeed, systemic—but no prospects for change though external pressure exist. Still, human rights groups are likely to expand their involvement with Cuba, Eastern Europe, China, and the Soviet Union. Firms which have been pressed into renouncing the "financing of apartheid" may also be called on the carpet for "financing totalitarianism."

With MNE home governments pursuing a mix of political, military, economic, and other interests in their foreign policies, it is probably safe to predict that inconsistency will remain a hallmark of their human rights policies. Government guidance to multinationals will continue to be wishy-washy, tangle-footed, hypocritical, and indecisive. Both in Western Europe and North America there seems to be growing conviction on the part of legislators that they, rather than the executive branches of government, should be calling the shots on foreign affairs. This may be most true in the United States, where legislators and people in general are perhaps less modest about their ability to determine what's good for other people, than in most other home countries of today's MNEs. This portends more, not fewer, attempts to meddle in the internal affairs of other nations, and so we are likely to see a variety of efforts aimed at prohibiting the use of government facilities for promotion of essentially private flows of trade, investment, and credit to nations allegedly violating human rights. Judging from current trends, legislators seem increasingly intent on mixing morality with money, and international economics with international politics. This could mean more frequent deviations from liberal trade and investment principles in the name of human rights.

In addition to long-distance political watchdogs in home governments, we are also likely to find nongovernmental pressure groups increasingly passing judgment—again from a comfortable distance—on the internal affairs of other nations. One sees an increasing tendency of groups at home to condemn the philosophical premises upon which other societies operate as less "moral" in large measure because they are different. Multinationals may thus be increasingly confronted with rigid and hubristic demands from groups at home to impose their ideals and values on others in their operations abroad. Such "cultural imperialism" could eventually lead to a good deal of contempt and cynicism toward the Western world in general, with the MNEs caught in the middle. One of the great advantages attributed to MNEs is their high degree of adaptability in operating profitably in different social, cultural, and economic systems. The danger is that home-country "cultural imperialism" of this sort will seriously reduce that adaptability and thus cut into one of the basic strengths of MNEs.

The issue of human rights highlights the growing thrust for morality in the conduct of world business. This thrust is likely to blossom into a broad-based concern over the impact of multinational corporate activities on both human needs and human rights. Development scholars and planners are already rapidly moving towards "basic human needs" as a cardinal yardstick in appraising national growth policies and even individual projects. Under the emerging ethics, multinational enterprise will increasingly be subjected to close and critical scrutiny and held accountable for its impact on this broader notion of human dignity incorporating both rights and needs.

Given this scenario, what guidelines might be useful to multinationals in coping with the human rights conflicts of tomorrow? In specific situations we believe that the contingency approach outlined in Chapters 2 and 3 of this volume, involving an informed and careful examination of the conflict situation—stakes, power, interests, and relationships—has much to contribute. In choosing a particular conflict-handling behavior the firm must factor in desired outcomes and notions of feasibility. In doing so, management must consider the personal values of corporate employees, the ranking of corporate objectives, the firm's stakes in the outcome, its vulnerability to internal and external pressures, and the limits or boundaries of effective action imposed by available resources, competitive consequences, legal constraints, and prevailing social norms. But no mechanistic formula can produce an automatic or unambiguous answer.

In relating to human rights and needs in a particular host nation, the enlightened multinational might be wise to strive in its actions to satisfy the injunction of the Hippocratic oath: "above all else do no harm." At a minimum, this entails an obligation to be informed about the impacts of corporate actions and to consider them in decision making. The notion of a "human rights/needs impact statement" is an idea that is already beginning to circulate for planning purposes within companies. MNEs may also find it in their best interests to keep a cool distance from governments which have gone beyond acceptable limits of decency in the treatment of their citizens. There certainly is a point when despotism, brutality, and oppression in a country become so morally repugnant and universally detested that routine business considerations should be set aside. "The Hitler exception" is how one top-level executive of a large American multinational labeled this notion.[216] Exceptional cases call for exceptional responses.

It is hard to envision how a close identification of multinationals with cruelty, deprivation of civil liberties, and human degradation could possibly be in their overall long-term interests. In the short run it may indeed be opportune to support or tolerate a repressive government that provides a favorable operating climate. But over the long-term a regime that relies upon force for its authority can be neither popular nor stable—Iran, Uganda, Nicaragua. It is axiomatic that repression breeds opposition and polarization. Firms closely connected with state terror, corruption, and enrichment of the elite at the expense of the population as a whole generally will not fare very well when the day of liberation arrives. But what is "short-term" and what is "long-term?" Certainly Eastern European human rights violations cannot be considered short-term in nature, and a strong argument can be made that MNE involvement leading to a betterment of human-needs conditions will eventually lead to liberalization in long-term repressive regimes. Paradoxically, multinationals' contributions in the latter area depend fundamentally on the existing political system, and so the very catalyst of economic betterment may not fare very well when the day of reckoning comes.

The creative energies of multinationals are best unleashed under the kind of strongly incentive-oriented system achieved thus far only under capitalism. Given the "inescapable connection between capitalism and democracy,"[217] it is our view that multinational corporate interests over the long term will be better served by a clear identification with human rights and democratic values than with the interests of repressive regimes. And in the matter of human rights, much of mankind does share a set of basic values that transcends social systems, stages of development, and national frontiers. Multinationals that choose to ignore this point ultimately do so at their own peril.

7 *MONKEYS IN THE MIDDLE*

By their very nature, MNEs are bound to become embroiled from time to time in conflicts between national states. Whether the issue is war, territorial disputes, division of tax revenues, or any of a host of similar issues, the multinational firm often finds itself trapped in the middle. Even worse, the MNE may become a means for one country to exert its power over another. Particularly the home countries of multinationals find it tempting to use their influence over corporate headquarters to influence the behavior of the firm's affiliates in one or more host countries. Conversely, host countries may use their influence over the operations of MNE affiliates to influence, via the parent firm, the actions of the home-country government.

In this chapter we shall examine four major areas of such extraterritorial application of political power via the multinational enterprise—international trade boycotts, antitrust policies, strategic and defense-related trade controls, and political conflict involving multinationals in the petroleum sector. In each instance, we shall consider the nature of the political conflict, how it affected the MNEs involved, and how the conflict management techniques used succeeded or failed in effectively containing the damage to the individual enterprise.

INTERNATIONAL BOYCOTTS

As we have seen in our two chapters on human rights, trade boycotts are often used by one or more countries against another in order to bring about changes in internal conditions more to the liking of the boycotting countries. Whether the issue is apartheid, Soviet treatment of political dissidents, or Ugandan repression, the objective is the same—to raise the economic costs of heinous domestic political behavior. As we have already noted, it is not clear how effective such boycotts are in achieving their intended objectives, and it sometimes seems that they in fact achieve precisely the reverse.

International boycotts, of course, go well beyond the goals of altering domestic political behavior to encompass general objectives of international relations. For decades the United States boycotted trade with the People's Republic of China. It still does with North Korea, Vietnam, Cambodia, Laos, and Cuba. Various black African countries boycott trade with South Africa. Arab countries boycott trade with Israel. Greece boycotts trade with Turkey. And the list goes on, involving different countries, for different reasons, and with different degrees of impact. In virtually all of them, the MNE takes its familiar position as the "monkey in the middle," raising serious problems for the firm.

International boycotts have been around for centuries, "although the word itself dates back only a hundred years—from the surname of the rent collector of the Earl of Erne, Captain Charles Cunningham Boycott, of County Mayo, Ireland. Notorious for his severity, he was singled out for punishment in 1879 and became the first target of the action which would forever afterward bear his name. No one would work for him, speak to him, or supply him with goods or services; ultimately, he was driven out of his home, and out of Ireland."[1] While the evidence seems to suggest that international boycotts are in fact far less effective than in the case of the unfortunate captain, one observer has suggested that they represent options employed by nations which feel "the need to do something, but not too much." They "keep the issue alive" and strengthen the idea that the receiver of sanctions is in some sense an outcast.[2]

Whereas "boycott" is a word widely applied to consumer, labor, and anti-trust actions as well, in terms of an individual or collective "refusal to deal" the word "embargo" is much more commonly used to describe a nation's refusal to export to or import from another country or countries. Interestingly, in Arabic the word for both boycott and embargo is the same. Neither is illegal.

Indeed, the United States has been described by a former State Department official as an "Olympic champion of political trade controls," employing extensively both "primary" and "secondary" boycotts or embargoes.[3] In partial compliance with United Nations resolutions, it has maintained a limited embargo against South Africa and a full one against Rhodesia. The Trading with the Enemy Act and Export Administration Act restrict certain United States goods or technology from entering certain Communist nations. Secondary-type sanctions have been maintained through the U.S. Foreign Assistance Act, the Battle Act, Public Law 480 and the Maritime Administration—again mostly employed against Communist nations. Like other countries, the United States has used blacklists and certification requirements to police its own boycotts, intended to achieve political ends. But whereas such long-standing political control of international trade has been an irritant and periodic source of conflict for multinationals, nothing has been as troublesome as the Arab boycott against Israel and its consequences.

Evolution of the Arab Boycott

The history, mechanics, and structure of the Arab boycott have been extensively documented and studied.[4] More than one boycott is involved. The first—or "primary"—boycott, declared initially by the seven members of the Arab League in late 1945, involves a refusal by Arab states to trade with Israel in any way. Choice of trading partners is each nation's sovereign right. However, the primary boycott is most commonly enforced by certification procedures which often brings Western multinationals into political conflict with home-country and/or Arab governments.

The most common form of certificate as part of a bid, purchase order, or letter of credit, is the so-called "negative certificate of origin." As a precondition to payment or letting a contract, a participating Arab government importer or bank requires a foreign exporter or contractor to certify that the goods are neither made in Israel nor contain Israeli-made components. Questions of morality, discrimination, and foreign intervention have been raised concerning this form of certification to enforce a primary boycott, often involving American MNEs. Some Arab nations do accept "positive certificates of origin"—statements as to product origin without reference to Israel.

In April 1950, the Arab League extended the boycott to include third parties that contribute significantly to Israel's economic and military strength. This "secondary" boycott is aimed at firms that invest in or do business with Israel. A Central Boycott Office (CBO) was established in Damascus, Syria, to coordinate boycott activities, and a "blacklist" was created as the principal instrument for enforcing the secondary boycott. As codified by the Arab League in 1954, a company—and usually its affiliates as well—is blacklisted: (a) if it maintains a plant, agency, office, or licensee in Israel; (b) if it serves as a partner, technical adviser, agent, or natural resources prospector in Israel; or (c) if it refuses, after warning, to reply to CBO questions.[5] No universal blacklist exists. Each Arab country separately approves any CBO non-binding recommendations on adding or deleting firms, and thus maintains its own list. The actual size of the Arab nations' respective blacklists can only be surmised, although a few, notably the Saudi Arabian list, have been published in the West. In February 1975 Senator Frank Church revealed a roster of 1500 blacklisted American firms.

Maintenance of Arab blacklists has been both capricious and confusing. Companies can be listed and de-listed almost at random. Burlington Industries, Kaiser, and General Tire & Rubber have all been de-listed while Coca-Cola, Ford, and Xerox remain on many blacklists. Today there is hardly a "Fortune 500" company that has not in some way become involved with the Arab boycott.

A "tertiary" or "extended secondary" boycott emerged from the 1954 secondary CBO boycott regulations. To discourage indirect Arab contributions to the Israeli economy, the CBO forbade the use of materials, equipment, or services of a blacklisted firm by a non-blacklisted firm in exports or to projects in an Arab country. One American manufacturer, for example, almost had its contract to supply buses to Saudi Arabia cancelled when it was discovered that the seats were manufactured by a blacklisted firm—the seats were replaced and the contract went through. However, such prohibitions do not apply to a foreign company's relationships outside the Arab world. The tertiary boycott, although most indirectly applied and least frequently enforced, has come under extensive attack by critics because of its extraterritorial implications. It is primarily found in tenders for major project contracts rather than in normal trade transactions.

Over the years the CBO has incorporated various new rules and exceptions into the basic boycott principles, presumably to avoid damaging Arab economies in the name of the boycott. It does not, for example, affect government-to-government sales, thus allowing Arab countries to buy military equipment from the same American and European companies that supply Israel. Hotel chains, public service companies, and tourist ships are exempt from the boycott. Participating countries may purchase pharmaceutical products and certain spare parts from blacklisted companies when no alternative supply sources are available—for example Saudi Arabia imports television spare parts from blacklisted RCA.

The boycott has also never applied to firms which conduct only import and export trade with Israel. Foreign firms may sell finished goods from their own production to both Israel and Arab countries as long as no codified boycott regulations are broken—John Deere and Burlington Industries fall into this category. A few companies even have investments in both the Arab countries and Israel: Hertz Rent-a-Car, a blacklisted RCA subsidiary, operates in Israel and Egypt. According to an official of the Israeli Ministry of Finance, "There are many examples where actual investments in Israel do not harm the companies which continue to do business with the Arabs. The boycott does cause some problems, but that is due to the American companies' lack of knowledge about it. They would find if they study the matter carefully that they can do business with all the countries of the Middle East."[6]

Until recently, the boycott was of relatively little significance to most companies. Occasionally one company or another would feel the effects of the boycott, but until 1977 only a few provisions in United States law concerning the boycott had been passed by Congress. The issue emerged prominently in the international spotlight during the mid-1970s, however. OPEC oil power gave the Arab League nations infinitely greater economic clout—the Middle East oil reserves, the extraordinary new financial power of the Arab states, and the emergence of the area as a growth market fundamentally altered the positions of all parties concerned both in the boycott and in the Arab-Israeli conflict, of which the boycott is an integral part. With the much larger Western stake in the Arab world, both MNEs and the general public—often through interest groups committed to Israel—have become more cognizant of boycott operations. Yet the boycott has been misinterpreted, misunderstood, and intertwined emotionally with political, social, ethnic, legal, and economic issues, particularly in the United States. By the mid-1970's, a United States MNE found complying with the secondary and/or tertiary elements of the Arab boycott could be faced with concurrent suits in federal and/or state courts as well as action by federal and state antidiscrimination authorities. The publicity that such litigation engenders in a highly emotional atmosphere could easily trigger domestic boycotts against company products and possible Congressional hearings.

In fact, the United States government over the last thirty years has demonstrated a conspicuous lack of support for multinationals that were struggling with trade sanctions of the Arabs. More intensive diplomatic pressure—or at least persuasion—might have been attempted, and could possibly have shored up those interest groups in the Arab countries that were prepared to continue dealing with American multinationals despite violations of the boycott rules. In contrast to the conspicuous lack of action by Washington when Ford, RCA, and Coca-Cola were all blacklisted in the latter part of 1966, the German government moved decisively on behalf of Volkswagen in 1973–1976 and the move ultimately proved successful. The United States government continued to allow foreign states to dictate the policies of its companies, to set conditions limiting their freedom of action, and to interfere in their freedom of commerce.

Anti-Boycott Pressures

Despite growing pressure from groups committed to Israel such as the Antidefamation League and the American Jewish Congress, and from members of Congress with large Jewish constituencies, no significant legislation to "punish" the Arab states or companies collaborating in the boycott was passed until 1977. The government did not act sooner in part because the United States itself engages in similar trade restrictions. Indeed, when Congress first considered legislation against the Arab boycott in 1965, the State and Commerce Departments opposed it partly because of fears that American restrictions on trade with Cuba and the People's Republic of China would be compromised. But more important was the fact that the boycott had negligible impact on American economic activity. Except for the oil companies there was relatively little American trade with the Middle East before 1973—for example, exports to the area in 1964 totalled a mere $200 million. Few American companies or banks were in a position to receive boycott-related requests accompanying purchase orders or letters of credit.

A 1965 amendment to the Export Administration Act remained the official United States policy on the boycott until 1977. According to the amendment, the government would "encourage and request" domestic companies to refuse any action which supported boycotts by foreign nations against another nation friendly to the United States, and recipients of boycott requests were required to notify the Department of Commerce.

American exports to the 18 Arab countries rose to $1 billion in 1971, $5.4 billion in 1975 and $6.9 billion in 1976, and the Commerce Department projected that they would exceed $10 billion in 1980, exclusive of consulting services and construction projects. Boycott-related requests by Arab countries and the CBO grew apace. For example, in the year ending in October 1976, 3477 American exporters, banks, freight forwarders, insurers and common carriers reported 169,710 boycott-related requests in connection with 97,491 transactions having a total value of $7.7 billion. The boycott also began to affect the financial community, and gradually public pressure mounted for a vigorous American government reaction. Proposed anti-boycott legislation was put forward in 1975 and 1976—some two dozen bills were introduced in Congress and eight different Congressional sub-committees held hearings on the matter. The Administration, joined by oil company representatives, opposed most of the proposed legislation, arguing that it would cause political and economic reprisals and turn the United States into a "second-rate economic power," as a Mobil Oil advertisement put it. Election-year politics and enactment of anti-boycott legislation in a half-dozen states also contributed to the pressure.

In response, and to forestall possible legislation, President Ford in November 1975 and again in October 1976 took executive action which not only strengthened reporting requirements and monitoring procedures, but also released Commerce Department reports for public inspection. As a result, Congress limited its own actions to an amendment of the 1976 Tax Reform Act, which denied specific tax benefits to American companies participating in secondary or tertiary boycott activities. Still, the business sector was not reassured. One executive was quoted as saying "We're goddamned scared of having our name linked with this boycott in any way. . . . What really seems to concern the business community isn't so much the new disclosure policy itself, but the growing anti-boycott sentiment if reflects."[7]

By the end of 1977 it was felt that the combined pressures of mandatory reporting of boycott activities to the government, proposed Congressional legislation to prohibit certain corporate activities in relation to the boycott, threat of loss of tax benefits, and threat of antitrust litigation by the government or private parties would serve as deterrents. The effects were not symmetrical, however, as medium and small American companies found it difficult to absorb the legal, advisory and administrative costs involved in understanding and coping with the anti-boycott measures. Many simply left the field. Even so, the Carter Administration in 1977 supported strict laws to prohibit boycott compliance, and a Louis

Harris poll published in early 1977 showed that a sizeable majority of the respondents favored strong anti-boycott laws as well as penalties on companies which complied with the Arab trade sanctions against Israel.

The State Department was once again joined by the oil companies in opposing more rigorous legislation—the chairman of the Arabian American Oil Company (Aramco), Frank Jungers, declared in an interview that business "will shift . . . from the U.S. to Western Europe or Japan or elsewhere."[8] Mobil Oil was again actively publishing newspaper advertisements against anti-boycott laws. Exxon joined with a mail campaign urging members of Congress to vote against the anti-boycott bills being introduced. But the Carter Administration recognized the new and determined mood of Congress. So did an important segment of the American business community. Chief executives of 170 major United States companies represented on the "Business Roundtable" met in March and April 1977 with the Anti-Defamation League and agreed on "legislative language" for an anti-boycott bill which President Carter would "strongly recommend."

A bill which amended the Export Administration Act was signed into law in June 1977. It explicitly prohibits (a) discriminatory business practices, (b) furnishing of information supporting the boycott, (c) attesting to negative certificates of origin, and (d) implementation of boycott-related letters of credit. A criminal penalty of up to $25,000 or one year imprisonment along with a "civil penalty" up to $10,000 can be imposed. The new law also contained exceptions to its prohibitions, allowing "unilateral selection" of carriers, insurers, and suppliers by an Arab customer, compliance with Arab laws forbidding imports of Israeli products into Arab countries, as well as "positive" certificates of origin. The term "United States person" used in the Act has been defined to include any United States resident or national, any American domestic concern, and any foreign subsidiaries or affiliates controlled by it. It also includes American branches of foreign business concerns. The extraterritorial implications of this legislation are still being studied by lawyers the world over.

Prior to the 1977 legislation, American multinationals were free to respond to the Arab boycott in a wide variety of ways. At one end of the range was RCA, which had no idea whether or not it would be de-listed if it withdrew its license from a small record-pressing operation in Israel but refused to do so in any case. As an RCA executive explained: "We're a worldwide communications company that has done business with China and Rumania, and we'd like to do business with the Arabs. But we are not going to end relations with Israel to get an Arab contract. This is a moral issue that we feel strongly about."[9] It was estimated that as a result of the blacklisting RCA lost about $9 million in Arab sales as well as routinely being cut out of contracts by companies that adhered to tertiary boycott demands.

Other MNEs with investments on one or the other side of the Middle East conflict have had to accept the fact that they are stuck with their choice. The oil companies, for example, have not and will not market any products bearing their labels in Israel. Some construction, engineering, and mining companies such as Kaiser and Bechtel also have large projects in the Arab world but nothing in Israel. Miles Laboratories, with subsidiaries and joint ventures in Israel, has never been active in Arab countries. Mobil Oil and Dresser Industries, with a great deal of business in Arab countries, became highly visible and politically active in their opposition to anti-boycott legislation.

Three blacklisted American multinationals, Coca-Cola, Ford and Xerox, began negotiating with the Arabs to be de-listed—the blacklistings had occurred because Coca-Cola licensed a bottling plant near Tel Aviv, an Israeli company annually assembles about 5000 Fords, and Xerox financed a documentary film about Israel. The ban is not total, since Coke is bottled and sold in Morocco, Tunisia, and Algeria, and Xerox copying machines are used in Egypt, although the companies have lost ground to competitors. De-listing discussions were primarily with the Egyptians, who have been eager for foreign investment, and joint projects were proposed which would contribute to Egypt's economic development in return for de-listing—the whole strategy became moot following the Egyptian-Israeli peace settlement. Although boycott rules do not permit de-listing simply because a company is willing to match its activity in Israel with some corresponding level of activity in the Arab world, some trade-offs of this kind have taken place.

Any negotiations undertaken by American multinationals have had to take into account the possibility of a strong domestic reaction, with pro-Israel groups organizing demonstrations and boycotts if, for example, a company were to try to back away from Israel in order to get into Kuwait or Saudi Arabia. Coca-Cola, Chevron and Rockwell International have been subjected to Jewish retaliation. And so any such agreements would presumably have to be palatable to Jewish opinion in the United States.

Bechtel

The United States government has thus far attempted to use antitrust law as a weapon against the Arab boycott on only one occasion, a suit filed in January 1976 against the Bechtel Corporation, with about $3.5 billion worth of business in 1974 and foreign contracts worth $450 million. At the time, the Ford Administration feared that direct anti-boycott legislation would anger the Arabs, yet its existing policy would not satisfy increasingly vocal pro-Israel groups in the United States in an election year. And so it sought refuge in its antitrust laws to deal with the boycott. The Justice Department charged Bechtel under Section 1 of the Sherman Act with implementing an agreement to refuse to deal with American subcontractors blacklisted by certain Arab countries and to require all of its American subcontractors to refuse similar dealings.

On the day the complaint was filed, Bechtel issued a statement calling the charges "totally unwarranted" and promised that they would be opposed vigorously.[10] Bechtel insisted that compliance with the laws of foreign governments, such as boycott laws, was not illegal in the United states and that the firm's policies were non-discriminatory and in compliance with existing law. Several days later an antitrust law specialist summed up the suit as a case "where two sovereigns each have jurisdiction and prescribe conflicting rules of law," and concluded that when litigation involved American defendants whose actions have harmed other Americans the resolution will be "that adherence to the boycott is illegal."[11]

In late April 1976 Bechtel filed a stiff multiple defense of its actions stressing the political dimensions of the case.[12] Bechtel's President, ex-Treasury Secretary George Schultz, summed up the defense as based on "the sovereign right of any country to stipulate what goods can be imported" and "of clients, whether Arabs or others, to review a list of bidders and strike those which are not preferred."[13]

A proposed consent decree was filed in mid-January 1977, which allowed the Justice Department to make its point public and Bechtel to agree to follow certain business practices without admitting wrongdoing of any kind. A Bechtel statement said that the company's initial reaction was to reject any agreement and to pursue the matter through legal channels "because we violated no laws and have not discriminated." But the issues involved in the suit had become "extremely emotional" and litigation would "result in widespread and polarized media coverage and prolonged public discussion," so that the best solution from Bechtel's point of view would be to work out a consent decree through negotiations with the Justice Department.[14] Although in early April Jewish groups protested against the proposed settlement, the proposed consent decree appeared to defuse the situation.

Bechtel's agreement to the proposed judgment notwithstanding, it subsequently attempted to withdraw its consent, citing several reasons for its change of mind. The company contended that the Arab boycott was beyond the scope of the Sherman Act because the boycott is political in nature, that the relief provided in the proposed decree was "overly stringent" and unnecessary in light of the enactment of the export Administration Amendments of 1977, and that the judgment "improperly" extended the reach of the antitrust laws extraterritorially.[15] Bechtel's arguments failed to sway the federal judge, however, and a final judgment with language identical to the earlier one was issued and signed in January, 1979.

The company had everything to lose and little to gain from an all-out defense of the lawsuit—a classic no-win situation.[16] Bechtel's mix of *competition* and *accomodation* produced an outcome that it can probably live with. The judgment prevents the company from refusing to deal with any U.S. blacklisted individuals or companies as subcontractors for any major construction projects. But if an Arab nation specifically and unilaterally selects a subcontractor using boycott principles and directs Bechtel to employ that choice, Bechtel will be allowed to do so. A company spokesman in 1979 commented: "With this decision, we have three laws—Internal Revenue Service, antitrust, and export administration law—governing the conduct of American companies doing business in the Middle East. The inconsistencies between these laws leave companies in a position where the most careful compliance with one law may involve you in conduct prohibited by another."[17]

Coca-Cola

In late 1964, Coca-Cola's management faced a critical policy decision on whether to grant a bottling franchise to its Israeli distributor, the Tempo Bottling Company of Israel, thereby antagonizing its Arab customers.[18] The following January, management decided that the demand prospects for Coke in Israel did not justify a bottling plant at that time, and declined the opportunity to offer a franchise. The potential Israeli market for Coke at the time (2.5 million people) was dwarfed by the 104.7 million population of the Arab League countries. The hot, dry climate and the anti-alcohol culture combined to make Arabs among Coke's heaviest consumers. Like all cola drinkers, however, they were vulnerable to defection in favor of a rival brand. In contrast, previous governments in Israel, to minimize foreign exchange problems, had denied Coca-Cola a bottling franchise in preference to local citrus-based drinks. The company also found Tempo Bottling Company a rather unsuitable partner—Coke filed a court suit in 1963 against Tempo for infringing upon its trademark, and was unhappy with Tempo for bottling other soft drinks. Dissatisfied with Coca-Cola's decision, Tempo asked the Anti-Defamation League in the United States to undertake an investigation. After a fifteen month study, the Anti-Defamation League in April 1966 released a report charging Coca-Cola with discriminating against Israel by cooperating with the Arab boycott.[19]

A few days later, James Farley, chairman of the Coca-Cola Export Corporation, vehemently denied the charge of complying with the boycott. He also contended that Coke's decision was based on (a) detailed economic and market surveys that indicated a low success potential in the Israeli market, (b) the fact that Tempo "had been found guilty in a Tel Aviv court of infringing the Coca-Cola trademark and bottle design", (c) the conclusion that a plant would not be "mutually profitable" to Tempo and Coke, (d) the fact that similar plant decisions had also been made in Jordan and Syria, (e) Coca-Cola's record as a goodwill ambassador for the United States by operating profitably at home and abroad, and (f) the view that Coke's decision was based solely on economic grounds and therefore violated neither United States statutes nor Congressional intent.[20]

In the meantime, Coca-Cola's decision as reflected in the Anti-Defamation League's report had created an uproar among American Jews. Despite the company's counter-arguments and the League's opposition to a consumer boycott of Coke in the United States, one of the shortest, most caustic and successful boycott actions took place in early April 1966. Bars, restaurants, and shops announced they were switching to rival colas. Mount Sinai Hospital in New York stopped serving Coke in its cafeteria. Nathan's Famous Hot Dog Emporium took full-page ads announcing it would no longer serve Coke. The company stood to lose the patronage of some 5.6 million American Jews. Within less than a week, Coca-Cola had lost an estimated $5 million in sales. Management was forced to reverse its decision, and on April 15 Coca-Cola granted a franchise to the Israeli Development Corporation. The one silver lining on the cloud was that Coke was able to bypass Tempo entirely.[21]

Shortly thereafter, the Central Boycott Organization gave Coca-Cola three months to "clarify" its concession arrangements, noting that more people consumed Coke in Arab countries than in the United States itself. Six months later, on November 20, 1966, the Arab League Boycott Conference in Kuwait voted unanimously for a ban by all Arab countries on dealings with Coca-Cola, but added that the "application of the ban is up to each member state of the Arab League."[22] A nine-month time limit was set to allow bottling plants to use up inventories of Coke syrup—ironically, the day before the conference opened a Coca-Cola advertisement placed in *Al Ahram* in Cairo announced the opening of its new Kuwait plant. The 29 franchised Coca-Cola bottlers in Arab countries were taken over by local imitators or by Coke's arch-rival, Pepsi-Cola. A Coca-Cola plant was built outside Tel Aviv and opened for business in February 1968, and today Coke is probably the most popular drink in Israel.

In mid-1975, Coca-Cola began "negotiating a joint venture for an agricultural project with the Egyptian government" in discussions that dragged on for the next three years.[23] In September 1977 the company signed an agreement with a number of Egyptian public enterprises to form a joint venture for the development of 15,000 acres of citrus groves near Ismailia. The long-anticipated agreement was described by a company spokesman as "a major breakthrough" whereby "we believe we can expect the support of the Egyptian government in our efforts to get off the boycott list." The spokesman stressed that the agreement "of course does not affect our ongoing business with Israel."[24] Nothing happened.

Frustrated in its inability to get off either the CBO or Egyptian blacklist, Coke management pressed on with additional plans for reentry into the Middle East markets. In March 1978 it was reported that Coca-Cola had made preliminary plans to undertake joint ventures with Saudi Arabia to build a $15 million canning plant, and with Egypt to establish a $4 million soft drink syrup plant. However both projects, whereby Coke would subsequently sell concentrate to each enterprise, remained contingent on the company's removal from the blacklist.[25]

By negotiating with the Saudis and the Egyptians, Coca-Cola continued a strategy of forging ties with both private and government groups in the Middle East. The stakes were high—a company official estimated that upon removal from the blacklist, Coca-Cola could "sell at least 100 million cases of soft drinks in the first full year of operation, an amount equivalent to 2% of the company's total current volume."[26] However, the Central Boycott Office on several occasions attacked both American multinationals and Egypt for such accords, indicating a growing sensitivity to de-listing publicity.[27] The resulting signals have been mixed. A customs official in Alexandria in March 1978 destroyed 12,000 cases of inbound Coca-Cola because of the boycott, yet in mid-May a "verbal agreement to resume Coke sales" in Egypt was reported, although "a date hasn't been set for Coke's reentry into the Egyptian market."[28] A low profile thus seemed to be emerging in future moves on reentry. Following the Egyptian–Israeli peace settlement, Coke received the green light and began distribution in July 1979.

Ford Motor Company

The Kuwait conference blacklisted Ford on the same day it banned Coca-Cola. The reason given was that the company had entered into a licensing agreement authorizing an Israeli firm to assemble British and American Ford trucks and tractors for the Israeli market, thereby reducing the cost of Israeli import duties on the finished product. Ford had previously announced plans in May 1966 and again in July to establish a car assembly operation in Israel as well. Ford dealers in Lebanon had warned their government in October that a boycott not only would put many of them out of the business but also deprive at least 6000 local workers of their jobs.[29]

Four days after the boycott was announced, it was reported that the Ford assembly plant in Alexandria, Egypt, with an estimated value of $3 million, had been seized by Egyptian customs authorities.[30] The alleged reason was that Ford owed $1.8 million in customs duties on components and parts assembled at the plant. Ford had been negotiating on the matter for the previous eighteen months. It was also reported that Egyptian officials had seized other Ford assets and property, and had frozen Ford bank accounts "until this matter is settled."[31]

Over the next several days Ford officials in Detroit, the Egyptian Embassy in Washington, and the U.S. State Department all denied that the plant had been seized or that the ongoing customs dispute with Ford was related to the Arab boycott. On December 1, it was reported that the Egyptian government had released all seized Ford property and bank accounts in return for a $1.15 million letter of guarantee by Ford for unpaid customs duties owed.[32] A few weeks later an announcement by Ford agreeing to pay overdue customs duties coincided with an announcement by the Central Boycott Office of a nine-month time limit to allow Arab plants to sell existing stocks of Ford vehicles and parts. By the end of 1967, Ford's Alexandria plant was being used for repair and maintenance of existing vehicles only, and an almost total ban on the sale of Ford vehicles in the Arab countries had begun.

Nearly a decade later, in October, 1975, a Ford Motor company delegation began negotiating the establishment of $230 million in "industrial projects" in Egypt.[33] As negotiations continued over the next two years, a serious open clash between Egypt and the CBO developed. The Egyptian government was determined to get blacklisted multinationals who promised to be large employers and exporters into the country with or without the Arab boycott. The more doctrinaire boycotters at the CBO were highly critical of such actions, which they viewed as an Egyptian sellout of boycott principles.

In October 1977, however, Ford and the Egyptian government signed a joint venture agreement to manufacture and assemble diesel engines and trucks in a $145 million plant near Alexandria. It was estimated that the facility "could be producing $90 million worth of trucks and diesel engines a year" by the mid-1980s, both for Egypt and for "Western markets as well as the Middle East and Africa."[34] Significantly, the agreement did not provide that Egypt had to work formally within the Arab League to get Ford de-listed.

The head of the CBO immediately blasted the agreement as "a disturbing violation" and threatened that any products from the joint venture "would be banned in Arab markets."[35] The boycott official was especially critical of Egypt for not imposing the same blacklist removal conditions on Ford as it had on Coca-Cola. Indeed, it may well be that Ford erred in not including such a clause in its final agreement with Egypt, so as to allow the CBO more of a chance to save face over violation of boycott principles.

Ford management obviously believed that Egyptian-made vehicles would find their way into other Arab countries normally stricter about enforcing the boycott. By negotiating directly with the Egyptians, Ford was thus on the verge of gaining reentry for an investment in Egypt much larger than its commitment in Israel—later stymied by the withdrawal of Arab capital following the Egyptian-Israeli peace settlement. As part of its new "open-door" investment policy, by late 1977 Egypt had approved over 50 projects with American companies, several of which were blacklisted. And there were signs that Saudi Arabia and even Syria were following Egypt's quest for Western investment and trade. So American multinationals investing in or trading with Israel may in the future be asked only to supply larger quantities of particular goods or services to an Arab nation in order to qualify for entry into Arab markets—if not for removal from official blacklists. Again, the Egyptian–Israeli peace settlement will no doubt significantly alter the ultimate outcome.

Mobil Oil

To gather public support for its position against the United States anti-boycott legislation, Mobil Oil Company issued a series of letters and advertisements during 1976 and 1977 in various print media, intending to convey to the public the repercussions of such legislation—loss of access to oil, loss of foreign revenues, loss of American status and the like.[36] These provoked considerable interest in the business community as well as counter-statements from such groups as the American Jewish Congress and U.S. Representative Benjamin Rosenthal, who drafted much of the anti-boycott legislation.

Mobil recognized that it was dealing simultaneously with a number of parties—the general public, the Jewish community, the CBO, Mobil stockholders and customers, business colleagues, supporters and opponents of the anti-boycott measures, the United States government, and Arab governments. It could hardly expect to win all of these games. Mobil hoped to win or play to a standoff those conflicts with parties who could most significantly affect the company's future economically or politically. Its strategy, of carrying out an open campaign in the press against pending anti-boycott legislation without attempting the impossible task of swaying public opinion over to the Arab side, could only enhance its standing with the Arabs and opponents of the legislation, while at the same time minimizing repercussions from pro-legislation groups. With significant crude oil interests in Saudi Arabia, Abu Dhabi, and Iran, Mobil's primary intent was to indicate to its Arab hosts a willingness to support their cause by making Americans more aware of their growing dependence on Arab oil. Mobil fought hard and openly against anti-boycott legislation, and could do no more. And indeed, Mobil felt no significant repercussions from either the United States government, the general public, the Jewish community, or other groups. Two news items: (1) Mobil shareholders in May 1977 soundly defeated a boycott compliance move; and (2) Egypt in February 1978 awarded Mobil a portion of its Sinai exploration rights.[37]

The Arab boycott represents a political conflict situation that has caught the MNE between political interest groups and nations which on occasion extend their extraterritorial reach. Multinationals that are successfully coping with the Arab boycott are politically astute—they know when to negotiate with governments and/or interest groups, and when to publicly speak out as pro-active lobbyists and modifiers of public opinion. Evidently, multinationals that are willing to listen to outside advice and have built a political strategy to confront the challenge of contradictory demands have been most successful in such conflicts.

Final Department of Commerce anti-boycott regulations were adopted in early 1978 to enforce the law, but do not seem to represent insuperable barriers to normal commercial relations between American multinationals and participants in the Arab boycott of Israel.[38] One observer summarizes them as having "a slight chilling effect on new Middle East ventures. But from every sign, existing business arrangements are holding up well because of legal loopholes and a new Arab willingness to bend boycott rules."[39] Saudi Arabia and Kuwait have been cited as having agreed to contract wording that would both appear to comply with CBO principles and yet omit direct references to the boycott that are forbidden by American law. As of mid-1979, no American company had been charged with violating the law, but the Commerce Department was actively investigating about 70 companies for possible breaches of the legislation.

Overall, the new United States anti-boycott rules have had a mixed impact on Arab investment and trade by American MNEs. American regulations have been reported as making it "doubly difficult" for American MNEs to operate in the three "hard-line" countries of Iraq, Libya, and Syria.[40] Yet in spite of fierce Japanese and European competitors in these countries, trade by United States firms has increased at a faster rate than trade with other Arab countries. In another group of Arab states—Kuwait, Qatar, and Oman—the situation has been described as "touch and go." They have taken a strict view on boycott policy but are generally friendlier to the United States and have made exceptions on a case-by-case basis. The situation is "less vexing" in a third tier of countries: Saudi Arabia, the United Arab Emirates, Bahrain, and Jordan. These nations, which have close ties with the United States diplomatically and economically, take care to administer their boycott policies in such a way that American MNEs are less likely to become embroiled in political conflict situations. In Egypt, of course, there is now an open door. A Commerce Department official noted in mid-1979 that "the ultimate impact of the law can't be determined right now, but it's fair to say that those who predicted a disastrous impact have been proven wrong."[41] As a result, and after months of quiet discussion, the Business Roundtable and B'nai B'rith's Anti-Defamation League, the American Jewish Congress and the American Jewish Committee all agreed in 1979 to support an extension, without modifications, of the controversial law.[42]

COMPETITION POLICY

One of the most conflict-prone areas facing multinationals, particularly American firms, is the extension overseas of national antitrust policy. As we shall see in the uranium cartel case discussed in Chapter 14, this has sometimes pitted the United States government against host countries as well as its own multinational enterprises. Its aggressive legal forays onto foreign soil, demanding documents, serving writs and hearing evidence, and the general posture that it has the right to command the cooperation of foreigners, have stirred up widespread protest. A number of Western governments have complained that the United States is infringing on their national sovereignty, sometimes with legal action barring their nationals from complying with American demands.

Charges of extraterritorial interference have been leveled by Canada, Britain, and the Netherlands over indictments by United States courts of American-owned affiliates for behavior that is considered entirely legal by the host governments. Antitrust decrees have forced United States parent companies to divest themselves of individual foreign affilitates or alter their activities in fundamental ways. One observer describes such political conflict as "a series of clashes between United States policy and that of other nations, in which the corporation has on occasion been something like the bird in a badminton game."[43] In this area, the decision whether or not to engage in particular transactions abroad is fraught with uncertainty regarding potential American antitrust consequences.

Many types of multinational corporate transactions may be subject to United State antitrust laws. For example, what antitrust consequences might be involved in a horizontal merger that takes place in a foreign country where the firm sells some or all of its output in the United States? Would it make any difference if the merger were mandated by the foreign government, or if it were simply permitted under the law of the foreign country? Suppose three American companies were planning separately to establish affiliates in a foreign market, but learned that the foreign government would permit only one foreign firm to enter. If two of these companies formed a joint venture in the foreign market and thereby precluded the third from entering, would this be illegal under the Sherman or Clayton Acts? What if an American company selling abroad agreed to accept payment conditioned on the expenditure of those funds in certain countries? What about the antitrust implications of a United States corporation agreeing with its foreign subsidiary not to export merchandise to the latter's domestic market because of a commitment it has made to its local competitors? Would it matter if the commitment had approval of the foreign government, or indeed was mandated by the foreign government? What if foreign manufacturers agreed to purchase standardized components from suppliers in their own country, thereby precluding a participating affiliate of a U.S. company from purchasing similar components from American suppliers? Do such actual or potential restraints on American commerce create United States antitrust problems and influence the behavior of the firm?

The legal basis for foreign intervention by the United States government derives mainly from the antitrust provisions of the Sherman and Clayton Acts, whose overseas impact has been broadened over the years by liberal judicial interpretations. These powers were significantly widened in 1976 by the Antitrust Improvement Act and the Foreign Sovereign Immunities Act, which gave the United States power to sue foreign governments as well as private companies for anticompetitive behavior and to demand evidence from third parties having business links in antitrust cases. In January of 1978 the Supreme Court ruled that foreign governments have the same rights as "persons" under American antitrust law and can now file suit under American antitrust statutes when they are injured by American corporate activities abroad.

Section 1 of the Sherman Act outlaws restrictive trade agreements, and Section 2 declares monopolies illegal. Because the Sherman Act has covered commerce "with foreign nations" since 1890, the application of the antitrust laws to international trade is not a new development. A prerequisite to extraterritorial jurisdiction and antitrust liability for acts committed abroad has been stated by the courts to be a "substantial effect" (or sometimes as a "direct and substantial effect") on the interstate or foreign commerce of the United States. This jurisdiction has often been challenged by defenses such as: (a) the "act of state" doctrine whereby United States courts will not sit in judgment of a foreign sovereign's conduct in its own territory, (b) the doctrine of foreign governmental compulsion and (c) other claims based on considerations of international comity.[44]

The Clayton Act of 1914, on the other hand, expands on the Sherman Act and regulates mergers—Section 7 applies to mergers both in the United States and abroad that substantially affect American foreign commerce. By mid-1973 the Justice Department had filed almost 250 antitrust cases involving foreign trade in some way. Not once did the government lose on the grounds that the suit was beyond the international scope of the statute.

The United States government has been consistent in its view that antitrust enforcement policy has two major purposes with respect to international commerce:[45] (1) to protect the American consumer by assuring him the "benefit of competitive products and ideas produced by foreign competitors as well as domestic competitors", and (2) to protect American export and investment opportunities against "privately imposed restrictions."[46] In judging antitrust issues, the courts proceed on the principle that competition is good *per se,* and that rule of reason therefore dictates that restraints are bad. This view frequently conflicts with foreign laws on competition and monopoly despite, for example, similarities between Articles 85 and 86 of the Treaty of Rome and United States antitrust legislation.[47] Broad extraterritorial application of American antitrust laws has resulted in key court cases covering many different dimensions of antitrust including mergers, access to information, licensing, patents, and technology. These have helped form a solid basis for the exercise of American extraterritorial jurisdiction.

Extraterritorial application of United States antitrust laws occur in three principal ways.[48] First, there is the possibility of prosecution of intrafirm conspiracy in the event of agreements made between an American parent and its foreign affiliate. An example is the prosecution of the Timken Roller Bearing Co. in 1951 for its agreement not to compete with its British and French affiliates in Europe and to prevent those affiliates from competing in the Western Hemisphere. Timken's affiliations overseas involved a large minority participation in British Timken, and a fifty-fifty ownership by Timken (United States) and Dewar (its partner in British Timken) in French Timken. In finding the agreement illegal the courts made clear that investment in an affiliated firm abroad does not necessarily provide reliable legal protection for a restrictive agreement. To avoid such outcomes, foreign affiliate operations may be incorporated separately giving management in the host country complete autonomy, or the parent may establish branch plants rather than subsidiaries in foreign countries and thus minimize managerial autonomy—either total control or no control at all—by the parent.

Second, a United States court may order an American multinational to divest itself of interests in a particular country. In 1950, United States courts ordered Alcoa to sell off its interests in Alcan, and in 1951 forced the termination of the joint ownership of Canadian Industries Ltd. by DuPont and Imperial Chemical Industries Ltd. (United Kingdom). Both divested themselves of their Canadian holdings despite the Canadian government's resentment of the American intrusion into Canadian affairs. In both cases it was suggested that competition increased in Canada as a result of the American court decisions. A study commissioned by the Justice Department in Ottawa failed to uncover any detrimental economic effects in either the Alcoa or DuPont cases.[49]

While there are not likely to be United States antitrust problems if an American MNE independently establishes its own branch, subsidiary, or affiliate abroad, this may not be the case if a joint venture is established overseas with the firm's competitors. In the early postwar period, four-fifths of the abrasives industry, including the Minnesota Mining and Manufacturing Company, combined to establish joint ventures in Canada, Germany and Britain to serve foreign markets instead of exporting from the United States. The common ownership arrangement was found by the courts to curtail or restrain the exports of each of the members, although there was the suggestion as well that joint ventures abroad by dominant American firms might also be illegal because of a tendency to dampen the domestic rivalry of the partners.

Third, American multinationals may be forbidden to acquire companies in particular host countries. Competition in the American market was the real issue in 1966 when United States courts prevented Schlitz Brewing Company from purchasing control of John Labatt, Ltd. in Canada. However, a decade later American antitrust officials did not proceed against the acquisition of British Aluminium by Reynolds Aluminum, although the former was about to build a large reduction plant in Quebec, because there appeared to be no substantial impact on American commerce.

Certainly a landmark case was a United States court action in 1968 against Gillette's purchase of Braun A. G. in Germany, the third largest manufacturer of electric razors in Europe. The complaint alleged that if the acquisition went through it would result in the elimination of Braun as a potential competitor in the American market. This was the first time that a United States court challenged an American multinational's acquisition of a foreign concern on the grounds of *potential* rather than actual reduction of domestic competition. According to an American antitrust lawyer, if the government won "a lot of companies are going to have to review their overseas merger policies."[50] However, Gillette was not deterred from buying up more of Braun stock. The original 1967 acquisition of 85% of Braun stock had increased to 92% by 1970.[51] Gillette agreed to keep the assets of the acquisition separate until the legal matter was resolved.

By the mid-1970s, American antitrust law was being applied overseas in "a new tempo of enforcement" which included: (a) probes into alleged illegal setting of uranium, phosphate, and ocean shipping prices by American and foreign competitors; (b) reviews of overseas licensing agreements of some two dozen MNEs as to whether their pricing or territorial arrangements unreasonably prevented overseas producers from selling in the United States; and (c) investigations of oil company reactions to the American two-tier pricing system for foreign crude as well as other aspects of their relations with oil-producing countries.[52] American antitrust officials assured Congressional questioners that "where there appears to be a substantial restriction of U.S. trade resulting from the merger, we will take appropriate action under antitrust laws."[53]

Perhaps the most striking political conflict situations now involve the efforts of host-country governments to rationalize and concentrate their industries. Independent oil tanker owners reportedly met in Norway with government sanction to launch a joint scheme to take tonnage out of service and prop-up disastrously low rates.[54] However, the plan was seriously weakened by American antitrust officials' views that any participating American oil companies would risk antitrust charges. The European Community has embarked on a series of cartel-like schemes to cushion the impact of severe recessions on output, employment, and profits in key industries, providing for production cutbacks, floor prices, import controls, market sharing, and rationalization of investments—oil refining, shipbuilding, synthetic fibers, steel, and possibly autos are involved. Subsidiaries of American multinationals have boycotted such arrangements on the grounds that they would violate United States antitrust law, despite the obvious weakening of the respective EEC policies.[55] According to a DuPont spokesman, "We were contacted but chose not to participate in any discussion, and we have not indicated we would cooperate with any agreement."[56] DuPont and Monsanto both cut back synthetic fiber manufacturing capacity in the EEC in the early part of 1977, and a tacit understanding that American multinationals operating in Europe would not capitalize on the synthetic fibers accord seemed to have been struck with their European competitors.[57]

Nevertheless, a number of American nultinationals have in effect called for exemption from United States antitrust laws in arranging business among foreign affiliates. For example, American-based construction and engineering firms would like to be able to join together in bidding on foreign contracts under the provisions of the 1918 Webb-Pomerene Act, which was passed to permit copper and other industries to form export associations that could compete against the foreign cartels of the time. However, the Justice Department has consistently rejected the idea even though foreign bidding on major construction contracts is commonly a joint government-industry affair abroad. The results have begun to be felt. For example, in July 1977 Alcoa and Reynolds Metals announced they would not go ahead with plans to build a joint $650 million aluminum smelter in Western Australia because of American government antitrust pressures. The state's premier angrily maintained that the United States should not be allowed to pursue its companies all over the world with its domestic antitrust laws. Alcoa and Reynolds both denied they had been approached by the Justice Department. An Alcoa spokesman said "there wasn't any U.S. government pressure" of a direct nature, but he did concede that "there are always antitrust considerations where there's a consortium involving competitors."[58]

A more highly publicized case was a 1977 bid for a Saudi Arabian telecommunications expansion project worth well over $3 billion. A consortium of Philips (Netherlands), L.M. Ericsson (Sweden), and Bell Telephone (Canada) beat out the two separate American bidders—ITT and AT&T's Western Electric— who were reportedly "stunned" at the outcome. Although influence-peddling by agents was a factor, all of the parties in the winning consortium were well-connected. The awarding of the contract seemed to depend upon the ability of the bidders to quickly and clearly respond to the Saudis directly and through their own governments. Both American bidders maintained that a United States consortium—or even more open and more accessible communications and coordination between them—would probably have led to a successful bid.

In July 1978 a White House task force announced a plan for a 12-point national policy to promote United States exports and remove obstacles to American businesses operating abroad. The task force reportedly listed several "options" in the antitrust field. One involved helping U.S. construction and engineering companies win more foreign contracts by allowing them to set up joint ventures without worrying about Sherman Antitrust Law violations. Another called for new government guidelines on how antitrust laws apply to international activities of American companies. However, it is doubtful that American antitrust considerations will diminish greatly as a source of conflict for multinationals. At a minimum, foreign governments increasingly involved in the conduct and ownership of business will be increasingly offended at interference by United States courts. As one observer put it, "antitrust law, and its application to conduct beyond the border of the legislating territory, is no longer solely an American aberration from good taste."[59]

To summarize, whereas an American multinational may operate within a foreign country's internal commerce, directly or through a subsidiary, it may incur antitrust liability if its activities restrain United States commerce. Second, American multinationals are generally subject to United States court orders for the production of documents or information in the possession of their foreign subsidiaries in antitrust suits, and should not depend on broad foreign prohibitions to protect such documents from scrutiny. Third, American multinationals should avoid participating in foreign cartels which may substantially affect American trade and closely watch their foreign subsidiaries in this regard, since they may be charged with constructive knowledge of their operations. Fourth, a product of territorial market division involving a foreign competitor is illegal also if it is accomplished by mutual patent licensing restrictions designed to implement a cartel arrangement. Fifth, Section 7 of the Clayton Act applies to mergers between American and foreign companies, and to potential as well as actual competition. The acquisition by a United States company of an actual or potential foreign competitor must be viewed accordingly, and minority stock holdings in an actual or potential foreign competitor also pose antitrust dangers. Finally, under present United States antitrust law a multinational may usually exercise its control over a foreign subsidiary in order to direct pricing and sales. But antitrust laws may apply to intra-corporate dealings where third parties are injured or monopolization is present.

POLITICAL CONTROL OF TRADE

Perhaps in no area has the problem of extraterritoriality been raised more frequently or more vehemently than in the field of East-West trade. Different nations have different rules governing trade with the Socialist countries of Eastern Europe and Asia, and this can result in serious problems for MNEs with affiliates in multiple host countries. Particularly for American multinationals, this has resulted in periodic outbreaks of conflict and will no doubt continue to do so. There are two facets to the problem of extraterritorial violation of host nation sovereignty in East-West trade. The first involves the application of home-country laws to MNE affiliates incorporated in host nations. The second results from differences in national policy objectives—the host nation may permit and in fact encourage its firms (including MNE affiliates) to trade with countries or in products that are discouraged or prohibited by the MNE's home country.

The United States government has for many years had the authority to prevent private transactions with "enemy countries," and to deny American goods or technology to any other country for foreign policy purposes. Although there are discriminatory import restrictions, such as denial of "most-favored nation" treatment to various Communist countries, export restrictions have been the cause of most extraterritorial conflicts and therefore of principal laws—the Trading with the Enemy Act of 1917 and the Export Control Act of 1949.[60] Under the former, the Treasury Department is empowered to prohibit "any person" over whom the United States has jurisdiction from entering into transactions with nationals of an enemy country. Under the Export Control Act, a license from the Commerce Department is required for the exports of technical data and products to such countries. Its purpose is to ensure that nothing of economic, military, or strategic significance is exported to Communist countries. Most exports come under "general licenses" which cover a specific list of nonstrategic commodities that can be traded without special clearance. However, a "validated license," describing the purchaser, the product, and its end-use as certified by the ultimate consignee, is required for all "strategic" exports. The Commerce Department maintains a "positive list" of products that are considered of a strategic nature and normally are not exportable to Communist nations. The State Department regulates exports of weapons.

The issue of extraterritoriality arises when goods are initially exported to a friendly country like Canada or France, yet the same restrictions are imposed for re-export as for direct export. The United States also follows components and technology through manufacture and assembly abroad under the same restrictions, which are binding on any person of any nationality. Difficulties of course arise when the foreign country has different concepts of strategic goods. In such circumstances, the country in which a product is assembled or manufactured may regard it as essentially national in origin, despite inclusion of some non-national components, and may well allow—perhaps even direct or encourage— its sale to buyers prohibited by the United States. Hence in a country like Canada, with a large number of American-owned plants, there is substantial scope for conflict over extraterritorial application of United States law.

Recognizing that unilateral controls on East-West trade would be largely ineffective, the United States entered into an agreement in 1950 with other NATO countries and Japan to establish more or less parallel controls over trade in strategic items. The Consultative Group Coordinating Committee (COCOM) has worked with varying degrees of effectiveness—agreement is reached voluntarily on items to be controlled—and the list is reviewed periodically. Agreement of all COCOM members is needed for exceptions. From 1971 to 1975 less than 1% of the $86 billion total COCOM exports to Communist countries were approved exceptions. The value of cases denied by COCOM was only 4% of the total of approved cases. Intelligence estimates suggest that only $150 million of Western embargoed goods were "illegally" shipped to the East between 1973 and 1977, compared with $150 billion in legal shipments of which about $45 billion was for machinery and equipment.[61] Most COCOM countries have placed less emphasis on exports of technology to Communist countries than has the United States.

Practically from the beginning there have been regular shrinkages in the COCOM list of controlled items, largely prompted by pressure from the European members to remove items in which they had developed commercial capabilities. Much discussion of export control issues has centered on exports of computers—computers and peripherals have accounted for more than half the total of COCOM approved exceptions. Other efforts to establish a common stand among exporters include the coordination of policies among suppliers of nuclear technology and equipment, as well as harmonization of policies among producers of conventional arms (see Chapter 13). In 1978 President Carter approved the recommendations of an American interagency task force to "streamline decision-making on sensitive export questions" under a new organization chaired by the President's science adviser.[62]

Pressures on MNEs to expand or reduce trade with Communist countries has waxed and waned with shifts in the policital climate. The optimism of détente in the early 1970s was replaced by the human rights conflicts of a few years later. Massive imports from the West to Eastern European countries were slowed by the inability of these countries to export and easily service foreign debt. American exports to the East have amounted to only a small fraction of the total Eastern imports and have mostly been farm products. This can partly be attributed to American import barriers and restrictions on Export-Import Bank lending. And the inefficiencies and rigidities of Eastern countries' planning systems, as well as high transactions and information costs, have also made trade difficult.

However, new techniques to stimulate East-West trade have been developed, including over 2000 reported "cooperation agreements" since the early 1960s. A 1977 EEC report summarized "industrial cooperation" as including: (a) licensing Communist countries to use Western technology, with royalty payments to the West in finished goods; (b) supply of complete plant or production lines, again with payment in finished goods; (c) coproduction and specialization; (d) subcontracting; (e) joint ventures, and (f) joint tendering, joint construction, and similar projects.[63] Similarly, compensation or "buy back" agreements have linked exports to the East with payment in kind, thus avoiding credit problems but raising potential competitive difficulties for the future.

Meanwhile, the United States has maintained its trade embargo on Cuba, but eased it somewhat in mid-1975 to allow foreign subsidiaries of American firms to sell goods to Cuba that contain 20% or less of American-made components. By mid-1977, sales of such goods totaled $330 million, including Ford and Chrysler autos built in Argentina. In early 1977 the Carter Administration eased passport restrictions on United States travelers to Cuba and relaxed a strict ban on financial transactions relating to American visitors. Such multinationals as Pepsico, Xerox, Boeing, Pillsbury, Control Data, Honeywell, and 3M soon dispatched executives to Havana for exploratory talks with officials of Cuban state trading agencies. Fishing rights and an antihijacking agreement have also been successfully concluded.

The most dramatic shift in East-West trade, of course, has involved the People's Republic of China, partly in resonse to intense pressure by multinationals. A trade embargo had existed since the Communist takeover in the late 1940s, but in 1969 the United States government began to permit imports by individuals and non-commercial organizations, and allowed foreign subsidiaries of American firms to export non-strategic goods. With the visit of President Nixon to China in 1972 and the death of Mao Tse-Tung in 1976, United States trade restrictions were gradually relaxed. The result was a shift in the status of Communist China from being essentially embargoed to being more accessible than even the Soviet Union and most of Eastern Europe. The final shift came in December 1978 when the United States established full diplomatic relations with

China and broke diplomatic ties with Taiwan. By that time, trade liberalization had already begun—in October 1976 President Ford approved the sale of two Control Data computers to China for oil exploration and seismic studies. The Soviet Union, on the other hand, was denied permission to buy Control Data's somewhat similar Cyber 76 for a United Nations-sponsored, worldwide weather forecasting system.[64] In June 1978 American officials quietly approved a Chinese request for airborne geological survey equipment using an infrared scanning system which they would not allow to be sold to the Soviet Union because of possible military use. In July 1978 the government denied a license to Sperry Univac to sell a computer system to Tass (see below), the Soviet news agency, although a month earlier the company was reportedly selling two similar Univac 1100 series machines to China.[65] By October 1978 preliminary negotiations were under way regarding an American role in launching a Chinese domestic communications satellite system.

American trade embargoes remain essentially intact with respect to Vietnam, Cambodia, and Laos, and are complicated by the shifting politics of the region as well as the new ties to China. However in mid-1977, Vietnam enacted a foreign investment code considered to be quite liberal and unexpectedly attractive. Three forms of investment were outlined: (1) joint ventures, (2) production specifically for export, and (3) development of natural resources. Foreign ownership rules were considered to be quite flexible, and Japanese, Canadian, and European firms have been negotiating with the Vietnamese government to tap what are believed to be significant offshore oil and natural gas reserves in the South China Sea.[66] Finally, the United States also maintains trade embargoes against Albania and North Korea.

In all such cases the political control of trade can clearly give rise to serious conflict for management of multinational enterprise, particularly if little or no coordination exists between the firm's home country and the governments of countries where its affiliates are located.

Firestone Tire and Rubber and Rumania

During 1964 an increasing number of organizations and individuals in the United States and Western Europe had begun to call for a concerted effort to raise the level of trade with Eastern Europe. As part of its policy of improving relations with those Communist countries that demonstrated independence from the Soviet Union, the American government entered into bilateral trade talks with the Rumanian government. In mid-1964 it agreed to grant export licenses for a number of industrial facilities in the fields of chemicals, petrochemicals (including two synthetic rubber plants), electric power, petroleum, and glass manufacturing.

During the next few months, with the encouragement of the United States government, the Rumanians approached several American companies to discuss the construction of a $10 million cracking plant and a $40-50 million synthetic rubber factory. A Rumanian trade delegation visited several American manufacturers, including Firestone and Goodyear. On October 22, 1964, it was reported that Goodyear had decided against building such a plant. In the company's own newsletter Goodyear later stated it had advised the State Department by letter as to its decision, citing as reasons the company's belief that the technical knowledge involved should not be made available to a Communist country because of its strategic value, and its feeling that the Rumanians might use increased synthetic rubber output to disrupt natural rubber prices. Firestone, on the other hand, on January 5, 1965 announced agreement on a preliminary contract to design and equip a synthetic rubber plant in Rumania.

Although it had acted entirely in accordance with government policy, in the months that followed Firestone found itself subjected to unusual competitive pressures and a nuisance boycott campaign conducted by a conservative political organization, the Young Americans for Freedom (YAF). In the spring of 1965 the organization picketed and distributed handbills outside Firestone stores in several large cities, attacking Firestone's decision by linking it to undermining American efforts in Vietnam. The YAF campaign apparently caught Firestone officials off-guard, and a number of franchised dealers either dropped their franchises or asked Firestone to get YAF off their backs. The company reacted by sending a public relations man and a Congressman from the Akron district to meet with YAF leaders and ·explain that the company was acting in the nation's best interests by following President Johnson's policy of "building bridges" to Eastern Europe.[67]

But on April 16, 1965 Firestone officials advised the State Department of the company's intention to terminate the Rumanian plant negotiations because of the unexpected extent and intensity of competitive pressures and political agitation. It also informed the Rumanians. A few days later State Department officials, taking care to maintain a position of noninvolvement, met with the Rumanian Ambassador to assure him that "the U.S. government still approved the sale of the synthetic rubber plants and had nothing to do with Firestone's decision." The meeting was not announced to the press—the State Department did not wish to appear to have a direct interest in the Firestone-Rumanian deal since it had previously been attacked by YAF for "ordering" Firestone to sell to the Communists.[68] But on April 20 Firestone issued a one-sentence announcement that it had terminated negotiations. No explanation was given for the company's decision.

Later Senator William Fulbright, in a speech on the Senate floor, was highly critical of the YAF, Goodyear, and the Administration. He charged that Goodyear had given its salesmen "right-wing" publications to use against Firestone prior to the latter's dropping out of the Rumanian transaction. And he noted that "our government has not always honored its responsibilities in connection with the foreign business activities of private organizations."[69] The Administration had failed to defend its own established policies, leaving an American MNE to solve the problem by its own efforts without government support. Without that support, Firestone was left alone to defend actions that were directly in accordance with government policy.

Firestone, however, had not associated its actions with government policy, and therefore was at a disadvantage in presenting to the American public its reason for accepting the project. While Goodyear was out in the open explaining to the public its reasoning for not accepting the project and pointing a finger at Firestone, the latter did nothing to defend itself nor did it explain to the public the conditions and terms of the contract. A forthright and continuing dialogue on the issues was entirely absent.

Firestone evidently perceived its position at the time to be characterized by relatively high stakes with power support from the two governments based upon their recently settled trade agreement. This support, however, was nonexistent or ineffective, and domestic competitive and political pressures soon forced Firestone to adopt an *avoidance* mode. Had the company developed a strategy that recognized and acted upon the need to broaden its relationships and interdependence with the United States government, it could possibly have salvaged the project. After Firestone announced its withdrawal, the Rumanian government started negotiating with German and British MNEs on the project. On July 26, 1965 Universal Oil Products Corporation, as the prime contractor, announced the completion of a $22.5 million petroleum refinery in Rumania. Accompanying the announcement was the statement by an official that the company "isn't trying to set foreign policy but is adhering to the policy of the federal government, which in June called for increased trade between the U.S. and Rumania."[70]

Chrysler, Ford, GM, and the Cuba Trade

After the United States imposed a full trade embargo against Cuba, the OAS, at American insistence, adopted a collective ban on trade and diplomatic ties with Cuba in 1962. Until the late 1960s the United States managed to curb trade with Cuba by foreign affiliates of American multinationals mainly because most foreign governments did not intend to challenge the restrictions. Canada—which does not belong to the OAS and had not joined in the economic quarantine of Cuba—maintained its traditional ties of close cooperation with the United States and most Latin American governments agreed with the political objectives of isolating Cuba. But in the early 1970s several OAS members began to question the usefulness of the embargo, and to regard the collective ban as unreasonable or outmoded. By the end of 1973 Mexico, Argentina, Peru, Colombia, and Venezuela had renewed trade ties with Cuba.

Like most of these countries, Argentina was concerned with increasing its exports, and efforts by the Peronist government to expand trade with Cuba in 1973-1974 was part of this drive. When it resumed diplomatic relations with Havana in 1973, Argentina offered $1.2 billion in credits to finance Cuban purchases of Argentine manufactures and farm products. Cuban trade missions that subsequently visited Buenos Aires proved to be most interested in transportation equipment to replace antiquated American-made motor vehicles and railroad equipment. And so, in the spring of 1974, the Argentine subsidiaries of the American "Big 3" auto manufacturers found themselves negotiating with the Cubans and bidding on some 42,000 autos and trucks that the Cubans planned to buy over the next three years. According to a Chrysler spokesman in Buenos Aires, "the only obstacle to signing a $25 million contract for the sale of 9000 cars is approval from Washington."[71]

The immediate issue was the right of Ford Motor Argentina, General Motors Argentina, and Chrysler Fevre Argentina to supply cars and trucks to Cuba from their local plants in the face of the United States embargo. The clash was a test of Argentine sovereignty and American foreign economic policy, involving the American practice of exporting some of its trade policies to other countries along with foreign direct investment by United states firms. If Washington backed down, another crack would be opened in the embargo on trade with Havana and possibly also the embargoes on North Vietnam, North Korea, and Communist China. Peron, on the other hand, intended to use the trade dispute as a weapon to attack the ostracism of Cuba by the OAS.

There is little doubt that the Argentine government had the power to compel the deliveries, if necessary. Although the subsidiaries were owned and controlled by their American parents, they were Argentine companies incorporated under Argentine law. The Argentines wanted Washington to concede that it had no right to put any export restrictions on the subsidiaries. When United States Treasury Secretary George Shultz said that the Administration was "still studying" the question in April 1974, Argentine Minister of Economy José Gelbard retorted that there was "nothing to study" and the national Parliament protested Shultz's "meddling in Argentina's internal affairs."[72]

American auto executives thus found themselves caught between two squabbling governments. On the one hand, the Argentine government could apply an array of legal and administrative pressures. On the other hand, the executives would be liable to fines or imprisonment under the U.S. Trading with the Enemy Act if they approved the Cuban sales without Washington's authorization. The attitude of the American auto makers was summed up by a GM executive: "General Motors subsidiaries in Argentina operate under the laws and policies of that country."[73]

On April 18, 1974 the United States Administration was forced to relax the embargo on Cuba temporarily by issuing export licenses to the Argentine subsidiaries of the three auto companies. Six days after the licenses were granted, the Argentine subsidiary of Chrysler signed a $24 million contract, and the Ford and GM subsidiaries soon followed suit. The State Department called this "an exception" and insisted that there was no change in America's hard-line policy toward Cuba. The Administration's decision reportedly was the result of both strong lobbying on the part of the auto manufacturers and prompting from the Argentine government.[74] By mid-September 1974 an estimated $74 million worth of vehicles had been shipped to Cuba from Argentina subsidiaries of Ford, Chrysler, and GM, although by May 1975 Argentina deliveries had fallen seriously behind schedule due to labor troubles, parts shortages, and rising costs. As a result, a direct state subsidy to the companies had to be made, on top of the previous liberal credit arrangements. On August 21, 1975 the United States government finally lifted the 13 year-old ban on Cuban sales by foreign subsidiaries of American multinationals. By combining a low profile with insistence on Argentine national sovereignty, the American automakers were able to see the issue resolved to their satisfaction.

Fruehauf-France and the China Deal

In October 1964 Berliet, the largest French truck manufacturer, asked the French affiliate of Fruehauf to bid on 200 truck trailers to be exported to an undesignated country. A month later Fruehauf-France was told that its bid had been accepted, with 60 trailers to be shipped to Communist China. The company began production in December 1964. By the end of that month, however, several American sources had notified the Treasury Department of the prospective exports to China.

As a result, the Treasury Department in early January 1965 requested additional information about the contract from Fruehauf Corporation in the United States. At that point, however, the parent was apparently still unaware of the contract between its French affiliate and Berliet. On January 18, 1965 Fruehauf-France received a letter from Fruehauf International asking for details on the contract and requesting that delivery be cancelled, if possible, in response to Treasury Department demands that delivery be delayed pending special authorization, yet to be negotiated. Four days later, Fruehauf-France advised Fruehauf International by letter as to contract details: The deal involved neither American parts nor American technology, similar vehicles could be manufactured by competitor French firms, financing arrangements had been made solely with French institutions, and costly penalties could be assessed if a cancellation took place and the scheduled initial delivery on February 15 were missed.

On January 29, Fruehauf-France received a second letter from Fruehauf International which ordered the French subsidiary to break the Berliet contract. Negotiations with the Treasury Department had failed, and as a result management faced the possibility that the Trading with the Enemy Act would be invoked if deliveries to Berliet were made. Berliet, asserting its contractual rights, threatened suit with full damages and penalties if the cancellation took place. At a special board meeting on February 12, the minority French directors of Fruehauf-France refused to cancel the contract and decided to go to court and ask for appointment of a receiver for the company long enough to ensure that the contract would be fulfilled. They argued that they were bound to the contract under French law, that heavy damages would be assessed against them if it were to be broken, and that injury would thus be caused to French stockholders of Fruehauf-France. The French court—reportedly pressured by the French government to deliver a fast and favorable verdict—quickly appointed a "provisional director" for 90 days, sufficient time to complete the order.

The American parent countered by trying to appoint an American to replace the managing director of Fruehauf-France. After a suit brought in a French court to block the appointment proved successful, Fruehauf appealed the verdict and lost. Fruehauf also offered to buy out one-third minority interest in France so that it could cancel the contract without French objection, but this too was blocked by the courts. Meanwhile,

Fruehauf again requested a license from the Treasury Department to permit the shipment. An official response was deliberately delayed, and, given the inability of Fruehauf to block the deal after the French court order, Treasury returned the license application without making a determination in the case. The contract was filled on schedule, and the provisional director resigned at the end of the three-month receivership period.

In this case United States political trade controls were frustrated in part because of the existence of a minority ownership in an MNE affiliate and in part because of the interference of the French government. While the competitive position of Fruehauf was compromised, the host government clearly prevailed because of the existence of minority shareholders. In such conflict situations there is clearly the desire on the part of host governments for minority holdings by local residents, while from the home-country's viewpoint wholly-owned affiliates provide greater control.

Moreover, Fruehauf was organized in a decentralized way, with affiliates operating largely independently of one another and the parent firm, and with little centralized control. Fruehauf could probably have avoided or more easily resolved the political conflict with stronger control over its affiliate, improved communications, and stronger identification of affiliates with central corporate goals and concerns.

Sperry, Dresser Industries, and Russian Sales

Several political incidents involving private citizens in Moscow occurred in the latter part of the summer of 1978 which affected Soviet-American relations. In the most publicized incident, two Soviet dissidents were brought to trial in Moscow and given harsh sentences. The Carter Administration perceived this as a direct provocation on the human rights issue. In addition, American newsmen were detained and in some cases expelled from the Soviet Union, and an International Harvester official was seized and jailed in Moscow on a currency violation.[75] Although he was subsequently tried and released, his treatment by the Soviets aroused considerable "anxiety" and some "condemnation" from American businessmen involved in East-West trade.[76] In response, the Carter Administration turned to trade controls.[77]

Beginning in late June 1978 White House officials pressed for a curb on the export of American oil production technology and equipment to the Soviet Union. This had been allowed since 1969 and 1972, respectively, except when judged to have direct military application. An interagency group headed by the Commerce Department approved numerous oil-related deals with the Soviets, including $545 million worth of oil equipment sales during 1977 and the first half of 1978. The group had recently approved a license to permit Dresser Industries to sell plans for a plant to produce drill bits, while another license for an advanced electron beam welder was "still before the panel."[78]

Immediately after the sentencing of the dissidents, United States government officials announced that the Administration would place all exports of oil technology and equipment to the Soviet Union under White House review. The sale of a Sperry Univac 1100 series computer to Tass, the Soviet news agency, was also cancelled.

Dresser's president and chief executive officer, James Jones, called the announcement "sheer idiocy. . . . Placing oil technology under government control will virtually hand American export business to foreign competitors on a silver platter."[79] Having waited for months for final government clearance on its Soviet oil deal, Dresser reportedly considered suing President Carter if the government cancelled its proposed sale. One company official remarked: "Most businessmen think a low profile is best; the soundest policy, they say, is to say nothing. We adamantly disagree and believe it is our responsibility as businessmen to speak out on issues that concern and effect us."[80] Dresser's combativeness was reflected in the periodic advertisements it had placed in newspapers to address assorted topics, including its opposition to both Arab boycott and questionable payments legislation.

Sperry's chairman and chief executive officer, J. Paul Lyet, on the other hand, greeted the action with a "Bah, humbug," but stressed that the company would accept the President's decision. "Sperry has always complied with the wishes of our government concerning where and with whom we should trade. . . . We will continue to follow that policy."[81] With respect to the future of Russian trade, he added, "we may find we can make better use of our efforts somewhere else."[82]

Faced with similar political restraints on their trade with the Soviet Union, the two firms thus embarked on separate paths. For Dresser, a lengthy and bitter sequence of events unfolded before final government approval. On August 7, 1978 Senator Henry Jackson wrote a personal letter to President Carter urging him to deny Dresser a license for its computerized electronic welding machine or at least to delay a decision. Two days later, despite strong appeals from national security adviser Zbigniew Brzezinski to delay action, the Commerce Department approved Dresser's export license for the welder—Commerce Secretary Juanita Kreps insisted that President Carter had personally cleared the decision, as had both the Defense and Energy Departments. The $144 million deal looked like it was about to go through.

A few days later, Energy Secretary Schlesinger, with close personal ties to Senator Jackson and great influence with President Carter on strategic matters, sent a "strong" memorandum to the President urging reconsideration. Brzezinski, meanwhile, asked Defense Secretary Brown to take a second look at the case. Brown called on the head of the Defense Science Advisory Board, who in turn asked J. Fred Bucy of Texas Instruments to put together a panel to review the issue. On August 25, 1978 the panel submitted a report recommending that the United States not export the drilling technology to protect the American technological lead.

Dresser's James Jones immediately issued a statement charging that "high government officials, particularly Energy Secretary James Schlesinger, National Security Adviser Zbigniew Brzezinski, and Senator Henry Jackson appear willing to go to any length to . . . kill the Dresser transaction as a symbol of their hard-line attitude." Jones went on to complain that panel head Bucy "is known to have a strong bias against the transfer of technology to the Soviet Union or to any other nation" and that the panel's negative finding was "preordained."[83] On August 29 the go-ahead on the electron beam welder reportedly was "being reviewed," and the Energy Department "was still studying strategic implications of the sale."[84] By mid-September, however, all government agencies had evidently "signed off" on the deal and final approval had been given.[85]

For Sperry, the final outcome was not as successful. At the urging of hardliners in the Senate and the National Security Council, the sale of the Sperry Univac computer to Tass was effectively killed despite complaints from Sperry and the State and Commerce Departments that Western Europe and Japan had plenty of similar computers for sale. By mid-August 1978, the United States had asked the British, French, Germans, and Japanese not to sell the Soviets a computer to replace the one that had been blocked. Carter, in announcing the cancellation for "security" reasons, may have been laying the groundwork for an American veto in COCOM negotiations. Yet the system to be sold was one of the smallest versions of the 10 year-old Univac 1100 series, and therefore considered easily able to meet COCOM restrictions. In addition, a nearly identical system, doubled for reliability and backup, had been sold and installed to handle the passenger reservation system of Aeroflot, the Soviet airline. Moreover, the system for Tass had at one time presented legitimate export-licensing problems because of a fast semiconductor memory, and at Washington's behest Sperry had "detuned" the machine to eliminate the advanced technology. And the company had announced plans to sell two similar computers along with related equipment and spare parts to China. So it seemed that if the Europeans and Japanese were to support the United States request it would have to be on the basis of politics rather than national security.

It was subsequently reported that both Britain's International Computers Ltd. and Germany's Siemens intended to approach Tass with an offer to replace the Univac machine. The French government clearly announced its refusal to go along with the American request on the grounds that France would not "subordinate" such sales to "political considerations."[86] In the spring of 1979 the Carter Administration finally gave Sperry the go-ahead. By that time, the French already had the contract sewn up—the computer to be supplied by CII-Honeywell-Bull. The Russians, annoyed by the American delays, were enticed by a more favorable pricing package and French willingness to sell a more advanced computer.[87]

Dresser, relying as it had in the past on a combination of bravado, threat, and leverage, maintained a rigid "competitive" position throughout the conflict period, fighting its battle "tooth-and-nail" and finally getting a favorable outcome after considerable "light-switch diplomacy" on the part of the Carter Administration.[88] Sperry Rand's position, characterized by reciprocity and a desire to maintain a good relationship with the government, moved towards "accommodation" under the heading "win a few, lose a few."

The four cases enumerated above represent only a few of the conflict situations encountered by American multinationals involving East-West trade. Other companies including Exxon, IBM, Rayonier, Boeing, Control Data, General Electric, and Studebaker-Worthington have become involved from time to time, usually with the United States government attempting to impose political trade barriers on other countries through the MNE parent-affiliate relationship. Most have concerned affiliates in Canada, and have focused on trade with China and Cuba, although the number and intensity of such conflicts have doubtless been reduced by new procedures under which an American subsidiary in Canada would ordinarily be exempted from export controls if the goods in question are of significant benefit to the Canadian economy, and if the order can be filled in Canada only by a firm whose parent is subject to United States control.[89]

The traditional extraterritorial application of political trade controls via MNEs has probably declined somewhat in recent years because of resistance by host-country governments and the emergence of a growing array of alternative sources of supply. It has given way to unilateral export controls concerned with the use of high-technology trade as a political lever. The degree of extraterritoriality thus appears to have declined, but the potential for conflict has not. In 1979 a deep and increasingly bitter split was developing both among United States Congressmen and businessmen over export controls.[90]

MULTINATIONAL OIL COMPANIES AND THE 1973 CRISIS

No other international political conflict involving MNEs was more acute than the 1973 oil crisis. The Arab oil embargo placed the large multinational oil companies in an extremely delicate position, having to somehow reconcile their positions in the producing areas—long-since eroded by nationalization, and increased government taxation and participation in decision-making—with the needs of their home countries, particularly the United States and the Netherlands.

The Immediate Background

With the establishment of OPEC in 1960, the governments of the oil exporting countries effectively constrained the actions of the multinational oil companies and provided an efficient forum for cooperative formulation of common objectives. The emergence of "radical" regimes in Iraq, Algeria, and Libya put both the more moderate governments and the oil companies on the defensive, and by 1973 the takeover of effective power by the OPEC host governments was nearly complete. At the same time, the growing dependence of the United States on imported oil changed the demand and supply conditions against which the bargaining was conducted.

As long as the Arab countries of OPEC had little cohesion and were in a weak position to exercise market control over oil supplies there was little fear that they could effectively use the "oil weapon" in their conflict with Israel. But as their position changed it became clear that if the deteriorating relations between Israel and the Arabs should come to open conflict, it was likely to bring a genuine crisis to the international oil industry as well. The October war brought these developments to a head. It triggered diverse responses from the producer countries, consuming countries, and multinationals.

By October 1973, OPEC included thirteen member countries spanning four continents, whose exports accounted for more than 85% of the world's oil trade. Seven of these Arab countries—Algeria, Iraq, Kuwait, Libya, Qatar, Saudi Arabia, and the United Arab Emirates—along with Bahrain, Egypt, and Syria formed the Organization of Arab Petroleum Exporting Countries (OAPEC). Non-Arab countries in OPEC included Ecuador, Gabon, Indonesia, Iran, Nigeria, and Venezuela. The OPEC producers, although comprising nations of different cultures, political systems, and levels of development, were linked by a number of common bonds, particularly a simultaneous striving toward "decolonization" and modernization. But only the Arab group within OPEC was directly concerned about Israel and the use of oil as a weapon in the political struggle. Nor was there unanimity within OAPEC as to the degree and manner in which the weapon should be used.

The seven giant oil multinationals—Exxon, Gulf, Mobil, Socal, Texaco, Shell, and British Petroleum—accounted in 1972 for 77.1% of total OPEC and 70.0% of world production. Frequently referred to as the "Seven Sisters," each MNE nevertheless has its own history, its own management and its own strategies.[91] Since it was generally assumed that the MNEs would automatically act on behalf of their home countries, there was widespread public dismay when they obeyed the embargo rules laid down by the Arab nations during the crisis period.

As far as the oil companies' home countries were concerned, cooperation during the embargo was meagre, as each government insisted on maintaining the widest possible room for maneuver. That goal persisted even as the dimensions of the embargo began to be apparent. Formal and informal economic and political ties among governments proved to be ineffective as each went its own way essentially in full-scale competition between the large consuming areas—the United States, Europe and Japan.

Of all the connections to be found in the world oil industry, the ties between the Saudis and Aramco—jointly owned by Exxon, Mobil, Socal, and Texaco—were probably the closest, exemplified by their mutual efforts to facilitate Saudi participation in the ownership of the company's properties. Incorporated in Delaware and based at Dhahran, Aramco is the world's largest oil producer. Both sides had sought an arrangement that would insulate Aramco-Saudi relations from events in the other oil producing countries. According to an Aramco vice-president, the Saudis were willing to leave Aramco's parents in control of most of the crude production, "especially if we could fuzz up the deal somehow" to prevent ready comparison with arrangements in other countries.[92] By 1973, Saudi Arabia possessed a third of the non-Communist world's oil reserves and practically all Saudi oil was produced from Aramco wells. Its concessions covered 93 billion barrels of proved reserves and each year it "proved up" more oil than it produced. By the strict letter of its contract with the Saudi government, Aramco owned concessionary rights to oil in the ground. In October 1972, the principle of 25% (subsequently raised to 60%) Saudi participation in Aramco assets was accepted.

Use of the Oil Weapon

Throughout the late spring and summer of 1973 the Arab nations with increasing frequency brandished the "oil weapon"—alternately described as an embargo directed at consuming nations "unfriendly" to the Arab cause or as a production cutback of a more general nature. In April the Saudis warned the United States that they would not acquiesce to Aramco's ambitious expansion program unless America altered its "pro-Israeli" stance. In May Aramco executives paid courtesy calls on King Faisal, who insisted that the United States government change its Mideast policy. At a second meeting he warned that Aramco might "lose everything." Corporate officials communicated the substance of both meetings to Washington. At the end of that month the same message was sounded by a former Secretary General of OPEC, who proposed a production "freeze" to force withdrawal of Israeli forces from the 1967 cease-fire lines.

On May 30, executives of Aramco's parent companies met with White House, State Department, and Defense Department representatives. The reaction in Washington, according to corporate correspondence, was "attentiveness," but the feeling there was that the King was "crying wolf"—the correspondence noted that "there is little or nothing the U.S. government can do or will do on an urgent basis to affect the Arab-Israeli issue." Corporate needs and American government policies were thus viewed as separate and distinct.

During the summer of 1973 the oil companies continued to take various actions that included a public statement by the board chairman of Socal expressing the need for the United States to conduct a foreign policy that would assure reasonable access to foreign oil.[93] Mobil published newspaper ads in a similar vein. Later in the summer, Aramco executives communicated their increasing apprehension regarding the possibility of a cutback and embargo to the government "at every opportunity."[94] They also assigned an Exxon representative to brief the State Department routinely on new developments. The Saudis subsequently indicated satisfaction with Aramco for its pro-Arab stand, and with its parent companies for being more pro-Arab than they had been before. An unidentified Saudi representative told J.J. Johnson, Aramco's vice-president for government relations, "We hope to reward you," a statement that Johnson interpreted as being the Saudis' promise to allow future growth in production.[95]

Meanwhile, Libya had embargoed Bunker Hunt Co. liftings of crude at the end of May and nationalized the company on June 11, justifying the action by asserting that the United States deserved a "good hard slap on its insolent face" for its support of Israel.[96] On July 19, Iraq threatened the use of embargoes and nationalizations as political weapons, and in August Libya took over 51% of the Occidental and Oasis groups, aiming at the more vulnerable independents. Saudi Arabian and Iranian output was boosted to compensate for the cutbacks in Libya as well as Kuwait.[97] In August, cables to its home offices from Aramco indicated that the Saudis were seriously considering limiting production for political reasons.[98]

On September 1, 1973 Libya nationalized 51% of the fields controlled by Mobil, Exxon, Shell, Texaco, and Socal, who immediately warned other companies not to buy "stolen oil," at least until fair compensation had been settled upon.[99] The New England Petroleum Corporation (Nepco), the largest single supplier of fuel oil to utilities such as Consolidated Edison in New York, was warned by Texaco and Socal of legal action if it continued to buy oil from the Libyan National Oil Company. The State Department also advised Nepco against using Libyan oil, suggesting that harm to American policy that would result—according to Nepco, the telephone call from Washington came a half-hour after comparable messages from the two companies. Another importer who had also bought Libyan petroleum found itself pressed by the companies, again with the support of the State Department, and decided it was expedient to go along. The Libyan crude was resold to Eastern Europe.[100] President Nixon followed on September 5, warning the OAPEC countries of the likely loss of markets and of other consequences if they raised prices, expropriated installations, or otherwise sought to emulate the actions of Iran a generation earlier. King Faisal of Saudi Arabia countered by expressing his concern and issuing warnings to the United States through interviews in various media.

A series of collective meetings by various participating groups during the crucial month of September generally failed to produce agreement on a common policy for the near-term future. Both OAPEC and the OECD, meeting separately on September 4, failed to reach a consensus as to how to use the "oil weapon" and how to devise an oil-sharing agreement, respectively. A meeting on September 12 of the four Aramco parents, to decide upon breaking down the shares of oil that the Saudis were to make available, also produced disagreement. Exxon, Texaco, and Socal favored a course of action that was unsatisfactory to "crude-short" Mobil, whose representatives informed them: "We are putting you on notice of our reserving the right to make our case individually with SAG (the Saudis) if the group effort fails."[101] At its 35th meeting a few days later on September 15, and after much agonizing, OPEC designated the "Persian Gulf Six" to negotiate collectively with the companies to revise prices beginning on October 8 in Vienna.

On October 6, the fourth Middle East war broke out, and two days later OPEC discussions with the oil companies began in Vienna as scheduled. The Iraqis nationalized Exxon and Mobil holdings in the Basrah Petroleum Company immediately following the outbreak of the war. In Europe, Italy and Spain imposed petroleum export restrictions while France tightened existing export controls. On October 9, Kuwait called for an emergency meeting of Arab oil ministers, while Aramco was directed to supply crude oil and petroleum products to fuel the Arab war effort. Even though the shipments were destined for other customers the Saudi office of Aramco informed their American parents that the request was a "matter of state priority" and that Aramco had "no alternative but to comply." In his first cable on this problem Aramco chairman

Frank Jungers informed them that "we can probably expect more of this as time goes on."[102] The first request was for Egypt; the second for Iraq.

The oil industry's negotiating team in Vienna, meanwhile, adjourned negotiations with the Persian Gulf Six on October 12, indicating that they had to consult their home governments regarding the steep OPEC price demands.[103] The board chairmen of the Aramco parents immediately sent a memorandum to President Nixon describing the "anger" and "irritation" of Arab governments over United States support of Israel. It warned that the Saudis would impose a cutback which could have a "snowballing effect that would produce a major petroleum supply crisis." They further warned that Japan and Western Europe could not "face a serious shut-in" of Persian Gulf oil because the world oil industry was operating "with essentially no spare capacity."[104] An October 12 State Department cable to a number of United States embassies abroad played down the possibility of a cutback.[105]

On October 15, Jungers cabled from Saudi Arabia that the Saudis were upset over what they believed to be the major role played by the United States on the side of Israel in the war, and that unless there was a major change in the tone of remarks coming from the highest level of the American government the companies could expect the imposition of a boycott. They maintained that the pressure for curtailment came mainly from Libya and Iraq, but that the effort was also being pushed hard by Kuwait (a major producer) and would, therefore, be very difficult to turn around.[106] That same day the State Department announced that the United States had begun to supply Israel with aircraft and equipment to replace her losses, while the Saudis reportedly told Western oil executives that they would cut crude production by 10% immediately and by 5% monthly in the future if the United States overtly undertook to resupply Israel. On October 16, before the embargo was announced, the Persian Gulf Six for the first time bypassed the negotiating table at Vienna and unilaterally raised posted prices—the companies learned from the newspapers that the host nations' prices were to be raised 70%.[107] While the oil companies were shocked, industrial country governments—absorbed in the issues of the Arab-Israeli war—seemed unaware of the significance of OPEC's actions.

On October 17, a conference of Arab oil ministers in Kuwait resolved to use the oil weapon in the struggle for the Arab cause. They agreed to a mandatory 5% cut each month and a recommended embargo on the United States. Iraq, largely isolated from the Arab community, opposed the decisions and withdrew. The remaining nine OAPEC countries approved the actions unanimously. Prior to the OAPEC meeting, King Faisal had sent an urgent message to President Nixon to cease resupplying Israel in the war, apparently with the intent of alerting world public opinion to the gravity of the Arab-Israeli conflict.

In the meantime, four Arab foreign ministers, who said they represented 18 Arab nations, submitted a general peace proposal to President Nixon and asked the United States to help mediate the Middle East conflict. That same day, the Pentagon announced plans to ask Congress for an extra $2 billion to replace American arms shipments being rushed to Israel. Immediately thereafter the Saudis announced over Radio Riyadh the 10% oil production cutback to put pressure on the United States to reduce its support for Israel.

Frank Jungers, Aramco's chairman and chief executive, was at home when the telephone rang. It was one of his staff with a message the whole world soon would hear. A broadcast over Radio Riyadh, the official Saudi radio, had just announced King Faisal's decision to reduce oil production 'immediately beginning today and until the end of November by 10 percent.' Without asking for further details, Jungers promptly ordered the well-heads shut in, not just 10 percent but a little more for good measure. 'The important thing,' Jungers said later, 'was to give the immediate image of being *with* the government, not trying to fight it' . . . With that act, the Arabian American Oil Co., became a little more Arabian and less American.[108]

When on October 19 King Faisal learned of the President's decision to ask Congress for an authorization of $2.5 billion for arms assistance to Israel, he decided to impose an embargo against the United States. The lack of preparation on the part of the United States and other industrial country governments left the oil multinationals as the only institutions capable of managing the production cutback and embargo. On October 21 Frank Jungers was summoned to a meeting where the Saudis announced a production cut of almost 25% from the level programmed for October.[109] They also announced (a) an embargo on shipments of oil to certain countries including the United States, (b) allocations to selected "exempt" countries of a quantity of oil equal to the average daily amount shipped to them between January and September, 1973, and (c) the allocation of the balance of the reduced Saudi production on a pro-rata basis to whatever countries remained. The Saudi production cutback and embargo was to last from October 18, 1973 to March 18, 1974.

Coping with the Oil Weapon

Aramco was warned by the Saudis that it would be dealt with harshly if all details of the program were not met, and its subsequent actions were subject to strict surveillance by the government.[110] Captains of ships loading Saudi crude were required to sign affidavits stating their destination and to report by cable to Aramco when they arrived. As an additional check, Saudi diplomats monitored public records of oil imports by country of origin. The oilmen were thus considered invaluable agents for administering the embargo and for policing all shipments and the ultimate destination of OPEC oil. In a cable on October 18 to the four Aramco parent companies, spelling out the Saudi embargo requirements, Frank Jungers reported that the Saudis were "entirely aware that this program would be very difficult to administer, but they are looking to Aramco to police it."[111] As George Keller of Aramco's board later explained, "the only alternative was not to ship the oil at all . . . obviously it was in the best interests of the United States to move 5, 6, 7 million barrels a day to our friends around the world rather than to have that cut off."[112]

At the end of October 1973 Saudi Arabia also asked Aramco to provide a rundown of petroleum products derived from Saudi oil that were being sold to the American military from refineries around the world. Aramco passed this request on to its parents in the United States, who evidently delayed two days before informing the Defense Department—Charles Peyton, president of Exxon International, later testified that he responded to the Saudi demand for military data for fear that if he did not the Saudi government might have retaliated by preventing the American companies from meeting "worldwide supply commitments" elsewhere.[113]

By early November 1973 the embargoes and cutbacks were firmly in place, and the net impact on crude production was approaching a 20% reduction. The rules of the game laid down by the Arabs had been made more concrete. The embargo applied to all exports to the United States, Canada, Holland, the Bahamas, Trinidad, the Netherlands Antilles, Puerto Rico, and Guam. As the embargo continued, transshipments to other European destinations via Holland and limited deliveries to Canada for domestic consumption were permitted. An "exempt" or "most favored" list of "friendly" nations was maintained, including France, Spain, the United Kingdom, Jordan, Lebanon, Malaysia, Pakistan, Tunisia, and Egypt. These countries were to receive 100% of their September 1973 supplies, notwithstanding the production cutbacks. Hence the remaining "neutral" countries were effectively cut back well over the announced percentages.

On November 4, OAPEC ministers reassembled in Kuwait to coordinate the embargo and production cutback. They raised the cutback to 25%—actually a 32% cut in Aramco's projected November production—but agreed to include the shut-in volumes for embargoed nations in this percentage. The purpose was to raise the smaller producers to the Saudi level and to establish a uniform calculating procedure. In addition, the embargo of the United States was expanded to include all indirect shipments as well as direct deliveries to the American market, including deliveries to refiners supplying American defense forces in Bahrain, Italy, and Greece. The "most favored" list was expanded at the same time.

In mid-November 1973 Saudi Arabia and Kuwait announced goals well beyond the previously agreed-upon 51% ownership participation level in ownership of oil production facilities. The Arab ministers also agreed to exempt on a one-time basis all the EEC nations (except Holland) from the scheduled 5% December cutback. At the Arab summit meeting held on November 26–28 in Algiers, the ministers decided that no producing nation would be expected to tolerate reductions of more than 25% in petroleum export earnings, and all consuming countries were classified into "most favored," "friendly," "neutral" or "hostile" categories. Following the summit, the Saudi and Algerian oil ministers made a trip to major European capitals to emphasize Arab demands for Israeli withdrawal and offer to restore production progressively in response to a staged Israeli pullback. In response to Secretary of State Kissinger's earlier reference to possible American countermeasures, the Arabs declared that any military intervention would simply induce them to destroy their oil facilities.

However, in early December Arab producers, with Saudi Arabia as leader and spokesman, began to give signs of relaxing their conditions, partly attributable to the active role as mediator that Washington had assumed in the Arab-Israeli conflict by that time. Relaxation of the embargo was effected in several stages. On December 9 the Arab oil ministers first accepted a new Saudi formula to link the lifting of the embargo with the adoption of a timetable for Israeli withdrawal from occupied Arab territories, including Jerusalem. On December 25 the ministers decided to decrease the 25% production cutback to 15% and cancel the 5% reduction scheduled for January. In the third stage, President Sadat began pressing for an early end of the embargo policy as a result of the conclusion, under United States auspices, of the Egyptian-Israeli disengagement agreement on January 17, 1974.

In early 1974 rumors of an impending end to the Arab embargo of the United States proliferated, and Henry Kissinger's intensive shuttle diplomacy finally bore fruit. On March 18, the Arab oil ministers decided to provisionally remove the embargo against the United States until June 1. The conclusion on May 29 of the Syrian-Israeli disengagement agreement opened the way for the permanent lifting of the embargo, although the Arab ministers warned that it could be reimposed if a new war broke out.[114] The curtailment of American petroleum supplies had lasted exactly five months.

While it seemed certain that the oil companies would obey the instructions of the producing nations, it seemed equally certain that the companies would be responsible for allocating the available oil not covered explicitly by these instructions. This responsibility, coupled with their operation of the physical facilities, placed the companies in the key role of managing the cutbacks and embargo. The American parents of Aramco, fearing the loss of the world's most valuable oil concession, dared not defy Saudi Arabia's wishes—they informed Washington of the actions they were taking to carry out the embargo and were neither ordered nor advised by the United States government to do otherwise.[115]

The oil companies faced a formidable task indeed. Each operated a complex chain of facilities, starting with the production of crude and ending with the delivery of a petroleum product to consumers. Each produced a hundred or more types of crude oil, differing both in impurities (such as sulfur) and the composition of the hydrocarbons, in refineries that likewise differed somewhat from one another. If a refinery designed to operate on a light Libyan crude oil were used to process a heavy Venezuelan crude, its capacity would be reduced, its equipment subject to corrosion, and its products of inferior quality.[116]

Managements normally solve the resulting supply problems with the aid of computers, taking into account the capabilities and constraints inherent in the system such as availability of tankers, quality of crude, capacity and processing capabilities of refineries, and products available for trade from other firms—and any constraints specified by management such as allocations of products to a given country. During the embargo, however, such allocation was often bypassed because instructions from the producing nations removed much of the companies' freedom of action and management wanted to exercise maximum control over those few decisions that were left to them. The resulting problems of supply and distribution were enormous. One manager remarked that he rebalanced his company's worldwide distribution system once a week during the height of the oil crisis. His company, operating dozens of refineries and over a hundred ships, was faced with continuous changes in production levels and demand schedules as well as, from time to time, changes in the quotas set by the Arabs.

The ability of the oil companies to control the flow of crude and final products had already caused uneasiness among consuming countries in the months prior to the embargo, and this concern approached panic during the embargo's early stages. Especially prevalent was the conviction of both the Europeans and Japanese that American oil companies were diverting "the bulk of their supplies to meet their U.S. shortfall."[117] It was also widely believed that since the Arabs had established priorities giving some countries proportionately more oil than others, this would result in substantial differences in impact. A report by the EEC stated: "The Middle East crisis has not affected all member countries in the same way, since at the start of the crisis two countries—and later three—enjoyed a privileged position: France, United Kingdom and Belgium."[118]

In allocating oil among the consuming nations the oil companies used a standard of "equal suffering," distributing the impact of any shortages more or less equally among the users in different markets. A standard of that sort clearly could not be precise, and therefore left considerable leeway in its application. American companies exhibited no signs of greatly favoring the American market, and BP (half-owned by the British government) showed little sympathy for its government's claims for preferred treatment.

From August 1973 to the height of the oil shortage in the United States (January–February 1974), American crude imports dropped 30%, and imports of Arab oil dropped from 1,200,000 barrels daily to only 19,000.[119] It was estimated that the five American oil companies diverted about 31% of their crude oil shipments during the embargo period to countries not included in their non-embargo destinations.[120] As expected, shipments of non-Arab oil to the United States and the Netherlands were increased to replace Arab crude, which in turn was shipped in greater quantities to Japan and the United Kingdom to offset reductions of non-Arab oil. Relatively little diversion occurred either to or from France and West Germany.

Whatever the exercise of government pressure might have achieved in general, it seems clear that pressure from home governments on the oil companies did not play a major role in determining the allocation of supply. Differences in treatment during the embargo appear to have resulted from a combination of random events and imperfections in data and in the measurement of the shortage. The patterns of oil distribution thus were essentially non-national, and anyone seeking confirmation of the view that it paid a country to have a multinational oil company based within its own jurisdiction would have found little support for such a hypothesis of favoritism.[121]

Given the circumstances, the MNEs on the whole did an efficient job of allocation during the embargo. As a Federal Energy Administration report concluded, "It is difficult to imagine that any allocation plan would have achieved a more equitable allocation of reduced supplies."[122] Nevertheless, the experience of the American oil majors in helping to manage the shortages of world oil during the embargo seems to have changed their view of the function that they might appropriately play in the future. Prior to the embargo, it would have been difficult to find an American oil company official who thought it was the responsibility of governments to allocate oil during such a conflict—they would probably have taken it for granted that the companies themselves would have that task. After the embargo was over, however, a number of company spokesmen, presumably worn by pressures and stung by the inevitable criticism that resulted from their handling of the situation, began to state that it was the responsibility of governments to determine such allocations.[123]

Probably as far back as the mid-1960s, in terms of our model of conflict management, the oil companies' historical *competitive* position was already being eroded by a powerful rising group of non-industrialized oil-producing governments. As management became cognizant of its long-standing relationships and growing interdependence with the producer nations, as well as their relative loss of power during the late 1960s and early 1970s, a gradual change in conflict behavior resulted. Reflecting a less assertive and more cooperative manner toward their host governments, the oil companies were forced to adopt a less *competitive* and more *compromising* behavior. By mid-1973, they found their position had further evolved from one of *compromise* to one of *accommodation*. Host government nationalization and participation policies were quickly eroding their power positions. They attempted to shore up their power during June–August 1973 by repeatedly but unsuccessfully asking the American government to move politically away from its support of Israel toward a more balanced position on the Arab-Israeli conflict.

After a summer of nationalizations of oil independents in the Mideast, the September 1973 nationalization by Libya resulted in a temporary, highly assertive reaction—the virtual domestic boycott of Libyan crude oil over the next few weeks was carried out by the MNEs with the full support of the United States government, but to no avail. As a result, the American oil companies quickly drifted back to a *compromise* behavior before the end of the month.

Today the oil companies still retain their ties and continue to negotiate with host governments.[124] They retain enormous leverage—in June 1974 an Exxon vice-president pointed out that no host government's oil company had ever made a major oil find. "No one in Government ever drilled at 3,000 feet of water. . . . Maybe some day governments will get all the expertise and we will be pushed out."[125] Offshore oil, with its complex exploration techniques, is sure to play a greater role in the international oil industry over the remaining years of the century. In the meantime, discussions on long-term supply contracts, service contracts, and management contracts go forward. Nevertheless, the oil companies remain vulnerable to politically-triggered supply disruptions, as the data in Table 7–1 show.

Just how vulnerable the multinational oil companies are to political conflict between countries became evident once again less than five years later with the Iranian crisis that began in 1978. The repeated and often violent demonstrations against the Shah triggered prolonged strikes in Iran's oil fields and severe cutbacks in production—to the extent that Iran itself was subject to a serious fuel shortage. Although not directly involved in nationalized Iranian production, the loss of a major source of crude forced the multinationals once again to restructure the logistics of supply. According to one American official, "At the moment, we are confident that the shortage is being spread as equitably as possible. There is no evidence that the system is not working."[126] Under the rules of the International Energy Agency, emergency intergovernmental reallocation procedures exist, but a requirement that this involve domestic steps such as rationing caused governments to prefer leaving the problem once again to the multinationals.

Companies like Socal, with ties to Aramco, were able to boost Saudi Arabian purchases enough to replace Iranian crude, but others were left with severe shortages, and BP had to inform customers of a 25% cutback in deliveries. Deliveries between oil companies and redirecting production from Kuwait, Alaska, Nigeria, Venezuela, and Indonesia helped to smooth out the burden. According to one observer, there is now ". . . widespread evidence to support most governments' belief that if they interfere with the companies' elaborate system they will be injecting political mechanisms into what is essentially a non-political process, and that will operate to almost everybody's detriment."[127]

Table 7–1 *Crude Oil Sources for Major Multinational Oil Companies*
(1977, in percent)

Company	Iraq	Kuwait	Saudi Arabia	Abu Dhabi	Oman	Libya	Qatar	Iran	Venezuela	Nigeria	Indonesia	Europe	Canada	U.S.A.	Asia	Other
BP	2	1	-	8	-	-	-	39	-	13	-	12	-	a	-	14
Shell	11	14	12	7	11	-	8	36	-	-	-	-	-	-	-	2
Exxon	-	-	28	-	-	3	-	9	21	-	-	2	6	23	6	2
Socal	-	-	66	-	-	-	-	5	-	-	12	-	3	12	-	2
Mobil	-	-	56	3	-	-	-	9	-	9b	-	2	5	15	-	1
Gulf	-	27	-	-	-	-	-	19	6	14	-	-	4	21	-	9b
Texaco	-	-	58	-	-	-	-	5	-	11	-	-	3	16	-	7

a Excludes Alaska.   Includes Angola.   *Source:* Oil Company Data.

EXTRATERRITORIALITY AND CONFLICT MANAGEMENT

In most of the ten cases examined here, the MNEs found themselves wedged between clashing actors in different nations whose interests were themselves in conflict — monkeys in the middle. As a result, the firms were compelled to simultaneously use different strategies to cope with different issues and/or actors in different countries. The inability of the firms to jointly and fully satisfy the concerns of both the home and host governments involved generally encouraged corporate efforts aimed at orchestrating middle-ground solutions. When such outcomes were not feasible, the MNEs reluctantly and painfully had to make clear choices, that is, to cooperate with one government and frustrate the interests of the other. Moreover, each of the cases generally reflected a change in stakes, power, interests, and/or relationships during the course of conflict, which called for sequential shifts of behavior. Most of the companies had perceived a loss of relative power before the conflict was fully resolved—in trying to remain *competitive* they were forced to soften their positions by making partial concessions to the governments involved, vis-à-vis *compromise* behavior. On the other hand, the Aramco case represented such a significant decline in power and polarization of home-host nation interests that movement went well beyond *compromise* to full *accommodation* with the Saudis. The Firestone and Mobil/Dresser cases represent somewhat exceptional patterns, with commitments to total *avoidance* and *competitive* behavior, respectively—in large measure, perhaps, as a function of the incompatibility of interests involved.

A few additional points should be noted as well. First, in emergencies that require the managing of complex transnational economic variables, governments will often respond either slowly or not at all. Unable to effectively monitor or supervise the activities of MNEs, governments may be tempted to leave the problem of management to the firms themselves. Whether this will continue for long periods depends on the technical complexity of the industry and on the national and transnational politics of control. But a crisis management role for MNEs and its attendant conflict seems inevitable. Second, the realization that MNEs cannot be used simply as extended arms of governments presumably means that they will hold "their" MNEs rather more at arms' length than in the past. And so the disposition of governments to support multinationals in international conflicts promises to be even more subdued in the future than it already is. And third, the ability of home-country government to require MNEs to be responsive to their interests when that conflicts with the interests of host governments has diminished. Increasing competition has reduced the discretion available to MNEs, and growing multinationality has reduced the relative concern of these firms for any individual market. At the same time, the diffusion of technology and the development of host-country capabilities has augmented their relative bargaining power, and eroded the ability of home countries to extend their influence via the MNE.

8 OWNERSHIP
AND CONTROL

A source of political conflict that invariably confronts multinational companies is ownership and control. The two issues can be separated. *Ownership* pressure is principally a political phenomenon. Apart from questions of socialism versus private ownership that almost always exist, *foreign* ownership raises fears of "domination" of the economy and society from abroad through the multinational's parent-affiliate relationship. Fundamental decisions that affect the local economy are made thousands of miles away at corporate headquarters by people not directly concerned with local conditions. And there is always the fear that home-country governments will try to influence the behavior of "their" MNEs on domestic or foreign policy issues in the host nation. All of these considerations in a climate of strong nationalism can generate powerful forces for local ownership especially in "sensitive" sectors like mining, telecommunications, and banking.

Control pressure is primarily an economic phenomenon, aimed at improving the relationship of benefits to costs in the involvement of multinational companies in host-country economies. Often ownership and control issues are intertwined, especially when governments decide that the latter cannot be achieved without the former. This chapter will deal with the various forms ownership and control pressure can take through the so-called "project cycle." We shall deal with entry, operating, financial, and terminal controls, wherein ownership issues enter primarily through nationalization, expropriation, and confiscation as the MNE-host country relationship evolves. Politically, governments cannot and will not allow the MNE totally free reign in its operations. *Laissez faire* in an era of giant firms and giant governments is simply no longer in the cards. Nor is it particularly desirable from the firm's own point of view. We shall argue that for MNE management, clear guidelines, which are stable and predictable over reasonable periods of time, yet adaptable in an orderly way to changing circumstances, are decidedly preferable to a high degree of regulatory uncertainty, even if it involves some reduction of economic freedom.

WHY CONTROL?

The effects attributable to MNE operations at the national level are many and varied. For host and home countries there are often serious implications for employment, labor-force composition, technology, trade, income, the natural environment, politics, business conduct, consumer interests, and other issues. Some of these will be viewed as beneficial and some not. To be sure, the individuals and groups who make up society will feel the benefits and costs in greater or lesser measure—a farmer, an auto worker, a college professor, and a union organizer in the garment industry will have very different attitudes on these costs and benefits, since each will be affected in a different way. So will people residing in different regions of a country or belonging to different ethnic, racial, or income groups. It is the job of the political system to reconcile the conflicting views and the political power their proponents represent into a coherent national policy on international trade and investment, just as it must on other controversial issues as diverse as nuclear power, national defense, welfare, or farm-support programs. The outcome at the national level, being the product of conflict, will itself inevitably be subject to dispute. And so even perfect corporate alignment with national policy positions is by no means a guarantee of freedom from conflict. But it does—depending on such factors as political stability and shifting coalitions of interests—contribute a critical degree of legitimacy to the firm's existence and operations that cannot be achieved in any other way.

From the point of view of a national state, therefore, the purpose of controls and pressures for national ownership is to achieve a closer correspondence between the effects of MNE activities and national policy objectives than would exist in their absence. This often means that the country tries to obtain for itself a greater share of the joint gains from MNE activities attributable to more efficient allocation of production and/or consumption activities. It may attempt to obtain greater tax revenues, more local production and employment, and the like, than it would get in an uncontrolled situation. In such cases controls may mean losses for the MNE, and we are thrown into a classic bargaining situation.

One problem with controls is that the outcomes often are not very clear either in prospect or even in retrospect. It is not easy to predict how MNE management will react to a given government policy initiative, whether or not it will bring about the desired result or whether, indeed, the opposite of the desired outcome might not be the final product. This brings out the critical importance of policy-makers' understanding what makes MNE management tick—how it behaves in terms of its own goal structure, how it reacts to external pressure when achievement of those goals may be compromised, and what alternatives may be open to it. Aside from generally consistent behavior of MNEs predicted by the overall goal of profit maximazation, which can be decomposed into a variety of constituent aspects—as we have done in Chapter 1, for example—it is important to bear in mind variations in the reactions of individual MNEs resulting from differences in leadership, organizational and competitive factors.

From the point of view of the MNE, controls also have certain advantages. They provide up-front indications of national preferences and priorities, serving as benchmarks for the long-run alignment of fundamental corporate policies. Even if they can be evaded or avoided, the burden of proof in departures from local behavioral norms falls on the firm. Nobody likes to be cast adrift in an uncertain setting where no behavioral guidelines exist, and where there are no indications whatsoever whether today's actions will be considered good or bad tomorrow. By providing external guidance for a firm to comply with—or ignore at its own peril—controls can play a useful uncertainty-reducing role. They also serve a conflict-deflecting function, since careful compliance with national controls can often shift conflict with the ubiquitous dissatisfied groups from the firm to the government for resolution. So reduced uncertainty over time and better guidance under existing circumstances are two benefits the MNE can expect from national controls, and these can partially offset the costs they may impose on the firm.

BOUNDARIES OF CONTROL

National control of the MNE is limited in two ways. The first is the bargaining leverage of each side. The second is the ability of the MNE to "escape" their effects. The greater the leverage of the individual MNE relative to the country in which it is operating, the less likely it is that effective controls can be established covering aspects of the firm's operations where actual or potential conflict exists. On the country's side, its bargaining power will be stronger: (a) the larger the internal market and the more rapid its rate of growth, (b) the more valuable to the firm are indigenous resources such as a stable, inexpensive, and well-trained labor force or a desirable natural resource base, (c) the more stable and favorable to foreign-owned firms are domestic political conditions—that is, the lower the perceived level of "sovereign risk," (d) the lower the economic and managerial costs of doing business locally, involving economic and social infrastructure (especially communications and transport), bribery, corruption, and political meddling, (e) the healthier the country's balance of payments outlook, promising adequate foreign exchange availability for profit remittances, (f) the more stable its external political relations, promising freedom from war, insurgency, or other externally-imposed violence, and (g) the larger the number of options available to the country for obtaining the "package" of services that the MNE in question promises, whether from one or more competing multinationals or from alternative independent sources such as foreign technical assistance, turnkey plants, and the like. These are "power" variables that fit into our conflict management model developed in Chapters 2 and 3.

From this we can infer that a country with a large, dynamic resource-rich economy, a stable and capable government with a high-quality infrastructure and low transactions costs, will be highly attractive to MNEs and other types of foreign business ventures, and thus can avail itself of a wide variety of control devices with significant bargaining leverage. A country that is uninteresting from a market or resources standpoint, that has a corrupt, inefficient, complex or hostile government, or that is threatened with internal or external political instability will be less attractive to MNEs. Having leverage or "power" requires having options, and such a country will have precious few. So control becomes largely a hypothetical issue, since the suitors among MNEs will be few and far between. Each country will have a distinct leverage profile comprising the various characteristics just mentioned. It is perhaps an indication of the complexity of this profile that government's ability to take stock of their own assets and liabilities in a bargaining context often seems limited, resulting in excessive or inadequate control and, perhaps as often as not, failure to successfully come to grips with basic regulatory problems affecting MNEs.

One the company's side, the power position that is the basis for control will be greater: (a) the greater its "packaged" technology, marketing, and management inputs, (b) the greater its prospective contribution to national employment, income, balance of payments, human-resource development, and related economic variables, as well as the more extensive its linkages to the remainder of the economy, (c) the greater the coincidence of the firm's prospective economic contributions and the direction of national political and economic planning, (d) the larger the number and the more relevant its activities in other countries as "showcases" for its prospective activities in the host country, and (e) the larger the number of options available to the firm in terms of investment opportunities and alternative ventures given its scarce capital and human resources. Again, each firm will have a particular profile in terms of its own sources of bargaining strength, and accurate perception on the part of management will determine its resistance to or acceptance of external controls within the context of our conflict management model.

The two sets of leverage are pitted against each other both in a *general* and *specific* context. That is, they figure into a country's overall ability to set terms and conditions for MNE operations more or less closely aligned with its own objectives. They also figure into its stance on a given MNE project: whether general policy measures will be applied strictly, not so strictly, or not at all. For example, the general policy may be that no foreign ownership of telecommunications facilities is allowed, yet a satellite communications firm may be allowed in on an equity basis with no questions asked. Or a commercial bank proposing a new branch may be told that existing banking services are quite adequate for the country's needs, and that it should conduct its business through correspondent relationships with local banks.

Some host countries may set explicit policy differentials among groups of projects. For example, a firm may apply for especially favorable "pioneer industry" status, involving tax concessions, guaranteed profit repatriation, and the like. Or it may fall into a "normal" category, or even an "undesirable" category where adequate local firms already exist and foreign firms are perceived as offering minimal net benefits—so they are either kept out or admitted only on a joint-venture basis with local firms.

HOME COUNTRY CONTROL

While the rationale for host country control of MNEs is clear, *home* countries are motivated by many of the same kinds of considerations—the coincidence of MNE operations with national economic and social policy objectives—yet the problems of control are very different. Presumably, policy objectives with respect to technology, trade, balance of payments, growth, and employment are quite similar for home and host countries. The home country has to decide whether activities of its firms abroad contribute to or detract from these objectives.[1] The answer once again depends on what would occur if the foreign activities were not permitted, and there is the very real question of effectiveness of home-country controls.

Attempts by MNE home countries to restrict the overseas activities of their firms have been rather sparse, presumably because the benefits of foreign investment are perceived as far exceeding their costs from a national point of view—pressure to the contrary from injured special-interest groups notwithstanding. The relative absence of home country controls of an economic nature may also reflect huge problems in making them work effectively, whether by attempts to regulate capital flows, trade flows, or technology transfers, short of drastic measures such as outright prohibition. Instead, home-country control has largely focused on political factors, such as the kinds of "monkey in the middle" issues discussed in Chapter 7, which have given rise to both conflict between

MNEs and their home governments, and inter-country conflict due to extraterritoriality in the application of national laws.

Nevertheless, capital export controls were imposed progressively on MNEs by the United States in the 1960s. In 1964 the Interest Equalization Tax was passed to reduce private portfolio capital outflows by reducing interest incentives. The following year a voluntary program of restricting loans to Western Europe was urged on American commercial banks. In 1966 the Foreign Investors Tax Act was imposed to encourage investments by foreign firms in the United States, and in 1968 the voluntary bank lending limits were made mandatory. All of this was accompanied by limits on United States foreign direct investments, at first voluntary (1965) and later mandatory (1968). Under the voluntary program, firms were requested to expand exports, repatriate liquid balances held abroad, increase profit remittances, reduce investment expenditures abroad, and finance a greater proportion of foreign capital spending offshore. The subsequent mandatory controls prohibited all foreign direct investments unless authorized by the Secretary of Commerce, restricting them to the average base level of 1965 under various computational formulas depending on the type of host country and the level of its economic development. Mandatory profit repatriation was lifted in mid-1968, but short-term liquid balances held abroad were restricted. Administration of the controls was vested in the Office of Foreign Direct Investments (OFDI) in the Commerce Department.

The OFDI controls primarily reflected balance of payments pressures on the dollar toward the end of the Bretton Woods system of fixed exchange rates. They clearly conflicted with host-country policies, for example, by urging maximum repatriation of profits and reliance on local financial markets. They stimulated the growth of offshore financial centers and the Eurodollar and Eurobond markets, neither of which was subject to extensive national control. From the United States point of view, any positive balance of payments effects of the OFDI program were essentially short-run, since today's capital outflows produce tomorrow's return flows of interest and dividends, and a certain amount of exports induced by foreign direct investment may also have been lost. But the impact on MNE operations does not appear to have been unduly severe in retrospect—foreign production of American-owned firms grew apace during the entire OFDI period. In any event, the controls were scrapped in 1973.

Another focus of home-country control has been taxation. In the United States, as we will discuss in Chapter 14, the emphasis has been to remove loopholes that permit deferral of taxes on corporate profits by levying them as earned rather than as remitted. Under existing conditions, the large number of tax shelters that exist around the world makes this, and the discovery of off-the-books slush funds, extremely problematic. But tax havens are sovereign states too, and so regulation and control tend to be significantly beyond national power and depend fundamentally on inter-governmental cooperation and agreement.

Home countries have also been concerned about disclosure of MNE operations abroad. True, they probably receive a greater amount of information than anyone else, through reports in compliance with governmental tax and securities laws. But information about production, trade, employment, technology transfer, and similar facets of MNE operations remains sparse indeed. Disclosure has its own pitfalls for MNEs quite apart from the improved information base available to the government for regulation and control purposes. A very significant problem is release of proprietary information to competitors by government agencies. For example, although the U.S. Freedom of Information Act prohibits release of "trade secrets and commercial or financial information obtained from a person (or company) and privileged or confidential," an increasing flow of proprietary information to competitors and opposing interest groups has in fact occurred.

Finally, home-country reaction to host-government policies that are viewed as distorting the international location of production is one possible factor underlying home-country controls. Investment incentives, subsidies, and other distortions that lure production away from some countries toward others and have no basis in comparative advantage can increasingly be expected to meet with opposition. And it is pointed out that host-country policies can increasingly deflect the MNE's interests away from its home country, so that in the divergence of economic interests between home and host countries its operations increasingly "tilt" toward the latter. In cases where the division of benefits comes close to zero-sum, this means that what the host country gains the home country loses (jobs, income, access to raw materials, exports, etc.) even if the MNE itself doesn't necessarily lose out in the process. Such cases may trigger direct inter-country conflict and the possibility of "investment wars" very similar to "trade wars" involving successive rounds of retaliation and counter-retaliation on tariffs and other commercial barriers.[2]

For both host and home countries the problem of "escape," next to leverage, sets a second boundary to effective control of the multinational enterprise. Throughout this book, the *avoidance* option always exists for the MNE in order to skirt conflict with host or home country governments. Sometimes this may be perfectly satisfactory, as when a firm relocates pollution-intensive production to less environmentally sensitive areas abroad. In other cases, as in tax avoidance, it may not be acceptable to one or more of the countries concerned, and plugging the holes depends fundamentally on cooperation between countries. Under such circumstances, either two countries must get together to agree on a set of controls, or effective control becomes a problem of multilateral agreement. The first option tends to generate conflict and bargaining between national governments, as in the negotiation of international tax treaties. The second option presupposes that countries have a great deal in common with each other when it comes to regulating the MNE which, as we shall see in Chapter 15, is often not the case.

Once an ownership and control policy has been decided upon in principle, at the national level what options are available to the host country for carrying out that policy? We can identify at least four sets of alternatives, or "pressure points," available: (1) control on entry, before a proposed project has gotten underway or an MNE commitment has been made; (2) controls on the operations of the MNE affiliate once it has gotten off the ground and is operating successfully; (3) financial controls on MNE affiliates, especially on earnings remittances, affecting their profitability from the standpoint of the parent; and (4) terminal controls which effect a phase-out of foreign participation in the local venture. All have their advantages and drawbacks, and all have been tried under widely varying conditions.

ENTRY CONTROLS

Perhaps the most conflict-resistant technique for national control of MNE operations is entry control. The host country sets the terms and conditions under which the MNE may operate within its national borders. It will normally establish some type of "gatekeeper" mechanism, such as registration and screening procedures. Foreign firms interested in entering a particular line of economic activity must first register with a "board of investments" or similar institution set up for that purpose. At the same time, the investing firm may be asked to disclose the nature of the investment, the source of financing, whether it is a new project or takeover of an existing firm, whether it will be wholly-owned or a joint venture, and similar details. If the country offers special incentives for certain types of investments, the firm will tend to apply for them at this point as well.

The proposal is carefully examined by the board in terms of its role in the national economic plan, its prospective effects on employment, competition, the balance of payments, and other important variables in order to determine the desirability of the project from a national point of view. It will then set the terms for entry, ranging from "permission denied," to essentially free rein, to major incentives for highly desirable projects. The response may include restrictions on location, financing, ownership, technology inputs, local sourcing of raw materials and intermediates, earnings repatriation, and the like. The critical point is, however, that the terms and conditions are set *before* the commitment to a project by the MNE, and there is at least the implicit assumption that these will remain constant over the life of the project.

Entry control has the advantage of minimum uncertainty and maximum freedom to negotiate on both sides. The country can determine how a particular venture fits into its plans, and may be able to select from among competing firms. The company can weigh the host country's offer in the light of its own alternatives and, once committed, be reasonably sure the rules of the game will not change in the near term—at least within the limits of political risk. So it can afford to be content with a relatively lower rate of return on invested capital, which in turn redounds to the benefit of the host country. Within the entry bargaining context, the firm may benefit from maximum negotiating leverage, since it is not yet committed and still has its options open—and the inevitable conflicts have not yet cropped up. Over the life cycle of a project, bargaining power may never again be as high for the firm as before it invests at all.

Conflict behavior in entry negotiations tends to be open and above-board for both sides. Each tends to adopt a *competitive* stance based on perceived advantages, yet is prepared to compromise up to a point. If negotiations fail, there is a clean end to conflict and both sides go about their business without lingering animosity or conflict-related repercussions. Indeed, there is nothing to prevent another set of negotiations between the same protagonists at some point in the future. And if both sides do a good job of forecasting future events, some of the more obvious conflicts arising over the life of the project can be resolved at the outset, or at least the ground-rules for resolving them can be established at that time. On the other hand, things do change—host-country needs and priorities, personalities, and political climate as well as company fortunes. Not everything can be anticipated. And conflict that arises as a result of thwarted expectations can sometimes be unusually intense.

The use of entry controls is widely dispersed. Argentina, Chile, Colombia, Cyprus, Greece, India, Indonesia, South Korea, Spain, Turkey, and Yugoslavia, among others, all require government approval before an investment can be made by a foreign firm. Restrictions on foreign ownership vary widely. Most countries restrict foreign investments in defense, public utilities, and the media. Argentina requires that, in the automobile industry, at least 51% of the capital of firms be owned by nationals, and a minimum of 80% of the directors and 90% of the professional and technical staff must be nationals living in Argentina. Spain generally requires prior approval for all projects where foreign ownership exceeds 50%, except that no such approval is required in the high-priority iron and steel, cement, food processing, and textile sectors. Spain also will not approve any project that proposes to restrict exports or access to technology. India's Foreign Exchange Regulation Act of 1974 (see below) requires all foreign affiliates to be 60% Indian-owned unless they produce exclusively for export. India has also had a very restricted but constantly-changing group of industries at the top of the priority list, where the general rule against majority participation by foreign firms can be waived. Moreover, any industrial license granted to a foreigner is predicated upon raising at least part of the equity capital within India. A 1972 Mexican law on foreign investment reserves the petroleum, petrochemicals, nuclear energy, electricity, railroads, telecommunications, and part of the mining sector exclusively for the government, and ownership of the media, road and air transport, forestry, and gas distribution is confined to Mexican citizens. In other sectors maximum percentages of foreign ownership are specified, all under the control of the National Commission on Foreign Investment and requiring all foreign participations in business be be recorded in a National Registry of Foreign Investments.[3]

Foreign ownership frequently becomes a factor in entry negotiations even in advanced countries. For example, the Libyan purchase of 10% of Fiat stock for $415 million at the end of 1976 triggered Communist and other demands for a parliamentary debate on the issue and prompted Fiat's chairman Giovanni Agnelli to inform Italy's President Giovanni Leone well in advance of announcing the transaction.[4] Especially controversial was the Soviet Union's alleged role in bringing the two sides together with a view to strengthening Fiat's ability to expand its Russian automobile activities.

In 1973, Japan for the first time permitted 100%-owned foreign investments after decades of protecting domestic industry from foreign-owned competition on its home turf—a policy attracting increasing criticism with Japan's growing export penetration of foreign markets and its own investment ventures in all parts of the world. Two provisions, however, block foreign takeovers of Japanese firms and require modifications of investments thought to have a "harmful" effect on Japan. Dow Chemical, for example, proposed construction of a chlorine plant, but was blocked by the Ministry of International Trade and Industry under pressure from domestic chlorine producers on the grounds that their older-style plants would be unable to compete. However, Dow did receive permission to go ahead with several other plants.

In 1967 the Japanese Ministry of International Trade and Industry informally announced "ten commandments" for foreign investors:

1. Invest in industries where a fifty percent equity is automatically approved, rather than in industries where a hundred percent is possible.

2. Avoid industries in which goods are produced mainly by medium to small factories.
3. Avoid restrictive arrangements with overseas parent companies or affiliates.
4. Cooperate with Japanese producers in the same industry in order to avoid "excessive competition."
5. Contribute to the development of Japanese technology.
6. Help promote Japanese exports.
7. Ensure that in a joint venture the number of Japanese directors reflects the percentage of Japanese equity participation.
8. Avoid layoffs and plant closures that might disrupt the Japanese labor market.
9. Cooperate in maintaining Japan's industrial harmony and help in the achievement of her economic goals.
10. Avoid concentrating investments in any particular industry or industries.

New investments in France must be approved by the Comité Interministeriel des Investissements Étrangers (CIIE), after an assessment of their prospective impact on the French economy. Regions where the new investment might be located are proposed. Subsidies or other aids are considered. No more than half of the needed capital can be raised locally, and the Ministry of Foreign Affairs must approve any project where over 20% of the equity is foreign-owned.

In Sweden, a law governs acquisition of domestic firms by foreign-based MNEs, backed by that country's all-powerful trade unions. A government spokesman maintains: "In the long run, the only solution regarding control of multinationals is by international cooperation. But this does not prevent Sweden from taking action now to protect Swedish interests."[5] For their part, Swedish industrialists have been concerned that such control would most likely be based on short-term political considerations, and not on basic competitive factors affecting the Swedish economy.

Entry controls to force more of the financing of affiliate operations offshore—and increase the net capital inflow—are used by various countries. One study claims that only 17% of the capital invested by United States–based firms in Latin America during the 1957–1965 period actually represented inflows from abroad, the rest being raised locally.[6] Australia is another country that sets entry limits on the amount of capital that can be raised locally.

Tariff policy is also used as an instrument to control MNEs at the entry level. As will be emphasized in Chapter 14, the promise of tariff protection can be used as an inducement for investments to serve the host country market. Similarly, foreign investment projects may be accorded duty-free treatment for capital equipment and inputs, provided that local raw materials are used in the production process. When production is for export, free-trade zone treatment or tariff drawbacks—rebating tariffs on inputs when the final product is exported—are sometimes provided. Even more narrowly, Singapore, which has rather liberal entry requirements, evaluates investment applications in part on the proportion of scientific and technical personnel to be included in the work force.

The Canadian Foreign Investment Review Act (FIRA) and the screening agency it created are perhaps the most comprehensive example of entry control. The Act is supposed to ensure that foreign investment projects benefit Canada. It is in part intended to discourage foreign takeovers of Canadian enterprises; to help ensure Canadian control of "future growth industries" like telecommunications, computer software, aerospace, electronics, and pharmaceuticals; and to keep close tabs on resource-extractive industries. Under the Act, purchase of at least 5% of the outstanding voting shares of a traded company or 20% of the equity in a privately held firm is defined as a takeover unless the purchaser can prove otherwise—acquisitions of over 50% are automatically considered takeovers. Any foreign investor proposing a takeover of an existing firm or establishing a business unrelated to his existing business in Canada is required to register with the agency, which applies 10 "tests" to the proposal including: (1) compatibility with domestic economic policies, (2) increased employment, (3) improved productivity, (4) improved industrial efficiency, (5) increased use of Canadian resources, parts, or services, (6) Canadian equity participation, (7) improved product variety, (8) enhanced technological merits, (9) expanded exports, and (10) new net investment. During a three-month period in 1975, 36 projects were submitted. Two passed all ten "tests", but most received five to seven points. Thirty were approved, although one of those approved scored only one point.

One of the two top scorers was a proposal by British retailer Marks & Spencer to take over Peoples Department Stores. "It undertook to open at least 25 new stores within the next five years and to ensure a high Canadian content in them. It promised to encourage the development of new yarns and fabrics by Canadian manufacturers and to promote exports of St. Michael products from Canada. It will set up a research group in Canada and give preference to Canadians at all levels of employment. The majority of the Boards of Directors of Peoples and its subsidiaries will be resident Canadians."[7] The other top scorer was Germany's Friedrich Krupp, which promised to double the capacity of the Canadian firm in which it planned to acquire a 50% interest. The firm would also become the exclusive licensee for Krupp materials-handling equipment in Western Canada.

Three sets of benefits were expected to derive from Canada's screening procedures applied at the entry level to foreign investments. First was the admittedly psychic benefit that decisions which affect the Canadian economy in a fundamental way would be made by Canadians. Second was the expectation of greater effectiveness of Canadian policy deriving from increased domestic ownership of industry and national control over foreign investment. Third was the possibility that a greater proportion of the joint gains from foreign investment would go to Canada, including the enhancement of domestic entrepreneurial activities.[8]

The Canadian policy was criticized heavily in political circles as well as in the media as not being sufficiently rigorous—a charge rebutted by government officials with statements such as "Our aim is not to stop foreign investment, but rather to get the best deal we can out of it."[9] Nationalists pointed out that foreign takeovers of Canadian firms were running at a rate of 170 per year and that 60% of Canadian manufacturing was foreign-controlled (over 90% in many industries). So there was some question whether this relatively mild form of entry control was the last word for Canada. On the contrary, by 1979 the policies of the Foreign Investment Review Agency had become even more lenient, in response to sluggish Canadian economic performance and more than $1 billion drop-off in United States net investment in Canada. FIRA had, in the view of some foreign firms, become a source of substantial irritation to foreign investors due to its lengthy deliberations and the resulting delays in getting projects underway. Even among Canadians, a debate began to rage over whether Canada's foreign investment controls, after five years of application, had "significantly benefited" Canada. One critic, the Premier of Manitoba, declared that FIRA symbolized a "prissy economic nationalism preached by a small band of misguided Canadians."[10]

An assessment of the experience of General Electric in France is a good way to nail down some of the points we have made here.

General Electric-Bull

During the 1960s, computer utilization grew much faster in Western Europe than in the United States, and was "regarded as a 'juicy pear' by those U.S. firms that could apply to it the technology and experience they had already acquired in the home market."[11] This strength, along with the failures and weaknesses of European computer firms, allowed American companies to establish a commanding position in Europe by the early 1960s. By the end of the decade, American computer MNEs were estimated to have carved out for themselves almost 80% of the European market, with IBM having a 52% market share.

In most European countries, the government has been the largest single user and purchaser of computers, accounting for perhaps 30–40% of the overall market and a much higher share of the larger computers and advanced systems. As a result, European governments in the 1960s began to view computers as a strategic industry requiring public-sector attention and support.

The French government seemed content during the 1950s not to intervene in the computer industry within its borders. A private firm, Compagnie des Machines Bull, had developed from a small punch-card machine producer in the 1930s and 1940s into a large, prosperous computer firm. Sales rose an average of 25% a year between 1953 and 1960, and profits peaked in 1961. Employment rose to around 11,000 workers, placing Bull among the top 30 employers in France. Bull held almost one-third of the French computer market during the 1950s and one-tenth of the total European market. Its performance swelled French national pride and excited the fancy of stock market speculators—it became "the Brigitte Bardot of French industry."

Despite these accomplishments, Bull suffered from a number of weaknesses in technology, finance, and management in the early 1960's. Development costs on its new, technically advanced but enormously expensive mainframe computer could not be recovered. The company lost confidence in its own design and engineering teams, and signed an agreement with RCA Corporation in 1961 to produce RCA machines in France. This project resulted in heavy tooling costs and little profit. Nor did Bull receive any financial support or special development contracts from the government. As a result, the company's borrowings increased as it went head-to-head against IBM in France—in mid-1963 the company arranged several large loans, only to find that the needed authorization had been refused by the government's Ministry of Finance. A family-dominated management considered by many observers to be conservative, disorganized, and inept compounded Bull's problems. Several company plants in France and its holding in Olivetti-Bull (Italy) were sold off. Bull also began giving discounts of as much as 35% to its foreign subsidiaries in order to compete with IBM. In October 1963 one of Bull's prime creditors, the Banque de Paris, forced two of its representatives into the firm. Conflict with the family-controlled board and management soon resulted, and the family began looking around for a completely new source of capital.

The General Electric Company had been selling computers in France since 1962, although its sales and service facilities were rather limited. Once GE made the decision in 1959 to enter the computer industry, it seemed almost inevitable that it would soon turn to the more open European market. By the end of 1963, it had already spent over $100 million on the development, manufacturing, and leasing of computers in the United States and was anxious to expand into overseas markets. As a latecomer (IBM, Honeywell,

NCR, and Sperry Rand had all set up European subsidiaries before World War II), GE preferred to take over established European computer firms rather than set up new facilities, perhaps also attributable in part to its lack of experience in overseas operations—in the early 1960s less than 10% of GE's total output was manufactured outside North America.

In December 1963 GE wrote to Bull's family-controlled board and renewed a 1962 offer that had been turned down, proposing to acquire a 20% stake in Bull's capital at the prevailing market price. In addition, financial and technical support was offered. By buying into Bull, GE would get a strong sales and service network in Europe that could be used to market both Bull equipment and GE's own computer line, as well as a strong line of peripheral equipment. Since the transaction required approval of the Ministry of Finance, upon accepting GE's offer Bull's board immediately sought government approval. The Finance Minister, in turn, took the proposal to Charles de Gaulle.

Reportedly angered over a United States embargo on computer sales to the French government's nuclear programs and over Chrysler's takeover of Simca, de Gaulle was not prepared to allow foreigners to grab another slice of "vital" French industry. After keeping GE and Bull waiting for more than a month, President de Gaulle flatly rejected Bull's "American solution." A Finance Ministry spokesman noted that the government "couldn't agree to the prospective acquisition of a part of [Bull's] capital by a foreign company."[12] Both GE and Bull declined comment on the government's action. Bull now had no option but to accept a "French solution"—a match between Bull and local banks and electronics firms arranged by the government.

It soon became apparent, however, that the company was in worse shape than anyone had suspected, and no members of the French rescue group wanted to carry such a large loser. There was also a widespread conviction inside and outside the company that nothing could save Bull short of turning over control to an organization with the capital and technical proficiency of a big firm like GE. According to a GE negotiator, "They felt that even if the necessary financing were forthcoming from French sources, this still wouldn't have been enough to make the company safe in the face of the onslaught of IBM competition. They had to have some stronger backing than that."[13] The government finally acknowledged this, and in late April 1964 completely reversed itself by accepting "in principle" a deal with GE.[14]

From May through July of 1964, GE and Bull discussed details leading to a final agreement. Given the deterioration in Bull's situation, GE's bargaining strength had improved markedly. It offered 25% less per share than it had offered earlier. Bull had to accept, and in late July GE agreed to pay $43 million for a 50% interest in the faltering company. Bull was to be reorganized as a holding company, with its operating assets spun off to form two new subsidiaries, a manufacturing company 49% owned by GE and a marketing company 51% owned by GE.[15] The agreement was immediately ratified by the government, less than four months after the Finance Minister had declared that the decision against GE participation was irrevocable.

It was chiefly the marketing operation that GE was seeking. It gave the company "access to the European data-processing market through the main entrance. . . . The main point is that we are acquiring a first-class distribution system. We will integrate production and distribution to make the best use of the strengths of both companies."[16] In August 1964, GE announced its entry into the mainframe computer field with its 600–series to be manufactured in Phoenix, Arizona, and simultaneously widened its European beachhead with a 75% interest in Olivetti's small data-processing division. Although all three ventures were losing money, GE seemed to feel than an infusion of cash and management would turn them around.

Since management control of Bull now rested with GE, an American executive was dispatched to France who had, in his own words, only "a brushing experience with Europeans."[17] Small groups of Americans were brought in discreetly to avoid arousing nationalist sentiments—by 1967, only 30 Americans were on Bull's payroll. In 1965, several administrative and production changes were made, which were generally well received by the French. Management structure was tightened. Production of unmarketable tabulating equipment was discontinued, and the company sailed optimistically through the rest of 1965 and into 1966.

Optimism soon faded, however. During the first 18 months of GE's involvement Bull lost $50 million, with heavier losses in the offing. "In the third quarter of 1966 it was apparent to us that targets were not being met. The figures were not satisfactory, and we decided to take substantial action to get back on target." [18] The company stopped hiring and began cutting back its payroll by attriton. Tension among French workers rose with news that GE had laid off several hundred employees in Phoenix and had run into serious problems with its 600–series computer. This touched off speculation in France that GE was going to drop out of the computer business and would soon scuttle the Bull venture.

In December 1966 rumors of possible massive layoffs began to circulate—GE headquarters in New York had recommended a personnel cut of 2500, or about 25% of Bull's French labor force—touching off widespread protests. In mid-December, the French Finance Minister, who had to approve any payroll cutbacks, authorized an immediate cutback of only 270 workers after reminding GE-Bull of an earlier promise to limit such cuts. The remaining personnel reduction would have to come about gradually through attrition. By the end of 1966, GE had also decided that its Gamma 140 computer line—which had been developed and designed by Bull before GE's participation—would be dropped due to rising costs and sluggish sales. By early January 1967, these announcements created a furor in France over "foreign domination."

GE-Bull had badly mishandled its relations with all the parties concerned. Workers' representatives had neither been informed nor consulted about the layoffs. Labor leaders and their unions thus reacted with anger, calling for a "democratic nationalization." The press headlined the "Deuxième Affaire Bull," stressing the layoffs and the scrapping of the French-designed Gamma 140 line as a blow to national pride. The French government decided—in response to both a renewed United States government computer embargo and the "second Bull affair"—to launch its *Plan Calcul*, designed to achieve a profitable, nationally-owned computer industry. The government no longer considered Bull a French firm, and would give it no future preference for government orders of R&D assistance. [19]

GE-Bull's reported operating losses totaled $73 million by early 1967. Overall, it was estimated that GE had sunk some $200 million into the venture. [20] The work force remained alienated and demoralized. The closing in early September of two Lyons plants which employed 600 workers, prompted a renewed union call for nationalization. [21] The dropping of the Gamma 140 line had seriously damaged the company's image and its overall product line lacked competitive punch. The second generation of GE computers, although improved, was vulnerable to competition and the one market GE-Bull had hoped to penetrate significantly, the French government, had been emphatically closed off. Some speculated that GE might cut its losses and run.

But GE stuck it out. Specialization of the product range, along with effective financial controls, finally resulted in squeezing out a 1969 net profit of slmost $650,000. A "ventures task force" of three vice presidents was appointed to appraise GE's future in three major and costly new businesses—computers, nuclear reactors, and jet aircraft engines. In early February 1970, it recommended that GE sell its computer business and devote its available resources to the nuclear, jet engine, and other enterprises more closely connected to the company's "core" electrical products. A half-billion dollar preliminary plan to move GE clearly into position behind IBM was rejected as "fraught with risk." [22] And so GE discreetly began to look around for a buyer for its computer business. The task force approached Control Data, Xerox, and Honeywell. A GE-Honeywell combination would have a combined computer "installed base" double that of either partner company, and the combination would thus be "undisputed No. 2" with some 10% of industry volume—for GE "an optimum fit with a well-managed and successful growth company."[23] In May 1970 GE and Honeywell announced an agreement to combine their computer assets in a new company that would be controlled and managed by Honeywell. Threats to the deal immediately developed in both the United States and France.[24] Within a few days Honeywell stock dropped 27% and the stock of Machines Bull declined 9%. A major threat was posed by the French government, which could at any time veto the transfer of GE's 66% interest in Bull—the initial 50% interest had increased as a result of subsequent capital contributions. The day prior to the announcement, GE's chairman flew to Paris to brief President Pompidou personally. A week after the announcement, with stock prices stabilizing and French press reporting favorably on the deal, the threat of French government rejection seemed to have faded.

In contrast to GE, Honeywell had emphasized profitability in its computer business, which in the mid-1960s had moved into the black and remained there. But with only 4% of the market Honeywell figured that it would take at least a 10% share to be tenable in the long-run—"Quite independently of GE, we came to the conclusion that an acquisition of another one of the so-called computer generalists was perhaps the best approach to the future."[25] The GE acquisition would extend both the company's computer line and customer base. GE-Bull appeared to have been an additional attraction. With well-established subsidiaries in many parts of Europe already, Honeywell would find Bull's extensive European marketing and manufacturing operations a welcome addition.

In October 1970 a new subsidiary, Honeywell Information Systems (HIS), was formed—81.5% owned by Honeywell, with the remaining 18.5% GE investment to be bought out by 1980—representing their combined computer operations. The next three years were increasingly profitable for HIS. Computer profits were estimated to have climbed from less than $3 million in 1970 to $30 million by the end of 1972. HIS experienced a significant dip in profitability during 1974 because of technical difficulties and weak demand for computers. In the meantime, Honeywell-Bull absorbed other Honeywell operations in most of Europe and went on to record increasing revenues and profits. Less affected by operating problems suffered by HIS in the United States, Honeywell-Bull had carved out a solid 18–20% share of the French market by the end of 1974 and was regarded as the most powerful overseas competitor for IBM.

Meanwhile, as part of its Plan Calcul, the French government had created a national competitor, Compagnie Internationale pour l'Informatique (CII), by combining three small computer firms. Built on a narrow base, CII failed to give the American multinationals much competition, and even with massive infusions of government capital it made no profit. Its share of the French market remained below 10%. When Honeywell took over GE's stake in Bull in 1970, some government officials were already advocating that it take over CII as well.[26] President Pompidou opted for a "European solution"—CII together with Siemens of Germany and Philips of Holland as a French-German-Dutch combine called Unidata—launched with much ceremony in mid-1973 as an attempt to keep American hands off what was left of the European computer market.[27]

Almost immediately, rumors began to circulate of a possible alliance between Honeywell-Bull and Unidata through a merger with CII.[28] The French government countered that such a proposal would be "acceptable" only if Honeywell-Bull severed most of its United States ties: "It is out of the question for Unidata to cooperate with Honeywell-Bull under the present financial circumstances."[29] Merger rumors continued through 1974 and into 1975 as both parties sensed that a merger could enhance their respective interests.[30] It promised to strengthen Honeywell-Bull's position in the European computer market by allowing it to obtain a share of French government business. It promised to relieve France of making substantial payments to an ailing CII whose capital needs were becoming an embarrassment to the national treasury. And it promised to neutralize the role of Unidata as something of a Trojan Horse—CII was selling almost no machines in its partners' home countries, but both partners were doing good business in France.

After more than a year of waffling over a "European solution" versus a "trans-Atlantic partnership," the French government in May 1975 decided on the latter, with CII to be absorbed into Honeywell-Bull.[31] Honeywell agreed to accept a 47% minority holding in the new group by selling 19% of its 66% stake in Honeywell-Bull to French interests for about $60 million. In return, Honeywell recorded a healthy gain on the transaction and, through the new company, was in line to receive French government grants of some $250 million plus $800 million in orders. In France, however, the announcement touched off a storm of protest. Communists called the deal "sabotage," while the Gaullists termed it a "deception." Unidata was pronounced on its "death-bed," and in September 1975 Philips pulled out of the group.[32]

By the end of 1975 a final agreement had been signed creating a merged company, CII-Honeywell-Bull, 53% owned by French interests and 47% by HIS. Years later, observers were still wondering whether the French government or Honeywell came out ahead on the deal.[33] For its part, Honeywell had to contend with several unexpected problems. The merger agreement gave the French a strong voice in the management of all Honeywell's computer operations, raising prospects of future conflicts over product strategy and planning, R&D spending, and similar critical decisions. French political factions began urging the government to boost its control over CII-Honeywell-Bull, either by increasing its share of Machines Bull or by outright takeover. After the March 1978 French election, Honeywell "was very relieved" by the outcome—according to the firm's president, "We would have lost our business" if the leftists had gained political control.

This case illustrates quite well the sources of MNE leverage and government entry control initiatives and how these many change. The American MNEs involved basically had few alternatives to the conflict management strategies they adopted. At GE, computers amounted to only about 5% of total company business. Top executives had neither the expertise nor the time to run the computer business well. "The trouble with GE," said an engineer who spent ten years there, "is that they think a manager can manage anything. That may be true on the level of washing machines, but it sure doesn't hold for computers."[35] GE's competence in technology and manufacturing was not sufficient to overcome its lack of management and marketing know-how overseas. As a result, it incorrectly perceived its initial relative power, as well as its interest interdependence and relationship quality with the French government. GE's behavior and its "learning curve" while operating in France remained mired in the lower left-hand corner of the grid developed in Chapter 3, hovering just above the *avoidant* mode.

At Honeywell, in contrast, computers accounted for more than one-third of the revenues. Management understood the computer business intimately. The 1970 deal with GE combined Honeywell's marketing skills with GE's technical abilities. Company executives called it "a textbook merger." Honeywell seems to have viewed its relative power position as well as its interdependence and relationship quality with the French government in much more realistic terms than GE. In terms of our model, Honeywell generally adopted an easy *compromise* mode during the 1970s in France.

The French government, fearing industrial dominance, technological dependence and disruption of its "indicative planning" by high-technology foreign MNEs, would not allow positive interest relationships to develop with foreign MNEs. A *collaborative* solution was thus precluded and the government too, was forced into compromise.

OPERATING CONTROLS

An alternative approach to national control of MNEs is to pursue a relatively liberal entry policy, without careful screening at the outset, but with controls on various facets of the firm's operations. The firm may be asked to reduce its equity holdings from a majority to a minority position, for example. Or it may be required to provide a minimum percentage of a product's total value locally, or to export a certain percentage of its production. Sometimes ingenious and complicated schemes are devised, as when firms are permitted $1 worth of imports for every $2 worth of exports—the foreign exchange can be used for needed inputs or capital equipment, or the firm might go into the profitable business of importing and distributing high-priced luxury goods.

Other operating controls include maximum price limits (for example, on products like drugs and gasoline), minimum price limits to protect locally-owned competitors, wage and credit controls, quantitative limits on the number of foreign workers or managers who may be hired, tax policies, environmental and plant safety restrictions, product quality controls and market restrictions, fringe benefit requirements, and many more. Presumably the firm can assess the environment in terms of operating controls *ex ante*, so it knows the rules of the game before it makes a commitment. But rules have a way of changing, and host countries that rely on operating controls are particularly subject to conflict with MNEs as a result of revisions of those controls over the life of investment projects. Operating controls thus may be more prone to conflict and more subject to change than entry controls. The greater uncertainty may require a higher return on investment in order to justify a particular MNE investment. At the same time, the MNE itself is committed, and so it is more vulnerable to external pressure and has less bargaining power than in an entry-type negotiating situation. On the other hand, the host country has to make sure that the pressures of operating controls do not drive the firm out—they must be progressive, so that the marginal cost of compliance to the firm is perceived to be lower than the losses associated with pulling out.

There is also the point that operating controls may well be inefficient from the host country's own point of view. Price and wage controls, rationing, and other direct controls clearly distort resource allocation, and this can be very costly indeed—costly enough to eat into the benefits the controls are supposed to achieve and possibly nullify them altogether. Often these negative effects are extremely difficult to identify and to measure, thus prompting the country to impose self-defeating controls that it could better do without. And there is the point that widespread and especially unstable operating controls have a way of souring a country's reputation as a place to invest, thus eroding its bargaining leverage for future investment projects by foreign-owned firms. On the other hand, operating controls are not cast in concrete, and can be altered over time as circumstances change, thus avoiding the rigidities inherent in entry controls.

Manning controls are one example of operating restrictions. Countries as diverse as Nigeria and Morocco have limits on foreign workers employed by MNEs, and in Indonesia three-fourths of all employees must be local nationals within five to eight years of start-up. In Argentina 85% of the combined scientific, technical, administrative, and managerial personnel must be local nationals. India and Turkey require periodic reports from foreign-owned firms about the number of nationals employed and progress made in the replacement of foreign managerial and technical staff.

Frequently, operating restrictions are used to encourage extension of linkages between the MNE and the local economy in order to improve the developmental benefits from foreign investment. Progressive local-content targets, which set the minimum percentage of total product cost that must be of local origin, have been used effectively by Mexico and other countries over the years. This is often backed up by measures to cut off imports of parts and components after the "adjustment period" has passed, although there is usually an escape valve in case local sourcing is impossible within the time available. Export incentives are sometimes tied to ownership limits. So, for example, in several countries 100% foreign ownership is allowed only on projects that export 100% of their output.

MNEs may also come into conflict with national macroeconomic policies, for reasons outlined in Chapter 14. For example in 1977 the H.J. Heinz affiliate in Britain decided to pay its workers 17–20% more, although this would exceed government pay limits and a 12-month interval required between raises. The workers skipped a previous allowed wage increase in the settlement, which the government termed "leapfrogging" and brought threats that all government procurement contracts held by H.J. Heinz would be cancelled and that the excessive cost of the contract would be deducted from the company's allowable profit ceiling.[36]

Banking is one industry that has increasingly come under tight national operating controls in many countries, presumably because the costs of such policies are relatively small and because close regulation of the financial sector by national authorities is considered essential. In 1972 Mexico, for example, considerably tightened up on foreign banks in part to get a handle on foreign indebtedness by Mexican firms. Representative offices of foreign banks were placed on the same regulatory basis as domestic banks and continued to be barred from commercial banking operations in Mexico. Foreign-owned financial institutions may not accept Mexican funds for placement abroad, must restrict domestic loans to those permitted by Mexican credit policies, and must provide the government with detailed monthly reports of operations. In addition, they must operate strictly within the confines of Mexican law, rather than their home-country regulations, and the government reserves the right to revoke the registration of foreign credit institutions at any time, at its own discretion.[37] Let's consider how operating controls look in the real world.

The Aluminum Companies in Jamaica

According to a recent Jamaican ambassador to the United States, "Gold is exciting. Oil is exciting. Copper is exciting. Why can't aluminum be exciting?"[38] It is, in a way. Over 90% of United States bauxite supplies are imported, mostly from Australia, Guinea, Guyana, and Jamaica. The latter country alone supplies over half of the total and in 1974 hosted about $800 million of American investment in bauxite and alumina production—a hefty amount for a country of only just over 2 million people. The American dependence on imports and Jamaican dependence on production and exports of the same commodity provided a ready-made stage for political conflict, with the multinationals caught in the middle.

By 1950, a dozen years before Jamaica won its independence from Britain, American aluminum companies headed by Alcoa, Kaiser, and Reynolds Metals had begun buying up bauxite reserves in Jamaica. Along with Anaconda, Revere, and Alcan, they owned and operated Jamaica's entire bauxite industry, which accounted for almost 40% of world production.

During the 1960s, Jamaican governments followed "open door" policies toward foreign direct investment and were anxious to avoid even the appearance of confrontation with MNEs. Taxes were low, and based only on "profits" which were kept low through transfer pricing of bauxite and alumina to the parent companies in the United States and Canada. Until 1974 Jamaica relied mainly on renegotiation of bauxite taxes and pressure to secure indigenous alumina plants to increase revenues and domestic value-added from the industry. At that time, Jamaica was receiving about $27 million in revenues annually—12% of gross domestic product, but around 40% of foreign exchange earnings—from 15 million tons of bauxite and alumina exports worth between $175 million and $350 million on the American market.

In 1972, political changes in Jamaica brought into office a left-of-center government, headed by Michael Manley, which was anxious not only to use the rhetoric of economic nationalism but also to demonstrate its commitment to national economic sovereignty over natural resources. The new government confronted a number of serious economic and social problems which required greater contributions from the extractive sector, yet renegotiation of contracts with all six companies over the years had not even been sufficient to cover price rises in imports. The companies, for their part, had committed large investments in the late 1960s to build three alumina plants, and with each of them drawing a significant share of raw materials from their Jamaican subsidiaries the companies' stakes in Jamaica were large indeed.

Prime Minister Manley suggested early in January of 1974 that the existing bauxite contracts should be renegotiated. The companies accepted this, and meetings with the government began in Kingston during mid-March. In the next ten weeks of secret negotiations, the companies and the government remained far apart on the question of higher taxes and royalties. Very little has been publicly reported as to what went on during those weeks of negotiations. One observer described the talks as "vitriolic," with Manley professing 'astonishment at the companies' attitude. They just would not offer a realistic figure."[39] Another observer, however, spoke of "a strange tone of cordiality" between parties, and noted that "both sides have much to lose by handling each other too roughly. . . . American industry observers generally were shocked by the breakdown in the talks because they expected the Jamaicans would give in, assuming the aluminum companies offered a substantial increase. They considered the island nation's dependence on bauxite almost as big a handicap as its reliance on oil."[40] By mid-May, with the talks deadlocked, the companies agreed to raise overall payments to the government from $25 million to $80 million annually, but the Jamaicans refused to go below $200 million. Manley broke off negotiations, and sent to Parliament a tax proposal that would produce $200 million from the companies.

The companies initially reacted indignantly to the unilateral demands of the Jamaican government. The two negotiators who represented the six companies warned that the higher Jamaican charges could make the country's bauxite uncompetitive on the world market, and could lead to significantly increased prices of aluminum products to consumers. They also threatened to submit the case to international arbitration by the International Center for the Settlement of Investment Disputes (ICSID) on the grounds that Jamaica's action "would break their existing long-term contracts."[41] On the other hand, a statement had been issued in Toronto by the Jamaican public information office immediately after the breakdown in talks which hinted at the possibility of future bargaining over revenue issues, with Jamaica ready to negotiate further to break the impasse, and both Alcoa and Kaiser were hopeful that negotiating room with Jamaica could be found.[42] However, the chief Jamaican negotiator in Kingston stressed that there would be no reduction in revenue demands.[43] Manley's proposal was approved by Parliament one week later in its original form.

With Jamaica the keystone of the bauxite producing countries' International Bauxite Association (IBA), formed in late 1973, the Kingston talks represented the first test of their ability to emulate OPEC with steep revenue increases and control of part of the extractive operations themselves. Significantly, the Jamaican government had also demanded that a second stage of the negotiations in Kingston consider the latter issue. Although there had been no prior talk of nationalizing bauxite and alumina properties, industry negotiators acknowledged that the Jamaicans had periodically brought up the possibility of purchasing an interest in company operations in their country.[44]

In the following months the companies repeatedly stressed their cooperation with Jamaican governments in returning mined land to productive farming and cattle raising. They repeated the argument that the higher tax would result in Jamaican bauxite becoming uncompetitive. By mid-June of 1973 Alcoa, Kaiser, and Reynolds, all of whom had international arbitration clauses in their contracts, asked the ICSID to begin arbitration proceedings on the tax boost, claiming damages for the equivalent amount of the tax increase.[45] The Jamaican government countered that it had withdrawn from that portion of the ICSID convention covering natural resources, and therefore would not participate in any such arbitration.[46] The companies were left with no legal recourse, and within a few weeks it had become evident that they would have to pay the new taxes under protest.

The conflict resumed a few months later, when negotiations concerning acquisition or participation began with the Jamaican government. It intended to negotiate repurchase of the surface rights to the land owned by the bauxite companies, and subsequently an equity stake in the companies' Jamaican affiliates themselves. The government's bargaining position was undermined by ample substitution possibilities for aluminum, ample alternative sources of supply, and dependence on extractive technologies supplied by the MNEs. At the beginning of October, Manley announced that his country had begun negotiations with the six bauxite companies regarding "majority government participation in their new operations." He went on to declare that he might "take a more flexible stance regarding existing operations."[47] A few weeks afterward, it was reported that Jamaica's Central Bank had been buying shares in Kaiser and Reynolds to hold as part of the country's external assets.[48] This form of "bauxite-dollar recycling" allowed Jamaica to acquire a position in the parent companies' stock and hence a stake in their future profitability. Company spokesmen praised these investment actions by the Jamaican government.

In late November, Kaiser became the first to reach tentative agreement with the government on a plan whereby Jamaica would have majority ownership in the company's existing mining operations and full ownership of all company lands. Under terms of the agreement in principle, the government would purchase 51% of Kaiser's mining interests in Jamaica. Kaiser would continue to manage the operations under the direction of an executive committee composed of equal numbers of company and government representatives. Kaiser agreed to sell its land to Jamaica at book value, and a leaseback arrangement would allow the company sufficient reserves to maintain bauxite production levels for 30 years.[49] The agreement with Kaiser was not surprising, since the company had a long history of cooperating with the Jamaican government in its development goals. Kaiser had, at considerable expense, a completely enclosed shipping and processing facility so as not to despoil nearby tourist centers with bauxite dust. It also had set up its own development corporation geared exclusively to promoting new Jamaican industries. Declaring that Kaiser "has no hangup over ownership," the company's president added that the agreement was "the beginning of a new and positive relationship" between his company and the Jamaican government.[50]

In December 1974, a somewhat similar tentative agreement was reached with Revere for the acquisition of its mining properties. In February 1975, the government began its negotiations with Reynolds for participation in bauxite mining and acquisition of company lands. However, reduced demand for aluminum and production cutbacks in the United States forced the Jamaican government to agree in June of 1975 to lower the minimum bauxite output on which Kaiser and Reynolds would have had to pay levies, and to delay negotiations on further takeovers. The depression of the aluminum market also forced Revere to suspend operations in Jamaica in August 1975. Under the bauxite tax law, however, the government ordered the firm to keep paying levies as if it were producing alumina at a rate of 190,170 tons a year. Incensed, Revere filed suit in a Jamaican court seeking to have the country's bauxite-production taxes declared invalid. The government, in response, expropriated Revere's bauxite mining and alumina processing facilities. (The company then sought $90 million from the Overseas Private Investment Corp. to cover its losses, but an arbitration panel in 1978 ruled that Revere only deserved $1.1 million since other American companies had been able to settle their tax disputes with the Jamaican government and continue operations there. Revere labelled the decision a "shocking injustice.")[51]

In early October 1976 Alcoa—the least dependent of the major American aluminum producers on Jamaican bauxite—reached final agreement with the government. Under the accord, the government would own 6% of a new joint venture to operate installations on the island, and would guarantee 40 years' supply of bauxite for Alcoa's Jamaican refining capacity. Alcoa's chairman hailed the agreement as "much more than just an understanding on bauxite levies. It establishes a new, stable relationship with the Jamaican government in a 40-year agreement with flexible financing arrangements."[52] Alcoa was to sell all of its mining and nonoperating lands to the government. In addition, the government would roll back the tax rate on bauxite produced in Jamaica by Alcoa from 8% to 7.5% calculated on the value of aluminum ingot prices, with taxes to be frozen until 1983—reducing the company's bauxite tax levies by $2.6 million per year at full capacity. With Kaiser and Reynolds expected to get similar tax treatment, the Jamaican government seemed to feel a need to insure that its future tax take would move in tandem with ingot prices and reflected an apparent concern that high bauxite taxes could put the island at a price disadvantage in competition with other sources of bauxite.

In early February 1977, Kaiser signed a final agreement with the Jamaican government. Patterned after the 1974 accord, it called for the government to purchase 51% of Kaiser's Jamaican bauxite mining interests and all of its mining as well as nonoperating properties. Kaiser would continue to manage the subsidiary's mining activities. The company would be assured of a 40-year supply of bauxite and a reduced 7.5% tax rate on production until 1983.[53] In April 1977 Reynolds became the final United States-based MNE to sign a long-term supply contract with the Jamaican government on terms very similar to those of Alcoa and Kaiser (Alcan of Canada reached an agreement with the government in late 1978).[54] Manley viewed the pacts as "setting the world an example of fair and successful partnership between poor Third World countries and giant multinational corporations."[55] The companies' problems were far from over, however. They faced a deteriorating economic and political situation in Jamaica, a heavy investment stake, dependence on Jamaican bauxite and alumina, and poor short-term alternative sources of supply. Indeed, in a bid to bolster its dwindling foreign exchange reserves the Jamaican government proposed in early March 1978 that the bauxite companies issue notes to the government (which it would resell) to cover an estimated $180 million of future bauxite tax payments.[56]

The Jamaican government, politically and economically weak by global standards, in this case was nevertheless successful in exploiting its position to secure higher returns on its bauxite deposits during the mid-1970s. The companies had always operated their wholly-owned foreign mining subsidiaries so as to undertake the more complex and higher value-added stages of processing at home. Intent on solving some of the more serious economic and social problems through a policy of political and economic nationalism, the Jamaican government clashed head on with an increasingly vulnerable aluminum industry. The sequence of preliminary and final settlements with each of the three American companies appeared to be partially dictated by differences in each company's degree of dependence on Jamaican bauxite—for example, 75% for Kaiser but only 15% for Alcoa—as well as the history of relations between the two sides.

Both sides felt compelled, because of the perceived high stakes and relative shift in power, to enter into direct talks with one another, so as to renegotiate the operating contracts. The companies had few alternatives in their conflict management strategies. In terms of our model, they all had similar strategies which tended generally to shift over the full negotiating period from an initially *competitive* stance, to a later *collaborative/compromise* mode and ultimately to a final *compromise/accommodative* mode. The flow of conflict management strategies can best be described by three events: (1) In mid-May 1974, the companies reportedly had "been issuing some not-so-subtle hints about what might happen" including "huge supplies of ore" in non-IBA countries, "numerous alternatives to bauxite," and touting their research efforts to make new ores competitive with bauxite, a task that gets easier as bauxite costs rise.[57] (2) By the end of June, the companies seemed to have realized that a new period had begun in which the government would play a more active role in investment, ownership, decision-making, taxation, and pricing—"The international company, which could be regulated, is being replaced in bauxite by the national government, which is above all sanctions. It is a very dangerous move on the part of the world to accept that."[58] (3) Nevertheless, the view that imposition by the host government of sharply increased bauxite taxes was tantamount to nationalization eventually seemed to fade—"In the long term, Jamaica and other countries will have to compete to increase their extraction capacity. The world will need new bauxite and aluminum plants in the 1980s. The question is where they will be built."[59] Part of the answer began to emerge in 1979 when aluminum producers cut back their bauxite mining and refining operations in Jamaica while stepping up their activities in other nations, such as Australia and Surinam. Jamaica, with the highest bauxite levy in the world, was losing its competitive edge. As a consequence, the government began designing incentive programs, such as lowering the bauxite levy for producers that increased their bauxite and alumina activities.[60]

FINANCIAL CONTROLS

Another option for host countries is to permit relatively liberal entry and impose minimal operating controls, thus giving the MNE a fairly free hand in terms of the activities it undertakes and how it handles its affairs, and then to apply a single set of controls on the "bottom line"—remittances of earnings. The firm may be able to set prices and incur costs according to market conditions, and its profits in local currency may likewise tend to be largely market-determined. But at that point financial controls are imposed, and only 10–15%, for example, of invested capital per year will be given clearance for securing the necessary foreign exchange to make the earnings remittance.

Financial control of this type has both advantages and disadvantages. It is comparatively simple, and avoids the array of bureaucrats and the economic inefficiencies and complexities associated with operating controls. It also avoids a good many of the kinds of conflicts that entry and operating controls are subject to. And it shares with entry controls the relative certainty of the rules of the game, which can be assessed and acted upon by MNEs prior to making a commitment.

On the negative side, financial controls lend themselves to avoidance and evasion. For example, the value of the initial capital contributed by the firm can be inflated through excessive valuation of capital equipment in order to boost the base upon which the remittance limit will be calculated. Firms may also repatriate funds via charges for technology, management fees, and other services, or they may achieve *de facto* repatriation through transfer pricing, discussed in Chapter 14. So instead of an allowed 10% return on equity, the firm may actually repatriate 20% or 30% through various channels.

The fact is that allocation of costs and profits within a large MNE system is bound to be set within limits that are to a certain extent arbitrary and that respond to international differences in tax rates, exchange controls, and other distortions. Hence observed prices and profit rates lose in value as targets for national policy in regulating MNEs, and ". . . the ability of MNEs to shift funds and profits internally represents a constraint on national policies, a constraint which must be observed if governments do not wish to encourage the growth of MNCs beyond levels justified by national conditions in goods and factor markets."[61]

Funds that cannot be repatriated sometimes force the MNE into totally unrelated activities, such as real estate, or cause it to buy up competitive or complementary firms—neither of which may be justified on economic grounds or is particularly desirable from the standpoint of public policy. Or the firm may try to repatriate blocked profits by converting them into goods or services for export at artificially low prices, or by over–invoicing imports from unrelated but cooperative firms, or engaging in questionable dealings on unofficial foreign exchange markets.

One way to avoid evasion of remittance controls at least partially is to use a different base. For example, a limit might be placed on total remittances of profits, license fees, and other payments as a percent of sales. Or profit remittances may be based on capital brought in from abroad only, and not on local borrowings—this may at least encourage capital inflows—although here again there is plenty of room to maneuver, especially if the MNE's capital contribution is in the form of equipment, whose value can be inflated.

The point is that profit remittance controls set up a powerful incentive to avoid them, which can lead to serious conflict in addition to eroding the effectiveness of the measures themselves. A final problem with reliance on financial controls, and perhaps the most serious one, is that they relate only to a single one of the many facets of MNE operations of concern to the host country. They may have little effect on employment, ownership, technology, and other dimensions that the host country may wish to influence from a policy perspective.

As one study recently pointed out, "If tax and financial systems provide incentives for certain types of behavior, MNCs should respond accordingly, within ethical and legal bounds. If they fail to do so, they are not behaving economically, at which point their very existence should be called into question."[62] In other words, the firm should behave in a *competitive* way when faced with attempts by host countries to impose financial controls, the burden resting with the country to remove the distortions underlying incentives for firms to undertake this kind of behavior. As long as countries have different tax systems, the incentives will always exist for MNEs to shift profits internationally for tax reasons, and the desirable goal of "tax neutrality" cannot be attained. Here again is a limit to the effectiveness of national control—the greater the exercise of national sovereignty, and the more it deviates from what other countries do, the greater will be the resulting distortions of international financial flows from this particular source.

Specifics of remittance policies vary widely from one country to the next. Colombia places a ceiling of 14% of invested capital. Greece limits repatriation of profits to 12% of the balance of capital not yet repatriated in previous years. Greece also permits firms engaged in exports to make larger remittances than firms that are not, up to a limit of 70% of export sales. Pakistan permits repatriation of foreign exchange costs that can be shown to have been incurred in achieving an appreciation of an investment. Chile permits companies to revalue local assets in accordance with exchange-rate changes, and permitted remittances are based on the revised asset values.

Brazil limits profit repatriation to 12% of registered capital, subject to a 25% withholding tax. Thereafter profit remittances are subject to taxes of 40–60%. Argentina likewise has a 12% limit, with excess profit remissions subject to taxes of 15–25%. Chile's ceiling is 14%, with no additional remissions allowed, and the investment itself must have been subject to prior government approval. Colombia and Peru likewise have a 14% limit. In some countries there are extensive delays in approval of profit remittances.

Financial controls and national ownership considerations are often closely interconnected, and it is sometimes difficult to ascertain the precise sources of ownership/control conflict. The experiences of Coca-Cola and IBM in India provide a good example.

Coca-Cola and IBM in India

The Coca-Cola Company came to India in the early 1950s and soon set up four bottling plants in major cities. By 1977, the Coca-Cola Export Corporation in India supplied syrup to 22 Indian-owned bottlers employing some 6000 people from a plant of its own. An estimated additional 200,000 people indirectly earned part of their livelihood selling Coke. Still, the 450 million bottles sold annually in India accounted for only one-fifth of 1% of the parent company's 1977 $3.1 billion of revenues from sales in some 137 countries.

After a four-year campaign against MNEs in general and Coca-Cola in particular, in early August 1977 the government in effect demanded that Coca-Cola turn over its ownership and "know-how" control to Indian investors by April 1978 or be expelled from India. The newly-elected Janata Party seemed eager to show that it would enforce the 1973 Foreign Exchange Regulation Act (FERA) more vigorously than the ousted Congress Party of Indira Gandhi. This turn of events was a far cry from the more tranquil days of the early 1950s, when Prime Minister Nehru sipped Coke as the cornerstone was being laid for an Indian Coca-Cola bottling plant.

More than three decades after its independence from Britain, India found itself still immersed in political debates about whether or not it should liberalize its economic development policies, with ideological considerations traditionally suppressing economic pragmatism. A modified form of socialism had increased state control over the economy and decreased the role of foreign capital—most of the $300 million United States private investment in India in 1977 was about 10 years old. Little new foreign investment was flowing in as a result of strict licensing procedures, corruption, stultifying bureaucracy, myriad controls, increasing government involvement in industry, and wavering socialist-oriented policies.

One of the most controversial controls on foreign investment is the Foreign Exchange Regulation Act. The Act was designed primarily to force British firms out of their lucrative middleman slot in the tea, jute, and fiber export industries—and replace them with companies that would repatriate fewer profits—by demanding that trading firms surrender majority control to Indian nationals. Hit hardest were a relatively small group of trading companies that had to convert entirely to Indian ownership. Foreign companies which produced highly-profitable "nonpriority" goods, such as soft drinks and cosmetics, were also vulnerable. Other foreign companies having sophisticated technology, manufacturing "priority" products such as capital goods, or exporting over 60% of their production could conceivably have a minimum Indian equity of only 26%. Under the Act, the more than 800 foreign companies operating in India at the time had to eventually reduce their equity ownership to 40%. But since the Act presented only broad outlines, negotiations began almost immediately between the individual foreign firms and the government over the terms on which foreigners would be allowed to operate in India. By the end of 1977, a total of 57 foreign firms had decided to close down their Indian plants and withdraw, rather than meet the FERA demands for local ownership.[63]

FERA was supposedly enacted in part to stem the flow of illegal profits remitted by MNE affiliates. The government claimed that since the early 1950s, Coca-Cola, with its more than $12 million investment, had remitted more than $12.5 million in profits to its parent company. It allegedly also found evidence that Coke was reaping 400% profit margins in its dealings with Indian bottlers.[64] Critics also charged that with the connivance of officials of the previous Congress Party government the company had managed to suppress competition and siphon off profits by bypassing government regulations. A Janata Party leader noted that FERA "came into effect in 1973, but Coca-Cola was not served with the notice to comply with the law. Only last April [1977] after the Janata Party took over, the notice was given.[65] Most of the bottlers, on the other hand, remarked that the government's treatment of Coca-Cola "smacked of political vendetta.[66]

Political conflict between Coca-Cola and the Janata Party government first came to public attention on August 8, 1977 when the newly installed Industry Minister, George Fernandes—a former socialist labor leader—spoke in Parliament of Coke's past and future.[67] In his view, the activities of Coca-Cola in India furnished "a classic example of how a multinational corporation operating in a low-priority, high-profit area in a developing country attains runaway growth and, in the absence of alertness on the part of the government concerned, can trifle with the weaker indigenous industry in the process."[68] Coca-Cola was given one year to transfer 60% of its equity to Indians and also transfer its "know-how" to the new Indian-controlled company.

The Coca-Cola Export Corporation, which supplied Coke concentrate to Indian bottlers, agreed to reduce its equity to 40%. But the parent company insisted that it be allowed to retain "quality control" and a liaison office in India to protect the confidentiality of its carefully guarded trade secrets in the formulation of its soft drinks. The Indian government told Coca-Cola that such conditions were "not acceptable," and Fernandes went on to explain that under such conditions the proposed Indian-controlled company would "merely function as a selling company of the concentrates, which would still be under the manufacturing control of the American company."[69]

The company's secret beverage formulas were clearly the crucial issue in Coca-

Cola's negotiations with the Indian government, and a spokesman in Atlanta noted that "the company has not been able to obtain Government agreement to a fundamental policy, which governs the company's operations worldwide. This refers to the company's insistence that it continually control and supervise the manufacturing of Coca-Cola through a local quality-control unit to insure the integrity and unvarying quality of its beverage." An Indian official of Coca-Cola added that the government did not seem to make any distinction between "technological knowhow and trade secret. . . . It looks like we have no choice but to wind up in India."[70]

On August 14, 1977, Coca-Cola announced that it had assigned a senior official, Anthony Young, to go to India and hopefully negotiate a way out of the secret formula impasse. Young noted upon arrival: "We don't think that the doors are shut on us. We have not been officially told that we should transfer our know-how."[71] The government responded with additional pressure tactics. Licenses to import ingredients for the concentrate were initially reported as "delayed," causing several Indian bottlers to suspend production because of a lack of supplies. By the beginning of September, the government reportedly had "denied" a license to import Coke concentrate for the year, resulting in the entire marketing operation virtually coming to an end.[72] In addition, Fernandes announced that government chemists had come up with a formula for a substitute cola beverage, which would be ready for sale by March 1978. The state-produced substitute would be named "77," officials explained, because 1977 was "the year of big changes," the end of the Indira Gandhi government and the end of Coca-Cola.[73]

The government's hopes of using the substitute as a drink which would be commercially exploitable, keep bottling plants running, and employment up, were dampened by two impending problems. One was how to deal with bottling plants that had been forced to shut down until March and had nothing to sell, with 6000 idle employees.[74] The other was how the copied Coke would sell. Observers noted that in the past Coke's ingredients had proved almost impossible to duplicate and that, in turn, India's consumers had learned how to distinguish between the ersatz Coke that is peddled everywhere in the Indian market and the "Real Thing."[75]

In the meantime, company negotiator Young continued to maintain that although the government considered the Coke formula technical know-how, "it is actually a proprietary trade secret, and there is a basic difference."[76] He hoped to persuade the government to reconsider its position, but altered his negotiating tactics from extolling the commercial and economic benefits of Coke to stressing the company's other activities in India—"We are the largest growers of citrus, tea and coffee. . . . We have the knowhow on agrochemicals and we can give our expertise on desalination of water. I want to tell Indian leaders that our presence will be useful to them."[77]

Industry Minister Fernandes immediately replied that he was having no second thoughts on the question of allowing the company to continue its operations in India. "Our policy toward multinationals is uniform. They must abide by the law of the land if they want to be in business here. They sell 450 million bottles for the whole year. It's not even one bottle per capita in a country of 600 million people."[78] By the end of 1977, Coca-Cola had withdrawn from India.

IBM traced its operation in India back to 1951, when Jawaharlal Nehru invited the company to set up an accounting-machine plant in Bombay. Nehru's strategy for building up India's industries involved fledging local firms operating in tandem with foreign companies. IBM went on to dominate the Indian computer industry as two rival computer companies—the state-owned Electronics Corporation of India and an affiliate of Britain's International Computers Limited—provided very weak manufacturing and servicing competition. IBM's wholly-owned Indian subsidiary employed only 800 people, and contributed only marginally to IBM's worldwide sales and profits. During the period 1951–1977 IBM installed nearly 1000 computer systems in India, mostly refurbished IBM 1401s initially used elsewhere. Its Bombay plant reconditioned used computers and at one point manufactured a medium-size computer with 20% local content for the domestic market and an inexpensive key-punch machine with 70% local content for export. However, from the early 1970s the Bombay plant produced only spare parts.

Under the leadership of Indira Gandhi, the Indian government urged IBM both to reduce its 100% ownership and to extend its computer design and manufacturing operations in India to the domestic as well as export markets. It is a fundamental policy at IBM, however, to maintain technological parity, which includes product designs and quality standards, in all of its overseas manufacturing operations. It had also been fundamental policy to maintain 100% ownership of manufacturing and servicing operations. Prior to the passage of FERA in 1973, many Indians viewed IBM's overseas design, manufacturing, and pricing policies as contributing to an essentially stagnant national computer industry—"IBM was trapped by its past, by a history that to many Indians reeked of near-colonial exploitation."[79] Others considered technical backwardness in the Indian computer industry primarily the result of flawed government policy—25 years of post-colonial defensiveness and self-pride combined with a centralized economic planning strategy, resulting in a protected, high-cost industrial sector with a narrow domestic market that could not be expanded.

Under FERA, IBM-India qualified as a trading company because it imported and sold computers in the Indian market. However, it hoped to gain an exemption from local-ownership requirements of FERA on the grounds that it was selling high technology that India badly needed, and therefore be qualified as a "priority" producer. Negotiations between IBM and the government of India began in 1975 and continued on and off until November 1977. Because the 1973 Act contained only broad outlines that allowed the negotiating parties considerable latitude, very few details of the various rounds of talks were reported or discussed with outsiders. IBM chairman Frank Cary in late 1977 remarked: "We have met many times with officials at all levels to discuss proposed changes in our operations in response to the FERA legislation."[80]

Both sides, although retaining some room for maneuver, seemed to have framed rigid positions. The Indian government considered IBM neither "substantially" engaged in export nor involved in sophisticated technology, and the company was therefore asked to reduce its equity holdings in the Indian operation from 100% to 40%.[81] By the end of 1976, India had not only prohibited IBM imports pending resolution of the dispute, but also had set up a public corporation for the apparent purpose of taking over IBM's computer maintenance and support functions.[82] IBM's only publicized offer, made in April 1976, proposed creating two companies. One company would have 40% of its equity parent-owned and would run IBM's data center (service bureau) operations in India. The second, fully IBM-owned, was to conduct marketing, maintenance, and manufacturing operations. Since under FERA companies manufacturing exclusively for export could be fully owned by foreign interests, IBM's Bombay plant would produce $100 million of data-processing equipment entirely for export over the following ten years. Other elements of the IBM proposal, designed to support India's technological capabilities, included establishing government-operated testing labs, setting up an IBM research center for government use, and making IBM patents available to Indian enterprises.

The company's proposal served as a basis for negotiations which continued for almost a year and a half. Both parties seemed to feel that they had "bent" their negotiating position as far as possible. The government conceded a "precedent" to IBM by allowing it to split its operations and run two companies which was done, according to an Indian official, to "accommodate" IBM in recognition of pioneering computer technology in India. The government contended there could be no further relaxation of the regulations for IBM alone. The company held that their April 1976 proposal already differed with its global policy of keeping all of its subsidiaries under 100% IBM ownership. But IBM's stance was weakened by the decision of Imperial Computer Ltd. to bow completely to the government's wishes and dilute its equity.[83]

In September 1977 the company was informed verbally by a government official that its proposal had been rejected. Pressure from the United States government through the

American ambassador in New Delhi, who warned that an adverse decision would affect the flow of American investment into India, proved ineffective.[84] The government gave "formal notice" rejecting IBM's proposal in early November. On November 15, IBM announced it would phase out essentially all of its manufacturing, marketing, and maintenance operations over a 180-day period and sell IBM equipment already on rental. Only a liaison office would remain in India to receive authorized requests for IBM products and services in the future.

The IBM and Coca Cola experiences in India are at once similar and different. The government's insistence on IBM's giving up 60% of its ownership ran up against the company's view that "such equity dilution would seriously impair its ability to manage an international high-technology company requiring sharing of resources and knowhow across national borders."[85] IBM considered it essential to maintain a powerful R&D program and high quality standards through a tight hold over its technology and marketing strategy. In the company's view, this basic objective can only be achieved through 100% ownership and control in the form of an integrated, global organizational structure. Given the trivial relative size of its Indian business, therefore, IBM's hard-line position could be expected. But weaker firms in the industry often see the world differently—in 1979, for example, representatives of Olivetti and Siemens were reportedly examining computer business opportunities in India associated with the vacuum that IBM's departure created.[86]

For India, FERA was politically popular and considered "fair." Many trading companies and low technology firms with tie-ins to Indian concerns, after initial reluctance, expressed a willingness to dilute their ownership. Because of public pressure, liberalization of FERA itself was virtually impossible and an easing of the policy would have to come through a less rigid implementation of the Act. The IBM case would set a pattern for future negotiations, and was intended to demonstrate a sense of firmness to both domestic and foreign critics. For IBM, it was important as a test of its determination to retain control through 100% ownership, particularly since problems of economic nationalism were beginning to appear for IBM in Brazil, Indonesia, Malaysia, Nigeria, and elsewhere.[87] If the policy was to survive, a firm stand in India was mandatory.

In terms of our model of conflict management, IBM's strategy over time would fall into the left-of-center triangular area formed by the *competitive*, *compromise*, and *avoidance* approaches. In the early negotiating period, IBM perhaps overestimated its relative "power" by staking out a fundamentally *competitive* mode. The government's 1976 insistence on a 60% equity share, coupled to its prohibiting IBM imports, undoubtedly induced the company to reduce its assertive stance and broaden its host-government relationship toward a *compromise* mode through its "two companies" proposal. At the same time, IBM's long-term stakes were rising due to stronger competition as well as evolving ownership pressures in other countries. As a result, IBM's 1976 move toward *compromise* was soon driven back to the *competitive-avoidance* axis. The remainder of 1976 and all of 1977 reflected a behavioral drift toward *avoidance*, which ended with IBM's November 1977 withdrawal announcement. For IBM, the short-term "stakes" in India were minimal and the long-term stakes throughout the developing world were all-important.

Two points seem especially worth noting. First, outcome stakes are not only determined within the context of the issue at hand, but also by strategic requirements and precedents relating to external factors. For IBM, the perceived gain/ loss was not measured in investment or sales terms in India, but rather in its strategy of maintaining ownership and control of its foreign affiliates. Second, by adopting a mixed behavior of publicly stressing *compromise* but privately emphasizing *competition/avoidance*, IBM was able to conclude its political conflict with the Indian government by accepting minimal short-term losses while at the same time neutralizing dangerous potential long-term external threats.

Coca-Cola, for its part, has subsequently indicated that it would like to return. In an April 1978 interview, a Coke official admitted that the company had been "deauthorized" in India, and added that he saw "nothing in the current environment" that might lead to Coke's return.[88] However, a future political change in government (the Janata Party government was indeed forced out in 1979), coupled with the company's emphasis on its other lines of activity such as citrus fruit and instant tea, could result in re-entry negotiations. Unlike the IBM case, here was a high-profile, low technology, consumer products multinational confronted by a newly elected socialist government intent on enacting its pre-election rhetoric. For over 90 years Coca-Cola has insisted that its "7X" formula remain a closely guarded secret known to no more than a handful of individuals —its success in exploiting brand loyalty based on insuring the absolute quality of its product. The Indian government, on the other hand, viewed the ouster of Coca-Cola as a political opportunity to bring into line recalcitrant foreign companies, embarrass its political opponents, and demonstrate its fundamental, rural-based, ethnocentric principles.[89]

As in the IBM case, all of the secondary characteristics in this instance played a visible role. Coca-Cola's success in the low-technology beverage industry depended on maintaining and protecting a strong trade name through quality control over its secret beverage formula which has been integrated into its global operating structure in 137 countries; its Indian business represented a marginal element. Also as in the IBM case, it was important to both sides to maintain a pattern of control. To make significant concessions or establish a precedent would be politically and/or economically costly and therefore unacceptable.

In terms of our conflict management model, Coca-Cola's strategy remained consistently close to the *competitive* mode on control over its secret formula until its withdrawal announcement in late 1977. In its earlier agreement to reduce its equity share to 40%, Coca-Cola clearly perceived its stakes as low to moderate, and therefore readily moved toward *compromise*. The trade secret issue, on the other hand, raised the stakes to such a high level that *compromise* or *cooperation* with the host government was virtually impossible. Additional pressures in the form of the nonrenewal of Coca-Cola's import license and development of a state-produced substitute drink proved ineffective.

Although Coca-Cola and IBM represent two entirely different industry sectors, both were basically committed to a *competitive* mode during the conflict period because of high stakes, determined more by technological control questions than by economic considerations.

TERMINAL CONTROLS

A fourth way of controlling MNE activities on the part of host countries is at the very end of their involvement, whether such disengagement is voluntary or not.

At one extreme is expropriation with compensation, where the foreign-owned enterprise is taken over by the host-country government. Compensation to foreign owners may be in full, by means of cash payments in hard currencies, in local currency with guaranteed convertibility, in government bonds, in products, or some combination of these. Compensation, like nationalization itself, may be instantaneous or phased-in over a period of months or years. The "fullness" of the compensation is, of course, in the eye of the beholder, and so the terms and conditions are generally the product of extended negotiations.

At the other extreme is expropriation without compensation, or confiscation, undertaken unilaterally by the host-country government. Often the case for non-compensation is based on past "excess profits" remitted by the firm, which generally equal or exceed the book value of the firm's assets. So there is nothing to be compensated.

Expropriation without compensation is clearly a conflict situation where national sovereignty is the determining variable and where the firm has very little power at all. It can fight, but in the end it loses. The defenses against uncompensated expropriation are both specific and general. There is the loss of the link between the MNE and the expropriated affiliate which, depending on the value of the "package" of services the MNE was providing at the time, will disappear after the expropriation. If market access, management skills, or technologies are important enough, then the cost to the host country can be very high indeed and the incentive to expropriate small. This doesn't mean it won't be done, since host countries can be notorious for over-estimating their own capabilities, especially when it comes to human resources. But the MNE can at least point to services that have value and without which the country will incur significant losses. This may be enough to promote adequate compensation and some continued profitable involvement by the firm on a non-equity basis. If it cannot find reasons why the host country might lose, the MNE is on a very weak footing indeed, and it's quite likely that the firm will not be able to prevent expropriation from happening.

Many countries have provided guarantees against expropriation, either for foreign-owned assets specifically or as part of a more general assurance that private industry will not be nationalized. Cyprus, Greece, Israel, Malta, Singapore, and Spain are among the countries providing such guarantees, sometimes as part of a package of incentives that contains tax holidays, tariff exemptions, and occasionally "most favored enterprise" provisions—which assure investors that if future foreign firms are given more favorable treatment, this will apply to the firm in question as well.

In a general sense, expropriation without compensation signals other firms that the same thing might happen to them, particularly if there is systemic political change in the wind heading away from a market system or private ownership of productive facilities. Despite governmental assurances to the contrary, sovereign risk rises, and to compensate for it firms require higher profits. This reduces the net benefits to the host country, and may in turn bring on pressures for additional MNE expropriations in the same or other sectors of the economy. There is also the matter of the U.S. Hickenlooper Amendment and other national measures in various MNE home countries, which could further increase the cost of uncompensated expropriations to the host country, and shift the focus of the conflict from the MNE alone to its home country. So uncompensated or inadequately compensated expropriation requires a great deal of thought in a long-term cost-benefit framework by countries contemplating such action. It is doubtful that this kind of careful analysis has in fact been done in very many of the expropriation cases on record.

MNEs can, of course, protect themselves against terminal controls in a variety of ways. They can subdivide the production process so that only a very small part is carried out in the country in question, and expropriation will do the country no good at all. Or sources of supply or export markets may be controlled by the firm with much the same results. Or the firm may go in as part of a consortium arrangement, not only to spread the risk but also to increase the cost of precipitous host-country action in terms of its relations with various foreign nations. Or it may go in on a joint basis with host country firms or governmental agencies in the first place, in order to reduce the net benefits of terminal-type actions. The best shield, though, still remains technological advantages that cannot be replaced by the host country after expropriation. Only rarely can companies any longer turn to their home governments for meaningful relief or protection from expropriation abroad.

More common than expropriation is nationalization or indigenization, where the host country requires the MNE to sell off its affiliates' assets, either to the government or to local investors. Nationalization may be phased in under gradual "fadeout" formulas, or it may be quite abrupt. The government may require total divestiture of assets, or only partial divestiture ending, for example, in minority participation in a joint venture. Although nationalization is perhaps somewhat milder than expropriation, there are still plenty of issues to argue in nationalization proceedings. Price is one point, especially when the buyer is the government, but also when forced divestiture threatens to result in fire-sale prices to private buyers familiar with the MNE's duress. Other bargaining points are the conditions under which the MNE will collaborate with the successor firm, and the price it will charge for its services—there are technology and the cost of licensed know-how, questions of market access, quality control, retention of proprietary technology, safeguarding trade secrets, and similar problems. All of these are bargaining-type solutions and, as in the case of Coca-Cola and IBM, the MNE will presumably take a relatively hard negotiating stance based on its relative leverage. MNE responses will of course vary, and views do change over time—firms that previously would not consider joint ventures are now ready to do so, perhaps because it is a good way to spread risk and reduce conflict, or perhaps because they realize the value to the host country of their particular "package" of services is perhaps no longer what it once was.

Asbestos and the Québec Government

A 1968 Report of the Canadian Task Force on the structure of Canadian industry observed that the "tendency inherent in direct investment to shift decision-making power in the private sector outside Canada has, on occasion, posed serious problems for those responsible for formulating Canadian policy, and has created widespread unease among Canadians as to the continuing viability of Canada as an independent nation-state. . . . The host country is likely to believe that the maintenance of its national independence and sovereignty and its capacity to carry out national policy require it to regard resident foreign subsidiaries as falling within its jurisdiction.[90] The Task Force found that, among the 743 largest Canadian corporations, 380 were foreign controlled (of which 221 were wholly-owned). The Report concluded that there was some correlation between the proportion of foreign control in an industry and the concentration of total output in a few firms.

On top of such national questions of ownership, Québec's asbestos mining industry had been a particular target of environmentalists, labor, and the provincial government because of its allegedly poor record in development, job creation, and worker health. Québec's asbestos operations, providing more than 40% of the non-Communist world's raw asbestos fiber, were controlled by five foreign-owned companies, four American and one British. Arguing that asbestos should logically be processed near the centers of consumption, the industry had been processing into finished products only 3% of the asbestos mined in Québec.

With the November 1976 election of the feisty separatist politician René Lévesque and the Parti Québecois, a lengthy political conflict developed between the provincial government and two American multinationals, General Dynamics and Johns-Manville. The beginnings of a new policy toward foreign investors had already been laid out in late January 1977, when Premier Lévesque addressed the Economic Club of New York. He stated that Québec had suffered too long from the institutionalized belief that "our economy could only be developed by outsiders." Foreign investment and technology was still needed and wanted, and no takeovers were contemplated with the exception of the asbestos industry. But some kind of control of asbestos was an "ultimate solution necessary" to correct poisonous working conditions and to gain full advantage from Québec's position as the world's greatest asbestos producer and exporter.[91] Asbestos stocks fell sharply in the wake of disclosure of Lévesque's takeover plan, but Johns-Manville issued a statement that the Premier's remarks were nothing new and that the extreme reaction of the financial community was uncalled for—"The premier's remarks pose no threat to the continued profitable operations of Johns-Manville's business in Québec."[92]

On February 1, 1977, it was reported that Johns-Manville had put its announced five year $77 million expansion of its asbestos mine and processing facility in Québec in limbo until after the provincial government completed its study of the possible nationalization of the asbestos industry. At a meeting between Johns-Manville president John McKinney and René Lévesque, it was made clear that the provincial government was considering buying a substantial interest in the asbestos industry "at a fair price." The goal of the provincial government was "to increase employment opportunities in Québec by converting up to 20% of the asbestos fiber produced or mined in the province to finished products."[93]

According to McKinney, the provincial government "thought that asbestos fiber was such an absolutely essential commodity that they had the world by the tail. . . . I can only describe the look on his face as rather sober when I told him that years ago it had occurred to Johns-Manville that the asbestos fiber industry might no longer exist someday" because of alternative products.[94] McKinney argued that high transportation costs would make Canadian production of many asbestos products uneconomical.

Additional pressure on the Québec government came with the announcement in mid-February of a major study covering "all the possibilities and conditions for an optimum development of a viable asbestos manufacturing industry in Québec" by the Québec Asbestos Mining Association, which represented the province's five foreign producers. Denying that the study had been undertaken to head off a previously announced Québec government study, a spokesman contended that it was designed partially to satisfy "the aspirations" of the Parti Québecois government to increase employment as well as to expand consumption of raw asbestos. It stressed that future processing facilities could be developed either privately, or jointly with the Québec government as a partner.

On February 21, the provincial government countered with an announcement that it was seeking to buy control of the Asbestos Corporation (54.6% owned by the St. Louis-based General Dynamics) as a step toward the province's control of the asbestos industry. The Asbestos Corporation, the second largest producer in the province, was singled out because it was the only one not integrated into manufacturing of asbestos products in Québec. Although no one had discussed a takeover with General Dynamics and it was not known whether it would be willing to sell, the government hoped to initiate discussions to that end. An industry observer at the time expressed doubt that General Dynamics would be willing to lose a subsidiary which had made a $21 million profit in the previous year on sales of $140 million (in 1977 Asbestos contributed about 15% of Dynamics' sales and about 25% of earnings). Indeed, on the following day a company spokesman noted that although General Dynamics "has been aware of the Premier's plans from previous utterances," it had "not been approached" and in fact "the first we knew of the actual intent was yesterday. . . . We read the newspapers too, you know."[95]

A week later the Québec Office of Natural Resources, in an apparent effort to soften the separatist government's earlier hard line, announced that the government would refrain from nationalizing the province's asbestos industry "if the mining companies involved cooperate with government aims to further local processing of asbestos to create more jobs."[96] All new industry developed had to contribute to processing capacity in the province, but nationalization was to be a last resort. Several days later, Johns-Manville announced that it planned to go ahead with its $77 million capital investment project in light of the provincial government's announcement.[97]

Over the next several months, Parti Québecois ministers made ambiguous and contradictory statements about how they would implement the party's objective of taking a degree of control over the asbestos industry. Finally, in late October 1977, the Québec government announced that it planned to take over, by negotiation or otherwise, the Asbestos Corporation. The announcement came hours after the Canadian federal government announced its own program which rejected such a takeover policy. The action appeared to be politically popular with a large part of the Parti Québecois' political constituency, but particularly so with the party's radical wing. But the essentially conservative local business community, already alienated by the government's drive for independence and by social and language measures, reportedly reacted with shock and dismay. The negative reaction was shared by asbestos industry spokesmen, who called the action "demoralizing," and by the financial community which considered such a policy "ill-timed" since it came in the midst of "general economic depression."[98]

In St. Louis that same day, the company called the Asbestos Corporation "a very valuable member of the General Dynamics family," adding that it had no desire to sell its interest—"We have dedicated a great deal of managerial effort to improving Asbestos's operations to assure its continued long-term growth and its expanding contribution to the economic health and well-being of the people of the Province of Québec."[99] The statement emphasized that the Québec government had not made an offer, nor had negotiations been scheduled. Québec officials countered that negotiations were under way, although no agreement had been reached. The Québec finance minister added that the government would make a bid for all public shares if it reached agreement with General Dynamics. "We are not looking for a minority position . . . We're shooting for all we can get." He also repeated Lévesque's earlier remarks that failure to negotiate an agreement with General Dynamics would "require a political decision."[100] By early December, a bill had been presented to the Québec Parliament authorizing $250 million in capital for a province-owned asbestos company that would undertake development, production, and marketing of asbestos, as well as transform the material into finished products.[101]

General Dynamics quickly set up standard takeover defenses: it lined up Lazard Frères & Co., the investment banking firm well known for spoiling unwanted courtships, more than doubled its dividend, and accelerated an exploration program to boost its proven mineral resources.[102] The company also hired outside consultants, who, under the supervision of Lazard Frères, were to place a value on Asbestos Corporation that could "be attested to, in court if necessary," and adopted a "vigorous defense" of its performance as majority shareholder of the company—"We're assuming that they're proceeding in a professional manner. If they are, we'll have something to discuss."[103] The government, in fact, hired Kidder, Peabody & Co. to produce a valuation of Asbestos Corp. and to act as the government's negotiator.

1978 began with the release in late January of the industry association study which had been undertaken to identify possibilities for the further development of an asbestos manufacturing industry in Québec. It concluded that the possibilities for expansion of manufacturing were limited to perhaps three products, representing an increase of about 7–8% and producing only about 400 jobs after a capital investment of $60 million. The study thus deemed unrealistic the government's projected goal of 20% manufacturing of finished products, which it was hoped would create an additional 20,000 jobs.[104] Undaunted, by the end of May the Québec government succeeded in getting legislation passed which set up its own company, National Asbestos Corporation, with authorized capital of $250 million. General Dynamics reiterated that it remained opposed to the sale of its controlling interest in Asbestos Corporation and that negotiations still had not begun— any initiative for the start of negotiations would have to come from the Quebec government.[105]

The evaluation studies of both sides were completed in the early Fall and the gaps between them were considerable. The Lazard Frères study valued the 55% General Dynamics holding in Asbestos Corporation at $154.5 million (Canadian), or $99.75 a share. This was more than double the $62 million, or about $42 a share indicated by the Kidder Peabody study for the provincial government.[106] The two valuation teams opened discussions in September to find reasons for the disparity and discovered that they had employed very different pricing assumptions. Discussions became "snagged" and the agents never got down to actual negotiations over a selling price.

Premier Lévesque announced in December 1978 that differences over the valuations were almost irreconcilable. On December 15, without having made a formal offer for the Asbestos Corporation shares, the government introduced expropriation legislation. Within a few months, political opponents and analysts were suggesting that Mr. Lévesque had "picked up a potato that's too hot to hold but too important to drop"—his government was "restrained on one side by its efforts to maintain a climate attractive to outside investors and on the other by its need for support from the radical ranks of its own party."[107] Lévesque was also worried that the radical expropriation action might unsettle voters and thus cause them to vote no on the forthcoming referendum on the government's proposal for Québec sovereignty.

The Premier had picked a hard target and cagey opponent in General Dynamics. One observer noted that the company's top management was "about as tough a bunch of hombres as you'd ever meet."[108] The chairman of Asbestos (and also an executive vice-president of General Dynamics), Mr. Guy Fiske, had been brought in from ITT in 1977 to build up General Dynamics' commercial business, of which asbestos was a major part. Without it, the company would remain highly vulnerable to governmental business. Fiske and General Dynamics thus chose to play a waiting game, which would include fighting the expropriation legislation in court if necessary. One executive of Asbestos noted: "We're hoping that is we wait long enough, Mr. Lévesque will be voted out of office."[109]

But the firm's strategy was not without high risks. By declining to accept a government price close to the $42-a-share level, the company was inviting expropriation which could leave it open to the full brunt of Canadian and American taxes if the payment was made in the absence of special arrangements. To counter this risk, General Dynamics announced in March 1979 that if it was expropriated as threatened, the revenue would be invested in Canadian natural resource industries, rather than paid out as a windfall dividend, so as to avoid the very high taxes.[110] Another element in the company's strategy was the assumption that the arbitration panel called for in the expropriation act would set a much higher share price than $42. Still another was the high-profile public criticism of the threatened expropriation would make the provincial govenment wary of ever carrying it out. As such, General Dynamics kicked off its campaign in late March with the assertion that if Asbestos was seized, Québec would "rightly be be perceived as an area hostile to the free-enterprise system."[111]

Growing criticism of the government's inaction from many Parti Québecois members forced the government to make a move in April. Québec Finance Minister Jacques Parizeau warned that he would request seizure of the Asbestos company if a forthcoming "very important" meeting with General Dynamics representatives failed to work out a purchase agreement.[112] General Dynamics, although still opposed to the sale, indicated to Québec that a formal offer "would be appropriate" at this time.[113] Mr. Fiske, however, noted: "They're the anxious buyer and we're the reluctant seller," and added that Québec would "have to do something to entice a merger."[114] But the negotiations which followed failed to arrive at a mutually acceptable price. As reported by Fiske, Québec "suggested a range of prices which was totally unacceptable . . . the top of the range wasn't even as high as book value."[115]

In early May the ruling Parti Québecois cabinet decided that it had no choice but to proceed with an expropriation bill. Still cautious, however, a government spokesman noted that "even if the law is sanctioned, that doesn't mean that it will be used," since negotiations with General Dynamics were continuing.[116] Guy Fiske termed the action "unfortunate," explaining that it obviously represented "a big-stick approach to get us to knuckle under."[117] He stressed that the negotiations so far had been "one-such" and that the company's actions would not be influenced by any such governmental maneuver. In .mid-May Fiske told the Asbestos annual meeting that "the expropriation of Asbestos Corporation would cause untold damage to the province in the marketplace of public opinion . . . such high-handed treatment of public property would cause great concern to the business and financial community."[118]

In private, however, General Dynamics proposed that it was prepared to form a joint venture with the Québec government in manufacturing operations that could create several thousand jobs.[119] The company was willing to comply with government demands that it increase asbestos fabrication in the province. But the private accommodation had come too late and the government was now more concerned about the effects of General Dynamics' public tactics. Premier Lévesque accused Dynamics of mounting an anti-Québec lobby and made it clear that his provincial government would not be swerved—he told the Québec assembly that "it is in the interest of Québec to proceed with this transaction in whatever form it takes to the final outcome."[120] Fiske remained stalwart, stressing that his company would "explore all possible legal avenues" to challenge the law, which he likened to "a gun in our backs."[121] He also warned that "any businessman who looks at Québec today should think twice."[122]

On June 20, 1979 the Québec legislature, by a vote of 59 to 35, gave its final approval to the expropriation legislation. The day after the law was perfunctorily signed by the Queen of England's representative, General Dynamics swiftly struck back. The parent and its subsidiary filed legal actions in Québec's Superior Court asserting that the expropriation law and legislation creating the provincially-owned National Asbestos Corporation were illegal, invalid, and beyond the powers of the Québec legislature. The companies specifically charged that only a French, and not a required English language version, of the bill had been approved, that a provincial government did not have the power to expropriate the assets of a federally incorporated company, that the expropriation would "sterilize" the company, and that such a forced takeover would not be in the public interest.[123] The companies asked for an injunction banning any action until the courts had decided on the merits of the case. A temporary injunction, the first one ever issued against a Québec government, was granted on June 27 but lifted one month later.[124] Lawyers close to the case stressed that a full examination of the issues would cover new legal ground in Canada and would take many years to complete. The arena of this protracted sparring match between highly assertive players thus shifted from the court of public and political opinion into the chambers of judicial wisdom.

The consistently *competitive* stance of General Dynamics in this case should be quite apparent, and is wholly consistent with the conflict management model we have developed. It is based on high stakes and relative power on the part of the company, coupled to an essentially zero-sum game and rather poor relationship quality throughout the duration of the conflict.

The Pattern of Takeovers

Table 8–1 provides a record of nationalization, expropriation, and confiscation, actions affecting American-based multinationals during the years 1962 to 1977 in various parts of the world. These include a number of well-known expropriation cases involving United States-based affiliates in Latin America. The revolutionary government of Peru in 1968 seized the oil properties of International Petroleum (Exxon), which began a process of takeovers of foreign firms including Cerro (mining), W.R. Grace (chemicals and paper), and Utah International (iron ore). The Allende government of Chile in 1971–1973 completed the takeover of the copper mining properties of Anaconda, Kennecott, and Cerro and then proceeded to expropriate ITT and Boise-Cascade (utilities) assets as well as manufacturing facilities operated by Ford Motor, Dupont, Dow, and Ralston-Purina. The Venezuelan government in 1974 nationalized both the iron ore and petroleum industries, including properties owned by U.S. Steel, Bethlehem Steel, Exxon, Mobil, and Texaco.

In Africa and the Middle East, the petroleum industry has been the principal target of expropriation actions. The governments of Nigeria, Algeria, Iraq, Kuwait, Libya, Morocco, Saudi Arabia, and Syria have nationalized the production and distribution facilities of such prominent petroleum MNEs as Exxon, Gulf, Mobil, Socal, and Texaco, as well as the holdings of French, Dutch, and British oil companies. In addition, foreign-owned assets in such diverse fields as banking, insurance, trade, and manufacturing have been brought under national control in Ethiopia, Sudan, Tanzania, Uganda, and Zambia.

Affiliates of American multinationals in Asia, although less subject to explicit expropriation actions, have encountered broad nationalization programs and a hardening of host government attitudes toward foreign investment. The insurance industry in India, the jute industry in Bangladesh, and petroleum and plantation properties in Indonesia are examples of broad nationalization programs instituted by Asian nations. Burma, Indonesia, Malaysia, and Singapore have enacted laws which prohibit or severely restrict foreign involvement in certain sectors of the economy. Other governments, such as India, Pakistan, the Philippines, Sri Lanka, and Thailand have adopted strict policies limiting foreign investors to minority participation in business ventures involving, besides Coca-Cola and IBM, such firms as Goodyear, NCR, Singer, and Union Carbide.

Over half of all takeover cases in Table 8–1 involved formal expropriation. Others have centered on forced sales, extra-legal interventions, and contract renegotiations. Formal expropriation was the dominant form of takeover during the entire period covered in Table 8–1. In many of these cases the United States government subsequently negotiated settlements with the host government involved that provide for compensation. In addition, some of the properties expropriated by the Allende (Chile) and Sukarno (Indonesia) governments have been restored to their private ownership since the overthrow of those regimes. Final settlement terms, compensation arrangements, and legal actions in many of the cases cited, however, have not been resolved at this writing.

Examination of the exercise of terminal controls by host country governments reveals several points. First, they are not random occurrences, but reflect distinct trends related to combinations of certain MNE and host country characteristics. Second, takeover cases have often resulted in political conflict that can be traced either to host government initiatives transmitted through affiliates to corporate headquarters, or direct contacts made between the host government and the parent firm. Third, takeovers have been described by some observers in terms of shifts in a kind of power whose nature does not involve open conflict but rather produces continuing tensions which can often be managed through compromise and accommodation, but which can also pass through a threshold where nationalization becomes inevitable.

The history of terminal controls in the 1960s and 1970s also holds a number of lessons: (1) The incidence of takeovers has risen markedly since the early 1960's. (2) A few high-incidence countries like Algeria, Chile, Indonesia, Libya, Peru, Tanzania, Uganda, and Zambia, undergoing radical transformations in economic and social policy, accounted for a disproportionate share of the takeovers. (3) The extractive sector is clearly the most vulnerable to takeovers, followed by manufacturing, financial services, and utilities. (4) Affiliates of large MNEs seem to be much more susceptible to takeovers than smaller firms. (5) Wholly-owned affiliates are more vulnerable than joint ventures with host-country firms. (6) Both very high and very low technology firms tend to be more susceptible to takeovers than firms which fall into the middle range. (7) Multinationals with a high degree of vertical integration on the supply and/or market side are less vulnerable to takeovers than are more integrated operations. (8) Greater MNE diversification across countries tends to reduce susceptibility to takeovers in individual host countries. (9) The "integrated global structure" increasingly adopted by MNEs can lead to greater susceptibility to takeovers than more fragmented managerial approaches. (10) Takeovers can be industry-wide and/or specifically targeted on a particular MNE, and both forms remain important, although sectors like mining and banking are especially susceptible by industry-wide actions while manufacturing is more subject to firm-specific actions.[125]

Certainly no event has triggered pressures for national ownership and control more strongly than the revelations about ITT's attempts to prevent Salvador Allende Gossens from gaining power in Chile—a case that is too well known and documented to be repeated here. The links between the CIA and ITT and their joint machinations to interfere in the Chilean political process, followed by Allende's impassioned pleas before the UN General Assembly, raised nationalist sentiment against MNEs to all-time highs. And the fact that other MNEs failed to come forward to renounce such interference in the political affairs of sovereign countries raised the spectre of sinister conspiracy and further intensified passions. Several criminal investigations of the ITT affair were initiated following the disclosures but had to be abandoned because of the possibility of revelations that would pose a threat to United States national security, the most recent one in 1979.[126]

The four alternative ownership-control strategies outlined in this chapter are

Table 8-1 *Takeovers of U.S. Foreign Direct Investment Interests by Type and by Countries, 1962-1977*

	SA	SB	UA	UB	UC	UD	VE	DL	TOTAL
OECD									
Australia		2						2	4
Canada		2			1		1	4	8
France		2					1	3	6
Italy		1					1		2
Japan								2	2
Netherlands		1							1
Spain								1	1
Switzerland		1							1
Turkey					1				1
United Kingdom							2	2	4
Total		9			2		5	14	30
AFRICA									
Benin	1		1						2
Central African Republic			2						2
Congo (Brazzaville)			2						2
Dahomey		1	2						3
Ethiopia			2						2
Ghana		1			1				2
Guinea		1							1
Liberia	1	1			2				4
Madagascar	1								2
Mauritania	1								1
Nigeria	1	5							6
Somalia	1		1		1				3
Sudan	2								2
Togo	1								1
Uganda	3								3
Zambia	1	1				1			3
Total	12	10	12	–	4	1	–	–	39
ASIA									
Bangladesh			2	1					3
Cambodia		2							2
Ceylon		2							2
India		4					1		5
Indonesia	5	1							6
Iran	1							1	2
Malaysia		1							1
Pakistan		1							1
Sri Lanka	1								1
Thailand							1		1
Total	7	11	2	1	–	–	2	1	24
LATIN AMERICA									
Antigua		1							1
Argentina	7	2	2					2	13
Bolivia	2	1							3
Brazil		1						2	3
Chile	17	12	1		1	5	1		37
Costa Rica	2								2
Ecuador	1	1			2		1		5
Guatemala		2							2
Guyana	1	1							2

Table 8-1

	SA	SB	UA	UB	UC	UD	VE	DL	TOTAL
					Takeover Type				
Honduras			2						2
Jamaica		3			5				8
Mexico	5	2						1	8
Panama	1	1							2
Peru	7	3	1						11
Puerto Rico		1							1
Surinam		1							1
Trinidad & Tobago	a	1							1
Venezuela	3		1		1	1	7		13
Total	46	33	7	–	9	6	9	5	115
NEAR EAST									
Abu Dhabi		1							1
Algeria	8								8
Egypt	1							1	2
Iraq	2								2
Kuwait	1	1							2
Lebanon						1			1
Libya	7	1	3		1				12
Morocco		4				1			5
Qatar		1							1
Saudi Arabia		2						1	3
South Yemen			2						2
Syria	1		2	1	2				6
Total	20	10	7	1	3	2	–	2	45
Grand Total	85	73	28	2	18	9	16	22	253

a21 oil companies nationalized in 1974.

Settled Takeovers

SA   Companies with majority or minority U.S. ownership which were formally expropriated or nationalized.

SB   Companies with majority or minority U.S. ownership whose contracts or concessions were cancelled or renegotiated or whose equity was bought out in part or in whole by public or private local interests.

Unsettled Takeovers

UA   Companies with majority U.S. ownership which have been formally expropriated or nationalized.

UB   Companies with minority U.S. ownership interest which have been formally expropriated or nationalized.

UC   Companies with majority or minority U.S. ownership interest whose contracts or concessions have been cancelled or are under renegotiation or which are being required to sell a part of their equity to local interests.

UD   Companies with majority or minority U.S. ownership interest which have been intervened or requisitioned.

VE   Miscellaneous unsettled takeovers involving companies with majority or minority U.S. ownership interest.

Other:

DL   Proposed bids/investments delayed or cancelled due to government action.

not, of course, mutually exclusive. All four can be and are used simultaneously. Yet different host countries rely on individual control techniques to a greater or lesser extent. The Philippines seems to prefer entry controls and the country has a rather well-developed institutional framework for doing so. India emphasizes operating controls, with government interference in virtually all facets of day-to-day corporate activities. Brazil has in the past seemed to prefer greater freedom and reliance on market mechanisms in MNE entry and operations, yet has maintained strict limits on earnings repatriation. Sri Lanka has until recently opted for terminal controls in nationalizing and expropriating foreign-owned tea plantations, with very little new investment coming in. Selective terminal controls have been used by countries as diverse as Chile, Venezuela, France, and Peru from time to time in specific sectors, not to mention Cuba, Angola, Mozambique, and similar countries undergoing drastic change in economic and political systems.

9 *QUESTIONABLE PAYMENTS*

The problem is as old as civilization itself. Aristophanes (450–385 B.C.) criticized Pericles in his comedy *The Clouds* for financial statements showing fuzzy disbursements identified only as being "expended for necessary purposes." Among the many Biblical references to questionable payments is the warning "Fire shall consume the tabernacles of bribery" (Job 4:34, c.325 B.C.). A more recent authority maintains "I generally avoid temptation unless I can't resist it" (Mae West in *My Little Chickadee*, 1940 A.D.). Such payments represent one of the most pervasive and complex issues in business and public policy today. In the 1970s, some 500 American-based companies, in an unprecedented "orgy of self-flagellation," told the Securities and Exchange Commission that they made a total of well over $1 billion in such payments.[1] The companies variously described them as unusual, illicit, dubious, improper, irregular, deviant, unaccountable, insensitive, unbusinesslike, illegal, or questionable—we prefer the latter and will hereafter use QPs to denote questionable payments.

These massive QP revelations, triggered by the same Watergate investigations that toppled Richard Nixon, have rocked the world. They have produced political turmoil in Japan, Italy, and Holland. They have caused large-scale investigations in Canada, Venezuela, Spain, West Germany, Brazil, Switzerland, Greece, Iran, and Egypt. They have led to the arrest and trial of Japan's former Prime Minister Kakuei Tanaka, the disgrace of Prince Bernhard in the Netherlands, the forced resignation of President Giovanni Leone in Italy, and the bloodless overthrow of the Chief of State of Honduras, General Oswaldo Lopez Arellano. They have pushed a few corporate executives to commit suicide, the most famous being Eli M. Black, Chairman of United Brands, who plunged from his 44th floor office in New York's Pan Am building early one winter morning in 1975. They have caused forced resignations or demotions, both here and abroad, of over a hundred executives—including senior managers at firms like Gulf Oil, Lockheed Aircraft, Ford Motor, Continental Oil, and Japan's Marubeni Trading Co. And at least 350 executives and public officials have been dragged through the doors of courtrooms around the world. The revelations have also caused damage to United States diplomatic relations, dismissals of numerous foreign defense ministers, cancellations of existing sales contracts, appropriations of American-owned property abroad, and changes in the military procurement decisions of allies. Not least important, they have severely eroded public confidence in the ethics and responsibility of corporate management and set in motion what may become a profound realignment in corporate governance.

Our purpose here is to develop a carefully-reasoned and balanced analysis of the QP issue, beginning with who pays what to whom, discussing both their effects on nations and companies and (perhaps most importantly) the fundamental reasons behind overseas corporate payoffs, and winding up with an assessment of policy approaches to the problem and an application of our conflict management model. Perhaps the strongest message that comes through is complexity. The social and economic factors underlying QPs—beginning with the inability of free markets to work effectively—are enormously complex. Yet measures which have emerged to deal with the problem often seem oblivious to this, and frequently concentrate only on the "immorality" of overseas payments no matter where they occur, for what purpose, and to whom paid.

WHAT, HOW, AND FOR WHOM?

First, let us define a little more precisely what QPs are, and identify the cast of characters—the givers and the takers, the two it takes to tango in the game of international payoffs.

Among the lucky QP recipients are heads of state, cabinet ministers, legislators, judges, mayors, generals, policemen, tax assessors, mailmen, customs inspectors, immigration officials, customs brokers, union bosses, lawyers, pollution control and health inspectors, purchasing agents, and appointments secretaries. As long as someone has the power to demand a little extra to do his job properly, or a lot extra *not* to do his job properly, he can be counted among prospective QP-takers. On the giving side are executives of international companies seeking benefits or avoiding damage to themselves or their firms. When caught, most have insisted they did it "for the good of the company."

A scanning of several hundred SEC-induced corporate confessions reveals at least six different motives, none of which is particularly surprising.[2] QPs are made to:

1. Procure or retain contracts for the sale of products or services,
2. Protect business assets by avoiding external interference or harassment,
3. Avoid taxes, tariffs, or exchange restrictions or settle disputes over such questions,
4. Secure favorable government treatment to which the firm *is not* otherwise entitled,
5. Expedite the performance of ministerial or official duties to which the firm *is* entitled, and
6. Influence or support the political process.

A recent study of over 100 New York, New Jersey, and Connecticut firms' SEC disclosures revealed nonexistent promotional, public relations, and advertising expenses, phantom legal and consulting fees, phony contributions to industry and trade associations, and purchases of undelivered goods as principal ways of generating corporate slush funds available for QP purposes. Often these were obscure to internal auditors and external auditing firms who, although suspicious, remained silent. The study indicated that the sample firms funneled over $65 million through secret accounts, with almost $200 million in payments involved in all. In the case of 40 firms, top management either was directly involved or was aware of QPs, and 23 firms admitted to multiple episodes.[3]

Cash is clearly the dominant form of QP. But non-cash payments are also prominent and may range from a new Mercedes Benz or Cadillac, jobs for relatives and protegés, rent-free villas on the Riviera, paid holidays at Alpine ski resorts to cases of aged whiskey, and seeing that officials somehow manage to find their way to the more exclusive Parisian bordellos—*chacun a son goût*. And whether in cash or in kind, QPs come in all shapes and sizes—direct or indirect, legal or illegal, overt or covert, volunteered or extorted, big-ticket or peanuts, on or off the corporate books, lump-sum or installments, prepaid or *post-facto*, ethical or unethical, inside or outside the host country, fictitiously or factually entered into corporate records. The variety boggles the mind, and attempts at neat QP typologies make little sense. Perhaps the best we can do is profile five basic kinds of QPs, recognizing that where one ends and another begins is eminently debatable.

Grease

Dash in West Africa. *Pot de vin* in France. *Mordida* in Mexico. *Baksheesh* in the Middle East. *Matabiche* in Zaire. *Bustarella* in Italy. *Kumshaw* in the Orient. Everywhere there are palms to be greased. These "lubricating" or facilitating payments are typically small sums of money—small bribes. They usually go to low-level government officials to perform their normal duties efficiently and expeditiously—duties that may be refused or delayed unless accompanied by small gratuities. Grease has been used to expedite or obtain work permits, visas, routine licenses and permits, customs clearance, hotel accommodations, police protection, mail delivery, foreign exchange authorizations, stevadoring, appointments with officials, even finding papers on cluttered desks. Grease surely accounts for at least 95% of all QPs made by MNEs, but in dollar value probably accounts for less than a quarter of the total.

Bribery

Bribery most often involves payment of relatively large dollar amounts to ranking public officials. The payments are voluntarily given or promised (often called "whitemail") to obtain specific benefits that an official has the authority and discretion to offer. Bribery seeks corrupt behavior from the recipient by deviating from the proper performance of his official duties through acts of commission or omission. The objective is to suborn the decision-making process for the briber's benefit by persuading the official to make decisions on grounds other than merit.

MNEs have used bribes to improperly influence many kinds of judicial, legislative, or administrative acts—to procure or maintain contracts or concessions, reduce tax assessments or settle tax liabilities, obtain product approvals or price increases, even to have corporate names removed from the Arab boycott list. United Brands offered $2.5 million, and paid the first half of it, to a Minister of Economy in Honduras to get a reduction in that country's banana export tax. It also paid $750,000 to Italian officials starting in 1970 to lift import restrictions on its products.[4] Philip Morris distributed $120,000 to various Dominican Republic legislators to get a law passed so that competitors would have to buy Virginia tobacco from its local affiliate.[5] Former Japanese Prime Minister Kakuei Tanaka allegedly received $1.6 million in bribes from Lockheed to encourage the purchase of Lockheed L-1011 Tristar jets by All Nippon Airways.[6] Such large-scale bribery has captured the lion's share of media attention. But within the overall context of QPs, explicit bribery has evidently not been very common among MNEs.

Extortion

The kissing cousin of bribery is extortion—blackmail as opposed to whitemail. The improper influence now comes from the receiving end. Payments are extracted from foreign firms under duress and coercion by corrupt officials by means of intimidation, threat of violence and abuse of public trust.

Reported cases of extortion of MNEs often involve threatened withdrawal of existing or potential contracts. Perhaps most frequently, however, extortion payments are made to protect assets—human, financial, and physical—from potential governmental injury, interference, or expropriation. For instance, Ashland Oil paid $190,000 to two high government officials in Gabon after being informed that "certain outstanding obligations" of very dubious validity had to be satisfied.[7] Translinear Inc., a Dallas real estate development company, told a Congressional subcommittee of extortinate demands for $250,000 leveled by Haitian officials in connection with an initial $3 million investment in the development of a port facility. The firm was told that things would become "unhealthy" if it chose not to cooperate. It refused, and was duly forced to terminate the project.[8]

Perhaps the most widely publicized case of extortion involved Gulf Oil in South Korea, strong-armed into making $4 million available to the Democratic Republican Party's election funds. Of this, $1 million was extracted in 1966 and another $3 million in 1970. Mr. S.K. Kim, financial chairman of the Party, had actually demanded $10 million and subjected Gulf's Chairman, Bob R. Dorsey, to severe personal abuse. According to Dorsey, his threats "left little to the imagination if the company would choose to turn its back on this request."[9]

Agents Fees

Another type of QP very much in evidence is exorbitant fees or commissions paid by MNEs to enterprising sales agents, consultants, lawyers, and marketers abroad. The concern is not with reasonable fees that are commensurate with the provision of necessary and legitimate commercial services, but with payments far out of proportion to services actually performed. Some portion of the fees may be used for bribery—with or without the principal's knowledge—or rebated to MNE executives for use as slush funds off the company's books. So the trick is to decide what "appropriate" agents fees really are.

From 1971 to 1973 the Northrop Corporation paid out more than $30 million in agents fees and commissions. A private report written by the public accounting firm of Ernst & Ernst disclosed that the big aircraft manufacturer had employed between 400 and 500 consultants and agents during that time—agents who were often members of royal families or closely associated with the military. Northrop's President, Thomas V. Jones, described the typical agent as "the stethoscope on the workings of government."[10] One rather well-heeled stethoscope with ties to the Saudi Arabian royal family was Adnan M. Khashoggi. He has provided marketing, consulting, and other services for Northrop, Lockheed, Rolls-Royce, General Tire & Rubber, Chrysler, Raytheon, and other MNEs—with fees often allegedly involving sizeable QP components. Boeing, which has reportedly paid out more than $50 million in questionable agents fees and other payments, evidently maintained an entire stable of well-paid consultants apparently including a prince, an ambassador, and officials of foreign governments or persons closely associated with them in countries such as Argentina, Brazil, India, Saudi Arabia, Libya, and the Sudan. [11]

Political Contributions

Lastly, there are contributions to politicians and political parties abroad. In many countries it is legal for corporations to make such contributions. As always, there is the *quid pro quo*. Contributions help make new friends and retain old ones, and maybe even soften up old enemies. Even if legal, such payments may still be questionable if not acknowledged or disclosed, and there is always the razor's edge between contributions that represent a legitimate interest in the political process and those patently aimed at improperly influencing government actions.

Political contributions in Italy have long been a corporate obligation. The experience of Exxon is illustrative. Its Italian subsidiary, Esso Italiana, funneled a total of $55.3 million to Italian political parties and government officials during the period 1963–1971. Contributions authorized by the parent firm averaged about $3 million per year, for a total of $27 million, and the rest was "siphoned out" of the company without authorization by the managing director of the Italian subsidiary ostensibly for political purposes. The company's payments were designed to "help bring about a political environment favorable to Esso Italiana's business interests." Some of these coincided in point of time with the acquisition of specific legislative benefits to the oil industry such as subsidies to offset the higher transportation costs caused by the closing of the Suez Canal in 1967, reductions of the manufacturing tax on petroleum products, and deferment of ENEL's (the government-owned electric utility) conversion to nuclear power. The contributions were made without disclosing the recipients, as was the custom, and most were camouflaged as payments to newspapers, publicity agencies, and others. All contributions were ordered stopped in 1972 (long before Watergate) by former Exxon Board Chairman J.K. Jamieson—that he meant business is attested to by the fact that heads did indeed roll.[12]

GAINS AND LOSSES

Having looked at the menu of QPs, we ought to examine their *effects*. Why all the excitement? Why have so many politicians, bureaucrats, reporters, educators, radicals, clergymen, lawyers, accountants, even investors and businessmen, been so worked up? Is it that the economic, social, political, and ethical effects of QPs are indeed profound? For any single QP, its consequences naturally depend on the specifics of the case. But we can assess in a general way their implications for nations and firms alike.

The Host Country

Harold M. Williams, a chairman of the SEC during the Carter Administration, said that "in the long run, honesty is not only the best business policy, but the only one compatible with the free market and with open competition. Corruption—whether it involves bribes to secure overseas contracts, illegal contributions to political candidates at home, or hampering the efficient function of the marketplace—results in higher prices, lessened responsiveness to the consumer, and lower quality of goods and services. Business corruption is not only inefficient, but it destroys the marketplace."[13]

William's thought can probably be defended in terms of modern Western societies. But applying them elsewhere may require some adaptation. For example, bribery in market economies may be contrasted with under-the-table deals in the Soviet Union. While damaging to the public interest in the West, "The Soviet deal, taking place in a centrally planned economy that is fundamentally inefficient, may sometimes—although not always—actually improve efficiency of production and distribution and thereby benefit the public."[14] In other countries such as India or Italy, where social systems are systemically chaotic, a certain amount of corruption accepted by all may be the thing that makes the system work tolerably well. And in a very poor developing country such as Indonesia, grease payments may (arguably) be a "second-best" way of getting a more equitable distribution of income. So QPs can be socially useful when they help to remove obstacles that themselves distort equity or efficiency in society.

But on the whole, the effects of most QPs in most host nations are pernicious. Bribes induce public officials to ignore established social priorities, or distort these priorities by allocating limited resources to purchases that are not the best, most appropriate, or least expensive. Payoffs thus raise the cost and lower the quality of goods and services purchased. They can lead to a deterioration in the country's balance of payments and inflate the burden of foreign borrowing used to buy imports. And they undermine nations' control over the activities of MNEs.

Large-scale extortion, political contributions, agents fees, and bribes can act to preserve existing class relationships to the detriment of society at large. Lockheed's disclosed bribes of $22 million were paid in 15 countries to fewer than 150 recipients.[15] To add insult to injury, a good deal of the money is funneled directly into foreign bank accounts and never even enters the local income and spending stream. For example, the Singer Company reported payments of $1.5 million to procure business in five countries between 1967 and 1976, all of which were made "to proprietors, agents or employees of customers, in each case by bank transfer to or for the benefit of the recipient in a country other than the country of his residence."[16]

Politically as well, QPs that induce public officials to violate their lawful duties are clearly subversive of sound government and political processes. They undermine the moral fabric of society—tolerance of corruption at high levels in industry and government inevitably fosters broader lawlessness. Perhaps most dramatically, disclosure of QPs sometimes has de-stabilizing political effects. Lockheed's bribery disclosures, for example, were a political bonanza for the opposition in Japan, Italy, and West Germany.[17] And Swedish economist Gunnar

Myrdal writes in his book *Asian Drama* that in developing nations corruption paves the way for authoritorian regimes, military takeovers, and totalitarianism—"the extent of corruption has a direct bearing on the stability of governments."[18]

The Companies

The effects of QPs on the multinational companies themselves are equally far-reaching. No doubt executives believe they are advancing corporate interests by spurring sales or protecting assets. A study in 1976 found that, on an average, the American businessmen interviewed believed that 10% of their international sales were risked if they stopped making QPs.[19]

Yet payoffs require enormous time and effort invested in what ought to be routine transactions governed by market forces, using up in the process the firm's scarcest single resource—managerial effort. They drive up its operating costs and, if everybody bribes, ultimately fail to provide hoped-for advantages. And once a company indicates a susceptibility to comply with demands for payoffs, it risks being considered an "easy mark," subject to permanent pressure for still more and larger payments.

For management, bribery involves some significant dangers. Exposure in the *host* country can cause retaliatory pressure on the company, even expropriation or nationalization. Exposure in the *home* country can induce stockholder suits, legal action by government regulatory agencies, and outright dismissal of those directly involved and their bosses. Often it leads to disclosure of proprietory information that can only help the firm's competitors. Slush funds, cooked books, and surreptitious behavior at top levels of management can result in fast-spreading corruption, employee demoralization, apathy, and loss of managerial control throughout the organization.

The use of QPs in a competitive setting may indicate that the firm is too lazy or too inefficient to compete on the basis of price, quality and service. By camouflaging such weaknesses, payoffs can easily land the firm in much greater trouble in the long run. Not least important, revelation of QPs leads to increased suspicion of the MNE *as an institution* around the world, and worsens a problem that is already quite serious.

The Home Countries

To the extent that QPs are employed by firms to win orders away from firms home-based in other countries, they undoubtedly pay short-term dividends to the multinational's home economy. In landing these foreign orders the MNEs are creating (or saving) the jobs of domestic workers and generating income— not, of course, if domestic competitors engage in QPs only to get an edge over each other. So even if major QPs do end up distorting international trade and production, imposing social and economic costs on host countries, the parent nation of the bribing MNEs may nevertheless reap substantial economic gains.

QPs can be consistent with a country's foreign policy objectives, such as supporting anti-Communist regimes or promoting foreign military sales. On the other hand, QPs can also undermine foreign policy. Indeed, MNEs stand accused of designing and implementing their own "corporate foreign policies," which may or may not coincide with objectives of the home government. Former Under Secretary of State George W. Ball notes that payoffs "give substance to the Communist myth that capitalism is fundamentally corrupt."[20]

Besides political strain that bribery revelations can exacerbate in many parts of the world, QPs made overseas are sometimes recycled back home. The $476,000 paid by Northrop to a retired Chief of Staff of the French Air Force was routed into illegal United States political contributions. Mr. Tongsun Park, the notorious distributor of QPs to American legislators and public officials, according to some reports obtained a good part of his financing from questionable commissions on both commercial and federally subsidized American rice sales to South Korea.[21] Although the company denied it, Mr. Park told both Department of Agriculture and Justice Department investigators that he also received "$1 million a month" in QPs from Gulf Oil.[22]

On the American political scene, many people believe that QPs by United States firms abroad reflect on the national honor, and that business behavior illegal or suspect at home ought not to be condoned overseas—even if accepted within the host country environment. That simplistic "moral imperialism" of this sort seems to play well to audiences in Peoria has not escaped the notice of astute American politicians, although the political dividends that Senator Frank Church (D-Idaho) hoped for in his ill-fated run for the Democratic Presidential nomination in 1976 did not quite pan out. Much more importantly, disclosure of overseas QPs tends to undermine public confidence in the private sector and encourages further regulation by politicians at least as vulnerable to public cynicism and distrust.

EXPLAINING QPs

Now that we know about QPs and their effects, we ought to find out how they come about. Social scientists would say that payoffs represent "learned behavior"—one way that organizations attempt to adapt themselves to their surrounding environments in terms of doing business. What seems to explain the enormous differences in the incidence of QPs between countries and between firms and industries? Only if we can answer this question can we hope to find sensible and effective ways of alleviating the problem.

Corporate payoffs can probably most often be explained by the inability of markets to work well. Efficient markets need a large number of buyers and sellers competing with each other. They also need freedom from artificial impediments, low transactions costs, good information, and products that are easily identified and priced so that people know what they are buying and selling and can tell when they are getting value for money.

QPs, in the economist's view, are the product of things that *prevent* markets from working efficiently—things that contribute to "market failures." Sometimes there are only a few sellers trying frantically to peddle their wares. Sometimes there are only a few buyers in a given market, or only a single one—as in government procurement. And there are all kinds of interferences with free markets as well: tariffs, taxes, price controls, foreign exchange restrictions, labor restrictions, and many more. Sometimes language or social-cultural barriers make it hard or even impossible to do business. All such obstacles to efficient markets give rise to incentives for QPs.

If the obstacles are real, as with language problems, hiring a local agent to get business done actually helps the market work, and payments for such services are both necessary and legitimate. But if the obstacles are artificial, thrown up by people abusing power positions on either the buying or selling side of the market, then QPs are clearly damaging. And if the obstacles are artificial but (like tariffs) are thrown up for one reason or another by public policy, then QPs may be good or bad—it all depends on the social usefulness of the market-distorting policy in the first place.

What can we in fact learn from the hundreds of voluntary or involuntary corporate confessions? Perhaps the first reaction is an inclination to agree with Walter Guzzardi, Jr., that ". . . taken as a whole, the revelations are baffling in their complexity, frustrating in their diversity, heavy with prolixity, and stubbornly resistant to conclusions."[23] This is partly because corporate confessions have almost always been incomplete. Under its "voluntary disclosure" program, the SEC allowed firms to withhold the names of recipients of QPs as well as the actual countries in which they were made. They did, however, state the amounts involved, the purposes of the various payoffs, whether corporate books were falsified, and whether top management was involved.[24]

When we add to the rather laconic "voluntary" corporate confessions the more detailed disclosures required of a number of multinational firms under the prodding of SEC legal action, some tentative patterns begin to emerge. And when we include the surveys and investigations of reporters and various business and public-interest organizations, some very strong QP patterns stand out. As shown in Exhibit 9–1, we believe potential causes of QPs can be found in features of the (1) host country, (2) home and third countries, (3) industry, and (4) company.

Host Country Pull

In 1783 John Gay wrote in his *Fables:* "Corruption's not of modern date, it hath been tried in ev'ry state." His terse conclusion still applies—MNEs as a group have so far disclosed making QPs in over 65 different countries. This is also true of individual firms. Tenneco, for example, admitted to questionable payments of $12 million in 24 different countries during 1970–1975.[25] Sterling Drug disclosed slightly more than $1.8 million of QPs in 21 foreign countries during the period January 1970 to June 1976.[26] The geographic distribution of QPs among host countries tells us a great deal about motivation. Long national traditions of business and government corruption, low levels of economic development, ambiguous rules of business conduct, statist political regimes, and a complex cultural environment all serve to encourage QPs.

Traditions of corruption. Business International Corporation, a private research outfit, concluded that ". . . the most important element by far in setting payment patterns is the attitude of the host country." Most multinationals con-

Exhibit 9–1
Explaining Questionable Payments of Multinational Corporations

Host country   Home and third country

Traditions of corruption	Coincidence of interests
Low levels of economic development	Regulatory failure
Legal/regulatory ambiguity	Ineffective watchdogs
Statist political regimes	Bank secrecy (gnomes)
Cultural complexity	Tax havens

Propensity to make
questionable payments

Competitive market structure	Competitive strength
Governmental sales	Inadequate internal control
Size of transactions	Management amorality
Government regulation	Multinationality

Industry   Company

cur, and in their SEC disclosure statements have usually included a phrase like "payments were made in accordance with local custom and tradition."

Standards of business conduct differ enormously in time and place. Lord Shawcross, chairman of a commission that examined corruption for the International Chamber of Commerce in Paris, claimed that there are today only twelve countries where corruption is "quite exceptional and is regarded with grave legal and social disapproval."[27] Since these "clean" countries are mainly in North America, Scandinavia and Northern Europe, we are talking about business and public corruption as a basic way of life in much of Asia, Africa, Latin America, and the Middle East, as well as Southern and (to a lesser extent) Eastern Europe. In practice, this often means payoffs are condoned or even encouraged, enforcement is lax, and unless it is a *cause célèbre*, penalties for those who get caught are often light.

American executives complain that the Middle East is the world's most vexing QP environment, with payoffs rampant in countries like Kuwait and Saudi Arabia.[28] These same executives point to South Korea, Indonesia, and Italy as examples of countries where heavy-handed and corrupt political practices are endemic. Where expectations for small and large QPs are deeply entrenched, many MNEs feel the need to "do as the Romans." At least in the perception of management, refusal to play along means business success will be elusive at best.

Low levels of economic development. With the exception of some very fat payoffs to prosperous Japanese and Europeans, QPs have been most pervasive in the poor countries of the world. Why? Some political commentators consider corruption as an inevitable product of economic backwardness. Harvard's Joseph

Nye notes that "corruption in developing countries is too important a phenomenon to be left to moralists."[29] Political scientist James C. Scott views corruption "as a sort of half-way house between violence and constitutionality, a means by which some of the new demands produced by rapid social change are accommodated within a political system whose formal institutions are inadequate to the task."[30]

Imperial Chemical Industries, second only to British Petroleum among Britain's largest firms, admitted to $2.4 million in QPs abroad over a four and one-half year period. It disclosed that no QPs at all were made in North America, Europe—except for one "minor" occasion in a Southern European country—Japan, or Australasia. With characteristic British understatement, ICI said that the QPs took place in "other areas of the world, in parts of which it is believed practices tend to be different" from the industrialized countries.[31] And what was ICI doing with the $2.4 million? Probably sharing the payroll expense of developing-country government bureaucracies. Most developing countries pay their public officials very poorly indeed, and it is often understood by all that they will make up the rest of their livelihood out of graft. Underpaid low-level bureaucrats, accustomed to and dependent on gratutities, have surely been the recipients of the vast majority of small and medium-size "grease" payments shelled out by MNEs.

Of course, large-size QPs also occur at top government levels in developing countries. In some, legislators have to kick-back up to half their paltry salaries to the political party that put them in office. To reimburse themselves, they put the arm on local firms and MNEs alike. And where politics are unstable, high government officials' tenure in office is often uncertain and brief. So they are strongly tempted to create offshore "retirement" funds that will tide them over or provide lifetime financial security when domestic political turmoil necessitates hasty departure. As often as not, the motto of newly-installed government officials is "my turn!" and so they get while the getting is good. The Swahili term for QP-recipients "wabenzi" (people who drive Mercedes Benz) says it all.

Ambiguous rules of the game. In developed and developing countries alike, an important stimulus to QPs is ambiguity in legal and regulatory systems. Virtually all nations have laws against corruption, bribery and extortion. But in dozens of countries these laws are obscure, untested, and unenforced. They leave wide gray areas as to the limits of legality. Without a clear definition of acceptable conduct, opportunities for abuse become legion. Under such conditions, "we should notice how easily men are corrupted and become wicked, although originally good and well-educated," said the Italian statesman and political philosopher, Niccolo Machiavelli, over 450 years ago.[32]

A more recent Italian observer, Luigi Barzini, provided further insight in his book, *The Italians*. He described his country's regulatory structure as a "tropical tangle of statutes, rules, norms, regulations, customs, some hundreds of years old, some voted last week by Parliament and signed to this very morning by the President." The Italian *bustarella* (stuffed envelope) is often the only way a foreign firm can cope with an unbelievable statutory and bureaucratic nightmare. Barzini says that Italian taxation is particularly chaotic, and quotes a local economist who calculated that "if every tax on the statute books was fully collected, the State would absorb 110% of the national income."[33] And so taxes are negotiable and the Italian style of business is to maintain three sets of books—

one for the tax assessor, one for the shareholder, and the other a real-world set of accounts for management decisions. Scores of MNEs have disclosed QPs in Italy designed to reduce tax assessments or to amicably settle tax liabilities.

Statist regimes. Theodore C. Sorenson writes ". . . bribe recipients have served in every kind of government on virtually every continent: anti-U.S. administrations and political parties as well as pro-U.S.; democracies as well as dictatorships; communist as well as noncommunist governments; and rich industrialized nations as well as poor and underdeveloped nations."[34] Corrupt politicians at high levels of government can be found almost everywhere—Gulf Oil found them in the United States, South Korea, and Bolivia, while Lockheed Aircraft uncovered them in Italy, Japan and the Netherlands.[35] Yet high-level political corruption may be more prevalent in some kinds of political or economic systems than in others.

Our reading of the evidence is that the prospects for bribery are brightest in political regimes that concentrate extensive economic, political, and social controls in the hands of the state at the cost of individual liberty and decentralized decisions. This includes tribal, militaristic, totalitarian, autocratic, and oligarchic states. Partial support for this view comes from the fact that an estimated 90% of all QPs have been paid in nations not included in the list of 21 (developed and developing) nations ranked "most free" by political rights in the Freedom House Comparative Survey discussed in Chapter 4.[36] In "less free" settings MNEs confront governments that hold essentially unlimited power. Civil servants are vested with discretionary authority to grant or withhold permits for almost every kind of commercial activity. Those at the seat of power see themselves as dispensers of privileges and exceptions, and the ordinary workings of consenual political processes or a free market cannot be relied upon to safeguard legitimate business interests. Constantly threatened with governmental interference in business affairs or afraid of worse things to come, MNEs are moved to dispense "good will" or yield to extortion to protect themselves. And on top of this are the inevitable grease or whitemail payments, based on political and social connections and necessary to obtain favorable treatment.

Cultural complexity. Cultures, says anthropologist Edward T. Hall, differ widely in the extent to which "silent language" and "hidden dimensions" govern the transmission of information and interpersonal relations. In some cultures human behavior is covert; in others it is quite open. Where covert behavior is the norm, it takes a good deal of getting used to ("contexting") to deal effectively with everyday life. In his book *Beyond Culture*, Hall finds relatively "high context" cultures in the Orient, around the Mediterranean, and in the Middle East. Relatively "low context" cultures include West Germany, Switzerland, the Scandinavian countries, and the United States. There is a strong correlation between "high context" cultures and high incidence of QPs by American firms abroad.[37]

"High context" cultures tend to have the following characteristics: (1) People tend to be involved in numerous activities with other people simultaneously. (2) Much information is implicit, rather than being explicitly stated. (3) Verbal agreements, rather than written contracts, are binding. (4) Bonds between individuals are strong and there is deep personal involvement of people with each other. (5) Great distinctions are made between insiders and outsiders. (6) Ingrained cultural patterns are slow to change. For the American or Northern European business executive psychologically attuned to his home "low context" environment, the reality of such a culture throws up formidable barriers to understanding and communication and, Hall warns, "it is sheer folly to get seriously involved with high context cultures unless one is really contexted."[38]

One way to get around the problem is the availability of "cultural bridges" —friendly local agents, consultants, or governmental officials who can make things happen. Of course, bridge-building in Saudi Arabia, Japan, or Italy is seldom provided gratis, and QPs are sometimes simply ways of avoiding the deep biases and inevitable blunders that pervade intercultural business encounters. Paid intermediaries may be the only way to penetrate a Moslem or Oriental culture. As Lockheed's president told a Senate Subcommittee, "The Japanese establishment is a close knit group of individuals in business and government. . . . U.S. companies need help."[39] In this case, help came in part from a $7.1 million cultural bridge named Yoshio Kodama—on the surface an ultra-right-wing nationalist, but behind the scenes a tremendously influential power broker with the leaders of the Japanese Liberal-Democratic political establishment.

Not all services of "cultural bridges" involve influence peddling, however. Local agents and consultants understand the social, economic, political, and psychological patterns of their countries and regions. The need for such intermediary services in places like the Middle East is compelling. Local government officials, typically suspicious and uneasy with foreign businessmen, will often insist on working with a compatriot they know. While the remuneration involved may appear questionable to American observers, it is at least in part legitimate payment for legitimate services.

Home Country Push

The American penchant for openness and disclosure has made sure that virtually all QP revelations so far have involved United States multinationals. There is absolutely no doubt that firms headquartered in France, West Germany, Japan, Canada, the Netherlands, Sweden, Switzerland, Belgium, the United Kingdom, and elsewhere are similarly involved. Yet with few exceptions there has been essentially no governmental or media pressure in these countries to expose foreign payments practices of their own firms.

We know that such Canadian corporations as Atomic Energy of Canada Ltd. and Polysar Ltd. made respective payments to promote the sale of nuclear reactors in South Korea and Argentina and chemical products in Europe.[40] British Petroleum and the Royal Dutch/Shell group of companies revealed in 1976 that each had made contributions to various Italian political parties from 1969 to 1973.[41] Over the years, allegations of payoffs by Dassault, the French aircraft maker, have been variously aired by the Dutch Parliament, a Swiss military tribunal, and the British press.[42] Back in 1968, the French armaments supplier Thompson-CSF was implicated in bribery of the commander in chief of the Lebanese armed forces to promote the sale of ground-to-air missiles.[43] Executives of large Japanese trading companies like Mitsubishi, Mitsui, and C. Itoh have been accused periodically of trying to bribe government officials, especially in the Asian countries like South Korea.[44] And in interviews on QPs with German executives, *Business International* researchers found that "companies dislike the practice, disapprove of it, but adjust to local requirements."[45]

In our view, conditions in the home countries of multinationals also have to be considered in attempting to find explanations for QPs—in the coincidence of economic interests between home-country governments and MNEs, in home-country regulatory failure, and in weakness of some of the legal and professional services provided to the MNE at home.

Coincidence of interests. From the available evidence, there seems to be a symbiotic relationship between many of the QPs undertaken by MNEs and the foreign economic policies of their home governments. In the United States, federal agencies have long been aware of QPs, and in essence have sanctioned them.[46] Overseas payoffs, especially in the arms and aerospace industries, have generally been considered good for balance of payments, jobs, national prestige, and political influence. Payoffs by extractive firms may help to assure reliable and reasonable access to imported supplies of basic materials and fuels. And there is always the political support of such strategic linchpins as the governments of South Korea, the Philippines, or Italy to be considered.

According to Senators Frank Church (D-Idaho) and Clifford J. Case (R-N.J.), the Pentagon must bear "some responsibility" for the bribery that has surfaced.[47] The Defense Department has for years authorized contractors to pay "reasonable" agents fees as part of the cost of their overseas sales. The contractors have been informed by government officials of the necessity for such fees and freely encouraged to pass them along to the Pentagon when it has acted as middleman in arms contracts. According to military procurement experts, the Defense Department has a particularly poor track record in controlling QP costs of its major contractors. In short, QPs seem to have been an integral part of "Pentagon Capitalism"—to borrow a phrase from Columbia University Professor Seymour Melman.[48]

We also need to remind ourselves that United States government agencies, particularly through CIA operations, themselves use clandestine payments as an instrument to promote legitimate American security interests. Millions of dollars have been funneled to scores of foreign leaders (such as King Hussein of Jordan) to obtain access to individuals, political gossip, and intelligence "penetrations."[49] Our political adversaries do likewise. According to President Jimmy Carter and Secretary of State Vance, such payments have been "proper, legal and appropriate."[50] In performing its assigned role, the CIA has been acquainted with and perhaps directly involved in some multinational corporate QPs. It works the other way too, as with ITT's notorious offer to subsidize the CIA to keep Salvador Allende from power in Chile.[51] *The New York Times* has reported that the CIA knew of bribes paid in Japan by Lockheed and had associated itself in one way or another with individuals like Kodama.[52] Harvard's Asian expert Jerome A. Cohen has suggested that the United States government did not want to see the names of Lockheed's Japanese QP-recipients exposed because the firm may have been "operating in intimate contact" with certain American government agencies.[53]

Some observers suggest this kind of symbiosis works even more effectively in MNE home nations such as France, West Germany, Britain, and Japan. The

French Defense Ministry, in its zeal to promote arms sales abroad, has apparently earned the nickname *la Ministère des Pots-de-vin*—the Ministry of Bribes.[54] Across the Rhine, Bonn's tax collectors permit resident corporations to deduct foreign bribes, known as *Sonderspesen* (special expenses) as long as they name the recipients.[55] QPs are also tax deductible in Britain, where the Bank of England supposedly has a complete private record of virtually every payoff made abroad by British firms.[56] In Japan almost all export sales of the kind that generate QPs are arranged with government export financing or other government support.[57] The home-country QP "push" can be powerful indeed, and by foreign standards American firms sometimes seem like babes in the woods.

Regulatory failure. Under American law it was not illegal for a corporate executive or his agent to bribe a foreign government official before 1978. Only when the businessman commited some other offense in the process of bribery, like tax evasion, did he run afoul of the law. Many critics point to a kind of "shut-eye sentry" attitude on the part of United States regulatory agencies prior to 1975 as a partial explanation for QPs. The IRS was especially criticized for failing to uncover illegal payments in its regular corporate audits; of being lax in enforcing the rule that money spent in violation of foreign laws is not a deductible business expense.[58]

It was reported that officials of the General Telephone and Electronics Company had protested to Export-Import Bank officials about alleged bribery of high-level Indonesian officials by the Hughes Aircraft Company to obtain contracts for a $160 million satellite communications system.[59] Eximbank conducted no inquiry into these allegations and in late 1974 proceeded to make more than $50 million in guaranteed loans for the project despite knowledge of the alleged payoffs. This same lack of concern has often been attributed to the State Department. Numerous MNE executives have testified on the futility of trying to get diplomatic assistance from American embassy officials around the globe when confronted with demands for extortionate QPs, with diplomats apparently consistent in taking the "hear no evil, see no evil" line.[60]

The Justice Department's Criminal Division was accused of being soft on corporate crime as a result of its preoccupation with organized crime.[61] It allegedly was not especially vigorous in pressing criminal charges in corporate bribery cases under securities, mail and wire fraud, bank secrecy, and perjury laws. And the SEC was itself chastised for unwillingness to establish an appropriate definition of QP "materiality" in regard to the integrity of management or investor interests, and for its aggressive crusade against payoffs only after-the-fact. Regulatory failure means there were few legal deterrents to QPs, and even moderately clever MNEs were able to circumvent legal constraints without much difficulty.

The watchdogs. The lack of effective control exercised over errant management by legal counsel, boards of directors, and accountants is another contributing factor in QPs. The SEC, for example, has acquired specific evidence of misconduct on the part of lawyers in the QP process.[62] A few seem to have played a part in directly facilitating QPs, but many more had knowledge of or condoned such activities. Effective checks have been precluded by the confidential attorney-client relationship.

Nor have corporate boards of directors fully exercised their fiduciary responsibility. "Outside" directors such as investment bankers, executives of other firms, or securities lawyers sometimes have not been sufficiently free from personal or business obligations affecting their independence of judgment, and others have been little more than "lullabyed puppets" of management. As the phrase goes "Keep them in the dark, water them well and cover them with horse manure."[63]

Some political activists see corporate auditors as simply another species of mushroom. According to Pullman Inc., the accounting firm of Arthur Young & Co. transmitted money to a foreign tax official on Pullman's behalf.[64] Merck & Company has disclosed that its outride auditor, Arthur Anderson & Co., failed to follow up information it was given about QPs overseas.[65] Coopers & Lybrand, auditors for Firestone Tire & Rubber Co., apparently knew of a special account maintained by one of the company's foreign subsidiaries to bribe officials in charge of setting maximum prices for tires, but the accountant's local partner did not insist upon a change in the improper accounting procedures being used.[66] Price, Waterhouse & Co., the United Brands accountant, was told about the famous Honduran bribe in January 1975, but one of its partners agreed to wait and see if it was uncovered in the company's European audit—it wasn't.[67]

Accounting firms and the corporations they audit rarely share such a cozy bed, but the fact remains that established accounting practice has not led to effective exposure of QPs. Audit procedures are performed on a random and partial basis, according to generally accepted accounting principles but without specific emphasis on discovery of misconduct on the part of company officials. Existing rules of thumb of financial "materiality" have usually excluded most QPs from their purview. And we have to keep in mind that corporate management has almost always deliberately attempted to hide fraud and illegality from their auditors. As one accounting authority has remarked: "People tend to think of auditors as detectives. They're not. They're accountants. We train them in debits and credits. Even if they look carefully, auditors will miss many, maybe even most, frauds."[68]

But a fundamental issue remains—that of true independence. Most of the "Big 8" accounting firms wear three sets of green eyeshades—auditing, tax advising, and management consulting. Critics argue that CPAs impair their independence as auditors when they simultaneously earn handsome fees from these very same clients for tax and management advice. Abraham J. Briloff sums it up this way: "These services are corruptive. They are distracting and contaminating to the independence of auditors. An accountant who is wooing this other business can potentially be bent, folded and mutilated by the client."[69]

Payoff-Prone Industries

Besides host-country pull and home-country push, firms in some industries seem to be more prone to QPs than others. The Council on Economic Priorities has found large-scale bribery to be particularly common among pharmaceuticals and health care, oil and gas, aerospace, chemicals, tire and rubber, and food products firms.[70] Subsequent surveys have added construction, communication, and shipping to the list.[71] But on dollar volume we estimate that roughly one-half of American QP disclosures so far have involved just two industries—aerospace and petroleum.

Competitive market structure. Especially in trying to explain large-scale QPs, the market structure within which the individual MNE operates seems to be critical. Most multinationals are in what economists call "oligopolistic" industries, with a relatively small number of firms competing tooth and nail for market-share. MNEs thrive in technology-intensive industries in which they have significant market power.

Oligopoly sometimes leads to collusion, and MNEs have occasionally coordinated their QP behavior. For instance, the "seven sisters" of the oil industry, or at least those operating in Italy such as Exxon, Gulf, British Petroleum, Shell, and Mobil, appear to have acted in concert in their political contributions. Company assessments were imposed by the industry's trade association—Unione Petrolifera Italiana—an arrangement apparently initiated by Esso Italiana's Managing Director during his long tenure as President of the association.[72] In Jamaica, Alcoa, Reynolds, and Kaiser apparently all made contributions to political groups.[73] In Mexico, six tire companies, including a Uniroyal subsidiary, made a $420,000 joint payoff in 1974 to get a price increase approved. The payment was arranged by the Rubber Industry Chamber, a trade association, and was apportioned among the companies according to market share.[74] Joint QP behavior tends to create a common cost structure and common exposure to risk for the participating firms. If everyone does a little, the relative position of the individual firms in the industry will not be upset.

Bribery can be viewed as a form of non-price competition. The evidence suggests that some American firms make such payoffs to get a competitive edge in industries where the products of competing companies are closely matched and the number of potential buyers is limited. Daniel Haughton of Lockheed testified that "we were many times in very stiff competition, and when you are in stiff competition, you have to try to meet the competition."[75] Lockheed's bribery in Japan, available evidence suggests, literally took orders away from both Grumman Aircraft and McDonnell-Douglas. Fierce sales competition can deteriorate into a rat race of corruption.

Government sales. One of the most important determinants of an industry's payoff incidence is its dependence on the procurement decisions of government officials. This affects aircraft, construction, and communication industries. Officials can simply pass the increased costs on to the taxpayer and camouflage shoddy merchandise. Unless there is an investigation, the chances of getting caught may be quite slim due to the frequent absence of effective supervision. Purchasers for private firms, on the other hand—while not immune to bribery— are much more easily found out when excessive prices or sub-standard products impair the firm's own competitiveness. Perhaps this is why several studies conclude that payments are less necessary and less common among companies in consumer product industries that conduct most of their business in the private rather than the public sector.[76]

Size of transactions. The size of a single transaction in the firm's overall business may also be an important factor in bribery. When individual transactions are huge, payoffs can easily be disguised in the price. The QPs usually represent only a tiny fraction of the overall deal. Whether it is the General Telephone and Electronics Corporation bidding for a $500 million telephone equipment order or Textron's Bell Helicopter Division bidding for $650 million in government contracts in Iran, or Cargill Inc. conducting massive grain sales to foreign countries, Westinghouse seeking a contract to build a $1.1 billion nuclear power plant in the Philippines, or Boeing, Northrop, Grumman, and Lockheed fighting it out for multibillion dollar aircraft contracts in the Middle East, the size principle is at work.[77]

For MNEs that depend heavily on one-shot big-ticket deals, the pressure for payoffs can be painfully intense. Sales are not continuous, and a large proportion of revenues each year depends on the procurement of just a few big contracts. Especially if the company is already on the rocks financially and one large contract can spell the difference between survival and disaster, management may be driven to unusual lengths. And the pressure gets even stronger in recessions—when business is bad and there is excess production capacity, firms will scramble desperately for sales to try to keep output levels up. Every little bit of business helps keep workers employed and profits from sinking quite as far, and the incentive to bribe is strong even after prices have been depressed by cut-throat competition.

Governmental regulation. Some industries are more subject to the whims of government bureaucrats than others. Industries that are closely regulated by government agencies abroad tend to be unusually subject to QP pressures. Take for example pharmaceuticals and health care products. So far virtually every major American firm in this industry has disclosed overseas payoffs, including such household names as American Cyanamid, Bristol-Myers, Johnson & Johnson, Pfizer, Revlon, and Upjohn. Payments in most cases have been made to secure registrations for new products, authorizations for price increases, import permits, and tax settlements.[78]

Other industries are equally dependent on governmental sanctions and services. Oil companies, for example, are vulnerable to unfavorable governmental policies that include nationalization and expropriation, award or revocation of drilling concessions, and tax changes. So it is not hard to understand why they resorted to QPs to obtain less unfavorable treatment in Libya, Bolivia, Ecuador, Venezuela, and elsewhere. Other big QP spenders in regulated industries can be found among tobacco firms—R. J. Reynolds, Philip Morris, Liggett, Lorillard, and others.[79] Perhaps the beverage industry can also be included. Pepisco disclosed $1.7 million in QPs over a five year period, while Coca-Cola reported a total of $300,000 in October 1976, which doubled to $600,000 in December of that year, and doubled again to $1.3 million in April 1977.[80]

Payoff-Prone Firms

Roderick Hills, former chairman of the SEC, pointed out that ". . . we find in every industry where bribes have been revealed that companies of equal size are proclaiming that they see no need to engage in such practices."[81] Why are some firms clearly more resistant to QPs than others, even within the same industry?

Competitive strength. Eric Hoffer once said "power corrupts the few, while weakness corrupts the many."[82] And so it is with QPs. MNEs having clearly superior technology and strong market position will usually find it less necessary. to engage in QP behavior than their less fortunate competitors. IBM, for example, has the luxury of being able to say "no" to extortionate demands of government officials. Yet in the same sector Burroughs, Control Data, Honeywell, Memorex, NCR, SCM, Sperry and Xerox, according to QP disclosures, have not been nearly so fortunate.[83]

Exclusive product technologies, unique engineering capabilities, market dominance, high visibility, and the ready access to customers and supplies are all sources of power that enable a firm to avoid QP pressures. Without them, it will be hard pressed to adopt a bold moral stance, and tempted or pressured to compete on grounds other than price, quality, and service. Especially the lack of clear *product* superiority can drive a firm to great lengths in efforts to influence the buyer's ultimate choice.

Inadequate internal control. A critical factor explaining the tendency for individual firms to engage in QPs seems to be the degree of control exercised by corporate headquarters over the behavior of its foreign affiliates. A large percentage of all QPs revealed involve cases where the parent firm either could not or chose not to exercise legitimate control or effective influence over its foreign units. Tight managerial control and oversight are easiest when affiliates abroad are wholly-owned subsidiaries—again IBM is probably the best example. When foreign affiliates are a potpourri of distributors, dealers, suppliers, subcontractors, licensees, agents, consultants, and joint ventures, headquarters control becomes difficult or impossible.

Paul Orrefice, former President of Dow Chemical's domestic operations, said in August of 1975 that he was "100 percent sure no one in Dow has made one payment. . . . I would fire anyone who did."[84] Dow steadfastly maintained a posture of uninvolvement for many months until, lo and behold, in March of 1977 Dow disclosed that it had made QPs totaling more than $3 million during the period January 1, 1970 to June 30, 1976. Why the embarrassing contradiction? Dow's degree of control seems to have been a bit flabby. Whereas total QPs made by the parent itself and its *wholly-owned* subsidiaries amounted to barely $200,000 over the period, the remaining $2.9 million were made by partially-owned foreign affiliates. Dow's QPs went for all of the usual things.[85] Yet sales of the subsidiaries involved in the QPs were only $27 million over the five and a half year period out of more than $22 billion in Dow's consolidated sales during that time—a 10.7% QP-to-sales ratio for the partially-owned subsidiaries versus .009% for the firm as a whole.[86]

Many other MNEs have suffered from limited control, especially where foreign sales agents are concerned. When asked about questionable commissions of more than $70 million in connection with aircraft sales, Mr. J. E. Prince, Senior Vice President and Secretary of Boeing, proclaimed: "Boeing cannot police the morality of the foreign businessmen or officials whom it hires as consultants or representatives. They're independent contractors, and we don't stick our noses into what they do."[87] The audit committee of General Telephone and Electronics attributed much of the responsibility for the firm's $2.2 million in QPs over a five year period to the relative autonomy of GTE International (a subsidiary), failure of its senior management officials to comprehend the foreign and domestic legal problems created by payoffs, and failure to bring them to the parent company's attention.[88] Exxon has placed much of the blame for its Italian fiasco on the frustration and circumvention of the system of internal control used in Italy prior to 1972—misguided trust had been placed in Esso Italiana's Managing Director who, on his own signature, had wide banking and guarantee authority. He was able to make millions in dubious payments and still keep them hidden from corporate and external auditors.[89]

In general, then, managerial control and oversight in MNEs may be better both if foreign affiliates are wholly-owned and their top management is staffed largely by citizens of the firm's home country. Paradoxically, on both issues MNEs are under heavy pressure to move the other way—to reduce the proportion of foreign ownership and to make more top management jobs available to nationals of the host country.

Management amorality. Views on business morality seem to differ widely among individuals in senior management slots, and this inevitably affects the firms they lead. Some have consistently thrown off the ubiquitous pressures and temptations to make QPs. Even without superior technology or strong market positions, some MNE executives have simply refused to engage in QPs of any sort whatever. They have sometimes paid a price, but consider the cost worthwhile.

Senior MNE management sets the moral tone that permeates the entire "culture" of the organization. Clearly, top executives of some MNEs have focused almost exclusively on the "bottom line," without worrying very much about how results are achieved and without exhibiting any deep-seated, consistent and long-term commitment to ethical business practice. In 1975 a study by the Conference Board found that 75% of the MNEs it surveyed did not have a written policy statement or even guidelines covering QPs abroad.[90] Top management failed to communicate a moral tone or clear, specific policy, whether formal or informal, to company employees worldwide.

Some top executives in effect allowed bribery to become a way of life in their companies. Senior managers countenanced, authorized, or actively participated in QPs at Gulf Oil, ITT, Northrop, 3M, United Brands, Continental Oil, General Tire & Rubber, American Ship Building, Avis, Textron, Firestone, and others.[91] Top-level management involvement and complicity in QPs affect the ethical climate within an organization like nothing else. After examining Senate testimony regarding Lockheed's foreign bribes, journalist Anthony Sampson concluded that, to most of the firm's executives, "Lockheed was Haughton. It was Haughton who inspired Lockheed men to go abroad to sell their planes with singleminded determination. And it was his drive and impatience that pressed them to use whatever hardselling methods they could employ, including bribery."[92] If Lockheed was Haughton, then Citicorp projects the character of Walter Wriston and ITT of Harold Geneen, and the critical importance of moral leadership in such strongly-led firms becomes clear.

Multinationality. A final company attribute that ought to be considered is the very fact of multinationality itself. Multinational firms, as compared to local firms, seem inherently more susceptible to QPs. Individual bribes are infinitesimal in relation to the firm's overall revenues, costs, and financial resources. MNEs also have unusual opportunities to engage in "off-the-books" and slush-fund financing, and the foreign manager can sometimes escape prosecution in the host country if he is exposed.

For the payoff recipient as well, MNEs have some distinct advantages. They may already be politically vulnerable in the host country, or their global logistical supply network may be very sensitive to disruptions in any one country. So serious losses due to strikes may be avoided by payoffs to local labor leaders or government officials—this has reportedly happened frequently in Southern Europe. Being heavily involved in international trade and payments, MNEs are sensitive to administrative obstacles that can be thrown up as well.

Particularly in developing nations, MNEs are viewed as having a greater ability to pay than local firms and—often most important—access to hard currencies that can be made available outside the country. Major General Ibnu Sutowo, former president (since arrested) of the Indonesian oil company Pertamina utilized this logic in part to shake down dozens of American, European, and Japanese MNEs for $1.11 million to set up his Ramayana restaurant in midtown Manhattan.[93] The distinctive options, risks, and strengths inherent in multinational operations have played a definite role in the QP process.

The Facilitators

The "Gnomes of Zürich" are important midwives of QPs. Secret bank accounts in Switzerland and elsewhere have figured prominently in QP confessions to the SEC, either as havens for slush funds, temporary funnels, money laundries, or final payoff repositories. The SEC charged in May 1977, for example, that Occidental Petroleum had set up two secret companies in Europe and funneled their profits into clandestine Swiss accounts and secret cash kitties for illegal campaign contributions.[94] Bank secrecy in a few nations has greatly facilitated the QP process throughout much of the world, especially in the developing countries. The "gnomes" have made it easy for bribees to avoid taxes and exchange restrictions on payoffs, possible criminal sanctions, and adverse public reaction, as well as establishment of nest eggs. Bribers have also benefited, since bank secrecy laws abroad usually make it almost impossible for agencies such as the SEC or IRS to uncover QPs, or to obtain a reliable accounting for relevant disbursements and receipts.

In addition to numbered overseas accounts, MNEs have also utilized dummy subsidiaries in tax havens and countries with lax regulatory systems to expedite QPs. Gulf Oil, for example, set up the Bahamas Exploration Co. Ltd. in Nassau in order to "launder" slush funds and pass them along to politicians.[95] Avis Inc., under SEC pressure, disclosed that it paid a check for $470,958 on February 3, 1975 to a short-lived "shell" company called Arbourage Financial Consultants in the tax haven of Jersey in the Channel Islands off the coast of France. A few days after the check was written, Italy reinterpreted its Industrial Credit Plan to allow Avis to take a series of tax deductions retroactive to 1968, and the company salvaged a bad financial year with a major windfall. An Italian tax adviser had negotiated, on behalf of Avis, approximately nine months with the Italian government to obtain the settlement.[96] The point here, however, is that nations which fly flags of corporate and financial convenience do serve as important facilitators in the QP process.

WHAT'S BEEN DONE ABOUT QPS?

It is hard to disagree with former President Ford, who concluded from the facts at hand in 1976 that it is extraordinarily difficult to determine where "true justice lies in this matter," and so "the issue may never be resolved to everyone's satisfaction."[97] Should the United States try to reform the world by trying to impose its law on other nations through MNEs? What kinds of payments are we going to consider acceptable and unacceptable? How much disclosure should our MNEs be forced to make? Will other nations go along and, if not, what competitive damage will we suffer? To what extent can we leave MNEs to police themselves? Can anything be done to narrow the profitable role of the third-country "gnomes" in QPs? Most important, what can be done to alleviate the kinds of market failures that give rise to QPs in the first place? These are the questions which have dominated the continuing debate.

The extensive laundry list of factors affecting QPs tells us that there are many ways in which the basic incentives that underlie payoffs could be restructured. Three general approaches stand out: (1) reduce the strength of motives, (2) increase the power of obstacles, and (3) eliminate facilitative resources that can be employed to overcome these obstacles. Any of these will change prospective costs and benefits facing those involved in QPs.

Setting the Standards for Policy

What rules of thumb suggest themselves in trying to identify equity and efficiency characteristics of different attempts to come to grips with this issue? Any potentially useful approach should be devised and enforced with care and precision, and must clearly discriminate between proper and improper behavior. Legitimate and socially useful business practices ought not to be inhibited. In making these distinctions the policy should be flexible so as to accommodate both unique circumstances in the short term and changing conditions in the long term.

Policies should be realistic in their assumptions. For instance, penny-ante grease is probably ineradicable. Attention should focus instead on curbing the most egregious kinds of QPs like major bribery and sordid extortion. Since unenforced or unenforceable laws create little more than disrespect, we ought to accept the real limitations of national sovereignty and corporate control. Much QP behavior is neither under complete control of the firm itself nor realistically subject to United States law, and overzealous approaches that attempt to reform mankind are doomed to failure.

We should also try to promote an equitable shouldering of the burdens of reform. The search for remedies should not focus exclusively on givers of QPs and ignore recipients, on American firms and ignore foreign-based enterprises, on MNEs and ignore smaller national enterprises, or on those which voluntarily disclose and ignore those remaining silent. And QP remedies should be credible enough to bolster public confidence in the integrity of corporate management in business as an institution.

Utlimately, though, establishing new obstacles or eliminating facilitative resources can never be much more than plugging holes in the dike. Permanent solutions must go to the heart of the matter—improving the ability of the market to do its job, using devices such as mandatory open competitive bidding on government contracts. Some obstacles to market efficiency (like language or cultural differences) can never be eliminated, and so the temptation to use this as an excuse to exploit monopoly positions by middlemen will always exist. Some obstacles, like foreign exchange restrictions, may be viewed as socially and economically necessary, and QPs that undermine them should rightly be attacked head-on. But aside from these exceptions we find it hard to think of cases where really solving the payoff dilemma does not depend on removing the underlying incentives related to market failures.

We can use these criteria to evaluate eight very different approaches that have been tried or proposed.

Forgive and Forget

The simplest approach advocated has been to do nothing. The logic here is that QPs have been such an entrenched part of international business, it is naïve to expect any real improvement in corporate or official behavior. Others have argued that the emotional storm of publicity and commotion of the mid-1970s has already helped to curb the most blatant abuses. Furthermore, the London *Economist* says, "the West has no overwhelming reason, of duty or self-interest, to play policeman for those who will not act as policemen for themselves."[98]

Who has wanted to forgive or forget? The large fraternity of corrupt public officials has of course seen anxious to get back to "business as usual." Yet perhaps the most dramatic proponents of this approach have been the denizens of Wall Street. The stockholding public and institutional investors have clearly been indifferent to the corporate QP disclosures. An SEC-sponsored statistical study of trading in the common shares of 75 companies right after such disclosures detected only faint signs of market reaction—a virtually imperceptible "blip" in stock price movements.[99] Most shareholders seem to have been bored by the whole affair, having overwhelmingly rejected proposals to guide management in this area in one company after another. But if shareholders have not been inclined to hold management accountable, many other groups have. What, then, have been the other options?

Host Country Reform

An approach widely pushed by the legal profession and multinational business executives has been to call for the comprehensive enactment in all countries of stringent and perhaps even uniform laws governing commercial and political corruption.[100] This approach would of course avoid adverse competitive consequences of unilateral action on the part of the United States. Unfortunately, we have seen precious little inclination to enforce existing laws on bribery in those countries where most of it has taken place, or to enact new laws. Lucrative patterns of corruption—often practiced for centuries—generate their own political constituencies and simply will not evaporate quickly.

Nonetheless, some progress has been made. Italy in 1974 passed a law on political contributions granting public subsidies of about $75 million per year to all political parties.[101] Brazilian legislators recommended drawing up a code of ethics for MNEs "so as to establish the rules of the game."[102] Two senior officials of the Swiss National Bank dropped a bombshell by recommending that anonymous accounts be abolished—its Vice President, Leo Schurmann, said numbered accounts were a "national embarrassment" and ought to be done away with.[103] Crown Prince Fahd of Saudi Arabia affirmed his government's determination to enforce a new regulation banning commissions, kickbacks, and payoffs by foreign weapons suppliers.[104] Iran's former Prime Minister Amir Abbas Hoveyda (who was executed after the Shah was ousted) denounced unethical foreign companies for exporting a "lack of morality" to Iran—a bit like carrying coals to Newcastle.[105] Despite the hypocrisy, Iran under the Shah did force Northrop and Grumman to atone for past questionable payments by paying stiff penalties.[106] A number of nations, including Egypt, Syria and Italy, have sentenced and jailed or even executed QP recipients.

While gradual and incremental progress in attacking corruption in host countries is welcome, more rapid alleviation of the problem has depended on actions in the MNEs' home countries.

Home Country Sunshine

Almost every other speech by SEC officials on the subject of QPs has included the famous maxim of Supreme Court Justice Louis D. Brandeis: "Publicity is justly commendable as a remedy for social and industrial disease. Sunlight is said to be the best disinfectant; electric light the most efficient policeman.[107] The SEC sold itself on the "prophylactic effects" of disclosure. In its view, business does not enjoy bribery and would be happy to have a defense against the arm-twisters of the world. And so disclosure would serve as a strong inhibitor to donor and recipient alike. The SEC wanted to see management forced to expose payoffs and then face whatever stockholder suits, public embarrassment, and governmental penalties followed, including prosecution of both United States firms and payoff recipients by foreign governments under their own laws. In April 1977 the SEC announced its intention to make public details on QPs and in May actually did so on 10 cases it had marked closed.[108]

Other sunshine advocates have been active as well. President Ford's Task Force on Questionable Corporate Payments Abroad, headed by Elliott Richardson, proposed more formal disclosure requirements.[109] So did Senator Frank Church in his proposed "Multinational Business Enterprise Information Act of 1976." The Internal Revenue Service posed its famous "Eleven Questions" concerning illegal activities to key executives of 1800 firms and required them to answer under penalty of perjury.[110] The "International Security Assistance and Arms Export Control Act of 1976" required reporting of political contributions and agents fees made or offered to secure the sale of defense-related materiel or services abroad—the Office of Munitions Control in the State Department issued detailed regulations to implement this statute. The Department of Defense went in for increased QP disclosure in cases where it plays the middleman role in arms sales.

Still, disclosure could not carry the whole burden. Theodore Sorensen, testifying on behalf of the criminalization approach, may have put it a bit strongly when he called the disclosure approach "a pitifully pallid response to a major moral crisis."[111] Sunshine does raise many technical and administrative questions. There is still no consensus on what constitutes "materiality," how much detail ought to be disclosed, or what should be done after disclosures. Henry Kissinger and others have argued that disclosure could jeopardize United States relations with its allies.[112] It could also cause severe harm to the innocent if inaccurate or premature. Certainly no other government has moved, or is so inclined, to expose the QP practices of its own firms. This bodes ill for American business abroad—disclosure may have already scared more potential customers into the arms of discreet foreign competitors than just about anything else.

Home Country Oversight

Some proposed that the QP problem could be adequately managed within the existing framework of United States law if American regulatory agencies took a more activist approach to enforcement. Others claimed that this would only work with a little help from friends such as boards of directors, auditors, and lawyers.

Ralph Nader proposed federal chartering of all corporations with $250 million or more in annual sales. He would restructure corporate management by removing all operating executives from corporate boards and replacing them with independent directors having their own staff and acting as internal watchdogs to prevent violations of law or disloyalty to shareholders. Others, such as management consultant Peter Drucker, have also called for a restructuring of the corporate director's role.[113] Stanley Sporkin, the aggressive chief of the SEC's Enforcement Division, declared that corporations should have their own "inspectors general" to monitor business ethics. He would like to see such "business practices officers" among corporate outside directors charged with blowing the whistle.[114]

Senator Lee Metcalf (D-Montana) focused specifically on the role of external auditors. An arbitrary and rather sloppy report produced by his staff concluded that the big accounting firms should come under stronger oversight by Congress to prevent conflict of interests.[115] Metcalf suggested that Congress consider a proposal that would require all companies to rotate their external auditors at least once every three years. And the Commission on Auditors' Responsibilities appointed several years ago by the American Institute of Certified Public Accounts, headed by Manuel F. Cohen (former chairman of the SEC) in March 1977 called for an increased role for auditors in detecting illegal and questionable acts on the part of their clients—including forty different recommendations for changing auditing and reporting procedures.[116]

In our view, boards that are more alert and auditors that are more independent have already made contributions to the QP problem, especially in conjunction with more vigorous regulatory enforcement. But there are still some important cost and benefit questions. Costs could could be astronomical if for example auditors were forced to explore every nook and cranny of their clients' businesses to try to catch all forms of management misconduct, all of it naturally well-hidden. Forced rotation of auditors would also entail drawbacks—"musical chairs" would not be conducive to the accumulation of knowledge about clients needed by CPAs to perform effective audits. And unless auditors and board members get their fees from sources other than the firm they are supposed to be watching, some suspicion of conflict of interest will always remain.

Home Country Criminalization

Senator William Proxmire sponsored a bill outlawing foreign bribes by American corporations and calling for fines up to $500,000 for each violation. After failing to achieve House passage of his bill in 1976 before the end of the 94th Congress, Proxmire reintroduced his "Foreign Corrupt Practices Act" (S.305) in January of 1977.[117] The bill was intended to make it a crime to corruptly offer or pay money to a foreign government official, politician, or agent to obtain or retain business for the corporation or to influence legislation or regulations of the government. It also was designed to make it illegal for a company to falsify its records to conceal such payments or to knowingly deceive auditors. And it provided that individual violators, such as corporate executives or directors, could be fined up to $10,000 and be jailed for up to five years. A similar, but narrower, "criminal penalties" bill (H.R. 3815) was introduced by Representative Eckhart in the House of Representatives in late February 1977 and referred to the Committee on Interstate and Foreign Commerce. This proposed "Unlawful Corporate Payments Act of 1977" was to prohibit corporations from using the means of interstate commerce to make any payment designed to influence corruptly a foreign official, political party, or candidate. Violators would be fined up to $1 million.[118]

The Carter Administration strongly supported this legislation and took an active role in raising the maximum fine for a corporation found guilty of overseas bribery from $10,000 to $500,000 in the Senate bill. Former Treasury Secretary Michael Blumenthal, perhaps leaning on his experience as head of the Bendix Corporation, testified that "paying bribes—apart from being morally repugnant and illegal in most countries—is simply not necessary for the successful conduct of business here or overseas." Because the business community had failed to come up with its own code of ethics against QPs, according to Blumenthal, the Carter Administration believed "strong government action in the form of further legislation" was needed.[119]

The Foreign Corrupt Practices Act (FCPA) was signed into law by President Carter on December 20, 1977, having been approved by a *unanimous* vote of both the House and Senate.[120] In its final version, it provides for fines of up to $1 million for firms found guilty of making payments to government officials or political organizations abroad for purposes of influencing government decisions. Executives and directors of such firms who are involved in or condone such activity face five years in prison and fines of up to $10,000 on each count. The law also prohibits falsifying corporate accounts in order to conceal questionable payments abroad, so that secret slush funds and large "miscellaneous" expense items will be more difficult to employ in supporting questionable payments. Firms are required to maintain detailed books and records and reliable systems of internal controls. Grease payments are basically exempt, although the dividing line between grease and other QPs remains unclear.

Outside the Administration, SEC, and the Congress, the criminalization approach has had few friends. Many have argued persuasively that this approach involves a dubious extension of American law to sovereign foreign countries, and that it (a) presents extraordinarily difficult enforcement problems, (b) fails to deal with those who solicit bribes, (c) fails to distinguish between lesser and greater bribes, (d) may seriously harm American foreign policy interests, (e) will turn the diplomatic corps into a kind of police force imposing United States standards on other countries, and (f) will make it harder for American firms to compete effectively with less scrupulous foreign firms—especially since no other government except Canada has chosen to follow the American lead.

Naturally, MNE executives have not been very happy about the criminalization approach either. One told *Business International:* "We are going after a flea with an elephant gun."[121] Charles Bowen, former Chairman of Booz Allen and Hamilton (a leading management consulting firm) reportedly characterized its proponents as "a bunch of pipsqueak moralists running around trying to apply U.S. puritanical standards to other countries."[122]

Enforcement problems abound. The FCPA says that it is illegal for American firms to "corruptly" make QPs abroad. This, like premeditation in murder, requires conviction on the basis of intent. Enforcement officials claim the Administration is fully prepared to extradite American executives to foreign countries to face charges of bribery, although how this will work when the countries demanding extradition have questionable legal systems and perhaps ulterior motives remains to be seen. And how are United States executives and directors charged with QPs at home or abroad to receive due process if they cannot deliver foreign witnesses in their own defense? The whole question of extraterritoriality in applying the law to foreign affiliates of United States-based MNEs remains unresolved.

While the FCPA has evidently had a salutary effect on American MNEs' questionable payments, its direction has sometimes varied from what was intended. Some United States firms have lost business to Japanese and European enterprises along the lines suggested earlier. Others have switched from being prime contractors to being subcontractors to firms headquartered in other countries to avoid QP involvement. Some have shifted production to foreign plants instead of exporting from the United States. Still others have convinced their overseas agents to act as principals and buy for their own account, reselling on the local market and shielding their American suppliers from involvement.

Home country criminalization has, however, provided ersatz morality, and removed a certain amount of ambiguity. It has also provided a strong legal basis for independent auditors, directors, and lawyers, as well as federal authorities, to insist on closer investigation of suspicious cases. And it has perhaps stiffened the resistance of American firms to extortionate demands for payoffs abroad. Observes economic journalist Leonard Silk, "criminalization, reinforced by mutual assistance agreements . . . [goes] to the heart of the problem of foreign bribery, not just to its periphery."[123] We doubt it. It has done nothing about the underlying incentives found in host nations to engage in QPs—it failed to recognize the complexity of the issue, and so its costs may well outweigh its benefits. A White House task force set up to study a range of export "disincentives," in fact, began a drive in 1979 to weaken or at least clarify the FCPA, on the grounds that it was costing American exporters as much as $1 billion a year in lost business.[124]

Multilateral Regulation

The obvious limitations of unilateral home-country approaches to eliminating QPs have given rise to calls for international cooperation in dealing with corrupt practices. The leading proponent of this approach has been the U.S. Department of State, which was able to cajole the Organization for Economic Cooperation and Development into adopting the following clause in its 1976 voluntary code of conduct for MNEs (see Chapter 15). "Enterprises should not render—and they should not be solicited or expected to render—any bribe or other improper benefit, direct or indirect, to any public servant or holder of public office."[125] The State Department also proposed in March 1976 that a multilateral agreement be negotiated within the United Nations to deter and disclose corporate wrongdoing, and that a cooperative structure with foreign law enforcement agencies be established. The UN Economic and Social Council established an eighteen-nation "Intergovernmental Working Group on Corrupt Practices" to examine the question in August 1976.[126] The United States also raised the issue in General Agreement on Tariffs and Trade (GATT) in Geneva, proposing an accord covering "bribery, indirect payments, kickbacks, unethical political contributions, and other such similar disreputable activities."[127] The GATT delegates politely heard the American delegate out, and then promptly got back to other business.

Almost everyone likes the international approach. Mark B. Feldman, Deputy Legal Adviser of the Department of State, said at the first meeting of the UN group: "Our experience has brought the conviction that the illicit payments problem can only be solved by collective international action based on a multilateral treaty to be implemented by national legislation."[128] The Association of the Bar of the City of New York recommended that the United States continue diplomatic initiatives in the United Nations and schedule talks with major industrial countries in an effort to negotiate bilateral or multilateral agreements.[129] Ex-SEC Chairman Roderick Hills testified in March 1977 that the United States ought to seek treaties with Japan, West Germany, and other industrial nations imposing common disclosure requirements on MNEs—he argued that such treaties "could practically wipe out the temptation to substitute competitive bribery for fair competition."[130]

Some argued before passage of FCPA that the international approach in part represented only an excuse for delay and inaction. As it turns out, the American effort to export its campaign against business bribery hasn't found many buyers at the United Nation. *The Wall Street Journal* reported that ". . . some foreigners view it as a mixture of woolly-minded idealism and hard-headed Yankee guile," and "there are signs that the search for ways to eliminate payoff competition could become as frustrating as the search for new international rules to govern the use of the seas, which has produced many conferences but few agreements."[131]

The prospects for a tough United Nations treaty are indeed slim—as of late 1979 the treaty was languishing in an inactive committee of the United Nations with very little possibility for early agreement even on a working draft. If an agreement does emerge, it could not be ratified in less than two years. Besides being unenforceable, it is likely that any such code would be so watered down to gaining general acceptance that in the end it would be all but useless. QPs are a political bombshell everywhere and, with the exception of Canada and Sweden, most nations seem disposed to let the Americans alone run with this particular hot potato.

Collective Self-Regulation

To steal some of the thunder from unilateral, bilateral, or multilateral governmental approaches to QPs, the Paris-headquartered International Chamber of Commerce prepared a self-regulatory international code of conduct to combat corrupt practices. In December 1975 the ICC established a distinguished *ad hoc* "Commission on Ethical Practices," headed by Lord Shawcross of the United Kingdom, to come up with a draft code. This code of "Ethical Practices in Commercial Transactions," adopted in November 1977, covers the gamut of corrupt payments, solicitation or acceptance of QPs, kickbacks, agents fees, political contributions, undisclosed transactions, secret accounts, restraints of trade, cooked books, financial statements and audits, conflicts of interest, commercial contracts, and company guidelines.[132] To quote from Article 2: "No enterprise may, directly or indirectly, offer or give a bribe in order to obtain or retain business, and any demand for such a bribe must be rejected." Another Article established an ICC Panel to interpret and oversee the guidelines, provide interpretation and clarifications, and consider alleged infringements of the Rules of Conduct.[133]

Skeptics, of course, have viewed such business codes as "prescriptions for doing nothing," and it is indeed hard to see how the ICC code could acquire teeth other than moral suasion. Executives in countries like France, who believe that QPs will remain a fact of life, are not likely to adhere very closely no matter what the code says. On the other hand, various American executives have told us that they put little stock in codes other than the ones companies formulate for themselves. The *Economist*, however, commented that "international agreement among businessmen is trebly desirable: first, because harmonization, regulated or not, is a significant part of any attempt to slow the rat race; second, because it would show a rightly skeptical world that business is at least trying; and third, because, albeit incompletely, it would work."[134]

Individual Self-Regulation

The last approach to the QP problem has been self-regulation by corporate management. Various techniques are available for internal cleansing, and many have already been applied in scores of MNEs. Some have established new codes of conduct or reaffirmed old ones that typically prohibit the use of company funds for political or illegal purposes. Others have improved internal reporting systems and controls. Exxon, for example, instituted uniform financial controls throughout the company and strengthened communications among its auditors.[135] A number of MNEs have established special audit committees composed of outside directors. Others have adopted stringent new policies governing the solicitation, use, and payment of international agents and consultants. A few have reorganized their operations to gain control. Lockheed announced, for example, that all of its international marketing activities, including the operations of the company's overseas offices, would be directed from the home office. Still other companies, such as Pitney Bowes, have demanded that key executives sign annual pledges that they have personally complied with their companies' ethical policies, and that to their knowledge all employees reporting to them have done likewise.

It is still too early to tell whether MNEs can effectively police themselves. Many of the company codes we have examined seem too vague and too public relations-oriented to be credible. A code by itself means little. Managers' views on the extent to which social and ethical concerns should intrude into business decision-making differ enormously. Many still think QPs are a normal and necessary feature of doing business in various parts of the world. To quote Mr. Proxmire, "a part of the private sector is [and will continue to be] a house of marked cards, composed of Kings of corruption, Jacks of all illicit trades, and Aces of political influence." As long as the motivational forces underlying such behavior remains, so too will the group of managers whose only motto is "don't get caught." For them, self-regulation will never be a viable substitute for external, strictly-enforced constraints. But in the end, we are forced to agree with Marcus Aurelius' sentiment that "a man should be upright; not be kept upright." Ultimately a major share of responsibility for reform does indeed fall on the business community itself. We see a genuine and strong willingness on the part of many MNEs to clean up their act, for bribery is indeed costly and corrupting. Corporate self-regulation—with plenty of external prodding—is perhaps the most practical and effective solution. It is not so much a matter of rules or procedures. Rather, in the words of the McCloy Committee which investigated the Gulf Oil case, it is "the tone and purpose given to the company by its top management."[136]

QPs AND CONFLICT MANAGEMENT

Nothing about QPs is simple or straightforward—neither the problem itself nor its prospective solution. The QP experience during the 1970s, however, does lend itself to some general observations regarding the ways in which MNEs have attempted to manage this breed of conflict. The experience dramatically reveals the necessity of sequentially and simultaneously utilizing different modes of handling conflict over time at home and abroad. This is best seen if we break the decade into three periods: the "undercover" period of 1970–1974, the "issue explosion" period of 1975–1977, and the "post–FCPA" period of 1978 onward. What has been witnessed, in large measure, is a massive transformation of MNE conflict management behavior from *host country accommodation* and *home country avoidance* during the early 1970s to *host country competition* and *home country accommodation* during the late 1970s. Let us examine this realignment in a bit more detail, keeping in mind that our discussion is highly generalized.

During the "undercover" period of 1970–1974, some MNEs having sufficient technical or other leverage, like IBM, were able to adopt successful *competitive* stances in regard to host country QP demands. Others with abundant market opportunities at their disposal or with especially strong-willed and moral top managements were able to forego business in vexing QP environments. Both sets of MNEs had no need to undertake major QPs and could assume a "take it or leave it" attitude with regard to host nation demanders of such payments. But most American MNEs, as the hundreds of corporate QP disclosures indicate, chose to simply do "as the Romans" during this early part of the decade, readily *accommodating* to extortion demands or triggering illicit behavior through bribes or secret political contributions in countless host nations. The "motivators" were strong, the "barriers" weak, and "facilitators" prolific. Where possible, of course, many MNEs attempted to bargain down outrageous QP demands, thus *compromising* with the host country QP recipients.

These behaviors in the host nations were simultaneously matched by considerable *avoidance* and some *collaboration* on the part of the MNEs back home. Tax authorities, outside auditors, shareholders, boards of directors, and the like were kept in the dark about the foreign QPs by means of a wide range of accounting ruses, including inflated expense accounts, off-the-balance-sheet slush funds, dummy subsidiaries in tax havens, secret bank accounts, money laundries, and so on. Conflicts were simply *avoided* by falsifying records and bypassing financial accountability systems. Much evidence has also emerged of home government complicity in many of the foreign payments in the early 1970s. The United States government often knowingly tolerated massive payments, viewing them as policy assets.[137] Some parts of the government, such as the Central Intelligence Agency, reportedly even encouraged such payments at times as a way of making, or helping, foreign friends of the United States. The coincidence of interests thus translated into occasional *collaboration* at home.

The foreign QP issue, as an outgrowth of the Watergate affair and associated SEC investigations of domestic political payments, exploded in 1975 and proceeded to attract headline attention well through 1977. Branches of the American government adopted, retrospectively of course, a high moral tone about the covert payoffs. Some classic *competitive* clashes ensued, such as between the Senate Subcommittee on Multinational Corporations and Gulf Oil, Northrop, Exxon, Mobil, and Lockheed. The Justice Department, SEC, and Internal Revenue Service unleashed a storm with either joint or rival investigatory or injunctive actions. Some American MNEs resisted, but most chose paths of *accommodation* and *compromise* in regard to the home government crackdown—there was, after all, safety in numbers in the admission of "sins." In exchange for a vague promise that participation would diminish the possibility of SEC action and an understanding that disclosures could withhold truly sensitive details, most American MNEs decided to cooperate with the SEC's "voluntary disclosure program." This *compromise* required each participating firm to appoint a special review committee of nonmanagement directors, to allow that committee (assisted by independent counsel and public accountants) to conduct a full investigation and report back to the full board of directors, to have the full board then issue appropriate corporate policies to terminate any illegal or questionable payments or accounting practices uncovered, and to file a final report on the entire matter with the SEC.

While the MNEs were busy *compromising* or *accommodating* to demands for disclosure and internal reform at home, they reportedly began to move away from the traditional *accommodation* approach overseas. Questionable practices in foreign operations were reassessed, QP plans were discovered and scotched, and controls or codes of conduct began to be promulgated for foreign subsidiary managements. The years 1975–1977 marked a difficult period of adjustment, involving movement towards QP conflict-handling modes of *avoidance* and *competition* on the part of MNEs in many host nations.

The Foreign Corrupt Practices Act, with its harsh penalties and perplexing pitfalls and loopholes, was signed into law in December 1977.[138] The intent of the new law was, of course, to force American MNEs into employing more uncooperative (*competing* and *avoiding*) modes of managing QP conflicts in foreign lands. The FCPA exempted, however, "grease" or accommodation payments made solely to expedite nondiscretionary official actions overseas, which naturally continue. To be sure, some United States-based MNEs have also continued to make payments, illegal under the FCPA, to foreign government officials to assist in obtaining or retaining business—particularly those confronted by English, French, German and Japanese companies unencumbered by extensions of home country morality—but are now using more ingenious or sophisticated methods such as changing QP distribution channels and using third parties to make the payments, so that the MNE's own books remain clean.[139] Other MNEs have pulled out of hazardous QP situations. AMF, for example, sold its Italian subsidiary Sasib, a manufacturer of cigarette machinery whose customers were mainly state-owned tobacco monopolies, at a bargain-basement price to a local Italian firm. As one reporter noted: ". . . When Sasib was no longer able to make payoffs—a fact of life . . . in the overseas tobacco world—the business lost its viability and AMF was forced to sell.[140] Other MNEs have pulled out of particularly sensitive areas such as Nigeria, Libya, Indonesia and South Korea.[141] But the bulk of American MNEs have reportedly halted making the kinds of QPs illegal under FCPA, at times with painful results. Abbott Laboratories lost a $2.5 million infant formula contract in a North African nation to a Dutch company when a payment request was refused.[142] And Dow and Union Carbide passed up a potential billion dollar petrochemical complex in the Philippines because a confidant of President Ferdinand Marcos had demanded a questionable fee of $3 million. When Dow kicked up a fuss, the government simply axed the project.[143] The firms reportedly hit hardest by the constraints imposed by FCPA have been the large international construction firms that deal mainly with foreign governments or government-run firms. Many such construction MNEs reported major losses attributable to the FCPA in 1979.[144] But in other industries, the general impression is that the competitive losses experienced in 1978–1979 were not as substantial as had been expected. The implication, therefore, is that much of the bribery of the early and mid-1970s may perhaps not have been necessary and that price, product quality, service, and reputation remain the fundamental keys to success in international business.

Back home, the post-FCPA period saw a reservoir of *competitive* struggles, with a task force of Justice Department and SEC lawyers probing the records of more than 50 firms in 1978–1979 for possible fraud charges and for MNEs still refusing to comply with SEC requirements to report QPs. The most heated battles during this period involved attempts on the part of such MNEs as ITT, Occidental Petroleum, Lockheed, Boeing, Textron and Dresser Industries to block the SEC from disclosing subpoenaed foreign payments information. ITT, for example, took its case all the way to the Supreme Court, claiming that disclosure of details of its $9 million in QPs could prompt foreign governments to take over the subsidiaries in question.[145] On another competitive front, many American firms began a behind-the-scenes lobbying campaign to press the Justice Department into issuing guidelines to clear up FCPA's "blatant ambiguities." The *compromise* mode was also put to use, with plea bargaining settlements involving the payment of fines reached between government agencies and firms such as Control Data, Gulf Oil, J. Ray McDermott, United Brands, Westinghouse, Lockheed, Tenneco and Pepsico. Control Data, for example, pleaded guilty in 1978 to three criminal charges and was fined $1.38 million; but the plea agreement specified that no foreign countries or recipients of the QPs would be disclosed.[146] Boeing's settlement with the SEC on charges that it had made $52 million in QPs also left key details cloaked in secrecy.[147] The behavior of most American MNEs in the post-FCPA era, however, reflected considerable *accommodation* to home government demands, with most American executives apparently in agreement with the basic purpose of the act and prepared to live with it.[148]

10 *MARKETING CONFLICT*

Should a drug banned in the United States be sold by United States companies abroad? Should the same marketing strategies and tactics that have proved successful in Western Europe, Japan, or North America be employed in developing countries? Are multinationals responsible for uncontrolled sales of prescription drugs in host countries, for the tendency of pharmacists to play doctor, or for people's habits of self-medication? What is the "appropriate" price of high-technology products in host countries when the manufacturing cost may only be a small fraction of that price? How far does the manufacturer's liability and accountability extend for the safety and effectiveness of his products, often used and misused under widely differing circumstances? These are typical of the kinds of questions that face marketers in a multinational environment where the rules of the game in sensitive areas like pricing and distribution, advertising and promotion, and product quality and safety are often ambiguous, contradictory, or rapidly-changing, and sometimes absent altogether.

To illustrate the full range of conflicts, perhaps no other industry has been subject to more criticism on the grounds of multinational marketing practices than the drug business. This runs the gamut from (a) lack of competition, with one-third of the world market served by the 10 largest drug firms; (b) excessive marketing expenditures, often 20% of sales, estimated in the United Kingdom alone to be twice the cost of training each physician; (c) excessive promotion and reliance on brand names, when generic equivalents may be far cheaper; and (d) safety issues and adequacy of testing; to (e) redundant drugs that are ineffective or whose therapeutic effects cannot be proved; (f) excessive promotion, oversubscription, and overreliance on drugs; (g) selling drugs in developing countries that are disallowed in industrialized nations; (h) excessive expenditures on "me too" drugs that simply copy competitors' products; and (i) drug overpricing, especially in poor countries.[1]

A 1975 Consumers Union report charged multinational drug companies with recommending drugs for much wider use in Latin America than is permitted in the United States, as well as incomplete or modified labeling, sales of drugs forbidden at home, recommending higher dosages than customary in the United States, and sales of drugs without prescription despite awareness of the fact by the companies.[2] In reply, the drug firms emphasize that they fully comply with labeling requirements in the countries in which the drugs are sold and that those requirements "may be more appropriate for those countries than standards established by the U.S. Food and Drug Administration. The practice of medicine in the United States is not necessarily regarded as the benchmark of medicine throughout the world, nor should it be. Product documentation will sometimes vary in individual countries to reflect local needs, economics, health conditions, and government regulations."[3]

In 1977, an estimated $7 billion in drugs were sold in the developing countries, adding up to 40% of their expenditures on health care. In 1978 the World

Health Organization (WHO) severely criticized the multinational drug companies for marketing pharmaceuticals in the developing world with little or no regard for needs, priorities, or abilities to pay of individual countries, with promotional activities artifically stimulating demand. WHO came up with a list of 209 generic drugs designed to meet the essential needs of most people in developing nations as a guide to governments in their planning. The move was strongly opposed by the International Federation of Pharmaceutical Manufacturers: "What the report disregards is the individuality of patients and pharmaceutical products. So-called similar drug products are often quite different in mode or speed of action, duration and speed of therapeutic activity, tolerability, side effects and other important respects."[4] Nevertheless, WHO maintained that the numbers and cost of drugs being marketed in developing countries are not proportionate to the resulting health-care gains. For example, an Indian government committee reported that 116 drugs would fulfill most of the country's health requirements, compared with 15,000 brands being marketed there.

A great deal of controversy has also developed in recent years in Brazil, whose over $1 billion annual drug sales make it the eighth largest pharmaceuticals consumer in the world. MNEs account for 80% of the total, with 14,700 brands of drugs being marketed. Aggressive marketing is alleged to cut seriously into household budgets, promote abuse of drugs, cause confusion among physicians, and encourage self-prescription based on formal promotion and hearsay. Many drugs are sold without prescription and people depend on advice from pharmacists. The government has neither the budget nor the skilled manpower to enforce drug laws, and a major share of the blame for these conditions is being placed on the multinational pharmaceutical firms. Indeed, recent testimony alleged that MNEs actually count on pharmacists to propagate drug sales. They are also alleged to promote drugs in Brazil that have been branded ineffective by the FDA in the United States.

According to WHO Director General Dr. Halfdan Mahler, "Products not meeting the quality requirements of the exporting country may be exported to developing countries that are not in a position to carry out quality control measures. While these practices may conform to legal requirements they are unethical and detrimental to health."[5] For their part, the drug companies contend that each country must make up its own mind as to the drugs it wants and needs, and establish regulatory machinery to enforce that position. Tropical diseases unknown in the United States, for example may well call for drugs for which there is no American market and hence no FDA approval.

In the Philippines, the Mead-Johnson subsidiary of Bristol-Myers has been alleged to corrupt the medical profession by inducing hospital administrators, pediatricians, and obstetricians to use its products exclusively. "In general, the allegations suggest a subversion of the medical profession's independence of judgment, grotesquely widening the rift between the rich and poor in the Philippines."[6]

In part because of such allegations, during the mid-1970s the drug industry in many developing countries came under increasingly tight control. In Mexico, for example, there were demands for creation of a state monopoly in the pharmaceuticals sector to take over from the foreign-owned drug firms. In Brazil there was growing pressure to foster a local industry to compete with multinationals through incentives and discriminatory treatment. Venezuela in 1975 instituted a "buy national" policy that gives preferences in government purchasing to drug firms that are at least 80% locally-owned. Argentina tightened controls on profit margins, royalties, product lines, imports, packaging, and advertising. Hong Kong, perhaps the last bastion of laissez-faire in the drug business, and Pakistan likewise tightened regulations substantially. Along with the emergence of such measures in developing nations, growing government restrictions were also forcing the pharmaceutical industry into a state of seige in developed countries, particularly in the EEC. One report explained growing public criticism and political pressure in Western Europe as follows: "If profit in any shape or form is already regarded with suspicion, criticism is bound to increase when the profit in question is made 'at the expense of the sick' and when, to cover the risks of research, it is also higher than the average in other industries."[7] Under heavy fire, drug companies from 14 European nations joined together in 1979 to form the European Pharmaceutical Manufacturers' Association in order to strengthen their lobbying efforts.

Whereas multinational marketing-related conflict in the drug industry is perhaps unusually intense, it is by no means an isolated case, as we shall see.

MULTINATIONAL MARKETING, CONSUMER INTERESTS, AND PUBLIC POLICY

Traditional views of marketing have focused on four so-called "controllable" variables—price, product, promotion, and distribution—emphasizing that the marketing function in corporations is simply to provide a product that is needed in the market at an acceptable price. With the aid of appropriate promotional devices such as advertising or personal selling, the product will presumably be purchased if it is conveniently available. In newer views of marketing, the focus has shifted from the product to the consumer and a direct appeal to the buyer's wants or desires. A typical definition of modern marketing is, "Those activities performed by individuals or organizations, either profit or non-profit, that enable, facilitate, or encourage exchange to the satisfaction of both parties."[8] Unfortunately, consumer satisfaction is a difficult concept to evaluate in a complex and dynamic environment, defying simple analysis. And so students of marketing have increasingly focused on six major variables: consumers, government, society, competition, science, and nature.[9] Each of these variables—called "uncontrollable" variables in terms of the traditional marketing function—poses new and often less manageable challenges to the marketer.

In the industrialized nations, the 1960s saw the birth of the so-called consumer movement, product technologies so sophisticated that their consequences are not always fully understood, changes in society's expectations, greater interaction between governments and the private sector, changes in the legal environment, and marketing on a global scale as corporations extended the sphere of their activities beyond national boundaries. A leading marketing theorist has proposed a "societal marketing concept" which attempts to incorporate the demands of the constantly changing external environment into the traditional concerns of marketing. It " . . . calls for a *customer orientation* backed by integrated marketing aimed at generating *customer satisfaction* and long-run *consumer welfare* as the key to attaining long-run profitable volume."[10] Yet terms such as "customer satisfaction" or "long-run consumer welfare" are not easily quantifiable or translatable into the language of the business world. And so " . . . the marketing concept is an idealistic policy statement for management, but relatively few companies are able—for whatever reason—to implement the concept and make it operational on a day-to-day basis."[11]

The problem of applying normative marketing theory to the actual marketing function of corporations continues to persist. The body of marketing theory has expanded rapidly, and includes such ideas as want-creation, de-marketing, and new concepts of accountability. Yet the marketer remains confronted with the task of selling in an uncertain external environment without many benchmarks to guide him:

> If an organization is to address fundamental issues instead of symptoms, it must identify and analyze them. Such a task is formidable. First, the basic issues are inherently difficult to understand. There is little established theory to guide the decision maker. Relevant empirical questions are usually unanswered. Issues tend to be dynamic and interrelated. The real problems are frequently not visible to the public. . . . The information systems of involved organizations are not oriented toward, or effective in, obtaining information that will enable such organizations to detect underlying social issues.[12]

Both marketing theory and marketing practice are thus confronted with the same challenges but have not yet managed to master them.

The problems marketers face in the domestic environment are greatly magnified as this reach extends into the global marketplace. One author has identified three types of marketing in the international environment: "international marketing (marketing across national boundaries); foreign marketing (marketing within foreign countries); and multinational marketing (coordinating marketing in multiple markets)."[13] Each of these will force the marketer to be concerned not only with the traditional marketing functions, but also to be "concerned with the question of how . . . international marketing operations can be designed to meet the needs and values of various stakeholders in countries with diverse sociocultural, economic, and political environments."[14] The marketer must adapt to an international environment in which "marketing is both a cause and effect of conditions within . . . the environment and culture."[15] Marketing is not a neutral activity. It informs, persuades, promotes, and induces change.

When marketers from industrialized nations turn to markets in developing countries the problems are not only different in degree but often in kind as well. Within the industrialized nations there at least exists a certain degree of commonality in the environment. In developing nations, the environment is often radically different, so that the marketer is sometimes unable to forecast the consequences of his actions. There is often a lack of reliable information. Regulatory processes may be nonexistent or unpredictable. Poverty and illiteracy are frequently present on a scale unknown to the industrialized nations. Confronted with this unfamiliar environment, the multinational marketer often appears to revert back to traditional marketing approaches—simply taking products that have been carefully designed to meet consumer needs and desires back home and marketing them as if they had been intended for developing-country markets all along. Rarely does one find situations in which a multinational corporation adapts its entire marketing strategy (including product development) to less developed countries, and the tendency to treat these countries as an extension of the industrialized marketplace creates very significant potential for conflict.

Besides the possibility, indeed likelihood, of marketing conflict facing multinationals in developing countries, two current trends are perhaps of equal importance. These are the rise of consumerism and the growing role of government regulation.

Consumerism

For the marketer, consumerism represents "a social movement seeking to augment the rights and power of buyers in relation to sellers."[16] According to Peter Drucker: "Consumerism means that the consumer looks upon the manufacturer as somebody who is interested, but who does not really know what the consumer's realities are."[17] And according to another observer, "Because of the lack of an overall philosophy and program of action, there is in a sense no real consumer movement. Consumerism is instead a conglomeration of separate groups each with its own particular concerns, which sometimes form temporary alliances on a particular issue."[18] But the somewhat confused state of the consumer movement does not mean that it is a temporary phenomenon. One authority compares the present consumer movement to the early labor movement, and predicts that consumerism too will become an "increasingly institutionalized force in United States society."[19]

A common threat is the focus on basic "rights" that are attributed to consumers: safety, quality, health, information, education, protection, truth, authenticity, and choice.[20] Three broad categories of consumerists have been identified—adaptionists, protectionists, and reformers—each of which is concerned with different areas of these rights. Adaptionists are concerned with consumer education, protectionists with health and safety issues, and reformers with increased information and political representation.[21] Exhibit 10-1 catalogues the major accusations consumerists have levied at the marketing practices of corporations. The issues range from detailed complaints such as "fake credit terms" to such esoteric issues as "creates needs" or "gives society false values."

Consumerism is not a new concept, but the consumer movement as it is understood today did not really emerge until the 1960s. The new consumerism is characterized by increasingly well-organized and relatively permanent coalitions of consumer advocates. Ralph Nader became the first "professional" consumer advocate and eventually built a complex and effective series of consumer groups into a powerful consumer coalition. "In the last ten years, Ralph Nader has become almost an industry himself. His principal organization is Public Citizen, a tax-exempt group supported largely by contributions that came to an estimated $1.1 million in 1977."[22] Nader's success was a powerful inducement to the development of other well-organized consumer groups and coalitions, although there are many other factors that contributed to the development of these groups as well. One author has identified several factors that appear to contribute to the establishment of consumer movements: levels of economic

Exhibit 10-1
Major Accusations Levied at Marketing Strategy Elements

Product Policy	*Communication Methods*
Product	manipulates consumers
proliferation of new products	creates needs
too many similar products	lies and deceives
false innovations	subliminal seduction
artificial differentiation	contributes to inflation
dangerous, defective, marginal products	promotes planned obsolescence
useless gadgets	causes mental pollution
	reduces free competition
Package	is of bad quality and morality
polluting packaging; dangerous; useless;	pushes the mass-consumption society to
expensive	excess materialism
deceitful packages; avoid possibility of	gives the society false values
comparison	smears the image of woman
labels do not provide adequate information	does not provide adequate information
inadequate warranties and service	pushes psychological not performance
contracts	characteristics of products
lacks precise indications of use	increases costs to oligopolistic
lacks description of ingredients	competitors
product dating	

Pricing Strategy	*Distribution Developments*
creating new products at higher prices	high pressure selling
profit maximizing	deceitful promotions
cartels	aggressive merchandising techniques
psychological pricing	new retailing methods push consumption
"call" prices	pushes high margin products
fictitious prices	does not weed out bad products
bad price / quality relation	bad after-sales service
fake credit terms	little in-store service
unreasonable margins	high value added for little effort
absence of unit prices	"basement" sales
fake price / quantity relationships	high-pressure door-to-door selling
positioning of products by price level	
fictitious promotions	

Source: Will Straver, "The International Consumer Movement," *European Journal of Marketing* 11 (No. 2, 1977), p. 97.

activity, social psychological variables, legal variables, political variables, and variables related to a country's marketing system. The most important factors, however, are the level of economic development and the level of education, both of which would seem to be preconditions to a sustained consumer movement.[23] And so consumerism as a phenomenon is associated more with industrialized than less-developed countries.

The relationship between consumerism and government is not always easy to determine. Legislation concerning product safety or questionable marketing practices is viewed as a governmental consumer-protection initiative, but piecemeal legislation on individual areas of concern does not necessarily represent a commitment to consumerism, broadly defined. And when governments do become involved in the more generalized consumerism movement—by supporting consumer organizations, for instance—the action is not always regarded with favor: "For example, French consumerists feel that the government tries to hamper their activities by supporting its own [consumer] institute."[24] In the United States the defeated Agency for Consumer Advocacy, which would have been empowered to represent consumers before other government agencies as well as to sue other agencies on behalf of consumers, was backed strongly by some consumer groups but rejected by other consumers as being yet another bureaucracy to further complicate an already bloated government.

In some countries, however, the consumer movement appears to have been fully incorporated into the political system. In Sweden, the leading consumer organization, the local equivalent of Consumers Union in the United States, operates under the Ministry of Commerce and is financially supported by the government. The government is also responsible for the Consumer Ombudsman and the Market Court, which provide redress on matters of misleading or abusive marketing practices. Consumer representation in the Market Court is a key element in the system.[25]

Other countries display a wide range of government participation in consumer activities. Britain had a Consumer Council within the government between 1962 and 1970. France has a tradition of state intervention in consumer affairs, sponsoring a number of consumer organizations and participating in their activities.[26] In the United States, all agencies of the Federal government were instructed to establish special departments of consumer affairs. In Germany, a broad coalition of consumer groups, including 32 national family, housewife, and religious associations, is financed by the government.[27]

In most countries, however, it is the private sector that is responsible for consumer initiatives. In 1971, there were over 60 consumer organizations in Europe, of which only 10 were associated with governments, with a total membership of 1.5 million.[28] In the United States, Consumers Union alone had an equal number of members, yet the organization represents only a small portion of all consumer group members. In Japan, an association of housewives (*Chifuren*) sponsored a boycott of television manufacturers for eight months after learning that Japanese television prices were higher than the prices of the same models in the United States.

Private consumer groups often seek the support of organizations with allied interests. In the United States, a number of Protestant and Catholic consumer groups joined their efforts under the aforementioned Interfaith Center for Corporate Responsibility (ICCR) in order to more effectively organize their protests. They also seek the support of professional groups who share similar concerns on specific issues, including the scientific community and charitable organizations. As a measure of the unpredictable nature of such coalitions it is interesting to note that an alliance consisting of Action for Children's Television, the National Association for Better Broadcasting, the Mexican-American Political Association, and the San Fernando Valley Fair Housing Council was formed to stop a Los Angeles television station from airing violent children's shows.

Consumer groups employ a wide range of tactics in order to make their demands felt. *Publicity* is a major tool, and a number of consumer groups have become quite adept at using news conferences or media events to bring their causes to a wider audience. Some corporations have shown themselves to be rather sensitive to adverse publicity which operates to the advantage of consumer groups. *Shareholder resolutions* represent another such tactic. The ICCR is a leader in the use of shareholder resolutions, and participation by major shareholders can be a decisive factor in the outcome of conflicts. *Boycotts* are somewhat more difficult to implement, but groups such as *Chifuren* in Japan have found that they can be extremely effective—the threat of a consumer boycott may be enough to force a company to reconsider its position in a conflict.

Consumer groups also may choose to sponsor *independent scientific studies* to force regulatory agencies to reconsider the safety of products. In the United States, groups such as the Environmental Defense Fund have been effective in using results from tests they sponsored to force government agencies to review the safety of products previously believed to be safe. Another tactic is simply to organize an effective *lobbying* campaign to pressure legislators to consider a consumer issue. It is difficult for legislators to ignore a well-organized letter-writing campaign from their constituents. Although action may not result directly, hearings may be held that serve the dual purpose of publicizing the issue to a wider audience and providing an information-gathering vehicle for possible further action.

Corporations have responded to the new environment of well-organized consumers in a number of ways. By 1975 over 300 corporations in the United States had established "consumer relations" departments.[29] While many of the early efforts were merely cosmetic—falling under the traditional public relations function—recent developments have given these departments more authority. By 1977 a 750-member Society of Consumer Affairs Professionals had been formed to exchange information. Some MNEs have extended the concept beyond the United States—for example, Coca-Cola decided to expand its consumers affairs departments to its subsidiaries overseas.[30] Others have responded by hiring well-known consumer affairs specialists—Bess Myerson, former Commissioner of Consumer affairs in New York City, was hired by Citibank and Bristol-Myers to handle various aspects of consumer affairs.[31] In this way they hope to better understand the nature of the consumer movement and simultaneously express their concern for consumer interests.

Consumerism has not emerged as a highly organized movement at the international level. Organizations such as the International Organization of Consumers Unions and the Bureau Européen des Unions de Consommateurs hold occasional conferences, but these are mainly informational. Ralph Nader has been instrumental in establishing Public Interest Research Councils in a number of countries. Characteristically, the international consumer movement displays more of the flexible qualities of its parent domestic movements than reliance on formal international organizations. But what is important is that consumer groups with similar interests are indeed receptive to the idea of assisting groups in other countries, if necessary.

For the multinational marketer, consumerism is becoming an unpredictable and often powerful force to consider. And since the consumer movement is an issue-oriented, spontaneous coalition effort, it is not easy to deal with. "The multinational business firm finds itself in an unenviable position. Not only must it live up to different consumerism standards in each country, but it must also be prepared to come closer to meeting these standards than domestic business. They are more visible, vulnerable, and more subject to criticism."[32] As we shall see, for multinationals it is becoming increasingly difficult to engage in some kinds of conflict with a growing and complex consumerism movement.

Government and Marketing

Governments influence marketing in a variety of ways that range from simple persuasion to formal regulatory agencies and legislation that is enforced through independent judicial systems. The underlying motive of such activities is to set the rules of the game. While government regulation is theoretically nondiscriminatory—since all participants are nominally subject to the same rules—governments are political creations and are often motivated by purely political considerations. For example, regulations are sometimes clarified by selective enforcement as a warning to all parties concerned. Companies selected to illustrate the applicability of a given law frequently maintain that they are in some way being discriminated against. And when the corporation is an MNE, this feeling may be even more pronounced and is often justified.

A major problem for multinational enterprise is that the regulatory environment varies considerably from country to country. Many regulations are difficult to interpret and not consistently enforced. In large parts of the world—especially in the Third World—there is a distinct absence of regulations and of mechanisms for enforcing them.

An element common to a number of countries, including industrialized nations, is that the regulatory environment can change abruptly. This may result from the arrival of a new and enthusiastic leadership in a regulatory agency, for example. And since multinationals are often the most conspicuous marketers in any given country, because of the size of their operations, they are likely candidates for action as the new leadership starts its campaign to see regulations vigorously enforced. Companies that have operated for years under traditionally accepted standards of conduct may suddenly find themselves in violation of narrowly interpreted rules or pathmark decisions widening the scope of the law. And within the regulatory process itself there is often a great deal of uncertainty. Disputes may arise among agency staff members about the proper interpretation of a vaguely worded mandate. The debates can lead to contradictory rulings on a given issue in the space of a few years.

In the discussion that follows, we shall consider three major types of marketing problems facing the multinational enterprise: the nature of the product that is being sold, pricing and distribution policies, and approaches to advertising and promotion. In each case, we shall discuss in some depth a major conflict involving multinationals that has surfaced in recent years.

PRODUCT CONFLICT

In 1974, Winthrop Laboratories' anabolic steroid, Winstrol, was restricted by the Food and Drug Administration (FDA) to treatment of aplastic anemia, pituitary dwarfism, and osteoporosis. However, the drug was being marketed in Brazil and Mexico as a remedy for poor appetite, fatigue and weight loss. Ciba-Geigy promoted its version of the same drug, Dianabol, as a remedy for thinness, underweight, appetite loss, lack of strength, general weakness, and growth disturbances in nursing infants, pre-school, and school-age children.[33]

In 1978, Union Carbide was marketing a new whole-body scanner outside the United States only since, for the time being, "new restrictions being placed on hospitals' purchases of major medical equipment is creating a regulatory morass in the U.S.," according to the company. (For purchases of equipment worth over $100,000, United States hospitals must get approval of health-care planning agencies.) The scanner sold for about $375,000.[34]

A drug used in the treatment of gout which was introduced by Ciba-Geigy in 1959 was found to reduce the incidence of heart attacks in tests conducted in Canada in 1975. After intensive investigation, Canada, South Africa, Switzerland, and Germany approved the use of the drug, Auturan, as a heart attack preventative. The United States and Britain refused to approve the drug for its new use pending further tests, although it is conservatively estimated that the drug could save 10,000–15,000 lives per year in the United States alone.[35]

In the early 1970's Ciba-Geigy sold Preludin (a reducing agent) and Ritalin (an antidepressant) in the United States although the drugs were banned in Switzerland "because of widespread use by young people who were injecting them like heroin," according to the company. Management maintained that United States controls over the availability of the drug made the potential for abuse less likely.[36]

In the early 1970's Libby McNeil & Libby sold 300,000 cases of cyclamate-sweetened canned fruit to customers in West Germany, Spain and other countries in Europe, the Far East, and the Caribbean during the 16 months following an FDA ban on the use of cyclamates in the United States.[37]

In April 1977, polychlorinated biphenyls (PCBs) leaked from damaged electrical equipment during a fire in a Ralston Purina animal-feed warehouse in Puerto Rico, contaminating 800,000 pounds of fishmeal, which was subsequently sold as poultry feed in the United States. When the contamination became known in 1978, hundreds of thousands of chickens and millions of eggs had to be destroyed, and since the contaminated Puerto Rican fishmeal was also sold to other mixers, more than 2.5 million pounds of additional feed had to be recalled. The FDA undertook an examination to determine if the feed had been sold negligently, with the company possibly held liable for the damage.[38]

In 1964, a Norwegian woman died from thrombosis resulting from use of Anovolar, a contraceptive pill manufactured by Schering A.G. of Germany. An Oslo court ruled that Schering was liable for compensatory damages, but on appeal a higher court ruled that Schering could not have *foreseen* the adverse side-effect at the time and overruled the lower court.[39]

A decade later, in 1972, a French consumer group, UDAF, sued the Morhange Company of Paris for criminal liability when several breastfed babies died or were permanently handicapped. The group charged that Morhange's talcum powder containing excessive amounts of hexachlorophene, which the mothers had used, was responsible for the deaths. Since Morhange was not financially able to indemnify the parents, charges were filed in 1976 against the supplier of hexachlorophene, Givaudan, a subsidiary of Hoffmann-La Roche.[40]

Wadkins, Ltd., an English machine-tool company, predicted that it would probably have to stop exporting its machines to the United States, which account for 5% of its $30 million in sales, after having its insurance rates increased 15 times between 1974 and 1977 as a result of several product-liability suits.[41]

In 1978, a French court awarded $1.5 million to the family of two victims of a 1974 crash of a McDonnell Douglas DC-10 aircraft flown by Turkish Airlines near Paris. There were 346 victims in the crash, all fatalities, and relatives of all of the victims have pursued legal action charging McDonnell Douglas and its subcontractors with product liability. Massive claims for compensation were also filed following the 1979 crash of an American Airlines DC-10 in Chicago which killed 273 passengers.[42]

These are but a few of the growing array of conflicts facing multinational companies related to the products and services that they sell around the globe. A central function of marketing is of course to provide a product that is appropriate to the needs of consumer or users. Internationally, the enormous variance in the environment within which consumers and users find themselves requires a high degree of sensitivity on the part of the marketing function of multinationals. It means adapting products to local conditions in order to maximize sales, and often the only way to do that effectively is to produce locally as well, particularly when an extended concept of "product" includes delivery conditions, financing terms, after-sales service, and warranty arrangements. Conflict often arises when a product is mismatched with respect to the receiving environment, as we shall again note in Chapter 13 with respect to "appropriate" product-related technologies.

Particularly in developing countries—or any society that is markedly different from that of the MNE's home country—products are sometimes viewed as eroding national cultural values and traditions, family spending patterns, political mechanisms and governmental control, and even external political relations. Soft drinks, transistor radios, motorbikes, jeans, tobacco products, and alcoholic beverages are among the products that are often mentioned in this regard. On the other hand, there have also been repeated cases where multinationals have successfully attempted to come to grips with the problem. General Motors' introduction of the Basic Transportation Vehicle (BTV) and the Ford Fiera's successes in developing countries are cases in point. Another example: As part of a 1976 settlement of the nationalization of its subsidiary, Cia. de Telefonos de Chile, ITT agreed to co-sponsor the "Chile Foundation" with the Chilean government. Its purpose is to develop technical innovations in food, nutrition, and electronics that relate directly to basic local needs and desires—ITT provides scientists and funds to the foundation.[43]

Perhaps the most serious sources of product-related conflict facing multinationals are safety, liability, and accountability. In many developed countries, *caveat emptor* is increasingly being replaced by a serious and often complex attempt to extend producer liability for damage to persons, property, and the environment resulting from the use—and often misuse—of products. Frequently the principle of "negative proof" is applied, whereby the producer must show beyond reasonable doubt that his products meet established safety norms before they can be sold, rather than placing the burden of proof on the regulators to show beyond reasonable doubt that products are indeed unsafe. Since legislative, regulatory, and legal systems covering the area of product safety differ widely among countries, this aspect of the marketing function in multinational companies can become complex indeed.

Among the most celebrated recent cases of product liability are those in the automobile industry. During 1977, for example, 18 million vehicles were re-called for defects in the United States, nearly triple the number in 1976. The process is usually quite lengthy, and may "start with news stories or car-owner complaints; then may cause lengthy government investigation and testing, con-sumer-group pressure for government action, resistance by the car's manufactur-er, an official finding of a safety defect, and a conflict between the company and Washington over planned repairs."[44] Perhaps the most dramatic case has been the Ford Pinto: the company decided to recall 1.5 million vehicles in June 1978 for fuel tank repairs after a year of negotiations about its propensity to catch fire after rear-end crashes. The fuel tank is allegedly easily crushed or punctured and separated from its filler pipe, and the initial defect finding pointed to 38 accidents, 27 deaths and 29 lawsuits or liability claims against Ford. In Septem-ber 1978 Ford was indicted by an Indiana grand jury on criminal charges of designing and building a dangerously faulty product "in reckless disregard of safety," in connection with a rear-end collison in which three girls were burned to death. The indictment charged three counts of "reckless homicide," and one count of "criminal recklessness," with a maximum fine of $35,000.[45] Similar problems faced the Firestone Tire and Rubber Company in connection with its "Firestone 500" steel-belted radial tire—10 million of such tires had to be re-called in 1978.

Even more serious is product marketing *in the absence* of clear-cut product safety guidelines or regulation, or any such external constraints whatsoever. With respect to product-safety initiatives, a recent study notes:

> It is clear that the degree of activity in industralized countries is increasing, although the exact nature of product safety initiatives varies. A look at the LDCs increases even further this diversity in product safety development. It is axiomatic to expect substantially different product safety pronounce-ments from the lesser developed countries even though their programs may not be rigorously enforced or formally institutionalized. Consequently, the complex subject of product safety development is viewed most effectively as a continuum rather than as conforming to any discrete categories or stages in a uniform process of development.[46]

National Regulation of Product Safety and Liability

The United States clearly represents the leading edge of the "continuum" re-ferred to above, and it may be instructive to briefly survey United States product safety regulations as representative of the existing or evolving environment in home countries of multinationals. The safety of products in the United States market is regulated by two Federal agencies, the Food and Drug Administration and the Consumer Product Safety Commission (CPSC). There are a number of other specialized agencies that handle product safety in particular sectors, al-though some of these were incorporated into the CPSC when it was formed in 1972.

The Pure Food and Drug Act of 1906 was passed in response to health scandals involving the food industry, and a major amendment to the Act was passed in 1938 as a result of scandal involving elixer of sulfanilamide in which 93 people were killed. Another legislative initiative was the "Delaney Clause" in a 1958 Amendment to the Food, Drug and Cosmetics Act, which requires the FDA to ban any food additive that has been shown to cause cancer in people or animals. The Act was further amended in 1962 as a result of the thalidomide tragedy (which we shall discuss below), and charged the FDA with responsibility not only for determining whether or not a drug is *safe*, but also whether it is *effective* in treating the conditions for which it is intended.[47]

By 1978 the FDA had become a highly controversial agency with a budget of $242 million and 7200 employees: " . . . The $10 billion a year market in prescription drugs made by 2500 companies is less than half the agency's regulatory responsibilities. It has legislative authority to oversee the products of 50,000 food companies that market $130 billion worth of goods. Add to the list cosmetics, medical devices such as eyeglasses, veterinary medicines fed to livestock and such other diverse products as microwave ovens and aerosol sprays."[48] Three examples of FDA decisions illustrate the kinds of controversy that surround the agency when it attempts to protect consumers from technological or scientific developments that often are not often fully understood.

In the mid-1970s acrylonitrile and polyester resins began to be test marketed by Coca-Cola and Pepsi-Cola as part of a five-year effort to find a lightweight plastic beverage container to replace the heavier and breakable glass bottles. In June 1975 the FDA reaffirmed its approval of acrylonitrile for use in soft drink bottles and Coca-Cola expanded its test marketing program.[49] In February 1977, the FDA reversed its decision and banned the use of acrylonitrile in beverage containers as a result of a new study which showed that the substance causes lesions and other growths in test animals:[50] "One of the tests involved leakage of acrylonitrile from the structure of the bottle under exposure to the desert temperature of 120 degrees Farenheit for six months. The other involved lifetime feeding to laboratory rats . . . equivalent to a human drinking thousands of quarts of soft drink daily."[51] Monsanto, the manufacturer of acrylonitrile bottles, applied for a stay of the FDA order in the U.S. Court of Appeals, charging that the tests were "exaggerated and ridiculous."[52] The court granted the stay, but the damage had been done. By October 1977, Coca-Cola had switched to a polyester bottle which was free of the difficulty, and Monsanto was forced to write off $18.5 million in plant and equipment used in making the acrylonitrile bottles.[53] Monsanto continued its challenge of the ban in court, however.

In 1969, the FDA banned the use of cyclamates, a low-calorie artificial sweetener, effectively killing off the 15 million pound per year industry. Abbott Laboratories, which held 65% of the United States market, contested the decision, maintaining that the original tests linking the sweetener to bladder cancer in rats were erroneous.[54] By 1970 consumption of saccharin, another artificial sweetener, had risen to 4.5 million pounds per year, partly because of the cyclamate ban, with 62% of the consumption in beverages.[55] Following a Canadian study showing that saccharin caused bladder cancer in rats, the FDA decided to ban its use as a food or beverage additive as well. The Canadian study was based on feeding rats the equivalent of a human drinking 800 12-ounce bottles of saccharin-sweetened soft drinks per day for life. Unlike the relative calm that followed the similar ban on cyclamate, this time the FDA was " . . . immersed in a wave of angry outbursts from the diet food and drink makers, groups representing diabetics and many Americans who believe that they should be allowed to continue using saccharin regardless of the opinions of Federal bureaucrats and even of possible health consequences."[56] Particularly incensed were the nation's 10 million diabetics. As a result of the controversy, the FDA proposed reclassifying saccharin as an over-the-counter drug which would allow its continued sale, although not as a food additive.[57] In October 1977, Congress voted an 18-month postponement of even the modified ban so that the matter could be studied further. When that law expired in 1979 the FDA's continued push for a ban was again strongly resisted, and bills were introduced to extend the Congressional moratorium on FDA action for another three years.[58]

Diethylstilbestrol (DES) is a growth hormone fed to an estimated 18 million cattle each year. As a result, cattle producers can get a better rate of weight gain per unit of feed. However, residues of the hormone build up in the tissue of cattle, and critics contend that they present a potential cancer hazard to humans when the slaughtered animals are eaten. In April 1971, tests conducted by the FDA found that 10 out of 2400 livestock tested contained DES residue, and several members of Congress and consumer activists demanded that the sale of DES be banned immediately.[59] FDA regulations at the time required DES to be withdrawn from cattle feed at least 48 hours before slaughter, but in August 1972 it decided to ban the use of DES entirely since new tests showed that the residue could be found in cattle up to seven days after DES was withdrawn from feed.[60] Three DES producers filed a court petition seeking a review of the ban.[61] In January 1974 the court ruled that the use of DES could continue because the FDA had not allowed sufficient time for the producers to comment when the ban was being proposed. It thereupon issued new regulations requiring that DES be withdrawn 14 days before slaughter. In January 1976 the FDA once again proposed a full ban on the use of DES in animal feed.[62]

As these brief examples indicate, the decisions made by the FDA can have an enormous impact on product markets within the United States, in some cases wiping them out altogether. Often they are fiercely contested by the affected industries. As one observer notes: "The Food and Drug Administration has a vital, but very difficult assignment. It is often required to make a decision on questions when no one knows the answers even though many stridently claim they do. In addition, the FDA must struggle with some poor laws, such as the Delaney Clause, which seeks to force simple answers to questions which are inherently complex. Consequently, the FDA sometimes makes mistakes, as it almost did with saccharin, until a stormwind of public opinion forced it to reconsider."[63] Overall, according to another observer, "Despite all its problems and defects, even some staunch critics say the FDA may be the best consumer protection agency in the world. Officials of the World Health Organization in Geneva say they regard it very highly and that 'nothing the FDA does escapes international attention.' Yet, if the agency is the best, it may be so by default. No other nation has citizens who not only desire safety in consumer goods but are also willing to spend a quarter of a billion dollars a year in such regulation."[64]

The Consumer Product Safety Commission was created by the Consumer Product Safety Act of 1972. With the exception of firearms, tobacco, boats, pesticides, aircraft, and products which fall under FDA authority the CPSC has the authority to " . . . ban, order the redesign of, or publicize the dangers associated with any product creating what it considers unreasonable risk of injury."[65] Congress also transferred authority of the Flammable Fabrics Act, the Hazardous Substances Act, the Poison Prevention Act, and the Refrigeration Safety Act to the new agency. Approximately two million companies in the

United States which account for $250 billion in sales fall under the jurisdiction of the Agency, which in 1977 operated with a staff of less than 1000 and a budget of under $40 million. According to a recent CPSC chairman: "Our statute does not say we are to make sure all consumer products are safe. Our responsibility is simply to remove unreasonable risk."[66] The Agency can impose civil penalties of up to $500,000 and jail terms of up to one year for failure to comply with its orders.

The CPSC has not had a particularly notable record of performance. In the first six years of its existence, the Agency had only promulgated safety standards for one product (swimming pools), and that took two years to accomplish. The Carter Administration seriously considered abolishing the CPSC, a threat that was not carried out, but that was indicative of the low regard in which it is held. The Agency has relied on industry cooperation in most cases, and any manufacturer, wholesaler, retailer, or distributor is required to report within 48 hours the existence of a substantial product hazard. Industry cooperation in the designing of product safety standards is encouraged. In general, the CPSC has the necessary authority to become an extremely important force in the regulatory environment relating to product safety. To date, it has been largely ineffective. But if, with new leadership, it begins to realize its potential, the impact could be dramatic.

A former commissioner of the FDA recently noted that "total consumer protection is an unrealistic dream . . . the costs would be staggering, hundreds of millions of dollars more, and the end result would be a bureaucracy that simply would not be tolerated by the public."[67] However, it is increasingly accepted that consumers ought to obtain compensation in the event that they are injured by poorly designed, negligently made, or inherently dangerous products. Product liability has only recently become a major source of concern: "As recently as two decades ago, only a few product-liability suits were filed each year. By 1965, the annual total had reached 50,000. A few years later, it had soared to half a million. Now, according to industry sources, the number is running at a rate of 1.5 million a year."[68] Again, the United States has perhaps the most stringent product-liability laws.

Changes in product-liability laws have extended the traditional negligence and breach-of-warranty doctrines to the concept of strict liability, whereunder ". . . an injured party need only prove that the product is defective and caused the injury. No longer does he have to prove the manufacturer has been careless. Further, strict liability has been extended to all products, not just to human consumables or to those products intended for intimate body use, as in the past."[69] As a result, the cost of obtaining insurance has greatly increased, and the problem has become so critical for some manufacturers that major revisions in the nature of this type of insurance have been proposed in Congress.[70] At the First World Congress on Product Liability, held in London during 1977, it was noted that "European based companies are being charged 10 times the normal premium for product liability insurance if they export to the U.S."[71]

Internationally, the United Nations Commission on International Trade (UNCITRAL) ". . . asked the U.N. Secretariat to continue its study of the question of the feasibility and desirability of drafting a uniform law on liability for damage caused by products involved in international trade."[72] The OECD has examined similar proposals. The Council of Europe has prepared a draft, "European Convention on Product Liability," which contains provisions that closely resemble strict United States liability doctrine.[73] The most significant development, however, is the EEC Commission's draft directive on product liability, which it sent to the Council of Ministers for approval in 1976 and which would introduce a new concept in product liability that goes beyond even the United States approach. Under the proposed directive, producers would be held liable for a period of ten years for any "development risk"—they would be responsible to consumers for damage resulting from a product, even though ". . . nobody could have recognized the injurious defect, because the product, according to the state of science and technology at the time when the producer put it into circulation, could be considered free from defects."[74] That is, even if it was impossible to know about a defect at the time the product was introduced, the producer is still liable.

Within this context of growing concern with product safety and changing concepts of producer liability and accountability in a multinational setting, it may be useful to consider two cases in greater detail for an understanding how product-related conflict can evolve.

Product Safety: The Tris Case

In 1972, the U.S. Consumer Product Safety Commission assumed jurisdiction over the Flammable Fabrics Act of 1953, shortly after the Secretary of Commerce issued flammability standards for children's sleepwear. As a result, United States production of flame retardants jumped from 175 million pounds in 1971 to over 300 million pounds in 1975.[75] Of all the flame retardants in existence at the time, one commonly known as "Tris" proved to be the most convenient and economical for use in garments. Other flame retardants had such undesirable properties as unpleasant odors or rough texture, and by 1967, Tris-treated fabrics were used in over 70% of all children's sleepwear.[76] However, a mutagenic screening test in March 1976 showed positive results, giving preliminary cause for concern that the chemical is a carcinogen.

In May 1976, the Environmental Defense Fund (EDF) filed a petition requesting the CPSC to require that labels of Tris-treated garments instruct purchasers to wash it three times before using it, to remove any excess Tris. The group did not seek a complete ban on Tris because "We can't be sure that the alternatives to Tris are safer, so by banning it we might be going from the fire into the frying pan."[77] The Chairman of the CPSC commented: "Based on what I've examined and on discussion with our biomedical science experts, I would doubt that there is a problem. There is a great leap from the tests to a conclusion that the chemical is a carcinogen."[78] However, by February 1977, the EDF obtained raw data from a National Cancer Institute test being conducted on Tris, and filed a new petition with the CPSC to immediately ban all Tris-treated clothing as an "imminent hazard to public safety."[79] Manufacturers had already been concerned enough about the potential problems of Tris to start work on developing substitutes. By the time the petition was filed, Tris-treated fabrics had fallen from 60% of the market to only 20%, with several major suppliers stopping production and apparel manufacturers halting its use.

When the official results of the National Cancer Institute study confirmed the EDF's analysis of the raw data, the CPSC started proceedings to ban the use of Tris in children's sleepwear. It announced a ban on the sale of all Tris-treated garments and all future production of Tris-treated clothing. Consumers were entitled to a refund for unwashed clothing that had been recently purchased—an enormous problem, with inventories of

Tris-treated garments estimated at 20 million items valued at $200 million—but the CPSC voted against recalling all 120 million garments already sold.

The decision was not well received. The EDF stated: "We are going back into court immediately because we want the Consumer Product Safety Commission to require retailers to repurchase all sleepwear now in the hands of consumers."[80] The American Apparel Manufacturers Association (AAMA) took its case to Federal Court in Washington, objecting to the retailers' having to bear the entire cost of the $200 million in recalled inventory, and in April a Federal judge ruled that the CPSC had acted "arbitrarily and capriciously."[81] The Court imposed a formula for sharing the costs of refunds—consumers would get a full refund for all unwashed Tris-treated clothing; retailers would collect the purchase price from the garment manufacturer; manufacturers would collect the cost of the Tris-treated fabric from the mills and the mills would collect the cost of the Tris from the chemical companies.[82]

The CPSC plan was beset with difficulties, including getting retailers to comply with the ban on sales. The EDF charged that retailers were trying to sell off their inventories as quickly as possible, and filed a lawsuit against F.W. Woolworth for selling Tris-treated clothing in violation of the ban. Woolworth insisted that it had officially stopped sales of Tris-treated sleepwear, but agreed to make sure the decision was clarified to all employees.[83] Consumers had no way of knowing whether or not the garments they were purchasing were Tris-treated or not, since the labels did not identify the nature of the flame-retardant used.

Spring Mills in North Carolina filed for an injunction against the CPSC order which would require the company to repurchase $2 million worth of sleepwear. The presiding judge granted the injunction, ruling that the CPSC "had violated its own rule-making procedures."[84] Indeed, the judge struck down the CPSC recall entirely and strongly criticized the agency: "In the present case, the Commission's action affects thousands of retailers, hundreds of manufacturers, millions of articles and many millions of dollars. The tragedy is that unlike an action where the property may be returned, the action of the CPSC has put the market in children's sleepwear in such a state of disarray that the CPSC itself has no estimate or idea of when the turmoil may end."[85] In the AAMA suit, the Federal Appeals Court refused to reinstate the CPSC ban, but it indicated that the CPSC had the right to pursue violators on a case by case basis. The CPSC immediately declared that anyone ". . . who persists in selling Tris-treated garments will be in violation of the Federal Hazardous Substances Act and will be subject to enforcement action by the Commission." The CPSC backed up its warning by filing separate lawsuits against R.H. Macy and Zayre Corp., two large retailers, to stop them from selling Tris-treated garments. An EDF study showed that in July 1977, 18% of all retailers continued to sell Tris-treated sleepwear.

While the domestic sales ban on clothing was in a state of confusion, the situation in regard to exports of banned inventories was equally uncertain. In October of 1977 the CPSC determined that it did not have the authority under the Federal Hazardous Substances Act to ban exports of Tris-treated sleepwear. Exports grew rapidly, and one company executive stated "I shipped it where it couldn't get back into this country. . . . But I got only $400,000 for my $2.5 million in goods."[86] Under pressure, from Congress and others concerned with "an export trade in death," the CPSC reversed its earlier ruling and decided that it did in fact have the authority to ban exports. The whole emotional affair led the United States Congress to investigate U.S. export policy as it affects products banned by U.S. regulatory agencies and to recommend a series of changes in that policy.[87]

Product Liability: The Thalidomide Case

By 1962, Thalidomide had become one of the most widely used tranquilizers in the world. It was believed to be completely non-toxic and virtually "suicide proof," and a reliable and safe sedative for children. The developers of the drug, Germany's highly respected Chemie Gruenthal, licensed the drug to a number of companies including Richardson-Merrell in the United States, Dainippon Pharmaceuticals in Japan, Astra Pharmaceuticals in Sweden, and Distillers Company (Biochemicals) Ltd. in Great Britain. Then the unforeseen side-effects of the drug became known—throughout the world, over 7000 children were born with a disfiguring abnormality called phocomelia after their mothers took the drug during pregnancy. In Germany, of the 5000 "Thalidomide babies" only 2000 survived, and 860 adults also suffered nerve damage as a result of other unanticipated effects. In virtually every country in which the drug was sold similar problems occurred.

In Britain, Distillers (Biochemicals) Ltd., was anxious to market Thalidomide as soon as it became aware of its existence. The management of Distillers apparently believed the drug was the answer to its search for a mind-altering drug of the type that Aldous Huxley had predicted would be developed to serve the same role as the traditional products of distillers and brewers. "So, incredible as it may seem, one of the factors that led to Thalidomide being marketed in Britain was the belief that it might become an alternative to whiskey."[88] Distillers signed a contract in July 1957 with Chemie Gruenthal, calling for Thalidomide to be marketed in the United Kingdom within nine months of the contract date. Because the company did not have sufficient time to test the drug fully, Distillers was forced to rely on the results of Chemie Gruenthal's own research, and in April 1958 began sales with the advice that it "can be given with complete safety to pregnant women . . . without adverse effect on mother or child."[89]

By March 1961, Distillers had sold nearly 64 million tablets of the drug and generally ignored mounting evidence linking Thalidomide to peripheral neuritis. In June 1961, a Sydney obstetrician working for Distillers' Australian subsidiary wrote the parent company advising them that he had strong evidence linking Thalidomide to birth defects—the letter did not arrive in London until November. By that time, a leading pediatrician in Germany had confronted the management of Chemie Gruenthal with similar evidence. When a German newspaper wrote a story on the findings, Chemie Gruenthal decided to withdraw the drug from the market. The following morning Distillers also decided to stop general sales of the drug, but continued to supply Thalidomide to hospitals for another year.[90] By 1962, Distillers had stopped all sales of the drug and indeed had sold its Biochemicals subsidiary to Eli Lilly.

The compensation problem first arose in 1962, when a writ was served on Distillers by the parents of a Thalidomide child. The suit charged Distillers with negligence. A coalition of British parents of Thalidomide children had already formed under the name, "Society for the Aid of Thalidomide Children," and similar coalitions would develop in other countries. Under British law, legal proceedings against Distillers would have to be initiated by the parents of a child within three years of the time the child was born, but of the estimated 430 British Thalidomide children only 70 had been represented in legal action by the time the statute of limitations had expired in 1965. It was generally agreed that Distillers was in a very strong legal position in regard to allegations of negligence, since drug safety laws only required a company to perform tests common to the industry at the time the drug was marketed, which did not include testing for possible teratogenic (deforming) effects of new drugs.

In 1968, Distillers made an out-of-court settlement with the parents of the 70 victims calling for compensation of 40% of the damages the children would have received had the parents won the lawsuit. The terms of the agreement called for the parents to release

Distillers from any further liability in the matter. According to the presiding High Court judge, "It would be folly to refuse such an offer. . . . The settlement was fair and just, in the interests of the infant plaintiffs and their parents, and it reflected great credit on all those who had taken part in negotiating it."[91] Unfortunately for Distillers, the publicity surrounding the settlement made the parents of other Thalidomide children in Britain aware of the possibility of obtaining compensation from the company, and over the next year 260 more parents applied to the Court for permission to file writs against Distillers. The Court had the power to set aside the statute of limitations, and duly granted the parents' requests. Within two years, Distillers compensated all but two of the original group of victims at a total cost of $2.4 million, but by 1970 Distillers was involved in negotiations with the parents of an additional 374 Thalidomide children who were not party to the first settlement.

Distillers' first formal offer to the new group of claimants was made in November 1971. Under the terms of the offer the parents and victims would receive a total of $10 million, conditional upon all of the parents accepting. Five parents were not agreeable to the terms, and after a court battle this effectively blocked the settlement. Despite a ban on stories about cases *sub judice*, the *London Times* decided to publish a series of articles to dramatize the personal and financial plight of the Thalidomide victims, many of whom were now entering their early teens. The first article, under the headline "Our Thalidomide Children: A Cause for National Shame," provoked intense national interest in the subject, and the story about the Thalidomide victims had become the leading British news item by Christmas 1972.

In November and December of 1972 anonymous posters started to appear around London condemning Distillers for their delay in compensating the Thalidomide victims. Featuring such graphic images as a withered hand in a martini glass, the posters were indicative of the powerful emotions that had been aroused. In December, the House of Commons debated the issue of compensation for victims: "If Distillers (Biochemicals) Ltd. had any friends in Commons, they did not speak up. . ."[92] The debates were intense and emotional, with the sympathies of the Commons clearly with the victims. In anticipation of the debate, Distillers raised its offer for compensation to $12 million. Buoyed by the evidence of public support, however, the parents of the victims were becoming more cautious about accepting the offer. On December 14, Distillers announced that it was raising its offer to $28.5 million. However, the parents were well aware that Commons considered no less than $50 million to be a reasonable offer.

In early 1973, "a group of rebel shareholders in the company . . . called for an extraordinary meeting of the shareholders to discuss possible removal of Distillers' Chairman Sir Alexander McDonald, who had been knighted only last year for 'services to exports.' " The charge: "failure to provide adequate compensation" for the Thalidomide children. Almost immediately, major shareholders began lining up to support the proposed meeting. Among them were Prudential Life Assurance Co. and Legal and General Assurance Society (Britain's two largest insurance companies), the General and Municipal Workers Union, and dozens of local authorities including those of London's boroughs and the cities of Birmingham and Manchester. Wrenson's, a chain of supermarkets, banned Distillers' goods from its shelves. On the London Stock Exchange Distillers' shares dropped a total of $70.5 million in value in nine days."[93] On the day after the meeting between the dissident shareholders and management, a director of Distillers' leading bank stated: "We made it clear that we wanted a solution to the problem, and we wanted it as soon as possible." There were also discussions with Ralph Nader about the possibility of a boycott of Distillers' products in the United States—a notable development due to the company's heavy reliance on the United States market for 35% of total sales.

Distillers then announced that it was raising its offer to $50 million, but that it would not be able to "contemplate any increase in the sums now offered." The terms of the offer were essentially agreeable to all parties to the conflict. Anti-Distillers agitation was stopped. The *London Times* noted, "No-one would doubt the resultant benefit to all which had arisen from the courageous stand taken in 1972 by a small minority of parents."[94] By May 1973 the Thalidomide conflict was essentially over in Britain, although there were still some compensation claims pending. The terms of the settlement were agreed on over a decade after the conflict began.°

PRICE CONFLICT

We touch on pricing policies of multinational companies several times in other chapters, in connection with tax and exchange-control avoidance, antitrust policy, restrictive business practices, and the cost of technology. Pricing is a central function of marketing, and can clearly be used in ways that reflect different conflict-handling modes. Pricing conflict can involve competitors, customers, public authorities, and other interest groups and institutions. Consider the following:

In 1973, Kellogg was found guilty of violating British monopoly laws because its profits on cereals were yielding a rate of return on capital that averaged 70% for the period 1960–1965 and 46% for the period 1966–1970. This return was found to be excessive, but Kellogg was not ordered to cut prices. Instead, it was warned that profits would be closely monitored in the future. The reluctance to order price cuts stemmed from British experience with Kodak in 1969—when Kodak was ordered to cut prices due to excess profits, it had the perverse effect of driving Kodak's competition in the United Kingdom out of business.

In the early 1970's Citroën was holding its dealers to an agreement not to export or allow parallel imports of Citroën cars. As a result, dealers could not sell the cars to neighboring countries. Citroën was attempting to make up reduced profit margins in France that resulted from government price control by maintaining higher prices in neighboring countries. The EEC ordered the company to discontinue the restrictions.

In 1978, the European Court of Justice upheld a 1975 EEC Commission ruling charging United Brands with abuse of dominant position in violation of EEC antitrust laws. Prices of bananas in the Common Market varied as much as 50% in six countries during the period 1971–1974, with the differentials not explained by cost factors. In its decision, the Court reaffirmed the Commission's ruling that a dominant position could be held with only 45% of the market. Prior EEC rulings had not considered anything below 50–70% of the market as dominant position. United Brands was ordered to pay a fine of over $1 million.

° In Sweden, Astra Chemicals was exonerated of negligence charges by the Swedish Medical Board, but in 1969 paid $10 million in compensation to victims. In Germany, criminal charges were filed against nine Chemie Gruenthal executives, but the 283-day manslaughter trial was suspended because of the 10-year time lapse between the events and any prospective outcome of the proceedings. Gruenthal eventually paid over 2000 victims about $29 million in compensation. In Japan, after an emotional meeting between Dainippon executives and parents, the firm paid over $20 million in compensation to almost 300 victims. In the United States, Richardson-Merrell never received FDA approval to market Thalidomide, but paid individual settlements to U.S. and Canadian victims of limited distribution of the drug. Evidently the company was able to avoid mass publicity and lawsuits by impounding and sealing records, making generous settlements, and isolating victims from each other.

Merck and Co. in 1973 agreed to reimburse the French government $10 million after being accused of overcharging for its anti-rheumatism drug, Indocin. The charges and the payments were conducted in private and with no publicity.[95]

In 1975, American Hoechst, Rhodia Inc., and Robeco Chemicals of New York were found guilty of price-fixing in regard to the import of three chemicals. The firms were given fines ranging from $25,000 to $45,000 and four of their managers were given jail sentences.[96]

Without any explanation, the Australian Pricing Bureau in 1976 ordered Pfizer's Australian subsidiary to cut prices on Vibramycin and Rondomycin by an average of 21%. The company was given 48 hours to comply with the order. The Australian pricing bureau is so secretive that its membership is not made public and it is not even known how many people serve on it.[97]

In 1975, the governments of India, Iran, South Vietnam, and the Philippines brought suit in St. Louis against American Cyanamid, Bristol-Myers, Upjohn, Pfizer, Squibb, and Olin Corp. for allegedly overcharging them for broad-spectrum antibiotics. Three years later the United States Supreme Court ruled that the countries had the required legal standing within the United States to bring suit.[98]

Such conflicts appear to be increasingly common as proprietary technology becomes a factor of growing importance in market behavior of multinational firms, and as governments play a growing role as regulators and purchasers of the goods and services that multinationals sell. This seems to be especially true in the pharmaceuticals industry, and perhaps no conflict has been more heated or prolonged than the one initially involving Hoffmann-La Roche and Britain's National Health Service.

Hoffmann-La Roche Versus the British Government

In the late 1960s and early 1970s, government health services throughout the world found the costs of administering national health plans skyrocketing. In a search for ways to reduce these costs, all aspects of health plans came under intense scrutiny. In Great Britain, Hoffmann-La Roche marketed its tranquilizers Valium and Librium through its Roche Products Ltd. subsidiary. By 1970, Valium and Librium accounted for 68% of the British tranquilizer market, producing revenues of $8 million for Roche Products. And so it was to be expected that Roche would come under increasing pressure to reduce the prices of Valium and Librium. The conflict emerged from a quiet but uneasy relationship between the Swiss firm and the British health authorities, and ultimately became a battle of "epic proportions, similar to such legendary upheavals as the break-up of Standard Oil Trust in the U.S.A."[99] As a result of this emerging conflict, the pricing practices of Hoffmann-La Roche would be challenged by officials in Japan, Australia, South Africa, Germany, Holland, Sweden, and Norway as well as by officials of the European Economic Community and various developing countries.

Under the British system, the cost of medicines prescribed by physicians is paid for by the National Health Service (NHS), which in turn is ultimately reimbursed by the Department of Health and Social Services (DHSS). Following a 1967 recommendation, the DHSS concluded a Voluntary Price Regulation System (VPRS) with all British pharmaceutical firms *except* Roche, which refused to provide any information on sales or costs. Hence DHSS was unable to determine whether or not the prices of Valium and Librium were "reasonable." Roche refused to lower the prices of its drugs, retaining the same prices at which the drugs had initially been introduced into the British market. However, Roche did agree to make $1.6 million in cash payments to the DHSS, with little or no publicity. In addition, DHSS forced Roche to submit annual financial statements starting in 1970, and to grant licenses for Valium and Librium to two British pharmaceutical firms, one of which was later taken over by Revlon, Inc. In all these matters Roche did not cooperate in any way with the United Kingdom health authorities, and acted only when it was forced to by statutory decree.

Given Roche's lack of cooperation, the DHSS in September 1971 referred the entire issue of Valium and Librium pricing to the Monopolies Commission (MONC), which for the next 18 months studied the question. During this period, Roche cut prices over 30% in response to the new competitors' pricing policies. Management also refused to provide MONC with any information on the allocation of centralized research and development costs or world-wide sales figures of Hoffmann-La Roche. The MONC report, released in April 1973, was highly critical of Roche, particularly noting its refusal to provide information and wide discrepancies between arm's-length prices for the raw materials used in Roche drugs and the transfer prices employed by the firm. The report recommended drastic cuts in the prices of both Valium and Librium.

Within 48 hours of the report's publication, the British Minister of Trade and Consumer Affairs ordered Roche to cut the price of Valium by 75% and Librium by 60% from 1970 levels. A copy of the report was forwarded to the EEC Commission for scrutiny. Roche was not given a chance to respond officially to the charges contained in the report, but was "invited" by the Secretary of State for Social Services to negotiate the repayment of "excess" profits earned since 1971. "Roche cannot have expected to come through the ordeal of inspection by the Monopolies Commission unscathed, but it is doubtful whether it anticipated quite the roasting it got."[100]

A few days later, the German Federal Cartel Office announced an official investigation of Hoffmann-La Roche's pricing practices—Valium and Librium prices in Germany were four times those in Britain—and the EEC Commission also expressed "interest" in the MONC report. After consultation with parent company officials in Switzerland, Roche announced that it would appeal the price cuts to the Special Orders Committee of the House of Lords, and indicated that the repayment of "excess" profits was "out of the question."[101] The company also ignored the request to negotiate on possible repayments. And management released a strongly-worded statement to the press charging the British government with unfair discrimination against Roche because it was foreign-owned, and accusing the government of abrogating its patents. One observer noted ". . . it is clear that Roche and its Swiss parent company, Hoffmann-La Roche of Basle, are preparing for a head-on clash with the government over the affair."[102]

For the first time in the company's history, a public news conference was held at Hoffmann-La Roche headquarters in Basle on April 28, 1973. According to the firm's chairman, "We refuse to repay one cent. In paying back I would admit I made immoral profits. The British Government has decided to dramatically interfere with the business practices of our firm. It has issued special rules with regard to just one company, thereby establishing a kind of special decree to one entity among many forming the pharmaceutical industry. We consider this lack of fair play against which we will fight."[103] He went on to indicate that, although he wished to avoid taking a threatening position toward the British government, the economics of the situation might require blocking Roche exports, drastic curtailment of planned research expenditures in Britain, and even transferring all operations out of Britain. "Health authorities all over the world will have to admit they can no longer continue with the unilateral interference that is now so fashionable and is motivated on purely political grounds. Once the first wave of sensation in the mass media has abated, it will be time for the soberminded to speak out."[104]

As the conflict spread, the situation in the United Kingdom became increasingly critical for the company.[105] Although a number of countries had begun investigations into Hoffmann-La Roche's pricing practices, decisions were likely to be postponed until the situation in Britain was resolved. Hence the company challenged the authority of the British government to order price cuts in every possible way. It appealed the decision through every available legal channel, hoping to neutralize the statutory powers of the health services. It reminded the British government that there would be economic consequences should the company be forced into reconsidering its investments in the United Kingdom. It even hinted that it was considering taking the British government to the European Court of Justice, thereby challenging the sovereignty of the government itself. This threat was widely disregarded, however, since a defeat in the European Court would subject Hoffmann-La Roche to antitrust prosecution in the EEC. According to one observer, all these efforts ". . . could take years and cost vast sums. But they would be insignificant compared to the revenue Roche would lose if other countries followed Britain's example. This is what Roche most fears. It is banking on being able to persuade other countries to hold their fire until its argument with the British government is settled."[106] Significantly, the patents on Librium and Valium were due to expire in 1975 and 1976, respectively. If Hoffmann-La Roche could manage to maintain its prices for a few more years, it would have succeeded in maintaining profit levels throughout the entire patent life, after which prices would in any case be expected to fall due to increased competition.

In June 1973, a British Special Orders Committee recommended that a select committee be set up in the House of Lords to review the matter. However, in an unusual move the House of Lords rejected the recommendation, and the Roche managing director charged the DHSS with political interference in this supposedly neutral forum.[107] Hoffmann-La Roche headquarters in Basle declared that it would "go to the High Court. It is a very unfair decision."[108] The company thereupon issued a writ against the DHSS charging that its decision to order price cuts was against the "laws of natural justice" and asked for damages in the event the suit succeeded. At about the same time, Hoffmann-La Roche announced its intention to *raise* the prices of Librium and Valium in defiance of the DHSS order—a maneuver designed to force the issue into court. DHSS sought an injunction against the announced intention to raise prices and Anthony Wedgewood Benn, speaking in Parliament, stated: "It is clear . . . that what is in effect a militant multinational monopoly is trying to exploit people who use the NHS."[109]

The next day Roche hinted that it had never meant the threat seriously, and the *Economist* surmised, "for the first time in this affair, the Roche company seems to be in retreat and in some confusion."[110] Further changes in Hoffmann-La Roche's attitude came a few days later, when it gave the Secretary of State for Trade and Industry the controversial secret information on company sales that had been the source of so much contention. After studying the documents, he indicated that there was nothing in the information that would cause the government to reexamine the findings of the MONC.

Along with these early indications of a change in Hoffmann-La Roche's attitude came some adverse legal developments. The Appeals Court supported the DHSS application for an injunction against any possible attempt on the part of Roche to raise prices. The only avenue left to the company was an appeal to the House of Lords—and from its previous experience, Roche doubtless concluded that chances for success were rather slim. In fact, the issue became lost for the next several years in the House of Lords, and the main challenge to the government in High Court was in the process of a lengthy litigation that would take years.

In 1974 the conflict in Britain became less visible as the court proceedings continued. Company officials were involved in meetings with authorities in a number of countries, and it appears that Hoffmann-La Roche had reevaluated its position in regard to the situation in the United Kingdom. According to one company spokesman, "We didn't mean to get into a fight with the British."[111] In May 1975, Librium went out of patent in Britain. Since the company was now fully involved in negotiations on drug pricing with a number of governments throughout the world, the original strategy of blocking the spread of the issue became less important. According to Chairman Adolph Jann, "We are like a chess player, compelled to play several boards simultaneously, against opponents with no clearly defined rules, but capable of interpreting them with wide discretion."[112] In Basle, the company even began regularly publishing a consolidated statement of earnings.

In late 1975 the British Department of Trade and Industry and Hoffmann-La Roche announced that an out-of-court settlement had been reached. As part of the agreement, Roche consented to repay excess profits of $28.4 million. However, the government agreed that due to cost increases, Roche was entitled to reduce that figure substantially, leaving the net settlement at $7.7 million. In addition, Roche agreed to join the Voluntary Price Regulation System: "We have discovered that the VPRS is a very reasonable and flexible system. We are very happy that what we have agreed is to settle as if we had been in the VPRS since 1970."[113] The settlement contained features that were agreeable both to the government and to Hoffmann-La Roche. The government had Roche Products participating in its VPRS and the company was left with a reasonable payment to the government.

In 1973, the *Manchester Guardian* had commented that the Roche inquiry should "warn governments of the dangerous opacity of the multinational companies."[114] In 1975, on resolution of the conflict, the *Sunday Times* pointed to "the almost total transformation of Roche from an enterprise uniquely secretive even for a Swiss company into a more or less responsible, open multinational corporation is an example of great world-wide significance.[115]

Meantime, however, Hoffman-La Roche was in hot water over drug pricing and marketing practices in a number of other countries as well, in addition to the EEC. In May of 1975, when the EEC antitrust suit against the company on vitamin pricing was in full swing, a former Hoffman-La Roche employee and star witness for the EEC, Stanley Adams, was arrested at the urging of Roche by the Swiss government and charged under industrial espionage laws with stealing documents from the company. The EEC put up a $10,000 bond to get Adams released on bail. He alleged that the company kicked back 5% "loyalty premiums" to regular customers, and in return expected to be kept informed on what competitors were doing. After Adams was convicted and jailed in Basle, his wife committed suicide. In July 1975 the EEC Commission formally charged Roche of violating Articles 85 and 86 of the Treaty of Rome, concerning market competition, by means of loyalty rebates and binding customers to exclusive arrangements with the company. A month later the restrictive business practices and kickbacks in the EEC market were said to have been stopped by the company. In June 1976, the Commission decided that Roche held a dominant position in the EEC for seven groups of vitamins, with market shares ranging from 47% to 95% and fined the firm 1.1 million Deutschemarks. Roche appealed the decision, but the European Court of Justice in February 1979 backed the Commission and toughened up EEC competition law on multinationals. As a result of the ruling, one legal observer noted that "Any company which is remotely in a dominant position in Europe will now need to revamp its entire attitude towards its distributors and suppliers."[116]

External Control of Pricing and Distribution

As the Hoffmann-La Roche case shows, multinational corporate conflict in the areas of pricing and distribution primarily pits the MNE against government authorities charged with ensuring that the market works—that producers are not able to abuse dominant positions in the market at the expense of purchasers, whether these are individuals or the government itself.

Yashica, the Japanese photo-optical firm, refused to deliver any further cameras to one of Germany's largest dealers, Doppheide and Kollow, after the latter refused to stop selling cameras at prices below those recommended by the manufacturer. The German Federal Cartel Office in 1972 ruled that the refusal was an infringement of German antitrust law and that attempts to enforce price recommendations through economic sanctions or the threat of such sanctions also constituted violations of the law. Yashica was fined. At about the same time Braun, the German subsidiary of Gillette, was also ordered to stop its retail price maintenance system on the grounds that the company could not legally prevent unauthorized re-imports of its products, without which it was impossible to enforce the system. Although the company decided to appeal the ruling, by June 1973 it had discontinued retail price maintenance.[117]

Such activity has also become common at the EEC level. Warner Bros. maintained the prices of its recordings more than 50% higher in Germany than in France through export restrictions and a retail price maintenance system. In 1973 the company was fined $60,000 by the EEC Commission for violation of Community antitrust provisions.[118] In 1972 the European Court of Justice upheld a 1969 Commission ruling that fined 10 chemical companies a total of $485,000 for violations of EEC antitrust laws. The Court ruled that "parallel pricing" policies utilized by the firms had the effect of creating five virtually isolated markets for dyestuffs within the EEC, with prices in the five areas differing by amounts not explained by cost factors. There was additional evidence of coordinated price progressions among the various companies. Although three of the firms were not based in the EEC at the time—Imperial Chemical Industries, Ciba-Geigy, and Sandoz—the Court ruled that their actions affected intra-EEC trade and thus fell under the jurisdiction of EEC antitrust law.[119]

A few years later, Commercial Solvents and its Italian subsidiary, Instituto Chemiotheripico Italiano were charged with violation of Article 86 of the Treaty of Rome for refusing to supply the base chemicals used in the manufacture of an anti-tuberculosis drug to another Italian company. The EEC Commission ruling was upheld by the European Court of Justice. The Court held that the nationality of the parent company was irrelevant because the effects of the restrictive practice was felt within the EEC, and Commercial Solvents was fined $120,000.[120] At about the same time, Beecham and Hoechst had an agreement that Beecham would supply Hoechst with unpacked ampicillin if Hoechst sold the drug only for human consumption and only in consumer-sized packaging. In addition, Hoechst was restricted to selling the ampicillin only in Germany and Austria. The EEC Commission filed a cease and desist order in 1976 and indicated that large fines would be imposed if the companies did not terminate the arrangement. Beecham and Hoechst complied with the order and amended their sales agreement.[121]

Elsewhere, the Parker Company had granted an exclusive license to M.N.C. Inc. (Canada) to distribute Parker pens outside the United States. Through its controlled distributorships and trademark licenses, M.N.C. monopolized the sale of Parker pens in Japan. Shriro Trading Co. requested permission to import the pens from Hong Kong independently but M.N.C. denied the request. In a subsequent lawsuit initiated by Shriro Trading, a Kobe District Court ruled in 1970 that M.N.C. could not prevent the Shriro from doing so.[122] In the United States, Anheuser-Busch restricted sales of its beer to only one distributor in the Bahamas in order to maintain prices in the Bahamian market. When wholesalers in the States tried to sell Anheuser-Busch beer to an independent Bahamian distributor, the company refused to allow the sales. In 1974 a court ruled that although the market lay entirely outside the United States, the restrictions imposed on American wholesalers were violations of United States antitrust law.[123] And in Scandinavia, several Swedish, Norwegian, and Finnish paper and paperboard manufacturers had an agreement not to sell in each others' markets. When the Ombudsman for Freedom of Commerce in Sweden ruled that the cartel constituted a restraint of trade, the members of the cartel agreed to terminate their agreements.[124]

Although antitrust laws such as the ones covering these conflicts have existed in the United States since the latter part of the nineteenth century, they are essentially a postwar phenomenon in much of the rest of the world. For the international marketer, antitrust laws introduce a climate of uncertainty, since the body of antitrust law and its applicability in a particular country is often not fully understood until after a major case—many times involving a multinational corporation—has been brought through a long process of litigation. Such laws are often applied selectively, and there is great variation in the amount of time and resources that antitrust authorities are either willing or able to devote to their consistent development. As of 1974, for example, the Brazilian antitrust authority, CADE, had only ruled in one case in its 12 year history.[125]

A great deal of attention has focused on the EEC's emerging body of antitrust law due to the large amount of business conducted by multinationals within the Common Market. The EEC Commission is empowered to enforce the antitrust provisions contained in Articles 85 and 86 of the Treaty of Rome, which prohibit practices that harm intra-EEC competition either through the use of restrictive practices or by abusing a dominant market position. On an operational level, the EEC Antitrust Directorate is one of only two agencies that are not required to have their activities approved by the Commission or national governments.[126] Consequently, the Antitrust Directorate is free to pursue antitrust violators without regard to political constraints that have hampered the functioning of so many EEC agencies. For multinational companies, the only recourse to the Directorate's rulings is an appeal to the European Court of Justice, and as we have seen, this often ends in failure.

EEC antitrust law has two major areas of concern—concentration and restrictive practices. Article 86, which covers abuse of dominant market position, is of importance to multinational firms because they often hold sizeable positions in markets and are by nature aggressive marketers. Characteristically, it is not always clear what constitutes a "dominant position," which itself is not prohibited but rather only *abuse* of that position. Restrictive business practices fall under Article 85 and cover five major classifications: (1) price-fixing, market sharing and quotas; (2) import and export cartels; (3) distribution agreements and resale price maintenance schemes; (4) exclusionary practices; and (5) joint R&D, standardization, and specialization.[127]

The marketer must not only be aware of the provisions of the Treaty of Rome, but he must also be concerned with the antitrust laws within each of the member states of the EEC. As we have seen, antitrust authorities such as Germany's Federal Cartel Office, France's Commission Technique des Ententes et des Positions Dominantes, and Britain's Monopolies Commission can be sources of serious problems for the multinational marketer in Europe.

In Japan, conflicts between multinational firms and antitrust authorities have been less apparent. "In Japan, the degree of power the antimonopoly law and its chief guardian, the FTC (Fair Trade Commission), wields in the world of Japanese Business is striking, especially in view of the fact that the basic law was artificially grafted onto a social structure which never embraced many of the ideals that served as the underlying base for the growth of this type of legislation in the West."[128] The Antimonopoly Act, passed in 1947, prohibits private monopolies, unreasonable restraints of trade, and unfair business practices. To date, there have been few cases of multinational firms being prosecuted under the Antimonopoly Act, largely as a result of their comparatively limited role in the Japanese economy. However, "the present outlook . . . is for the FTC to play a key role in the life of all business marketing in Japan during the 1970s. This role may be strengthened by the prognosis for change in the traditional Japanese marketing patterns and the gradual relaxation of control over the activities of foreign businesses by other Japanese government agencies."[129] The basic elements of Japanese antitrust law are modeled after United States antitrust law. It will be interesting to watch future developments in Japanese antitrust activity as multinational corporations become an increasingly competitive part of the Japanese economy.

Antitrust laws in the developing countries do not form any consistent pattern. If such laws exist at all, they are selectively enforced. This uncertain legal climate can present problems for the multinational corporation, since there are often few reliable guidelines to define acceptable conduct.

Antitrust laws in the Eastern Bloc nations represent the opposing end of the spectrum. "Practices which our countries would condemn as criminal or civil antitrust violations are there enshrined as the natural and desirable approach to all economic activity. Attempts to monopolize, combinations in restraint of trade, price-fixing, refusal to deal, division of markets, reciprocal purchase decisions, and exclusion of competitive products, far from being legislatively proscribed, are constitutionally protected principals of public policy."[130] Trade with Eastern Bloc nations can thus present perplexing antitrust issues.

To sum it all up, one author notes: "All over the world, from Australia to West Germany, antitrust laws are being revised, extended, and strengthened. This trend is making business increasingly complicated and bewildering for the multinational corporation. . . .While the intricacies of antitrust have become a special field for specialist lawyers, executives making the deals that antitrust is concerned with can hardly afford to ignore the subject."[131]

PROMOTION CONFLICT

A major source of marketing conflict for multinational companies involves the promotion of products in markets that are subject to widely divergent constraints. Promotional techniques that are perfectly acceptable in some countries may be viewed as counterproductive with respect to national economic, social, or political goals in other countries. What seems perfectly reasonable in one time and place may appear irresponsible in another, and the MNE may be called on the carpet as a result. A few representative conflicts follow:

In 1978, a rather eye-catching Finnair ad in the United States was withdrawn after the National Organization for Women (NOW) objected to its headline that the sauna was discovered when a Finn "locked his wife in the smokehouse, set it on fire, beat her soundly with birch leaves, and discovered she loved it." NOW objected to the reference to wife-beating. Puzzled, Finnair agreed to withdraw the ad.[132]

In 1973, the Swedish Academy of Fine Arts sought an injunction against Levi Strauss to stop an advertisement that showed a pair of Levis jeans being "created" by God— superimposing a pair of jeans onto a photograph of Michaelangelo's "Creation" from the Sistine Chapel. The injunction was sought under Swedish copyright laws which "prohibits the display of an artistic work in a manner that violates cultural interests."[133]

Four years later, Levi Strauss was the plaintiff in lawsuits filed in San Francisco, London, Hong Kong, Belgium, Switzerland, and the Netherlands seeking $5 million in damages against an international group of counterfeiters of Levis jeans. A former employee allegedly set up a company under the name "Levi Strauss & Co. Taiwan" with several other businessmen to make jeans. The company had produced 110,000 pair of jeans before the crackdown. In 1978 Levi Strauss persuaded a number of other MNEs such as Samsonite, General Electric, General Mills, Munsingwear, Pierre Cardin, Walt Disney Productions, and A.T. Cross to join forces via a new International Anti-Counterfeiting Coalition to press for stiffer regulations of bogus goods worldwide.[134]

Philips N.V. introduced a new electric shaver into the German market in 1972 as the first major effort to cut into the commanding control of the German shaver market by the Braun subsidiary of Gillette. A Philips advertisement claimed the shaver "could be used like a wet razor." Braun sued Philips, contending that the ads were misleading and promoted an unjustified claim of uniqueness. The court ruled in Braun's favor. Braun had also won an earlier court decision against Philips in October 1971 in which Philips had claimed world leadership for electric razors. The court ruled that Philips could not make that claim in Germany.[135]

A few years later in the United States, Matsushita Electric Industries Corp., makers of Panasonic television sets, was charged in 1976 with misleading advertising by the Federal Trade Commission for claiming its televisions were "the easiest, least time consuming and least expensive" to repair. Matsushita supported its claim with independent tests, but the FTC disagreed that the tests supported the claim.[136]

Later the same year in Holland, Theodorus Niemeyer—wholly-owned by the British-based Gallagher Group—and British-American Tobacco (BAT) reached a gentleman's agreement not to use "nicotine-poor" in cigarette ads. When Niemeyer started a comparative ad campaign to show their Roxy-Dual cigarettes were lower in nicotine than BAT's brands, BAT took Niemeyer to court for misleading advertising. BAT won the case and Niemeyer was ordered to cease and desist from showing the ads or face a heavy fine.[137]

In 1978, General Foods was fined $4300 in France for wrongful advertising in claiming that its instant beverage, Tang, had the taste of freshly squeezed orange juice. The complaint was filed by two French soft-drink and fruit juice producer associations.[138]

And in the United States Anheuser-Busch, the nation's leading brewer, filed a complaint with the FTC against Philip Morris's Miller subsidiary for misleading advertising. Miller acquired exclusive rights to Germany's Löwenbräu beer in 1974 and marketed the product in bottles only slightly different from the original. However, Miller changed the formulation of the Löwenbräu beer from 100% malt to only 75% malt. Anheuser-Busch maintained the Miller ads misled the public into thinking the beer was from Germany. The FTC decided to allow the companies to settle their differences in advertising privately, rather than through the FTC edict. Under pressure from the U.S. Treasury Department's Bureau of Alcohol, Tobacco and Firearms, however, Miller changed its Löwenbräu advertising to make it clearer that the beer is made in the United States.[139]

The Regulatory Setting

Of the major forms of promotion—advertising, personal selling, publicity, and sales promotion—advertising is subject to the most restrictive regulatory environment internationally, and represents a continuum with respect to degree of control or consistency of application. The United States has a relatively unrestricted advertising climate, although even here the situation is becoming increasingly difficult. Advertising is also one of the few marketing practices that is subject to rather tight government regulation and control in a number of developing countries not otherwise noted for an especially restrictive marketing environment.

Part of the reason why advertising is so heavily regulated is because of its highly exposed position. Advertising relies on television as a major vehicle for reaching its audiences, and outside the United States there is almost always state monopolization or at least some state ownership of television transmission. With government control of broadcasting comes governmental control over the content of advertisements that are permitted. In Canada, for example, advertising directed at children is banned outright on the government channel. The government also restricts the amount of time the commercial channel may devote to such advertisements, and all scripts and storyboards must obtain government approvals before the commercials are aired.[140]

Other countries have similar restrictions. "Germany, Switzerland and New Zealand don't allow TV ads on Sunday. In Austria, France, Germany, Holland, Italy, and Switzerland, commercial time is strictly limited and therefore sold on an allocation basis."[141] In Italy, it is forbidden to advertise luxury goods on television. In Germany, any of the seven state governments can prohibit a television advertisement that it opposes for "moral or ethical" reasons. Also in Germany it is essentially prohibited to mention the name of a competitor in any advertisement. Some countries ban all comparison advertising and others forbid advertisements that mention a competitor's prices. Such control takes effect before the advertisements even get on the air, and government authority is unassailable.

Another reason advertising in particular seems to come under high degree of government control is that it is relatively simple to regulate. It does not require a large bureaucracy of highly trained specialists or sophisticated information systems to look at a commercial and decide whether or not it can be seen on television or heard on radio. In Venezuela, a Superintendency of Advertising has a broad mandate to approve advertising content both locally generated and foreign, as well as authority to dictate how much a company may spend on advertising.[142] In France, under the Energy Conservation Act of 1974, supplemental enabling legislation was passed "to forbid all advertising . . . which is of a nature to favor an increase in the consumption of energy."[143] It is extremely difficult to control energy comsumption, but quite easy to ban advertisements that promote energy consumption. Critics of this type of regulation point to the failure of the American ban on cigarette T.V. advertising to reduce the level of smoking. However, such restrictions are an easily-accomplished, relatively inexpensive way for the government to show its constituency that it is taking action on a particular issue.

Some countries take a less restrictive view of advertising. A few favor industry self-regulation as a workable means of insuring the fairness in advertising. In Holland, "self-regulation is administered through an Advertising Code Commission made up of volunteers from advertising associations, consumers' organizations, newspaper and magazine publishers, and advertising agencies and consultants."[144] Although the Commission cannot impose penalties, it can ban advertisements from the media and blacklist anyone that ignores the ban. In Britain, the Advertising Association, consisting of four industry members, eight public members, and an independent chairman, is responsible for approving all television advertisements. In France, the Bureau pour la Vérification de la Publicité has a government representative on its board and performs a similar function.

The diversity of regulatory environments found among the European countries alone presents difficulties even for the EEC Commission as it attempts to harmonize member-state advertising regulations through its proposed "directive on misleading and unfair advertising." The directive went through four drafts during two years, and a final version was presented to the Council of Ministers for approval in March 1978.[145] There has been continuing controversy over the proposal and action was expected to take some time.

In the United States the main government agency concerned with advertising regulation is the Federal Trade Commission (FTC), although there are several agencies that have authority over specific types of advertising. Until 1970, the FTC focused on localized instances of blatantly misleading advertising.[146] Thereafter, it took a much more active role in examining the limits of its authority, which covers unfair and deceptive acts or practices in commerce. "Corrective advertising" was introduced into the FTC regulatory tools, as well as requirements that advertisers substantiate all claims with objective evidence. The Agency is also beginning to explore some of the larger issues associated with advertising, especially practices that fall under the broadly defined category of "unfair" advertising. The FTC does not enjoy the position of power held by regulatory agencies in other countries, and each time it explores a new area it is immediately surrounded with controversy, with final decisions frequently subject to litigation. For example, a recent FTC proposal to ban advertising to children—first studied in the early 1970s—will have to go through a lengthy process of public discussion before the agency makes a ruling. When the FTC finally acts in 1981, the decision will be fiercely contested in court by advertisers.[147] Whereas most countries can implement such a decision almost by government fiat, as in Canada, the FTC can take 15 years for an issue to be studied, discussed, and implemented.

Industry self-regulation has become a feature of the United States advertising environment since 1972. If a complaint is submitted from any source about a national advertising campaign, the advertisement is reviewed by the National Advertising Division (NAD) of the National Council of Better Business Bureaus (NCBB). If a company disagrees with an unfavorable ruling by the NAD, the matter is referred to the National Advertising Review Board (NARB), made up of leading members of the advertising industry. If an accord is not reached after the appeal to the NARB, the Board will simply publish its findings and send the matter to the FTC for its consideration. The procedure has been judged relatively effective thus far, but since there are no longer many instances of blatantly misleading advertisements, this success is not surprising. And it is questionable whether the review procedure is capable of adjudicating some of the more sophisticated controversies that are developing on "unfair" advertisements.

Although self-regulation coexists with government control, the trend is clearly toward increasing government control. According to one observer," . . . advertisers are unable to comprehend the present trends in regulation. Through costly experience, advertisers have learned that the same ad will have different meanings for the same person in different situations. . . . Equipped with this experience, advertisers cannot understand questions like, 'What is the meaning of this ad?'"[148] Advertisers will be increasingly confronted with such questions as control becomes more extensive. For their part, advertisers contend that " . . . regulators and other government employees do not appreciate the presence of this uncertainty, nor do they understand the mechanisms that cause it."[149] Still, the trend worldwide is toward more regulation, not less.

Whatever one thinks about government control of the media and advertising, the rules of the game are at least relatively clear-cut in each country. Hence multinationals are able to adapt to the regulatory environment and operate more or less successfully within it. This is far less true, however, of other techniques of sales promotion. And when these rules are unclear, ambiguous, or non-existent, the potential for major conflict becomes evident.

The Infant Formula Controversy

"In 1866, in the little town of Vevey, a baby was on the point of death because he could not tolerate any food. The family doctor was a friend of Henri Nestlé, and knew about his experiments with a new complete food for infants. The doctor begged him to give the food to the dying baby. Nestlé agreed, and the baby lived."[150] A century later, the Swiss-based multinational Nestlé Alimentana, S.A., was the center of a massive conflict concerning the marketing of infant formula in developing countries, and a song was making the rounds (sung to the tune of "I'll Never Fall in Love Again"): "What do they get when they take the bottle/They get enough germs to catch Marasmus/Nestlé may win but the babies all lose . . . I'll never buy from Nestlé again/No, I'll never buy from Nestlé again."[151]

It is widely agreed that, in general, breast feeding provides the most satisfactory form of nutrition for infants. Mother's milk provides resistance to disease, requires no preparation, and is free. Yet evidence shows a decline in breast feeding throughout the developing world in favor of infant formula—generally acknowledged to be a safe, high-quality product. Opponents to the use of infant formula in the developing countries have argued that it contributes to malnutrition, diarrea, and death among infants, and that consumers are incapable of using the product properly because of the pervasiveness of poverty and illiteracy. For their part, proponents of infant formula have noted that infant mortality in developing countries is actually declining, that the product itself is safe, and that the companies who manufacture and sell it cannot be held responsible for the conditions of poverty and illiteracy in which it is used. Several specific practices have been at issue.

First, infant formula producers have employed a variety of promotional techniques in the highly competitive battle for a share of this market. Critics have condemned the employment of milk nurses or mothercraft personnel (saleswomen dressed in nurse-like uniforms) by the companies. They maintain that these nurses are no more than sales agents, disguised as members of the medical profession who (especially when they are on commission) cannot be relied upon to discuss breast feeding impartially while under retainer to the infant formula companies. The industry has responded to these charges by emphasizing the need for such nurses to educate consumers on the proper use of infant formula in the absence of adequate official health personnel in developing countries.

Second, many companies have provided free samples of infant formula to clinics and hospitals. Critics contend that when mothers receive free samples they become dependent on continued use of the product, since the lactation process of the mother becomes easily disrupted with the discontinuation of breast feeding. Eventually the mother can no longer obtain the free samples, but by then she is "hooked" on the product. Yet the income of her family may well be insufficient to afford proper quantities of infant formula to insure the health of the child. By "stretching" infant formula to fit meagre family budgets, malnutrition can easily result. The companies have argued that the samples are given only to the health professionals, absolving management of further responsibility.

Third, manufacturers have long supplied health professionals in developing countries with benefits such as furniture and air conditioners for clinics and free formula for physicians' wives. Critics content that these benefits have had the effect of compromising the independence and integrity of the doctors and nurses involved. The companies have insisted that they retain their independence.

Finally, there has been the matter of advertising infant formula. Not all companies have employed advertising, but those that have insist that they stress the benefits of breast feeding and that as with any consumer good, are necessary to establish brand awareness. They are also considered to serve an educational role. Critics maintain that advertisements have been designed to induce mothers to believe that healthy babies depend on infant formula, and that this "modern" form of feeding carries with it elevated social standing.

During the early 1970s the decline of breast feeding in developing countries and the possible economic, social, and health effects of aggressive promotion of infant formula began to be discussed among nutrition specialists. In 1972 and 1973 the United Nations Protein Advisory Group (PAG) sponsored a series of conferences on the problem, attended by several of the leading infant formula manufacturers, and drew attention to the concern felt by the participants about the situation.[152] In March 1974 a pamphlet entitled "The Baby Killer" was published in London by the British charitable organization "War On Want," which examined in detail the general issue and provided specific examples of allegedly harmful promotional practices employed by the industry, with Nestlé mentioned prominently.[153] The company had no reaction to the pamphlet. In May 1974 a

Swiss activist group made up of teachers, clergy, and students, translated the pamphlet into German. The group known as the Third World Action Group (TWAG) made a decision to change the title of the pamphlet to "Nestlé Kills Babies," and added a new introduction that was highly critical specifically of Nestlé. The group also prepared posters to promote the pamphlet and drafted an open letter to Nestlé repeating the allegations contained in the introduction to the pamphlet.

Nestlé responded in July 1974 with a lawsuit against TWAG charging the group with libel. The suit contained four specific charges, directed at the title, the introduction, and the text itself, and attracted the attention of the world press. Although Nestlé announced its intention not to comment on the suit until the hearings—scheduled for November 1975—were underway, TWAG soon afterward released a 40-page document titled "Does Nestlé Kill Babies? An Attempt by a Multinational Company to Silence a Political Development Action Group: Provisional Report of a Suit," which contained testimonial evidence against the promotional practices of the infant formula manufacturers. The publicity surrounding the Nestlé lawsuit induced the World Health Organization to adopt a resolution calling for a review of the entire infant formula issue. In the United States, Consumers Union sponsored the publication of a book titled *Hungry for Profits*, which included a study of the promotional practices of the leading American infant formula manufacturers.[154] Armed with the information contained in that volume, several church groups in the United States filed shareholder resolutions with Abbott Laboratores, American Home Products, and Bristol-Myers to cease and desist from the offending marketing practices.

Nestlé vs. TWAG. The Nestlé libel suit in Berne was held in a series of three sessions in 1975 and 1976. Just prior to the hearings, an industry association called the International Council of Infant Formula Industries (ICIFI) was formed to produce a voluntary code of ethics concerning the promotion of infant formula. Almost simultaneously, TWAG held a major press conference with the British author of "The Baby Killer."

Once the hearings were underway, Nestlé announced that it was quite confident that the company's promotional practices were both morally and ethically sound. Nestlé could only assume resonsibility for seeing that its advertising did not contain any misleading statements, and could not be held accountable for conditions of poverty or illiteracy that might lead to abuse of its products. With regard to TWAG, Nestlé's managing director stated, "No-one has the right to accuse us of killing babies. No-one has the right to assert that we are pursuing unethical and immoral sales practices, . . . this is why we have brought libel actions against them. . . . Even in these troubled times which we are living through, we fail to see the obligation for a firm to allow its good reputation to be so tarnished."[155] He went on to accuse TWAG of using the issue of infant malnutrition as a way "to attack one of those capitalist multinational creations in the hope of convincing a sufficient number of dupes" by means of "lies, distortions, and false allegations."

Just prior to the end of the hearings in June 1976, a 20-page Nestlé press release entitled "Infant Feeding as Seen by Nestlé" provided positive testimonial support from authorities on infant nutrition to counter the adverse testimonial support that TWAG had been using in their own press releases. The company acknowledged that there were a number of credible witnesses involved on the other side of the controversy, but that these well-intentioned individuals had misperceived the real problem. It posed the question, "What is the purpose of the attacks by TWAG? Again we are indebted to the authors for the answer: 'the image of the multinational exploiting the poverty of the Third World mothers makes good copy for a radical charity.' In other words, these people make use of any issue which helps to discredit industry, regardless of whether it happens to be the truth or not."[156] Indeed, TWAG had stated in an earlier publication that "the multinational companies have been criticized by the public for a long time, but it has hardly come to concrete investigation in court. It is all the more vital in the political debate that the problem arising from the introduction of Western consumption into developing countries should be openly discussed."[157]

The conflict between Nestlé and the Third World Action Group ended rather abruptly on June 24, 1976 when the Company dropped three of its four charges against TWAG—the only charge left for the court to rule on was the allegedly libelous title of the TWAG pamphlet. Nestlé explained that the charges were dropped "merely to simplify proceedings" and to avoid another four years of litigation. The Court awarded the case to Nestlé, although the presiding judge noted that his decision" . . . was not an acquittal of Nestlé. . . . The company must reconsider its advertising policies if it wants to avoid being accused of immoral conduct."[158] It levied only token fines against the defendants and TWAG decided not to appeal the decision, apparently satisfied with the comments made by the judge. A letter from the Nestlé Managing Director to company employees after the trial made it clear that Nestlé would not consider any changes in its promotional policies for infant formula in developing countries despite the court's admonishments. "Our products are indispensable to many children. Consequently we cannot give up effective advertising. . . . We must affirm that we have full confidence in the ethical basis of our actions."[159] Thus ended the Nestlé-TWAG conflict. Little was accomplished for either side, but promotion of infant formula was now a matter of international attention. Nestlé management emerged from the conflict confident of the propriety of its promotional policies, and with a lingering suspicion that those opposed to the promotion of infant formula in developing countries were using the issue for essentially political motives.

The infant formula controversy in the United States. In the 1950s and 1960s a number of American companies developed infant formula products as the postwar "baby-boom" unfolded, and as many as 75% of all American infants born in some years received formula. However, as the birth rate declined during the late 1960s, manufacturers were forced to look to overseas markets to maintain sales momentum.[160] Abbott Laboratories concentrated on Canada, Europe, and North Africa; American Home Products focused on Latin America, Europe, and South East Asia; while Bristol-Myers looked to Puerto Rico, Jamaica, and the Bahamas. A number of church groups, alarmed by the various infant formula allegations, initiated shareholder resolutions directed at the companies, initially concentrating their efforts to force disclosure of information on the promotion of infant formula in developing countries. In January 1975, top officials of Bristol-Meyers met with representatives of the Interfaith Center on Corporate Responsibility to discuss the stockholder resolution filed with their company.

Throughout 1975, similar meetings were also held between ICCR representatives and officials of Abbott and American Home Products. In April, the Ford and Rockefeller Foundations joined in support of the ICCR demands that Bristol-Myers divulge information on the Company's sales of infant formula in the Third World, and management agreed to publish a special report on the subject. Titled "Infant Formula Practices of the Bristol-Myers Company in Countries Outside the U.S.," the report was not well received—a leading nutrition specialist closely allied with opponents of the marketing practices of infant formula companies condemned it as being "inadequate and evasive."[161]

Nine infant formula manufacturers met in Switzerland in May 1975 as members of the International Council of Infant Formula Industries to develop a code of ethics regarding the promotion of infant formula (see Exhibit 10-2). Instead of prohibiting many of the controversial promotional practices, they emphasized the need to use existing practices responsibly. Bristol-Myers refused to participate in the ICIFI meetings at all. Abbott decided that the code was too lenient, and preferred to devise its own more stringent code of marketing ethics. The Abbott code ruled out the use of mass media advertising entirely, although it allowed the use of mothercraft nurses and free samples. In an assessment of the actions taken by the various infant formula manufacturers, one observer indicates that the orientation of the various companies helps explain their behavior with regard to ethical codes. Abbott, American Home Products, and Bristol-Myers were essentially drug companies that promoted infant formula in a manner similar to the way ethical drugs were sold, relying more heavily on promotion to hospitals and physicians where they were already well established. Nestlé, on the other hand, is a food processing company that has used mass media advertising as an integral part of its overall marketing plans. The ICIFI code meetings were dominated by Nestlé which, not unexpectedly, insisted on allowing the use of mass media advertising. Abbott, not feeling compelled to use this means of promotion, was agreeable to banning its use.[162]

As a result of the various meetings with church officials, shareholder resolutions were withdrawn at American Home Products and Abbott. The Bristol-Myers resolution was in fact voted upon, but received only a small percentage of shareholder support. In 1976, ICCR continued to exert pressure on company officials by filing new shareholder petitions.[163] In spite of a number of meetings between ICCR representatives and Bristol-Myers management, the Company's 1976 proxy statement included a resolution to ensure that its products were "not promoted where chronic poverty or ignorance could lead to misuse."[164] On the day before the Bristol-Myers annual meeting, four church groups led by the Sisters of the Precious Blood filed suit against the Company for false and misleading statements in management's recommendations to shareholders in the proxy statement. Bristol-Myers tried to have the suit summarily dismissed, but it was allowed to proceed. For the remainder of the year, ICCR was actively involved in accumulating evidence from developing countries to support the Sisters' lawsuit. ICCR shareholder resolutions introduced at Abbott and Bristol-Myers received 1.7 and 3.5% of the ballots, respectively, in 1976—the American Home Products resolution was withdrawn after discussions with company officials. In July, representatives of activist groups in eight countries concerned with the promotion of infant formula met in Switzerland and issued a joint resolution to continue the struggle. In August, Representative Michael Harrington introduced a joint resolution into the U.S. House of Representatives calling

Exhibit 10–2

Zurich, November 1975

Code of Ethics and Professional Standards for
Advertising, Product Information and Advisory
Services for Breast-Milk Substitutes

In recognition that sound nutrition during infancy is essential for normal growth and development, the members of the INTERNATIONAL COUNCIL OF INFANT FOOD INDUSTRIES subscribe to the principles and the primacy of the medical and paramedical professions' roles in supervising the dietary intake of infants. These principles affirm that the milk of healthy mothers is the preferred form of nutrition for normal infants, and support the recommendations of the United Nations Protein-Calorie Advisory Group and of the World Health Organization.

Breast-milk substitutes meet essential needs when used appropriately in the feeding of infants. Breast-milk substitutes are intended to supplement breast-milk and for use when mothers cannot or elect not to breast feed for medical or other reasons.

Therefore, the members of the INTERNATIONAL COUNCIL OF INFANT FOOD INDUSTRIES hereby pledge that:

1) As providers of essential supplies for infant nutrition, the members of ICIFI accept responsibility for the diffusion of information which supports sound infant feeding practices and for services consistent with the application of this Code.
2) Product information for the public will always recognize the milk of healthy, well-nourished mothers as the feeding choice with the recommendation to seek professional advice when a supplement or alternative may be required.
3) Product labelling will affirm breast feeding as the first choice for the nutrition of normal infants.
4) Product claims will reflect scientific integrity without implication that any product is superior to the breast milk of healthy mothers.
5) To insure optimal nutritional intake, explicitly worded instructions and demonstrations for product use will be provided for the hygienic and correctly measured preparation of breast-milk substitutes.
6) In cooperation with health authorities, professional communications and educational materials will be provided to caution against misuse and to inform mothers on the importance of methods for obtaining safe water for the preparation of breast-milk substitutes.
7) Members' personnel will observe professional ethics and established rules of conduct in medical/nursing centres, maternities, and physicians' offices and in all contacts.
8) Members will employ nurses, nutritionists, and midwives whenever possible to perform mothercraft services. When professionally trained personnel are not available, high educational standards and experience commensurate with prevailing conditions will be required. Training of these staffs will be in keeping with scientific standards for infant nutrition to emphasize the importance of breast-feeding and the appropriate use of breast-milk substitutes.
9) Individual contacts by mothercraft personnel and issuance of complementary supplies of breast-milk substitutes will be in consultation with medical or nursing personnel in the institution or the area.
10) Mothercraft personnel will support doctors' and nurses' prerogatives in counselling mothers on infant feeding and will not discourage mothers from establishing or continuing breast-feeding.
11) Nurses' uniforms will be worn only by persons who are professionally entitled to their use. The attire worn by mothercraft personnel will bear the identification of the respective ICIFI member. It is recommended that an ICIFI emblem be worn.
12) Compensation of mothercraft personnel will be on a basis of ICIFI except when precluded by the laws or regulations of a given country.
13) Adherence to this Code will be obligatory on all members of ICIFI except when precluded by the laws or regulations of a given country.

Companies adopting the Code: Nestlé of Switzerland, Wyeth International of the United States, Unigate of Britain, Dumex of Denmark, and four Japanese firms Meiji Milk, Morinaga Milk, Snow Brand Milk and Wakado.

for an investigation into the promotion of infant formula and any possible relevance the matter might have to the U.S. Agency for International Development.

Conflict diffusion. During 1977 the infant formula controversy became more complex, and could no longer be defined in terms of two somewhat isolated conflicts—Nestlé in Europe and the three major suppliers in the United States. In January, a new coalition was formed. Activist groups involved with the issue in major American cities joined with several campus-related groups to form a new coalition called the Infant Formula Action Coalition (INFACT), under the leadership of the Third World Institute at the University of Minnesota. This new group worked in close cooperation with the ICCR and another church group, the Clergy and Laity Concerned (CALC) which already was involved in a number of international human rights issues (see Chapters 5 and 6). With the expansion in the number of participants in the conflict, it became more difficult to define the specific conflicts under consideration.

ICCR again filed shareholder resolutions in 1977 with the major American infant formula manufacturers.[165] For the first time, Borden (a powerful force in the powdered milk business) received an ICCR shareholder resolution. ICCR also became more adamant in its demands. Systematically visiting countries where infant formula was being marketed, ICCR representatives pinpointed discrepencies between the promotional policies as communicated to them by the company management and their personal observations. Borden was typical of the emerging credibility gap. ICCR had been assured by Borden officials that its milk product Klim was not promoted for infant use. Tape recordings of advertisements for Klim in a number of developing countries flatly contradicted this, and led to the filing of an ICCR shareholder resolution with the company. According to ICCR's supporting statement,

> For the past two years, church shareholders have been questioning companies that market milk and formulas for infants in developing countries. This concern stems from that fact that the promotion of bottle feeding is causing women who could safely and healthfully breast feed to turn away from it. However, bottle feeding is associated with higher rates of mortality, malnutrition, and disease. Dr. Michael Latham, professor of nutrition at Cornell, has said 'placing an infant on a bottle [in developing countries] might be tantamount to signing that baby's death certificate.' Last year, our management told church representatives in a meeting that Klim milk was not promoted for infant milk. However, copies of ads and radio commercials disprove that statement. As shareholders, we are concerned both with candid disclosure and the proper use of our Company's products.

American Home Products had assured ICCR officials that milk nurses were being phased out. Skeptical, the 1977 ICCR shareholder resolution with the company demanded that management publish a timetable for the withdrawal of the nurses. Abbott Laboratories also was the target of a shareholder resolution in 1977 in spite of the concessions made in earlier years. A typical shareholder resolution is reproduced in Exhibit 10–3.

In February 1977, Borden responded to ICCR pressure and agreed to withdraw all promotion of Klim for infants in the developing countries, and the

Exhibit 10-3

Abbott Laboratories

(Infant Formula Shareholder Resolution)

WHEREAS church shareholders, institutional investors, international agencies, nutritional and health specialists have become increasingly concerned with the effects of infant formula malnutrition;

WHEREAS Congress has recently taken action to investigate the role of U.S. based corporations involved in the problem;

WHEREAS many developing countries such as Malaysia, Guyana, and Nigeria are initiating breast feeding campaigns and/or restricting imports and advertising;

THEREFORE, BE IT RESOLVED THAT the Board of Directors make the following changes in our corporation's policies and practices for developing and underdeveloped countries:

1. That management limit free samples given to health care institutions to that quantity sufficient only for use with infants whose mothers are unable to breast feed or whose health is otherwise endangered;
2. That management phase out mothercraft personnel and Abbott nurses;
3. That management terminate any distributorship which persists in using mothercraft personnel;
4. That management prohibit any inducement directed toward health care professionals or government agencies specifically designed to motivate use of Abbott infant formula with babies who have no medical need for the product;
5. That management distribute the Abbott Code of Marketing Ethics for Developing Countries, including the above revisions, annually to all health care institutions and government agencies in all countries where Abbott infant formula is promoted and/or marketed.

AND BE IT FURTHER RESOLVED THAT the Board of Directors provide a full, written report to the shareholders within four months of the date of the 1977 annual meeting showing the implementation and use of the Abbott Code of Marketing Ethics for the corporation, particularly illustrating the procedure for resolving conflict between actual distribution practices and the guidelines in the Code, provided that the cost of preparing this report shall be limited to an amount deemed reasonably by the Board of Directors.

Statement of Security Holder: "Our corporation's decision to market infant formula in developing countries carries with it the obligation to take all reasonable means to see that the product is used safely. Without effective guidelines, Abbott's promotion of infant formula through health care professionals can have the detrimental effect of persuading mothers to use artificial feeding under circumstances where breast feeding would be both safer for the infant and more economical for the family.

Directing formula primarily to babies in medical need of it and separating the sales function from the nursing function through the termination of mothercraft personnel and Abbott nurses are two concrete steps our corporation should take to reduce mothers' access to formula where it is almost impossible to use it safely. Furthermore, we wish our corporation to state clearly that it offers no inducement used specifically to secure the recommendation of infant formula through medical or government authorities.

While Abbott has a forward-looking Code of Marketing Ethics, that code has not been widely distributed in the countries where infant formula is marketed. Maximum distribution would have great potential for influencing the infant formula industry.

Finally, we believe shareholders should be informed about how management is making the Code of Marketing Ethics for Developing Countries work."

ICCR resolution was withdrawn. In March, Abbott consented to major revisions in their code of ethics and agreed to take all mothercraft nurses out of uniform. The ICCR shareholder resolution was withdrawn. In May, the Sisters of the Precious Blood lawsuit against Bristol-Myers was dismissed by the judge on a technicality not related to the underlying issues.[166] The decision was appealed by the Sisters, and in an unusual move the SEC agreed to file an *amicus curiae* brief on behalf of the Sisters.

In July 1977, INFACT called for a national boycott of all Nestlé products in the United States—under the slogan "Crunch Nestlé Quick"—as a protest over the promotion of its infant formula in the Third World. This new conflict appeared to be a greater threat than the earlier conflict with TWAG in Switzerland. Nestlé's sales in the United States at the time were over $2 billion, and according to *Fortune* "expansion in the U.S. has been made a top priority company policy. . . . In the next few years it aims to push the U.S. share of Nestlé's worldwide sales from just over 20 percent to nearly a third. This means more than doubling U.S. sales."[167] In contrast, Nestlé's sales of infant formula represented only $300 million, or less than 7% of its worldwide total. A potential American boycott of Nestlé products would be difficult to ignore.

Nestlé began to request meetings with various groups involved in the boycott initiative. The reaction of the activists engaged in the series of meetings was interesting: "The Nestlé representatives, who had initiated the meeting, appeared shaken by our conviction and expertise. . . . Apparently they thought the whole campaign was 'handed down' from New York and that all they had to do was go around telling the 'truth' to nip the boycott in the bud."[168] Nestlé management continued to be convinced of the propriety of their marketing practices. The company's reaction was as follows: "Nestlé disagrees with the charges offered by critics. Infant formula as it is now promoted is not harmful. Nestlé does not need to change its policies at all; all it has to do is tighten those policies up. . . . Governments ask Nestlé to sell products in their countries."[169] The Company had not reevaluated its long-standing position, and very little genuine communication appeared to be taking place during the course of these meetings.

In January 1978, the Sisters of the Precious Blood lawsuit against Bristol-Myers was settled out of court.[170] The Company agreed to publish a special report to stockholders defining the position of both sides in the lawsuit, including some of the evidence presented during the trial. In addition, the Company agreed to stop all advertising in infant formula directed to consumers and agreed to withdraw all mothercraft nurses from Jamaica.

In March, ICCR decided to start a national campaign to solicit support for its shareholder resolution demanding that American Home Products establish a 15-member corporate committee to review its policies on promotion of infant formula. Although sales of this product represent less than 2% of the company's total revenues, management opposed the resolution because it refused to believe that its products are competing with breast milk, only with "less nutritious products," making the review committee unnecessary.[171]

INFACT held its first nationwide boycott demonstrations in April 1978. Protesters demonstrated and sang outside Nestlé headquarters in White Plains, New York and demonstrated at a number of other sites, including the Swiss embassy and offices of American Home Products. Among the protest songs was the following (sung to the tune of *Auld Lang Syne*): "We use no Nestlé products here, Cause they have a cruel campaign,/Selling formula to Third World folks/And the babies go down the drain./There's no refrigeration there,/The mother's milk soon dries,/And the baby sucks this rotten stuff,/And it soon gets sick and dies . . . /Nestlé knows damn well what's going on,/There are protests everywhere,/But the ads still run and the profits rise,/And the Nestlé gang don't care./So we read the labels carefully,/Where the Nestlé brands appear,/And we tell the world the reason why,/And we use no Nestlé here." As the boycott plan developed, endorsers included the largest political organization in Minnesota (the Democratic Farmer-Labor Party), Ralph Nader, Cesar Chavez, Gloria Steinem, Dr. Benjamin Spock, various church groups, as well as state and local agencies. Demonstrations included an "Infant Formula Action Day," a "Nestea Party" in Boston, telegram and letter-writing campaigns, fasts, and other public events.[172]

On May 23, Senator Ted Kennedy's Subcommittee on Health and Scientific Research held a session on the promotion of infant formula. Representatives of many of the parties involved in the conflict were given a chance to air their opinions. During the hearings, American Home Products management revealed for the first time that it was withdrawing mothercraft nurses from all markets, a major concession. Nestlé was represented by the President of Nestlé Brazil, who stated that the "United States Nestlé Company has advised me that their research indicates this is actually an indirect attack on the free world's economic system. A worldwide church organization with its stated purpose of undermining the free enterprise system is at the forefront of these activities."[173] The statement was greeted with laughter and incredulity.

In June and July 1978, the controversy over the marketing of infant formula in the Third World received the attention of major television programs in the United States. On one such occasion, the INFACT representatives stated his group's objectives as follows: "The goal of the Nestlé boycott campaign and of the entire Infant Formula Coalition is to get the multinationals to stop promotion of infant formula. We're not asking them to pull out of the countries. We're simply asking them to stop the promotion."[174]

In 1978–1979 many developing nations, including Botswana, Brazil, Guyana, India, Indonesia, Jamaica, Malaysia, Papua New Guinea, Sri Lanka, and Tanzania, either launched or strengthened programs supporting breast-feeding and discouraging the use of bottle-feeding. Church groups in 1979 submitted shareholder resolutions asking Abbott and American Home Products to establish infant formula review committees, and Bristol-Myers to end a range of specific promotional practices. Votes in favor of the resolutions at the firm's spring annual meetings amounted to 4.9% at Abbott, 3.2% at American Home Products, and 3.8% at Bristol-Myers. INFACT's boycott of Nestlé products, meanwhile, attracted growing attention from national news media, secured further endorsements from a wide range of institutions, and inspired thousands of protest letters to flow into Nestlé's offices each month. The boycott also spread worldwide, with active efforts emerging in Canada, the Netherlands, Switzerland, Sweden, Norway, Britain, West Germany, and Japan.

Nestlé had issued a set of "policy changes" in early 1978—dealing with such issues as labels, educational materials, monitoring of advertising, home visits by nurses, and color of nurses uniforms—only to find them labeled by INFACT and others as "cosmetic at best."[175] Nestlé's policy statement still condoned all four methods of promotion that the boycott sought to end: direct consumer advertising, free samples, milk nurses and promotion to the medical profession. The company later announced, however, that it would "suspend" use of the first method. Critics saw this as representing only a temporary change, however, and discovered evidence that it was not being enforced in nations such as Malaysia.

Nestlé denied that the boycott was injuring sales, but certain evidence indicated otherwise: conferences were moved out of Stouffer (a U.S. subsidiary) hotels, Norwegian cheesemakers ended their United States distribution contract with Nestlé, and the company stepped up public relations and promotional efforts in the United States with more cents-off coupons, store displays and media advertising. The direct involvement of Nestlé's top management also indicated concern over damage to the firm's reputation.[176] Arthur Furer, president and chief-executive officer of Nestlé S.A., reportedly flew to the Vatican in October 1978 to ask for an end to Catholic support of the boycott in the United States—he was unsuccessful. Furer, along with other group-level Swiss vice presidents and the president of the Nestle U.S.A. also participated in boycott negotiations with the powerful National Council of Churches. But the Council's Governing Board concluded that the company was unwilling to make needed official policy changes and so voted to endorse the boycott in November. *Business Week* reported in April 1979 that Nestlé had 15 people in the U.S. working on boycott matters, that a public relations firm had been engaged to publicize the company's story, that Nestlé had sent letters to 300,000 clergymen, and that line and marketing executives, rather than public relations officials, were now being sent to meetings with the boycotters.[177]

The company's strategy during 1979—the "International Year of the Child"—appeared to be one of deflecting attention from its promotion practices by endorsing a conference on infant feeding to be held in Geneva by the World Health Organization and the U.N. Children's Fund. Nestlé proclaimed that the conference represented the ultimate and only responsible forum for debate—the hope was that the Third World officials, health personnel, corporate executives and industry critics attending the meeting would finally agree upon a set of guidelines for marketing infant formula that could be followed by all MNEs vying for the $1.5 billion formula market in the developing world. At the conference, which met in October 1979, it was agreed that mothers should begin breast feeding as soon as possible after birth and continue for as long as possible, that they should be given instruction on breast feeding during pregnancy, and that "breast milk from other sources" should be the first alternative to mother's milk. Marketing of infant formulas should not discourage breast feeding, and this applies to all advertising and sales promotion to the public—marketing to medical personnel should be limited to "factual and ethical information". An ICIFI spokesman commented that "This is an extraordinary concession for an industry like ours. . . . Anything that is a direct sales promotion is out".[178] In response, INFACT decided to continue the Nestlé boycott for the time being, pending clarification by the company as to how it intended to carry out the conference recommendations. Meantime, the World Health Organization began work on a code of conduct dealing wth the marketing of breast milk substitutes.

CONCLUSIONS

International marketing conflict thus runs the gamut of issues from product to price to promotion and distribution, from consumerists to governments to church groups in external protagonists, and from developed to developing countries in location. It may be convenient to view the international marketing environment as a number of continua. Typically, one country or regional group will be the "leading edge" of a particular continuum, as with antitrust in the United States or consumerism in Sweden. The developing countries will usually (but not always) be at the opposite extreme, with virtually no control over many market-related activities. Between these extremes lie marketing-oriented public policies and private pressures that are in a constant state of evolution.

The tendency in this complex environment is toward increasingly difficult conditions for the multinational marketer. Antitrust in Europe, in the space of a decade, has approached the antitrust environment in the United States in terms of its well-developed and strictly enforced body of law. Japan has the necessary mechanisms in place but has not, to date, relied on them to a significant extent. Most of the Third World countries have a long way to go in countering abuses of market positions.

Advertising regulation is tough throughout the world. In countries in which television is state-owned, government control is pervasive. Many countries rely on some form of self-regulation, but the trend is for more government involvement in the regulatory process. With the disappearance of virtually all blatantly misleading advertisements in many countries, regulators have begun to focus on more abstract objections to advertising—advertising to children may be deemed "unfair"; advertising may induce "undesirable" social behavior; it may induce "questionable" cultural changes, and the images used in advertising may be "deceptive" although the copy is "acceptable." For the multinational marketer the problems are enormous, and already most companies have all but abandoned the idea of globally coordinated advertising in favor of locally produced material. But as we have seen, the problems persist.

The allegation that multinationals' marketing practices have eroded host-country culture has been extended to the concept of "self-colonization," especially by means of mass-media advertising and the popular shows these make possible. Moreover, employees who work for multinationals' local affiliates are exposed constantly to home-country influences and parent-firm "sociocultural investments," which they then carry out into the local business system and society as a whole. Planned obsolescence, emphasis on branding and packaging, and the emphasis on sales rather than workmanship are alleged to reinforce these tendencies, as well as the international activities of ad agencies—which often dominate host-country advertising industries.[179]

Product safety and liability likewise present costly and difficult problems for the multinational marketer. Given the variety of product liability standards at the national level and the uncertainty surrounding product safety initiatives, some multinationals have decided to establish tough internal controls of product development and safety. But these may be costly and are far from universal. And even extreme internal controls may not be able to avoid some problems of product liability.

Finally, consumerism has evolved into a permanent feature of the external marketing environment. While the consumer movement is characterized by temporary coalitions related to specific issues, there are increasingly well-organized groups of a more permanent nature that have been willing to absorb new issues of interest and work in new ways to challenge corporate marketing practices. For the multinational marketer, consumerism can present a range of problems for marketing policies from specific practices to general social concerns.

In terms of our contingency model of conflict management, MNE behavior in marketing-related conflict situations has run the gamut from *accomodation* to *competition*, from *collaboration* to *avoidance*, as the stakes and relative power of the firms and the amount of interest interdependence and quality of relations between the contending parties have varied or changed over time. Recall Distillers' behavior in the Thalidomide tragedy. Initially there were only 70 victims involved, the company was in a strong legal position, the stakes were relatively modest, and the British government was displaying cold hostility to Thalidomide families. Both the company and the families were interested in a quick settlement of the compensation claims, and so the stage was set for Distillers to buy out the families for a pittance. But when additional parents joined the battle, the company's stakes rose dramatically. Distillers was still in a relatively powerful position, and continued to deny any negligence and legal obligation to compensate the victims. Nearly eight years had gone by since the children were born, and all of them required special, and often expensive, care. Most of the parents were desperate for some financial relief, but a few others were more concerned with principles of justice and fairness. The greater heterogeneity of interests, along with the much larger size of the new group of parents, made bargaining much more difficult. Yet, a precedent had already been established—the company had acknowledged a moral responsibility to compensate the victims in some manner as evidenced by its willingness to negotiate with the parents in the absence of an established legal responsibility. Both Distillers and the parents had a common interest in seeing the matter resolved, but the higher stakes and more divergent goals moved the company to a more *competitive* stance.

But in the end, according to one observer, Distillers was "brought down from the peaks of corporate greed and inhumanity by an *ad hoc* coalition spurred by the *Sunday Times*, and including not only some political leaders (former prime minister Harold Wilson was one) and even Ralph Nader, but arrestingly, insurance companies with large stockholdings in Distillers."[180] Distillers' management, with its power base severely eroding, could not afford to antogonize its opponents further. The stakes were no longer defined so much in terms of the cost of reaching a settlement. Rather, failure to reach a settlement might potentially be more costly—especially if a boycott in the United States was launched or if the boycott movement in Britain gained momentum. Distillers now shared a common interest with the parents in seeing the situation resolved as soon as possible in a manner externally perceived as "socially responsible." Distillers was forced from a *compromise-competitive* mode of behavior to one of *compromise-accommodation*.

Or recall the Hoffman-La Roche drug pricing case in Great Britain. The company's stand was highly *competitive* throughout most of the battle, with rapidly deteriorating relations between Roche and the Department of Health and Social Services occurring in the opening phases of the conflict, and extremely high stakes in the outcome perceived by the company—both within the United Kingdom and elsewhere—if a precedent were set. The stakes rose further as the German Federal Cartel Office took up the case (and years later did order big price cuts) and other governments followed suit. All sides saw the pricing issue as essentially a zero-sum game, with interest totally opposed. Eventually the stakes declined as the company's tranquilizers were going out of patent. The move toward *compromise* began with its willingness to provide information about its operation. It had also become clear that Roche's power position was declining in virtually every arena in which the conflict had emerged, and that continued uncooperative behavior might inspire European governments to pounce on other market practices or product lines of the company. So the move toward *compromise*, however reluctant, was perhaps preordained.

No end was in sight for a cease-fire in the infant formula case in 1979, but differences in corporate conflict management behavior are interesting to note. Firms based in the United States, in comparison to Nestlé, were generally more vulnerable to legal and shareholder action in the United States, more willing to acknowledge the legitimacy of church and action group concerns, more accustomed to dealing with citizen challenges to business authority, and less obsessed with maintaining methods of mass-marketing. Thus they were willing to *compromise* on disclosure and *accommodate* on certain promotion practices time and again, while Nestlé continued to view the matter as an illegitimate attack on the free enterprise system. We should note that Nestlé's stakes in the developing countries in general, and the infant formula business in particular, were the highest of any of the firms involved. In 1978–1979, however, it appeared that Nestlé was beginning to feel the heat of the broad-based boycott campaign. With the massive adverse publicity damaging its corporate image—just at a time when the company had chosen to rapidly expand its American business—it seemed that Nestlé's hard-nosed *competitive* stance was beginning to give way to a stream of concessions aimed at *compromise*.

Many MNEs are increasingly planning for *compromise, accommodation,* and even *collaboration* in their international marketing efforts. For example, Gillette has established a new position of Vice President, Product Integrity:

> . . . He is directly responsible for the safety and quality of all 850 Gillette products. He can yank them off the market anytime they fail to meet standards he sets. He can veto new product introductions, quash advertising claims, order packaging changes, derail proposed acquisitions, and otherwise upset the best-laid plans of executives far senior to him . . . and can overrule any research scientist, quality control expert, plant manager or marketing executive in any Gillette division anywhere in the world."[181]

It seems clear that multinationals will have to start exploring ways to better manage conflicts within the external marketing environment once they occur. It will not always be possible to anticipate some of them, but once a conflict develops management must begin to explore ways of better analyzing the key variables involved. Only when these variables have been correctly isolated can the corporation begin to explore ways of manipulating the most important variables in order to bring the conflict outcome as nearly as possible in line with corporate objectives. By allowing marketing-related conflicts to evolve without any clear sense of how to manage them, the firm may find itself involved in controversies of immense proportions, far beyond the initial conflict situation. The consequences, in terms of diverting the attention of key executives from more appropriate concerns and the expenditure of major financial resources to counter controversy that has gone out of control, can be significant indeed.

11 *LABOR RELATIONS*

One of the key arenas of multinational corporate conflict involves labor relations and, more broadly, the management of human resources. The firm must become adept at bargaining over wages and working conditions in many different social, political, and economic settings, a situation giving rise to labor problems that vary enormously internationally. Generally this means labor relations are best conducted by management of local affiliates according to local rules of the game, with a maximum of negotiating flexibility left to affiliate management. There are times, however, when conflict with labor arises precisely *because* the firm is multinational. What about the MNE's ability to break a strike by serving markets from foreign plants? Whose "ability to pay" counts in wage bargaining, the local affiliate's or the multinational's as a whole? How do expatriate employees in MNE affiliates affect labor relations in host countries? There are also times when management of the multinational runs into entirely new human resource problems. Employment of disadvantaged groups in host countries has been a major concern for European firms in the United States and American firms in South Africa, for example. What about the burgeoning "industrial democracy" movement centered in Europe, which strikes at the very heart of the way multinationals do business in important countries like West Germany? And what about multinational unions—do they represent a major new force for MNEs to contend with?

In this chapter we shall focus particularly on these "new" kinds of conflict issues, discussing only briefly the traditional questions of collective bargaining in a multinational setting. To begin, let us briefly review the kinds of settings within which MNEs must conduct negotiations with labor.

NATIONAL BARGAINING

It is clear that multinationals have to become skilled at bargaining with unions that come in a bewildering array of shapes and sizes. The United States has its traditional industrial and craft unions and adversary collective bargaining, with union representation dropping from 35.5% of non-agricultural employees in 1954 to 25.8% in 1976—the only real union gains being among public-sector employees. American unions have traditionally been nonpolitical and interested only in the welfare of their own members, and have exerted political influence mainly by lobbying and campaign contributions, again with an eye toward passage of legislation favorable to union causes.

In France only 20% of the work force is unionized, with the largest union being the communist *Confédération Générale du Travail* (CGT), mainly in the engineering, chemicals, gas, and electric industries, and railroads. There is also the socialist *Confédération Democratique du Travail* (CFDT), especially strong in the high-technology industries, and there are strong civil service and teachers unions. Socialist and communist unions favor far-reaching nationalization of industry. Short protest strikes are quite common, but modest union funds generally preclude long strikes.

Germany has about 8.5 million unionized employees among its 24 million workers, almost all belonging to 16 industrial unions that are members of the federation of unions—*Deutscher Gewerkschaftsbund* (DGB), committed to private enterprise and democracy. There is no closed shop, the unions have substantial funds, and strikes have to be approved by 75% of the membership. Generally, strikes are called against all firms in an industry at the same time, although recently the United States pattern of selecting individual targets seems to be catching on. They bargain with employers' associations, with the outcome generally applying to all firms in an industry. Unions have also become major employers themselves, owning a major bank (*Bank für Gemeinwirtschaft*) and a large building society (*Neue Heimat*). They have major political influence through the ruling Social Democratic Party (SPD), 80% of whose legislative representatives are union members. Union policies seem increasingly removed from the rank and file, and strongly influenced by professional bureaucrats at union headquarters with little or no shop-floor experience or contact. In part, this may be responsible for a growing ideological thrust of German unions toward co-management and co-ownership of enterprises, with the unions themselves holding the reins of power.

Italian unions represent between 30% and 50% of the labor force, with three unions dominant—the Christian Democrat CISL, the Socialist and Republican UIL, and Communist CGIL—all originally heavily influenced by outside contributions from American unions and Eastern European governments. There are no closed shops and the unions are usually rivals except in the chemicals and engineering industries. The unions are relatively poorly financed, but strikes are plentiful. Italy has the worst strike record in the EEC.

In Holland there are three unions, Socialist, Catholic, and Protestant, which work relatively closely together. Bargaining occurs once a year for all industries at a central level with employer representatives. The outcome usually applies to all industries as well, although recently some differentiation has occurred between weak and strong sectors. Dutch unions are wealthy, and strikes are rare. In neighboring Belgium, over 70% of workers are unionized by two unions, one Socialist and one Christian, which are rivals at the plant level but often work together in bargaining centrally with employers in a "common front." Wages are generally indexed to the cost of living.

Britain has 495 different unions, which represent half the work force. The Trades Union Congress (TUC) represents 110 of these unions and about 10 million workers. The public sector, coal, railroads, utilities, and steel are almost totally unionized, and unionization is also heavy in manufacturing and engineering firms. Union funds are adequate to support industry-wide strikes, and bargaining tends to be done at the firm level. The system of shop stewards and weak links between central unions and employees frequently leads to unauthorized walkouts.

A recent ILO study found that strikes in the United Kingdom accounted for 788 working days lost per year for every 1000 employees during 1967–1976. For the United States the figure was 1050, and for Canada 1900. However, these data do not include slowdowns and refusals to work overtime, or the much more disruptive effect of unauthorized strikes, which cannot be anticipated. Switzerland and Sweden had the least number of days lost due to strikes.[1]

In Japan, company-based unions ensure that bargaining occurs at the firm level or even at the plant level. Wages are based largely on seniority, age and education, and employment is guaranteed until compulsory retirement at age 55. In recessions, workers are kept on the payroll in larger firms, although overtime and temporary workers may be reduced and short-time may be used to cut wage bills. Japanese firms also tend to be overstaffed with administrative workers. Unions are usually interested entirely in the welfare of their own members, and the 33% of the workforce that is unionized is considered privileged. Subcontracting to nonunionized small firms ensures that in recessions a significant part of the burden is carried by the nonunionized sector. Increasingly, however, company unions are represented by industry-wide federations in bargaining. Particularly in recent rounds of wage bargaining in Japan, the tradeoffs between lifetime job security and the flexibility required in a mature industrial economy are becoming increasingly clear—overstaffing during recessions means higher costs and less money available for raises.[2]

These few examples should suffice to make the point that collective bargaining by multinationals has to be carried out according to rules of host countries. In some cases bargaining is at the plant level. In others it is at the company level. In still others it is at the industry or even sector level, with the MNE represented in employers' federations just like local firms. This heterogeneity virtually demands that negotiations be left largely to local management which understands the system and can work efficiently within that system. In many countries, where industry-wide bargaining is the rule, the relevant outcomes are beyond MNE management's power in any case, except to the extent that they can influence the employers' association's bargaining position. All management can do is live with the outcome and perhaps react to it in reorienting corporate strategies. In other countries, where individual firm bargaining is possible, local managers again are in the best position to represent the firm effectively, and only broad guidelines are provided by corporate headquarters.

At the same time, the flexibility of the system within which conventional bargaining on wages and working conditions takes place is undergoing change in many host countries, and this may affect the ultimate degrees of freedom available to multinationals in reacting to labor-market developments. For example, throughout much of Europe layoffs are becoming increasingly costly for the business firm. For instance, in January 1976 the Timex watch company laid off part of its work force in Portugal because of "production failures," and its plant was promptly occupied by workers calling for government intervention to determine whether the layoffs were justified. About the same time, a Bulova Watch Company decision to close a plant in Switzerland led to a 10–day sit-in by workers, forcing the company to submit its proposal to an outside accounting firm to see whether closure was justified. All of the workers involved would have received jobs at another Bulova plant, but objected to being "uprooted."[3]

Social payments in many layoff cases are extremely high. In 1977 the Badger subsidiary of Raytheon Company decided to close its Antwerp office. Termination claims of its 241 employees came to $5.5 million, far exceeding the $2.5

million in company assets. The company was declared bankrupt, resulting in an action by Belgian unions to accuse Raytheon of failure to uphold the new Organization for Economic Cooperation and Development (OECD) code of conduct on multinational companies (see Chapter 15) in an attempt to collect severance pay (unions have since then dragged more than 20 cases of apparent MNE code transgressions up before the OECD Committee on Multinationals).[4] Similar difficulties with layoffs in Europe have hit Raytheon in Sicily, Richardson-Merrill, Ingersoll-Rand, General Foods, Singer, TRW, Gould, Harris, and White Motor in Italy. "You must treat people as a fixed investment," says one American manager in Europe. A consultant adds, "if you are getting out, sell as a going concern. Cancel intra-company debt, knock down the price, stump up your liability, and severance pay (one twelfth of the last year's pay for every year in service), anything to find a buyer. It will cost a bomb, but every month of labor trouble will cost more, as the plant deteriorates and the balance sheet begins to look more and more awful!"[5] It is this sort of reduced flexibility that, at the national level, threatens to erode one of the multinational's basic sources of strength: the ability to alter its operations in response to market changes on either the output or the input side, and "escape" from consequences that might be inimical to the interests of the firm. Another such threat comes from the multinationalization of labor.

MULTINATIONAL BARGAINING

The rise of the multinational enterprise has not been paralled by a corresponding rise in international labor organizations. Unions have been very active indeed in expressing their concern over MNE activities. Problems relating to jobs displacement, erosion of labor bargaining power, transfers of production, negotiating authority of affiliate managers, lack of information about MNE operations, and affiliate versus corporate ability to pay have been around for a long time, but principally as a matter for *national* unions in attempting to influence national legislation and controls affecting the MNE. They have not, however, led to significant *international* labor actions despite isolated but vocal efforts to move events in this direction.

Employment Displacement

A major issue, perhaps the most important one, concerning organized labor in the United States is the effect of multinational enterprise on jobs. We shall discuss this issue and the conflicting evidence surrounding it in more detail in Chapter 14. Whether significant employment displacement can be ascribed to multinationals or not—and our view is that under most plausible assumptions it cannot—it seems clear that the net effect has indeed been to erode the power of the unions.

We shall note in our later discussion that even if no net jobs displacement (or even net jobs creation) can be ascribed to MNEs, it is certain that they have been responsible for a considerable "churning" of employment patterns. That is, MNE activities may have destroyed on balance lower-skill, lower-wage, and blue-collar jobs even as they have created higher-skill, higher-wage, and white-collar jobs. If the degree of unionization is higher in the former group than among the latter, then a certain degree of built-in union antagonism toward multinationals is a natural result. Organized labor in the United States since 1970 has been virulently anti-multinational enterprise precisely for this reason, and labor's legislative proposals have generally included mandatory import controls, increased taxation of foreign earnings, capital controls to discourage foreign investment, and even technology controls to regulate the transfer of know-how between the United States and the rest of the world by way of MNEs.

Reduced Strike Vulnerability

An important advantage that MNEs are alleged to have over other firms in bargaining with labor unions at the local level is reduced vulnerability to strikes and plant shutdowns. In the first place, the existence of the firm itself is not imminently threatened by even the largest and most costly of strikes brought by a union at the local level. Whereas a local firm might be threatened with extinction under such circumstances, the MNE affiliate can look forward to reopening for business afterward, with survival assured by financial support of the parent firm. Hence the ability of unions to block financial receipts is far more limited.

Secondly, the MNE's "downside risk" associated with strike action can also be limited by the ability to serve the market from plants in other countries. To the extent that this can be done in sufficient volume at reasonable cost levels, the losses in market-share and overall corporate profits attributable to a strike in a local affiliate can be substantially reduced. This greatly enhances the affiliate's ability to "ride out" a strike and to take a far tougher bargaining stance. The firm's ability to accomplish this naturally depends on the existence of "duplicate" output in other plants. Few firms appear to follow "dual sourcing" strategies specifically for this reason, but in many industries the existence of multiple plants producing the same or similar goods is quite common.

On the other hand, for firms whose production is integrated transnationally—with output in some plants serving as inputs for others—the company's bargaining power with respect to local unions may be considerably less. Strikes or job actions can do far more damage to the firm than their quantitative importance would make it appear. Again, "dual sourcing" can be used by firms in order to insure against such loss of leverage, while attempts by unions to persuade their counterparts in other nations dealing with the firm to refuse overtime or even undertake sympathy strikes will increase the bargaining leverage of the union. The evidence appears to be that multinationals in most industries have extensive duplicative production in different countries. As one observer notes, "The key is production flexibility to serve different and changing product market conditions. This implies local production autonomy except where the return to the MNE for standardized production and intra-firm exports is greater than the market loss associated with the inability to meet varied market conditions."[6] The question at any given point in time is how much incremental output can be pulled out of the system or diverted from other markets in order to support the struck affiliate.

Transfer of Production

Unions frequently claim that bargaining power of multinationals is greatly enhanced, compared with non-multinational firms, by their ability to threaten shifts of production to foreign plants in the absence of what the company considers reasonable labor conditions. Especially in free-trade areas like the EEC, where access to the domestic market of any member country from any other is guaranteed, this threat has to be taken seriously by the union side.

Especially in the automobile industry, where the same manufacturing process is often undertaken in multiple plants in different regions, production transfer is a real possibility. The most famous example was the threat by Henry Ford II in 1971 to progressively move automotive operations from the United Kingdom to the United States, Spain, and the Continent unless product quality and labor productivity showed significant improvements in Ford's British plants. The threat produced union outrage and government bluster. Ford today, however, is probably the most successful of British automobile firms. By 1977, it had even decided (with ample government subsidies) to locate a new Fiesta engine plant in South Wales after considering a number of attractive rival sites in other countries. Chrysler also made a similar threat in the early 1970s, vowing to shift production to France unless the British company's abysmal record of product quality and frequent work stoppages improved—in the end, Chrysler sold all of its British and continental European manufacturing operations to Peugeot–Citroën for $230 million and a 15% interest in the French automaker. Before the purchase was consumated, Chrysler trade unionists from Britain, France, and Spain met under the auspices of the Geneva–based International Metalworkers' Federation, and pledged international pressure, including "industrial action," to prevent any job losses as a result of the takeover.[7] And General Motors clearly had that option with respect to its Continental plants, especially through increased reliance on its Opel subsidiary in Germany. Perhaps not coincidentally, British Leyland, without the "disengagement option" available to the American auto manufacturers, has the worst labor relations and performance record in the industry. And at the same time, *de facto* disengagement was occurring by way of the marketplace as imports from Japan and Continental Europe made ever larger inroads on the British automobile market—to the point where the government encouraged a "voluntary" export restraint agreement with Japanese auto firms.

The production-transfer option exists in other sectors as well—in machinery and equipment, electronics, and consumer durables industries in particular—and clearly presents unions with limits on bargaining power. But as long as international markets are allowed to function, these limits would to a large extent exist in any case. Favorable wage and working conditions that are "excessive" by international standards and are not offset by differential productivity gains will clearly lead to competitive shifts in the marketplace through increased imports and/or reduced exports. So the jobs would be lost in any case, whether through multinational corporate shifts in production or market losses in competitiveness. And the more competitive the market in which the MNEs find themselves, the more alike the two effects will be. This does not deny, of course, that the threat of production shifts cannot be used by the multinational to keep labor costs competitive.[8]

Negotiating Authority

Another common complaint of labor unions against multinationals in a bargaining context is that local MNE officials are not given sufficient negotiating authority by corporate headquarters. In effect, union spokesmen do not have an opportunity to present their case directly to the corporate executives who have the ultimate say. At the same time, the facts may be "filtered" by local management, errors of fact or interpretation may creep in, and cultural differences may influence behavior. As a result, the bargaining process may lose in efficiency, with conflicts that are far more costly to both sides than need be.

A recent assessment of labor relations in American-based MNEs in the automobile industry showed substantial autonomy in industrial relations on the part of affiliate management. Evidently the view is that only on-site management can effectively align labor policy with local social, cultural, and economic conditions. In rare cases, usually where special expertise was required, headquarters intervened to set policy at the affiliate level.[9] In a 1975 Conference Board study, out of 134 American MNEs operating abroad and 34 foreign MNEs operating in the United States, 27% required headquarter's approval of local agreements that had cost implications for the firm but only 18% were concerned with the specific type of agreement negotiated. The remaining 73% of the firms evidently left matters entirely in the hands of affiliate managers within an overall profit-center type of managerial framework.[10] So within the general constraint of affiliate profitability the lack of negotiating authority does not appear to be a major problem.

Lack of Information

Unions bargaining with multinationals often charge that they have inadequate access to information about the financial strength of the MNE affiliate involved. Whereas the firm as a whole may provide consolidated balance sheet and profit-loss statements on a regular basis, this is insufficient for effective bargaining. Moreover, such affiliate profit and loss figures as are provided to union officials may be distorted by transfer pricing practices of the firm. While in many countries industry-wide bargaining practices and alignment of wage rates to local labor market conditions may reduce ability-to-pay criteria in bargaining, the fact that MNEs frequently pay higher wages and offer better working conditions than competing local firms means that the issue continues to be important.

For example, in the late 1960s a major union information-gathering exercise was aimed at Philips N.V. in Holland by the European Metal Committee of the International Metal Workers Federation (now the European Metalworkers Federation). Data were collected at the plant level from local union representatives in six European countries. Based on that information meetings were held with headquarters management on such topics as production switching, job security, worker retraining, the impact of transfer pricing on profit sharing plans, inter-country differences in wages, and working conditions. As a result of this exercise the union was able to enter into agreements with management that would have been impossible without adequate information. However, it depended on international cooperation among unions.[11] In another case, in 1969 General Electric was requested to supply information on its global operations by the International Union of Electrical Workers, in support of a proposed contract clause forbidding relocation of operations from the United States to foreign operations. GE refused to comply, and the company was upheld by the National Labor Relations Board.[12]

Ability to Pay

Unions frequently claim that the "ability to pay" of the multinational as a whole should be considered in labor bargaining at the affiliate level, and not merely the profitability of the affiliate itself. However, when affiliate profitability is felt to exceed overall corporate profitability, this logic is usually reversed in the bargaining process by the union side. A further point that frequently arises is that the ability to pay of the MNE on grounds other than profitability invariably exceeds that of the individual affiliate, and so bigger settlements are in any case possible. This raises the issue of conflict between "profit center" approaches to management and the more comprehensive view of unions in an affiliate bargaining context.

An interesting case involved the French Saint Gobain company, employing over 100,000 people in 143 plants and 12 countries in 1969. Fighting a takeover bid from another French glassmaker, management revealed that overall corporate profits and reserves were considerably larger than what had been previously known. Saint Gobain's American union had failed to come to terms with the company. Management argued that affiliate profitability was too poor to permit a substantial settlement, and the union claimed that the company's overall profits were what counted. The revised profit disclosures substantially strengthened the union's bargaining leverage and, after working for some time without a contract, Saint Gobain's workers went out on a 26-day strike, after which the company settled with considerably more generous terms than its final offer in the initial round of bargaining.[13]

Multinational Union Organization

If labor is convinced that multinationals are "bad" for their members and bad for the labor movement as a whole under the existing state of affairs, there are essentially two choices. The first approach is to work at the national level to alter the regulatory framework of the MNE. This may involve imposition of fair labor standards, negotiating dispute settlement procedures, closed and union shops, checkoffs, and other measures belonging to the standard repertoire of organized-labor activity but often varying considerably from one country to the next. But these measures are essentially symmetrical as between multinationals and domestic firms, and do nothing to alleviate the allegedly disproportionate bargaining power possessed by the MNC.

In addition, this approach includes measures to curb and regulate the activities of multinationals themselves, including taxation, investment controls, controls on earnings remissions, and other devices discussed in detail in Chapter 14. In MNE home countries, it generally involves attempts to retain union jobs that otherwise might be displaced. In most countries, it may involve rules requiring mandatory unionization for foreign firms, disclosure requirements, increased labor usage, limits on earnings repatriation, and the like. The national approach is limited by the essentially limited span of national control over MNEs. Excessive pressure may elicit responses by the multinational that can throw the baby out with the bathwater. For this reason strong anti-union coalitions tend to form in opposition to union proposals for stiffer national regulations, and sometimes even the unions back off when the full consequences of their proposals become evident.

A second approach is to extend the union's own span of control—in effect, to create multinational unions to bargain collectively with multinational corporations. Conceptually, this approach has a number of advantages, attacking a number of "evils" associated with MNEs as seen from the union perspective. For example, it could provide improved flow of information about corporate operations worldwide and influence decisions to transfer production. It could increase the damage done to the firm as a result of strikes by interrupting the firm's overall financial flows and servicing of struck markets from non-struck plants. It could also guarantee local management authority to negotiate by direct discussions with headquarters management, and ensure that overall corporate "ability to pay" is considered in labor negotiations.

Despite such possible advantages, multinational unionization has been an abject failure. Why? First, like governments, unions in home and host countries, and among different home and host countries, have different ideas about what they want to get out of multinationals. Home-country unions, for example, want to prevent the export of jobs while host-country unions are all in favor of production shifts in their direction as long as they are able to organize the workers. Second, attempts by home-country unions to extend their scope of operations are often viewed as "labor imperialism" by host-country unions and hence are to be resisted. Third, there are wide ideological differences between unions which cannot be bridged as easily as the multinationals' legendary ability to work within alien ideological systems. Finally, unions work in different ways in different countries, running the gamut from strongly political unions, religion-oriented unions, and confrontive hard-bargaining unions to unions interested in co-determination and corporate ownership and unions representing whole sectors of the national economy. Legislative differences also tie each union to the particular national environment in which it operates—for example, on the legality of various forms of strikes, job actions, and boycotts. One observer has in fact noted that "trading off" benefits for domestic workers in support of foreign unions' objectives may be illegal for United States unions under the terms of their mandates to exclusively represent their members.[14] For all of these reasons, labor's attempts to develop effective multinational action programs have gone nowhere. On the relationship between multinational corporations and trade unions one observer notes: ". . . there are as many union systems as there are states, and even within specific states, ideological splits and other areas of conflict serve to divide them. In addition, relevant union organizations exist at the state, regional and international levels, and at each level there are some unions encompassing only a simple trade or industry, and others that are comprehensive, embracing many types of industries and skills, such as the AFL-CIO."[15]

There are, nevertheless, three international confederations of trade unions: (1) The International Confederation of Free Trade Unions (ICFTU), a non-

Communist federation consisting of 48 million members with headquarters in Brussels, to which many European unions belong but whose influence is less important in developing countries; (2) The World Federation of Trade Unions (WRTU), a Communist federation with 134 million members, headquartered in Prague, but with only a small following outside the Communist countries; and (3) The World Confederation of Labor (WCL), also located in Brussels, a confessional Christian union federation with only 15 million members but best represented around the world with nine organizations in Asia, 28 in Latin America, 21 in Africa, and one in North America. Of greater significance for multinationals are the specialized international trade union bodies covering a particular industry or a group of more or less related industries—the so-called International Trade Secretariats (ITS), autonomous agencies having working relations especially with the ICFTU. Finally, some very important national labor organizations do not have international affiliations, including Sohyo, the big Japanese union, and the AFL-CIO in the United States.

The evolution of the European Economic Community has stimulated the development of a number of European labor organizations, among whose duties are the protection of workers against adverse effects of multinationals. The European Confederation of Free Trade Unions (ECFTU) is a comprehensive union organization composed of the non-Communist and non-confessional unions, which perceives itself essentially as a regional lobbying organization representing the interests of unions in the deliberations and decisions of the EEC Commission and Council of Ministers. In the case of cross-border mergers, the ECFTU has sought to obtain required preliminary consultation between union and management whenever employment stability is threatened, and the maintenance of existing agreements for unions affected is by a merger. With respect to the proposed European Company Law, ECFTU attempted unsuccessfully to have the "Comité de Surveillance" composed of workers, shareholders, and the public (in equal proportion) established for each firm. It proposed that for each company, a permanent committee of trade union representatives from each plant of the company be established, which could meet regularly with management.[16] Finally, the European Trade Union Confederation (ETUC), which began operation in 1973 in Brussels after 18 months of negotiations, represents 29 million members in the EEC and associated nations.

For the most part, international union activity has been limited to the objective of establishing lines of communication between MNE headquarters and the unions involved, synchronization of expiration dates of labor contracts, improvement of data availability on company operations, and a certain amount of cooperation among unions. Only rarely have stronger measures appeared on the scene, including boycotts and picketing, organization of sympathy strikes, and direct international collective bargaining. Reported actions include United Auto Workers intervention with GM headquarters at the behest of a local union on a 1975 plant closure in Switzerland, and protests by affiliates of the International Union of Food and Allied Workers (IUF) in various countries during a 1971 dispute with local Coca-Cola bottlers on the closing of an Italian plant.

Much of the direct activity in attempts to get MNEs to bargain transnationally has centered on actions of the ITS. The International Metalworkers Federation (IMF) has sponsored the creation of "world company councils" at such firms as Ford, Volkswagen, and General Electric whose mandate is "recognition of the right to organize, upwards harmonization of wages and social benefits, adequate relief time, the vacation bonus, suitable pension levels, worker protection against technological obsolescence, and reduction of working time."[17] In addition to the IMF, the International Federation of Chemical, Energy and General Workers Unions (ICEF), and the International Transport Workers Federation (ITF) are relatively active.

Among the International Trade Secretariats, the IMF is the largest, and has played a role in trying to bring international union activity to the automobile industry. In 1968, for example, Ford workers at Genk, Belgium were pushing for wage parity with workers at the Antwerp plant and went on strike. The IMF claimed to have enlisted British, German, and American union support of the Genk workers' action, although it is unclear exactly what was accomplished. It also protested Ford plans to develop major operations in Spain on the grounds that this would displace workers elsewhere in Europe. Ford rejected a request to discuss product planning and its impact on jobs and working conditions on the IMF's European affiliated unions. As one observer noted, "apparently, Ford does not wish to impair its local bargaining relationships to demands for multinational collective bargaining, or to jeopardize the managerial perogatives of making decisions on investment and production deployment".[18]

The IMF also tried to initiate substantive discussions with N.V. Philips, the Dutch multinational in the electrical industry. Philips had had a number of meetings with union representatives from the EEC countries to discuss various labor problems, but rejected a meeting to discuss wages. It also refused to allow an IMF observer to attend the meetings.[19] When Honeywell's French computer subsidiary Honeywell-Bull was struck by repairmen in January 1973, the company asked British and German workers to step in until the strike was settled. As a result of efforts by the IMF secretariat in Geneva—which let it be known that Honeywell was trying to break the strike—they refused, and not long thereafter the company settled. Among other actions: United States rubber workers interceded with Goodyear in 1973 to settle a strike at its Turkish plant; French workers at Rhône-Poulenc S.A. refused to handle goods destined for shipment to the company's strike-bound British affiliate; and German Ford workers ostensibly refused to work overtime in order not to undermine the position of striking Ford workers in England. [20]

In April 1976 the United Rubber, Cork, Linoleum, and Plastic Workers (URW) struck Goodyear, Firestone, Uniroyal, and B.F. Goodrich (all major multinational producers) in the United States. Contrary to union expectations, only 45% of American tire production was affected—output of non-union plants and non-struck firms was maintained together with continued supplies by management and supervisory personnel in struck plants. The ICEF secretariat in Geneva promised to assist the URW by coordinating boycotts, instigating refusals to work overtime in foreign plants, and monitoring imports, with Firestone the target company. The results were marginal. According to one study, "there have been no international boycotts, no monitoring of shipments by European or Japanese union members, no cooperation with the International Transport Workers' Federation nor with the American longshoremen and maritime unions to prevent tire imports into countries where rubber plants are on strike, and no sympathy actions in 1976, claims to the contrary notwithstanding."[21] This nevertheless did not prevent the ICEF from claiming "this appeal met with an active and enthusiastic response from ICF affiliates throughout the duration of the lengthy URW strike. In fact, the sustained solidarity of ICEF rubber affiliates during the long strike constituted an important advance in ICEF's action program against multinationals."[22]

The Akzo Case

In April of 1972, management of the Dutch multinational chemical giant Akzo announced plans to close five synthetic fiber plants of its Enka Glanzstoff (EG) subsidiary, laying off some 5700 employees at Breda and Emmercampascum in the Netherlands, Fabelta in Belgium, Wuppertal-Barmen in Germany, and Feldmühle in Switzerland. Management stressed that "measures for a further concentration of manufacturing facilities are of vital importance for the group's [Akzo] survival."[23] Union and works council response was quick and severe, with each group appealing to their government and EEC authorities to intercede and protect their jobs. The pressure was especially strong in the Netherlands, where an agreement was reached to form a study group—Committee of Outside Experts (COE)—comprised of Akzo, Enka, works council, and trade union representatives.

In August of 1972, COE issued its report condoning the Akzo management's action on business grounds but condemning them on social grounds. They proposed that rationalization be spread throughout the company to spare any closings, and that governments or industry as a cartel allocate synthetic fiber production.[24] Management agreed to consider the COE report. However, with Switzerland not a member of the EEC, they had already closed down the Feldmühle plant. On September 18, the employees at Breda, led by the Netherlands Catholic Trade Union Federation (NKU), seized the plant and held it for one week. Management thereupon agreed to forestall any further plant closings, to achieve output reductions throughout the company, and to sell a majority interest in its Belgian facilities to the government. Employment in fibers was reduced by 6800 in 1972 without further closures.[25] But by 1973, due to pickup in demand for fibers, Enka requested importation of Spanish workers, thus confirming in the workers' minds the validity of the decision not to close down plants.

The years 1973 and 1974 marked a period of relative calm between Akzo and its employees, except for charges by trade union officials that Akzo was transferring production outside Europe in order to exploit cheap labor elsewhere, and nonspecific demands for the company to sit down with international union delegates or face international action. The calm was broken in August 1975 by issuance of a report by McKinsey & Company, commissioned by Akzo management, forecasting dire consequences for the company's future unless certain fiber operations were curtailed. Based on these findings, Enka announced a severe restructuring plan aimed at ending redundancies in the company's Dutch, Belgian, West German, and Austrian fiber plants. The following reactions occurred in rapid succession:

1. Twenty-eight delegates (15 from Holland, 9 from Belgium, and 4 from Germany) met with Akzo representatives at Arnhem to protest the McKinsey report and demand greater access to information on the company. No results were forthcoming.[26]

2. Unions scheduled another joint meeting for September. Both unions and management met informally with the Dutch Ministry of Economic Affairs which was determined to stay neutral.

3. On September 6, unions promised to decide whether Enka was in poor enough shape to start cutting back. They rejected cutbacks.

4. On September 19, Enka announced a restructuring plan involving the loss of 4000–6000 jobs over the next two years.

5. In early October, unions met in Düsseldorf and decided that the Enka plans were unacceptable due to misleading estimates of potential losses through 1980. On October 10, unions tried for EEC support and failed.

6. On October 29, Enka announced firm plans to cut nearly 6000 jobs through normal attrition shortly after union-management talks broke off. ICF scheduled November 7 to decide on international action, and on October 30th Teamsters met to discuss actions against the company in the United Kingdom to get Enka back to the bargaining table.

7. International retaliation failed as Dutch works councils voted to support the restructuring plan. Only a small Protestant union withheld support.

By year-end 1975, Akzo had initiated the restructuring program, with over half of the 6000 job losses occurring at Dutch plants in Arnhem and Emmen by the following procedures:

No replacement of workers lost through natural attrition;

Workers transferred wherever possible to other Enka factories in the same country;

Part wages until pension age reached for the older workers;

Help in transferring workers to other Akzo factories in the same country;

Assistance in finding jobs with firms outside the Akzo group;

Every possible facility to be offered by the Akzo Central Staff Affairs Bureau;

Full use to be made of every possibility for temporary employment both inside and outside the Akzo group;

Special cases to receive special consideration;

All redundant workers to receive the full legal compensatory wages and allowances; and study of new products that could be made in factories to be closed.[27] In addition, in the final stages of restructuring, a reorganization of the Enka Board of Management was to include three German and two Dutch members, a move approved by unions and works councils in July 1976.

Having established the Akzo World Council in 1972, the ICEF secretariat in Geneva claimed much of the credit for the results, even though the organization evidently had little to do with them. Nevertheless, these claims were printed as fact by the media, giving rise to the view that the formation of multinational labor organizations and international collective bargaining was well on its way to success.

One study notes that ". . . there is apparently widespread belief that the ICEF has been involved in a large number of successful confrontations with multinational concerns. . . . Undoubtedly, ICEF's greatest asset and major accomplishments have been [ICEF Secretary-General Charles Levinson's] fantastic public relations abilities. He has envisioned the potential of multinational bargaining, and by sparking the idea, probably brought it closer. . . . He has made his name synonymous with international unionism without any demonstrable record of action."[28] Despite the fact that ICEF international action against Akzo layoffs in 1975 failed as individual national unions settled separately, Levinson noted, "the Enka experience was an important step forward for us. Two years from now, if we get in a similar position, we will do better. You can't expect to step in and have the company play dead at once." By 1978 the Enka case, along with parallel problems faced by most major synthetic fiber producers, had become the official business of the EEC with a plan for what amounted to a European fiber cartel. By 1981, 20% of capacity was to be retired with a net loss of 15,000 jobs by means of production quotas for each firm set at 1976 base-period market shares. With combined losses of $1 billion in 1977, European fiber producers welcomed the EEC initiative despite grave misgivings of Community antitrust authorities and failure of DuPont and Monsanto to become involved on United States antitrust grounds.[29]

Prospects for International Bargaining

A study of 134 American multinationals, using United States and Canadian data only, revealed that 10% of the firms had labor actions taken against them across national frontiers while 14% reported that their employees were involved in international union action short of actual bargaining. The remaining 76% reported no multinational labor activity at all. On the other hand, the percentages for non-American multinationals were 21% and 24% respectively, somewhat higher than for American firms.[30]

Jack Jones, secretary general of Britain's powerful Transport and General Workers Union and Lane Kirkland, now president of the AFL-CIO have stated that they do not see multinational unionism getting very far. "I personally don't see the feasibility of international collective bargaining" said Jones, preferring instead to concentrate on increased exchanges of information. "Combined international bargaining isn't possible," added Kirkland. "We often can't get joint bargaining by unions in one company in the United States or even common contract expiration dates."[31]

The close alignment between unionism and national identity can be seen in periodic efforts of Canadian unions to disengage from their parent unions in the United States. In 1974 the Canadian Labor Congress, allied with the AFL-CIO, passed rules under which American-based international unions must allow Canadians to elect their own officers who will represent Canadian membership and set national policy, affiliate with international labor secretariats, and concentrate on participation in Canadian national affairs. Despite major disadvantages including exclusion from United States jobs, inadequate pension funds, and major dues increases, the nationalistic attraction proved very strong indeed. Meanwhile, American multinationals operating on both sides of the border had to decide whether the old rules of the game, involving identical pay and fringes, still held.[32]

One recent study of the impact of multinationals on bargaining in Germany and the Netherlands shows little evidence of any real consequences: "The strengths of the respective union movements, the highly integrated and institutionalized nature of the industrial relations systems and the general socio-political climate in the two countries clearly constrain the potential for direct adverse effects." Instead, prospects for conflict seem to center on "the unilateral supranational decision-making powers of (multinationals), and the lack of transparency in decision-making processes and financial operations."[33] Nevertheless, one writer suggests

. . . that in the long run, international unionism might not be dead; it could be very much in the cards, especially if the employees concerned and their own plant leadership decide to break out of their "national orbits." . . . While two of the three historic economic *incentives* to national unionism—avoidance of regional job loss and countering the whipsaw capability of multiplant firms—also exist on an international scale, the third and possibly most important—the need to resist competitive reductions in industrywide wage levels—has not been experienced for over a generation. Moreover, the whipsaw power of some large international firms has been subject to self-restraint by the need to differentiate product lines to meet local market requirements and also, although within limits, as part of a constrained "low-profile" policy. Thus, while some characteristics of the international economic climate operate to lower barriers to the development of international unionism, other environmental characteristics have prevented the emergence of an historically proven incentive.

Finally, where incentive is strong—where it is prompted by fear of job loss in relatively high-wage countries—an *alternative* to international unionism is also relatively strong. Job bargaining . . . is designed to restrain investment patterns directly to avoid job loss rather than indirectly through international coordination of wage determination on the union side. The job-bargaining alternative relies heavily for its effectiveness on governmental authority and the political process. Hence national authority, which underlies many of the obstacles to international unionism, also underlies a powerfully attractive alternative in jurisdictions of potential job loss. Thus, at least in the short run, any countervailing union power to the international corporation is likely to be neither so wide in geographic scope nor so private in origin as might have been contemplated in the past decade.[34]

According to the ICEF's Charles Levinson, what the unions want is eventually to influence multinationals in their investment planning: "Traditional wage bargaining is just arguing about sharing the pie. We want a voice in baking the pie. . . . The object of the international union isn't to stop multinational investment. We couldn't stop it if we wanted. Our objective is to enclose it in a framework of collective bargaining so that all the sacrifices don't fall on the workers."[35]

For their part, multinational companies have been cautious in approaching the activities of the international union organizations. Says one MNE spokesman, "We will probably be dealing with the ICEF eventually. But for the time being we want to resist getting into any position where we have to explain why we do things differently in one country or another. That leads directly to cross-border bargaining. Nor do we want to talk about investment plans. It's extremely dangerous." And foreseeing a power struggle between national unions and their international secretariats, he says ". . . we want to see how power relationships are going to develop within the unions first."[36]

In the view of one MNE spokesman, the reason why multinational unions will not get as far as multinational companies is that they are essentially political entities which immediately clash with the fact of national sovereignty as soon as, for example, international bargaining is attempted. Inflation and unemployment rates differ between countries, and a set of union goals and strategies acceptable in one might not be acceptable in another. The same is true of national structural, social, and political objectives. Even in the EEC, the greatest impediment to multinational bargaining is the sovereignty of the national state. "Genuine multinational bargaining will take place in Europe when the European Community becomes the sovereign state of Europe."[37] In one recent study of the impact of MNEs on union power, the author concludes that most of the problems that arise ". . . can be solved within the national industrial relations system without disadvantages to the unions, despite the transnational structure of the MNE. The main approach followed for this purpose is integration of MNEs into local systems and practices, a goal in which unions and government join and one which generally meets with the inclination of multinational management."[38] Nevertheless, concern of national and local unions with job displacement and worker participation in decision making are national pressures that will exist whether or not international unionism makes any headway.

On balance, it seems rather apparent that the day of multinational bargaining between labor and management remains rather far in the future, all things considered, if indeed it ever materializes. The institutional constraints are simply too great and there is little on the horizon that would indicate a change in these constraints. And there is the fundamental point that national union interests often do not coincide, indeed conflict with each other, which seriously inhibits even the most rudimentary forms of coordination and cooperation in all but a few exceptional cases. In short, multinationals have little to fear from international unionism, since the arena of conflict lies primarily within the labor movement itself.

INDUSTRIAL DEMOCRACY

Movements for "industrial democracy" have evolved into a significant source of actual or potential conflict for multinationals. This is particularly so for firms based in the United States, where the industrial democracy idea has been considered both by management and organized labor to be fundamentally inferior to hard-nosed profit-maximizing behavior of management coupled with equally hard-nosed and adversary collective bargaining by labor. Both sides have viewed industrial democracy as unnecessary, counterproductive and, at worst, a threat to the private-enterprise, market-oriented form of economic organization. In Europe, however, in part because skepticism about the performance of free markets and because socialist pressures are much stronger than they are in the United States, the industrial democracy movement has made a great deal of headway during the past decade or so.

Essentially, the industrial democracy movement has three major dimensions: (1) increasing employee participation in company ownership and profit-sharing, (2) direct employee participation in managerial decision-making; and (3) humanizing the workplace. Many American firms, of course, have significant employee-participation programs in the form of stock-purchase plans, stock options, profit sharing for different groups of employees, and "shop-floor" decision-making by employees, but management is still considered fundamentally a concern of professional managers and the shareholders who employ them. Working conditions are considered fundamentally an object of collective bargaining and (increasingly) government regulation. It can be persuasively argued that collective bargaining in the United States is, in fact, a form of industrial democracy and shared decision-making. But other forms of participation by employees in management do not fit well into the American labor relations tradition.

Employee Ownership and Profit-Sharing

In the mid-1970's, financial participation of employees in the equity of their firms and profit-sharing as a major component of industrial democracy was relatively uninteresting to workers in Belgium, Ireland, Italy, the Netherlands, Norway, and the United Kingdom, as well as in the United States, Canada, and Japan. But in Germany, France, Sweden, and Denmark things were different.

In Denmark, a proposed law would have required that a central employee fund be set up by each firm to which the company would have to contribute stock. The proposal was shelved.

In Germany, "asset-formation" *(Vermögensbildung)* was considered a central theme of the ruling political parties' concept of a "social market economy." Originally, the government's proposals for industrial democracy included a plan whereby companies would put aside 10% of profits into an asset pool for employees in the form of company stock. Companies could pay cash instead, but would be charged a 10–15% tax surcharge. The asset pool would be frozen for at least seven years. However, the proposal was withdrawn at a relatively early stage of the debate and has not been resurrected as worker accumulation of capital is progressing under other (voluntary) programs.

In Sweden, legislation allows state-sponsored pension funds to invest in company stock—for example, in 1974 they acquired 4.5% of Volvo stock—and some labor leaders saw this as the initial step toward far-reaching union ownership of industry. Swedish unions in 1978 were pushing legislation that would require firms to turn over 20% of pretax profits each year, in cash or in stock, to the national federation of unions.

In France, a 1967 *"intéressement"* law passed with strong Gaullist support provides that any firm with over 50 employees set aside about half of any profits in excess of 5% return on net worth into a financial pool for workers. Depending on the arrangement between the company and its employees, these funds may be invested in company stock, loans to the company, bank accounts, mutual funds or other financial assets. A 1973 law also provides tax benefits for employee stock purchases. These statutes appear to be widely ignored, however.

In the Netherlands, the unions in 1978 proposed an "excess profits tax" requiring companies to hand over to unions part of their profits in the form of company stock. However, there is some question about what "excess" profits are. And industry has argued that such profits ought to be paid to company workers directly, rather than to the unions as shares in the firm.[39]

The British government has also been toying with the idea of mandatory profit-sharing. A proposal in 1978 would allow companies to provide pretax funds to a trustee, who would buy stock in the firm and distribute it to individual employees. The share distributions would not be taxable, but would have to be held for a least five years. A recent survey revealed strong support for profit-sharing among both senior managers and workers, but very little interest in linking profit-sharing to the ownership of company stock. The same survey showed that only about half of the employees thought that profit-sharing would make them work any harder.[40]

To a considerable extent, the movement toward employee participation in corporate ownership and profits reflects two important elements. One is the old Marxist notion that the wage rate tends to be well below the marginal product of labor, that capital is really nothing more than the result of past labor, and that workers are thus entitled to a larger share of the fruits of their labor. Both worker participation in ownership and mandatory profit-sharing move in this direction. Unlike the collectivization of Eastern Europe, which throws out the "carrots" of individual and corporate material gains and has to replace them with the "sticks" of a command-type planned economy, Western European programs for employee ownership would focus on the firm itself. Firms would continue to be privately owned, in part by their own workers, and operate under market competition. The better a particular firm does, the better its employees do. To redress perceived inequities in the distribution of income and wealth, therefore, this type of socialization of capital is supposed to be "carrot-oriented" and avoid the fundamental, stultifying inefficiencies of the central planning model.

The second idea is that employee ownership interests would actually enhance corporate efficiency and profitability by giving a worker a direct stake in the "bottom line." The attitudes of employee shareholders to risk-taking—and to corporate policies that could affect them adversely as workers even as it benefits them as shareholders—remain in an open question. So does the real significance of a small stake in corporate profits for individual effort and initiative on the job. As a result, employee ownership has made slower progress than some other aspects of industrial democracy. It is also highly politicized, since many such schemes vest ownership rights not with the firms' own workers but with the unions, thus being viewed as primarily a power-grab by the unions and their increasingly self-perpetuating bureaucrats.

Humanizing the Workplace

A second major thrust of the industrial democracy movement has been to improve working conditions of employees. This often involves demands for flexible working hours, continuing education, improvements in the quality of the working environment, job enrichment, restructuring of work flow, increased worker responsibility and initiative, and the like.

To a large extent, such pressures of course coincide with management aims of increased worker productivity, not only as a direct result of the reforms themselves but also because of employee participation in their design and implementation. "As behavioral scientists have insisted for decades, to the degree that employees see themselves as co-determining the renewal of their own work, they will contribute motivation and means for real success."[41] The idea here is that employee motivation extends beyond pay alone, and to the extent that these other sources of motivation can be tapped, the enterprise itself will tend to benefit as well as the workers.

On the other hand, many reforms that comprise the objective of humanizing the workplace are costly, either in financial terms or in reduced operating efficiency or in increased risk. And so the basic question for management is whether or not the benefits exceed the costs for individual components of the humanization "package" of demands. Because in many countries there is the feeling that for management the perceived costs of humanization exceed the perceived benefits, this objective has become a powerful motive for the direct involvement of employees in managerial decision-making.

One of the major thrusts of the "humanization" movement in recent years has been workplace innovation—the attempt to upgrade workers' tasks into ones that are more creative and satisfying for the individual and lead to a higher level of worker motivation, greater productivity, reduced absenteeism, and reduced strike activity. "Increasingly better-educated Western workers protest against having to carry out short, fragmented jobs on an assembly-line day-in and day-out. They protest by not turning up to work, by leaving or (in Britain, France, and Italy) by going on strike."[42] Moreover, new approaches to production, moving away from the assembly line, could lead to greater versatility in production, higher levels of quality, elimination of backup assemblers, and reduced vulnerability to temporary snafus that could shut down an entire line.

Certainly the most widely publicized experiment along these lines is the Volvo assembly plant at Kalmar, Sweden. Computer controlled car carriers move between 28 groups of 15–20 people each, who perform major assembly tasks and have the impression of doing a complete job from start to finish. Buffer systems provide teams with 10-minute breaks between work cycles of 20–30 minutes. Saab-Scania has implemented much the same approach at its Södertälje engine plant, where worker teams of 3–4 essentially assemble complete engines in stationary bays. Renault has tried short assembly lines subdivided into three groups of 18–20 people assigned to major assembly tasks at its Douai plant, a system also attempted by Fiat at its Cassino plant.

Experience has been mixed. Costs at Volvo's Kalmar plant have been about 10% higher than at conventional plants. The system requires about 10% more space. Capital costs are 10–30% greater. Required inventories are greater, production planning is more complex, and training takes longer. Man-hours required for assembly are about the same. Absenteeism is about the same, but product quality has declined. Swedish workers seem to prefer the system, although Detroit auto workers preferred the assembly line after spending several weeks at Kalmar. Renault finds productivity up 20% in group-work on components assembly. Morale at all plants seems to have gone up. The Singer Company has also experimented with group assembly in its plant at Karlsruhe, Germany, resulting in an increase in output and improvement in quality. Other firms experimenting with such approaches include Volkswagen, Olivetti, Bosch, Siemens, and Daimler-Benz.

Besides tedium, "humanization" seems to have a good deal to do with the actual hours spent at work. Growing numbers of white-collar workers are resisting demands to work overtime, and increasingly the watchword even among higher-level executives seems to be "get the job done and go home."[43] Among the rank and file, there is growing pressure for a shorter work-week in most of the industrial countries where MNEs operate. In the United States, the United Auto Workers in 1976 negotiated a new "paid personal holiday" plan that gave auto workers up to seven personal holidays in 1979, which could be scheduled flexibly but well in advance so as not to disrupt production schedules.[44] But the concept of a four-day week, even one retaining 40 hours of work, has met with very little success. More successful has been "flexi-time" work scheduling, pioneered to a large extent in Europe, usually in white-collar jobs. By giving workers several hours leeway regarding when they start and stop work, flexi-time has caught on relatively widely despite the careful attention required for the scheduling process itself.[45]

Worker Participation in Management

At first glance, the movement in Europe toward employee participation in managerial decisions might appear to be little more than a surrogate for employee participation in ownership—as pressure toward increased socialization of enterprise. It is not. Worker participation is an amorphous concept based on the notion that individuals ought to have more say about what they do and how they do it at the workplace, with the objective of promoting industrial peace. In other forms of social organization, including academic and government institutions, collegial governance is a long-standing tradition. But in corporations, as in the military, democracy has been considered inimical to the fundamental mission of the organization, with a top-down command structure viewed as essential. It is this concept that worker participation challenges, with employees considered "stakeholders" in the enterprise with interests that extend well beyond the traditional realm of pay and working conditions.[46]

As far as management is concerned, the "stakeholder" concept embodies both positive and negative aspects. In the United Kingdom, Italy, and France, for example, traditional systems of labor relations have been so bad that management sometimes is not entirely hostile to new departures that may lessen labor conflict and its costs to the enterprise. In Germany, the Netherlands, and Sweden, where labor relations have traditionally been good, worker participation is often viewed as a means of keeping them that way. Sometimes worker participation can have the effect of increasing union control over its membership, and in other circumstances it can have precisely the opposite effect. Either can serve the aims of management under appropriate conditions. And shop-floor democracy, with each worker being encouraged to involve himself in problems of direct concern to him, is a form of worker participation that has long been accepted and welcomed.

On the other hand, worker participation, to the extent that it alters management decisions, has the potential of seriously affecting the profitability of the enterprise. New technologies that displace jobs or alter working conditions may be resisted, delayed, or adopted only with costly add-ons. Foreign investment opportunities may be put off or passed up because of concern about the effects on employees, with possible serious long-term consequences for the firm. To the extent that worker participation means that corporate decisions depart from profit maximixing criteria, it pits the interests of the employees directly against the interests of shareholders and, by inference, involves a *de facto* expropriation of ownership interests.

The meaning of worker participation in management decisions varies widely internationally. In Germany codetermination (*Mitbestimmung*) means employee representation on a company's supervisory board and the use of Works

Councils. In Denmark the same term (*Medbestemmeke*) means any method of diffusing decision-making power within a business firm. The same is true in Norway and Sweden. In England it usually means management-initiated alterations in the work process in response to perceived worker desires, but in France it is intertwined with political confrontation and Gaullist promises to combat the "alienation of man in modern society." And in Ireland, Italy, and the United States it means virtually nothing.

As a fundamentally European phenomenon, worker participation has a number of distinct roots. One is an increased level of educational achievement among workers, leading to diminished acceptance of menial jobs and decisions from above. Another is rising income, shifting attention to non-wage dimensions of work. And there are governmental measures to insure full employment and provide far-reaching unemployment benefits, which in turn focus worker attention more on job satisfaction.

Germany. Worker participation or codetermination had its origins in the coal and steel industry in the early 1950s with laws giving workers and stockholders an equal voice in a company's supervisory board (*Aufsichtsrat*). A "neutral" member, selected by both sides, votes only in case of a tie. A board of 11 members, for example, will consist of two labor representatives selected by the Works Council (*Betriebsrat*) of the company and three named by the union (one of whom must be a nonemployee representing the "public interest"), plus five shareholder representatives (one of whom must be an "independent personality") and the jointly-selected "neutral" member. The *Aufsichtsrat* normally deals only with major policy issues, reviews financial statements, and appoints the Management Board (*Vorstand*) which actually runs the firm. Under the 1951 coal and steel law, one member of the *Vorstand* must also be appointed by the Works Council to specialize in personnel and social matters. None of the *Vorstand* members may serve on the *Aufsichtsrat*.

In 1952, the coal and steel model was extended by law to all German firms with over 500 employees, except that only one-third of *Aufsichtsrat* members were assigned to worker representatives. But in 1976, after six years of debate, a new law was passed that extended *Mitbestimmung* on a more powerful basis to firms with over 2000 employees (over 650 companies in all, including some 30 affiliates of American multinationals employing over 200,000 people).

Under the 1976 law (which fully came into effect in the summer of 1978), the number of stockholder and employee representatives in an *Aufsichtsrat* must be equal. The number of *Aufsichtsrat* members depends on the size of the company, with a minimum of 12 and a maximum of 20. Twelve or sixteen-member boards must have two union representatives, and twenty-member boards must have three union delegates on the labor side of the table. The remaining nonshareholder representatives must be employees of the firm itself, proportionally chosen from blue-collar and white-collar ranks, with the white-collar contingent again divided between "ordinary" and "supervisory" employees (at least one from each). The Board chairman has a double vote, and in case of a tie, his second vote decides the issue. The chairman is elected by a two-thirds majority of the *Aufsichtsrat*—but in case no two-thirds majority is forthcoming on the first vote, the stockholder representatives have the final say. Moreover, the "supervisory" employee delegate is generally expected to be employer-oriented. Hence the 1976 law does *not* provide full "parity" for the labor side—parity would have meant, in view of many, an end to free collective bargaining and would have undermined the right to private property guaranteed under the German constitution.

Exercise of worker democracy under *Mitbestimmung* is still subject to debate. A key factor is the role of the *Betriebsrat*, or Works Council, which by law must be established in each firm, and in each separate location of the same firm having more than five employees. The *Betriebsrat* is elected by the employees, and besides representing worker interests to management is charged under a 1972 law with such shop-floor issues as working conditions, hours, payroll, and vacation scheduling. The *Betriebsrat* has veto rights on hiring, transfers, and firing, and must be consulted on planning and plant facilities. Employees also have the right to see their personnel files and to comment on the contents. All companies with over 100 employees must also have an Economic Council (*Wirtschaftsrat*), appointed by the *Betriebsrat*, whom management must provide with current information on the company's financial, marketing, investment, and organizational status as well as information on planned changes in the company's operations. Finally, the workers may appoint one member of the *Vorstand* to work on personnel matters. So even in the absence of *Mitbestimmung* at the Board level a substantial amount of participatory decision-making was accorded German workers.[47]

How stable codetermination will be remains to be seen. German *Mitbestimmung*, for example, ignores the possibility that the shareholder side of the *Aufsichtsrat*—possibly comprising small stockholders, representatives of large banks, and in some cases government representatives with strong links to organize labor—may not in fact vote in unison. This happened in the delayed decision of Volkswagen to set up an assembly plant in the United States: the labor side of its *Aufsichtsrat* was effectively "over-represented" with representatives of the Federal Government and the State of Lower Saxony sitting on the shareholder side of the table. In that battle, VW chairman Rudolf Leiding, an abrasive but successful manager who masterminded the company's post-beetle marketing strategy, was abruptly dismissed by a coalition of labor and Social Democrat party representatives on Volkswagen's *Aufsichtsrat*.[48]

In mid-1977 30 German industry associations and nine major industrial firms—led by the late Hanns Martin Schleyer who was kidnapped and murdered by terrorists a few months later—went to court to try to get the codetermination law overturned. They challenged the constitutionality of the law on the grounds that it deprived management and shareholders of control over company assets, thereby depriving individuals of the right to private property which is constitutionally guaranteed. They also charged that *Mitbestimmung* undermined management's power in collective bargaining with unions who sit on both sides of the table and thus see all the cards in management's hand. In March 1979 the challenge was thrown out by the Federal Constitutional Court, ruling that the law did not infringe on property rights because shareholders still had a slight voting edge, but making clear that *Mitbestimmung* had gone far enough.

Sweden. Among all European countries Sweden was perhaps the most fertile ground for the industrial democracy movement, with its extremely high income and education levels together with a long history of social experimentation.

Works Councils were established as early as 1946 and are mandatory for all firms with over 50 employees. Both labor and management are represented—often with several subcommittees dealing with questions like leisure-time activities, health, and safety—with positive results for shop-floor participation in decision-making largely at management's own initiative.

Although Swedish unions have not concentrated as heavily as their German counterparts on Board representation, a 1973 law does require all firms with over 100 employees to have representatives on supervisory boards *if* the labor side takes the initiative. Worker representatives are selected by the unions, mostly from the firm's own employees. Swedish employers have not shown strong resistance to this program, and both unions and employers mount training programs to prepare workers for board membership. In addition, a 1973 law gives the head of each company's safety committee, who is appointed by the union, the right to participate in planning new facilities, changing existing facilities, and shutting down facilities considered dangerous to worker safety. A new codetermination law went into effect in 1977 and requires management to consult with labor before making any major operating decisions affecting employees. This includes, for example, the selection of subcontractors on construction jobs. If there is a dispute, the union's position prevails while the matter is being thrashed out at a higher level between employer and union organizations.

France. The student-worker revolt of 1968 is often interpreted on the labor side as a concerted, if spontaneous, attack on narrow, dead-end jobs and exclusion of workers from corporate decisions. Works Councils had already been created by government order in 1945 for firms with over 50 employees. The councils are controlled by the unions, which possess the exclusive right to propose candidates for Works Council membership on the first ballot. The Councils have control over various social matters, receive financial information on company operations, may offer an opinion on financial matters to shareholders, and may appoint two observers to attend Board meetings. Independent unions also exist at the firm level.

This law has been widely ignored by both unions and management. Unions have been concerned that making use of their participatory powers could interfere with wage bargaining, while management in its authoritarian tradition was not anxious to do more than absolutely necessary under the law. Many French firms do not even have Works Councils. However, in 1968 additional legislation was passed to strengthen the rights of unions in companies. In 1971 a new law required companies to spend 1% of their total wage bill on training. And a 1973 law granted workers protection against arbitrary dismissal. More recently, a French government report recommended that workers be given one-third of the seats on company Boards. This was rejected outright by management, as well as by the unions which have traditionally favored nationalization over worker participation. The unions termed the plan "a trap of class collaboration."[49] Says a French union representative, "French unions are not German unions. We believe in keeping some distance between management and labor. Codetermination is not something we are striving for."[50]

United Kingdom. British discovery of codetermination lagged some years behind the Continent, and it was not until January 1977 that the debate reached a high pitch with the presentation of the so-called Bullock Report. Chaired by Oxford historian Lord Allan Bullock and composed predominantly of labor sympathizers, a 10-man committee proposed that the Boards of all British firms with over 2000 employees—including British affiliates of foreign-owned MNEs—contain equal worker (unionized) and stockholder representation, provided that one-third of all employees want such a change. Equal numbers of both groups would select an uneven number of outsiders. Shareholders would in effect lose control of the Board.

The Bullock Report predictably triggered major support from the labor side, especially the powerful Trades Union Congress (TUC), and vehement opposition from management. "The reactions to the proposals within the business community were the fiercest the Government has experienced in years—fierce enough to suggest that industry might finally withdraw its support of the Government's arduous efforts to rebuild the economy."[51] By intentionally discriminating against white-collar employees, it also attracted the opposition of this large and growing segment of the population. Consequently, the Bullock Report was shelved. In retrospect it essentially boiled down to an exercise in TUC power, in substantial disregard of other elements of British society—where only half of all workers are unionized and only half of the latter belong to the TUC—under the guise of industrial democracy.

Nevertheless, treading a thin line between the resulting widespread hostility and its own political obligations to the TUC, the Labor Government produced a "white paper" in 1978 suggesting that:

1. Workers be given the right to be involved in Board-level decisions, but not by actual Board membership.
2. A representation committee comprised of all unions in a company be formed to discuss strategic planning decisions with management.
3. After several years, the representation committee may nominate representatives to the Board if a ballot among employees shows this is what they want.
4. Refusal by management to accept employee Board members would result in a "fallback" strategy that would force the company to allow employees to fill one-third of the seats.
5. The decision on a single-tier or two-tier Board would be left to the company and committee to agree on—but barring agreement, a two-tier structure would be mandated with employee representation restricted to the top Board.
6. All firms, including banks, insurance companies, and affiliates of multinationals would be covered.[52]

Several British firms have moved voluntarily on worker participation in hopes of avoiding labor trouble. In 1975, for example, Imperial Chemical Industries established a dialogue with shop stewards concerning investment planning. Albright & Wilson, a subsidiary of Tenneco, did likewise by means of committees representing its 14 divisions, who consult with management on matters of safety, training, and job organization. And British Oxygen Co., Ltd. has provided financial data to workers.[53] This collaborative response to increased pressure for worker participation, it was felt, was probably superior to outright confrontations and would pay off handsomely in reduced labor strife. By the end of 1979, there were renewed efforts to come to grips with the participation issue in Britain, not along the lines of the divisive Bullock Report, but through some form of application of the successful German use of Works Councils to deal with shopfloor issues.

Among other European countries, the Netherlands passed a law in 1971 requiring all firms with over 100 employees to set up Works Councils, consisting of 7-25 members. Management is compelled to consult with them on major issues such as mergers, plant closures, and changes in personnel policies, and Works Council consent is necessary on pension schemes, profit sharing plans, and safety and health measures. Members of the Works Councils are normally immune from firing and get time off for education and training. Other laws give workers the right to demand an investigation if they suspect company mismanagement or if they suspect that financial statements are misleading. All firms with over 100 employees must also have a Supervisory Board which appoints management and sets major policy directions. Board membership is composed of shareholder, worker, and management representatives—once established, the Board chooses its own members. In 1978, Dutch unions also proposed "parity" membership on Supervisory Boards as well as direct participation of Works Councils in additional areas of corporate decision-making, investment and personnel decisions. The Dutch Parliament, in response, approved legislation in October of that year giving the Councils the right to contest management decisions that affect personnel. The legislation also extended the councils' advisory roles to such matters as takeovers, intercompany cooperation, investments, and hiring of new employees. However, the Dutch law does not apply to foreign subsidiaries in Holland or to Dutch firms that have more employees abroad than at home. A recent Dutch study found that Works Councils are fairly easily manipulated by management, that controversial issues often are not brought up, and that elected members are often reluctant or lack sufficient knowledge to disagree with management. One Dutch observer notes: "The labor unions are ambiguous towards codetermination. On the one hand, they want to exert more influence in companies. On the other hand, they are afraid that they will lose control over workers who become too identified with management."[54]

Austria closely follows the German *Mitbestimmung* model, with substantial *de jure* participation at both the Works Council and Supervisory Board levels. Norway requires "Company Councils" for all firms with over 200 employees which, with one-third employee representation, appoint management and are involved in major financial and policy decisions. Similar developments have occurred since the early 1970's in Luxembourg, Switzerland, and Denmark, but with each system having its own unique characteristics. In 1976, a constitutional amendment was put to Swiss voters which would have provided for worker participation at the Board level, but was soundly defeated. Italian unions have had much the same antagonistic stance toward codetermination as the French, and an effort by the Italian government in 1977 to give the unions participation in management of the country's state-owned enterprises was spurned as an invitation to share in "co-managing disaster."[55]

With so many of its member countries moving towards codetermination, it was inevitable that the European Economic Community would get into the act as well. A new draft statute for European companies, designed to replace national incorporation with EEC incorporation to facilitate doing business in the Common Market, was produced in 1974. This proposal included two institutions designed to promote codetermination in firms incorporated under EEC auspices: (1) a European Works Council to represent all employees of the company, and (2) a Supervisory Board with labor representation. Given the differences of view on codetermination among EEC countries, the second proposal in particular led to heated debate—that one-third of Board members should represent shareholders, one-third employees, and one-third should be selected jointly by both groups. Conservative groups in the European Parliament felt that worker representation must be restricted to one-third, while Socialists argued that one-third in no sense represented codetermination. Communist groups argued that the proposal co-opted the workers. As a result, it failed to be approved by the European Parliament and may have to be redrafted from scratch in the future.[56]

While codetermination is basically alien to American union and management philosophy, bits and pieces of worker participation are being tried, at least at the shop floor level. One of the leaders has been General Motors, motivated by a damaging three-week wildcat strike at its Lordstown, Ohio assembly plant over what workers called "dehumanizing" working conditions. Both the United Auto Workers and GM initiated a far-reaching job enrichment program designed to cut absenteeism, improve productivity, and above all boost morale. Several reported experiments along these lines have taken place in other firms as well.[57]

General Foods even went so far as to open a new dog-food factory in Topeka, Kansas, designed to be run largely under worker supervision. But the company, which once heralded the experiment as a major success, later apparently ran into serious trouble. According to one report, "The problem has not been that the workers could not manage their own affairs as that some management and staff personnel saw their own positions threatened because the workers performed almost too well."[58] By creating animosities and uncertainty the success of the system was seriously compromised.

The most prominent United States initiative in codetermination occurred in 1976, when the United Auto Workers broke with the traditional union position and requested as part of its initial bargaining position to put two representatives on Chrysler's Board of Directors. The proposal was quickly dropped, however, at an early stage of the negotiations, although Chrysler and the union agreed to increase job enrichment and consultation efforts at the plant level. The UAW demand was triggered by Chrysler's own initiative in the United Kingdom, when it tried to buy labor peace with its 54 British unions in 1975 by offering to let labor share in management.[59] The proposal was resurrected in 1979, as part of the Chrysler rescue plan.

As in the United States, codetermination is not now in the cards in Japan. In part this is due to the high level of workplace participation that is a traditional component of the highly successful Japanese industrial model. In 1975, some weaker Japanese firms were considering codetermination as an alternative to labor's demands for 15–20% annual wage increases—an idea rejected by most managers as an attack on the very basis of Japanese capitalism. "If that's the price that companies have to pay, let the unions have their 20% increase in wages."[60]

Multinationals and Industrial Democracy

It should be clear by now that the push for industrial democracy poses one of the principal challenges to multinational enterprise in the human resource area. Carried to its conclusion, for example, mandatory profit-sharing via company stock would eventually put MNE affiliate ownership in the hands of employees or host-country unions and spell the end of the multinational enterprise and foreign direct investment as we know it today. It would also, of course, spell the end of private enterprise in its traditional form and trigger a fundamental re-structuring of the economy and of society. For this reason employee ownership has made the least headway of all, even in countries like Germany that have gone a long way toward worker participation in management. Even so, it re-mains a danger.

In contrast, humanization of the workplace is not something that managers of multinationals should consider a fundamental threat. Frequently, initiatives in this direction are as much in the interests of the firm as of the workers, yielding improved efficiency, reduced absenteeism, reduced waste, and the like. And where humanization pressures are not in the interest of the firm they can be dealt with in a straightforward bargaining framework with labor representa-tives.

The most serious threat for the immediate future clearly lies in codetermina-tion, which for multinationals means losing control, to some degree, over affiliate operations. Nor are the stakes trivial. In 1974, for example, 70 of the 200 largest American companies had affiliates in Germany, and 260 of the "Fortune 500" had operations there. Six of these affiliates were among Germany's top 50 com-panies, and 18 were among the top 200.[61] Even in the earliest stages of the debate over German codetermination the multinationals were vocal in their opposition. The American Chamber of Commerce in Frankfurt, for example, sought a legal opinion on the compatibility of Germany's *Mitbestimmung* law with German obligations under international law, which found that such incom-patibility did indeed exist with the German-American Friendship Treaty of 1954. This treaty normalized postwar relations between the two countries, and protects the rights of United States-based firms against actions by third parties. The initiative by the Chamber triggered a vociferous counterattack by German labor and government officials, charging interference in the internal affairs of a sovereign state. "We are no banana republic!" exclaimed one German labor leader. By the end of 1979 the Opel board had been expanded from 6 to 20 members, with half representing an increasingly militant labor force. Worker members pressed to veto appointment of a new personnel chief, and repeatedly brought up for discussion issues as diverse as improved pension plans and better plant ventilation—"worker spokesmen are pushing GM to justify Opel's whole investment program, contending that improvement of working conditions should get increased capacity and product improvement."[62]

Avoidance of the German codetermination law by both indigenous firms and multinationals has sometimes been possible. For example, the largest European coffee producer, Jacobs A.G.—a Swiss-based holding company but with most of its production facilities in Germany—split its production of instant coffee be-tween the German market and the export market. The result was that it was able to cut the payroll at its Bremen plant from 2800 to 2000, thus falling below the employee limit at which the *Mitbestimmung* law applies.[63] The business interests of the giant Flick group were similarly split into smaller units to avoid the law. Yet avoidance can easily be blocked by future legal changes.

So MNEs have been forced to find ways of accommodating to codetermination in one form or another, and the incidence of conflict could possibly increase. For example, General Motors in 1977 made a decision to invest $2 billion in three German plants of its Opel affiliate over a six-year period, yet did not advise its Works Council on the matter. According to one local labor leader, "if such heavy investment is to get rid of overtime, then we support it. But if it is to increase productivity far above the average, we are not happy. After all, Opel has 60,000 people in Germany. Any big increase in productivity without a corresponding increase in cars sold would put thousands of our people out of work."[64] In more general terms, it is conceivable that employee representatives on Boards may be able to obstruct major investment and divestment decisions, dividend remittances, and personnel decisions on top management, as well as possibly transfer pricing and financing decisions.

Multinationals may be especially vulnerable to codetermination because the ownership and management interests are foreign-oriented—that is, to the parent firm—while worker representatives on Boards are entirely oriented to the host country of the affiliate. According to a recent study, the *Aufsichtsrat* of the typical German affiliate of a American multinational has less than 50% German membership, and its principal function is to rubber-stamp management decisions. With managers themselves serving at the pleasure of headquarters, the Board essentially plays a peripheral role, with the important lines of authority running between the *Vorstand* and corporate headquarters. All of this changes with codetermination, and the adaptation is far more radical for the German affiliate of a foreign-based multinational enterprise than for the typical German company, whose *Vorstand* is closely linked to its *Aufsichtsrat* and whose management is accustomed to operating in a collegial and consultative manner.

Clearly, in multinationals the interests of the affiliate and the corporation as a whole will differ from time to time. Traditionally, headquarters prevails. But under codetermination the affiliate's Board could conceivably block headquarters wishes on such issues as reinvestment of earnings in the affiliate itself versus remission of earnings to headquarters for investment somewhere else, although the basic decisions are made by the *Vorstand*. And since Boards almost always appoint management and establish salaries, ". . . it is easy to see that—given some disposition to horse-trading on the part of local management—the parent multinational could lose its most effective check-rein on unruly executives, namely the power to fire."[65]

Codetermination also provides a potentially convenient entry into multinational companies for the international trade unionists discussed earlier. In 1977, for example, Charles Levinson, Secretary General of the International Federation of Chemical, Energy, and General Workers Union (ICEF) was nominated to the *Aufsichtsrat* of the German DuPont affiliate by the local chemical union. As a vociferous critic of MNEs, Levinson expected to use his position to obtain access to data on global DuPont operations and to further international unionism's cause. Similarly, international trade unionists were nominated for board membership at German affiliates of ITT, Ford, and Philips.[66]

Another problem is that long-winded negotiations with employees can seriously hamper foreign competition, especially if the consultative and approval bureaucracy gets out of hand. As one Swedish management representative notes: "We can run into situations where the decision making process will take so long we shall lose our competitiveness with companies in other countries. You can't say when you are sitting in negotiations abroad. 'This seems very fine, but I have to telephone my trade union at home to ask if it's acceptable or not.' It is impossible."[67]

On the other hand, proponents of codetermination have pointed to the German iron and steel sector. One recent study of the German codetermination experiment in the coal and steel sector concludes:

There is little or no evidence of widespread negative outcomes concerning organizational effectiveness or economic progress. Indeed, a credible argument can be made that industrial enterprise has been made more efficient and effective as a result of participation. Technological and organizational change has not been impeded, entrepreneurial risk may have been reduced, and modern methods for the management of human resources have been initiated. . . . Participation at the supervisory and management board level has not destroyed collective bargaining, nor has it made trade unions redundant. Despite participation in enterprise decisions, employee organizations, which exclusively look after the needs of the workers, continue to play a vital role in German society.[68]

The idea is that codetermination need not spell the decline and fall of the firms involved, although the iron and steel industry—with massive government intervention and cartelization in Europe—may not be the best example. But the unions claim that a major side-benefit of the system is that it helps keep management on its toes. Labor members of Boards will tend to be serious participants in discussions, to do their homework, and to stress accountability, requiring better information and planning systems at the affiliate level. Not coincidentally, they also collect sizeable directors fees, and particularly among union officials who sit on multiple Boards the establishment of a new élite seems well underway.

Whatever the case, it is clear that multinationals will have to adapt their management styles to the requirements of codetermination if satisfactory involvement in countries like Germany and Sweden, and possibly most of Western Europe, is going to continue. Management of local affiliates is going to have to look more like the management of local firms and less like received management doctrines handed down by the parent firm.[69] Management styles will have to become more cooperative and collegial. Long-range planning will have to take account of more limited strategic and tactical options, and will have to be more carefully done. Top-management personnel policy will have to become more careful and long-range in nature, with emphasis on consistency and de-emphasis on *ad hoc* hiring and firing. Works Councils will have to be carefully cultivated by management. Planning and control systems will have to be overhauled to ensure accountability to newly-objective Supervisory Boards. Bylaws and articles of incorporation will have to be updated and tightened. And companies will have to show a willingness to help new Supervisory Board members to essentially learn their jobs. In short, with respect to our conflict-management model it seems clear that an element of *compromise* and *cooperation,* coupled with a vigorous and even aggressive defense of corporate interests, is most appropriate.

To date, the European experience with codetermination has not borne out the worst predictions of its detractors. As one international labor expert in Geneva put it: "Codetermination has not prevented Germany from becoming Europe's leading industrial power and the wealthiest nation in Europe."[70] Nevertheless, in the end, codetermination's drawbacks may outweigh its advantages by calcifying the economic decision process at the firm level and, together with various other types of social legislation, inducing a rigidity or "economic sclerosis" that will be extremely costly in the long run. If that happens, then the confrontive and rather loose United States system may, despite its drawbacks, ultimately come out ahead. Certainly the mushrooming foreign direct investments in the United States during the late 1970s are partly attributable to foreign MNEs' betting in this direction—a flight from socialization of the economic process. But in the meantime, profitable involvement under changing conditions of corporate governance remains possible.

EXPATRIATE EMPLOYEES

Multinationals are frequently accused of altering the employment composition in host countries by introducing workers from overseas. Sometimes this particular problem has been a major source of multinational corporate conflict. During the mid-1960s, when anti-MNE sentiment ran high in Western Europe, American multinationals were even accused of stimulating boom conditions in national economies that led to "over-full" employment which in turn required the importation of millions of "guest workers" from Italy, Spain, Yugoslavia, Greece, Turkey, Morocco, and other countries. These guest workers created a variety of social stresses in ethnically relatively homogeneous societies that proved difficult to resolve. Unquestionably there was a link between American direct investment in Europe and the guest worker phenomenon, but to employ this argument as an indictment of multinational enterprise is rather far-fetched, and in any case it apparently disappeared as soon as "over-full" employment began to be replaced by unemployment in Germany, France, the Benelux countries, and elsewhere in Western Europe.

More usual are two distinct lines of argument. The first is that multinationals tend to use foreign labor as opposed to domestic labor, thereby exacerbating domestic unemployment problems. The second is that multinationals tend to rely heavily on expatriates—both home- and third-country nationals—for top management talent in host-country affiliates, thereby placing a ceiling on the aspirations and achievements of indigenous managers.[71]

At its 1973 peak, 6 million guest workers were employed in Western Europe (excluding Commonwealth workers in the United Kingdom). By the end of 1976, about 2 million of these—plus 100,000 out of an estimated half million illegals—had lost their jobs. In November 1973 Germany cut off all further immigrant labor permits; France followed in July 1974. But once in, guest workers are difficult to get rid of. Italian workers cannot be expelled from Common Market partner countries. Others may fail to have their work permits renewed, but often this takes time.

In 1977 the French government hatched a scheme to give each guest worker willing to depart a "bonus" of $2000, at an estimated cost of $3.8 billion or about 1% of French GNP. The German government made a low-interest loan to a Turkish automotive parts plant to lure workers home, using a $17 million fund to help would-be Turkish entrepreneurs working in Germany set up businesses in their native country. But because Turkish workers are entitled to the same generous unemployment benefits as their German colleagues, the initial results were poor.[72] In Switzerland, the number of seasonal foreign workers allowed in was sharply cut back, even though a referendum that would have expelled most foreign laborers was defeated in 1974. Immigrant workers must physically leave Switzerland at the end of their current permit and can be denied re-entry at the discretion of the Swiss authorities.

Such reductions in immigrant labor are not easy to undertake, despite the undeniable argument that in times of recession their social costs rise substantially and the benefits derived from their presence dwindles. A decade of foreign workers in substantial numbers clearly skews the employment structure of the work force. Host-country nationals move to higher-skill, higher-pay jobs, leaving work in construction, sanitation, tourism, and other critical sectors largely in the hands of immigrants. To reverse this process appears to be almost impossible, at least in the near term, thereby "locking-in" the guest workers. This was well understood by the voters in the Swiss referendum, for example, since expulsion would have done major damage to the national economy.

At the company level as well, reversal of immigrant worker flows is by no means painless. Ford Motor Company's German affiliate had great difficulty adding 2500 semi-skilled people to the work force in 1977 in Cologne, where 20,000 people were out of work locally, because of a scarcity of foreign workers and the unwillingness of unemployed Germans drawing high benefits to return to work.[73] At Renault in France some assembly lines are manned almost entirely by immigrants, and as French policy on foreign workers tightened, both Renault and Citroën had to consider moving factories to the provinces because non-immigrant labor would be virtually impossible to employ for semi-skilled automobile assembly.[74] Moreover, in the view of some economists, the plentiful and cheap foreign labor during the boom period deflected management attention from important innovative cost-cutting and capital investment, thus reducing labor productivity and holding down wage costs below what they otherwise would have been. Expulsion of foreign workers would presumably eliminate this problem, but not without possibly significant adjustment costs.

Added to the guest worker problem is the dilemma of illegal immigrants. In 1977 Europe had well over 700,000 illegals, or 0.8% of the labor force, despite close monitoring of the labor market. A recent study put the number of illegal aliens in Milan alone at 80,000, the largest group hailing from the northern Ethiopian province of Eritrea, with another estimated 120,000 in Rome. Most live in squalor, in constant fear of arrest and deportation, and those fortunate enough to find work are often exploited by local employers.[75]

The problem is of course far more severe in the United States, which does not have the kind of carefully controlled migrant labor policy, ranging from immigration through employment to eventual repatriation, that exists in most European countries. In 1977 an estimated 3.8 million jobs were held by illegal aliens, who suffered some of the same pressures as their European counterparts. They tend to be highly motivated and willing to work at low wages, thus competing head-to-head with domestic disadvantaged groups and contributing significantly to the unemployment problem—if it can be shown that in their absence the jobs would be filled by American workers. To meet the challenge, the Carter Administration proposed an amnesty program permitting many illegals to remain permanently, thus protecting industries that have grown dependent on them, reducing downward pressure of illegals on wages and working conditions—and predictably stimulating illegal immigration.

To a large extent, the problem of expatriate workers has not concerned multinationals disproportionately. They have benefited symmetrically with local firms from the influx of guest workers in Europe, and have had to share symmetrically in the problems of their repatriation. They have not been directly involved in the migration process more heavily than local firms, nor have they evidenced a larger proportion of immigrant workers among their employees. Regarding illegal aliens, it is probably fair to say that MNEs have been far less involved than local firms simply because those industries most prone to using illegals tend to be subject to minimal MNE involvement. Multinationals do, of course, transfer labor directly within the corporate structure, but this labor tends to be highly skilled engineering and technical workers on limited-term assignments who comprise a tiny fraction of the total. However, on occasion there have been problems. In 1973 Bell Helicopter International transferred large numbers of pilots and technicians to Iran, where they had trouble adjusting to local conditions, with negative results for the company's training program for Iranians. In 1977 employees of a South Korean construction firm in Saudi Arabia rioted over wages and working conditions, incurring the displeasure of the Saudi government.[76] But these examples stem not from imported labor competing with local workers, but from adjustment problems faced by workers in great demand in host countries.

Perhaps a more serious problem and source of conflict for multinationals is expatriate executives. On the one hand, host countries welcome foreign executives as part of the MNE "package" of services that the firm typically contributes. On the other hand, nationals of the host countries see expatriate managers as an impediment to their own professional advancement. In 1972 a Conference Board study found that 267 major United States-based firms employed 3455 Americans abroad, but a 1975 study of 213 companies showed that the total number of expatriates Americans employed by these same firms abroad had risen to 5300. Efforts to send people abroad who are especially well-suited and adaptable to foreign business environments continue. And demand for overseas assignments continues to be strong—despite adverse tax changes—helped by high levels of compensation and rapid promotion. Many MNEs attempt to maintain equality between executive salaries at home and abroad, cost of living adjustments and fringe benefits for foreign-based executives often add up to an attractive package. On the other hand, some of the most promising executives seek overseas assignments only for the short term, afraid of missing out on promotion opportunities at home.

Resentment among local employees builds, however, when expatriate employees occupy the most desirable jobs in host-country affiliates. Besides creating conflict within the enterprise itself, this problem tends to cause friction with the local political environment, especially since the disgruntled employees are likely to be at the upper end of the talent and influence range. In earlier years, such resentment was compounded because remuneration levels of expatriate executives were far higher than those of local recruits doing very similar jobs. With the decline in the value of the dollar and rapid increases in executive salaries abroad, however, this problem has eased considerably in many countries where MNEs are intensively involved. Moreover, in the early 1970s many American firms cut back pay differentials for overseas assignments considerably—"hellholes aren't so hellish . . . a man is safer in Central Africa than in Central Park."[77] As a result, local executives often caught up with and sometimes passed American expatriates in levels of remuneration.

American multinationals in particular have tried to keep expatriate presence at a minimum in affiliates abroad. The reasons are clear. First, it makes good business sense to staff with local managers—many personnel managers are convinced "that foreigners can perform the job not only more cheaply but also better than transplanted Americans."[78] To maintain an expatriate executive overseas often costs a firm twice what it costs to maintain the same individual at home. So there is a strong financial incentive to keep the expatriate presence to a minimum, especially with the growing supply of well-trained host-country executives in many areas. On the other hand, many host countries provide strong protection for fired executives—sometimes up to two years' notice plus large cash payments—and this speaks for using American executives under the supposition that they have no such protection, although recent court decisions in countries like Belgium have ruled that such protection extends to expatriates as well.

On balance, the result is that American multinationals in most industries try to limit expatriate presence in affiliates to perhaps the managing director, the chief financial officer and one or two others, although frequently no Americans at all are found on affiliate executive staffs. For example, in the early 1970's numerous United States firms like Coca-Cola, Citibank and IBM as well as British, Dutch, French, and German multinationals in Japan turned over all management jobs to Japanese. The reasons given included better familiarity with local business customs, reduced friction with the external environment, reduced cost, and of course language. Still, there are limits. As one Citibank executive noted, "We worry that in turning over a bank to nationals, we run a risk that it will become a closed operation. They could run it so we would not know what was going on."[79] And there is often a tradeoff between the ability to operate well in the local environment and the ability to communicate well with executives at corporate headquarters.

Non-American multinationals have also tried to limit the presence of expatriates in foreign affiliates. For example, Nestlé's Swiss manager in the Ivory Coast in 1972 was given the dual task of turning over his job to an Ivorian as soon as possible and to fully "indigenize" management over a five-year adjustment period. At that time there were two Ivorians among Nestlé's thirteen local managers, and both were trainees. By 1977 there were 20 Ivorians among 33 managers. The recruitment and selection process was not easy and very time consuming, but by 1980 Nestlé expected to have 37 locals and eight Europeans among its Ivory Coast managers, with the European contingent ultimately to be cut to five individuals. "Because 90% of our Nescafé is exported, we need good quality control to maintain international standards. . . . We want cross-fertilization of the staff. We want to allow Ivorians to travel to other Nestlé companies and Europeans to travel here. But once we have a general manager, a marketing manager, and a finance manager who are Ivorian, the goal of having a local company will have been accomplished."[80]

Still, foreign-based MNEs seem to have been somewhat less successful in indigenizing local management than have American-based firms. Perhaps this is in part because it is easier to find locals fluent in English than in German, French, Swedish, or Japanese. Certainly Japanese multinationals staff their foreign affiliates very heavily with expatriates. This has caused some problems. For instance, as one report notes, "many Americans who work for Japanese companies in the United States are complaining that the path to promotions is blocked because they are not Japanese citizens. The unhappy employees are charging reverse discrimination that often leaves them with markedly lower pay and fringe benefits."[81] This pattern has led to court action under the Civil Rights Act of 1964, as well as to considerable personnel friction at the company level. Of the 30 top managers in the United States at C. Itoh & Co., a large Japanese trading house, 29 were Japanese—C. Itoh (USA) was sued in 1975 by three American citizens on charges of unlawfully depriving them of their civil rights as a result of discrimination and blocked opportunities (the case was still in court as of summer 1979). For their part the Japanese firms seemed insensitive to the whole thing, citing the 1948 Treaty of Friendship for Commerce and Navigation which permits them to send technical and managerial staff to the United States. They also cited the greater difficulty and longer learning process involved in getting to know a Japanese firm. But the heavy Japanese expatriate presence in affiliates around the world, together with often far superior wages and fringe benefits, is sure to create growing problems for Japanese multinationals in the years ahead. Of the Japanese response, one observer notes "Some companies are trying to change their ways to avoid problems down the road. But most just won't change until they are forced to."[82]

Even with American and other multinationals that are sensitive to the expatriate management issue, there are still limits to the progress of local employees. Even if the usual one or two "key" affiliate slots often occupied by expatriates are not a problem, it is not very likely that advancement to top managerial ranks in the parent company is in the cards. There are, of course, some exceptions. One is Colin Marshall, a one-time ship's purser with extensive international experience with Hertz who became European manager with Avis and rose to chief executive officer of the parent firm. But Marshall is a self-described internationalist and probably owed a good part of his rise to the highly results-oriented policies of Avis's parent company at that time, ITT.[83] However, other foreigners have made it to the top of American corporations as well, and gradually some corporate boards of directors are opening up to senior managers in foreign operations as well as to outside directors who are from abroad.[84]

The problem of expatriate workers and management remains a serious source of potential conflict for multinationals. On the labor side, they clearly have to follow a strategy of accommodation to host-country policies, and generally this will suffice. On the management side, however, MNEs need to undertake voluntary actions to produce greater "indigenization." As we have said, most American multinationals have sought to achieve this goal insofar as possible, with rather positive results in ameliorating conflict. Many European and particularly Japanese multinationals, on the other hand, still have a long way to go.

DISADVANTAGED GROUPS

The United States is not the only country in the world with a serious problem concerning disadvantaged minorities and other groups in the labor force. The French-Canadian problem, the Malay/Chinese problem in Malaysia, the Basque problem in Spain, and many others around the world point to the need for multinationals to carefully weigh the needs of disadvantaged groups in hiring, job assignment, remuneration, and promotion policies. And foreign firms can easily run into problems in the United States. Volkswagen encountered minority employment problems when it set up its new assembly plant in New Stanton, Pennsylvania, for example. On the one hand, local residents wanted first crack at jobs. On the other hand, blacks in Pittsburgh and Allegheny County, some 35 miles away, demanded a proportionate share of the jobs under "affirmative action" criteria. With blacks making up 6.9% of the region's population, a Pittsburgh civil rights organization, the Volkswagen Coalition, demanded 25% of the jobs at New Stanton and picketed the plant site. The company had turned over preliminary employment screening to the Pennsylvania Bureau of Employment Security, but refused to divulge specifics of its own personnel policy. For their part, residents of the area adjacent to the plant were concerned about VW's influence on the basically rural nature of their communities, especially about the possible influx of "blacks from Pittsburgh and Detroit" as part of the company's workforce.[85]

Labor practices are, however, a two-edged sword. On the one hand, ignoring needs of disadvantaged groups may breed serious conflict with the affected groups themselves as well as with host governments. On the other hand, it is sometimes the case that particular groups are disadvantaged precisely because of government policies intended to keep them that way. In that case, efforts to promote their interests in labor practices may breed serious conflict with government and the issue for the multinational comes very close to the kinds of human rights problems considered in Chapters 5 and 6.

Improving Labor Practices in Repressive Nations

Perhaps no other issue concerning labor relations and multinational enterprise has raised as much controversy as the employment concerns of nonwhites in South Africa. It is also an area where MNEs have extensively altered their behavior patterns in response to outside criticism. The focus has been on a wide range of South African labor policies and practices—wage levels, worker representation, working conditions, training, fringe benefits, employment opportunity, equal pay for equal work, the right to strike, recruitment, selection, promotion, and so on. More generally, the charge has often been that multinationals acquiesce to the wishes of a repressive regime and take advantage of the resultant inequitable labor systems.

One of the basic tactics of activist groups on this issue has been to force MNEs to disclose information on employment and labor relations practices. "Ethical investors" are strong believers in disclosure as a relatively gentle approach which appeals to the broad range of institutional investors. And so shareholder resolutions calling for disclosure at annual meetings typically garner much higher voting percentages than those demanding specific changes in corporate policy or practice. Disclosure is considered to serve both prophylactic and curative functions. Information presumably enlightens the firm's shareholders and allows them to vote on resolutions, make decisions on buying, holding, or selling securities, and decide on courses of action in negotiating with or otherwise pressuring management to bring about operational changes. The process of information-gathering also focuses the time and attention of management on the issue in question, and with this awareness often comes substantial change. Disclosure is certainly a powerful mechanism for dealing with corporate practices that are inimical to human rights. When exposed to public view such practices, to borrow a phrase from Justice Felix Frankfurter, exhibit "a shrinking quality."

Perhaps the foremost disclosure campaign on MNE labor practices was organized by the Church Project on U.S. Investments in Southern Africa during 1972–1976. This coalition of Protestant denominations employed disclosure resolutions as its main tool of raising public awareness and learning more about the operations of American corporations in Southern Africa. Resolutions calling for disclosure on labor practices and other data were filed with eight companies in 1972: General Motors, General Electric, Gulf, Goodyear, IBM, AMAX, Newmont, and Mobil Oil.[86] IBM and Mobil acquiesed, agreeing to issue reports, and the proxy materials were thus withdrawn. General Motors, after a series of public relations efforts aimed at staying one step ahead of the churchmen—a personal inspection visit to South Africa by former Chairman Richard C. Gerstenberg and special presentations to institutional investors—finally agreed to provide the information in late 1972.[87]

In 1973, the Project filed disclosure resolutions with 12 multinationals, of which only Burroughs Corporation agreed to make the information available without a proxy fight. IBM, which had enjoyed considerable publicity mileage during 1972 for its agreement to make the requested disclosure without a stockholder vote, turned out to be a target again in 1973 because "in the end," according to the churchmen, "IBM disclosed only a portion of the information."[88] Although opposing the resolutions, Eastman Kodak, Ford Motor, ITT, Texaco, 3M, and Xerox all decided to provide the information. Targets in 1974–1976 included Engelhard Minerals, Newmont Mining, Union Carbide, IBM, Gillette, Goodyear, and Phelps Dodge. By 1976, twenty companies had prepared special reports on their employment practices and operations in South Africa for the benefit of shareholders: General Motors, Ford Motor, Chrysler, Mobil, Union Carbide, International Harvester, IBM, Burroughs, Citicorp, AMAX, Weyerhaeuser, Colgate-Palmolive, 3M, Pfizer, Eastman Kodak, Caterpillar, ITT, General Electric, Caltex, and Xerox.[89] A few easily and quickly accommodated to the request. Others had at first resisted but in time negotiated an acceptable compromise. Still others, such as Goodyear and Newmont, perhaps believing that disclosure of information would put them at a competitive disadvantage or—as critics charged—fearing disclosure of practices truly worthy of condemnation, had refused to give in to pressure for disclosure.

South African Labor and Codes of Conduct.

On February 28, 1977, the Reverend Leon Sullivan, the prominent black minister of the Zion Baptist Church of Philadelphia and a board member of General Motors, accompanied by Frank Cary, Chairman of IBM, and Thomas A. Murphy, Chairman of GM, visited the office of South African Ambassador Roelof Botha in Washington, D.C. They presented him with a statement endorsed by GM, IBM, American Cyanamid, Burroughs, Caltex, Citicorp, Ford Motor, International Harvester, 3M, Mobil, Otis Elevator, and Union Carbide. The statement affirmed the following operating principles which the twelve multinationals agreed to support in their South African facilities:[90]

(1) Nonsegregation of the races in all eating, comfort and work facilities.

(2) Equal and fair employment practices for all employees.

(3) Equal pay for all employees doing equal or comparable work for the same period of time.

(4) Initiation and development of training programs that will prepare, in substantial numbers, blacks and other nonwhites for supervisory, administrative, clerical and technical jobs.

(5) Increasing the number of blacks and other nonwhites in management and supervisory positions.

(6) Improving the quality of employees' lives outside the work environment in such areas as housing, transportation, schooling, recreation and health facilities.

We agree to further implement these principles. Where implementation requires a modification of existing South African working conditions, we will seek such modification through appropriate channels.

We believe that the implementation of the foregoing principles is consistent with respect for human dignity and will contribute greatly to the general economic welfare of all the people of South Africa.

Rev. Sullivan had worked for 18 months to get the twelve firms to join in his campaign. After preliminary discussions with top executives in late 1975, he had met formally with 16 chairmen of multinationals with South African operations during January 1976 at the IBM Country Club in Sands Point, Long Island. Several smaller meetings with the companies and consultations with the Carter Administration and and the South African embassy followed before the principles were formally adopted, and key wording was reportedly changed at the request of Ambassador Botha.[91] The code was publicly announced by Rev. Sullivan on March 1, 1977. Three months later he announced that 21 more American-based companies had endorsed the principles, and that he hoped for the support of companies in other countries: "I want international support for the maximum impact possible . . . this movement must be a tide, not a ripple."[92] On September 14, Sullivan announced that still another 21 firms had accepted the code. By June 1979 almost half of the 280 American firms operating in South Africa had agreed to implement the principles.[93]

Although agreeing that the principles represented worthy goals, a variety of observers and activist groups subjected them to bitter criticism. The London *Economist* commented that the gesture represented "little more than a cosmetic reaction to public criticism."[94] South Africa's *Financial Mail* titled its article on the Sullivan initiative "a damp squib" (a firecracker that fizzles), stating that "two main points must be made about the manifesto. The first is that it is more significant for what it leaves out than for what it says. The second is that signing statements of principle, however worthy, on one side of the Atlantic is one thing; putting them into practice on the other is another. . . . The most obvious omission is the question of trade union rights for Africans. Not only does continuing refusal by U.S. (and other) companies to recognize African unions constitute a perpetuation of racial discrimination. Equally important, many of the problems which the manifesto seeks to tackle arise in large part from the fact that Africans are denied collective bargaining rights."[95]

The Interfaith Council on Corporate Responsibility accused the participating corporations of engaging in a "whitewash for apartheid," stressing that the principles were merely a warmed-over and indeed weaker version of recommendations that the State Department had produced for American investors in 1974, that they did not deal with the central ways in which multinationals strengthen apartheid, and that the issue at this time was "black political power" and "not slightly higher wages or better benefits or training programs, unless these lead to basic social change."[96] The American Committee on Africa labeled the endorsement of principles "an exercise in triviality," charging that "the corporations have deliberately avoided confronting apartheid by treating it primarily as a problem of workplace racial discrimination."[97] The Multiracial Trade Union Council of South Africa stated that the United States code "smacks of paternalism."[98] Other observers stressed that "the Sullivan Principles have no goals or quotas, for example, for the ratio of black managers or for closing the average wage gap between blacks and whites. Even if the Sullivan Principles were faithfully carried out by all corporations (and many U.S. corporations have yet to sign them) you would still have a situation where 95 percent of the executive jobs were held by whites and where the average black wage still lagged considerably behind white wages."[99] In their view, one had to be careful of propaganda attempts to convince Americans that "important changes" were taking place when, in fact, the moves were only serving to desegregate "the deck chairs on the Titanic."[100]

Responses to this sort of criticism by some of the signatories varied. Chairman Frank Cary of IBM replied that "we support the six principles because they are consistent with our own objectives in our operations in South Africa. I think support of the principles is constructive. It commits a company to progress, and it gives employees and others a standard by which to measure a company's progess."[101] A Ford Motor Company spokesman announced:

We believe that the Statement of Principles is an appropriate and responsible step by affiliates of U.S. companies toward achieving constructive change in South Africa . . . we recognize that reasonable men and women may differ over the most appropriate means to achieve commonly shared objectives. In our opinion, the Statement of Principles represents a realistic approach to a complex and difficult problem. We take the principles seriously, and intend to implement them. Future investment and expansion decisions regarding our operations in South Africa will include an assessment of the progress which Ford Motor Company is able to make with respect to these principles.[102]

In September of 1977 the Foreign Ministers of the nine EEC countries agreed to a code of conduct for EEC firms operating in South Africa. This code, proposed by the British Foreign Secetary, went far beyond the Sullivan statement and urged companies to recognize black trade unions and to practice collective bargaining.[103] Although this code has no statutory force and relies on moral suasion, the reaction of European companies was sharply critical. West Germany's *Bundesverband der Deutschen Industrie* (BDI) warned that "a general politicization" of international trade would put in question Germany's reputation as a reliable partner; the Dutch Industry Federation saw the code's call for union encouragement as a political document with "elements which have no place in business life" and warned that business should not get involved in "a political-ethical decision."[104] But in late 1978 the EEC began exerting strong pressure for the voluntary code to be extended to other countries of the OECD. And in 1979 the British government revealed the first statistics generated by the code—only eight of the 109 British companies reporting had recognized black unions. Lonrho, the British conglomerate, reportedly had more black workers on poverty in South Africa than any other British MNE.[105]

In response to the EEC code and criticism from human rights groups in the United States, Rev. Sullivan announced in 1978 that he proposed to expand his six principles to include a provision that black workers be free to form or belong to government-registered unions. Other new guidelines would bar job fragmentation and restrictions on apprenticeships for blacks. Rev. Sullivan also said he was instituting a periodic reporting program for the subscribing companies in order to have "some measurable way of determining just what progress was being made."[106] In a survey of code performance published in April 1979, Arthur D. Little Inc. gave 66 companies a nod of approval, 16 a slightly lower grade, and the remainder no grade at all.[107]

The core issue in 1979, on both sides of the Atlantic, was that of black African trade union recognition by MNEs operating in South Africa. Ford Motor had been the first American company to recognize an illegal black labor union, the United Automobile, Rubber & Allied Workers Union. With this move in 1977, it thus joined such European firms as Metal Box, Unilever, SKF Industries, and Volkswagen in moving toward normal collective bargaining arrangements with black employees. But for most MNEs, dealings with African unions has amounted to little more than lip service.[108] Most have been content to function with government-approved consultative in-company works and liaison committees, and have not viewed it as their responsibility to promote union development.

The long-standing policy of the minority white government in South Africa until 1979 was to refuse statutory protection for black unions, on the grounds that such groups "would quickly become lightning conductors for nationwide strikes and political unrest."[109] But pressures exerted by foreign labor organizations, the Sullivan and EEC codes, and perhaps most importantly, the shortage of skilled labor (especially in manufacturing), led to some new thinking in 1979. A 14-member Wiehahn Commission, appointed by South Africa's Labor & Mines Minister, in early 1979 proposed dramatic changes in the country's race laws: granting of legal recognition to black trade unions and abandonment of statutory job discrimination.[110] The Commission's pragmatic view was that economic survival could only be assured by a free market rather than a racial approach to the use and movement of labor. In early May the South African government accepted, in principle, most of the proposals and began preparing appropriate legislation to submit to Parliament. The Commission's report stirred intense debate and tremendous backlash from right-wing white labor leaders and Afrikaner traditionalists, including a protest strike by the white mine workers' union.

The result was predictable. The Commission's recommendations were watered down considerably in the legislation that was proposed to Parliament on May 22. The draft bill outlawed racially mixed unions, excluded migrant and commuter blacks from union membership (three-quarters of the black working population), and gave existing unions the right to veto legal recognition of new unions.[111] A labor spokesman for the opposition in Parliament accused the government of "surrendering to white, right-wing trade unions," while the Federation of South African Trade Unions, mainly a black organization, condemned the draft bill as "thwarting the development of black or integrated trade unions."[112] *Business Week* concluded that the goal of the legislation was to "create a privileged minority of black workers with restricted union rights in an effort to bring the inevitable black union movement under government control."[113]

Labor Conditions in Developing Nations

Labor practices of multinationals with respect to disadvantaged groups in places other than South Africa have also drawn increasing outside attention and criticism. For example, in 1975 the National Council of Churches sponsored a shareholder resolution at Gulf & Western Industries, asking for information about the company's operations in the Dominican Republic, and in September 1976 representatives of 12 Protestant and Catholic church organizations held an "Interfaith Inquiry on Gulf & Western's Role in the Dominican Republic."[114]

In 1977, a resolution on disclosure of Dominican Republic operations was withdrawn after agreement was finally reached with the company. Del Monte was asked in 1976 for information on labor displacement and cash cropping in its foreign and domestic operations. In response, the company prepared a report on its land ownership, certain leasing arrangements, and labor practices in Mexico, Kenya, and the Philippines. In 1977, another activist group charged that Del Monte "has benefited greatly from martial law in the Philippines. Marcos has exempted much of the agricultural land owned by foreign corporations from his 'land reform' program and has banned strikes by workers on agribusiness plantations. The Philippine government has been more than willing to force its own people off the land in order to encourage production of export crops. . . . Del Monte's operations in the Philippines is evidence that hunger and poverty are the darker side of corporate profits."[115] The firm was asked to establish a Philippines Review Committee to study wages, trade unionization, and land acquisition. Other agribusiness firms asked to disclose data on labor practices, primarily in their Central American operations, have included United Brands, Rosario Resources, and Castle & Cook. The latter MNE was asked by church groups in 1979 to develop a "code of minimum standards which the company will require of its labor operations worldwide."[116]

In the manufacturing sector, Motorola was presented with resolutions in 1975 and 1976, asking for disclosure of its labor practices in South Korea. Originating from a concern about the health and working conditions of the firm's primarily young female employees, the resolution asked for disclosure on the number, nationality, sex, and marital status of employees, as well as wages, medical facilities, and employee benefits.[117] In 1978 Church Women United asked Mattel Toy Corporation for information on the Taehyup Company in Seoul, Korea which manufactured Barbie dolls, Marie Osmond dolls, and related products under contract to Mattel. The churchwomen cited a ten-hour day, limited break time, no annual holidays, low starting wages, and injurious working conditions, which put into question "management's sensitivity to human rights." The shareholder resolution asked for a "statement of corporate policy regarding minimum wage and labor conditions in Mattel's foreign operations and companies with which we do major business." The resolution was withdrawn when the company approved a statement on employee relationships and announced it would require its principal foreign suppliers to confirm their adherence to the standards outlined in the statement.[118]

Coca-Cola in Guatemala. In a more controversial case, it became known in 1976 that Coca-Cola's bottler in Guatemala City, Embotelladora Guatemalteca (owned by a Houston lawyer), had engaged in unusual actions against employees exercising their right to union representation. The attempt to organize a union was met with stiff opposition:

> The crack anti-riot platoon of the Guatemalan National Police and a mobile unit of military police came to support Coca-Cola's franchisee. The right-wing terrorist group La Marro Blanca was also involved. Workers were locked out of the factory as the company attempted to fire 154 employees and replace them with scabs. Two workers were machine-gunned and others were severely injured during the months of struggle. Several workers were kidnapped and then later appeared in the custody of the secret police. The management of the bottling plant, knowing that by law Guatemalan workers can organize in one company only and not across an industry, reorganized the company into eight separate firms.[119]

In 1977 the Sisters of Providence proposed a stockholder resolution that asked Coca-Cola "to demonstrate its commitment to worker rights abroad as well as within the United States" by terminating its franchise agreement with Embotelladora Guatemalteca unless the bottler recognized the union. Coca-Cola argued that it was not the owner of the Guatemalan firm and had no control over its labor practices. A complicated agreement was reached, however, whereby Coca-Cola would investigate the charges of repressive action in return for a withdrawal of the resolution.

In 1978 the Sisters were joined by three other church groups in filing a new resolution asking the company to establish "minimum labor standards which the company will require of its franchised bottlers worldwide." The groups reasoned that "through franchises, Coca-Cola avoids many production and marketing problems, which are the principal responsibility of bottlers. While providing these benefits to the company, franchises permit independent bottlers to conduct questionable labor practices beyond the immediate jurisdiction of the company. Such practices damage Coca-Cola's good name and sales."[120] This resolution was also withdrawn after the church sponsors visited Guatemala in 1978 to see conditions in the bottling plant and to meet with Coca-Cola representatives, the local bottler and workers. The shareholders also witnessed the signing of an agreement between the bottler and the workers, which was designed to settle the labor problems. But the violence instead escalated. In late 1978 and early 1979 two union leaders were reportedly murdered while making deliveries in Coca-Cola trucks, police riot squads were called to the plant, all union officials were "condemned to death" by a rightist paramilitary organization, and two of the union's chief lawyers were abducted.[121]

Five church groups in the United States again filed a resolution asking Coca-Cola to adopt a "code of minimum labor standards" that could be required of its franchise operations worldwide." The company's management urged defeat of the proposal as "an improper and unnecessary intrusion by the company into the business affairs of its independent bottlers."[122] The soft drink concern's annual meeting in May 1979 was dominated by the church shareholders and shaken by accounts of violence and repression. Testimony was offered by Israel Marquez, the former secretary-general of the franchise bottler's union in Guatemala who had been forced into exile after several attempts on his life. He told the meeting that "in Guatemala, crime is referred to as Coca-Cola," and he pleaded for "immediate help so blood no longer flows through the Coca-Cola plant."[123] Corporate officials declined to respond to the charges and merely restated its position that such allegations involving independent bottlers were none of its business. More than 98% of the company's shareholders agreed.

Older Workers

Attitudes towards older workers are changing rapidly in many of the countries in which multinationals operate. In many nations there are significant pressures from labor unions and governments to reduce the age at which a worker may retire on a pension that is adequate to provide for his or her remaining years. Pushed by the "demonstration effect" of early retirements in the public sector, there are growing demands for increased fringe benefits via actuarially sound, vested, and often portable retirement plans that make the availability and incentives of older, experienced workers increasingly questionable, particularly in some of the advanced industrial countries like Canada, Germany, and the United Kingdom where multinational corporate activity has been most intense.

In part, this has been triggered by persistent unemployment among the young. For example, in France an early retirement plan was announced in 1977 whereby workers between 60 and 65 years of age are granted 70% of their last salaries until they reach 65, with firms expected to replace them with younger workers. However, initial worker response proved negligible—instead of a predicted 75,000 workers in the metallurgical trades taking advantage of the plan, less than 200 did so in the first three months, presumably because of cost of living problems and a prohibition on part-time employment.[124] Belgium, Finland, and Ireland have had similar early retirement programs.

Whether this can be sustained through a shifting demographic structure where an increasingly small number of younger workers must support a growing burden of early retirees remains to be seen, and may present a critical social problem of the future in many of these countries. According to a recent OECD study, "If the fertility rate continues to drop as it has done over the last 10 years, the financial burden for pensions will be spread over a smaller number of working people and it will become more and more difficult to increase the number of those drawing pensions by systematically lowering the pensionable age."[125] Multinationals will have to bear part of this burden in the form of higher operating costs and possibly increased bargaining conflict. But by and large, for MNE management it is a problem of tough *bargaining, accommodation* to local requirements, or *avoidance* of countries where such costs are excessive, but not one where a great deal of voluntary behavior is called for.

No less difficult from the MNE's point of view is the pressure toward *elimination* of mandatory retirement that is building in many countries. This has been most dramatic in the United States itself, perhaps because service beyond a given age has been considered a relatively normal occurence in many other countries or because the retirement age itself was not as rigorously established or enforced elsewhere. With the coming of "gray power" in the United States, pressure to raise the mandatory retirement age peaked in 1977 in the form of an amendment to a 1967 law on age discrimination which permits (but does not require) workers to retire at age 70 instead of 65, with some exceptions. The intent of pressure in this direction stems from a recognition that individuals are ready for retirement at different ages, and that this decision should be made by the individual himself or arrived at by mutual agreement, so that a mandatory retirement age is in effect discriminatory.

There are, of course, problems. Not least are narrowed opportunities for younger workers, limited opportunities for women, minority workers, and other disadvantaged groups, terminating older employees not working up to par, and possibly reduced receptivity to new ideas and approaches in various areas of corporate activity. But the discriminatory attributes of mandatory retirement probably outweigh these considerations. Certainly this has been felt in nonretirement age discrimination cases. For example, in 1978 the U.S. Department of Labor filed suit against Boeing for violating fair labor standards by discriminating on the basis of age among engineers from 45 to 60 years of age in promotions, layoffs, and salaries. The company felt the suit represented "questionable tactics."[126]

To some degree, extended retirement and age discrimination problems are countered by the trend to early retirement, mentioned earlier, and can be further eased by offers to "sweeten the pot" and "buyouts" of employees prior to mandatory retirement. To some extent, too, the problem will tend to resolve itself as demographic change stimulates demand for older workers in many industrial countries including the United States in the 1980s and 1990s. And not least important, those older workers who continue to be productive represent a valuable known resource. What seems clear is that companies will have to use much more sophisticated measures to ascertain appropriate retirement policy on an individual basis, with careful attention to "functional age" versus chronological age in retention or termination.[127]

Female Employment

As in the United States, the role of women in the labor force is undergoing substantial change in many of the countries where multinationals operate. And perhaps more importantly, views on the subject differ widely. The environment ranges from Iran, where the "family code" alows a man to murder a female relative who has dishonored him; to Bangladesh, where infant marriages have been common; to Ghana, where women run a major part of domestic commerce; and to the Sudan and much of Africa, where women are responsible for a large share of agricultural production. As one observer notes, "The problems of women in America are serious ones, but it is a question of awareness. I wonder what will happen when women in some of these other countries become aware."[128]

For multinationals, the problem initially is one of adapting to local patterns of female participation in the work force and of discarding home-country stereotypes. For instance, Swedish women have traditionally branched out into all segments of employment, and industry has been very receptive to experimentation along these lines.[129] In France, on the other hand, the advancement of women at the workplace is viewed by some observers as little more than tokenism,[130] although an active feminist movement appears to be emerging. In developing countries, the employment of women also varies widely. Ceylonese women were recruited during colonial times to keep wages low, and the reliance on migrant labor in Southern African mines excluded women from the workplace entirely. Elsewhere, the output of modern factories producing light manufactures and textiles has displaced female employment in cottage handicraft industries, pushing women still further into the periphery of the local economy.[131] Conditions are positive for women in the Philippines, for example, where virtually no limits are set, but this is the exception. In general, pressure for and genuine achievement of progress at the workplace for women is probably greatest in the Communist countries, followed at some distance by the Anglo-Saxon developed market-economy countries as a relatively recent phenomenon. They are somewhat less well developed in the remainder of Western Europe—perhaps less so in Italy, France, Belgium, Spain, and Portugal than in Germany, the Netherlands, and Scandinavia. They are far behind in most developing countries of Latin America, Asia, and Africa.

Multinationals face the problem of operating in local labor markets according to local rules of the game. Yet they are often under considerable pressure to stretch those rules from feminist activists at home and, more importantly, by economics. MNEs have brought about far-reaching, mostly beneficial, changes in utilization of the female labor force in countries like South Korea, Taiwan, Singapore, and Malaysia through labor-intensive assembly and manufacture requiring high levels of patience or agility. Feminists frequently view these developments as "exploitative," especially given the generally low wages, but relative to their alternatives in the local environment the effects are frequently highly beneficial not only for the women but for their families as well—and for local economic policymakers.

Even more problematic for MNEs is the transnational employment of women in executive and technical jobs. Saudi Arabia, for example, does not permit unaccompanied women into the country, although this is an exception. Thus far, as one observer notes, " . . . there still aren't many women in foreign posts. U.S.-based companies—which by most accounts are leading the trend—are only beginning to send women abroad, and most of these women are in what one describes as lower-middle-management positions. Much of the activity has been concentrated in a few fields, such as banking, which generally have led in promoting women at home. It's all so new that neither women's groups nor international organizations have data on the number of women in international management."[132]

Difficulties persist, but the fact that a woman works for a multinational evidently helps greatly to overcome local prejudices in the sense that she is viewed as a representative of the firm pure and simple and must be dealt with if business is going to get done. In many cases such "resistance" has reportedly been minimal, and it may well be that the multinational is actually serving in a limited way to break down barriers to female employment abroad—at least in the higher managerial levels. It may also be that in many countries businessmen are more willing to deal with foreign women than they are with local ones. A recent ILO study of female employment in the United Kingdom, France, Belgium, and Sweden finds that despite noises to the contrary the increase in female employment has not been paralleled by an extension of job responsibility. And old habits die hard—of London's financial district one female attorney at Rank-Xerox says "The City is the last bastion. . . . I had my bun pinched more times than when I was on Italian Riviera."[133]

A consideration of three quite different settings of female employment, the United States, Japan, and Europe may be instructive. In the United States, 53% of all women between the ages of 18 and 65 were in the labor force, accounting for 39% of the labor force as a whole and 48% of the unemployed during 1977, as compared with 28% and 27% respectively thirty years earlier. Only 2.3% of all workers classified by the Bureau of the Census as "officials, managers, and proprietors" are women, however. Under pressure from women's groups, equality of opportunity legislation, "affirmative action" and anti-discrimination activities of the government, court decisions and, not least important, good business sense this has been changing with doors increasingly open to women in higher levels of management.

For example, the American Telephone and Telegraph Company responded to all of these pressures in 1973 when it completely overhauled all of its salary and promotion policies—guaranteeing equal pay for equal work and placing women in jobs of increasing managerial responsibility, and increasing numbers of men in telephone operator and secretarial jobs—after signing an agreement with the Labor Department and the Equal Employment Opportunity Commission (EEOC). Still, change takes time, and in 1978 only three women had made it to AT&T's sixth (out of 10) level of management and 1077 women were at the third level or above out of a total of over 384,000 women employed—half the work force of the company. Moreover, the company had to contend with its three major labor unions, which went to court to challenge the program on the grounds that the affirmative action initiative abrogates worker seniority rights under negotiated contracts—"affirmative action overrides" were used to promote women and minorities with less seniority over the heads of more experienced male employees. All of this has required an enormous compliance monitoring apparatus, with all employees classified by gender, race, or ethnic group into 10 categories, with ultimate quantitative group-representation goals in each of 14 job categories negotiated with the EEOC. Despite implementational problems, the AT&T experience is considered by the government to be a model, to be followed by other firms in their personnel policies. One result at AT&T has been an actual reduction of 29,000 in female employment as the implementation of quantitative goals took hold.[134]

Other firms, in efforts to meet overall quantitative goals, have staffed entire departments with women in so-called "velvet ghettos." Such selective staffing is also evidently due to problems in finding qualified women for line management responsibility and "a lingering desire to keep women out of mainline posts."[135] Nevertheless, public affairs, advertising, and similar departments typically do not lead to top management responsibility, and this particular approach is increasingly coming under fire as a way of meeting affirmative action goals with respect to women.

Such preoccupations of American managers remain far removed from the concerns of their counterparts in Japan, where labor relations are more aligned with people's inclination to belong to social groups and cooperate rather than to act individually and compete. Teamwork and *esprit de corps* are the watchwords, resulting in a system of lifetime employment, flexible wages depending on corporate performance, and individual remuneration levels based on "social rank" or experience through to retirement. Intra-firm labor mobility is provided by extensive retaining programs and inter-industry mobility is in part provided by the cross-industry organization of the *Zaibatsu*. This results in a degree of employee loyalty to the firm that is unknown in the West, and in the words of one observer, "work has no meaning outside the social context in which it occurs."[136]

As might be expected, the role of women reflects this social context, and very few even attempt to climb the corporate ladder. While many Japanese firms are heavily dependent on female labor (46% of Japanese women hold jobs), essentially " . . . all executive-level positions remain closed to women—particularly industrial and banking conglomerates (such as Mitsubishi and Mitsui) which control the bulk of Japan's capital. . . . The men at the top of Japan's hierarchies, now mostly in their 50's and 60's, were reared on an ancient Japanese maxim: *danson johi*—revere the man, despise the woman."[137] And so the distaff side of Japanese management is sparse indeed. Equal pay for equal work exists, but since salary goes with the individual rather than with the job women end up earning much less than men. Moreover, there are restrictions on women working overtime and at night. Low-cost female labor evidently benefits the profitability of many Japanese firms—a 1977 study by Nomura Securities shows an interesting positive relationship between a company's share price on the Tokyo Stock Exchange and the percentage of women in its work force.[138] As one observer notes, "There are no women at the president or vice-president level in advertising, banking, or manufacturing firms that have at least 1000 employees."[139] Women are expected to leave the job after marriage, so corporations are reluctant to bid for them on graduation from universities and to provide expensive on-the-job training. Since this is essentially the only route to higher-level management responsibility, women are systematically excluded.

Evidently, women's attitudes represent an equally formidable barrier, with work viewed as largely a social experience and a time to locate a desirable husband in a society that is strongly conformist. In return, women have virtually complete supremacy in the home. The system is unlikely to change rapidly, and programs such as "affirmative action" in the United States remain for the distant future.

In Europe, as noted earlier, a heterogeneous picture exists. On the one hand, there are comments like "Of course there's a place for women in business. They're good at all things that are too boring for machines."[140] On the other hand, there is plenty of national legislation guaranteeing equal pay for equal work, a principle that is also embodied in the Treaty of Rome which founded the European Common Market. The United Kingdom is the only country with equal opportunity laws sufficiently powerful to prevent sex discrimination in employment advertising. In Germany, women reportedly earn one-third less than men on average, with women tending to be classified as "light workers" and rarely seen in managerial jobs. In Italy, only 26.5% of the labor force is composed of women and less than 1% of corporate managerial employees are female, with a sizeable proportion of these owning their own firms. Reasons cited include the attitudes of male colleagues and inadequate transportation, housing, social conditions, day care centers, and domestic service.[141] Moreover, the Italian practice or paying executives despite long periods of absence is given as a reason for avoiding women in managerial posts, since this might be used to cover childbearing and extended periods in the home.

Multinationals are affected by pressures to bring women into higher-level jobs in a number of ways. Militant women's rights groups may exert pressure for expanded opportunities for women in the firm's global operations. This may run counter to strong resistance to women business executives in many countries, although as noted earlier this frequently is not an insurmountable barrier even in the most closed societies. However, this pressure may extend to the "exploitation" of women in production jobs abroad, particularly low-skill jobs in low-wage countries. Here MNEs need to take an assertive position and point out the nature of the alternatives for the women involved, together with providing important fringe benefits such as company health care, recreation, day-care centers, cultural programs, transportation, and the like.

In the end, it is ability that counts, and MNEs are increasingly anxious to tap the female labor pool for higher-level management positions—wherein American firms are clearly in the lead. For example, in Europe and Japan a disproportionately large number of women work for American and Canadian multinationals, and this appears to have influenced European competitors to do likewise. Dow Chemical Europe implemented the American parent's equal opportunity policy, increasing the proportion of women in junior and middle management ranks from 3% in 1972 to 9% in 1976.[142] Especially the United States commercial banks in Europe employ a relatively large number of women officers, and some European banks have followed suit.

It seems safe to predict that women's rights pressure will continue, and that the United States will continue to lead in this respect. It follows that American multinationals will have an easier time complying with and even anticipating such pressure abroad, while foreign-based MNEs may have to overcome a greater degree of internal resistance to women managers in order to avoid possibly serious conflict in their American operations. However, in 1970 the Bank of Tokyo started training women for overseas assignment in recognition of this need, and there is evidence that others are doing likewise.[143]

To summarize, employment of disadvantaged groups poses a serious problem for multinationals. Foreign-based firms operating in the United States have frequently run into equal-opportunity and affirmative action problems on a variety of grounds. At the same time, multinationals based in the United States and operating abroad face different kinds of problems in countries where the racial or ethnic minority often has the economic power, where equality of opportunity programs do not exist, and where particular disadvantaged groups are actually persecuted under government policy.

Similarly, labor policies with respect to older workers and women may pose a problem for MNEs. Here again, however, American multinationals may be in the position of having had to deal with these problems at home before encountering them abroad, while foreign-based firms may have a rather more difficult time of it.

CONCLUSIONS

Managing human-resource problems in terms of our conflict-management model clearly runs a very broad gamut indeed. The stakes of the firm in a given labor conflict can vary between very low, as when in a strike-threat situation there exists substitute capacity in one of its plants abroad, to very high if the threatened plant manufactures inputs that could affect the company's worldwide market position. Similarly the quality of the relationship between the firm and its labor pool can vary between conflict-prone, as with American automotive MNEs in England, to conflict–free, along the lines of the traditional German or Japanese labor relations models. Both the stakes and the relationship quality, then, vary enormously among both countries and issues. For this reason, the conflict-management patterns and outcomes will certainly differ from case to case.

In standard collective bargaining conflict, the firm can usually be expected to take an initially *competitive* stance, either on its own or as part of an employers' confederation bargaining collectively with a union. The same is true on questions of multinational unionism, where the aim is to close off some to the options the MNE has available; hence the stakes for the firm are extraordinarily high. On the other hand, with respect to disadvantaged groups and the employment of expatriates in host countries the stakes may be relatively lower and the degree of interest interdependence greater, so that a certain amount of *compromise* and even *accommodation* may be called for.

The problem of industrial democracy appears to call for a mixed response. Codetermination can trigger everything from withdrawal and complete *avoidance* to *accommodation* and learning to live with the system, even though the consequences for MNE decision making can substantially exceed those for local firms. With respect to employee ownership the same reaction spectrum is available, possibly tilted somewhat more to the *avoidance* side after an assertive battle to stave off this development has been fought and lost. On humanizing the workplace, on the other hand, a *collaborative* position can frequently best serve the interests of the firm.

12 THE NATURAL ENVIRONMENT

Environmental conflict is perhaps one of the most difficult issues confronting multinationals. The frequency and intensity of conflict over ecological issues seems bound to increase as three broad trends continue to unfold in the years ahead: First, *the pool of environmental resources* over which disputes occur is likely to diminish in size. Second, *the views of firms and other parties* on how these resources should be used are likely to grow more incompatible. And third, *the ability of environmentalists* and others to interfere with corporate objectives is likely to continue to expand.[1]

If these trend assessments are broadly correct, multinationals in a number of industries, particularly chemicals, energy, metals, mining, and transportation, will face major challenges in the coming decades.

Consider the following sample of environmental conflict "classics" involving multinational enterprise:

The Alyeska Pipeline Service Co. vs. a unique coalition of environmental groups insisting on preservation of American's last frontier, Alaskan natives demanding settlement of land claims, and lawmakers pressing for hefty taxes on North Slope oil. The conflict over the Trans-Alaska Pipeline ended only when the Arab oil embargo jolted Congress into passing a right-of-way bill in 1973. Due in large measure to the environmental delays, the pipeline opened in 1977 five years behind schedule at a cost ten times higher than its original estimate. At $9.3 billion it became the most expensive private construction project in history.[2]

Montedison vs. French and Italian fishermen and public officials concerned about damage to the tourism and fishing industries caused by the company's dumping of titanium dioxide wastes into the Mediterranean Sea. Protests during the course of this long-running dispute of the 1970s involved rioting in the streets of Corsica, seizure of the Corsican Deputy Prefect, blockades by fishermen of the port of Ajaccio, dynamiting of Italian ships, plant shutdowns, lawsuits asking for 60 million French francs in damages, a court trial in which Montedison's President and other senior officials were convicted of pollution charges and given three month suspended jail sentences, and much squabbling in Brussels over the need for uniform EEC standards on TiO_2 waste disposal.[3]

Olympic Refineries, Inc. (Greek-owned) **vs. citizens of Durham, New Hampshire,** over plans for a $600 million oil refinery. Olympic's hard sell saturation campaign of radio spots, newspaper advertising, television shows, and junkets for legislators failed to convince residents that the refinery meant cheaper energy, lower taxes, more jobs, and no harm to the coastal environment. At a special public meeting on the refinery in

March 1974, they rejected the project by a nine to one margin despite heavy pressure from the state government to accept it. The "Greeks bearing gifts" were told by Yankee opponents to "go back to Scorpio."[4]

Shell Oil Co. vs. the Oil, Chemical and Atomic Workers Union (OCAW) who went on strike at Shell's six United States refineries in January 1973 because of the company's refusal to accept health and safety contract provisions already agreed to by eleven major oil firms. OCAW's call for a national consumer boycott against Shell products during the strike was endorsed by most of America's large environmental action groups. The four month strike and attempted boycott, however, failed to significantly harm Shell's production and profitability, and concessions were eventually wrung from OCAW on the wording of health and safety clauses in the settlement.[5]

Chemische Werke München (CWM) vs. citizen groups and public officials in at least eight German or French towns where CWM proposed establishing a new lead stearate plant. Stymied by Bavarian authorities from expanding its complex in a suburb of Munich, CWM (part-owned by Degussa) went on the road to find a new plant site. After little luck in Germany, CWM focused on France. But fears regarding toxic lead emissions blocked its first choice in St. Avold. The company received central government authorization for its next choice in Marckolsheim in the Alsace region, but local town council members resigned in protest over the project while local environmentalists and farmers orchestrated a five-month occupation of CWM's plant site. When the Ministry of Industry in Paris changed its mind about the project a half-year later, CWM went back to site-shopping. But French environmental groups such as "Pollution Non" and "Les Amis de la Terre" shadowed the firm, convincing small towns approached by CWM in Brittany and Lorraine to refuse the project. Rejected in France, CWM returned home and continued its ill-fated search in places such as Kiel and Braunschweig.[6]

Braskraft vs. Brazilian environmental groups and regulators in 1977–1978 over construction of a $200 million cellulose plant in a rural location. Such a battle was hardly imaginable back in 1972 when Brazil fervently championed the view at the UN Stockholm Conference on the Human Environment that "poverty is the worst pollution" and that environmental protection's principal impact would be to slow the development of Third World nations. Brazil's planning minister even observed hopefully that his country could "become the importer of pollution." Such attitudes were short-lived. New industrial zoning laws were designed in 1977 to effectively block new or expanded heavy industry in Brazil's developed urban areas, and environmental coalitions even began to target their fire on projects in rural areas. The Braskraft venture (affiliated with the Continental Group) was long delayed by the government's refusal to accept three successive drafts of the firm's environmental impact statement, even though company officials maintained the plant met current U.S. Environmental Protection Agency standards. While waiting, Braskraft was forced to dismiss workers already hired for the operation.[7]

The consequences of the environmental challenge for multinationals are profound. As dramatized in our sample of conflicts, these include interminable delays, skyrocketing construction costs, growing regulatory constraints on managerial decision-making, wasted planning efforts, forced relocations of productive capacity, plant shutdowns, and technical modification, as well as banned products, lost markets, fines and compensation payments, tarnished reputations, losses of good-will, dissolution of trust, and even civil disobedience or violence. But it is not environmental conflict itself that is dangerous, but rather its mismanagement. Dealing with this problem in a reasonably coherent national setting is one thing. Dealing with it in a multinational setting is another matter altogether.[8] Expectations with regard to protection of health and the environment differ widely in intensity, substance, and durability, both between countries and over time. Multinationals thus are faced with varied "zones of discretion" in the timing and strength of their responses across the range of nations in which they operate with a unified management structure.[9] And actions in one country frequently expose management to scrutiny and potential conflict in others.

THE SETTING

The scale, pervasiveness, and variety of environmental despoliation at present differ widely among nations, and so do the substance, intensity, and timing of national environmental policies.[10] Exhibit 12–1 provides a generalized sequencing model of environmental issues and policy-formation that attempts to explain this fundamental lack of homogeneity in national environmental problems and public policies designed to deal with them.[11]

Environmental Problems

Most environmental problems can be traced to *economic activities* (Box 1) involving extraction, production, distribution, consumption, and disposal of goods and services—activities that either directly, or indirectly through the generation of residuals, change *natural conditions* (Box 2). These typically constitute "common property resources." They cannot, or can only imperfectly, be reduced to private ownership. They can, however, be viewed as asset-like stocks which produce streams of varied and useful services—intangible (scenic views and recreational amenities), functional (waste assimilation, nutrient cycling, pest control, and climate regulation), and tangible (flows of life-sustaining material resources such as water, air, and minerals). All natural systems possess a capacity to assimilate, to some degree, most forms and types of residuals through natural mechanisms of transport, transformation, and storage. Economic activities may diminish the capacity of natural systems to perform their waste disposal and other vital roles, or the volume of residuals generated may exceed that capacity. The significance of these environmental changes in human terms, however, will depend heavily on interactions of these changes with *human conditions* (Box 3). For example, degradation in air quality may be more serious if it occurs in a densely rather than sparsely populated region. Likewise, soil erosion will have a greater impact if it occurs in a region where arable land is in short rather than abundant supply.

The *character of environmental problems* (Box 4) within any given geographic area thus depends on the changes in natural conditions and interactions with human conditions induced by economic activity. Given inter-country variations in each of these dimensions, the resulting characteristics of environmental

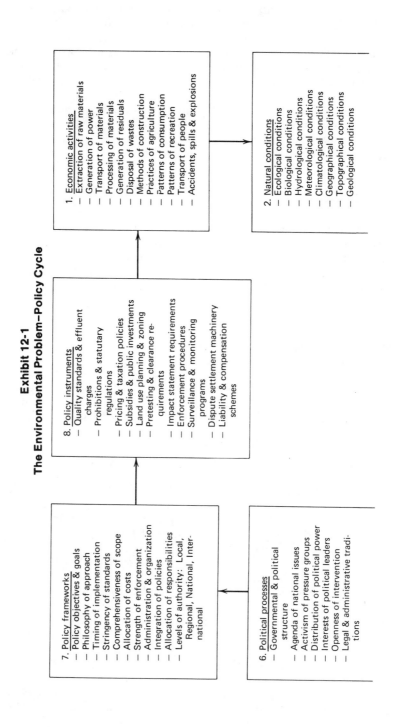

Exhibit 12-1
The Environmental Problem–Policy Cycle

1. Economic activities
   – Extraction of raw materials
   – Generation of power
   – Transport of materials
   – Processing of materials
   – Generation of residuals
   – Disposal of wastes
   – Methods of construction
   – Practices of agriculture
   – Patterns of consumption
   – Patterns of recreation
   – Transport of people
   – Accidents, spills & explosions

2. Natural conditions
   – Ecological conditions
   – Biological conditions
   – Hydrological conditions
   – Meteorological conditions
   – Climatological conditions
   – Geographical conditions
   – Topographical conditions
   – Geological conditions

8. Policy instruments
   – Quality standards & effluent charges
   – Prohibitions & statutory regulations
   – Pricing & taxation policies
   – Subsidies & public investments
   – Land use planning & zoning
   – Pretesting & clearance requirements
   – Impact statement requirements
   – Enforcement procedures
   – Surveillance & monitoring programs
   – Dispute settlement machinery
   – Liability & compensation schemes

7. Policy frameworks
   – Policy objectives & goals
   – Philosophy of approach
   – Timing of implementation
   – Stringency of standards
   – Comprehensiveness of scope
   – Allocation of costs
   – Strength of enforcement
   – Administration & organization
   – Integration of policies
   – Allocation of responsibilities
   – Levels of authority: Local, Regional, National, International

6. Political processes
   – Governmental & political structure
   – Agenda of national issues
   – Activism of pressure groups
   – Distribution of political power
   – Interests of political leaders
   – Openness of intervention
   – Legal & administrative traditions

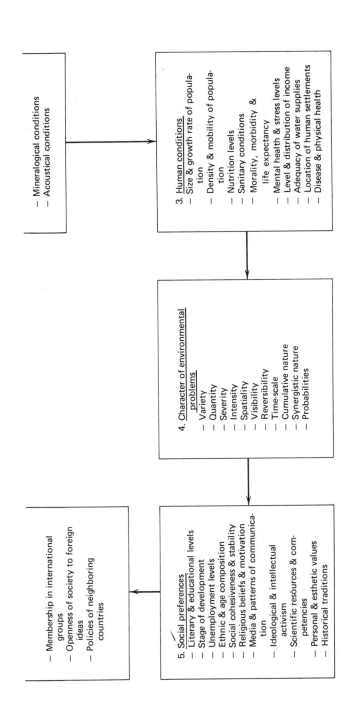

- Mineralogical conditions
- Acoustical conditions

3. Human conditions
- Size & growth rate of popula-
  tion
- Density & mobility of popula-
  tion
- Nutrition levels
- Sanitary conditions
- Morality, morbidity &
  life expectancy
- Mental health & stress levels
- Level & distribution of income
- Adequacy of water supplies
- Location of human settlements
- Disease & physical health

4. Character of environmental
   problems
- Variety
- Quantity
- Severity
- Intensity
- Spatiality
- Visibility
- Reversibility
- Time-scale
- Cumulative nature
- Synergistic nature
- Probabilities

5. Social preferences
- Literary & educational levels
- Stage of development
- Unemployment levels
- Ethnic & age composition
- Social cohesiveness & stability
- Religious beliefs & motivation
- Media & patterns of communica-
  tion
- Ideological & intellectual
  activism
- Scientific resources & com-
  petencies
- Personal & esthetic values
- Historical traditions

- Membership in international
  groups
- Openness of society to foreign
  ideas
- Policies of neighboring
  countries

427

problems found within different nations exhibit correspondingly wide variations. These make themselves felt in a number of ways. Environmental problems may be reversible or irreversible, more or less certain, temporary or cumulative, independent or synergistic, and short or long in the time scale between cause and effect. The order of gravity may extend from losses in amenities to problems that seriously threaten human health, genetic stock, and the sustaining capacity of entire ecological systems. The areas affected by the environmental damage may be local, regional, national, multinational, or global.

The majority of environmental problems are local in nature with little or no spillovers to other regions, and therefore are capable of local solution. Some of the most serious and intractable environmental problems, however, may be truly global in nature and affect the biosphere as a whole—for example, pollution of the oceans, build-up of carbon dioxide in the atmosphere and particulate content in the stratosphere, mobility and persistence of pesticide residues, and the like.[12]

Environmental Policies

The translation of existing or expected environmental problems into corrective or preventive environmental policy depends heavily on social and political factors. Environmental problems within any nation are perceived, interpreted, and given priorities in accordance with existing *social preferences* (Box 5). Environmental quality is a matter of social choice and societies may differ, quite legitimately, in their views as to what constitutes an "acceptable" level of environmental quality. Societies afflicted with widespread malnutrition and disease, high infant mortality, low life expectancy, high illiteracy levels, and endemic unemployment are not likely to place the same value on degradation of the natural environment as societies in which these kinds of problems have been overcome. This means that identical objectively-perceived environmental damage may receive quite different social weightings in different societies. These relative social weightings then enter into the *political process* (Box 6), where their transformation into policy action depends on the structure, representativeness, accessibility, prevalent ideology, and other features of the national political system. Differences in interest-group pressures and political machinery will often lead to differences in the assessment and selection of feasible policy alternatives. Since policy structures among nations are highly variegated and imperfect, this means that identical social weightings applied to the same environmental issue in different countries may not in fact result in, the same selections of policy alternatives.

What generally emerges from the political process is a *framework of environmental policy* (Box 7) that explicitly or implicitly outlines the objectives to be sought, the approach and timetable to be followed, and organizational arrangements to be employed. The framework will reflect differences in the balance between centralized and decentralized authority (Japan versus Australia), comprehensiveness or fragmentation in administrative structures (Denmark versus Italy), balance between executive and legislative control (France versus Canada), relative strengths in staffing of environmental ministries (Netherlands versus Brazil), preferences for the "case-by-case" or "blanket" approaches (United

Kingdom versus United States), and allocation of environmental costs to taxpayers or consumers (Sweden versus West Germany).

Implementation of the policy framework will involve the selection, development, and use of different kinds of *environmental policy instruments* (Box 8). Nations typically will utilize some combination of prohibitions, standards, charges, tax schemes, land use controls, clearance requirements, subsidies, hearing procedures, and the like in their attempts to carry out environmental policy. Such controls provide incentives and disincentives for decision makers at the operating level of the economy—"carrots and sticks" that serve to guide the choice of inputs, processes, and outputs of environment-affecting activities, thus coming back full-circle to *economic activities* (Box 1).

Variance in Approaches

Multinationals thus operate in a heterogeneous world of environmental problems and policies—sovereign nations are going about the business of environmental and health protection at different speeds, with different degrees of rigor, using different techniques. Variations in environmental policy "climates" follow in part from intercountry differences in levels of industrialization and standards of living. A great deal of policy is already in place in some of the highly industrialized nations. It is just beginning to emerge in others. In still others—particularly in the least developed—it probably will be some time in coming. Other policy differences exist mainly because of variations in political and social philosophies. The ways in which the United Kingdom and the United States approach problems of air and water pollution, for example, are illustrative. The British approach to environmental problems is pragmatic, consensual, specific, gradual, and flexible, while the American approach tends to be doctrinaire, controls-oriented, general, abrupt, and rigidly juridical. Both the British and American approaches appear to work tolerably well, but probably neither would work if applied in the other nation. Such radically different approaches to essentially similar problems reflect different traditions of business-government relations, philosophies of collective intervention, patterns of industry competition, and degrees of sophisitication on the part of public officials.

There are, nevertheless, a number of forces at work that may significantly reduce the extent of environmental-policy diversity over time.[13] There is some evidence, for example, that the demand for improved environmental quality (which may involve a cost in terms of reduced availabilities of other goods and services) is a positive and relatively sensitive function of income. If this is true, then one can expect some convergence in environmental standards as levels of real per-capita income rise among certain countries. In certain cases, such as the European Economic Community, attempts at regional harmonization of member-nation environmental policies are beginning to get underway. International organizations such as the United Nations Environment Programme (UNEP) and the Organization for Economic Cooperation and Development (OECD) are beginning to exert an influence on the setting of national policy agendas, mainly by increasing general awareness of pollution problems. Finally, environmental policy innovations—such as environmental impact statements, toxic substances control legislation, and coastal zoning acts—which emerge in one nation are often diffused and adopted by other nations. Although such mechanisms are beginning to work in the direction of greater homogeneity in national environmental programs, they have yet to exert a great deal of influence and the environmental setting in which multinationals operate remains highly diverse.

POLLUTION HAVENS

The main source of controversy regarding multinationals and the human environment centers precisely on whether they should be permitted to exploit this diversity in environmental conditions, values, priorities, and policies around the world. Typical questions include the following: Should "locational flight" on the part of hazardous industries to "pollution havens" be allowed? Should the overseas projects of multinationals be subject to advance environmental review and clearance back in their home countries? Should nations such as the United States attempt to impose their health and safety standards on the rest of the world? If not, how can exports to Third World nations of products which are labeled unfit for domestic use be justified? Should developing countries be used as both environmental dumping and testing grounds by multinationals?

Businessmen and economists argue that if differences in national norms are the result of international variations in environmental assimilative capacities and/or social preference patterns, and if transboundary effects are absent, then little *a priori* justification can be provided for environmental controls on the overseas activities of multinationals by their home governments. Such extension of home-country standards would merely frustrate the efficient allocation of environmental resources, reduce social welfare at the global level, and infringe upon the sovereignty of host nations.[14] But many consumer and environmental groups, along with certain government agencies, argue that there is "only one Earth" and that advanced nations such as the United States have no choice but to become the "environmental policemen or scientists of the world." In their view the ecosphere will be saved from destruction only if home-country foreign policy is "environmentally oriented."[15]

Legislation to limit the right of American companies to market products abroad that are labeled hazardous and restricted in the United States has been proposed throughout this decade. The affected industries have typically argued that their export marketing activities are in conformance with the laws of the foreign importing nations, that many United States health and safety regulations are unwarranted, and that some products, such as pesticides, are so badly needed abroad that the benefits of use far outweigh any harm that might result.[16] As noted in Chapter 10, these views have usually prevailed, although things are beginning to change under legislation such as the Toxic Substances Control Act of 1976. So far, over 500 consumer, drug, pesticide, and chemical products have been banned from the American market, but many, including such pesticides as aldrin, DDT, chlordane, heptachlor, leptophos, and mirex, have still been exported.

An interagency working group formed by the Carter Administration to develop policy on this issue identified numerous conflicting policies among the statutes affecting exports: "Eight laws permit export of banned products, and conflicts arise out of three laws that require approval by a foreign government; three that require notification of the foreign power; and, at the other extreme, two laws that give the regulatory agency authority to ban such exports; and two laws that ban such exports."[17] In October of 1978 the House Committee on Government Operations recommended that export provisions relating to banned products should be strengthened, and called for legislation that would permit the agencies to issue outright export bans on dangerous products, while setting specific guidelines for other goods that are prohibited for sale in the United States.[18] In the same month, the House Subcommittee on Commerce, Consumer and Monetary Affairs recommended a series of legislative changes for increased data collection on hazardous exports, conspicuous labeling, and required communication of the hazardous nature of such exports to importing foreign governments.[19] And in January 1979 President Carter handed environmentalists a major victory by issuing an executive order requiring federal agencies to undertake environmental reviews of government actions associated with the export of products that are prohibited or strictly regulated in America because of their toxic or environmental effects.[20]

It is too early to tell how such executive and legislative initiatives will affect American exports. But the trend clearly seems to be in the direction of stricter home-country controls over sales of hazardous products abroad, and United States-based multinationals are going to find it more difficult to compete with foreign companies not encumbered by such restraints. And as with other issues involving the extension overseas of domestic values—such as human rights and questionable payments—the likelihood of conflict will grow as American multinationals begin to experience serious losses as a result of being "monkeys in the middle" of environmental diversity.

Environmentalists in the United States have also been concerned about transfers abroad of environmentally damaging technologies and capital investment. For example, various groups launched a major campaign in the mid-1970s to establish a "global reach" for the National Environmental Policy Act (NEPA) of 1969, which requires "all agencies of the Federal Government" to write detailed environmental impact statements (EIS) in advance of "major Federal actions significantly affecting the quality of the human environment." Controversy raged over whether environmental impact statements should apply to federal export licenses, permits, approvals, and other export-related actions by agencies like the Nuclear Regulatory Commission, Export-Import Bank (Eximbank), Agency for International Development (AID), and the Overseas Private Investment Corporation.[21]

Environmental groups achieved a steady stream of favorable rulings that included (1) a court decision that the interests of Canadian environmentalists in the Trans-Alaska pipeline were protected by NEPA, (2) an agreement by the Atomic Energy Commission to prepare an "umbrella" environmental impact statement on the American nuclear power export program, and (3) an out-of-court settlement whereby AID agreed to prepare a programmatic impact statement on its pest-control activities and to prepare an environmental statement for any AID activity having a significant effect on the United States environment or on the "global commons."[22] In early 1977, the Natural Resources Defense Council and the Audubon Society filed suit in the U.S. District Court for the District of Columbia to force Eximbank to file environmental impact statements according to United States law on the more than $20 billion in export projects that it finances. Among the projects cited in the suit were a 400-mile railroad in central Gabon and a 650-mile transmission line in southern Zaïre, both of which according to the Conservation Foundation would "disrupt tropical forest ecosystems, endanger scientifically valuable species and other wildlife, and induce damaging development."[23]

The efforts of environmental groups were further boosted in 1977 when the White House Council on Environmental Quality (CEQ) issued a memorandum that the EIS requirement of NEPA applied to all significant effects of proposed federal actions on the quality of the human environment, including those within the jurisdiction of other nations and those outside the jurisdiction of any nation.[24] The CEQ based its proposed regulations in part upon section 102 (2) (F) of NEPA, which requires all agencies of the Federal Government to recognize the "worldwide and long-range character of environmental problems and, where consistent with the foreign policy of the United States, lend appropriate support to initiatives, resolutions, and programs designed to maximize international cooperation in anticipating and preventing a decline in the quality of mankind's world environment."[25] To bolster its case, the CEQ cited such projects as a 1976 Eximbank authorization for a $277 million loan, along with further loan guarantees of $367 million, to enable the Philippines to buy a Westinghouse Electric nuclear reactor. No environmental impact assessment was performed by Eximbank, which would otherwise have called attention to the fact that the reactor was to be sited in an earthquake zone near five volcanoes—the CEQ exposé eventually caused United States agencies to delay necessary approvals, the International Atomic Energy Agency to investigate the reactor site, and Philippines President Ferdinand Marcos to suspend construction in 1979 until he was convinced the plant "posed no danger to the public."[26]

The CEQ's draft provisions were vigorously opposed in 1978, however, by the Departments of State, Defense, Agriculture, Commerce, and Treasury, as well as American exporters. Some of the agencies were concerned about the foreign policy implications of "dictating" environmental terms to other nations, and saw few gains in exporting such "pettifoggery."[27] Others, noting a study by the General Accounting Office showing that preparation of environmental impact statements delayed projects by 31 months on average, alleged that the preparation time lags would cause the United States to lose export sales and investment opportunities in other countries by preventing prompt delivery, stalling contracts, and offending trading partners.[28] As a result of such resistance, the Carter Administration in 1978 dropped the idea that an EIS be filed with *all* applications for export licenses. Under a carefully hedged executive order finally issued in January of 1979, all government agencies were required to prepare environmental impact assessments on Federal actions that: (1) have an effect on the global environment, including air, water, or Antarctica; (2) involve facilities that are either prohibited or strictly regulated in the U.S., such as nuclear reactors; (3) affect natural or ecological resources that have worldwide importance, such as endangered species; and [as noted previously], (4) involve products such as pesticides that are prohibited or strictly regulated in the U.S. because of their toxic and environmental effects."[29] Only about 5% of American government assisted sales overseas would require environmental reviews under these provisions.

A related issue concerns the location of hazardous industries abroad to circumvent restrictive environmental or occupational health laws at home.[30] In 1975 the Maryland Public Interest Research Group charged that the United States was selectively exporting hazardous industries to developing nations, and recommended that Congress enact tariffs or outright bans on hazardous imports from countries that do not have adequate worker protection laws.[31] The National Institute of Occupational Safety and Health also acknowledged the problem of "runaway shops," and a bill was introduced in Congress to establish a commission on unemployment caused by the dispersion of hazardous industries to other parts of the world—asserting that such dispersion creates unemployment and balance of payments problems in the United States and that the American industries that do comply with domestic regulations are therefore faced with unfair competition.[32]

In 1978 a research report on the export of hazardous industries financed by organized labor, environmental groups, and Congress's Office of Technology Assessment found that the "flight from regulation" was either in progress or just around the corner in industries including asbestos products, arsenic, zinc, mercury, benzidene dyes, and pesticides.[33] The study recommended that the United States: (1) monitor potential exports of hazardous manufacturing facilities by American companies, (2) help create an international "hazard export information service," (3) make sure that direct United States government assistance is not provided to the export of workplace or environmental hazards, (4) ensure that environmental assessments are made by international organizations that finance development projects with United States aid, and (5) impose sanctions to make the hazard export business less attractive to American firms.[34]

But the charge that multinationals are relocating abroad on a significant basis for environmental or health reasons is far from proven.[35] There is as yet only very limited evidence of cross-border locational shifting by MNEs in response to national differences in environmental policy climates and concomitant pollution-control or health/safety costs.[36] Certain copper smelters, petroleum refineries, and asbestos, ferroalloy, and vinyl chloride plants have reportedly been constructed abroad rather than in the United States for environmental reasons. A number of petrochemical complexes and chemical plants originally slated for West Germany and the Netherlands have evidently been re-sited in Belgium, France, and Spain. And some recent Japanese pollution-intensive investments have reportedly been channeled to developing nations in Southeast Asia and Latin America. But the evidence, viewed on a world scale, certainly does not suggest massive locational shifting thus far. As we shall see, locational spillovers that have occurred seem to stem from blockage or exclusion of preferred sites in various developed nations, and not from an opportunistic search for low-cost environmental locations on the part of MNEs. A number of jurisdictions in the United States, Japan, the Netherlands, West Germany, Australia, the United Kingdom, and elsewhere have begun to discourage the location of new pollutive industry, and MNEs which have met locational impasses in such regions have simply been forced to resort to alternative foreign locations where the "ecology-growth tradeoffs" are different.

A number of "delaying" and "limiting" factors may explain why a large flow of MNE investment in response to intercountry variations in environmental standards has not yet materialized. Consider first the factors which may account for a delay in the appearance of cross-border shifting: (1) Many MNEs have chosen in recent years to expand, to the extent possible, at existing sites rather than face the social and ecological problems often associated with "greenfield" plant sites. (2) Intranational rather than international shifting is still feasible in a number of countries—for example, to the South in the United States, the North in the Netherlands, the West in Australia—and represents an option that a number of MNEs have utilized. (3) The steep rise in cost and uncertain availability of energy and petrochemical feedstocks has created a great deal of confusion in plant siting and has added importance to energy supply as a site selection factor, and the "environmental backlash" induced by the energy crisis has sometimes led to a significant decline in the amount of opposition to new refineries, pipelines, offshore terminals, and the like. (4) Recession conditions during the 1970s in both North America and Western Europe led to cancellations and postponements of proposed investments by MNEs, while conditions of high unemployment led to shifting environmental priorities and less opposition to new plant construction in some regions. (5) Lead-times in the planning of new projects such as petrochemical complexes, aluminum smelters, and open-pit mines often extend for five to ten years, so that locational outcomes of many of the project planning decisions taken during the years when the awareness of environmental policy differentials among nations became evident may not yet have surfaced.

At the same time, a number of other factors may fundamentally limit the potential scope for environmentally-induced locational shifts: (1) An MNE emphasis on strategic and competitive factors under oligopoly conditions implies that foreign direct investment flows are likely to be rather insensitive to variations in environmental costs in different locations. (2) Reduced environmental or occupational health costs from investing abroad may be counterbalanced by other considerations—labor availability and quality may be poor, supporting infrastructure may be lacking, market size may be inadequate, transport costs may be prohibitive, political and expropriation risk may be too high, and so on. (3) Locational flexibility of many kinds of MNE investments is limited and the freedom to seek out low-cost environmental locations may be constrained by such factors as access to deep-water port facilities, complementary industrial facilities, location of ore bodies and energy resources, or global logistics, and transportation networks. (4) The extended time horizons and managerial perceptions associated with new foreign investments may be biased against locational shifting—MNE executives may expect substantial convergence to occur among national pollution standards over the next ten years and, with plant lives extending anywhere from 15 to 40 years, this means that high-cost technical remedies would have to be applied in the future to all plants constructed today without stringent environmental controls. (5) Pollution-intensive industries at the same time tend to be energy-intensive, capital-intensive, technology-intensive, industrial-market-intensive, and transport-intensive as well; hence the importance of pollution control as a cost element may be relatively small.

The emergence of environmental and occupational health cost differentials among nations thus represents a shift *at the margin* in the locational calculus of MNE investment. The significance of this shift for inducing "real-world" migration, however, can be properly appraised only within the complete structure of costs, risks, and returns which are considered when investment decisions are made. We believe the most critical factor in the entire equation is environmental opposition to new plant-siting in the developed countries.

PATTERNS OF ENVIRONMENTAL CONFLICT

In order to get a factual handle on the emergence of environmental conflict facing multinational companies, we conducted a systematic and detailed search of the literature covering the years 1970–1978.[37] The survey identified 587 environmental battles, focusing on the chemical process industry, which represents a small and high-profile subsample of an estimated 10,000 major environmental conflicts that took place in the developed market-economy countries during those years. The composition of the sample is summarized in Table 12–1.

Of the 587 conflicts surveyed, 62% occurred in the United States, of which 31% took place in the Northeast, 21% in the Southeast, 21% in the Southwest, 18% in the Midwest, and 10% in the Far West.[38] Outside America, environmental conflicts were reported in 22 nations, with the top ten being the Netherlands, United Kingdom, West Germany, Japan, Italy, France, Belgium, Canada, Spain, and Sweden. The first five nations listed accounted for 62% of the reported non-American environmental disputes.

Table 12–1 also reveals that 59% of the battles were fought over environmental aspects of facilities already in existence, while 6% involved expansions of facilities at existing production locations, and the remaining 35% involved new "greenfield" plant proposals. Disputes over new proposals were particularly evident in the oil refinery, nuclear power, transport and storage facility, and mineral mining sectors. Over the years, there was a definite shift in focus from existing to greenfield projects in environmental conflicts both in the United States and overseas, but it was more dramatic in the United States, where conflicts over expansions and greenfield projects rose from a 13% share in 1970–1971 to a 53% share in 1974–1975. This largely reflects the fact that pollution problems at many existing operations were apparently corrected as a result of citizen group and governmental pressure.

Data on facility ownership is also presented in Table 12–1. Of the facilities involved, 86% were wholly-owned by a single firm and the remainder were joint ventures, of which two-thirds were foreign investments. Twenty-four percent of all the environmental battles surveyed involved foreign investors—49% of all the conflicts which emerged overseas, but only 8% of those occurring in the United States—attributable mainly to American firms investing in Western Europe in the chemical, petroleum, and nonferrous metal sectors. The percentage of conflicts involving foreign investments outside America rose substantially during the period, perhaps linked to the more general debate over multinationals with opponents who find criticism of the adverse environmental impacts to be an increasingly powerful and "socially-respectable" tool of protest. A final dimension revealed in Table 12–1 is that after an initial bulge during the "age of discovery" period of 1970–1971, the amount of reported conflict has remained steady.[39]

The Issues

Many kinds of issues are at stake in environmental conflicts, which have an important bearing on the intensity of the struggle, its duration, and the general difficulty of reaching agreement. We considered the following eight topical categories:

Table 12-1 Composition of Environmental Conflict Sample (587 conflicts; 1970–1978 scanning; % rounded off)

Type of Facility	Percentage of Total	Location		Facility Nature			Facility Ownership				Year of Conflict Emergence			
		U.S. %	Non-U.S. %	Existing %	Expansion %	New Proposal %	Foreign %	Domestic %	Wholly-Owned %	Joint Venture %	1970-1971 %	1972-1973 %	1974-1975 %	1976-1978 %
Petrochemical	10	31	69	37	17	46	37	63	75	25	32	12	23	33
Oil Refinery	9	55	45	30	8	62	36	64	83	17	51	26	13	10
Nonferrous Metal	6	61	39	55	3	42	33	67	78	22	31	31	28	10
Ferrous Metal	5	85	15	89	4	7	7	93	96	4	32	32	31	5
Pulp and Paper	4	95	5	95	0	5	10	90	100	0	59	23	6	12
Nuclear Power	7	90	10	37	3	60	5	95	84	16	35	16	19	29
Electric Utility	2	91	9	50	10	40	0	100	73	27	50	0	37	13
Transport Storage	7	76	24	16	3	81	24	76	63	37	31	11	35	23
Mineral Mining	8	86	14	36	5	59	17	83	83	17	21	24	39	16
Inorganic Chemical	20	49	51	75	4	21	22	78	94	6	36	30	2	14
Organic Chemical	17	40	60	72	8	20	30	70	93	7	22	26	20	32
Other	6	63	37	67	10	23	23	77	90	10	25	21	11	43
Total Sample	100	62	38	59	6	35	24	76	86	14	33	24	22	21

1. **Air Quality** (pollution, visibility, odor).
2. **Water quality** (degradable/nondegradable/persistent residuals).
3. **Land use** (landscape, scenery, wilderness, erosion, solid waste).
4. **Biota** (vegetation, wildlife, biological effects, ecological balance).
5. **Minerals** (fuel, nonfuel).
6. **Human health and safety** (disease, noise, radioactivity, accidents, genetic and reproductive effects).
7. **Social resources** (recreation, residential, cultural, lifestyle, congestion, boomtowns).
8. **Economic resources** (property values, tax, income, employment).

The last three represent *primary issues* in the sense of being disputed in terms of manifest or direct human impacts, while the first five can be viewed as *secondary issues*, that is, those not necessarily or not yet translated into matters of direct human impact.

Table 12–2 shows that the three most frequent types of issues were water quality (present in 54% of all the conflicts), air quality (38%), and human health (31%). Air quality was the most frequent issue in conflicts over petrochemical plants, oil refineries, nonferrous metal facilities, ferrous metal plants, and electric utilities. Water quality issues, in comparison, were at stake in a majority of the pulp and paper sector disputes, transportation and storage projects, inorganic chemical plants, and organic chemical facilities. Land use and minerals issues were especially prominent in mining project conflicts. Biotic impact issues were evident in 50% of the transportation and storage facility conflicts, while human health and safety concerns were found most frequently in battles over organic chemical plants, nonferrous metals facilities, and nuclear power plants. Social and economic impact issues were present most often in disputes over oil refineries, electric utilities, transport and storage facilities, and minerals mining. Water quality and human health were frequently at issue in the case of existing facilities, while expansions and new proposals more often involved issues of air pollution, land use change and social/economic impact. Expansion proposals generate fewer issues than "greenfield" proposals, and this may explain why many chemical process firms in the United States in recent years have chosen the route of expanding, if at all possible, at existing manufacturing sites.[40] Such expansions appear to attract less public attention and opposition, and thus often stand a better chance of clearing social and environmental hurdles.

Air quality was the most frequent issue in the American Southwest; water quality in the Northeast; human health in the Midwest; and land use, mineral base, and social and economic impacts in the Far West. The variations reflect both the different types of facilities involved in conflicts and environmental resources under particularly heavy pressure within the five regions. At the same time, air quality was a more frequent issue in environmental battles overseas than in the United States, and was particularly prevalent in disputes in the heavily congested industrial areas of Germany, Belgium, and the Netherlands. Water quality was more frequently an issue in Japan and America than elsewhere. Environmental conflicts in densely populated and heavily industrialized Japan also exhibited the highest frequencies in land use, biota, human health, and social/economic issues.

Environmental conflicts involving foreign investors were disproportionately characterized by air quality and human health issues, and less so by water quality. This is in line with the high concentration of foreign direct investments in

Table 12-2 Issues in Environmental Conflict (587 conflicts; 1970–1978 scanning; % rounded off and means)

	Types of Issues								Mean Number of Issue Types
	Air	Water	Land	Biota	Minerals	Human Health	Social	Economic	
1. All Conflicts	38	54	15	20	3	31	13	19	1.9
2. Type of Facility									
Petrochemical	65	39	11	9	0	37	11	11	1.9
Oil Refinery	57	41	26	11	4	13	30	22	2.1
Nonferrous Metal	79	36	27	27	6	46	6	27	2.6
Ferrous Metal	72	40	0	4	0	16	4	8	1.5
Pulp and Paper	20	90	0	10	0	0	20	0	1.2
Nuclear Power	5	47	13	11	3	45	5	26	1.8
Electric Utility	82	9	9	0	0	27	27	18	1.7
Transport & Storage	11	61	19	50	6	28	33	42	2.5
Mineral Mining	15	49	59	15	17	0	27	24	2.1
Inroganic Chemical	43	60	8	30	0	34	9	25	2.0
Organic Chemical	33	60	9	21	1	56	9	16	2.0
Other	31	55	10	31	0	31	14	10	1.9
3. Nature of Facility									
Existing	32	63	7	21	1	33	6	16	1.8
Expansion	67	18	6	6	3	42	12	6	1.6
New Proposal	44	43	30	21	6	25	26	26	2.2

4. Location of Facility

United States	31	59	16	18	3	22	14	18	1.8
Northeast	28	66	14	20	4	20	18	17	1.9
Southeast	17	63	20	23	1	21	16	16	1.8
Midwest	28	66	3	9	2	30	6	16	1.6
Southwest	50	43	19	18	4	26	11	22	1.9
Far West	30	49	27	21	6	6	21	24	1.8
Overseas	51	46	13	23	1	45	11	21	2.1
Japan	33	67	27	54	0	88	21	58	3.2
West Germany	70	26	24	13	0	39	12	9	1.9
Belgium/Neth.	62	40	12	6	2	38	4	6	1.7
France	41	53	4	35	0	18	13	29	2.1
United Kingdom	47	38	8	21	0	53	8	21	2.3

5. Ownership of Facility

Foreign	58	42	20	21	4	38	18	22	2.2
Domestic	33	57	14	20	2	29	12	19	1.9

6. Time of Emergence

U.S.

1970-71	27	73	7	16	2	18	9	12	1.6
1972-73	35	51	14	8	3	19	10	14	1.6
1974-75	34	38	27	27	9	29	21	23	2.1
1976-78	32	48	20	17	2	38	12	15	1.9

Non-U.S.

1970-71	54	46	14	16	0	37	11	18	2.0
1972-73	40	63	9	44	0	48	14	35	2.5
1974-75	56	33	18	18	7	47	9	18	2.1
1976-78	50	42	18	13	0	50	8	8	1.9

new projects for petrochemical, oil refinery, nonferrous metal, inorganic, and organic chemical plants sited in European locations. Foreign investment battles, as a result, also typically involved more types of issues than domestic investment battles, perhaps due to nationalistic or anti-foreign sentiment. Dow Chemical, for example, confronted interactive nationalistic and environmental resistance in a number of its overseas conflicts, including a stymied insecticide factory at Lejona (Spain), cancelled petrochemical complexes at Le Verdon (France), and Redcliffs (Australia), delayed expansion of a chlorine-caustic complex at Stade (West Germany), delayed synthetic resins and agricultural chemicals plant in Aiichi prefecture (Japan), and blocked chlorine-caustic soda plant at Toma Komai, Hokkaido Island (Japan). Nationalism and environmentalism can thus feed on each other, making multinational corporate conflict management much more complex.

Table 12–2 also shows that the issues involved in environmental battles have been changing, both in the United States and abroad. Water quality issues in the United States declined dramatically in prominence—from being involved in three quarters of all disputes in 1970–1971 to only 38% in 1974–1975 and to 48% in 1976–1978. The decline can perhaps be traced to considerable progress in cleaning up water pollution problems at existing facilities under the Federal Water Pollution Control Act Amendments of 1972, the most expensive and far-reaching effort ever undertaken by Congress in the field of environmental protection. Land use issues, on the other hand, have been on the rise, as have human health and safety issues in environmental disputes—the increased emphasis on health hazards, particularly in the area of environmental carcinogens, has been of major importance in the United States in recent years. In other countries, one sees declines in the frequency of water quality, biota, and social/economic resource issues since the 1972–1973 period, and an increase in human health concerns.

The Opponents

Multinationals have confronted many types of opponents in environmental disputes, who can be classified into nine categories: 1) foreign governmental body; 2) national governmental body; 3) regional governmental body; 4) local governmental body; 5) national environmental group; 6) regional or local environmental group; 7) local resident; 8) local industry; and 9) social action group. These different types of opponents can be further classified for purposes of analysis into *governmental* vs. *non-governmental* and *local* vs. *non-local* groupings. The results of our survey are given in Table 12–3. National governmental bodies such as the United States Environmental Protection Agency, British Department of the Environment, or Swedish Environment Protection Board were involved as opponents in one half of the disputes. Regional bodies were present in 44% of the conflicts and local governmental bodies in 26%. Local residents were active in more than a third of the cases and local industries such as fishermen, farmers, housing developers, and tourist facility operators in 11%. Regional or local environmental groups were opponents in about one quarter of the cases, while national environmental groups appeared in 14% of the disputes. Social action groups got involved in 8% of the conflicts. Foreign governmental bodies appeared only in cases where cross border environmental effects were involved. Table 12-3 reveals a division of labor among opponents in waging conflict against different types of industrial facilities. It also shows that the average number of opponent types involved per battle varied by type and nature of facility.

Existing-facility disputes attracted the most involvement of national and regional governmental bodies, with national agencies or ministries involved in 57% of all such battles. "Greenfield" conflicts, on the other hand, attracted higher percentages of all other types of opponents. Local governmental bodies, environmental groups, residents, and social action groups, in particular, targeted much of their fire on new projects. Environmental groups both at the national and local levels, for example, exhibited about four times as much involvement in conflicts over proposed as against existing facilities. They appear to devote the bulk of their energies to opposing perceived adverse environmental consequences related to the future rather than the present, which may be explained by their relatively greater power to oppose change than to effect corrections of existing problems.

Disputes in the United States attracted dramatically higher involvement of national and regional government agencies compared with almost all other countries—the key exception being Japan. Environmental battles in Western Europe were much more a local affair, with considerably higher involvement of local governments and residents in disputes. Conflicts involving foreign direct investment, perhaps in large measure because of their predominantly European location and "greenfield" character, attracted a disproportionately large involvement of local governmental bodies, environmental groups, residents, industries, and social action groups.

The Tactics

Environmental opponents pressed business firms with a wide range of tactics on practically every front: at construction sites, in the hearing rooms, in the courts, at shareholder meetings, in the media, on the streets, in city councils and regional and national legislatures, as well as in the appointive bureaucracies of government at every level. Tactics can be classified in many ways, but the distinction between "regulatory" and "social" tactics is particularly helpful. *Regulatory tactics* involve governmental opponents through legal and administrative action, while *social tactics* encompass nongovernmental pressure such as private legal action, petitions, demonstrations, lobbying, media campaigns, civil disobedience, and violence.

What determines the tactics used by opponents of corporations in environmental battles? The nature of the issues giving rise to conflict are particularly important. So are the opponents' ideology, leadership, resources, degree of organization, past experience in waging conflict, and their perception of the relevant audience's reactions. The nature of the preexisting relationship between the opponents and the corporation may influence the choice of tactics, and so will the kinds of tactics employed by the corporation. For example, corporate reliance on a strategy of power and tactics of threat, coercion, and deception is likely to elicit resistance, alienation, and similar types of countertactics on the

Table 12-3 Opponents in Environmental Conflict (587 conflicts; 1970-1978 scanning; % rounded off and means)

	Types of Opponents									Mean Number of Opponent Types
	Foreign Govtl. Body	National Govtl. Body	Regional Govtl. Body	Local Govtl. Body	National Envtl. Group	Regional/ Local Envtl. Group	Local Residents	Local Industry	Social Action Group	
1. All Conflicts	2	51	44	26	14	24	36	11	8	2.2
2. Type of Facility										
Petrochemical	0	20	35	39	6	35	52	7	7	2.0
Oil Refinery	4	46	41	33	15	41	57	15	7	2.6
Nonferrous Metal	6	42	58	36	6	18	30	18	12	2.3
Ferrous Metal	0	67	78	22	7	11	26	4	11	2.3
Pulp and Paper	0	70	50	0	5	5	20	0	5	1.5
Nuclear Power	3	71	29	13	37	40	37	11	13	2.7
Electric Utility	0	64	36	0	27	18	46	9	9	2.1
Transport & Storage	8	58	45	40	42	47	45	13	13	3.1
Mineral Mining	3	50	43	23	38	38	30	3	5	2.3
Inorganic Chemical	2	55	44	28	7	17	36	22	5	2.0
Organic Chemical	0	45	44	25	8	18	38	7	12	2.0
Other	7	52	48	28	3	14	48	3	7	2.1
3. Nature of Facility										
Existing	2	57	49	18	6	11	30	10	6	1.9
Expansion	0	37	29	34	6	26	37	0	3	1.7
New Proposal	4	44	39	38	28	45	44	15	13	2.7

4. Location of Facility

										Mean
United States	1	59	54	17	15	22	30	7	7	2.1
Northeast	1	60	54	19	13	28	36	8	5	2.2
Southeast	0	62	53	12	16	15	24	7	5	2.0
Midwest	2	64	41	16	5	18	27	3	8	1.9
Southwest	1	53	56	22	18	28	28	7	7	2.2
Far West	6	56	71	12	32	15	32	9	9	2.4
Overseas	4	38	27	40	11	28	45	17	10	2.2
Japan	0	71	29	13	0	4	71	50	8	2.5
West Germany	0	22	26	48	9	22	48	4	4	1.8
Belgium/Neth.	6	28	31	55	2	39	47	4	4	2.1
France	18	41	12	47	12	24	59	29	12	2.5
United Kingdom	3	42	12	55	24	36	52	9	9	2.4

5. Ownership of Facility

										Mean
Foreign	4	35	34	42	15	34	46	16	15	2.4
Domestic	2	56	47	21	13	21	33	9	6	2.1

6. Time of Emergence

										Mean
U.S.										
1970–71	1	61	52	12	7	17	26	8	4	1.9
1972–73	0	56	52	14	10	19	18	1	3	1.8
1974–75	2	61	54	19	25	19	29	7	10	2.3
1976–78	2	54	51	18	11	21	41	5	6	2.1
Non-U.S.										
1970–71	5	40	21	46	11	37	53	12	12	2.3
1972–73	0	37	19	44	12	21	44	33	5	2.1
1974–75	10	35	27	46	15	21	40	14	13	2.3
1976–78	3	39	33	25	11	36	36	11	14	2.0

part of its opponents. In our survey, the use of social tactics was highly correlated with conflicts involving new proposals while regulatory tactics were more often employed when the conflicts involved existing facilities.

Table 12–4 shows that regulatory tactics in the form of administrative actions occurred in two-thirds of all the conflicts sampled. Some examples are the order given to Bayer-Rickman by the Brugge (Belgium) town council to shut down its vitreous enamels plant because of excessive fluorine emissions; the stipulation given to DuPont in 1975 by the U.S. Environmental Protection Agency that it terminate ocean disposal of liquid acid wastes from its titanium pigments plant at Edgemoor, Delaware, and the revoking of Sefanitro's permit by local authorities, after construction had already begun, for a fertilizer ammonia plant in the heavily industrialized area of Bilbao, Spain. Governmental legal actions were observed in one-third of all the disputes, but were employed in 65% of the ferrous metals conflicts. They include the raft of lawsuits by state and local governments against Union Carbide because of its lagging pollution control at ferroalloy plants in Ohio and West Virginia, a suit filed by Allegheny County and the State Department of Environmental Resources in 1972 to force U.S. Steel to use the "best technology available" to clean up pollution from the world's largest coking plant at Clairton, Pennsylvania, and notices of more than 1000 air pollution violations against Kaiser Steel's Fontana mill in southern California—which led the company to agree in 1977 to a major cleanup plan and to pay the federal Environmental Protection Agency (EPA) and the California Air Pollution Control Fund $1 million each, and the County of San Bernardino $100,000, in settlement of environmental lawsuits. Without admitting liability, Kaiser's objective was to avoid both prolonged litigation and EPA's blacklist of companies with which the federal government will not do business.

Private legal actions were undertaken in a fourth of all the disputes. They were most prevalent in the electric utility, nuclear power, minerals mining, and pulp and paper sectors. Examples include (a) a class-action suit filed against International Paper by Vermont landowners charging that their Lake Champlain property had been damaged by discharges from the firm's Ticonderoga, New York, pulp mill, (b) a plea to the U.S. Court of Appeals in Washington by the Saginaw Intervenors (an anti-nuclear group) to revoke a construction license granted to Consumers Power Co. for a nuclear plant at Midland, Michigan, from which Dow Chemical was scheduled to buy large amounts of power and steam, and (c) a Sierra Club suit against the Secretary of the Interior in 1973 demanding that he consider regional as well as local impacts of coal development in the northern Great Plains coal belt, thus bringing to a halt the development programs of AMAX and Wyodak Resources Development, and the coal mining operations of Exxon, Atlantic Richfield and Kerr-McGee in Wyoming's Powder River Basin.

Demonstrations were carried out in 8% of all the conflicts (twice as high in the nonferrous metal and nuclear power sectors), while petitions and referenda were reported in 4% of the conflicts, with most of them occurring in oil refinery cases. For example, a number of petitions opposing plans of Cromarty Petroleum Co., a subsidiary of National Bulk Carriers of New York, for an oil refinery at Nigg Point in Scotland were circulated in the surrounding communities and helped induce a full public inquiry. Opponents took their grievances directly to politicians, government bureaucrats, business executives, and/or corporate shareholders in 11% of the cases, especially in the oil refining, nuclear power, and minerals mining industries. A classic case arose in 1970 when the Episcopal Diocese of Puerto Rico became concerned about the economic and environmental effects of proposed copper mining and smelting by Kennecott and AMAX. At its request, 14 representatives of six denominational investors that together held $7.5 million of the two companies' stock traveled to San Juan in early 1971 to hold open hearings on the impact of the mining project. As a result of the hearings, the *ad hoc* Interfaith Committee on Social Responsibility recommended that the companies postpone the project because of the dangers such mining would cause to the "health and well-being of the people of Puerto Rico."[41] At corporate headquarters the church groups held talks with management and filed shareholder resolutions asking each firm to adopt a charter amendment requiring the company to bear the financial costs of environmental damage caused by any new operation, and that management report to shareholders on efforts taken by the company to prevent such damage. Although both shareholder resolutions were defeated at the companies' 1971 annual meetings, the precedent of using proxy resolutions to challenge management policy in the environmental field was firmly established. Church groups since then have gone on to submit proxy resolutions on nuclear power to General Electric and Westinghouse; on the effects of coal stripmining to American Electric Power, Pittston, Continental Oil, General Dynamics, Gulf Oil, Standard Oil of California, Standard Oil of Indiana, Shell, Tenneco, AMAX, and Exxon; on the environmental impact of the B-1 bomber to General Electric; on worker health and safety problems to Kerr-McGee and J.P. Stevens; and on community health and safety dangers stemming from nuclear weapons production to Bendix, DuPont, Monsanto, General Electric, and Union Carbide, to cite a few.[42]

Vigorous press campaigns were initiated by opponents in 12% of all the environmental battles surveyed, but were twice as frequent in the nuclear power and oil refinery cases. The long and acrimonious battle between Shell Oil and the State of Delaware over plans for an oil refinery is one case where a high-volume press campaign by opponents won the day. The Governor of Delaware, Russell W. Peterson (who later became head of the National Audubon Society),campaigned vigorously against the project—"As far as I'm concerned, even if Shell can build a plant 100 percent free of pollution, I'm still opposed. . . . Jobs are very important to our people, but so is the overall quality of life . . . we can afford to be selective."[43] The controversy precipitated the passage of Delaware's 1971 Coastal Zone Act, which bans heavy industry such as refineries, paper mills, and steel mills from a strip about two miles wide along the State's coast within which Shell's refinery site was located. According to Shell, "faced with the prospect of extensive litigation to challenge the validity of the arguably invalid provisions of the Act, or awaiting a long-term shift in the pendulum of hysteric public opinion generated by Mr. Peterson's shameful and disreputable 'To Hell With Shell' campaign, Shell naturally chose not to exacerbate the then clearly inhospitable climate in Delaware . . . [and] was forced to seek an alternate site in the Delaware Valley."[44]

The least frequent type of tactic observed in the environmental conflicts was that of violence. "Ecological terrorism" occurred in only 2% of all the disputes and was concentrated mainly in the nuclear power, transport and storage, and organic chemical sectors, as shown in Table 12–4. Examples would include the

Table 12–4 Tactics of Opponents in Environmental Conflict (587 conflicts; 1970–78 scanning; % rounded off and means)

				Types of Opponent Tactics					Mean Number of Tactics Types
	Govtal. Legal Action	Govtal. Admin. Action	Private Legal Action	Demon-stration	Petition-Referenda	Lobbying	Press Campaign	Violence	
1. All Conflicts	32	67	26	8	4	11	12	2	1.6
2. Type of Facility									
Petrochemical	27	64	23	5	5	11	9	0	1.5
Oil-Refinery	20	66	27	10	17	27	22	0	1.9
Nonferrous Metal	22	70	26	19	4	7	19	0	1.7
Ferrous Metal	65	69	8	4	4	4	8	0	1.6
Pulp and Paper	40	55	35	0	0	5	10	0	1.5
Nuclear Power	19	75	36	17	11	17	22	3	2.0
Electric Utility	36	55	55	9	0	9	0	0	1.6
Transport & Storage	22	76	32	8	5	11	16	8	1.8
Mineral Mining	28	72	36	6	0	17	0	1	1.6
Inorganic Chemical	33	73	18	11	3	8	9	1	1.6
Organic Chemical	29	68	25	8	0	7	15	4	1.6
Other	36	61	29	7	0	21	14	4	1.7
3. Nature of Facility									
Existing	44	62	26	7	1	5	7	2 }	
Expansion	7	83	21	3	7	14	7	0	1.5
New Proposal	14	75	27	11	7	21	21	2	1.8

4. Location of Facility

United States	39	64	30	4	3	8	6	1	1.6
Northeast	43	62	25	5	6	9	8	0	1.6
Southeast	36	65	31	3	1	10	4	0	1.5
Midwest	59	51	30	5	2	5	5	2	1.6
Southwest	16	77	28	4	2	4	4	2	1.4
Far West	38	69	47	0	0	9	9	3	1.8
Overseas	18	73	18	16	6	16	22	3	1.7
Japan	39	70	39	48	0	0	17	4	2.2
West Germany	11	72	28	6	6	11	22	0	1.6
Belgium/Neth.	18	84	5	13	11	16	8	3	1.6
France	23	62	31	23	15	31	16	0	2.0
United Kingdom	13	63	17	7	7	17	23	0	1.5

5. Ownership of Facility

Foreign	19	70	18	13	10	22	22	3	1.8
Domestic	36	66	28	7	2	8	8	2	1.6

6. Time of Emergence

U.S.									
1970–71	54	53	26	2	2	6	6	1	1.5
1972–73	39	67	23	3	1	6	1	0	1.4
1974–75	26	71	38	2	3	7	3	2	1.5
1976–78	26	70	34	7	4	4	5	0	1.5
Non-U.S.									
1970–71	20	78	16	20	7	20	22	7	1.8
1972–73	19	68	24	24	5	8	19	9	1.8
1974–75	13	74	5	13	10	23	26	3	1.6
1976–78	3	77	13	7	0	17	27	3	1.2

destruction of boats in Montedison's titanium dioxide waste dumping affair mentioned earlier, the "knee-capping" of local authorities and bombing of Hoffmann-La Roche offices and home of a senior Roche executive after the Seveso tragedy (see below), bombings at Electricité de France reactor sites, sabotage at the Alaska oil pipeline, and a bloody battle between 5000 riot police and 30,000 anti-nuclear protestors in 1977 at the site of the new Super-Phénix breeder reactor at Creys-Malville in southeast France. The fear of violent tactics was reflected in the precautions taken by Nordwestdeutsche Kraftwerke at its Brokdorf reactor site: "Behind what must be one of the most impregnable fortifications this side of the East-West German border, work has begun on building West Germany's latest nuclear power station. Much of the perimeter of the 75-acre site, at Brokdorf in the marshlands of the lower Elbe, is screened by a concrete wall 10 feet high, surmounted by coils of barbed wire. The rest, regarded as 'strategically observable,' is girdled by a ditch 10 feet wide and filled with water. Approach roads to the site are patrolled by dozens of policemen and the compound itself is guarded by 600 men from a private security organization and by 30 dogs."[45]

Table 12–4 also provides data on the mean number of different types of tactics employed in various classes of environmental battles. Also provided are data on tactics according to nature, location, and ownership of facility, as well as time of conflict emergence. Some key points to note are the strong association of regulatory tactics with existing facilities and social tactics with new proposals, and high relative frequency of private legal actions in the Far West of the United States, where a number of national environmental groups are headquartered. The litigious nature of American society is also dramatically revealed in the much higher relative use of governmental and private legal actions in United States as compared to overseas conflicts. The frequency of government legal action in America, however, has been steadily declining in favor of administrative methods.

The Resolution Mechanisms

Various methods of dispute settlement (or termination) have been employed in the field of environmental conflict. Nine different resolution mechanisms were observed and coded in our study. They can be grouped into a smaller number of categories based on the relative amount of external participation in the resolution process. Such outside intervention was at a maximum level when *public resolution mechanisms* (that is, legislation, vote, public hearing) were employed; moderate level when traditional *third party resolution mechanisms* (that is, unilateral governmental decision, adjudication, arbitration/mediation) were utilized; and very low level when *private resolution mechanisms* (that is, bargaining/negotiation, joint problem-solving, private decision) were relied upon. Many environmental battles in our sample involved only one of the above mechanisms, but others involved two or more of them in sequential or simultaneous combination. Figure 12–2 provides a contingency framework regarding constructive environmental conflict resolution being developed by the authors. Consistent with the viewpoint expressed throughout this book, we believe there is "no one best way" to manage environmental disputes. The focus must be on contingencies

Exhibit 12-2

Constructive Management of Environmental Conflict: A Contingency Model

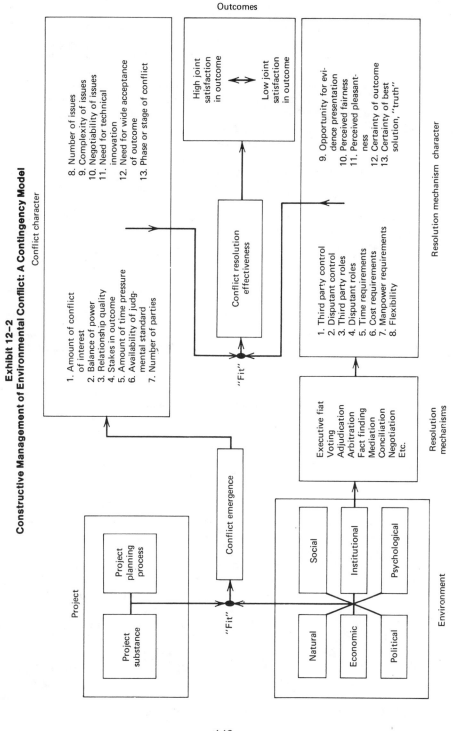

Outcomes

Conflict character

1. Amount of conflict of interest
2. Balance of power
3. Relationship quality
4. Stakes in outcome
5. Amount of time pressure
6. Availability of judgmental standard
7. Number of parties

8. Number of issues
9. Complexity of issues
10. Negotiability of issues
11. Need for technical innovation
12. Need for wide acceptance of outcome
13. Phase or stage of conflict

High joint satisfaction in outcome ↔ Low joint satisfaction in outcome

Conflict resolution effectiveness

"Fit"

Resolution mechanism character

1. Third party control
2. Disputant control
3. Third party roles
4. Disputant roles
5. Time requirements
6. Cost requirements
7. Manpower requirements
8. Flexibility

9. Opportunity for evidence presentation
10. Perceived fairness
11. Perceived pleasantness
12. Certainty of outcome
13. Certainty of best solution, "truth"

Resolution mechanisms

Executive fiat
Voting
Adjudication
Arbitration
Fact finding
Mediation
Conciliation
Negotiation
Etc.

Project

Project planning process

Project substance

Conflict emergence

"Fit"

Environment

Natural
Economic
Political
Social
Institutional
Psychological

449

which combine to suggest that most appropriate mechanisms of conflict management. (The notion of "appropriateness," of course, frequently differs as between
private and public policy perspectives, and whether it is defined in terms of the
outcomes of environmental conflict or in terms of the processes of conflict resolution, or both.)

Exhibit 12–2 shows that conflict avoidance can be viewed primarily as a
matter of attaining compatibility or an optimal "fit" between industrial projects
and the external settings into which they are injected, or already situated. In
terms of both physical characteristics and planning processes utilized, environmental disputes arise when projects are incompatible in the eyes of concerned
parties with their receiving environments. If such incompatibility exists, the
emergence of environmental conflicts is a foregone conclusion, and their effective resolution depends on the appropriateness of the resolution mechanisms that
are utilized. Effective conflict resolution can thus be viewed as a function of the
match or fit between procedure and dispute, and the basic question is "what
kinds of environmental conflicts are likely to be best handled by what resolution
mechanisms, alone or in sequential or simultaneous combination?"[46]

Table 12–5 provides data on resolution mechanisms that were employed the
587 chemical process industry environmental disputes in our sample. Autocratic
government decision-making and courtroom adjudication were each employed
in more than a third of all the conflicts. Public hearings, bargaining, private
decisions, and joint problem-solving were each evident in at least 10% of all the
disputes. The least-used mechanisms were legislation, voting, and arbitration/
mediation. The use of different resolution mechanisms varied according to the
type, location, nature, ownership, and timing of projects. For example, unilateral
decisions by government bureaucrats in such forms as sanctioning an environmental impact statement, authorizing a development, or approving a plan for
regulatory compliance were evident in 36% of all the conflicts, but were employed in two-thirds of the disputes in the highly-regulated electric utilities
sector. A case in point was the negative decision in 1973 by Rogers Morton,
Secretary of the Interior, on plans by Southern California Edison, San Diego Gas
and Electric, and Arizona Public Service Co. for a $3.5 billion, 3000-megawatt
coal-fired power complex on the Kairparowits Plateau in southern Utah. The
secretary, whose approval was required because the plant was to be built on
federal land, held that "the environmental problems on the plateau cannot be
overcome."[47] The project, however, was revived a few years later but abandoned
by the backers because of massive environmental protest as well as cost and
demand uncertainties.

Adjudication, often in the form of protracted litigation, was employed in
37% of the conflicts, but was resorted to in one out of every two battles over pulp
and paper and ferrous metal facilities. Other forms of third-party intervention,
such as arbitration and mediation, were very rarely utilized in the kinds of
industrial project disputes considered in our survey. The most common public
resolution mechanisms involved were public hearings or inquiries, which were
employed in 21% of the disputes. The frequency of their use, however, was
about twice as high in oil refinery and transport and storage battles. Legislation,
at local, regional, and national levels, was called into play in helping to resolve
8% of all the disputes, but was approximately three to four times more frequent
in the nuclear power and transport and storage sectors.

Citizen voting was also occasionally resorted to in those two sectors, as well as in cases of petrochemical plants and oil refineries. Examples are the unexpected negative vote by Austrians in a 1978 national referendum on whether to start up the already-constructed $595 million nuclear power plant at Zwentendorf on the Danube, and rejection by Long Beach, California voters of a proposition challenging a lease Standard Oil (Ohio) had made with the city regarding the company's proposed 500,000 bbl./day terminal to receive Alaskan oil for movement to the Gulf and Midwestern states by pipeline—Sohio cancelled this project in 1979, citing "endless government permit procedures" which served to erode the project's once–attractive economics.[48]

Direct bargaining and negotiation among the disputing parties, unassisted by third parties, was employed in 17% of all the battles in the sample, but was evidenced in a third of all the nonferrous and ferrous metal disputes. An example was bargaining between local fishermen, government authorities, and the consortium of Alcan, Pechiney, and Instituto Nacional de Industria resulting in relocation of the consortium's proposed alumina-aluminum complex in 1975 from Villagarcia, Spain to a site further inland.[49] Joint problem-solving only transpired in 10% of the cases as a whole, but was two to three times as common in the inorganic chemical, nonferrous metal, and pulp and paper sectors. A good example drawn from the mineral mining sector would be the "Experiment in Ecology" launched by AMAX during the late 1960s in the planning of its Henderson molybdenum mine in Colorado. A hybrid committee of company executives and representatives from local citizen groups was created and met periodically throughout the entire course of planning to discuss, monitor, and make suggestions about the development of the ore body.[50] Finally, private decisions, typically in the form of the corporation unilaterally deciding to shut down a facility or cancel new projects, were the way in which 15% of the disputes were resolved—25% of the organic, and 20% of the inorganic chemical facility conflicts were handled in this way.

Compared to the experience overseas, environmental dispute management in the United States was characterized less by autocratic governmental decision-making or bargaining/negotiation, and more by adjudication, legislation, and voting. It is interesting, however, to note the close similarity between the American and French conflict-resolution patterns, Japan's high use of autocratic decision-making (52% of all cases) and bargaining (67%), and Britain's pervasive use of public hearings and inquiries (57%). West Germany's relatively high use of unilateral private decisions (26%) and relatively low average number of resolution mechanisms used per battle may be indicative of rigidity in that country's dispute settlement system. This may explain the recent rapid rise of *Bürgerinitiativen* (citizen's initiative groups), as well as the relatively high presence of violence and flamboyant tactics such as marches and plant site occupations in Germany's recent environmental conflicts, particularly in the nuclear power sector.

The way in which environmental battles are resolved also seems to have been changing over time. In the United States there has been a rise in (1) autocratic decision-making, perhaps reflecting the stronger powers vested in administrative agencies in recent times, (2) citizen voting, indicating a rise in single-issue politics and the level of distrust of Americans in their elected representatives, and (3) public hearings, probably as a product of increased participatory activism

Table 12–5   Resolution Mechanisms Used in Environmental Conflict (587 conflicts; 1970–78 scanning; % rounded off and means)

				Types of Resolution Mechanisms						Mean Number of Resolution Mechanism Types
	Autocratic Govtal. Decision	Adjudication	Legislation	Vote	Public Hearing	Arbitration Mediation	Bargaining/ Negotiation	Joint Problem Solving	Private Decision	
1. All Conflicts	36	37	8	4	21	1	17	10	15	1.5
2. Type of Facility										
Petrochemical	33	33	2	10	21	2	21	7	10	1.4
Oil Refinery	51	15	10	12	37	0	15	12	12	1.6
Nonferrous Metal	33	44	4	4	30	0	33	19	11	1.8
Ferrous Metal	31	50	8	0	12	0	31	8	12	1.5
Pulp and Paper	13	50	0	0	13	0	13	31	19	1.4
Nuclear Power	42	42	21	18	27	3	0	3	12	1.7
Electric Utility	67	44	0	0	11	11	11	11	11	1.7
Transport and Storage	38	35	35	8	43	3	16	5	8	1.9
Mineral Mining	27	38	9	3	12	3	18	12	21	1.4
Inorganic Chemical	34	33	1	1	13	1	20	18	20	1.4
Organic Chemical	36	30	4	0	19	1	16	16	25	1.5
Other	48	32	4	0	16	0	12	8	20	1.4
3. Nature of Facility										
Existing	32	46	4	1	10	2	19	16	16	1.5
Expansion	43	14	4	0	36	0	18	4	14	
New Proposal	42	25	14	9	35	1	13	9	15	1.6

4. Location of Facility										
United States	30	46	10	6	19	1	13	14	11	1.5
Northeast	33	43	9	9	26	0	14	17	9	1.6
Southeast	24	48	4	4	18	2	13	16	14	1.4
Midwest	22	69	13	4	9	4	7	20	11	1.6
Southwest	33	30	7	6	20	0	13	6	16	1.3
Far West	38	50	22	0	19	3	16	13	9	1.7
Overseas	46	17	5	2	23	2	24	10	22	1.5
Japan	52	33	0	0	10	10	67	0	14	1.9
West Germany	42	21	5	0	21	0	16	0	26	1.3
Belgium/Neth.	49	16	5	3	16	0	24	19	14	1.5
France	33	42	17	8	25	0	17	8	17	1.7
United Kingdom	23	10	7	3	57	0	10	7	27	1.4
5. Ownership of Facility										
Foreign	44	20	7	4	36	2	18	11	20	1.6
Domestic	33	42	8	5	16	1	16	13	14	1.5
6. Year of Emergence										
U.S.										
1970-71	25	55	6	2	11	0	5	12	15	1.3
1972-73	33	44	10	5	16	3	18	16	14	1.6
1974-75	24	42	12	6	24	2	14	18	10	1.5
1976-78	41	36	9	11	27	2	18	11	5	1.6
Non-U.S.										
1970-71	50	28	4	0	17	0	15	13	26	1.5
1972-73	46	17	3	0	20	3	34	0	11	1.4
1974-75	47	16	12	3	38	0	28	16	28	1.9
1976-78	31	10	0	7	28	0	10	14	28	1.2

453

and broadened acceptance of the notion of pre-project environmental impact assessment. Contrary to popular impressions, however, the relative amount of litigation in American industrial environmental disputes seems to have been falling (from 55% in 1970–1971 to 36% in 1976–1978), and the field of battle appears to be moving from the courtroom to the hallways of government agencies, town hall meeting rooms, and local ballot boxes. Some of the same patterns have been evident overseas, although the use of autocratic governmental decision-making and bilateral bargaining has been declining.

The Outcomes and Durations

We now come to the outcomes of the environmental battles. As of the mid-1978 closing date of our survey, more than 40% of the sample conflicts were still going on. The data in Table 12–6 thus reflect intermediate outcomes reported for unresolved conflicts as well as both intermediate and final outcomes for disputes fully terminated or resolved. Final and/or intermediate outcomes were reported for 80% of the conflicts. The figures on duration, however, are limited to cases which had ended by the survey cut-off date.

For purposes of analysis, the outcomes of environmental conflict can be grouped into three categories: (1) Certain outcomes were generally of greater benefit to the *opponents* than the corporations involved, and would include fines and compensation, jail sentences, shut downs and capacity reductions, blockages, and postponements. (2) Other outcomes can be viewed as representing *compromises* offering partial satisfaction to each of the contesting parties, and would include delays, project modifications, and relocations. (3) Still other outcomes would generally indicate victory for the *corporation,* manifested in project approvals and go-aheads. What determines the outcomes of environmental conflicts? The answer to this vital question is unfortunately not yet in hand on either a theoretical or empirical basis. Whether a conflict ends in a clear victory for one side, or a compromise, obviously depends upon many aspects of the conflict process. Scholars have noted dozens of interacting variables which serve to shape the magnitude and distribution of conflict outcomes. The outcomes shown in Table 12–6, for example, can perhaps be traced to characteristics of the parties involved, nature and magnitude of the goals in contention, nature of the issues at stake, past and anticipated relationship between the parties, strategies and modes of conflict behavior engaged in, differential power or resources among the parties, presence and influence of audiences, availability and use of third parties, and character of the resolution mechanisms employed.[51]

The outcomes of the conflicts contained in our sample survey varied considerably according to type of facility involved. Fines or compensation for damage were paid by corporations in 15% of all the disputes, but were more prevalent in the nonferrous metal and inorganic chemicals sectors. There were, for example, Allied Chemical's payments of more than $20 million in damage settlements and pollution fines as a result of its Kepone pollution ordeal at Hopewell, Virginia, General Electric's settlement of $7 million for PCB research and waste-treatment facility construction that terminated the New York State Department of Environmental Conservation's proceedings against the company's PCB pollution of the Hudson River, and Chisso's staggering multi-million dollar payments of compensation to Minamata disease victims and fishermen in Japan. Jail sentences for corporate executives were involved in only 1% of the sample cases and were mainly found in Italy—such as three month sentences ordered for Montedison's top executives after conviction on Scarlino titanium dioxide waste dumping pollution charges, and jail sentences for the owners, two directors, and the company physician of the Cirie dyestuffs factory of Industria Piemontese dei Colori di Anilina after a court found the officials guilty of "manslaughter and injury" in regard to cancer deaths.

Shutdowns or reductions in output on a temporary or permanent basis were outcomes in 19% of all the battles, and were most prevalent in the nonferrous metals, pulp and paper, and chemicals sectors. Blockages of projects occurred in 17% of all the sample conflicts, although about half of all the oil refinery conflicts ended in this manner. Three percent of all the battles ended with the firm postponing its planned project, although it was as high as 18% in the minerals mining sector. Delays of at least six months for the proposed plans of a corporation occurred in 27% of all battles, but over 40% of the nuclear power, minerals mining, electric utility, and transportation and storage conflicts were marked by delays. They were quite pervasive (65%) and often highly involved in the transportation and storage sector.

Technical modifications in projects represented the most frequent outcome, resulting in 37% of all the sample battles. About 60% of the ferrous metal, pulp and paper, and inorganic chemical facility conflicts were resolved in this way, often involving the addition of millions of dollars of pollution control gear at existing facilities. Site relocations, either attempted or realized, were the result in 8% of the 587 conflicts, and they were three times as prevalent in the oil refinery and nonferrous metal sectors. An example in the refining industry is Gulf Oil's move from Zelo Buon Persico to Bertonico near Milan, Italy after encountering considerable anti-foreign sentiment and ecological opposition. An example in the nonferrous metals sector is the ten-year aluminum smelter siting saga of Alumax, a joint venture of AMAX, Mitsui, and Nippon Steel. Rising power costs, tough pollution control regulations, and a scarcity of industrial land forced Japan's aluminum companies in the early 1970s to step up their search for overseas investment sites. This brought Mitsui and Nippon to join AMAX in its attempt to construct a new smelter in the northwest corner of the United States. An effort to site a smelter at an economically depressed seacoast town, Warrenton, Oregon, was blocked by restrictive fluoride emission standards. In 1974 the consortium switched to Umatilla, a port on the Columbia River in eastern Oregon, only to find its construction plants stalled by its own supporters back in Warrenton and a court ruling that Alumax's power contract with the Bonneville Power Administration was unenforceable until the agency submitted an environmental impact statement on its future plans for the entire Northwest region—an effort which would take two to three years to accomplish. As a result, Alumax redirected its site acquisition search and in 1979 finally announced its choice of a site in the Newcastle area of New South Wales, Australia.[52]

Table 12–6 also shows corporate victories in about a third of the nuclear power, transport and storage, and mineral mining sectors. Opponent victories of the kinds just described were more frequent in the petrochemical, oil refinery, ferrous metals, electric utility, and organic chemical sectors. Compromise outcomes were generally most frequent in the nonferrous metals, pulp and paper,

Table 12-6 Outcomes and Duration of Environmental Conflict (587 conflicts; 1970–1978 scanning; % rounded off and means)

	Types of Outcome										Mean Duration of Conflict (Years)
	Fine or Compensation	Jail Sentence	Shutdown or Capacity Reduction	Delay	Technical Modification	Approved	Blocked	Postponed	Relocated	Established	
1. All Conflicts	15	1	19	27	37	22	17	3	8	7	1.6
2. Type of Facility											
Petrochemical	15	0	2	38	26	38	23	6	11	11	1.6
Oil Refinery	10	0	2	22	17	22	49	2	24	2	1.7
Nonferrous Metal	13	3	23	26	26	13	13	3	29	13	1.8
Ferrous Metal	35	0	17	9	61	9	4	0	0	0	2.7
Pulp and Paper	8	0	33	0	58	17	0	0	0	0	1.8
Nuclear Power	3	3	17	41	24	41	17	0	0	7	1.7
Electric Utility	10	0	0	50	30	0	40	0	0	0	2.0
Transport and Storage	3	0	3	65	21	35	24	3	6	27	2.1
Mineral Mining	3	0	21	44	18	29	15	18	3	8	1.3
Inorganic Chemical	23	1	32	13	59	17	8	0	5	1	1.5
Organic Chemical	19	4	33	28	45	15	10	3	7	7	1.6
Other	9	0	17	22	44	26	26	0	13	17	1.3
3. Nature of Facility											
Existing	27	2	32	6	54	9	3	0	2	2	1.6
Expansion	3	0	3	50	28	31	22	3	3	13	1.7
New Proposal	1	1	4	53	17	37	34	7	18	14	

4. Location of Facility

United States	16	1	19	24	36	22	16	2	4	6	1.8
Northeast	22	2	13	14	47	17	18	1	7	7	1.8
Southeast	16	0	18	24	28	22	11	0	4	4	1.4
Midwest	17	0	29	23	43	17	6	0	0	6	1.8
Southwest	15	0	26	23	28	23	16	8	5	7	1.7
Far West	0	0	10	55	28	35	28	0	3	7	2.3
Overseas	13	2	19	32	39	22	18	4	14	9	1.5
Japan	55	5	32	5	68	9	0	0	0	3	1.2
West Germany	0	0	14	57	9	17	30	0	17	13	1.8
Belgium/Neth.	4	0	10	37	47	24	8	4	10	8	1.4
France	6	0	7	13	33	13	53	7	13	17	1.2
United Kingdom	3	0	16	41	28	44	19	16	9	0	1.6

5. Ownership of Facility

Foreign	5	1	15	44	26	25	28	7	17	10	1.7
Domestic	17	1	20	22	41	20	13	2	6	6	1.6

6. Year of Emergence

U.S.											
1970-71	19	0	20	11	43	10	12	1	4	1	1.9
1972-73	9	2	26	19	26	17	17	2	6	6	2.0
1974-75	12	0	12	33	26	33	19	2	0	2	1.7
1976-78	23	2	23	33	30	19	12	7	7	5	1.1
Non-U.S.											
1970-71	13	4	18	22	46	20	20	4	11	6	1.8
1972-73	15	0	23	36	44	26	5	3	13	23	1.3
1974-75	2	0	7	44	27	22	37	5	22	5	1.3
1976-78	6	3	22	38	25	28	13	6	16	6	1.2

and inorganic chemicals industries. Moreover, the bulk of all fines and compensation, jail sentences, shut downs, and technical modifications arose in connection with existing facilities, while most of the delays, blockages, postponements, relocations, approvals, and establishments were associated with expansions and new proposals. Opponents were generally most successful in achieving their aims in the case of existing facilities and least successful in the case of expansions. Overall, 54% of all the conflicts over existing facilities ended with technical modifications, while production shut downs occurred in 32%, and fines or compensation were paid in 27% of the cases. More than 53% of all the new-project battles involved delay, while 34% of them were blocked and 18% relocated. The aggregate economic cost of these outcomes, while impossible to estimate accurately, has surely been enormous.

The international data in Table 12–6 show that Japan led in the frequency of fines or compensation, jail sentences, shut downs, and technical modifications, all reflecting the severe problems with pollution from existing facilities. Delays and site relocations were most frequent in West Germany, while blocked projects occurred most often in France. Although projects were delayed 41% of the time in Britain as a result of that country's public inquiry system, the rate of eventual approval was twice the American average, indicating a relatively favorable climate for new investment in the chemical process industries. It is also interesting that local firms encountered a higher incidence of fines and technical modifications than did foreign-owned enterprises, while the latter experienced two to three times as much delay, relocation, postponement, and blockage. These higher frequencies may in part be explained by foreign firms' relative lack of sensitivity to local political and social influences. The presence of anti-foreign sentiment, as described earlier, as well as the multinational's greater flexibility in choosing investment locations, may also be reflected in these less satisfactory conflict outcomes for the firms involved.

The mean duration for all of the "terminated" conflict cases represented in Table 12–6 was 1.6 years, with the range for battles in the 1970s extending from 1 to 8 years. The duration data, while missing the effects of the still unresolved battles, reveal some interesting patterns. Ferrous metal, electric utility, and transport and storage sector conflicts lasted longer on average than those in other facility sectors. Battles over expansions and new proposals were slightly more protracted than those over existing facilities, but the time difference was much more pronounced overseas than in the United States. The average dispute in America lasted three tenths of a year longer than the average overseas conflict, while Japan and France—perhaps because of close business-government relations and centralization of government power—exhibited the shortest time delays in resolving or terminating the environmental conflicts. Foreign investors experienced slightly longer battles than indigenous investors.

The Interrelationships

Table 12–7 shows a matrix of intercorrelations that reflect the relationship between all pairs of composite variables on issues, opponents, tactics, resolution mechanisms, and outcomes involved in environmental conflict that have been discussed here.[53] A summary description of the experience of foreign as com-

Table 12-7 *Matrix of Correlation Coefficients Between Composite Variables in Environmental Conflict (587 conflicts; 1970–1978 scanning; zero-order correlations)*

Columns are numbered to match the row order (lower-triangular matrix):
1 Foreign Investment · 2 New Proposal · 3 Time of Emergence · 4 Primary Issues · 5 Secondary Issues · 6 Number of Issues · 7 Governmental Opponents · 8 Nongovernmental Opponents · 9 Local Opponents · 10 Nonlocal Opponents · 11 Number of Opponents · 12 Social Tactics · 13 Regulatory Tactics · 14 Number of Tactics · 15 Public Resolution Mechanisms · 16 Third Party Resolution Mechanisms · 17 Private Resolution Mechanisms · 18 Number of Resolution Mechanisms · 19 Opponent Outcomes · 20 Compromise Outcomes · 21 Corporate Outcomes · 22 Duration

	1	2	3	4	5	6	7	8	9	10	11	12	13	14	15	16	17	18	19	20	21	22
Foreign Investment	1.0																					
New Proposal	.31**	1.0																				
Time of Emergence	.12**	-.10*	1.0																			
Primary Issues	.10**	.10*	-.06	1.0																		
Secondary Issues	.10*	.08*	-.05	.12**	1.0																	
Number of Issues	.13**	.13**	-.04	.75**	.73**	1.0																
Governmental Opponents	.05	.05	-.01	.16**	.25**	.29**	1.0															
Nongovernmental Opponents	.17**	.33**	-.10*	.46**	.23**	.48**	.16**	1.0														
Local Opponents	.25**	.32**	-.09*	.44**	.23**	.46**	.30**	.87**	1.0													
Nonlocal Opponents	-.15**	-.04	-.01	.16**	.23**	.27**	.79**	.28**	.09*	1.0												
Number of Opponents	.09*	.21**	-.06	.44**	.31**	.52**	.68**	.82**	.80**	.65**	1.0											
Social Tactics	.16**	.21**	.03	.38**	.15**	.38**	.20**	.66**	.61**	.23**	.60**	1.0										
Regulatory Tactics	-.10**	-.16**	.03	.00**	.11**	.07*	.47**	-.05	.00	.40**	.22**	-.11**	1.0									
Number of Tactics	.09*	-.10*	-.01	.35**	.20**	.39**	.44**	.58**	.55**	.42**	.67**	.85**	.43**	1.0								
Public Resolution Mechanisms	.14**	.36**	-.02	.22**	.11**	.23**	.30**	.44**	.40**	.32**	.49**	.41**	.02	.38**	1.0							
Third Party Resolution Mechanisms	.07	-.11**	.09*	.02	.03	.05	.22**	.06	.07	.21**	.18**	.17**	.28**	.30**	-.12**	1.0						
Private Resolution Mechanisms	.04	-.12**	.10*	.16**	.12**	.18**	.16**	.09*	.10*	.14**	.15**	.13**	.09*	.17**	-.12**	-.24**	1.0					
Number of Resolution Mechanisms	.08*	.09*	.00	.28**	.18**	.32**	.48**	.41**	.40**	.47**	.57**	.48**	.27**	.58**	.52**	.44**	.46**	1.0				
Opponent Outcomes	.01	-.15**	.01	.23**	.15**	.25**	.15**	.15**	.16**	.13**	.20**	.27**	.10*	.29**	.04	.14**	.22**	.27**	1.0			
Compromise Outcomes	.14**	.21**	.00	.09*	.14**	.14**	.30**	.17**	.25**	.18**	.29**	.18**	.08*	.20**	.12**	.10*	.11*	.22**	-.25**	1.0		
Corporate Outcomes	.07	.34**	-.18**	.03	.12**	.11*	.02	.16**	.12**	.07	.13**	.13**	.06	.09*	.13**	.03	-.12**	.03	-.25**	.09*	1.0	
Duration	.03	-.02	-.26**	.13**	.13**	.17**	.31**	.29**	.24**	.33**	.40**	.29**	.16**	.36**	.19**	.18**	.09	.33**	.07	.11*	.07	1.0

* p ≤ .05
** p ≤ .01

pared to domestic investors in regard to environmental conflict during the period 1970–1978 might be drawn from Table 12–7 as follows: Those foreign direct investments which became enmeshed in disputes were more often new proposals than existing facilities. In contrast to the battles of indigenous firms, they emerged slightly later in time and on average entailed slightly more primary and secondary issues. Foreign investor battles were positively associated with the presence of nongovernmental and local opponents and negatively associated with the involvement of nonlocal opponents—the number of opponents confronted on average was a bit higher for foreign firms than for domestically-owned firms. The tactics employed by the opponents were more often social than regulatory in kind, and also somewhat more numerous than those brought to bear against indigenous firms. The number of resolution mechanisms utilized was also a bit higher; foreign investors experienced more decision-making in the form of public resolution processes than did domestic firms; and compromises emerged slightly more often in the case of foreign investments.

Some of the strongest associations uncovered in the entire study were those bearing upon the magnitude (size, intensity, and duration) of environmental conflict. Table 12–7 shows, for example, that the number of opponents in a battle was strongly and positively associated with the number of issues, tactics, and resolution mechanisms involved in a dispute, as well as its duration. In a predictive sense this means that knowledge with regard to any one of these variables carries information about the others. For example, this would suggest that the wider and deeper the environmental impacts of an industrial facility, the more numerous and diverse the actors which emerge in opposition and the tactics which they correspondingly bring to bear against the firm. This may, in turn, necessitate the use of more methods of conflict resolution. And channeling conflicts sequentially or simultaneously through a greater range of resolution mechanisms may eat up more time and thus lengthen the duration of the dispute.

Perhaps our most important descriptive finding is that many of the items in Table 12–7 appear to fall into clusters corresponding to two distinct types of environmental conflict. One seems to represent a "social conflict," and the other might be described as "regulatory conflict." Patterns in the intercorrelation matrix in Table 12–7, particularly in regard to opponents, tactics, and resolution mechanisms, suggest that different sets of variables tend to hang together. The two types of conflict pose different management challenges for the corporation. Primary issues (for example, health and safety, economic, and social impact) of deep concern to nongovernmental and local opponents tend to be most prominent in social conflict, while secondary issues of environmental quality (for example, air and water pollution) of concern mainly to governmental and nonlocal opponents tend to be more prevalent in regulatory conflict. Tactics such as demonstrations, lobbying, and press campaigns are confronted by firms planning new proposals in social conflict, while governmental legal and administrative actions as applied to existing facilities characterize regulatory conflict.

Social conflicts tend to encompass more issues, opponents, tactics, and resolution mechanisms than do regulatory disputes. And the two types are dealt with in different ways—public resolution mechanisms are almost exclusively found in social conflict while third-party mechanisms are mainly employed in regulatory disputes. Compromise and opponent outcomes appear to result in both types of disputes, but corporations generally fail to win regulatory battles, although they have better luck in the social ones. Foreign investors in this decade have had to confront the social variety of environmental conflict more often than the regulatory kind.

THE SEVESO INCIDENT

Our discussion of environmental conflict facing multinational companies would not be complete without a more in-depth analysis of at least one major case, in order to convey a sense of the "pathology" of such disputes. Our case begins on Saturday, July 10, 1976, at a small chemical plant just outside the Italian town of Seveso, about 13 miles north of Milan. The plant belonged to ICMESA (Industrie Chimice Meda Societa Anonyma), a company owned by Givaudan of Switzerland, a large supplier of cosmetic products and hexachlorophene. Givaudan, in turn, is a wholly-owned subsidiary of Hoffmann-La Roche.

A production run of 2, 4, 5-trichlorophenol (TCP), an intermediate used in the manufacture of bactericides and herbicides, had supposedly been shut down at the ICMESA plant at 6 A.M. Saturday for the weekend, with power off and dials set to cooling. The reaction employed in producing TCP is highly exothermic, that is, one in which a temperature increase is caused by chemical activity within the reaction vessel. It is also one in which small quantities of a by-product, 2, 3, 7, 8-tetrachlorodibenzo-para-dioxin (TCDD), "dioxin" for short, could be produced. At the normal working temperature of 170–180°C the quantities of TCDD produced are small, but higher temperatures could create conditions for the formation of substantial quantities. TCDD is one of the deadliest substances known—just one gram (.035 ounces) of the poison, according to scientists, is capable of killing thousands of people.

For reasons still unknown, the ICMESA batch reactor used in making TCP overheated shortly after noon on July 10, with the temperature jumping to 450–500°C.[54] At 12:37 P.M. the safety valve installed to prevent the reactor from rupturing blew, and part of the contents of the reactor were blasted through a relief pipe leading directly into the open air. An estimated 500 kg. of TCP and from 1 to 11 lbs. of TCDD were released—some early press estimates of the amount of TCDD released went as high as 132 lbs.[55] A slight breeze blew the thick grey cloud southward over Seveso and several neighboring communities in the heavily populated outskits of Milan. About 95% of the highly toxic TCDD in the drifting plume was thought to have fallen in a cone shaped area some two kilometers long and 700 meters wide, affecting the homes of 739 people. Many of the residents saw the cloud or smelled its pungent, medicinal odor. But noxious vapors were nothing new in the heavily polluted industrial area and at first little attention was paid to it.

A day after the gas escaped, ICMESA's production manager assured local mayors that there was nothing to worry about, and merely advised local health authorities that local fruit and vegetables should not be eaten.[56] On Monday (July 12) the plant, with the exception of a small area cordoned off around the defective reactor vessel, resumed normal operations. The plant manager also sent a formal letter to the local authorities confirming the gas release, although nothing was apparently known or stated about the presence of appreciable amounts of TCDD. Within days, household pets in the area began to bleed at the nose and mouth, and then died. Vegetation withered, almost 80,000 domestic fowl died, and so did hundreds of pigs and cattle, as well as wild birds and insects. On the afternoon of July 15, Hoffmann-La Roche rather vaguely informed local authorities that a highly toxic material might have escaped, again without mentioning TCDD.[57] Residents began to complain of blistering, acute diarrhea, dizziness, headaches, and liver and kidney pains. Children suffering from burning skin rashes (chloracne) were admitted to local hospitals where doctors were puzzled by the malady. Workers at the

ICMESA plant grew suspicious and demanded a meeting with management. When all their efforts were rebuffed, the 210 employees went on strike.

On the weekend of July 17–18 Hoffmann-La Roche finally revealed that TCDD had been released and advised hospitals of its significance. ICMESA's managing director and plant manager were charged under Italian law with culpable negligence in causing a disaster, and placed under house arrest. They were held for 12 hours and then released. Results of an analysis of soil and plant samples carried out by Givaudan at its laboratory in Dubendorf, near Zurich, prompted the company to warn the chief of the Lombardy regional health administration 13 days after the accident occurred that the situation was "extremely serious" and that an immediate evacuation of the most contaminated area was necessary. The statement shattered the optimism of Italian authorities who, according to one government official in Rome, had been trying to "down-play the event to avoid scaring tourists."[58] From July 23 on, Hoffmann-La Roche "offered full assistance, but it was mostly cold-shouldered by the Italian authorities, which had understandably become rather distrustful of it. The authorities then went on to make their own blunders."[59]

Truckloads of Italian soldiers began arriving in Seveso on the morning of July 25 to isolate an area within a 500-meter radius of the factory. ICMESA provided an initial 100 million lire (about $120,000) for relief efforts on the same day. The sale and consumption of vegetables, fruit, milk, and meat produced locally were banned, and residents were advised to abstain from sexual intercourse if any of these had recently been consumed. Local authorities ordered the immediate evacuation of all residents from a 37 acre area south of the factory, and on July 27, 179 people were finally evacuated amid much confusion and bitter protest. The evacuees were housed, at the expense of Givaudan, in a large and luxurious apartment and hotel complex just north of Milan. Police were given orders to shoot on sight anyone trying to loot the evacuated homes. The evacuation zone was extended a number of times in the next few days, with the result that more than 700 people were removed from 267 acres of land—an area which became known as Zone A. Thousands of other residents in surrounding areas with lower recorded average TCDD soil concentrations were allowed to stay, but advised to take a range of severe precautions.

Late on the night of July 28 a powerful bomb exploded outside the offices of Hoffmann-La Roche in Rome's fashionable Pavioli district. Credit was claimed by a leftist group and the explosion caused severe damage but no injuries. Smoldering resentment also began to be expressed in public demonstrations against the company and local authorities for their slowness to react or attempted coverup, and in wall posters with slogans such as "IN SEVESO, AS IN VIETNAM, THE KILLERS ARE THE SAME." Ecology groups called for boycotts of Hoffmann-La Roche products. The Italian and European press went wild with headlines such as "Deformity Terror in Italy," "A Chemical Hiroshima," "Poison Cloud Ravages Italy," and "Le Vietnam en Italie." The link to Vietnam arose from charges that the ICMESA plant was secretly engaged in production of poison gas or defoliants for NATO military use. Press attention focused heavily on the widespread use of TCP in the herbicide base 2, 4, 5-trichlorophenoxy acetic acid (2, 4, 5-T). This compound, in the form of "Agent Orange," had been in widespread use by the United States Air Force as a defoliant during the Vietnam war. Givaudan in a statement on July 27 flatly repudiated the charges and stressed that its trichlorophenol was "used exclusively in the production of hexachlorophene, a bactericide utilized for bodycare," in the United States and in Switzerland.[60] The American embassy in Rome also denied that ICMESA was involved in any NATO or United States defense contracts. These statements, however, could not be confirmed by authorities because order books had vanished from ICMESA's offices after the explosion.

By mid-August some 30 firms in the area had been closed down, more than 500 people treated for skin rashes and internal complaints, and 855 persons evacuated from their homes with little more than the clothes on their backs. The dioxin cloud, declared the regional health minister, had become "our own little Hiroshima."[61] Reports suggested that TCDD might be thousands of times more dangerous to fetuses than teratogen, the deforming agent in thalidomide (see Chapter 10). Dozens of Seveso women decided to seek special permission for abortions and Justice Ministry officials in Rome quickly declared them exempt from Italy's strict anti-abortion laws. Subsequent abortions stirred nationwide controversy in Italy, with the Vatican condemning them on doctrinal grounds and instead urging adoption of deformed children. In the highly charged atmosphere the technical director of ICMESA was arrested and jailed on August 12 and the Managing Director and Plant Manager rearrested, all on charges of culpably causing a disaster. A week later there were reports that the Italian government was thinking of taking legal proceedings against the management of Givaudan as well.

Seveso elevated environmental concerns to new levels in Italy, and predictably touched off a xenophobic attitude toward multinationals. MNEs were widely denounced for poisoning not only Seveso, but the world's environment.[62] And the central government in Rome was blamed for having allowed Italy to become "the dumping ground of the MNEs," through the absence or lack of enforcement of environmental, health, and safety laws.[63] Hoffmann-La Roche was viewed as one among hundreds of foreign firms that had chosen Italy to produce potentially dangerous intermediates with a high pollution risk for export back to affiliates in countries like Switzerland or Germany where environmental regulations were more tightly observed. In fact, Givaudan at one point openly admitted that it had chosen Italy for the manufacturing of products involving TCDD because it could not obtain permission to do so in Switzerland.[64] And once established in Italy, the company's Seveso plant was indeed treated with leniency by public health and judicial authorities; such treatment was reportedly assisted by the company's practice of paying nearby farmers not to report damage to livestock grazing near the plant.[65]

After the Seveso accident, Italian officials checked chemical plants in and around Milan; and over 300 were found to be breaking regulations. They announced that Seveso would accelerate the tightening of Italy's notoriously lax pollution laws. As one bureaucrat put it, the disaster would inspire Italy to shed its image of "doing the dirtiest work for all the dirtiest industries in Europe."[66] And Seveso became the rallying point for stiff local opposition to at least a dozen proposed chemical plants and nuclear power stations.

The Seveso backlash extended far beyond the Italian borders. In early August 1976, Coalite & Chemical Products Ltd. shut down its TCP unit at Bolsover in the United Kingdom, and Bayer suspended production of TCP at Leverkusen, Germany, until the exact cause of the ICMESA accident could be identified. That left Dow Chemical as the only remaining major Western producer of TCP. Dow maintained that a Seveso-type accident would be impossible at its Midland, Michigan unit, and that controls and safety devices would contain any toxic emissions.[67] Among Europe's governments, Seveso induced the United Kingdom to urge its chemical industry to improve safety standards, Germany to tighten up its controls on dangerous chemicals in the Ruhr, and Sweden to recommend a total ban on herbicides containing dioxin. The EEC began studying ways to improve enforcement of industrial safety measures throughout Europe. And in Brazil, the São Paulo State Environmental Protection Agency prohibited the production, formulation, and use of dioxin-containing materials, thereby blocking some output at Dow Chemical's recently completed $6 million agricultural chemicals plant at Franco da Rocha.[68]

In Italy the frustration and bitterness continued to mount. In early October a group of Zone A evacuees scuffled with police, scaled barbed wire and attempted to reoccupy their homes. Local officials were forced to call on Prime Minister Andreotti to send in additional troops to "isolate, defend and protect" the polluted zone.[69] Talks about damages were also held between Hoffmann-La Roche and Italian officials. The liability of the company was being closely watched by other chemical process MNEs. "What Hoffmann-La Roche does will set the standard in these matters for years," commented an industry observer.[70] Despite advice from its lawyers that Roche was not legally responsible for ICMESA because the firm was not a direct subsidiary, the company announced at an early stage that it would pay all costs and damages incurred that were not covered by insurance. The mission of Rudolph Rupp, a member of Roche's worldwide engineering staff, in October meetings in Milan was to fight to keep the earlier commitment from becoming a blank check. At the start of those meetings, Italian authorities estimated direct damage to industry, commerce, and agriculture at $78 million. The negotiations moved slowly, with Roche remaining tight-lipped about its compensation plans. The first concrete result emerged on December 2, 1976 when Givaudan paid the Lombardy region the sum of $2.4 million in damages, most of it reportedly covered by corporate insurance.[71]

Italian authorities reported in the spring of 1977 that new and dangerous levels of dioxin had been discovered in an area south of the contaminated site at Seveso, and 600 schoolchildren from surrounding regions were now also showing evidence of suspected chloracne. These discoveries called into question the regional government's handling of decontamination procedures. Public outcry over the government's bureaucratic foot-dragging grew, and plans to construct an incinerator for destruction of dioxin were stymied by fierce local opposition. Nearly a year after the accident "a cloud of misfortune still hangs over the small town. Citizens are plagued with newly developing deformities; dioxin-contaminated foliage and [60,000] animal carcasses still have not been disposed of; the contamination has spread to areas outside Seveso; and legal actions against ICMESA are proceeding slowly."[72]

Each plan to decontaminate the area adjacent to the plant became embroiled in controversy between central regional and local authorities on the one hand, and between Hoffmann-La Roche and Italian officials on the other. Roche complained in June that matters were not receiving a realistic appraisal because of "alarmist new reports" in the Italian press which were causing unnecessary anxiety among the inhabitants. The company strongly opposed local plans to remove and incinerate the top soil in the agricultural area, claiming that this would involve "not inconsiderable risks." Based on advice from a British consulting firm with TCDD decontamination experience, Roche instead was pushing an alternative scheme involving the growth of natural surface vegetation to accelerate the breakdown of the chemical.[73] The intrusion of politics, "pushing scientific and medical concerns aside," made progress inordinately slow.[74]

On the legal front, ICMESA's local managers had been criminally prosecuted, but no determination of civil damages had been made by mid-1977. The regional government, frustrated by delays, began pressing the courts to place responsibility on Hoffmann-La Roche. But this was considered by some to be impossible, since there was no precedent under Italian law whereby a foreign parent of an Italian company had been held responsible for civil damages incurred by the affiliate. In the case of Seveso, the estimated damages as of June 1977 were set by the government at $132 million. Givaudan, however, saw the damages totalling only about $30 million.[75] Amid the quarrel, an investigation into who was responsible for the accident and who should pay for the clean-up was finally begun by the Italian Parliament.

A few Italians saw no need to await the investigations results or compensation. In June the local health officer, Dr. Giuseppe Ghetti, was shot in the legs—"knee-capped" in the language of Italian terrorism. On the first anniversary of the Seveso incident, the Swiss home of Rudolf Rupp in Basel was bombed. The terrorist group called "Commando 10th of July" took responsibility and threatened other Roche executives with more of the same. In a tirade against the firm and "its poisonous products," the terrorists declared that Rupp was just a small fish and that the bombing was only "a first warning to others with more responsibility in the company."[76]

Hoffmann-La Roche chose this time to adopt a higher profile stance. After months of providing little information on any aspect of the accident, the company began to make cautiously optimistic statements on both the progress of decontamination and on the evaluation of potential health risks to people in the area—"not surprisingly, Givaudan and Hoffmann-La Roche officials, who are confronted not only with an enormous public relations problem but with the prospect of criminal and civil court proceedings, have struck a positive note in their public pronouncements. The company has sought to combat what it regards as false or exaggerated press reports."[77]

In October 1977 more dioxin was found on school grounds in four communities previously believed uncontaminated by the July 1976 reactor explosion. In early 1978 a group of 5000 people in the Seveso area brought a class action suit against the regional authorities of Lombardy, alleging neglect and dereliction of duty after the explosion and during the decontamination operations.[78] By April the authorities conceded that two-thirds of Zone B (the large and populous area south of Zone A) was probably still contaminated and that residents there should have been evacuated.[79] One observer concluded that "the authorities must take the blame . . . for failing to take early decisions on decontamination, which might have avoided months or years of needless exposure to TCDD."[80]

In June 1978 Roche reported that scientific findings now permitted "the confident assumption" that the population of Seveso had been exposed to only small amounts of dioxin and that no "serious and permanent" damage to health had occurred.[81] At the same time however, the possibility of "belated consequences" could not be ruled out— "that the population of the Seveso area was spared grave damages is due to the fact that we compelled the authorities to take the seemingly harsh and unpopular measure of evacuating the population from the contaminated area."[82] Roche also reported that civil suits had been filed against it, but that settlements had been reached with most people who suffered from the dioxin contamination and with all the businesses affected by the disaster. Press reports set the company's pay-out at $17 million (which rose to $25 million by mid-1979). The eventual cost of decontamination alone, however, was now being estimated by government officials at $140 million.

Precise plans for decontamination, however, were still in doubt due to public fears. Regional government authorities had devised a plan during the summer whereby shipments of thousands of tons of dioxin-contaminated material—such as soil, plants, animal carcasses and building materials—would be sent from Seveso to the Herfa-Nevrenrode salt mines in the West German state of Hesse. But when news of the disposal plan hit the media, there were immediate cries of protest in both Germany and Italy. Local environmentalists in Hesse protested that the mine wasn't safe, mainly because there had been an earthquake in the area in 1953. In Italy, the deputy mayor of Seveso declared: "The population would never permit dioxin-contaminated material from Seveso to be moved from Zone A. Dust would be raised and there would be a serious risk of fresh pollution."[83] The reactions sent governmental planners back to the drawing board in search of other possible solutions.

A summary report of the Seveso inquiry by the Italian Parliament was released in August 1978 and turned up charges against ICMESA, its parent companies, and certain public officials. Among the investigator's findings:

1. ICMESA's TCP production carried greater risks than methods used by other producers due to the absence of automatic measuring and control systems as well as automatic shut-down systems.

2. ICMESA was producing 33 toxic substances for which all necessary permits had not been obtained, and under law should not have been produced in urban areas.

3. The plant's owners did not initiate security measures that might have prevented the explosion.

4. Workers responsible for temperature control during the TCP reaction process were unaware of the dangers involved in production, and they had received no real training.

5. ICMESA let 27 hours pass before it advised the local authorities that a toxic cloud had escaped from the factory and it was not until a week after the disaster that the

director Givaudan's Swiss laboratory informed public authorities and evacuation of residents got under way.

6. Public officials were also lax, and ten of them must appear in court to answer charges that they bear some responsibility.[84] Hoffmann-La Roche declined comment on the findings in 1978, noting that it did not want to prejudice legal proceedings under way in Italy.

The full version of the Italian Parliamentary Commission Report was finally made available to interested parties in 1979. An investigation by *Nature* magazine revealed that the claims of Roche were more accurate than those of the Commission's report. The Commission was charged with omitting some vital evidence in its report—apparently to cover-up delays by Italian authorities in ordering the initial evacuation. A spokesman for Roche concurred, describing the Commission's report as telling a "twisted tale."[85] Roche, by February 1979, had settled all but a few of the 6000 civil claims for damages against it—the hope was that prompt settlement of claims would avoid a higher bill if the criminal court case went against the company. That criminal prosecution, considering whether or not Givaudan was negligent in its maintenance of the trichlorophenol reactor and whether it could have informed people more quickly of the dangers they faced after the accident, was moving at a snail's pace through the clogged Italian judiciary. Scientists appointed to conduct the judicial inquiry, however, placed responsibility for the accident on ICMESA and its parent Givaudan in a court report in 1979. Meanwhile, local authorities reported that the rate of serious birth malformations in the Seveso area had increased significantly from 1977 to 1978.[86]

MANAGING ENVIRONMENTAL CONFLICT

As might be expected, observers have had a field-day pointing out the many lessons of Seveso, that is, failure to apply systematic risk identification, provide adequate safety measures, properly train plant workers, disclose information to health authorities, engage in adequate disaster planning, thoroughly research the safety of dioxin, and legislate and enforce pollution laws.[87] Let us now return, however, to the broader challenge of environmental conflict facing multinationals.

Undoubtedly the most important observation to be drawn from our survey is that environmental conflict appears here to stay—the number of reported battles per year has remained relatively constant since 1972 despite energy crises and recessionary conditions. We suspect that the frequency of environmental conflict, as measured by the percentage of all new industrial projects that encounter environmental opposition in the industrial countries, has been rising steadily throughout the decade. We have also stressed that the focus of conflict has been shifting from old to new targets, from existing pollution problems to potential environmental impacts, and from "band-aid" remedies to preventive or risk-reduction measures. The character of conflict in nations such as the United States, United Kingdom, Japan and West Germany has thus turned increasingly "social" as compared to "regulatory." The issues at stake have been changing, with land use and human health concerns, for example, rapidly on the rise as central matters in contention. The range of human emotions giving rise to environmental opposition has definitely widened, and the name of the game is no longer simply ecology, but rather overall quality of life.

The environmental opponents confronting multinationals can no longer be viewed as naïve and elitist fanatics, radicals, or bird-lovers—the environmental movement over the years has broadened its base, improved its political stature, established social legitimacy, become bureaucratized, and attracted the support of prominent scientists and politicians. The environmental opponent of today is simply anyone who is or feels threatened by an industrial activity—people almost anywhere now seem to be capable of turning into effective protesters in short order, although growing armies of governmental bureaucrats in many nations have increasingly taken on this role, equipped with extensive discretionary powers. But citizen trust in both corporations and government has waned, with the result that the use of public resolution mechanisms, such as votes and hearings, has been on the rise in a number of countries around the world, and high levels of frustration among opponents have at times also driven the action into the streets and onto the sites of proposed facilities. The results of all this for multinationals have often been painful and expensive—delays, fines, shut-downs, technical modifications, relocations, and blockages have translated into billions of dollars of incremental costs. And foreign direct investors as compared to indigenous firms have been the victims more frequently of such opponent-oriented and compromise outcomes.

Environmental conflict has been spreading internationally as well as interregionally, with most battles in the early part of the decade concentrated in heavily industrialized parts of America, Britain, Germany, the Netherlands, and Japan, but later emerging in virtually every other developed nation—and more recently emerging, albeit sporadically, in rapidly industrializing developing nations such as Brazil. They are rarely isolated events. Waves of battles often follow environmental disasters of many types—major spills, explosions, collisions, and industrial accidents like the Seveso case. The crisis atmosphere attracts extensive media coverage and arouses public concern. Public confidence in the competence of industry and government declines and environmental opposition is triggered. Along with geography, we should also note that environmental conflict is spreading industrially to include a broader range of industrial facilities—very few corporate projects now seem immune to potential environmental opposition. The focus of conflict has also spread among the various phases of production. Where it was once concentrated mainly on extractive and manufacturing processes, today other phases such as transportation, storage, fabricating, distribution, product use, and product disposal are often the focus.

It seems certain that variance in environmental policies will continue to prevail from nation to nation as a consequence of differences in natural and human conditions, social preferences, political processes, and so on. The same is true of the frequency and character of environmental conflicts. Multinationals will continue to confront diversity in the types of issues, opponents, tactics, resolution mechanisms, and outcomes in their environmental battles. Certain areas will continue to be more conflict prone than others. Still, some convergence in conflict patterns, particularly among the developed market economy countries of Western Europe, North America, and the Pacific Basin, will probably emerge. And MNEs may increasingly find themselves enmeshed in environmental conflicts that have a distinctly transnational structure—that is, with groups or government agencies at home over environmental impacts associated with corporate activities overseas.

These patterns and trends, in comparison with current MNE behavior, point to the need for new managerial approaches and adjustments.[88] The conventional project planning process has not paid sufficiently careful attention to environmental consequences, nor has it included meaningful citizen participation. The key to conflict management is to adopt environmentally oriented planning in which inputs and means related to environmental concerns, values, processes, conditions, and interrelationships are continuously and carefully taken into account.[89] Accomplishing this will require injection of a range of expertise and techniques that heretofore have generally not been employed. The involvement in planning of a variety of professionals with different but relevant backgrounds such as ecology, biology, sociology, and political science, will help to inculcate awareness of environmental concerns. The use of systematic techniques for predicting, describing, and evaluating environmental consequences will also be necessary if the information acquired is to be properly organized for effective use in project design. It will also require a much broader and more extensive participation in the planning process by those who will be affected by the project decisions made. Although adapting the corporate planning process to permit meaningful external participation will not be easy, the benefits of doing so will be large.

The call for environmentally-oriented planning can be viewed as a plea for more *collaborative, compromising,* and *accommodative* corporate handling of environmental conflicts according to the model proposed in this book. This is not to say that *avoidance* and *competitive* behavior will always be ineffective. And it is clear that increasing environmental opposition to new manufacturing investment in many developed countries is merely reinforcing shifts toward a greater service orientation. Environmental opposition is a factor in favoring increased relocation of industrial production to developing countries—which may have both lower environmental preferences and greater assimilative capabilities than the advanced nations. Along with flight or *avoidance,* power-oriented, *competitive* behavior by MNEs to force their opponents into submission may at times be very appropriate in regard to certain environmental issues.

The prevailing view, however, is that society in nations such as Germany or the United States has become too adversary and legalistic in dealing with problems of the environment. Many point to the extravagant costs of litigation, the endless time it consumes, and the antagonism that it generates. Others maintain that the trial-by-battle procedure of the courts distorts the search for truth and impedes the discovery of reasonable remedies.[90] All subtleties are forced into rigid and artificial choices of yes-or-no, either-or, and guilty-or-innocent. Verdicts and sentences in environmental cases are at times unfair or interminably delayed. The growing dissatisfaction with the use of adversary and legislative procedures as vehicles to jointly pursue growth and environmental objectives has led to a search for new ways to resolve environmental conflicts. Substitutes now being actively considered or experimented with include increased reliance upon arbitration, mediation and conciliation, creation of impartial science courts and neighborhood justice centers, and the like.[91] Institutional changes such as one-stop permit systems and pre-approved site banks are also coming into play. The underlying belief is that methods of third-party assistance and joint problem-solving have been under-utilized in the environmental arena. Removing disputes from the traditional legal framework will not be a panacea, but we believe that multinational corporate decision–makers, as well as environmentalists and government agency officials, may all stand to gain by so doing.

Managing environmental affairs and conflicts in most MNEs today is typically viewed as a strictly local problem. Given international diversity, some degree of fragmentation in the way in which MNEs go about environmental management in different nations will continue to be appropriate and, indeed, necessary. But a number of the trends reviewed above appear to be working in favor of more standardization in global environmental management policy and practice. They imply that MNEs should be able to draw upon environmental conflict management strategies, practices, technologies, and ideas that have been acquired, developed, and tested in one or several of the nations at the forefront of environmental policy, and apply them in an increasing number of comparable situations on a global basis. By doing so, MNEs may be able to achieve leverage or tactical advantage over local firms in the host nations. Major gains may accrue from ensuring a continuous flow of environmental conflict know-how and experience within the multinational corporate system, and encouraging local managers to draw from that flow as needed.

13 *TECHNOLOGY*

Technology is both a key to the economic power and influence of the multinational enterprise on the world enconomy, and a source of a great many of the conflicts that surround it. In recent years, technology has become a central arguing point for those who support the MNE and those who are its principal detractors. And it follows that technology has become a tool for those who would place increased controls, at both the national and international levels, on the operations and effects of multinational firms. In this chapter we shall discuss the role of technology and technological transfer within the organizational structure of the MNE, with specific reference to its potential for conflict and ways of managing it constructively.

DEFINITIONS, FORMS, AND EFFECTS

Of the three most important determinants of economic growth—labor, capital, and technology—the latter is easily the most elusive. Labor can be more or less easily identified and measured. We know—or can find out within acceptable margins for error—who is working, and how much time is being put in per year, quarter, or month. The underlying statistics on population, labor force participation rates, and average hours worked per person are gathered regularly through census and other statistical undertakings. Similarly, capital—the physical stock of buildings, machinery, and other productive assets available in an economy—is regularly kept track of with the help of national accounts statistics, periodic censuses of business and industry, and surveys of business plant and equipment expenditures. To be sure, there are problems of sampling, valuation, depreciation, and the like, but most countries with a reasonable capability in economic statistics can ascertain the size of, and changes in, the national capital stock. Natural resources, which might be viewed as a separate factor of production, are often considered the product of the labor and capital needed to bring them into production. Again, measurement is relatively easy.

No so with technology. Economists know that economic growth depends in large measure on growth in labor and capital inputs, and advances in technology. We can measure growth in output in terms of real GNP, and as noted we can measure the increases in labor and capital inputs that are partly responsible. Yet when we relate output to these two inputs a significant part of production growth invariably remains unexplained. This "residual" or unaccounted-for variance in economic growth is usually attributed to technological progress. Technology is viewed as the prime determinant of the *efficiency* with which labor and capital resources are used in the production process. This approach avoids the problem of trying to measure technological inputs directly, but it gets us no nearer to the problems of defining and accounting for the precise role that technology plays in the growth process.

Nor is it trivial. Estimates of the factors affecting economic growth show that output in such advanced countries as the United States has in fact risen substantially faster than labor and capital inputs combined. Economies of scale—production units of larger size combining labor and capital inputs more efficiently—might be responsible for part of this difference, but technological advance clearly contributes a very major part indeed.[1]

At the firm level, organized research and development (R&D) projects have been estimated to account for about 40% of productivity increases in the United States, and to contribute perhaps one-fourth to one-third of overall technological progress. And the rate of return on R&D investment is high. A recent estimate places it at 25–27%, or about twice the rate of return on investment in plant and equipment.

The measurement problems become clear when we define technology as "useful knowledge"—anything that allows us to attain a greater amount of production or consumer satisfaction with the existing stock of labor and capital. We can perhaps identify four distinct types of technology:

1. **Process technology,** applied directly in production activities to increase the efficiency of workers and/or machines.
2. **Product technology,** which is aimed at consumer goods of higher quality that yield greater satisfaction or capital goods that yield higher rates of output per unit of labor, capital, or raw materials employed.
3. **Applications technology,** which bridges products and processes by developing new ways to use existing capital or consumer goods, or adapting these to different technical environments to yield improvements in economic efficiency.
4. **Management technology,** which includes the knowledge of how to combine different resources to efficiently produce goods and services, and how to distribute and market these outputs to the final consumers or users—"marketing technology" is sometimes separated out as a possible fifth component of technology.

Defined this broadly, the measurement problems become obvious. How do we measure the economic value of a safer car, a faster milling machine, an automated transfer process? How about a more effective labor relations program that reduces wildcat walkouts, an improved managerial decision process, or a more effective merchandise display for supermarket shelves? Some measurement attempts have focused on the number of patents awarded. But what about patents that are never utilized because the invention has no economic value, and what about old patents that were useless when invented but find new applications now? And patents capture only a small fraction of the overall advancement in "useful knowledge" that promotes economic efficiency. An alternative might be research and development expenditures. But here we are trying to measure technological change by the resources devoted to it (measuring outputs by inputs) and there is an enormous amount of slippage between the two in terms of unsuccessful experiments, useless innovations and the like. And what about the individual inventor working in his garage or basement, and therefore unlikely to be accounted for in R&D statistics? The fact is there are no good ways of measuring technical change. This doesn't mean that attempts to do so are worthless; it simply means they are unlikely to explain a great deal of the unexplained variance in growth attributed to technological progress.

There are two additional complicating factors. One is that technology in its abstract or "disembodied" form is again only part of the story. A great deal of technology can only be applied effectively when it is "embodied" either in human beings or in machines. It takes people to know things and to come up with and implement new ideas. Better-trained people are more likely to do so than ignorant people. Society can and does invest in "human capital" through education and training—in effect injecting technology or useful knowledge into human beings who will eventually be in a position to apply that knowledge in the productive process. But without people the knowledge is useless. Similarly, a better machine can't be realized without investment in the machine itself—technology embodied in capital investment. So the ways in which technology enters into the production process are themselves rather complex.

The second point is that the production of technology—the process of invention and innovation—is often long and drawn-out, and its path tortuous. Things get invented as the product of time, effort and money invested by individuals, businesses, and governments. The new idea then has to be "scanned" for possible commercial applications either by the inventor or by outsiders. Sometimes this is almost instantaneous—as when invention comes in response to a specific and immediate need—and sometimes it is an exceedingly long and tedious process —an invention in search of a need. Once a potentially useful application is found there is usually an "innovation" phase, where the new idea is adapted to the realities of the marketplace, or to the economics of existing production processes—a feasibility analysis. Again, this may be almost instantaneous, or it may take years. Then there are applied research, prototype development, trial runs, or pilot production that have to be gone through, further extending the time before the new idea actually makes itself felt in real output and income. Finally, tooling and construction or adaptation of existing plant may have to be undertaken.

For important postwar innovations, the average time needed from invention to the beginning of commercial development has been 10 years, and from that stage to full start-up and manufacturing another five years, according to recent studies.[2] And often there are spinoffs, ancillary applications of a new product or process that can compound its economic effects or lead to entirely new avenues of technological innovation.

The point is that the term "technology" is nothing nice and neat. It is a complex, messy, and often ambiguous concept. True, technology can be bought and sold, but only in part. Without understanding fully the nature of a particular technology the buyer sometimes gets a good deal less than he bargained for— sometimes nothing at all. Using and shopping for a new technology often requires almost as much knowledge as replicating the technology itself.

It is this inherent technological complexity that is partly responsible for the conflict in this domain which surrounds the multinational enterprise. Lawyers, politicians, even businessmen often act as though technology is different from what it is. Many have never seen a shop floor, and few have technical backgrounds. Even those who do often end up defining technology in ways that are much too restrictive and removed from reality. And so the policies they come up with to deal with what they perceive to be technological problems often fail to work, sometimes backfire, and almost always lead to conflict.

Finally, it is important to mention the proprietary nature of technology, which is invariably interwoven with the economics of entrepreneurship and risk-taking. The inventor or innovator makes an investment in technology—often cash, generally time and effort, and always the product of previous investment in human capital and native intelligence. The individual invests his own resources and assumes risk, or the firm that employs him does so. The innovator or his firm makes decisions on the costs of the research and development effort and the discounted value of the expected returns, which in many cases is subject to a very high degree of risk. Sometimes, but not always, government policies will effect this risk/return calculus, such as permitting tax deductions or tax credits for R&D expenditures, guaranteeing a market for the final product, providing subsidies or low-cost loans, and the like. But in the main, innovation and technological advance must meet the tests of the market, and often it takes a market-regulated "trigger" toset the whole process in motion.

Expected returns on innovation will be positive, of course, only if the new product or process can be protected in some way from imitation by others. This protection leads to a widening of cost-price margins for the innovating firm—profits, which represent the returns on the research on the research and development resources expended. The firm or individual thus "appropriates" the technology—it becomes proprietary, and is regarded as an asset no different from employees or machinery. It is a different kind of asset, though, in that it is capable of being appropriated by competitors and thus brings about an erosion of the returns on the investment. And so patents, copyrights, and trademarks have been devised to protect the innovators' monopoly rights for varying periods of time against competitors' incursions. What cannot be protected in this way is jealously guarded as "trade secrets" and just as vigorously sought after by competitors in ways that range from simple emulation to industrial espionage. Society recognizes the nature and importance of industrial and intellectual property, and the need for a positive and fair rate of return on these assets to induce further creative and innovative activity. Yet because taking away the monopoly rents by copying an innovation is somehow not quite the same thing as stealing a machine, the appropriation and protection of technology have become hot topics of debate particularly in an international context—and a source of continuing conflict.

There are major international variations in the development of new knowledge, again only partially reflected in patents. For instance, a recent study of the global exchange of patents shows that 95% of all international inventions originated in just 12 countries in the mid-1960s. The United States leads with a 41.3% share of all exported inventions, followed by West Germany (15.7%) and the United Kingdom (9.3%), France (6.2%), Switzerland (5.0%), and Japan (4.7%). But relative to their economic size, such small countries as Switzerland and the Netherlands show a substantial lead over the United States. The principal destinations for American patented technology are Canada, Britain, West Germany, Japan, France, Australia, the Netherlands, Belgium, Mexico, and Sweden, in that order of importance. The United States is the primary destination for patented innovations originating in Britain, Japan, and Canada, but ranking much further down for the other main technology exporters.[3]

TECHNOLOGY AND THE MULTINATIONAL ENTERPRISE

The multinational firm is inexorably involved in the technology issue for a number of reasons. In the first place, today's MNEs are themselves important sources of both invention and innovation. Being predominantly large firms, they have the resources to throw into significant R&D efforts and—especially where economies of scale are involved and it takes a large number of specialists from many fields working with expensive equipment to come up with new developments—may thus add to the overall rate of technical progress. MNEs also have a built-in market "trigger," which keeps the pressure on R&D in terms of the direction of effort and the evaluation of innovations as they develop. Moreover, the MNE tends to be very good at adopting inventions that materialize outside the firm, adapting them to fit the firm's needs in the various markets it serves and the different production requirements it faces. And because it operates globally, its net is cast far wider than national firms in terms of possible external technological infusions.

To carry this view a bit further, we noted in Chapter 1 that the MNE can be viewed as a kind of "information factory." Its affiliates all over the world absorb information about markets, costs, competition, and technologies and transmit it to corporate headquarters, where it is collected, sorted out, stored, analyzed, and evaluated. Useless information is thrown out, while information that promises a profit potential is retained and later possibly applied throughout the MNE network. Whether this information is of a technical nature or not, it is quite obviously "useful knowledge" and thus comes under the rubric of technology. Such assimilated technology is also appropriated by the firm for its own use, and it serves to enhance the value of the MNE "package" of services (described in Chapter 14) and the price (economic rent) charged for that package. So the possession of an enormous stock of technical, administrative, sourcing, marketing, and informational know-how—both disembodied and embodied in machines and human beings—can give the multinational firm a decisive competitive edge over purely national enterprises and at the same time allows it to make a net economic contribution in the international economy.

An even broader view of the symbiotic relationship between technology and the MNE links the two directly in terms of the efficiency of international transactions. Traditionally the free and open market has been the principal transactions medium between independent buyers and sellers. Markets need many buyers and many sellers, low transactions costs, easily available and low-cost information, and relatively homogenous products to work well. Under such conditions, market transactions tend to be the most efficient. To take into account uncertainty about shifts in market price over time, futures markets and long-term contracts have developed to help buyers and sellers reduce business risk. For centuries market mechanisms were equal to the task of efficient international transactions.

Technology has changed all that. It has made many internationally traded goods and services so complex that many of the market-efficiency criteria often do not hold—there are often few buyers and sellers, high transactions costs, and extremely limited market information, again because of the proprietary nature of technology. When technology itself is being traded it may indeed be impossible for the seller to describe what is to be sold to the potential buyer without divulging its substance and rendering it worthless. One would hardly describe the markets for main-frame computers, gas turbine engines, or electronic components as meeting very many of the market-efficiency criteria noted above. And so intra-firm dealings, between parent and affiliates of a given MNE, which avoid the market altogether and use the corporate managerial hierarchy to provide many of the policing functions of the market, may actually be more efficient from a transactions standpoint and avoid some of the weaknesses of the market in an age of high technology.[4]

So technology can be viewed simultaneously as a product of MNEs, as an input into the MNE productive structure and a source of its competitive strength, and as a characteristic of international transactions that enhances the "institutional comparative advantage" of the MNE in relation to alternative transactions media.

As an international organization, the MNE is deeply involved in the process of inter-country technology transfer or diffusion. Useful knowledge that is generated in-house or acquired from outside and "processed" by the MNE in the way described above is applied in the firm's operations in other countries. From a national point of view, technology may thus be exported by the MNE—that is, made available to other countries for which a return may or may not be received. It may also be imported by way of the MNE as part of the "package" of services, for which a return will probably have to be paid. In the first instance, MNE technology transfer provides a new agent of growth to the importing country without detracting from the sources of growth in the exporting country. It does, however, have economic and social effects that can be profound indeed, and can represent a critical determinant of the welfare effects of MNE operations as well as a source of serious conflict.

TECHNOLOGY TRANSFER: FORMS AND COMPETITIVE EFFECTS

Just as the process of technological change is exceedingly complex, so too is the international transfer of technology. First of all, as we noted above, the MNE generates a good deal of its own technology internally. This can occur both at the headquarters and affiliate level, in home countries and in host countries, although in-house research and development by most MNEs is conducted very largely at home. There are exceptions, like IBM, where significant R&D operations are carried on in host countries as well. And such American–based MNEs as Kodak, Exxon, Hoover, Johnson & Johnson, Ford, General Motors, Gillette, and Sperry are prominent for maintaining overseas R&D facilities, while such European firms as Hoffmann-LaRoche, Shell, Philips, SKF, Unilever, British Petroleum, Ciba-Geigy, Bayer, and Pechiney have research activities of various sizes in the United States.

But in the main, the need to exploit economies of scale in research and development activities, the desire to keep close managerial tabs on R&D activities and guard the proprietary nature of results, and the need for a highly-skilled and stable technical labor force keep research and development activities close to home. In all, only about 6% of all R&D expenditures by United States-based MNEs are undertaken abroad. In the mid-1960s a study by the Stanford Research Institute of 200 large American firms showed that about half had R&D activities abroad, but most spent less than 4% of their research budgets overseas.[5]

Secondly, the MNE absorbs useful knowledge from its environment in both home and host countries. The techniques include buying up firms with desired technologies, licensing from other firms, copying and industrial espionage, and such mundane techniques as subscribing to technical journals and going to professional meetings. They also include recruiting technology embodied in people from local universities and from other firms, and buying technology-intensive capital equipment. And they include contract research let out to consulting firms, academic investigators, and others, as well as government research made available to contractors or to industry in general. Once assimilated and evaluated, external innovation can be applied throughout the MNE's operations in accordance with the dictates of competitive behavior.

Again, the international technology transfer process is itself complex. It may be embodied in finished products or parts and components shipped between parent and affiliates, or between affiliates. It may be embodied in employees, such as production managers, quality control specialists, or financial executives, who have learned how to do things and are transferred internationally within the MNE complex. Then there is international travel, where information is exchanged in company sales, production or management meetings, and exchanges of technical memoranda or correspondence. Intrafirm licensing, usually by the parent to its affiliates, of product and process technology is also important. Sometimes the MNE transfers technology that it does not even use itself. The case of Heinz, Del Monte, and Dole has been cited, in terms of their ability to get independent growers in various countries to produce fruit and vegetables of uniform size and quality. At the same time, they provide growers with bulk-purchased low-cost seeds, chemicals and fertilizers, and long-term purchasing commitments which remove a good deal of the market uncertainty.[6]

Often, too, technology is licensed to unaffiliated foreign firms. Examples abound. Cummins Engine shares its diesel technology with Komatsu, the Japanese earthmoving equipment manufacturer, under licensing agreements. The Amdahl Corporation has licensed highly sophisticated computer technology compatible with IBM equipment to the Japanese Fujitsu Ltd., which in turn has transferred it to other countries through cooperative production arrangements. Japan already has a wholly-owned manufacturing subsidiary of IBM and a 49%-owned affiliate of Sperry, as well as a 50-50 partnership between Control Data Corporation and C. Itoh & Company, a major Japanese trading house. Other United States computer firms like Honeywell, RCA, and General Electric have been limited to licensing arrangements in Japan. Technology transfer to unaffiliated firms abroad can be motivated by financial weakness of the technology-generating MNE and its inability to underwrite the further development of the technology it has generated or to fully exploit its market potential. Or, as part of its R&D effort, a firm may uncover technologies it does not wish to use itself, in which case it may find it advisable to farm them out to foreign firms.

As noted, the interaction between the MNE parent and its affiliates, and the technological environments within which they lie, are both continuous and bi-directional. Technology is disseminated by the firm to its environment, as well as being absorbed from it. And technological accumulation can be not only an effect of foreign direct investment, but also a cause of it. Pharmaceutical, chemical, and electronics firms have a history of casting their nets widely, seeking equity interests in firms that possess or are working on promising new technologies. SKF, the giant Swedish bearings manufacturer, bought up a medium-size American firm some years ago to gain a very effective toehold on the market for gas turbine engine bearings. According to one recent survey, 6.0% of the French firms investing in the United States hope to repatriate management and marketing know-how. The German electrical equipment manufacturer Robert Bosch GmbH took a 9.3% equity interest in the Borg-Warner Corporation and a 25% interest in American Microsystems, Inc. in part to tap into the R&D base of these firms. And Italy's Olivetti for years was said to maintain a regular professionally-staffed "listening post" in the United States to assure continued access to American know-how for the parent firm.

There is no doubt that the MNE serves as an effective conduit for technology transfers internationally, both from parent and subsidiary and vice-versa. An important factor in the success of technology transfer is the sophistication and skill of the recipient enterprise. Here the MNE has a decided advantage in being able to control this critical factor if the recipient is its own affiliate. Another important element is sustained effort over an extended period of time, and again firm-to-firm relationships under the MNE umbrella give it a distinct advantage over technology transfers between unrelated national enterprises. Transfer of managerial technology is often a good deal more difficult than other types of know-how, since it is critically dependent on the nature of the receiving cultural and social environment.[7]

A recent study dealing with the pharmaceuticals and semiconductor industries, concludes that "the large MNC . . . is not necessarily the best institution for technology creation, however, it frequently brings ideas and people world-wide together, sometimes creating a most productive environment for technology creation."[8] At the same time, small progressive firms often play an important peripheral role by providing a significant challenge to the MNE.

Another study has shown that international technology transfer both involves substantial resource costs and varies widely from one firm to the next and between industries. These costs appear to be lower with accumulated skills, embodiment of technology in capital equipment, long production runs, repetitive applications of the same technology, and the sophistication and maturity of the partner in cases of licensing or joint ventures.[9] In interfirm technology transfer, project planning is important. So is plant design and supervision. Then there are production control and plant support systems to be designed and implemented. There are production start-up problems. And there are management support and continuing infusions of product and process improvements originating abroad.

There are also limitations in the ability of MNEs to put together feasible technological packages. One of the most dramatic failures was Litton Industries' attempt to develop backward regions of Greece in the 1960s, abandoned by mutual agreement a little over two years after it got going. Litton viewed itself as a leader in solving "the problems of tommorrow" using the systems approach and yet ignored even the most elementary lessons of economic development in its approach to the problem.[10]

The international competitive and trade effects of MNE technology transfer can be very significant indeed. The well-known factors that underlie a country's international competitiveness include labor and capital costs, natural resources, and technology. Countries that have invested heavily in technology generally have strong international competitive position in high-technology products and services. There is a "technology gap" between them and the rest of the world which underlies their trade performance—technology is indeed exported, but mostly after it has been embodied in exportable products and services. It thus provides the basis for that country's export performance.

Exports of technology by way of the MNE put the know-how in the hands of competitors abroad in two ways. First, technology is made available to MNE affiliates directly for overseas production in the local market, for export to third countries, or for export back to the MNE home country, assuming the principal factors of production are cheaper abroad.[11] Second, local firms in host countries are forced to step up their own R&D effects in an effort to keep up with the MNE affiliate—a sort of "imitation cycle" that puts unaffiliated foreign firms in an improved international competitive position.

A recent study of the "imitation cycle" in the semiconductor and pharmaceuticals industries shows that "the rate of diffusion or imitation of technology may have been marginally influenced by rivalry amongst MNCs. . . . Moreover, rivalry amongst companies within the same country can bring about transfers as well as that between companies in different countries. Therefore, the impact on host countries of the MNC may be considerable since local companies, to service the market, generally must compete locally with rival foreign firms, which base their technologies on much larger and more highly developed markets."[12]

In assessing the economic effects of the technology transfer, it can be argued that a distinction has to be made between standardized technology available from multiple sources and advanced "frontier technology" where the proprietary value is very high. Another important distinction is between the transfer of technology itself and transfer of the knowledge of how to push ahead the frontier of technology.

The effect of technology exports on the home country's international competitive position seems to be of particular concern with respect to "front end" technology. According to J. Fred Bucy, President of Texas Instruments: "Today our toughest competition is coming from foreign companies whose ability to compete with us rests in part on their acquisition of United States technology. . . . The time has come to stop selling our latest technologies, which are the most valuable things we've got."[13] The problem with "front end" technology transfer is that it gives recipient countries a state-of-the-art springboard from which to move ahead of the home country. An example is, the aforementioned arrangement between Amdahl and Fujitsu—"In return for its investment of about $23 million in Amdahl Corp., Fujitsu has received the know-how it needs to help close the technology gap between it and the U.S. computer industry."[14] In an environment where the Japanese government is making massive support efforts to drive its computer industry ahead of its American rivals, such transfers can have a very significant impact indeed.

With respect to product-related technology, the process of transfer and its effects is described by the so-called "product cycle" theory of international trade[15] A new product is developed initially for the domestic market, where it is tested, put into pilot production and initially marketed. The product then achieves an export market, which is in the early phases of development even as the domestic market matures. Technology then migrates, via the MNE itself and by imitiation, to the importing countries. These take up production which in turn displaces home-country exports. Eventually, overseas production of the product may also displace domestic exports to third countries, and it may ultimately be exported back to the technology-source country itself. A second stage of the cycle may then develop as the product matures in the first-stage host country and the technology is transferred to second-stage host countries, for example, developing nations. And so competitiveness shifts geographically as a result of international technology transfers, and production migrates accordingly, with implications for trade, consumer welfare, employment, balances of payments, and other economic variables.

While such transfers may indeed narrow international technology gaps between nations, the benefits flowing back to the innovating country are not inconsiderable. They include lower-cost imports, expanded export markets for complementary products, as well as receipts of payments for the technology employed overseas. Nevertheless, there are negative implications for certain export categories, associated production, and jobs. And some have argued that technology diffusion via MNEs no longer follows classic product-cycle lines, now that frontier-type technology which is itself useful in generating new products is increasingly being made available to foreign manufacturers via MNEs.

American labor was sufficiently concerned about this that explicit provisions for the control of technology exports were built into the highly restrictive Hartke-Burke trade legislation, discussed in Chapter 14, which was proposed a number of times in the early 1970s. One study of 25 cases of technology transfer concludes that the United States economy will gain in engineering, design, and R&D employment and output, but will lose in manufacturing employment as a result of know-how exports, especially in the automobile, aircraft, consumer electronics, and chemicals industries. It also concludes that a recent move toward export of "front-end" technology can lead to a significant shortening of the technology gap and an erosion of the United States competitive position[16] Indeed, technologically lagging countries have sometimes actively encouraged joint ventures and consortium arrangements with MNEs from leading countries to accelerate this transfer. The United States Congress has been concerned as well about American affiliates of foreign MNEs tapping into the national technology base. Between the operations of United States-based firms abroad and foreign firms abroad and foreign firms in America, a double-barrelled technology drain was suspected.

Yet even in a period of technological "gap" between the United States and Europe there have been significant return transfers of technology—Bic disposable pens and lighters from France; the Harrier VTOL fighter, the Pilkington float glass process, and Wilkinson stainless steel razor blades from the U.K.; drugs from Switzerland; steelmaking technology from Austria; Lego toys from Denmark; electric appliances from Holland; soft contact lenses from Czechoslovakia; and many more. Indeed, American firms like National Patent Development Corporation and DGA International have done very well by specializing in the brokerage of offshore technology for the American market.

From a managerial point of view, conflicts surrounding the economic consequences of technology transfer are—as in the jobs issue discussed in Chapter 14—a problem for MNEs as a group. Rarely is an individual firm singled out as a particularly troublesome exporter of technology. The counter-argument has to be made in terms of the return-flows of benefits to the home country and the "alternative scenario" of imitation and technological diffusion that could have occurred even without the existence of the MNE. At the same time, the flexibility to apply various technologies internationally in ways most appropriate to the firm is critical to management's objectives. And so, in terms of our conflict management model, such conflicts clearly call for uncooperative behavior, with little justification or need for compromise on the part of management in justifying its actions to home-country policymakers.

TECHNOLOGY ADAPTATION

From a host-country point of view, imported technology can be a bane as well as a boon. To be sure, process-related technology infusions can increase the degree of efficiency with which productive factors are employed, and hence raise the capacity of an economy to produce output and generate income. But they also can affect the *proportions* of resources used in the productive process. They are "resource-saving," by reducing the amount of raw materials, energy, labor, or capital needed to produce a given level of output. With rare exceptions, materials- and energy-saving technologies could be considered beneficial unless the one requires greatly increased amounts of the other, or if the new technologies are particularly pollutive or otherwise socially disruptive.

On the other hand, there is considerable scope for conflict concerning the relative shifts in the use of labor and capital brought about by new production technology. Process innovation may either be "neutral" (saving the same relative amounts of capital and labor), or it may be labor-saving or capital-saving. Much process-related technological advance in the industrial countries has been labor-saving in nature, simply because labor has been the expensive factor of production, and continued upward pressure on wages has both stimulated this type of technological progress and guaranteed that labor would receive an appropriate share of the dividends. Labor-saving technologies have not only dominated production processes, but have also caused products to be designed for easier labor-saving manufacture, and they have influenced quality control procedures and related support services.

Few problems arise when labor-saving production technologies are transferred between industrial countries faced with the same general productive-factor scarcities. Among other things, the MNE may contribute to general capital-intensive production worldwide by insisting on uniform global product quality which is not necessarily the best available, but rather is viewed as consistently "reliable." A labor-saving innovation is ultimately as welcome in France, Germany, or Japan as it is in the United States, although the institutional ways of "digesting" it may vary from one country to the next and be subject to different degrees of conflict. This is not true, however, for transfer of labor-saving technologies to the developing countries, where mass unemployment and underemployment generally constitute the number-one economic and social problem.

Multinationals have frequently been accused of transferring "inappropriate" technology to the developing countries. "Appropriateness" in product technology may be defined in terms of the ease with which a product can be manufactured with labor-intensive techniques. Or the extent to which it is "luxurious" beyond the needs of the host society, as opposed to the simple "essentials" at substantially lower cost.

If a given product is produced capital-intensively at home, the MNE tends to build a capital-intensive plant abroad using state-of-the-art technology that it knows how to work with and that will produce products of acceptable and uniform quality. What this means in a developing-country context is that the project adds relatively few jobs, thus contributing little to the employment problem, but uses up plenty of capital—which is in scarce supply locally and which the host country will have to service in terms of returns on the investment and making available the necessary scarce foreign exchange for repatriation of profits, fees, and other charges. Even worse, if the firm's products are better or its costs lower, MNE production will gain in market share relative to local firms, which may well be supplying competitive products in more labor-intensive ways. If this happens, then the MNC technological infusion actually can make the unemployment problem worse, by causing layoffs in (labor-intensive) competing firms that exceed the absorption of workers by its own (capital-intensive) production.

The available evidence suggests that some part of technology transfer by MNEs to the developing countries undoubtedly has this effect. One study notes that firms do not adapt technology in developing countries because the gains are so small—due to imperfect competition in both factor and product markets—and because manufacturing costs may be small relative to the value of the final product. So their use of productive factors ends up differing relatively little from locally-owned firms subject to the same kinds of forces.[17]

In any case, technology adaptation to local conditions is easier said than done. One reason for non-adaptation of technology may simply be familiarity with tried and true methods. Even when adaptation is justified by the economics of the case, the firm employs the same techniques as it does elsewhere, with perhaps some bias toward the newest technologies available. Lack of local competitive pressure—perhaps due to protection against imports—may also justify such economic irrationality. Moreover, even under local conditions it may not be cheaper to produce labor-intensively. Despite the fact that developing-country labor is cheap, it may be very expensive to use in production because of low productivity, thus justifying labor-saving technologies. And labor-intensive technologies may require complementary inputs, like extra raw materials to compensate for waste, which may be in scarce supply locally. There is also the point that substantial amounts of research and development may be required to make the established technology more labor-intensive, and the returns on that incremental R&D may be small, zero, or even negative. In adapting production technology to local conditions, product uniformity and quality may be difficult or impossible to maintain as well.

At the limit, production technology may not be adaptable at all—for example, there are no apparent technologies for extruding synthetic fibers labor-intensively—that is, the labor and capital proportions for some types of technology are effectively "locked in," with little or no scope for substituting one for the other. Several studies have noted that production of powders, liquids, and other nondurables tend to be less technology-adaptable than durables, and that complex, large-size, and very precise tasks are likewise less suitable to labor-intensity.[18] The best that can be done in such cases is to undertake ancillary activities like materials-handling, packaging, shipping, and various accounting and administrative tasks in more labor-intensive ways than would be true in the MNE's home country.

"Inappropriate" technology has become a hot political issue in various developing countries and particularly in international organizations like the United Nations, where bureaucrats are sufficiently far removed from the realities of production technology to view the issue in the abstract. Yet despite the spotty record of adapting production technology to developing-country conditions there is little evidence that MNEs have performed any worse in this respect than locally-owned firms. As noted, for MNE management the degrees of freedom are limited. Where possible, some labor-capital substitution can often be undertaken in the production process itself, especially with a certain amount of additional R&D, at a cost which may be less than the cost of conflict that could otherwise result. For example, Ford Motor was found to use more inspectors, single-hand as opposed to multiple-hand wrenches, and generally older technology in some developing-country operations than in advanced-country plants.[19] On the other hand, attempts to achieve technology adaptation by purposely introducing obsolescent capital equipment requiring more labor—to service the machines and/or to maintain them—have led to even more acrimonious conflict with local officials wanting only the newest and best technologies. But peripheral activities do lend themselves to easier adaptation, as noted, often without significant sacrifice in operating performance or product quality. Here, then, is a case where a certain degree of *compromise* or even *accommodation* in MNE conflict management seems possible and perhaps even desirable from the standpoint of the firm's own interests.

Techniques of successful technology adaptation, uncovered by a study of foreign pharmaceutical firms in India, include importing foreign managers or sending local managers abroad for intensive training, adequate compensation of foreign nationals, great care in selecting foreign personnel, providing local managers with key positions, granting considerable autonomy to local affiliates, and accepting local ownership on a joint venture basis.[20]

To try to encourage this, many developing country planners have proposed the creation of uniquely suited technologies of their own, particularly through national and regional research and development centers that would work on innovations designed specifically to meet local needs. The rationale is also to reduce the economic and balance of payments cost of imported technology, discussed in the next chapter. And there is a point that labor-intensive (capital-saving) technologies simply do not have significant markets in the advanced countries, and so there is little incentive for MNEs to direct research and development effort toward the kinds of technologies especially suited to conditions of economic backwardness. Hence there are felt to be substantial benefits to be derived from technological exchanges among developing countries themselves, and between them and labor-abundant command-type economies like the People's Republic of China. Whether such ventures are doomed to re-invent the wheel, or produce substitutive technologies at far higher costs than would have to be paid for imported MNE technology remains to be seen. Still, the fact that the developing countries are even considering such potentially high-risk, high-cost ventures testifies to the importance they attach to the effects of technology on their particular social and economic needs.

The "appropriateness" of technology applies to products as well as processes. Cases of successful product adaptation to developing-country conditions that have been cited include a low-cost communications system by Northrup, a small tractor by Ford, and special drugs for tropical diseases by Pfizer.[21] On the other side of the coin is the infant-formula case involving Nestlé and other food-products MNEs that has already been discussed in Chapter 10. New product technologies involving radio, television, motorcycles, drugs, and myriad others have sometimes had profound effects on the economies and societies of developing countries. Again the demand is for "appropriate" technologies, and for products embodying those technologies. So MNEs are frequently called to account for product-related technological mismatches. Yet who is to decide what is "appropriate?" And extensive product adaptation may not be justified by the smallness of the market.

MNEs are guided by market demand—individuals willing and able to pay the price for new-product technologies. If an alternative arrangement other than the market is to decide "what" is to be produced, then it is up to the local political system to implement such an arrangement by prohibiting or taxing production and imports, discouraging consumption, and so on—running the risk, of course, of smuggling, illicit production, and other products of human ingenuity. Or joint ventures can be attempted to assure products that meet local needs. In one such experiment, General Motors agreed to design and build a 100,000 annual capacity truck plant in Poland, including training of Polish production workers and managers, under a joint venture with Polmot, the state automotive enterprise. GM shares design and engineering technology, and thus supplies the entire MNE "package," in return for 15,000 trucks per year marketed under the GM label abroad.

Even when product adaptation is undertaken, there may be major problems. For example, "appropriate" motor vehicles for developing countries should be simple, reliable, rugged, fuel-efficient, easy to maintain and manufacture with low skills, and inexpensive. On the basis of this perfectly rational view, "basic transportation vehicles" like the Ford Fiera were designed and put into production in developing countries by various automotive MNEs. Yet often the results proved less useful than expected—for example, because of the practice in developing countries of paying no attention whatsoever to vehicle load limits when piling on people and goods. In many cases, a conventional American style pick-up truck would have done the job better and, in the long run, more cheaply.

On the other hand, there are sometimes major markets to be opened up through technology adaptation. General Electric, for example, sold several small, compact, steam-generating power plants to Jamaica, Trinidad, and other developing countries—far better suited to their needs than conventionally-sized plants.[22]

In general, aside from the kind of sensitivity to consumer interests discussed earlier, it seems to us that MNE management of conflict related to product technology calls for relatively straightforward competitive or avoidant behavior with some willingness to compromise or accommodate in the labor-capital substitution area where this can be achieved within reasonable cost and quality limits.

TECHNOLOGICAL DEPENDENCE

We have already noted the concern of host countries about "technological dependence," again with particular reference to the developing nations. The allegation is that MNEs do their research and development at home, something that appears to be quite true. Such concentration of research and development activities is of serious concern to the developing countries—with an estimated share of global R & D expenditures by MNEs of only around 1%. This means that any new technologies are apt to arise in the MNE home countries or other advanced nations and exported under proprietary conditions, with developing host countries locked into a position of permanent import-dependence for technology.

Furthermore, the fact that technology is imported with virtually no local R&D by MNEs means that employment opportunities for research-oriented graduates of local universities and technical schools may be extremely restricted. They are thus encouraged either to emigrate directly or to be shifted to research-oriented activities abroad within the personnel structures and manning needs of the MNEs themselves. This induced "brain drain" is viewed as detrimental to long-term growth and economic viability.

Another thing the developing host countries lose is the external spinoffs from active domestic R&D programs. This includes the kinds of interactions between research shops and their technological environments, mentioned earlier, and ultimately a self-sustaining research community that will serve as an ongoing support function to the economy as a whole. Europeans complained about this sort of phenomenon—a wide and growing technology "gap" with the United States coupled to a troublesome brain drain—for years in the 1960s and early 1970s. But eventually things changed. The United States grew disenchanted with major technological feats like the space program and skeptical about technological progress in general. Additional blame for a slowdown in American technical progress is placed on a no-risk, super-cautious attitude on the part of management and society in general. According to one survey ". . . from boardroom to research lab, there is a growing sense that something has happened to American innovation. Some say it is in rapid decline. Others claim it is taking new forms. Either way, the country's genius for innovation is not what it used to be."[23] Indeed, United States spending on R&D has declined dramatically—from 1953 to 1961 it increased at an average annual rate of 13.9% (adjusted for inflation) for government and 7.7% for nongovernment. For the period 1961–1967 these annual growth figures were 5.6% and 7.4% respectively, and from 1967–1975 they sank to 3% and 1.8%, according to National Science Foundation statistics. European economic growth and the prosperity of European firms, meanwhile, permitted the kinds of large-scale, well-equipped research complexes and remuneration levels needed to keep scientists and technicians at home.

So the issue has largely died down in Europe and certainly in Japan, but it remains more alive than ever with respect to the developing countries. The ability of even the most advanced among them—like Mexico, Brazil, Hong

Kong, Taiwan, and South Korea—to develop a broad R&D base in the foreseeable future appears very slim indeed. In 1973, only 1% of all patents and 14.5% of all trademarks were held by developing-country residents, with with a comparable percentage of the R&D activities of multinational firms undertaken there.[24]

Despite the difficulties, arguments for maintaining overseas R&D commitments by MNEs include (1) more effective commercialization of products in the local environment, (2) more effective adaptation of production techniques, design and technical service facilities, (3) lower cost of recruiting and equipping foreign researchers, (4) possibility of preemptive use of local R&D talent by competitors, (5) access to government contracts, where technological independence in defense-related areas is a concern, (6) some nations are better at some kinds of R&D than others, and so there is a case to be made for specialization in research internationally, and (7) the size of cultural and social gaps between countries, requiring at least an R&D listening post.

Arguments for R&D *centralization,* on the other hand, include (1) economies of scale and "critical mass", (2) avoidance of duplication of effort, (3) absence of need for offshore R&D as long as listening posts can be maintained and foreign researchers can be brought to the central research facility, (4) absence of a scientific and technical infrastructure abroad, (5) absence of skilled manpower and/or scientific equipment, (6) problems of co-opting scarce local technical talent in the face of equal needs by local firms and public agencies, and (7) closed-mouthedness of many foreign scientific communities, relative to those at home.[25]

From a managerial point of view relatively little can be done, because of the peculiar economics and logistics of R&D operations just mentioned, and because of the thin technological manpower base and "knowledge industry" that will realistically take decades or generations to develop in poor countries. Yet because of the validity of the complaint and the seriousness of the problem a policy of *collaboration* or *accommodation* clearly seems desirable and is in the long-term self-interest of the firm. The question is how this can be brought about. One possibility is increased adaptation-oriented research and development at the local level with respect to both products and processes. Aside from possible efficiencies and market gains, this has the potential of killing two birds with one stone—stimulating local R&D activity and improved adaptation of products and processes to developing-country conditions. And it would ease the chronic net balance of payments burden the developing countries ascribe to technology imports by potentially cutting these back somewhat and possibly permitting the export of new products particularly to other developing countries.

Beyond that, in a few developing nations a considerable supply of (often underemployed) scientific and technical manpower exists. ITT has established research efforts in Mexico, and Pfizer has done so in Brazil and Kenya. India is perhaps the most outstanding example. It would appear that MNE "captive" think tanks involved in basic research might operate cost-effectively here, with the results of that research and its further development downstream into marketable products and processes carried out in the MNE home country. Under the right conditions, the results could indeed be mutually beneficial, and contribute to a more efficient global allocation of R&D activity.

TECHNOLOGY PRICING

One of the most serious conflicts between MNEs and host countries in the sphere of technology involves pricing. We have seen that technology is the product of investment in research and development, and investment that must be amortized—costed out and built into the price of the goods and services it helps to produce. As a result, there is frequently a wide margin between the direct manufacturing cost of high-technology products and their market price. The "price" of MNE technology may be difficult or impossible to identify in the first place, since it is often built into other aspects of a complex product or project.

Gross profit on technology covers both R&D amortization, a return on the firm's willingness to accept risk, and an element of pure profit. High-technology firms consistently point to the need for the cash flows from high gross cost-price margins to provide the resources needed to underwrite new research and development efforts. And a healthy net profit is needed to attract further debt and equity capital into the firm. What appears exorbitant to outsiders appears eminently reasonable to management, for in its absence both the firm itself and society at large would be worse off. In any case, a monopoly return made possible by the proprietary nature of technology is part of the system.

It does seem to be true that charges for technology are often not particularly well related to the value of that technology. Often rules of thumb are used with no specific relation to the technology actually in question. Some technology is supplied free. In other cases no systems at all are used to price technology, and returns are assumed to be embodied in the overall profit rate. Sometimes shipments of intermediates from the parent to the affiliate incorporate the price of the technology.

Argument about the "appropriate" size of the cost-price margin is a permanent feature of corporate external conflict in many high-technology industries. What price is appropriate for a life-saving drug that a sick person would move heaven and earth to obtain? What is appropriate when a large share of its sales is to national health insurance plans where government is the sole buyer? Often there are economic answers and political answers, with wide gaps in between. The need for judgment and bargaining is ubiquitous.

In the bargaining process, the developing country "will be in a better position if (1) it has a large and growing economy, (2) it knows the terms of agreements made by the MNC in other countries, (3) it understands the benefits and costs to the MNC of the sale of this technology, and (4) it investigates other alternatives that it may have open."[26]

Beyond such general technology pricing issues, the developing countries maintain that MNEs systematically overcharge them for the technology they purvey. Their argument rests on equity grounds—that the limited ability to pay of developing countries should entitle them to a lower price for technology than that charged to buyers in advanced countries. Research and development costs ought to be recaptured in the advanced countries and not in the developing world. The question is whether "need creates entitlement" in technology pricing. Certainly the firm itself is in a poor position to make this decision.

Restrictive business practices may also serve to inflate the cost of imported technology if the affiliate is forbidden to exploit its full market potential—for example, by not being permitted to export—thus raising the effective cost of technology per unit of output. Table 13–1 lists the kinds of limitations that an UNCTAD survey identified as being of major concern to developing countries regarding the transfer of technology. Restrictive business practices in the field of technology include prevention of exports produced under license, prevention of trademarked imports, "field of use" restrictions limiting application of licensed technology, prevention of licensees from acquiring competing technologies, "tied" procurement of raw materials from the licensing firm, and "grant-back" clauses requiring licensees to supply to the licensor without cost any improvements to the technology it has undertaken.

Some developing and developed host countries have themselves acted to reduce gross returns on technology to MNEs. Price ceilings on drugs, for example, put the firm in a quandary. On the one hand, it is clearly failing to recover a pro rata share of R&D costs and profits from such sales. On the other hand, is it good business to forego sales when the ceiling price is still well in excess of direct manufacturing costs? Depending on the actual level of the permissible price, many firms would be sorely tempted to proceed with production and marketing under such conditions. And so the conflict becomes a matter of bilateral pressure, with the host country anxious to obtain the technology as cheaply as possible (preferably free) and the firm having to make a decision on its reservation price and then stick to it.

A different approach—theft of intellectual property—is illustrated in the area of copyrights by Taiwan's long-time refusal to sign the Universal Copyright Convention. Taiwanese publishers have printed thousands of titles in recent years—including encyclopedias, textbooks, and even a Boeing 707 flight manual.[27] They and other book pirates in South Korea, Iran, and Pakistan thus expropriate intellectual property with apparent impunity.

The same kind of conflict over the equity of technology pricing in developing countries arises in other areas as well, but in a vastly more complex form. We have emphasized the importance of the MNE "package" of capital, labor, technology, marketing, and management as bearing the essence of the firm's contribution in a host-country setting and the critical role of "useful knowledge," as defined here, in that package. The price charged by the MNE for the package, after subtracting an appropriate return for the use of finance capital under conditions of risk, is in essence the price it charges for technology—a price that is paid in a variety of different ways as we have seen. Moreover, access to that technology is continuous. In fields where technical progress is rapid, products and processes as well as managerial practices tend to be updated on a regular basis. Again the question is what a "fair" price for this technology really is under conditions of economic underdevelopment. Countries increasingly understand that "free" is not the answer, and attempts to force the issue by expropriation and nationalization have frequently led to technical and managerial obsolescence in a surprisingly short period of time. Meanwhile, the MNE's reservation price is difficult to determine even for corporate management itself. How much impairment of earnings through host-government actions is it willing or able to stand before throwing in the towel and calling it quits? And if it does pull up stakes, how much impairment of host-country interests is likely to result both in

Table 13-1 *Pattern of Limitations on Access to Technology by Developing Countries*

Type of limitation	Replies as to whether the country faced the specified limitation	
	Yes	*No*
1. Tied purchases of imported inputs, equipment, and spare parts	Argentina, Chile, Cyprus, Ecuador, Greece, Iran, Malta, Mexico, Nigeria, Pakistan, Peru, Sri Lanka, Turkey	Rep. of Korea
2. Restriction of exports (total prohibition, partial limitation, geographical constraint)	Argentina, Chile, Cyprus, Ecuador, Greece, Iran, Malta, Mexico, Nigeria, Pakistan, Peru, Sri Lanka, Turkey	Singapore
3. Requirement of guarantees against changes in taxes, tariffs, and exchange rates affecting profits, royalties and remittances	Cyprus, Nigeria, Turkey	Greece, Iran, Malta, Mexico, Singapore
4. Limitation of competing supplies by: (i) restriction of competing imports	Cyprus, Greece, Mexico, Nigeria, Peru	Iran, Rep. of Korea, Malta, Pakistan, Singapore, Turkey
(ii) preventing competition for local resources	Greece, Malta, Mexico	Iran, Rep. of Korea, Nigeria, Pakistan, Singapore
(iii) obtaining local patents	Ecuador, Malta, Nigeria	Greece, Iran, Singapore
5. Constraints limiting the dynamic effects of the transfer: (i) excessive use of expatriate personnel	Argentina, Malta, Mexico, Nigeria, Peru, Turkey	Singapore
(ii) discouragement of the development of local technical and R&D capabilities	Argentina, Ecuador, Greece, Malta, Mexico, Nigeria, Turkey	

Source: UNCTAD, *Major Issues Arising from the Transfer of Technology to Developing Countries* (New York: UNCTAD document TD/B/AC.11/10/Rev. 1, 1974), p. 19.

the short run and over the long term? The answers to these questions will determine the bargaining leverage of the two sides, and will ultimately determine the outcome on technology pricing.

Partly because of their lack of leverage, the developing countries have demanded a revision of the international patent system. They also want a legally binding code of conduct for "fair" prices and terms for technology transfer—greater disclosure, guarantees of "complete" technology, limits on royalty payments, time limits on licensing argreements, "preferential" treatment for developing countries, and outlawing restrictive business practices. Moreover, they want economic assistance in developing their own R&D programs, particularly for technological adaptation, and greater exchanges of technical information outside the framework of the MNE. Critics of the developing countries' position point out that tough controls would simply drive firms away, and possibly induce them to raise prices even further because of the increased risk. And there are clearly differences between such sweeping demands and the "druthers" of individual developing countries like Singapore, which are perfectly happy to continue doing business under existing conditions.

The issue of technology pricing thus essentially boils down to the pricing of MNE services themselves. If that pricing took place in an open market it would be a straightforward question of supply and demand. But it does not, as we have seen. So the problem enters the realm of nonmarket conflict, beset by a wide variety of economic and political complexities. In our view management's behavior ought to be essentially *competitive* in a tough bargaining context. It must be prepared to give way under pressure within that context, to *compromise*. But it cannot *avoid* the problem, nor are its interests generally served by *collaborative* or *accommodating* behavior.

BARRIERS TO TECHNOLOGY TRANSFER

As an institution whose very existence depends on international transmission of useful knowledge, and as the most important single conduit for international technology flows, it follows that the MNE is extraordinarily sensitive to governmental measures that interfere in this process. Fortunately for the multinational firm, international flows of useful knowledge do not lend themselves very well to external control—certainly less well than international flows of trade and finance. In large part, this is simply due to the variety of forms technology transfer can take, and to the complexity and alternatives available in the transmission mechanisms themselves.

Nevertheless, attempts are made periodically for economic or political reasons to restrict technology transfer. We have already mentioned the interest of organized labor in the United States in restricting technology outflow in order to save jobs. Indeed, the proposed Hartke-Burke legislation of the early 1970s contained provisions for just such restrictions in the form of a so-called Office of Technology Transfer, intended to monitor and control exports of useful knowledge. This would have required permits for licensing production abroad, and regular assessments of the economic effects of technology transfer. Whether such an agency would have had much effect remains an open question, as does the possible reaction of other countries to a United States initiative in this direction.

The principal case of home-country restrictions on technology transfer has been motivated by political and military considerations in dealings with Communist countries—see Chapter 7. Technology embodied in products has been controlled both unilaterally by the United States through an export license scheme administered by the Office of Export Control of the Department of Commerce, and multilaterally in the form of the Consultative Committee on East-West Trade (COCOM) under NATO, which maintains a "negative list" of sensitive products. The force of unilateral American technological restrictions on

East-West trade has weakened in recent years as an increasing number of western industrialized countries have developed sophistication in advanced technologies. At the technological frontiers in such industries as electronic data processing, however, unilateral United States restraints remain effective. We have seen how, in mid-1977, the federal government blocked the sale of a $13 million Cyber 76 computer to the Soviet Union, ostensibly to be used for weather forecasting, by the Control Data Corporation. Earlier Soviet emulation of the IBM 360 series computers indicated a significant lag in Soviet technology for both defense and civilian purposes, and provided a national security justification for a continued ban on advanced technology transfers in this field.

Outright military technology sales have also been subject to government control, despite the desire of large defense contractors to exploit promising export markets. Besides the proliferation of advanced military equipment, what concerns governmental policymakers is the ability of recipient countries to assimilate new technologies. If they cannot, as occured in Iran, for example, it may require a large contingent of support personnel for extended periods of time, raising a variety of potential political problems. And there is the problem of technological leakage resulting from lax host-country security systems. Again in 1977, the United States Administration refused to sell Iran its sophisticated AWACS airborne mission control system, partly for fear that one such aircraft might fall into enemy hands and severely compromise American national defense interests—the wisdom of the decision became evident with the overthrow of the Shah less than two years later.

But experience shows how hard it is to control the flow even of highly sensitive technology unless there is basic agreement among all supplier countries on the issues in question. Nobody has a monopoly on brains, or on the ability to expend resources for the creation of new knowledge. So sooner or later there will always be alternatives. But in this sensitive area MNE managers caught in the middle of political conflict have typically found it necessary to *accommodate* to home government demands—and thus to simultaneously be uncooperative with regard to host nation interests.

THE NUCLEAR TECHNOLOGY IMBROGLIO

Perhaps in no other area of international technology transfer have economic interests clashed so violently with political interests as in the nuclear field, where multinationals are caught squarely in the middle. At stake was an enormous market for nuclear power reactors in all parts of the world, a market whose growth prospects became even more buoyant as a result of the oil crisis of the mid-1970s and the growing scarcity of fossil fuels. And the nuclear industry is a high-technology one, which makes it attractive to both the supplier countries in terms of their future technological competitiveness and leadership, and to the recipient countries in terms of their own technological objectives. Also at stake, however, are the consequences of nuclear proliferation—which are closely associated with the availability of plutonium from reprocessed reactor wastes and development of fast breeder reactors—the consequences of which could be horrendous. To these are added concerns about the safety of nuclear reactors themselves and environmental worries about their direct ecological effects and indirect problems of nuclear waste disposal. The conflicting economic, environmental, safety, and geopolitical interests have been locked in battle for well over a decade, and the end is nowhere in sight. Extremely long gestation periods and serious technical and scientific uncertainties mean that decisions taken now have largely unknown consequences for the future. Given the stakes, the result has been a debate characterized more by heat than light even at the highest policy levels. Much of the debate has focused on Brazil.

In the early 1970s Brazil was beset by energy worries. Its extensive hydroelectric capabilities were deemed inadequate, and are located far from the main population and industrial centers. Domestic fossil fuels were lacking, and the 1973 oil crisis had a major adverse impact on the country. So Brazil turned decisively to the nuclear option—"promoting an articulated utilization of the country's water resources with nuclear energy," implemented "in the medium term by complementing hydroelectric stations with nucleoelectric ones, and in the longer run (the 1990's) by utilizing nuclear energy in an increasingly preponderant manner."[28] The Brazilian government decided on light water/enriched uranium reactors, and in 1972 Westinghouse was chosen to supply the first unit, Angra 1, with a capacity of 600,000 kw. At the time, the United States was the exclusive possessor of uranium enrichment capacity for reactor fuel and dominated the nuclear technology export market, with two-thirds of all international sales of atomic power plants in 1974.

The Export-Import Bank played an important role in financing American nuclear power plant sales abroad, and government people even participated in sales negotiations—as a German newspaper put it: "No matter where a plant is being planned, American diplomats agitate as if they were employees of the American firms."[29] So the fact that Brazil turned to the United States for its first nuclear power reactor seemed to be in that country's best interest, combining attractive contract terms with excellent technology and favorable delivery conditions.

But there were clouds on the horizon as well. Throughout the early 1970s growth in demand for enriched uranium fuel was rapid and closely related to burgeoning reactor sales. Yet American uranium enrichment capacity lagged seriously behind the demand expansion, and there was the prospect that future allocations of available supplies would have to be selective. There was also the distinct possibility that the United States enriched uranium monopoly could eventually be used to exert political pressure on recipient countries. In 1974 such fears seemed justified when the U.S. Atomic Energy Commission suspended the signing of new delivery contracts for future supplies of enriched uranium. The European Atomic Energy Community (Euratom) and other countries—including Brazil—were counting on these supplies and had even partially paid for them in advance. Another temporary American embargo in 1975 had a similar effect, alerting countries around the world to the implications of excessive external supply dependence for reactor fuel on the United States. In 1976 Canada imposed an uranium embargo on Euratom as well. And in April 1978 there was an embargo on American fuel shipments to Euratom as a result of a new United States nuclear export bill (see below), which required renegotiation of previous agreements governing nuclear sales abroad—enforcing stricter safeguards and greater control over final disposition of nuclear fuel. Such incidents appeared to show that reactor fuel supplies could easily be used to exert economic and political pressure on fuel-dependent countries.

Brazil had already been following a strategy of supplier diversification for many imported products in order not to rely too heavily on any one nation, as was the case in its nuclear relationship with the United States. The American suspension of new fuel supply orders in 1974 strengthened this conviction and added a new dimension: since Brazil was felt to have significant uranium deposits, it should attempt to obtain the enrichment technology that could eventually assure nuclear fuel self-sufficiency.

Meantime, the factors that had made the United States the world's most attractive nuclear power plant and fuel exporter underwent significant changes. Nuclear technology-transfer and diffusion occurred over a period of years, and countries like West Germany, France, and Canada not only absorbed American technology but developed their own and were eager to sell it. For example, Framatome of France and Kraftwerk Union of Germany (KWU)—affiliated with Siemens—both assimilated Westinghouse nuclear technology under licensing arrangements and went on to compete with United States firms. Against American competitors, Framatome soon won contracts for two 925 megawatt plants in Iran (later cancelled by the Iranian government in 1979) and two 925 megawatt plants in South Africa.[30] Because domestic orders during the mid-1970s were sluggish in most of these countries resulting from a combination of economic setbacks and public opposition, the reactor manufacturers concentrated on exports in an effort to absorb excess production capacity. Competition grew fierce for such markets as Brazil, Iran, and Mexico.

Besides Germany and France, Italy, Sweden, Japan, and Canada all began to compete in the world market. Britain had the capability, but remained inactive. The Soviet Union sold to members of the Eastern bloc. One observer noted in 1978 that "of the eight contracts signed on the international market during the last two years, the United States landed only one, a Westinghouse order from the Philippines that is now being reviewed by the Government and may yet be cancelled. GE has not closed a deal since 1974, although the company got a letter of intent last year from Spain for one reactor. Neither of the two other domestic manufacturers—Combustion Engineering and the Babcock & Wilcox Company—has ever won a foreign order."[31] In 1977 twelve new power reactors were ordered worldwide at a cost of about $1 billion each. None went to American manufacturers, with the principal losers being Westinghouse and General Electric. Westinghouse did, however, manage to land the first two 1978 reactor orders, from South Korea.

Although the United States continues to be the world's most important enriched uranium supplier, other countries are creating or expanding their uranium enrichment capacity. "Until recently, the United States was supplying some 95% of the enriched uranium used by EEC reactors. But now the Community has started to buy enriched uranium from the Soviet Union, which is less fussy about the terms. Almost half of the EEC's enriched uranium this year will come from the Soviet Union. . . .The Anglo-Dutch-German Urenco consortium is building two plants in Holland and Britain, and the French-Italian-Spanish-Belgian-Iranian consortium is building a plant in France. By next year, these plants should be able to supply 25% of the EEC's needs."[32] West Germany had also begun to make its own "jet-nozzle" enrichment technology available to countries like Brazil and South Africa, locations of uranium ore deposits, in an attempt to eliminate the uncertainty of nuclear fuel availability for its own reactors by increasing the number of possible suppliers. The Soviet Union had also become an important supplier of enriched uranium to Western Europe.

In the United States, the long-standing export-oriented political alliance of nuclear manufacturers and government began to dissipate under the attack of antinuclear, environmentalist, and nonproliferation forces. "The time required for licensing began to stretch out longer and longer. The increased scope and complexity of government regulation not only slowed down the official licensing process, but also provided additional opportunity for opponents of nuclear energy to obstruct and delay."[33]

In a 1975 speech, Senator Abraham Ribicoff summarized the situation as follows:

> Hard economic times and the high price of oil have combined to establish a desperate need to sell and a desperate need to buy nuclear power reactors. Nothing less than balanced international payments and energy self-sufficiency are at stake. The resulting cutthroat nuclear competition is leading to the spread of plutonium reprocessing and uranium enrichment facilities. The capability to produce nuclear explosives is spreading "like a plague" in the words of the Inspector General of the International Atomic Energy Agency, who is responsible for detecting the diversion of peaceful nuclear materials to weapons development. . . .In truth, the United States must assume a major share of the responsibility for the present nuclear proliferation problem. We pioneered the civilian nuclear power technology, made it available to other nations through our Atoms for Peace program, and still clearly dominate the worldwide nuclear power industry. Closer attention should have been given to safeguards over the years, particularly to safeguards conditions on the re-exports of U.S. nuclear technology by nations like France and West Germany.[34]

In April 1977 the Carter Administration deferred indefinitely the construction of spent-fuel reprocessing units and the fast breeder reactor, a move intended to establish compatibility between American foreign policy on avoiding nuclear weapons proliferation and controlled development of the domestic nuclear industry.

> Fast breeders are advanced nuclear reactors that convert uranium into plutonium and produce more plutonium than they burn. While the Soviet Union, France, Japan, and other nations are pressing ahead with breeder technology, President Carter has insisted on a restructuring of the American breeder program to eliminate, bypass, or delay the commercial use of plutonium. . . .Plutonium, a man-made element, can be used to manufacture nuclear weapons. Opponents of a 'plutonium economy' fear that commercial use of the toxic and dangerous substance would lead to a spread of nuclear armaments and cause extremely long-lasting environmental hazards.[35]

In 1977 President Carter also offered to buy and store spent reactor fuel from United States and foreign sources if the latter agreed to forego reprocessing.

Also of major concern to the American government were security lapses in the shipment of nuclear materials between countries, export of laser technology that could make possible extraction of bomb-grade material from low-grade uranium, material losses in normal use that are unaccounted for in audits, and administrative inadequacies in the machinery of the International Atomic Energy Agency (IAEA).[36]

Besides suspending or slowing American progress on the fast breeder reactor and fuel reprocessing, the Carter Administration also prohibited American firms from exporting "sensitive technology"—spent-fuel reprocessing and uranium enrichment techniques. With regard to nuclear exports financed by the Eximbank, "since 1974, the bank has had to allow Congress to review, and even to veto, all such exports . . . Congressman Clarence C. Long introduced legislation barring the bank from financing any nuclear exports at all."[37] In short, economic interests were suppressed in favor of political interests.

Another significant development was the U.S. Nuclear Antiproliferation Act, proposed in 1977 and passed by the House and the Senate in 1978, which laid out much stricter rules for granting export licenses. It tied export policy to the domestic decision of deferring nuclear fuel reprocessing. The six basic criteria contained in the bill refer to the importing country's willingness to: (1) Place all United States-source materials under international safeguards; (2) Refrain from using United States-source materials or technology to build a nuclear explosive device, peaceful or not; (3) Keep United States-source materials protected from theft or terrorism; (4) Give the United States a veto of the re-export of United States-source material; (5) Give the United States a veto over plans to reprocess United States-origin spent fuel; and (6) Apply these same conditions to any other materials produced using United States-source technology.[38]

The Act was not well received abroad.

> All governments in possession of U.S.-supplied enriched uranium must now obtain Washington's permission in advance if the uranium is to be sent anywhere for reprocessing. Moreover, the non-proliferation law is retroactive and can apply to thousands of tons of enriched uranium that the U.S. has shipped abroad to old and trusted customers in the past. Twenty-six agreements with other countries can be called back for renegotiation—and the U.S. could cut off all further nuclear supplies if the recipient governments are unwilling to accept the new American controls. . . . With considerable justification, they complain that instead of seeking to build or improve on the existing machinery, the Carter Administration promulgated a policy that lumps everybody together as potential cheaters and seems to regard the world as ruled by a bunch of Idi Amins.[39]

In April 1978 the United States embargoed deliveries of enriched uranium to the EEC because the latter did not agree to meet the new American non-proliferation safeguards, that is, that no uranium should be reprocessed without permission from the United States. This affected about half the uranium used in the EEC. All member countries except France agreed to renegotiate the supply contracts. The fundamental difference of view was that the Carter Administration wanted to avoid nuclear fuel reprocessing because of the resulting production of plutonium, while the Europeans felt it better to reprocess than to store the spent fuel indefinitely.[40] However, renegotiation of the agreement did in fact begin in July of 1978.

As the American government forced retrenchment, the Europeans continued to offer prospective buyers competitive technologies, and the governments of

France and West Germany showed no signs whatsoever of following the American lead. Indeed, things moved the other way:

> Governments have clearly subsidized domestic and international power sales of their vendors by means of no-interest or low-interest loans, loan guarantees, absorption of research and development costs, preferential access to and pricing of fuels and reprocessing services, etc. . . . The German government, for example, underwrote the success of a Siemens sale to Argentina by giving the Argentine government a five year no-interest loan, and balance-of-payments considerations. France managed to sell a reactor unit in Spain in return for loans covering 90 percent of its cost and agreeing to represent Spanish interests in the Common Market.[41]

And as one observer noted:

> Europeans and Japanese may be our best friends in the world; they are also our major industrial rivals. The commercial stakes involved in nuclear technology are enormous. Europeans will not willingly leave themselves dependent upon America for nuclear technology or fuel, especially with Congress demonstrating how easy it is to tear up long-standing commitments. We do have a common interest with Europe in preventing proliferation to unstable parts of the world, but we only obscure that interest by seeming to link non-proliferation to industrial subordination. The net result, many in Europe believe, is a strong boost to European independence—not quite, presumably, what the Administration had in mind.[42]

In view of the events, it is hardly surprising that Brazil's desire for supplier-diversification and nuclear self-sufficiency, through the purchase of the complete fuel cycle, complemented Germany's interest in penetrating nuclear export markets. The temporary American nuclear fuel supply interruption of 1974 and the emerging obstructionist United States policy on nuclear exports were important factors in negotiations between Brazil and Germany and the eventual completion of the deal in June 1975 covering: (1) Uranium exploration of 73,000 square kilometers of Brazilian territory with guaranteed delivery of 20% of any ore found to Germany initially and increasing later on, the joint exploration company being 51% Brazilian-owned. (2) Construction of a pilot enrichment plant by 1981 in Germany and a full-scale one subsequently built in Brazil using Germany's experimental "jet-nozzle" technology. (3) Pilot and subsequent commercial fuel fabrication plants built in Brazil by the Germans but 70% Brazilian-owned. (4) Development of a 100% Brazilian-owned pilot nuclear fuel reprocessing plant under a technical assistance agreement with a German consortium. (5) Two 1300 megawatt pressurized water reactors (Angra 2 and 3) and options for six more by 1990, with construction and component manufacture increasingly taken over by Brazilian firms—70% by 1980 and 90% by 1990.[43]

The last two areas were the cause of great unhappiness for the American government because of the proliferation danger. But from Brazil's point of view they were essential. Still, "the centerpiece of the deal is the sale to Brazil of between two and eight giant reactors, together worth from $2 billion to $8 billion, that would accelerate her nuclear energy program toward the goals of

10,000 megawatts of electricity generating capacity of 1990 and of producing 41 percent of her total energy supply by 2010."[44]

Facing a major competitive reduction in nuclear exports, United States-based suppliers tried to pressure the federal government to change its views on reprocessing and uranium enrichment technology transfers. A Westinghouse spokesman declared before Congress: "The U.S. government is proposing to attach a permanent veto power over nuclear fuel processing in Iran, as a pre-condition for sale of U.S. nuclear reactors. Other vendors from Germany and France are already selling without such conditions. The result is obvious—the U.S. sold no reactors to Iran, despite an Iranian desire to buy a large number." (Not five years later, these same companies were thanking their lucky stars).[45] Indeed, a few weeks before the official signing of the agreement between West Germany and Brazil—and even as United States government officials were trying to torpedo the deal—the Bechtel Corporation sent a letter to the Brazilian Minister of Mines and Energy stating: "There has been a most recent decision by the Energy Research and Development Administration to encourage Uranium Enrichment Associates (UEA)° to seek potential sites for enrichment plants outside the U.S.A. One of the locations which is most promising is Brazil, with the abundant hydro potential in the Amazon Basin. Because of ERDA's support, UEA can offer Brazil the entire gamut from development of the mine, ore processing, enrichment, fuel processing, through the design of and construction of the nuclear power plants themselves."[46] Secretary of State Henry Kissinger quickly pressured Bechtel to withdraw the offer.

Certainly the United States position on nuclear energy has been eroded in recent years by events beyond its control, and the Brazilian deal with Germany was one of the symptoms. David Calleo wrote, in *The New York Times*:

> In an era of détente, when no one's security was seriously threatened, and of cheap oil, when nuclear energy seemed an expensive toy, our non-proliferation policy had a relatively easy time. . . . The oil crisis has radically changed the situation. Europeans fear a serious oil shortage by the 1990's, particularly as the American appetite grows unchecked. Hence, several European countries press forward in nuclear power, in programs that need 10 to 15 years lead time. . . . Our present policy toward nuclear proliferation springs from a certain "bipolar" model of how the world should be organized. In this view, only the United States and the Soviet Union should be nuclear powers, and their relations stabilized in détente. Our allies should be given confidence that we not only will protect them but also not take economic advantage of our protector's role. . . . Our present policy is still based on the bipolar model. It lumps together Valery Giscard d'Estaing, Helmut Schmidt, the Shah of Iran, the Palestine Liberation Organization, the Red Brigades, and Idi Amin. It causes us to treat the major European states like banana republics and further inflames their fears of commercial domination. As a consequence, it divides us from those countries that ought to be our closest allies, above all in preventing proliferation where it is really dangerous.[47]

°Uranium Enrichment Associates is a consortium organized by Bechtel for construction of uranium enrichment plants by private companies, previously a government monopoly.

Brazil has consistently viewed the nuclear Non-Proliferation Treaty (NPT) with considerable skepticism, and has refused to sign it despite continuous pressure to do so. In defense of their position Brazilian spokesmen frequently refer to the 1967 signing and later ratification of the Nuclear Arms Proscription in Latin America Treaty (NAPLAT)—which bans the manufacturing, testing, utilization, and storage of nuclear weapons throughout Latin America and provides that nuclear countries cannot use or threaten to use nuclear weapons against the signatory nations—"In order that the NAPLAT become effective, we depend, at the moment, on the nuclear powers' acceptance of such obligations."[48] The Brazilian stand was that it would be willing to participate in efforts seeking nuclear non-proliferation provided they involve commitments by both nuclear and non-nuclear states.

The NPT proposes to legitimize an unacceptable power distribution because it resulted from the stage of military nuclear technology application the states had reached at the time of its signing. As a consequence of this stratification, the treaty requires strict control, by the International Atomic Energy Agency, over the spread of peaceful utilization of the atom, while, with regard to militarily nuclear countries, it does not create any barriers to nuclear arms vertical proliferation, evidence being the continuous growth and development of their nuclear arsenals. In addition, as for the security aspect, the NPT does not provide for an effective protection system for the militarily non-nuclear countries.[49]

Whereas the NAPLAT is understood as "a non-armament treaty," with Latin American nations voluntarily renouncing nuclear weapons, the NPT is understood "to disarm the disarmed," in that it discourages proliferation among the non-nuclear countries but does nothing about proliferation among the nuclear nations.[50]

Ford Administration negotiators worked hard to induce the Germans to cancel their nuclear deal with Brazil. However, "while U.S. newspapers and politicians urged the Ford Administration to pressure Bonn into rescinding or modifying the Brazilian deal, Washington's negotiating position was severely undermined by its inability to offer other nations an alternate source of reactor fuel."[51] A major concern was the emergence of a nuclear rivalry between Brazil and Argentina, which has made considerable strides in nuclear technology over the past several decades. Perceiving that cancellation was not possible, the American negotiators suggested changes which were accepted by the two countries involved, and when the agreement between West Germany, Brazil, and the IAEA was signed it included much stricter controls and safeguards than any previous nuclear sale to any country that has refused to sign the Non-Proliferation Treaty. This did not prevent the Carter Administration from once again attacking the deal in 1977, this time putting pressure on both ends of the contract with official visits to both Brazil and Germany and seriously straining American relations with the two countries. It was met by a harsh reaction from Brazil, which accused the United States of intervening in its internal affairs, and a reiteration on the part of Germany that it had not violated international obligations and that, in fact, the modified agreement had been previously approved by the Ford Administration. The renewed *ex post facto* United States pressure was also greeted with widespread cynicism abroad, and (paradoxically) viewed as the expected reaction of a country that had just lost billions of dollars in exports: "U.S. objections to the nuclear deal were widely interpreted as reflecting the disappointment of American suppliers who had sought the contract."[52]

The Carter Administration then announced, after pressure to have the deal called off was obviously leading nowhere, that it would refuse to supply the nuclear fuel necessary to operate the German reactors in Brazil. This seemed the strongest leverage available after the negotiations had been successfully concluded. However, given the existence of alternative nuclear fuel supplies, American bargaining power was limited in this area as well—Urenco will guarantee uranium fuel for Brazil's second and third 1,200-megawatt nuclear power plants after obtaining safeguards from the Brazilians against the misuse of plutonium produced by the nuclear fuel cycle. Brazil indicated that it would agree to a system for storing nuclear wastes before the deliveries start in 1981.[53]

Although United States nuclear policy no longer called the shots and was powerless to prevent the Brazilians and Germans from pursuing their own interests, all problems were not over. By late 1978 the Brazilian nuclear program had encountered some major difficulties. The site for the one Westinghouse and two KWU power stations south of Rio de Janeiro had been selected without serious geological survey, and was showing critical stresses requiring extensive modifications of construction plans. Cooling system problems postponed startup of Angra 1 from 1976 to 1979. Civil engineering contracts on the project were let without competitive bidding, resulting in enormous cost overruns. There were unresolved questions about the effectiveness of the German "jet-nozzle" nuclear enrichment technology. And there were complaints about gaps in German willingness and ability to transfer critical know-how to Brazilians: "Scientists believe that Brazil will end up like a skillful mechanic that can change atomic car parts but has no idea how to make the engine."[54]

Safety problems continued to be raised as well, notably focusing on 71 fires at Angra 1 during a five-month period in 1977. These incidents touched off debate in Brazil about management of the nuclear energy program.

> The Brazilian fires also underscore charges made recently, first secretly, then publicly, by IAEA experts that third-world buyers often lack the experience and training they need to make responsible safety decisions . . . Developing nations, however, tend to see these new safety warnings as just another attempt by developed nations to tie strings to the nuclear technology they sell. They also maintain that any safety lapses they experience should be largely blamed on the advanced nations' technological secretiveness and not on their own shortcomings. . . . Had the rich nations fulfilled their obligation to share nuclear know-how fully and to properly train third world technicians, the nuclear safety issue would be moot.[55]

Uncertainty about the reliability of the United States as a fuel supplier had the expected reaction in other countries besides Brazil. In 1978 President Carter overruled the Nuclear Regulatory Commission, which refused to issue an export license for nuclear fuel after India exploded a nuclear device and banned international inspectors from its nuclear facilities. The export control law prohibits fuel shipments to all countries that do not permit inspection after 24 months unless the President or Congress makes an exception. In this case the President hopes that continued fuel shipment would prompt the Indians to accept international safeguards. Canada, which provided some of the materials used by India in bomb manufacture, ceased all shipments. For its part, India insisted that failure by the United States to deliver the fuel would constitute a breach of contract and would free India to pursue other options.[56] "Far from buckling under, [former Prime Minister] Desai has reacted to this threat by asking Indian scientists to press ahead with their experiments to produce a substitute for the enriched uranium from America. A new technology, now being tested at the reprocessing plant at Tarapur, involves fabricating fuel roads from a mixture of locally produced natural uranium plus plutonium extracted from spent fuel. If the spent fuel is taken from India's indigenously developed reactors, it would not be subject to American or Canadian safeguards."[57]

Another case in point is Japan, which has likewise decided to shift rapidly away from the American position and into breeder technology. A pilot reprocessing plant was built recently with French assistance, but enriched uranium supplies were cut off by the Carter Administration. A compromise was reached whereby some fuel was provided in order to encourage the Japanese to rethink the whole breeder issue. Instead, they moved in precisely the opposite direction and opted for the entire nuclear fuel cycle, contracting with both France and the United Kingdom for spent-fuel reprocessing in the 1980s and moving full speed ahead on their own reprocessing facilities for late in the decade. At the same time, they moved to diversify sources of enriched uranium away from the United States and toward new possibilities in Niger and Australia.[58] Australia, after protracted internal debate, had moved towards becoming a major supplier of uranium with a safeguard accord signed by Finland. Additional accords were under negotiation with the EEC, Japan, Iran, Sweden, Austria, and the Philippines. However, the Australian position on reprocessing was similar to that of the United States.[59]

Meantime, Combustion Engineering and Atomics International, a unit of Rockwell International, were negotiating with the French Atomic Energy Commission for licensing of breeder technology. It was clear that American policy in this area would stop technical progress domestically, and the two firms wanted to be in position to tap into the superior French know-how when and if the course of events made this feasible. General Electric and Westinghouse also joined the negotiations.[60]

At a 1977 Nuclear Suppliers Group meeting, American delegates sought to obtain agreement on restraints on future exports of nuclear technology. They failed miserably, and in the end considered themselves lucky to fend off a French attempt to disband the entire organization. However, at a January 1978 meeting of the Group agreement was reached on a new code which would allow them to continue selling nuclear power equipment but would still provide safeguards against its use in weapons production.[61]

There was also some concrete movement towards safeguards. In France's original package sale to Pakistan, the whole nuclear fuel cycle was covered, as it was in Germany's deal with Brazil. The so-called "sweeteners"—reprocessing and enrichment technologies—were included in both contracts. As noted, American firms could not offer such technologies but were pressing to do so in order to survive. The Carter Administration's position was that the United States would not reverse its export policy, but instead will pressure other countries to adhere to common nuclear export criteria. With regard to reprocessing technology, the two main competitors—France and Germany—announced their adherence, but nothing was decided on enrichment. "In December 1976, France announced that it would henceforth not export reprocessing plants, and Germany made a similar announcement in June 1977. So other than the arrangements with Pakistan and Brazil, there is now general supplier agreement about the undesirability of further transfers of reprocessing plants."[62]

According to one observer, however, President Carter's nuclear nonproliferation policy was clearly doomed to failure.

His big success in curbing the advance of high-technology nuclear activity in the interest of non-proliferation has been at home. He has cut back sharply on the development of the nation's first commercial fast-breeder power-reactor project at Clinch River, Tennessee, and cancelled the building of our only large-scale commercial nuclear-reprocessing plant at Barnwell, South Carolina. . . . The rest of the world, on the other hand, continues to move ahead in all three kinds of nuclear development that Carter set out to check: commercial reprocessing to extract plutonium from spent fuel rods, the development of plutonium-fed, fast-breeder nuclear-power reactors, and the proliferation of new facilities and processes for producing enriched uranium.[63]

The Carter offensive against nuclear power did initiate a comprehensive International Fuel Cycle Evaluation Study, with representatives from 52 countries attempting to find technical safeguards to prevent the weapons-proliferation phenomenon in the future. Scheduled for completion in late 1980, the study was evidently expected by the Carter Administration to point up the dangers inherent in the nuclear fuel cycle and to move France, Germany, and other suppliers toward the restrictive United States view. But the outcome could also go the other way. According to one observer, "The study will be called upon, among other things, to reply to the objections leveled against fuel reprocessing and breeder reactors which are considered by some to be both too hazardous from the standpoint of proliferation and not really justified in the economic sense. It will act as an honorary board of judges that could eventually, or so many of us think, rehabilitate these parts of the fuel cycle by demonstrating that they are capable of being protected against risks of proliferation and are also indispensable for the full-scale development of nuclear energy."[64] In any case, it will go far either to vindicate United States policies or to condemn them as a serious error with lasting economic and political consequences for the country.

SUMMARY

Technology, defined as "useful knowledge," is the very lifeblood of the multinational enterprise.[65] Without proprietary know-how, the MNE has little reason for existence. For this reason, in terms of our conflict management model, technology-related conflicts frequently involve high stakes for the firm, whether it is IBM, Coca-Cola, Westinghouse, or Sperry. Depending on the firm involved and its competitive position in the industry, the MNE's power may be high or low. Since loss of proprietary technology or an inadequate return on R&D may turn conflicts in this area into zero-sum games, interest interdependence is often negative and conflict management is biased toward the *competition-avoidance* axis of our model—the firm either fights like hell or chooses not to participate in arrangements that might compromise its source of technological strength.

This does not mean that there is no room for *compromise, collaboration* or *accommodation* in technology-related conflicts. Efforts by MNEs like General Electric, General Motors, and Philips to adapt technology specifically to host-country conditions, and by IBM to undertake R&D in a variety of host nations, shows that there is at least some room for maneuver in an area that is critical to the survival of the multinational enterprise. And given the emergence of trans-national political struggles over barriers to technology transfer—as typified in the nuclear imbroglio above—MNEs may increasingly find themselves playing third party intervention roles in the hope of orchestrating compromises between conflicting governments. Should such efforts fail, the companies will naturally be forced to simultaneously *accommodate* to the demands of one government, while *competing* with or *avoiding* those of the other.

14 *ECONOMICS AND FINANCE*

Economic conflict is fundamental to the character of the multinational enterprise. Yet it is often vastly different from the classic market-type conflict that students learn about in textbooks, where large numbers of fiercely competitive firms compete tooth and nail for a large and free market composed of equally competitive buyers. Many MNEs are enormous in size and operate in markets where there are only a few competitors of more or less equal size and power. As we have already seen in previous chapters, governmental regulations bear on virtually all aspects of the firm's behavior in the marketplace—its decisions on pricing, product quality, disposition of profits, labor relations, acquisition of finance capital, health, safety and environmental standards, and many others. Big Labor and Big Capital play a major role on the resource side, often behaving like monopolists. Products are frequently amazingly complex, and sometimes consist only of disembodied technology—useful knowledge which can be bought and sold much like anything else. Adam Smith would surely have been bemused by the way today's multinational giants do battle in the global marketplace, and by management's contemporary views on winning and losing.

Despite all of this, MNE management's bottom line remains maximum long-term shareholder wealth, a goal that requires careful attention to achieving the largest possible after-tax earnings per share with minimum risk to the survival and stability of the enterprise. Notwithstanding "revised" behavioral views of managerial goals based on such targets as maximum firm size and growth, personal power, prestige among peers, and social status, modern managers can ignore their age-old responsibility to the material well-being of company shareholders only at their own peril. History is replete with sagging price-earnings ratios, hostile takeover bids, bankruptcy or near-demise of formerly robust firms, wholesale reshufflings of top management teams, and selective "pruning" among corporate leadership by disgruntled boards of directors. So eventually the signals on corporate profitability come through loud and clear. And not to be ignored are the keen-eyed securities analysts, observing and interpreting every move management makes for their clients, the individual and institutional investors whose collective actions can make or break corporate fortunes.

SOURCES OF ECONOMIC CONFLICT

How does the management of multinational enterprise, operating under this sort of unambiguous mandate from the shareholder community, develop the goal structure that drives the actions of the firm in the various settings in which it operates? What are the main components of that complex set of goals? And what kinds of economic conflict with home and host governments, with rivals and economic interest-groups in home and host countries, and with the guardians of the international economic order evolve out of multinational corporate management's pursuit of its economic objectives?

Identifying MNE Objectives

There are at least six more or less distinct objectives that MNE management needs to focus on in order to carry out its shareholder mandate.

First, it must seek out large and growing markets for its products. Corporate fortunes are closely linked to taking advantage of existing but unexploited markets and opening up entirely new ones. And markets should be growing rapidly, not stagnating or declining. The market-exploitation objective may mean heavy corporate emphasis on new-product development, modification of existing products, or shifts in the location of production to be nearer to changing sources of final demand.

, Second, MNE management prefers to operate in a market that is less than perfectly competitive, where profit margins are wide and yield a favorable return on invested capital and human resources. This may mean achieving a position of market dominance through superior product or process know-how that cannot easily be appropriated or copied by competitors. But it may also mean collusion with other firms in the industry, lobbying for protective government shielding from competitive imports, negotiating an exclusive concession in a national market with a country's government, driving out existing or potential competitors through predatory practices, and the like. In a related vein, the firm may try to artificially depress wage rates or other input costs to boost profits by using its power as a dominant purchaser of the productive factors in question.

Third, the MNE needs to keep a watchful eye on costs—labor and capital, raw materials, and environmental resources. When labor is far cheaper or more productive in one country than another the firm may want to shift all or part of a given production process from one to the other, in order to obtain a competitive edge over its global competition or to prevent rivals from encroaching on its market share. This may well mean plant shutdowns in the United States or Germany or the United Kingdom and the transfer of production to Taiwan or Malaysia or Mexico. For example, in 1972 the Royal Typewriter Company (a division of Litton Industries) cited growing pressure from foreign competition as the reason for moving the bulk of its production from Hartford, Connecticut to foreign plants, laying off 1500 local employees. Its competitor, Sperry, had already moved all but electric typewriter production from the United States to sites in Holland, Italy, and Brazil, although SCM Corporation continued to produce typewriters in the United States. In another industry, the Bendix Corporation in 1972 moved automobile ignition systems manufacturing from New York to Mexico, being unable to make a profit at its American plant because of competitive pressures.[1] Similarly, when capital costs are lower in some financial markets than in others, the firm will have an incentive to take up financing where it is relatively cheapest, all things considered. And cost can often be lowered by concentrating all or part of the production process at a single location, and serving the global market from there, in order to reap favorable economies of scale.

Fourth, the multinational firm will seek to avoid risk and uncertainty in its global operations whenever it can. This includes the risk of exchange-rate fluctuations, the political risk of expropriation or nationalization, war and insurrection, the business risk of supply or transportation disruptions or industrial espionage, and the labor-related risk of strikes, wildcat work stoppages and slowdowns, sabotage and violence. In each case, management will try to protect itself however it can—by shifting production, by diversifying assets, by subdividing production processes, by financial and foreign-exchange manipulations, and by pressing for changes in public policies.

Fifth, management will try to avoid artificial barriers that governments throw up for various economic and social reasons, which inhibit or threaten the firm's efficiency. For example tariffs, quotas, and other trade barriers may prevent or impede a company's access to a particular national market, inducing it instead to set up shop inside the protected area in order to avoid the impact restrictions. For instance, John Deere went into Europe in the 1950s to avoid the competitive disadvantages of an 18% tariff rate, one of many American multinationals reacting to tariff changes associated with the creation of the European Common Market. Japanese MNEs, finding that trade restrictions increasingly impede their access to major markets, have taken in growing numbers to production offshore in Southeast Asia, especially the countries of Thailand, Singapore, Malaysia, Indonesia, and the Philippines. Such sectors as textiles, steel, bearings, television, calculators, tires, machine tools, cameras and watches have been especially involved, both in production for local Asian markets and for export into the Western industrialized countries—partly under the United Nations Generalized System of Preferences, which affords poor countries especially favorable tariff treatment in access to United States, EEC, Japan, and other major markets.[2] Thus, Common Market import restrictions on bearings and steel, and American restrictions on television sets could in part be successfully avoided by Japanese firms through offshore production.

Apart from trade barriers, exchange restrictions of various types may also influence corporate behavior if they impede the remission of earnings from a particular MNE subsidiary back to the parent firm. In such cases there is the incentive for management to try to repatriate the blocked funds through "transfer pricing"—exporting to other company units at less than full value or importing from them at inflated prices—or overcharging for technology or other services provided by the company to the beleaguered affiliate.[3] Like trade and product markets, financial markets are also subject to a variety of distortions and risks centering on taxes, credit restrictions, and exchange rates. The MNE has advantages over local firms in each of these areas by internalizing financial transfers to circumvent such impediments and to reduce the overall level of risk.

Finally, MNE management has to focus on after-tax return on stockholder equity, and this means using whatever loopholes are available to minimize its overall tax burden. Since the firm operates in both high-tax and low-tax countries, it means lodging as little profit as possible in the former and as much as possible in the latter. It also means using tax havens like the Bahamas, the Grand Cayman Islands, and Switzerland to tax-shelter corporate profits, particularly if MNE home countries like the United States do not levy taxes on corporate profits until these are repatriated.

These six elements—exploitation of markets, restricted competition, cost reduction, moderation of risk, avoidance of trade and financial barriers, and avoidance of taxes—translate the underlying management objective of maximum shareholder wealth into global corporate economic policy and behavior. Each element may be assigned a different weight by management at different times under different circumstances. Yet each is always present, as part of a network of incentives that underlies both the benefits and the sources of conflict that surround the economic dimensions of multinational corporate operations.

Identifying National and Group Objectives

Countries that are the home bases and the hosts of multinational enterprise likewise have a specific set of economic objectives—goals that are determined by local political processes which to the outsider are often obscure, and which can differ substantially both in time and in space. To complicate matters further, national economic objectives, being a political product, inevitably fail to satisfy various *group* interests. Farmers, textile workers, environmentalists, pipe-nipple manufacturers, and consumer advocates all have their own "druthers," some of which invariably depart from the official economic policy of the government toward multinationals. So even if bilateral dissonance between the economic objectives of MNEs and government policymakers can be ironed out, there is still plenty of room for conflict with vocal and often powerful national interest groups.

National economic objectives are usually rather straightforward in their principal dimensions. In the United States, for example, the Employment Act of 1946 mandates the President to focus as his principal economic policy targets on the maintenance of full employment, price-level stability, international payments balance, and an acceptable rate of economic growth. Other countries have comparable aggregate policy goals, whether codified or not, that spell out the economic stewardship of the government. Politically, the "jobs" issue is almost always the most sensitive. Inflation becomes a political problem above some "threshold" level of tolerance which varies internationally—for example between Germany and Brazil as possible low and high extremes in terms of willingness and ability to live with inflation. Economic growth, usually defined in terms of real income per capita, is an underlying theme everywhere because it underlies long-term trends in human material welfare. No matter what the rhetoric about "quality not quantity" and "small is beautiful," governments ignore the growth objective only at their own very distinct peril—nothing foments political change more effectively than the absence of hope for a better life among the masses. The things that contribute to growth, such as the formation of physical capital like buildings and machinery, infrastructure facilities such as schools, telecommunications, roads and hospitals, and technological advancement, are of critical concern in this context. And finally, for many countries the balance of payments represents a central element in the achievement of economic targets as a determinant of real resources from abroad that can be absorbed in the growth process.

Apart from such basically ubiquitous aggregate governmental targets, there are others which are often much more specific and which may or may not be important in any particular national context. One is income distribution between rich and poor, involving the structure of the tax system and often a bewildering array of transfer payments between income groups in cash or in kind. Another is regional balance, and the geographic distribution of industry and population throughout the country. Then there are economic problems surrounding disadvantaged racial or ethnic groups, which are important political considerations in countries like Malaysia. Resources and environmental policy, consumer protection, occupational safety and health, public versus private ownership of industry, economic aspects of military security, trade and investment relations with other countries, science and technology policy—all may assume major significance at one time or another in different countries of the world. That is, all may be built into the national objectives that a government may be trying to achieve through public policy.

As we have noted, groups within countries have their own peculiar sets of goals. Labor groups are interested in jobs, union membership rolls, wage rates, job security, working conditions and fringe benefits. Consumer advocates worry about truth in advertising, packaging, and lending, as well as prices, product safety and quality, the use of trademarks and warranties, and the like. Environmentalists are concerned with the social costs of private and public economic activities related to water and air pollution, solid waste, noise, and loss of amenities. Local entrepreneurs competing with MNEs like to focus on "unfair" competitive advantages and predatory business practices on the part of their foreign-owned business rivals. Ethnocentric and nationalist interest-groups oppose foreign ownership of national firms and industries as a matter of principle, while socialists are often obsessed with private ownership of enterprises, whether domestic or foreign. Everyone has an axe to grind in one way or another. And since public policy is by definition a consensual process, the satisfaction obtained by individual interest-groups in the form of national policy is necessarily partial. So there is invariably a good deal of potential for economic conflict between MNEs and interest groups that is quite separate and apart from possible broader conflict between the MNE and public policy at the national level.

The Shape of Economic Conflict

The outlines of economic confrontation between the multinational enterprise on the one hand, and home and host countries on the other, should already be apparent. Pursuit of the firm's economic objectives targeted on maximum long–term shareholder wealth—remembering all the things management needs to do in pursuit of that goal—inevitably clashes with the national and group interests we have just described. There is no way of getting around such economic conflict, which after all is the very essence of international trade and competition and the source of the benefits that international specialization contributes to economic welfare.

Take jobs, for instance. A German-based MNE finds it is cheaper to assemble transistor radios in Penang, Malaysia than in Stuttgart. It shuts down the assembly lines in West Germany and opens a new plant in Penang, exporting parts and components and bringing back the finished product. Perhaps 1000 jobs are destroyed in Stuttgart and 1200 jobs are created in Penang. Somebody benefits (consumers, shareholders, Malaysian workers) and somebody gets burned (German workers, local Malaysian employers, competitors in the industry). How badly do the losers get hurt? It all depends on how easy it is for them to adjust to the economic dislocation involved. Still, the incidence of benefits and costs invariably differs, and so conflict is inevitable—conflict which is targeted on the MNE as the catalyst in the international relocation of production. Yet much the same result might have emerged if the MNE did not exist, if local firms in Malaysia (or South Korea or Taiwan or Japan) had eventually captured a comparable share of the transistor radio market. So the root of conflict is between the German workers and the Malaysian workers—or more generally, between the expensive factor of production and the cheap factor internationally. The MNE is caught in the middle as an accelerator and amplifier of economic change. In the end, everybody benefits. But in the meantime there are disruptions and costs to be borne and there are vital questions about their seriousness and who has to bear them.

So economic conflict surrounding the MNE is more than the conventional maelstrom of competition and survival in the marketplace—though in an era of government regulation and control, and subsidization and ownership, even this is increasingly interlaced with complexity. Rather, it involves clashes on a variety of levels between actors whose fundamental economic interests point in different directions: the MNEs themselves, national macroeconomic and structural policy, and the special concerns of national or regional interest-groups. The simple fact that the multinational firm optimizes *transnationally* while the others are forced to optimize *nationally* guarantees that economic conflict will rise to the surface.

DIMENSIONS OF ECONOMIC INTERACTION

The linkages between the MNE and national economies are at least as complex as they are important. Consider Exhibit 14–1, which illustrates in a simple way the economic linkages that exist between a parent MNE and one of its affiliates, as well as the linkages between each of these and their respective national economies—the home-country and host-country economic environments.

In terms of direct parent-affiliate linkages, the following are most important: The parent provides its foreign affiliate with (1) finance capital to procure productive assets and maintain working-capital balances, (2) manage and marketing know-how, including access to markets and sources of supply of raw materials and intermediate inputs, (3) technology related to products, processes, and applications, and (4) goods and services transferred on an intercompany basis—capital, equipment and materials as well as possibly marketing, transport, and other services. This is the renowned MNE "package." It comprises a bundle of ingredients, including the critical element of entrepreneurship and risk-taking, whose totality is supposed to be *greater* than the sum of its constituent parts. This net increment is the real contribution of the multinational firm, that elusive element that the host country or its entrepreneurs could not easily acquire by simply buying the main components of the MNE "package" on the open market and attempting to produce comparable results independently at competitive cost.

In return, the MNE affiliate supplies the parent with (1) goods and services on an intercompany basis, (2) in some cases technological innovations that have

Exhibit 14-1

Interactions Between an MNE and Home and Host Economies

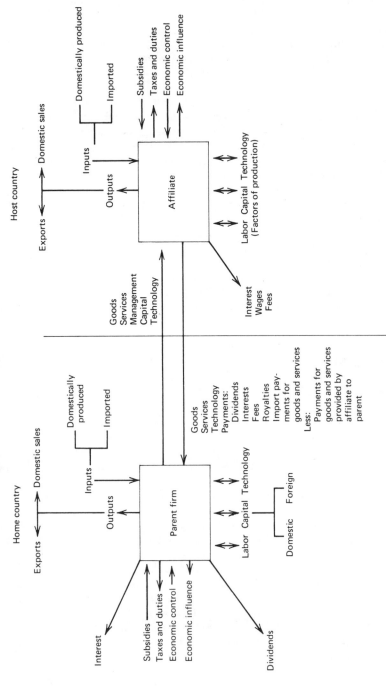

been developed abroad and can be used effectively in parent-company or third-country operations, and most importantly (3) payments back to the parent in the form of net remissions for intercompany goods and services sales, dividends on capital investment, interest on intercompany loans, fees and royalties on licensed technology. This latter constitutes the overall return to the parent for the "package" of services the MNE provides. It is clear that the returns take a variety of different forms, and a singularly important question is whether that return is commensurate with the real economic value of the MNE "package" to the host country.

At the same time, both parent and affiliate are tied into their respective national economies in a variety of ways. On the host-country side, labor and capital (particularly loans) are taken up locally, and so is technology that may be useful in affiliate operations. At the same time, the affiliate supplies some capital to the local market (principally working capital balances) as well as technology that gets copied by local competitors or is embodied in the products the firm sells on the market. And the affiliate may also be a supplier of labor when layoffs occur or when workers change employers. For each of these productive agents acquired by the MNE affiliate, payments are made to the local economy.

The affiliate itself produces goods or services, some of which are exported and others sold locally, and acquires material inputs that again may be imported or produced locally. The MNE affiliate also pays taxes and other fiscal charges to the host government, and may benefit from subsidies the latter provides. It is also subjected to, and may try to influence, the system of economic controls that prevails locally. Note that each of the factors of concern to economic policymakers in the host country, from jobs to balance of payments, is affected by the MNE affiliate's operations.

The MNE parent has similar linkages with the home country's economic environment with respect to labor, capital, technology, goods and services inputs and outputs. There are some differences, though. For example, dividends are paid out domestically to shareholders (most of whom are legal residents of the home country) whereas in the affiliate's case any dividends tend to go abroad to the parent firm. Borrowed capital may either be taken up locally or in international capital markets—for the affiliate it tends to be local credits or intercompany loans from the parent. But the critical issue, and the one that generates most of the conflict between the MNE and its economic environment, is what gets done where and under what conditions in the multinational network of parent and affiliates. The decisions are made at corporate headquarters level in accordance with the firm's own economic interests. But their effects send ripples and waves through each of the national economies touched by the enterprise.

International integration of production in some MNEs has gone very far indeed within such networks of affiliates. For example, in the late 1970s Ford's Fiesta had its engines assembled in Valencia, Spain; engine blocks made in Dagenham, England; carburetors in Northern Ireland; transmissions and axles in Bordeaux, France; and body stampings in Saarlouis, Germany; with final assembly in Valencia, Saarlouis and Halewood, England for both the European as well as the American markets.

PROBLEMS OF IMPACT ASSESSMENT

Before taking a look at the various forms taken by economic conflict surrounding the MNE, it is vitally important to keep one thing in mind. In attempting to discern the impact the MNE has on any single aspect of economic life, no matter what it is, one has to run the world twice—once the way things *actually* went, and again the way things might have gone if the MNE *as an institution* had not existed. It is not enough to say that 10,000 jobs have been created or destroyed in a particular country by the activities of MNEs. We know (or think we know) what actually happened to employment. We *need* to know what would have happened without the MNE. Would the jobs have been created or destroyed anyway? That is, would employment trends have been any different without the multinational? If not, then clearly there are no MNE effects to worry about and no need to come up with policy proposals to deal specifically with them.

There are two aspects of any discernible MNE effect that need to be identified. One is the quantitative effect at a given point of time. The other is the actual time-path of adjustment. Since there is no way to run the world twice through a given stretch of time, the non-MNE "alternative scenario" has to be based on *assumptions* which serve as a plausible underpinning for the way things might have gone. If the issue is MNE export of jobs through offshore production in the color television industry and one can defend the proposition that "our Japanese competitors would have wiped us out anyway," then a good case can be made for a zero net MNE effect on jobs. This hardly makes the displaced workers any happier. But the job losses cannot be laid at the multinationals' doorstep unless it can be shown that the inevitable displacement was much more *abrupt* and more *disruptive* as a result of the MNEs—in other words, that the time-path of adjustment was itself more damaging. So the assumptions are critical, and any assessments of the economic effects of multinational corporations have to be carefully measured against the quality of the assumptions and the intellectual honesty of the investigator.

But there is a second side to the MNE impact-assessment coin. Once a plausible alternative scenario has been ascertained and a net MNE effect determined, the next question is "so what?" How should the MNE impact be interpreted? Herein lies the fundamental importance of the needs and preferences of national and group interests noted earlier. It is impossible to tell whether or not a particular set of effects ascribed to multinational companies will be a source of economic conflict until an accurate assesment has been made of the social and group preferences that prevail within the home or host country.

Finally, we have emphasized the complexity of the economic interactions between the MNE and its environment. In a particular case, some of these may be considered good and others bad—a typically mixed bag. The good may outweigh the bad, or vice-versa, depending on what is considered more or less important in the local setting. And so precisely the same set of perceived MNE effects on the national economy may render the multinational's presence desirable in one country and undesirable in another, or desirable in a particular country now and undesirable later on. It all depends on the political rank-ordering of economic objectives, which can differ internationally as well as change through time. It also depends on the options available locally to replace the "package" of services the MNE provides. The essential point is not to prejudge. What appears to be a favorable picture to outsiders can easily be viewed as unfavorable (or vice-versa) to those who ultimately have to make the hard choices in devising their own policies on the involvement of multinational firms in the national economy.

DIMENSIONS OF ECONOMIC CONFLICT

There are at least seven distinct dimensions of actual or potential economic conflict between the MNE and the national settings within which it finds itself. The issues include employment, capital formation, real output and income, market behavior, international payments, national economic policy, and economic instability. Another very important issue is technology—so important, in fact, that we have discussed it separately in the previous chapter.

Employment and Location of Production

Perhaps the most sensitive area is jobs, an issue we have touched on briefly before. For the MNE home country, the question is: "Have the overseas production activities of our multinationals destroyed or 'exported' jobs?" For host countries the question is: "Have multinationals operating here contributed to the more efficient use of the nation's human resources and/or added to the supply of labor as a factor of production, especially in areas where domestic shortages have been a problem?" Let us take the home-country case first.

Foreign activities of MNEs in the *extractive* (e.g., mining) and *services* (e.g., banking) industries are not usually viewed in their home countries as having negative domestic employment effects. The reason is that in most cases such activities for obvious reasons could not have been carried out at home. Besides, overseas operations may generate a demand for domestically-made goods (aircraft, mining equipment, transport vehicles) and, in the extractive sector, provide sources of supply of imported raw materials, which in turn make it possible to expand industrial employment at home. And in both sectors overseas activities generate managerial jobs in accounting, finance, marketing, and administration at home that would not otherwise exist. So neither the extractive nor services sector is particularly susceptible to conflict involving the export of jobs.[4]

Not so for manufacturing. Here, overseas production by MNEs to take advantage of lower production costs or market proximity is alleged to displace workers previously producing for export or, alternatively, to displace workers producing for the domestic market by offshore production and subsequent captive-importation for home-market sale. As we said before, it all depends on the assumptions. If foreign MNE production is "aggressive," without competitive threat and undertaken simply to reduce costs and enhance profits, then clearly there is a displacement of domestic production workers. If it is "defensive," in order to save established foreign or domestic markets from encroachment by lower-cost or better-situated overseas suppliers, then clearly overseas production will not on balance involve displacement of production jobs.[5] This may also be true if the foreign activity involves a "takeover" by an MNE of a firm in a host country which previously served the local market—thus displacing few if any home-country exports, at least in the near term—and if it opens up an entirely new market that home-country production did not previously serve.

The following quotation illustrates the "defensive" position quite nicely: "If Procter & Gamble had not gone to Algeria, for example, Unilever would have preempted the local soap business. If Caterpillar Tractor had not gone to Britain, Vickers might today be that country's leading producer of bulldozers. If Squibb had not gone into Italy, it would have surrendered the Italian market to Hoffmann-La Roche."[6] Also typical of the "defensive" view is the following quotation from the president and chief executive officer of a large American electrical equipment MNE: "Our overseas operation slowed down the growth of companies like Philips, Siemens, Olivetti, Bull, and Telefunken. If we hadn't been over there, those companies would have made a lot more money, would have greatly expanded their research effort, and would now be making much better calculators, accounting machines, and punch-card systems. As a result, the United States market would be flooded with their products." Or take the view of Ellwood Curtis of John Deere: "If the U.S. farm-tractor companies had not taken a part of the European market, Deutz in Germany, Fiat in Italy, and Zetor in Czechoslovakia would now be challenging us not only in their home markets, but also in the United States."[7]

So "aggressive" shifts in production locations by multinationals tend to be displacive of home-country production jobs, while similar developments undertaken for "defensive," takeover, or new-market reasons do not. From an international trade point of view, the former tend to displace exports and/or stimulate imports, on balance, while the latter do not. One detailed study estimated that American foreign direct investment generated $12 billion in exports and $3 billion in imports in 1970, assuming none would have occurred without the foreign investment and ignoring export-displacement effects.[8]

Two further points: First, even the "aggressive" relocation of production abroad may not be complete, and may involve the continued production and export of components and parts from the home country. The same is true of "defensive" production abroad, where continued supply of parts and components—which might not exist if markets were lost to foreign competitors—actually produces a net *gain* in production jobs in relation to the alternative scenario. Second, there are nonproduction jobs to be considered as well, and it is clear that the existence of foreign production affiliates (for whatever reason) stimulates home-country white-collar employment in finance, accounting and control, research and development, communications, sales support, and the like. These must be netted out against possible negative effects on production jobs in order to ascertain the overall employment impact of MNE operations on home countries. So MNEs both create *and* destroy jobs, but the effects on labor markets in home countries will vary by occupation, industry, region, and skill level. And evidence that domestic employment by MNEs is in fact growing is no protection against the job-displacement argument, since employment might have increased *even more* without foreign investment.

Studies of job displacement and creation in the United States have come up with estimates that vary enormously—again, based on different sets of assumptions. Research undertaken by the AFL-CIO purports to show a net job loss of 1.2 million, albeit ignoring any positive efforts on nonproduction jobs and relying heavily on "offensive" assumptions. AFL-CIO analysts have argued that a net loss of 500,000 job opportunities could be directly ascribed to MNE operations by aggressively transferring production technology overseas and producing goods there that displace either United States exports or domestic sales. Another AFL-CIO estimate calculated the net job loss at around 900,000 for 1966–1971.

In contrast, the U.S. Department of Commerce has estimated a net *gain* of 600,000 jobs based on a questionnaire survey.[9] The Commerce Department study found that majority-owned United States affiliates abroad sold 72% of their output in host countries, 22% in other countries and 7% re-exported to the United States. Another study sponsored by the Department of Commerce, with the aid of more "defensive" assumptions and fully considering nonproduction employment, came up with a net job creation of 0.7 million.[10] This latter analysis of firms in the paper, chemicals, tire, wire cable, automobile, oil, and electronics industries found that only 10% of the American firms' foreign production was exported back to the United States. Another study estimated that 260,000 jobs were created, on net, as a result of American MNEs' foreign direct investment.[11] Yet another one, by the U.S. Tariff Commission, estimated the range of employment effects to be from plus 500,000 to minus 1.3 million, depending on the assumptions.[12] In between are perhaps a half dozen assessments showing a wide variety of results and using equally diverse methodologies and assumptions.

One evaluation of the employment effects concludes that "the question of jobs and the MNCs can be most fruitfully viewed as a normative domestic political squabble over distributive shares of income in the U.S., and can be analyzed using the tools employed in the economics of pork-barrel politics," and that the vastly different findings in this literature "are just logical conundrums hatched from the sloppy language employed in the redistributive arguments."[13]

Perhaps the best guess is that, overall, job gains and losses resulting from the production activities of the American multinationals abroad probably cancel each other out—with perhaps a slight "tilt" to the side of job creation—under reasonably plausible assumptions. This "wash" nevertheless hides a great deal. It may obscure a significant "churning" of the labor force. Production workers lose while management workers gain. Low-skill workers lose while high-skill workers gain. And there are important structural effects such as net displacement of jobs in paper, plastics, industrial chemicals, household appliances, textiles and apparel and transportation, but net job creation in electrical machinery, office equipment, drugs, and instruments.[14] Some regions lose while others benefit. So even if MNE activities have had no *net* displacive employment effects, there may still have been considerable pressure exerted on labor markets, and the hardship endured by individual displaced workers—which is, after all, the relevant measure of adjustment cost—cannot be ignored. Finally, there is always the question we raised earlier—whether the MNE makes this adjustment more rapid and disruptive, possibly raising the adjustment burden that must be borne by the displaced workers.

Organized labor remains implacable. In general, it seems clear that American union leaders have felt that their flexibility and influence has been threatened by MNEs. Its response has been to push for restrictive legislation bearing on the MNE, perhaps best illustrated by the Hartke-Burke bill, introduced in several sessions of Congress during the early 1970s. Among its major features were the following:

1. Establishment of a powerful new government agency to administer country-by-country import quotas based on 1965–1969 levels of trade.
2. Repeal of the foreign tax credit.
3. Mandatory straight-line depreciation of all property outside the United States computed on the useful life of assets.
4. Authorization of the President to prohibit direct and indirect exports of capital, and to prohibit holders of United States patents from manufacturing abroad or licensing others to do so.
5. Stricter mark-of-origin rules for all foreign products sold in the United States.[15]

The United Auto Workers' position on trade in the early 1970s would have required licenses for all foreign investments by American firms, including reinvestments, a "competitive promotion tax" on companies for refusal to compete with imports to be imposed on firms making profits while import-competition prevailed, and criminal penalties for "speculating against the dollar."[16]

Similar job-displacement controversies have occurred in Germany, Switzerland, Sweden, the United Kingdom, France, Canada, Japan, the Netherlands, and other major MNE home countries. As we have already noted in Capter 11, Volkswagenwerk A.G. in Germany, with a supervisory board heavily laden with labor representatives, debated for over two years before deciding that "defensive" considerations were paramount in the American market, so that building production facilities in Pennsylvania would indeed save German jobs.

In our model of MNE conflict, the jobs issue for the individual firm would generally lead us toward a *competitive* mode in management behavior: (a) the firm often has enormously high stakes in being free to allocate production rationally based on international competitive factors—under extreme defensive conditions its very survival may be at stake; (b) it is in a relatively powerful position so long as it is capable of closing plants and laying off workers; and (c) its resources in terms of options and information regarding alternative production sites are significant. In terms of its own mandate, management cannot avoid the issue and it can afford to accomodate only at significant cost to the firm and its shareholders. Management can, however, *collaborate* or *compromise* if its relationships with labor are good and there is compatibility of interests in the long term health of the enterprise—as in the VW case. From a conflict-management point of view, therefore, the outcome will tend to fall in the upper *competition-compromise–collaboration* triangle of our model. The costs of conflict can be reduced by pushing the outcome toward *collaboration* to the extent possible by finding ways to reemploy displaced workers within the firm, providing retraining and other forms of adjustment assistance, and affording adequate severance terms to those who ultimately have to be let go.

Conflict management relating to *host-country* employment issues is perhaps a bit easier. In the first place, the host country tends to gain jobs—no matter what assumptions apply—from the group of MNEs that operate within its borders. Whether a given firm initiates operations "offensively" or "defensively" is of little concern. And depending on the economic, social, and political dimensions of the host country's unemployment or underemployment problem, this gain by itself may be enough to overwhelm all other potential sources of conflict and give the multinational a very strong hand indeed.

Furthermore, MNEs have been shown to have various beneficial "indirect" labor-market effects in host countries. These range from on-the-job training and formal in-plant educational programs for their own employees, and those of suppliers and customers, to company nutrition/health programs and other fringe benefits that help upgrade labor quality.[17] To the extent that workers leave to join other firms or start their own businesses, the resulting investment in "human capital" disseminated through employee turnover can have rather broad beneficial effects on the national labor force. Such qualitative benefits are hard to measure, but they are undoubtedly an important facet of MNE operations in many host countries, particularly the less-developed ones.

This hardly means that the labor-market effects of MNEs in host countries are free from conflict, however. On the contrary, by paying higher wages and providing better working conditions than competitive and other local firms, MNEs have frequently been accused of "unfair" labor-market competition, of skimming the cream off the local labor force and thereby impeding the competitive position of indigenous enterprises. Here the conflict is with group interests, rather than national interests, and it seems to us that the firm can often take an uncooperative stance without compromising its position or otherwise attempting to "manage" the conflict.

MNEs have also been accused of creating "over full" employment, of contributing to a national labor shortage in countries like Germany or Singapore, forcing governments to permit an influx of more or less permanent "guest workers," with or without their families, who bring with them a variety of social and economic problems with which the host country must deal—not least of which is trying to expel them in case of economic slowdown. Once again, however, this is not usually a matter for discretionary corporate conflict management. The labor-market and immigration rules have to be set by the government itself after weighing the various benefits and costs, and the MNE has to play the game according to those rules—that is, to follow a strategy of straightforward accommodation.

Host-country conflict has also arisen in relation to possible labor-market instability and (as in MNE home countries) job displacement.[18] Henry Ford in 1972 threatened to progressively relocate his company's automotive production from the United Kingdom to other countries. Ford's reaction eventually made Germany instead of Britain the major center of European operations, with the British operations concentrating on parts and components and commercial vehicles. To insure against British labor disruptions the company initially went to "double sourcing" of parts and components, later abandoned as excessively costly.[19] Chrysler threatened to pull out of the United Kingdom altogether in 1975 for much the same reason—an unreliable labor force and excessively low productivity—but was persuaded to stay by a massive government infusion of capital, only to sell out to Peugeot-Citroën a few years later. Whether or not labor-market conditions are directly involved, MNE relocation of production raises the same kinds of issues in host countries as it does in home countries. But in host countries MNE managers may have a bit more leverage in finding an optimum conflict-management stance between outright *competitive* behavior and intransigence on the one hand, and *collaborative* or *accomodative* behavior on the other.

Lastly, host countries are sometimes concerned with the income distributional aspects of MNE employment effects—that certain inequities may arise within or between occupation or income groups as a result of multinational corporate operations. Here again, it is government's responsibility to design and implement its own income distribution policy by means of taxes, transfers, or other tools of income policy, and not the role of MNE management. So conflicts that arise from this source could legitimately be tackled in a predominantly *competing* or *avoiding* way by management.

The potential for conflict between *labor groups* in different countries on MNE employment issues may also be important, as became clear during the aforementioned Hartke-Burke debate in 1972–1973, when the prospect of protectionist legislation with union backing in the United States severely disturbed organized labor abroad. One American union warned that future strategy would "require a careful balance between the nationalistic interests of American members on the one hand and a non-nationalistic concern for all of the people of the world on the other."[20]

To summarize, home-country jobs are a real source of conflict for MNE management, both for individual companies and for the multinationals as a group. Without the ability to rationalize production globally, the unique advantages of the multinational firm and much of its net contribution to society will disappear. And so, despite sometimes bitter conflict and acrimony there is really not very much room for *compromise* on the basic issue of the location of production internationally. There is plenty of room, on the other hand, for *accommodation* at the local level in facilitating the process of adjustment for affected workers. Conflict involving the jobs issue in host countries tends to be less serious than in home countries, and generally involves behavioral rules that have to be set by government policy; there is relatively little MNE management can or should do to ameliorate conflict—unlike the kinds of human-resource and industrial-relations conflicts discussed in Chapter 11 or the technology aspects covered in Chapter 13.

The Capital Problem

A very basic question is whether MNE operations in home and host countries contribute to the three fundamental ingredients of economic growth—labor, capital, and technology. With regard to labor, we have already seen that the MNE itself affects the local supply of labor in a rather small way through intrafirm personnel transfers. Indirectly, though, MNE job creation and displacement in different countries can encourage international migration, and thus influence the size of the labor force in national economies. But more importantly, we have already noted that MNEs may influence the *quality* of labor in a positive way through training and related activities, and this may well be their principal contribution to the human-resource base of economic growth. While there is relatively little prospect for conflict concerning MNE impacts on overall labor-force size, the same is certainly not true of technology as an agent of growth—both disembodied "useful knowledge" and that embodied in human beings and capital equipment, as we have seen. This leaves the impact of MNE activities on the physical capital stock of home and host countries—its effects on overall savings, investment, and capital-allocation efficiency.

The simple view of foreign investment through MNEs is that what is invested in one place cannot be invested someplace else. By investing abroad, MNEs do not invest at home, and thus help economic growth in host countries and hinder it in home countries. With a smaller capital stock, productive capacity and real output in the home country cannot be pushed as far, but a larger capital base allows it to be pushed farther in the host (capital-receiving) countries.

Robert Gilpin is one who worries about MNE misdirection of home-country resources.[21] Drawing an analogy with the British case a century earlier, he argues that MNE capital exports allow the domestic economy to atrophy. Companies have looked for easy sources of profit abroad, while neglecting difficult economic issues at home and increasing national economic vulnerability. He proposes a government effort to stimulate new domestic investment in the United States, specifically by means of stepped-up research and development, opening up new profit opportunities to reduce incentives to invest abroad.

But presumably the rate of return on the invested capital is in fact higher in the host countries than in the home country; otherwise the MNEs would not have undertaken the foreign investment in the first place. And the profit component of the value of incremental output in the host countries eventually gets repatriated, thus boosting real income in the home country and sharing the economic benefits of a more efficient global allocation of capital between both sides.

So while it may be true that foreign investment hurts potential output in home countries, this damage is unlikely to be as great as it appears because the repatriated earnings have to be deducted from any net loss. And MNE capital inflows benefit potential output in host countries, but some of this has to be given up to service the imported capital. Globally, however, output capacity based on a more efficiently allocated capital stock will invariably rise—that is, host-country productive capacity will rise by more than home-country capacity falls, because of the differential productivity of capital between the two. This conclusion stands whether we are talking about the direct export of capital from home to host country or whether the capital is raised in third countries or international financial markets—the latter results in a broader distribution of the gains from improved capital-allocation efficiency.

What if the MNE investment hadn't been made? One possibility is that somebody else (perhaps a rival MNE) would have undertaken the investment anyway and the net contribution of our investment to the capital base and to growth in the host country is zero. Or nothing would have happened, and we can be credited with the full contribution. Again, it depends on your assumptions.

One study of the MNE in the foreign investment process concludes that it is indeed difficult to tell whether such investment adds to or supplants local investment in host countries: "Whether or not [foreign direct investment] supplements or possibly even stimulates local investment opportunities can only be deduced by summing up the net effect of foreign competition on local investment plans throughout the economy."[22] Other studies seem to show that MNE investments in developing countries are principally determined by supply factors (e.g., raw materials, wage rates) while investment in developed countries depend more on demand factors (e.g., market size, growth).

What if MNE capital spending in a particular host country involves no infusions at all? That is, suppose the capital is borrowed locally by the foreign-based MNE. In the first place, efficiency still rises—otherwise the MNE couldn't have bid the capital away from other uses—and so does output and income. In economists' terminology, the capital-output ratio falls, which is good. Some of the gains go to the local savers in the form of higher interest payments, and some go to the MNE in the form of profit. There is no "alternative scenario" because if local entrepreneurs or rival MNEs could have made the same or a higher-yield investment by tapping local savings they presumably would have done so. So the MNE in question can claim the full amount of the efficiency gain in the use of local capital resources.

This does not make local competitors for capital any happier, of course. Indeed, one of the problems arising out of this seemingly conflict-proof issue is the complaint by local firms that the MNE affiliates have "preferred access" to local capital because of their "superior borrowing ability." This covers the aforementioned ability to pay a higher return, the often relatively large size and stability of the local MNE affiliate, and the explicit or implicit guarantee of the parent firm standing behind its subsidiary. Each of these elements is alleged to confer upon the MNE affiliate lower-cost credit, and preferred treatment in the queue of prospective borrowers if there is credit rationing. Local firms often view this "crowding-out" effect as a source of conflict with multinationals. In addition, the MNEs have access to international credit markets and intercompany loans which may not be accessible to local firms. In its more extreme form, the argument accuses the multinationals of "draining" local financial markets for their own ends.

So long as there is effective competition in local credit markets, MNE management can refute such self-serving allegations without difficulty in a purely confrontive manner. From an efficiency point of view, capital should flow to those who offer higher returns and/or lower risk. Besides, there is some evidence that MNE affiliates often supply as much or more credit to local financial institutions as they drain from them.[23]

Finally, there is the question whether MNE activities actually increase the rate of saving and investment. To the extent that saving is positively related to prospective returns and negatively related to the degree of riskiness of how these savings are held, and to the extent that MNEs raise overall returns by applying capital more efficiently and cut risk by diversifying operations and enhancing operational stability, some positive effect is possible. But it has not yet been pinned down in studies that have been undertaken, and in any case it is likely to be relatively small. It is certainly not a significant source of conflict for management to contend with.

Ownership of Capital

Quite apart from the economic arguments surrounding the interrelationships of savings, investment, and MNEs, there is a closely related political issue as well—one that was discussed in much greater detail from a political perspective in

Chapter 8. This is that foreign ownership of capital is itself somehow bad. Even worse, foreign-based MNEs can buy up a host nation's resources with their own money when they finance the investment locally. So the nation can expect to benefit far less from foreign-owned capital than from locally-owned capital, and foreign investment thus takes on essentially "exploitative" characteristics. This charge is frequently intermeshed with socialist views in particular host countries, where private ownership of the means of production is considered exploitative (therefore damaging to society), and foreign ownership is viewed as doubly bad.

Without debating the pros and cons of public versus private ownership, it is of course true that foreign ownership involves payments to investors and lenders abroad while local ownership does not. This burden is the price that has to be paid for the MNE "package" of services provided. Whether this payment is excessive or exploitative depends on the real economic benefits the host country gets, and what its alternatives are—that is, whether it could get the same set of benefits cheaper in other ways. Again, note the critical importance of assumptions!

Foreign ownership of domestic industry has become an especially sensitive issue with the build-up of petrodollars since 1973, and the oil exporters' efforts to invest some of these funds by means of equity holdings in major firms. Kuwait's purchase of 14.6% of Daimler-Benz, Libya's buying into Fiat, and Iran's purchase of 25% of Krupp Steel raised eyebrows but went through. Other investments, especially in real estate, have been even more sensitive—as for example the purchase by a group of Kuwaitis of Kiawah Island off the coast of South Carolina to build a resort. And the hue and cry raised in the United States blocked Iran's proposed financial deal involving ownership of 13% of Pan American World Airways stock. Still, no explicit foreign-ownership restrictions yet exist in the United States, except on farmland at the state level. But prime defense contractors like Lockheed, Grumman, and General Dynamics, of which there are 10, as well as perhaps 20 additional major defense-oriented firms would probably be placed off-limits if the foreign-ownership issue arose in the United States. In contrast, we noted in Chapter 8 that the Canadian Gray Report argued in 1973 that major control of national industry by foreign firms (80% of them American) inhibited the development of an innovative and internationally competitive economy. Thereupon the Canadian parliament passed the Foreign Investment Review Act to control investment inflows, albeit producing no noticeable changes in subsequent investment patterns.

The fact remains that foreign ownership is a source of conflict that pervades and compounds all of the other dimensions of MNE conflict. Economically, conflict over foreign ownership *per se* makes little sense—what gets bought must be paid for, in one way or another. But it is a fact of life that management must contend with. Fortunately, there are plenty of ways of *accommodating* the demand for local ownership. This may involve joint ventures with local firms, individuals, or government agencies, turnkey projects, management contracts, tripartite ventures and international consortia, or barter trade arrangements. The possibilities are many.

The point is that demands for local ownership generate opportunities for conflict management through *compromise* and *accommodation*. The outcomes often cost MNEs little or nothing, and they may not generate any real economic benefits for host countries. The pie cannot be sliced any differently. But conflict, and its associated uncertainties and costs, may be reduced with a net economic gain for both sides.

Growth and Development

Growth and development do not necessarily go hand in hand. Abu Dhabi has had enormous economic growth, measured in per capita real income, but relatively little development. Development means that a variety of economic sectors advance in a reasonably balanced way, producing for export or the local market or both, generating broad linkage–effects into upstream and downstream sectors as well as throwing off resources to support social overhead, which in turn supports the development process. We thus have feeder and user industries developing, as well as the banking and financial sector, transport and distribution services, schools, hospitals, rail and road systems, telecommunications, and a competent civil service, all together providing a dynamic job market for the local labor pool and (not incidentally) improving income distribution.

The question here is whether MNE operations really do contribute significantly to the economic development process as defined in this way. The answers depend on a lot of things discussed elsewhere in this book, including technology transfers, research and development, human resources, and the like. But one of the most important measures of how MNEs contribute to development focuses on the backward and forward linkages. That is, are there close and supportive ties to the local economy—the local sale of products that can be serviced by indigenous firms, wage and salary payments that encourage retail sales and services, purchases from local suppliers and raw-materials producers, and so on? These are often difficult to identify in terms of their relative developmental contributions, but they are certainly important considerations.

In developing countries MNEs inevitably lay additional claim to local resources which could be in extremely restricted supply. So more limited investment opportunities may be provided for local entrepreneurs, which could in turn result in foreign investment being substituted for domestic investment, with the latter being driven out of the country or being less efficiently employed at home.

Potentially least beneficial is the industrial or extractive MNE "enclave," where imported inputs are manufactured or assembled for export, or where local minerals are extracted for sale abroad. Labor, raw materials and perhaps capital are the only locally-procured resources. And while the economic benefits to the host country may be very substantial indeed, the contribution to "development" as we have defined it may be rather small.

The fact is that the difference between growth and development is not all that clear in the minds of many government planners. Consider for example the developing countries' strident insistence on commodity price-rigging à la OPEC as an answer to many of their problems. Or the increasingly urgent warnings by the World Bank that development planners had better pay more attention to the diffusion of benefits and improved income-distribution at home. But as development policy becomes more sophisticated—in countries like Mexico and Brazil it is already very advanced; and in India perhaps even a bit too sophisticated— MNEs will be under growing pressure to improve their developmental linkages in an affirmative way.

These linkages have another important potential impact. That is to create new opportunities for local entrepreneurs to appear and fill the new demands that have been created. This may involve greater local sourcing of inputs, greater emphasis on the local market in promoting sales and adapting products to local requirements, and similar measures to enhance the diffusion of benefits. Here certainly is one source of MNE conflict that lends itself to a corporate strategy based on *compromise* and *accommodation*.

Market Behavior

Few aspects of economic conflict surrounding MNEs are as sensitive as their effects on competition—going beyond the international political dimensions of antitrust policy discussed in Chapter 7. Has the development of the multinational firm, on balance, increased or reduced the level of market competition prevailing in national economies? Has it led to a greater role for the free market, or has it caused increasingly restrictive competitive conditions involving oligopolies, local monopolies, cartels, and restrictive business practices?

The MNE's interest necessarily lies in global allocation of markets, output and profits, and this may well inhibit its competitive behavior in any single national market. "The question is whether the MNE, in its interaction with host markets, is directly responsible for 'inadequate competition.' If the MNE is primarily a 'mature international oligopolist' . . . then the apparent thrust of conduct is directed towards stability within markets, behind barriers to entry. . . . Under these conditions, the mechanism which ensures maximum host-country gains is not MNE competition nor competitiveness but the bargaining positions and relative strength of the host-country government vis-a-vis the MNEs."[24]

The Uranium Cartel Case

Perhaps the most dramatic antitrust involvement by multinationals in recent years is the great uranium cartel scandal that began in 1972 and continued into the 1980s. A 1976 House Commerce Subcommittee investigation appeared to show that the dramatic rise in the price of uranium on the world market (from $6 per pound in 1972 to $41 in 1976) was brought about by an international cartel which had been rumored in the nuclear industry for years. The uranium price increases also happened to coincide with the OPEC-induced oil price rise. An environmental action group, Friends of the Earth, had released correspondence and documents purporting to show that such a cartel existed, and an investigation was subsequently taken up by the Justice Department. These documents were obtained from Mary Kathleen Uranium Ltd., an Australian affiliate of Rio Tinto-Zinc. They appeared to indicate that the cartel first met on February 1, 1972 in Paris, and involved various uranium companies as well as government representatives from Australia, South Africa, France, and Canada. According to one of the Mary Kathleen letters, "This club, comprising virtually all the Free World producers of U_3O_8 with the exception of the U.S.A., was set up last year to regulate sales of U_3O_8 with a view to improving prices."[25]

According to a subsequent New York State investigation of the cartel, RTZ originally approached the Canadian government with plans for the arrangement and won its approval. The cartel was evidently shaped during a preliminary meeting in Paris sponsored by the French Atomic Energy Commission, and at a subsequent secret meeting in Johannesburg, South Africa, in June 1972. Each participant was awarded a share of "available free world utility demand" under a two-tier price system. The French agency's role apparently was "to relay communications to members of the cartel, thereby providing in some instances a way around certain antitrust restrictions against direct producer contacts. To disguise the true purpose of the cartel, elaborate security measures were taken, including 'burying' of the Paris office within France's AEC.''[26] Documents that became available in 1977 indicated quite clearly that the cartel was active at least from 1972 to 1974. Companies identified with the cartel maintained, however, that United States firms were excluded so that American antitrust law could not have been violated.

Nevertheless, it became known that a Gulf Oil Company subsidiary, Gulf Minerals Canada, had been actively involved in the cartel. Gulf's chairman said that its Canadian affiliate had been forced to join the cartel by the Canadian government. He denied that this violated American antitrust law, or that it had anything to do with the rapid rise in uranium prices.[27] Apparently the Canadian government had indeed pressured Gulf and Germany's Uranerzbergbau to join the cartel, since the two firms were jointly developing Saskatchewan's Rabbit Lake uranium deposit.[28] The Canadian government denied that it had forced Gulf to join the cartel, although a spokesman did acknowledge that it had "urged" Gulf to participate—reiterating that the cartel did not affect Canadian or American prices and was made necessary in the first place by United States restrictions on access to uranium supplies.[29] The Canadian government evidently withdrew from the cartel in early 1975.[30]

In a letter to the U.S. Atomic Energy Commission dated February 14, 1972, the Canadian embassy in Washington had advised that the Paris cartel meeting had been held as "a general discussion on possible price stabilization mechanisms." Apparently the AEC and its successor in the U.S. Department of Energy took no action.[31]

A 1977 staff study of the House Commerce Committee's Subcommittee on Oversight and Investigation concluded that the cartel's activities had a direct impact on American utility purchases during the 1972–1975 period. The implication was that, contrary to Gulf's declaration, the cartel did have a significant effect on United States uranium prices. According to Committee Chairman Albert Gore, "The evidence we have so far tells a rare story of price-fixing, bid-rigging, and market allocation."[32] However, the Committee failed to determine precisely what that impact was.

Eventually the case turned into the largest civil lawsuit in United States history. The key elements were: (a) 27 utilities charging Westinghouse Electric Corp. with reneging on uranium supply contracts, with a majority of the disputes contested in a Richmond, Virginia court; (b) Westinghouse charging Gulf and 16 other domestic and 12 foreign uranium producers in a Chicago court with allegedly conspiring to fix uranium prices and to force middlemen like Westinghouse out of the market, and seven of the 29 defendants filing counterclaims against Westinghouse charging the company with monopolistic practices; and (c) four uranium producers suing in New Mexico to break contracts signed with Gulf's affiliate, General Atomic, for delivery of uranium at low prices because of Gulf's connection with the cartel. For good measure, the Justice Department brought suit, after a lengthy but unproductive grand jury investigation, on criminal misdemeanor charges of price fixing for Gulf's cartel activities.

Westinghouse versus the utilities.

Westinghouse had signed long-term contracts for the supply of uranium to 27 utilities using its nuclear power plants. Faced with an eight-fold price increase, the company announced in September 1975 that it was repudiating its fixed-price supply obligations under the "commercial impracticability" clause of the U.S. Uniform Commercial Code. The utilities thereupon sued Westinghouse for about $2 billion for breach of contract—an amount equal to three-quarters of the company's total equity. The company reacted by suing 17 American and 12 foreign uranium producers with conspiracy to illegally raise uranium prices and to restrict supplies in ways that were both artificial and illegal. The suit sought triple damages. Foreign uranium producers reacted angrily to the Westinghouse suit and the Justice Department investigation—Australia's Pancontinental Mining termed the charges ridiculous and "an unwarranted interference in Australian affairs."

Several attempts to reach out-of-court settlements with Westinghouse's uranium suppliers failed in 1977.[33]

The real questions in the utilities' suit were: Did Westinghouse do everything it could to fulfill the contracts before it cancelled? And did an international uranium cartel really prevent Westinghouse from honoring the contracts? "Did an unlawful cartel force up U.S. uranium prices? If so, is that an adequate excuse for Westinghouse to bow out of its supply agreements, when it failed early on to cover its commitments by entering into long-term contracts with producers?"[34] The judge had the power to order Westinghouse to deliver all, part, or none of the uranium.

The Justice Department tried to compel seven RTZ executives to testify in the Westinghouse civil suit, with the evidence possibly being used later in a criminal investigation by a grand jury of the uranium cartel. Hearings at the United States embassy in London produced only "fifth amendment" pleas from the executives. In response, the Justice Department promised immunity from prosecution and got a court order to compel the executives' testimony. However, the House of Lords, serving as Britain's highest court, rejected the bid as an outright infringement on British sovereignty and an investigation of "the activities of companies not subject to the jurisdiction of the United States."[35]

U.S. Attorney General Griffin Bell stated: "We are obligated to do all that we reasonably can to prosecute foreign private cartels which have the purpose and effect of causing significant economic harm in the United States in violation of antitrust laws."[36] In response, the governments of Canada, France, Australia, and the United Kingdom, among others, tended to emphasize the limits to the applicability of national law. Indeed, some passed legislation to prevent compliance with American antitrust investigations. The sovereignty problems raised by the case have yet to be resolved. According to one Gulf official:

> When Gulf was forced by power of subpoena to surrender certain documents pertaining to the cartel to Congress, we were severely criticized by the Canadian government. The Canadian government's sensitivity to this issue is more understandable when it is recognized that one of the reasons it helped form the uranium marketing arrangement was in response to the United States government's efforts to control the uranium market by banning the use of foreign uranium in U.S. reactors. . . . Gulf is convinced that its participation in the uranium marketing arrangement was within the strictures of the law.[37]

The Canadian government replied to the Justice Department investigation with "a hurried law forbidding the removal from Canada of any information relating to uranium marketing from 1972 to 1975."[38] A report at the time stated: "The Canadians are currently and, we believe, effectively pressuring the U.S. Department of State with threats of Canadian retaliation against the Alaskan pipeline if the uranium investigation surfaces as a criminal inquiry."[39]

By August 1977 Westinghouse had made out-of-court settlements with three of the utilities, but if that pattern continued the total amount could add up to more than $1 billion. A consolidated trial of ten other contract disputes began in Richmond, Virginia, in September 1977 with 800 witnesses, 75 lawyers and 4000 exhibits waiting to make an appearance. Court employees were even sent to New York to pick up pointers from people associated with the massive Justice Department suit against IBM. Westinghouse's counsel suggested that the outcome be decided by a softball game between attorneys for both sides, but this was rejected by counsel for the utilities, who claimed they were not up to it![40] The utilities used terms like "mismanagement" and "reckless speculation" in describing Westinghouse behavior, while the company called the charges "wild allegations" and blamed a "concerted boycott" by the uranium cartel. The utilities claimed Westinghouse got into the deal without having adequate "cover" in long-term uranium supplies, and that the company was "furnished explicit details about the cartel's activities in 1976 even as it was still signing contracts with utilities."[41] The judge hoped that the two sides would settle out of court during the trial, so that the hearings would not have to run their full course.

Additional evidence emerged in late 1977. In a 1972 letter, one Gulf lawyer had written to another, "the more intricately the Canadian government and any of its agencies or departments becomes and remains in this uranium matter, the better the degree of protection for Gulf." A Canadian government official wrote, "the consensus finally reached was that if the club was to survive as a viable entity, it would be necessary to delineate where the competition was and the nature of its strength as a prelude to eliminating it once and for all." And another Gulf memorandum stated: "My inclination is that Gulf representatives should always record their strong objection and total disagreement with any such predatory cartel action affecting or intended to affect American trade or commerce. I don't think that recorded expressions of this sort will hurt Gulf as far as the Canadian government is concerned, because surely that government will recognize the unique hazard presented as far as Gulf is concerned. . . . There is the further practical consideration that Gulf's recorded objection and disagreement will in all likelihood just be noted and overridden by other cartel members."[42]

Westinghouse reached out of court settlements with Alabama Power Company and Texas Utilities Services, Inc., in the Fall of 1977. The judge continued to press for such settlements during 1978, stating that "nobody has got a locked case here."[43] He even berated the utilities for holding out for 100 cents on the dollar—"They're just plain fools. No other way to say it." But a spokesman for one of the utilities called the case "a contest between the utilities' rate payers and Westinghouse stockholders."[44] For its part, Westinghouse began building up its liquidity position by more than $500 million to have the cash on hand to buy amounts of uranium that might be required in settlements or court decisions. The company's chairman, Robert E. Kirby, decided in mid-1978 to take personal charge of negotiating the multibillion-dollar uranium claims in hopes of extracting his company from the toughest jam in its history.[45] The company's directors created a new position of vice chairman and chief operating officer in order to give Kirby more time to participate in settlement discussions with top officers of the many utilities involved.

The decision to turn the disputes from "litigation lane" to "negotiation avenue" began to pay dividends by the Fall of 1978, with a major settlement reached with Houston Lighting & Power Co., whereby Westinghouse agreed to pay the utility a combination of equipment, services and cash valued by Houston at $350 million.[46] One observer commented on the strategy as follows: "Executives were better suited than the court to resolve the disputes. If the court forced Westinghouse to pay cash damages, the financial drain would not only cripple Westinghouse but also jeopardize completion of the nuclear-power plants it was building for the utilities. The goal of the management negotiators was to devise a *business* solution to the lawsuits—one that the court, limited to traditional contract remedies, was not able to produce."[47]

In late October the Federal judge ruled that Westinghouse had to honor its uranium fuel contracts with the seven utilities still party to the consolidated suit. Westinghouse's Kirby was "naturally disappointed" with the stinging courtroom defeat, but added that as a result of the ruling "we may get more settlements."[48] The judge reiterated his strong desire that the cases "should be settled as business problems by businessmen."[49] The ruling, however, meant that the utilities were now in the driver's seat and that Westinghouse would need to sweeten its existing offers if more out of court settlements were to follow before court-awarded damages were determined.

Westinghouse, via face-to-face negotiations reached settlements with Sydkraft, OKG and Statens Vattenfallsverk of Sweden, and with Virginia Electric & Power Co., Wisconsin Electric Power Co., and the Tennessee Valley Authority in the United States, during the first seven months of 1979. By mid-July it had thus settled ten of the original uranium-supply contract lawsuits, accounting for more than 55% of the total uranium originally claimed by all the utilities, and resulting in a recorded cumulative extraordinary loss before income taxes of $497.8 million.[50] According to the firm, settlement of the remaining uranium litigation still was a "No. 1 management priority."[51]

United Nuclear versus General Atomic.

In 1977, United Nuclear Corp. sued General Atomic Co. (jointly owned by Gulf and a subsidiary of Royal Dutch/Shell) in Santa Fe, New Mexico, alleging that it had entered into low-priced uranium supply contracts with United Nuclear while Gulf had inside information on upward uranium price pressures due to cartel operations. The suit sought to nullify the deal. At stake was compensation ranging from $250 to $280 million—officially, United Nuclear sought release from the contracts and damages of $2.3 billion. General Atomic filed a counterclaim seeking performance under the contracts and damages of $2 billion. Gulf used the same arguments employed in the Westinghouse suit (see below) to bolster its position—that it was forced to join the cartel, that the cartel had no effect, and that in any case it did not apply to the United States and Canada. United Nuclear claimed that Gulf's German partner, Uranerz Canada, did not in fact join the cartel and that "Gulf representatives sometimes played a key role in cartel meetings abroad . . . on one occasion even helping write price and other marketing regulations."[52] After a month of hearings, Gulf sought to submit the dispute to arbitration, its attorneys allegedly having moved at a snail's pace to prevent United Nuclear's attorneys from introducing evidence related to the cartel.

Early in 1978 General Atomic petitioned the New Mexico Supreme Court to halt the case and to remove the presiding judge. "United Nuclear's success has put Gulf in a potentially dangerous legal position . . . the case in Santa Fe could result in findings that might leave Gulf defenseless not only in New Mexico but also in cases elsewhere in the country involving the uranium cartel."[53] One way to reduce that danger was to remove the judge. The petition was denied, but General Atomic was granted several extensions to answer the allegations because documents demanded by the judge were in Canada and prevented from release under Canadian law. But in March 1978 the judge awarded a declaratory default judgement to United Nuclear and dismissed General Atomic's countersuit. "General Atomic Company has followed a conscious, willful and deliberate policy throughout this litigation . . . in cynical disregard and disdain of the Rules of Procedure . . . of concealing rather than in good faith revealing the true facts concerning the international uranium cartel in which Gulf Oil Corporation was involved."[54] General Atomic called the decision "outrageous and unprecedented."

The potential damage to Gulf was substantial. The judge found (a) that the Canadian government "encouraged" but in no way "required" Gulf to participate in the cartel, (b) that Gulf acted intentionally to monopolize New Mexico uranium reserves, (c) that this was in furtherance of the "cartel conspiracy," and (d) that Gulf was aware that the cartel would raise United States prices substantially.[55] United Nuclear celebrated its victory in full-page ads in major newspapers. Whereas the judge did not immediately make an award, voiding the contracts meant an estimated $900 million to United Nuclear.

Gulf appealed to the U.S. Supreme Court, and was turned down after arguing that United Nuclear management had contradictory ideas about whether or not the cartel in fact served to raise prices—in a memorandum to his board of directors, the chairman of United Nuclear had written: "The public impression . . . would suggest that uranium prices are not economic but rather are the direct result of cartel activities. This as we all know is not true . . . uranium prices are the direct result of economic forces coming to bear in a somewhat belated fashion."[56] Gulf also obtained a friend-of-the-court brief from the Canadian government stating that it was Canadian law that prevented General Atomic from producing the documents demanded by the court. The Canadian Government and General Atomic both contended the New Mexico judge had "contravened established principles of international comity and of U.S. law which required deference to the laws and national policies of Canada."[57] Westinghouse, meanwhile, prepared to introduce the

New Mexico verdict into its proceedings against Gulf and other uranium producers in Chicago (see below) and Exxon was preparing a new suit against Gulf and General Atomic for fraud and antitrust violations in a similar uranium supply agreement with Exxon's nuclear unit.[58]

In the end, United Nuclear was awarded the relatively modest sum of $8.3 million in damages from General Atomic, but against that amount prepayments by General Atomic for undelivered uranium were netted out, leaving a balance of only $236,425. However, a defendant cross-claimant in the suit, a unit of American Electric Power, won $160 million for undelivered uranium from General Atomic. The company appealed to the New Mexico Supreme Court.[59] In June 1978 that court vacated the lower court ruling, opening the way to an upset of the default judgement against General Atomic which thereupon revived its long-standing push for arbitration that had been supported by the U.S. Supreme Court in its earlier decision on the case. The company named former Secretary of Labor Willard Wirtz as arbitrator, but United Nuclear said it would fight arbitration.[60] Throughout the dispute Gulf's General Atomic partner, Royal Dutch/Shell, maintained a very low profile, although a dispute did eventually surface as to who would have to pay any future damages resulting from the cartel suits. Shell in August 1978 expected "Gulf to be fully responsible for any economic impact of the uranium litigation on General Atomic, which might result from antitrust allegations against Gulf."[61] Shell formally pulled out of the uranium and light-water reactor fuel supply business of General Atomic in 1979, receiving about $60 million from Gulf to cover the loss of profit Shell would have earned had it remained in this aspect of their ill-fated partnership.[62]

Westinghouse versus Gulf, et al.

In October 1976, Westinghouse brought suit in U.S. District Court in Chicago charging 17 domestic and 12 foreign uranium producers with creating an international cartel that forced up the price of uranium from $8/lb. to more than $40 over a two-year period. The dispute shaped up to be "one of the thorniest legal imbroglios in years."[63] The goal of Westinghouse was to prove that the 29 defendants conspired to force the price up and block the company from obtaining uranium at prices that would permit it to fulfill its contracts. By doing so, Westinghouse hoped to be able to recover in damages the money that it would have to pay to honor its utility contracts, as reviewed above. The clash between Westinghouse and its Pittsburgh neighbor Gulf, one of the 29 defendants, attracted particular attention.

Gulf Chairman McAffee in late 1977 lashed out at Westinghouse for its attempts to hide its "greed or managerial mistakes" by raising the uranium cartel issue as a smokescreen. Westinghouse retorted "If anybody is hiding behind a smokescreen it is Gulf Oil, which has consistently refused to make available cartel documents."[64] According to McAffee,

> "Westinghouse is trying to mitigate a terrible business judgement error. One can't berate them for that, unless and until they begin to hurt someone else—mainly us. . . . We've made mistakes in our time, but I don't think any this big. Basically, we don't believe in playing the market in any area where we don't know what we're doing. We'd never speculate. When you speculate, you know, you're gambling. I've got no reason to quarrel with Westinghouse or anyone else who wants to gamble—so long as they take the penalty if they're wrong."

But according to Westinghouse Chairman Kirby, "This was one of the massive ripoffs of all times, and from what I've seen, it was directed from Pittsburgh."[65] According to one observer:

> In a sense, Gulf has far more at stake than its neighbor. To Westinghouse, the case of the cartel is mostly a matter of money. A lot of money, to be sure, but after out-of-

court settlements and tax write-offs, perhaps only $300 million or so. To Gulf however, its past tainted by political payoffs and the ouster of a disgraced chairman [see Chapter 9], its present marred by earnings setbacks and a round of belt-tightening, and its future clouded by critics of multinational oil companies who would force the company out of the uranium business, the cartel dispute is a matter of reputation on a grand scale.[66]

The financial and human-resource expenditures were considerable. Besides lawyers and General Atomic people, Gulf had 50 employees working on cartel problems. And then there were the legal fees. According to McAffee, "Every time I think of them I get sick to my stomach. It's several million dollars a year."[67] Westinghouse's 1977 legal fees were $25 million, and Chairman Kirby spent most of his time on the uranium litigation. "I've given instructions to the rest of the corporation to go about business. But it's distracting whether I order them to ignore it or not. . . . I think we were caught in a web that no one understood. If I knew then what I know now, there are things I would have done differently. But I didn't know the cartel was operating."[68] For him, the utilities' suit created a cloud over the company's future. . . . "We've got to get out from under this cloud because it impacts our future ability to borrow money and it impacts the stock price. In certain cases, it still causes some big foreign customers to be nervous about the fact that the viability of Westinghouse hasn't been totally proven as long as this is hanging over our head."[69]

Gulf, in addition to its battles with Westinghouse, United Nuclear, Shell and so on, also had to contend with the Justice Department. But the evidence developed by the House Subcommittee and grand jury investigations of the international uranium cartel was inadequate, in the view of the Administration's Antitrust Chief, to show that any violations by Gulf continued after December 21, 1974, the day before an act of Congress made price-fixing a felony, with a maximum fine of $1 million and possible imprisonment.[70] Gulf got away with merely pleading no contest to a misdemeanor charge of conspiring to fix uranium prices and paying a fine of $40,000. Senator Howard Metzenbaum, chairman of the Senate Antitrust Subcommittee, called the Justice Department's handling of the case "truly disappointing" and labeled the $40,000 fine against Gulf as "tantamount" to getting off without a fine; the Justice Department assistant attorney general countered that he "didn't think we could win a felony prosecution."[71]

Back on the Westinghouse front, Gulf had meanwhile retaliated by charging in a suit that Westinghouse had monopolized the uranium, nuclear fuel, and power reactor business, asking treble damages for Gulf losses amounting to "hundreds of millions of dollars." Westinghouse charged that the Gulf suit was "totally without merit" and was "merely an effort to direct attention from the Westinghouse conspiracy suit in Chicago."[72] Similar counterclaims, however, were filed by Atlas Corporation, Anaconda Company, Kerr-McGee Corporation, Homestake Mining Company, Western Nuclear, Inc., Getty Oil Company, and Utah International Inc. All claimed that Westinghouse illegally tied contracts for low-priced uranium to its nuclear reactors to induce utilities to buy from Westinghouse rather than from its competitors.[73] The Federal judge in April 1979 denied a motion by Westinghouse to dismiss these charges.

Along with counterclaims, Westinghouse had its hands full with respect to the refusal of most of the foreign defendants, and their governments, to cooperate in pretrial activity. A few of the foreign uranium producers attacked the Chicago tribunal as a "Kangaroo Court," while foreign governments of those producers denounced the proceedings as a "serious infringement" on their countries' sovereignty and as "inimical" to their national interests.[74] Nine of the 12 foreign defendants (Anglo-American Corporation of South Africa, Conzinc Rio Tinto of Australia, Mary Kathleen Uranium of Australia, Nuclear Fuels of South Africa, Pancontinental Mining Ltd. of Australia, Queensland Mines Ltd. of Australia, Rio Algom of Canada, Rio Tinto-Zinc of Britain and RTZ Services Ltd. of Britain) chose routinely to ignore summonses and resist requests for documents, thus taking full advantage of their government's protection against American antitrust prosecution.[75] As of May 1979 all nine had failed to respond to the price-fixing charges. The three foreign producers which had responded were Denison Mines Ltd., Noranda Mines Ltd., and Gulf Minerals Canada Ltd. (the unit of Gulf Oil Corporation), all of Canada.

Westinghouse won a default judgement against the nine non-responding foreign producers. The company also offered evidence that some of them were moving assets out of the United States, in violation of an injunction by the judge against such moves, in attempts to protect their property from being attached by Westinghouse. As a result, Westinghouse was able to block payments from subsidiaries and customers in the United States destined for Rio Algom Ltd. and Mary Kathleen Uranium Ltd. Attaching the assets of the foreign defendants, however, was a risky strategy. As one American lawyer saw it: "The foreign firms could retaliate by attaching assets Westinghouse owns overseas. Or they could make life so miserable for them (through taxation and other penalties) that Westinghouse couldn't afford to carry on business in those countries anyway."[76]

Another lawyer observing the entire affair in mid-1979 noted that Westinghouse was "fighting an uphill battle all the way."[77] The "lawyers' full employment case," as the Federal judge described it, was set for trial in September 1980. The consensus was that it could take at least a decade before all the motions, counterclaims, and appeals were finally decided. Nonetheless, Westinghouse attorneys were confident. As one declared, "I don't think there's any question we'll win in Chicago court," but "maybe we'll only inherit the wind."[78]

The Multinationals and Antitrust

Whereas the Gulf-Westinghouse uranium case is perhaps atypical in terms of the issues involved, it does raise a variety of questions that are present in other cases as well. Consider, for example, the French Bic company, which could not reach agreement with the U.S. Federal Trade Commission on the domestic competitive implications of acquiring the American Safety Razor Company from Philip Morris Inc. in 1977. As a result, a plant at Virginia was threatened with closure and a major loss of jobs. Sometimes large international firms have committed outright fraud to raise profits in the face of stiff competition. For example Cook Industries, a large grain dealer, was found guilty of short-weighting grain shipments, and was sued by the United States Government for $25 million and the government of India for $35 million.[79] Pleas of no contest were made by other large firms like Bunge and Continental Grain.

Then there is the case of Pittsburgh Corning Europe, which was fined $100,000 for fixing prices of ceramic insulation under Common Market antitrust action in 1973. Continental Can got into a major antitrust action after being charged with seeking to dominate the European metal-packaging business. In that case, Continental Can argued that, since its headquarters lay outside the EEC, it was not subject to the jurisdiction of the EEC or the European Court of Justice. Many other Common Market antitrust actions have involved American firms, allegedly partly for political reasons. But actions have also been taken against European firms such as Switzerland's Sandoz and Ciba-Geigy, and Britain's Imperial Chemical Industries, and their attempt to fix dyestuff prices. And the British Rank-Xerox organization, 51% owned by Xerox Corporation, was held to be a monopoly by the British Monopolies and Mergers Commission after a three-year study. The Commission attributed the monopoly to "innovative and technical dominance rather than elimination of competitors," and maintained that "being in a monopoly position which was an inevitable result of its success" should not be the subect of criticism. the Rank Xerox monopoly was not considered to be against the public interest.[80]

Anti-competitive practices, of course, are by no means limited to MNEs. In 1972, for example, Consumers Union charged that a "conspiracy" existed between United States officials and steel firms for "unreasonable restraint of trade" in establishing import quotas for certain kinds of steel. [81] There is indeed some evidence of MNE monopoly power in recent studies of firm size. For example, MNE affiliates tend to be larger than competitive local firms. in countries where a high degree of MNE activity is found, there also tends to be a high degree of concentration in the affected industries. There tends to be more concentration in high-technology than low-technology industries, and the former attract MNEs far more than the latter. A counter-argument is that, if one considers both traded and domestically-produced goods in a global market context, then MNEs have served to substantially enhance competition among firms, rather than reduce it. Even if barriers to entry by new firms in a given market are high, other MNEs can and do compete effectively.

As we said at the beginning, from the standpoint of profit maximization less competition is better than more, and this is a natural component of management's complex of objectives. Within a particular economy, this is the same for the MNE affiliate as for a comparable local firm. Both prefer less competition if they can find a way to bring it about and get away with it. The allegation is, however, that the MNE is better able to realize its anti-competitive drives than are local firms. The reason is that it is part of a large firm that can sustain operating losses within a given affiliate for a period of time while it out-competes local firms at bargain-basement prices. Such predatory behavior made possible by MNE cross-subsidization can later lead to a much greater degree of monopoly power for the surviving firm.

For example, despite regionally high unemployment, prospective major local sourcing of component parts (70%), and significant export of local production (50%), a proposed Hitachi television factory in northern England was bitterly opposed by local industry and trade unionists because it "could be part of a wider strategy by Japanese manufacturers to destroy the British set-making and components sectors. . . . If the Hitachi factory is established we shall have introduced a Trojan horse into our own electronics industry. For a temporary advantage we will have allowed ourselves a permanent disadvantage."[82] How much of this was a true concern for effective competition and how much was self-serving argumentation by British competitors pushing their Luddite views is hard to tell. Some of the propaganda was extreme—"Hitachi, from the country that gave you Pearl Harbour." Hitachi's response was to leave the scene and search for a site in another EEC or EFTA country, still with completely free access to the British market.

Besides cross-subsidization, local MNE affiliates are frequently viewed as having access to the kinds of superior technology that give multinationals much of their market advantage. In one view, monopoly power of the MNE tends to derive from its technology, its "packaging" function, and its ability to coordinate actions closely on an inter-firm basis. This and the superior general information base available to MNE affiliates from corporate headquarters are often alleged to bias their operations toward monopolistic market conduct, with inflated profit margins the end result. Yet much depends on local conditions. For example, domestic protective policies will tend to stimulate entry of additional foreign firms. And the absence of an effective antitrust policy will tend to reduce competitive behavior.

Few MNEs have been accused of abusing technical monopoly power more regularly than pharmaceuticals firms.[83] As we have already noted in Chapter 10, Swiss-based Hoffmann-La Roche has frequently been in hot water over abuse of a powerful market position in the United Kingdom, Costa Rica, and elsewhere.[84] In the same sector, a series of suits by the governments of India, Iran, the Philippines, and South Vietnam charged that American Cyanamid, Bristol-Myers, Squibb, Olin-Mathieson, and Upjohn colluded to drive up the price of tetracyclene (an antibiotic) patented in 1955. The suit came on top of private law-suits in the United States involving more than $100 million in awards. Meanwhile, suits by South Korea, Spain, and Kuwait had been withdrawn, but cases brought by Germany and Colombia were still pending. All were brought under the U.S. Clayton Act.[85]

Sometimes MNEs can gain an environment of reduced competition as a concession to help attract investment on the part of the host government. This may involve a promise that no other MNEs will be allowed to operate in the protected market for a specific length of time, coupled with high import barriers to keep out competition from foreign suppliers on "infant industry" grounds. Precisely this happened in the case of a Dow Chemical plant in pre-Allende Chile, a venture that was later nationalized by the Marxist government and then returned to Dow after Allende was overthrown. Such "sweetheart" exclusivity arrangements are rarely the source of conflict at the outset, with the government figuring that a monopolistic industry is better than no industry at all. But as time passes the economic costs of monopoly inevitably become increasingly apparent, and often lead to acrimonious conflcit.

Antitrust policy can also be used by private firms doing battle in takeover bids and raids. For example, when in 1975 the French Société Imetal, controlled by French financier Baron Guy de Rothschild, offered to buy shares of the Copperweld Corporation, Copperweld management filed suit for an injunction against Imetal on the grounds that its offer violated United States antitrust and securities laws. Part of the reasoning was that another American-based MNE, AMAX, held shares in Imetal and that the required disclosures of this fact had not been made to Copperweld shareholders. Copperweld workers, in a virtually unprecedented action, went on record opposing the Imetal move with large demonstrations and picketing in Washington, D.C. and New York—their placards read "Keep Copperweld American" and "Go Home Frenchie." After assurances about employment security and management continuity at Copperweld after the takeover, the legal actions were dismissed and Imetal's takeover was successfully consummated.

Monopoly elements are also involved in restrictions that parent firms put on their local affiliates in terms of what can be sold where. For example a Ghanaian plant of XYZ Company may not be allowed to export to the Ivory Coast, because under XYZ's global strategy that particular market is to be served from the firm's Italian plant. This may be fine for the MNE, but it certainly runs counter to the host country's desire to increase manufacturing for export to foreign markets. Sometimes such "restrictive business practices" are initiated by the MNE's home government, which for political reasons may want to restrict trade with particular countries (see Chapter 7). Exhibit 14–2 outlines the principal types of restrictive business practices, categorized into horizontal, vertical, and exclusionary measures.

A great deal of uncertainty remains about the overall effects of MNEs on competitive market conditions. Much depends on how competitiveness is measured (number of firms, firm size, market share, cost-price margins, etc.) and how the "market" is defined. International mergers and takeovers have certainly been substantial. BP and Sohio, Gillette and Braun, Litton Industries and Adler, Matsushita and Motorola's TV operations, Nestlé and Libby, Bayer and Wyandotte are just a few examples. Yet some studies seem to suggest that MNEs may have increased rather than decreased competition in certain host countries, particularly the advanced industrial countries.[86] The MNE is able to overcome various barriers to entry (such as capital or technology requirements) that local firms might not be able to achieve, thus increasing competition. Once in, however, the MNE may try to create even greater barriers to entry by rival firms. Yet, sometimes even major MNEs fail to crush a local market. Nabisco closed its German Xox baking operation after 13 years of trying to compete with established local firms and $25 million in losses.

MNEs have occasionally also been accused of periodically causing *excessive* competition. The scenario goes like this: One MNE sets up a plant in a particular host country. Other MNEs, keeping their eye on global or regional market shares, follow suit. Pretty soon, lo and behold, we have 10 MNE affiliates competing tooth and nail for a market that can support at most three or four plants at efficient levels of production. Then there is the inevitable shakeout, and the survivors end up with a cozy market-sharing agreement or some other form of restricted competition. One study concludes that "there is ample evidence . . . that under certain conditions MNE entry has created fragmented host-country markets with attendant excess capacity. The conditions which commonly stimulate this inappropriate entry, however, are related to inappropriate host-government policies, particularly protection policies geared to industrialization."[87]

Competitive behavior is thus a regular source of MNE conflict. Many multinationals work under an oligopolistic market structure at home, and allegedly carry the competitive behavior they are used to over into host countries. Often, as in the case of American multinationals, they are subject to strict antitrust laws at home which are far more rigorous than those encountered in host countries. While they may be able to get away with more anti-competitive activity abroad than at home, even perfectly legal overseas collusion can lead to antitrust trouble at home. The antitrust problem thus takes on both economic and legal dimensions that are not at all unambiguous in many instances, as in the Gulf uranium case discussed above.

It has certainly become clear that United States-based MNEs remain well within reach of American antitrust law, even in their international operations, when competitive restraints actually or potentially affect the United States market. This includes (a) criminal investigations into uranium, phosphate and ocean shipping price-fixing, (b) restrictions by MNEs built into licensing and territorial divisions, to ascertain whether exports to the United States are inhibited, and (c)

Exhibit 14–2
Categories of Restrictive Business Practices

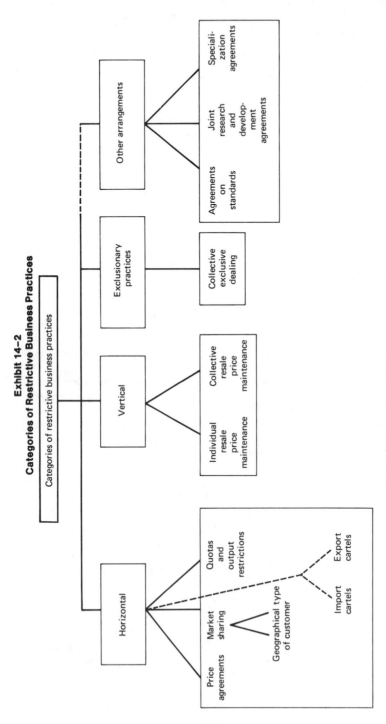

Source: Susane Brun, "Antitrust Policy in Europe", *Journal of World Trade Law* (September 1975).

relationships of multinational oil companies with oil-producing countries. Highest priority goes to market-allocation issues. And under a new "sovereignty immunity" law passed in 1977, commercial activities of foreign governments are potentially just as subject to American antitrust action as are MNEs. Still, MNE actions to get foreign governments to restrict competition are not covered, although American firms may not comply with foreign decrees affecting competition in the United States.[88]

In January 1977 the Justice Department issued guidelines for MNE operations abroad. Companies were urged to get an Antitrust Division opinion before joining any cartel overseas. The Justice Department would also challenge any foreign cartels, joined by American firms, whose formation occurs without official sanction by foreign governments. Agreements with foreign firms that operate in the United States or are *potential* entrants into the American market would also come under scrutiny. The guidelines also dealt with granting exclusive distributorships abroad, the formation of joint research projects overseas, and joint manufacturing ventures. However, they did not cover Federal Trade Commission enforcement policies under the Federal Trade Commission Act or the Clayton Act, thereby failing to remove yet another major source of uncertainty. In the late 1970s new proposals for anti-merger legislation were put forward by Senator Ted Kennedy and the Federal Trade Commission in the United States, designed to replace economic criteria with political criteria governing permissible firm size. Since this legislation would bear on American multinationals' operations abroad as well as foreign MNE's operations in the United States, its economic (and extraterritorial) implications were serious indeed.

In terms of our model, it is difficult to ascertain where MNE management ought to come out on the issue of competitive behavior. On the one hand, the MNE's stakes in the outcome are often high. Yet its power position is indeterminate, and depends in part on the relative power of home and host country antitrust authorities. The firm may also be highly resourceful, having fought antitrust battles at home and elsewhere before. So the outcome is likely to fall somewhere on the *competitive-accommodation* spectrum, where *accommodation* is interpreted as simple *compliance* with local or host-country antitrust regulations. The firm may wish to take advantage of gaps in the antitrust net, but the result may be sharp conflict whose consequences can eventually take the form of nationalization or expropriation.

Finally, it ought to be noted that domestic antitrust conflict can easily influence the MNE's own growth strategy. For example, in 1972 ITT was effectively blocked from making further acquisitions in the United States when it acquired the Hartford Fire and Casualty Insurance Company—including divestiture of ITT's Avis car-rental subsidiary. This meant that further growth of ITT, at least by acquisition, would have to be international rather than domestic, and forced the firm onto an even more multinational growth path than it was on already.

International Payments

The contribution of MNE operations to home and host country balances of payments has been a more or less permanent source of conflict, at least for many of the host countries involved. The fact that the currencies of many of the MNE home countries are now floating has dramatically reduced conflict there. Gone are the days when capital exports would be discouraged or inhibited, as under the U.S. Interest Equalization Tax and Office of Foreign Direct Investment controls of the 1960s. Instead, exchange rates are at least partly allowed to take up the shock of international investment flows, and payments are allowed to adjust accordingly. But many MNE host countries continue to maintain exchange rates that are pegged against certain other currencies, finding it economically or politically impossible to let the value of their currencies be determined by the market. For many of them, this means elaborate exchange control systems, where hard-currency earnings are carefully doled out for imports and other expenditures on the basis of a certain set of priorities. Such countries are often heavily in debt to foreign lenders, and their balance of payments trends are carefully watched as indicators of debt-service capability and international credit-worthiness. For them, the balance of payments effects of MNE operations can be of vital importance.

These effects can be spelled out quite easily. First, capital investments by MNE parents in foreign affiliates show up as a minus on home country and a plus on host country balance of payments. The repatriated earnings on that investment have the reverse effect. The former effect is immediate, the latter occurs over the life of the project. Eventually, the cumulative total of remitted earnings is likely to exceed the initial capital investment. Such flows can assume large proportions. For example, during 1966–1976 Volkswagen reportedly repatriated $100 million in profits from its Brazilian affiliates, and another $100 million in technical fees. In 1975 alone, technical and management fees paid by Brazilian MNE subsidiaries to their parents amounted to $223 million, compared with $237 million in profit remittances.[89] Leading and lagging international payments by MNEs can also have balance of payments effects—that is, delaying payment to suppliers in countries whose currencies are depreciating and speeding them up where currencies are on the rise. Further pressure on remissions comes from Financial Accounting Standards Board Rule 8 (discussed below), encouraging American multinational firms to squeeze cash out of affiliates in weak-currency countries and send it home.

Second, new MNE projects usually require imported capital equipment, and this shows up as a minus on the host country's balance of payments. If that equipment is bought in the MNE home country, it appears as a balance of payments plus there. Both appear fairly soon after the initial investment is made.

Third, there are usually continuing trade effects which enter the balance of payments. For the host country this may mean more or less permanent imports of parts, components, and raw materials to service the project, as well as payments for licenses, fees, and other such disbursements. On the other hand, the project may supply locally products that were formerly imported at much higher foreign-exchange costs, or it may produce for export and thus earn foreign exchange, both representing balance of payments gains. For the home country the reverse may be true, with the MNE producing abroad things that were formerly exported (minus), or formerly produced at home and now imported from the foreign affiliate (also minus). On the other hand, the home country may have found an excellent export market for parts, components, and raw materials (plus). For a given home or host country's balance of payments, the net impact of the induced trade effects depends entirely on the project in question.

Finally, there are more indirect effects. In the host country a new MNE investment hopefully provides jobs and output. The resulting income boost, especially if it is well diffused throughout the economy, will generate demands for more imports of both consumer and industrial goods—with negative balance of payments implications. Or the MNE affiliate may drive out local firms whose production had a smaller "import content" (hence adversely affecting the balance of payments), or which were more export-oriented while MNE exports are kept in check by parent company global marketing policies. The possibilities are many, and once again it is very difficult to pin down the MNE's balance of payments effects unless the "alternative scenario" is known, which once again has to be based on a more or less arbitrary set of assumptions. The same holds true for the indirect balance of payments effects on MNE home countries of such things as induced exports generated by income expansion abroad.

The overall balance of payments effects of MNE operations represent a composite of all of these initial and continuing, direct and indirect, straightforward and contingent relationships. Conflict arises from government's desire for maximum balance of payments contribution (or minimum cost) and the firm's desire for maximum efficiency or minimum cost in its production and trade patterns. Both the government and the company have a number of weapons available to achieve their ends.

Government can refuse to allocate foreign exchange for various purposes, including certain imports, service payments, and earnings remissions. It can try to stimulate exports, or to link the two together by such schemes as allowing $1 of imports or earnings remissions for every $2 of exports that the local MNE affiliate generates. It can put a lid on profit remittances by limiting them to a particular fixed percentage of invested capital. It can administratively pressure the firm to source inputs in the host country through progressive "local-content" requirements, or to export a minimum percentage of its output. It can force MNEs to actually bring in investment capital from abroad (as opposed to raising it locally) as a condition of setting up shop. The possibilities are impressive.

For its part, the MNE can find ways to get around government restrictions. It can avoid exchange controls by "transfer pricing"—by overpricing imports or underpricing exports in interaffiliate transactions to help get profits out—a variant on the tried-and-true practice of over-invoicing imports and under-invoicing exports to avoid exchange controls in trade between independent buyers and sellers. But when interfirm trade consists of components, parts, and other items for which no good market-reference prices exist, the chances are sometimes not too bad. Transfer pricing, of course, may be checked by local partners in the event of joint ventures, or by labor members on supervisory boards in the event of codetermination. And not to be ignored, MNE division managers often resist practices that make their financial results look poor and others' look good.[90] In 1979, the OECD drew up a voluntary code aimed at curbing the use of transfer pricing by MNEs to reduce their tax liabilities.

Other ways of coping with blocked profits include swaps of parts and raw materials among affiliates of the same firm, investment in unrelated domestic businesses (e.g., Volkswagen's large farming business and GM's coffee plantations in Brazil), and overvaluation of investment is imported machinery in order to increase the capital base on which allowable profit remissions are computed—including buying up failed companies for a pittance and keeping them on the books at original value. The MNE can also fight a war of nerves with the government, and threaten to pull out altogether if this or that exchange restriction is not relaxed.

Countries' international financial problems can have a severe impact on MNEs' local affiliates. One classic example is Turkey. In a severe payments bind due to a pre-election spending binge, the Turkish government cut virtually all foreign exchange allocations for imports of raw materials and spare parts while foreign trade-financing dried up as a result of government misuse of trade credits. A moratorium was placed on all remittances of profits and other payments. Prices of foreign firms were subject to strict controls. On top of all this, a lira devaluation of 20–30% was in the offing in mid-1977 and, under the circumstances, numerous foreign-based firms were considering closing up shop.[91] Thereafter things got even worse.

Ideological factors can play a role as well. As part of a general indictment of the American-based Marcona Corporation, Peru in 1976 charged it had taken its profits offshore in sales and shipping, while its Peruvian iron-ore mines showed losses. Overseas Marcona affiliates allegedly charged the mining company 4% sales commissions and fines for loading delays. Under its former left-wing government, Peru carved out several sectors for national ownership. Accordingly, it expropriated Marcona iron-ore properties without payment because of "not replacing and maintaining capital equipment and not establishing proven reserves of iron ore."

In terms of our conflict-management model, the balance of payments problems surrounding MNE operations do lend themselves to some measure of *compromise*. There clearly is sufficient room to maneuver in several areas, where a *quid pro quo* can be negotiated. But the principal conflict remains, and *competitive* behavior is likely to predominate, at least initially.

Foreign Exchange Markets

A final international payments conflict affecting MNEs is their alleged destabilizing effect on foreign exchange markets. A 1973 study by the U.S. Tariff Commission estimated that $268 billion in short-term assets were held by MNEs and other private institutions at end-1971, over twice the value of international reserves held by central banks and international financial institutions. Hence, the study contends, "it is clear that only a small fraction . . . needs to move in order for a genuine crisis to develop," with MNE funds flows focusing "with telling effcect on a crisis-prone situation—some weak currency which repels funds and some strong ones which attracts them."[92]

And so, with short-term working capital balances, payables, and receivables arising in a variety of curriences which tend to fluctuate against each other, the MNE is alleged to take an essentially speculative role. Currencies expected to rise in value will attract MNE cash balances, lending, and short-term investments, while currencies expected to decline will induce MNEs to draw down their short-term asset holdings and to borrow. Whether one is speculating or just protecting assets, the idea is to buy low and sell high. The charge is that by sloshing around "hot money," MNEs make exchange rates more unstable. In the process, they increase the degree of risk in international transactions and hence the cost of international business, thereby reducing the efficiency of the international economy.

For example, in 1972 Richardson-Merrill Inc.—the American pharmaceutical MNE—had a Dutch subsidiary that needed to borrow $500,000 for one year. It could do so locally at 7.5%, costing a total of $37,500 in interest charges. Meanwhile, Richardson-Merrill's Swiss subsidiary had excess cash, which it could invest locally at about 5%, or $25,000 in interest receipts. Parent-company financial officials in the United States brought the two together to work out a mutually advantageous deal.[93] Central monitoring and control such as this, together with the cooperation of financial institutions, can wring the uneconomic "float" out of intercompany payments, reduce foreign exchange exposure, and reduce net interest costs. In the process, money flows internationally and influences exchange rates.

Yet there is very little evidence that MNEs actively speculate in foreign exchange markets. The Tariff Commission study cited earlier found in 1973 that "only a small fraction" of corporate treasurers speculate offensively in foreign currencies. What is perhaps the definitive study on the subject seems to show that they seriously sub-optimize in their international financial dealings—one study estimated that if MNEs had exploited all of the financial opportunities for borrowing, investing, foreign exchange, and the like, they could have increased their 1972 earnings of $12 billion by about one-third. It also found, incidentally, that the multinational oil companies were much better at international money management that MNEs in other industries.[94]

For their part, virtually all MNE executives deny taking "offensive" speculative positions in foreign exchange markets. In 1973, for example then GM Vice-Chairman Thomas A. Murphy said, "Let me state unequivocally and in the strongest possible terms that General Motors has not and will not speculate in the world money markets."[95] A spokesman for Hercules, Inc. was quoted as saying, "We are not in the foreign exchange business, but we always like to be on the right side of currency realignments."[96] Still another prominent chief executive officer of a manufacturing MNE is quoted as saying: "Our concern is productivity, not currency exchange. We do not exploit local financial situations because we feel we're there [in other nations] forever. We wouldn't do anything that might make a government feel we weren't a real contributor to its economy."[97]

ITT lost nearly $50 million in 1974 on "defensive" foreign exchange dealings. Thereafter, most multinationals apparently decided to live with the volatile earnings reports that exchange rate shifts bring about. But the problem got worse in 1976 when the Financial Accounting Standards Board issued Rule 8, which requires United States companies to translate all foreign assets and liabilities into dollars and to reflect exchange gains and losses each quarter. As a result, many firms tried to balance fixed assets in a given country with liabilities like bank borrowings. Many firms, like TRW, restructured their entire foreign debt as a result, with controlling foreign exchange exposure assuming top management priority.[98] Others have made extensive use of forward (future) exchange markets and currency swaps to cover exposure.

The fact is that "destabilizing" MNE foreign exchange operations are most likely under fixed exchange rates or "dirty floating," where adjustments are dependent on policy action by governments. Once the exchange rate has become unrealistic and an alteration appears in the offing, preemptive moves by MNEs can help to hasten this action in an atmosphere of currency crisis.[99] In this context, "defensive" speculation is of course no different from "offensive" speculation, in terms of its effects. So the potential for conflict remains. Yet the international rules of the game in monetary affairs are the responsibility of national governments, not corporations. And so in this respect it seems to us that *avoidance* or *accommodation*-oriented behavior is appropriate, with little need for more assertive conflict management on the part of the firm.

National Economic Policy

Multinationals are often accused of making more difficult the execution of economic policy by national governments. By virtue of their multinationality they are alleged to be able to do things that local firms cannot, in terms of compliance or avoidance of national economic policy measures. At least three issues are involved: taxation, regional policy, and macroeconomic control.

Taxation. As noted at the beginning of this chapter, MNE management must focus on after-tax return on investment and this means reducing the overall tax burden on its global operations to whatever minimum is sustainable over the long term. In home countries like the United States, where foreign taxes paid can be credited against domestic tax liability and taxes can be deferred until earnings are repatriated, the argument is that the tax system favors foreign over domestic investment. While the "tax credit," provision simply insures neutrality by placing a ceiling of the domestic rate on foreign earnings (except if host-country taxes are higher than American rates), the tax-deferment provision clearly "tilts" in favor of foreign earnings. Tax reform to eliminate the tax credit provision would result in double taxation, while elimination of deferment would restore symmetry—both would increase MNE tax burdens. MNE conflict behavior in the tax area is likely to be uncooperative, in view of the importance of taxes in corporate financial performance. But *compromise* is possible, especially by yielding on the issue of deferment.[100]

The aforementioned Hartke-Burke bill would have both eliminated tax deferment and replaced the foreign tax credit with a deduction, thus ensuring double taxation of foreign income.[101] Even after the demise of Hartke-Burke with enactment of the Trade Act of 1974, the AFL-CIO continued to press for MNE tax increases, closely relating their arguments to the jobs-export issues discussed earlier. Senator Frank Church declared that tax policy "has been so tilted in favor of overseas rather than domestic investment that I sometimes wonder why any multinational corporation, given the choice, invests in the United States at all."[102] Thus far, nothing has happened, except for some changes in the limits on foreign tax credits from a global to a country-by-country basis. Given all the excitement, it seems all the more surprising that a 1973 Senate Finance Committee staff study would show that American multinationals paid taxes to foreign governments at a rate as high as 51% of earnings abroad.[103]

In host countries the problem is tax-avoidance. Especially in high-tax countries, the incentive is to keep profits as small as possible so there is little left to tax. This can be done, as in the case of exchange control avoidance, by means of transfer pricing. If the MNE plays its cards right, and if it has a large enough volume of inter-affiliate transactions, it ought to be able to lodge its profits to a significant extent in low tax countries. And if tax deferment is provided by the home country, this could make a significant contribution to the overall profitability of the enterprise. In any case, there is a reduction of the overall tax burden on the firm *and* a shifting of taxes paid among the MNE host countries, and between them and the home country of the parent firm.

One provocative study purports to show that transfer pricing from developing country affiliates to developed country parents occurs despite the fact that home-country tax rates exceed those in host countries. It explains this as a way to disguise local profitability to ease political pressure, to improve the firm's bargaining position on various host-country concessions, to avoid exchange controls, and to get a larger share of profit in joint ventures.[104]

Tax authorities, of course, have attempted to reduce avoidance by applying "constructed" values to intercompany transactions. But what is a proper "arms length" price? Cost plus "reasonable" profit? What is reasonable? How are research and development and other overhead costs to be accounted for? How about "market value"? What market? When? At what exchange rates? These kinds of questions show that transfer pricing is indeed a complex issue, where companies or countries can make just about any case they want to.

Tax havens, of course, facilitate avoidance by MNEs. Banks have also made heavy use of tax havens in recent years. An example is New York bank operations in the Bahamas.[105] By booking Eurocurrency loans through the Bahamas, banks can avoid New York City and State taxes and London bank taxes—in the traditional Eurocurrency centers—since bank income from foreign sources is not subject to state and local taxation. Not incidentally, offshore booking of loans also takes them outside the preview of United States regulatory authorities. The New Hebrides are another such tax haven. This group of 80 Pacific islands with 80,000 people is jointly administered by France and the United Kingdom, and in 1972 had over 700 companies officially registered. As in the Bahamas, little or no tax is levied. In this case, France and Britain were unable to agree on a tax system, so there has never been a tax code. "All that is required for public consumption is any kind of nameplate on the door. There are some 200 nameplates at Melanesia International Trust Co., in which Irving Trust Co. of New York and Crocker National Bank of San Francisco have an interest."[106]

Switzerland, of course, has been the traditional tax haven for MNEs, as well as for individuals. In 1977 Swiss banks announced an agreement to prevent the improper use of numbered accounts, to ensure that a client's identity is properly established, and to prevent abuse of bank secrecy. This includes "the opening or management of accounts and deposits of which the legal owners are unknown, the acceptance of funds of which the fraudulent origin can be recognized by the bank and assistance during operations involving flight of capital [from countries with exchange restrictions] and fiscal fraud." Bankers must require clients to specify the origin of funds where illegal actions are suspected, and obligates them to refuse "active assistance in the illegal transfer of capital or in fraudulent maneuvers on the part of their clients to the detriment of Swiss or foreign authorities, particularly to the detriment of fiscal authorities."[107]

Tax conflict is as much a battle between countries as it is between the MNE and any single country. Certainly the MNE can lower its local tax burden by taking its profits offshore. But these profits are eventually taxed in other countries, albeit at lower rates, and ultimately they are taxed in the home country. In any case, a study of 39 United States-based MNEs shows that transfer pricing to save United States taxes is well below what the potential would appear to indicate. It cites as "blocks" (a) sharp-eyed customs agents, (b) standard formulas on transfer pricing forced on management by the sheer complexity of the large number of affiliates, (c) difficulties in changing existing formulas without alerting the IRS, and (d) inadequate experience on the part of some firms in recognizing potential gains.[108]

An ultimate solution to the conflict of tax avoidance rests with governments and their ability to come up with tax compacts that at once close loopholes and represent agreement on the sharing of revenues. For management of MNEs, whereas tax avoidance represents purely *competitive* behavior—taking advantage of the existing systems very real weaknessess—the ultimate solution will require *accommodating* behavior, although the path from one to the other may well lead through various interim *compromise* solutions.

Regional and structural policy. Another dimension of public policy of concern to, and possible conflict with, MNE management is regional policy in host countries. Frequently there is a policy of industrial decentralization, to force industry out of areas (usually the capital city) where the costs of crowding, pollution, and congestion are already excessive. Or the policy may favor "backward" regions where there are local unemployment or industrialization problems, and where the concern is for greater parity with the more advanced parts of the country. In either case the locational preferences of the MNE may conflict with those of the government, and the firm may be especially vulnerable because it is foreign-owned and because it may be in a position to decide on new plant sites from scratch without significant historical geographic commitment.

A good example is the French case in the early 1960s, where the government was pushing a policy of industrial decentralization into the provinces, and at the same time did not look kindly on foreign-owned firms. When pressure was applied to prevent new ιocations or plant-expansions in the Paris area, some of the affected MNEs simply relocated to other EEC countries like Belgium or Germany, thus causing France to lose both the investments and the jobs. The policy was soon relaxed. But here again is a conflict situation where *compromise* probably represents the appropriate behavior. The MNE can compromise by backing off partially from its locational demands, while government can provide investment incentives to bear part of the costs.

Sometimes investments aids to implement the government's regional policy can run into opposition abroad. For example France's Michelin Tire Manufacturing Company was lured to underdeveloped Nova Scotia by Canadian government tax incentives and low-interest loans. In 1973 the United States Treasury viewed these aids as subsidies, and imposed countervailing duties of 6.6% against imports of Michelin tires from Canada.[109]

Sometimes, too, host government economic goals are themselves in conflict. For example, in late 1976 a proposal by Digital Equipment Corporation of the United States to build a plant employing 1000 in an economically depressed area of France was rejected by the French Government because it would increase competition for CII-Honeywell-Bull, the principal domestic computer manufacturer.[110]

Structural issues fall into the same category. Government may favor employment of certain disadvantaged economic groups. Or particular industries like steel or chemicals, or sectors like high-technology or labor-intensive manufacturing, may be favored by government structural policy. In all of these potential conflicts the same points hold—the MNE is disproportionately subject to conflict and there is ample room for *compromise* and *accommodation* in its solution.

Even within MNC home countries, conflict related to possible structural effects has recently been raised in a rather dramatic way. MNEs are alleged to "Latin Americanize" the United States—to undermine a healthy, diversified, dynamic economy and turn it into a weak and dependent one. This is the alleged result of the ever-increasing influence of MNE managers in economic decisions, aided by interlocking financial relationships with the large banks and working on cozy terms with the national government. This results in more economic concentration and less competition, exports of jobs, erosion of union power, fewer opportunities for the disadvantaged, worse income distribution, and a concentration of wealth and power in the hands of a few. All of this, in turn, leads to periodic shortages and class antagonisms, ultimately pointing to some sort of unstated cataclysm.[111]

This sweeping neo-Marxist view begins from an ideological perspective, typically tends to reject research findings that do not corroborate the underlying hypotheses, and almost always fails to consider the complexity of the analysis— the "running the world twice" we have consistently emphasized here. Such *caveats* have not, however, prevented the World Council of Churches from accepting "research" reports along these lines and officially calling for a "crusade against the multinationals." MNEs are held responsible for "underdevelopment and stagnation in Third World economies, exploitation of natural resources and cheap labor, the amassing of vast wealth and power without adequate control and responsibility, and the operation of intensive technology against the best interests of host countries. . . . They see the shortcomings of the combines as economic sins from which mankind must be cleansed."[112] The economic illiteracy of the churchmen is astounding, but this will hardly make the added source of conflict any less biting—particularly when such arguments are raised in emotional and righteous tones by spokesmen representing church-held blocks of shares at MNE annual meetings.

Macroeconomic control. There are, on the other hand, some legitimate arguments involving adverse aggregate economic effects of MNEs in host countries. For example, it is argued that MNEs may be able to "escape" domestic credit restraints by making use of intercompany loans and resorting to international credit markets—options not available to locally-owned enterprises.[113] So when national monetary authorities decide it's time to put on the monetary brakes in order to dampen the pressures of inflation, with a view to getting firms to cut back on investment spending, local firms are forced to comply while MNE affiliates go right on investing. Depending on the size of the MNE sector in the national economy, this could lead to significant slippage in national monetary control and contribute possibly important competitive advantages to the foreign-owned sector.

MNEs have been accused of exerting an inflationary influence in other ways as well. They tend to be high-productivity, high-wage employers. Average money-wage inflation depends in part on wage increases in those sectors where productivity is growing fastest through the so-called "wage transfer mechanism," which can seriously increase wage-push in the lagging sectors that is unmatched by productivity gains. So an egalitarian wage philosophy of "me too" can easily lead to upward wage pressure. Moreover, MNE affiliates are themselves often linked into a complex international supply network and can ill afford disruptive strikes, and so are often anxious to pay higher wages for productivity gains—or even in excess of productivity gains. Finally, MNEs are closely linked with the burgeoning Eurodollar market: Without MNEs the market's growth would undoubtedly have been much slower, and without the Euromarkets MNE financing might not be as easily obtainable. The unregulated nature and enormous size of this market is argued by some to have significant world inflationary potential.

In all these areas, however, policymaking is in the hands of governments, not corporations. Inflationary pressures from whatever source are validated by government expansion of the money supply, and this is a tap that only governments can close. With respect to aggregate economic policy it seems clear that, despite the conflicts raised, MNE management should take an *avoidance* or *compliance* oriented conflict-management position and wait for governments to design and implement appropriate techniques of economic control.

QUESTIONS OF RISK AND LEVERAGE

To conclude, economic conflict is inevitable in multinational corporate operations—whether the issue is job displacement, income distribution, capital formation, anti-competitive behavior, balance of payments, or tax avoidance. And conflict-management strategy for management runs the gamut of *accommodating*, *avoiding*, *competing*, *collaborating*, and *compromising* behavior, as we have seen.

The outcome of economic conflict hinges in large part on ecomomic leverage—what can the country offer that the MNE needs (and vice versa), and what are the options each of the two parties has at its disposal. Company leverage will be larger (1) the greater the economic value of the "package" of services it can provide, (2) the broader the options it has available, and (3) the fewer the options available to the home or host country involved. The latter's leverage will be greater, in turn, (1) the larger is its national market and the more rapidly it is growing, (2) the more valuable are local resources and the more conducive the local business climate, and (3) the larger the number of viable options it has available and the smaller the number of options open to MNE management. Such basic economic elements determine bargaining power in what is likely to be a positive-sum game where both sides can gain, but where the argument is about the relative size and character of the respective gains.

Heavy leverage in favor of the firm can lead to a situation of competitive bidding among prospective host countries where the eventual "lucky winner" ends up giving the sought-after MNE sweetheart terms and conditions that are highly skewed in the firm's favor. Tax holidays, low interest loans, cash grants, duty-free status, guaranteed labor peace and similar concessions are part and parcel of such a "sweetheart" deal. The firm's gets the lion's share of the pie. Still, such an arrangement may well be worthwhile for the country in the light of its particular bargaining power and social needs. Such an ultra-hard bargain may not be too favorable for the MNE over the longer term, however. Bargaining power changes with shifting needs, priorities and options. So do governments. And in the end an excessively competitive MNE negotiating strategy at the outset may boomerang into forced accommodation under extreme duress.

Countries, too, need to take such factors into account in plotting strategy. A critical question is how stable the foreign firms are likely to be. An electronics plant that can pack its belongings and be out of the country in 48 hours may be less valuable to the host country than a tire and rubber operation with a permanent commitment to the country, even if all of the other ecomomic costs and benefits are perceived to be identical. In deciding what kind of "portfolio" of MNEs it would like to attract, the host country must look at the *risks* as well as the *returns* of each prospective new project. The promise of stability, in turn, gives the MNE added bargaining leverage.

Another source of risk is the speed of adjustment. MNEs are highly sensitive to what goes on in the rest of the world. If fundamental conditions of production change in favor of other countries the firm may be able to close plants and shift production in a matter of months. In the absence of MNEs it would take years for a comparable local firm to lose its markets to imports and be driven out of business. And what if there is a recession abroad, cutting demand for the MNE's worldwide production? Might it not have to shut down local affiliate plants completely? Might it not shut these down before closing home-country plants without worrying too much about the local consequences? All of these things have to be watched carefully as sources of risk to host countries. Speed of economic change is especially important in the disruption of labor markets, so that the MNE by its very nature may impose significant incremental adjustment costs on national economies.

We have seen that MNE economic conflict covers an extremely broad spectrum of both very specific and amazingly sweeping topics, some of which MNE management can do something about with constructive conflict management and some of which it cannot. Certainly ideological broadsides against private or foreign ownership cannot be effectively refuted by the firm's own actions. Neither can sweeping charges that the "market" is being fundamentally unfair in an international welfare sense—that free markets basically favor the rich countries and are inimical to the poor, as argued in the New International Order demands raised in the mid-1970s by the developing countries. The MNE is inexorably intertwined with the operation of markets, and so these demands also call for "economic and technological independence" by developing countries and reduced involvement on the part of multinationals. Whether such a commitment will be honored more in the breach than in the practice, as now seems to be the case, remains to be seen. But there is little the individual MNE can itself contribute to resolution of the debate.

15 MULTINATIONAL CONFLICT MANAGEMENT

We have now come full-circle in this volume. We began with an assessment of the nature of multinational corporate conflict by tracing its impact on five rather different multinationals during a ten-year span—Hoffmann-La Roche, ITT, Rio-Tinto Zinc, Dow Chemical, and Gulf Oil. We proceeded to outline a "contingency" approach to conflict behavior, which we believe can be used by MNE management to diagnose individual conflicts and their principal components as they affect the firm, and to develop from that diagnosis corporate conflict-management strategies that appear to make sense. And we examined a series of major types of non-market conflicts in terms of our model, in each case developing an in-depth analysis of the nature of the problem and how it interacts with the domain of the multinational corporate manager. We come now, in this concluding chapter, to a summing-up and identification of some managerial initiatives that seem to suggest themselves.

THE CHALLENGE OF CONFLICT

We have seen that conflict is inevitable in multinational corporate operations. At base, this is because the goals of MNE managers assigned the task of making optimum use of corporate resources on a global basis clash with countries and interest groups whose goals point in fundamentally different directions and who are confined to seeking their own objectives within the confines of the national state. But more than this, the multinational enterprise is often caught up in conflicts not of its own making—between countries or groups whose interests cut across countries—which can affect the vital interests of the firm. We have stressed throughout that it is not conflict itself that is dangerous for the multinational firm, but rather its mismanagement.

The range of conflict facing the MNE is amazingly broad. Terrorism presents a unique set of problems that fall well outside the domain of managerial competence and often generate secondary conflict with national governments. How should firms like Akzo, Owens–Illinois, or Fiat react when they are confronted with situations threatening the lives of their managers—when they are used as pawns in violent struggles between insurgent groups and host country governments? Human rights present equally perplexing problems: MNE management is often caught in the middle of conflict between its home-country stakeholders and host-country governments over the alleged cruel, unjust, and repressive behavior of those governments. As companies like Polariod and others have discovered at considerable cost, what interest-groups and government at home demand is not necessarily in the best interests of the oppressed in the host nation of concern and certainly runs counter to the directives of the government there.

The linkages between "human rights" and "human needs" are indeed complex, and so the answers sought by the firm are not nearly as straightforward as those often proposed by human-rights groups. The very complexity of the issue makes it exceedingly difficult to build a credible defense of corporate actions without appearing to argue for oppression.

Political conflict facing the NME can be equally perplexing. Ford and Coca-Cola were caught in the middle of the Arab boycott against Israel, and a great many multinationals have been affected by counter-moves like the American anti-boycott legislation. Political conflict of a different kind was behind problems of national ownership like those faced by IBM in India, Nigeria, Indonesia, Brazil, and elsewhere. And conversely, the political activities of ITT with respect to Chile in the early 1970s has led to major damage to the interests of multinationals around the world.

Questionable payments pose a different kind of issue that has moral, political, as well as economic dimensions for companies like Exxon, Lockheed, and Union Carbide. And criminalization in the form of the 1977 Foreign Corrupt Practices Act, which the United States government adopted as the "solution" to the problem, has done little to eliminate the demand for "QPs." As with other areas of extraterritoriality, the strategies adopted by MNEs to cope with the problem will have less to do with a true resolution of the underlying causes than with compliance with rather simplistic extensions of home-country laws to their overseas operations.

Marketing-related conflict presents MNEs with a wider range of behavioral discretion, simply because the rules of the game are less clear-cut. The problems of Nestlé in the infant-formula business, for example, could perhaps have been severely reduced by greater managerial sensitivity to the social needs of the market. Similarly, a great deal of scope exists for managerial discretion in the labor relations field, despite pressures for codetermination and improved job satisfaction that go well beyond the traditional scope of bargaining over wages and fringe benefits. Companies like Volvo have found significant payoffs in anticipating and reacting to the emergence of conflict relating to human resources. And MNEs like General Motors have been wise to seek accommodation with major shifts in labor relations such as codetermination in Germany.

Conflict relating to the natural environment is a relatively new issue that has taken on major dimensions for companies like Hoffman-La Roche and Dow Chemical, whether it derives from accidental damage such as the Seveso incident or relates to the ecological consequences of existing plants or new projects and products. The costs of environmental policy in expanded capital commitments, operating expenses, project delays, and outright cancellations are only now becoming apparent in industrial countries and will increasingly affect worldwide MNE operations in the years to come.

Closer to the market, but still often well beyond the conventional scope of management decision-making, are conflicts related to the technological and economic impacts of the MNE on home and host countries. Questions relating to the "appropriate" technologies have bedeviled companies, especially with regard to their activities in developing host countries. Such companies as General Electric, Philips, and Celanese face real problems in their attempts to tailor product and process technologies to local conditions where social needs and relative supplies of capital and labor frequently differ fundamentally from those at home. Perhaps even more troublesome is the question of a "fair" price of technology to be charged by companies like Merck and Bayer on products sold in national markets around the world where "ability to pay" enters into the political dialogue of conflict. And in another economic area, that of attempting to optimize production and sourcing patterns, companies like Zenith, John Deere, and Volkswagen will inevitably run into conflict with national and interest-group concerns over employment, the balance of payments, income distribution, and similar divergent worries of their respective constituents.

The consequences of conflict for the multinational firm are serious indeed. As we noted at the outset, competitive success in the 1980s and 1990s may be determined more by the ability to construct a corporate "technology of conflict management" than by the traditional performance criteria of the marketplace. In our view, firms that can deal effectively with each of the issues discussed here may end up by most measures as the most profitable and the ones with the brightest growth outlook. This presupposes that poor conflict management is costly to the firm in terms of price and product-competitiveness, delayed decisions on product or process innovations, increased costs, frustrated development strategies, and perhaps above all, diverted managerial resources. We have repeatedly stressed that managerial time and attention, among the most valuable and scarce resources available to MNEs, are extraordinarily sensitive to nonmarket conflict. Each of the issues we have discussed chews up managerial resources at a ferocious rate—resources that should properly be employed in other ways to secure the future of the enterprise. Perhaps for this reason alone the careful development of a contingency-oriented conflict-management system seems fully justified.

INTERNATIONAL POLITICS AND CONFLICT MANAGEMENT

The uniqueness of conflict management in a multinational corporate setting derives in large measure from the absence of a coherent, cohesive set of laws, behavioral norms, and guidelines such as usually exist at least to some degree at the national level. Nor does the problem boil down to simply complying with heterogeneous sets of national controls wherever the firm operates. For one thing, there is the question of political legitimacy. MNEs frequently operate in countries where domestic political mechanisms are highly imperfect. There are now only two dozen or so political democracies left on earth. All other countries have some form of dictatorship or one-party regime that often resort to different degrees of authoritarian control with varying levels of public support. The people who are the MNE's employees, customers, and suppliers in such countries may often consider their own interests more closely aligned with the firm's than with the government's. And so it may be wrong to assume that a particular conflict is with the entire host society as expressed by government policy. Rather, it may be with the local power élite, a particular political party, or an ideological perspective that may or may not be broadly shared. The MNE's own position in the conflict may in fact represent the views of significant social groups and perhaps even the majority of the population. This may or may not be good for the firm from the point of view of bargaining and leverage. It certainly raises the degree of politicization of the MNE and the skepticism and perhaps fear with which national political leaders sometimes view multinationals.

Internationally as well, it has frequently been argued that MNEs can serve as a significant force for reducing the kinds of international conflict, based on nationalism, that can lead to war. One need only recall the origins of the European Economic Community in the 1950s, where a powerful political argument favoring the Treaty of Rome held that creation of an economically integrated Europe would at last ameliorate the long-standing hostility between Germany and France. Economic interdependence was viewed as a key to reduced political enmity. Once the EEC was formed it was the American multinationals that first regarded Europe as an integrated market and brought about the very kind of economic linkages among member countries that promised to reduce political conflict.[1] And so it is possible to argue that the MNE can indeed be a constructive force for political integration through trade, finance, and technological diffusion precisely *because* it is not impregnated with the kind of nationalism that has been so divisive and destructive in the past. This may be reinforced by the MNE's own fusion of people from many countries in a common business undertaking, which can itself serve to support international political integration.

There are, of course, opposing views. One is the role of the MNE as an instrument of national policy—a means of extending home-country influence for national economic and political purposes. Especially from the vantage point of developing countries, the MNE can sometimes appear to be a vehicle for neo-imperialism on the part of its home government with the result that often "poverty is the product."[2] National officials, for their part, worry about political independence and its economic prerequisites, and politicians are not happy about what they view as erosion of effective national sovereignty, no matter what the potential dividends in terms of economic gains or reduced international conflict. They often react xenophobically to perceptions of foreign influence, especially in an environment where the profit motive itself is suspect and where there are already strong socialist tendencies. The MNE affiliate is a foreign firm in a foreign environment, and can expect to face different conflict management problems from those confronting a local firm in a local environment. Perhaps most troublesome of all, the MNE's available options, including its ability sometimes to adopt a "take it or leave it" attitude, are viewed as giving the firm excessive leverage and, therefore, excessive power.

We come full circle in political relations between East and West. Here the MNE is frequently viewed as a powerful instrument for reducing political tensions. The chronic technological and managerial backwardness of the Communist countries, and the ability of the MNE to undertake major technical projects successfully, provide the key. The MNE "package," bought under a variety of alternative arrangements, is inordinately effective in breaking the kinds of bottlenecks such a system throws up, so effective that there is a willingness to pay a political price for access to it. On the other hand, some observers worry that this sort of role will increasingly involve MNEs in the international political system and in what is called the "interstate violence system," with consequences for the individual firm that are difficult to predict.[3]

The international political climate within which the MNE exists is both complex and ambiguous. The basic source of conflict resides in the essence of the MNE, that is, with its global view. The MNE confronts policymakers with a national view, and nobody has an international political mandate that corresponds to the operational scope of the firm. Some contend that this is inevitable, and that similar conflicts would exist even in the absence of the MNE.[4] There is such a thing as an "optimal economic area" which, from a static efficiency point of view, encompasses the whole world in a system of free trade. Then there is an "optimal political area," determined by such factors as effective exercise of voting franchise, delivery of social services, provision for collective defense, and the like. Lastly, there is an "optimal cultural area," a product of common racial or ethnic stock, language, and similar factors. It is not hard to conclude that the size of the optimum economic area exceeds that of the optimum political area, which in turn exceeds that of the optimum cultural area. And so there are constant conflicts among the second "pair" (e.g., the Welsh or Québecois or Basque regional independence movements) and among the first pair (e.g., Commission versus national authority within the EEC, and free trade versus protectionism). The fact is that we have political areas in the form of nations which may not even be "optimal" in a political sense, and even less so in a cultural and economic sense. The MNE operates across all three dimensions. And if preservation of the power of the state means preventing erosion of *status quo* sovereignty in either direction, it essentially means that measures will be sought to curb the activities of institutions which threaten to erode that sovereignty—including multinational enterprise.

The political-cultural conflict is arguably less troublesome in general, but certainly less troublesome for the MNE, than political-economic conflict. The mere fact that most "optimum cultural areas" are incapable of economic survival drives them to the larger context of the modern national state. And there are scale economies in social and economic infrastructure and defense expenditures that have the same effect. A variety of policy options such as regional self-governance in various dimensions can also be used to defuse hostility and promote reconciliation on the part of national governments. Finally there is the point that both national and multinational firms are involved in regional economies, which reduces the differential vulnerability of the MNE. None of this, however, prevents the MNE from being used as *vehicle* in various separatist attacks against national states, especially through terrorism.

The problems seem far more acute in political-economic conflict, and the policy options are less clear-cut. Two general resolutions suggest themselves. One would be to reduce the economic dimension to the narrower political one of the national state using the instruments of autarky—tariffs, quotas, investment controls, technological independence, and the like, all affecting the MNE, as discussed in Chapters 8 and 14. Some observers see this as the right way to go—to encourage firms to integrate their activities horizontally across industry lines *within* a country rather than within an industry *between* countries. The former is admitted to carry with it a certain amount of economic sacrifice, but is viewed as paying significant dividends in political independence.[5] Whether or not one accepts such arguments, the tradeoff between political independence and economic welfare becomes quite clear, especially for small countries. Yet the fact is that we don't know what values to attach to either dimension, and this makes it difficult to talk about such tradeoffs in more than an abstract way.

The second possible resolution is to extend the political dimension to begin to encompass the larger optimum economic area. Attempts in this direction have been made in the European Economic Community—besides trade, for example in antitrust, agriculture, labor, and regional policy—and in a more limited way in other economic groupings as well. Such experiments show how difficult it is to extend political control beyond the bounds of the national state. National sovereignty, especially in countries large enough to have options, is not easily overcome even when everyone agrees on the ultimate objectives, and it is far more problematic when they do not.

WHYS AND HOWS OF INTERNATIONAL CONTROL

At the national level, control of business enterprise takes a wide variety of forms. There are laws governing the character of corporations and defining their scope of activities. Antitrust policy regulates competitive behavior in the marketplace. Securities and banking laws and enforcement agencies prevent abuses of the financial system. There are labor laws, environmental regulations, food and drug laws, and many more, in addition to private groups (such as labor unions and the consumer movement) that provide "countervailing power" in a national environment to the potential excesses of the business sector. All coexist in a dynamic, uneasy, but generally robust equilibrium of shifting coalitions and adaptation to changing economic and political circumstances. Business would often like things to be a bit more favorable, but so would each of the other interest-groups.

At the international level no such system of controls and countervailing pressures exists. Behaviorally, MNEs represent managerial systems that operate on a global scale, but from a legal and regulatory standpoint they are really private "clusters of firms of diverse nationality joined together by ties of common ownership and responsive to a common management strategy."[6] Laws and regulations bear on individuad affiliates in these clusters. None of them bear on the clusters themselves. Only intergovernmental agreements, generally on a bilateral basis, and regional approaches like the Common Market and to a far lesser extent the Andean Pact, begin to move beyond this exclusively national frame of reference.

Regulation and control of MNEs has certainly been a growth industry in recent years. It has also been highly politicized—the game of controlling multinationals "is serious indeed. . . . But the game is also deeply cynical, because all the players know the multinationals are being whipped for everybody's faults as well as their own—and that the 101 restrictions that might be placed on them will ultimately give way, as often as not, to imperatives that may be economic, political, or, quite frequently, less respectable than either."[7]

There are basically two sets of initiatives in international control of the MNE. Both have the avowed objective of permitting the firm to operate profitably in an international legal and regulatory setting of less ambiguity and uncertainty, and both allow it to make its contribution to national and global economic efficiency and welfare with minimum external interference while at the same time steering the treacherous course between conflicting national interests.

The first involves the creation of international institutions to identify common areas of interest between MNEs, home countries, and host countries, and to set rules of conduct by international agreement. The experiences of the General Agreement on Tariffs and Trade (GATT) in setting the rules for commercial policy and the International Monetary Fund (IMF) in financial affairs serve as models. GATT is perhaps the more appropriate model in this respect—one which incorporates national rights and obligations, adjudication of disputes, and avenues of relief in the event of economic injury. In addition to these functions, a "GATT for international investment" could be an effective forum for harmonizing policy in specific areas such as taxation, nationalization, exchange restrictions, and so on.

Perhaps the most ambitious example in this vein is the proposal for a "General Agreement for the International Corporation" (GAIC), covering competition policy, exchange control, securities regulations, export controls, and taxation under a set of universally-agreed principles.[8] The agency's findings in cases of conflict would be subject to mutual agreement and accepted voluntarily by the signatories. A legalistic arrangement of this sort has the advantage of being resistant to the kinds of eroded effectiveness that can plague less formal institutions after a time, and has the added advantage of "stability and predictability."[9] On the other hand, in 1973 at a conference in Düsseldorf, West Germany, delegates from government, industry, and academia concluded that a GATT-type organization for international investment simply is not in the cards. As one delegate stated: "The discussion has clearly shown that there isn't any possibility whatsoever of organizing an institution which might really exercise some control. The companies, the home-base nations and the subsidiaries' 'host' countries all are unwilling to accept an international agency that would tell them what to do."[10]

The second option is somewhat looser, involving agreement on codes of conduct to govern the behavior of MNEs in each of its major dimensions. Such codes would provide standards or norms of behavior to serve as voluntary guidelines for the MNE, with moral suasion the primary enforcement mechanism. In addition, a voluntary code would underpin or justify national policies to regulate the MNE, and increase the country's leverage in a bargaining context. Mandatory codes of conduct would have the same effects to a greater degree and, in addition, cut down the options available to the firm—although they would require enforcement machinery and a greater degree of international agreement than voluntary codes. Codes may be all-encompassing "good citizenship" guidelines covering virtually all aspects of MNE operations, or they may be fairly narrow, covering only taxation or bribery or technology transfer, for example. They may be global, negotiated under broad auspices like the United Nations, or they may be regionally-oriented. If international laws or institutions governing foreign investment are not practicable, then codes of conduct are viewed as a second-best alternative. Codes of conduct have long had support in the private sector as well as among governments, if only to reduce international business risk and bring a certain amount of order out of the chaos of uncoordinated national policies.

A final point concerns disclosure. One of the principal contributing factors to conflict involving the multinational enterprise is the flow of information. We have frequently emphasized the critical importance of information to the MNE. Without the technical and managerial knowledge, as well as information on markets and supply factors, that characterizes multinational firms, their advantage over non-MNEs would largely disappear. Indeed, the MNE is often viewed as an "information factory," scooping up knowledge wherever it can and acting or reacting accordingly. Yet the return flow of information is not nearly so free. Partly, this is because of the proprietary nature of many kinds of information within a highly competitive (especially nonprice competitive) framework. Partly it is because one of the main lessons of effective bargaining is not to lay too many cards on the table. And partly it is because information collection and disclosure is a costly process, which is not encouraged by management when there is no prospect of a return or benefit.

Nevertheless, it appears to many observers that there is an excessively one-way flow of information between the MNE and its environment—with few if any disclosure requirements in host countries, and disclosure in home countries often limited to extremely broad annual reports. This adds an air of mystery to the external image of the MNE that can only contribute to an environment of hostility. Greater disclosure, this view holds, would substantially reduce the risk of conflict, to the point where the benefits of increased disclosure would greatly exceed the costs to the firm. Whether this is true or not, it seems clear that disclosure has become a major aspect of the more recent initiatives toward international control of the multinational enterprise.

Existing international agreements covering foreign direct investment are sparse. They include the Paris Convention of 1883 and the Inter-American Convention on Inventions, Patents, Designs and Models of 1910 in the technology area; the OECD Code of Liberalization of Capital Movements (1961) and Code of Liberalization of Current Invisible Operations (1961); and the World Bank-sponsored Convention on the Settlement of Investment Disputes between States and Nationals of Other States (1966), which by 1978 had been ratified by 70 countries and is intended to ease the flow of capital particularly to developing countries by facilitating conflict resolution. Neither the Latin American countries nor a number of others have signed the latter, however, on the grounds that national courts should have sole jurisdiction in disputes involving multinational firms.

Over the years a variety of other initiatives have dealt with the design of international rules for MNEs. The Havana Charter (1947) would have served this role, but was torpedoed by the United States Congress.[11] Hemispheric initiatives got nowhere, pitting the Hickenlooper Amendment mentality in the United States against the Calvo Doctrine of the Latin American countries, which asserted unconditional rights of national sovereignty to be preeminent over international obligations. The International Chamber of Commerce tried repeatedly to formulate voluntary guidelines beginning in 1949 which generally were unacceptable to governments, and so did the United Nations General Assembly and Economic and Social Council (ECOSOC), often adopting strongly pro-developing nation positions. For example, the "Charter of Rights and Duties of States," approved in 1974 by a General Assembly vote of 120 to 6 with 10 abstentions, generally reflects the viewpoints of socialist and developing countries, and asserts complete national sovereignty in questions of nationalization, expropriation, and ownership transfer of foreign property. It acknowledges no obligation on the part of host countries. It affirms that nations have permanent and full control over their resources and wealth, and over economic activities undertaken inside their borders. It also asserts the right of countries to organize export cartels, and to share fully in technological advance no matter what the source of innovation. No guarantees are given on the safety of foreign investment or on the provision of prompt and adequate compensation under international law in the event of expropriation or nationalization. However, the Charter has no legal force.[12]

At a regional level, EEC efforts have concentrated on the development of an effective anti-trust policy under Article 85 of the Treaty of Rome, and a "European companies law" to assure consistency and increased disclosure for all firms operating in the EEC. The European Parliament has also come up with draft MNE guidelines, called the Lange-Gibbons Code. Aspects of guidelines for multinationals are contained in the EEC's association agreement with developing countries under the Lomé Convention.[13] In Latin America, the Andean Pact contains provisions dealing with MNE in its Decision 24, which covers the use of patents, trademarks, technology transfer, and restrictive business practices, as well as a "fadeout provision" which demands a local majority holding in MNE affiliates (with first option going to governments) during a 15–20 year adjustment period. It also specifies preferences, in Decision 46, for local home-grown multinationals. Finally, the Organization of American States has also developed a draft set of guidelines for MNEs, published in 1975, that strongly reflect the Calvo Doctrine.[14]

Several codes of conduct have been addressed to technology transfer, including a draft code produced by the Pugwash Conference on Science and World Affairs and one developed by the United Nations Conference on Trade and Development (UNCTAD), both highly favorable to developing countries and viewed as inimical to MNE and host-country interests.[15] In 1975 the International Confederation of Free Trade Unions (IFCTU) likewise came up with a code of conduct favorable to labor,[16] as did the International Labor Office (ILO) of the United Nations in 1976,[17] both notably without active United States participation and hence without hope of implementation. Such essentially anti-MNE code-making was paralleled by blistering attacks in such groups as the so-called Non-Aligned Countries and the World Council of Churches.[18]

Perhaps the most comprehensive program for influencing the behavior of MNEs through international measures grew out of the events in 1972 involving ITT and its involvement in the internal political affairs of the Republic of Chile. The ITT revelations prompted the government of President Salvador Allende Gossens to demand a United Nations inquiry into the conduct of multinational enterprises. As a result, the Secretary General in 1973 appointed a Group of Eminent Persons, composed of 20 individuals with presumed expertise in the field, to investigate the role of MNEs with particular reference to the developing countries and to submit recommendations for action by ECOSOC. After extensive hearings that included representatives from business, labor, governments, and academia, the Group submitted its report in mid-1974.

While the report contained numerous memoranda of reservation and dissent by individual members of the Group, it did recommend that a Commission on Transnational Corporations be created as an advisory body to ECOSOC. The staff functions of the Commission are provided by the Centre on Transnational Corporations, located in New York, and intended to serve as an information clearing-house on MNEs. Its mandate includes research into the political, economic, and social effects of MNEs, technical cooperation programs at the request of national governments, and studies designed to define the concept of MNEs. The first order of business of the new Commission was to initiate work on an international agreement for an MNE code of conduct.

In 1978 the Commission endorsed a recommendation on increased MNE disclosure by 14 international experts, including the establishment of a permanent accounting body under United States auspices.[19] Minimum disclosure would include (a) balance sheet, income, and funds statements for the MNE parent company and each major subsidiary as well as on a consolidated basis for the firm as a whole, (b) data on sales and earnings, accounting policies, and ownership on a geographical and product-line basis, and (c) nonfinancial data on employment, production, transfer pricing, significant new processes and products, new investments, mergers and acquisitions, and environmental impacts, particularly at the affiliate level. Work on the Code of Conduct continues at the United Nations.

More rapid progress was made in the Organization for Economic Cooperation and Development (OECD), whose members constitute the home nations for virtually all of the world's multinational companies. The result was an agreement in 1976 by the OECD Ministerial Council on "Guidelines for Multinational Enterprises," a set of voluntary and not legally binding principles.[20] The document's intent is to maximize the positive contributions of MNEs while reducing the chances of conflict. It also recognizes the responsibility of governments to treat both domestic and foreign-owned firms in an equitable manner, in accordance with contractual obligations and international commitments. It encourages the establishment of international machinery for the settlement of disputes, and applies both to privately-owned and state-owned enterprises.

The OECD code encourages disclosure by MNEs of production structures, ownership of affiliates, and geographical patterns of operation. Sales and operating results should be shown both in terms of their geographical distribution, including country-by-country reporting, and by major lines of business. The same breakdown should be provided for new investments, overall sources and uses of funds, geographic distribution of employees, employee remuneration, and research and development expenditures. Finally, a statement should be provided on intra-firm pricing policies and accounting practices.

In the area of competition policy, MNEs are requested not to restrain competition by abusing a real or potential dominant position in the marketplace. They are asked to allow purchasers, distributors, and licensees the freedom to resell products, and to refrain from discriminatory pricing that would discourage competition—including the use of intercompany pricing for this purpose. MNEs are encouraged to cooperate and consult with governments on issues relating to competition, and to refrain from participating in or otherwise promoting the restrictive effects of cartels.

MNEs should also cooperate with national tax authorities and comply with tax laws and regulations, and should not use transfer pricing for purposes of tax avoidance. They should take into account national balance of payments and exchange rate objectives in their commercial and financial transactions. Indeed, MNEs should conduct their affairs generally in accordance with national economic and social objectives, in return for which they are assured of commercial freedom and nondiscrimination consistent with sound business practice. Bribes and other improper payments should not be made, although political contributions are permissable unless they are illegal. Also, MNEs should refrain from "improper" political activities.

With respect to science and technology, MNEs ought to accommodate their operations to the objectives of host countries, and promote the diffusion of technology on fair and reasonable terms. On employment and labor relations, MNEs should support collective bargaining consistent with local practice, respect employees' right to organize and provide facilities and assistance for this purpose, and supply information needed for labor negotiations. Moreover, they should not threaten to transfer operations while engaged in labor negotiations, and should ensure that management representatives in local labor negotiations are authorized to make decisions and binding commitments. They should also observe labor standards at least as strict as those observed by local firms, train local labor, refrain from discrimination in employment practices unless this is consistent with government policy, and minimize adverse effects of changes in operations on employees.

A Committee on International Investment and Multinational Enterprises was established to report periodically to the OECD on implementation of these guidelines, and solicit the views of business and labor advisory groups. In cases of conflicts with regard to the interpretation of individual issues, an appropriate procedure for their resolution was devised, wherein the affected firms could be invited to present their views—although the conclusions of such reviews would not be binding on individual firms.

While the OECD guidelines are voluntary, there is strong pressure on MNEs to comply. For one thing, the business-sector inputs into the deliberations were so effective right from the beginning that the guidelines are widely regarded as the best MNEs could hope for. Moreover, because codes of MNE conduct have been under discussion in ILO, UNCTAD, OAS, and ECOSOC as well—all of which are clearly less favorably inclined toward the MNE than OECD member governments—close adherence to the OECD guidelines could forestall more onerous measures in some of these other organizations. MNEs also hoped that the guidelines would partly erase the image of corruption that had emerged during the United States questionable payments disclosures discussed in Chapter 9. Not least important was the view that the guidelines might be a step toward a real policy covergence—the MNEs, encouraged by their industry associations and home governments, would declare company adherence to the guidelines while host governments would look to these same guidelines in the formulation of their own policies toward multinational enterprise.

Overall, the OECD guidelines are probably the most promising initiative thus far among the many attempts to exert a modicum of control over the multinational enterprise. There is a real attempt to set standards of conduct that home and host countries, MNEs, and organized labor alike can accept in a part of the world that attracts the overwhelming majority of multinational corporate activities. There is also an attempt to deliver symmetry in rights and obligations by the various parties and to increase security for the MNE itself. Moreover, the OECD guidelines may in time become accepted practice for MNE conduct and may pave the way to the broader agreement sought by the UN Commission on Transnational Corporations that will encompass the developing countries as well.

The outlook for binding, enforced international rules governing MNEs is not bright. National interests between home and host countries, and among host countries, differ enormously. There are continuing conflicts about the symmetry of rights and obligations, about the voluntary or binding nature of any such rules, and about the problem of disclosure. From the standpoint of MNE management, international controls represent a decidedly mixed bag. There are advantages in the reduced ambiguity and greater clarity they might contribute with respect to appropriate conduct in various important areas such as environmental management and questionable payments. There are also advantages to the firm in being able to point to international agreements to justify its policies with respect to national governments. There are advantages if international accords reduce disagreements between countries, where otherwise the MNE could be caught in the middle with conflict on both sides. And there are obvious advantages in any agreements that spell out the obligations of host countries toward foreign investment and reduce the incidence of capricious and arbitrary behavior by governments that contributes so much of the "political" or "sovereign" risk in international operations of companies. On the other hand, disadvantages include information costs and losses of confidentiality implied by increased disclosure, and the reduced flexibility and bargaining leverage that international control might bring with it. More of the joint gains from MNE activities may thus go to host countries and fewer to the firm itself, with possible damage to overall corporate profitability.

With respect to our conflict management model, international regulation reduces the degree of freedom a firm has available in selecting its conflict strategy. *Avoidance* will become a less readily available option, and constraints will be placed on *competitive* behavior. So solutions on our conflict-resoltuion plane will tend to move toward *compromise* and *accomodation.* But at the same time the variance in results, or risks, associated with any given management strategy will also tend to be less. And so it is impossible to conclude before the fact that a certain degree of international control is necessarily worse for the interests of the firm than a freer but more chaotic and risky environment. Much depends on the precise nature of international controls. But as we have seen, no binding agreements of GATT-type institutions are likely to emerge soon. More probable are non-binding codes, as in the OECD, that combine some MNE guidance and reduced risk in a flexible package whose benefits may well outweigh the costs to the multinational enterprise. They also leave plenty of room for conflict emergence and conflict management on the part of multinational firms. "Where the law ends" in international control of MNEs is not very far from the starting gate.

THE CONTINGENCY APPROACH REVISITED

It is useful at this point to summarize once more the contingency approach to multinational conflict management that we developed in Chapters 2 and 3, and that we subsequently employed in assessing managerial behavior in each of the substantive conflict issues we have discussed. In essence, we have advocated careful and comprehensive diagnosis of MNE conflicts within the specific context in which they occur. This diagnosis should include four major dimensions:

1. The stakes of the firm in the conflict outcome.
2. The firm's power and options in relation to its opponents.
3. The interest interdependence between the firm and its opponents, or whether the conflict is zero-sum or not.
4. The quality of the relationship between the two sides.

These four dimensions were mapped ordinally onto a grid such as Exhibit

15–1, and used to identify conflict-management strategies and tactics that make sense—both in a static situation and when one or more of the variables shift over time.

Depending on the conflict diagnosis, MNE management's strategic or tactical positioning can range from total non-cooperation to full compliance with the desires of its opponents on the one hand, and from a passive and unassertive stance to highly aggressive behavior on the other. Combinations of the various behavioral positions thus comprise competition (assertive/uncooperative), avoidance (unassertive/uncooperative), accommodation (unassertive/cooperative), collaboration (assertive/cooperative) and various degrees of compromise. We have seen that in conflict situations where corporate stakes are extremely high, where relationship quality with opponents is poor, where the game is essentially zero-sum, and where the firm has relatively little real power, the obvious solution is typically to throw in the towel and pull out. We have seen that in other situations where both corporate power and stakes are high, yet where relation-

Exhibit 15–1
Determinants of Appropriate Conflict Behavior

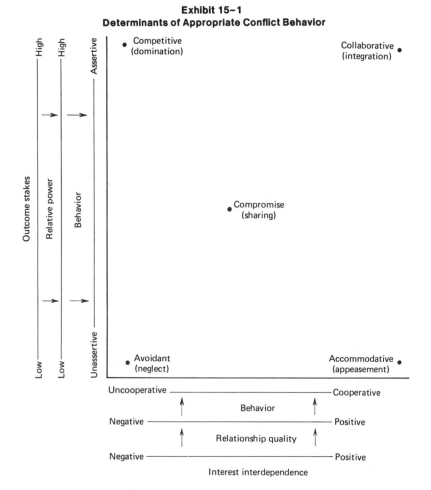

ship quality is poor and interest interdependence is low, that high profile competitive behavior aimed at achieving domination may make sense.

Of course, most of the cases we have examined were not nearly so "polar" in nature. Recall IBM/India, Polaroid/South Africa, Coca-Cola/Egypt, and Roche/Britain, for example, where management's diagnoses of the four determining variables were complex affairs and where choices among alternative conflict-handling modes were difficult to make. It is also important to recall that conflicts have a life of their own, so that each of the determining variables often move through a range of values and the appropriate conflict management modes change accordingly. In Chapter 8 for example, we saw how company and host-country leverage or power can shift over the life-cycle of a project. Competitive or collaborative behavior at the beginning may well move through a range of compromises as country priorities change and the company's contributions are viewed differently, and towards the end of the cycle the most appropriate modes may be full accommodation to the country's wishes or even total withdrawal.

The existence of international rules or codes of conduct, as we have seen, affects each of the conflict management variables just identified. It precludes some options, for example, and thus both facilitates the job of diagnosis and cuts into the firm's power or leverage. More than that, it can spell out rights and obligations on both sides, and can thus cut into the probability of conflict emergence in the first place. But we have also emphasized that a coherent, cohesive set of rules of the game are unlikely to emerge anytime soon, if ever. And so the task of conflict management by multinational corporate executives will remain and, if anything, will grow. Firms that do well in the 1980s and 1990s will perforce have mastered the art of conflict management in a multinational setting.

IMPLEMENTATION OF CONFLICT MANAGEMENT

Accepting the logic and value of our "contingency approach" to constructive conflict management is one thing; executing such an approach effectively and efficiently on the part of MNE management is another. How can the model best be translated from theory into practice? How can implementation of constructive conflict management best be encouraged or facilitated? The answers, we believe, lie in creating a conducive management environment *within* the firm. This, in turn, depends vitally on two systems—the *incentive system* under which managers operate, and the *task system* necessary for carrying out conflict management itself. Given the appropriate "carrots and sticks," MNE senior management has numerous "points of leverage" at its disposal for shaping corporate behavior. Some of the more important variables bearing upon the organizational climate for constructive conflict management are shown in Exhibit 15–2.

Ultimately, constructive conflict management must be a deeply-ingrained facet of the MNE's corporate personality—shared in, believed in, and acted upon at every level. It is required at local, regional, and national as well as international levels. It must be done on a project, program, operating unit, divisional, and corporate-wide basis. In short, it represents an integral part of the normal planning and decision-making process, if only because conflict manage-

Exhibit 15-2
Incentives and Task Systems for Constructive Conflict Management

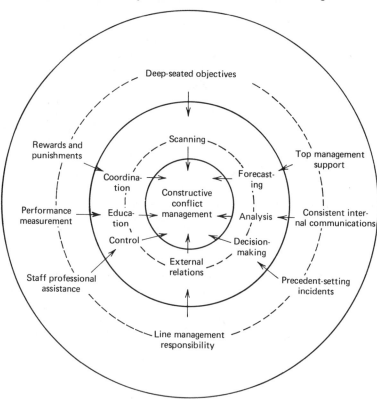

ment performed separately is not likely to be very successful. Consequently, constructive handling of external conflict must gain strong and consistent support at the highest levels of management. Without this support the middle managers most directly involved are likely to waver in the care and attention they devote to this function. Senior managers need to communicate clearly and forcefully how much constructive conflict management means to the firm—one effective way of doing this is to use creatively a conspicuous incident (e.g., an investment project that has been blocked due to obviously poor conflict management) as a corporate learning experience. Top management can intervene in the incident, using it to set a well established precedent on the need for wise conflict management.

We believe conflict management should be primarily a "line" function, with responsibility and authority clearly in line management hands. A sure route to disaster is to leave conflict management strategies and tactics totally in the hands of staff specialists and then issue them to line managers as directives. Staff professionals can, of course, play a useful support role to the line organization— assisting in external scanning, forecasting, analysis, external relations, and so on—but line managers must themselves make and direct the implementation of conflict management decisions. The point is that conflict management is not something that can be carried out by only one part of the organization or be turned on and off. To be effective, conflict management must be a continuous and major element in the line manager's decision system. And this will happen only when these managers clearly perceive that their careers depend on it. Additionally, the function of conflict management must be tested by periodic measures of performance. A formal mechanism for doing so would be to use conflict management criteria in rewarding executives. MNEs must build contributions to conflict management objectives into the specific job responsibilities of each operating manager, set targets for accomplishment, measure performance, and use organizational "carrots and sticks" to reinforce behavior. Middle and lower-level managers, in other words, should come to perceive that what is good for the company on effective conflict management is also good for themselves.

Our attention now shifts from the outer to the inner ring of Exhibit 15-2, the primary tasks essential to effective *implementation* of conflict management by MNE management: scanning, forecasting, analysis, decision-making, external relations, control, and education must all take place in a coordinated way.

Scanning

The multinational's ability to constructively manage nonmarket conflict depends on its expertise in scanning, selecting, transmitting, and interpreting information related to the potential emergence and actual character of conflict.[21] Conflicts do not always present themselves as obvious and objective realities, and become known only through processes of enactment by which perceptions, attention, and interpretation on the part of managers come to define the relevant challenges.[22] MNEs will be victimized by perceptions that ignore or distort critical conflict-related factors—poor diagnosis. Accurate and sensitive external scanning mechanisms are thus essential, and "opportunistic surveillance" is required, particularly when conflict conditions are turbulent.[23] At the same time, the MNE must remain sensitive to the cost of information, and in theory should not go beyond the point where the incremental cost of additional information exceeds the marginal benefit pay-back of reduced risk applied to possible conflict-related losses.

Much of the scanning activity can be performed by staff "boundary-spanning" personnel. The MNE can establish multiple scanning units or scanning centers that have within them a variety of interests, backgrounds, and types of expertise—political science, sociology, ecology, law, economics. Staff specialists can be assigned to selectively search for external information; to summarize, filter, and put it into usable form; to communicate it to the organizational units that need it; and to store it for future use.[24] Formal intelligence and conflict management information systems can be developed. Staff members can maintain a regular liaison with legislators, industry associations, political organizations, consumer and environmental groups, academic institutions, and the like. Information specialists can be assigned to monitor the media. Social, political risk, and quality of life indicators can be systematically tracked.[25] Thought leaders or "strategic elites" in host countries can be surveyed concerning their perceptions on evolving notions of appropriate corporate and MNE behavior. [26] Public opinion polling can be employed on a conflict-specific or more general basis.[27]

Forecasting

Forecasting is at the heart of constructive conflict management. Many of the most serious problems confronting MNEs stem from their inability to predict or assess the potency and demands of various interest groups, how these demands conflict, and how they may constrain the organization's actions. Risk (which can be calculated) and uncertainty (which cannot) are determined in large measure by the level of forecasting capability of the organization. As forecasting techniques improve, uncertainty and risk diminish. Consistently accurate forecasts of conflict potential, future legal requirements, coalition formation, political instability, and the like will, of course, never be possible because of the costs of time and information needed. Conflict management will thus be faced with difficult decisions on how to allocate resources. Deciding which matters should receive attention, and in what detail, depends on the professional judgments of experienced executives, on the time pressures and resources at hand, on the specific concerns of external interest groups as identified by scanning, and ultimately on the corporate stakes perceived to be involved. The use of sensitivity analysis and relatively simple techniques of systems description such as cross-impact matrices and network diagrams may help to identify the most critical factors and interrelationships.[28]

The techniques of forecasting available to the MNE are plentiful, and should be selected in relation to their capabilities and applicability to the issues involved.[29] The techniques can be classified into nine categories: single variable extrapolation, theoretical limit envelopes, dynamic models, mapping, multivariate interaction analysis, unstructured expert opinion, structured expert opinion, structured inexpert opinion, and unstructured inexpert opinion.[30] Scenario generation, brainstorming, and the Delphi technique may be particularly useful in conflict management forecasting when operating line managers are themselves directly involved in the exercise. Commitment to the forecasts may be low if the activity only involves specialized experts using sophisticated methodological approaches and terminology unfamiliar to the line managers who must eventually use the information.

Analysis

The MNE's ability to manage conflict effectively will also depend on its expertise in formulating specific alternatives as well as evaluating differences among them. The task of generating conflict management strategies and tactics is essentially a creative process. The ability to reformulate conflict challenges and develop alternative solutions depends on the availability of cognitive resources—as one observer has stressed:

Ideas are important to the creative resolution of conflict, and any factors that broaden the range of ideas and alternatives cognitively available to the participants in a conflict will be useful. Intelligence, the exposure to diverse experiences, an interest in ideas, a preference for the novel and complex, a receptivity to metaphors and analogies, the capacity to make remote associations, an independence of judgment, and the ability to play with ideas are some of the personal factors that characterize creative problem solvers. The availability of ideas is also dependent upon such social conditions as the opportunity to communicate with and be exposed to other people who may have relevant and unfamiliar ideas (i.e., experts, impartial outsiders, people facing similar or analogous situations), a social atmosphere that values innovation and originality and encourages the exchange of ideas, [and] a social tradition that fosters the optimistic view that, with effort and time, constructive solutions can be discovered or invented to problems that initially seem intractable."[31]

In conflict management, emphasis must be placed on discovering and inventing alternative sets of means and alternative sets of effects. The MNE's planners must be able to identify "alternative scenarios of desired futures," both from the company's and the public's point of view. They must also be able to display differences (or "trade-offs") among the alternatives. In coping with political risks, for example, the relative advantages and disadvantages of risk avoidance, risk transfer, risk retention, and risk reduction would have to be considered.[32] The idea is to make as clear and explicit as possible the consequences of implementing one alternative set of actions rather than others. This forms the basis for subsequent evaluation that makes sense.

A range of techniques can be utilized in the display and evaluation of alternatives. The display of differences in impacts among alternative conflict management strategies, for example, can be accomplished with cross-impact matrices, narrative scenarios, trade-off balance sheets, procedural flow charts, and factor profiles. A number of management science techniques may be useful in evaluating the displayed alternatives and their impacts.[33] The critical path method (CPM) can be used to chart the different steps of all possible branches of a conflict, and to aid selection of the "optimum path." The Program Evaluation and Review Technique (PERT) can be employed to "probabilistically" analyze uncertain data, times and relationships. Cost-effectiveness procedures can be used to analyze and compare several courses of action that might accomplish a single desired objective. Formal "decision analysis" may provide a logical framework for assessing alternatives when multiple objectives are involved.[34] Game-theoretic reasoning can be employed to explicate the strategic features of a conflict situation.[35] Risk measurement, constraint-setting, and various weighting procedures may also be useful in evaluating and ranking alternatives on the basis of their desirability.

Decision-Making

The essence of MNE conflict management according to our contingency scheme, of course, is expertise in choosing among the five basic types of conflict-handling behavior. Decision-making should be facilitated by sound scanning, forecasting, and analysis. But all three of these "input" tasks are subject to limitations—critical elements may be overlooked, various developments may be unpredictable, and analyses may quickly become obsolete if there is rapid change. Decisions in conflict management are thus unlikely to be simple and straightforward products of earlier evaluation.

Decision-making in MNE conflict situations cannot be rigid. Rather, the process must be fast, fluid, and flexible. Timing is often of the essence. Decisions must be made quickly in order to keep pace with the changing situation. Delays to seek more data or to reduce risk may only serve to create "paralysis through analysis." Because of unpredictability, decisions and plans must be reversible—they cannot be cast in concrete. If one can't forecast, then all one can do is be quick on your feet. Instead of relying on a single plan with perhaps one or two variations, a whole battery of contingency plans and alternate scenarios should probably be developed. Then when surprises or unexpected snags occur, the MNE can be ready with a preplanned action alternative. Conflict management requires escape valves—options must be kept open as much as possible. Flexibility, combined with seasoned and balanced judgment, is thus a highly valued component in the constructive management of external conflicts in multinational corporate operations.

Another characteristic of decision-making that may be desirable in conflict situations is that of participation. Certain decisions may call for wide participation, open communication channels, and influence centered in expertise rather than in formal authority. Increased participation may, of course, work against the ability to react quickly to changing conditions. On the other hand by reducing uncertainty, consultative decision-making—both internally and externally—may reduce the need for such flexibility. External participation in conflict management decision-making can produce benefits such as more immediate and accurate judgement regarding local systems, "reality testing" of the assumptions used by internal planners, early warning signals regarding various alternatives, and smoother relations with outside interest groups.[36] But external participation is not all "wine and roses"—there are some very real limitations and potential dangers.[37]

External Relations

External relations are the primary vehicle for implementing conflict management. The firm's ability to successfully manage conflict will depend vitally on its expertise in representing itself, communicating with, and exerting influence over relevant external groups and organizations.[38] Activities can be undertaken to maintain or improve the organization's credibility and legitimacy. Other activities can be engaged in to "enlist the support and/or negate the opposition" of other actors in the firm's environment.[39]

To the extent that the MNE can obtain social support, political legitimacy, and a favorable corporate image in the minds of those making up the external environment, it may see payoffs in terms of easier acquisition of resources and conflict outcomes. MNEs cannot leave their reputation and legitimacy to chance—they must actively and judiciously attempt to manage their images, particularly in conflict situations. This does not mean "P.R. gimmickry," but rather effective communications with various constituencies—particularly with home and host governments.[40]

There are many techniques of external representation, communication, and influence that can be used in conflict management.[41] Some of the more important include lobbying, advocacy advertising, press releases, charitable donations, trade association publications, outsiders on boards of directors, political contributions, and so on. In specific cases of conflict the techniques might include presentations to community organizations, informal small-group meetings, information brochures, material for mass media, responses to public displays and models, open-house events, trips for reporters or regulators to inspect facilities, and the like. Such techniques vary in terms of cost, level of contact achieved, ability to handle specific interests, degree of two-way communication, and amount of time required. Packaging an external relations program, either on an ongoing or conflict specific basis, is probably one of the most important tasks of effective management.

Control

A control system is an important adjunct to the decision-making system in conflict management. The MNE must be able to monitor and control its performance in achieving its objectives. Control is essential mainly because external demands change over time—stakes, power, relationship quality, and interests in regard to conflict issues are dynamic. Deviations from plan also occur through faulty internal communications and managerial oversight. So control is necessary in conflict management to enable the MNE executives to anticipate problems and to take corrective actions when plans are not being met.

The process of control includes a number of aspects. The results desired in conflict management must first be defined and control standards established that relate to time, money, people, or issues. This is where multinational corporate codes of conduct in relation to external issues and standards of behavior can be useful.[42] The next step is to identify reliable indicators of conflict management performance. Operational auditing and reporting procedures can then be used to measure performance of subsidiaries, units, and divisions according to these indicators. Although still in their developmental stage, this is where corporate social accounting and auditing methods may eventually prove useful.[43] Actual performance can be judged against predetermined yardsticks and, if performance is out of line, corrective action can be recommended. Control is thus a process of trying to make events conform to plans. The idea is to prevent disasters—to monitor performance on a regular basis, rather than waiting until undesirable consequences have piled up. In this way, remedial conflict management action can be initiated early.

Control over the conflict management behavior of line MNE managers can be exercised through a variety of personal and/or impersonal means in addition to those suggested above. Small-group conferences, direct person-to-person interaction, informal consultation, personal surveillance, executive performance evaluation, centralization of key decisions in conflict, and so on represent personal controls. Impersonal means would include budgets, schedules, and formal policies, procedures and rules.

Education

Success in conflict management will naturally rest on the MNE's expertise in ensuring that its current and future managers have knowledge, attitudes, and skills suitable for conflict management. This is especially critical in regard to middle-level line managers. In many MNEs these executives frequently find it difficult to understand the mentalities of politicians and citizen groups. They often regard questioning and criticism of their activities as unreasonable. They often feel allegiance to their traditional missions and sometimes feel that they have an inalienable right to continue doing what they have always done. And they are loath to make proposals public before all anticipated problems have been solved, principally because they do not wish to look foolish. Finally, they are sometimes insensitive to the role and information needs of external relations specialists in the planning process. In sum, these kinds of characteristics are likely to be dysfunctional during an age when extra-organizational relations is an important key to multinational corporate effectiveness.

A profile of the line manager who can best cope with an era of external turbulence and conflict is beginning to emerge from the studies of several psychologists and organizational scientists. The following might apply: "(1) they must have attitudes directed toward inquiry and novelty rather than the particular content of the job; (2) they must be willing to remain flexible so that changing circumstances can be handled in whatever way is most appropriate; (3) they must have the proclivity to commit themselves to the active pursuit of complexity and variety, and to actions whose consequences are uncertain and ambiguous; and (4) they must have a high tolerance of ambiguity and a high degree of independence."[44] Conflict management requires executives who are creative, willing to take risks, patient and persistent, and comfortable in spanning organizational boundaries.

Conflict management requires a combination of knowledge, attitudes, and skills. Knowledge is rooted in the intellect and consists of retained observations, facts, and interrelationships. Attitudes are often emotionally rooted and consist of predispositions to act and react in predictable ways. Skills pertain to the ability to do things, to use knowledge, to mobilize resources, and to accomplish specific tasks. The MNE must compare the capacities of its current managers with a profile of managerial characteristics it feels are necessary for constructive conflict management. Based on this gap analysis it can then formulate management development objectives and programs to bridge the identified gaps in knowledge, attitudes, and skills.

Conflict management knowledge can be transmitted to managers through a variety of techniques in both in-house and external programs. These include lectures, discussions, films, slide/videotape packages, corporate-wide seminars and conferences, selected readings, manuals and pamphlets, and newsletters. Programmed learning packages consisting of audio and visual materials can be designed to meet the knowledge requirements of effective conflict management. Attitudes of managers in relation to conflict management can be modified through role palying, sensitivity training, and other forms of laboratory experience. Conflict management skills can be developed through conflict simulations, negotiation exercises, and use of the incident and case method. Programs which integrate knowledge-, attitude-, and skill-change objectives can also be developed.

Coordination

We come now to the final and most critical task. The MNE's ability to constructively manage external conflict will depend in the final analysis on its expertise in bringing about "unity of effort" in the performance of all of the tasks described above. Conflict management poses severe coordination problems. A lot of people have to be involved. A wide array of professional disciplines need to be synthesized. Internal and external resources of many types have to be mobilized. Relationships have to be worked out between different levels of management, between staff and line personnel, between the company and its joint venture partners, between internal executives and external consultants, between different divisions and regions, and so on.

Conflict management thus requires a complex pattern of task specialization and internal differentiation. Such specialization can create problems of communication, waste and duplication, internal disagreement, and ineffectiveness if organizational sub-units work tangentially to one another or even at cross purposes. To minimize these problems, mechanisms of integration are needed. Coordination in conflict management may involve written rules and policies, schedules, and system of controls and information flows, as well as personal consultation, ad hoc coordinating groups, overlapping committee memberships, temporary problem-solving bodies, cross-functional "linking-pins," and perhaps matrix structures. Given the dynamic nature of conflicts confronting MNEs, it would appear that flexible rather than highly formalized methods of coordination and information sharing should be used. This generally means a large amount of face-to-face participation in discussions and decision-making, with an emphasis on close lateral relations among the participants involved, instead of formal links up and down hierarchies or through periodic formal meetings. Unity of effort is probably the real key to success in effective conflict management.

ADAPTING THE ORGANIZATION

The foregoing policy guidelines and operational tasks associated with the conflict management function were couched in terms relevant to any level of the corporate organization—plant, national subsidiary, product or area division, and in regional or world headquarters. But how should conflict handling policy and practice be linked among those levels? Stated another way, how should conflicts on any one issue be managed on a multinational basis? Should the MNEs global pattern of conflict management behavior in regard to that issue be characterized in a relative sense by "unification" (headquarters intervention, system-wide interchange, and uniformity in policy and practice), or by its opposite, "fragmentation."[45] We believe that real gains in effectiveness for the MNE as a whole can be derived from systematically adopting globally unified patterns of conflict management on some issues, largely fragmented patterns on to others, and mixed patterns of conflict management on still others. The key managerial challenge, of course, lies in determining how much fragmentation or unification makes sense with respect to the issue at hand. Exhit 15–3 provides an analytical framework which can be employed on an issue- and enterprise-specific basis for exactly this purpose.[46]

External Environment

The dashed line in Exhibit 15–3 represents the boundary between the internal organization system of the MNE and the environment in which it operates. This environment, from the standpoint of conflict emergence, consists of what we might call "public policy climates" in the home nation of the enterprise, and in each of the host countries where it has existing or prospective operations. These climates can be viewed as interrelated systems of preferences, pressures, actions that characterize interest groups (governmental and nongovernmental) with respect to the particular issue in question (e.g., pollution control, minority employment, product safety, political contributions, appropriate technology, transfer pricing, etc.). The process by which societies generate these policy climates is typically long and complex, and varies from one issue to the next.

Individual units of a MNE confront individual public policy climates in the nations or regions where they operate. The MNE as a worldwide system faces the complete collection of policy climates in which it has current or potential operations. This amalgam of climates—and the forces, demands, and influences they incorporate—exhibits various analytical dimensions, or points of contrast, or relevance to the functioning of the MNE. Although climates may vary along many dimensions, we have here selected four that seem particularly relevant to dealing with issues of conflict in the course of international business operations. These are (1) dynamic-static, (2) unstable-stable, (3) heterogeneous-homogeneous, and (4) independent-interdependent.[47] The first two pertain primarily to the nature of econditions within individual nations, while the second pair relates to conditions among different nations. Each dimension should be viewed as a continuum, rather than as a dichotomy.

Dynamic-static. This dimension can be viewed as the degree to which policy climates related to a given issue are changing. As environmental influences become more dynamic the organization must become more receptive to change because strategies and plans, by necessity, will be tentative and subject to continual redesign. Bureaucratic structures and processes will inhibit the firm's ability to detect, diagnose, and adjust to rapidly-changing nonmarket demands, whereas open channels of communication, decentralized decision-making, and a predominance of situational expertise seem more appropriate in the face of rapid change. As has been noted, successful firms in changing environments tend to have "organic" or flexible structures and management styles.[48]

Unstable-stable. This dimension can be viewed as the degree to which policy climates bearing upon a given issue are unsteady or steady in their rate of change. The concern here is with the "variability" of change.[49] High turbulence means that important factors influencing notions of acceptable corporate behavior are changing unpredictably in value and that the set of critical factors involved is also changing. Such instability and induced uncertainty makes the task of designing conflict management strategies and

Exhibit 15–3
Framework for Analyzing MNE Conflict Management

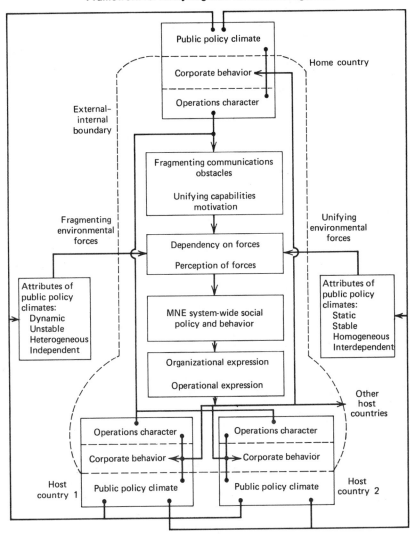

tactics in regard to any given issue very complex, difficult, and frustrating. Research shows that perceived irregularity and looseness in the pattern or rate of environmental change tends to magnify internal problems of coordination and control, gives rise to buffering mechanisms for reducing or structuring the uncertainty, induces greater decentralization in the locus of decision-making, encourages increased differentiation in the orientation of managers, and encourages a more adaptive and organic organizational structure.[50]

Heterogeneous-homogeneous. This dimension can be viewed as the degree to which policy climates concerning a given issue are dissimilar or similar in kind. With increasing heterogeneity comes a larger number of critically important factors that have to be taken into consideration in centralized decision-making. The challenge is that of diversity, not only with regard to the substance of policy climates, but also with respect to the rapidity and stability of change in those climates. The organizational response is typically differentiation. Firms functioning in complex or heterogeneous environments generally seek to identify homogeneous segments or "subenvironments" and to establish decentralized, semi-autonomous operating units and corresponding strategies, policies, management styles, and techniques to deal with them.[51]

Independent-interdependent. This dimension can be viewed as the degree to which policy climates in nations are sensitive to developments in, and reactions from, policy climates in other nations. Advances in communication and transportation, personal mobility, economic interdependence, development of regional and supranational institutions, and emergence of transcultural interest groups all serve to increase the volume of transactions between, and interpenetration among, different policy climates.[52] Interdependence increases the probability that corporate actions in one nation will be exposed to scrutiny and entangled with reactions of governments and interest groups in others. This interconnectedness makes partial analysis and unilateral action on a given issue by an MNE affiliate in a single policy climate unwise. Interdependence of interests across cultures thus encourages reductions in affiliate autonomy on conflict management.

As shown in Exhibit 15–3, we postulate that *dynamism, instability, heterogeneity,* and *independence* associated with the collection of various policy climates in which the MNE operates represent *fragmenting forces.* These attributes on a given issue tend to limit the potential for MNE system-wide unification in conflict management, and push the MNE toward custom-tailoring or adaptation to local policy environments. Confronted with dynamic policy climates, the ability to quickly and efficiently perceive and adjust to rapid changes will tend to be inhibited by centralization. When the change in the various climates is erratic and unstable, the viability of headquarters-devised or executed policies will be constrained by high levels of unpredictability. Given heterogeneous climates, the feasibility of centrally-determined and standardized corporate policies will tend to be burdened by the large amount of critically important information necessary for decision-making. And the absence of international interest-linkages and demands, by virtue of policy-climate independence, implies that decision-makers need not fear repercussions of their actions elsewhere around the world. All of these elements permit organizational and operational *differentiation* in corporate approaches to managing a given conflict.

With similar logic, we suggest that *static conditions, stability, homogeneity,* and *interdependence* associated with the policy climates surrounding a given issue represent *unifying forces* as noted in Exhibit 15–3. These attributes encourage system-wide interchange of capabilities relevant to managing the particular types of conflict encountered, with essentially easier central formulation of strategies, policies and response-patterns. With low rates of change in policy climates, the need for direct contact and quick adjustment tends to be reduced, and with stability in the rates of change, predictability is enhanced—the MNE knows reasonably well what conditions it will face in the future. With homogeneous policy climates, fewer categories of information are necessary for effective decision-making at headquarters level. The resultant simplicity and certainty permits organizational and operational *integration*—cost savings can be gained by avoiding duplication of effort and leverage can be achieved over purely domestic firms by applying conflict management experience acquired elsewhere. In addition, policy-climate interdependence may also demand multinational coordination and standardization, given the organization's high vulnerability to transnational repercussions and conflicts.

Internal Organization

Our focus in the framework now shifts to the internal organizational system of the MNE, the components lying inside the broken line in Exhibit 15-3. For analytical purposes we show a simple MNE structure consisting of operations in its home country and two host countries, along with a notation indicating the potential role of third-country affiliates. Operations in all countries are directly linked, and constitute the overall MNE system. In discussing system-wide features it is helpful to envisage the existence of an international headquarters—a central point of potential coordination and administration conceptually separate from home-country domestic operations. Each MNE may be characterized in terms of its growth, profitability, size, tradition, structure, product diversity, geographical dispersion, communications system, capital intensity, pollution-intensity, and so forth. This profile will determine its internal strengths and weaknesses, and its dependence on—and perception of—external influences as discussed below.

Just as we saw fragmenting and unifying forces arising out of policy climate conditions, so too will an MNE experience fragmenting and unifying pressures within its own organizational system. Depending on the corporate profile, the MNE will have what might be called an "internal fragmentation-unification balance." The "balance" of particular concern here is one that relates to managing a specific conflict issue such as pollution control or governmental sales policy in repressive nations. MNEs must contend with a variety of fragmenting "communications gaps."[53] These internal communication difficulties arise from the absence of common values, norms, and expectations among managers in different nations, from tendencies toward ethnocentric attitudes, from psychological impediments to cross-cultural understanding, and from obstructions and deficiencies in the flow of information within the MNE system attributable to distance and conditions of shared ownership. These communications obstacles place limits on the depth of understanding corporate headquarters can have of its affiliates and on that which the affiliate management can have of headquarters. They give rise to transactions costs in system-wide interchange, and engender a compulsion for local adaptation in regard to managing conflict.

Tending to offset such communication difficulties are internal forces that push MNEs toward unification in organization and operations. These consist of the technological and managerial capabilities available throughout the MNE system, and the potential economies and efficiencies inherent in an integrated global structure.[54] Capabilities relevant to managing a specific type of conflict can be most effectively drawn upon and transmitted across borders—and economies of scale by means of specialization most efficiently realized—when the activities and behavior of national subsidiaries exhibit a high degree of uniformity and are integrated through international coordination within the firm. Many observers of the MNE contend that inherent in the basic rationale of its existence is a tendency toward integration and uniformity. As one has stated, "the justification for a MNE is to exploit the synergy of being multi-national."[55]

Internal-External Interaction

We have now examined the relevant "fragmenting" and "unifying" forces—both those bearing on the MNE from external policy climate sources and those existing within the MNE as an organization. MNE policy and behavior in a specific conflict issue area such as worker participation, kidnapping, or bribery, we submit, should be a function of the interaction of the internal and external balance of fragmenting and unifying forces. This interaction in an actual experience, however, will be modified by dependency and perception variables as shown in Exhibit 15–3.

Dependency on the unifying and fragmenting forces will tend to be a function of the MNE's "domain"—or existing and desired arena of activity.[56] Dependency on the environment can be viewed in terms of constraints.[57] Constraints on resource or support acquisition are related to the degree to which the MNE relies on specific elements of the environment for goal attainment, and on the extent to which these elements affect each other. Two critical variables are the nature of the MNE's operations, and the spatial dispersion of these operations. An office-machines MNE, for example, may have a high degree of autonomy from policy climate pressures and constraints regarding pollution control, whereas a petroleum MNE may be quite subordinate to and dependent on them. Goal attainment will also depend on such external pressures to a greater degree in some national settings than in others—e.g., anti-bribery pressures will be stronger in the United States than in Italy, human rights demands heavier in Sweden than Brazil, or worker participation requirements more extensive in Germany than in Britain. The MNE's overall level of dependency on the issue of pollution control, for example, could be viewed as a product of its pollution-intensity and a weighted average of the policy climate pressures existing in the nations where it has pollution-intensive operations.

The impact on the MNE of external forces bearing upon a given issue will also be a function of *perception* both at the affiliate and system-wide levels. External forces lack inherent meaning or information value until they penetrate the organization's boundaries and are perceived and structured by management. Environmental forces likely to be influential are those that are "enacted"—created through the process of attention.[58] In addition, it has been observed that firms differ in their ability to perceive, search for, evaluate, and act upon information in their environments.[59] This focus on the process of attention means that the same "objective" external pressures may appear different to different MNEs. One scholar, in fact, has observed that "the same environment one organization perceives as unpredictable, complex and evanescent, another organization might see as static and easily understood."[60] It is clear that managerial perceptions and organizational information-processing systems, as we noted above, are critical in determining how a given MNE—both at the subsidiary and overall system level—will adjust to external forces. In a prescriptive sense, it is obvious that accurate perception to minimize distortions in interpreting and acting upon external pressures is central to constructive conflict management.

To summarize, each MNE is likely to have a different "options-matrix" reflecting the unique profile that determines what it can do under different circumstances. The two essential points are that environmental pressures will not be deterministic,[61] and that managerial perceptions and actions will have a strong influence on the organization's response. We hypothesize that the interaction of organizational and environmental unification-fragmentation balances, as modified by dependency and perception factors, should determine a MNE's policy relating to any particular conflict issue. As illustrated in Exhibit 15–3, this policy will find expression in both organizational and operational realms. Whether system-wide policy in a given issue area should be characterized by global unification rather than localism—that is, a high degree of headquarters intervention, system-wide interchange, and uniformity in policy and practice among subsidiaries in different nations—is directly related to perceived dependence on unifying (and inversely related to perceived dependence on fragmenting) external forces. It should also be a positive function of the motivation to exploit task-related internal system-wide capabilities and a negative function of associated communications obstacles. Moreover, the behavior of a given MNE affiliate should be a function of a tripartite interaction between the character of the unit's own operations (size, ownership, type of production, management competence, and so forth), the "pull" of pressures exerted by the local environment, and the "push" of guidance and resources exerted from above by system-wide policy.

It is important to emphasize once again the contingency logic incorporated in the foregoing analytical framework. The model is issue- and enterprise-specific—a given MNE's global policy and conflict handling behavior on a specific issue should depend on unique internal and external situational and circumstantial factors. The emphasis on specific contingencies and managerial perceptions implies that it is difficult to appraise whether existing patterns of MNE behavior on the many different issues considered in this book have been "optimal" according to our scheme. But it is possible to crudely rank-order the general conflict management behavior of MNEs observed in the twelve topical chapters in the book along the fragmentation-unification continuum.

Perhaps the most fragmented patterns of behavior have been in the areas of labor relations (Chapter 11), marketing (Chapter 10), and environmental protection (Chapter 12). The prevailing view in these areas has been "polycentric"—local conflicts have usually been dealt with by local personnel using local techniques.[62] Headquarters guidance, control, and intervention have not been very powerful, purposeful, or cohesive. Few MNEs have attempted to develop consistent sets of corporate objectives and standards applicable to worldwide operations in these areas. In line with our model, it is tempting to suggest that the highly diversified policy and practice observed in these three kinds of conflict has been encouraged by perceived dependence on fragmenting external forces and perhaps also by the presence of obstacles to system-wide conflict management, skill-transfer, and communications. Although this seems reasonable, it is clear that our observations do not represent more than inferential evidence.

At the other extreme, the behavior of MNEs has probably been most unified with respect to political conflict (Chapter 7), technology (Chapter 13), and economics/finance (Chapter 14). Corporate behavior in all three areas has involved considerable headquarters intervention and coordination, standardization or uniformity in policies and practices around the globe, and much interchange of strategies, systems, and people among MNE affiliates. These appear to be areas where the efficiencies of integration and cross-border resource transmission have been significant sources of competitive advantage or necessities of global corporate optimization. Our model suggests that this is encouraged by perceived dependence on unifying forces and by motivation to exploit system-wide conflict management capabilities.

Finally, we should note that MNE behavior in the remaining conflict areas—terrorism (Chapter 4), human rights (Chapters 5 and 6), national control (Chapter 8), and questionable payments (Chapter 9)—have generally been marked by mixes of fragmentation and unification, with perhaps some movement over time in the latter direction. A number of these have of course emerged rather recently, and corporate behavior patterns in response to them are still very unsettled. Using our model, it is probably true that MNEs are receiving mixed signals regarding these issues from external forces around the world. Pressures on human rights and questionable payments, for example, are very much heterogeneous (thus recommending fragmentation), but they are also interdependent in the sense that corporate behavior overseas is increasingly monitored and reacted to back home (thus recommending unification).

CONFLICT MANAGEMENT IN THE YEARS AHEAD

It is customary in all books like this to close with some crystal-ball gazing. We've tried to look ahead on many specific areas of conflict in previous chapters. But what general trends seem to be shaping the challenge of conflict management as it will confront MNEs in the 1980s and beyond? The outlook is, of course, fuzzy. It appears to shape up, however, as a "future of contradictions"—a nonmarket environment facing MNEs that will be characterized by often incompatible factors bearing upon corporate objectives and policies. A few trends which may work in almost dramatically opposed directions may be noted.

The importance of the nation state and nationalism may continue to grow, but so will world economic interdependence. New struggles between countries over shares in the benefits produced by international investment have already emerged, yet effective international dispute settlement machinery and "rules of the game" between governments seem to be slow in coming. The power balance between MNEs and host nations may continue to shift in favor of host nations, but at the same time, home countries may increasingly assert their powers in the form of political controls over outward technology transfer, investment, and trade. At the same time that MNEs may confront increased regulation by host country governments, they are likely to be also menaced by the growth of enterprises owned, directed and supported by those governments—the combat with these foreign state-controlled MNEs, some even based in developing nations, is bound to be quite unequal. Most developing nations appear steadfast in their desire for a "New International Economic Order," but their demands for a more "equitable" share of global prosperity are coming at a time when they need the

MNE as much as ever and when developed nations are in no mood to make concessions as a result of unemployment, inflation, and energy problems. Two-thirds of the world's population continues to confront poverty, malnutrition, disease, illiteracy, poor-housing, unemployment, and misery, yet the pool of resources required to meet basic human needs seems to be shrinking as a result of natural resource scarcities, rapid population growth, declining foreign aid, and the like.

The contradictions continue. The push of technology in telecommunications, computers, and travel will continue to shrink time and space, and produce increasingly universal standards of behavior, but cultural homogenization appears to be increasingly resisted by groups seeking ethnic, religious, and cultural identity. The new importance given to maintaining local values may translate into more frequent charges of "cultural imperialism" against MNEs in host nations—yet pressure groups at home seem intent on forcing MNEs to carry home-grown values abroad, particularly regarding ethical and moral dimensions of corporate policy. Industrial democracies are scheduled to experience lower long-term growth rates in the 1980s with serious implications for social peace, yet environmental and social resistance to new industrial investment that would contribute to output and income is not likely to disappear. Government regulation and direct intervention in business is worldwide and increasing, yet the legitimacy, relevance, and competence of big government in many countries is deteriorating in the eyes of their citizens. Employees will continue to demand a greater say in how their companies are run, but at the same time, myriad outside interest groups continue their struggle to have a say in corporate governance. The demands for participation, accountability, and transparency will tend to be both internal and external, and minority shareholders are likely to pursue their direct challenges to corporate managements on social issues. We can also expect, however, that majority stockholders will grow increasingly restive if corporate executives continue to concede their power to make moral choices to vocal minorities engaged in pressure tactics.

We could go on, but the fact that MNEs will in part create, collide with, and be victimized by contradictions in the 1980s and beyond should be clear. The central task of conflict management on the part of multinationals will be to cope with such contradictions.[63] The opposing trends imply a continuation of conflict, a loss of autonomy, greater environmental turbulence, and perhaps even a serious threat to survival for the MNE as we now know it.

Tensions surrounding the MNE will remain and perhaps intensify—the multinational enterprise will continue to be under fire. Tensions will center both on rational conflict of interest over such things as disclosure, standards of behavior, control and ownership of foreign affiliates, and also on "irrational" reactions by governments and interest-groups. The MNE will continue to arouse instinctive nationalistic distrust and resistance. The pathological "love-hate" relationship is not likely to disappear. Perhaps most importantly, we may increasingly find MNEs being used as political tools, hostages, and bargaining chips by competing sovereignties. As we have repeatedly emphasized, the risks of being caught between conflicting parties is serious and growing. So multinational corporate managers are going to find themselves spending a considerable portion of their time dealing with conflict, and its management will become increasingly important to the MNE's effectiveness.

Many of the trends also imply that MNEs are going to see their wings severely clipped in certain respects—the flexibility they have had in the past is bound to decline. The mixture of emerging law, regulation, government intervention, trade union/employee power, and citizen lobby pressure can only translate into increased external control. Resultant accountability, increased transparency, and reviews of corporate governance will mean less autonomy. But accommodation or compliance to the burgeoning demands is not going to be a satisfactory answer if the demands are themselves in substantial conflict—compliance with some demands would naturally mean noncompliance with others. The MNE cannot allow itself to become completely "other directed." To survive, it must seek to avoid being controlled. It must engage in a constant struggle to retain autonomy and discretion. In cases of illegitimate or conflicting demands it must begin returning the fire to avoid decimation.

The trends imply increasing turbulence. A more uncertain and unstable environment may emerge for the MNE. The key factor here is interdependence, and shifts in the external environment are increasingly going to come from anywhere without notice, to produce consequences unanticipated by those initiating the changes and those experiencing the results. Interdependence, of course, can as easily be a source of cooperation as of conflict. But when everything is connected to everything else, the capacity to adapt and innovate will become more important than ever for the MNE. Greater coordination between firms will also be needed to cope with the uncertainties created by interdependence.

In sum, we believe multinationals will have to show far more political-social savvy in the years ahead in order to ensure survival and success—a true "technology of conflict management." Under fire, the conflict management challenge confronting MNEs boils down to finding the path, to borrow from Henry Adams, "of running order through chaos, direction through space, discipline through freedom, unity through multiplicity."[64]

NOTES

CHAPTER 1

1. Raymond Vernon, in an early work entitled *Sovereignty at Bay* (New York: Basic Books, 1971) provides an excellent overview. His *Storm Over the Multinationals: The Real Issues* (Cambridge: Harvard University Press, 1977) provides a later reassessment. A popular antagonistic view is contained in Richard J. Barnet and Ronald E. Müller, *Global Reach: The Power of the Multinational Corporations* (New York: Simon & Schuster, 1974). A more objective presentation can be found in C. Fred Bergsten, Thomas Horst, and Theodore H. Moran, *American Multinationals and American Interests* (Washington, D.C.: The Brookings Institution, 1978).

2. Jean-Jacques Servan-Schreiber, *The American Challenge* (New York: Athenaeum, 1968); Robert Heller and Norris Willatt, *The European Revenge* (New York: Scribner's, 1975).

3. Lawrence G. Franko, *The European Multinationals* (London: Harper & Row, 1976).

4. For surveys of some of these, see John H. Dunning (ed.), *Economic Analysis and the Multinational Enterprise* (London: George Allen & Unwin, 1974); Peter J. Buckley and Mark Casson, *The Future of the Multinational Enterprise* (New York: Holmes & Meier, 1976); Yair Aharoni, *The Foreign Investment Decision Process* (Boston: Division of Research, Graduate School of Business Administration, Harvard University, 1966); Richard E. Caves "International Corporations: The International Economics of Foreign Investment," *Economica* 38 (February 1971), pp 1–27, Charles P. Kindleberger, *American Business Abroad* (New Haven: Yale University Press, 1969); and Raymond Vernon, *The Economic and Political Consequences of Multinational Enterprise: An Anthology* (Boston: Division of Research, Graduate School of Business Administration, Harvard University, 1972).

5. For this view of organizational effectiveness see Jeffrey Pfeffer and Gerald R. Salanick, *The External Control of Organizations: A Resource Dependence Perspective* (New York: Harper & Row, 1978).

6. For one of the earliest expressions of this perspective see Lewis A. Coser, *The Functions of Social Conflict* (New York: Free Press, 1956).

7. This discussion is drawn from Ingo Walter, "A Guide to Social Responsibility of the Multinational Enterprise," pp. 146–192 in Jules Backman (ed.), *Social Responsibility and Accountability* (New York: New York University Press, 1975). For a discussion of environmental variability, complexity, hostility, heterogeneity, and interdependence in the context of international business see: Thomas N. Gladwin and Vern Terpstra, "Introduction," pp. xi–xxiv in Vern Terpstra, ed., *The Cultural Environment of International Business* (Cincinnati: South-Western, 1978).

8. See Morton Deutsch, *The Resolution of Conflict: Constructive and Destructive Processes* (New Haven: Yale University Press, 1973).

9. Aimée L. Morner, "Dow's Strategy for an Unfriendly New Era," *Fortune* (May 1977), p. 312. Also see *The Dow Chemical Company 1977 Annual Report* (Midland, Michigan: Dow, 1978); *Form 10-K Annual Report to the SEC for the Fiscal Year Ended 31 December 1977 for The Dow Chemical Company* (Midland, Michigan: Dow, 1978); and Don Whitehead, *The Dow Story: The History of the Dow Chemical Company* (New York: McGraw-Hill, 1968).

10. Morner, "Dow's Strategy . . .," p. 314.

11. Anthony J. Piombino, "Profile of a Global Enterprise: Dow," *Chemical Week* (27 August 1975), pp. 21–30 and William F. Fallwell and William F. Storck. "Chemical Earnings Continue Strong Gains," *Chemical and Engineering News* (14 May 1979), p. 13. Also see Lee Smith, "Dow vs. DuPont: Rival Formulas for Leadership," *Fortune* (10 September 1979), pp. 74–84.

12. See Craig Thompson, *Since Spindletop: A Human Story of Gulf's First Half Century*

(Pittsburgh: Gulf Oil, 1951); "Gulf Oil Corporation/75 Years," a special issue of *The Orange Disc* **22** (1976); "Gulf Oil Corporation," *Petroleum Press Service* (January 1973), p. 8; *Gulf Oil Corporation 1977 Annual Report* (Pittsburgh: Gulf Oil, 1978); and "Gulf Fact Sheet 1977–78," (Pittsburgh: Gulf, 1977).

13. "Gulf 1978 Annual Meeting," *The Orange Disc* (May–June 1978), p. 15. Also see Jack H. Morris, "Bouncing Back: Gulf Oil Corporation, Once 'A Big Barrel of Money,'" *The Wall Street Journal* (22 February 1973), pp. 1 & 9; David Oates, "Gulf Oil Seeks a High Profile," *International Management* (July 1975), pp. 18–22; Michael C. Jensen, "Gulf: Its Troubles Get Deeper," *The New York Times* (4 January 1976), pp. F1 & 11; and "Gulf Oil Goes Back to What It Knows Best," *Business Week* (31 January 1977), pp. 78–80.

14. N.R. Kleinfield, "Geneen Leaving ITT Helm, with Admirers and Critics," *The New York Times* (23 December 1977), p. D1.

15. See Anthony Sampson, *The Sovereign State of ITT* (New York: Stein and Day, 1973); "The Clubby World of ITT," *Time* (27 March 1972), p. 86; "ITT: A Mixed Machine," *Time* (14 May 1973), p. 92; "Harold Geneen's Tribulations," *Business Week* (11 August 1973), pp. 102–110; and "ITT: The View from Inside," *Business Week* (3 November 1973), pp. 46–63.

16. Nigel Rowe, "ITT Replies," *The Guardian* (7 February 1975), p. 11.

17. *International Telephone and Telegraph Corporation 1977 Annual Report* (New York: ITT, 1978); and *A Report of the 1978 ITT Annual Shareholder's Meeting* (New York: ITT, 1978).

18. "A Drug Giant's Pricing Under International Attack," *Business Week* (16 June 1975), pp. 50–56. See also James H. Leonhard, "F. Hoffmann-La Roche," pp. 327–343 in Raymond Vernon and Louis T. Wells, Jr., *Manager in the International Economy* (Englewood Cliffs, N.J.: Prentice Hall, 1976); and "Roche," in Jonathan Love (ed.), *Jane's Major Companies of Europe* (New York: Franklin Watts, 1977) p. C176.

19. "A Drug Giant's Pricing Under International Attack," p. 52.

20. See Heller and Willat, *The European Revenge*, Chapter 8; "Hoffmann-La Roche's Rigid Stance in the U.K. Harms Image of Multinational Firms," *Business Europe* (14 September 1973), pp. 289–291.

21. David Avery, *Not on Queen Victoria's Birthday: The Story of the Rio Tinto Mines* (London: Collins, 1974).

22. Cited in Richard West, *River of Tears: The Rise of the Rio Tinto-Zinc Mining Corporation* (London: Earth Island Ltd., 1972), p. 23.

23. "Statement by the Chairman Sir Mark Turner," Annual General Meeting, *The Rio Tinto-Zinc Corporation Limited Annual Report and Accounts 1977* (London: RTZ, 1978).

24. Cited in West, *River of Tears*, p. 23.

25. Our methodology consisted of systematically scanning every issue of a range of newspapers and periodicals (*The New York Times, The Wall Street Journal, The Economist, Business Week, Chemical Week*, and *European Chemical News*) for the period 1969 through mid-1978 and pulling out every item pertaining to a conflict in which any of the firms were involved. The clippings were then supplemented by data from annual reports, Form 10-K reports to the SEC (for U.S. based firms), and a range of books and articles written about the firms. Files were created for every single conflict discovered. Data on each conflict was then coded for the firm involved, issues involved, the year of conflict emergence, the nation in which the dispute took place, the opponents involved, the tactics utilized by the opponents, and where possible, the outcomes of resolved or terminated cases.

26. For a review of theory and empirical research regarding the role of issues in conflict see Jeffrey Z. Rubin and Bert R. Brown, *The Social Psychology of Bargaining and Negotiation* (New York: Academic Press, 1975), Chapter 6.

27. "Sharp-Tongued Foreigner," *Forbes* (1 June 1976), p. 23.

28. See Avery, *Not on Queen Victoria's Birthday*.

29. Richard West, "British Multinational in Hot Water," *Business and Society Review* (Spring 1975), p. 78.

30. See Mira Wilkins, *The Maturing of Multinational Enterprise: American Business Abroad from 1914 to 1970* (Cambridge, Mass.: Harvard University Press, 1974), Chapter IX, "The Paradox of Oil."

31. For reviews of this controversy see S. Prakash Sethi, *Up Against the Corporate Wall*, 1st ed. (Englewood Cliffs, N.J.: Prentice-Hall, 1971), pp. 236–266; and Robert Heilbroner (ed.), *In the Name of Profit* (New York: Doubleday, 1972).

32. Sampson, *The Sovereign State of ITT*, p. 24.

33. See David Vogel, *Lobbying the Corporation: Citizen Challenges to Business Authority* (New York: Basic Books, 1978).

34. See Barnet and Müller, *Global Reach*.

35. See Robert Ackerman and Raymond Bauer, *Corporate Social Responsiveness: The Modern Dilemma* (Reston: Reston Publishing Co., 1976).

36. Harold S. Geneen, *International Telephone and Telegraph Corporation 1962 Annual Report* (New York: ITT, 1963).

37. West, "British Multinational in Hot Water," p. 76.

38. From the *Sunday Times* of 12 March 1967 cited in West, *River of Tears: The Rise of the Rio Tinto-Zinc Mining Corporation*, p. 12.

39. "EEC Drug Price Curbs Harmful," *Financial Times World Business Weekly* (30 October 1978), p. 12.

40. "Hidden Costs at Dow," *The Wall Street Journal* (25 May 1978), p. 24 and "Rapid Wrap-Up," *Chemical Week* (14 February 1979), p. 18.

41. "No Time To Sit Back," *Chemical Week* (28 June 1978), p. 17; and "He's Not One to Shy Away from Controversy," *Chemical Week* (16 August 1978), p. 46.

42. Jensen, "Gulf: Its Troubles Get Deeper," pp. F1 & 11.

43. See Nigel Rowe, "How ITT Solved Its Own Corporate Communications Riddle," *Industrial Advertising and Marketing* (Autumn 1975), reprint.

44. *Gulf Oil Corporation 1976 Annual Report* (Pittsburgh: Gulf, 1977).

45. Priscilla S. Meyer, "The New Order: ITT Chief Hamilton Seeks to Shed Parts of 'Geneen Machine'," *The Wall Street Journal* (11 October 1978), p. 34.

46. "A Drug Giant's Pricing Under International Attack," *Business Week* (16 June 1975), p. 50.

47. Quote of Richard Tanner Pascale of Stanford University in N.R. Kleinfield, "Geneen Leaving ITT Helm, With Admirers and Critics," *The New York Times* (23 December 1977), p. D5.

48. On the functionality of conflict see Lewis Coser, *The Functions of Social Conflict* (New York: Free Press, 1956); Morton Deutsch, "Toward an Understanding of Conflict," *International Journal of Group Tensions* 1 (January–March 1971), pp. 42–54; Jay Hall, "Decisions, Decisions, Decisions," *Psychology Today* 5 (November 1971), pp. 51–54, 86–87; Joe Kelly, "Make Conflict Work for You," *Harvard Business Review* 48 (July–August 1970), pp. 103–113; Joseph A. Litterer, "Conflict in Organizations: A Re-Examination," *Administrative Science Quarterly* 12 (September 1967), pp. 296–320.

49. See Irving L. Janis, *Victims of Groupthink* (Boston: Houghton Mifflin, 1972).

50. Jayne Baker Spain, "Communication in a Crisis," *Across the Board* 15 (June 1978), pp. 84–85.

CHAPTER 2

1. Fremont Kast and James Rosenzweig, "General Systems Theory: Applications for Organization and Management," *Academy of Management Journal* (December 1972), p. 463.

2. See Thomas L. Ruble and Kenneth W. Thomas, "Support for a Two-Dimensional Model of Conflict Behavior," *Organizational Behavior and Human Performance* 16 (June 1976), pp. 143–155.

3. Robert R. Blake and Jane S. Mouton, *The Managerial Grid* (Houston, Texas: Gulf Publishing Co., 1964). See also Robert R. Blake, Herbert A. Shepard, and Jane S. Mouton, *Managing Intergroup Conflict in Industry* (Houston, Texas: Gulf Publishing Co., 1964).

4. Kenneth W. Thomas, "Conflict and Conflict Management," pp. 889–935, in Marvin D. Dunnette (ed.), *Handbook of Industrial and Organizational Psychology* (Chicago: Rand McNally, 1976).

5. This categorization scheme is adopted from Thomas, "Conflict and Conflict Management," p. 900.

6. Most discussions have been in the context of interpersonal or intergroup relations. See: Robert R. Blake and Jane S. Mouton, "The Fifth Achievement," *The Journal of Applied Behavioral Science* 6 (October–December 1970), pp. 413–426; Blake and Mouton, *The Managerial Grid;* Ronald J. Burke, "Methods of Resolving Superior-Subordinate Conflict: The Constructive Use of Subordinate Differences and Disagreements," *Organizational Behavior and Human Performance* 15 (July 1970), pp. 313–329; Hans J. Thamhain and David L. Wileman, "Conflict Management in Project Life Cycles," *Sloan Management Review* 16 (Spring 1975), pp. 31–50; Ronald J. Burke, "Methods of Resolving Interpersonal Conflict," *Personnel Administration* (July–August 1969), pp. 48–55; Kenneth W. Thomas "Toward Multi-Dimensional Values in Teaching: The Example of Conflict Behaviors," *The Academy of Management Review* 2 (July 1977), pp. 484–489; P.R. Lawrence and J.W. Lorsch, *Organization and Environment: Managing Differentiation and Integration* (Boston: Division of Research, Graduate School of Business Administration, Harvard University, 1967); R.E. Walton and R.B. McKersie, *A Behavioral Theory of Labor Negotiations* (New York: McGraw-Hill, 1965); J. Hall, *Conflict Management Survey* (Conroe, Texas: Teleometrics International, 1969); Mary P. Follett, *Dynamic Administration: The Collected Papers of Mary Parker Follett*, edited by H.C. Metcalf and L. Urwick (New York: Harper, 1941); C.J. Lammers, "Tactics and Strategies Adopted by University Authorities to Counter Student Opposition," pp. 171–198, in Donald Light, Jr. and John Spiegel (eds.), *The Dynamics of University Protest* (Chicago: Nelson-Hall, 1977); and Rensis Likert and Jane Gibson Likert, *New Ways of Managing Conflict* (New York: McGraw-Hill, 1976).

7. Mike Muller, *The Baby Killer* (London: War on Want, March 1974); Iain Carson, "Consumers Try to Tilt the Scales," *Vision* (April 1976), pp. 49–52; "Nestlé," *Business and Society Review* (Fall 1976), p. 80; "The Formula Flap," *Time* (16 February 1976), p. 57; Ann Crittenden, "Baby Formula Sales in Third World Criticized," *The New York Times* (11 September 1975), pp. 55 and 61; and Douglas Clement, "Nestlé's Latest Killing in the Bottle Baby Market," *Business and Society Review* (Summer 1978), pp. 60–64.

8. "Westinghouse, Utilities Square Off," *Chemical Week* (21 September 1977), p. 28; "Issues on Trial in the Westinghouse Suits," *Business Week* (26 September 1977), pp. 125 and 131; "The Uranium Dilemma: Why Prices Mushroomed," *Business Week* (1 November 1976), pp. 92 and 97; Tim Metz, "Panel Finds Cartel Had a Direct Impact on Uranium Purchases by U.S. Utilities," *The Wall Street Journal* (15 August 1977), p. 3; and "Westinghouse Presses Its Case," *Chemical Week* (25 July 1979), pp. 25–26.

9. Jerry Landauer, "State Department May Help Boeing Keep 'Consultants' Secret in Payoffs Inquiry," *The Wall Street Journal* (28 December 1976), p. 4; "SEC Clashes With Boeing Co. Over Payments," *The New York Times* (17 December 1976), p. D1; Jerry Landauer, "U.S. Says Some Boeing Co. Consultants Are Officials of Foreign Governments," *The Wall Street Journal* (7 January 1977), p. 3; "Court Bars SEC From Forcing Boeing to Disclose 18 Consultants," *The New York Times* (1 March 1977), p. 47; and "How Boeing Passed $52 Million Under the Table," *Business and Society Review* (Winter 1978–79), pp. 36–40.

10. Emergency Committee for American Trade, *The Role of the Multinational Corporation in the United States and World Economy* (Washington, D.C.: ECAT, 1972); Richard L. Barovick, "The Washington Struggle Over Multinationals," *Business and Society Review*, No. 18, (Summer 1976), pp. 12–19.

11. "No Fizz Without Fuss," *The Economist* (20 August 1977), pp. 95–96; "Coca-Cola Ordered by India to Disclose Formula for Drink," *The Wall Street Journal* (10 August 1977), p. 11; Kasturi Rangan, "India Demands 'Know-How' and 60% Share of Coca Cola Operation," *The New York Times* (9 August 1977), p. 45; "India Stands Firm Against Coca-Cola," *The New York Times* (5 September 1977), p. 22; "India May Swallow Coke," *Time* (22 August 1977), p. 44.

12. "Unions Are Gearing for Multinational Action Against Chemical Giants," *Chemical Week* (25 October 1972), p. 37; Paul Kemezis, "A Multinational vs. United Unions," *The New York Times* (2 November 1975), pp. 1 and 6; "A Multinational Talks Back," *Chemical Week* (8 December 1975), p. 10; "Multinationals: Bargaining on an International Scale," *Business Week* (27 October 1975), pp. 38–39; Paul Kemezis, "Unions: Setback Abroad," *The New York Times* (1 February 1976), p. 3; "Akzo Threads Its Way Back to Profits," *Chemical Week* (2 November 1977), pp. 31–32.

13. United Church of Christ Center for Social Action, *The Oil Conspiracy* (New York: Interfaith Center on Corporate Responsibility, June 1976); Robert D. Hershey, "Mobil Denies It Had Secret Plan for Supplying Oil to Rhodesia," *The New York Times* (18 September 1976), p. 28; Fred Armentrout, "Mobil's Oily 'No Comment' on Rhodesia," *Business and Society Review* (Spring 1977), pp. 52–55; and "U.S. Can't Determine Whether Mobil Oil Broke Rhodesian Ban," *The Wall Street Journal* (18 May 1977), p. 2. Tami Hoffman and Reed Kramer, "U.S. Oil and the Embargo of Rhodesia," *New York Times* (26 January 1979), p. 25.

14. John Costello and Terry Hughes, *The Concorde Conspiracy* (New York: Scribner, 1976); Richard Witkin, "Supreme Court Lifts Kennedy Ban on SST; Jet Due in Tomorrow," *The New York Times* (18 October 1977), pp. 1 and 28; and Clyde H. Farnsworth, "French Leader in U.S.; Asks Concorde Entry," *The New York Times* (16 September 1977), p. 8.

15. See Bertram H. Raven and Arie W. Kruglanski, "Conflict and Power," pp. 69–109, in Paul Swingle, ed., *The Structure of Conflict* (New York: Academic Press, 1970).

16. See James T. Tedeschi, "Threats and Promises," pp. 155–191, in Swingle, *The Structure of Conflict*. See also Thomas C. Schelling, *The Strategy of Conflict* (New York: Oxford University Press, 1960).

17. See R. Stagner and H. Rosen, *Psychology of Union-Management Relations* (Belmont, California: Brooks/Cole Publishing Co., 1965); and Blake, Shepard and Mouton, *Managing Intergroup Conflict*.

18. "Coping with Terrorism in Argentina," *Business Week* (9 March 1974), pp. 40–42; Juan de Onis, "Businessmen Under the Gun in Argentina," *The New York Times* (22 February 1976), p. F3; Susan Heller Anderson, "An Agent 007 for the Businessman Abroad," *The New York Times* (23 October 1977), p. F3; and "Terrorism is Changing Executives' Lives," *The New York Times* (29 October 1977), pp. 1 and 6.

19. Deborah Rankin, "Control Data Plans No Expansion of Its South African Investment," *The New York Times* (26 October 1977), p. D3.

20. Vasil Pappas, "Payoff Aftermath: Crackdown on Bribery Hasn't Damaged Sales, Big Companies Report," *The Wall Street Journal* (28 February 1977), pp. 1 and 8; "Business Without Bribes," *Newsweek* (19 February 1979), pp. 63–64; and "U.S. Firms Say '77 Ban on Foreign Payoffs Hurts Overseas Sales," *The Wall Street Journal* (2 August 1979), pp. 1 and 19.

21. "Worker Participation: Jacob's Escape Ladder," *The Economist* (8 October 1977), p. 102.

22. Herbert E. Meyer, "Business Has the Jitters in Québec," *Fortune* (October 1977), pp. 238–244; Robert S. Cameron, "Outward Bound: Firms Leaving Québec as Two Divisive Issues Generate Uncertainty," *The Wall Street Journal* (30 September 1977), pp. 1 and 30; Henry Giniger, "New Era in Québec's Industry," *The New York Times* (25 October 1977), pp. 55 and 57; "An English-Speaking Rush to Leave Québec," *Business Week* (22 August 1977), pp. 62–64; and Leonard Anderson, "Business Pressure Building Steadily to Leave Québec," *The Wall Street Journal* (18 May 1979), p. 14.

24. "Australia: It Fears Becoming a Second Canada," *Business Week* (20 May 1972), pp. 46–47; "Economic Nationalism Flares Up in Australia: Why ITT Postponed Takeover Offer," *Business Asia* (November 1972), p. 137.

25. Quotes drawn from Dudley Hunt, "Refineries, Other Noxious Industries in Coastal Zone," *The Wilmington Morning News* (13 May 1974), p. 25; "State Funds Can Buy Land to Block Refineries, Mills," *The Wilmington Evening Journal* (11 February 1971), pp. 1 and 3; Mr. Abrams, "Thinking Out Loud: Peterson Misstates Facts About Shell," *The Wilmington Evening Journal* (14 May 1974), p. 23.

26. David Tobis, "How Coca-Cola Keeps Its Corporate Image Bubbly," *Business and Society Review* (Summer 1977), pp. 71–74.

27. The collaborative mode has also been labeled as "problem solving" by Blake, Shepard, and Mouton, *Managing Intergroup Conflict in Industry;* "integrative bargaining" by Richard E. Walton and Robert B. McKensie, *A Behavioral Theory of Labor Negotiations* (New York: McGraw Hill, 1965); "integrating" by Mary P. Follett, *Dynamic Administration;* and "confronting" by Lawrence and Lorsch, *Organization and Environment.*

28. "Inventing Backwards: Some Firms Simplify Products for Markets in Poor Countries," *The Wall Street Journal* (27 May 1969), p. 1; "Tough, Cheap Trucks for the Third World," *Business Week* (27 May 1971), p. 15; "Detroit's Low-Gear Drive in Asia," *Far Eastern*

Economic Review (15 July 1974), pp. 58–61; and Thomas N. Gladwin, "Technology and Material Culture," pp. 175–218, in Vern Terpstra, ed., *The Cultural Environment of International Business.*

29. "World Roundup: Sweden," *Business Week* (18 April 1977), p. 67 and "New Wage-Earner Fund Proposal Sparks Debate in Sweden," *Business Europe* (31 March 1978), pp. 103–104.

30. "Justice Will Guide Multinationals on Antitrust Problems," *Chemical Week* (11 June 1975), p. 12.

31. "The Trade Union Jet-Set," *The Economist* (15 October 1977), pp. 89–90; Neil Ulman, "Multinational Firms Face a Growing Power: Multinational Unions," *The Wall Street Journal* (23 April 1973), pp. 1 and 14.

32. Thomas N. Gladwin, *Environment, Planning and the Multinational Corporation* (Greenwich, Conn.: JAI Press, 1977), Chapter VIII; "Chemical Companies Team Up for Early Warning on More VCMs," *Chemical Week* (29 January 1975), pp. 44–45; Jack N. Behrman and William Gilbert Carter, *Problems of International Business Cooperation in Environmental Protection* (New York: Fund for Multinational Management Education, November 1975).

33. Isaiah A. Litvak and Christopher J. Maule, "Foreign Corporate Social Responsibility in Less Developed Economies," *Journal of World Trade Law* 9 (March/April 1975), pp. 121–135; "Kissing the Hand You Just Bit," *Forbes* (15 June 1977), pp. 64–65; H. Crookell, "Alcan in Guyana," Case WCTs 11007-WIBM 141, (London, Ontario: The University of Western Ontario, 1971).

34. "In Indonesia, Mining Is Only Half the Job," *Chemical Week* (1 September 1976), pp. 26–31.

35. Jonijane Paxton, "An Experiment in Ecology—AMAX/Henderson: Meeting the Environmental Challenges," *Editorial Alert* (July 1974); "Bucking the Pessimistic Trend in Mining," *Business Week* (2 August 1976), pp. 32–39; "Openness, Cooperation—Keys to the AMAX Environmental Program," *Engineering and Mining Journal* (September 1972); "The Henderson Project," *Mining Magazine* (August 1975), pp. 90–96.

36. This notion of "integrative bargaining" is advanced by Walton and McKersie, *A Behavioral Theory.*

37. Processes of creative thinking underlie the entire collaborative effort. See Deutsch, *The Resolution of Conflict*, pp. 360–363; G.M. Prince, *The Practice of Creativity* (New York: Harper & Row, 1970); C.W. Taylor, *Climate for Creativity* (Elmsford, N.Y.: Pergamon Press, 1972); and Gary A. Steiner, *The Creative Organization* (Chicago: University of Chicago Press, 1965).

38. "Bank of America Will Stop Assisting the Arab Boycott," *The New York Times* (4 November 1976), p. 8 and Milton R. Moskowitz, "The Bank of America's Rocky Road to Responsibility," *Business and Society Review* (Summer 1977), pp. 61–64.

39. Juan de Onis, "Businessmen Under the Gun in Argentina," *The New York Times* (27 February 1976), p. F3.

40. "France: Trying to Placate a Hostile Labor Force," *Business Week* (25 April 1977), p. 44 and "World Roundup: France," *Business Week* (2 May 1977), p. 41.

41. Robert D. Hershey, Jr., "SEC Charges Indonesia Oil Chief in Shakedown of Big U.S. Concerns," *The New York Times* (3 February 1977), pp. 1 and 55, and Burt Schorr, "Indonesian Restaurant Shows How Firms Can Succumb to Threats to Foreign Stakes," *The Wall Street Journal* (13 October 1977), p. 13.

42. "Exxon Consents to SEC Charges It, Aide Made $56.5 Million in Overseas Payoffs," *The Wall Street Journal* (28 September 1977), p. 48. Also see Edward G. Harness, Sir Richard Dobson, and Jack F. Bennett, *Determination and Report of the Special Committee on Litigation* (New York: Exxon Corporation, 23 January 1976).

43. Thomas E. Mullaney, "12 Big U.S. Concerns in South Africa Set Equality in Plants," *The New York Times* (2 March 1977), p. D1; "21 More U.S. Companies Backing Antiracist Code for South Africa," *The New York Times* (21 June 1977), p. 44; "21 More Concerns Back South African Equality," *The New York Times* (15 September 1977), p. D16; Timothy Smith, "Whitewash for Apartheid from Twelve U.S. Firms," *Business and Society Review*, (Summer 1977), pp. 59–60; and "Reforms in South Africa," *Business Week* (18 June 1979), p. 158.

44. "Johnson & Johnson's Research Laboratory Meets Brazilian Demands for Local R&D," *Business Latin America* (25 November 1971), pp. 373–374.

45. "Ian Clark: The Scourge of North Sea Oil Men," *Business Week* (1 November 1976), pp. 45–46; James R. Nicolson, *Shetland and Oil* (London: William Luscombe, 1975); Pamela L. Baldwin and Malcolm F. Baldwin, *Onshore Planning for Offshore Oil: Lessons from Scotland* (Washington, D.C.: The Conservation Foundation, 1975); and "Sullen Woe, Again," *The Economist* (2 September 1978), p. 102.

46. William D. Hartley, "Talking It Over: More Concerns Willing to Enter Negotiations on Holder Resolutions," *The Wall Street Journal* (23 March 1977), pp. 1 and 32.

47. Timothy Smith, "Whitewash for Apartheid from Twelve U.S. Firms," *Business and Society Review* (Summer 1977), pp. 59–60.

48. "South Africa: Multinationals Are Caught in the Middle Again," *Business Week* (24 October 1977), pp. 49–50; "Black Labor Union Recognized by Ford," *The New York Times* (20 August 1977), p. 6.

49. See: Ruth Leeds Love, "The Absorption of Protest," in W.W. Cooper, H.J. Leavitt, and M.W. Shelly, eds., *New Perspectives in Organizational Research* (New York: John Wiley, 1964).

50. "France: Seizing Control of Technical Industries," *Business Week* (17 May 1976), p. 47, and "France: A Setback in Trying to 'Frenchify' Phones," *Business Week* (21 November 1977), p. 68.

51. Michael C. Jensen, "Dissident Stockholders Begin to Get Somewhere at Last," *The New York Times* (16 May 1977), pp. 43 and 46 and "Tenneco Inc. Agrees With Jewish Group About Arab Boycott," *The Wall Street Journal* (18 March 1977), p. 28.

52. "Financing Troubles for VW's New Plant," *Business Week* (5 July 1976), p. 26; "Why VW Must Build Autos in the U.S." *Business Week* (16 February 1976), pp. 46–51; "Pollution May Kill VW's Rabbit Plant," *Business Week* (7 March 1977), p. 26; John Vinocur, "The Americanization of VW," *The New York Times* (9 October 1977), Section 3, pp. 1 and 4; "Black Groups Accuse VW of Discrimination," *The New York Times* (26 October 1977), p. D15; "VW of U.S. and UAW Agree Tentatively on Terms to Settle Pennsylvania Dispute," *The Wall Street Journal* (20 October 1978), p. 4.

53. E. Patrick McGuire, "The Terrorist and the Corporation," *Across the Board* 14 (May 1977), pp. 11–19; "Kidnappers Release Fiat Aide in France, Held for 3 Months," *The New York Times* (12 July 1977), p. 3; and "French Cops and Revolutionary Robbers," *The Economist* (16 July 1977), pp. 51–52.

54. "Goodyear vs. Goodrich Tussle in Netherlands Points Up Pitfalls of Joint Ventures," *Business International* (20 May 1970), pp. 169–170; "Goodrich May Lower Its European Profile," *Business Week* (20 July 1976), pp. 51–52; "B.F. Goodrich: Quick Getaways," *The Economist* (7 August 1976), pp. 60–61; and "Getting Out of Dutch," *Chemical Week* (27 October 1976), p. 23.

55. "AMC-Arab Joint Venture," *The Wall Street Journal* (14 October 1977), p. 46; "Coca-Cola and Egypt Agree to Form Venture," *The Wall Street Journal* (8 September 1977), p. 16; Marvine Howe, "Coca-Cola and Egypt Plan Joint Venture," *The New York Times* (8 September 1977), p. 8; "Ford Motor Says Egypt Approved a Joint Venture," *The New York Times* (8 September 1977), p. 8; "Arabs to Ban Products of Ford Made in Mideast," *The New York Times* (4 November 1977), p. D9; "Arab League Boycott Chief Lashes Out at Egypt for Joint Venture with Ford," *The Wall Street Journal*, (4 November 1977), p. 14; and "Middle East: The High Initial Costs of a Peace Treaty," *Business Week* (2 April 1975), pp. 38–40. Also see: "Coke is Returning to Egyptian Market After 12-Year Ban," *Wall Street Journal* (17 July 1979), p. 29; "Search for Aid as Confidence Wanes," *World Trade Weekly* (3 September 1979), pp. 37–38; and "Egypt's Surprising Cash Flow," *Business Week* (24 September 1979), pp. 86–90.

56. "No Fizz Without Fuss," *The Economist* (20 August 1977), pp. 95–96; Kasturi Rangan, "India Agrees to Deal that Allows IBM to Stay in Country," *The New York Times* (11 September 1977), p. 13; "Tea Instead of Sympathy," *The Economist* (24 September 1977), p. 100; Kasturi Rangan, "New Delhi Official Says IBM Told India It Is Leaving," *The New York Times* (1 October 1977), pp. 25 and 29; "Reshaping IBM," *The Economist* (29 October 1977), pp. 92–93; and N.R. Kleinfield, "IBM to Leave India and Avoid Loss of Control," *The New York Times* (16 November 1977), p. D1 and 12.

57. Stephen Young and Neil Hood, "Multinational and Host Governments: Lessons from the Case of Chrysler U.K.," *Columbia Journal of World Business* 12 (Summer 1977), pp. 97–106; and

"The Multinational That Wanted to be Nationalised: A Case History of the Chrysler Rescue," *Multinational Business*, (March 1976), pp. 1–18.

58. For a good collection of articles see I. William Zartman (ed.), *The 50% Solution* (Garden City, N.Y.: Anchor Books, 1976).

59. This distinction is from Kenneth E. Boulding, *Conflict and Defense: A General Theory* (New York: Harper, 1962).

60. See: H.H. Kelley, "A Classroom Study of the Dilemmas in Interpersonal Negotiations," in K. Archibald (ed.), *Strategic Interaction and Conflict: Original Papers and Discussion* (Berkeley, California: Institute of International Studies, 1966).

CHAPTER 3

1. See Charles P. Kindleberger, *American Business Abroad: Six Lectures on Direct Investment* (New Haven: Yale University Press, 1969).

2. See Raymond Vernon, *Storm Over the Multinationals; The Real Issues* (Cambridge, Mass.: Harvard University Press, 1977); Raymond Vernon and Louis T. Wells, Jr., *Manager in the International Economy*, 3rd edition, (Englewood Cliffs, N.J.: Prentice-Hall, 1976); John Fayerweather, *International Business Management: A Conceptual Framework*, (New York: McGraw Hill, 1969); and John Fayerweather and Ashok Kapoor, *Strategy and Negotiation for the International Corporation: Guidelines and Cases* (Cambridge, Mass.: Ballinger, 1976).

3. Kasturi Rangan, "New Delhi Official Says IBM Told India It Is Leaving," *The New York Times* (1 October 1977), pp. 25 and 29.

4. Sanford Rose, "Why the Multinational Tide Is Ebbing," *Fortune* (August 1977), p. 114.

5. Edward Cowan, "U.S. vs. Big Oil—A Legal Snarl," *The New York Times* (17 July 1977), Section 3, pp. 1 and 7.

6. Cited in Joseph S. Nye, Jr., "Multinational Corporations in World Politics," *Foreign Affairs* 53 (October 1974), p. 169.

7. David N. Smith and Louis T. Wells, Jr., *Negotiating Third-World Mineral Agreements* (Cambridge, Mass.: Ballinger, 1975), p. 14.

8. John Thibaut and Laurens Walker, *Procedural Justice: A Psychological Analysis* (Hillsdale, N.J.: Lawrence Erlbaum, 1975), p. 7.

9. "Decision costs" are a function, among other things, of the time and effort required by a decision-making or conflict resolution procedure. See J.M. Buchanan and G. Tullock, *The Calculus of Consent* (Ann Arbor: University of Michigan Press, 1962).

10. Experimental research on the impact of time limits is reviewed in Jeffrey Z. Rubin and Bert R. Brown, *The Social Psychology of Bargaining and Negotiation* (New York: Academic Press, 1975), pp. 120–124.

11. This theme is stressed by Morton Deutsch, *The Resolution of Conflict: Constructive and Destructive Processes* (New Haven: Yale University Press, 1973), pp. 84–85.

12. J.W. Thibaut and H.H. Kelley, *The Social Psychology of Groups* (New York: John Wiley, 1959).

13. J.R.P. French, Jr. and B.H. Raven, "The Bases of Social Power," in D. Cartwright, ed., *Studies in Social Power* (Ann Arbor: University of Michigan Press, 1959). Also see Bertram H. Raven and Arie W. Kruglanski, "Conflict and Power," pp. 69–109, in Paul Swingle (ed.), *The Structure of Conflict* (New York: Academic Press, 1970).

14. Deutsch, *The Resolution of Conflict*, p. 395.

15. For studies of coalition formation see: T.A. Caplow, "A Theory of Coalitions in the Triad," *American Sociological Review* 21 (1956), pp. 489–493; W.A. Gamson, "A Theory of Coalition Formation," *American Sociological Review* 26 (1961), pp. 373–382; J.M. Chertkoff, "A Revision of Caplow's Coalition Theory," *Journal of Experimental Social Psychology* 3 (1967), pp. 172–177; and J.M. Chertkoff, "Coalition Formation and Function of Differences in Resources," *Journal of Conflict Resolution* 15 (1971), pp. 371–383.

16. These are the predictions of Rubin and Brown, *The Social Psychology of Bargaining and Negotiation*, pp. 64–80.

17. Cited in Vernon and Wells, *Manager in the International Economy*, p. 15.

18. Joseph Collins, "Britain is Awarded Ford Engine Plant in Stiff Competition," *The New York Times* (10 September 1977), pp. 31 and 35; and "Ford, or How to Invest More and Pay Less," *The Economist* (17 September 1977), pp. 123–124.

19. Theodore H. Moran, "Transnational Strategies of Protection and Defense by Multinational Corporations: Spreading the Risk and Raising the Cost for Nationalization in Natural Resources," *International Organization* **27** (Spring 1973), pp. 273–287.

20. See Smith and Wells, *Negotiating Third-World Mineral Agreements*.

21. Raymond Vernon, *Storm Over the Multinationals*, pp. 171–172.

22. See Clinton F. Fink, "Some Conceptual Difficulties in the Theory of Social Conflict," *The Journal of Conflict Resolution* **12** (December 1968), p. 448.

23. Deutsch, *The Resolution of Conflict*, p. 20.

24. Deutsch, *The Resolution of Conflict*, p. 20.

25. Joseph S. Nye, Jr., "Multinational Corporations in World Politics," *Foreign Affairs* **53** (October 1974), p. 168.

26. Vernon, *Storm Over the Multinationals*, pp. 193–194.

27. See Thomas, "Conflict and Conflict Management," p. 915.

28. Rubin and Brown, *The Social Psychology of Bargaining and Negotiation*, p. 56.

29. For a good discussion of the combined effects of goals and means interdependence see Bertram H. Raven and Jeffrey Z. Rubin, *Social Psychology: People in Groups* (New York: John Wiley, 1976), Chapter 5.

30. Deutsch, *The Resolution of Conflict*, p. 365.

31. "In hoc Signo," *The Economist* (13 August 1977), p. 58.

32. William Graham Sumner, *Folkways* (Boston: Dover Publications, 1906), p. 13.

33. Carlton J.H. Hayes, in *The Dynamics of Nationalism*, Louis L. Snyder (ed.) (Princeton, N.J.: D. Van Nostrand, 1964), p. 2.

34. For a good framework see John Fayerweather, "A Conceptual Scheme of the Interaction of the Multinational Firm and Nationalism," *Journal of Business Administration* **7** (Fall 1975), pp. 67–89.

35. Richard D. Robinson, *International Business Management: A Guide to Decision Making* (New York: Holt, Rinehart and Winston, 1973), p. 1.

36. Margaret Mead (1937),

37. Georg Simmel, *The Web of Group Affiliations (1908)*, translated by K.H. Wolff (New York: Free Press, 1955), p. 34.

38. Anatol Rapoport, "Game Theory and Intergroup Hostility," pp. 368–375, in M. Berkowitz and P.G. Bock (eds.), *American National Security: A Reader in Theory and Policy* (New York: Free Press, 1965).

39. Some of these situations are suggested in Kenneth W. Thomas, "Toward Multi-Dimensional Values in Teaching: The Example of Conflict Behaviors," *The Academy of Management Review* **2** (July 1977), p. 487.

40. See R. Fisher, "Fractionating Conflict," in R. Fisher (ed.), *International Conflict and Behavioral Science: The Craigville Papers* (New York: Basic Books, 1964).

41. Alonzo L. McDonald, "The MNE: Monkey in the Middle," *The McKinsey Quarterly* (Spring 1977), pp. 15–31.

42. "Venezuela Owens Move Creates Dismay," *The New York Times* (8 April 1977), p. 55.

43. "Pay Policy: Ford's Prayer," *The Economist* (8 October 1977), pp. 123–124. Also see "Cracks in the Pay Ceiling," *The Economist* (15 October 1977), p. 115; and "The Brothers Do Their Duty," *The Economist* (22 October 1977), pp. 89–90.

44. For duPont see "U.K. Lobbies for duPont Acrylic Fibers Plant," *Chemical Week* (12 October 1977), p. 47 and "Dupont to Phase Out Production of Orlon at Netherlands Plant," *The Wall Street Journal* (20 October 1977), p. 3. For Metal Box see "Arab Boycott: Rally Round Which Flag," *The Economist* (25 June 1977), pp. 84–85. For Volkswagen see "Brazil Has Second Thoughts about Multinationals," *Multinational Business*, No. 3 (September 1975), pp. 18–27. For South Africa see "Multinationals are Caught in the Middle Again," *Business Week* (24

October 1977), pp. 49–50 and "Black-Chip Investment?," *The Economist* (26 November 1977), pp. 47–48.

45. For reviews of trading-with-the-enemy cases see Jack N. Behrman, *National Interests and the Multinational Enterprise: Tensions Among the North Atlantic Countries* (Englewood Cliffs, N.J.: Prentice-Hall, 1970); David Legton-Brown, "The Multinational Enterprise and Conflict in Canadian-American Relations," *International Organization* 28 (Autumn 1974), pp. 733–754; Isaiah A. Litvak, Christopher J. Maule, and R.D. Robinson, *Dual Loyalty: Canadian-U.S. Business Arrangements* (Toronto: McGraw-Hill, 1971); and Malcolm Levin and Christine Sylvester, *Foreign Ownership* (Don Mills, Ontario: Paperjacks, General Publishing Co., 1972).

46. Louis R. Pondy, "Organizational Conflict: Concepts and Models," *Administrative Science Quarterly* 12 (September 1967), pp. 296–320.

47. For a discussion of "superordinate" goals see Muzafer Sherif, "Superordinate Goals in the Reduction of Intergroup Conflict," *The American Journal of Sociology* 63 (January 1958), pp. 349–356.

48. See Smith and Wells, *Negotiating Third-World Mineral Agreements;* Theodore H. Moran, *Multinational Corporations and the Politics of Dependence* (Princeton: Princeton University Press, 1974); Raymond F. Mikesell, ed., *Foreign Investment in the Petroleum and Mineral Industries: Case Studies in Investor-Host Country Relations* (Baltimore: The Johns Hopkins Press for Resources for the Future, 1971); and Zuhayr Mikdashi, *The International Politics of Natural Resources* (Ithaca, N.Y.: Cornell University Press, 1976).

49. Carlos F. Diaz Alejandro, "International Markets for Exhaustible Resources, Less Developed Countries, and Multinational Corporations," pp. 269–298 in Robert G. Hawkins, ed., *The Economic Effects of Multinational Corporations* (Greenwich, Conn.: JAI Press, 1979).

50. See Rubin and Brown, *The Social Psychology of Bargaining and Negotiation*, Chapter 9: "Social Influence and Influence Strategies."

51. "The Trade Union Jet-Set," *The Economist* (15 October 1977), p. 89.

52. "Black-Chip Investment," *The Economist* (26 November 1977), pp. 47–48; and Michael C. Jensen, "Polaroid Severs Business Links to South Africa," *The New York Times* (23 November 1977), pp. D1 & 16.

53. "California Standard and Texaco Settle Dispute With Libya," *The Wall Street Journal* (26 September 1977), p. 6.

54. Marvine Howe, "Portugal, Ending Long Opposition, to Allow Production of Coca-Cola," *The New York Times* (18 January 1977), p. 26.

CHAPTER 4

1. For a profile of the ERP see Charles A. Russell, James F. Schenkel, and James A. Miller, "Urban Guerrillas in Argentina: A Select Bibliography," *Latin American Research Review* 9 (Fall 1974), pp. 53–89.

2. Agis Salpukas, "Ford Will Pay $1-Million To Halt Argentine Terror," *The New York Times* (24 May 1973), pp. 1 and 3.

3. "Ford Maps Aid for Hospitals in Yielding to Argentine Rebels," *The New York Times* (25 May 1973), p. 2.

4. *Ibid.* See also "Businessmen Hit Ford Deal With Guerrillas," *Washington Star-News* (25 May 1973), p. 7.

5. Jonathan Kandell, "Argentine Guerrillas Vow More Attacks," *The New York Times* (28 May 1973), p. 3.

6. Jonathan Kandell, "U.S. Concern Resisting Argentine Rebels," *The New York Times* (2 June 1973), p. 13.

7. "A Ford Executive Slain in Argentina," *The New York Times* (23 November 1973), pp. 1 and 13; and Jonathan Kandell, "Ford Company Protects Argentine Staff," *The New York Times* (30 November 1973), p. 6.

8. "Ford Executives Arrive," *The New York Times* (2 December 1973), p. 3.

9. "Exxon is said to Agree to Pay $10-Million Argentine Ransom," *The New York Times* (13 December 1973), p. 2.

10. Jonathan Kandell, "Argentine Guerrillas Promise to Step Up Attacks," *The New York Times* (15 February 1974), p. 6.

11. The *Herald* report is quoted in Jonathan Kandell, "Exxon Manager Yet to be Freed," *The New York Times* (15 March 1974), p. 5.

12. "Argentinians Shut Daily for Exxon Ad on Ransom Fund," *Advertising Age* (18 March 1974), pp. 1 and 77.

13. "Ransomed U.S. Oilman Rejoins Family," *The New York Times* (1 May 1974), p. 2.

14. Neil Amdur, "U.S. Oilman Tells of Ordeals of Kidnapping in Argentina," *The New York Times* (3 May 1974), p. 2.

15. Russell, Schenkel, and Miller, "Urban Guerillas in Argentina," p. 89.

16. Directorate of Intelligence, U.S. Central Intelligence Agency, "International Terrorism in 1976," RP77-10034U (Washington, D.C.: CIA, July 1977).

17. Russell's statistics are reported in: Judith Miller, "Washington & Business: A Seminar on Threat of Terrorism," *The New York Times* (5 January 1978), pp. D1 and 5. The U.S. State Department Working Group to Combat Terrorism has also published a series of chronologies and supplements covering the period 1970 to present entitled "Significant International Terrorist Incidents." Edward F. Mickolus, in the Office of Regional and Political Analysis, International Issues Division of the U.S. Central Intelligence Agency, has created a comprehensive computerized data bank called ITERATE (International Terrorism: Attributes of Terrorist Events). This data set can be obtained from the Inter-University Consortium for Political and Social Research, Box 1248, Ann Arbor, Michigan, 48106. For the Rand data base see Brian M. Jenkins and Janera Johnson, "International Terrorism: A Chronology, 1968–1974," (Santa Monica: Rand Corporation, R-1597-DOS/ARPA, March 1975). Also see: A.O. Sulzberger, Jr. "Data on Terrorism is New Venture's Product," *New York Times* (15 January 1979), p. D1 and 6.

18. David L. Milbank, "International and Transnational Terrorism: Diagnosis and Prognosis," PR 76 10030 (Washington, D.C.: U.S. Central Intelligence Agency, April 1976), pp. 12–13.

19. Directorate of Intelligence, "International Terrorism in 1976," p. 4.

20. Academic analysis of terror has become a growth industry. For bibliographies see: Guy D. Boston, *et. al.*, *Terrorism: A Selected Bibliography*, 2nd edition (Washington, D.C.: National Criminal Justice Reference Service, March 1977) and Edward F. Mikolus, *Annotated Bibliography on Transnational and International Terrorism*, PR 76 10073U (Washington, D.C.: U.S. Central Intelligence Agency, December 1976). Some recent books are: J. Bowyer Bell, *A Time of Terror: How Democratic Societies Respond to Revolutionary Violence* (New York: Basic Books, 1978); J. Bowyer Bell, *Transnational Terror* (Washington, D.C.: American Enterprise Institute, Study 17, September 1975); Anthony M. Burton, *Urban Terrorism: Theory, Practice and Response* (New York: The Free Press, 1975); Christopher Dobson and Ronald Payne, *The Carlos Complex: A Study in Terror* (New York: G.P. Putnam's Sons, 1977); Roland Gaucher, *The Terrorists: From Tsarist Russia to the O.A.S.* (London: Seeker and Warburg, 1968); Frederick J. Hacker, *Crusaders, Criminals, Crazies: Terror and Terrorism in Our Time* (New York: W.W. Norton, 1976); Ernst Halperin, *Terrorism in Latin America* (Beverly Hills: SAGE Publications, 1976); Edward Hyams, *Terrorists and Terrorism* (New York: St. Martins Press, 1974); James Kohl and John Litt, *Urban Guerrilla Warfare in Latin America* (Cambridge: MIT Press, 1974); Walter Laqueur, *Terrorism* (Boston: Little, Brown & Co., 1977); Robert Moss, *The War for the Cities* (New York: Coward, McCann & Geoghegan, 1972); Albert Parry, *Terrorism: From Robespierre to Arafat* (New York: Vanguard Press, 1976); Richard Clutterbuck, *Kidnap & Ransom: The Response* (London: Faber and Faber, 1978); Paul Fugur and Jerry V. Wilson, *Terrorism: The Executive's Guide to Survival* (Houston: Gulf Publishing, 1978); Christopher Dobson and Ronald Payne, *The Terrorists: Their Weapons, Leaders and Tactics* (New York: Facts on File, 1979); Jan Schreiber, *The Ultimate Weapon: Terrorists and World Order* (New York: William Morris, 1978); Paul Wilkinson, *Terrorism and the Liberal State* (New York: Halsted, 1978); Eugene Victor Walter, *Terror and Resistance: A Study of Political Violence* (New York: Oxford University Press, 1969); Francis M. Watson, *Political Terrorism: The Threat and the Response* (Washington, D.C.: Robert Bluce Co., 1976); and Paul Wilkinson, *Political Terrorism* (New York: John Wiley & Sons, 1974).

For anthologies see the Winter 1976 issue of *ORBIS*, the Spring 1977 issue of *Stanford*

Journal of International Studies, and Spring/Summer 1978 issue of the *Journal of International Affairs.* See also David Carlton and Carlo Schaerf (eds.), *International Terrorism and World Security* (New York: John Wiley & Sons, 1975); M. Cherif Bassiouni (ed.), *International Terrorism and Political Crimes* (Springfield, Ill.: Charles C. Thomas, 1975); Johan Neizing (ed.), *Urban Guerrilla* (Rotterdam: Rotterdam University Press, 1974); and Yonah Alexander (ed.), *International Terrorism: National Regional and Global Perspectives* (New York: Praeger, 1976).

Finally, no subject is complete without its own journal: *Terrorism: An International Journal* (published at the State University of New York at Oneonta).

21. Kerry L. Milte, "Prevention of Terrorism Through the Development of Supra-National Criminology," *The Journal of International Law and Economics* **10** (August–December 1975), p. 522.

22. See Paul Wilkinson, "Three Questions on Terrorism," *Government and Opposition* **8** (Summer 1973), pp. 290–312.

23. Brian M. Jenkins, "International Terrorism: A New Mode of Conflict," p. 14 in Carlton and Schaerf, eds., *International Terrorism and World Security.*

24. Jordan J. Paust, "Terrorism and the International Law of War," *Military Law Review* (Spring 1974), pp. 3–4. Emphasis added.

25. See Carlos Marighella, "Minimanual of the Urban Guerrilla," pp. 67–115, in Jay Mallin, ed., *Terror and Urban Guerrillas* (Coral Gables, Fla: University of Miami Press, 1971); Laqueur, *Terrorism,* pp. 49–53; and Thomas Perry Thornton, "Terror as a Weapon of Political Agitation," pp. 71–99 in Harry Eckstein, ed., *Internal War: Problems and Approaches* (New York: Free Press of Glencoe, 1964).

26. Laqueur, *Terrorism,* note on p. 79.

27. See Frederick J. Hacker, *Crusaders, Criminals and Crazies.*

28. Laqueur, *Terrorism,* Chapter 1, "The Origins" and Chapter 2, "The Philosophy of the Bomb." Also see Part 2: "History" of Parry, *Terrorism: From Robespierre to Arafat.*

29. "The Terrorist Impulse," *The Wall Street Journal* (8 October 1977), p. 16.

30. J. Bowyer Bell, "Trends on Terror: The Analysis of Political Violence," *World Politics* **29** (April 1977), p. 478.

31. Abdul A. Sard and Luis R. Simmons (eds.), *Ethnicity in an International Context* (New Brunswick, N.J.: Transactions Press, 1976).

32. See Christopher Hewitt, "Majorities and Minorities: A Comparative Survey of Ethnic Violence," (in special issue on "Ethnic Conflict in the World Today"), *The Annals,* **433** (September 1977), pp. 150–160.

33. Laqueur, *Terrorism,* p. 220.

34. Ernst Halperin, *Terrorism in Latin America* (The Washington Papers, Volume IV, No. 33), (Beverly Hills, Calif.: SAGE Publications, 1976), pp. 51–52.

35. Ted Robert Gurr, *Why Men Rebel* (Princeton: Princeton University Press, 1970), p. 319.

36. Paul Hofmann, "Italians Fearful as La Dolce Vita Turns Perilous," *The New York Times* (18 July 1977), pp. 1 and 10.

37. See "War Without Boundaries," *Time* (31 October 1977), pp. 28–45.

38. "War Without Boundaries," pp. 28–45.

39. Laqueur, *Terrorism,* p. 206.

40. This is the phrase of Paul Oestreicher, Chairman of the British Section of Amnesty International. See Paul Hofmann, "Made in Germany: The Urban Terrorists," *The New York Times* (25 September 1977), p. 26.

41. See Ralf Dahrendorf, "Baader-Meinholf: How Come? What's Next?" *The New York Times* (20 October 1977), p. 23.

42. See Jillian Becker, *Hitler's Children: The Story of the Baader-Meinhof Terrorist Gang* (Philadelphia: J.B. Lippincott, 1977).

43. "Ghosts of the Past," *The Economist* (29 October 1977), pp. 11–12.

44. For a profile of the JAR see Andrew H. Malcolm, "Japanese Red Army's Hijackings and Its Demands Said to Reflect Political and Financial Desperation," *The New York Times* (30 September 1977), p. 3.

45. David G. Hubbard, *The Skyjacker: His Flights of Fantasy* (New York: Collier, 1973).

46. See Eugene H. Methvin, *The Riot Makers: The Technology of Social Demolition* (New Rochelle, N.Y.: Arlington House, 1970), and *The Rise of Radicalism: The Social Psychology of Messianic Extremism* (New Rochelle, N.Y.: Arlington House, 1973).

47. "The Terrorist Impulse," *The Wall Street Journal* (28 October 1977), p. 16.

48. See: "War Without Boundaries," *Time* (31 October 1977), pp. 28–45.

49. Laqueur, *Terrorism*, p. 120. See also Constance Holden, "Study of Terrorism Emerging as an International Endeavor," *Science*, 203 (5 January 1979), pp. 33–35.

50. Bernard-Henri Levy, "The War Against All," *The New Republic* (11 February 1978), p. 15.

51. Carlos Marighella, "Minimanual of the Urban Guerrilla."

52. C. L. Sulzberger, "Terror Without a Philosophy," *The New York Times* (22 October 1977), p. 21.

53. Thomas Perry Thornton, "Terror As A Weapon of Political Agitation," pp. 83–84.

54. Robert Moss, *The War for the Cities*, p. 36.

55. Peter Weiss, "Joe McCarthy is Alive and Well and Living in West Germany: Terror and Counter-Terror in the Federal Republic," *New York University Journal of International Law & Politics* 9 (Spring 1976), p. 67.

56. David Fromkin, "The Strategy of Terrorism," *Foreign Affairs* **53** (July 1975), p. 693.

57. Fromkin, "The Strategy of Terrorism," p. 693.

58. "Venezuela Owens Move Creates Dismay," *The New York Times* (8 April 1977), p. 55. For the outcome see "Abducted American Freed in Venezuela," *The New York Times* (1 July 1979), p. 7.

59. Juan de Onis, "Businessmen Under the Gun in Argentina," *The New York Times* (22 February 1976), p. F3 and "Ransom in Print," *The Economist* (9 December 1978), pp. 12–13.

60. "The Company Pays," *The Economist* (1 April 1972), p. 34.

61. "The Price of an Ambassador," *The Economist* (20 June 1970).

62. Paul Hofmann, "West German Banks Limit Cash to Thwart Terrorists," *The New York Times* (27 November 1977), p. 4.

63. Laqueur, *Terrorism*, p. 90.

64. "Curbing Terrorism," *Atlas World Press Review* (January 1978), p. 31–37. See also Richard Clutterbuck, *Kidnap & Ransom: The Response*.

65. For a detailed look at "Kidnap Inc." in operation see: Curtis Bill Papper, "Kidnapped" *The New York Times Magazine* (20 November 1977), pp. 42ff.

66. See W.F. May, "Terrorism as Strategy and Ecstacy," *Social Research* **41** (Summer 1974), pp. 277–298.

67. Laurent Tailhade quoted in Bell, *Transnational Terror*, p. 1.

68. Frantz Fanon, *The Wretched of the Earth* (New York: Grove Press, 1967).

69. See Paul Wilkinson, *Terrorism and the Liberal State* (London: Macmillan, 1977).

70. Milbank, "International and Transnational Terrorism: Diagnosis and Prognosis," pp. 1–2.

71. Peter Calvert, *A Study of Revolution* (Oxford: Clarendon Press, 1970).

72. Laqueur, *Terrorism*, p. 109.

73. Brian M. Jenkins, "International Terrorism: A New Kind of Warfare," (Santa Monica: The Rand Corporation, P-5261, June 1974), p. 4.

74. Andrew J. Pierre, "The Politics of International Terrorism," *ORBIS* 19 (Winter 1976), p. 1259.

75. David L. Milbank, "International and Transnational Terrorism: Diagnosis and Prognosis," p. 20. See also Suzanne Weaver, "The Political Uses of Terror," *Wall Street Journal* (26 July 1979), p. 18.

76. Walter Laqueur, "West Germany's Terrorist Onslaught," *The Wall Street Journal* (1 September 1977), p. 8.

77. "School for Scandal," *The Economist* (14 May 1977), pp. 73–74.

78. Paul Hofmann, "Italy Accuses Priest, 11 Others of Helping to Recycle Ransom," *The New York Times* (21 January 1978), p. 3.

79. John B. Wolf, "Controlling Political Terrorism in a Free Society," *ORBIS* 29 (Winter 1976), p. 1291.

80. See R.W. Apple, Jr., "A Loose Alliance of Terrorists Does Seem to Exist," *The New York Times* (23 October 1977), Sect. 4, p. 1. See also Claire Sterling, "The Terrorist Network," *Atlantic Monthly* (November 1978), pp. 37–47.

81. "International Terrorism in 1976," p. 1.

82. "Terrorism: The Companies in the Guerrillas' Sights," *The Economist* (1 June 1974), pp. 42–43.

83. "Terror Through the Mails," *The Economist* (23 September 1972), pp. 15–16.

84. "Some Poisoned Israeli Oranges Discovered in Europe," *The New York Times* (2 February 1978), p. 2.

85. Fromkin, "The Strategy of Terrorism," pp. 689 and 692.

86. Milbank, "International and Transnational Terrorism: Diagnosis and Prognosis," p. 3.

87. "Kidnapping: Growth Industry," *The Economist* (16 June 1973), p. 79, and "Living in Fear," *Newsweek* (11 June 1973), p. 93.

88. "Coping with Terrorism in Argentina," *Business Week* (9 March 1974), p. 40.

89. Juan de Onis, "Businessmen Under the Gun in Argentina," *The New York Times* (22 February 1976), p. F3.

90. W. David Gibson, "Looking Out for Top Executives," *Chemical Week* (20 July 1977), pp. 33–34.

91. Paul Hofmann, "Terror and the Executive Suite," *The New York Times International Economic Survey* (February 5, 1978), p. 13.

92. "Bombs in New York City Kill 1, Injure 8; Threats Force Evacuations of Buildings," *The Wall Street Journal* (4 August 1977), p. 5.

93. See Ina Selden, "Italy is to Expand Its Secret Service to Fight Terrorism," *The New York Times* (31 July 1977), p. 6, and Paul Lewis, "Business Leaders in Germany Hiding," *The New York Times* (18 September 1977), p. 18.

94. Roy Reed, "In Ulster, Economy is Hurt by Terrorism," *The New York Times* (16 March 1977), pp. D1 and 9. See also Philip Revzin, "Ulster Conflict Enters Ninth Year With Economy and Politics Stagnant, but Security is Improved," *The Wall Street Journal* (23 August 1977), p. 42.

95. Walter Laqueur, "West Germany's Terrorist Onslaught," *The Wall Street Journal* (1 September 1977), p. 8.

96. Bernard-Henri Levy, "The War Against All," *The New Republic* (11 February 1978), p. 17.

97. Carlos A. Astiz, "U.S. Policy and Latin American Reaction," *Current History* (February 1978), p. 50.

98. "Curbing Terrorism," *Atlas World Press Review* (January 1978), pp. 31–37.

99. Fritz Stern, "The Pressures of Liberalism and Terrorism in West Germany," *The New York Times* (30 December 1977), p. 25.

100. Milbank, "International and Transnational Terrorism: Diagnosis and Prognosis," p. 6.

101. Paul Johnson, "The Seven Deadly Sins of Terrorism," *The New Republic* (15 September 1979), pp. 19–21.

102. Paul Hofmann, "Bonn Defends Anti-Terror Plan," *The New York Times* (20 September 1977), p. 2.

103. See Declan Costello, "International Terrorism and the Development of the Principle of Aut Dedere Aut Judicare," *The Journal of International Law and Economics* 10 (August–December 1975), pp. 483–501; Robert G. Bell, "The U.S. Response to Terrorism Against International Civil Aviation," *ORBIS* 19 (Winter 1976), pp. 1326–1343; Thomas M. Franck and Bert B. Lockwood, Jr., "Preliminary Thoughts Toward an International Convention on Terrorism," *The American Journal of International Law* 68 (January 1974), pp. 69–90; and Laqueur, *Terrorism*, Chapter 5 and conclusion.

104. Laqueur, *Terrorism*, pp. 225.

105. Wilkinson, "Three Questions on Terrorism," p. 311.

106. Advertisement for "Advanced International Conference and Seminar on Terrorism and

Countermeasures," co-sponsored by the Federal Bar Association, Washington, D.C. and the Center for the Study of Human Behavior, held at the Caribe Hilton Hotel, San Juan, Puerto Rico, September 26–27, 1977 (in *Wall Street Journal*, 4 August 1977), p. 5.

107. Lynn Adkins, "Terrorism: How to Manage a Crisis," *Dun's Review* (January 1978), pp. 96–100. See also Paul Hofmann, "Terror and the Executive Suite;" "The Wages—and Profits—of Fear," *Time* (10 July 1978), pp. 54–57; and John Huey, "Spread of Terrorism Spreads Good Cheer at Ex-Sleuth's Firm," *The Wall Street Journal* (15 January 1979), pp. 1 and 22.

108. E. Patrick McGuire, "Safeguarding Executives Against Kidnapping and Extortion," *The Conference Board Record* 11 (June 1974), p. 58.

109. "Terrorism is Changing Executive's Lives", *The New York Times* (29 October 1977), pp. 1 and 6.

110. See E. Patrick McGuire, "The Terrorist and the Corporation," *Across the Board* 14 (May 1977), pp. 11–19.

111. W. David Gibson, "Looking Out for Top Executives," *Chemical Week* (20 July 1977), pp. 33–34.

112. E. Patrick McGuire, "Safeguarding Executives Against Kidnapping and Extortion," *The Conference Board Record* 11 (June 1974), p. 57.

113. "Terrorism: The Companies in the Guerrillas' Sights," *The Economist* (1 June 1974), pp. 42–43.

114. See "Terrorism is Changing Executives' Lives," *The New York Times* (29 October 1977), pp. 1 and 6; W. David Gibson, "Protection: More Than a Man at the Gate," *Chemical Week* (27 July 1977), pp. 26–28; and E. Patrick McGuire, "When Bombing Threatens," *The Conference Board Record* 8 (September 1971), pp. 57–63.

115. "The Wages—and Profits—of Fear," *Time* (10 July 1978), p. 54.

116. "Terrorism: The Companies in the Guerrillas' Sights," p. 43.

117. "Terrorism: The Companies in the Guerrillas' Sights," p. 42.

118. "Violence in Argentina Cripples Petrochemicals," *Chemical Week* (29 October 1975), p. 20.

119. "Kidnapping: Growth Industry," *The Economist* (16 June 1973), pp. 78–79.

120. Susan Heller Anderson, "An Agent 007 for the Businessman Abroad," *The New York Times* (23 October 1977), p. F3.

121. Lynn Adkins, "Terrorism: How to Manage a Crisis," *Dun's Review* (January 1978), p. 100.

122. Adkins, "Terrorism," p. 100.

123. See Edward F. Mickolus, "Negotiating for Hostages: A Policy Dilemma," *ORBIS* 19 (Winter 1976), pp. 1309–1325.

124. See Richard Clutterbuck, *Kidnap & Ransom: The Response;* Lynn Adkins, "Terrorism: How to Manage A Crisis," *Dun's Review* (January 1978), pp. 96–100; E. Patrick McGuire, "Safeguarding Executives Against Kidnapping and Extortion," *The Conference Board Record* 11 (June 1974), pp. 56–64; David A. Baldwin, "Bargaining With Airline Hijackers," pp. 404–429 in I. William Zartman (ed.), *The 50% Solution* (Garden City, N.Y.: Anchor Books, 1976); Brian M. Jenkins, "Hostage Survival: Some Preliminary Observations," p. 5627 (Santa Monica, Calif.: The Rand Corporation, April 1976); Elmer H. Adkins, Jr., "Protection of American Industrial Dignitaries and Facilities Overseas," *Security Management* 18 (July 1974), pp. 14, 16 and 55; D.M. Allbach, "Countering Special-Threat Situations," *Military Police Law Enforcement Journal* 2 (Summer 1975), pp. 34–40; Ric Blackstern and Richard Engler, "Hostage Studies," (Arlington, Va.: Ketron Concept Paper, Ketron Inc., 8 January 1974); "Extortion," *Assets Protection* 1 (Summer 1975), entire issue; Judith Miller, "Bargain with Terrorists?" *New York Times Magazine* (18 July 1976), pp. 7, 38–42; Richard Clutterbuck, *Living With Terrorism* (London: Faber, 1975); H.T. Mahoney, "After a Terrorist Attack: Business as Usual," *Security Management* 19 (March 1975); and Jonathan Wahl, "Responses to Terrorism: Self-Defense or Reprisal?" *International Problems*, 5 (1–2, 1973), pp. 28–33.

125. Mickolus, "Negotiating for Hostages: A Policy Dilemma," pp. 1319–20.

126. Laqueur, *Terrorism*, p. 221.

127. "Terror," *The New Republic* (29 October 1977), p. 2.

128. See Mason Willrich and Theodore B. Taylor, *Nuclear Theft: Risks and Safeguards* (Cambridge, Mass.: Ballinger, 1974). Also see: Brian M. Jenkins, "The Potential for Nuclear Terrorism," P-5876 (Santa Monica, Calif.: The Rand Corporation, May 1977).

129. Laqueur, *Terrorism*, p. 232.

CHAPTER 5

1. "Rights Can't Be Only Goal, Carter Says," *The Los Angeles Times* (20 September 1977).

2. For a review and critique of four meanings see Irving Kristol, "The 'Human Rights' Muddle," *The Wall Street Journal* (20 March 1978), p. 12.

3. Maurice Cranston, *What Are Human Rights?* (New York: Taplinger Publishing Co., 1973), p. 1.

4. See U.S. Department of State, Bureau of Public Affairs, *Human Rights: Selected Documents*, No. 5, (Washington, D.C.: Department of State, 1977).

5. Much attention has been given to the role of the UN and other international organizations in the field of human rights. See: Commission to Study the Organization of Peace, *Some Aspects of the International Protection of Human Rights* (New York: Commission to Study the Organization of Peace, 1977); Richard P. Claude (ed.), *Comparative Human Rights* (Baltimore: Johns Hopkins University Press, 1976); Allessandra L. del Russo, *International Protection of Human Rights* (Washington, D.C.: Lerner Law Book Co., 1971); Jack Fraenkel, et. al., *The Struggle for Human Rights* (New York: Random House, 1975); James Frederick Green, *The United Nations and Human Rights* (Washington, D.C.: Brookings Institution, 1956); Ernst B. Haas, *Human Rights and International Action* (Stanford, Calif.: Stanford University Press, 1970); Ian McGregor, *Human Rights* (London: Batsford, 1975); A.H. Robertson, *Human Rights in the World* (Manchester, England: Manchester University Press, 1972); Egon Schwelb, *Human Rights and the International Community* (Chicago: Quadrangle Books, 1964); Louis B. Sohn and Thomas Buergenthal, *International Protection of Human Rights* 4 volumes (New York: Bobbs-Merrill, 1973); United Nations, *The United Nations and Human Rights* (New York: U.N., 1973); and Vernon VanDyke, *Human Rights, the United States, and the World Community* (New York: Oxford University Press, 1970).

6. See U.S. Department of State, *Human Rights, Selected Documents*.

7. See Appendix C in Cranston, *What Are Human Rights?*.

8. "The Push from Ulster," *The Economist* (26 November 1977), p. 15.

9. See Robert K. Goldman, *The Protection of Human Rights in the Americas: Past, Present, and Future* (New York: New York University Center for International Studies, 1972).

10. Irving Louis Horowitz, "On Human Rights and Social Obligations," *Transaction/Society* 15 (November—December 1977), p. 26.

11. Horowitz, "On Human Rights," p. 27.

12. Abdul Azis Said, "Pursuing Human Dignity," *Transaction/Society* 15 (November—December 1977), p. 35.

13. Cranston, *What Are Human Rights?*, pp. 81 and 21.

14. Kenneth L. Adelman, "The Black Man's Burden," *Foreign Policy*, No. 28 (Fall 1977), p. 89.

15. Jahangir Amuzegar, "Rights, and Wrongs," *The New York Times* (29 January 1978), p. 17.

16. Leonard Silk (interviewer), "McNamara on the Largest Issue: World Economy," *The New York Times* (2 April 1978), p. E3.

17. "What Are Human Rights?" *The Wall Street Journal* (25 November 1977), p. 4.

18. Kristol, "The 'Human Rights' Muddle."

19. Cranston, *What Are Human Rights?*, pp. 54 and 65.

20. Cranston, *What Are Human Rights?*, p. 68.

21. Office of International Justice and Peace, United States Catholic Conference, *Human Rights— Human Needs: An Unfinished Agenda* (Washington, D.C.: United States Catholic Conference, January 1978); Patricia Weiss Fagen, *Basic Needs and Human Rights* (Washington, D.C.:

Center for International Policy, January 1978); Peter Weiss, *Human Rights and Vital Needs* (Washington, D.C.: Institute for Policy Studies, September 1977); Peter Henriot, *Human Ethics for a Sustainable Society: Linking Human Rights and Basic Needs* (Washington, D.C.: Center of Concern, October 1977); Morris D. Morris and Florizelle B. Liser, *The PQLI: Measuring Progress in Meeting Human Needs* (Washington, D.C.: Overseas Development Council, August 1977); and John McHale and Magda Cordell McHale, *Basic Human Needs: A Framework for Action* (Edison, N.J.: Transaction Books, 1977).

22. For a sophisticated assertion of this logic see Amuzegar, "Rights, and Wrongs," p. 17.

23. John Richardson, Jr., and Raymond D. Gastil, "A Full Stomach Alone Does Not Make a Man Free," *The New York Times* (25 February 1978), p. 21.

24. Quoted by William Kintner, "A Program for America: Freedom and Foreign Policy," *ORBIS* (Spring 1977), pp. 139–156.

25. See Bernard Gwertzman, "U.S. Rights Report on 105 Lands Is Bleak Except for a Few Gains," *The New York Times* (10 February 1978), pp. 1 & 14.

26. See Raymond D. Gastil, "The Comparative Survey of Freedom—IX," *Freedom at Issue*, No. 49 (January—February 1979), pp. 3–14.

27. See Gastil, "Comparative Survey," for a listing of the criteria of freedom employed.

28. Gastil, "Comparative Survey," p. 11.

29. See Raymond D. Gastil, "The Comparative Survey of Freedom—VIII," *Freedom at Issue*, No. 44 (January 1978), p. 11.

30. Donald M. Fraser, "Freedom and Foreign Policy," *Foreign Policy*, No. 26 (Spring 1977), pp. 140—141.

31. Estimates use data on U.S. Direct Investment Position Abroad as of 1976. See Obie G. Whichard, "U.S. Direct Investment Abroad in 1976," *Survey of Current Business* (August 1977), pp. 32–55. Calculations by J.F. Truitt of The University of Washington using the political rights measure found only 73% of U.S. FDI in the "Free" category and at least 10% in the "not Free" one.

32. R. Keith Miller, "Our Selective Morality," *Newsweek* (3 April 1978), p. 17.

33. Senator Dick Clark, *U.S. Corporate Interests in Africa*, Report to the Committee on Foreign Relations, United States Senate, January 1978 (Washington: U.S. Government Printing Office, 1978), p. 5.

34. See Kurt Finsterbusch and C.P. Wolf (eds), *Methodology of Social Impact Assessment* (Stroudsberg, Pa.: Dowden, Hutchinson & Ross, 1977) and Thomas N. Gladwin and Michael G. Royston, "An Environmentally-Oriented Mode of Industrial Project Planning," *Environmental Conservation* 2 (Autumn 1975), pp. 189–198.

35. For some expressions of these views see: "Banking on Apartheid," *Africa*, No. 59 (July 1976), pp. 28–31; Tom Wicker, "Investing in Apartheid," *The New York Times* (6 December 1977), p. 39; Richard H. Ullman, "Human Rights and Economic Power: The United States Versus Idi Amin," *Foreign Affairs* 56 (April 1978), pp. 529–543; Clyde Ferguson and William R. Cotter, "South Africa—What is to be Done?" *Foreign Affairs* 56 (January 1978), pp. 253–274; Dick Clark, "Against Financing Apartheid," *The New York Times* (21 February 1978), p. 31; Jack Nelson, "Del Monte in the Philippines," *CALC Report* (September 1977), pp. 9–10; Tim Smith, "South Africa: The Churches vs. the Corporations," *Business and Society Review*, No. 15 (Fall 1975), pp. 54–64; Barbara Rogers, "Apartheid for Profit," *Business and Society Review*, No. 19 (Fall 1976), pp. 65–69; "The Republic of the Philippines: American Corporations, Martial Law, and Underdevelopment," CIC Brief, *Corporate Examiner* (September 1973), pp. 3a–3d; Joel Rocamora, "Martial Law and Underdevelopment," *Southeast Asia Chronicle* (December 1977), pp. 25–31; "Assembly Factories in Haiti," *Haiti Report* (Spring 1976), pp. 1–8; and Centre on Transnational Corporations, *Activities of Transnational Corporations in Southern Africa and the Extent of their Collaboration with the Illegal Regimes in the Area*, Report to the Secretariat Commission on Transnational Corporations, U.N. Economic and Social Council, E/C.10/26, April 6, 1977 (New York: U.N., 1977).

36. Naom Chomsky and Edward S. Herman, "The United States versus Human Rights in the Third World," *Monthly Review* 29 (July–August 1977), pp. 30–31.

37. For some expressions of these views see: Ray Vicker, "Experiment in South Africa: Some U.S. Firms Ignore Urgings to Leave, Instead Seek to Upgrade Status of Blacks," *The Wall Street*

Journal (22 September 1971), p. 28; Richard R. Leger, "On the Spot: U.S. Firms' Operations in South Africa Cope with Varied Pressures," *The Wall Street Journal* (16 March 1977), pp. 1 and 33; "Doing Business with a Blacker Africa," *Business Week* (14 February 1977), pp. 64–80; Desaix Myers, III, *Labor Practices of U.S. Corporations in South Africa* (New York: Praeger, 1977); and Senator Dick Clark, *U.S. Corporate Interests in Africa*, Report to the Committee on Foreign Relations, U.S. Senate, January 1978 (Washington, D.C.: U.S. Government Printing Office, 1978).

38. Letter to the Editor from John E. Purcell, *Foreign Affairs* 56 (April 1978), p. 654.

39. "Simple Morality Play," *The Wall Street Journal* (7 April 1972), p. 6.

40. Jennifer Davis, "U.S. Corporations Support Apartheid," (Washington, D.C.: Coalition for a New Foreign and Military Policy, September 1976).

41. Clark, *U.S. Corporate Interests in Africa*, p. 6.

42. See Foreign Affairs and National Defense Division, Congressional Research Service-Library of Congress, *Human Rights in the International Community and in U.S. Foreign Policy, 1945–76*. Prepared for the Subcommittee on International Organizations of the Committee on International Relations, House of Representatives, July 24, 1977 (Washington, D.C.: U.S. Government Printing Office, 1977).

43. See Robert Keatley, "Human Rights and Diplomatic Pitfalls," *The Wall Street Journal* (22 March 1977), p. 22. Also see: Donald P. Kommers and Gilbert D. Loescher, eds., *Human Rights and American Foreign Policy* (Notre Dame: University of Notre Dame Press, 1979).

44. "Pitfalls of Morality," *The New Republic* (29 October 1977), p. 13. See also "The Plot Against Human Rights," *The New Republic* (9 December 1978), p. 11; and David Hawk, "Human Rights at Half-Time," *The New Republic* (7 April 1979), pp. 21–23. Also see: Stanley Hoffmann, "Rights and Dipomacy," *New York Times* (31 December 1978), p. E15.

45. See Dana D. Fischer, "The International Protection of Human Rights," pp. 44–55, in David A. Kay (ed.), *The Changing United Nations: Options for the United States* (New York: Academy of Political Science, 1977). See also "UN Widens Rights Inquiry", *The Interdependent* (May 1978), p. 5.

46. Office of International Justice and Peace, United States Catholic Conference, *Human Rights–Human Needs: An Unfinished Agenda* (Washington, D.C.: U.S. Catholic Conference, January 1978), p. 20.

47. Report of the Committee on Social Responsibility Investments of The Episcopal Church to the Executive Council, The 64th General Convention (17 September 1973), p. 4.

48. Programme Unit on Justice and Service, World Council of Churches, "Report of the Geneva Consultation on a Proposed Action/Reflection Programme on Transnational Corporations," June 13–18, 1977 (Geneva: World Council of Churches, 1977), p. 2.

49. Don Morton, *Partners in Apartheid* (White Plains, N.Y.: Printcraft for the Council for Christian Social Action, United Church of Christ, 1973), p. 44.

50. See Corporate Information Center, National Council of Churches, *Church Investments, Corporations and Southern Africa* (New York: Friendship Press, 1973).

51. "Multinationals: In hoc Signo," *The Economist* (13 August 1977), p. 58.

52. For partial listings see: American Friends Service Committee, *Action Guide on Southern Africa* (Philadelphia: American Friends Service Committee, December 1976), and Coalition for a New Foreign and Military Policy, *Citizen's Action Guide to Human Rights* (Washington, D.C.: Colition for a New Foreign and Military Policy, 1978).

53. For a profile of the ACOA see: Derek Reveron, "Small Group of Activists Puts Pressure on Big Firms to Get Out of South Africa," *The Wall Street Journal* (23 February 1978), p. 48.

54. Clyde Ferguson and William R. Cotter, "South Africa—What is to be Done?" *Foreign Affairs* 56 (January 1978), pp. 253–274.

55. See *Don't Buy ITT* and *Don't Buy Hostess*, (Dayton, Ohio: IT&T Boycott, South Africa Committee, Congregation for Reconciliation, 1977). See also *Don't Buy Del Monte Sardines*, (Philadelphia,: Philadelphia Namibia Action Group, 1976).

56. "Sticking to Principle," *The Wall Street Journal* (12 October 1972), p. 14.

57. "University to Sell U.S. Stock with South Africa Ties," *South Africa/Namibia Update* (29 June 1977), p. 2.

58. For a survey of campus positions see Edward B. Fiske, "South Africa is New Social Issue for College Activists," *The New York Times* (15 March 1978), p. 22. See also The South Africa Catalyst Project, *Anti-Apartheid Organizing on campus . . . and Beyond* (Palo Alto: South Africa Catalyst Project, 1978).

59. "695 Anti-Apartheid Demonstrators Arrested in California Sit-ins," *South Africa/Namibia Update* (8 June 1977), p. 2.

60. See "Churches & Corporate Responsibility: International," (CIC Brief), *The Corporate Examiner* (May 1976), pp. 3A–3D; and Prexy Nesbitt, "Anti-Apartheid Activities in the United States of America," *Centre Against Apartheid Notes and Documents* (New York: United Nations, December 1977).

61. George W. Shepherd, Jr., *Anti-Apartheid: Transnational Conflict and Western Policy in the Liberation of South Africa* (Westport, Conn.: Greenwood Press, 1977), p. 146.

62. Letter to the authors from William R. Davis, Treasurer, The United Church of Canada (Toronto, Ontario), 23 February 1978.

63. "Churches and Corporate Responsibility: International," p. 36.

64. For a case history of negotiations between the United Church of Christ and First National Boston Corporation on the issue of South African loans see Mitchell C. Lynch, "Proxy Plea: Holder Groups Press Issue of South Africa at Annual Meetings," *The Wall Street Journal* (30 March 1978), pp. 1 and 25. See also Mitchell C. Lynch "Church Groups Press South African Issue in Executive Suites, with Softer Demands," *The Wall Journal* (22 June 1978), P. 15.

65. William D. Hartley, "Talking it Over: More Concerns Willing to Enter Negotiations on Holder Resolutions," *The Wall Street Journal* (23 March 1977), pp. 1 and 32.

66. See Eleanor Craig, *A Shareholders' Manual: For Church Committees on Social Responsibility in Investments* (New York: Interfaith Center on Corporate Responsibility, 1977). See also David Vogel, *Lobbying the Corporation: Citizen Challenges to Business Authority* (New York: Basic Books, 1978). See also "Latin America: More Human Rights, Less U.S. Clout," *Business Week* (17 September 1979), p.60.

67. For legislative histories see Foreign Affairs and National Defense Division, Congressional Research Service, Library of Congress, *Human Rights in the International Community and in U.S. Foreign Policy, 1945–76*, Prepared for the Subcommittee on International Organizations of the Committee on International Relations, House of Representatives, July 24, 1977 (Washington, D.C.: U.S. Government Printing Office, 1977).

68. See Center for International Policy, *Human Rights and the U.S. Foreign Assistance Program* (Washington, D.C.: Center for International Policy, 1977).

69. See Center for International Policy, "Foreign Aid: Evading the Control of Congress," *International Policy Report* (Washington, D.C.: Center for International Policy, January 1977).

70. Center for International Policy, "Foreign Aid," p. 10.

71. "Export-Import Bank: Stop Financing of Apartheid," (Washington, D.C.: Washington Office on Africa, 1977); and "House Approves Curbs on Credit Guarantees Involving South Africa," *The Wall Street Journal* (5 June 1978), p. 6.

72. See Center for International Policy, "OPIC: Insuring the Status Quo," *International Policy Report* (Washington, D.C.: Center for International Policy, September 1977).

73. Tom Wicker, "The High Cost of Repression," *The New York Times* (2 December 1977), p. 27; and William Goodfellow and James Morrell, "Why Chile Doesn't Lose and When It Loses Aid," *The Philadelphia Inquirer* (28 July 1977), p. 11A.

74. Center for International Policy, "World Bank Sets $2.9 Billion in Loans to Human Rights Violators for Fiscal Year 1979," *Research Study* (Washington, D.C.: Center International Policy, 1977).

75. Leonard Silk (interviewer), "McNamara on the Largest Issue: The World Economy," *The New York Times* (2 April 1978), p. E3.

76. Ann Crittenden "Congress Changes Its Views on International Lending Agencies," *The New York Times* (27 May 1979), p.E 5.

77. Ann Crittenden, "Role of Ex-Im Bank in South Africa Gets Growing Criticism," *The New York Times* (9 February 1978), pp. D1 and 9. See also James Morrell and David Gisselquist, "How the IMF Slipped $464 million to South Africa," *Special Report* (Washington, D.C.: Center for International Policy, January 1978).

78. "Human Rights Unite the IMF's Foes," *Business Week* (27 February 1978), p. 117.

79. "Aid: First Promise to Be Good," *The Economist* (18 February 1978), p. 64.

80. See: Pranay Gupte, "Apartheid Assailed by U.N.'s Assembly," *The New York Times* (15 December 1977), and Pranay Gupte, "U.N. Assembly Votes to Seek Oil Embargo Against South Africa," *The New York Times* (December 17, 1977), p. 9.

81. Barry Newman, "Namibia: A Major Test for the U.N.," *The Wall Street Journal* (24 March 1972), p. 10.

82. Kathleen Teltsch, "U.N. Council Orders Arms-Sale Sanctions Against South Africa," *The New York Times* (5 November 1977), pp. 1 and 7.

83. Ray Vicker, "An End of Rhodesian Sanctions?" *The Wall Street Journal* (4 November 1971), p. 16.

84. See Yoko Kitazawa, *From Tokyo to Johannesburg* (New York: Interfaith Center for Corporate Responsibility, 1975).

85. "Nigeria Rejects Firms Tied to South Africa," *South Africa/Namibia Update* (2 November 1977), p. 3.

86. "Canada Will End Business Operations in South Africa," *The Wall Street Journal* (20 December 1977), p. 27. See also "Several Countries Move Toward Restrictions on Business in South Africa," *Business International* (5 May 1978), p. 142.

87. "Code of Conduct Adopted" *European Community* (November–December 1977), p. 44.

CHAPTER 6

1. Valerie Heinonen, *Church Proxy Resolutions: January 1977* (New York: Interfaith Center on Corporate Responsibility, January 1977), p. 61. See also Isabel Letelier and Michael Moffitt, "How American Banks Keep the Chilean Junta Going," *Business and Society Review* (Spring 1979), pp. 42–51.

2. Senator Dick Clark, *U.S. Corporate Interests in Africa*, Report to the Committee on Foreign Relations, United States Senate, January 1978 (Washington: U.S. Government Printing Office), pp. 12–13. See especially Section 2 of this report entitled "International Credit and South Africa," pp. 17–79. For background see also Special Committee Against Apartheid, "Role of Recent Loans in Strengthening the Apartheid Regime in South Africa," (New York: United 10 November 1976) and Corporate Data Exchange, *U.S. Bank Loans to South Africa* (New York: Corporate Data Exchange, 1978).

3. American Committee on Africa, "A Summary Report on the Bank Campaign" (New York: American Committee on Africa, 1970), p. 1.

4. "Banking on Apartheid" (CIC Brief), *The Corporate Examiner* (October 1976), p. 3A.

5. "The Frankfurt Documents—Secret Bank Loans to the South African Government" (CIC Brief), *The Corporate Examiner* (July 1973), pp. 3A–3D.

6. David Halsan, "Role of Shareholder Action in Opposing Loans to South Africa," (New York: Centre Against Apartheid, June 1976).

7. For some excerpts of the Congressional Hearing see "Banking on Apartheid," p. 3D.

8. "Churches & Corporate Responsibility: International" (CIC Brief), *The Corporate Examiner* (May 1976), p. 3D.

9. "Churches & Corporate Responsibility," p. 3B

10. "Banking on Apartheid," *Africa*, No. 59 (July 1976), p. 28.

11. See Martin Bailey, *Barclays and South Africa* (London: Haslemers Group and Anti-Apartheid Movement, 1975).

12. Prexy Nesbitt, "Anti-Apartheid Activities in the United States of America," (New York: Centre Against Apartheid, December 1977), p. 8.

13. Heinonen, *Church Proxy Resolutions: January 1977* p. 77.

14. George Dugan, "Church Group Acts Over South Africa," *The New York Times* (11 November 1977), p. 6.

15. Gene Jones, "South Africa: Bank Campaign Gains Momentum," *CALC Report* (July–August 1977), pp. 6 and 21.

16. Michael C. Jensen, "The American Corporate Presence in South Africa," *The New York Times* (4 December 1977), p. 1F.

17. Tendayi Kumbula, "U.S. Banks Target of Apartheid Critics," *Los Angeles Times* (30 September 1977), p. 4.

18. Jensen, "The American Corporate Presence," p. 9F.

19. "European American Bank Bars Loans to South Africa," *South Africa/Namibia Update* (2 November 1977), p. 3.

20. "Bank in South Africa Drops Defense Bonds," *The New York Times* (16 December 1977), p. 7.

21. Letter from Timothy H. Smith and Michael J. Clark, Interfaith Center on Corporate Responsibility, New York (June 1977).

22. "Corporate Social Responsibility Challenges—Spring 1978," *The Corporate Examiner* 7 (February 1978).

23. See Mitchell C. Lynch, "Proxy Plea: Holder Groups Press Issue of South Africa At Annual Meetings," *The Wall Street Journal* (30 March 1978), pp. 1 and 25; and "Bank's Shareholders Fail in Effort to Bar South African Loans," *The Wall Street Journal* (31 March 1978), p. 22.

24. "Citicorp, Citing Apartheid, Halts Loans to South Africa Government, State Firms," *The Wall Street Journal* (13 March 1978), p. 6.

25. Michael C. Jensen, "South Africa Loans Barred by Citibank," *The New York Times* (11 March 1978), pp. 1 and 31.

26. "Chemical Bank Has Ban on Loans to South Africa," *The Wall Street Journal* (22 March 1978), p. 8.

27. "Bank America to Continue to Do Business in South Africa," *The New York Times* (23 March 1978), p. D9.

28. "Virtue of Necessity," *The Economist* (1 April 1978), p. 75.

29. "Barclays in Nigeria: Political Banking," *The Economist* (1 April 1978), p. 75.

30. Charles J. Elia, "Major Platinum Source Could be Disrupted if South Africa Strife Worsens, Study Says," *The Wall Street Journal* (21 October 1977), p. 39.

31. Fred Armentrout, "Mobil's Oily 'No Comment' on Rhodesia," *Business and Society Review* (Spring 1977), pp. 52–55.

32. "Realism on Rhodesia," *The Wall Street Journal* (30 November 1971), p. 18.

33. Corporate Information Center–National Council of Churches, *Church Investments, Corporations and Southern Africa* (New York's Corporate Information Center, 1973), p. 136.

34. Corporate Information Center, *Church Investments, . . . ,* p. 139–140.

35. Barry Newman, "Imports of Chrome From Rhodesia Stir Increased Opposition," *The Wall Street Journal* (19 April 1972), p. 28; "Chrome Row Wide Open," *Chemical Week* (3 May 1972), p. 17; and "Chrome Imports Okayed," *Chemical Week* (10 May 1972), p. 16.

36. "Corporate Social Responsibility Challenges—Spring 1976," *The Corporate Examiner* (February 1976), p. 8.

37. See: Graham Hovey, "Vance Begins Drive to End U.S. Imports of Rhodesia Chrome," *The New York Times* (11 February 1977), pp. 1–10; "Ban on Chrome From Rhodesia Cleared by House," *The Wall Street Journal* (15 March 1977), p. 2; and "Ban on Chrome From Rhodesia Voted by Senate," *The Wall Street Journal* (16 March 1977), p. 4.

38. See "The Door is Closing on Chrome," *Business Week* (21 February 1977), pp. 29–30; Gene Smith, "Steelmakers' Opposition to Banks on Rhodesian Chrome Softening," *The New York Times* (18 February 1977), p. D9; and Victor K. McElheny "Technology: Ways to Overcome a Chromium Embargo." *The New York Times* (5 April 1978), pp. D1 and 13.

39. "Morality Means Majority Rule," *The Economist* (19 March 1977), p. 25.

40. "Byrd Amendment: 'Our Rulers Reek of Munich'," (letter to the editor), *The New York Times* (25 March 1977), p. 24.

41. John F. Burns, "Rhodesia Calm on Chrome Move," *The New York Times* (18 February 1977), p. D1.

42. Center for Social Action of the United Church of Christ, *The Oil Conspiracy: An Investigation*

into How Multinational Oil Companies Provide Rhodesia's Oil Needs (New York: Center for Social Action, 1976).

43. Center for Social Action, *The Oil Conspiracy*, p. 36.

44. "Mobil Oil," *Business and Society Review*, No. 19 (Fall 1976), p. 80.

45. For a summary of these hearings see "U.S. Corporate Interests in Africa," Report to the Committee on Foreign Relations, United States Senate, by Senator Dick Clark, Chairman of Subcommittee on African Affairs (Washington, D.C.: U.S. Government Printing Office, January 1978), pp. 173–232.

46. Robert D. Hershey, Jr., "Mobil Denies It Had Secret Plan for Supplying Oil to Rhodesia," *The New York Times* (18 September 1976), p. 28. Also see: Fred Armentrout, "Mobil's Oily 'No Comment' on Rhodesia," *Business and Society Review* (Spring 1977), pp. 52–55.

47. "U.S. Can't Determine Whether Mobil Oil Broke Rhodesia Ban," *The Wall Street Journal* (18 May 1977), p. 2 and "Mobil Absolved by U.S. of Violating Embargo," *The New York Times* (18 May 1977), p. D15.

48. "Corporate Social Responsibility Challenges—Spring 1977," *The Corporate Examiner* 6 (March 1977), p. 6.

49. "Lonrho—Sues Big Oil Companies, Charges They Supply Rhodesia," *The New York Times* (2 June 1977), p. D9. See also "Dividends From Blowing the Whistle on 'Oilgate' ", *Business Week* (23 October 1978), p. 64.

50. "Africa Puts the Pressure on the Oil Sanctions Buster," *New African* (June 1977), p. 489. See also "Zambia Sues 17 Big Oil Companies," *The New York Times* (24 August 1977) p. D3.

51. See "When Sanctions, Bust," *The Economist* (9 September 1978), pp. 11–13; "Dividends from Blowing the Whistle on Oilgate," p. 64; Stan Luxenberg," American Oilgate," *The New Republic* (3 February 1979), pp. 17–21; and "After Bingham," *The Economist* (23 December 1978), pp. 10–11.

52. "Africa Puts the Pressure on the Oil Sanctions Busters," p. 489.

53. "Nigeria Rejects Firms Tied to South Africa," *South Africa/Namibia Update* (2 November 1977), p. 3.

54. "Nigerians Move to Take Over All of BP's Interests," *The Wall Street Journal* (1 August 1979), p. 12.

55. Pranay Gupte, "Rhodesia's Oil Suppliers Assailed," *The New York Times* (22 November 1977), p. 8.

56. "Corporate Social Responsibility Challenges—Spring 1978," *The Corporate Examiner* 7 (February 1978), p. 7.

57. See Michael T. Klare, *Supplying Repression* (New York: The Field Foundation, 1977), p. 50; and "Olin Is Charged With Arms Sales to South Africa," *The Wall Street Journal* (15 March 1978), p. 8.

58. Robert E. Tomasson, "Olin Corporation Indicted for Shipping Arms to South Africans," *The New York Times* (15 March 1978), pp. D1 and 5.

59. Robert E. Tomasson, "Judge in Arms Case Orders Olin to Pay $510,000 in Charity," *The New York Times* (31 March 1978), pp. D1 and 7. See also Robert E. Tomasson, "Olin's Arms Penalty: 'Donation' Plus Fine," *The New York Times* (2 June 1978), p. D1; and Nicholas M. Horrock, "Olin Deal Reported on Arms Shipments," *The New York Times* (6 March 1979), p. A7.

60. Philadelphia Namibia Action Group, "The People vs. Del Monte," and "Don't Buy Del Monte Sardines" (Philadelphia: P.N.A.G., 1977).

61. Sister Valerie Heinonen, *Church Proxy Resolutions: January 1978* (New York: Interfaith Center on Coporate Responsibility, January 1978), p. 84.

62. Richard H. Ullman, "Human Rights and Economic Power: The United States Versus Idi Amin," *Foreign Affairs* 56 (April 1978), p. 539.

63. Ullman, "Human Rights and Economic Power," p. 529.

64. John de St. Jorre, "The Ugandan Connection," *The New York Times Magazine* (9 April 1978), p. 28.

65. Franklin H. Williams, "Idi Amin's Achilles' Heel," *The New York Times* (14 August 1977), p. E17.

66. See John de St. Jorre, "31 in House Propose Severing Commercial Ties With Amin," *The Washington Post* (23 October 1977), p. G5; Jack Anderson and Less Whitten, "Ugandans Get

Pilot Training in U.S." *The Washington Post* (7 November 1977); and de St. Jorre, "The Ugandan Connection," pp. 27ff.

67. Ullman, "Human Rights and Economic Power," p. 532

68. "News Release," Congressman Don J. Pease, Washington, D.C., (25 November 1977). See also Jack Anderson and Les Whitten, "Some Coffee Drinkers and Amin," *The Washington Post* (23 November 1977).

69. Williams, "Idi Amin's Achilles' Heel."

70. See H.R. 11758, H.R. 11756, and H.R. 11759 in the House of Representatives, 95th Congress, 2nd Session.

71. Congressman Don J. Pease, "Statement on Uganda Trade Ban Legislation," *Congressional Record—House* (22 September 1977), p. H.9838.

72. de St. Jorre, "The Ugandan Connection," p. 82.

73. de St. Joree, "The Ugandan Connection" p. 84.

74. Ullman, "Human Rights and Economic Power," p. 538.

75. Anderson and Whitten, "Some Coffee Drinkers."

76. Ullman, "Human Rights and Economic Power," p. 529.

77. de St. Jorre, "The Ugandan Connection," p. 86.

78. *Washington Post* (14 November 1977).

79. Congressman Don J. Pease, "The Case Against Idi Amin," *Congressional Record* (Extension of Remarks) (21 February 1978), p. E720. See also "Another Cup of Coffee", *The New Republic* (13 May 1978), pp. 7–8.

80. Shirley A. Jackewicz, "Krugerrand, Other Gold-Coin Sales Are Brisk in U.S. on Inflation Fears," *The Wall Street Journal* (31 March 1978), p. 26.

81. "3 City TV Stations Stopping Ad on Coin From South Africa," *The New York Times* (5 November 1977), p. 27.

82. Derek Reveron, "Pamphlet Power: Small Group of Activists Puts Pressure on Big Firms to Get Out of South Africa," *The Wall Street Journal* (23 February 1978), p. 48.

83. Tom Herman, "Global Report: South Africa Coins Target of Protest," *The Wall Street Journal* (30 January 1978), p. 6.

84. "3 TV Stations Reject Krugerrand Ads," *South Africa/Namibia Update* (24 November 1977), p. 2.

85. Herman, "Global Report."

86. Herman, "Global Report."

87. Jackewicz, "Krugerrand."

88. "Engelhard Markets Krugerrand Competitor," *South Africa/Namibia Update* (29 June 1977), pp. 2–3.

89. Michael T. Klare, *Supplying Repression* (New York: The Field Foundation, December 1977), pp. 7, 8–9.

90. Klare, *Supplying Repression*, p. 43. See also Michael T. Klare, "Pointing Fingers," *The New York Times* (10 August 1977), p. 19; and Michael T. Klare and Nancy Stein, "Exporting the Tools of Repression," *The Nation* (October 1977), pp. 365–370.

91. "The Commerce of Death" (CIC Brief), *The Corporate Examiner* (June 1976), pp. 3A–3D.

92. Jonathan Kandell, "European Arms Exports Growing," *The New York Times* (2 April 1978), pp. 1 and 4.

93. See Klare, *Supplying Repression*, for a review of these programs.

94. Klare, *Supplying Repression* pp. 41, 48, 49.

95. "President is Urged to Stop Plane Deal With South Africans," *The New York Times* (19 December 1977), p. 9.

96. Heinonen, *Church Proxy Resolutions—January 1977*, pp. 57–59.

97. Heinonen, *Church Proxy Resolutions—January 1978*, p. 21.

98. Heinonen, *Church Proxy Resolutions—January 1978*, p. 80.

99. See Corporate Information Center, *Church Investments*, . . . pp. 100–107.

100. See Corporate Information Center, *Church Investments*, . . . ; Don Morton, *Partners in*

Apartheid (New York: United Church of Christ, 1973), pp. 26–27; and Richard Leonard, *Computers in South Africa: A Survey of U.S. Companies* (New York: The Africa Fund, 1978).

101. Smith, "South Africa: The Churches vs. the Corporations," *Business and Society Review*, No. 15 (Fall 1975), p. 58.

102. Myers, *Labor Practices of U.S. Corporations in South Africa*, p. 18.

103. Minutes to the 1975 Annual Meeting of Shareholders of International Business Machines Corporation.

104. Tim Smith, "South Africa: The Churches vs. the Corporations," p. 59.

105. Clark, *U.S. Corporate Interests in Africa*, p. 224.

106. Letter to the Editor from Frank T. Cary, Chairman of IBM, *The New York Times* (11 December 1977), p. 16F.

107. Laurie Nadel and Hesh Wiener, "Would You Sell a Computer to Hitler?" *Computer Decisions* 9 (February 1977), p. 23; and "Corporate Action News," *The Corporate Examiner* (March 1979), p. 1.

108. See Umni Glaz, "The Silicon Curtain," *Computer Decisions* 9 (September 1977), pp. 30–33.

109. See Becky Barna, "How to Export a Computer," *Computer Decisions* 9 (September 1977), pp. 48–52.

110. Robert Ellis Smith, "The Kremlin Wants Our Computers," *Computer Decisions* 9 (September 1977), pp. 22–26.

111. Smith, "The Kremlin Wants Our Computers," p. 26

112. Laurie Nadel, "CDC Meets the Press," *Computer Decisions* 9 (September 1977), p. 38.

113. Nadel and Wiener, "Would You Sell a Computer to Hitler?" pp. 22.

114. Nadel and Wiener, "Would You Sell a Computer to Hitler?," p. 26.

115. "U.S., Churches Score Gestapo Computers," *Computer Decisions* 9 (March 1977), p. 4.

116. "U.S., Churches Score Gestapo Computers," p. 65

117. Hesh Wiener, "Why Police States Love the Computer," *Computer Decisions* (Summer 1977), p. 42.

118. Heinonen, *Church Proxy Resolutions–January 1978*, p. 87.

119. Centre on Transnational Corporations, *Activities of Transnational Corporations in Southern Africa and the Extent of their Collaboration with the Illegal Regimes in the Area*, E/C.10/26 (New York: United Nations Economic and Social Council, 6 April 1977) p. 4.

120. Corporate Information Center, *Church Investments, . . .* p. 88.

121. "Gulf Oil and Portugal: Partners in Colonialism" (CIC Brief), *The Corporate Examiner* (April 1974), p. 3B.

122. See "Gulf Oil and Portugal," p. 3A. See also Committee of Returned Volunteers/New York, *Gulf Oil Corporation: A Study in Exploitation* (New York: Committee of Returned Volunteers, 1970); American Committee on Africa, *Why We Protest Gulf Oil in Angola* (New York: American Committee on Africa, June 1973); Center for Social Action of the United Church of Christ, *Gulf in Colonial Angola—An Update* (New York: United Church of Christ, April 1974); Toronto Committee for the Liberation of Portugal's African Colonies, *Larceny by Proxy: Gulf Oil (Canada) Ltd. and Angola* (Toronto, Ontario: Committee for the Liberation of Portugal's African Colonies, undated); "Gulf Oil in Cabinda," *Africa Today* (July–August 1970), p. 20; "Gulf Oil: Portuguese Ally in Angola" (CIC Brief), *The Corporate Examiner* (December 1972), pp. 3A–3D; and United Nations, *Foreign Economic Interests and Decolonialization* (New York: U.N. Office of Public Information, 370–69–15406, 1969).

123. For a chronology of the actions against Gulf see: Corporate Information Center, *Church Investments, . . . ,* pp. 97–98.

124. See Stephen B. Farber (Special Assistant to the President of Harvard University), "Gulf and Angola," *Harvard University Gazette* (6 October 1972).

125. "On Doing Business in Cabinda," *The Orange Disc* (June 1972), p. 17.

126. Statement of Council for Christian Social Action, United Church of Christ (28 August 1972).

127. "Gulf Oil and Portugal: Partners in Colonialism," p. 3A.

128. "Portugal: The Major's Home in New Oil Sites," *Business Week* (23 March 1974).

129. David Binder, "Gulf Undecided on Continuing Oil Payments to Angola," *The New York Times* (21 December 1975).

130. David Binder, "Gulf Oil Cuts Off Angola Operation," *The New York Times* (23 December 1975), pp. 1 and 7.

131. Michael T. Kaufman, "Angolan Leftist Charges U.S. with Economic War," *The New York Times* (31 January 1976), pp. 1 and 17.

132. "Gulf's Private Oil Diplomacy in Angola," *Business Week* (1 March 1976), p. 18.

133. "Gulf's Private Oil Diplomacy in Angola," p. 18.

134. Leslie H. Gelb, "U.S. Backing Gulf's Ties with Victorious Angolans," *The New York Times* (21 February 1976), pp. 1 and 6.

135. Committee on International Relations, *Resources in Namibia: Implications for U.S. Policy*, Hearings before the Subcommittee on International Resources, Food and Energy of the Committee on International Relations, House of Representatives, 94th Congress, June 10, 1975 and May 13, 1976 (Washington, D.C.: U.S. Government Printing Office, 1976), p. 16.

136. Barry Newman, "Newmont, AMAX Face Mounting Pressure to Take Stand in Namibia Political Hassle," *The Wall Street Journal* (7 February 1972), p. 7.

137. Winifred Courtney and Jennifer Davis, *Namibia: U.S. Corporate Involvement* (New York: American Committee on Africa, 1972), p. 30. Also see: *Tsumeb: A Profile of U.S. Contribution to Underdevelopment in Namibia* (New York: Corporate Information Center, 1973); Roger Murray, et al., *The Role of Foreign Firms in Namibia: Studies on External Investment and Black Workers' Conditions in Namibia* (London: Africa Publications, 1974); Neville Rubin, *Labour and Discrimination in Namibia* (Geneva: International Labour Office, 1977); and Edward C. May, *Report on the Wingspread Conference on Namibia* (Racine, Wisconsin: The Johnson Foundation, 1976).

138. Newman, "Newmont, AMAX Face Mounting Pressure . . .," p. 7.

139. Barry Newman, "Namibia: A Major Test for the U.N.," *The Wall Street Journal* (24 March 1972), p. 10.

140. Newman, "Namibia: A Major Test," p. 10.

141. Proxy Statement, AMAX Inc. (6 April 1972).

142. Committee on International Relations, *Resources in Namibia*, p. 42.

143. Centre on Transnational Corporations, *Activities of Transnational Corporations in Southern Africa*, pp. 34 and 36.

144. "AMAX Says Issue of South African Firm Can't Be Solved in Court," *The Wall Street Journal*, (23 August 1973), p. 21.

145. See Anthony J. Hughes, "Interview with Martti Antisaari, United Nations Commissioner for Namibia," *Africa Report* **22** (November–December 1977), pp. 18–21.

146. Corporate Information Center, *Church Investments*, p. 206.

147. See: Tim Smith, "South Africa: The Churches vs. the Corporations," *Business and Society Review*, No. 15 (Fall 1975), pp. 60–61.

148. "Namibia, Foreign Companies Are Running Scared," *Business Week* (5 May 1975).

149. "World Roundup: South Africa," *Business Week* (24 November 1975), p. 40.

150. "Banking on Apartheid," *Africa* No. 59, (July 1976), p. 31.

151. "New African Leaders Will Drive Tough Bargains," *Chemical Week* (13 October 1976), p. 52.

152. Philadelphia Namibia Action Group, "Newmont Mining Corporation is An Unequal Opportunity Exploiter," (Philadelphia: Namibia Action Group, 3 May 1977).

153. "The Great Majority Rule Hoax," Advertisement of the Club of Ten, *The New York Times* (28 March 1978), p. 13.

154. "The Political Threat to Business in South-West Africa," *Business Week* (4 June 1979), p. 84.

155. The Christian Institute of South Africa, "Investment in South Africa," (Statement of 10 October 1976 by H. Kleinschmidt).

156. See Ann Crittenden, "Teachers Wield Their Proxies," *The New York Times* (19 March 1978), Section 3, pp. 1 and 13.

157. Louis Harris, "Apartheid Unjustified," *The Harris Survey* (15 December 1977), p. 1.

158. See Barbara Rogers, "The Expansion of Foreign Oil Companies in South Africa," (New York: Interfaith Center on Corporate Responsibility, March 1976) and Anton R. Lovink, "U.S. Corporate Expansion in South Africa," CIC Brief, *The Corporate Examiner* (April 1976), pp. 3A-3D.

159. Lovink, "U.S. Corporate Expansion in South Africa," *op. cit.*, p. 3D.

160. Heinonen, *Church Proxy Resolutions: January 1977*, p. 88.

161. Heinonen, *Church Proxy Resolutions: January 1977*, p. 88.

162. Heinonen, *Church Proxy Resolutions: January 1978*, p. 67.

163. United Nations, Special Committee Against Apartheid, "Present Economic Situation in South Africa and the Importance of Urgent International Action" (UN. A/AC. 115/L.456).

164. Myers, *Labor Practices of U.S. Corporations in South Africa*, p. 18.

165. "Doing Business With a Blacker Africa," *Business Week* (14 February 1977), p. 70.

166. General Motors Corporation, *1976 General Motors Public Interest Report* (Detroit, Michigan: General Motors, April 1977), p. 51.

167. Deborah Rankin, "Control Data Plans No Expansion of its South African Investment," *The New York Times* (26 October 1977), p. D3.

168. "G&W Won't Invest More," *South Africa/Namibia Update* (14 December 1977), p. 3.

169. From General Assembly Resolution 3448 (XXX), adopted at the 2433rd plenary meeting, on 8 December 1975.

170. Andrew Brewin, Louis Duclos, and David MacDonald, *One Gigantic Prison: The Report of the Fact-Finding Mission to Chile, Argentina and Uruguay* (Toronto, Canada: The Inter-Church Committee on Chile, November 1976), p. 77.

171. "Fifth Anniversary Issue," *The Corporate Examiner* (September 1976), p. 6.

172. "Corporate Social Responsibility Challenges—Spring 1976," *The Corporate Examiner* (February 1976), p. 7.

173. General Motors Corporation, *1976 General Motors Public Interest Report* (Detroit, Michigan: G.M., April 1977), p. 46.

174. Heinonen, *Church Proxy Resolutions: January 1977*, pp. 63-64.

175. General Motors Corporation, *1976 Public Interest Report*, pp. 46-48.

176. Advertisement reprinted in "World of Work," *UAW Solidarity* (30 September 1977), p. 22.

177. "Exxon Unit Sets Bid for 87% of Chile's State Copper Firm," *The Wall Street Journal* (21 December 1977), p. 5, and "Exxon Unit Says Two Copper Mines Are Bought in Chile," *The Wall Street Journal* (29 December 1977), p. 3.

178. "Goodyear's Chilean Unit Buys the Assets of Major Tire Firm," *The Wall Street Journal* (10 January 1978), p. 2.

179. See: "Chilean Investments," *Business Week* (13 February 1978), p. 40, and "Chile's Junta Flouts Carter on Human Rights," *Business Week* (13 February 1978), pp. 52–54.

180. "Buying into Chile," *Chemical Week* (15 March 1978), p. 25.

181. "World Roundup: Chile," *Business Week* (17 April 1978), p. 56; and "Foreigners Again Say 'Si' to Investment in Chile," *Business Week* (21 May 1979), p. 55.

182. See: Ray Vicker, "Experiment in South Africa: Some U.S. Firms Ignore Urgings to Leave, Instead Seek to Upgrade Status of Blacks," *The Wall Street Journal* (22 September, 1971), p. 28; Investor Responsibility Research Center, *U.S. Business and South Africa: The Withdrawal Issue* (Washington, D.C.: Investor Responsibiltiy Research Center, 1977); Corporate Information Center, *Church Investments . . .*, pp. 17–27; Morton, *Partners in Apartheid*; World Council of Churches, "Programme to Combat Racism," *Time to Withdraw* (New York: World Council of Churches, January 1973); "The Withdrawal Debate: U.S. Corporations and South Africa" (CIC Brief), *The Corporate Examiner* (June 1973), pp. 3A–3D; Richard A. Jackson (ed.), *The Multinational Corporation and Social Policy: Special Reference to General Motors in South Africa* (New York: Praeger, 1974); The Africa Fund, "U.S. Business in South Africa: Voices for Withdrawal," (New York: The Africa Fund, 1977); Herman Nickel, "The Case for Doing Business in South Africa," *Fortune* (19 June 1978), pp. 60–74; and Tom Wicker, "Should American Business Pull Out of South Africa?," *The New York Times Magazine* (3 June 1979), pp. 31ff.

183. "Heading for the Exit in South Africa," *The New York Times* (2 April, 1978), p. E18.

184. General Motors Corporation Minutes to 1971 Annual Meeting of Shareholders, and "Fifth Anniversary Issue," *The Corporate Examiner* (September 1976), p. 1.

185. Charles B. Camp and Walter Mossberg, "GM Meeting is Tepid Despite Ingredients for Epic Confrontation with Reformers," *The Wall Street Journal* (22 May, 1972), p. 4.

186. Lena Williams, "NAACP Calls for Total Pullout by U.S. Businesses in South Africa," *The New York Times* (20 January, 1978), p. 2.

187. See "Corporate Social Responsibility Challenges—Spring 1977," *The Corporate Examiner* (March 1977), and "Corporate Social Responsibility Challenges—Spring 1978," *The Corporate Examiner* (March 1978).

188. General Motors Corporation, *1976 Public Interest Report*, p. 50, and Jensen, "The American Corporate Presence in South Africa," p. 1f.

189. Jensen, "The American Corporate Presence in South Africa," p. 1f.

190. Jensen, "The American Corporate Presence in South Africa," p. 1f.

191. Jennifer Davis, "General Electric in South Africa: Partners in Apartheid," (New York: Interfaith Center on Corporate Responsibility, 1977).

192. James C. Conden, "G.E. Ducks Out on a Debate " *The New York Times* (10 April, 1977), p. F15.

193. John F. Burns, "Ford Defends Role in Africa," *The New York Times* (20 January, 1978), p. 2.

194. John F. Burns, "Many Blacks in South Africa, Despite Job Restraints, Want Foreign Companies to Stay," *The New York Times* (18 January, 1978), p. 3.

195. See Jeremiah J. O'Connell, "Polaroid Corporation Case," pp. 825–844 in Charles E. Summer and Jeremiah J. O'Connell, *The Managerial Mind*, 3rd edition (Homewood, Ill.: Richard D. Irwin, 1973); and Colin Cruz, "The Polaroid Experiment in South Africa," (Boston, Mass.: Intercollegiate Case Clearing House, 9-376-639).

196. O'Connell, "Polaroid Corporation Case," p. 829.

197. "Letters to the Editor," *The Wall Street Journal* (8 February, 1971).

198. Quoted in "Polaroid and South Africa," (Cambridge, Mass.: Africa Research Group, 1971).

199. George M. Houser, "The Polaroid Approach to South Africa," *The Christian Century* (24 February, 1971).

200. George M. Houser, "Polaroid's Dramatic Withdrawal from South Africa," *The Christian Century* (12 April, 1978).

201. See Beryl Unterhalter, "The 'Polaroid Experiment' in South Africa—A Progress Report," *Vanderbilt Journal of Transnational Law* 6 (Fall 1972), pp. 109–120.

202. "Polaroid Ends Its 'Experiment' in South Africa," *South Africa/Namibia Update* (14 December, 1977), p. 3

203. "Polaroid Ends Its 'Experiment 'in South Africa," p. 3.

204. Houser, "Polaroid's Dramatic Withdrawal."

205. Houser, "Polaroid's Dramatic Withdrawal."

206. See "Chrysler Said to Seek Pretoria Sale," *The New York Times* (23 September, 1976), p. 63; "Business This Week," *The Economist* (15 April, 1978), p. 85; Michael C. Jensen, "The American Corporate Presence in South Africa," *The New York Times* (4 December, 1977), Section 3, pp. 1 and 9; and "Exodus from South Africa," *The Economist* (5 August 1978), p. 80.

207. "South Africa: Black-Chip Investment," *The Economist* (26 November 1977), p. 48.

208. Charles J. Elia, "South Africa Crackdown on Blacks Supporters Intensifies Pressure on U.S. Firms to Respond," *The Wall Street Journal* (5 December 1977), p. 41.

209. Anthony Lewis, "State of Violence: II," *The New York Times* (8 December 1977), p. 23.

210. "Rights Can't Be Only Goal, Carter Says," *The Los Angeles Times* (20 September 1977).

211. "Rights and Wrongs About Sanctions," *The Economist* (5 November 1977), pp. 87–88.

212. See Bernard Gwertzman, "U.S. Reports Political Prisoners Freed Abroad," *The New York Times* (26 October 1977), p. 3; David Vidal, "Military Regimes in South America Looking Less

Harshly on a Return to Some Form of Civilian Rule," *The New York Times* (25 November 1977), p. 12; David Hawk, "Human Rights at Half-Time," *The New Republic* (7 April 1979), pp. 21–23; and Tom Wicker, "A Modest Success," *The New York Times* (23 July 1978), p. E19.

213. See Kenneth L. Adelman, "The Black Man's Burden," *Foreign Policy*, No. 28 (Fall 1977), p. 89.

214. For one survey, see Jerry Flint, "Economic Reprisal on U.S. Rights Stand Believed Unlikely," *The New York Times* (25 March 1977), p. D1 and 5. See also "Eximbank Veto of Credit for Argentine Sale Blackens US–LA Relations," *Business Latin America* (26 July 1978), pp. 233–234; and "The Plot Against Human Rights," *The New Republic* (9 December 1978), p. 11.

215. Hawk, "Human Rights at Half-Time," p. 21.

216. Karen Elliott House, "Uneven Justice? U.S. Officials Worry Over Inconsistencies in Human Rights Plan," *The Wall Street Journal* (11 May 1978), pp. 1 and 18.

217. Anthony Lewis, "State of Violence: II," *The New York Times* (8 December 1977), p. 23.

218. See "Capitalism, Socialism, and Democracy: A Symposium," *Commentary* (April 1978), pp. 29–71.

Chapter 7

1. Walter H. Nelson and Terence C.F. Prittie, *The Economic War Against the Jews* (New York: Random House, 1977), p. 25.

2. Adam Roberts, "Do Economic Boycotts Ever Work?," *New Society* (11 September 1975), p. 579.

3. Andreas F. Lowenfeld, "Sauce for Gander...the Arab Boycott and United States Political Trade Controls," *Texas International Law Journal* 12 (No. 1, 1977).

4. Details of the history of the Arab boycott may be found in the following: Dan S. Chill, *The Arab Boycott of Israel* (New York: Praeger, 1976); Nelson and Prittie, *The Economic War Against the Jews*; U.S. Congress, House Committee on Interstate and Foreign Commerce and Subcommittee on Oversight and Investigations, *The Arab Boycott and American Business*, 1976; Walter Guzzardi, Jr., "That Curious Barrier on the Arab Frontiers," *Fortune* (July 1975), pp. 82–85; and Nancy Turck, "The Arab Boycott of Israel," *Foreign Affairs* (April 1977), pp. 472–493.

5. See Turck, "The Arab Boycott," p. 475.

6. "Israel is in the Mideast, Too," *Industry Week* (4 October 1976), p. 58.

7. See various references in *Newsweek* (25 October 1976).

8. Discussed in detail in *Events* (London, 14 January 1977).

9. Guzzardi, "That Curious Barrier," p. 170.

10. "U.S. Sues Concern in Arab Blacklist Case," *The New York Times* (17 January 1976) p. 5.

11. Lawrence R. Velval, "Antitrust and the Arab Boycott," *The Wall Street Journal* (27 January 1976), p. 6.

12. Answer, *United States vs. Bechtel Corporation*, Civil No. C-76–99 (N.D. California filed 16 January 1976), reprinted in 762 *Antitrust and Trade Regulation Report* (BNA) F-2 (4 May 1976).

13. "Business Bridles at Antiboycott Bills," *Business Week* (27 September 1976), p. 38.

14. "U.S., Bechtel Reach Accord on Boycott Case," *The Wall Street Journal* (11 January 1977), p. 14.

15. "Judge Signs Judgment Barring Bechtel from Participating in Arab-Led Boycott," *The Wall Street Journal* (16 January 1979), p. 14.

16. "World Trade: Will a Boycott Backfire on Bechtel?" *Business Week* (15 December 1975), p. 32.

17. "Judge Signs Judgement Barring Bechtel," p. 14.

18. Irving Spiegel, "Coca-Cola Refuses Israelis A Franchise," *The New York Times* (8 April 1966), p. 1.

19. Spiegel, "Coca-Cola Refuses Israelis," p. 1.

20. Thomas Buckley, "Coca-Cola Grants Israeli Franchise," *The New York Times* (16 April 1966), p. 1.

21. Buckley, "Coca-Cola Grants Israeli Franchise," p. 1.

22. Thomas F. Brady, "Arabs Vote to Bar Ford, Coca-Cola," *The New York Times* (21 November 1966), p. 1.

23. "Coca-Cola Links Aid to Egypt Citrus Firms, Return to that Nation," *The Wall Street Journal* (12 August 1977), p. 29.

24. "Coca-Cola and Egypt Agree to Form Venture," *The Wall Street Journal* (8 September 1977), p. 16.

25. "Coke Aims to Get Off Boycott List, Slates Jobs in Two Arab Nations," *The Wall Street Journal* (30 March 1978), p. 17.

26. "Coca-Cola is Pressing Efforts to Uncork Arab Markets," *The New York Times* (29 March 1978), p. 1.

27. "Arab League Boycott Chief Lashes Out At Egypt for Joint Venture with Ford," *The Wall Street Journal* (4 November 1977), p. 14.

28. "Coke's Breakthrough into the Arab World," *Business Week* (10 April 1978), p. 40; and "Coca-Cola Gets Accords to Resume Egypt Sales," *The Wall Street Journal* (10 May 1978), p. 20.

29. Brady, "Arabs Vote to Bar Ford, Coca-Cola," p. 1.

30. "U.A.R. Ford Plant is Reported Seized," *The New York Times* (25 November 1966), p. 1.

31. "U.A.R. Ford Plant," p. 1.

32. "Ford Equipment Released by Cairo," *The New York Times* (1 December 1966), p. 63.

33. See references in the *Sun Times* [Chicago, Illinois], (21 October 1975), p. 18.

34. "Back to the Pyramids," *The Economist* (5 November 1977), p. 106; and "Ford Motor Says Egypt Approved a Joint Project," *The Wall Street Journal* (31 October 1977), p. 15.

35. "Arab League Boycott Chief Lashes Out," p. 14.

36. Mobil Corporation advertisements in *The New York Times* (16 September 1976), p. 39; (27 September 1976), p. 14; (30 September 1976), p. 41; (14 October 1976), p. 37; (24 October 1976), p. 15; (28 April 1977), p. 29; and letters to the editor in *The New York Times* (24 September 1976), p. 24; (28 September 1976); and (22 April 1977), p. 26.

37. "Mobil Shareholders Defeat Boycott Compliance Move," *The New York Times* (6 May 1977) p. 9.

38. "Congress Eases Final Antiboycott Rules," *Chemical Week* (25 January 1978), p. 19; and "Rules to Enforce Arab Boycott Laws Win Endorsement," *The New York Times* (28 January 1978), p. 27.

39. "Antiboycott Law: A Quiet Success," *U.S. News and World Report* (26 June 1978). See also "World Roundup," *Business Week* (3 April 1978), p. 44.

40. "Boycott Impact Varies in Arab Lands," *The Wall Street Journal* (3 April 1978), p. 6; and Steven Rattner, "Israeli Boycott Losing Its Grip," *The New York Times* (12 June 1978), p. D2.

41. Robert S. Greenberger, "Firms Supporting Arab Boycott of Israel Face First Legal Actions by Washington," *The Wall Street Journal* (23 April 1979), p. 2.

42. Judith Miller, "Antiboycott Law Gains Support," *The New York Times* (13 March 1979) pp. D1 and 5.

43. George W. Ball, ed., *Global Companies* (Englewood Cliffs, N.J.: Prentice-Hall, 1975), p. 48.

44. For more details on such jurisdictional questdions see "Antitrust Guide for International Operations," *Mergers and Acquisitions* (Spring 1977).

45. See Antitrust Division of Justice Department's January 1977 "Antitrust Guide for International Operations" reprinted in *Mergers and Acquisitions* (Spring 1977). Also January 1973 and May 1973 speeches reprinted in 5 CCH Trade Regulation Report, para. 50, 161 at 55, 283; and 50, 169 at 55, 300 (1974).

46. "Antitrust Guide for International Operations," p. 17.

47. Jack N. Behrman, *National Interests and the Multinational Enterprise* (Englewood Cliffs, N.J.: Prentice-Hall, 1970), pp. 115–6; and Robert T. Jones, "Executive's Guide to Antitrust in Europe," *Harvard Business Review* (May–June 1976), pp. 106–118.

48. Many of the details of these cases were found in Kingman Brewster, *Antitrust and American Business Abroad* (New York: Arno Press, 1976), especially pp. 26–30 and pp. 45–51.

49. I.A. Litvak and C.J. Maule, "Conflict Resolution and Extraterritoriality," *Journal of Conflict Resolution* (September 1969), p. 315.

50. William M. Carley, "Trustbusters Challenge U.S. Firms' Dealings with Concerns Abroad," *The Wall Street Journal* (30 July 1970), p. 1.

51. Richard Barovick, "International Antitrust . . . Washington Style," *Business Abroad* (September 1979), p. 10.

52. "The Antitrust Aim Overseas," *Business Week* (14 March 1977), pp. 100–101.

53. Hearings before the Senate Committee on the Judiciary on "International Aspects of Antitrust" (April–August 1966), Part 1 and Appendix, Part 2 (1967), p. 491.

54. Jean Ross-Skinner, "Antitrust Tensions With Europe," *Dun's Review* (May 1978), p. 104.

55. Ross-Skinner, "Antitrust Tensions," p. 105.

56. See "The Common Market's Rush Into Cartels," *Business Week* (27 March 1978), p. 107.

57. See "Textiles: An EC Cartel to Save Its Ailing Fiber Industry," *Business Week* (6 March 1977), p. 44.

58. "Aluminum Firms Drop Consortium Bid in Australia," *The Wall Street Journal* (7 July 1977), p. 4.

59. Seymour J. Rubin, "Multinational Enterprises and National Sovereignty: A Skeptic's Analysis," *Law and Policy in International Business* 3, (No. 1, 1971), pp. 1–14.

60. Three other important export control acts are: the Munitions Control Act, which prohibits the sale of munitions without approval of the State Department; the Battle Act, which provides for a cutoff of aid funds if a foreign country permits exports of strategic items to prohibited destinations; and the Agricultural Trade Development and Assistance Act, which prohibits the sale of agricultural products to most Communist countries.

61. *Report to the Congress in Response to Section 24 of the International Security Assistance Act of 1977* (21 August 1978), pp. 26–28.

62. *Report to the Congress*, pp. 25–26.

63. See "East-West Industrial Cooperation," *The Economist* (6 August 1977), pp. 56–57.

64. See William C. Norris, "High Technology Trade with the Communists," *Datamation* (January 1978), pp. 99–103.

65. See John T. Norman, "Plan for a National Export Policy is Sent to President by Administration Officials," *The Wall Street Journal* (26 July 1978), p. 3; and Phillip H. Wiggins, "Computer-Sale Bar Irks Sperry," *The New York Times* (26 July 1978), pp. D1 and 7.

66. For further details see: "Welcome Foreign Capitalists (Even American Ones)," *The Economist* (5 March 1977), pp. 91–92.

67. See *Akron Beacon Journal* (8 and 14 May 1965).

68. *Washington Evening Star* (8 May 1965).

69. See *Congressional Record* (26 July 1965); and "Universal Oil Products Proceeds on Building Refinery for Rumania," *The Wall Street Journal* (27 July 1965), p. 23.

70. "Universal Oil Products Proceeds," p. 23.

71. "A Showdown Over the Ban on Cuban Trade," *Business Week* (13 April 1974), p. 80.

72. "A Showdown," p. 80.

73. H. J. Maidenberg, "U.S. Move on Trade with Cuba Acknowledges Present Practice," *The New York Times* (22 August 1975), p. 8.

74. See "Cuban Countdown," *The Economist* (4 May 1974), p. 59.

75. See David K. Shipler, "Soviet Police and Détente," *The New York Times* (17 June 1978), p. A6.

76. "Moscow's Uneasy Americans," *Business Week* (3 July 1978), p. 25 and 28; Craig Whitney, "Soviet Questioning American Executive," *The New York Times* (1 August 1978), p. 8.

77. See "Using Trade to Influence Russia," *Business Week* (24 July 1978), p. 181; and "The Rising Sentiment Against Sales to Russia," *Business Week* (11 September 1978), pp. 57 and 60.

78. See Richard Burt, "Carter Aides Favor Ban on Oil Equipment for Soviet," *The New York Times* (27 June 1978), p. A3.

79. *The New York Times* (21 July 1978), p. D1.

80. *The New York Times* (21 July 1978), p. D1.

81. Wiggins, "Computer Sale Bar Irks Sperry," p. D1.

82. "Sperry Rand Efforts to Market to Soviets Face Uncertainties," *The Wall Street Journal* (26 July 1978), p. 3.

83. "The Rising Sentiment Against Sales to Russia," pp. 57 and 60.

84. "Exports of Oil Technology to Russia is Reexamined," *The Wall Street Journal* (30 August 1978), p. 9.

85. Greg Conderarci, "Sale of Oil-Pipe Gear to Soviets is Cleared by Administration," *The Wall Street Journal* (28 September 1978), p. p. 14.

86. "Worldwide," *The Wall Street Journal* (17 August 1978), p. 1.

87. "Can Computers Kill," *The Economist* (28 April 1979), pp. 56-57; and "A Honeywell for the Russians," *World Business Weekly* (18 June 1979), pp. 14–16.

88. George P. Shultz, "Light-Switch Diplomacy," *Business Week* (28 May 1979), pp. 24–26.

89. See Kingman Brewster, Jr., *Law and United States Business in Canada* (Montreal: Canadian-American Committee, 1960), p. 26.

90. See Raymond Vernon, "The Fragile Foundations of East-West Trade," *Foreign Affairs* (Summer 1979), pp. 1035–1051; Jonathan B. Bingham and Victor C. Johnson, "A Rational Approach to Export Controls," *Foreign Affairs* (Spring 1979), pp. 894–920; Collection of articles on "Trade, Technology and Leverage," *Foreign Policy* (Fall 1978), pp. 63–106; and "Export Controls Split Business," *Business Week* (7 May 1979), p. 36.

91. See Anthony Sampson, *The Seven Sisters* (New York: Bantam Books, 1975) for a detailed look at each of the seven oil MNEs.

92. See Allan T. Demarre, "Aramco is a Lesson in the Management of Chaos," *Fortune* (February 1974), p. 58.

93. Otto N. Miller, "To Our Stockholders" *Standard Oil Company of California* (26 July 1973).

94. U.S. Senate, *Hearings before the Subcommittee on Multinational Corporations of the Committee on Foreign Relations, Multinational Petroleum Companies and Foreign Policy*, 93rd Congress (20 June 1974), p. 429.

95. U.S. Senate, *Hearings*, p. 531.

96. William D. Smith, "Libya Intensifies Oil Restrictions," *The New York Times* (14 August 1973), p. 43.

97. U.S. Senate, *Hearings*, pp. 268 and 318.

98. U.S. Senate, *Hearings*, pp. 541–542.

99. U.S. Senate, *Hearings*, pp. 318–319.

100. U.S. Senate, *Hearings*, pp. 29–58, 316–325 and 682–687.

101. U.S. Senate, *Hearings*, pp. 528–529.

102. U.S. Senate, *Hearings*, p. 515.

103. U.S. Senate, *Hearings*, pp. 216–217.

104. U.S. Senate, *Hearings*, pp. 546–547.

105. U.S. State Department Confidential Cable 202315 (12 October 1973), p. 3.

106. U.S. Senate, *Hearings*, p. 515.

107. U.S. Senate, *Hearings*, p. 217.

108. Demarre, "Aramco is a Lesson in the Management of Chaos," pp. 58, and 60–63.

109. U.S. Senate, *Hearings*, p. 515.

110. Federal Energy Administration, *U.S. Oil Companies and the Arab Oil Embargo: The International Allocation of Constrained Supplies* (Washington, D.C., 1975) p. 2.

111. U.S. Senate, *Hearings*, pp. 515–517.

112. U.S. Senate, *Hearings*, p. 418.

113. "Oil Hearings Raise the Loyalty Question," *Business Week* (27 April 1974), pp. 45-46.

114. OPEC oil cutback/embargo warnings have been raised on several occasions subsequently for a variety of reasons. Most recently, the Associated Press reported an OPEC threat "to cut oil

supplies to industrialized nations if they don't make it easier for OPEC to get into producing and selling gasoline." See *New York Post* (10 October 1978), p. 4.

115. U.S. Senate, *Hearings*, p. 515.

116. U.S. Senate, *Hearings*, p. 46.

117. As discussed in *The Economist* (December 1973), p. 1.

118. *Directorate-General for Energy, Commission of the European Communities*, "Chronological Summary of Developments in the Oil Crisis Which Have Affected Community Supplies," XVII/110/73–E, p. 6.

119. *U.S. Department of Commerce*, "Imports Commodity by Country," various monthly issues and news releases, CB 74–83 (8 April 1974).

120. Federal Energy Administration, *U.S. Oil Companies*, Appendix II.

121. For an excellent review see Raymond Vernon, ed., "The Oil Crisis: In Perspective," special issue of *Daedalus* **104** (September 1975).

122. Federal Energy Administration, *U.S. Oil Companies*, p. 10.

123. For example, see the statement of Emilo G. Collado, Director and Executive Vice-President of Exxon, U.S. Senate, *Hearings*, p. 5.

124. See "International Oil Firms Find OPEC Still Needs Their Technology, Skill," *The Wall Street Journal* (17 October 1978), pp. 1 and 20.

125. Emilo Collado testimony before the Church Committee (unpublished). Pemex's recent oil find in Mexico seems to have made this statement obsolete.

126. Steven Rattner, "Oil Firms Get Another Chance to Play God," *The New York Times* (7 January 1979), p. E4.

127. Rattner, "Oil Firms Get Another Chance," p. E4.

CHAPTER 8

1. For a good survey see Robert G. Hawkins and Bertram Finn, "Regulation of Multinational Firms' Foreign Activities: Home Country Policies and Concerns," *Journal of Contemporary Business* (Autumn 1977), pp. 7–30.

2. See C. Fred Bergsten, "Coming Investment Wars?" *Foreign Affairs,* **53** (October 1974), pp. 135–152.

3. "From Control of Foreign Investment to Total Investment Programming" *Comercio Exterior* (1 February 1973), pp. 3–5.

4. See Alvin Shuster, "Libya Buys 10% of Fiat Company for $415 Million," *The New York Times* (2 December 1976), p. 1 and 73; Alvin Shuster, "Fiat's Libyan Deal Held Aid to Soviet; Moscow Role Seen," *The New York Times* 11 December 1976), p. 27 and 31; Alvin Shuster, "Fiat Chairman Under Criticism for Libya Deal," *The New York Times* (19 December 1976), p. 24; and "What Fiat Will Do with Libya's Money," *Business Week* (14 March 1977), pp. 97–99.

5. "Sweden: A Lid on Expansion of Multinationls," *Business Week* (2 March 1974), p. 32.

6. Ronald E. Müller, "Poverty is the Product," *Foreign Policy* (Winter 1973–74).

7. "What's Good for Canada," *Foreign Trade* (5 August 1975), p. 11.

8. A.E. Safarian and Joel Bell, "Issues Raised by National Control of the Multinational Corporation," *Columbia Journal of World Business* (December 1973), pp. 7–18.

9. Canadian Trade Minister Jean-Luc Pepin, quoted in *U.S. News and World Report,* (15 May 1972).

10. John Urquhart, "Canadians Are Questioning Usefulness of Screening Investments by Foreigners," *The Wall Street Journal* (6 March 1979), p. 17.

11. Y.S. Hu, *The Impact of U.S. Investment in Europe* (New York: Frederich A. Praeger, 1973), p. 96.

12. "France Vetoes GE Bid to Buy Minority Share of Computer Producer," *The Wall Street Journal* (6 February 1964), p. 4. See also Thomas R. Bransten and Stanely H. Brown, "Machines Bull's Computer Crisis," *Fortune* (July 1964), p. 155 and Hu, *The Impact of U.S. Investment in Europe,* pp. 136–137.

13. "Business Around the Globe," *Fortune* (September 1964), p. 59.

14. See references in *Newsweek* (27 April 1964), p. 88.

15. Referred to in detail in *Newsweek* (3 August 1964), p. 65.

16. "Business Around the Globe," p. 59.

17. For a complete review see Gregory H. Wierzynski, "GE's $200-Million Ticket to France," *Fortune* (June 1967), pp. 92–95, 159–162.

18. Wierzynski, "GE's $200-Million Ticket," p. 159.

19. Wierzynski, "GE's $200-Million Ticket," p. 161.

20. Wierzynski, "GE's $200-Million Ticket," p. 93.

21. "Takeover of French Computer Firms Urged," *The Wall Street Journal* (6 September 1967), p. 13.

22. "GE Chairman Says It Wasn't IBM Moves that Drove GE Out of Computer Business," *The Wall Street Journal* (10 December 1975), p. 16; Scott R. Schmedel, "Why and How GE Left Computer Field: The Road is Marked in IBM Trial Record," *The Wall Street Journal* (12 January 1976), p. 26. Both give a detailed description of this task force in reference to the IBM antitrust suit.

23. "GE Chairman Says It Wasn't IBM," p. 16.

24. "GE and Honeywell Test Their Match," *Business Week* (30 May 1970), pp. 30–31.

25. "Honeywell Tries to Make Its Merger Work," *Business Week* (26 September 1970), pp. 93 and Gene Bylinsky, "Happily Married in Computers," *Fortune* (April 1973), p. 91.

26. "The French Lesson That the British Won't Learn," *The Economist* (17 May 1975), p. 87.

27. See "Dutch, French, German Computer Firms Agree on Broad Joint Venture," *The Wall Street Journal* (5 July 1973), p. 5.

28. "Multinationals: A French Rebuff for Honeywell-Bull," *Business Week* (8 September 1973), p. 35.

29. "Multinationals: A French Rebuff," p. 35.

30. K. Ames Smithers, "Honeywell Denies Rumor It Plans to Quit Computer Industry After Poor 1974 Year," *The Wall Street Journal* (27 December 1974), p. 4; and "French Computers: Un-Unidata?," *The Economist* (29 March 1975), pp. 105–106.

31. "France Set to Allow Computer Firm Tie to Honeywell-Bull," *The Wall Street Journal* (6 May 1975), p. 22 and "The French Lesson that the British Won't Learn," *The Economist* (17 May 1975), pp. 87–88.

32. "Goodbye to a Chimera," *Time* (26 May 1975), p. 75.

33. "Corporate Strategies," *Business Week* (27 March 1978), p. 71.

34. "Honeywell Forecasts Modest Rise in Results for 1st, 2nd Quarters," *The Wall Street Journal* (28 March 1978), p. 18.

35. Wierzynski, "GE's $200-Million Ticket," p. 93.

36. Robert D. Hershey, Jr., "Heinz in a Pickle with Britain for Wage Rises Over Guidelines," *The New York Times* (16 August 1977), p. 49.

37. "Mexico Issues Rules Tightening Controls on Foreign Financing," *The Wall Street Journal* (26 April 1972).

38. Statement by Ambassador Douglas Fletcher as reported in "The Frustration Facing Aluminum Makers," *Business Week* (16 February 1974), p. 116.

39. *Time* (8 July 1974), p. 46.

40. "Jamaica Proposes Bauxite Legislation to Produce $200 Million Over 13 Months," *The Wall Street Journal* (17 May 1974), p. 3.

41. "Jamaica Proposes Bauxite Legislation," p. 3.

42. "Alcoa to Increase Aluminum Ingot Price 6.3% June 3," *The Wall Street Journal* (20 May 1974), p. 4.

43. *Wall Street Journal* (20 May 1974), p. 4.

44. *Wall Street Journal* (17 May 1974), p. 3.

45. "Three Big U.S. Firms Seek Arbitration of Jamaica's Bauxite Mining Tax Boost," *The Wall Street Journal* (18 June 1974), p. 10; "Aluminum Firms' Jamaican Dispute to be Arbitrated,"

The Wall Street Journal (25 June 1974), p. 12; and "Bauxite May Go to Court," *Chemical Week* (26 June 1974), p. 13.

46. "Three Big U.S. Firms Seek Arbitration," p. 10.

47. "Balk on Bauxite Tax," *Chemical Week* (9 October 1974), p. 15.

48. "Jamaica Buys Shares of Kaiser Aluminum," *The Wall Street Journal* (29 October 1974), p. 44; and "Jamaican Government is Buying Small Stake in Reynolds Metal Co.," *The Wall Street Journal* (30 October 1974), p. 41.

49. "New Bauxite Partners," *Chemical Week* (27 November 1974), p. 19; "Jamaican Move on Kaiser Equity Unveils Government's Aim" *Business Latin America* (4 December 1974), pp. 387–389; and "Jamaica Reaches Major Accords With Two Bauxite Producers," *Business Latin America* (9 April 1975), p. 119.

50. "Jamaica Reaches Major Accords," p. 119.

51. See: "New Bauxite Deal," *Chemical Week* (18 June 1975), p. 24; "Bauxite Leverage is Less," *Chemical Week* (15 October 1975), p. 22; "Revere Copper Sues to Invalidate Taxes Levied in Jamaica on Bauxite Production," *The Wall Street Journal* (14 January 1976), p. 4; and "Revere Copper Calls Expropriation Award of $1.1 Million Unjust," *The Wall Street Journal* (29 August 1978), p. 44.

52. "Bauxite Producers Opt for Stability," *Business Week* (1 November 1976), p. 27.

53. "Kaiser Aluminum Pact on Bauxite Mining Signed with Jamaica," *The Wall Street Journal* (3 February 1977), p. 11.

54. See "Reynolds Metals to Sell Jamaica Certain Holdings," *The Wall Street Journal* (1 April 1977), p. 7; and "Alcan Says Jamaica Will Get 7% Interest in Bauxite Operation," *The Wall Street Journal* (26 September 1978), p. 20.

55. "Reynolds Metals to Sell Jamaica Certain Holdings," p. 7.

56. Gay Sands Miller, "Minimum Price for Base Grade Bauxite is Set at Meeting of 10 Producing Nations," *The Wall Street Journal* (8 December 1977), p. 13 and Gay Sands Miller, "Jamaica Proposes Aluminum Firms Issue Notes to It," *The Wall Street Journal* (6 March 1978), p. 7.

57. See references in *Wall Street Journal* (17 May 1974), p. 3.

58. Referred to in *Business Week* (16 February 1974), p. 116.

59. "Bauxite Producers Opt for Stability," p. 28.

60. Amal Nag, "Long An Advocate of High Bauxite Prices, Jamaica Tries to Moderate the Ore's Levy," *The Wall Street Journal* (18 May 1979), p. 7.

61. Donald R. Lessard, "Transfer Prices, Taxes and Financial Markets: Implications of Internal Financial Transfers Within the Multinational Corporation," in Robert G. Hawkins (ed.), *The Economic Effects of Multinational Firms* (Greenwich, Conn.: JAI Press, 1979) pp. 101-124.

62. Lessard, "Transfer Prices, Taxes and Financial Markets."

63. See "Reaction is Mixed as IBM Departs," *The New York Times* (12 December 1977), p. 59.

64. See "Coca-Cola Ordered by India to Disclose Formula for Drink," *The Wall Street Journal* (10 August 1977), p. 11.

65. "India Stands Firm Against Coca-Cola," *The New York Times* (5 September 1977), pp. 22–23.

66. "India Stands Firm Against Coca-Cola," pp. 22–23 and "Sweet Stuff," *Nation* (17 September 1977), pp. 228–229.

67. Kasturi Rangan "India Demands 'Know-How' and 60% Share of Coca-Cola Operation," *The New York Times* (9 August 1977), p. 45.

68. Rangan, "India Demands 'Know-How,'" p. 45.

69. Rangan, "India Demands 'Know-How,'" p. 45. Also see "No Fizz Without Fuss," *The Economist* (20 August 1977), p. 95.

70. Rangan, "India Demands 'Know-How,'" p. 45.

71. "Coca-Cola Executive in India to Discuss Official Demands," *The New York Times* (15 August 1977), p. 44.

72. "India Stands Firm Against Coca-Cola," p. 22.

73. "India Chooses '77' Name For Its Coke Substitute," *The New York Times* (25 August 1977), p. D9.

74. "India Coca-Cola Bottlers Seek Import Permission," *The New York Times* (3 September 1977), p. 26.

75. "India May Swallow Coke," *Time* (22 August 1977), p. 44.

76. "India Chooses '77' Name," p. D9.

77. "India Stands Firm Against Coca-Cola," p. 22.

78. "India Stands Firm Against Coca-Cola," p. 22.

79. Vin McLellan, "Why IBM Must Withdraw from India in June," *Datamation* (April 1978), p. 181. The *Datamation* article is primarily based on negative comments from ex-IBM-India employees who now work for the state-owned manufacturing or service companies. Also see "Reaction is Mixed as IBM Departs," *The New York Times* (12 December 1977), p. 59.

80. IBM "Corporate News Bulletin," dated 15 November 1977.

81. "IBM Announces Plan to Curtail India Operations," *The Wall Sreet Journal* (16 November 1977), p. 48; and "Tea Instead of Sympathy," *The Economist* (24 September 1977), p. 110.

82. See McLellan, "Why IBM Must Withdraw from India in June," p. 181; and Kasturi Rangan, "India Agrees to Deal That Allows IBM to Stay in Country," *The New York Times* (11 September 1977), p. 12.

83. "Indianisation: Tea Instead of Sympathy," *The Economist* (24 September 1977), p. 100.

84. Professor M. G. K. Menon, chairman of the Indian Electronics Commission and the most "influential" ministerial advisor on the IBM case contended: "What might have been feasible is that if IBM could have relaxed the 100% and said we're willing to come down anywhere below 74%... Above 74 is very difficult. It would have to have been backed up by really unusual offers.... But from 74 it would have been very possible." From McLellan, "Why IBM Must Withdraw from India in June," p. 184. Also see "How Companies Comply with India's FERA and Keep Control," *Business Asia* (24 February 1978), pp. 59–62.

85. Kasturi Rangan, "New Delhi Official Says IBM Told India It Is Leaving," *The New York Times* (1 October 1977), p. 29; and "IBM Withdraws from India," *Time* (28 November 1977), p. 92.

86. "India Beckons Europes Computer-Makers," *World Business Weekly* (2 April 1979), p. 52.

87. See Angeline Pantages, "Erosion Extends Around the World," *Datamation* (April 1978), p. 182; "Reshaping IBM," *The Economist* (29 October 1977), pp. 92–93; "Foreign Firms Excluded from Brazil's Drive to Build Minicomputers," *Business Latin America* (4 January 1978), pp. 1–2; "IBM Says It Resolved Dispute Over Control of Indonesian Activities," *The Wall Street Journal* (20 December 1977), p. 26; and "IBM Says Nigeria Accepts Business Plan," *The Wall Street Journal* (6 November 1978), p. 22.

88. "A Market Thirst, Never Quenched," *The New York Times* (9 April 1978), Sec. III, p. 1. See also "How Companies Comply With India's FERA and Keep Control," *Business Asia* (24 February 1978), pp. 59–62.

89. See "Coke is Right," *The Wall Street Journal* (10 August 1977), p. 14.

90. "Foreign Ownership and the Structure of Canadian Industry," report prepared for the Privy Council Office, Ottawa (January 1968), pp. 21 and 49.

91. "Québec Premier Doesn't See Takeover, Except Possibly of the Asbestos Industry," *The Wall Street Journal* (26 January 1977), p. 10.

92. "Some Stocks, Bonds, Canadian Dollar Fall After Lévesque Speech," *The Wall Street Journal* (27 January 1977), p. 8.

93. "Johns-Manville Delays Expansion for Québec Asbestos," *The New York Times* (1 February 1977), p. 43.

94. "At Johns-Manville, It's Back to Basics." *Business Week* (31 October 1977), p. 77.

95. Henry Giniger, "Québec Government Plans Bid for the Asbestos Corp." *The New York Times* (22 February 1977), p. 45; and "Dynamics Denies Talk of Asbestos Takeover," *The New York Times* (23 February 1977), p. D5.

96. "Official Says Québec Unlikely to Takeover Asbestos Operations," *The Wall Street Journal* (1 March 1977), p. 7.

97. "Johns-Manville Sets $77 Million to Spur Québec Asbestos Plant, *The New York Times* (8 March 1977), p. 52.

98. For reactions see Henry Giniger, "New Era in Québec's Industry," *The New York Times* (25 October 1977), p. 55.

99. Henry Giniger, "Québec Threatens U.S.-Held Company With a Takeover," *The New York Times* (22 October 1977), p. 27; and "Québec Plans to Take Control of Asbestos Firm," *The Wall Street Journal* (24 October 1977), p. 12.

100. Giniger, "Québec Threatens U.S.-Held Company." Also see "Québec Hopes to Bid for Asbestos' Shares If Parent Agrees," *The Wall Street Journal* (25 October 1977), p. 15; and "Québec Eyes Asbestos," *Chemical Week* (2 November 1977), p. 20.

101. "Québec Introduces Legislation to Set Up Asbestos Company," *Chemical Week* (7 December 1977), p. 56.

102. Frederick Rose, "Québec's Plan to Purchase Asbestos Corporation Remains Stalled by Province's Inaction," *The Wall Street Journal* (27 March 1979), p. 10.

103. David P. Garino, "General Dynamics Hires Firms to Place Value on Asbestos Unit Sought by Québec," *The Wall Street Journal* (29 November 1977), p. 12.

104. "Asbestos Industry Terms Expansion in Québec Unlikely," *The New York Times* (23 January 1978), p. D2.

105. Henry Giniger, "Québec Sets Up Company to Widen Asbestos Stake," *The New York Times* (25 May 1978), p. D3.

106. Rose, "Québec's Plan to Purchase Asbestos Corporation," p. 10.

107. Rose, "Québec's Plan to Purchase Asbestos Corporation," p. 10.

108. Rose, "Québec's Plan to Purchase Asbestos Corporation," p. 10.

109. Rose, "Québec's Plan to Purchase Asbestos Corporation," p. 10.

110. "General Dynamics Unit Gives Plan in Takeover," *The Wall Street Journal* (28 March 1979), p. 16.

111. "General Dynamics Unit Gives Plan," p. 16.

112. "Québec Moves Closer to Expropriation of Asbestos Unit of General Dynamics," *The Wall Street Journal* (6 April 1979), p. 12.

113. "General Dynamics, Québec Meet to Mull a Formal Offer for Firm's Asbestos Unit," *The Wall Street Journal* (13 April 1979), p. 10.

114. "Québec Moves Closer to Expropriation of Asbestos Unit," p. 12.

115. "Québec's Expropriation of Asbestos Corporation Moves Nearer as Cabinet Proceeds on Bill," *The Wall Street Journal* (3 May 1979), p. 10.

116. "Québec's Expropriation of Asbestos Corporation," p. 10.

117. "Québec's Expropriation of Asbestos Corporation," p. 10.

118. "Asbestos Corporation Officer Says Québec's Bid for Takeover Hurts Province in Market," *The Wall Street Journal* (10 May 1979), p. 16.

119. Henry Giniger, "General Dynamics Fails in Québec Asbestos Bid," *The New York Times* (12 May 1978), p. 29.

120. Giniger "General Dynamics Fails," p. 19.

121. "Québec Moves Nearer to Expropriating General Dynamics' Asbestos Corporation Unit," *The Wall Street Journal* (21 June 1979), p. 20.

122. "Québec Business Holds Its Breath," *Business Week* (28 May 1979), p. 54.

123. "General Dynamics' Asbestos Sues Québec Charging Expropriation Law is Invalid," *The Wall Street Journal* (25 June 1979), p. 16.

124. "Québec Purchase of Asbestos Firm Blocked by Court" *The Wall Street Journal* (28 June 1979), p. 17.

125. See J. Frederick Truitt, "Expropriation of Foreign Investment: Summary of the Post World War II Experience of American and British Investors in the Less Developed Countries," *Journal of International Business Studies* (Autumn 1970), pp. 21–34; Richard D. Robinson, "Expropriation," pp. 412–427 in his *International Business Management: A Guide to Decision Making* (Hinsdale, Ill.:Dryden Press, 1978); David G. Bradley, "Managing Against Expropriation," *Harvard Business Review* (July–August 1977), pp. 75–83; Robert G. Hawkins, Norman Mintz, and Michael Provissiero, "Government Takeovers of U.S. Foreign Affiliates," *Journal of International Business Studies* (Spring 1976), pp. 3–16; Franklin R. Root, "The Expropriation

Experience of American Companies," *Business Horizons* (April 1968), pp. 69–74; James K. Weekly, "Expropriation of U.S. Multinational Investments," *MSU Business Topics* (Winter 1977), pp. 27–36; and Stephen J. Kobrin, "Firm and Industry Factors Which Increase Vulnerability of Foreign Enterprise to Forced Divestment: A Cross-National Empirical Study," Sloan School of Management Working Paper #1022–78 (October 1978).

126. Nicholas M. Horrock, "ITT–Chile Case Closed," *The New York Times* (8 March 1979), p. D1.

Chapter 9

1. This represents our estimate as of July 1979. For earlier estimates see The Council on Economic Priorities; "Corporate Payoffs: The Tally So Far," *Business and Society Review*, No. 19 (Fall 1976), pp. 54–57; Robert D. Hershey, Jr., "Payoffs: Are They Stopped or Just Better Hidden," *The New York Times*, (9 January 1977), p. 23; Vasil Pappas, "Payoff Aftermath: Crackdown on Bribery Hasn't Damaged Sales, Big Companies Report," *The Wall Street Journal* (28 February 1977), pp 1 and 18.

2. For an extensive discussion of motives see Edward D. Herlihy and Theodore A. Levine, "Corporate Crisis: The Overseas Payment Problem," *Law and Policy in International Business* 8 (No. 3, 1976), pp. 547–629. See also Neil H. Jacoby, Peter Nehemkis and Richard Eells, *Bribery and Extortion in World Business* (New York: Macmillan, 1977) and Tom Kennedy and Charles E. Simon, *An Examination of Questionable Payments and Practices* (New York: Praeger, 1978).

3. Deborah Rankin, "Accounting Ruses Used in Disguising Dubious Payments," *The New York Times* (27 February 1978), p. D1.

4. Robert D. Hershey, Jr., "United Brands Bribe Called Aberration," *The New York Times* (11 December 1976), pp. 29 and 31. See also Peter Nehemkis, "Business Payoffs Abroad: Rhetoric and Reality," *California Management Review* 18 (Winter 1975), pp. 5–20; Thomas McCann, *An American Company: The Tragedy of United Fruit* (New York: Crown, 1976); and Arnold H. Lubasch, "Guilty Plea in Foreign Bribe Case," *New York Times* (20 July 1978), p. D3.

5. Deborah Sue Yeager, "Internal Philip Morris Filings Outline Payoffs by Dominican Republic Affiliate," *The Wall Street Journal* (28 December 1976), p. 2.

6. "Tanaka Will Go On Trial January 1977 on Lockheed Bribery Charges," *The New York Times* (26 November 1976), p. A13; and Henry Kamm, "Tanaka, on Stand, Denies Accepting Bribery by Lockheed," *The New York Times* (28 January 1977), p. A4.

7. *Report of the Special Committee of the Board of Directors of Ashland Oil, Inc.* (26 June 1975); and Ann Crittenden, "Business Bribes Abroad: A Deeply Etched Pattern," *New York Times* (20 December 1976), pp. D1 and 3.

8. Robert M. Smith, "Bribe Requests in Haiti Alleged," *The New York Times* (3 March 1976), pp. 51 and 54.

9. See John J. McCloy, Nathan W. Pearson, and Beverly Matthews, *The Great Oil Spill, The Inside Report: Gulf Oil's Bribery and Political Chicanery* (New York: Chelsea House, 1976) Section on South Korea, pp. 93–122. See also "South Korea May Plan to Regain 75% Stake in Gulf Oil Venture," *The Wall Street Journal* (20 December 1976), p. 28.

10. Cited in Nehemkis, "Business Payoffs Abroad," p. 15. Also see Robert Lindsey, "The New Adventures of Tom Jones," *The New York Times* (19 September 1976), Section 3, p. 1 and 11.

11. Jerry Landauer, "U.S. Says Some Boeing Co. Consultants Are Officials of Foreign Governments," *The Wall Street Journal* (7 January 1977), p. 3; "SEC Clashes with Boeing Co. Over Payments," *The New York Times* (17 December 1976), p. D1; and Jerry Landauer, "Influential Allies: Boeing Co.'s Friends in Some Arab States Helped in Plane Sales," *The Wall Street Journal* (28 June 1978), pp. 1 and 29.

12. Edward G. Harness, Sir Richard Dobson, and Jack F. Bennet, *Determination and Report of the Special Committee on Litigation* (New York: EXXON Corporation, 23 January 1976); William D. Smith, "Exxon's Study of Payoffs in Italy Finds No Basis for Action Against Its Officers," *The New York Times* (31 January 1976), pp. 33 and 37; Robert Smith, "Exxon's Italian Payments Tied to Specific Benefits, *The New York Times* (17 July 1975), p. 1; "Exxon Says Donations in Italy Exceeded $46 Million," *The Wall Street Journal* (17 July 1975); and

William M. Carley, "How Exxon Official Agonized over Making '71 Italian Contribution," *The Wall Street Journal* (14 July 1978), pp. 1 and 27.

13. Robert Lindsey, "A New Chairman for the SEC," *The New York Times* (3 April 1977), p. F7.

14. *The Wall Street Journal* (27 January 1976), p. 8.

15. Jerry Landauer, "Lockheed Chairman Prepares to Confront SEC Over Disclosing Payoff Recipients," *The Wall Street Journal* (17 May 1977), p. 4; "The Lockheed Mystery (Cont'd.)," *Time* (13 September 1976), pp. 31–32; Joel Seligman, "Crime in the Suites," *MBA* (June 1976), pp. 23–31; *SEC v. Lockheed Aircraft Corporation;* Civil No. 76.0611, (D.D.C. filed 13 April 1976).

16. "Singer Panel Finds Dubious Payments," *The New York Times* (5 March 1977), pp. 25–26.

17. See Alvin Shuster, "Post-Lockheed Picture Not At All Clear," *The New York Times* (20 March 1977), p. 2; "The Lockheed Mystery (Cont'd.)," pp. 31–32; "An Aftershock of the Lockheed Affair," *Business Week* (12 April 1976), p. 43; "Japanese Business After Lockheed," *The Economist* (18 September 1976), pp. 88–89; Michael Blaker, "Japan 1976: The Year of Lockheed," *Asian Survey* **17** (January 1977), pp. 81–90; "Payoffs: The Growing Scandal," *Newsweek* (23 February 1976), pp. 26–33; Paul Kemezis and Richard Halloran, "Disclosures by Lockheed Shake Dutch and Japanese," *The New York Times* (7 February 1976), pp. 1, 8 and 9; "Italian Panel Urges 2 Ex-Aides be Tried in Lockheed Scandal," *The New York Times* (30 January 1977), pp. 1 and 4; Alvin Shuster, "Italian Government Faces Threat From the Lockheed Bribe Case," *The New York Times* (3 March 1977), p. 2; Alvin Shuster, "2 Former Italian Defense Chiefs to Stand Trial in Lockheed Case," *The New York Times* (11 March 1977), p. 6; "Scandal on Lockheed Shakes Germany, Too," *The New York Times* (12 September 1976), p. 14; and "Bonn Socialists Pressing Investigation into Charges Linking Foes to Lockheed," *The New York Times* (30 September 1976), p. 2.

18. Gunnar Myrdal, *Asian Drama* (New York: The Twentieth Century Fund, 1968). See also Geoffrey B. Shields, "The Cumshaw Pot," *Harvard Magazine* **78** (June 1976), pp. 27–31; and Juan de Onis, "Scandal and Arrests Embroil Argentina," *The New York Times* (15 May 1977), p. 17.

19. Business International Corporation. *BI Public Policy Study, Questionable Corporate Payments Abroad: Patterns, Policies, Solutions* (New York: Business International Corporation, October 1976). For some contradictory evidence, however, see Vasil Pappas, "Payoff Aftermath: Crackdown on Bribery Hasn't Damaged Sales, Big Companies Report," *The Wall Street Journal* (28 February 1977), pp. 1 and 8.

20. U.S. Congress, Senate, Committee on Banking Housing and Urban Affairs, *Hearings, Foreign and Corporate Bribes*, 94th Congress, 2nd Session (1976), pp. 41–42. See also Leonard Silk, "To Bribe or Bribe Not," *The New York Times* (26 October 1976), p. 39.

21. "Beware of Koreans Bearing Gifts," *The Economist* (27 November 1976), pp. 49–50; William Robbins, "A Korean Lobbyist With Global Links," *The New York Times* (17 November 1976), p. A18; and Anthony Marro, "The Korean Probes Are Still Very Much Alive," *The New York Times* (10 April 1977), p. E 4.

22. Nicholas M. Horrock, "Gulf Oil Disputes Korean's Claim It Pays Him $1 Million a Month," *The New York Times* (3 November 1976), pp. 45 and 47.

23. Walter Guzzardi, Jr., "An Unscandalized View on Those 'Bribes' Abroad," *Fortune* (July 1976), p. 180.

24. For criticism of the SEC disclosure program see Gordon Adams and Sherri Zann Rosenthal, *The Invisible Hand: Questionable Corporate Payments Overseas* (New York: Council on Economic Priorities, 1976).

25. Robert M. Smith, "Tenneco Reports 'Sensitive' Gifts in U.S. and Abroad," *The New York Times* (15 February 1976), pp. 1 and 34; and "Payments Suit Settled," *Chemical Week* (25 February 1976), p. 14.

26. "Sterling Drug Payments," *The Wall Street Journal* (10 March 1976), p. 4.

27. *London Financial Times* (26 March 1976), as quoted in U.S. Senate, *Hearings, Foreign and Corporate Bribes*, p. 57.

28. Ann Crittenden, "Business Bribes Abroad: A Deeply Etched Pattern," *The New York Times* (20 December 1976), pp. D1 and 3. For an opposing view see Brendan Jones, "Middle East Deals: Bribery Held Pointless," *The New York Times* (9 September 1975), pp. 53 and 58.

29. Joseph S. Nye, "Corruption and Political Development: A Cost-Benefit Analysis," *The American Political Science Review* 61 (No. 2, 1967), p. 427.

30. James C. Scott, "An Essay on the Political Functions of Corruption," *Asian Studies* 5 (No. 3, 1967), pp. 501–523. Reprinted in Claude E. Welch, Jr., ed. *Political Modernization*, 2nd edition (Belmont, California: Duxbury Press, 1971), p. 315. See also James C. Scott, *Comparative Political Corruption* (Englewood Cliffs, N.J.: Prentice-Hall, 1972).

31. Robert D. Hershey, "Imperial Chemical Admits to Paying Questionable Fees," *The New York Times* (9 September 1976), p. 57.

32. Niccolo Machiavelli, *The Discourses,* cited in Richard Halloran, "Influence Peddling, a Global Industry," *The New York Times* (14 November 1976), Section 4, p. 1.

33. Luigi Barzini, *The Italians* (New York: Grosset & Dunlap, 1964). See also Felix Kessler, "Bribery of Politicos is Routine in Italian Business; It Brings Results, and, Now, A Crackdown of Sorts," *The Wall Street Journal* (4 April 1972), p. 34.

34. Theodore C. Sorenson, "Improper Payments Abroad: Perspectives and Proposals," *Foreign Affairs* 54 (July 1976), p. 720.

35. Michael C. Jensen, "Gulf: Its Troubles Get Deeper," *The New York Times* (4 January 1976), pp. 1 and 11; McCloy, Pearson, and Matthews, *The Great Oil Spill;* "The Big Payoff," *Time* (23 February 1976), pp. 6–11; "Lockheed's Iceberg," *The Economist* (24 February 1976), pp. 13–14; "Holland's Crown Jewel," *The Economist* (4 September 1976), p. 15; "Dutch Officials Name Bernhard in Bribery Case," *The New York Times* (9 February 1976), p. 1; Alvin Shuster, "Rome Aide Denies Link to Lockheed," *The New York Times* (15 February 1976), p. 1; and Alvin Shuster, "Post-Lockheed Picture Not at All Clear," *The New York Times*, (20 March 1977), p. 2.

36. Raymond D. Gastil, "The Comparative Survey of Freedom—IX," *Freedom at Issue*, No. 49 (January–February 1979), pp. 1–14.

37. Edward T. Hall, *Beyond Culture* (Garden City, N.Y.: Anchor Books, 1977). Also his *The Silent Language* (Garden City, N.Y.: Doubleday, 1959) and *The Hidden Dimension* (Garden City, N.Y.: Doubleday, 1966).

38. Hall, *Beyond Culture*, p. 127. Raymond Vernon argues in correspondence that the cultural issue is substantially more complex than this: "I've seen some exceedingly persuasive stories which suggest that foreigners got into the QP problem in Thailand by misinterpreting some subtle indigenous practices—practices that required persons of lesser rank to buy the attention of those of higher rank as a matter of hierarchical practice. My interpretation of mordida in Mexico follows similarly complex lines of explanation, lines that carry one back to the concept of the absolute monarchy and the rights of its agents."

39. See: "Japanese Business After Lockheed," *The Economist* (18 September 1976), pp. 88–89; Karl Dixon, "Japan's Lockheed Scandal: Structural Corruption," *Pacific Community* 8 (January 1977); Richard Halloran, "Lockheed's Operation in the Tight-Knit World of Japanese Politics," *International Herald Tribune* (8 March 1976), p. 6; and Howard F. Van Zandt, "Learning to do Business with Japan, Inc.," *Harvard Business Review* 50 (July–August 1972), pp. 83–92.

40. "Chief Auditor in Canada Questions Use of Funds to Promote Atom Sales," *The New York Times* (24 November 1976), p. 2; "Canadian Government Again Involved in Case on Foreign Payments," *Wall Street Journal* (29 November 1976), p. 14; "Foreign Payoffs," *Business Week* (13 December 1976), p. 38; Robert Trumbull, "Canada's Parliament Opens Inquiry on Payments to Aid Reactor Sales," *The New York Times* (3 December 1976), p. A16; and Robert Trumbull, "Canada Acts to Bar Illegal Deals by Agencies Abroad," *The New York Times* (18 December 1976), p. 3.

41. "Italy Said to Probe BP, Shell Political Fund," *International Herald Tribune* (12 April 1976), p. 1; "Payments Continued," *Chemical Week* (21 April 1976), p. 24; and "Italian Oil Scandal: Big Deal," *The Economist* (17 April 1976), p. 86.

42. Clyde H. Farnsworth, "The Scandal in Dassault's Missing Dossier," *The New York Times* (26 September 1976), Section 3, pp. 1 and 5; "The Prince and the Probers," *The Economist* (14 February 1976), p. 52; "Colombia Sets Inquiry," *The New York Times* (21 February 1976), p. 36.

43. Egan, "Global Payoff Survey," *Washington Post* (22 June 1976), p. 1.

44. Richard Halloran, "Influence Peddling, A Global Industry," *The New York Times* (14 November 1976), Section 4, p. 1; and Jerry Landauer "U.S. Business Made Payments in Korea, Helped Reelect Park, House Panel Alleges," *The Wall Street Journal* (2 November 1978), p. 7.

45. Business International Corporation, *BI Public Policy Study.*

46. "Bribes and Payoffs—The U.S. Congress Reaches Out Its Long Arm," *Multinational Business* No. 4 (December 1975), pp. 31–37; and Jerry Landauer, "Documents on Textron's Iran Link Show U.S. Officials Arguiesced in Such Payoffs, "*The Wall Street Journal* (17 February 1978), p. 6.

47. For a thorough discussion of the mercantilist view see Robert Gilpin, *U.S. Power and the Multinational Corporation* (New York: Basic Books, 1975).

48. Seymour Melman, *Pentagon Capitalism: The Political Economy of War,* 1st edition (New York: McGraw-Hill, 1970).

49. Charles Mohr, "U.S. Tries to Minimize the Impact of Report on CIA Aid to Hussein," *The New York Times* (19 February 1977), pp. 1 and 9; Richard Halloran, "Influence Peddling, A Global Industry," *The New York Times* (14 November 1976), Section 4, p. 1; James M. Naughton, "Morality Has Always Had Its Limits in the Spy Business," *The New York Times* (27 February 1977), Section 4, p. 1.

50. Anthony Marro, "CIA Money Flowed, but U.S. Aides Insist It was for Intelligence," *The New York Times* (1 March 1977), p. 8; and Anthony Marro, "CIA Considers Much of Its Money Well Spent," *The New York Times* (6 March 1977), p. E3.

51. S. Prakash Sethi, "The ITT Affair (B): Interference in the Chilean Presidential Elections," pp. 122–178 in his *Up Against the Corporate Wall: Modern Corporations and Social Issues of the Seventies,* 3rd edition (Englewood Cliffs, N.J.: Prentice Hall, 1977).

52. Ann Crittenden, "CIA Said to Have Known in 50's of Lockheed Bribe," *The New York Times.* See also Jerry Landauer, "Lockheed Chairman Prepares to Confront SEC Over Disclosing Payoff Recipients," *The Wall Street Journal* (17 May 1977), p. 4.

53. Jerome Alan Cohen, "Japan's Watergate: Made in USA," *The New York Times Magazine* (21 November 1976), pp. 37 ff.

54. Jerry Landauer, "Proposed Treaty Against Business Bribes Gets Poor Reception Overseas, U.S. Finds," *The Wall Street Journal* (28 March 1977), p. 11.

55. Landauer, "Proposed Treaty Against Business Bribes," p. 11.

56. Nossiter, "A Part of Britain's Third World Business Deals," *Washington Post* (22 February 1976), p. 9, cited in Edward D. Herlihy and Theodore A. Levine, "Corporate Crisis: The Overseas Payment Problem," *Law and Policy in International Business* 8 (No. 3, 1976), p. 565.

57. Jerry Landauer, "Proposed Treaty Against Business Bribes," p. 11.

58. For a discussion of IRS concerns and actions see Edward D. Herlihy and Theodore A. Levine, "Corporate Crisis: The Overseas Payment Problem," *Law and Policy in International Business* 8 (No. 3, 1976), pp. 547–629.

59. Seymour M. Hersh, "Hughes Aircraft Faces Allegation that It Used Bribery in Indonesia," *The New York Times* (25 January 1977), pp. 1 and 14; "Proxmire Investigates Bribery in Indonesia," *The New York Times* (26 January 1977), p. A9; David A. Andelman, "Indonesia Opens Inquiry on Charge of Huge Payoffs," *The New York Times* (4 February 1977), p. A3.

60. See for example the testimony of Bob R. Dorsey, former chairman of Gulf Oil before the U.S. Senate Subcommittee on Multinational Corporations. Reprinted as "Gulf Oil Corporation," pp. 369–397 in John Fayerweather and Ashok Kapoor, *Strategy and Negotiation for the International Corporation* (Cambridge, Mass.: Ballinger, 1976).

61. "Corporate Crime," *The New York Times* (9 September 1975), editorial page; Michael C. Jensen, "Corporate Corruption is Big Business," *The New York Times* (14 September 1975); Robert D. Hershey, Jr., "Special Task Force Will Press Charges in Corporate Bribes," *The New York Times* (14 October 1976), p. 53.

62. See statement of Mr. Sporkin of the SEC in *The Wall Street Journal* (8 April 1976).

63. Robert Lindsey, "A New Chairman for the SEC," *The New York Times* (3 April 1977) p. F7. See also "The Changing Fashion in Company Directors," *Business Week* (14 March 1977), p. 32; and Burt Schorr, "Corporate Directors Scored for Lax Scrutiny of Management's Acts," *The Wall Street Journal* (10 April 1978), pp. 1 and 24.

64. Robert D. Hershey, Jr., "Pullman Payouts Abroad Widened," *The New York Times* (23 October 1976), p. 41.

65. Richard Phalon, "Payments Abroad Reported by Merck," *The New York Times* (18 December 1975), p. 72. See also *SEC Current Report*, Form 8-K, Merck & Co., Commission File No. 1-3305 (December 1975) and *SEC Current Report*, Form 8-K, Merck & Co. (February 1976).

66. Robert D. Hershey, Jr., "Firestone Inquiry Finds Officer Ran $1.16 Million Fund," *The New York Times* (24 December 1976), p. D1.

67. "Price Waterhouse Knew United Brands Paid Bribe but Didn't Require Disclosure," *The Wall Street Journal* (3 December 1976). See also "United Brands Co. Switches to Arthur Young as Auditor," *The Wall Street Journal* (6 May 1977), p. 40.

68. "Why Everybody's Jumping on the Accountants These Days," *Forbes* (15 March 1977), p. 43.

69. "Should CPAs be Management Consultants," *Business Week* (18 April 1977), p. 70.

70. Adams and Rosenthal, *The Invisible Hand:*

71. Business International Corporation, *BI Public Policy Study;* and U.S. Securities and Exchange Commission. *Report of the Securities and Exchange Commission on Questionable and Illegal Corporate Payments and Practices*, submitted to the Senate Banking, Housing and Urban Affairs Committee (12 May 1976).

72. Nehemkis, "Business Payoffs Abroad," pp. 5–20.

73. "They Paid and Paid," *Chemical Week* (21 July 1976), p. 17; Robert D. Hershey, Jr., "Alcoa Asserts a U.S. Envoy Solicited Payment Abroad," *The New York Times*, (15 July 1976), p. 11.

74. "Uniroyal Enjoined From Future Illegal Overseas Payments," *The Wall Street Journal* (28 January 1977), p. 2. See also Robert D. Hershey, Jr., "SEC Sues General Tire; Company Agrees to Settle," *The New York Times* (11 May 1976), pp. 45 and 52; "SEC Charges Supported by General Tire's Inquiry," *The New York Times* (16 October 1976), p. 35.

75. Robert M. Smith, "Haughton Expects U.S. Curbs on Payments," *The New York Times* (3 September 1976), pp. 53 and 56.

76. See for example Business International Corporation, *BI Public Policy Study.*

77. "SEC Complaint Says General Telephone Made a Questionable Payment in Iran," *The Wall Street Journal* (28 January 1977), pp. 2 and 22; "Cargill Inc. Discloses 'Unusual Payments' of About $5 Million," *The Wall Street Journal* (18 March 1977), p. 26; Pranary Gupte, "Grumman's 'Fees' to Iran Beg Questions," *The New York Times* (23 February 1976), pp. 37–38; "All in the Normal Course of Selling Aeroplanes," *The Economist* (24 January 1976), pp. 87–88; Thomas W. Lippman, "Ex-Aide of Egyptair Accused of Taking Boeing Kickbacks," *International Herald Tribune* (26 January 1977), p. 2; Seymour M. Hersh, "Jets for Iran: Did Grumman Influence U.S.?," *The New York Times* (18 September 1976), p. 26; Robert M. Smith, "Lockheed Documents Disclose a $106-Million Saudi Payout," *The New York Times* (13 September 1975), p. 31; Ron Cooper, "Clearing Payoff Storm, Northrop Chief Keeps Firm Hand on Controls," *The Wall Street Journal* (15 December 1976), pp. 1 and 31; and Barry Kramer, "Marcos Sets Review of Philippine Award for Nuclear Power Plant Westinghouse Builds," *The Wall Street Journal* (16 January 1978), p. 10.

78. For a listing of drug firms making QPs see Adams and Rosenthal, *The Invisible Hand*. See also Clare M. Reckert, "Cyanamid Role Cited," *The New York Times* (6 March 1976), p. 31; Robert D. Hershey, Jr., "Revlon Admits Big Payments Overseas," *The New York Times* (5 October 1976), p. 67; "Syntex Says $259,000 in Dubious Payments Made by Foreign Units," *The Wall Street Journal* (17 November 1976), p. 48; "Questionable Payments Made by Carter-Wallace," *The New York Times* (16 November 1976), p. 66; "Searle Concedes Bribe Payments," *The New York Times* (10 January 1976), pp. 31 and 36; and "Abbott Labs Paid $500,000 Abroad," *The New York Times* (10 March 1976), pp. 53 and 59.

79. Robert D. Hershey, Jr., "R.J. Reynolds Tells SEC of Payments," *The New York Times* (11 September 1976), pp. 1 and 28; "Philip Morris Says Investigation Showed 'Questionable' Payments," *The New York Times* (16 December 1976), p. 86; "Liggett Discloses Dubious Payments of About $182,000," *The Wall Street Journal* (26 November 1976), p. 6.

80. "Pepsi Co. Investigation Discloses $1.7 Million in Dubious Payments," *The Wall Street Journal* (13 December 1976), p. 8; "Coca-Cola Payments," *The New York Times* (9 October 1976), p. 31; "Coca-Cola Co. Doubles Dubious Payments Total," *The Wall Street Journal*, (6 December 1976), p. 28; "Coca-Cola Again Raises Dubious-Payments Total," *The Wall Street Journal* (4

April 1977), p. 15; and "Coca-Cola Gives Details of Questionable Payments That Totaled $1.3 Million, *The New York Times* (11 August 1977), p. D9.

81. U.S. Congress, Senate, Committee on Banking, Housing and Urban Affairs, *Hearings Prohibiting Bribes to Foreign Officials,* 94th Congress, 2nd Session, (1976), p. 4.

82. Eric Hoffer, *The Passionate State of Mind, and Other Aphorisms,* 1st edition (New York: Harper, 1955), p. 41.

83. See Adams and Rosenthal, *The Invisible Hand.* See also "Control Data Concedes Questionable Payments," *The New York Times* (9 October 1976), p. 31; "Memorex Lists Payments of $504,000 Made Abroad," *The New York Times* (2 October 1976), p. 37; "NCR Cites Deals Abroad," *The New York Times* (2 March 1977), pp. 43 and 47; Michael C. Jensen, "Payments Abroad Disclosed by SCM," (5 May 1976), pp. 59 and 63; "Xerox Notes Improper Payments of $375,000 in 7 Foreign Nations," *The New York Times* (14 May 1977), p. 29; and "Sperry Rand Reports Some Disbursements Were Foreign Payoffs," *The Wall Street Journal* (13 June 1979), p. 3.

84. *The Washington Post* (29 August 1975), p. 6. cited in Edward D. Herlihy and Theodore A. Levine, "Corporate Crisis: The Overseas Payment Problem," *Law and Policy in International Business* 8 (No. 3, 1976), p. 568.

85. "Dow Chemical Finds Dubious Payments of Some $3.1 Million," *The Wall Street Journal* (28 March 1977), p. 11.

86. "SEC Is Investigating Dow Chemical Reports on Dubious Payments," *The Wall Street Journal* (26 April 1977), p. 3.

87. Vasil Pappas, "Payoff Aftermath: Crackdown on Bribery Hasn't Damaged Sales, Big Companies Report," *The Wall Street Journal* (28 February 1977), pp. 1 and 18.

88. See Burt Schorr, "GTE's Offer of 5 Million Shares Delayed by U.S. Demand for More Payoffs Data," *The Wall Street Journal* (14 December 1976), p. 36; and "New Details on GTE Philippine Payments Disclosed in SEC Suit Against 3 Concerns," *The Wall Street Journal* (13 January 1977), p. 9.

89. Harness, Dobson, and Bennett, *Determination and Report of the Special Committee on Litigation.*

90. James R. Basche, Jr., *Unusual Foreign Payments: A Survey of the Policies and Practices of U.S. Companies* (New York: The Conference Board, 1976). See also Michael C. Jensen, "Many U.S. Executives Reported in Favor of Overseas Bribes," *The New York Times* (13 February 1976), pp. 45 and 49.

91. For some examples see Morton Mintz and Jerry S. Cohen, "Corporate Bribery," pp. 133–155 in their *Power, Inc.: Public and Private Rulers and How to Make Them Accountable* (New York: Viking Press, 1976); Ron Cooper, "Clearing Payoff Storm, Northrop Chief Keeps Firm Hand on Control," *The Wall Street Journal* (15 December 1976), pp. 1 and 31; Steven Rattner, "Conoco Ousts Two in Payments Cases," *The New York Times* (16 December 1976), pp. 77 and 86; "Avis Says Audit Study Discloses $425,000 in Improper Payments," *The New York Times* (10 November 1976), p. D14; Robert D. Hershey, Jr., "Firestone Inquiry Finds Officer Ran $1.16 Million Fund," *The New York Times* (24 December 1976), p. D1; "Gulf Board Approves a Restitution Plan for 6 Past Officers," *The New York Times* (24 September 1976), p. D1; and Judith Miller, "Study of Questionable Payments Accents Involvement of Officers," *The New York Times* (25 February 1978), pp. 27 and 29.

92. Anthony Sampson, "Lockheed's Foreign Policy: Who, in the End, Corrupted Whom?" *New York Magazine* (15 March 1976), p. 56 (quoted in Joel Seligman, "Crime in the Suites," *MBA* (June 1976), p. 31). See also David Boulton, *The Grease Machine* (New York: Harper & Row, 1979).

93. Robert D. Hershey, Jr., "SEC Charges Indonesia Oil Chief in Shakedown by Big U.S. Concerns," *The New York Times* (3 February 1977), pp. 1 and 35; "Indonesia Oil Company May Close Restaurant," *The New York Times* (6 February 1977), p. 5; "Ex-Pertamina Head, Other Former Aides Placed Under Arrest," *The Wall Street Journal* (28 February 1977), p. 15. Raymond Vernon suggests that the opposite argument might be made just as easily. That is, in view of the very limited information available on this subject, one could make the case that MNEs have greater defensive capabilities than similarly situated local firms.

94. Robert Lindsey, "SEC Documents Charge Occidental With Secret Deals," *The New York*

Times (4 May 1977), pp. D1 and 15 and "SEC Ties Occidental Petroleum Corp to Illegal Payments," *The Wall Street Journal* (4 May 1977), p. 17.

95. "The Cautionary Tale of Gulf Oil," *Multinational Business* (March 1976), pp. 43–44.

96. Priscilla S. Meyer, "Audit Aftermath: Avis's Payoff Inquiry Has a Lingering Effect as Questions Remain," *The Wall Street Journal* (15 March 1977), pp. 1 and 37; and "Avis Inc. Discloses $470,958 Payment Studied by the SEC," *The Wall Street Journal* (3 May 1977), p. 38.

97. "Ford Crusades Against Corruption Abroad," *Multinational Business* (June 1976), pp. 37–38.

98. "Corporate Corruption: What's to be Done?," *The Economist* (3 April 1976), pp. 38–39. See also "Bribery: Pure but Not too Pure," *The Economist* (22 May 1976), p. 105.

99. Frederick Andrews, "Management: Wall Street Winks at Bribery Cases," *The New York Times* (12 November 1976), p. D5.

100. See for example The Association of the Bar of the City of New York (Ad Hoc Committee on Foreign Payments), *Report on Questionable Foreign Payments by Corporations: The Problem and Approaches to a Solution* (14 March 1977); Commission on Ethical Practices, International Chamber of Commerce, "Ethical Practices in Commercial Transactions" (Report submitted by the Commission to the 7th Session of the Executive Board of the ICC, Document No. 192/36); and "Most Firms in Study Say They Practice U.S. Ethics Abroad," *The Wall Street Journal* (5 May 1977), p. 44.

101. Michael C. Jensen, "Bribery Dilemma Grows," *The New York Times* (25 January 1976), pp. 44–45.

102. Jensen, "Bribery Dilemma Grows," pp. 44–45.

103. "Swiss Banking Secrecy: Candu and Can't," *The Economist* (19 March 1977), p. 94.

104. Jensen, "Bribery Dilemma Grows," pp. 44–45.

105. Eric Pace, "Iranian Assails Unethical Foreign Concerns," *The New York Times* (3 March 1976), pp. 43 and 48.

106. "All in the Normal Course of Selling Aeroplanes," *The Economist* (24 January 1976), pp. 87–88; and Eric Pace, "Northrop Rebate Reported in Iran as an Atonement," *The New York Times* (23 February 1976), pp. 1 and 36.

107. Louis D. Brandeis, *Other People's Money* (New York: Frederick A. Stokes, 1914), p. 92.

108. Robert D. Hershey, Jr., "Files by SEC Show Slush Funds in Use Decades Before Watergate," *The New York Times* (18 May 1977), pp. 1 and D16; Michael C. Jensen, "Reporters Rush for 28 Cartons of Political Payments Data," *The New York Times* (18 May 1977), p. D16; Robert D. Hershey, Jr., "SEC to Open Files on Bribery at Corporations," *The New York Times* (30 April 1977), p. 29. See also James M. Naughton, "The New American Information Revolution," *The New York Times* (10 April 1977), p. E4; "SEC Proposal Seeks to Inform Holders of Dubious Payments," *The New York Times* (20 January 1977), p. 17; Robert D. Hershey, Jr., "SEC in Effect Ends Its Lenient Program on Illicit Payments," *The New York Times* (7 March 1977), p. 39; Jerry Landauer, "Lockheed Chairman Prepares to Confront SEC Over Disclosing Payoff Recipients," *The Wall Street Journal* (17 May 1977), p. 4.

109. "A Tough Bribery Probe?" *Time* (12 April 1976), pp. 71–72. See S. 3741 and H.R. 15149, bills developed by the Task Force and entitled "Foreign Payments Disclosure Act." These bills were not considered as such in hearings in either the Senate or House in the 94th Congress.

110. Robert J. Cole, "IRS to Require Companies to Answer 11 Bribe Questions," *The New York Times* (8 April 1976), p. 60; and Sanford L. Jacobs, "Eleven Questions Get Results, Stir Company Ire," *The Wall Street Journal* (25 April 1977), p. 18.

111. "Statement of Theodore C. Sorenson before The House of Representatives Interstate and Foreign Commerce Committee, Subcommittee on Consumer Protection and Finance," (21 September 1976), p. 5.

112. Jerry Landauer, "State Department May Help Boeing Keep 'Consultants' Secret in Payoffs Inquiry," *The Wall Street Journal* (28 December 1976), p. 4.

113. Ralph Nader, Mark Green, and Joel Seligman, *Taming the Giant Corporation* (New York: W.W. Norton & Co., 1976); Frederick Andrews, "Management: The First Draft of a New Constitution For Corporations," *The New York Times* (22 April 1977), pp. D1 and 3; Elizabeth M. Fowler, "Management: Defining Role of a Corporate Director," *The New York Times* (25

March 1977), p. D3; and "The Changing Fashion in Company Directors," *Business Week* (14 March 1977), p. 32.

114. "Official of SEC Urges Corporate Post on Ethics," *The Wall Street Journal* (17 March 1977), p. 25; "The SEC Focuses on Executive 'Perks'," *Business Week* (18 April 1977), p. 52 and 54; and "SEC Enforcement Aide Asks Laws to Rectify Some Corporate Abuse," *The Wall Street Journal* (5 May 1977), p. 3.

115. See "Internal Reforms by Accountants Urged as Senate Hearings Open; Bill Not Likely," *The Wall Street Journal* (20 April 1977), p. 18; "Should CPAs be Management Consultants," *Business Week* (18 April 1977), pp. 70–73; "CPAs Suggest the Watchdogs They Want," *Business Week* (23 May 1977), pp. 94–96; and Joshua Ronen, "Who Should Audit the Auditors?" *The New York Times* (8 May 1977), p. 14.

116. Robert D. Hershey, Jr., "Wider Auditor Role in Company Affairs to be Advocated," *The New York Times* (9 March 1977), pp. D1 and 11; and "A Sharper Definition of the Auditor's Job," *Business Week* (28 March 1977), pp. 55–56.

117. U.S. Congress, Senate Committee on Banking, Housing and Urban Affairs, S. 305 Report No. 95-114: "Foreign Corrupt Practices and Domestic and Foreign Investment Disclosure Acts of 1977," 95th Congress, 1st Session (introduced by Senator Proxmire on 18 January 1977). See also "Senate Unit Clears Bill Outlawing Bribery Abroad and Setting Fines Up to $500,000," *The Wall Street Journal* (7 April 1977), p. 3; and "Senate Approves Bill Making Foreign Bribes by U.S. Firms a Crime," *The Wall Street Journal* (6 May 1977), p. 13.

118. U.S. Congress, House of Representatives, H.R. 3815, "Unlawful Corporate Payments Act of 1977," 95th Congress, 1st Session (introduced by Representative Eckhardt on 22 February 1977).

119. "Blumenthal Backs Corporate Bribe Ban, Discloses Probe of 8 Multinational Firms," *The Wall Street Journal* (17 March 1977), p. 2.

120. Public Law 95-213, "Foreign Corrupt Practices Act of 1977," passed and signed into law as an amendment to the Securities Exchange Act of 1934. See also Hurd Baruch, "The Foreign Corrupt Practices Act," *Harvard Business Review* (January–February 1979), pp. 32–50.

121. Business International Corporation, *BI Public Policy Study*.

122. *The Wall Street Journal* (9 July 1976), cited in Richard L. Barovick, "The SEC Unleashes a Foreign Payoffs Storm," *Business and Society Review* (Fall 1976), p. 49.

123. Leonard Silk, "To Bribe or Bribe Not," *The New York Times* (26 October 1976), p. 39.

124. Jerry Landauer, "SEC Suit Against International Systems for Millions in Payoffs Readied," *The Wall Street Journal* (26 June 1979), p. 6; Philip Taubman, "U.S. Seen Clarifying Bribery Law," *The New York Times* (28 May 1979), pp. D1 and 6; and Jerry Landauer, "Antibribery Law Uncertainties Persist, Despite President's Call for Clarification," *The Wall Street Journal* (30 May 1979), p. 12.

125. Organization for Economic Cooperation and Development, *International Investment and Multinational Enterprises: Guidelines for Multinational Enterprises* (Paris: OECD, 1976), p. 14.

126. Jerry Landauer, "Proposed Treaty Against Business Bribes Gets Poor Reception Overseas, U.S. Finds," *The Wall Street Journal* (28 March 1977), p. 11.

127. Landauer, "Proposed Treaty Against Business Bribes," p. 11.

128. Statement of Mark B. Feldman before the U.N. ECOSOC Intergovernmental Working Group on Corrupt Practices (15 November 1976), *The Department of State Bulletin*, **75** (1976), pp. 696–698.

129. The Association of the Bar of the City of New York, *Report on Questionable Foreign Payments*. See also Robert J. Cole, "City Bar Opposing a U.S. Law to Ban Payments Abroad," *The New York Times* (14 March 1977), pp. 43 and 45.

130. "Blumenthal Backs Corporate Bribe Ban, Discloses Probe of 8 Multinational Firms," *The Wall Street Journal* (7 March 1977), p. 2.

131. Landauer, "Proposed Treaty Against Business Bribes," p. 11.

132. "Corruption is Bad," *The Economist* (19 March 1977), pp. 88–89. See also "Business Against Bribery," *The Economist* (26 November 1977), p. 86.

133. International Chamber of Commerce, "Extortion and Bribery in Business Transactions," Paris: ICC, 1977.

134. "Corruption is Bad," *The Economist*, pp. 88–89.

135. "How Companies React to the Ethics Crisis," *Business Week* (9 February 1976), pp. 78–79; and "CPI Firms Tackle 'Payments' Problem," *Chemical Week* (19 May 1976), pp. 20–21.

136. See Myles L. Mace, ed. "John J. McCloy on Corporate Payoffs," *Harvard Business Review* 54 (July–August 1976), pp. 14 ff.; and Byron E. Calame, "At Gulf Oil Nowadays, a 'Questionable' Deal is One to be Shunned," *The Wall Street Journal* (25 January 1977), pp. 1 and 37. See also Christopher D. Stone, *Where the Law Ends: The Social Control of Corporate Behavior* (New York: Harper & Row, 1975).

137. See "Government Complicity in Payments?" *The Wall Street Journal* (17 October 1978), p. 26; and David Ignatius, "Foreign-Bribery Trials May Show U.S. Knew of Some Payments," *The Wall Street Journal* (5 October 1978), pp. 1 and 32.

138. See "The Antibribery Bill Backfires," *Business Week* (17 April 1978), p. 143; John S. Estey and David W. Marston, "Pitfalls (and Loopholes) in the Foreign Bribery Law," *Fortune* (9 October 1978), pp. 182–188; and Hurd Baruch, "The Foreign Corrupt Practices Act," *Harvard Business Review* (January–February 1979), pp. 32–50.

139. See Paul Lewis, "European Businessmen Don't Take Their Morality So Seriously," *The New York Times* (5 March 1978), p. E2; David Ignatius, "Some U.S. Firms Are Still Paying Bribes Overseas, Despite Law, Investigators Say," *The Wall Street Journal* (21 July 1978), p. 4; and Burt Schorr, "Questionable Payments Drive Stimulates Competition, Tough Internal Controls," *The Wall Street Journal* (23 June 1978), p. 34.

140. "How AMF Got Burned on Payoffs," *Fortune* (9 April 1979), p. 82.

141. See "U.S. Firms Say '77 Ban on Foreign Payoffs Hurts Overseas Sales," *The Wall Street Journal* (2 August 1979), pp. 1 and 19.

142. "Business Without Bribes," *Newsweek* (19 February 1979), pp. 63–64.

143. Fox Butterfield, "U.S. Law Against Bribes Blamed for Millions in Lost Sales in Asia," *The New York Times* (26 June 1978), p. D1 and 10.

144. "U.S. Firms Say '77 Ban on Foreign Payoffs Hurt Overseas Sales," pp. 1 and 19.

145. Burt Schorr, "ITT Says Possible SEC Suit May Prompt Foreign Takeover Order for Some Units," *The New York Times* (27 March 1978), p. 3; and "Supreme Court Clears Way for Release of SEC Complaint Alleging ITT Payoffs," *The Wall Street Journal* (31 October 1978), p. 5.

146. "Control Data Corp. Penalized $1,381,000 After Pleading Guity to Foreign Bribe," *The Wall Street Journal* (27 April 1978), p. 17.

147. "Boeing's Accord with SEC on $52 Million in Payoffs Keeps Some Key Details Secret," *The Wall Street Journal* (31 July 1978), p. 4.

148. "How Firms Can Minimize Their Vulnerability to U.S. Corrupt Practices Law," *Business International* (17 November 1978), pp. 362–364.

CHAPTER 10

1. "Profits in Pills," *The Economist* (5 June 1976), pp. 62–63; "Drug Law Reforms Proliferate in Congress," *Chemical and Engineering News* (4 June 1979), p. 22; and "Europe's Drugmakers Open Attack on Price Controls," *Chemical Week* (16 May 1979), pp. 33–34.

2. Robert J. Ledogar, *Hungry for Profits* (New York: IDOC/North America, 1975).

3. Robert M. Smith, "Multinational Drug Firms Assailed for Sales Techniques," *The New York Times* (17 August 1975), p. 3.

4. Lawrence K. Altman, "The Drugs in Developing Countries Now Cause Worry," *The New York Times* (12 March 1978), p. E7; and "WHO, Third World Take on Global Drug Firms," *The Interdependent* 5 (November 1978), p. 6.

5. Quoted in Jonathan Kandell, "Drug Marketers Stir Bitter Debate in Brazil," *The New York Times* (14 November 1976), p. L3.

6. Mike Muller, "Selling Health—Or Buying Favor?," *New Scientist* (3 February 1977), p. 266.

7. "EEC Drug Price Curbs Harmful," *World Business Weekly* (30 October 1978), p. 12.

8. Burton Marcus, *Modern Marketing* (New York: Random House, 1975), p. 4.

9. Marcus, *Modern Marketing*, p. 4.

10. Philip Kotler, "What Consumerism Means for Marketers," *Harvard Business Review* (May–June 1972), p. 106.

11. Hiram C. Barksdale and Bill Darden, "Attitudes Toward the Marketing Concept," *Journal of Marketing* (October 1971), p. 36.

12. Marcus, et al., *Modern Marketing*, p. 55.

13. Vern Terpstra, *International Marketing* (Hinsdale, Ill.: The Dryden Press, 1978), p. 5. See also Ulrich Wiechmann and Lewis G. Pringle, "Problems That Plague Multinational Marketers," *Harvard Business Review* (July–August 1979), pp. 118–124.

14. Stuart S. Malawar, "International Law, European Community Law and the Rule of Reason," *Journal of World Trade Law* (January–February 1974), p. 71.

15. Sidney J. Levy and Gerald Zaltman, *Marketing, Society and Conflict* (Englewood Cliffs: Prentice Hall, Inc., 1975), p. 113.

16. Kotler, "What Consumerism Means for Marketers," p. 48.

17. Peter Drucker, "Consumerism In Marketing," Speech to National Association of Manufacturers, April 1969.

18. Robert O. Herrmann, "Consumerism: Its Goals, Organization and Future," *Journal of Marketing* (October 1970), p. 56.

19. Kotler, "What Consumerism Means For Marketers," p. 49.

20. Will Straver, "The International Consumer Movement," *European Journal of Marketing* 11 (No. 2, 1977), p. 95.

21. Herrmann, "Consumerism," p. 57.

22. Linda Charlton, "Ralph Nader's Conglomerate Is Big Business," *New York Times* (29 January 1978), p. E3.

23. Straver, "The International Consumer Movement," p. 101.

24. Straver, "The International Consumer Movement," p. 114.

25. Adrien Sapiro and Jacques Lendrevie, "On the Consumer Front in France, Japan, Sweden, U.K., and the U.S.A.," *European Business* (Summer 1973), p. 48.

26. "Big Fight Over How to Protect the Consumer," *U.S. News and World Report* (26 January 1976), p. 40.

27. Straver, "The International Consumer Movement," p. 120.

28. "Europe's Consumer Uprising: It's More Profitable to Surrender, *Vision* (April 1971), p. 19.

29. "Disgruntled Customers Finally Get a Hearing," *Business Week* (21 April 1975), p. 138.

30. "Corporate Clout for Consumers," *Business Week* (12 September 1977), p. 148.

31. "Bess Myerson's Advocacy A Business Matter Now," *The New York Times* (10 June 1977), Sec. 4, p. 1.

32. Ralph M. Gaedeke and Udo Udo-Aka, "Toward the Internalization of Consumerism," *California Management Review* (Fall 1974), p. 87.

33. Ledogar, *Hungry for Profits*, p. 29.

34. "Union Carbide Introduces Scanner for Entire Body," *The Wall Street Journal* (28 June 1978), p. 4.

35. "A Drug Not On the Market," *The Economist* (3 June 1978), p. 93.

36. Stanford N. Sesser, "Many U.S. Companies Sell Products Abroad That Are Barred Here," *The Wall Street Journal* (11 February 1971), p. 17.

37. Richard Martin, "Gillette's Giovaccini Rules on Quality, Safety of 850 Products," *The Wall Street Journal* (2 December 1975), p. 17.

38. "PCB Incident With Fish Meal Still Before FDA," *Feedstuffs* (17 July 1978), p. 1.

39. Iain Carson, "Consumers Try to Tilt the Scales," *Vision* (April 1976), p. 51.

40. Carson, "Consumers Try to Tilt the Scales," p. 50; and "Offering Indemnities," *Chemical Week* (16 August 1978), p. 18.

41. "A Liability Threat to U.S. Bound Exports," *Business Week* (14 March 1977), p. 42.

42. Carson, "Consumers Try to Tilt the Scales," p. 51.

43. "ITT Forms Foundation with Chilean Government to Help Meet Social Goals," *Business Latin America* (22 November 1976), p. 371.

44. Albert R. Karr and Leonard M. Apcar, "Government Pressure Propels Auto Recalls Toward a New High," *The Wall Street Journal* (16 August 1978), p. 1.

45. "Ford Motor Indicted in a Criminal Case over Pinto Accident," *The Wall Street Journal* (14 September 1978), p. 2.

46. Steven E. Permut and James A. Firestone, "Consumer Product Safety in the International Market Place," *Columbia Journal of World Business* (Winter 1977), p. 80.

47. Richard D. Lyons, "FDA is Caught Between Demand for New Goods and Public Safety," *New York Times* (13 March 1977), p. 57

48. Richard D. Lyons, "FDA May Be Ultimate Challenge to Carter's Pledge on Reorganization and Consumer Aid," *The New York Times* (14 March 1977), p. 24.

49. "Bottle Wins Battle," *Chemical Week* (25 June 1975), p. 18.

50. "FDA Reverses Position on Use of Plastic Bottles for Beer and Soft Drinks," *The New York Times* (12 February 1977), p. 29.

51. Victor K. McElheny, "The Dispute Over Plastic Bottles," *The New York Times* (13 April 1977), Sec. 4, p. 1.

52. "FDA Bans on Plastic Coke Bottle May Be Suspended," *Chemical Week* (16 March 1977), p. 18.

53. Victor McElheny, "Plastic Bottles: Where the Bottle Stands," *The New York Times* (9 November 1977), Sec. 4, p. 1.

54. "Sugar Substitutes, Seek Sweet Smell of Success," *Chemical Week* (6 November 1974), p. 37.

55. "Sweetener in Trouble," *Chemical Week* (9 February 1972), p. 12.

56. Richard D. Lyons, "Proposed Saccharin Ban and Its Underlying Logic Prompt National Debate," *The New York Times* (21 March 1977), p. 42.

57. "Saccharin Can Be Sold For Now," *Business Week* (25 April 1977), p. 38.

58. Richard D. Lyons, "Depth and Finesse of Lobbying Against Saccharin Ban Expected to Result in 18-month Delay," *The New York Times* (5 October 1977), p. 18; and Joann S. Lublin, "Saccharin-Ban Moratorium Ends Today, But Sweetener Isn't About to Disappear," *The Wall Street Journal* (23 May 1979), p. 10.

59. "Washington Newsletter," *Chemical Week* (20 October 1971), p. 27.

60. "Washington Newsletter," *Chemical Week* (9 August 1972), p. 10.

61. "Washington Newsletter," *Chemical Week* (27 September 1972), p. 10.

62. "Hormonally Active Substances in Food," *CAST Report #66* (March 1977), p. 33.

63. P.J. Wingate, "Reason to Applaud: FDA Handling of the Nitrite Problem," *The Wall Street Journal* (8 September 1978), p. 14.

64. Lyons, "FDA May Be Ultimate Challenge to Carter's Pledge," p. 24.

65. Paul H. Weaver, "The Hazards of Trying to Make Consumer Products Safer," *Fortune* (July 1975), p. 133.

66. "What the Government Can—and Cannot—Do to Protect the Public. Interview with S. John Byington," *U.S. News and World Report* (24 October 1977), p. 33.

67. Lyons, "FDA May Be Ultimate Challenge to Carter's Pledge," p. 24.

68. "The Urge to Sue—Growing Hazard for Business," *U.S. News and World Report* (23 August 1976), p. 41.

69. Lawrence A. Benningson and Arnold I. Bennigson, "Product Liability; Manufacturers Beware!," *Harvard Business Review* (May–June 1974), p. 122.

70. "Insurers Are Seeking Changes in Coverage for Product Liability," *The Wall Street Journal* (19 January 1978), p. 8.

71. "Alarm Over Liability," *Chemical Week* (2 February 1977), p. 18.

72. "Product Liability: Toward Increasing International Control," *European Report* (23 April 1975), p. 1.

73. J.G. Fleming, "Draft Convention on Products Liability (Council of Europe)," *American Journal of Comparative Law* 23 (1975), pp. 729–737.

74. "Proposal for a Council Directive Relating to the Approximation of the Laws, Regulations, and Administrative Provisions of the Member States Concerning Liability for Defective Products," Commission of the European Community (23 July 1976), p. 4. See also Eric Morgenthaler, "Common Market Nations Likely to Adopt Harsher Product-Liability Codes for Firms," *The Wall Street Journal* (3 March 1977), p. 36.

75. Arlene Blum and Bruce N. Ames, "Flame Retardant Additives as Possible Cancer Hazards," *Science* (7 January 1977), p. 17.

76. "Ban Asked on Children's Sleepwear: Is There a Risk of Cancer?," *The New York Times* (9 February 1977), p. 25.

77. "Flame Retardant Sleepwear: Is There a Risk of Cancer?," *The New York Times* (10 April 1976), p. 32.

78. "Flame Retardant Sleepwear," p. 32.

79. "Flame Retardant Sleepwear," p. 32.

80. Nadine Brozan, "U.S. Bans a Flame Retardant Used in Children's Sleepwear," *The New York Times* (18 April 1977), p. 14.

81. "Around the Nation," *The New York Times* (29 April 1977), p. 14.

82. "Court Orders Chemical Concerns and Stores to Share Tris Burden," *The New York Times* (4 May 1977), Sec. 4, p. 1.

83. "Tris Ban Violation Laid to Woolworth," *The New York Times* (18 May 1977), Sec. 4, p. 2.

84. "Judge May Bar Consumer Unit On Ban Of Tris," *The New York Times* (24 May 1977), p. 47.

85. "Judge Strikes Down Safety Ban on Tris," *The New York Times* (24 June 1977), p. 9.

86. "Banned at Home—But Exported," *Business Week* (12 June 1978), p. 152.

87. Committee on Government Operations, U.S. House of Representatives, *Report on Export of Products Banned by U.S. Regulatory Agencies* (Washington, D.C.: U.S. Government Printing Office, 1978).

88. Philip Knightley, "The Story Nine Judges Banned," *Sunday London Times* (31 July 1977), p. 10. See also The Insight Team of the Sunday Times of London, *Suffer the Children: The Story of Thalidomide* (New York: Viking, 1978).

89. Alvin Schuster, "Better As Is Than Not At All," *The New York Times* (29 April 1973), p. 14.

90. Knightley, "The Story Nine Judges Banned," p. 11.

91. Marcel Berlins, "Britain's Thalidomide Children: A Ten Year Diary," *The London Times* (18 November 1972), p. 14.

92. "The Commons Will Be Watching Very Carefully What Goes On," *The Economist* (2 December 1972), p. 23.

93. "The Thalidomide Affair," *Time* (22 January 1973), p. 26.

94. Marcel Berlins, "£20 M Thalidomide Settlement Approved," *The London Times* (31 July 1973), p. 1.

95. Clyde H. Farnsworth, "Drugs in Europe: Collision of Interest," *The New York Times* (21 March 1976), Sec. 3, p. 1.

96. "Chemical Importers, Managers Get Fines, Jail for Price Fixing," *The Wall Street Journal* (26 September 1975), p. 2.

97. "Aussie Firms in Price Clash with Government," *Business Asia* (19 March 1976), p. 90.

98. "Washington Newsletter," *Chemical Week* (19 February 1975), p. 10 and "Court Allows Suits by Foreign Nations in Antitrust Cases," *The New York Times* (12 January 1978), Sec. 4, p. 1.

99. James Poole, "Both Roche and DTI Need a Tranquilizer," *The Sunday London Times* (1 July 1973), p. 62. See also "A Drug Giant's Pricing Under International Attack," *Business Week* (16 June 1975), pp. 50–56.

100. "Now Look Who Needs Tranquilizers," *The Economist* (14 April 1973), p. 82.

101. Patricia Tisdall, "Roche Ready to Answer 'Excessive' Price Claim," *The London Times* (24 April 1973), p. 15.

102. Malcolm Brown, "Drugs Cut Unfair and Punative Says Firm," *The London Times* (28 April 1973), p. 1.

103. Malcolm Brown, "Swiss Drug Group Refuses to Pay 'Excess' Profits," *The London Times* (28 April 1973), p. 1.

104. Brown, "Swiss Drug Group Refuses to Pay," p. 1.

105. "The Lords and La Roche," *The London Times* (9 June 1973), p. 13.

106. "Oh, Lordy," *The Economist* (2 June 1973), p. 88.

107. "Roche Appeals to Whitehall to Play Fair," *The London Times* (27 June 1973), p. 26.

108. Malcolm Brown, "The Lords Reject New Inquiry On Swiss Drugs," *The London Times* (23 June 1973), p. 1.

109. "MPs Back to the Hilt Possible Injunction On Defiant Drug Firm," *The London Times* (28 June 1973), p. 9.

110. "If You Can't Get Your Librium On the NHS, Try a Drop of Scotch," *The Economist* (30 June 1973), p. 83.

111. "Trouble Ahead for the Drugmakers?," *Dun's Review* (February 1975), p. 66.

112. "Trouble Ahead for the Drugmakers?," p. 66.

113. "Trouble Ahead for the Drugmakers?," p. 66.

114. "Hoffmann-La Roche's Rigid Stance in the U.K. Harms Image of Multinational Firms," *Business Europe* (4 May 1973), p. 289.

115. James Poole, "How Roche Finally Got Its Clean Bill of Health," *The Sunday London Times* (16 November 1975), p. 1.

116. "Roche Case Changes Antitrust Picture," *World Business Weekly* (26 February 1979), p. 59.

117. "German Cartel Office Creates Dilemmas for Japan's Orderly Marketers," *Business Europe* (18 August 1972), p. 264; and "German Trustbusters Zero In On Braun's RPM Scheme," *Business Europe* (2 February 1973), p. 41.

118. "Common Market Trustbuster Is Eager for Action," *The New York Times* (29 January 1973), p. 41.

119. "New EEC Antitrust Regulation Reshape Distribution Agreements," *Business Europe* (28 July 1972), p. 240; and "EEC Court Prepares Final Verdict in Important Dyestuffs Case," *Business Europe* (8 October 1971), p. 363.

120. "European Court of Justice Upholds EEC-Commercial Solvents Ruling," *Business Europe* (15 March 1974), p. 86.

121. "EEC Trustbusters Push Their Legal Power to Intervene," *Business Europe* (10 September 1976), p. 289.

122. Mitsuo Matsushita and Eugene H. Lee, "Antimonopoly Regulation of Marketing," in Robert J. Ballon, ed., *Marketing in Japan* (Tokyo, Sophia Univ., 1974), p. 58–59.

123. "Legal Developments in Marketing," *Journal of Marketing* (July 1975), p. 87.

124. "Sweden Adopts EEC Ruling on Restrictive Practices," *Business Europe* (19 October 1973), p. 336.

125. "Brazil's First Antitrust Ruling," *Business Latin America* (9 October 1974), p. 324.

126. "Brazil's First Antitrust Ruling," p. 324.

127. Susanne Brun, "Antitrust Policy in Europe: The Emergence of Strict Enforcement?," *Journal of World Trade Law* (September–October 1974), p. 479.

129. Matsushita and Lee, "Antimonopoly Regulation of Marketing."

129. Matsushita and Lee, "Antimonopoly Regulation of Marketing," p. 67.

130. Samuel J. Pisar, "Crossroads for the Multinationals," *The Wall Street Journal* (26 June 1974), p. 18.

131. Robert T. Jones, "Executive's Guide to Antitrust in Europe," *Harvard Business Review* (May–June 1976), p. 106.

132. "Advertising for Trouble," *Business Week* (20 March 1978), p. 63.

133. "International Outlook," *Business Week* (14 April 1973), p. 44.

134. "How Levi's Cracked a Ring of Counterfeiters," *Business Week* (5 September 1977), p. 27; and "They Join Forces to Keep Copycats from Cashing In," *Chemical Week* (11 October 1978), pp. 35–36.

135. "German Courts Strictly Define Truth in Advertising," *Business Europe* (11 August 1972), pp. 251–252.

136. "Matsushita, FTC Staff Agree to Settle Charge Against Misleading Ads," *The Wall Street Journal* (27 May 1976), p. 3.

137. "Aggressive Advertising Can Generate Market Shares and Litigation Costs," *Business Europe* (3 December 1976), p. 389.

138. "French Court Fines Unit of General Foods on Ads," *The Wall Street Journal* (19 May 1978), p. 8.

139. Burt Schorr, "FTC Wants Anheuser-Busch and Miller to Settle Conflict Through Advertising," *The Wall Street Journal* (21 July 1978), p. 10. See also Bill Abrams and David P. Garino, "War Between Miller and Anheuser-Busch Stays Hot, Worrying Other Beer Makers," *The Wall Street Journal* (14 March 1979), p. 48.

140. "Coming: A New Era in Multinational Marketing," *Grey Matter* 48 (No. 3, 1977), p. 3.

141. "Coming: A New Era in Multinational Marketing," pp. 1–3.

142. "Venezuelan Advertising Bill Would Further Restrict Firm's Operating Freedom," *Business Latin America* (25 February 1976), p. 63.

143. Daniel Yergin, "France's Tough Energy Program Puts the Heat on the Admen," *Fortune* (17 July 1978), p. 106.

144. "European Advertising: Self-Regulation is the Trend," *Business Europe* (12 November 1976), p. 366.

145. "Not Persuaded," *Economist* (18 March 1978), p. 56–57; and Candare Denning, "Consumer Reports, EC Style," *European Community* (November–December 1978), pp. 44–45.

146. Thomas G. Krattenmaker, "The Federal Trade Commission and Consumer Protection," *California Management Review* (Summer 1976), p. 94.

147. Donald Dunn, "If the Product is the Problem Do You Censor the Ad?," *Business Week* (3 April 1978), p. 90; and "Curbs on TV Ads to Kids Are Opposed by Congress," *The Wall Street Journal* (14 September 1978), p. 37.

148. "Industry Fights Back: The Debate Over Advocacy Advertising," *Saturday Review* (21 January 1978), pp. 20–24.

149. Francesco M. Nicosia, "Industry Viewpoint in Advertising," *California Management Review* (Winter 1974), p. 9.

150. From "Documentation for the Press," (Berne: Nestlé Alimentana S.A., June 1976).

151. From "Songsheet for the Nestlé Boycott Campaign," *Infant Formula Action Packet* (April 1978).

152. "PAG Recommendations for the Promotion of Processed Infant Food for Vulnerable Groups" (PAG Statement #23), *PAG Bulletin*, 2 (28 November 1973).

153. Mike Muller, *The Baby Killer* (London: War on Want, 1974).

154. Ledogar, *Hungry for profits*.

155. Dr. A. Furer, "Nestlé and Baby Food in the Third World," (Nestlé Press Release 1975), p. 3.

156. "Libel Proceedings Nestlé Alimentana Against Arbeitsgruppe Dritte Welt," (Nestlé Press Release, June 1976).

157. "SAFEP Press Release #1," (November 1974), p. 7.

158. "Nestlé Wins Libel Suit on Third World Pamphlet," *The New York Times* (25 June 1976), Sec. 4, p. 7.

159. Letter from A. Furer to All Nestlé Staff (2 July 1976), p. 2.

160. James E. Post, "Strategy and Orientation of Patterns of Corporate Response to Social Conflict," (Boston University School of Management Working Paper, 1977), p. 11.

161. "The Story So Far," *New Internationalist*, April 1977.

162. Post, "Strategy and Orientation of Patterns of Corporate Response," pp. 15–16.

163. Discussed in *The Corporate Examiner* 5 (No. 2, February 1976), p. 1.

164. Ann Crittenden, "Infant Formula at Issue," *The New York Times* (3 April 1977), Sec. 3, p. 15.

165. See discussion in *The Corporate Examiner* 6 (No. 3, March 1977), p. 1.

166. "Sisters Appeal Bristol Meyers Decision," *INFACT* (August 1977), p. 2.

167. Robert Ball, "Nestle Revs Up Its U.S. Campaign," *Fortune* (13 February 1978), p. 80.

168. "News From Chapters and Friends," *CALC Report* (November–December 1977), p. 21.

169. "Minutes CALC/Nestle Meeting-Union Theological Seminary, 14 February 1978," (New York: Clergy and Laity Concerned, 1978).

170. "Bristol-Meyers Says It Settled a Lawsuit Over Infant Formula," *The Wall Street Journal* (28 January 1978), p. 32.

171. "Infant Formula: A Proxy Issue," *The New York Times* (9 April 1978), p. 8.

172. "Chronology: The Infant Formula Controversy," *INFACT* (April 1978), pp. 1–6.

173. "Infant Formula Abuse," *MacNeil-Lehrer Report Transcript* (12 June 1978), and "Into the Mouths of Babes," *CBS Reports Transcript* (5 July 1978), p. 7.

174. "Infant Formula Abuse;" and "Into the Mouths of Babes."

175. "Has Nestlé Really Changed?" *INFACT Newsletter* (Winter 1978), p. 5.

176. "The Need for the Boycott," *INFACT Newsletter* (February 1979), p. 8.

177. "A Boycott Over Infant Formula," *Business Week* (23 April 1979), pp. 137–140.

178. Victor Lusinchi, "Baby Food Industry Agrees to a Curb On the Promotion of Infant Formulas", *The New York Times*, October 4, 1979, p. 12.

179. Karl P. Sauvant, "His Master's Voice," *Ceres* (September–October 1976), pp. 27 ff.

180. Morton Mintz, review of *Suffer the Children: The Story of Thalidomide* by the Insight Team of the *Sunday Times of London*, in *The New Republic* (21 April 1979), p. 30.

181. Richard Martin, "Gillette's Giovacchini Rules on Quality Safety of 850 Products," *Wall Street Journal* (12 December 1975), p. 1.

Chapter 11

1. International Labor Organization statistics.

2. See "Japanese Managers Tell How Their System Works," *Fortune* (November 1977), pp. 126–138; "Japan's Unions: Struggle Time," *The Economist* (14 April 1979), p. 82; and "Tough Times Erode Worker–Company Tie," *World Business Weekly* (18 December 1978), p. 56.

3. Marvine Howe, "U.S. Plant Seized in Lisbon Dispute," *The New York Times* (27 January 1976), p. 9.

4. "Belgium Hits Badger for Shutting an Office," *Business Week* (28 March 1977), p. 32; and "Ways of Making Multinationals Talk," *The Economist* (9 December 1978), p. 89.

5. "Over Here," *The Economist* (10 September 1977), p. 70.

6. Duane Kujawa, "Collective Bargaining and Labor Relations in Multinational Enterprises: A U.S. Public Policy Perspective," pp. 25–50 in Robert G. Hawkins, (ed.) *The Economic Effects of Multinational Corporations* (Greenwich, Connecticut: JAI Press, 1979).

7. See International Labour Office, *Multinationals in Western Europe: The Industrial Relations Experience* (Geneva: ILO, 1975).

8. Duane Kujawa, *International Labor Relations Management* (New York: Frederick A. Praeger, 1971).

9. Kujawa, *International Labor Relations.*

10. David C. Hershfield, *The Multinational Union Faces the Multinational Company* (New York: The Conference Board, 1975), p. 12.

11. I.A. Litvak and C.J. Maule, "The Union Response to International Corporations," *Industrial Relations* (February 1972), pp. 318–327.

12. Kujawa, "Collective Bargaining and Labor Relations," pp. 25–50.

13. "Labor Shaping Up for Global Conflicts: U.S.-European Threat to S. Gobair," *Business International* (18 April 1969), p. 121; and Herbert R. Northrup and Richard L. Rowan," Multina-

tional Bargaining Approaches in the Western European Flat Glass Industry," *Industrial and Labor Relations Review* (October 1976), pp. 32–46.

14. Kujawa, "Collective Bargaining and Labor Relations."

15. Kujawa, "Collective Bargaining and Labor Relations."

16. David H. Blake, "Trade Unions and the Challenge of the Multinational Corporation," *Annals of the American Academy of Political and Social Science* (September 1972), p. 4.

17. Blake, "Trade Unions and the Challenge of the Multinational," p. 41.

18. Kurt H. Decker, "Multinational Collective Bargaining: Myth or Reality," *Vanderbilt Journal of Transnational Law* (Winter 1976), p. 123.

19. Richard L. Rowen and Herbert R. Northrup, "Multinational Bargaining in Metals and Electrical Industries: Approaches and Prospects," *Journal of Industrial Relations* (March 1975), pp. 1–29.

20. Neil Ulman, "Multinational Firms Face a Growing Power: Multinational Unions," *The Wall Street Journal* (23 April 1973), p. 1.

21. Herbert R. Northrup and Richard L. Rowen, "Multinational Union Activity in the 1976 U.S. Rubber Strike," *Sloan Management Review* (Spring 1977), p. 25.

22. P. Revson, "How a Union Leader Stays Busy Keeping Strikers' Spirits Alive," *The Wall Street Journal* (8 July 1971), p. 1.

23. Herbert R. Northrup and Richard Rowen, "Multinational Collective Bargaining Activity: The Factual Record in Chemical, Glass and Rubber Tires," *Columbia Journal of World Business* (Summer 1974), pp. 49–63.

24. "Akzo Men Told Fibers Weakness Perils Company," *Chemical Week* (4 September 1972).

25. Akzo, *Annual Report*, 1972, p. 9.

26. "Enka Plans to Restructure Despite Cross-Border Union Resistance," *Business Europe* (31 October 1975), p. 345.

27. "Enka Plans to Restructure," p. 346.

28. Paul Kemezis, "Unions: Setback Abroad," *The New York Times* (1 February 1976), p. 3.

29. "Common Market Gets Fiber Act Together," *Chemical Week* (22 February 1978), p. 27.

30. Hershfield, *The Multinational Union*.

31. "Business Forum in Europe Hears Labor News It Likes," *The Wall Street Journal* (1 January 1978), p. 34.

32. "Canada's Unions Start to Defect," *Business Week* (15 June 1974), p. 98. See also Leonard Zeher, "Canadian Union Leaders are Striving to Break Ties With Powerful U.S.-Based Internationals," *The Wall Street Journal* (29 December 1972), p. 20

33. Gerard B. Bomers and Richard B. Peterson, "Multinational Corporations and Industrial Relations," *British Journal of Industrial Relations* (March 1977), p. 53.

34. Lloyd Ulman, "Multinational Unionism: Incentives, Barriers, and Alternatives," *Industrial Relations* (February 1975), pp. 29–30 (italics added).

35. Quoted in Neil Ulman, "Multinational Firms Face a Growing Power," p. 1.

36. Quoted in Ulman, "Multinational Firms Face a Growing Power," p. 14

37. G.B. McCulloch, "Multinational Bargaining: An MNC Perspective," (New York: Exxon Corporation, Mimeographed, 1977).

38. Hans Gunter, "Erosion of Trade Union Power Through Multinational Enterprises?," *Vanderbilt Journal of Transnational Law* (Fall 1976), p. 79 .

39. "Profit-Sharing, of a Sort," *The Economist* (29 April 1978), p. 91.

40. "Profit-Sharing Yes, Ownership No," *The Economist* (11 March 1978).

41. Jeremiah J. O'Connell, "Industrial Democracy," (Geneva: Centre d'Etudes Industrielles, Mimeographed, 1975), p. 4.

42. "Another Way of Making Cars," *The Economist* (25 December 1976), p. 68

43. Gerarda Evans, "Volvo Pulls the Plug on the Assembly Line," *Business and Society Review* (Summer 1977), pp. 25–26.

44. "Detroit Inches Closer to a Four-Day Week," *Business Week* (13 February 1978), p. 85.

45. "Europe Likes Flexi-Time Week," *Business Week* (7 October 1972), p. 80.

46. For a general discussion, see Kenneth F. Walker, "Workers' Participation in Management—Problems, Practice and Prospects," *International Institute of Labor Studies Bulletin* (No. 12, 1974).

47. See Klaus E. Agathe, "Mitbestimmung: Report on a Social Experiment," *Business Horizons* (February 1977), pp. 5–14 for a recent discussion of the German case.

48. "Codetermination: A Setback," *Business Week* (19 January 1976), p. 73.

49. Jonathan Kandell, "Workers' Movement Falters in Europe," *The New York Times* (5 January 1978), p. D3.

50. Michel Rolant, quoted in "Worker Democracy is Losing Its Appeal," *Business Week* (24 April 1978), p. 46.

51. Peter T. Kilborn, "Power of British Trade Unions: Signs of Resistance Appear," *The New York Times* (2 February 1977), p. 3.

52. "Never Mind Bullock, What About the Workers?," *The Economist* (29 April 1978), p. 123.

53. "Hardhats in U.K. Boardrooms?," *Chemical Week* (2 July 1975).

54. Professor Joop Ramondt, quoted in Jonathan Kandell, "Workers Movement Falters in Europe," *The New York Times* (5 January 1978), p. D1.

55. Kandell "Workers Movement Falters," p. D3.

56. See European Countries, *The Protection of Workers in Multinational Companies* (Brussels: EEC, 1976).

57. A.H. Raskin, "The Workers in the Executive Suite," *The New York Times*, (4 January 1976).

58. "Stonewalling Plant Democracy," *Business Week* (28 March 1977), p. 78.

59. A.H. Raskin, "Unions and a Voice in Management," *The New York Times* (15 November 1975), p. 47.

60. "Codetermination: When Workers Help Manage," *Business Week* (14 July 1975), p. 134.

61. George S. McIsaac and Herbert Henzler, "Codetermination: The Hidden Noose for MNCs," *Columbia Journal of World Business* (Winter 1974), pp. 67–74.

62. "Workers on Boards of German Companies: Are They a Threat to the Multinational Investor in Germany?," *Multinational Business* (December 1974). See also "West Germany: The Worker Dissidents in Opel's Boardroom," *Business Week*, 23 July 1979, p. 79.

63. "Jacob's Escape Ladder," *The Economist* (8 October 1977), p. 102.

64. Quoted in Roy Hill, "How Effective are Works Councils?," *International Management* (October 1977), p. 18.

65. McIsaac and Henzler, "Codetermination," p. 70.

66. "The Trade Union Jet Set," *The Economist* (15 February 1977), p. 89.

67. Quoted in David Oates, "How Far Will Worker Power Go?," *International Management* (February 1977), p. 12.

68. Roy J. Adams and C.H. Rummel, "Workers' Participation in Management in West Germany," (McMaster University, Faculty of Business, Research Series, No. 117), pp. 48–49.

69. See McIsaac and Henzler, "Codetermination," pp. 72–74.

70. *U.S. News and World Report* (10 May 1976).

71. "Black Market in Black Labor," *L'Espresso* (4 October 1977).

72. "A Plan to Lure Guest Workers Home," *The Economist* (20 September 1976), p. 46.

73. "Going Soft?," *The Economist* (16 July 1977), p. 55.

74. "Merci, et Au Revoir," *The Economist* (7 August 1977), p. 62.

75. "What Illegal Aliens Cost the Economy,'" *Business Week* (13 June 1977), p. 86.

76. Elizabeth M. Fowler, "Management: Picking Those to Go Abroad," *The New York Times* (18 February 1977), p. D1.

77. Alfred L. Malabre, Jr., "Firms Cut Pay Extras of Overseas Managers, Use More Foreigners," *The Wall Street Journal* (1 August 1973), p. 1.

78. Malabre, "Firms Cut Pay Extras," p. 1.

79. "When in Japan, Put a Japanese at the Top," *Business Week* (18 November 1972), p. 41.

80. Sandra Salmans, "Africans Get a Taste for the Top," *International Management* (October 1977), p. 39.

81. Nathaniel C. Nash, "Americans Hit Japanese on Promotions," *The New York Times* (31 May 1977), p. 39. See also S. Prakash Sethi and Carl L. Swanson, "American Subsidiaries of Foreign Multinationals and U.S. Civil Rights Laws—Can Alien Executives Be Treated Differently Than American Executives?" (Working Paper No. 79–02, Center for Research in Business and Social Policy, The University of Texas at Dallas, 1979.)

82. Nash, "Americans Hit Japanese on Promotions," p. 57.

83. Jay Palmer, "An Englishman is No. 1 at Avis," *The New York Times* (6 February 1977), p. 5.

84. "Boardrooms Open the Door to Foreigners," *Business Week* (19 August 1972), p. 60.

85. "Why Tension Grows Around VW's New Plant," *Business Week* (6 February 1978), pp. 106–108.

86. See Corporate Information Center, *Church Investments, Corporations and Southern Africa* (New York: Friendship Press, 1973).

87. See Laurence G. O'Donnell, "The Power of the Pulpit: Churchmen's Effort to Get Data From GM Points Up a New Force on Corporations," *The Wall Street Journal* (19 May 1972), p. 26.

88. "Churches File Resolutions at 12 U.S. Firms for Fuller Disclosure of South Africa Ties," *The Wall Street Journal* (17 January 1973), p. 4.

89. Tim Smith, "South Africa: The Churches vs. the Corporations," *Business and Society Review* (Fall 1975), p. 56.

90. See Thomas E. Mullaney, "12 Big U.S. Concerns in South Africa Set Equality in Plants," *The New York Times* (2 March 1977), p. D1.

91. Jennifer Davis, "Too Little, Too Late: The U.S. Corporation Employment Manifesto for South Africa," (New York: The Africa Fund, 1977).

92. "21 More U.S. Companies Backing Antiracist Code for South Africa," *The New York Times* (21 June 1977), p. 44.

93. "21 More Concerns Back South African Equality," *The New York Times* (15 September 1977), p. D16; and "Reforms in South Africa," *Business Week* (18 June 1979), p. 158.

94. "South Africa: Black-Chip Investment," *The Economist* (26 November 1977), p. 48.

95. "A Damp Squib Unless . . . ," *Financial Mail* (4 March 1977), p. 632.

96. Timothy Smith, "Whitewash for Apartheid from Twelve U.S. Firms," *Business and Society Review* (Summer 1977), pp. 59–60.

97. Davis, "Too Little, Too Late."

98. "Common Market Endorses Code for Companies," *South Africa/Namibia Update* (12 October 1977), p. 3.

99. Letter to the Editor from Clyde Ferguson and William R. Cotter, *Foreign Affairs* **56** (April 1978), p. 659.

100. Clyde Ferguson and William R. Cotter, "South Africa: What is to be Done," *Foreign Affairs* **56** (January 1978), p. 274.

101. "Why Are We in South Africa," *Business and Society Review* (No. 23 Fall 1977), p. 57.

102. "Why Are We in South Africa," p. 58.

103. "Code of Conduct Adopted," *European Community* (November–December 1977), p. 44; and "The European Community and South Africa," *Commission of the European Communities: Information* (November 1977), pp. 16–17.

104. "South Africa: Multinationals Are Caught in the Middle Again," *Business Week* (24 October 1977), p. 49; and "German, Dutch Business Turn Down EEC Code," *South Africa/Namibia Update* (2 November 1977), p. 4.

105. "Black Wages," *The Economist* (17 February 1979), p. 92; and "Push for South African Code Extension," *World Business Weekly* (27 November 1978), p. 60.

106. "Guides for U.S. Concerns in South Africa Widened," *The New York Times* (6 July 1978), p. D5.

107. "Why Pretoria is Giving Black Workers a Break," *Business Week* (18 June 1979), p. 130.

108. See Desaix Myers, III, *Labor Practices of U.S. Corporations in South Africa* (New York: Praeger, 1977), pp. 99–108.

109. "South Africa: Multinationals Are Caught in the Middle Again," *Business Week* (24 October 1977), p. 49.

110. Daniel I. Fine, "Pretoria's Turn Toward More Liberal Racial Policies," *Business Week* (23 April 1979), p. 65.

111. "South African Labor Revision Proposal Leaves Many Old Racial Barriers Intact," *The Wall Street Journal* (25 May 1979), p. 12.

112. "South African Labor Revision Proposal," p. 12.

113. "Why Pretoria is Giving Black Workers," p. 130.

114. See "Gulf & Western in the Dominican Republic," (CIC Brief) *The Corporate Examiner* (October 1975), pp. 3A–3D; and "Gulf & Western in the Dominican Republic: II," (CIC Brief) *The Corporate Examiner* (November–December 1976), pp. 3A–3D.

115. Jack Nelson, "Del Monte in the Philippines," *CALC Report* (September 1977), pp. 9–10.

116. See Valerie Heinonen, *Church Proxy Resolutions: January 1978* (New York: Interfaith Center on Corporate Responsibility, 1978); and "Corporate Social Responsibility Challenges—Spring 1979," *The Corporate Examiner* (February 1979), p. 4.

117. "Corporate Social Responsibility Challenges—Spring 1976," *The Corporate Examiner* (February 1976), p. 7.

118. "Church Women United Asks MATTEL for Information on Korea," *The Corporate Examiner* (March 1978), p. 1; and "MATTEL Shareholder Resolution Withdrawn," *The Corporate Examiner* (June 1978), p. 4.

119. David Tobis, "How Coca-Cola Keeps Its Corporate Image Bubbly," *Business and Society Review* (Summer 1977), p. 74.

120. Heinonen, *Church Proxy Resolutions: January 1978*, p. 10.

121. "Guatemalan Union Leader Attends Coca-Cola Annual Meeting," *The Corporate Examiner* (May 1979), pp. 1 and 4.

122. Jim Montgomery, "Coke Holders Urge Creation of a Code of Labor Standards," *The Wall Street Journal* (13 April 1979), p. 18.

123. "Coke Dissidents Say Guatemala Franchisee Violent, Repressive," *The Wall Street Journal* (8 May 1979), p. 20.

124. "Early Retirement is Gaining Throughout Western Europe," *The New York Times* (4 December 1977), p. 1.

125. Quoted in "Early Retirement is Gaining Throughout Western Europe," p. 64.

126. "Boeing Accused of Bias Against Older Workers," *The Wall Street Journal* (20 March 1978).

127. "What is the Right Retirement Age?" *Chemical Week* (19 October 1977).

128. "She Studies Societies that Brutalize Women," *The New York Times* (28 March 1978), p. 39.

129. "Swedish Women Enjoy Doing Men's Jobs," *International Management* (October 1977), p. 9.

130. See Simone de Beauvoir, "Still the Second Sex," *Le Monde* (10 January 1978).

131. Maggie Black, "The Third World: Development First?," *New Internationalist* (October 1977).

132. Eric Morgenthaler, "More U.S. Firms Put Females in Key Posts in Foreign Countries," *The Wall Street Journal* (16 March 1978), p. 1.

133. Morganthaler, "More U.S. Firms Put Females in Key Posts," p. 1

134. Georgette Josen, "Women Got Big Gains in '73 AT&T Job Post, but Sexism Cry Persists," *The Wall Street Journal* (28 February 1978), p. 1.

135. "PR: 'The Velvet Ghetto of Affirmative Action," *Business Week* (8 May 1978), p. 122.

136. William M. Wallace, "Two Approaches to Human Labor," *The Wall Street Journal* (30 March 1972), p. 10.

137. Tracy Dahlby, "In Japan, Women Don't Climb the Corporate Ladder," *The New York Times* (18 September 1977), p. 11.

138. "Women at Work," *The Economist* (6 August 1977), p. 77.

139. Tomoko Shihata, as quoted in "Women at Work," p. 77.
140. "European Women: Heading for the Executive Suite," *Dun's Review* (October 1976), p. 80.
141. Sergio Ferrari, "The Italian Woman Executive," *Management International Review* (October 1977), p. 16.
142. "European Women: Heading for the Executive Suite," p. 82.
143. "Labor: Japanese Women Joint the Lib Movement," *Business Week*, (10 April 1971), p. 70.

Chapter 12

1. For a discussion of these assumptions of growing resource scarcity, goal incompatibility, and interference capability see Thomas N. Gladwin, "The Management of Environmental Conflict: A Survey of Research Approaches and Priorities," Working Paper 78–09, Graduate School of Business Administration, New York University, January 1978.

2. See James P. Roscow, *800 Miles to Valdez: The Building of the Alaska Pipeline* (Englewood Cliffs, N.J.: Prentice Hall, 1977).

3. See P. Schmidt, D. Friedberg, "Ecologia Concreta: Il Caso Scarlino," (address to the Milan Rotary Club, 22 February 1974); "Montedison TiO₂ Plant Faces Closure," *European Chemical News* (23 February 1973), p. 6; "Suits Name Montedison," *International Herald Tribune* (17 February 1976), p. 1; "EEC Proposals Still Threaten Titanium Dioxide Industry," *European Chemical News* (7 May 1976), p. 27; and "To Sea or Not to Sea with TiO₂ Wastes," *Chemical Week* (8 December 1976), pp. 65–67.

4. See "The New England Oil Rush," *Business Week* (9 March 1974), p. 130; and Daniel Ford, "The Refinery That Ran Aground," *The Nation* (4 May 1974), pp. 561–564.

5. See "Labor: New Allies Among Environmentalist," *Business Week* (24 February 1973), p. 86; "How Much is Strike Hurting Shell?," *Chemical Week* (9 May 1973), p. 16; "Tentative Agreement is Signed in Four-Month Shell-OCAW Strike," *Chemical Week* (23 May 1973), p. 15; "Score One for Shell," *Chemical Week* (30 May 1973), p. 15; and Anthony J. Piombino, "When the Safety Sleuth Comes to Call," *Chemical Week* (6 June 1973), pp. 41–52.

6. See "Plump und Einfallslos," *Manager Magazin* (7 July 1975), pp. 24–29; Solange Fernex, "Non-Violence Triumphant," *The Ecologist* **5** (October 1975), pp. 372–376; and "CWM Plant Site Moves to Germany," *European Chemical News* (14 March 1975), p. 6.

7. See "Brazil Starts to Clean Up Its CPI Act," *Chemical Week* (4 October 1978), pp. 35–36; "Brazilian Antipollution Step," *Business Latin America* (14 June 1978), p. 186; "Brazil Zoning Plan Could Shift Investments to Undeveloped Areas," *Chemical Week* (4 January 1978), p. 35; "Turn to Pollute," *The New York Times* (23 February 1972), p. 38; Claudio de Moura Castro, "Heirs to an Infinite Land?" *Mazingra* (No. 7, 1978), pp. 58–62; and "Developing Countries Have Become Less Reticent on Environmental Problems," *Business International* (13 April 1979), pp. 116–117.

8. For a conceptual framework regarding the process of responding to heterogeneous policy environments see Thomas N. Gladwin and Ingo Walter, "Multinational Enterprise, Social Responsiveness, and Pollution Control," *Journal of International Business Studies* **7** (Fall–Winter 1976), pp. 57–74.

9. See Robert W. Ackerman, "How Companies Respond to Social Demands," *Harvard Business Review* **51** (July–August 1973), pp. 88–98.

10. For discussions regarding environmental problem and policy diversity see: Ingo Walter, *International Economics of Pollution* (London: Macmillan and New York: Halsted-Wiley, 1975); Ingo Walter, ed., *Studies in International Environmental Economics* (New York: Wiley-Interscience, 1976); Ingo Walter, "Implications of Environmental Policies for the Trade Prospects of Developing Countries: Analysis Based on an UNCTAD Questionnaire," (Geneva: United Nations Conference on Trade and Development, 1976); Charles Pearson and Anthony Pryor, *Environment North and South: An Economic Interpretation* (New York: Wiley-Interscience, 1978).

11. This section draws from Thomas N. Gladwin and Ingo Walter, "Multinational Enterprise and the Natural Environment: Diversity in Challenge and Response," Working Paper #75–101, Graduate School of Business Administration, New York University (December 1975).

12. For reviews of critical environmental problems see Sterling Brubaker, *To Live on Earth: Man and His Environment in Perspective* (Baltimore: The Johns Hopkins Press, 1972); Lynton K. Caldwell, *In Defense of Earth: International Protection of the Biosphere* (Bloomington: Indiana University Press, 1972); Institute of Ecology, *Man in the Living Environment: A Report on Global Ecological Problems* (Madison: The University of Wisconsin Press, 1972); David A. Kay and Eugene B. Skolnikoff, (eds.), *World Eco-Crisis: International Organizations in Response* (Madison: The University of Wisconsin Press, 1972); Clifford S. Russell and Hans H. Landsberg, "International Environmental Problems: A Taxonomy," *Science* **172** (25 June 1971), pp. 1307–1314; and Maurice F. Strong, "Progress or Catastrophe: Whither Our World?," *Environmental Conservation* **2** (No. 2 Summer 1975), pp. 83–88.

13. For a review of trends in this area see Thomas N. Gladwin, "Environmental Policy Trends Facing Multinationals," *California Management Review* **20** (Winter 1977), pp. 81–93.

14. Such global efficiency arguments are explored in Walter, *International Economics of Pollution;* and Pearson and Pryor, *Environment North and South.*

15. For an early survey see Eugene V. Coan, Julia N. Hills, and Michael McCloskey, "Strategies for International Environmental Action: The Case for an Environmentally Oriented Foreign Policy," *Natural Resource Journal* **14** (January 1974), pp. 87–102.

16. See "Export Ban on Banned Products Proposed," *Chemical Week* (31 March 1971), p. 15; and Stanford N. Sesser, "Many U.S. Companies Sell Products Abroad that are Banned Here," *The Wall Street Journal* (11 February 1971), pp. 1 and 17.

17. "Double Standard on Exports," *Chemical Week* (19 July 1978), p. 19. See also "Products Banned in U.S. Being Exported," *Chemical and Engineering News* (6 November 1978), p. 19 and "Banned at Home—But Exported," *Business Week* (12 June 1978), p. 152.

18. "New Export Policy for Hazardous Goods?" *Chemical Week* (25 October 1978), p. 24; and Committee on Government Operations, U.S. Congress, *Report on Export of Products Banned by U.S. Regulatory Agencies* (Washington: U.S. Government Printing Office, 4 October 1978).

19. "Products Banned in U.S. Being Exported," p. 19.

20. "Environmental Pinch on Exports," *Chemical Week* (17 January 1979), p. 17; "A Priority for Exports over the Environment," *Business Week* (22 January 1979), p. 26; and "Impact Statements Now Required for Exports," *Chemical and Engineering News* (15 January 1979), p. 8.

21. See "Reviewed Controversy over the International Reach of NEPA," Comment in *Environmental Law Reporter* 7, p. 10205.

22. For a review see "A Growing Worry: The Consequences of Development," *Conservation Foundation Letter* (January 1978), p. 5.

23. "A Growing Worry," p. 5.

24. "U.S. Agencies Resist Environmental Limits Overseas," *The New York Times* (19 January 1978), p. A7; and "International Application of NEPA Explained by CEQ Spokesman," *Pollution Control Guide* (17 April 1978), pp. 198–199.

25. "Administrative Survey: October 1976 to September 1977," *Law and Policy in International Business* **10** (No. 1, 1978), p. 226.

26. Tom Wicker, "Looking Before Leaping," *The New York Times* (20 June 1978), p. A17; and "Nuclear," *World Business Weekly* (25 June 1979), p. 11.

27. Tom Bethell, "Exporting Pettifoggery," *Harpers* (October 1978), pp. 34–37.

28. "U.S. Proposes Extension of Environmental Rules to International Arena," *Business International* (10 March 1978), pp. 75–76.

29. "Impact Statements Now Required for Exports," *Chemical and Engineering News* (15 January 1979), p. 8.

30. The "pollution haven" issue has been examined conceptually in Ingo Walter "Environmental Control and Patterns of International Trade and Investment: An Emerging Policy Issue," *Banca Nazionale del Lavoro Review* (March 1972); pp. 3–27; Walter, *International Economics of Pollution;* Pearson and Pryor, *Environment North and South;* William J. Baumol, "Environmental Protection, International Spillovers, and Trade," Wicksell Lectures 1971, (Upsala: Almquist and Wicksell, 1971).

31. "Exporting Pollution: What Does It Cost U.S.?", *Not Man Apart* (mid-February 1976), p. 3.

32. "Exporting Pollution," p. 5.

33. "Controls Too Tough?," *Chemical Week* (5 July 1978), p. 15; Helen Dewar, "Dirty Industries Export Plant," *International Herald Tribune* (30 June 1978); David R. Obey, "Export of Hazardous Industries," *Congressional Record* (29 June 1978), pp. E3559–3567; and Barry Castleman, "How We Export Dangerous Industries," *Business and Society Review* (Fall 1978), pp. 7–14.

34. Barry I. Castleman, "The Export of Hazardous Factories to Developing Nations," (7 March 1978), available from the Natural Resources Defense Council, Washington, D.C., pp. 27–29.

35. This section draws from Thomas N. Gladwin and Ingo Walter, "Multinational Enterprise, Social Responsiveness, and Pollution Control," *Journal of International Business Studies* 7 (Fall–Winter 1976), pp. 57–74.

36. See Thomas N. Gladwin and John G. Welles, "Environmental Policy and Multinational Corporate Strategy," in Ingo Walter, ed., *Studies in International Environmental Economics;* Anthony Yezer and Amy Philipson, "Influence of Environmental Considerations on Agriculture Decisions to Locate Outside of the Continental United States," prepared by the Public Interest Economics Center for the CEQ, 1974 (mimeo.); E. Dennis Conroy, "Will 'Dirty' Industries Seek Pollution Havens Abroad?," *SAIS Review* 18 (Fall 1974), p. 48; "Corporate Investment and Production Decisions: Does Environmental Legislation Play a Role?" *Multinational Business* (No. 3, 1978); Francisco Szekely, "Pollution for Export," *Mazingira* (No. 3/4, 1977), pp. 68–75; Gabriele Knödgen, "Environment and Industrial Siting," (draft discussion paper, International Institute for Environment and Society of the Science Center Berlin, May 1979); Donald Reynolds, "Pollution Control and Plant Location in the Primary Aluminum Industry," (unpublished PhD dissertation, Graduate School of Business Administration, New York University, 1973); and Charles Pearson, "Implications for the Trade and Investment of Developing Countries of United States Environmental Controls" (Geneva: United Nations Conference on Trade and Development, 1976).

37. Quantitative studies have come to dominate analyses of social conflict, particularly in regard to collective violence, strike activity and, racial disturbances. Major research of this kind with regard to environmental conflict was undertaken by the authors, with the support of the Rockefeller Foundation. A team of researchers at New York University systematically scanned a range of industrial and environmental magazines for the period 1970–1978 and pulled out every item pertaining to an environmental conflict. Files were created for every separate conflict, and information on the type of facility, timing, location, participants, issues, tactics, outcomes, and so on involved in each were coded using a standardized format. A particular type of issue, for example, was deemed to be present and coded as such only if the collection of articles assembled on the conflict explicitly mentioned the issue as being in contention among the disputing parties. Data as of 1979 had been collected on approximately 3000 disputes. To facilitate descriptive and statistical analysis, parts of the data base were computerized. The data reported on in this chapter represents our "Chemical Process Industry Data Set" which includes information on 587 industrial facility environmental disputes—every one mentioned in *Chemical Week Magazine* and/or *European Chemical News* during the period 1 January 1970 through 30 June 1978 (i.e., 442 weeks of coverage). The assistance of Patrick P. McCurdy, Editor-in-Chief of *Chemical Week*, and Kenneth Krieger, Judith Ugelow, Deborah Halliday, C.V. Pappachan, Greg Kiviat, and Fred Wise is gratefully acknowledged.

38. Over time, the share accounted for by the Northeast and Midwest declined markedly (the combined share of these two regions in 1970–1971 was 59%; in 1976–1978 it was 38%). This shift in the location of conflict in the U.S. to the South and West is in accordance with the shift of industry in general in that direction.

39. It should be noted that our scanning operations revealed a significant lag in media reporting of conflicts, with coverage apparently dependent upon the disputes reaching some threshold level of media-attracting intensity. For this reason, the 1976–mid-1978 share of 21% is somewhat understated (scanning since the computer data-base cut-off date of July 1978 has indeed revealed three dozen battles which emerged in 1977 and early 1978 but did not make it into the data-base).

40. See John M. Winton, "Plant Sites 1975: Social Concerns Are Complicating the Choosing," *Chemical Week* (23 October 1974), pp. 33–52; "Plant Sites 1976," *Chemical Week* (22 October 1975), pp. 27–55; John M. Winton, "Plant Sites 1977: It's North's Move," *Chemical Week* (10 November 1976), pp. 35–55.

41. David Vogel, *Lobbying the Corporation: Citizen Challenges to Business Authority* (New York: Basic Books, 1978), p. 164.

42. See "Corporate Social Responsibility Challenges—Spring 1978," *The Corporate Examiner* 7 (February 1978), pp. 1–8 and other issues of the *Examiner* detailing proxy resolutions filed each year.

43. "Where Pollution Control is Slowing Industrial Growth," *U.S. News and World Report* (23 August 1971), p. 49.

44. Mr. Abrams, "Thinking Out Loud: Peterson Misstates Facts About Shell," *The Wilmington Evening Journal* (14 May 1974), p. 23.

45. "Don't Tell Us Nuclear Power Is Safe, We Don't Like It," *The Economist* (13 November 1976), p. 63.

46. For a fuller discussion see Thomas N. Gladwin, "The Management of Environmental Conflict."

47. "Energy: Beauty and the Beast," *The Economist* (1 May 1976), p. 38. The project has been resurrected twice since that time. See Molly Ivins, "New Environmental Fight Looms Over Developing Coal-Rich Utah Area," *The New York Times* (12 March 1979), p. A14.

48. "Nuclear No," *The Economist* (11 November 1978), pp. 54–55; "Austria: Anti-Nuclear Vote Will Hurt Economy," *World Business Weekly* (13 November 1978), pp. 53–55; and "Voters Clear the Way for Sohio, Set Up Roadblocks for Nukes," *Chemical Week* (15 November 1978), p. 24.

49. "Environmental Protection: Constraints, Costs and Ways to Cope," *Business International* (14 November 1975), pp. 361–363.

50. See Jonijane Paxton, "An Experiment in Ecology—AMAX/Henderson: Meeting the Environmental Challenges," *Editorial Alert* (July 1974), p. 33.

51. For a review of theory and empirical research on some of these dimensions see Jeffrey Z. Rubin and Bert R. Brown, *The Social Psychology of Bargaining and Negotiation* (New York: Academic Press, 1975).

52. "Japan: There's No More Room to Smelt Aluminum," *Business Week* (3 May 1976), p. 63; "How Aluminum's Strategy Risks a Shortfall," *Business Week* (26 February 1979), pp. 109–114; and "Alumax Inc. to Build Plant in Australia for $500 Million," *The Wall Street Journal* (20 April 1979), p. 5.

53. The measures for the interval scale data represent zero-order Pearson's product-moment correlation coefficients (ranging from −1 to +1) which assume symmetric and simple linear associations.

54. "Probers Detail Dioxin Damage," *Chemical Week* (9 August 1978), p. 20.

55. C.J. Temple, "Seveso: The Issues and the Lessons," *Foresight: The Journal of Risk Assessment* (October 1976), p. 5. See also Tessa Namuth, "A Dioxin Plague in Northern Italy," *Business and Society Review* (Winter 1976–77), pp. 29–31.

56. "Italy: Our Own Hiroshima," *Newsweek* (16 August 1976), p. 8.

57. "Seveso: Lessons from an Escape," *The Economist* (17 June 1978), p. 104.

58. "The Costly Aftermath of a Poison Cloud," *Business Week* (11 October 1976), p. 33.

59. "Seveso: Lessons from an Escape."

60. "L'Affaire de Seveso: Un Communiqué de la Société Genevoise," *Tribune de Genève* (27 July 1976), p. 8.

61. "Italy: Our Own Hiroshima," p. 8.

62. "The Costly Aftermath of a Poison Cloud," p. 33. Also see "Politics Complicates Italy's New Environmental Concern," *Business Europe* (2 June 1978), pp. 169–170.

63. Federice Bugno, "Apriamo il Libro Nere degli Avvelenatori," *Tempo*, No. 32 (15 August 1976), p. 68.

64. Christina Lord, "Seveso Fallout: Poison Cloud Effects, Known and Unknown, Linger," *European Community* (November–December 1976), p. 4.

65. "Poison Gas: Fatal Carelessness," *The Economist* (31 July 1976), p. 64; and "The Hazards of Dioxin and 2, 4, 5–T," *Chemical and Engineering News* (18 June 1979), p. 36.

66. Philip Revzin, "Chemical Fallout: A Year After Tragedy, Seveso, Italy, Residents Debate the Dangers," *The Wall Street Journal* (29 June 1977), p. 1.

67. "Tack on Toxin Assayed," *Chemical Week* (18 August 1976), p. 14. For Dow's regulatory problems in regard to dioxin see Thomas Whiteside, "The Pendulum and the Toxic Cloud," *The New Yorker* (25 July 1977), p. 30–55.

68. "More Dioxin Bans Are Coming Up," *Chemical Week* (27 April 1977), p. 33.

69. "Italy Asked to Use Troops to Seal Polluted Region," *The New York Times* (13 February 1977), p. 7.

70. "The Costly Aftermath of a Poison Cloud," p. 33.

71. "Swiss Concern Pays $2.4 Million for Harm Chemical Caused in Italy," *The New York Times* (3 December 1976), p. 9.

72. "Dioxin Aftermath," *Chemical Week* (1 June 1977), p. 15.

73. "Roche Reports Good Progress on Seveso Decontamination," *European Chemical News* (17 June 1977), p. 34.

74. Revzin, "Chemical Fallout: A Year After Tragedy," p. 1.

75. Revzin, "Chemical Fallout: A Year After Tragedy," p. 1.

76. "Seveso Reprisal: Home Bombed," *Chemical Week* (20 July 1977), p. 15.

77. John Walsh, "Seveso: The Questions Persist Where Dioxin Created a Wasteland," *Science* **197** (9 September 1977), p. 1065.

78. Paul Hofmann, "Company Says '76 Blast in Italy Caused Little Injury," *The New York Times* (25 June 1978), p. 4.

79. "Dioxin Lingers On," *Chemical Week* (12 April 1978), p. 22.

80. "Seveso: Lessons from an Escape," p. 108.

81. Hofmann, "Company Says '76 Blast in Italy Caused Little Injury," p. 4.

82. Hofmann, "Company Says '76 Blast in Italy Caused Little Injury," p. 4.

83. "Disposal in Doubt," *Chemical Week* (30 August 1978), p. 13.

84. "Probers Detail Dioxin Damage," *Chemical Week* (9 August 1978), p. 20.

85. Alastair Hay, "Italian Commission Covered Up Seveso Delays," *Nature* **277** (22 February 1979), p. 589.

86. See "Study Blames ICMESA for Dioxin Disaster," *Chemical Week* (14 February 1979), p. 13; "Faulty Reporting of Seveso Birth Defects?" *Chemical Week* (28 February 1979), p. 24; and Philip Revzin, "Chemical Cloud Still Casts Long Shadow Over Seveso, Italy," *The Wall Street Journal* (10 July 1979), pp. 1 and 34.

87. See "Dioxin Fears Spread to More Plants—Coalite, Bayer Close," *European Chemical News* (13 August 1976), p. 4–6; Temple, "Seveso: The Issues"; Whiteside, "The Pendulum and the Toxic Cloud," p. 30–55; "The Cost of Avoiding Another Seveso," *The Economist* (14 August 1976), p. 73; "Seveso: Lessons from an Escape," p. 108; Peter Harnik, "The Lessons of Seveso," *Sierra Club Bulletin* (May/June 1979), pp. 77–78; and Thomas Whiteside, *The Pendulum and the Toxic Cloud* (New Haven: Yale University Press, 1979).

88. See Thomas N. Gladwin, "Environmental Policy Trends Facing Multinationals," *California Management Review* **20** (Winter 1977), pp. 81–93; John G. Welles, "Multinationals Need New Environmental Strategies," *Columbia Journal of World Business* (Summer 1973), pp. 11–18; and International Chamber of Commerce, *Environmental Guidelines for World Industry* (Paris: I.C.C., 1974).

89. See Thomas N. Gladwin and Michael G. Royston, "An Environmentally Oriented Mode of Industrial Project Planning," *Environmental Conservation* (Autumn 1975), pp. 189–198; and Thomas N. Gladwin, *Environment, Planning and the Multinational Corporation* (Greenwich, Conn.: JAI Press, 1977).

91. See Anne Strick, *Injustice for All* (New York: Putnam, 1978); Special issue on "Conflict Resolution," *Environmental Comment* (May 1977); John H. Noble, John S. Banta and John S. Rosenberg, *Groping Through the Maze* (Washington, D.C.: The Conservation Foundation, 1977); Herbert Kaufman, *Red Tape: Its Origins, Uses and Abuses* (Washington, D.C.: Brookings, 1977); Donald L. Horowitz, *The Courts and Social Policy* (Washington, D.C.: Brookings, 1977); and "The Chilling Impact of Litigation," *Business Week* (6 June 1977), pp. 58–64.

92. See Jane E. McCarthy, "Resolving Environmental Conflicts," *Environmental Science and Technology* **10** (January 1976), pp. 40–43; "Removing the Rancor from Tough Disputes,"

Business Week (30 August 1976), pp. 50–51; RESOLVE, Center for Environmental Conflict Resolution, *Environmental Mediation: An Effective Alternative*, A Report of a Conference Held in Reston, Virginia, 11–13 January 1978, (Palo Alto, California: RESOLVE, 1978); Donald B. Straus, "Mediating Environmental, Energy, and Economic Tradeoffs," *The Arbitration Journal* 32 (June 1977), pp. 96–110; Lawrence E. Susskind, James R. Richardson, and Kathryn J. Hildebrand, "Resolving Environmental Disputes: Approaches to Intervention, Negotiation, and Conflict Resolution," Environmental Impact Assessment Project, Laboratory of Architecture and Planning, Massachusetts Institute of Technology, June 1978; Gerald W. Cormick, "Mediating Environmental Controversies: Perspective and First Experience," *Earth Law Journal* 2 (August 1976), pp. 215–224; and Michael O'Hare, "Not on My Block You Don't: Facility Siting and the Strategic Importance of Compensation," *Public Policy* 25 (Fall 1977), pp. 407–458.

CHAPTER 13

1. See Edward F. Denison, *Accounting for United States Economic Growth, 1929–1969* (Washington, D.C.: The Brookings Institution, 1974); and his *Why Growth Rates Differ* (Washington, D.C.: The Brookings Institution, 1967).

2. See Edwin G. Mansfield, *Economics of Technological Change* (New York: W.W. Norton, 1968); and his *Research and Innovation in the Modern Corporation* (New York: W.W. Norton, 1971).

3. D. A. Was, "The Global Exchange of Patents: An Analysis of Patent Statistics," *Idea* (1970). Also see "U.S. Maintains Technological Advantage," *Chemical and Engineering News* (16 October 1978), pp. 18–19.

4. See Jean-Pierre Hennart, "A Technology Theory of the Multinational Corporation" (unpublished Ph.D. dissertation, University of Maryland, 1977).

5. Michael J. Thomas, "The Location of Rearch and Development in the International Corporation," *Management International Review* 15 (January 1975), pp. 35–41.

6. See Hal Mason, *Strategies of Technology Acquisition* (New York: UNITAR, 1975).

7. Yoshi Tsurumi, "Myths that Mislead U.S. Managers in Japan," *Harvard Business Review* (July–August 1971), pp. 118–127. Also see Richard Howe, "America Learns from Europe," *Vision* (June 1975), pp. 37–39.

8. Arthur W. Lake, "Technology Creation and Technology Transfer in Multinational Firms," pp. 137–187 in Robert G. Hawkins, ed., *The Economic Effects of Multinational Corporations* (Greenwich, Conn.: JAI Press, 1979).

9. D. J. Teece, "Technology Transfer by Multinational Firms: The Resource Cost of Transferring Technological Know-How," *The Economic Journal* 87 (June 1977), pp. 242–261.

10. William W. McGrew, "Litton's Noble Experiment," *Columbia Journal of World Business* 7 (January–February 1972), pp. 65–75.

11. This argument is very well presented in Harry G. Johnson, "Technological Change and Comparative Advantage: An Advanced Country Viewpoint," *Journal of World Trade Law* (January–February 1975), pp. 1–14.

12. Lake, "Technology Creation and Technology Transfer by Multinational Firms," in Hawkins, *The Economic Effects*, pp. 137–187.

13. Herbert E. Mayer, "Those Worrisome Technology Exports," *Fortune* (22 May 1978), p. 106.

14. Mayer, "Those Worrisome Technology Exports," p. 106.

15. See Raymond Vernon, "International Investment and International Trade in the Product Cycle," *Quarterly Journal of Economics* 80 (May 1966), pp. 190–207. Also William Gruber, Dileep Mehta and Raymond Vernon, "The R&D Factor in International Trade and International Investment of United States Industries," *Journal of Political Economy* 75 (February 1967), pp. 20–37.

16. Jack Baranson, "Technology Exports Can Hurt Us," *Foreign Policy* (May 1977), pp. 197-226. Also see series of articles on "Trade, Technology and Leverage," *Foreign Policy* (Fall 1978), pp. 63–106.

17. See Hal Mason, "The Selection of Technology: A Continuing Dilemma," *Columbia Journal of World Business* 9 (Summer 1974), pp. 29–34.

18. See Richard W. Moxon, "The Cost, Conditions and Adaptation of MNC Technology in Developing Countries," pp. 189–233, in Hawkins, *The Economic Effects.*

19. Jack Behrman and Harvey Wallender, III, *Transfer of Manufacturing Technology Within Multinational Enterprises* (Cambridge, Mass.: Ballinger, 1976).

20. Barry Richman and Melvyn Copen, "Management Techniques in the Developing Countries," *Columbia Journal of World Business* 8 (Summer 1973), pp. 49–58.

21. See Moxon, "Cost, Conditions and Adaptation." See also Richard J. Howe, "Inventing Backwards: Some Firms Simplify Products for Markets in Poorer Countries," *The Wall Street Journal* (27 May 1969), pp. 1 and 16; "Appropriate Technology: The Sometimes Bumpy Road from Theory to Practice," *Business International* (26 January 1979), pp. 29–30; and Vern Terpstra, "Multinationals and Appropriate Technology," Working Paper #179, Graduate School of Business Administration, The University of Michigan (May 1979).

22. "Multinationals: GE's Rich Market in Poorer Nations," *Business Week* (2 December 1972), p. 40.

23. "The Breakdown of U.S. Innovation," *Business Week* (16 February 1976), pp. 56–68.

24. "Poor Nations Demand Change in Getting Technology from Rich," *The New York Times* (24 June 1976), p. 45.

25. See also Thomas, "The Location of Research and Development."

26. Moxon, "Cost, Conditions and Adaptation."

27. "American Publications Pour Off the Presses in Taiwan, But That Doesn't Help the Authors," *The Wall Street Journal* (4 May 1971).

28. *O Programa Nuclear Brasileiro* (Brasilian: Official Publication, 1977).

29. Quoted in *Die Zeit* (20 June 1975).

30. David Calleo, "Faulting Nuclear Diplomacy," *The New York Times* (7 June 1978), p. 23.

31. Anthony J. Parisi, "U.S. Reactor Makers' Recovery in Doubt After 4-Year Market Dip," *The New York Times* (7 March 1978), p. 59. President Ferdinand Marcos ordered construction halted on the Westinghouse nuclear power project because of safety fears in June 1979.

32. "Watch that Uranium," *The Economist* (25 February 1978), p. 45.

33. Juan Cameron, "Where Does the President Stand on Nuclear Energy?" *Fortune* (27 March 1978), pp. 99–106.

34. Quoted in Norman Gall, "Atoms for Brazil, Dangers for All," *Foreign Policy* (Summer 1976), pp. 156–157.

35. Paul Hofmann, "40 Countries Review Plutonium Options," *The New York Times* (17 December 1977), p. 5.

36. Paul L. Leventhal, "The Plumbat Affair," *The New York Times* (30 April 1978), p. E19.

37. Quoted in *The New York Times* (12 February 1978).

38. See Sarah Miller, "A Nuclear Difference," *European Community* (May–June 1978), pp. 30–33.

39. Don Cook, "How Carter's Nuclear Policy Backfired Abroad," *Fortune* (23 October 1978), p. 125.

40. "Nuclear Fuel Exports to Common Market Halted by U.S. Over Dispute on Contracts," *The Wall Street Journal* (3 May 1978), p. 6.

41. Richard Barber Associates, Washington, D.C., unpublished study.

42. David Calleo, "Faulting Nuclear Diplomacy," *The New York Times* (7 June 1978), p. 23.

43. Norman Gall, "Atoms for Brazil, Dangers for All," *Foreign Policy* (Summer 1976), p. 160.

44. Gall, "Atoms for Brazil," p. 160.

45. Gall, "Atoms for Brazil," p. 160. See also "Iran to Halt Purchases of Nuclear Gear From West, Use Funds for Social Welfare," *The Wall Street Journal* (11 October 1978), p. 14; and "Iranian Moves Indicate Government Will Halt Nuclear Energy Plans," *The Wall Street Journal* (4 June 1979), p. 10.

46. Gall, "Atoms for Brazil," p. 160.

47. David Calleo, "Of Atoms and Allies," *The New York Times* (18 June 1978), p. E19.
48. *O Programa Nuclear Brasileiro*, p. 22.
49. *O Programa Nuclear Brasileiro*, p. 22.
50. See references in *Journal do Brasil* (11 June 1978).
51. Gall, "Atoms for Brazil," p. 167.
52. Gall, "Atoms for Brazil," p. 167.
53. Charles Batchelor, "Holland Checks Brazil's A-Plans," *Financial Times* (5 August 1978), p. 2.
54. "Brazil's Megawatt Megalomania," *The Economist* (7 October 1978), p. 93.
55. Elizabeth Sullivan, "Nuclear Exports: Unsafe at Any Price?" *The Interdependent* 5 (June 1978), p. 1.
56. "A Nuclear Gamble on India," *The New York Times* (1 May 1978), p. A20. See also Graham Hovey, "Carter Orders Sale of Uranium to India for Power Facility," *The New York Times* (28 April 1978), p. 1; and Tad Szulc, "How India Got the Bomb," *The New Republic* (22 July 1978), pp. 19–21.
57. "Nuclear DIY," *The Economist* (29 April 1978), p. 81.
58. Cook, "How Carter's Nuclear Policy Backfired," p. 130.
59. "Australia Will Sell Uranium to Finland," *The New York Times* (21 July 1978), p. 4.
60. "Will the French Sell Reactors in the U.S.," *Business Week* (17 April 1978), p. 36; and "To France for Reactors," *Business Week* (12 March 1979), p. 32.
61. Richard Burt, "15 Nations Set Atom Code," *The New York Times* (12 January 1978), p. 1.
62. Gall, "Atoms for Brazil," p. 158.
63. Cook, "How Carter's Nuclear Policy Backfired," p. 124.
64. Cook, "How Carter's Nuclear Policy Backfired," p. 136. See also David J. Rose and Richard K. Lester, "Nuclear Power, Nuclear Weapons and International Stability," *Scientific American* 238 (April 1978), pp. 45–57; Edmund Faltermayer, "Keeping the Peaceful Atom from Raising the Risk of War," *Fortune* (9 April 1979), pp. 90–96; and Victor Gilinsky, "Plutonium, Proliferation and the Price of Reprocessing," *Foreign Affairs* 57 (Winter 1978–79), pp. 374–386.
65. See Robert G. Hawkins, ed., *Technology Transfer and Economic Development* (Greenwich, Conn.: JAI Press, in press); Jack Baranson, *Technology and the Multinationals: Corporate Strategies in a Changing World Economy* (Lexington, Mass.: Lexington Books, 1978); and Denis Goulet, *The Uncertain Promise: Value Conflicts in Technology Transfer* (New York: IDOC/North America, 1977).

CHAPTER 14

1. "Hartke, Javits Dispute Widsom of Curbs on Imports, Investing," *Industry Week* (3 April, 1972), p. 13.
2. For a complete discussion, see Tracy Murray, *Trade Preferences for Developing Countries* (London: Macmillan, and New York: Halsted-Wiley, 1977).
3. See Donald R. Lessard, "Transfer Prices, Taxes and Financial Markets: Implications of Internal Financial Transfers Within the Multinational Corporation," pp. 101–124, in Robert G. Hawkins, ed., *The Economic Effects of Multinational Corporations* (Greenwich, Connecticut: JAI Press, 1979).
4. An exception is merchant shipping, where operation under foreign flags of convenience permit hiring lower-cost foreign crews. But the "multinationality" of this industry is open to doubt. And there is always the question whether the cost of domestic crews would permit competitive operations—if not, of course, no jobs would materialize anyway. American maritime unions know this, and have concentrated their efforts on obtaining cargo preference legislation to preclude foreign competition in certain export (grain) and import (petroleum) trade, as well as all domestic intercoastal shipping, and lobbying for subsidies to U.S. shipbuilding and the merchant shipping industry itself. Despite the enormous costs to consumers, special-interest legislation along these lines has fared well with the Administration and in Congress.

5. This of course is not true if the overseas production is "defensive" against other home-country MNEs acting "offensively" to better compete in foreign markets. Here the multinationals' actions have to be considered collectively as a group, which after all is the case when it comes time to make public policy regarding the issue of production displacement and exports of jobs.

6. Sanford Rose, "Multinational Corporations in a Tough New World," *Fortune* (August, 1973), pp. 52–56+.

7. Rose, "Multinational Corporations," p. 55.

8. Susan B. Foster, "Impact of Direct Investment by United States Multinational Companies on the Balance of Payments," *Federal Reserve Bank of New York Monthly Review* (July, 1972), pp. 166–177.

9. See Nat Goldfinger, "The Case for Hartke-Burke," *Columbia Journal of World Business* (Spring, 1973, pp. 22–25.

10. Robert B. Stobaugh and Associates, *U.S. Multinational Enterprises and the U.S. Economy; A Research Study of the Major Industries That Account for 90 Per Cent of U.S. Foreign Direct Investment in Manufacturing* (Cambridge, Mass., Harvard Business School, 1972).

11. H. Tell, "Offshore Production by American Multinational Corporations" (Unpublished Ph.D. dissertation, New York University, 1976).

12. U.S. Tariff Commission, *Implications of Multinational Firms for World Trade and Labor* (Washington, D.C.: GPO, 1973).

13. Stephen P. Magee, "Jobs and the Multinational Corporation: The Home Country Perspective; pp. 1–15 in Hawkins, *The Economic Effects*.

14. Stobaugh and Associates, *U.S. Multinational Enterprises*.

15. *Foreign Trade and Investment Act of 1972* (S. 2592).

16. "A Campaign for Protectionist Trade Action," *Business Week* (20 May 1972), p. 70.

17. Cf. Louis T. Wells, Jr., "More or Less Poverty? The Economic Effects of the Multinational Corporation at Home and in Developing Countries," pp. 70–98 in Carl H. Madden (ed.), *The Case for the Multinational Corporation* (New York: Frederick A. Praeger, 1977).

18. There is some interesting new evidence that certain MNEs are able to provide significantly greater employment stability in host countries than local firms. By lending workers on temporary assignments in other Latin American divisions, for example, the Otis Elevator Company in Uruguay has been able to help maintain employment levels economically even in times of a depressed local construction industry.

19. "Ford Thinks European," *The Economist* (14 August, 1976), pp. 66–67. In 1977, however, Ford decided to locate a major new engine plant in Wales, rather than elsewhere in Europe, apparently viewing the labor-cost advantages as outweighing the possibly disruptive effects of chronic walkouts the U.K. automobile industry has been experiencing.

20. "Import Curbs Could Hurt U.S. Labor's Ties to Unions Abroad, AFL–CIO Officials Say," *The Wall Street Journal* (27 February, 1973), p. 4

21. Robert Gilpin, *Power and the Multinational Corporation* (New York: Council on Foreign Relations, 1975).

22. R. E. Caves and G. L. Reuber, *Capital Transfers and Economic Policy: Canada* (Cambridge, Mass: Harvard University Press, 1971).

23. James Riedel, "Economic Dependence and Entrepreneurial Opportunities in the Host Country-MNC Relationship," pp. 235–253 in Hawkins *The Economic Effects*.

24. Thomas Parry "Competition and Monopoly in Multinational Corporation Relations with Hose Countries," pp. 63–94 in Hawkins *The Economic Effects*.

25. "The Uranium Dilemma: Why Prices Mushroomed," *Business Week* (1 November 1976), p. 92.

26. "French Connection," *Chemical Week* (27 July 1977), p. 16.

27. "French Connection," p. 16.

28. "Gulf Oil Corporation," *Business and Society Review* (No. 22, Summer 1977), p. 80.

29. "Canada says Gulf Oil Unit Wasn't Forced to Join Uranium Body," *The Wall Street Journal* (17 October 1977), p. 6.

30. Tim Metz, "Panel Finds Cartel Has a Direct Impact on Uranium Purchases by U.S. Utilities," *The Wall Street Journal* (15 August 1977), p. 3.

31. Byran E. Calame, "Canada Told U.S. About Uranium Cartel 10 Days After Top Producers Met in 1972," *The Wall Street Journal* (1 November 1977), p. 10.

32. Six opposition members of the Canadian Parliament filed an action in Ontario Supreme Court designed to compel the government to disclose information on the cartel. Robert Turnbull, "Information Sought on Uranium Cartel," *The New York Times* (27 August 1978), p. 27.

33. "Uranium Firms Sued," *Chemical Week* (27 October 1976), p. 23.

34. "Issues on Trial in Westinghouse Lawsuits," *Business Week* (26 September 1977), p. 125.

35. "Britain Puts Up Its Fence," *The Economist* (10 December 1977), p. 77.

36. "U.S. Vows to Pursue Foreign Violators of Antitrust Laws," *International Herald Tribune* (10 August 1977), p. 5.

37. William E. Moffet, "Letter to the Editor," *The New York Times* (12 July 1977), p. 28.

38. "The Uranium Dilemma: Why Prices Mushroomed," *Business Week* (1 November 1976), p. 97.

39. "French Connection," p. 16.

40. "N-Power Cost at Stake in Suit," *Denver Post* (11 September 1977), p. 12E.

41. "Utilities Open Case Against Westinghouse on Uranium Contracts," *The Wall Street Journal* (17 September 1977), p. 23.

42. Tim Metz, "New Data Due Today on Uranium Cartel Likely to Increase Pressure on Gulf Oil," *The Wall Street Journal* (8 December 1978), p. 12.

43. "Pushing for Settlements," *Chemical Week* (5 July 1978), p. 16.

44. "Uranium Suit Nears Settlement," *Chemical Week* (14 June 1978), p. 19.

45. "Westinghouse's Kirby Leads the Defense," *Business Week* (10 July 1978), p. 24.

46. "Westinghouse Settles Another Uranium Suit," *Chemical Week* (11 October 1978), p. 17.

47. Stephen Solomon, "A Businesslike Way to Resolve Legal Disputes," *Fortune* (26 February 1979), p. 82.

48. "Westinghouse, Set Back in Court, Is Seen Boosting Efforts to Settle Uranium Cases," *The Wall Street Journal* (30 October 1978), p. 10.

49. "Westinghouse: A Blow in the Uranium Wars," *Business Week* (13 November 1978), p. 40.

50. "Westinghouse Reports $79.1 Million Loss," *The New York Times* (13 July 1979), p. D2.

51. "Westinghouse to Seek Extension of Hearing in Uranium-Fuel Case," *The Wall Street Journal* (26 April 1979), p. 38.

52. Tim Metz, "Gulf Oil Enters Important Legal Struggle in Suit Relating to Uranium Cartel Role," *The Wall Street Journal* (1 October 1977), p. 15.

53. Anthony J. Parisi, "General Atomic Seeking Removal of Judge in Suit Against Gulf Oil," *The New York Times* (9 January 1978), p. D3.

54. Anthony J. Parisi, "Judgment Awarded to United Nuclear on Uranium Pricing," *The New York Times* (3 March 1978), p. D1.

55. "United Nuclear Wins Judgement Uranium Case," *The Wall Street Journal* (3 March 1978), p. 6.

56. Anthony J. Parisi, "Gulf Charges Uranium Monopoly by Westinghouse," *The New York Times* (10 May 1978), p. D1.

57. "Justices Let Stand Ruling United Nuclear Won Against Partnership of Gulf-Shell," *The Wall Street Journal* (16 May 1978), p. 5.

58. "Exxon Plans Suit Against Gulf Oil, General Atomic," *The Wall Street Journal* (11 April 1978), p. 10.

59. "AEP Unit Wins $160 Million Damages Award," *The Wall Street Journal* (18 May 1978), p. 14.

60. Anthony J. Parisi, "General Atomic Names Agent for Arbitration," *The New York Times* (6 June 1978), p. D12.

61. "Gulf to Try to Cover Uranium Shortage At Affiliate With Its Canadian Resources," *The Wall Street Journal* (7 August 1978), p. 8.

62. "Gulf Pays Shell in N-Fuel Dispute," *World Business Weekly* (26 March 1979), p. 14.

63. George Getschow, "Westinghouse Finds It Has Its Hands Full in Uranium-Cartel Suit," *The Wall Street Journal* (4 May 1979), p. 1.

64. "Westinghouse Greed Alleged by Gulf Oil," *The New York Times* (2 December 1977), p. D9.

65. "Westinghouse Greed Alleged," p. D9.

66. Anthony J. Parisi, "The Great Uranium Flap," *The New York Times* (9 July 1978), p. F1.

67. Parisi, "The Great Uranium Flap," p. F1.

68. Parisi, "The Great Uranium Flap," p. F1.

69. Byran E. Calame, "Westinghouse Seeks End to Cloud Caused by Suits Over Uranium Supply Contracts," *The Wall Street Journal* (7 June 1978), p. 17.

70. Edward Cowan, "Uranium Price Trial Ruled Out," *The New York Times* (27 March 1979), p. D1.

71. "Justice Department's Handling of Gulf Case Criticized by Senator," *The Wall Street Journal* (27 March 1979), p. 7.

72. "TVA Sues Gulf and 12 Others, Charging Uranium Conspiracy," *The New York Times* (19 November 1977), p. 34.

73. "Westinghouse Presses Its Case," *Chemical Week* (25 July 1979), p. 25.

74. Getschow, "Westinghouse Finds It Has Its Hands Full," p. 1 and 29.

75. Getschow, "Westinghouse Finds It Has Its Hands Full," p. 29.

76. Getschow, "Westinghouse Finds It Has Its Hands Full," p. 29.

77. Getschow, "Westinghouse Finds It Has Its Hands Full," p. 29.

78. "Westinghouse Presses Its Case," p. 26.

79. Lewis Berman, "Ned Cook in the Agonies of Confession," *Fortune* (May 1977), pp. 340–354.

80. "Xerox Subsidiary Holds Monopoly, U.K. Unit Rules," *The Wall Street Journal* (17 December 1976).

81. "Steel Input Quotas Assailed as Violation of Sherman Act in Consumers Union Suit," *The Wall Street Journal* (25 May 1972), p. 13.

82. "Hitachi Bid to Build Television Plant in Britain, Creating Jobs, Provokes a Storm of Opposition," *The Wall Street Journal* (1 November 1977), p. 46.

83. *Financial Times* (27 July 1977), p. 11.

84. "More Tales of Hoffmann," *The Economist* (2 August 1975), pp. 36–40.

85. "High Court to Scan Triple-Damage Plea of Foreign Nations," *The New York Times* (19 April 1977), p. 64.

86. Parry, "Competition and Monopoly," pp. 63–94.

87. Parry, "Competition and Monopoly," pp. 63–94.

88. "The Antitrusters Aim Overseas," *Business Week* (14 March 1977), pp. 100–102.

89. "The Ticklish Task of Repatriating Profits," *Business Week* (6 September 1976), pp. 77–78.

90. James Shulman, "When Price is Wrong—by Design," *Columbia Journal of World Business* (May–June 1967), pp. 69–76.

91. "Stung by Turkey's Foreign Exchange Crisis," *Business Week* (4 July 1977), p. 55.

92. Tariff Commission, *Implications of Multinational Firms.*

93. "More Concerns Tighten Management of Funds Abroad to Trim Costs," *The Wall Street Journal* (19 May 1972), p. 1.

94. Robert Stobaugh and Sidney Robbins, *Money and the Multinational Corporation* (New York: Basic Books, 1974).

95. "Business Learns to Live With Crisis," *Business Week* (10 March 1973), pp. 36–39.

96. "How a Multinational Firm Protects Its Flanks in Monetary Dealings," *The Wall Street Journal* (20 August 1971), p. 1.

97. "How a Multinational Firm Protects Its Flanks," p. 1.

98. "Bitter Exchange: New Translation Rule for Currency, *The Wall Street Journal* (8 December 1976), pp. 1 and 34.

99. See Lessard, "Transfer Prices, Taxes and Financial Markets," pp. 101–124 in Hawkins, *The Economic Effects.*

100. Cf. Thomas Horst, "The Theory of the Multinational Firm: Optimal Behavior Under Different Tariff and Tax Rates," *Journal of Political Economy* (September–October 1971), pp. 1059–1072. See also his "American Taxation of Multinational Firms," *American Economic Review* (June 1977), pp. 376–389.

101. For a discussion, see George F. James, "MNCs and the Foreign Tax Credit," *Columbia Journal of World Business* (Winter 1974), pp. 61–66.

102. Quoted in Brendan Jones, "Should Multinational Companies' Taxes be Raised?" (13 August 1975), p. 45.

103. "The Multinationals Win Some Points," *Business Week* (3 March 1973), p. 19.

104. Constantine V. Vaitsos, *Intercountry Income Distribution and Transnational Enterprises* (Oxford: Claredon Press, 1974).

105. "Citibank Fund to Lead in Shift of Loans to Tax Havens," *The New York Times* (4 March 1977), p. A.1.

106. "Pacific's New Haven," *The Wall Street Journal* (13 October 1972), pp. 1 and 17.

107. "Swiss Banks Set Accord to Prevent Misuse of Numbered Accounts," *The Wall Street Journal* (3 June 1977).

108. See their *Money and the Multinational Corporation.*

109. "Canada Protests Plan by U.S. to Surcharge Michelin Tire Imports," *The Wall Street Journal* (22 January 1973), p. 23.

110. "Digital Equipment Plant in France is Turned Down," *The New York Times* (4 December 1976), p. 137.

111. The best example is Richard Barnet and Ronald Müller, *Global Reach* (New York: Simon and Schuster, 1974).

112. *Manchester Guardian* (29 July 1977), p. 1.

113. Cf. R. G. Hawkins and D. Macaluso, "Multinational Corporate Operations and Domestic Credit Restraint," *Journal of Financial and Quantitative Analysis* (September 1977), pp. 89-97.

Chapter 15

1. See Finn B. Jensen and Ingo Walter, *The Common Market: Economic Integration in Europe* (Philadelphia: Lippincott, 1965).

2. See Richard Barnet and Ronald Müller, *Global Reach* (New York: Simon & Schuster, 1975).

3. See Robert O. Keohane and Joseph Nye, *The Politics of International Economics* (Washington, D.C.: Brookings, 1976).

4. See Charles P. Kindleberger, "Size of Firm and Size of Nation," in John H. Dunning (ed.), *Economics Analysis and the Multinational Enterprise* (London: George Allen & Unwin, 1974).

5. See S. Hymer and R. Rowthorn, "Multinational Corporations and International Oligopoly: The Non-American Challenge," Chapter 3 in Charles P. Kindleberger (ed.), *The International Corporation* (Cambridge, Mass.: MIT Press, 1970).

6. See Raymond Vernon, *Sovereignty at Bay* (New York: Basic Books, 1971), Chapter 1.

7. *The Economist* (14 November 1974), p. 68. See also Karl P. Sauvant and Farid G. Lavipour, *Controlling Multinational Enterprises: Problems, Strategies, Counterstrategies* (Boulder, Colo.: Westview Press, 1976).

8. Paul M. Goldberg and Charles P. Kindleberger, "Toward a GATT for Investment: A Proposal for Supervision of the International Corporation," *Law and Policy in International Business* (Summer 1970), pp. 295–325.

9. Robert O. Keohane and Van Doorn Ooms, "The Multinational Firm" in C. Fred Bergsten and Lawrence Krause (eds.), *World Politics and International Economics* (Washington, D.C.: Brookings, 1975).

10. "Multinationals Face Disorderly Struggle Over Foreign Controls, Conference Finds," *The Wall Street Journal* (1 August 1973).

11. United Nations Conference on Trade and Employment held at Havana, Cuba, from 21 November 1947 to 28 March 1948, *First Act and Related Documents*, United Nations publications No. 1948. II.D.4.

12. See United Nations Commission on Transnational Corporations, *International Codes and Regional Agreements Relating to Transnational Corporations* (New York: U.N. document E/C.10/9/Add. 1, 3 February 1976).

13. Henri Schwamm, "Origin, Nature, Economic and Political Significance of Codes of Conduct," in European Centre for Study and Information on Multinational Corporations, *Codes of Conduct for Multinational Enterprises* (Brussels: ECSIM, 1977). See also "Codes of Conduct for Multinational Corporations," *Business International* (29 December 1978), pp. 410–411 and "Multinationals: An EC Policy," *European Community* (March–April 1979), p. 12.

14. OAS document CP/GC-656/76 corr. 1 (26 February 1976), Appendix 1. Also OAS document CP/GC-656/76 corr. 1 (26 February 1976) and CP/CG-699/766 (30 April 1976).

15. Pugwash Conference, "Draft Code of Conduct on Transfer of Technology," *World Development* (April–May 1974).

16. USA-Business and Industry Advisory Committee on International Investment and Multinational Enterprise, *A Review of Standards and Guidelines for International Business Conduct* (New York: USA-BIAC, 1975).

17. International Labour Organization, *Multinational Enterprises and Social Policy* (Geneva: ILO, 1973), Part II, Paragraph 141. Also ILO, *International Principles and Guidelines on Social Policy: For Multinational Enterprises: Their Usefulness and Feasibilities* (Geneva: ILO, 1976), p. 25.

18. Stanford Research Institute, *International Business Principles: Codes* (Stanford: SRI, 1975).

19. United Nations, *International Development Strategy* (New York: U.N., 1971). See also Resolution 3201 (S-V10) and Resolution 3281 (XXIX).

20. Organisation for Economic Cooperation and Development, *Guidelines for Multinational Enterprises* (Paris: OECD, 1976). See also "Rules for Firms—and Governments," *The Economist* (31 March 1979), pp. 60–61.

21. See John Hargreaves and Jan Davman, *Business Survival and Social Change* (New York: Halsted-Wiley, 1975); and Robert W. Ackerman and Raymond A. Bauer, *Corporate Social Responsiveness: The Modern Dilemma* (Reston, Va.: Reston Publishing, 1976). External scanning by MNEs, however is currently rudimentary in character. See W. J. Keegan, "Multinational Scanning: A Study of the Information Sources Utilized by Headquarters Executives in Multinational Companies," *Administrative Science Quarterly* (September 1974), pp. 411–422; and John S. Schwendiman, *Strategic and Long-Range Planning for the Multinational Corporation* (New York: Praeger, 1973).

22. See Karl E. Weick, *The Social Psychology of Organizing* (Reading, Mass.: Addison-Wesley, 1969).

23. The notion of "opportunistic surveillance" is from James D. Thompson, *Organizations in Action* (New York: McGraw-Hill, 1967). See also "International Companies Use a Select Breed to Monitor the Environment," *Business Europe* (19 May 1978), pp. 153–154.

24. The informational roles of boundary-spanners are discussed in Howard Aldrich and Diane Herker, "Boundary Spanning Roles and Organizational Structure," *The Academy of Management Review* 2 (April 1977), pp. 217–230; and J. Stacy Adams, "The Structure and Dynamics of Behavior in Organizational Boundary Roles," pp. 1175–1190 in Marvin D. Dunnette (ed.), *Handbook of Industrial and Organizational Psychology* (Chicago: Rand McNally, 1976).

25. See Raymond A. Bauer (ed.), *Social Indicators* (Cambridge, Mass.: MIT Press, 1966); Burkhard Strumpel, *Economic Means for Human Needs: Social Indicators of Well-Being and Discontent* (Ann Arbor: Survey Research Center, Institute for Social Research, The University of Michigan, 1976); Kenneth C. Land (ed.), *Social Indicator Models* (New York: Russell Sage Foundation, 1975); and Leslie D. Wilcox, *et al.*, *Social Indicators and Societal Monitoring: An Annotated Bibliography* (Amsterdam, N.Y.: Elsever Scientific Publishing Company, 1973).

26. See John Fayerweather, "Elite Attitudes Toward Multinational Firms: A Study of Britain, Canada and France," *International Studies Quarterly* 16 (December 1972), pp. 472–490;

Fund for Multinational Management Education, *Private Investment in Latin America: A Survey of Elite Attitudes* (New York: FMME, 1976); Joseph LaPalombara and Stephen Blank, *Multinational Corporations and National Elites: A Study in Tensions* (New York: The Conference Board, 1976).

27. See Thomas A. Heberlein, "Some Observations on Alternative Mechanisms for Public Involvement: The Hearing, Public Opinion Poll, The Workshop and the Quasi-Experiment," *Natural Resources Journal* 16 (January 1976), pp. 197–212; and G. Peninous, M. Holthus, D. Kebschull, and J. Attali, *Who's Afraid of the Multinationals? A Survey of European Opinion Toward Multinational Corporations* (Brussels: European Centre for Study and Information on Multinational Corporations, 1978).

28. See Richard N.L. Andrews, "A Philosophy of Environmental Impact Statement," *Journal of Soil and Water Conservation* 28 (1973), pp. 197–203; Thomas G. Dickert, "Methods for Environmental Impact Assessment: A Comparison, pp. 127–143, in Thomas G. Dickert and Katherine R. Domeny (eds.), *Environmental Impact Assessment: Guidelines and Commentary* (Berkeley: University Extension, University of California, 1974).

29. Erich Jantsch, "Forecasting and the Systems Approach: A Critical Survey," *Policy Sciences* 3 (1972), pp. 475–498; J.C. Chambers, S.K. Mullick, and D.D. Smith, "How to Choose the Right Forecasting Technique," *Harvard Business Review* (July–August 1971); O.D. Duncan, "Social Forecasting: The State of the Art," *The Public Interest* 17 (Fall 1969), pp. 88–110; Martin V. Jones, "The Methodology of Technology Assessment," *The Futurist* (February 1972); H.W. Landford, *Technological Forecasting Methodologies: A Synthesis* (New York: American Management Association, 1972); and T.P. Merritt, "Forecasting the Future Business Environment—The State of the Art," *Long Range Planning* (1974), pp. 54–62.

30. Don Lebell and O.J. Krasner, "Selecting Environmental Forecasting Techniques from Business Planning Requirements," *The Academy of Management Review* 2 (July 1977), pp. 373–383.

31. Morton Deutsch, *The Resolution of Conflict: Constructive and Destructive Processes* (New Haven: Yale University Press, 1973), p. 362.

32. See Bruce Lloyd, *Political Risk Management* (London: Keith Shipton Developments, 1976); Robert D. Stobaugh, Jr., "How to Analyze Foreign Investment Climates," *Harvard Business Review* (September–October 1969), pp. 100–108; "Risk Managers: Ready for Anything," *International Management* (July 1977), pp. 22–25; Norman A. Baglini, *Risk Management in International Corporations* (New York: Risk Studies Foundation, 1976); Stephen Goodman, "How the Big Banks Really Evaluate Sovereign Risks," *Euromoney* (February 1977), pp. 105–110; Dan H. Haendel, Gerald T. West, and Robert G. Meadow, *Overseas Investment and Political Risk* (Philadelphia: Foreign Policy Research Institute, 1975); F.T. Haner, "Business Environment Risk Index," *Best's Review* (Property/Liability ed.), (July 1975), pp. 47–50; R.J. Rummel and David A. Heenan, "How Multinationals Analyze Political Risk," *Harvard Business Review* 56 (January–February 1978), pp. 67–76; Lar S.H. Thunell, *Political Risks in International Business* (New York: Praeger, 1977); and Stephen J. Kobrin, "Political Risk: A Review and Reconsideration," Working Paper #998–78, Sloan School of Management, MIT (May 1978).

33. See Allen V. Kneese, "Management Science, Economics and Environmental Science," *Management Science* 19 (June 1973), pp. 1122–1137.

34. See H. Raiffa, *Decision Analysis* (Reading, Mass.: Addison-Wesley, 1969); and R.L. Keeney and H. Raiffa, *Decisions with Multiple Objectives* (New York: Wiley, 1976).

35. See Steven J. Brams, *Game Theory and Politics* (New York: The Free Press, 1975).

36. See Richard Warren Smith, "A Theoretical Basis for Participatory Planning, *Policy Science* 4 (September 1973), pp. 275–295.

37. For some provocative propositions on the negative consequences of participation see Walter A. Rosenbaum, "The Paradoxes of Public Participation," *Administration and Society* 8 (November 1976), pp. 355–383. For different forms and degrees of external participation see Sherry R. Arnstein, "A Ladder of Citizen Participation," *Journal of the American Institute of Planners* 35 (July 1969), pp. 216–224; and Alden Lind, "The Future of Citizen Involvement," *The Futurist* 9 (December 1975), pp. 316–328.

38. See Phyllis S. McGrath, *Managing Corporate External Relations' Changing Perspectives and Responses* (New York: Conference Board, 1976); Phyllis S. McGrath (ed.), *Business Credibility: The Critical Factors* (New York: Conference Board, 1976); Jean J. Boddewyn, "External Affairs: A Corporate Function in Search of Conceptualization and Theory," *Organization and*

Administrative Science 5 (Spring 1974), pp. 67–111; David H. Blake, *Managing the External Relations of MNCs* (New York: Fund for Multinational Management and Education, 1977); and C.N. Aguilar, "External Affairs at the World Headquarters Level of the U.S. Based Industrial Multinational Enterprise," (PhD dissertation, Graduate School of Business Administration, New York University, 1974).

39. See Jean J. Boddewyn, *Corporate External Affairs: Blueprint for Survival* (New York: Business International, 1975).

40. See Jack N. Behrman, J.J. Boddewyn, and Ashok Kapoor, *International Business—Government Communications: U.S. Structures, Actors and Issues* (Lexington, Mass.: Lexington Books, 1975); Orville L. Freeman, "Communication: Key to Corporate Survival," (New York: Business International, 1976); Jayne Baker Spain; "Communication in a Crisis," *Across the Board* (June 1978), pp. 82–88; "Why Multinationals Need a High Profile," *International Management* (June 1977), pp. 14–17.

41. See International Business–Government Counsellors (IBGC), *Multinational Government Relations: An Action Guide for Corporate Management* (Washington, D.C.: IBGC, 1977); Business International, *A Public Policy Program for the Multinational Corporation* (New York: Business International, 1977); Public Affairs Council, *Selected Proceedings of PAC Conference on Multinational Public Affairs* (Washington, D.C.: Public Affairs Council, 1976); S.P. Sethi, *Advocacy Advertising and Large Corporations* (Lexington, Mass.: D.C. Heath, 1977); and Boddewyn, *Corporate External Affairs.*

42. See Stanford Research Institute, *International Business Principles—Company Codes* (Menlo Park, California: Stanford Research Institute, 1976); Public Affairs Council, *Codes of Conduct* (Washington: Public Affairs Council, 1975); U.S. Business and Industry Advisory Committee to the OECD, *U.S. Corporate Response to OECD Guidelines: Examples of Voluntary Cooperation* (New York: USA-BIAC, 1978); and European Centre for Study and Information on Multinational Corporations (ECSIM), *Codes of Conduct for Multinational Companies—Issues and Positions* (Brussels: ECSIM, 1977).

43. See David H. Blake, William C. Frederick, and Mildred S. Myers, *Social Auditing: Evaluating the Impact of Corporate Programs* (New York: Praeger, 1976); John Humble, *The Responsible Multinational Enterprise* (London: Foundation for Business Responsibility, 1975); John Humble, *Social Responsibility Audit: A Management Tool for Survival* (New York: Amacom, 1973); Raymond A. Bauer and Dan H. Fenn, Jr., "What is a Corporate Social Audit?," *Harvard Business Review* (January–February 1973), pp. 37–48; and Meinolf Dierkes and Rob Coppock, "Europe Tries the Corporate Social Report," *Business and Society Review* (Spring 1978), pp. 21–24.

44. Phillip L. Hunsaker, William C. Mudgett, and Bayard E. Wynne, "Assessing and Developing Administrators for Turbulent Environments," *Administration and Society* 7 (November 1975), pp. 312–327.

45. Our framework in this section relies with some modification on Fayerweather's conceptual scheme of fragmentation and unification in dealing with multi-country strategic and administrative issues. See John Fayerweather, *International Business Strategy and Administration* (Cambridge, Mass.: Ballinger, 1978).

46. An early version of this analytical framework appeared in Thomas N. Gladwin and Ingo Walter, "Multinational Enterprise, Social Responsiveness, and Pollution Control," *Journal of International Business Studies* 7 (Fall–Winter 1976), pp. 57–74. Also see Thomas N. Gladwin and Vern Terpstra, "Introduction," in Vern Terpstra (ed.), *The Cultural Environment of International Business* (Cincinnati: South Western, 1978), pp. xi–xxiv.

47. These dimensions of the external environment of the organization have been treated theoretically and empirically by: Jeffrey Pfeffer and Gerald R. Salancik, *The External Control of Organizations: A Resource Dependence Perspective* (New York: Harper & Row, 1978); Robert B. Duncan, "Characteristics of Organizational Environments and Perceived Environmental Uncertainty," *Administrative Science Quarterly* 17 (September 1972), pp. 313–327; Fred E. Emery and Eric L. Trist, "The Causal Texture of Organizational Environments," *Human Relations* 18 (February 1965), pp. 21–32; Paul R. Lawrence and Jay W. Lorsch, *Organization and Environment: Managing Differentiation and Integration* (Boston: Division of Research, Graduate School of Business Administration, Harvard University, 1967); Shirley Terrebery, "The Evolution of Organizational Environments," *Administrative Science Quarterly* 12 (March 1968), pp. 590–613; James D. Thompson, *Organization in Action* (New York: McGraw

Hill, 1967); and William R. Dill, "The Impact of Environment on Organizational Development," in Sidney Mailick and Edward H. van Ness (eds.), *Concepts and Issues in Administrative Behavior* (Englewood Cliffs, N.J.: Prentice Hall, 1962), pp. 94–109.

48. See Tom Burns and G.M. Stalker, *The Management of Innovation* (London: Tavistock Publications, 1961); and Richard N. Osborn and James G. Hunt, "Environment and Organizational Effectiveness," *Administrative Science Quarterly* 19 (June 1974), pp. 231–246.

49. See John Child, "Organizational Structure, Environment and Performance—The Role of Strategic Choice," *Sociology* 6 (January 1972), pp. 1–22; Ray Jurkovich, "A Core Typology of Organizational Environments," *Administrative Science Quarterly* 19 (September 1974), pp. 380–394; and Kjell-Arne Ringbakk, "Strategic Planning in a Turbulent International Environment," *Long Range Planning* 9 (June 1976), pp. 2–11.

50. See Michael Aiken and Jerald Hage, "Organizational Interdependence and Intraorganizational Structure," *American Sociological Review* 33 (December 1968), pp. 912–930; Pradip N. Khandwalla, "Environment and Its Impact on the Organization," *International Studies of Management and Organization* 2 (Fall 1972), pp. 297–313; and Lawrence and Lorsch, *Organization and Environment*.

51. See Thompson, *Organization in Action;* Khandwalla, "Environment and Its Impact"; and Lawrence and Lorsch, *Organization and Environment*.

52. See Peter J. Katzenstein, "International Interdependence: Some Long-term Changes and Recent Changes," *International Organization* 29 (Autumn 1975), pp. 1021–1034; and Robert O. Keohane and Joseph S. Nye, Jr., "International Interdependence and Integration," in Fred I. Guenstein and Nelson W. Polsby (eds.), *Handbook of Political Science, Volume 8: International Politics* (Reading, Mass.: Addison-Wesley, 1975), pp. 363–414.

53. John Fayerweather, *International Business Management: A Conceptual Framework* (New York: McGraw Hill, 1969).

54. Fayerweather, *International Business Management*.

55. David P. Rutenberg, "Planning for a Multi-national Synergy," *Long Range Planning* 2 (December 1969), pp. 24–26.

56. This has been noted by Sol Levine and Paul E. White, "Exchange as a Conceptual Framework for the Study of Interorganizational Relationships," *Administrative Science Quarterly* 5 (March 1961), pp. 583–601.

57. See Thompson, *Organization in Action*.

58. See Ingo Walter, "Social Responsibility and the Future of Multinationals: Guidance Without Rules," *Intereconomics* (May 1976), pp. 141–145.

59. See Dill, "The Impact of Environment on Organizational Development."

60. See William H. Starbuck, "Organizations and Their Environments," pp. 1069–1123, in Marvin D. Dunnette, ed., *Handbook of Industrial and Organizational Psychology* (Chicago: Rand McNally, 1976).

61. Arguing the role of "strategic choice," Child maintains that managers in large organizations such as MNEs possess some discretion in guiding their organizations along different courses in response to perceived environmental pressures and constraints. MNEs have a certain degree of latitude in choosing whether to (a) adapt to external forces, (b) select new domains so as to reduce the degree of dependence, or (c) attempt manipulation of external forces. See Child, "Organizational Structure, Environment and Performance."

62. See Howard V. Perlmutter, "The Tortuous Evolution of the Multinational Corporation," *Columbia Journal of World Business* 4 (January–February 1969), pp. 9–18.

63. Managing contradictions has also been viewed as the central task of U.S. foreign policy. See: Thomas L. Hughes, "Carter and the Management of Contradictions," *Foreign Policy* (Summer 1978), pp. 34–55.

64. From Henry Brooks Adams, *The Education of Henry Adams* (1907).

INDEX

AAMA, 346
Abbott Laboratories, 52, 328, 342, 362-364,
  366, 368, 369
Ability to pay, 382
Abourezk, James, 147
Abraham and Straus, 185
Abrams, B., 579, 624, 633
Absenteeism, 116
Accommodation, 47, 58, 214, 293, 372, 373,
  538
Accommodation payments, 328
Accommodative mode, 81, 214
Accountability, 69
Account withdrawals, 154
Ackerman, R. W., 577, 630, 642
ACLI Sugar Co., 183
Acrow Steel, 92
Acrylonitrile, 342
Action for Children's Television, 19, 366
Adams, G., 612, 615, 616
Adams, Henry, 574, 645
Adams, J. S., 642
Adams, R. J., 627
Adams, Stanley, 353
Adaptionists, 334
Adelman, K. L., 590, 602
Ad Hoc Committee for Chilean Solidarity, 33
Adjudication, 450
Adjustment, 510, 543
Adkins, L., 589
Adkins, E. H., 589
Adler, W., 531
Administrative and legal tactics, 37
Advance planning, 124
Advertising, 358
  direct consumer, 370
  fairness in, 359
  regulation, 359, 371
  and television, 358
Advertising Association, 359
Advertising Code Commission, 359
AEC, France, 521, 522
Aeroflot, 245
Aerospace industry, 312
AFL-CIO, 49, 77, 383, 384, 388, 513, 538
Africa, European colonialism in, 193

education, 208
  liberation groups, 208
Africa, American Committee on, 150, 155, 161
African, Caribbean, Pacific (ACP) associates
  of EEC, 163ff
African Chrom Mines Ltd., 176
African Commission on Human Rights, 133
Arrican Development Fund, 162
African National Congress, 209
Agathe, K. E., 627
Agency for Consumer Advocacy, 336
Agency for International Development, 161
Agents fees, 300, 302, 310
Agnelli, Giovanni, 265
Aguilar, C. H., 644
Agricultural projects, 229
Aharoni, Yair, 575
AID, 187, 431
Aiken, M., 645
Aircraft, 156
Air France, 50, 74, 113
Air Products and Chemicals, Inc., 56
Air quality, 437
Akzo, 49-51, 69, 71, 77, 84, 105, 110, 155, 386,
  387, 544
Akzo Central Staff Affairs Bureau, 387
Akzo v. labor unions, 49-50
Akzo restructuring, 386
Akzo World Council, 387
Alabama Power Co., 524
Albright & Wilson, 398
Albrecht, Susanne, 101
Alcan Aluminium Ltd., 53, 56, 84, 155, 234,
  275, 277
Alcan, Pechiney, and Instituto Nacional de
  Industria, 451
Alcoa, 51, 88, 234, 236, 275-278, 313
Aldrich, H., 642
Alexander, Y., 586
Alfa Romeo, 112
Algemene Bank Nederland, 155, 174
Al Fatah, 12
Allbach, D. M., 589
Allende Gossens, Salvador, 16, 33, 205, 292,
  293, 310, 530, 552
Alliance for National Liberation, 105

Allied Chemical Co., 24, 56, 454
Allis Chalmers, 53
All Nippon Airways, 299
Alejandro, C. F. Diaz, 584
Altman, L. K., 619
Alumax, 455
Alyeska Pipeline Serviced Co., 423
Alyeska Pipeline Service Co. v.
    environmental groups, 423
AMAX, 57, 73, 75, 77, 196-200, 410, 444-445,
    451, 455, 530
AMAX v. Colorado Open Space
    Coordinating Council, 57
Amdahl, Corp., 476, 478
Amdur, H., 585
American Airlines, 340
American Apparel Manufacturers Associa-
    tion (AAMA), 346
American banks, 168, 169
American Baptist Convention, 149
American Bar Association, 120
American black community, 194
American Chamber of Commerce, 401
American churches, 168
American Committee on Africa, 150, 155, 161,
    168, 170, 182, 185, 187, 193, 201, 209,
    412
American Cyanamid, 59, 202, 314, 350, 411,
    530
Americans for Democratic Action, 150
American Electric Power, 445, 526
American Friends of Brazil, 150
American Friends Service Committee, 150,
    161, 177
American Gold Prospector, 186
American Hoechst, 350
American Home Products, 362-364, 366, 368,
    369
American Institute of Certified Public
    Accountants, 321
American Jews, 229
American Jewish Congress, 17, 61, 75, 224,
    231, 232
American Motors, 63
American Safety Razor Co., 528
American Ship Building, 316
American uranium, 491
Ames, B. N., 622
Amerada Hess, 194
AMF, 328
Amherst College, 155
Amin, Idi Dada, 182-184, 187, 494, 496

Amin regime, 165
Amnesty International, 118, 142, 151, 156
Amoco, 194
Amoco Argentina, 92
Amsterdam-Rotterdam Bank N.V., 153, 169,
    174, 216
Amungme tribe, 77
Amuzegar, J., 590, 591
Anaconda, 48, 275, 292
Andelman, D. A., 614
Anderson, Jack, 17, 33, 596, 597
Anderson, L., 579
Anderson, S. H., 579, 589
Andreotti, P., 463
Andrews, F., 617
Andrews, R. N. L., 643
Audubon Society, 431
Anglican Church of Canada, 169
Anglo-American Corp., 527
Anglo-Iranian Oil Co., 51, 88
Angola, 154, 156, 194
Angolan independence, 195
Angola Solidarity Committee, 150
Angry Brigade, 100
Anheuser-Busch, 354, 357, 358
Anovolar, 339
Anti-Apartheid Movement, 150, 169, 212
Anti-apartheid, 154, 185-188
Antibiotics, overcharging for, 350
Anti-boycott, 224ff, 226, 231
Anti-colonial wars, 193
Anti-competitive practices, 529
Anti-Defamation League of B'nai B'rith, 21,
    224, 226, 228, 229, 232
Anti-Distillers agitation, 348
Anti-libertarian trends, 118
Antioch College, 154
Antitrust, decrees, 233
    in developing countries, 356
    in Eastern bloc, 356
    guidelines and MNEs, 55-56
    law, 227, 355, 531
    liability, 237
    multinationals and, 235, 528
    policies, 221, 530, 552
Antitrust Improvement Act, 233
Automation Industries Inc., 52, 54
Apartheid, 150, 163, 164, 168, 170, 173, 182,
    185, 188, 189, 200-202, 204, 206, 207,
    209, 217, 221, 412
Apartheid, Committee on, 148
Apartheid, Committee of Conscience

Against, 168
Apcar, L. M., 621
Apex Textile Co., 110
Appeasement, 58
Apple, Jr., R. W., 588
Applications technology, 471
Arab blacklists, 223, 299
Arab boycott, 222, 226, 227, 244
Arab embargo, 196, 246, 253
Arabian American Oil Co., *see* Aramco
Arab investment and trade, 232
Arab-Israeli conflict, 224, 226, 248, 250, 255
Arab League Boycott Conference, 229
Arab League Council, 133, 223, 224, 228, 229
Arab oil, 231, 249
Arab Revolutionary Army, Palestinian
        Commando, 114
Arab states, 222, 226, 248
Aramco, 226, 247-253, 255
Araskog, Rand V., 8
Arbourage Financial Consultants, 317
Archibald, K., 582
Arellano, Oswaldo Lopez, 297
Argen Information Systems, 124
Argentina, 157, 163
    Coca-Cola and, 91-92
    Exxon and, 92
    Ford executives murdered in, 92
    sovereignty, 242
Argentina People's Revolutionary Army, 97
Argimiro Gabalden Revolutionary
        Command, 82, 103
Aristophanes, 297
Arizona Public Service Co., 450
Armco Steel, 59
Armed assault, 112
Armed Forces of National Liberation for
        Puerto Rico (FALN), 112
Armed Forces Movement, 195
Armed Front of National Resistance,.104
Armenian Liberation Front, 102
Armentraut, F., 579, 595, 596
Arms and ammunition, 157, 164
Armstrong, Lord, 170
Arnstein, S.R., 643
Arthur Anderson & Co., 312
Arthur D. Little Inc., 413
Arthur Young & Co., 312
ASARCO, 73
Asbestos, 291ff
Asbestos Corp., 289-290
Ashland Oil, 300

Ashton project, 22
Asian Development Bank, 162
Assassination, 96, 113
Assertiveness, 46, 66, 213
Association of the Bar of the City of New
        York, 324
Astiz, C. A., 588
Astra Pharmaceuticals, 347, 349
Atoms for Peace, 493
Atlantic Richfield, 59, 68, 117, 444
Atlas Corp., 527
Atomic Energy of Canada Ltd., 309
Atomic Energy Commission, 431, 491, 522
Atomics International, 499
AT&T, 236, 419
Attali, J., 643
A.T. Cross Co., 357
Attention, terrorists and, 103
Audit procedures, 312
Aufsichtsrat, 395, 396, 402
Aurelius, Marcus, 326
Australia, 150
Australian Labour Party, 33
Australian Pricing Bureau, 350
Austria, 399
Autocratic states, 308
Automation Industries Inc., 52, 54
Automobile industry, 341, 380, 381
Auturan, 339
Avery, D., 576
Avis, 316, 317, 408, 533
Avoidance mode, 47, 52, 80, 88, 123, 213, 241,
        257, 263, 279, 284, 328, 372, 538

Baader-Meinhof Gang, 97, 100, 108, 109, 112
Babcock & Wilcox Co., 492
Baby Killer, 361
Backman, J., 575
Badger, 377
Baglini, N. A., 643
Bahamas, 539
Bahamas Exploration Co. Ltd., 317
Bailey, M., 594
Balance of payments, 31, 261, 262, 264, 302,
        533, 534-535, 536
Baldwin, D. A., 589
Baldwin, M. F., 581
Baldwin, P. L., 581
Ball, George W., 304, 603
Ball, R., 625
Ballon, R. J., 623
Banco Angola, 195

Bank, 154, 155, 167, 170
  Canadian, 167
  secrecy, 317
Bankers Trust Company, 168
Banking, 274
Bank für Gemeinwirtschaft, 376
Bank of America, 58, 60, 92, 105, 110, 114, 130,
    167, 168, 170, 173, 174, 175, 214
  Arab boycott of Israel and, 58
Bank of England, 311
Bank of Italy, 92
Bank of Montreal, 53, 174
Bank of Tokyo, 421
Banque de Paris et Pays-Bas (BNP), 59
Banta, J. S., 634
Barclays Bank, 153, 169, 175, 200
Barclays International, 174
Baranson, J., 635, 637
Barbes, R., 636
Bargaining, 64, 260, 380
Barksdale, H. C., 620
Barlow Rand Ltd., 212
Barna, B., 598
Barnet, R. J., 575, 577, 641
Barovick, R. L., 578, 604, 618
Barre, Raymond, 51, 58
Barricade and hostage, 110
Barrientos, 18
Barriers, trade and financial, 504, 505
Baruch, H., 618, 619
Barzini, Luigi, 307, 613
Basche, Jr., J. R., 616
BASF, 2
Basrah Petroleum Co., 249
Bassiouni, M. C., 586
Batchelor, C., 637
Bauer, R., 577, 642, 644
Baumol, W. J., 631
Bauxite industry, 275
Bauxite tax law, 277
Bavarian Motor Works (BMW), 208
Bavinck, Jan, 112
Bay Area Air Pollution Control District, 22
Bayer A. G., 463, 475, 531, 546
Bayer-Rickman, 444
Beame, Abe, 116
Beard, Dita D., 17
Beauvoir, S. de, 629
Bechtel Corporation, 226, 227, 228, 496
Becker, J.B., 586
Bedell, Berkley, 147
Beecham Group, 354ff

Begin, Menachem, 96
Behavioral process view, 3
Behavioral "zones," 79
Behn, Sosthenes, 7, 26
Behrman, J. N., 580, 584, 603, 636, 644
Belgium, 150
Bell Canada, 53
Bell, Griffin, 523
Bell, J. B., 585, 586, 606
Bell, R. G., 587, 588
Bell Helicopter, 183, 187, 314, 406
Bell Telephone, 236
Bell Telephone Manufacturing Co. of
    Antwerp, 17
Bendix Corporation, 113, 322, 445, 503
Benn, Anthony Wedgewood, 352
Bennett, J. F., 580, 611, 616
Benningson, A. I., 621
Benningson, L. A., 621
Bergsten, C. F., 575, 606, 641
Berkowitz, M., 583
Berk Pharmaceuticals Ltd., 23
Berlins, M., 622
Berman, L., 640
Bernhard, Prince, 297
Betaald Antwoord, 155
Bethell, T., 631
Bethlehem Steel, 61, 292
Bewegung 7. Juni, 100
Biko, Stephen, 149, 185
Bill of Rights, 132, 134
Binder, D., 599
Bingham, J. B., 605
Bingham Commission, 180
Biota, 437
Bipolar model, 496
Black, Eli M., 297
Black, M., 629
Black African Trade Union, 413
Black Caucus, 161
Blacklist, 223
Blackmail, 300
Black Mountain Mineral Development
    Co., 212
Black Panther Party, 97
Black's civil rights groups, 151
  consciousness, 149
  employees, 166, 208
  and MNEs, 151, 154, 166, 177, 201, 208, 209,
    413
  organizations, 151, 177, 194, 201
  trade unions, 413

Black September, 109, 113
Blackstern, R., 589
Blake, D. H., 626, 644
Blake, R. R., 577, 578, 579
Blaker, M., 612
Blank, S., 643
Blocked profits, coping with, 535
Blore, Geoffrey B., 178
Blum, A., 622
Blumenthal, Michael, 322
B'nai B'rith, 232
Bock, P. G., 583
Boddewyn, J. J., 643, 644
Bodyguards, 121
Boeing Co., 48, 49, 51, 67, 74, 84, 187, 239, 246, 300, 314, 315, 328, 329
Boeing Co. v. U.S. Securities and Exchange Commission (SEC), 48-49
Boise-Cascade, 292
Bombing, 112
Bomers, G. B., 626
Booker McConnell Ltd., 56, 57, 77
Bonneville Power Administration, 455
Booz Allen and Hamilton, 323
Borden, 366
Borg-Warner Corporation, 202, 477
Born, Jorge, 105
Born, Juan, 105
Bosch, 393
Bos Kalis/Westminister Dredging Group, 155
Boston, G. D., 585
Boston Coalition for the Liberation of Southern Africa, 185
Boston University, 154
Botha, Roelof, 411
Bougainville Separatist Movement, 14
Boulding, K. E., 582
Boulton, D., 616
Bowen, Charles, 323
Boycott, 153, 164, 250, 337
    Bechtel and, 227
    Captain, C. C., 221
    Coca-Cola and, 228-230
    Ford Motor and, 230-231
    Mobil Oil and, 231-232
    primary, 222
    secondary, 222, 223
    tertiary, 137, 223
Brandt, Baron Charles Victor, 113
Brady, T. F., 603
Bradley, D. G., 610
Brams, S. J., 643

Brandeis, Louis D., 320, 617
Brandeis University, 154
Bransten, T. R., 606
Brascan, 155
Braun A. G., 235, 354, 357, 531
Brazil, 149, 155, 157, 162, 491, 497
    American Friends of, 150
    drug industry feud in, 373
    and foreign R&D, 59
    nuclear program, 498
Brazilian-German negotiations, 495
Breast feeding, 360, 361
Breeder technology, 499
Brewin, A., 600
Brewster, K., 604, 605
Bribery, 299, 302, 303, 307, 308, 310, 311, 312, 314, 316, 319, 323, 324, 326, 327, 328
Brigate Rosse, 100
Briloff, Abraham J., 312
Brinco Co. Ltd., 16
Bristol Myers, 19, 53, 314, 331, 337, 350, 362, 363, 364, 368, 369, 530
British Aluminium, 235
Britain, 150, 155, 156, 165, 166, 174, 274, 391
    Higher Court, 348, 352
    House of Commons, 348
    House of Lords, 351, 352, 523
British Department of Trade and Industry, 353
British Department of the Environment, 440
British Department of Trade, 180
British Monopolies and Mergers Commission, 528
British American Tobacco, 52, 92, 357
British Airways, 50, 53, 74, 113
British Insulated Callender Cables, 23
British Leyland, 212, 380
British Oxygen Co., Ltd., 398
British Petroleum, 2, 51, 59, 60, 75, 88, 166, 176, 178, 180, 247, 254, 255, 307, 309, 313, 475, 531
British Steel Corporation, 202
British Timken, 234
Brown, B. R., 576, 582, 583, 584
Brown, M., 622, 623
Brown, Harold, 245
Brown, S. H., 606
Brown-Boveri, 56, 57
Brozan, N., 622
Brubaker, S., 631
Brun, S., 623
Brzezinski, Zbigniew, 245

BSN-Gervais Danone, 56
Buchanan, J. M., 582
Bucher, Giovanni, 104
Buckley, P. J., 575
Buckley, T., 603
Bucy, J. Fred, 245, 478
Buergenthal, T., 590
Bugno, F., 633
Bull, (Comp. des Machines Bull), 268, 269, 270, 271, 512
Bullock, Lord Allan, 398
Bullock Report, 398
Bulova Watch Co., 377
Bundesverband der deutschen Industrie (BDI), 413
Bunge, 528
Bunge and Born Ltd., 105
Bunker Hunt Co., 248
Bureau of Alcohol, Tobacco and Firearms, 358
Bureau of the Census, 419
Bureau pour la Vérification de la Publicité, 359
Burke, R. J., 578
Burlington Industries, 223
Burmah Oil, 59
Burns, T., 645
Burns, J. F., 595, 601
Burroughs Corporation, 59, 190, 214, 315, 410, 411
Burt, R., 604, 637
Burton, A. M., 585
Business, 302, 355, 486
Business International Corporation, 305, 310, 323, 329
Business Roundtable, 232
Bustarella, 307
Butterfield, F., 619
Byington, J. S., 621
Bylinsky, G., 607
Byrd Amendment, 165, 177, 215
Byrd, Harry F., 177

Cabinda, 195
CADE, 355
Cadillac Gauge, 187
Caetano government, 195
Calamé, B. E., 619, 639, 640
CALC, Human Rights Coordinating Center, 150
CALC, U.S. Power and Repression Program, 150
Caldwell, L. K., 63
California, University of, 154
  UCLA, 178
Callaghan, M., 83
Calleo, D., 496, 636, 637
Caltex Oil Co., 59, 114, 179, 201, 410, 411
Calvert, P., 587
Cambodia, 240
Cameron, R. S., 579
Camp, C. B., 601
Campaign for a Democratic Foreign Policy, 150
Campaign for Political Prisoners in Indonesia, 150
Campora, Dr. Hector J., 90, 91, 92
Canada, 150, 166, 169
  government, 161, 166, 523
  industry, 53, 287
  United Church Board of, 155
Canadian Foreign Investment Review Act (FIRA), 266
Canadian Imperial Bank of Commerce, 169, 174
Canadian Industries Ltd., 234
Canadian Labor Congress, 388
Canadian Pacific, 53
Canadian Task Force on the Churches and Corporate Responsibility, 200, 287
Canteen Corporation, 24
Capital, 470, 516
  equipment imported, 534
  export controls, 262
  intensive firms, 68
  investments, 534
  ownership of, 518
  socialization of, 392
  transfers abroad of, 431
Capitalism, 77, 102
Capitulation, 125
Caplow, T.A., 582
Caransa, Maurits, 106
Cargill Inc., 314
Carley, W. M., 604, 612
Carlton, D., 586
Carlton, L., 620, 586
Carnegie Foundation, 151
Carson, I., 578, 620
Carson Pirie & Scott, 185
Cartels, 521, 525
Carter, James E., 24, 51, 131, 133, 147, 148,

156, 162, 163, 177, 187, 205, 216, 217, 225, 226, 239, 244, 245, 246, 302, 310, 322, 344, 406, 411, 430, 431, 432, 493, 494, 497, 498, 499, 500

Carter Administration, 157, 162

Carter, W. G., 580

Cartwright, D., 582

Cary, Frank T., 63, 189, 190, 191, 283, 411, 412, 598

Case, Clifford J., 310

Casson, M., 575

Castle & Cook, 415

Castleman, B., 632

Castro, Fidel, 108

Caterpillar Tractor Co., 188, 410, 512

Causen, A. W., 174

Caveat emptor, 340

Caves, R. E., 575, 638

Celanese Corporation, 545

Central Boycott Office (CBO), 223, 225, 229, 230, 231, 232

Central Michigan University, 17

Central National Bank, 169

Central planning model, 392

Centre Europe-Tiers Monde, 150

Center for International Policy, 150, 162

Center for Science in the Public Interest, 20

Center for Social Action of the United Church of Christ, 50, 156, 178, 180, 193

Centre on Transnational Corporations, 148, 552

Cerro Corporation, 292

Cessna Aircraft, 187

Chambers, J. C., 643

Chomsky, N., 591

Charter of Rights and Duties of States, 551

Chase Manhattan Bank, 168, 172, 173, 215, 216

Chavez, Cesar, 369

Chemical Bank, 114, 168, 174

Chemical Industry Institute of Toxicology (CIIT), 56

Chemicals and fertilizers, 156

Chemie Gruenthal, 347, 349

Chemische Werke München (CWM), 424

Chertkoff, J. M., 582

Chevron, 227

Chevron Oil Italiana, 113

Chicago, Central National Bank of, 169

Chicago, First National Bank of, 168

CHIFUREN, 336, 337

Child, J., 645

Chile, 149, 151, 155, 157, 163, 204

G.M., in, 204

reconstruction, 162

University of, 191

Chill, D. S., 602

China, 165

and Fruehauf-France, 243-244

Chisso Chemical, 454

Christian Churches, 207

Christian Concern for Southern Africa, 150

Christian Democrat CISL, 376

Christian Institute of South Africa, 201

Chrysler Corporation, 62, 63, 64, 68, 69, 72, 212, 239, 242, 243, 269, 300, 380, 400, 410, 515

Chrysler Fevre Argentina, 115, 242

Church, Frank, 77, 304, 310, 320

Church, actions, 174

groups, 149, 155, 177, 194, 202, 205

leaders, 154

Church of England, 170

Church Project on U.S. Investment in Southern Africa, 15, 149, 189, 410

Churches and Corporate Responsibility, Task Force on, 150

Churches, Corporate Information Center of the U.S. National Council, 168

Churches, National Council of, 149, 189, 191

Churches, World Council of 149, 150, 155 (see also WCC)

Church Women United, 18, 415

Churchill, Winston, 132

Churchill Falls Labrador Corporation, 16

CIA, 16, 26, 33, 72, 94, 95, 106, 108, 110, 112, 118, 195, 293, 310, 327

Cia de Telefonos de Chile, 340

Ciba-Geigy Co., 338, 339, 354, 475, 528

CII-Honeywell-Bull, 61, 246, 249, 271, 272, 540

Cirie, 455

Citibank, 92, 168, 170, 172, 173, 174, 337, 407

Citicorp, 2, 59, 123, 168, 170, 174, 175, 215, 216, 316, 410, 411

Cities Service, 54, 117, 123, 194

Citizen lobbies, 33, 451

Citroën, 349, 405

City National Bank, 169

Civil rights groups, 151

Civil wars, 195

Clark, D., 142, 147, 148, 201, 591, 592, 594, 596, 598

Clark, Ian, 59

Clark, M. J., 595

Claude, R. P., 590
Clayton Act, 233
Clement, D., 326
Clergy and Laity Concerned (CALC), 150,
      161, 173, 366
Clutterbuck, Major General Richard L., 105,
      585, 587, 589
Craig, E., 593
Cranston, Alan, 147
Crittenden, A., 578, 593, 599, 611, 612,
      614, 624
Cranston, M., 131, 132, 590
Creative issue-control, 82
Creditanstalt-Bankverein, 169
Credit Lyonnais, 113
Credit Suisse, 62
Crime, 105
Criminalization, 320, 321, 322
Crisis management, 121, 125ff, 127
Crocker National Bank, 173, 174, 539
Cromarty Petroleum Co., 444
Crookell, H., 580
Cruz, C., 601
Coalite and Chemical Products Ltd., 463
Coalition for a New Foreign and Military
      Policy, 150, 156, 161
Coalition formation, 71
Coan, E. V., 631
Cola beverage, substitute, 282
Coca-Cola, 49, 51, 55, 57, 63, 64, 68, 74, 77, 88,
      91, 92, 116, 123, 130, 224, 227, 228, 229,
      230, 280, 282, 284, 285, 287, 292, 314,
      337, 342, 384, 407, 415, 416, 500, 545,
      557
   Arab customers of, 228
   and Guatemala, 415
   quality control, 281
   secret beverage formula, 281
Coca-Cola Export Corporation, 228, 280, 281
Code of Hammurabi, 132
Codes of Conduct, 148, 411, 550, 557
Codetermination, 394, 397, 401, 402, 403, 422
   and American unions, 400
Cohen, J. A., 310, 614
Cohen, J. S., 616
Cohen, Manuel F., 321
Cohesiveness, internal, 42
Cole, R. J., 617, 618
Colgate-Palmolive Co., 55, 410
Collaboration, 55ff, 192, 372, 373
Collaborative mode, 81, 86, 213
Collaborative/compromise mode, 278

Collado, E. G., 606
Collective bargaining, 377, 413
Collective self-regulation, 325
Collins, J., 583
Collusion, 313
Colonialism, 148, 150, 193, 213
Colorado Open Space Coordinating
      Council, 57, 77
Colt Industries, 181, 187
Columbia University, 154
Comalco, 17
Combustion Engineering, 53, 492, 499
Comité Contre le Colonialisme et
      l'Apartheid, 150
Comité de Surveillance, 384
Comité Interministeriel des Investissements
      Etrangers (CIIE), 266
Commando 10th of July, 14, 464
Commerce Department, U.S., 190, 224, 225,
      232, 238, 244, 245, 262, 513
Commercial bodies, 33
Commercial risk, 161
Commercial Solvents, 354
Commissioners of the Church of England, 15
Commission on Auditors' Responsibilities,
      321
Commission on Transnational Corporations,
      552
Commission Technique des Ententes et des
      Positions Dominantes, 355
Committee Against Racial Exploitation, 150
Committee for Socialist Revolutionary
      Unity, 62
Committee of Conscience Against
      Apartheid, 168
Committee of Outside Experts (COE), 386
Committee of Returned Volunteers, 193
Committee of 24, 148
Committee on Apartheid, 148
Committee on International Investment and
      Multinational Enterprises, 554
Committee on Interstate and Foreign
      Commerce, 322
Committee to Oppose Bank Loans to South
      Africa, 170
Committee on the Elimination of Racial
      Discrimination, 148
Common's Committee (U.K.), 166
Communications, 37, 168
Communist CGIL, 376
Communist countries, 190, 238, 239, 240, 308
Community organizations, 168

Compagnie des Machines Bull, 268. *See also* CII-Honeywell-Bull

Compagnie Française des Pétroles, 51, 88

Compagnie Internationale pour l'Informatique, *see* CII-Honeywell-Bull

Company Councils, 399

Comparative Survey of Freedom, 136

Compensation, 286

Competition, 47, 48, 213, 235, 257, 264, 313, 328, 372, 521, 531
    approach, 284
    behavior, 87, 531, 533
    bidding, 542
    bribery, 324
    market structure, 313
    mode 80, 213, 284, 285, 514
    policy, 232-237, 553
    reduced, 530
    stance, 264
    strength, 314

Compromise, 47, 61, 285, 293, 373
    accommodation, 372
    approach, 284
    mode, 81, 215, 329, 372

Compromise/accommodative mode, 278

Computer Decisions (article), 191

Computers Sciences Corporation, 187

Computers, 253, 270
    facilitating repression through, 190
    and Latin America, 191
    products, 189
    and University of Chile, 191
    utilization, 268

Concorde (at Kennedy International Airport), 50-51

Conden, J. C., 601

Conderarci, G., 605

Confédération Française Democratique du Travail (CFDT), 58, 376

Confédération Géneral du Travail (CGT), 58, 375

Conference Board, 316, 381

Conference of Presidents of Major American Jewish Organizations, 18

Confiscation, 258, 286, 292

Conflict, arena of, 1ff
    avoidance, 450
    two dimensions of, 46ff
    benefits of, 42
    challenge of, 544
    cost of, 40

handling modes, 86
    management, 4, 45, 66, 257, 298, 468, 500, 536, 544, 546, 555, 557, 564, 572
    marketing-related, 545
    mismanagement of, 43ff
    site of, 72

Congress, U.S., 157, 161 162, 165, 224, 225, 226, 251, 321, 323, 342, 343, 344, 346, 423, 440, 479, 494, 495, 496, 499, 514, 523, 525, 551
    Office of Technology Assessment, 433

Congressional Black Caucus, 147, 161, 177

Conroy, E. D., 632

Consolidated Edison, 249

Conservation Foundation, 432

Consolidated Zinc, 9

Consultative Group Coordinating Committee (COCOM), 238, 245, 489

Consumer, 153, 334, 372
    advocates, 506
    coalition, 334
    and government, 335
    interests, 332
    movement, 332, 334, 336
    relations, 337
    tactics, 336

Consumer Council, 336

Consumers Power Company, 444

Consumer Product Safety Commission (CPSC), 341, 343, 344, 345, 346

Consumers Union, 330, 336, 362, 529

Continental Baking, 19

Continental Can, 528

Continental Grain, 528

Continental Group, 424

Continental Illinois, 168, 170, 173, 174, 175, 185, 215

Continental Oil, 59, 117, 199, 297, 316, 445

Contingency approach, 6, 97, 555, 557, 571

Control Data Corporation, 52, 54, 69, 74, 153, 187, 190, 191, 204, 214, 239, 240, 246, 270, 315, 329, 476, 490

Controllable variables, 332

Conversion, 55

Conzinc Rio Tinto, 527

Conzinc Rio Tinto of Australia, 17, 22

Cook, D., 636, 637

Cook Industries, 528

Cooper, R., 615, 616

Cooper, W. W., 581

Cooperativeness, 46, 213

Coopers and Lybrand, 312

Coordination, 565
Copen, M., 636
Copperweld Corporation, 51, 530
Coppock, R., 644
Cormick, G. W., 635
Cornell University, 155, 366
Corporate activities, 136
  communications, 155
  control, 318
  crime, 311
  fines, 322
  operations, 115
  payoffs, 304
Corporate Information Center of the
     National Council of Churches, 149
Corruption, 305, 307
  commercial and political, 319
Corso-Insa, 205
Coser, L. A., 575, 577
Costello, D., 588
Costello, J., 579
Cost reduction, 503, 504-505
Cotter, W. R., 591, 592, 628
Council for Christian Social Action of the
     United Church of Christ, 14, 193, 194
Council for Namibia, 148, 196
Council for Scientific and Industrial
     Research, 189
Council of Europe, 133, 148, 344
Council on Economic Priorities, 312
Council on Environmental Quality (CEQ),
     432
Council on Hemispheric Affairs, 150
Counter-Information Services, 15
Counter-insurgency, 187
Courtney, W., 599
Cowan, E., 582, 640
Cuban National Liberation Front, 102, 103
Cuba, trade embargo, 242, 243
Cultural bridges, 308, 309
Cummins Engine Co., 476
Cunningham, Captain Charles, 221
Curtis, Ellwood, 512
Customers, loss of, 115
Cyclamates, FDA ban on, 339, 342

Dahlby, T., 629
Dahrendorf, R., 586
Daimler-Benz, A. G., 104, 113, 393, 519
Dainippon Pharmaceuticals, 347, 349
Darden, B., 620
Dartmouth College, 155
Dassault, 309

Davis, J., 592, 599, 601, 628
Davis, W. R., 593
Davman, J., 642
DDSA Pharmaceuticals Ltd., 23
Death squads, 118
Decker, K. H., 626
Déclaration des Droits de l'Homme et du
     Citoyen, 132
Declaration of Independence, 132
Defense, U.S. Department of, 245, 248, 251,
     310
Defensive position, foreign exchange, 512,
     537
de Gaulle, Charles, 269
Degussa, A. G., 424
Delaney Clause, 342, 343
Delaware, 1971 Coastal Zone Act, 445
Del Monte, 153, 182, 414, 476
De-listing discussions, 227
Demarre, A. T., 605
Demerara Bauxite Company, 56
Democracies, 107, 164, 308
Democratic Farmer-Labor Party, 369
Democratic Foreign Policy, Campaign for a,
     150
Democratic nationalization, 270
Demonstrations, 154, 168, 444
De Nascimento, Lopo, 196
Denison, E. F., 635
Denison Mines Ltd., 48, 528
Denmark, 161
Denning, C., 624
den Uyl, Joop, 50
Department of Agriculture, U.S., 304, 432
Department of Commerce, U.S., 231, 432,
     489, 513
Department of Defense, U.S., 187, 320, 432
Department of Energy, U.S., 522
Department of Health and Social Services
     (DHSS), U.K., 23, 350, 351, 352, 372
Department of State, U.S., 324, 432, 523
Department of Treasury, U.S., 432
Dependencia, 3, 570
Depersonalization, 96
Desai, A., 499
Descamisades Peronistas Montoñeros, 12
Desirability, in conflict management, 66, 74
De Spinola, Antonio, 195
d'Estaing, Valery Giscard, 496
Détente, 239
Detroit, City National Bank of, 169
Deutsch, M., 575, 577, 580, 582, 583, 643
Deutsche Bank, 169

Deutscher Gewerkschaftsbund (DGB), 376
Deutz, A. G., 512
Developed countries, 332
Developing countries, 161, 331, 488, 520
  labor in, 414
  risk in, 345
Dev Genc, 109
Dewar, H., 234, 632
DGA International, 479
Diamond Shamrock Company, 56, 206
Dickert, T., G., 643
Dictatorships, 308
Dierkes, M., 644
Diethylstilbestrol (DES), 343
Diggs, Charles, 177
Digital Equipment Corporation, 540
Dill, W. R., 645
Direct bargaining and negotiation, 451
Direct investment, 165, 275, 287
Direct parent-affiliate linkages, 507
Disadvantaged groups, 409
Disclosure, of MNE operations, 262, 321, 324,
  410, 550
Discrimination, 154, 222
Discrimination, Prevention of and Protection
  of Minorities, UN Subcommittee, 148
Disputada de las Condex, 205
Distancing, 55
Distillers Company (Biochemicals) Ltd.,
  346-348, 372
Diversification, 3
Divestiture, 206, 234
Dixon, K., 613
Dobson, C., 585, 616
Dobson, Sir R., 580, 611
Dole Pineapple, 476
Domeny, K. R., 643
Domestic antitrust conflict, 533
Domination, 80
Dominican Republic, 162, 414
Domestic International Sales Corporation
  (DISC), 49
Doppheide und Kollow, 353
Dorsey, Robert R., 7, 18, 300, 614
Douglas Aircraft, 105, 313, 340
Dow Chemical Company, 6, 7, 9, 12, 14-26,
  36, 37, 40-44, 52, 54, 56, 104, 186, 205,
  265, 292, 315, 328, 373, 421, 440, 444,
  463, 530, 544, 545
  v. Bay Area Air Pollution Control District,
    22
  v. Brazilian Industrial Development
    Council, 24

  v. Central Michigan University, 17
  v. Chilean Government, 16
  v. DSM (Dutch State Mines), 23
  v. Federal Trade Commission, 19
  v. Ina Industrija Nafte of Zagreb, 25
  v. Iranians Bank, 25
  v. Italian Communist Party Economist
    Eugenio Peggio, 23-24
  v. Japanese chlorine and caustic soda
    producers, 23
  v. Lejona Associations, 22
  v. Local Brindisi prosecutor, 25
  v. Medical Committee for Human Rights,
    14
  v. Michigan State University, 15
  v. Occupational Safety and Health
    Administration, 21
  v. plant maintenance workers, 21
  v. Popular Resistance Organized Army, 14
  v. Province of Ontario, 22
  v. São Paulo State Environmental
    Protection Agency, 22
  v. Securities and Exchange Commission,
    18
  v. United Steelworkers Local 12075, 20
Doyle Dane Bernbach, 185
Drake, Tom, 92
Dresdner Bank A.G., 101, 113, 116
Dresser Industries, 226, 244, 245, 246, 257,
  328
Drucker, P., 321, 334, 620
Drug industry, 330
Dual sourcing, 379
Duclos, L., 600
Dugan, G., 594
Duncan, O. D., 643
Duncan, R. B., 644
Duncan, Sir Val, 9, 40
Dunlop Pirelli, 56
Dunn, D., 624
Dunnette, M. D., 577, 642, 645
Dunning, J. H., 575, 641
Du Pont Company, 6, 53, 56, 83, 113, 122,
  234, 236, 292, 388, 402, 444, 445
Dutch Industry Federation, 413
Dutch Ministry of Economic Affairs, 386
Dutch State Mines, 23
Dutch unions, 399
Dynamic-static climate, 566

Earnings remissions, controls, 382
Eastern Europe, 249
Eastman Kodak, 2, 56, 188, 410

East-West political relations, 547
East-West trade, 237, 239, 244, 246
Eckhart, R., 322, 618
Eckstein, H., 586
Ecological terrorism, 445
Economic activities, 425, 429
Economic and Social Council (ECOSOC), 551
Economic Club of New York, 288
Economic conflict, 502, 542
  dimensions of, 511
  shape of, 506
Economic development, levels of, 306
Economic effects of MNEs, 541
Economic goals, 540
Economic growth, 146, 470, 505, 516
Economic interactions, dimensions of, 507
Economic interdependence, 572
Economic leverage, 542
Economic nationalism, 275
Economic resources, 437
Economics, and finance, 24, 502
Economic tactics, 37
Economy, 117
ECOSOC, 552, 554
Education, 564
EEC, 19, 40, 148, 163, 166, 235, 236, 239,
    252, 253, 255, 328, 332, 345, 349, 350,
    351, 352, 353, 354, 355, 384, 386, 387,
    388, 390, 404, 413, 414, 423, 429, 448,
    495, 504, 528, 529, 540, 547, 549, 552
  Antitrust Directorate, 19, 355
  antitrust law, 355
  code of conduct for MNEs, 413
  Commission, 163, 359
  Council of Ministers, 359
  Hoffmann-LaRoche suit, 353
Eells, R., 611
Effective power, 71
Effective response, 127
EFTA, 529
Egan, R., 613
Egypt, 227
  industrial projects, 230
  investment and Arab boycott, 62-63
Egyptian-Israeli disengagement agreement, 252
Egyptian-Israeli peace settlement, 227, 231
EIS, 431, 432
El Al, 113
Electricité de France, 104, 114, 448
Electronics Corporation of India, 282

Elia, C. J., 595, 601
Eli Lilly, 347
El Salvador, 157
Embargo, 175, 213, 222, 247, 248, 250, 251,
    252, 253
Embotelladora Guatemalteca, 415
Emergency Coalition for Human Rights in
    South Africa, 151
Emergency Committee for American Trade
    (ECAT), 49, 69, 71, 77
Emery, F. E., 644
Emigration, 165
Empain, Baron Edouard-Jean, 106
Empain-Schneider, 106
Employee ownership, 391, 392, 422
Employee profit-sharing plans, 55
Employment, 261, 264, 513
  displacement, 378
  guidelines, fair, 166
  and labor relations, 553
  of women, transnational, 418
Employment Act of 1946, 505
End Loans to South Africa (ELTSA), 150,
    155, 169, 174
ENEC, 300
Energy, 168
Energy Department, U.S., 245
Energy Research and Development
    Administration (ERDA), 496
Enforcement problems, 323
Engelhard Minerals and Chemicals
    Corporation, 186, 410
Engler, R., 589
English Bill of Rights, 132
Enka Glanzstoff (EG), 49, 386, 387, 388
Entry control, 264, 296
Environment, 22, 405
  oriented planning, 468
  policies, 428, 429
Environmental conflict, 423, 435, 466, 467
Environmental Defense Fund, 337, 345, 346
Environmental disputes, 440
Environmental groups, 431, 441
Environmental impact statements, 431, 432
Environmentalism, 440, 506
Environmental opponents of MNEs, 466
Environmental Protection Agency, U.S., 22,
    62, 440, 444
Episcopal Church, 149, 155, 188, 200, 206
Episcopal Churchmen for South Africa, 198,
    199
Equal Employment Opportunity

Commission, (EEOC), 419
Equal Rights Amendment, 134
Ericsson, L. M., 67, 236
Eritrean Liberation Front, 102
Erne, Earl of, 221
ERP, 91, 93, 94, 104
European Covenant for the Protection of
    Human Rights and Fundamental
    Freedoms, 133
Ernst & Ernst, 300
Esso Argentina, 62, 93, 94
Esso Italiana, 301, 313, 316
Estel Steel Corporation, 155
Estey, J. S., 619
ETA (Basque terrorist organization), 102,
    108
Ethical practices, in commercial
    transactions, 325
Ethiopia, 157
Ethnic violence, 99
Europe, 155, 169
  layoffs in, 377
European American Bank, 168, 169, 174
European Atomic Energy Community
    (EURATOM), 491ff
European Commission on Human Rights,
    133, 148
European Community, see EEC
European Confederation of Free Trade
    Unions (ECFTU), 384
European Court of Human Rights, 133, 148
European Court of Justice, 19, 352, 353,
    354, 355, 528
European Economic Community, see EEC
European independence, 495
European Metal Committee of the
    International Metal Workers
    Federation, 381
European Metalworkers Federation, 381
European Parliament, 400, 552
European Pharmaceutical Manufacturers'
    Association, 332
European Trade Union Confederation
    (ETCU), 384
Euskadi ta Azkatasuna, see ETA
Evacuation, 462
Evans, G., 626
Evasion, tax and exchange control, 279
Ex-Cell-O Corporation, 187
Excessive competition, 531
Exchange rates, 534
Exchange restrictions, 504

Executive life, 115
Executive security, 121
Exiles, 150
Eximbank, 161, 162, 165, 197, 239, 311, 431,
    432, 491
  credits, 165, 197
  financing, 161
  lending, restrictions on, 239
Expatriate employees, 404
Expatriate executives, 406
Expert influence, 71
Export Administration Act, 225, 228
Export Control Act of 1949, 238
Export-control laws, 84, 498
Export Control, Department of Commerce,
    489
Export Controls, 238, 246, 354
Export Development Corporation, 161
Export financing, 161
Export-Import Bank, see Eximbank
Exports of technology by way of the MNE,
    478
Expropriation, 258, 292, 296, 300, 303, 309,
    314, 407, 487, 533
  actions, 292
  bill, 291
  compensation, 286
  legislation, 290
External environment, 566
External relations, 562
Extortion, 300, 302, 307, 308, 318
  payments, 328
Extraterritoriality, 221, 238, 257, 262
Exxon Chemical, 56
Exxon Corporation, 2, 7, 54, 59, 60, 62, 68,
    93, 123, 203, 226, 246, 247, 248, 249,
    255, 292, 300, 313, 315, 327, 444, 445,
    475, 526, 545
Exxon International, 251
Exxon Minerals International, 205

Face-standard, 14
Facilitators, in OPs, 317
Facility security, 123
Fairchild, 187
Fair competition, 324
Fairbanks-Morse, 84
Falconbridge, 155
Falconbridge Nickel Mines, 200
Fallwell, W. F., 575
FALN, 116
Fahd, Crown Prince, 320

Fair Trade Commission (Japan), 356
Faltermayer, E., 637
Fanon, Franz, 160, 587
Farber, S. B., 598
Farley, James, 228
Farm-support programs, 259
Farnsworth, C. H., 579, 613, 622
Fascist Volksunie, 116
Fast breeder reactor, 493
Fatah, 97, 105
Fayerweather, J., 582, 583, 614, 642, 644, 645
FBI, 121
FDA, 330, 331, 338, 339, 341-344, 349, 374
Feasibility, 66, 74
Fedayeen, 105
Federal Appeals Court, 346
Federal Cartel Office, German, 355
Federal Energy Administration, 254
Federal Laboratories, 187
Federal Trade Commission, 19, 49, 68, 74,
    357, 358, 359, 360, 528, 533
Federation of South African Trade Unions,
    414
Federation of West German Industries, 102
Feisal, King, 248, 249, 250, 251
Feldman, Mark B., 324, 618
Female employment, 417
Female labor, in Europe, 420
  Japanese firms, 420
Fenn, Jr., D. H., 644
Ferguson, C., 591, 592, 628
Fernandes, George, 49, 281, 282
Fernex, S., 630
Ferrari, S., 630
Ferrochrome, 176
Fiat, 64, 84, 94, 112-114, 116, 123, 204, 265,
    393, 512, 519, 544
Fiat Concord, 104
Fiat France, 62
Fiduciary responsibility, 311
Filipino People, Friends of, 150
Finance, South African Ministry of, 168
Financial Accounting Standards Board,
    537
Financial condition, 69
Financial controls, 278
Financing, 105
Fine, D. I., 629
Fink, C. F., 583
Finnair v. National Organization of Women,
    357
Finn, B., 606

Finsterbusch, K., 591
Firestone Tire and Rubber Company, 53, 54,
    77, 88, 92, 110, 205, 240, 241, 257,
    312, 316, 341, 385
Firestone, J. A., 621
Firms, payoff-prone, 314
First National Bank of Boston, 52, 153, 169,
    170, 173-175
First National Bank of Chicago, 168, 170,
    173-175, 185
First National Bank of Louisville, 169
First World Congress on Product Liability,
    344
Fischer, D. D., 592
Fisher, R., 583
Fiske, E. B., 593
Fiske, Guy, 290, 291
Flame retardants, U.S. production of, 345
Fleming, J. G., 621
Fletscher, D., 607
Flexible response, 125
Flick Konzern, 402
Flight from regulation, 433
Flint, L., 602
Fluor Corporation, 154, 188
FNLA (National Front for Liberation of
    Angola), 195, 196
Folger Coffee Company, 183, 184, 214
Follett, M. P., 578, 579
Fonda, Jane, 17
Food and Drug Administration, *see* FDA
Foote Minerals Company, 177
Ford Argentina, 90, 91, 92, 242
Ford, D., 630
Ford Foundation, 128, 151, 364
Ford, G., 16, 147, 195, 218, 225, 227, 240,
    320, 497
Ford II, Henry, 207, 380, 515
Ford Middle East Company, 63
Ford Motor Company, 52, 55, 57, 59, 60, 63,
    64, 73, 74, 82-84, 90-92, 113, 123, 130,
    154, 187, 188, 202, 207, 223, 224, 227,
    230, 231, 239, 242, 292, 297, 340, 341,
    380, 384, 385, 402, 405, 410-413, 475,
    482, 483, 545
Ford Pinto, 341
Ford U.K., 83
Forecasting, 560, 561
Foreign aid, bilateral, 156
  bill, U.S., 161
Foreign Assistance Act of 1961, 157
Foreign Assistance Act of 1973, 157

Foreign banks, 168, 274, 302
Foreign bribes, 322
Foreign cartels, 237
Foreign Corrupt Practices Act (FCPA), 49, 322, 328
Foreign debt, 239
Foreign exchange, 273, 319
  markets, 536, 537
Foreign Exchange Regulation Act of 1973 (FERA), 280, 281, 283, 284
Foreign intervention, 222
Foreign investments, 164, 198, 227, 261, 265, 266, 274, 281, 292, 517
  code, 240
  direct, 262, 404
Foreign Investment Review Agency (FIRA), 267
Foreign investors, 265
Foreign Investors Tax Act, 262
Foreign marketing, 333
Foreign military sales disclosure, 187
Foreign oil, 248
Foreign ownership, 265, 519
Foreign policy, 150, 157, 186, 303
Foreign Sovereign Immunities Act, 233
Formal expropriation, 292
Foster, S. B., 638
Foundations, 151, 155
Fowler, E. M., 617, 627
Fractionating, of issues, 82
Fraenkel, J., 590
Fragmenting forces, 568
Framatome, 61, 492
Frame, Alistair, 9
France, 132, 164, 268, 397, 540
  "interessement" law, 391
  investments in, 266
Frankfurt Documents, 168, 169
Frankfurter, Felix, 410
Frank and Hirsch Pty Ltd., 208, 209
Framkin, A., 587, 588
Franko, L. G., 575
Fraser, D. M., 591
Fraser, Dan, 147
Frederick, W. C., 644
Freedom House, 136, 137, 151, 213, 308
Freeman, O. L., 644
Freeport Indonesia Inc., 56
Freeport Minerals Corporation, 56, 57, 73, 77
Free Trade Unions, International Confederation of, 151

French, J. R. P., 582
French Ministry of Finance, 269
French Ministry of Foreign Affairs, 266
French Timken Company, 234
Friedberg, D., 630
Friedrich Krupp, 267, 519
Friends Committee on National Legislation, 150
Friends of Haiti, 150
Friends of the Earth, 521
Friends of the Filipino People, 150
Front de Libération du Québec, 102, 112
Front for the Liberation of the Enclave of Cabinda, 113
Frozen Food Industries Ltd., 53, 69
Fruehauf Corporation, 84, 243
Fruehauf-France, 243
Fruehauf International, 243
Fugur, P., 585
Fujitsu Ltd., 476, 478
Fulbright, William, 241
Fundamental freedoms, 164
Furer, Arthur, 370, 624
Furriers Joint Council, 171, 172

Gaedeke, R. M., 620
Gall, N., 636, 637
Gallagher Group, 357
Gamson, W. A., 582
Gandhi, Indira, 280, 282, 283
Garfield, President, 96
Garino, D. P., 610, 624
Gastil, R. D., 591, 613
GATT, 324, 549, 550, 555
Gay, John, 305
Gelb, L. H., 599
Gelbard, Jose, 242
Geneen, Harold S., 8, 37, 42, 316, 577
General Accounting Office, 432
General Agreement for the International Corporation (GAIC), 550
General and Municipal Workers Union, 348
General Assembly, 164
General Atomic, 522, 525-527
General Biscuit (Antwerp), 24
General Dynamics, 288-292, 445, 519
General Electric Co., 67, 130, 187, 188, 207, 212, 246, 268-270, 272, 357, 380-382, 384, 410, 445, 454, 476, 483, 492, 499, 501, 545
General Electric-Bull, 268-272
General Foods, 183, 184, 214, 357, 378, 400

General Mills, 357
General Motors Corporation, 2, 52, 54, 55, 57, 59, 60, 91, 92, 114, 123, 155, 188, 202, 204, 206, 207, 215, 242, 243, 340, 380, 384, 400-402, 410, 411, 475, 483, 501, 535, 537, 545
General Motors Argentina, 242
General Motors Chile, 205
General Motors France, 58
General Telephone and Electronics, 51, 112, 311, 313, 315
General Tire & Rubber Co., 205, 223, 300, 316
Georgetown University Center for Strategic and International Studies, 120
Gerber, Fritz, 8
Germany, Federal Republic of, 150, 164, 391
Germans, 165, 196
German-American Friendship Treaty, 401
German DuPont, 402
German Federal Cartel Office, 351, 354, 373
Germany's Mitbestimmung law, 401
German Mitbestimmung model, 399
Gerstacker, Carl, 7
Gerstenberg, Richard C., 410
Getschow, G., 640
Getty Oil, 199, 527
Getty, J. Paul, 110
Gibson, W. D., 588, 589
Gillette, 235, 354, 357, 373, 410, 475, 531
Gilinsky, V., 637
Gilpin, Robert, 517, 614, 638
Giniger, H., 579, 609, 610
Giovanelli, Luis, 90
Giscard d'Estaing, Valéry, 51
Gisselquist, D., 593
Givaudan, 339, 461-464, 466
Gladwin, T. N., 575, 580, 591, 630-634, 644
Glaverbel, 56, 57
Glaz, 598
Ghetti, Giuseppe, 464
Global strategy, 66
Gnomes of Zurich, 317
Goal interdependence, 74
Goucher, R., 585
Goldberg, P. M., 641
Gold fields of South Africa, 212
Goldfinger, N., 638
Goldman, R. K., 590
Goodfellow, W., 593
Goodman, S., 643
Goodrich, B. F., Co., 62, 64, 72, 74, 88, 113, 385

Goodyear, 53, 54, 61, 62, 113, 205, 207, 240, 241, 292, 385, 410
Gore, Albert, 522
Gould, 378
Goulet, D., 637
Government, 107, 108, 313, 535
    actions, 156
    aid, 128
    and marketing, 338
    non-governmental groups, 440
    policymaking, 542
    regulation, 314, 334
    relations, 116
    role of, 119
Grace, J. Peter, 115
Grace, W. R., Company, 115, 292
Graduate unemployment, 99
Grease payments, 322
Green, J. F., 590
Green, M., 617
Greenberger, R. S., 603
Group of Eminent Persons, 552
Groupement d'Intérèt Economique pour la Commercialisation de l'Uranium, 48
Growth, and development, 261, 520
Gruber, W., 635
Grumman, 313, 314, 320, 519
Gruppo Lepetit S. A., 23, 25
GTE International, 315
Guardian Royal Exchange Assurance, 212
Guatemala, 157
Guatemalan National Policy, 415
Guenstein, F. I., 645
Guerrilla war, 196
Guest workers, 404, 515
Guidelines for Multinational Enterprises, 553
Guinea, independence of, 195
Guinea Information Centre, 150
Gulf Oil Corporation, 6, 7, 9, 12, 14-22, 24-26, 29, 34, 36, 37, 40-42, 44, 45, 48, 54, 61, 68, 122, 153, 154, 156, 193-196, 198, 202, 214, 215, 247, 292, 297, 300, 304, 305, 308, 313, 316, 317, 326, 327, 329, 410, 445, 455, 522-528, 531, 544
    v. *American Jewish Congress*, 17
    v. *Anti-Defamation League of B'nai B'rith*, 21
    v. *Black Students at Harvard University*, 15
    v. *Bolivian Government*, 18
    v. *Carter Administration*, 24
    v. *Church Women United*, 18

v. *Conference of Presidents of Major American Jewish Organizations,* 18
v. *Council for Christian Social Action of the United Church of Christ,* 14-15
v. *Federal Trade Commission,* 19
v. *Ford Administration,* 16
v. *Italia Nostra,* 22
v. *"A Jewish Militant,"* 14
and Justice Department, 527
v. *Loretto Literary and Benevolent Institution,* 21
mismanagement at, 44
Gulf Boycott Coalition, 193, 194
Gulf Minerals, Canada, 522, 528
v. *Nelson Bunker, Herbert and Lamar Hunt,* 24-25
v. *Pan African Liberation Committee,* 15
v. *RASD,* 13
v. *Rozenburg Municipality,* 22
v. *Senate Foreign Relations Subcommittee on Multinational Corporations,* 18
v. *Senate Judiciary Committee on Administrative Practice and Procedure,* 20
v. *Southern Africa Task Force of the United Presbyterian Church in the U.S.A.,* 15
v. *Weather Underground,* 13
v. *Westinghouse Electric Corporation,* 25
Gulf Oil Angola, 193
Gulf & Western Industries, 59, 204, 414
Gunter, H., 626
Gupte, P., 594, 596, 615
Gurr, T. R., 586
Guzzardi, Jr., W., 602, 612
Gwertzman, B., 591, 601

Haack, Robert W., 52
Haas, E. B., 590
Habeas Corpus Acts, 132
Hacker, F. J., 585, 586
Haendel, D. H., 643
Hage, J., 645
Hague Convention, 119
Haiti, Friends of, 150
Halesmere Group, 150, 180
Hall, Edward T., 308, 309, 613
Hall, J., 577, 578
Halliday, D., 632
Halling Vicker Corp., 154
Halloran, R., 612, 613, 614
Halperin, Ernst, 99, 585, 586

Halsan, D., 594
Hamilton, Jr., Hyman C., 8, 42
Hampshire College, 154
Haner, F. T., 643
Hangerton, Daniel, 313, 316
Harkin, Tom, 147
"Harkin amendment," 157, 162
Hargreaves, J., 642
Harness, E. G., 580, 611, 616
Harnik, P., 634
Harris Corp., 183
Harris, Louis, 201, 225, 226, 378, 599
Harrington, Michael, 147, 364
Hartford Fire and Casualty Insurance Company, 533
Hartke-Burke Bill, 49, 69, 77, 489, 514, 516, 538
Hartley, W. D., 581, 593
Hartmann, Alfred, 8
Harvard University, 154, 155, 194
Havana Charter, 551
Hawk, D., 592, 602
Hawkins, R. G., 584, 606, 608, 610, 625, 635, 636, 637, 638, 641
Hay, A., 634
Hayes, C. J. H., 583
Hazardous industries abroad, 433
Hearst, Patty, 110, 112
Heath, E., 83
Heberlin, R. A., 643
Heenan, D. A., 643
Heilbroner, R., 577
Heinonen, V., 594, 596, 597, 598, 600, 629
H. J. Heinz, 274, 476
Heller, R., 575, 576
Hemispheric Affairs, Council on, 150
Henderson molybdenum mine, 57
Hennart, J.-P., 635
Henriot, P., 591
Henzler, H., 627
Hercules, Inc., 56, 537
Herker, D., 642
Herlihy, E. D., 611, 614, 616
Herman, E. S., 591
Herman, T., 597
Herrema, Dr. Tiede, 105, 110
Herrmann, R. O., 620
Hersh, S. M., 614, 615
Hershey, Jr., R. D., 579, 580, 596, 607, 611, 613, 614, 615, 616, 617, 618
Hershfield, D. C., 625, 626
Hertz, 223, 408
Heterogeneous-homogeneous climate, 567-568

Hewitt, C., 586
Hexachlorophene, 339
Hibernia Bank, 113
Hickenlooper amendment, 72
High context cultures, 308
High standard, 187
High technology, 67
High-technology trade, 246
Hijacking, 113
Hildebrand, K. J., 635
Hill, R., 627
Hills, J. N., 631
Hills, Roderick, 314, 324
Hitachi, 529
Hitachi T.V., England, 529
Hitler, Adolf, 101, 184, 191
Hoechst, A. G., 354
Hoffer, Eric, 314, 616
F. Hoffman-La Roche & Company A.G.,
    2, 6, 8, 9, 12, 14, 19, 20, 21, 22, 23,
    24, 26, 34, 37, 40, 42, 43, 44, 45, 69,
    77, 104, 339, 350, 351, 352, 353, 372,
    373, 448, 461, 462, 463, 464, 465, 466,
    475, 512, 530, 544, 545, 557
    v. "Action for Children's Television," 19
    v. British Government, 350
    v. Canadian health authorities, 20
    v. "Commando 10th of July," 14
    v. Department of Health and Social
        Security, 23
    drug pricing in Great Britain, 372
    v. EEC Antitrust Directorate, 19
    v. Government of Brazil, 19
    v. International Federation of Chemical
        and General Workers' Unions, 20
    v. Lombardy Regional Authorities and
        Area Residents, 22
    and media, 351
    v. Montclair Chapter of National
        Organization for Women, 21
    out-of-court settlements, 353
    v. Secretary of State for Social Services,
        24
    v. U.K. Monopolies Commission, 19
    Voluntary Price Regulation System, 353
    v. Zenith Laboratories, 23
Hoffmann, P., 586, 587, 588, 589, 634, 636
Hoffman, S., 592
Hoffman, T., 579
Holden, C., 587
Holland, 150, 155
Hollandse Beton Groep, 155

Holtaus, M., 643
Home country accommodation, 326
Home country avoidance, 326
Home-country control, 261-263
Home-country jobs, 516
Home-country push, 309
Home-country resources, misdirection of,
    517
Home-country sunshine, 320
Home-country unions, 383
Homestable Mining Company, 527
Honeywell-Bull, 271, 272, 385
Honeywell Inc., 61, 64, 67, 115, 239, 268,
    270, 271, 272, 315, 385, 476
Honeywell Information Systems (HIS),
    271, 272
Hood, N., 581
Hoover Corp., 475
Horowitz, D. L., 634
Horowitz, I. L., 590
Horrock, N. M., 596, 611, 612
Horst, T., 575, 641
Host country, 302, 305
    accommodation, 326
    competition, 326
    conflict, 515
    control, f.f., 264
    employment, 514
    reform, 319
Hostess Products, 20
Host-government policies, 263
House, K. E., 602
House Banking Committee, 161, 163
House Commerce Committee, 522
House Committee on Government
    Operations, 431
House Committee on International
    Relations, 157
House International Relations Committee,
    184
Houser, F. M., 209, 601
House Subcommittee on African Affairs,
    177
House Subcommittee on Commerce,
    Consumer and Monetary Affairs,
    431
Houston Lighting & Power Company, 523
Hovey, G., 595, 637
Hoveyda, Amir Abbar, 320
Howe, M., 581, 584, 625
Howe, R. J., 635, 636
Hubbard, D. G., 587

Huey, J., 589
Hughes, A. J., 599
Hughes Aircraft, 51, 311
Hughes, T. L., 579, 645
Hughes Tool Company, 59
Humanization movement, 393
Human resources, management of, 375
Human Rights Committee, 148
Human Rights Coordinating Center, 150
Human conditions, 425
Human health and safety, 437
Human rights, 14, 130, 147, 148, 149, 150,
    155, 182, 185, 186, 187, 190, 191, 193,
    201, 204, 205, 206, 213, 219, 221, 410,
    413, 431, 544
  abuse of, 137
  action groups, 217
  activists, 168, 169
  and computers, 188
  campaigns, 161
  challenge of, 217-220
  codes of conduct, 166
  condemnations, 164
  conflicts, 167, 213, 214, 239
  definition of, 131
  evolution of, 134
  issue, 130, 244
  managing challenge of, 212
  and multinationals, 142, 175
  and President Carter, 147
  resolutions and condemnations of, 164
  status of, 136
  tactics of, 151
  violations, 137, 157
Humble, J., 644
Hunt, D., 579
Hunt, Herbert, 24
Hunt, J. G., 645
Hunt, Lamar, 24
Hunt, Nelson Bunker, 24, 88
Hunsaker, P. L., 644
Hussein, King, 310
Hutchinson, John, 178
Hu, Y. S., 606
Huxley, Aldous, 346
Hymer, S., 641
Hyams, E., 585

IBM Corporation, 2, 59, 63-65, 67, 69, 73,
    89, 92, 112, 124, 153, 187, 189-192,
    213-215, 246, 268, 270, 271, 280,
    282-285, 287, 292, 315, 326,

407, 410, 412, 475, 476, 490, 500, 501,
    523, 545, 557
  and India, 63, 283ff
ICMESA (Industrie Chimice Meda Societa
    Anonyma), 22, 461-466
Ideological factors, 536
Ideology, 96
Ignatius, D., 619
Illegal governments, collaborating with,
    192ff
Illegal immigrants, 405
Illegal profits, 281
ILO, 148, 204, 376, 419, 552, 554
  study on strikes, 376
  see also United Nations International
    Labour Organization
IMF, see International Metalworkers
    Federation
Immigrant labor, reductions in, 405
Impact assessment, 510
Imperial Chemical Industries, 53, 234, 307,
    354, 398, 528
Imperial Computers Ltd., 283
Imperialism, 3, 77, 95
Imperial Smelting Corporation, 20
Import restrictions, discriminatory, 237
INA, 175
INA Industrija Nafte, 25
Inappropriate technology, 481, 482
Incendiary attack, 114
Incentive system, 557
Income distribution, 505, 516
Independence, Rhodesia's unilateral
    declaration of, 165
Independent-interdependent climate, 568
India, 498ff
  Coca-Cola and IBM in, 49, 280-285
  computer industry, 282
Indiana University, 154
Indianapolis, Trust Company of, 169
Indigenization, 287
Indirect labor-market effects, 515
Indirect payments, 324
Individual self-regulation, 325
Individual terrorism, 118
Indocin, 350
Indonesia, 150, 157, 162
Industrial decentralization, 540
Industrial democracy, 390, 401ff, 422
Industrialized nations, 308
Industria Piemontese dei Colori di Anilina,
    455

Industries, 312, 511
Infant Formula Action Coalition
　　(INFACT), 366, 368-370
Infant formula, benefits, manufacturers,
　　361
　　case, 373ff
　　code of ethics for promotion, 364
　　controversy, 360, 363
　　free samples of, 361
　　producers, 361
　　promotion of, 361, 369
Infant Formula Coalition, 369
Inflation, 505, 541
Information, costs, 239
　　lack of, 381
Informational influence, 71
Ingersoll-Rand, 378
Instituto Chemio Theripico Italiano, 354
Insurance, 69, 122
Insurance companies, 155
Intellectual property, theft of, 487
Inter-American Commission on Human
　　Rights, 133, 148
Inter-American Development Bank, 162
Interdependence and centralization, 107
Interest Equalization Tax, 262
Interest groups, 506
Interest interdependence, 74ff
Interfaith Center on Corporate
　　Responsibility (ICCR), 149, 169,
　　173, 193, 201, 204, 207, 336, 337, 363,
　　364, 366, 368
Interfaith Committee on Social
　　Responsibility, 445
Interfaith Council on Corporate
　　Responsibility, 412
Intergovernmental Working Group on
　　Corrupt Practices, 324
Internal control, inadequate, 315
Internal-external interaction, 570
Internal differentiation, 565
Internal fragmentation-unification balance,
　　569
Internal organization, 569
International agreements, 551
International Anti-Counterfeiting Coalition,
　　357
International approaches, 324
International Atomic Energy Agency, 432,
　　493, 494, 497, 498
International bargaining, prospects for, 388
International Bauxite Association (IBA),
　　276

International business, 319
International Center for the Settlement of
　　Investment Disputes (ICSID), 51,
　　275, 276
International Chamber of Commerce, 306,
　　325, 551
International Chemical Workers
　　Federation, 84
International Commission of Jurists, 151,
　　156, 199
International Committee of the Red Cross,
　　151
International Computers Ltd., 245, 282
International Confederation of Free Trade
　　Unions (ICFTU), 151, 383, 552
International conflict, 547
International control, 549
International Council of Infant Formula
　　Industries, (ICIFI), 362, 364
International Court of Justice, 88, 197, 198
International Covenant on Civil and
　　Political Rights, 133
International Covenant on Economic,
　　Social and Cultural Rights, 133
International credits, 168
International Defense and Aid Fund for
　　Southern Africa, 151
International Development, Agency for,
　　161
International Development Association,
　　162
International development and food
　　assistance, 157
International Energy Agency, 255
International Federation of Chemical,
　　Energy and General Workers Union
　　(ICEF), 20, 50, 385-387, 389, 402
International Federation of Pharmaceutical
　　Manufacturers, 331
International Finance Corporation, 162
International Financial Institutions Act of
　　1977, 162
International financial problems, 536
International Fuel Cycle Evaluation Study,
　　500
International Gold Corporation, 185
International B. F. Goodrich Europe B.V.,
　　62
International Harvester, 59, 244, 410, 411
International institutions, 549
International Investment and Multinational
　　Enterprises, Committee on, 554
International Justice and Peace of the U.S.

Catholic Conference, 150
International labor organizations, 378
International League for Human Rights, 151, 156
International Longshoreman and Warehouse Workers Union, 151
International marketing, 333
International marketing conflict, 371ff
International metalworkers Federation (IMF), 20, 21, 56, 87, 134, 380, 384, 385, 549
International Monetary Fund, 161-163
International Narcotics Control Program, 187
International oil industry, 255
International organizations, 148
International Organization of Consumers Unions, 337
International Organizations, Subcommittee on, 157
International Paper Corporation, 444
International patent system, revision of, 488
International payments, 533
International petroleum, 292
International Petroleum Industry Environmental Conservation Association (IPIECA), The, 56, 57
International Policy, Center for, 150, 162
International politics, 546
International political climate, 547
International relations, 221
International Relations, House Committee on, 157
International Rescue Committee, 151
International rules, 551, 554, 557
International Security Assistance and Arms Export Control Act of 1976, Section 301 of, 157
International sports community, 164
International technology, 477
International trade, 4, 184, 222, 259, 303, 317, 413, 506
  boycotts, 221. See also Boycotts
International Trade Secretariat (ITS), 384, 385
International transactions, 474
International Transport Workers Federation (ITF), 385
International unionism, 388, 389
International Union of Electrical Workers, 382
International Union of Food and Allied

Workers (IWF), 20, 384
International variations, 473
International Year of the Child, 370
Intourist, 190
Invention and innovation, 472
Investigators findings, 465
Investments, 151, 165, 223, 226, 259, 264, 273, 281, 518
  aids, 540
  controls, 382
  policies, 143, 231
  restrictions, 165, 166
Investment Corporation, Overseas Private, see OPIC
Investor Responsibility Research Center, 151, 212
IRA, 105, 109, 110
Iranians Bank, 25
Iranian Sky Cavalry Brigade, 187
Ireland, 150, 221
Irgun Zvai Leumi, 96
Irish Republican Army, 97, 102
IRS, 41, 197, 228, 317, 320, 327, 540
Irving Trust, 168, 539
Ismailis, 96
Israel, 164, 222, 226, 247, 250
  discriminating against, 228
  Tempo Bottling Company of, 228
Israel Can Co., 83
Israeli-Arab relations, 247
Israeli Development Corporation, 229
Italia Nostra, 22
Italian companies, 165
Italian Parliamentary Commission, 466
Italian taxation, 307
Italy, 164
Itoh & Company, C., 59, 309, 408, 476
ITT, 6, 7, 8, 9, 12, 14-24, 26, 29, 33, 34, 37, 40-47, 51-54, 61, 64, 67, 69, 72, 77, 92, 104, 114, 115, 136, 153, 188, 212, 214, 236, 290, 292, 293, 310, 316, 328, 340, 402, 408, 410, 485, 533, 537, 544, 545, 552
  v. Australia, 53
  v. Belgian Government, 17-18
  Boycott Committee, 33
  v. Brazilian Government, 23
  v. Center for Science in the Public Interest, 20
  v. Chilean President Salvadore Allende, 16
  v. Church Project on U.S. Investments in Southern Africa, 15

v. Columnist Jack Anderson, 17
v. Congregation of the Passion, et al, 18
v. Descamisados Peronistas Montoneros, 13
v. Environmental Protection Agency, 22
v. Federal Trade Commission, 19
v. French Government, 24
v. General Biscuit Co., 24
v. International Metalworkers Federation, 21
v. International Metalworkers Federation and International Union of Food, Drink and Allied Workers' Associations, 20
v. Justice Department, 24
v. Portuguese Government, 16
v. Republic of Chile government, 552
v. Securities and Exchange Commission, 18-19
v. Senate Foreign Relations Subcommittee on Multinational Corporations, 16
v. Unidentified Terrorists (Milan), 14
v. Unidentified Terrorists (Rome), 14
v. United Presbyterian Church, U.S.A., 15
v. Weather Underground, 13
Ivins, M., 633

Jackewicz, S. A., 597
Jackson, Henry, 245
Jackson, R. A., 600
Jackson-Vanik Amendment, 165
Jacobs, A. G., 52, 401
Jacobs, S. L., 617
Jacoby, N. H., 611
Jamaica, aluminum companies in, 274-278
Jamaican bauxite, 277
James, G. F., 641
Jamieson, J. K., 300
Janata Party, 136, 280
Janis, J. L., 577
Jann, Adolf W., 8, 42, 352
Jantsch, E., 643
Japan, 165, 169, 400, 499
  antimonopoly Act, 356
  antitrust law, 356
  banks, 165
  Chlorine and Caustic Soda Producers Association, 23
  expatriate presence, 408
  Ministry of International Trade and Industry, 265

multinational firms, 165
  Red Army, 97, 109
Japan Airlines, 113
Japan Soda Industry Association, 23
Jenkins, B. M., 585, 586, 587, 589, 590
Jensen, M. C., 576, 577, 581, 584, 595, 601, 613, 614, 616, 617
Jensen, F. B., 641
Jet aircraft engines, 270
Jewish community, 231
Jewish Defense League, 102
Jewish groups, 228
Job (biblical), 297
Job actions, 379
Job bargaining, 389
Job displacement, 506, 511, 513, 514, 515
John Deere, 223, 504, 512, 546
John Labatt, Ltd., 235
Johns-Manville, 288, 289
Johnson & Johnson, 59, 60, 314, 475
Johnson, H. G., 635
Johnson, J. J., 248
Johnson, J., 585
Johnson, Lyndon B., 241
Johnson, Paul, 118
Johnson, V. C., 605
Joint ownership, 69
Jones, B., 612, 641
Jones, G., 595
Jones, Jack, 388
Jones, James, 244, 245
Jones, M. V., 643
Jones, R. T., 603, 623
Jones, Thomas V., 300
Josen, G., 629
Jungers, Frank, 226, 250, 251
Junta de Coordinación Revolucionaria, 94, 109
Jurists, International Commission of, 151, 156
Jurkovich, R., 645
Justice Department, U.S., 17, 24, 55, 227, 228, 234, 236, 304, 311, 327, 328, 329, 522, 523, 527, 533

Kaiser Aluminum, 17, 23, 51, 88, 223, 226, 275, 276, 277, 278, 313
Kaiser Steel, 444
Kamm, H., 611
Kandell, J., 584, 585, 597, 619, 627
Kapoor, A., 582, 614, 644
Karr, A. R., 621
Kashoggi, Adnan M., 300

Kast, F., 577
Katjavivi, Peter, 200
Katzenstein, P. J., 645
Kaufman, H., 634
Kaufman, M. T., 599
Kaunda, Kenneth, 180
Kay, D. A., 592, 631
Keatley, R., 592
Kebschull, D., 643
Keegan, W. J., 642
Keeney, R. L., 643
Kefauver, Estes, 26
Keller, George, 251
Kelley, H. H., 582
Kellogg, F. F., 349
Kelly, J., 577
Kemezis, P., 578, 612, 628
Kennecott Copper, 16, 51, 73, 88, 202, 292, 445
Kennedy, Edward, 147, 181, 191, 369, 533,
    611
Keohane, R. O., 641, 645
Kerr-McGee, 444, 445, 527
Kessler, F., 613
KGB, 190
Khandwalla, P. N., 645
Kickbacks, 324
Kidder, Peabody & Co., 290
Kidnapping, 110
    Argentine Montoñero guerrillas, 58
    executives, 52
    insurance policies, 122
    victims, 62
Kilborn, P. T., 627
Kim, S. K., 300
Kimberly Clark, 207
Kindleberger, C. P., 575, 582, 641
Kirby, 526
Kirby, Robert E., 524, 527
Kirkland, Lane, 388
Kissinger, Henry, 196, 252, 253, 321, 496
Kitazawa, Y., 594
Kiviat, G., 632
Klare, M. T., 596, 597
Kleinfield, N. R., 576, 577, 581
Klintner, W., 591
Kneese, A. V., 643
Knightley, P., 622
Knödgen, G., 632
Knowledge, 564
Kobrin, S. J., 611, 643
Koch, Edward, 147
Kodak, 52, 92, 115, 123, 188, 349, 475
Kodama, Yoshio, 309, 310

Kohl, J., 585
Komatsu, 476
Kommes, D. P., 592
Korea, 415
Korry, Edward M., 33
Kotler, P., 620
Kraftwerk Union (KWU), 492, 498
Kramer, B., 615
Kramer, R., 579
Krasner, O. J., 643
Krattenmaker, T. G., 624
Kraus, L., 641
Kreps, Juanita, 245
Krieger, K., 632
Kirstol, Irving, 135, 590
Krugerrand, 153, 154, 185, 214
Krupp Steel, 267, 519
Kruglanski, A. W., 579, 582
Kujawa, D., 625, 626
Kumbula, T., 595
Kurds, 102
Kuwait, 229, 230
KWU, *see* Kraftwerk Union

Labor, 470, 516
    bargaining, 151, 382
    groups, 506
    imperialism, 383
    market instability, 515
    relations, 20, 375
    saving technologies, 480
Labor Department, U.S., 419
Labor Government, 398, 516
Laissez faire, 258
Lake, A. W., 635
La Marro Blanca, 415
Lammes, C. J., 578
Land, Edwin H., 208
Land, K., 642
Land, use, 437
Landauer, J., 578, 611, 614, 617, 618
Landford, H. W., 643
Landsberg, H. H., 631
Lanusse, Alejandro, 90, 104
Laos, 240
LaPalombara, J., 643
Laqueur, W., 117, 128, 585, 586, 587, 588,
    590
Latham, Michael, 366
Latin America, North American Congress on,
    150
Lavipour, F. G., 641
Law of the Twelve Tables, 132

Lawrence, P. R., 578, 579, 644, 645
Lazard Frères & Co., 289, 290
League of Nations, 196
Leavitt, H. J., 581
Lebanese Socialist Revolutionary
        Organization, 110
Lebel, D., 643
Leddy, Thomas, 163
Ledogar, R. J., 619, 620, 624
Lee, E. H., 623
Legal and General Assurance Society, 348
Leger, R. R., 592
Legislators, U.K., 177
Legitimate influence, 71
Legton-Brown, D., 584
Leiding, Rudolf, 396
Lejona Associations, 22
Lendrevie, J., 620
Lenin, V. I., 109
Leonard, R., 598
Leone, Giovanni, 265, 297
Leonhard, H. H., 576
Leshinsky, Harry, 115
Lessard, D. R., 608, 637, 641
Lester, R. K., 637
Letelier, I., 594
Leventhal, P. L., 636
Lévesque, René, 53, 288, 289, 290, 291
Levin, M., 584
Levine, S., 645
Levine, T. A., 611, 614, 616
Levinson, Charles, 50, 387, 389, 402
Levi Strauss & Co. Taiwan, 357
Levy, B. H., 587, 588
Levy, S. J., 620
Lewis, A., 601, 602
Lewis, P., 588, 619
Libby McNeil & Libby, 339, 531
Liberal unions, 151
Liberation, wars of, 150
Liberation movements, S. African, 150
Liberty to the Captives, 150
Librium prices, 350
Libya, producers agreement, 25
    Texaco and Standard Oil of California, 88
Libyan crude oil, boycott of, 249, 255
Libyan National Oil Co., 249
Liggett, 314
Light, Jr., D., 578
Lightweight plastic beverage containers, 342
Likert, J. G., 578
Likert, R., 578

Lind, A., 643
Line manager, profile of, 564
Link, George, 114
Lindsey, R., 611, 612, 614, 616
Lippman, T. W., 615
Liser, F. B., 591
Litigation, 37
Litt, J., 585
Litterer, J. A., 577
Litton Industries, 477, 503, 531
Litvak, I. A., 580, 584, 604, 625
Living and social patterns, 116
Llambi, Benito, 92
Lloyd, B., 643
Lloyds International Exchange Bank of
        London, 94
Loans, 161, 163, 168, 169
    to Chile, 168
    Citicorp's halt to, 174
    to S. Africa, campaign against, 174
Lobbying, 156, 337
Local management, indigenizing, 408
Local ownership, 440, 519
Locke, John, 132
Lockheed Aircraft Co., 52, 67, 69, 297, 299,
        300, 302, 308, 309, 310, 313, 314, 316,
        325, 327, 328, 329, 519, 545
    foreign bribes, 316
Lockwood, B. B., 588
Lockwood, Charles A., 110
Loescher, G. D., 592
Lombardy Regional Authorities, 22
Lomé Convention, 163, 552
London Committee for Freedom in
        Mozambique, Angola and Guinea,
        193
London Stock Exchange, 348
Long, Clarence C., 494
Longshoremen's Union, 154
Lonrho Trading Co., 180
Lord, C., 633
Loretto Literary and Benevolent
        Institution, 21
Lorillard, 314
Lorsch, J. W., 578, 579, 645, 646
Love, J., 576
Love, R. L., 581
Lovink, A. R., 600
Lovins, Amory, 22
Lowenfeld, A. F., 602
Lubasch, A. H., 611
Lublin, J. S., 621

Lufthansa German Airlines, 114, 115
Lusinschi, V., 625
Luxemberg, S., 596
Lyet, J. Paul, 244
Lynch, M. C., 593, 595
Lyons, R. D., 621

McAfee, Jerry, 7, 40, 42, 526, 527
Macaluso, D., 641
McCann, T., 611
McCarthy, J. E., 634
McCloy, J. J., 611, 613
McCloy Committee, 326
McCloskey, M., 631
McCulloch, G. B., 626
McCurdy, P. P., 632
McDermott, J. Ray, 329
McDonald, A. L., 583
McDonald, Sir Alexander, 348
MacDonald, D., 600
McDonnell-Douglas Corp., 105, 313, 340
Mace, M. L., 619
McElheny, V. K., 595, 621
McGovern, George, 147
McGrath, P. S., 643
McGregor, I., 590
McGrew, W. W., 635
McGuire, E. P., 581, 589
McHale, J., 591
McHale, M. C., 591
Machiavelli, Niccolo, 307, 613
Machinery and equipment, 156-157
Machines Bull, 271, 272
McIsaac, G. S., 627
McKee Tecsa, 94
McKersie, R. B., 578, 579, 580
Mackey International Airlines, 115
McKinley, President, 96
McKinney, John, 288
McKinsey & Company, 50, 386
MacLeish, Archibald, 147
McLellan, V., 609
McNamara, Robert S., 135, 162, 163
Macroeconomic control, 538
Macy, R. H., 346
Madden, C. H., 638
Magee, S. P., 638
Magna Carta, 132
Mahgoub, Mohammed, 63
Mahoney, H. T., 589
Mahler, Dr. Halfdan, 331
Maidenberg, H. J., 604

Mailick, S., 645
Malabré, Jr., A. L., 627
Malawar, S. S., 620
Malcolm, A. H., 586
Mallin, J., 586
Management amorality, 316
  technology, 471
  time and attention, 41
  worker participation, 394
Mandatory codes of conduct, 550
Mandatory retirement, 417
Mandela, Winnie, 209
Manley, Michael, 272, 276, 277
Mansfield, E. G., 635
Manufacturers Hanover, 168, 170, 172, 173,
  174, 175, 215
Manufacturing, 511
Mao Tse-Tung, 239
Marcona Corp., 536
Marcos, Ferdinand, 328, 414, 432
Marcus, B., 619, 620
Margnac, 112
Marighella, Carlos, 102, 586, 587
Maritime Administration, 222
Market behavior, 521
  demand, 483
  dominance, 72, 503
  exploitation, 504
  industrialized versus developing
    countries, 333
  mechanisms, 296
  market position, 355
Market court, 336
Marketing, 19ff
  conflict, 330ff
  function, 333
  practices, 333, 371
  problems, 338
  theory, 333
Marks & Spencer, 267
Marquez, Israel, 416
Marro, A., 612
Marshall, Colin, 408
Marston, D. W., 619
Martin, R., 620, 625
Marubeni Trading Company, 297
Mary Kathleen Uranium Ltd., 521, 527, 528
Maryland National Bank, 153, 169
Maryland Public Interest Research Group,
  433
Marxist theory, 3
Mason, H., 635, 636

Mason, Roy, 117
Massachusetts, 154, 156, 208
Le Matériel Téléphonique, 24, 61
Matheson, Hugh, 9
Matsushita, M., 531, 623
Matsushita Electric Industries Corp., 357
Mattel Toy Corp., 415
Matthews, B., 611, 613
Maule, C. J., 580, 584, 604, 625
Maxwell House, 183, 184
May, E. C., 599
May, W. F., 587
Mayer, E., 635
Mays Department Stores, 185
Mead, Margaret, 78, 583
Mead-Johnson, 331
Meadow, R. G., 643
Measurement problems, 471
Medbestemmeke, 395
Media coverage, 107
Medical Committee for Human Rights, 14
Medical profession, 370
Meidner, R., 55
Mehta, D., 635
Melanesia International Trust Company, 539
Mellon (family), 7
Melman, Seymour, 310
Memorex Corp., 315
Menon, M. G. K., 609
Mercedes-Benz, 58, 60. *See also* Daimler-Benz A.G.
Merchants National Bank and Trust Company, 169
Merck & Company, 312, 350, 546
Merrill Lynch, 175, 185, 214
Merritt, T. P., 643
Merszei, Zoltan, 7, 23
Metal Box Company, 83, 413
Metcalf, Lee, 321
Metcalf, H. C., 578
Methodist Church, 170
Methvin, E. H., 587
Metz, Franz, 58, 104
Metz, T., 578, 639
Metzenbaum, Howard, 527
Mexican-American Political Association, 336
Mexico, 274
Meyer, H. E., 579
Meyer, P. S., 577, 617
MFN (most-favored-nation) status, 165
Michaelangelo, 357

Michelin, 540
Michigan State University, 15
Mickolus, E. F., 585, 589
Microsystems, Inc., 477
Middle East, 229
    conflict, 226
    oil independents, 255
    policy, 248
    war—4th, 249
Midland Bank, 156, 169, 174, 216
Mikdashi, Z., 584
Mikesell, R. F., 584
Milbank, D. L., 585, 587, 588
Miles Laboratories, 19, 226
Militaristic states, 308
Military aid, 157
    Assistance Program, 161
    buildup, 168
    hardware, 156
    technology sales, 490
    weapons, 164
Milk nurses, 361, 370
Miller, A., 357, 358
Miller, J. A., 584, 585, 589, 616
Miller, G. S., 608
Miller, O. N., 605
Miller, R. K., 591
Miller, S., 636
Milte, K. L., 586
Minnesota Mining and Manufacturing (3M) Company, 235. *See also* 3M Company
Mintz, M., 616, 625
Mintz, N., 610
Mitbestimmung, 394, 396
Mitsubishi, 59, 309, 420
Mitsui, 59, 309, 420, 455
Mixed modes, 215
Mixed strategies, 82
MLW Worthington, 84
MNC Inc. (Canada), 354
Mobil Oil, 7, 24, 50, 51, 59, 68, 77, 112, 116, 117, 156, 176, 178, 179, 180, 181, 214, 225, 226, 231, 247, 248, 249, 257, 292, 313, 327, 410, 411
Moffet, W. E., 639
Moffit, M., 594
Mohr, C., 614
Molina, Edgar R., 90
Molly Maguires, 96
Monopolies Commission (MONC), 351, 355
Monopoly elements, 530

Monopoly power, 530
Monsanto, 56, 59, 236, 342, 388, 445
Montclair Chapter of National
    Organization for Women, 21
Montedison, 69, 114, 423, 448, 455
Montgomery, J., 629
Montoñeros, 103, 104, 105, 109, 112, 118
Montreal, Bank of, 169
Montreal Convention, 119
Moores, Frank, 16
Moral imperialism, 304
Morality, 222
Moram, T. H., 575, 583, 584
Morgan Guaranty Trust Company, 168,
    170, 172, 173, 206
Morgan, J. P., 170, 174, 175
Morgenthaler, E., 622, 629
Mohange Company, 339
Morner, A. L., 575
Moro, Aldo, 122
Morrell, J., 593
Morris, J. H., 576
Morris, M. D., 591
Morton, Dan, 592, 597, 600
Morton, Rogers, 450
Mosadegh, Muhammad, 26
Moskowitz, M. R., 580
Moslem International Guerrillas, 113
Moss, R., 585, 587
Mossberg, W., 601
Motorola Inc., 124, 153, 188, 207, 415, 531
Motorola Teleprograms Inc. (MTI), 124
Motor vehicles, 157
Mount Sinai Hospital, 229
Moura Castro, C. de, 630
Mouton, J. S., 577, 578, 579
Moxon, R. W., 636
Mozambique, 165, 195
Mozambique Information Centre, 150
MPLA (Popular Movement for the
    Liberation of Angola), 195, 196
Mudgett, W. C., 644
Mullaney, T. E., 580, 628
Muller, M., 578, 619, 624
Muller Pharmacy, 209
Müller, R. E., 575, 576, 606, 641
Mullick, S. K., 643
Multilateral aid programs, 163
Multilateral foreign aid and credits, 162
Multilateral regulation, 324
Multinational affiliates, 507, 518
    bargaining, 378, 390
    conflict management, 565

conflicts, 555
dummy subsidiaries, 317
French control, 61
markets, 503
impact of, 388
indispensibility of, 73
invent backwards, 55
operations abroad, Justice Department
    guidelines for, 533
objectives, 503
opponents, 30
origin, 1
"package," 507
parent, 509
policy climates, 566
ruthless behavior, 43
technology transfer, 475
theories of, 2
unions, 382, 388, 389
Multinationality, 316
Multinational banks, 168
Multinational marketing, 332, 333
Multinational oil companies, 246
Multi-party systems, 33
Multiracial Trade Union Council of South
    Africa, 412
Munsingwear, 357
Murray, R., 599
Murray, T., 637
Murphy, Thomas A., 411, 537
Muzorewa, Abel, 178
Myers, III, D., 592, 598, 600, 629
Myers, M. S., 644
Myerson, Bess, 337, 620
Myrdal, Gunnar, 301, 302, 612

NAACP (National Association for the
    Advancement of Colored People),
    151, 171, 207
Nabisco, 531
Nadel, L., 598
Nader, Ralph, 321, 334, 337, 348, 369, 372,
    617
Nag, A., 608
Naidoo, Indrus, 209
Namibia, 153, 154, 155, 164, 165, 196
    AMAX in, 196
    council for, 148
    natural resources, 199
    Newmont Mining in, 196
    resource exploitation in, 196
    strike of black workers, 197
Namibia Support Committee, 150

Namuth, T., 633
Narodnaya Volya, 96
Nash, N. C., 628
Nathan's, 229
National antitrust policy, 232
  bargaining, 375
  control, 280
  defense, 259
  economic policy, 505, 538
  macroeconomic policies, 274
  policy, MNE as instrument of, 547
  sovereignty, 286, 318
  unionism, 388, 389
National Advertising Review Board
  (NARB), 360
National Advertising Division (NAD), 359
National Asbestos Corp., 290, 291
National Association for Better
  Broadcasting, 336
National Association of Broadcasters, 185
National Association of Manufacturers, 49
National Audubon Society, 445
National Bank of Argentina, 112
National Black Coalition on Southern
  Africa, 151
National Bulk Carriers, 444
National Cancer Institute, 345
National Cash Register, 55, 269, 292, 315
National Chile Center, 150
National Coffee Association, 184
National Commission on Foreign
  Investment, 265
National Council of Better Business
  Bureaus (NCBB), 359
National Council of Churches, 149, 172,
  189, 190, 370, 414
National Development Bank, 110
National Institute of Occupational Safety
  and Health, 433
Nationalism, 78, 267, 278, 303, 440, 547,
  572
National Labor Relations Board, 382
National Liberation Alliance, 104
Nationalist Liberation Front (FLN), 96
Nationalization, 246, 249, 255, 258, 286,
  287, 289, 292, 293, 296, 314, 376, 487,
  533
National Patent Development Corp., 479
National Registry of Foreign Investments,
  265
National Science Foundation, 484
National Security Council, 245

National Supplies Procurement Act, 165
NATO (North Atlantic Treaty
  Organization), 238, 462, 489
Natural conditions, 425
  environment, 423, 545
  resources, 73, 275
Natural Resources Defense Council, 431
Naughton, J. M., 614, 617
Negative proof, principle of, 340
Negative relationship, 77
Negotiating authority, 381
Nehru, Jawaharlal, 280, 282
Nehemkis, P., 611, 615
Neizing, J., 586
Nelson, J., 591, 629
Nelson, W. H., 602
Neo-Marxist views, 541
NEPA, 431, 432
Ness, E. H. Van, 645
Nesbitt, P., 593, 594
Nestlé Alimentana, S.A., 48, 51, 56, 68, 77,
  183, 184, 360, 361, 362, 363, 364, 366,
  368, 369, 370, 373, 407, 531, 540
Nestlé Brazil, 369
Netherlands, 391, 399
Netherlands Catholic Trade Union
  Federation (NKU), 386
Neue Heimat, 376
New England Petroleum Corp. (Nepco),
  249
New England Power Company, 156
New York State Department of
  Environmental Conservation, 454
New left, decline of, 100
Newman, B., 594, 595, 599
Newmont Mining, 130, 154, 196, 197, 198,
  199, 200, 213, 410
Newmont Mining Namibia, 193
Nicaragua, 157, 168
Nickel, H., 600
Nicolson, J. R., 581
Nicosia, F. M., 624
Niehous, William F., 82, 116
Nigeria, 166
Nippon Steel, 455
Nixon, R., 147, 239, 249, 250, 297
Nobel Peace Prize, 1977, 151
Noble, J. H., 634
Nomura Securities, 420
Nonaligned countries, 552
Noncommunist governments, 308
Nongovernmental actions, 153

Nongovernmental organizations, 151
Nongovernmental pressure groups, 218
Nonproduction jobs, 512
Nonproliferation policy, 496
Noranda Mines Ltd., 48, 155, 528
Nordwestdeutsche Kraftwerke, 448
North American Congress on Latin
　　America, 150
Northrop Corp., 187, 188, 300, 304, 314,
　　316, 320, 327, 483
Northrup, H. R., 625, 626
North Sea oil pipeline, 112
Northern Telecom, 53
Norman, J. T., 604
Norris, W. C., 604
Norton Company, 202
Norway, 399
Nossiter, R., 614
Nuclear deal, Germany-Brazil, 497
　　exports, 496
　　industry, 490
　　nonproliferation policy, 500
　　power, 259, 496
　　proliferation, 490, 496
　　reactors, 270
　　safeguards, 499
　　safety problems, 498
　　technology, 239, 499
　　terrorists, 128
Nuclear Arms Proscription in Latin
　　America Treaty (NAPLAT), 497
Nuclear Fuels, 527
Nuclear nonproliferation treaty (NPT),
　　497
Nuclear Regulatory Commission, 431, 498
Nuclear Suppliers Group, 499
Nuclear technology imbroglio, 490
Nufcor, 48
NOW (National Organization for Women),
　　357
Nye, Jr., J. S., 306, 582, 583, 613, 641, 645

OAS, see Organization of American States
OAS General Assembly, 148
OAS Convention, 119
Oates, D., 576, 627
Obasanjo, Lt. Gen. O., 180
Oberlin College, 154
Obey, D. R., 632
Objectives, identifying, 42, 505
Obsolescing bargain, 85

Occidental Petroleum Corporation, 72,
　　194, 317, 328
Occidental and Oasis groups, 249
Occupational Safety and Health
　　Administration, 21
O'Connell, J. J., 601, 626
O'Donnell, L. G., 628
OECD, see Organization for Economic
　　Cooperation and Development
OECD Committee on Multinationals, 378
Oestreicher, P., 586
Offensive speculation, 537
Office of Export Administration, 190
Office of Export Control, 483
Office of Foreign Direct Investment
　　(OFDI), 262, 534
Office of Munitions Control, 320
Office of Technology Assessment, 433
Office of Technology Transfer, 489
O'Hare, M., 635
Ohio Conference of the United Church of
　　Christ, 193
Ohio University, 154
Oil, 168
　　companies, 226, 246, 249, 253
　　conspiracy, 178
　　crisis, 246, 496
　　embargo, 164
　　imports, 251
　　offshore, 255
　　reserves, Middle East, 224
　　and Shetland inhabitants, 59-60
　　weapon, 247, 248, 249, 250, 251, 252, 253,
　　254, 255
Oil Chemical and Atomic Workers Union
　　(OCAW), 424
Oil Service Company, 114
OKG, 524
OKHELA, 178
Oligarchic states, 308
Oligopolistic industries, 313
Olin Corporation, 176, 181, 214, 350, 530
Olivetti, 2, 284, 393, 477, 512
Olivetti-Bull, 268
Olympic Refineries, Inc., 423
Ooms, V. D., 641
OPEC, see Organization of Petroleum
　　Exporting Countries
Opel, 380, 401, 402
Operation Namibia, 150
Operating controls, 273, 296
Opponents, 37, 440

Opposition, when to work with, 74
Optimal cultural area, 548
Optimal economic area, 548
Optimal political area, 548
Options, 69
Options-matrix, 571
Oreffice, Paul F., 7, 17, 40, 315
Organization, disruption, 42
  and operations, 569
  religious and academic, 188
Organization for Economic Cooperation
    and Development (OECD), 249,
    324, 344, 378, 413, 416, 429, 535, 551,
    553, 554, 555
Organization of American States, 18, 133,
    148, 242, 552, 554
Organization of African Unity, 183, 196
Organization of Arab Petroleum Exporting
    Countries (OAPEC), 247, 249, 250,
    252
Organization of Petroleum Exporting
    Countries (OPEC), 68, 71, 89, 108,
    162, 224, 246, 247, 248, 249, 250, 251,
    276, 520, 521
Oregon, University of, 154
Organized crime, 311
Organized labor, 513
Origin, negative certificate of, 222
Origin, positive certificates of, 222
Osborn, R. N., 645
Otis Elevator Co., 59, 91, 92, 123, 411
Outcomes and Durations, 454
Overfull employment, 515
Overseas payoffs, 304, 310, 322
Overseas R&D, arguments for, 485
Overseas Private Investment Corporation
    (OPIC), 16, 69, 162, 278, 431
Owen, Dr. David, 180
Ownership, 258
Ownership and control, 258ff
Ownership-control strategies, 293
Owens-Illinois, 82, 83, 103, 116, 544

Pace, E., 617
Page Airways, 183
Palmer, J., 628
Pan African Liberation Committee, 15,
    193, 194
Pan American World Airways, 113, 114,
    519
Panasonic, and misleading advertising, 357
Pancontinental Mining Ltd., 522, 527

Pantages, A., 609
Pappachan, C. V., 632
Pappas, V., 579, 611, 612, 616
Papper, C. B., 587
Parallel pricing, 354
Parent firm, government assistance of,
    72
Parisi, A. J., 636, 639, 640
Parizeau, Jacques, 291
Parker Co., 354
Parry, A., 585
Parry, T., 638, 640
Parti Quebecois, 53, 288, 289, 291
Pascale, R. T., 577
Paust, J. J., 586
Payne, R., 585
Paxton, J., 580, 633
Payments, 317
Payments and fees, 41
PDFLP, 105
Peace Corps, 161
Pearson, C., 630, 631, 632
Pearson, N. W., 611, 613
Pease, Don J., 184, 597
Pechiney, 475
Peggio, Eugenio, 23, 24
Peninous, G., 643
Pension funds, 151, 155
Pennsylvania Bureau of Employment
    Security, 409
Pentagon, 250, 310
People's Bicentennial Commission, 50, 77,
    179
People's Coalition Against ITT, 33
Peoples Department Stores, 267
People's Revolutionary Army (Argentina)
    (Ejercito Revolucionario del Pueblo-
    ERP), 90, 104, 105, 109, 116, 118
Pepin, J. L., 606
Pepsico, 94, 99, 229, 239, 329, 342
Pericles, 297
Perlmutter, H. V., 645
Permanent Arab Commission on Human
    Rights, 133
Permut, S. E., 621
Peron, Isabel, 52, 118
Peron, Juan, D., 90, 91, 92
Peronist Armed Forces (Fuerzas Armadas
    Peronistas-FAP), 92
Perperin, Frank, 17
Persian Gulf Six, 249, 250
Perez, President, 82

Pertamina, 317
Peterson, R. B., 626
Peterson, Russell W., 53, 77, 445
Petroquimica, 16
Petroquimica Argentina (PASA), 115, 123, 124
Petroquimica Chilena, 206
Peugeot-Citroen, 64, 94, 113, 380, 515
Peyton, Charles, 251
Pfeffer, J., 575, 644
Pfizer, 314, 350, 410, 483, 485
PFLP, 105
Phalon, R., 615
Pharmaceuticals and semiconductors, 477
Phelps Dodge, 198, 202, 207, 212, 410
Phelps-Stokes Fund, 151, 183
Philadelphia Namibia Action Group, 200
Philip Morris, 299, 314, 357, 528
Philippines, 157, 162, 163, 414
Philippines Review Committee, 415
Philips, N. V., 2, 56, 57, 87, 104, 112, 155, 236, 271, 272, 357, 381, 385, 402, 475, 501, 512, 545
Phillips Petroleum, 59, 199, 207
Phillips-Van Heusen Corporation, 33
Philipson, A., 632
Phocomelia, 347
Pierre, A. J., 587
Pillsbury, 239
Pinochet, Augusto, 162, 206
Piombino, A. J., 575, 630
Pirelli, 114
Pisar, S. J., 623
Pitney Bowes, 326
Pittsburgh Corning Europe, 528
Pertamina, P. N., 59
Plants, shut-down of, 115
PLO, 496
P.L. 480-Food for Peace, 161
Plotting strategy, 543
Pittston, 445
Polaroid Corporation, 87, 188, 208, 209, 212, 214, 215, 544, 557
Polaroid Revolutionary Workers' Movement (PRWM), 87, 208, 209
Polarization, 116
Polisario guerrillas, 113
Policy, standards for, 318
Political activists, 312
  campaign for, 150
  conflict, 221, 545, 548
  contributions, unethical, 301, 302, 324

frustration, 100
legitimacy, 546
marketing practices, 373
prisoners, 151, 164
process, 428
repression, 103
risk, 161, 264
Soviet treatment of, 221
system, 336
trade controls, 246
weapons, 249
Politicians, 33
Politics, 16ff, 105, 117
Pollution havens, 430
Polmot, 483
Polyester resins, 342
Polychlorinated biphenyls (PCBs), 339
Polysar Ltd., 309
Polsby, N. W., 646
Pompidou, Georges, 271
Pondy, L. R., 584
Ponto, Jürgen, 101, 108, 116
Poole, J., 622, 623
Popular Front for the Liberation of Palestine, 102, 109, 112, 113
Popular Movement for the Liberation of Angola, 16
Popular Resistance Organized Army, 14
Port Authority of New York and New Jersey, 50
Portugal, 165
  coup in, 195
  colonialism, 193, 194
  government, 195
Positive relationship, 77
Post-FCPA period, 328
Post, J. E., 624
Poultry feed, 339
Precedents, 69
Preludin, 339
Press, 151
Pressure groups, 213
Price, 349ff
Price, Waterhouse & Co., 313
Price-fixing, 350
Pricing and distribution, external control of, 353
Prince, G. M., 580
Prince, J. E., 315
Princeton University, 154
Pringle, L. G., 620
Prittie, T. C. F., 602

Private consumer groups, 336
Private legal actions, 444
Private individuals, 168
Private ownership, 519
Private organizations, 149
Probe International, 120
Process technology, 471
Proctor & Gamble, 183, 512
Product, 338
   adaptation, 483
   cycle, 2, 478-479
   liability, 340, 344
   related conflict, sources of, 340
   safety, 341, 371
   Thalidomide Case, 347-349
   Tris Case, 345
   technology, 471
Production, employment and location of, 511
   geographic dispersion of, 72
   international integration of, 509
   transfer, 380
Products Roche, 20
Profits, loss of, 115
   maximization, 529
   repatriation, 280
   sharing, 391
Project cycle, 258
Promotion, 356
Protectionism, 334
Protestant denominations, 149
Provissiero, M., 610
Provos, 102
Proxmire, William, 322, 326, 618
Proxy resolutions, 155, 445
Prudential Life Assurance Co., 348
Pryor, A., 630, 631
Psychopathology, 101
Public image, 41
Public policy, 332, 566
Publicity, 336
Puerto Rico, 339, 445
Public Citizen, 331
Public Interest Research Council, 337
Public Safety Program, 187
Pugwash Conference on Science and World Affairs, 552
Pullman Inc., 312
Purcell, J. E., 592
Pure Food and Drug Act, 341

Qaddafi, Moamer, 108

Québec, asbestos mining in, 287
Québec Asbestos Mining Association, 288
Québec Office of Natural Resources, 289
Queensland Mines Ltd., 48, 527
Questionable payments, 17-19, 244ff, 297, 431, 545
   and conflict management, 326
   and Dow Chemical, 315
   explaining, 304
   disclosures, 319
   factors affecting, 318
   motives for, 298
   rules of game, 307
Quimica Chilena, 16

Racal, 212
Racial discrimination, 209
Racial Discrimination, Committee on the Elimination of, 148
Racial equality, 161
Racial Exploitation, Committee Against, 150
Racism, 170, 173, 201, 207
Racism, Fund to Combat, 150
Radio Riyadh, 250, 251
Raiffa, H., 643
Ralston-Purina, 292, 339
Ramondt, J., 627
Ramayana Restaurant, 59, 75, 317
Ranchey, Alberto, 100
R & D, see Research and Development
Rangan, K., 577, 581, 582, 608, 609
Ranger Export Development Company, 48
Rank-Xerox, 419, 528, 529
Rankin, D., 579, 600, 611
Rapoport, A., 583
RASD, 12
Raskin, A. H., 627
Rate of return, 517
Rattner, S., 603, 606, 616
Raven, B. H., 582, 583
Rayonier, 22, 84, 246
Raytheon Company, 300, 377, 378
RCA Corp., 137, 223, 224, 226, 268, 476
Recessions, 99, 314, 377
Reckert, C. M., 615
Red Army Faction, 100, 101, 102, 103, 105, 115, 122
Red Brigades, 97, 102, 103, 496
Red Cross, International Committee of the, 151

Reed International, 212
Reed, R., 588
Referent influence, 71
Reformers, 334
Regional balance, 506
Regional policy, 538, 540
Regulation and control of MNEs, 549
Regulatory agencies, 33
Regulatory conflict, 460
Regulatory failure, 311
Regulatory setting, advertising and the, 358-360
Regulatory tactics, 441, 444
Relationship with the opposition, 46
Relationship quality, 77
Relative deprivation, 99
Relative power, 70
Religious groups, 167, 188, 189, 192, 193
Religious organizations, 168, 177
Relocating abroad, MNE, 433
Remittance controls, 279
Remington Arms, 187
Renault, 393, 405
Renault-Peugeot, 204
Repatriation, profit, 279
Repressive nations, buying from, 182ff
    expanding in, 200ff
    labor practices in, 409
    lending to, 167ff
    selling to, 186
    withdrawing from, 206ff
Repressive technology, 186
Republican National Convention, 17
Research and Development, 471, 475, 484, 485
Research Institute for Endemic Diseases, 59
Resolution mechanisms, 448
Resource losses, 40
Restricted competition, 504
Retail price maintenance systems, 354
Retirement programs, early, 416
Reuber, G. L., 638
Révelli-Beaumont, Luchino, 62ff
Revere, 275, 276, 277
Reveron, D., 597
Revlon, Inc., 314, 351
Revolutionary Force, 112
Revson, P., 626
Revzin, P., 588, 633, 634
Reward influence, 71
Reynolds, D., 632

Reynolds Metals, 51, 88, 235, 236, 275, 276, 277, 313
Reynolds, R. J., 314
Rhodesia, 151, 154, 155, 156, 164, 165
    Mobil Oil and, 178ff
Rhodesian chrome, 154, 156, 165, 176ff
Rhodesian Chrome Mines Ltd., 176, 178
Rhodesian Information Service, 177
Rhodia, Inc., 350
Rhône-Poulenc S.A., 385
Ribicoff, Abraham, 493
Riccardo, John, 63ff
Richman, B., 636
Richardson, Elliott, 320
Richardson, Jr., J., 591
Richardson, J. R., 635
Richardson-Merrell, Inc., 347, 349, 378, 537
Riedel, J., 638
Rights, Civil and Political, International Covenant on, 148
Rights, economic-social-cultural, 134
Rights, political-civil, 134
Rin, Naomi Baruj de la, 90
Ringbakk, K.-A., 645
Rio Algom Ltd., 527, 528
Rio Medical Association, 374
Rio Tinto Zinc, 6, 9, 12, 14-17, 20, 22-29, 34, 36, 40, 41, 44, 45, 48, 73, 130, 200, 521, 523, 527, 544
    v. aboriginal tribesmen, 22
    v. authors Richard West and Amory Lovins, 22
    v. Bougainville Separatist Movement, 14
    v. Church Commissioners of the Church of England, 15
    v. Counter Information Services, 15
    v. Government of Papua New Guinea, 24
    v. Indonesian Government, 25
    v. Kaiser Aluminum, 23
    v. Local Press, 17
    v. Newfoundland Government, 16
    v. South-West Africa People's Organization, 17
    v. Trades Union Congress, 20
    v. U.S. Justice Department and U.S. District Court in Richmond, 16-17
Risk, avoidance, 504
    insurance, 161
    and leverage, 542
    moderation of, 505
Ritalin, 339

Roan Selection Trust, 73
Robbins, S., 640
Robbins, W., 612
Robeco Chemicals, 350
Robert Bosch GmbH, 477
Roberts, A., 602
Robertson, A. H., 590
Robinson, R. D., 583, 584, 610
Rocamora, J., 591
Roche, James M., 206
Roche Products Ltd., 350, 351, 352
Rockefeller, David, 172, 173
Rockefeller Foundation, 151, 364
Rockwell International Corp., 41, 113, 187,
    191, 227, 499
Rogers, B., 591, 600
Rolls-Royce, 300
Rolant, M., 627
Roman Catholic bishops, 149
Roman Catholic communities, 149
Rondomycin, price cut of, 350
Ronen, J., 618
Root, F. R., 610
Rose, D. J., 637
Rose, F., 610
Rose, S., 582, 678
Rosario Resources, 415
Roscow, J. P., 630
Rosen, H., 579
Rosenberg, J. S., 634
Rosenbaum, W. A., 643
Rosenthal, Benjamin, 231
Rosenthal, S. Z., 612, 615, 616
Rosenzweig, J., 577
Ross-Skinner, J., 604
Rothschild, Guy de, 530
Rothschild interests, 26
Rote Armee Fraktion, *see* Red Army
    Faction
Rowan, R. L., 625, 626
Rowe, N., 576, 577
Rowland, President Tiny, 180
Rowthorn, R., 641
Royal Bank of Canada, 53, 169, 174
Royal Dutch Shell, 155, 309, 525, 526
Royal Typewriter Company, 503
Royston, M. G., 591, 634
RTZ, *see* Rio Tinto-Zinc Ltd.
RTZ Services Ltd., 527
Rubber Industry Chamber, 313
Rubberfabriek Vredestein N.V., 62, 64, 88
Rubin, J. Z., 576, 582, 583, 584, 633
Rubin, Neville, 599

Rubin, S. J., 604
Ruble, R. L., 577
Rumania, Firestone Tire & Rubber and,
    240-241
Rummel, C. H., 627
Rummel, R. J., 643
Rupp, Rudolf, 14, 463, 464
Russell, Dr. Charles A., 94, 95, 584, 585
Russell, C. S., 631
Russel, Vincente, 12
Russian Sales, Sperry Rand, Dresser
    Industries and, 244-246
Russians, 165
Russo, A. L. del, 590
Rutenberg, D. P., 645

Saab-Scania, 393
Sabotage, 114
Sadat, Anwar, 63, 252
Safarian, A. E., 606
Saginaw Intervenors, 444
Said, A. A., 590
Saiga, 105
Saint Gobain, 382
Saks International, 183
Salanick, G. R., 575, 644
Sallustro, Dr. Oberdan, 104, 105, 116
Salmans, S., 628
Salpukas, A., 584
Samuelson, Victor E., 62, 93, 94
Sampson, Anthony, 33, 316, 576, 577, 605,
    616
Samsonite, 357
Sanctions, 184
    busting, 175, 181
    circumventing of, 175
    Rhodesian and S. African, 175
San Diego Gas and Electric Co., 450
Sandinist Front of National Liberation, 102
Sandoz, 354, 528
San Fernando Valley Fair Housing
    Council, 336
Sauvant, K. P., 625, 641
São Paulo State Environmental Protection
    Agency, 22, 463
SAPAC Corporation Ltd. (Société
    Anonyme de Produits Alimentaires
    et de Cellulose), 8
Sapiro, A., 620
Sard, A. A., 586
Sasib, 328
Saudi Arabia, 247, 248
Saudi Arabian National Guard, 187

Saudi crude, 251
Saudi oil, 251
Saving, 518
Scanning, 559, 561
Schaerf, C., 586
Scheel, Walter, 119
Schelling, T. C., 579
Schenkel, J. F., 584, 585
Schering, A. G., 339
Schlesinger, James, 245
Schleyer, Dr. Hanns-Martin, 102, 105, 122, 128, 396
Schlitz Brewing Co., 235
Schlossberg, Harvey, 101
Schlumberger, 59
Schmedel, S. R., 607
Schmidt, Helmut, 101, 496
Schmidt, P., 630
Schmitema, Fritz, 104
Schorr, B., 580, 614, 616, 619, 624
Schurmann, Leo, 320
Schuster, A., 622
Schwamm, H., 642
Schreiber, J., 585
Schwelb, E., 590
Schwendiman, J. S., 642
Science and technology, 553
SCM, 315, 503
Scott, James C., 307, 613
SDS, 100
Seagram Company, Ltd., 202
SEC, 33, 48, 51, 52, 59, 60, 67, 74, 84, 155, 198, 297, 298, 302, 304, 306, 311, 314, 317, 319, 321, 322, 324, 327-329, 368
Secretary of State, 157
Securities and Exchange Commission, *see* SEC
Security briefings, 122
Security management, 121
Sefanitro, 444
Selden, I., 588
Selective terminal controls, 296
Self-colonization, 371
Seligman, J., 612, 616, 617
Senate, U.S., 494
Senate Antitrust Subcommittee, 527
Senate Finance Committee, 538
Senate Foreign Relations Committee, 50, 201
Senate Foreign Relations Subcommittee on African Affairs, 179
Senate Foreign Relations Subcommittee on Multinational Corporations, 16, 18

Senate Judiciary Subcommittee on Administrative Practice and Procedure, 20
Sensitive technology, exporting of, 494
Separatism-nationalism, 99
Sequential utilization, 84ff
Servan-Schreiber, J. J., 575
Sesser, S. N., 620, 631
Sethi, S. P., 577, 614, 628
Seven Sisters, 113, 247
Seveso backlash, 463
Seveso, decontamination, 464, 465
Seveso incident, 461ff
Shah of Iran, 187, 255, 320, 490, 496
Shapp, Milton J., 62
Shareholder resolutions, 164, 170, 174, 198, 206, 337
Sharpeville, S. Africa, 168
Shawcross, Lord, 306, 325
Shell Oil Co., 24, 53, 54, 56, 59, 68, 75, 77, 88, 112, 117, 156, 176, 178, 180, 247, 249, 313, 424, 445, 527, 575
   v. *Delaware*, 53-54, 445
   v. *OCAW (Oil, Chemical, and Atomic Workers Union)*, 424
Shelly, M. W., 581
Shepherd, Jr., G. W., 593
Shepard, H. A., 577, 579
Sheraton Corporation of America, 17, 92ᵗ
Sherif, M., 584
Sherman Act, 227, 233, 236
Shetland County Council, 59, 75
Shields, G. B., 612
Shibata, T., 630
Shipler, D. K., 604
Shiro Trading Co., 354
Shulman, J., 640
Shultz, George P., 227, 242, 605
Shuster, A., 606, 612, 613
Sicarii, 96
Siemens, A. G., 245, 271, 284, 393, 492, 512
Sierra Club, 444
Silk, Leonard, 323, 590, 593, 612, 618
Simon, C. E., 611
Simca, 269
Simmons, L. R., 586
Simmel, G., 583
Singer, 292, 302, 378, 393
Sinn Fein, 96
Sisters of the Precious Blood, 364, 368
Sisters of Providence, 415
Skandinaviska Enskilda Banken, 55, 57, 74
SKF, 2, 56, 57, 60, 413, 475, 477

Skills, 564
Skolinikoff, E. B., 631
Sloganeering, 116
Smith, Adam, 502
Smith, D. D., 643
Smith, D. N., 582
Smith, Gene, 595
Smith, Ian, 177, 178, 180
Smith, L., 575
Smith, R., 611
Smith, R. E., 598
Smith, R. M., 611, 612, 615, 619
Smith, R. W., 643
Smith, T., 580, 581, 591, 599, 628
Smith, T. H., 595
Smith, W. D., 605, 611
Smith College, 154
Smith & Wesson, 187
Smithers, K. A., 607
Snyder, L. L., 583
Social conflict, 460
Social conscience, 104
Social consequences, 116
Social Democratic Party (SDP), 376
Social disorientation, 103
Social inequalities, 99
Social issue life cycle hypothesis, 36
Social justice, 104
Social payments, 377
Social pluralism, 99
Social preferences, 428
Social relations, crude law of, 77
Social resources, 437
Social tactics, 441
Socialism, 77, 281
Socialist countries of Eastern Europe, 190
Socialist and Republican UIL, 376
Societal marketing concept, 332
Société Générale de Banque S.A., 169
Société Imetal, 51, 530
Society for the Aid of Thalidomide
    Children, 347
Society of Consumer Affairs Professionals,
    337
Sohn, L. B., 590
Solarz, Stephen, 147
Solomon, S., 639
Sohio, 531
Sohyo, 384
Solzhenitsyn, Aleksandr, 190
Somoza, Anastasio, 102
Sorenson, Theodore C., 308, 321, 613, 617

South Africa, 148-151, 153-156, 161,
    163-165, 168, 170, 188, 196, 200, 206,
    208, 209, 409, 413
  army, 196
  Blacks, 201, 206, 217
  Cape Town oil refinery in, 201
  Cessna aircraft in, 187
  coal, 156
  Church Project on U.S. Investments in,
    410
South Africa, Christian Concern for,
    150
  Committee for Liberation of, 150
  Committee of the Congregation for
    Reconciliation, 153
  Emergency Coalition for Human Rights
    in, 151
  End Loans to, 150, 155
  Eximbank financing of, 161
  Expansion in, 201ff
  government of, 168, 169, 249
  hearings on, 179
  IBM and, 189ff
  and international banks, 175
  International Defense and Aid Fund for,
    151
  investment in, 201, 202
  loans to, 173ff
  Midland Bank limits loans to, 174
  National Black Coalition on, 151
  Olin Corporation in, 181
  profits in, 208
  and Rev. Sullivan's six principles on, 59
  Task Force of the United Presbyterian
    Church, 15, 194
  withdrawal campaign, the, 206
South African Institute on Race Relations,
    209
South African Ministry of Finance, 168
Southern California Edison, 450
Southern Christian Leadership Conference,
    194
Southern Company, 182
South Korea, 157, 162
South Moluccans, 97, 102, 115, 116
South-West African Peoples' Organization
    (SWAPO), 17, 149, 196
South-West Africa, U.S. investment in, 197
Soviet-American relations, 244
Soviet Constitution, 134
Soviet Union, 165, 190, 244
Soweto, uprising in, 164, 207

Spain, J. B., 577, 644
Sporkin, Stanley, 321, 614
Spontis, 102
Special Committee for U.S. Exports, 49
Spent-fuel reprocessing units, 493
Sperry, 191, 269
Sperry Univac, 240, 244-246, 315, 475, 476, 500, 503
Spiegel, I., 602
Spiegel, J., 578
Spock, Benjamin, 369
Spring Mills, 346
Squibb, 350, 512, 530
Stagnation, conflict and, 42
Stagner, R., 579
Stakeholder concepts, 394
Stakes, 66ff
Stalker, G. M., 645
Standard Bank, 200
Standard Brands, 53
Standard Elektrik Lorenz, 21
Standard Electrica S.A., 23
Standard Oil of California, 7, 61, 68, 88, 180, 181, 199, 201, 202, 207, 247-249, 255, 292, 445
Standard Oil of Indiana, 68, 92, 445
Standard Oil (Ohio), 451
Standard Oil Trust, 350
Stanford Research Institute, 476
Stanford University, 154
Starbuck, W. H., 645
State Department, 16, 157, 187, 222, 224, 226, 230, 238, 240, 241, 243, 248-250, 311, 320, 412
State Department, Coordinator for Human Rights and Humanitarian Affairs, 157
State Department of Environmental Resources, 444
State terrorism, 118
Statens Vattenfallsverk, 524
Statist regimes, 308
Stauffer Chemical, 56, 370
Steel production, 168
Stein, N., 597
Steinem, Gloria, 369
Steiner, G., 580
Stellenbosch Mines, 202
Stereotyped views, 43
Sterling, C., 588
Sterling Drug, 305
Stern, F., 588

Stevens, J. P., 445
St. Jorre, J. de, 596, 597
Stobaugh, R. B., 539, 638, 640, 643
Stock divestitures, 154, 164
Stockholder equity, 504
Stone, C. D., 619
Storck, W. F., 575
Strang, M. F., 631
Straus, D. B., 635
Straver, W., 620
Strick, A., 634
Strikes, 317, 376, 379
Structural issues, 540
Studebaker-Worthington, 246
Student groups, 151, 168
Studies, independent scientific, 337
Strümpel, B., 642
Subcommittee on Health and Scientific Research, 369
Subcommittee on Multinational Corporations, 327
Successful technology adaptation, 482
Suharto, General, 57
Sukarno, President, 292
Sullivan, E., 637
Sullivan, Rev. Leon, 59, 60, 71, 75, 77, 84, 161, 189, 206, 207, 411-414
Sulzberger, C. L., 587
Sulzberger, Jr., A. O., 623
Summer, C. E., 601
Sumner, W. G., 583
Sun Oil, 194
Super-Phénix, 448
Supreme Court, 233, 328, 525, 526
Susskind, L. E., 635
Sutowo, Major General Ibnu, 60, 317
Swanson, C. L., 628
SWAPO, 200
Swarthmore College, 155
Sweden, 161, 165, 266, 396
  company stock in, 391
Swedish Academy of Fine Arts vs. Levis Strauss, 357
Swedish Environment Protection Board, 440
Swedish Medical Board, 349
Swift & Co., 104
Swingle, P., 579, 582
Swint, John A., 92
Swissair, 112
Swiss National Bank, 320
Switzerland, 150, 539

Sydkraft, 524
Sylvania, 92
Sylvester, C., 584
Sylvester, Stanley, 104
Symbionese Liberation Army, 112, 133
Sympathizers, 108
Syria, Damascus, 223
Syrian-Israeli disengagement agreement, 253
Szekely, F., 632
Szulc, T., 637

Taehyup Company, 415
Tailhade, L., 587
Taiwan, 162
    copyrights and, 487
Tanaka, Kakuei, 297, 299
Tariff Commission, 513, 536, 537
Tariff policy, 266
Task Force on Questionable Corporate
    Payments Abroad, 320
Task Force on the Churches and
    Corporate Responsibility, 150, 169
Task specialization, 565
Task system, 557
Taubman, P., 618
Taxation, 262, 382, 538
Tax credits, 197, 538
Tax deferment, 538
Tax avoidance, 505, 538
Tax havens, 539
Tax Reform Act of 1976, amendment of, 226
Tax revenues, 221
Taylor, C. W., 580
Taylor, T. B., 590
TCDD, 461, 462
Teachers Insurance and Annuity
    Association—College Retirement
    Equities Fund (TIAA-CREF), 201
Techniques, alternative, 561
Technological and economic impacts, 545
Technological dependence, 484
Technological parity, 283
Technological restrictions, unilateral
    American, 489
Technology, 23, 261ff, 470, 500, 516, 573
    adaptation, 480
    appropriateness of, 483
    disembodied, 471-472
    exports, effects of, 478
    four distinct types of, 471
    gross profit on, 486

and MNEs, 474
    pricing, 486, 487
    production of, 472
    proprietary nature of, 472
    return transfers of, 479
Technology transfers, barriers to, 489
    codes of conduct, 552
    forms and competitive effects, 475
    office of, 489
    restrictions on, 489
    study of 25 cases, 479
Tedeschi, J. T., 579
Teece, D. J., 635
Telefunken, 512
Tell, H., 638
Teltsch, K., 594
Temple, C. J., 633, 634
Tempo Bottling Company, 228, 229
Temporal urgency, 69
Tenneco, 61, 64, 75, 305, 329, 445
Tennessee Valley Authority, 524
Terminal controls, 285, 287, 293
Terpstra, V., 575, 580, 620, 636, 644
Terrebery, S., 644
Territorial disputes, 221
Territorial power, 102
Territorials, 103
Terrorism, 13, 37ff, 90, 100, 101, 135, 544
    challenge of, 94
    coping with, 119
    definition of, 95
    effects of, 114
    facilitators of, 106
    forms of, 109
    origins of, 97
Terrorist, ecstasy and, 106
    extortion, 125
    objectives, 101
Terrorist International, 109
Texaco, 7, 54, 68, 88, 100, 113, 117, 180,
    181, 201, 202, 207, 247, 249, 292, 410
Texas Instruments, 245, 478
Texas Utilities Services, Inc., 524
Textron, 183, 187, 188, 314, 316, 328
Thais, Union of, 150
Thalidomide babies, 347
Thamhain, H. J., 577
Theodorus Niemeyer, 357
Thibaut, J., 582
Third parties, 34
Third World Action Group (TWAG), 48,
    77, 362, 363, 368
Third World governments, 164

Third World Institute, 366
Thomas, K. W., 577, 578, 583, 636
Thomas, M. J., 635
Thompson, C., 575, 635
Thompson, J. D., 642, 644
Thomson CSF, 24, 61, 309
Thonnessen, Werner, 21
Thornton, T. P., 586, 587
3M Company, 207, 239, 316, 410, 411
Thunell, L. H., 32, 646
Timex, 377
Timken Roller Bearing Company, 234
Tisdall, P., 622
Tobis, D., 579, 629
Tokyo Convention, 119
Tokyo Stock Exchange, 420
Tomasson, R. E., 596
Toronto Committee for the Liberation of
    Portugal's African Colonies, 193
Toronto Committee on the Liberation of
    Southern Africa, 150, 174
Toronto Dominion Bank, 169, 174
Total, 59, 179, 180
Totalitarianism, 303
Totalitarian states, 308
Tourism, 117
Trade, 261
    barriers, 504
    controls, 221, 237, 244
    effects, 534
    embargoes, 164, 239, 240
    restrictions, 224
Trades Union Congress (TUC), 20, 376
Trade Unions, World Federation of, 151
Trading with the Enemy Act, 84, 238, 243
Trans-Alaska Oil pipeline, 112, 115
Transactions, size of, 313
Trans Alpine Oil, 112
Transax, 92
Transliner Inc., 300
Transnational Corporations, Centre on,
    109, 148
Transnational Corporations, Commission
    on, 552
Transnational networks, 109
Transport and General Workers Union, 388
Transportation, 168
Treasury Department, U.S., 199, 238, 243,
    244
Treaty of Rome, 353, 354, 355
Tribal states, 308
Trist, E. L., 644
Trumbull, R., 613

Trust Company of North Carolina, 169
TRW, 378, 537
Tsumeb Corp. Ltd., 197, 199, 200
Tsurumi, Y., 635
TUC, 398
Tufts University, 154
Tullock, G., 582
Tupamaros, 103, 104, 108, 118
Turck, N., 602
Turkish Airlines, 340
Turkish People's Liberation Front, 113
Turnbull, R., 639
Turner, Sir Mark, 9
Two companies proposal, 284

Udo-Aka, U., 620
UDAF, 339
Uganda, 165
    missionaries in, 184
    repression, 221
    coffee boycott, 182
Ugandan Coffee Connection, 182
Ugandan Coffee Marketing Board, 183
Ugelow, J., 632
Ullman, L., 597, 626
Ullman, N., 580, 626
Ullman, Richard H., 183, 591, 596
Uncontrollable variables, 332
Undercover period, 326
Underdeveloped nations, 308
Unidata, 271, 272
Unifying forces, 568
Unilever, 2, 155, 413, 475, 512
Union, 177
    Belgian, 376
    British, 376
    German, 376
    in Holland, 376
    in France, 375
    Italian, 376
    Japanese, 377
    opposition to, 415
    socialist and communist, 376
    talks and MNEs, 56
Union Carbide, 6, 52, 56, 59, 130, 176, 177,
    178, 202, 207, 213, 215, 292, 328, 339,
    410, 411, 444, 445, 545
Union Carbide Rhomet Ltd., 176
Union de la Gauche, 54
Union del Pueblo, 112
Union information-gathering exercise, 381
Union Minière, 51

Union Oil, 59

Union of Thais, 150

Unione Petrolifera Italiana, 313

Uniroyal, 313, 385

UNITA (National Union for the Total
Independence of Angola), 195, 196

Unitarian Universalist Association, 167

United Auto Workers, 151, 172, 204, 384,
393, 400, 514

United Automobile, Rubber and Allied
Workers Union, 413

United Brands, 51, 72, 297, 299, 312, 316,
329, 415
violation of EEC antitrust laws, 349

United Church Board for World Ministry,
50, 52, 74, 177, 179, 181, 200

United Church Board of Canada, 155

United Church of Christ, 149, 169, 178,
179, 199
Center for Social Action, 156, 194

United Methodist Church, World Division
Board of Global Ministries of the,
201

United Dominions Trust, 212

United Fruit, see United Brands, 72

United Kingdom, 150, 166, 168, 169
Codetermination in, 397
Monopolies Commission, 19, 77

United Methodist Church, 149, 168

United Nations, 2, 36, 41, 133, 142, 148, 151,
156, 164, 165, 168, 175, 178, 180, 181,
183, 193, 196, 197, 198, 200, 222, 240,
324, 550, 552, 553
Association, 197
Charter, 132
Childrens Fund, 370
Commission on Human Rights, 148ff, 148,
204
Commission on International Trade
(UNCITRAL), 344
Commission on Transnational
Corporations, 554
Convention, 120
Council for Namibia, 130, ff., 199
Conference on Trade and Development
(UNCTAD), 487, 552, 554
Economic and Social Council, 164, 324
Environment Programme (UNEP), 56, 57,
429
Food and Agricultural Organization
(FAO), 148

General Assembly, 16, 33, 132, 133, 164,
177, 193, 196, 197, 199, 201, 204, 293,
551
Genocide Convention, 133
International Labor Organization (ILO),
148
Protein Advisory Group (PAG), 361
Resolution 385 (re: S. Africa), 200
Scientific and Cultural Organization
(UNESCO), 148
Security Council, 164, 176, 181, 197, 198,
200
Stockholm Conference on the Human
Environment, 424
system, 148
World Health Organization (WHO), 148

United Nuclear, 525, 526, 527

United Presbyterian Church, U.S.A., 15, 149,
156, 188

United Radio, Electrical and Machine
Workers Union, 172

United Red Army, 100

United Rubber, Cork, Linoleum, and Plastic
Workers (URW), 385

United States, 150, 151, 153, 155, 157, 161,
163, 165, 168, 169, 222
Agency for International Development,
366
aid, 161
Air Force, 462
Air Force Directorate of Counter-
Intelligence, 94
anti-boycott rules, 232
antitrust law, 234, 236
Catholic Conference, 149, 150
Chamber of Commerce, 49
coffee companies, 183
Congress, 162, 165
Constitution, 132
Court action versus Gillette-Braun, 235
Court of Appeals, 49, 342, 444
Department of Justice, 33, 55
Department of Labor, 417
Department of State, 49
District Court in Richmond, 16
expatriate employees in, 405
Federal Trade Commission (FTC), 359
foreign intervention, 233
fuel suppliers, 498
Government, 147, 165, 227
House of Representatives, 364

Justice Department, 16, 57
Labor Department, 21
moral imperialism, 157
Nuclear Antiproliferation Act, 494
National Council of Churches, 168, 169
nuclear policy, 498
oil shortage, 254
organized labor in, 378
Overseas Private Investment Corp., 33
Senate Foreign Relations Committee, 168
Senate Foreign Relations Subcommittee on
    African Affairs, 169
Senate Foreign Relations Subcommittee on
    Multinational Corp., 33
Soviet trade agreement of 1972, 165
State Department, 26, 51, 84, 166
trade embargo on Cuba, 239
Tariff Commission, study by, 536
Trade Act of 1974, Title IV of, 165
Treasury Department, 41, 50, 156, 161,
    176, 179, 340, 358
Universal Copyright Convention, 487
Universal Declaration of Human Rights, 132,
    164, 198
Universal Oil Products Corp., 241
Universities, 155
University faculties, 151
Unstable-stable climate, 566-567
Unterhalter, B., 601
Upjohn, 314, 350, 530
Uranerzbergbau, 522
Uranerz Canada, 525
Uranerzgesellschaft, 48
Uranium, 491, 492, 522
    U.S. embargo of, 494
Uranium Cartel Case, 521
Uranium Enrichment Association (UEA), 496
Urenco, 492, 498
Urquhart, J., 606
Uruguay, 157, 163
URW, 386
Urwick, L., 578
United States Steel Corp., 130, 292, 444
United Steelworkers, 20
United Steelworkers Local 12075, 20
Utah International Inc., 292, 527

Valium prices, 350
Vaitsos, C. V., 641
Vance, Cyrus R., 51, 184, 197, 310
VanDyke, V., 590

Van Zandt, H. F., 613
Variance, in conflict approaches, 429
Velval, L. R., 570
Vernon, R., 575, 576, 582, 583, 605, 606, 613,
    616, 635, 641
Vibramycin, price cut of, 350
Vicker, R., 591, 594, 600
Vickers, 512
Vidal, D., 601
Vienna, 249
Vietnam, 240
Vietnam war, 186
Vinnell Corporation, 187
Vinocur, J., 581
Violence, 95, 106, 114
Virginia Electric and Power Company, 524
Vitamin pricing, 353
Vogel, D., 577, 593, 633
Volkswagen, 2, 61, 62, 64, 68, 73, 83, 224, 384,
    393, 396, 409, 413, 514, 534, 535, 546
Vorstand, 395, 402
Vorster government, Soweto reaction to, 151
Vorster, John, 164, 207
Voluntary codes, 550
Voluntary Price Regulation System (VPRS)
    of DHSS, 350
Volvo, AB, 56, 57, 391, 393, 545

Wabenzi, 307
Wachovia Bank and Trust, 169
Wadkins, Ltd., 339
Wahl, J., 589
Walker, K. F., 627
Walker, L., 582
Wallace, W. M., 629
Wallenberg, 55
Wallender, III, H., 636
Walsh, J., 634
Walt Disney Productions, 357
Walter, E. V., 585
Walter, I., 575, 630, 631, 632, 641, 644, 645
Walton, R. E., 578, 579, 580
War, and MNEs, 221
Warner Bros., 354
Was, D. A., 635
Washington, D.C., 150, 161
Water quality, 437
Watson, F. M., 585
Weapons availability, 106
Weather Underground, 12, 100, 102, 109
Weaver, P. H., 621

Weaver, S., 587
Webb-Pomerene Act, 1918, 236
Weekly, J. K., 611
Weick, K. E., 642
Weiss, P., 587, 590, 591
Welch, Jr., C. E., 613
Welfare, 259
Welles, J. G., 632, 634
Wells Fargo Bank, 168, 169, 175
Wells, Jr., L. T., 576, 582, 583, 584, 638
West, G. T., 577, 643
West German Confederation of Employers
    Associations, 102
West, Mae, 297
West, Richard, 22, 576
Western Electric Company, 236
Western Europe, 149, 153, 163
Western governments, 164
Western Nuclear, Inc., 527
Westinghouse Electric Corp., 16, 25, 48, 51,
    64, 67, 69, 84, 314, 329, 432, 445, 491,
    492, 496, 498, 499, 500, 522, 528
  v. Gulf, 526
  out-of-court settlements, 523-524
  v. utilities, 48, 522
Weyerhaeuser Company, 212, 410
White, P. E., 645
Whichard, O. G., 591
Whitehead, D., 575
Whitemail, 299, 308
White minority rule, 206
White Motor Company, 378
Whiteside, T., 634
Whitney, C., 604
Whitten, J., 596, 597.
WHO, 148, 330, 331, 343, 362, 370
Whole-body scanner, 339
Wicker, T., 591, 593, 600, 602, 631
Wiechmann, U., 620
Wiehan Commission, 414ff
Wiener, H., 598
Wierzynski, G. H., 607
Wiggins, P. H., 604, 605
Wilcox, L. D., 642
Wileman, D. L., 578
Wilkie, David W., 92
Wilkins, M., 576
Wilkinson, P., 585, 586, 587, 588
Willatt, N., 575, 576
Williams, Franklin H., 183, 596, 597
Williams, Harold M., 302
Williams, L., 601

Willrich, M., 590
Wilson, Harold, 63, 372
Wilson, J. V., 585
Winchester International, 181, 187
Wingate, P. J., 621
Winstrol, 338
Winthrop Laboratories, 338
Winton, J. M., 632
Wirtz, Willard, 526
Wisconsin Electric Power Company, 524
Wisconsin, University of, 154
Wise, F., 632
Witkin, R., 632
Wolf, C. P., 591
Wolf, J. B., 588
Wolff, K. H., 583
Woolworth, F. W., 346
Worker participation, in Germany, 392,
    395, 422
Working Group Betaald Antwoord, 150, 169
Workplace, humanization of the, 401
Works Councils, 397, 399
World Bank, 134, 135, 161, 162, 163, 520, 551
World Bank, International Centre for the
    Settlement of Investment Disputes, 88
World company councils, 384
World Confederation of Labor, (WCL), 384
World Council of Churches, 1, 77, 149, 150,
    155, 169, 174, 541, 552
World Court, 198, 200
World Federation of Trade Unions
    (WFTU), 151, 384
World Health Organization (WHO), 330-331
World monetary system, 163
World revolution, 102
World Student Christian Federation, 168
World Trade Institute, 120
World War I, 196
World War II, 132
Wriston, Walter, 316
Wrenson's, 348
Wyandotte Chemical Co., 531
Wynne, B. E., 644
Wyodak Resources Development, 444

Xerox Corporation, 223, 227, 239, 270, 315,
    410, 528
XOX Company, 531

Yashica, 353, 354
Yeager, D. S., 611
Yergin, D., 624

Yezer, A., 632
Young Americans for Freedom, 53, 77, 88, 190, 241
Young, Andrew, 216
Young, Anthony, 282
Young, S., 581

Zaibatsu, 55, 420
Zaltman, G., 620
Zartman, I. W., 582, 589

Zayre Corporation, 346
Zebra Associates, Inc., 194
Zeher, L., 626
Zengakuren, 100
Zenith Corporation, 546
Zenith Laboratories, 23
Zetor, 512
Zimbabwe Solidarity Committee, 150
Zion Baptist Church of Philadelphia, 59, 411